Collecting TOYS

IDENTIFICATION & VALUE GUIDE

EDITED BY ELIZABETH STEPHAN

Published by

**krause
publications**

700 E. State Street • Iola, WI 54990-0001
Telephone: 715/445-2214

Please call or write for our free catalog.
Our toll-free number to place an order or obtain a free catalog is 800-258-0929
or please use our regular business telephone 715-445-2214
for editorial comment and further information.

Library of Congress Catalog Number: 99-61890
ISBN: 0-87341-749-6

Printed in the United States of America

TABLE OF CONTENTS

EDITOR'S NOTE

When Richard O'Brien compiled the first edition of *Collecting Toys* it was the only toy price guide available, but things have changed. Over the years, numerous toy price guides appeared on the market, yet none cover the same obscure topics and categories covered by O'Brien. While other guides concentrate on the newer, collectible toys, O'Brien always focused on the older, more obscure toys. After years of editing *Collecting Toys*, O'Brien and handed the reins to Krause Publications, the largest publisher of hobby periodicals and books.

Although *Collecting Toys* is considered by many to be the bible of toys, it has, in the past, been difficult for the novice collector to use. Hopefully you will find the reorganized ninth edition of *O'Brien's Collecting Toys* easier to navigate. Readers will also benefit from the extended table of contents, updated prices and expanded appendices.

Other changes made include chapters organized by manufacturer or type of toy; the addition of several chapters—Dollhouses and Miniature Furniture, Lionel Trains, Vintage Hot Wheels and Yo-yos; and several chapters were created from the Miscellaneous Chapter—Catalogs and Bell Toys, for instance.

Comments of numerous collectors and dealers were considered when editing this book. People wondered at the purpose of the number code at the beginning of many listings. Because these number had no relation to the toy or toy company, they were deleted.

A Word on Pricing

As with all price guides, the values listed here should be used as a guide only. Please understand, the prices given in *O'Brien's Collecting Toys* are seller prices—the price a dealer would sell the item for, not what a dealer will pay for the toy. Remember, a dealer needs to make a profit when reselling a toy.

Condition is key when buying and selling any collectible, the same is true in the world of toys. You will find anywhere from one to four pricing categories in *O'Brien's*. When only one price is listed it is for an item in C10, or Mint-in-Box, condition. One category, Erector Sets, even boasts four pricing categories. Contributor W.S. Harrison felt this was necessary to represent the numerous incomplete sets found by collectors. You will find that most categories have the tried and true O'Brien pricing system—C6, C8 and C10.

Also note that values given in picture captions are for items in C10 condition, unless otherwise noted.

Thank You

I would like to extend my thanks to all of the new contributors to this new edition *O'Brien's Collecting Toys* as well as express my gratitude to the long-term contributors for their patience and guidance—Stan Alekna, Charles Best, Ray Brandes, Jim Buskirk, Jim and Patsy Carlson, Kent M. Comstock, Reid Covey, Perry Eichor, John Gibson, Jim Harmon, Bill Harrison, Judy Izen, Michele Karl, Dave Leopard, Richard McNary, John Murray, Mark Rich, Leo Rishty, Aaron Roy, Conrad Schwager, Ron Smith, John K. Snyder, Jr., Marcie Tubbs, David Welch and Randy Welch. I hope I haven't forgotten anyone—there were a lot of people who helped in this new edition!

This book wouldn't have been possible without all of the people working behind the scenes. Stacy Bloch, Cheryl Mueller, Ethel Thulien of Book Production put this monster of a book together. After working long weeks and long hours the book was finally done. Great job guys! Also, *Toy Shop* editor Sharon Korbeck, *Toy Shop* associate editor Mike Jacquart, and *Toy Cars & Vehicles* associate Merry Dudley were a valuable resource. Not only did they assist in background information and pricing, they were able to pull together and gather many of the photos you see in this book.

Elizabeth A. Stephan
Editor
stephane@krause.com

ON THE COVER

ACTION FIGURES

Adventure heroes and superheroes are everywhere, on comic pages, television and movie screens, and, of course, in toy store aisles. The action figure likenesses produced by numerous toy companies are among today's hottest collectibles.

Action figure collecting is one of the fastest growing and potentially largest collectibles areas since the baseball card boom of the 1980s. A stroll through the toy section of any store is proof enough. Plus, it is a given that a percentage of today's teen and preteen action figure buyers will become collectors, and their potential numbers are huge. Action figures could bring more collectors into the hobby than G.I. Joe, Hot Wheels and model kits combined.

Hundreds of figures are for sale currently, and they are commonplace in toy stores. In some places action figures are literally climbing the walls. Why collect them if they can be bought directly from current store shelves? For many collectors, that's exactly how the collecting frenzy begins.

For many action figure collectors, time began in the 1960s. While boys had played with toy soldiers for hundreds of years, these were typically iron or lead figures with no movable parts. The same held true for the hard plastic Marx figures of the 1950s. By definition, however, the term "action figure" was born in the 1960s.

That decade also saw American culture and technologies come of age in ways that changed countless aspects of everyday life, including how toys would be made and sold.

Heroes from the TV screen

By the late 1950s, television had replaced the dinner table and parlor radio as the family hearth. The sturdy cabinet in the living room captivated with a power only hinted at by radio and which has never been challenged since. It was a working window not only into a wide world of people and places, but also, increasingly, of neat things to buy. Youngsters clustered on the floor, soaking up the names and lore of their new friends and heroes—Wonder Woman, Superman, Batman, G.I. Joe.

From 1961 to 1963, toy makers watched with envy and despair as Mattel's Barbie, aided by TV, took the world of girls' toys by storm. Of course, no one would dream of selling dolls to boys, so this barrier seemed insurmountable. But wheels of industry would not be easily stopped, and the simple solution to this dilemma ranks as one of the greatest marketing spins of all time. If boys won't play with dolls, why not rename them "action figure"?

Hasbro's first test of G.I. Joe, the male answer to Barbie, debuted at New York's International Toy Fair in early 1964. Toy Fair is where buyers, retailers and manufacturers meet to view upcoming lines—and in the process, make or break a toy's success.

Buyers met the twelve-inch G.I. Joe with both hopes and reservations. They wanted to believe that a successful "Barbie for boys" had been created, but as much as Hasbro touted Joe as "America's Movable Fighting Man," the buyers still heard "doll."

Virtually no orders were generated at Toy Fair, so in June, with no fanfare or ad support, Hasbro released the new toy into the New York test market. Every test store sold out within a week and the invasion of America was on. By year's end, G.I. Joe had earned Hasbro $17 million, in spite of sales lost to product shortages.

G.I. Joe was the first true-articulated action figure for boys, but he wouldn't be alone for long. A.C. Gilbert introduced James Bond figures in 1965, but for the first time in his career, Ian Fleming's super spy failed in his mission. Marx also entered the ring with the Best of the West series, but G.I. Joe had seemingly limitless arsenal of battle-geared appeal.

The first reasonably successful challenge to G.I. Joe came from Ideal's Captain Action. While Joe's identity was well established, Captain Action was a man of many faces. Ideal designed Captain Action to establish not only his own identity, but also to capitalize on those many popular superheroes. Joe was just Joe, but Captain Action figures and sets could become Spider-Man, Batman, the Phantom, Green Hornet and others. Today, Captain Action figures and sets command the second highest prices in the action figure market, second only to classic G.I. Joes.

Ideal's brief foray into the world of superhero action figures paved the way for many to come. While G.I. Joe was forced to temper his image and soften it from the quintessential military Green Beret Joe of 1967 into the Adventure Team Joe of 1970, superheroes were largely immune to the Vietnam protests that forced Joe's change of mission. By 1969, Ideal tired of Captain Action's complex licensing agreements and discontinued the series, but another company was waiting in the wings. It was Mego.

Mighty Mego

In 1972, Mego released its first superhero series, the six-figure set of Official World's Greatest Super Heroes. These eight-inch tall cloth and plastic figures were joined by twenty-eight others by the time the series ended ten years later. Mego supplemented this superhero line with licensed film and TV characters from, most notably, *Planet of the Apes, Star Trek* and *The Dukes of Hazzard,* as well as historic figures representing the Old West and the World's Greatest Super Knights.

Another milestone in action figure history took place in 1977. Out of nowhere, George Lucas' *Star Wars* had become a worldwide smash, but nobody except Kenner had bothered to secure rights to merchandise toys. When Kenner realized the magnitude of Star Wars' potential, it rushed toys through production, but it didn't have time to get action figures on the shelves by Christmas. Instead, Kenner essentially presold the figures as the mail-order Early Bird set.

By Christmas 1978, the line had grown to seventeen figures and the first wave of a deluge of accessories and related toys. The Star Wars figures also established a third standard size for action figures. G.I. Joes and Captain Action were twelve-inch figures, Mego figures measured eight inches, and Kenner's Star Wars figures were just 3-3/4-inches tall. Their tremendous popularity cemented that size as a new standard that holds to this day.

Next came the six-inch figure, set by Mattel's highly successful and lucrative 1981 Masters of the Universe series. This series was the first to be reverse licensed; in other words, Mattel made the toys first, and then sold the licensing to television and film, not the other way around. Mattel also upped the manufacturing ante by endowing the figures with action features such as punching and grabbing movements, thus enhancing their play value and setting another standard in the process.

Action figures are big business, and hot series like Star Trek and McFarlane's Spawn are now regularly ranked in the top twenty best selling lines by industry trade magazines. An enduring character identity is a key to the continued demand and future appreciation. Star Trek has proven itself a worthy long term franchise and is joining the ranks of Star Wars as the blue chip stocks of the action figure market.

The action figure aisles are now attracting more adults, and they are not always buying for their kids. More adults today buy action figures as collectibles and investments. And those investments will in years hence feed the needs of tomorrow's collectors—the ones who are now sitting on the floor playing with Captain Picard, Batman and Spawn.

Contributors: Action Figures—Anthony Balasco, Figures, P.O. Box 19482, Johnston RI 02919. Star Wars—Chris Fawcett, cfawcett@ix.netcom.com. G.I. Joe—Vincent Santelmo. P.O. Box 789, New York, NY 10021; Dale Wormer, The Joe Depot, P.O. Box 228, Kulpsville PA 19443-0228.

ACTION JACKSON

(Mego, 1974)

8" Figures

	C8	C10
Action Jackson, Black version	25	60
Action Jackson, blond, brown, or black beard	15	30
Action Jackson, blond, brown, or black hair	15	30

Accessories

	C8	C10
Parachute Plunge	5	15
Strap-On Helicopter	5	15
Water Scooter	5	15

Outfits

	C8	C10
Air Force Pilot	7	15
Army Outfit	7	15
Aussie Marine	7	15
Baseball	7	15
Fisherman	7	15
Football	7	15
Frog Man	7	15
Hockey	7	15
Jungle Safari	7	15
Karate	7	15
Navy Sailor	7	15
Rescue Squad	7	15
Scramble Cyclist	7	15
Secret Agent	7	15
Ski Patrol	7	15
Snowmobile Outfit	7	15
Surf and Scuba Outfit	7	15
Western Cowboy	7	15

Play Sets

	C8	C10
Jungle House	40	85
Lost Continent Play Set	40	85

Vehicles

	C8	C10
Adventure Set	40	85
Campmobile	40	85
Dune Buggy	30	60
Formula Racer	30	60
Mustang	30	60
Rescue Helicopter	40	85

	C8	C10
Safari Jeep	40	85
Scramble Cycle	20	40
Snowmobile	15	30

ALIENS

(Kenner, 1979)

	C8	C10

18" Figure

Alien	200	500

AMERICAN WEST

(Mego, 1973)

	C8	C10

8" Figures

Buffalo Bill Cody, boxed	40	75
Buffalo Bill Cody, carded	40	100
Cochise, boxed	40	75
Cochise, carded	40	100
Davy Crockett, boxed	70	110
Davy Crockett, carded	70	140
Shadow (horse), carded	70	140
Sitting Bull, boxed	45	90
Sitting Bull, carded	45	125
Wild Bill Hickok, boxed	40	75
Wild Bill Hickok, carded	40	125
Wyatt Earp, boxed	40	75
Wyatt Earp, carded	40	125

Play Sets

Dodge City Play Set, vinyl	100	200

ARCHIES (MARX, 1975)

	C8	C10
Archie	15	75
Betty	15	75

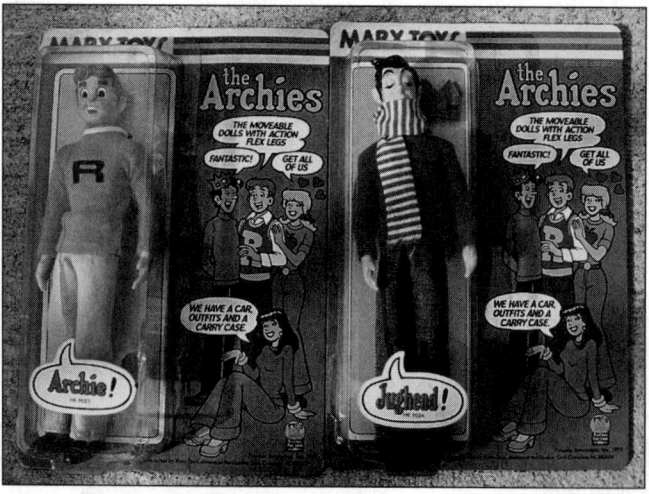

Left to Right: Archie, $75; Jughead, $75

	C8	C10
Jughead	15	75
Veronica	15	75

ASTRONAUTS

(Marx, 1969)

	C8	C10
Jane Apollo Astronaut	35	75
Johnny Apollo Astronaut	35	75
Kennedy Space Center Astronaut	35	75

BANANA SPLITS (SUTTON, 1970)

	C8	C10
Bingo the Bear	45	125
Drooper the Lion	45	125
Fleagle Beagle	45	125
Snorky the Elephant	45	125

BATTLESTAR GALACTICA

(Mattel, 1978-79)

	C8	C10

12" Figures

Colonial Warrior	20	55
Cylon Centurian	20	55

3-3/4" Figures, 1978, Series 1

Commander Adama	15	30
Cylon Centurian	15	40
Daggit (brown)	15	30
Daggit (tan)	15	30
Imperious Leader	15	30
Ovion	12	25
Starbuck	15	30

Colonial Warrior, Battlestar Galactica, $55

Chief Cherokee, Best of the West, $90

3-3/4" Figures, 1979, Series 2	C8	C10
Baltar	30	75
Boray	30	75
Cylon Commander	55	110
Lucifer	55	110

BEST OF THE WEST

(Marx, 1960s)

	C8	C10
Figures		
Bill Buck, 1967	100	200
Brave Eagle, 1967	45	90
Buckboard w/Horse and Harness	35	75
Chief Cherokee, 1965	45	90
Daniel Boone, 1965	100	200
Davy Crockett	100	200
Fighting Eagle, 1967	45	90
General Custer, 1965	40	80
Geronimo and Pinto	40	80
Geronimo, 1967	45	90
Jamie West, 1967	32	65
Jane West, 1966	40	80
Janice West, 1967	32	65
Jay West, 1967	32	65
Johnny West Covered Wagon, w/horse and harness	35	75
Johnny West w/Comanche	80	125
Johnny West, 1965	40	80
Josie West, 1967	32	65
Pancho Horse, for 9" figures, 1968	20	40
Princess Wildflower, 1974	50	100
Sam Cobra, 1972	45	90
Sheriff Garrett, 1973	40	80
Thunderbolt Horse	35	75
Zeb Zachary, 1967	40	80

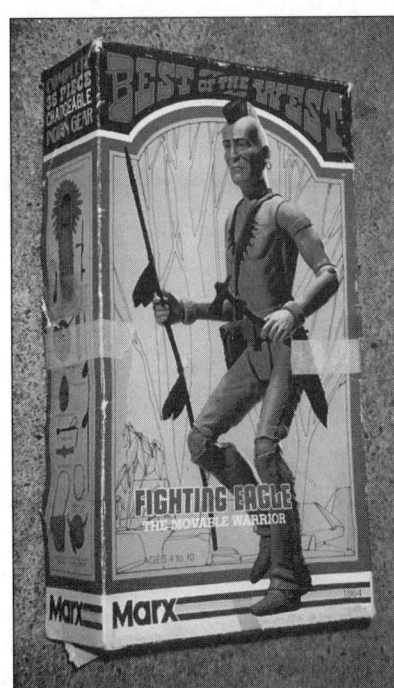

Fighting Eagle, Best of the West, $90

Jane West, Best of the West, $80

Johnny West, Best of the West, $80

BLACK HOLE

(Mego, 1979-80)

	C8	C10

12" Figures

Captain Holland	25	50
Dr. Alan Durant	25	50
Dr. Hans Reinhardt	25	50
Harry Booth	30	60
Kate McCrae	35	80
Pizer	25	50

3-3/4" Figures

Captain Holland, 1979	10	20
Dr. Alan Durant, 1979	10	20
Dr. Hans Reinhardt, 1979	10	25
Harry Booth, 1979	10	25
Humanoid, 1980	70	135
Kate McCrae, 1979	10	25
Maximillian, 1979	17	40
Old B.O.B., 1980	60	120
Pizer, 1979	15	25
S.T.A.R., 1980	60	120
Sentry Robot, 1980	25	60
V.I.N.cent., 1979	30	60

BUCK ROGERS

(Mego, 1979)

	C8	C10

12" Figures

Buck Rogers	30	80
Doctor Huer	30	60

Buck Roger, $80

	C8	C10
Draco	30	60
Draconian Guard	30	60
Killer Kane	30	60
Tiger Man	30	80
Walking Twiki	30	60

3-3/4" Figures

Ardella	6	15
Buck Rogers	20	40
Doctor Huer	6	15
Draco	6	15
Draconian Guard	10	20
Killer Kane	6	15
Tiger Man	6	15
Twiki	20	30
Wilma Deering	12	25

3-3/4" Play Sets

Star Fighter Command Center	35	100

3-3/4" Vehicles

Draconian Marauder	25	50
Land Rover	20	40
Laserscope Fighter	20	40
Star Fighter	25	50
Starseeker	30	60

Dr. Evil, Captain Action, $1,200

CAPTAIN ACTION

(Ideal, 1966-68)

	C8	C10

12" Figures

	C8	C10
Captain Action, box photo, 1966	200	900
Captain Action, parachute offer on box, 1967	275	1150
Captain Action, photo box, 1967	200	1250
Captain Action, w/blue-shirted Lone Ranger on box, 1966	200	900
Captain Action, w/red-shirted Lone Ranger on box, 1966	200	900
Dr. Evil, 1967	300	1200

Aqualad, Captain Action, $900

	C8	C10

9" Figures

	C8	C10
Action Boy, 1967	275	650
Action Boy, w/space suit, 1968	350	825

Accessories

	C8	C10
Action Cave Carrying Case, vinyl, 1967	400	700
Directional Communicator Set, 1966	110	300
Dr. Evil Sanctuary, 1967	600	750
Jet Mortar, 1966	110	300
Parachute Pack, 1966	100	225
Power Pack, 1966	125	250
Quick Change Chamber, Cardboard, Sears Exclusive, 1967	750	900
Silver Streak Amphibian, 1967	500	1000
Silver Streak Garage, w/Silver Streak Vehicle, Sears Exclusive	400	500
Survival Kit, 20 pieces, 1967	125	275
Vinyl Headquarters Carrying Case, Sears Exclusive, 1967	200	500
Weapons Arsenal, ten pieces, 1966	110	225

Action Boy Costumes

	C8	C10
Aqualad, 1967	300	900
Robin, 1967	300	1200
Superboy, 1967	300	1000

Captain Action Costumes

	C8	C10
Aquaman, 1966	160	600
Aquaman, w/flasher ring, 1967	180	750
Batman, 1966	225	1000
Batman, w/flasher ring, 1967	250	1100

Green Hornet with Flasher Ring, Captain Action, $5,500

	C8	C10
Buck Rogers, w/flasher ring, 1967	450	2700
Captain America, 1966	220	900
Captain America, w/flasher ring, 1967	225	900
Flash Gordon, 1966	200	1250
Flash Gordon, w/flasher ring, 1967	225	1000
Green Hornet, w/flasher ring, 1967	1500	5500
Lone Ranger, blue shirt, w/flasher ring, 1967	300	1500
Lone Ranger, red shirt, 1966	170	1350
Phantom, 1966	150	875
Phantom, w/flasher ring, 1967	175	900
Sergeant Fury, 1966	200	1000
Spider-Man, w/flasher ring, 1967	550	6000
Steve Canyon, 1966	150	1000
Steve Canyon, w/flasher ring, 1967	175	1200
Superman, 1966	200	1200
Superman, w/flasher ring, 1967	225	1300
Tonto, w/flasher ring, 1967	375	1100

CHiPs

(Mego, 1979)

3-3/4" Carded Figures & Accessories

	C8	C10
Jimmy Squeaks	5	15
Jon	10	20
Launcher w/Motorcycle	25	50

Ponch, CHiPs, $20

Motorcycle, CHiPs, $75

	C8	C10
Motorcycle (boxed)	5	30
Ponch	8	20
Sarge	10	25
Wheels Willie	5	15

8" Carded Figures & Accessories

	C8	C10
Jon	20	50
Motorcycle	30	75
Ponch	15	40
Sarge	25	50

CLASH OF THE TITANS

(Mattel)

4" Figures

	C6	C8	C10
Thallo	10	16	45
Calibos	10	16	45
Charon	12	25	60
Perseus	9	15	50
Pegasus	9	15	55
Kraken	30	75	150
Perseus/Pegasus Set	12	25	50

COMIC ACTION HEROES

(Mego, 1975)

3-3/4" Figures

	C8	C10
Aquaman	30	60
Batman	20	50
Captain America	20	50
Green Goblin	22	55
Hulk	20	50
Joker	20	50
Penguin	20	50
Robin	20	50
Shazam	20	50

Batgirl, Comic Heroine Posin' Dolls, $4,500

DEFENDERS OF THE EARTH

(Galoob)

5-1/2" Figures

	C6	C8	C10
Flash Gordon (20)	7	11	20
Garax (18)	7	11	18
The Phantom (22)	7	11	22
Ming (20)	7	11	20
Mongor (95)	10	15	95
Mandrake (20)	7	11	20
Lothar (20)	7	11	20
Flash's Swordship (30)	10	15	30
Garax's Swordship (40)	10	15	40

DIE-CAST SUPER HEROES

(Mego, 1979)

6" Figures

	C8	C10
Batman	30	75
Hulk	25	65
Spider-Man	30	75
Superman	30	75

DUKES OF HAZZARD

(Mego, 1981-82)

3-3/4" Carded Figures

	C8	C10
Bo Duke	8	15
Boss Hogg	8	20

	C8	C10
Spider-Man	20	50
Superman	20	45
Wonder Woman	20	40

Accessories

	C8	C10
Collapsing Tower, w/Invisible Plane and Wonder Woman	50	125
Exploding Bridge w/Batmobile	75	150
Fortress of Solitude w/Superman	100	200
Mangler	55	110

COMIC HEROINE POSIN' DOLLS

(Ideal, 1967)

12" Boxed Figures

	C8	C10
Batgirl	1000	4500
Mera	600	3000
Supergirl	600	3000
Wonder Woman	600	3000

COMMANDER POWER

(Mego, 1975)

Figure w/Vehicle

	C8	C10
Commander Power w/Lightning Cycle	20	40

Luke Duke, Dukes of Hazzard, $30

	C8	C10
Cletus	15	30
Cooter	15	30
Coy Duke	15	30
Daisy Duke	12	25
Luke Duke	8	20
Rosco Coltrane	15	30
Uncle Jesse	15	30
Vance Duke	15	30

3-3/4" Figures w/Vehicles

	C8	C10
Daisy Jeep w/Daisy, 1981, boxed	25	50
General Lee Car w/Bo and Luke, 1981, boxed	25	50

8" Carded Figures

	C8	C10
Bo Duke	15	30
Boss Hogg	20	40
Coy Duke (card says Bo)	25	50
Daisy Duke	25	50
Luke Duke	15	30
Vance Duke (card says Luke)	25	50

FLASH GORDON

(Mego, 1976)

9" Figures

	C8	C10
Dale Arden	35	70
Dr. Zarkow	55	110
Flash Gordon	55	110
Ming	30	60

Play Sets

	C8	C10
Flash Gordon Play Set	55	125

FORT APACHE FIGHTERS

(Marx, 1960s)

	C8	C10
Captain Maddox, 1967	35	70
Fighting Eagle and Comanche	50	100
Fighting Eagle, 1967	35	70
General Custer, 1967	35	70
Geronimo, 1967	35	70

G.I. JOE

Figure Sets

12" Hall of Fame Figures

	C6	C8	C10
Ace, Fighter Pilot, 1993, No. 6837	15	20	25
Cobra Commander, Cobra Leader, 1992, No. 6827	20	30	35
Destro, Weapons Manufacturer, 1993, No. 6839	15	20	25

Cover of Hasbro's 1965 G.I. Joe Catalog

	C6	C8	C10
Duke, Master Sergeant, 1991, No. 6019	25	35	45
Duke, Master Sergeant, 1992, No. 6826	20	30	35
Grunt, Infantry Squad Leader, 1993, No. 6111	5	10	25
Gung-Ho, Dress Marine, 1993, No. 6849	15	20	25
Heavy Duty, Heavy Ordnance Specialist, 1993, No. 6114	15	20	35
Rapid Fire, Commando, 1993, No. 6924	35	50	60
Rock 'n Roll, Heavy Weapons Gunner, 1993, No. 6128	15	20	25
Snake Eyes, Commando, 1992, No. 6828	20	30	35
Stalker, Ranger, 1992, No. 6829	20	30	35
Storm Shadow, Ninja, 1993, No. 6848	15	20	25
Talking Duke, Talking Battle Commander, 1993, No. 6117	25	35	50

3-3/4" Series #1, Cobra

	C6	C8	C10
Cobra, Infantry Soldier, 1982, No. 6423	25	55	110
Cobra Commander, mail order; Commanding Leader, 1982	25	55	110
Cobra Officer, Infantry Officer, 1982, No. 6424	25	55	110
Major Bludd, mail order; Mercenary w/card, 1982, No. 6426	10	25	50

Short Fuse, 3-3/4" Series #1, G.I. Joe, No. 6402, $75

	C6	C8	C10
Gung-Ho, Marine, 1983, No. 6414	12	30	65
Rock 'n Roll, reissue, 1983, No. 6408	15	30	65
Scarlett, 1983, No. 6407	30	80	165
Short Fuse, reissue, 1983, No. 6402	15	30	65
Snake Eyes, reissue, 1983, No. 6404	40	80	165
Snow Job, Arctic Trooper, 1983, No. 6412	15	25	50
Stalker, reissue, 1983, No. 6401	25	45	90
Torpedo, Navy S.E.A.L., 1983, No. 6413	12	30	65
Tripwire, Mine Detector, 1983, No. 6410	15	30	65
Zap, reissue, 1983, No. 6405	15	30	60

3-3/4" Series #3, Cobra

	C6	C8	C10
Baroness, Intelligence Officer, 1983-84, No. 6428	40	85	175
Cobra Commander, mail order; Enemy Leader w/Hood, 1983-84, No. 6425	10	20	40
Fire Fly, Saboteur, 1983-84, No. 6432	40	85	175
Scrap Iron, Anti-Armor Specialist, 1983-84, No. 6431	15	30	60
Storm Shadow, Ninja, 1983-84, No. 6429	35	75	150

3-3/4" Series #3, G.I. Joe

	C6	C8	C10
Blow Torch, Flamethrower, 1983-84, No. 6421	10	20	40
Duke, First Sergeant, 1983-84, No. 6422	15	25	50
Mutt, Dog Handler w/Dog, 1983-84, No. 6416	10	25	50
Recondo, Jungle Trooper, 1983-84, No. 6420	15	25	50
Rip-Cord, H.A.L.O. Jumper, 1983-84, No. 6418	10	25	50
Road Block, Heavy Machine Gunner, 1983-84, No. 6419	15	25	50
Spirit, Tracker w/Eagle, 1983-84, No. 6417	15	25	50

3-3/4" Series #4, Cobra

	C6	C8	C10
Buzzer, Mercenary, 1984, No. 6433	10	25	50
Crimson Guard, Elite Trooper, 1984, No. 6450	15	30	60
Eel, Frogman, 1984, No. 6448	15	30	60
Ripper, Mercenary, 1984, No. 6434	15	30	60
Snow Serpent, Polar Assault Trooper, 1984, No. 6449	15	30	60
Tele-Viper, Communications Trooper, 1984, No. 6447	15	30	60
Tomax, Crimson Guard Commander w/Xamot, 1984, No. 6063	30	65	125
Torch, Mercenary, 1984, No. 6435	15	30	60

3-3/4" Series #4, G.I. Joe

	C6	C8	C10
Air Tight, Hostile Environment Trooper, 1984, No. 6439	20	40	85
Alpine, Mountain Trooper, 1984, No. 6443	15	25	50
Barbecue, Fire Fighter, 1984, No. 6445	10	25	50

3-3/4" Series #1, G.I. Joe

	C6	C8	C10
Breaker, Communications Officer, 1982, No. 6403	20	35	75
Flash, Laser Rifle Trooper, 1982, No. 6406	20	35	75
Grunt, Infantry Trooper, 1982, No. 6409	20	35	75
Rock 'n Roll, Machine Gunner, 1982, No. 6408	20	35	75
Scarlett, Counter Intelligence, 1982, No. 6407	40	85	175
Short Fuse, Mortar Soldier, 1982, No. 6402	20	35	75
Snake Eyes, Commando, 1982, No. 6404	40	85	175
Stalker, Ranger, 1982, No. 6401	25	35	100
Zap, Bazooka Soldier, 1982, No. 6405	20	35	75

3-3/4" Series #2, Cobra

	C6	C8	C10
Cobra, reissue, 1983, No. 6423	25	50	100
Cobra Commander, reissue, 1983, No. 6425	25	50	100
Cobra Officer, reissue, 1983, No. 6424	25	50	100
Destro, Enemy Weapons Supplier, 1983, No. 6427	25	50	75
Major Bludd, 1983, No. 6426	15	30	65

3-3/4" Series #2, G.I. Joe

	C6	C8	C10
Airborne, Helicopter Assault Trooper, 1983, No. 6411	15	35	75
Breaker, reissue, 1983, No. 6403	15	30	65
Doc, Medic, 1983, No. 6415	10	20	45
Duke, mail order; Master Sergeant, 1983	10	25	40
Flash, reissue, 1983, No. 6406	15	30	65
Grunt, reissue, 1983, No. 6409	15	30	65

	C6	C8	C10
Bazooka, Missile Specialist, 1984, No. 6438 10		25	50
Dusty, Desert Trooper, 1984, No. 6442 10		25	50
Flint, Warrant Officer, 1984, No. 6436 10		25	50
Footloose, Infantry Trooper, 1984, No. 6444 10		25	50
Lady Jaye, Covert Operations Officer, 1984, No. 6440 25		50	100
Quick Kick, Silent Weapons Martial Artist, 1984, No. 6441 20		40	85
Shipwreck, Sailor and Parrot, 1984, No. 6446 15		25	50
Snake Eyes, Commando and Wolf, 1984, No. 6437 30		60	125
Tripwire, Mine Detector, 1984, No. 6102 20		35	75

3-3/4" Series #5, Cobra

	C6	C8	C10
B.A.T. , Battle Android Trooper, 1985, No. 6456 10		15	35
Dr. Mindbender, Master of Mind Control, 1985, No. 6461 10		15	35
Monkey Wrench, Mercenary, 1985, No. 6460 10		15	35
Viper, Infantry Trooper, 1985, No. 6473 10		15	35
Zandar, Zartan's Brother Mercenary, 1985, No. 6457 10		15	35
Zarana, reissue w/earrings, 1985, No. 6472 30		65	125
Zarana, Zartan's Sister Mercenary, 1985, No. 6472 10		15	35

3-3/4" Series #5, G.I. Joe

	C6	C8	C10
Beach Head, Ranger, 1985, 6463 10		15	30
Dial Tone, Communications Expert, 1985, No. 6471 10		15	30
Hawk, Commander, 1985, No. 6468 10		15	30
Ice Berg, Snow Trooper, 1985, No. 6466 10		15	30
Leather Neck, Marine Gunner, 1985, No. 6458 10		15	30
Life Line, Rescue Trooper, 1985, No. 6465 .. 10		15	30
Low-Light, Night Spotter, 1985, No. 6459 .. 10		15	30
Main Frame, Computer Specialist, 1985, No. 6462 10		15	30
Road Block, Heavy Machine Gunner, 1985, No. 6467 10		15	30
Sci-Fi, Laser Trooper, 1985, No. 6469 10		15	30
Sgt. Slaughter, Mail order; Drill Instructor, 1985 10		15	30
Wet-Suit, Navy S.E.A.L., 1985, No. 6470 15		20	40

3-3/4" Series #6, Cobra

	C6	C8	C10
Big Boa, Troop Trainer, 1986-87, No. 6484 ... 5		10	20
Cobra Commander, Cobra Leader w/Battle Armor, 1986-87, No. 6474 10		15	30

G.I. Nurse, Action Girl Series, No. 8060, $4,000

	C6	C8	C10
Cobra-La Team, Three-figure set, 1986-87, No. 6154 20		40	75
Crocmaster, Reptile Trainer, 1986-87, No. 6487 10		15	30
Crystal Ball, Hypnotist, 1986-87, No. 6479 .. 5		10	20
Raptor, Falconer, 1986-87, No. 6485 5		10	20
Techno-Viper, Battlefield Technician, 1986-87, No. 6490 5		10	20

3-3/4" Series #6, G.I. Joe

	C6	C8	C10
Chuckles, Undercover M.P., 1986-87, No. 6482 3		5	10
Crazy Legs, Air Assault Trooper, 1986-87, No. 6475 10		15	30
Falcon, Green Beret, 1986-87, No. 6476 10		15	30
Fast Draw, Mobile Missile Specialist, 1986-87, No. 6488 10		15	25
Gung-Ho, Marine in Dress Blues, 1986-87, No. 6486 10		15	25
Jinx, Ninja Intelligence Officer, 1986-87, No. 6480 10		15	25
Law & Order, M.P. w/Dog, 1986-87, No. 6478 10		15	25
Outback, Survivalist, 1986-87, No. 6483 5		10	20
Psych-Out, Deceptive Warfare Trooper, 1986-87, No. 6477 5		10	20

Right to Left: Action Soldier, Action Soldier Series, No. 7500, $350; Action Sailor, Action Sailor Series, No. 7600, $350; Action Marine, Action Marine Series, No. 7700, $375; Action Pilot, Action Pilot Series, No. 7800, $600

	C6	C8	C10
Secret Mission: Brazil, Toys R Us set w/four figures, 1986-87	75	150	300
Sgt. Slaughter Set, Three-figure set, 1986-87, No. 6153	10	25	50
Sneak Peek, Advanced Recon Trooper, 1986-87, No. 6491	10	15	30
Tunnel Rat, Underground Explosive Expert, 1986-87, No. 6481	5	10	20

30th Salute Series

	C6	C8	C10
30th Salute Black Action Soldier, 1994, No. 81271	55	100	150
Action Marine, 1994, No. 81047	45	60	80
Action Pilot, 1994, No. 81046	50	75	125
Action Sailor, 1994, No. 81048	60	80	100
Action Soldier, 1994, No. 81045	25	50	95
Green Beret Lt. Joseph Cotton, mail order, 1994	75	125	175

Action Girl Series

	C6	C8	C10
G.I. Nurse, Red Cross hat and arm band, white dress, stockings, shoes, crutches, medic bag, stethoscope, plasma bottle, bandages and splints, 1967, No. 8060	1750	2000	4000

Action Marine Series

	C6	C8	C10
Action Marine, fatigues, green cap, boots, dog tags, insignias and manual, 1964, No. 7700	125	145	375
Marine Medic Series, Red Cross helmet, flag and arm bands, crutch, bandages, splints, first aid pouch, stethoscope, plasma bottle, stretcher, medic bag, belt w/ammo pouches, 1967, No. 90711	325	425	3250

	C6	C8	C10
Talking Action Marine, 1967, No. 7790	175	200	850
Talking Adventure Pack and Tent Set, 1968, No. 90711	275	325	3250
Talking Adventure Pack w/Field Pack Equipment, 1968, No. 90712	275	325	3250

Action Pilot Series

	C6	C8	C10
Action Pilot, Orange jumpsuit, blue cap, black boots, dog tags, insignias, manual, catalog and club, application, 1964, No. 7800	130	165	600
Talking Action Pilot, 1967, No. 7890	190	245	1500

Action Sailor Series

	C6	C8	C10
Action Sailor, White cap, denim shirt and pants, boots, dog tags, navy manual and insignias, 1964, No. 7600	125	225	350
Navy Scuba Set, Adventure Pack, 1968, No. 7643-83	300	450	3250
Talking Action Sailor, 1967, No. 7690	200	330	1250
Talking Landing Signal Officer Set, Talking Adventure Pack, 1968, No. 90621	325	350	3500
Talking Shore Patrol Set, Talking Adventure Pack, 1968, No. 90612	200	450	3500

Action Soldier Series

	C6	C8	C10
Action Soldier, Fatigue cap, shirt, pants, boots, dog tags, army manual and insignias, helmet, belt w/pouches, M-1 rifle, 1964, No. 7500	100	175	350
Black Action Soldier, 1965, No. 7900	450	800	2500
Canadian Mountie Set, Sears exclusive, 1967, No. 5904	850	1500	4000
Desert Patrol Attack Jeep Set, Desert Fighter figure, jeep w/steering wheel, spare tire, tan tripod, gun and gun mount and ring, black antenna, tan jacket and shorts, socks, goggles, 1967, No. 8030	400	1250	2000
Forward Observer Set, Sears exclusive, 1966, No. 5969	200	375	750
Green Beret, Field radio, bazooka rocket, bazooka, green beret, jacket, pants, M-16 rifle, grenades, camouflage scarf, belt pistol and holster, 1966, No. 7536	275	400	3000
Machine Gun Emplacement Set, Sears exclusive, 1965, No. 7531	150	275	1250
Talking Action Soldier, 1967, No. 7590	85	135	825
Talking Adventure Pack, Bivouac Equipment, 1968, No. 90513	275	325	3000
Talking Adventure Pack, Command Post Equip., 1968, No. 90517	275	375	3000

Astro Locker, G.I. Joe, $375

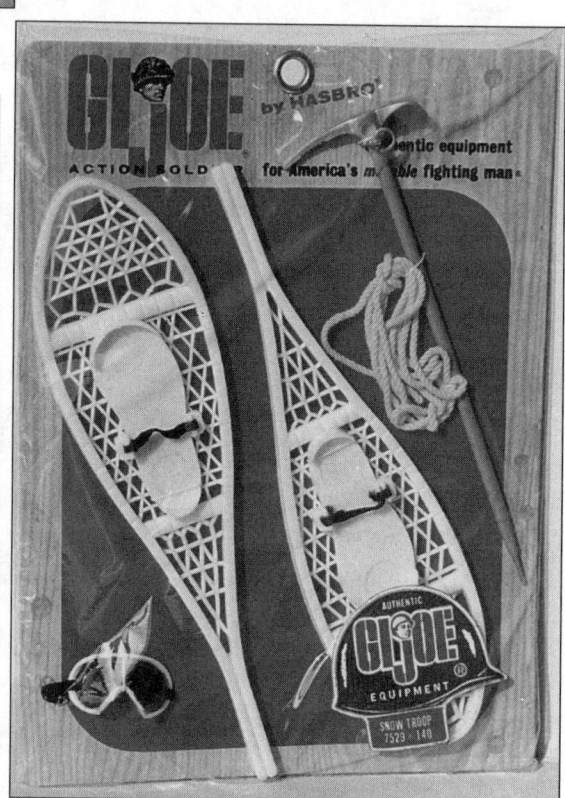

Action Soldier Snow Troop Set, 1966, $150

*Scarlett, Counter Intellligence, 3-3/4"
Series #1, $175*

Left to right: Land Adventurer, No. 7401, 1970, $200; Sea Adventurer, No. 7402, 1970, $245; Air Adventurer, No. 7403, 1970, $300; Black Adventurer, No. 7404. 1970, $375; Man of Action, No. 7500, 1970, $225

Left to Right: Land Adventurer, No. 7905, 1969, $1,000; Negro Adventurer, No. 7905, 1969, $2,750; Aquanaut, No. 7910, 1969, $3,000; Talking Astronaut, No. 7915, 1969, $1,000

Left to Right: Action Sailor No. 7600, 1964, $350; Australian Jungle Fighter, No. 8205, 1996, $2,500; Japanese Imperial Soldier, No. 8101, 1966, $2,700; Air Force Security Set, No. 7815, 1966, (doll not included), $590; Navy Attack Set, No. 7607, 1964, (doll not included), $425; Annapolis Cadet, 1967, $1,350; Green Beret, No. 7536, 1966, $3,000

Black Action Soldier, Action Soldier Series, No. 7900, $2,500

	C6	C8	C10
Talking Adventure Pack, Mountain Troop Series, 1968, No. 7557-83	375	650	3500
Talking Adventure Pack, Special Forces Equip., 1968, No. 90532	275	500	3500

Action Soldiers of the World

	C6	C8	C10
Australian Jungle Fighter, action figure w/jacket, shorts, socks, boots, knife, flamethrower, entrenching tool, bush knife, bush hat, belt, "Victoria Cross" medal, knuckle and sheath, 1966, No. 8105	250	400	2500
Australian Jungle Fighter, Standard set w/action figure uniform, no equipment, 1966, No. 8205	150	275	1200
British Commando, Standard set w/no equipment, 1966, No. 8204	150	275	1750
British Commando, Deluxe set w/action figure, helmet, night raid green jacket, pants, boots, canteen and cover, gas mask and cover, belt, Sten sub machine gun, gun clip and "Victoria Cross" medal, 1966, No. 8104	300	425	2500
Foreign Soldiers of the World, Talking Adventure Pack, 1968, No. 8111-83	750	825	5000

	C6	C8	C10
French Resistance Fighter, Standard set w/action figure and equipment, 1966, No. 8203	125	225	1250
French Resistance Fighter, Deluxe set w/figure, beret, short black boots, black sweater, denim pants, "Croix de Guerre" medal, knife, shoulder holster, pistol, radio, sub-machine gun and grenades, 1966, No. 8103	200	250	2250
German Storm Trooper, Standard set w/no equipment, 1966, No. 8200	275	325	130
German Storm Trooper, Deluxe set w/figure, helmet, jacket, pants, boots, Luger pistol, holster, cartridge belt, cartridges, "Iron Cross" medal, stick grenades, 9MMSchmeisser, field pack, 1966, No. 8100	275	425	2500
Japanese Imperial Soldier, Deluxe set w/figure, Arisaka rifle, belt, cartridges, field pack, Nambu pistol, holster, bayonet, "Order of the Kite" medal, helmet, jacket, pants, short brown boots, 1966, No. 8101	425	675	2700
Japanese Imperial Soldier, Standard set w/equipment, 1966, No. 8201	300	325	1425
Russian Infantry Man, Deluxe set w/action figure, fur cap, tunic, pants, boots, ammo box, ammo rounds, anti-tank grenades, belt, bipod, DP light machine gun, "Order of Lenin" medal, field glasses and case, 1966, No. 8102	275	400	2250
Russian Infantry Man, Standard set w/no equipment, 1966, No. 8202	315	400	1250
Uniforms of Six Nations, 1967, No. 5038	750	950	2500

Adventure Team

	C6	C8	C10
Air Adventurer, w/Kung Fu grip, 1974, No. 7282	95	125	325
Air Adventurer, includes figure w/Kung Fu grip, orange flight suit, boots, insignia, dog tags, rifle, boots, warranty, club insert, 1970, No. 7403	120	375	300
Air Adventurer, life-like body figure, uniform and equipment, 1976, No. 7282	75	100	200
Black Adventurer, w/life-like body and Kung Fu grip, 1976, No. 7283	85	125	225
Black Adventurer, includes figure, shirt w/insignia, pants, boots, dog tags, shoulder holster w/pistol, 1970, No. 7404	125	150	375
Bulletman, 1976, No. 8026	50	75	150
Eagle Eye Black Commando, 1976, No. 7278	85	125	250
Eagle Eye Land Commander, 1976, No. 7276	65	80	150

	C6	C8	C10
Eagle Eye Man of Action, 1976, No. 7277 ... 65		80	165
Intruder Commander, 1976, No. 8050 50		75	150
Intruder Warrior, 1976, No. 8051 50		75	175
Land Adventurer, 1976, No. 7280 35		50	150
Land Adventurer, w/life-like body and Kung Fu grip and uniform set, 1974, No. 7280 50		65	225
Land Adventurer, 1976, No. 7270 20		50	180
Land Adventurer, includes figure, camo shirt and pants, boots, insignia, shoulder holster and pistol, dog tags and team inserts, 1970, No. 7401 45		75	200
Man of Action, includes figure, shirt and pants, boots, insignia, dog tags, team inserts, 1970, No. 7500 50		75	225
Man of Action, figure w/life-like body and Kung Fu grip, 1974, No. 7284 45		75	200
Man of Action, 1976, No. 7274 25		45	175
Mike Powers/Atomic Man, figure w/"atomic" flashing eye, arm that spins hand-held helicopter, 1975, No. 8025 20		45	150
Sea Adventurer, includes figure, shirt, dungarees, insignia, boots, shoulder holster and pistol, 1970, No. 7402 45		70	245
Sea Adventurer, 1976, 7271 40		75	250
Sea Adventurer, w/life-like body and Kung Fu grip and uniform w/equipment, 1974, No. 7281 55		75	225

	C6	C8	C10
Sea Adventurer, 1976, No. 7281 55		85	200
Secret Mountain Outpost, 1975, No. 8040 50		85	150
Talking Adventure Team Black Commander, w/Kung Fu grip, 1974, No. 7291 85		350	750
Talking Adventure Team Black Commander, 1973, No. 7406 150		225	600
Talking Adventure Team Commander, includes figure, two-pocket green shirt, pants, boots, insignia, instructions, dog tag, shoulder holster and pistol, 1970, No. 7400 65		125	400
Talking Adventure Team Commander, w/Kung Fu grip, 1974, No. 290 75		200	500
Talking Astronaut, 1970, No. 7590 90		175	650
Talking Black Commander, 1976, No. 7291 125		300	600
Talking Commander, 1976, No. 7290 75		115	500
Talking Man of Action, 1976, No. 7292 75		120	525
Talking Man of Action, w/life-like body and Kung Fu grip, 1974, No. 7292 75		200	650
Talking Man of Action, shirt, pants, boots, dog tags, rifle, insignia, instructions, 1970, No. 7590 75		125	350

Adventures of G.I. Joe

	C6	C8	C10
Aquanaut, 1969, No. 7910 175		550	3000
Negro Adventurer, Sears exclusive, includes painted hair figure, blue jeans, pullover sweater, shoulder holster, and pistol, plus product letter from Sears, 1969, No. 7905 450		750	2750
Sharks Surprise Set w/Frogman, w/figure, orange scuba suit, blue sea sled, air tanks, harpoon, face mask, treasure chest, shark, instructions and comic, 1969, No. 7980 125		300	750
Talking Astronaut, hard-hand figure w/white coveralls w/insignias, white boots, dog tags, 1969, No. 7615 85		275	1000

Battle Corps

	C6	C8	C10
Alley-Viper, 1994, No. 81089 3		5	10
Beach-Head, 1994, No. 81088 3		5	10
Dialtone, 1994, No. 81002 3		5	10
Flint, 1994, No. 81001 3		5	10
Ice-Cream Soldier, 1994, No. 81004 3		5	10
Life-Line, 1994, No. 81007 3		5	10
Major Bludd, 1994, No. 81012 3		5	10
Metal-Head, 1994, No. 81005 3		5	10
Night Creeper Leader, 1994, No. 81098 3		5	10
Shipwreck, 1994, No. 81003 3		5	10
Snow Storm, 1994, No. 81097 3		5	10
Stalker, 1994, No. 81008 3		5	10
Viper, 1994, No. 81006 3		5	10

Talking Black Commander, Adventure Team, No. 7291, $600

G.I. Joe Extreme

	C6	C8	C10
Ballistic, 1995, No. 81168................ 5		6	8
Ballistic, 1995, No. 81209................ 7		8	10
Freight, 1995, No. 81176................. 5		6	8
Inferno, 1995, No. 81179................. 5		6	8
Iron Klaw, 1995, No. 81177............. 5		6	8
Iron Klaw (Deluxe), 1995, No. 81208.... 7		8	10
Lt. Stone, 1995, No. 81161............. 5		6	8
Lt. Stone (Deluxe), 1995, No. 81207 7		8	10
Lt. Stone vs. Iron Klaw, Super Deluxe, 1995, No. 81295 10		15	20
Metalhead, 1995, No. 81167............ 5		6	8
Metalhead (Deluxe), 1995, No. 81206.... 7		8	10
Sgt. Savage, 1995, No. 81162.......... 5		6	8

Shadow Ninja

	C6	C8	C10
Bushido, 1994, No. 81147............. 5		10	25
Night Creeper, 1994, No. 81146....... 5		10	25
Nunchuck, 1994, No. 81145........... 5		10	25
Slice, 1994, No. 81144............... 5		10	25
Snake-Eyes, 1994, No. 81141 5		10	25
Storm Shadow, 1994, No. 81142........ 5		10	25

Star Brigade/Cobra

	C6	C8	C10
Cobra Astro-Viper, 1993, No. 81105 5		10	25
Cobra Blackstar, 1994, No. 81057......... 5		10	25
Cobra Commander, 1994, No. 81056........ 5		10	25
Cobra TARGAT, 1993, No. 81106........ 5		10	25

Star Brigade/G.I. Joe

	C6	C8	C10
Carcass, 1994, No. 81061............. 5		10	25
Countdown, 1993, No. 81102......... 5		10	25
Countdown, 1994, No. 81119......... 5		10	25

Super Joe, No. 7503, $70

	C6	C8	C10
Duke, 1994, No. 81052.................. 5		10	25
Effects, 1994, No. 81054................ 5		10	25
Lobotomaxx, 1994, No. 81058......... 5		10	25
Ozone, 1993, No. 81103............... 5		10	25
Ozone, 1994, No. 81127............... 5		10	25
Payload, 1994, No. 81117............. 5		10	25
Payload, 1993, No. 81101............. 5		10	25
Predacon, 1994, No. 81059............ 5		10	25
Roadblock, 1994, No. 81118........... 5		10	25
Roadblock, 1993, No. 81104........... 5		10	25
Sci-Fi, 1994, No. 81053............... 5		10	25
Space Shot, 1994, No. 81055.......... 5		10	25

Super Joe

	C6	C8	C10
Gor, 1977, No. 7510 40		70	130
Luminos, 1977, No. 7506............. 45		70	130
Super Joe, 1977, No. 7503............ 20		35	70
Super Joe (Black), 1977, No. 7504.... 35		50	100
Super Joe Commander, 1977, No. 7501 25		45	75
The Shield, 1977, No. 7505........... 40		65	125

Uniform/Equipment Sets

3-3/4" Series #1, G.I. Joe

	C6	C8	C10
F.L.A.K., Attack Cannon, 1982, No. 6075 ... 20		45	90
H.A.L., Heavy Artillery Laser w/Grand Slam, 1982, No. 6052 20		45	90
J.U.M.P., Jet Pack w/Platform, 1982, No. 6071 20		45	90
M.M.S., Mobile Missile System w/Hawk, 1982, No. 6054 20		45	90

3-3/4" Series #2, Cobra

	C6	C8	C10
Headquarters Missile-Command Center, w/three figures, 1983, No. 6200............. 65		125	250
S.N.A.K.E., One-Man Battle Armor, 1983, No. 6083 10		25	50

3-3/4" Series #2, G.I. Joe

	C6	C8	C10
Battle Gear Accessory Pack #1, 1983, No. 6088 10		20	40
Headquarters Command Center, 1983, No. 6020 40		85	175
Jump, Jet Pack and Platform w/Grand Slam, 1983, No. 6065 25		50	100
Pac/Rats Flamethrower, Remote Control Weapon, 1983, No. 6086-1 10		25	50
Pac/Rats Machine Gun, remote Control Weapon, 1983, No. 6086-2 10		25	50
Pac/Rats Missile Launcher, remote Control Weapon, 1983, No. 6086-3 10		25	50
Whirlwind, Twin Battle Gun, 1983, No. 6074 10		25	45

	C6	C8	C10
3-3/4" Series #3, Cobra			
A.S.P., Assault System Pod, 1983, No. 6070	15	30	60
C.L.A.W., Cobra Covert Light Aerial Weapons, 1983, No. 6081-1	15	30	60
S.N.A.K.E., ne-Man Armored Suit (white), 1983, No. 6081-2	10	25	50
3-3/4" Series #3, G.I. Joe			
Battle Gear Accessory Pack #2, 1983, No. 6092	10	20	40
Bivouac, Battle Station, 1983, No. 6125-1	10	25	35
Machine Gun Defense Unit, 1983, No. 6129-2	10	20	40
Manta, mail order; Marine Assault Nautical Air Driven Transport, 1983	10	20	35
Missile Defense Unit, 1983, No. 6129-1	10	15	25
Mortar Defense Unit, 1983, No. 6129-3	10	15	25
Mountain Howitzer, 1983, No. 6125-3	10	15	25
Parachute, mail order; Parachute Pack w/Working Parachute, 1983	5	10	20
Watchtower, 1983, No. 6125-2	10	15	25
3-3/4" Series #4, Cobra			
Cobra Bunker, 1984, No. 6125	5	15	25
Flight Pod, One-Man Bubble Pod, 1984, No. 6081	5	15	25
Night Landing, Mini Battlefield Vehicles Assortment, 1984, No. 6085	5	15	25
Rifle Range, 1984, No. 6129	5	15	25
3-3/4" Series #4, G.I. Joe			
Air Defense, 1984, No. 6125-2	10	15	25
Ammo Dump, 1984, No. 6129-1	10	15	25
Battle Gear Accessory Pack #3, 1984, No. 6092	5	10	15
Bomb Disposal, 1984, No. 6085-2	10	15	25
Check Point, 1984, No. 6125-1	10	15	25
Forward Observer, 1984, No. 6129-2	10	15	25
Tactical Battle Platform, 1984, No. 6021	10	20	40
Weapon Transport, Battlefield, 1984, No. 6085-1	10	15	25
3-3/4" Series #5, Cobra			
Battle Gear Accessory Pack #4, 1985, No. 6096	5	10	15
Surveillance Port Playset, 1985, No. 6130	15	30	75
Terror Drome, Armored Headquarters w/Fireball Jet and A.V.A.C., 1985, No. 6003	75	150	300
3-3/4" Series #5, G.I. Joe			
Outpost Defender Mini Play Set, 1985, No. 6130	5	10	15
3-3/4" Series #6, Cobra			
Earth Borer, 1986, No. 6133-3	5	10	15

	C6	C8	C10
Mountain Climber, 1986, No. 6133-7	5	10	15
Pom-Pom Gun Pack, 1986, No. 6133-8	5	10	15
Rope Crosser, 1986, No. 6133-5	5	10	15
3-3/4" Series #6, G.I. Joe			
Antiaircraft Gun, 1986, No. 6133-1	5	10	15
Battle Gear Accessory Pack #5, 1986, No. 6677	5	10	15
Helicopter Pack, 1986, No. 6133-2	5	10	15
Mobile Command Center Play Set, 1986, No. 6006	25	50	100
Rope Walker, 1986, No. 6133-4	5	10	15
S.L.A.M., Strategic Long-Range Artillery Machine, 1986, No. 6172	10	15	30
Vehicle Gear Accessory Pack #1, 1986, No. 6098	5	10	15
Action Marine Series			
Beachhead Assault Field Pack Set, M-1 rifle, bayonet, entrenching shovel and cover, canteen w/cover, belt, mess kit w/cover, field pack, flamethrower, first aid pouch, tent, pegs and poles, tent camo and camo, 1964, No. 7713	100	175	325
Beachhead Assault Tent Set, Tent, flamethrower, pistol belt, first-aid pouch, mess kit w/utensils and manual, 1964, No. 7711	100	200	475
Beachhead Fatigue Pants, 1964, No. 7715	15	30	200
Beachhead Fatigue Shirt, 1964, No. 7714	20	30	225
Beachhead Field Pack, Cartridge belt, rifle, grenades, field pack, entrenching tool, canteen and manual, 1964, No. 7712	40	65	150
Beachhead Flamethrower Set, reissue, 1967, No. 7718	15	30	225
Beachhead Flamethrower Set, 1964, No. 7718	15	30	125
Beachhead Mess Kit Set, 1964, No. 7716	25	40	275
Beachhead Rifle Set, reissue, 1967, No. 7717	30	50	225
Beachhead Rifle Set, Bayonet, cartridge belt, hand grenades and M-1 rifle, 1964, No. 7717	30	50	150
Communications Field Radio/Telephone Set, reissue, 1967, No. 7703	35	60	275
Communications Field Set, 1964, No. 7703	35	50	175
Communications Flag Set, Flags for Army, Navy, Air Corps, Marines and United States, 1964, No. 7704	200	250	475
Communications Poncho, 1964, No. 7702	35	50	250
Communications Post and Poncho Set, Field radio and telephone, wire roll, carbine, binoculars, map, case, manual, poncho, 1964, No. 7701	125	175	475

	C6	C8	C10
Dress Parade Set, Marine jacket, trousers, pistol belt, shoes, hat, M-1 rifle and manual, 1964, No. 7710 125	225	450
Dress Parade Set, reissue, 1968, No. 7710 125	225	750
Jungle Fighter Set, reissue, 1968, No. 7732 450	700	2750
Jungle Fighter Set, Bush hat, jacket w/emblems, pants, flamethrower, field telephone, knife and sheath, pistol belt, pistol, holster, canteen w/cover and knuckle knife, 1967, No. 7732....... 450	700	3500
Marine Automatic M-60 Machine Gun Set, 1967, No. 7726 35	75	325
Marine Basics Set, 1966, No. 7722............... 55	85	275
Marine Bunk Bed Set, 1966, No. 7723 55	80	375
Marine Bunk Bed Set, reissue, 1967, No. 7723 55	80	475
Marine Demolition Set, reissue, 1968, No. 7730 50	100	450
Marine Demolition Set, mine detector and harness, land mine, 1966, No. 7730 50	100	350
Marine First Aid Set, First-aid pouch, arm band and helmet, 1964, No. 7721 45	85	125
Marine First Aid Set, reissue, 1967, No. 7721 45	85	225
Marine Medic Set, reissue, 1967, No. 7720 25	40	225
Marine Medic Set, w/crutch, etc., 1965, No. 7720 25	40	125
Marine Medic Set w/stretcher, First-aid shoulder pouch, stretcher, bandages, arm bands, plasma bottle, stethoscope, Red Cross flag, and manual, 1964, No. 7719 175	300	850
Marine Mortar Set, 1967, No. 7725............. 60	80	350
Marine Weapons Rack Set, 1967, No. 7727 75	145	625
Paratrooper Camouflage Set, netting and foliage, 1964, No. 7708........................ 20	35	65
Paratrooper Helmet Set, 1964, No. 7707..... 20	40	85
Paratrooper Parachute Pack, 1964, No. 7709 30	80	125
Paratrooper Small Arms Set, reissue, 1967, No. 7706 30	75	225
Tank Commander Set, reissue, 1968, No. 7731 325	500	1525
Tank Commander Set, includes faux leather jacket, helmet and visor, insignia, radio w/tripod, machine gun, ammo box, 1967, No. 7731.................. 325	500	1750

Action Pilot Series

	C6	C8	C10
Air Academy Cadet Set, deluxe set w/figure, dress jacket, shoes, and			
pants, garrison cap, saber and scabbard, white M-1 rifle, chest sash and belt sash, 1967, No. 7822 225	450	1250
Air Academy Cadet Set, reissue, 1968, No. 7822 225	450	1150
Air Force Basics Set, reissue, 1967, No. 7814 30	55	275
Air Force Basics Set, 1966, No. 7814 30	55	200
Air Force Mae West Air Vest & Equipment Set, 1967, No. 7816 85	125	325
Air Force Police Set, reissue, 1967, No. 7813 70	150	325
Air Force Police Set, 1965, No. 7813............ 70	150	250
Air Force Security Set, Air Security radio and helmet, cartridge belt, pistol and holster, 1967, No. 7815 275	350	590
Air/Sea Rescue Set, reissue, 1968, No. 7825 325	550	2500
Air/Sea Rescue Set, includes black air tanks, rescue ring, buoy, depth gauge, face mask, fins, orange scuba outfit, 1967, No. 7825 325	550	2500
Astronaut Set, Helmet w/visor, foil space suit, booties, gloves, space camera, propellant gun, tether cord, oxygen chest pack, silver boots, white jumpsuit and cloth cap, 1967, No. 7824 100	200	3000
Astronaut Set, reissue, 1968, No. 7824...... 100	200	1250
Communications Set, 1964, No. 7812.......... 55	100	225
Crash Crew Set, fire proof jacket, hood, pants and gloves, silver boots, belt, flashlight, axe, pliers, fire extinguisher, stretcher, strap cutter, 1966, No. 7820..... 125	250	450
Dress Uniform Jacket Set, 1964, No. 7804 .. 40	65	250
Dress Uniform Pants, 1964, No. 7805 20	35	200
Dress Uniform Set, Air Force jacket, trousers, shirt, tie, cap and manual, 1964, No. 803 225	450	3000
Dress Uniform Shirt & Equipment Set, 1964, No. 7806 25	40	200
Fighter Pilot Set, reissue, 1968, No. 7823 .. 400	650	2650
Fighter Pilot Set, working parachute and pack, gold helmet, Mae West vest, green pants, flash light, orange jump suit, black boots, 1967, No. 7823 400	650	2500
Scramble Communications Set, reissue, 1967, No. 7812 35	75	250
Scramble Communications Set, Poncho, field telephone and radio, map w/case, binoculars and wire roll, 1965, No. 7812 35	75	175
Scramble Crash Helmet, helmet, face mask, hose, tinted visor, 1964, No. 7810 65	90	125

	C6	C8	C10
Scramble Crash Helmet, reissue, 1967, No. 7810	65	90	225
Scramble Flight Suit, gray flight suit, 1964, No. 7808	50	300	225
Scramble Flight Suit, 1967, No. 7808	50	75	400
Scramble Parachute Set, 1964, No. 7811	20	40	150
Scramble Parachute Set, reissue, 1967, No. 7809	20	40	250
Scramble Set, Deluxe set, gray flight suit, orange air vest, white crash helmet, pistol beltw/.45 pistol, holster, clipboard, flare gun and parachute w/insert, 1964, No. 7807	125	225	950
Survival Life Raft Set, Raft w/oar and sea anchor, 1964, No. 7802	45	90	325
Survival Life Raft Set, Raft w/oar, flare gun, knife, air vest, first-aid kit, sea anchor and manual, 1964, No. 7801	75	125	550

Action Sailor Series

	C6	C8	C10
Annapolis Cadet, reissue, 1968, No. 7624	275	375	1350
Annapolis Cadet, Garrison cap, dress jacket, pants, shoes, sword, scabbard, belt and white M-1 rifle, 1967, No. 7624	275	375	1350
Breeches Buoy, reissue, 1968, sword, scabbard, belt and white M-1 rifle, No. 7625	325	425	1450
Breeches Buoy, yellow jacket and pants, chair and pulley, flare gun, blinker light, 1967, No. 7625	325	425	1500
Deep Freeze, reissue, 1968, No. 7623	250	375	1500
Deep Freeze White boots, fur parka, pants, snow shoes, ice axe, snow sled w/rope and flare gun, 1967, axe, snow sled w/rope and flare gun, No. 7623	250	375	1600
Deep Sea Diver Set, reissue, 1968, No. 7620	325	425	2000
Deep Sea Diver Set, Underwater uniform, helmet, upper and lower plate, sledge hammer, buoy w/rope, gloves, compass, hoses, lead boots and weight belt, 1965, No. 7620	325	425	2000
Frogman Scuba Bottoms, 1964, No. 7604	20	35	100
Frogman Scuba Tank Set, 1964, No. 7606	25	40	100
Frogman Scuba Top Set, 1964, No. 7603	25	45	125
Frogman Underwater Headpiece, face mask, swim fins, rubber suit, Demolition Set scuba tank, depth gauge, knife, dynamite and manual, 1964, No. 7602	175	250	1500
Landing Signal Officer jumpsuit, signal paddles, goggles, cloth head gear, headphones, clipboard (complete),			

	C6	C8	C10
binoculars and flare gun, 1966, No. 7621	225	350	575
Navy Attack Helmet Set, shirt and pants, boots, yellow life vest, blue helmet, flare gun binoculars, signal flags, 1964, No. 7610	35	75	150
Navy Attack Life Jacket, 1964, no. 7611	20	45	120
Navy Attack Set, life jacket, field glasses, blinker light, signal flags, manual, 1964, No. 7607	60	125	425
Navy Attack Work Pants Set, 1964, No. 7609	25	40	150
Navy Attack Work Shirt Set, 1964, No. 7608	25	40	175
Navy Basics Set, 1966, No. 7628	25	55	125
Navy Dress Parade Rifle Set, 1965, No. 7619	35	65	125
Navy Dress Parade Set, Billy club, cartridge belt, bayonet and white dress rifle, 1964, No. 7619	45	80	175
Navy L.S.O. Equipment Set helmet, headphones, signal paddles, flare gun, 1966, No. 7626	40	80	150
Navy Life Ring Set U.S.N. life ring, helmet sticker, 1966, No. 7627	25	45	150
Navy Machine Gun Set, MG and ammo box, 1965, No. 7618	40	80	175
Sea Rescue Set, life raft, oar, anchor, flare gun, first-aid kit, knife, scabbard, manual, 1964, No. 7601	95	135	500
Sea Rescue Set, reissued w/life preserver, 1966, No. 7622	95	135	500
Shore Patrol, reissued w/radio and helmet and shoes, 1967, No. 7612	1000	2000	3500
Shore Patrol, dress shirt, tie and pants, helmet, white belt, and holster, billy club, boots, arm band, sea bag, .45, 1964, No. 7612	500	1000	2000
Shore Patrol Dress Jumper Set, 1964, No. 7613	75	125	225
Shore Patrol Dress Pant Set, 1964, No. 7614	40	75	175
Shore Patrol Helmet and Small Arms Set, white belt, billy stick, white helmet and .45 pistol, 1964, No. 7616	40	75	150
Shore Patrol Sea Bag Set, 1964, No. 7615	25	50	125

Action Soldier Series

	C6	C8	C10
Adventure Pack w/12 items, Adventure Pack Footlocker, 1968, No. 8006.83	75	125	600
Adventure Pack w/12 items, Adventure Pack Footlocker, 1968, No. 8005.83	75	125	600
Adventure Pack w/14 pieces, Adventure Pack Footlocker, 1968, No. 8008.83	75	125	600

	C6	C8	C10
Adventure Pack w/16 items, Adventure Pack Footlocker, 1968, No. 8007.83 75		125	600
Adventure Pack, Army Bivouac Series, 1968, No. 7549-83 225		450	3500
Air Police Equipment, gray field phone, carbine, white helmet and bayonet, 1964, No. 7813 40		95	200
Basic Footlocker, wood tray w/cardboard wrapper, 1964, No. 8000 35		75	125
Bivouac Deluxe Pup Tent Set, M-1 rifle and bayonet, shovel and cover, canteen and cover, mess kit, cartridge belt, machine gun, tent, pegs, poles, camouflage, sleeping bag, netting, ammo box, 1964, No. 7513 115		225	450
Bivouac Machine Gun Set, machine gun set and ammo box, 1964, No. 7514 25		40	125
Bivouac Machine Gun Set, reissue, 1967, No. 7514 25		40	225
Bivouac Sleeping Bag, zippered bag, 1964, No. 7515 20		30	125
Bivouac Sleeping Bag Set, mess kit, canteen, bayonet, cartridge belt, M-1 rifle, manual, 1964, No. 7512 25		30	150
Combat Camouflaged Netting Set, foliage and posts, 1964, No. 7511 25		40	85
Combat Construction Set, orange safety helmet, work gloves, jack hammer, 1967, No. 7572 325		400	575
Combat Demolition Set, 1967, No. 7573 65		100	525
Combat Engineer Set, pick, shovel, detonator, dynamite, tripod and transit w/grease gun, 1967, No. 7571 125		175	625
Combat Fatigue Pants Set, 1964, No. 7504 15		25	110
Combat Fatigue Shirt Set, 1964, No. 7503 20		30	125
Combat Field Jacket, 1964, No. 7505 45		65	325
Combat Field Jacket Set, Jacket, bayonet, cartridge belt, hand grenades, M-1 rifle and manual, 1964, No. 7501 65		100	525
Combat Field Pack and Entrenching Tool, 1964, No. 7506 25		45	125
Combat Field Pack Deluxe Set, field jacket, pack, entrenching shovel w/cover, mess kit, first-aid pouch, canteen w/cover, 1964, No. 7502 75		125	325
Combat Helmet Set, w/netting and foliage leaves, 1964, No. 7507 20		35	75
Combat Mess Kit, plate, fork, knife, spoon, canteen, etc., 1964, No. 7509 20		45	85

	C6	C8	C10
Combat Rifle and Helmet Set bayonet, M-1 rifle, belt and grenades, 1967, No. 7510 55		100	325
Combat Sandbags Set, three bags per set, 1964, No. 7508 10		40	85
Command Post Field Radio and Telephone Set, Field radio, telephone w/wire roll and map, 1964, 7520 35		70	135
Command Post Field Radio and Telephone Set, reissue, 1967, No. 7520 35		70	400
Command Post Poncho, on card, 1964, No. 7519 30		45	225
Command Post Poncho Set, Poncho, field radio and telephone, wire roll, pistol, belt and holster, map and case and manual, 1964, No. 7517 85		125	400
Command Post Small Arms Set, Holster and .45 pistol, belt, grenades, 1964, No. 7518 30		60	100
Dress Parade Adventure Pack, Adventure Pack w/37 pieces, 1968, No. 8009.83 750		1250	3500
Green Beret and Small Arms Set, 1966, No. 7533 85		110	300
Green Beret and Small Arms Set, reissue, 1967, No. 7533 85		100	425
Green Beret Machine Gun Outpost Set, Sears exclusive w/two figures and equipment, 1966, No. 5978 225		450	1500

Green Beret Machine Gun Outpost Set, Action Soldier Series, No. 5978, $1,500

	C6	C8	C10
Heavy Weapons Set, mortar launcher and shells, M-60 machine gun, grenades, flak jacket, shirt and pants, 1967, No. 7538	175	325	1750
Heavy Weapons Set, reissue, 1968, No. 7538	175	325	1500
Military Police Duffle Bag Set, 1964, No. 7523	25	40	85
Military Police Helmet and Small Arms Set, reissue, 1967, No. 7526	35	75	250
Military Police Helmet and Small Arms Set, 1964, No. 7526	35	75	125
Military Police Ike Jacket, Jacket w/red scarf and arm band, 1964, No. 7524	40	60	125
Military Police Ike Pants, Matches Ike jacket, 1964, No. 7525	20	30	100
Military Police Uniform Set, includes green or tan uniform, black and gold MP Helmet, billy club, belt, pistol and holster, MP armband and red tunic, 1967, No. 7539	450	1650	3500
Military Police Uniform Set, reissue, 1968, No. 7539	450	900	3000
Military Police Uniform Set, includes Ike jacket and pants, scarf, boots, helmet, belt w/ammo pouches, .45 pistol and holster, billy club, armband, duffle bag, 1964, No. 7521	450	1650	3000
Mountain Troops Set, snow shoes, ice axe, ropes, grenades, camouflage pack, web belt, manual, 1964, No. 7530	90	175	350
Sabotage Set, reissued in photo box, 1968, No. 7516	125	250	1700
Sabotage Set, dingy and oar, blinker light, detonator w/strap, TNT, wool			

Military Police Uniform Set, Action Soldier Series, No. 7521, $3,000

	C6	C8	C10
stocking cap, gas mask, binoculars, green radio and .45 pistol and holster, 1967, No. 7516	125	250	2000
Ski Patrol Deluxe Set, White parka, boots, goggles, mittens, skis, poles and manual, 1964, No. 7531	170	350	1250
Ski Patrol Helmet and Small Arms Set, 1965, No. 7527	35	75	135
Ski Patrol Helmet and Small Arms Set, reissue, 1967, No. 7527	75	125	250
Snow Troop Set, reissue, 1967, No. 7529	20	45	225
Snow Troop Set, snow shoes, goggles and ice pick, 1966, No. 7529	20	45	150
Special Forces Bazooka Set, 1966, No. 7528	35	45	225
Special Forces Bazooka Set, reissue, 1967, No. 7528	35	45	325
Special Forces Uniform Set, 1966, No. 7532	200	375	1000
West Point Cadet Uniform Set, Dress jacket, pants, shoes, chest and belt sash, parade hat w/plume, saber, scabbard and white M-1 rifle, 1967, No. 7537	250	475	1500
West Point Cadet Uniform Set, reissue, 1968, No. 7537	250	375	1200

Action Soldiers of the World

	C6	C8	C10
Australian Jungle Fighter Set, 1966, No. 8305	25	50	250
British Commando Set, Sten submachine gun, gas mask and carrier, canteen and cover, cartridge belt, rifle, "Victoria Cross" medal, manual, 1966, No. 8304	125	200	325
French Resistance Fighter Set, shoulder holster, Lebel pistol, knife, grenades, radio, 7.65 submachine gun, "Croix de Guerre" medal, counter-intelligence manual, 1966, No. 8303	25	50	275
German Storm Trooper, 1966, No. 8300	125	175	325
Japanese Imperial Soldier Set, field pack, Nambu pistol and holster, Arisaka rifle w/bayonet, cartridge belt, "Order of the Kite" medal, counter-intelligence manual, 1966, No. 8301	175	275	625
Russian Infantry Man Set, DP light machine gun, bipod, field glasses and case, anti-tank grenades, ammo box, "Order of Lenin" medal, counter-intelligence medal, 1966, No. 8302	175	220	325

Adventure Team

	C6	C8	C10
Adventure Team Headquarters Set, Adventure Team play set, 1972, No. 7490	50	125	200
Adventure Team Training Center Set, rifle rack, logs, barrel, barber wire, rope ladder, three tires, two targets, escape slide, tent and poles, first aid kit, respirator and mask, snake, instructions, 1973, No. 7495	75	125	225
Aerial Reconnaissance Set, jumpsuit, helmet, aerial recon vehicle w/built-in camera, 1971, No. 7345	75	125	225
Attack at Vulture Falls, Super Deluxe Set, 1975, No. 7420	75	150	275
Black Widow Rendezvous, Super Deluxe Set, 1975, No. 7414	125	200	350
Buried Bounty, Deluxe Set, 1975, No. 7328-5	10	25	85
Capture of the Pygmy Gorilla Set, 1970, No. 7437	100	175	325
Challenge of Savage River, Deluxe Set, 1975, No. 8032	100	175	350
Chest Winch Set, reissue, 1974, No. 7313	10	15	75
Chest Winch Set, 1972, No. 7313	10	15	40
Command Para Drop, Deluxe Set, 1975, No. 8033	200	300	550
Copter Rescue Set, blue jumpsuit, red binoculars, 1973, No. 7308-3	15	20	30
Danger of the Depths Set, 1970, No. 7412	100	175	325
Danger Ray Detection, magnetic ray detector, solar communicator w/headphones, two-piece uniform, instructions and comic, 1975, No. 7338-1	45	90	225
Dangerous Climb Set, 1973, No. 7309-2	20	35	75
Dangerous Mission Set, green shirt, pants, hunting rifle, 1973, No. 7608-5	20	35	75
Demolition Set, armored suit, face shield, bomb, bomb disposal box, extension grips, 1971, No. 7370	20	45	125
Demolition Set, w/land mines, mine detector and carrying case w/metallic suit, 1971, No. 7371	75	100	250
Desert Explorer Set, 1973, No. 7309-5	20	40	80
Desert Survival Set, 1973, No. 7308-6	20	40	80
Dive to Danger, Mike Powers set, orange scuba suit, fins, mask, spear gun, shark, buoy, knife and scabbard, mini sled, air tanks, comic, 1975, No. 8031	150	250	450
Diver's Distress, 1975, No. 7328-6	35	70	125

	C6	C8	C10
Drag Bike Set, three-wheel motorcycle brakes down to backpack size, 1971, No. 7364	25	65	125
Eight Ropes of Danger Set, 1970, No. 7422	125	225	375
Emergency Rescue Set, shirt, pants, rope ladder and hook, walkie-talkie, safety belt, flashlight, oxygen tank, axe, first aid kit, 1971, No. 7374	45	75	150
Equipment Tester Set, 1972, No. 7319-5	15	20	40
Escape Car Set, 1971, No. 7360	30	60	85
Escape Slide Set, 1972, No. 7319-1	15	25	40
Fangs of the Cobra, Deluxe Set, 1975, No. 8028-2	125	200	375
Fantastic Freefall Set, 1970, No. 7423	125	200	375
Fight For Survival Set, w/blue parka, 1970, No. 7431	300	550	2500
Fight for Survival Set, brown shirt and pants, machete, 1973, No. 7308-2	20	30	45
Fight for Survival Set w/Polar Explorer, 1969, No. 7982	250	450	850
Fire Fighter Set, 1971, No. 7351	20	30	55
Flying Rescue Set, 1971, No. 7361	35	60	85
Flying Space Adventure Set, 1970, No. 7425	400	600	1000
Footlocker, green plastic w/cardboard wrapper, 1974, No. 8000	35	70	225
Green Danger, 1975, No. 7328-4	30	45	60
Hidden Missile Discovery Set, 1970, No. 7415	100	200	450
Hidden Treasure Set, shirt, pants, pick axe, shovel, 1973, No. 7308-1	15	25	40
High Voltage Escape Set, net, jumpsuit, hat, wrist meter, wire cutters, wire, warning sign, 1971, No. 7342	40	75	150
Hurricane Spotter Set, slicker suit, rain measure, portable radar, map and case, binoculars, 1971, No. 7343	55	80	175
Jaws of Death, Super Deluxe Set, 1975, No. 7421	325	500	650
Jettison to Safety, infrared terrain scanner, mobile rocket pack, two-piece flight suit, instructions and comic, 1975, No. 7339-2	85	200	275
Jungle Ordeal Set, 1973, No. 7309-3	15	25	45
Jungle Survival Set, 1971, No. 7373	15	25	45
Karate Set, 1971, No. 7372	35	70	125
Laser Rescue Set, reissue, 1974, No. 7311	20	35	100
Laser Rescue Set, hand-held laser w/backpack generator, 1972, No. 7311	20	35	45
Life-Line Catapult Set, 1971, No. 7353	15	25	40
Long Range Recon, Deluxe Set, 1975, No. 7328-3	10	20	35

	C6	C8	C10
Magnetic Flaw Detector Set, 1972, No. 7319-2	10	20	30
Mine Shaft Breakout, sonic rock blaster, chest winch, two-piece uniform, netting, instructions, comic, 1975, No. 7339-3	70	125	250
Missile Recovery Set, 1971, No. 7340	40	55	85
Mystery of the Boiling Lagoon, Sears, pontoon boat, diver's suit, diver's helmet, weighted belt and boots, depth gauge, air hose, buoy, nose cone, pincer arm, instructions, 1973	150	200	225
Night Surveillance, Deluxe Set, 1975, No. 7338-2	35	45	90
Peril of the Raging Inferno, fireproof suit, hood and boots, breathing apparatus, camera, fire extinguisher, detection, meter, gaskets, 1975, No. 7416	85	150	275
Photo Reconnaissance Set, 1973, No. 7309-4	20	30	45
Race for Recovery, 1975, No. 8028-1	20	35	125
Radiation Detection Set, jumpsuit w/belt, "uranium ore," goggles, container, pincer arm, 1971, No. 7341	30	50	85
Raging River Dam Up, 1975, No. 7339-1	60	90	150
Rescue Raft Set, 1971, No. 7350	15	20	65
Revenge of the Spy Shark, Super Deluxe Set, 1975, No. 7413	50	175	400
Rock Blaster, sonic blaster w/tripod, backpack generator, face shield, 1972, No. 7312	10	20	35
Rocket Pack Set, reissue, 1974, No. 7315	10	20	50
Rocket Pack Set, 1972, No. 7315	10	20	75
Sample Analyzer Set, 1972, No. 7319-3	10	20	45
Search for the Abominable Snowman Set, Sears, white suit, belt, goggles, gloves, rifle, skis and poles, snow shoes, sled, rope, net, supply chest, binoculars, Abominable Snowman, comic book, 1973, No. 7439.16	110	175	350
Secret Agent Set, 1971, No. 7375	30	55	175
Secret Courier, 1975, No. 7328-1	45	65	135
Secret Mission Set, 1973, No. 7309-1	45	65	135
Secret Mission Set, Deluxe Set, 1975, No. 8030	65	95	200
Secret Mission to Spy Island Set, comic, inflatable raft w/oar, binoculars, signal light, flare gun, TNT and detonator, wire roll, boots, pants, sweater, black cap, camera, radio w/earphones, .45 submachine gun, 1970, No. 7411	75	125	250
Secret Rendezvous Set, parka, pants, flare gun, No. 1973, 7308-4	10	20	35
Seismograph Set, 1972, No. 7319-6	10	20	35

Sky Dive to Danger, Upper Deluxe Set, Action Soldiers of the World, No. 7440, $325

	C6	C8	C10
Shocking Escape, escape slide, chest pack climber, jumpsuit w/gloves and belt, high voltage sign, instructions and comic, 1975, No. 7338-3	25	65	125
Signal Flasher Set, large back pack type signal flash unit, 1971, No. 7362	15	30	50
Sky Dive to Danger, Super Deluxe Set, 1975, No. 7440	90	150	325
Solar Communicator Set, reissue, 1974, No. 7314	10	20	95
Solar Communicator Set, 1972, No. 7314	10	20	35
Sonic Rock Blaster Set, 1972, No. 7312	10	20	35
Sonic Rock Blaster Set, reissue, 1974, No. 7312	10	20	35
Special Assignment, Deluxe Set, 1975, No. 8028-3	30	55	135
Thermal Terrain Scanner Set, 1972, No. 7319-4	25	35	50
Three-in-One Super Adventure Set, Danger of the Depths, Secret Mission to Spy Island and Flying Space Adventure Packs, 1971, No. 7480	550	975	1250
Three-in-One Super Adventure Set, Cold of the Arctic, Heat of the Desert and Danger of the Jungle, 1971, No. 7480	250	400	750
Thrust into Danger, Deluxe Set, 1975, No. 7328-2	45	55	175
Trouble at Vulture Pass, Sears exclusive, Super Deluxe Set, 1975, No. 59289	75	125	325
Turbo Copter Set, strap-on one man helicopter, 1971, No. 7363	15	35	65

	C6	C8	C10
Undercover Agent Set, trenchcoat and belt, walkie-talkie, 1973, No. 7309-6 15		30	35
Underwater Demolition Set, hand-held propulsion device, breathing apparatus, dynamite, 1972, No. 7310 15		20	40
Underwater Demolition Set, reissue, 1974, No. 7310 10		20	75
Underwater Explorer Set, self propelled underwater device, 1971, No. 7354 15		30	60
Volcano Jumper Set, jumpsuit w/hood, belt, nylon rope, chest pack, TNT pack, 1971, No. 7344 45		80	250
White Tiger Hunt Set, hunter's jacket and pants, hat, rifle, tent, cage, chain, campfire, white tiger, comic, 1970, No. 7436 80		125	275
Windboat Set, back pack, sled w/wheels, sail, 1971, No. 7353 10		25	55
Winter Rescue Set, Replaced Photo Reconnaissance Set, 1973, No. 7309-4 40		75	150

Adventures of G.I. Joe

	C6	C8	C10
Adventure Locker, Footlocker, 1969, No. 7940 80		165	350
Aqua Locker, Footlocker, 1969, No. 7941 90		180	375
Astro Locker, Footlocker, 1969, No. 7942 90		180	375
Danger of the Depths Underwater Diver Set, 1969, No. 7920 140		275	500
Eight Ropes of Danger Set, diving suit, treasure chest, octopus, 1969, No. 7950 110		225	525
Fantastic Freefall Set, includes figure w/parachute and pack, blinker light, air vest, flash light, crash helmet w/visor and oxygen mask, dog tags, orange jump suit, black boots, 1969, No. 7951 150		325	675
Flight for Survival Set w/o Polar Explorer, reissue, 1969, No. 7982.83 150		300	500
Hidden Missile Discovery Set, 1969, No. 7952 70		135	400
Mouth of Doom Set, 1969, No. 7953 125		250	550
Mysterious Explosion Set, basic, 1969, No. 7921 60		125	425
Perilous Rescue Set, basic, 1969, No. 7923 150		300	500
Secret Mission to Spy Island Set, basic, 1969, No. 7922 110		225	450

G.I. Joe Action Series, Army, Navy, Marine and Air Force

	C6	C8	C10
Basic Footlocker, 1965, No. 8000 50		75	175
Footlocker Adventure Pack, sixteen pieces, 1968, No. 8000.83 65		135	450
Footlocker Adventure Pack, twenty-two pieces, 1968, No. 8002.83 70		145	450
Footlocker Adventure Pack, fifteen pieces, 1968, No. 8001.83 65		135	450
Footlocker Adventure Pack, 15 pieces, 1968, No. 8002.83 65		135	450

Super Joe

	C6	C8	C10
Aqua Laser, 1977, No. 7528-1 10		20	30
Edge of Adventure, 1977, No. 7518-2 10		20	35
Emergency Rescue, 1977, No. 7518-3 10		20	30
Fusion Bazooka, 1977, No. 7528-3 10		20	30
Helipak, 1977, No. 7538-2 10		20	30
Invisible Danger, 1977, No. 7518-1 10		20	35
Magna Tools, 1977, No. 7538-1 10		20	30
Path of Danger, 1977, No. 7518-4 10		20	30
Sonic Scanner, 1977, No. 7538-3 10		20	30
Treacherous Dive, 1977, No. 7528-2 10		20	30

Vehicle Sets

	C6	C8	C10

3-3/4" Series #1, Cobra

	C6	C8	C10
C.A.T., Motorized Crimson Attack Tank, 1982 15		25	55

3-3/4" Series #1, G.I. Joe

	C6	C8	C10
M.O.B.A.T., Motorized Battle Tank w/Steeler, 1982, No. 6000 30		65	125
R.A.M., Rapid Fire Motorcycle, 1982, No. 6073 15		25	55
V.A.M.P., Multi-Purpose Attack Vehicle w/Clutch, 1982, No. 6050 20		35	70

3-3/4" Series #2, Cobra

	C6	C8	C10
Cobra Glider, Attack Glider w/Viper, 1983, No. 6097 35		75	150
F.A.N.G., Fully Armed Negator Gyro Copter, 1983, No. 6077 10		20	45
H.I.S.S., High Speed Sentry Tank w/H.I.S.S., 1983, No. 6051 25		50	100

3-3/4" Series #2, G.I. Joe

	C6	C8	C10
A.P.C., Amphibious Personnel Carrier, 1983, No. 6093 15		25	50
Dragon Fly XH-1, Assault Copter w/Wild Bill, 1983, No. 4025 25		50	100
Falcon, Attack Glider w/Grunt, 1983, No. 6097 30		75	150

	C6	C8	C10
Polar Battle Bear, Sky Mobile, 1983, No. 6072	15	25	50
Sky Striker XP-14F, F-14 Jet and Parachute w/Ace, 1983, No. 6010	35	75	150
Wolverine, Armored Missile Vehicle w/Cover Girl, 1983, No. 6048	25	50	100

3-3/4" Series #3, Cobra

	C6	C8	C10
Rattler, Ground Attack Jet w/Wild Weasel, 1983-84, No. 6027	25	50	100
Stinger, Night Attack Jeep w/Cobra Officer, 1983-84, No. 6055	20	40	80
Swamp Skier, Chameleon Vehicle w/Zartan, 1983-84, No. 6064	30	55	125
Water Moccasin, Swamp Boat w/Copperhead, 1983-84, No. 6058	20	40	80

3-3/4" Series #3, G.I. Joe

	C6	C8	C10
Attack Cannon (FLAK), 1983, No. 7444-3	5	10	15
Attack Vehicle (VAMP), 1983, No. 7444-1	15	35	70
Battle Tank (MOBAT), 1983, No. 7444-4	15	25	50
Heavy Artillery Laser (HAL), 1983, No. 7444-2	10	15	25
Killer W.H.A.L.E., Armored Hovercraft w/Cutter, 1983, No. 6005	30	65	125
Mobile Missile System (MMS), 1983, No. 7444-5	10	15	30
RAM, HAL & VAMP, three-piece, die-cast set, 1983, No. 74450	10	20	40
Rapid-Fire Motorcycle (RAM), 1983, No. 7444-6	15	20	30
S.H.A.R.C., Submersible High-Speed Attack & Recon Craft w/Deep Six, 1983, No. 6049	25	50	100
Sky Hawk, V.T.O.L. Jet, 1983, No. 6079	10	15	30
Slugger, Self-Propelled Cannon w/Thunder, 1983, No. 6056	15	25	50
Vamp Jeep w/H.A.L., Attack Vehicle w/Heavy Artillery Laser Cannon, 1983, No. 6680	20	35	75
Vamp Mark II, Desert Jeep w/Clutch, 1983, No. 6055	25	40	80

3-3/4" Series #4, Cobra

	C6	C8	C10
Ferret, All-Terrain Vehicle, 1984, No. 6069	10	15	30
Moray, Hydrofoil w/Lamprey, 1984, No. 6024	15	25	50
Motorized Crimson Attack Tank, MOBAT Tank, 1984, No. 6687	30	60	125

	C6	C8	C10
Sentry and Missile System, Sears, w/H.I.S.S. Tank, Cobra Commander, Officer and Soldier, No. 1984, 6686	75	150	250

3-3/4" Series #4, G.I. Joe

	C6	C8	C10
A.W.E. Striker, All-Weather Environment Jeep w/Crankcase, 1984, No. 6053	15	25	50
Armadillo, One-Man Mini-Tank, 1984, No. 6078	10	15	35
Bridge Layer, Bridge Laying Trank w/Toll Booth, 1984, No. 6023	15	25	50
Mauler, Motorized Tank w/Heavy Metal, 1984, No. 6015	15	25	50
Silver Mirage, Motorcycle w/Sidecar, 1984, No. 6076	10	15	35
Snowcat, Snow Half-Track Vehicle w/Frost-Bite, 1984, No. 6057	15	25	50
U.S.S. Flagg, Aircraft Carrier w/Admiral Keel Haul, 1984, No. 6001	125	250	500

3-3/4" Series #5, Cobra

	C6	C8	C10
Air Assault, Air Vehicle, 1985	10	15	25
Air Chariot, Vehicle w/Serpentor "Cobra Emperor," 1985, No. 6062	15	20	55
Ground Assault, Land Vehicle, 1985	10	20	25
Hydro Sled, 1985, No. 6099-2	10	15	25
Jet Pack, One-Man Jet Set, 1985, No. 6099j-1	10	15	25
Night Raven S-3P, Surveillance Jet w/Drone Pod and Strato Viper, 1985, No. 6014	20	35	70
Stun, Split Attack Vehicle w/Motor Viper, 1985, No. 6041	10	20	35
Swamp Fire, Air/Swamp Transforming Vehicle w/Color-Change, 1985, No. 6068	10	15	30
Thunder Machine, Compilation Vehicle of Spare Parts w/Thrasher, 1985, No. 6042	10	20	35

3-3/4" Series #5, G.I. Joe

	C6	C8	C10
Conquest X-30, Super-Sonic Jet w/Slip Stream, 1985, No. 6031	15	30	65
Devil Fish, High-Speed Attack Boat, 1985, No. 6066	10	15	30
H.A.V.O.C., Heavy Artillery Vehicle Ordinance Carrier w/Cross-Country, 1985, No. 6030	10	15	35
L.V.C. Recon Sled, Low-Crawl Vehicle Cycle, 1985, No. 6067	10	15	30
Tomahawk, Troop Transit Helicopter w/Lift Ticket, 1985, No. 6022	15	30	65
Triple T, One-Man Tank w/Sgt. Slaughter, 1985, No. 6061	10	25	50

	C6	C8	C10

3-3/4" Series #6, Cobra

	C6	C8	C10
Buzz Boar, Underground Attack Vehicle, 1986-87, No. 6087-3	5	10	15
Dreadnok Air Skiff, Mini-set w/Zanzibar, 1986-87, No. 6070	10	20	30
Dreadnok Cycle, Compilation Cycle w/Gunner Station, 1986-87, No. 6171	5	10	20
Maggot, three-in-one tank vehicle w/W.O.R.M.S. driver, 1986-87, No. 6029	10	15	35
Mamba, Attack Copter w/removable pods w/Gyro-Viper, 1986-87, No. 6026	10	15	30
Pogo, Ballistic Battle Ball, 1986-87, No. 6170	5	10	20
Sea Ray, Combination Submarine/Jet w/Sea Slug, 1986-87, No. 6040	10	20	40
Wolf, Arctic Terrain Vehicle w/Ice Viper, 1986-87, No. 6039	10	20	45

3-3/4" Series #6, G.I. Joe

	C6	C8	C10
Coastal Defender, Mini-Vehicle w/accessories, 1986-87, No. 6087-2	5	10	15
Crossfire-Alfa, Radio Control Vehicle w/Rumbler, 1986-87, No. 6004-1	25	50	100
Crossfire-Delta, Radio Control Vehicle w/Rumbler, 1986-87, No. 6004-2	25	50	100
Defiant Space Shuttle Complex, Space shuttle, space station, crawler, 1986-87, No. 6002	75	350	525
Persuader, Laser Tank w/Backstop, 1986-87, No. 6038	10	15	35
Radar Station, 1986-87, No. 6133-3	5	10	15
Road Toad, Tow Vehicle w/accessories, 1986-87, No. 6087-1	5	10	15

Action Pilot Series

	C6	C8	C10
Crash Crew Fire Truck Set, 1967, No. 8040	950	1700	3500

Official Sea Sled and Frogman Set, Action Sailor Series, No. 5979, $650

Military Staff Car, Irwin, Action Solider Series, No. 5652, $750

	C6	C8	C10
Official Space Capsule Set, space capsule, record, space suit, cloth space boots, space gloves, helmet w/visor, 1966, No. 8020	175	225	350
Official Space Capsule Set w/flotation, Sears exclusive w/collar, life raft and oars, 1966, No. 5979	200	325	700

Action Sailor Series

	C6	C8	C10
Official Sea Sled and Frogman Set, Sears, w/figure and underwater cave, orange scuba suit, fins, mask, tanks, sea sled orange and black, 1966, No. 5979	175	325	650
Official Sea Sled and Frogman Set, w/o cave, 1966, w/o No. 8050	150	300	550

Action Soldier Series

	C6	C8	C10
Amphibious Duck, Irwin, 1967, No. 5693, 26" long	175	375	700
Armored Car, Irwin, friction powered, 1967, w/o No. 5397, 20" long	150	300	500
Helicopter, Irwin, friction powered, 1967, No. 5395, 28" long	150	300	500
Jet Fighter Plane, Irwin, friction powered, 1967, No. 5396, 30" long	225	475	800
Military Staff Car, Irwin, friction powered, 1967, No. 5652, 24" long	200	400	750
Motorcycle and Sidecar, Irwin, khaki, w/decals, 1967, No. 5651, 14" long	75	150	325
Official Combat Jeep Set, Trailer, steering wheel, spare tire, windshield, cannon, search light, shell, flag, guard rails, tripod, tailgate and hood, w/o Moto-Rev Sound, 1965, No. 7000	200	375	550
Official Jeep Combat Set, w/Moto-Rev sound, No. 7000, 1965	225	400	650
Personnel Carrier/Mine Sweeper, Irwin, 1967, No. 5694, 26" long	300	350	700

Adventure Team

	C6	C8	C10
Action Sea Sled, J.C. Penney, Adventure Pack, 1973, 13"	25	40	85
Adventure Team Vehicle Set, 1970, No. 7005	50	75	225
All Terrain Vehicle, 1973, No. 23528, 14"	50	75	125
Amphicat, Irwin, scaled to fit two figures, 1973, No. 59158	35	55	125
Avenger Pursuit Craft, Sears exclusive, 1976	100	175	275
Big Trapper, w/o action figure, 1976, 7498	75	105	325
Big Trapper Adventure w/Intruder, w/action figure, 1976, No. 7494	100	150	425
Capture Copter, w/o action figure, 1976, No. 7480	80	175	325
Capture Copter Adventure w/Intruder, w/action figure, 1976, No. 7481	110	200	350
Chopper Cycle, J.C. Penney's, 1973, No. 59114, 15"	30	50	100
Combat Action Jeep, J.C. Penney's, 1973, No. 59751, 18"	50	65	125
Combat Jeep and Trailer, 1976, No. 7000	80	135	550
Devil of the Deep, 1974, No. 7439	80	135	325
Fantastic Sea Wolf Submarine, 1975, No. 7460	60	100	175
Fate of the Troubleshooter, 1974, No. 7450	50	125	225
Giant Air-Sea Helicopter, J.C. Penney's, 1973, No. 59189, 28"	50	125	225
Helicopter, 1976, No. 7380	50	90	300
Helicopter, yellow; w/working winch, 1973, No. 7380, 14"	50	90	150
Mobile Support Vehicle Set, 1972, No. 7499	85	150	325
Recovery of the Lost Mummy Adventure Set, Sears exclusive, 1971	125	250	425
Sandstorm Survival Adventure, 1974, No. 7493	125	200	300
Search for the Stolen Idol Set, 1971, No. 7418	120	225	350
Secret of the Mummy's Tomb Set, w/Land Adventurer figure, shirt, pants, boots, insignia, pith helmet, pick, shovel, Mummy's tomb, net, gems, vehicle w/winch, comic, 1970, No. 7441	175	300	600
Sharks Surprise Set w/Sea Adventurer, 1970, No. 7442	175	325	550
Signal All Terrain Vehicle, J.C. Penney's, 1973, 12"	30	65	125

	C6	C8	C10
Sky Hawk, 1975, No. 7470, 5-3/4' wingspan	65	100	175
Spacewalk Mystery Set w/Astronaut, 1970, No. 7445	225	300	550
Trapped in the Coils of Doom, J.C. Penney's exclusive, 79-59301, 1974	250	300	550

Adventures of G.I. Joe

	C6	C8	C10
Sharks Surprise Set w/Frogman, 1969, No. 7980	175	325	650
Sharks Surprise Set w/o Frogman, 1969, No. 7980.83	150	300	550
Spacewalk Mystery Set w/Spaceman, 1969, No. 7981	150	375	650
Spacewalk Mystery Set w/o Spaceman, reissue, 1969, No. 7981.83	125	275	550

Super Joe

	C6	C8	C10
Rocket Command Center, 1977, No. 7570	50	100	200
Rocket Command Center, Super Adventure Set including Gor, 1977, No. 7571	60	115	225

HAPPY DAYS

	C6	C8	C10
(Mego, 1978)			
Fonzie, boxed		30	60
Fonzie, carded		30	75
Potsie, carded		30	75
Ralph, carded		30	75
Richie, carded		30	75

Ralph, Happy Days, $75

	C6	C8	C10

Play Sets

Fonzie's Garage Play Set, 1978 .... 60 150

Vehicles

Fonzie's Jalopy, 1978 .... 40 80
Fonzie's Motorcycle, 1978 .... 40 80

HARTLAND

	C6	C8	C10

9-1/2" Figures

	C6	C8	C10
Annie Oakley, No. 823	90	200	450
Bill Longly, No. 827	240	400	700
Brave Eagle, No. 812	140	300	600
Bret Maverick	100	175	350
Buffalo Bill, No. 819	140	250	500
Bullet, No. 700	40	65	125
Cheyenne, No. 818	85	125	350
Chief Thunder Cloud, No. 813	125	275	500
Cochise, No. 816	60	90	300
Colonel Randal Mackenzie, No. 829	400	800	1200
Dale Evans, No. 802	70	100	300
Davy Crockett	185	350	450

Paladin, Hartland, $400

General George Washington, Hartland, flag not shown, $300

	C6	C8	C10
General Custer, No. 814	70	100	450
General George Washington, No. 815	90	150	300
General Robert E. Lee, No. 808	90	135	300
Gil Favor	250	450	700
Hoby Gilman, No. 825	135	270	600
Jim Bowie, No. 817	140	250	500
Jim Hardie, No. 864	110	300	300
Johnny Yuma	325	600	950
Josh Randle, No. 828	290	480	700
Lone Ranger, old/chaps, No. 801	80	120	300
Lucas McCain, No. 826	110	180	500
Major Seth Adams, No. 824	90	200	400
Matt Dillon, No. 822	85	130	300
Paladin, No. 866	90	150	300
Roy Rogers, No. 806	90	135	450
Sgt. Lance O'Rourke, No. 804	140	250	400
Sgt. Preston, No. 804	140	250	300
The Lone Ranger, newer, No. 801	80	120	300
Tom Jeffords, No. 821	110	180	600
Tonto, No. 805	60	90	300
Turfking & Jockey	100	175	350
Western Champ, extra large, No. 801P	90	200	300
Western Champ, No. 801P	90	150	300
Wyatt Earp, No. 809	90	135	300

Famous Gunfighter Series

	C6	C8	C10
Bat Masterson, No. 769	270	300	450
Bret Maverick, No. 762	90	150	300

Roy Rogers, Hartland, $115

Indiana Jones, Adventures of Indiana Jones, $100

	C6	C8	C10
Chris Colt, No. 761	90	150	400
Clay Holister, No. 763	125	190	400
Dan Troop, No. 767	140	300	600
Jim Hardie, No. 764	125	200	400
Johnny McKay, No. 768	240	400	750
Marshall Wyatt Earp, No. 709	90	150	300
Paladin, No. 766	175	375	400
Vint Bonner, No. 765	180	325	550

8" Western Wranglers (Riders are Removable)

	C6	C8	C10
Alkali Ike, No. 611	75	125	250
Cactus Pete, No. 612	75	125	250
Comanche Kid, No. 613	75	125	250

5-1/2" Western Horse and Riders (Hats and Riders are Removable)

	C6	C8	C10
Bret Maverick	35	80	115
Cheyenne	35	80	115
Gill Favor	35	80	115
Jim Hardie	35	80	115
Johnny Yuma	35	80	115
Lucas McCain	35	80	115
Matt Dillon	35	80	115
Paladin	35	80	115
Roy Rogers	35	80	115
The Lone Ranger	35	80	115
Tonto	35	80	115
Wyatt Earp	35	80	115

INDIANA JONES, ADVENTURES OF

	C8	C10

(Kenner, 1982-83)

	C8	C10
Belloq	10	25
Belloq in Ceremonial Robe, in mailer box	6	15
Belloq in Ceremonial Robe, on card	200	500
Cairo Swordsman	8	20
Convoy Truck	15	35
German Mechanic	15	35
Indiana Jones	50	100
Indiana Jones in German Uniform	20	45
Indiana Jones, 12"	125	250
Map Room Set	20	50
Marion Ravenwood	70	175
Sallah	20	45
Streets of Cairo Set	18	45
Toht	5	15
Well of Souls	30	75

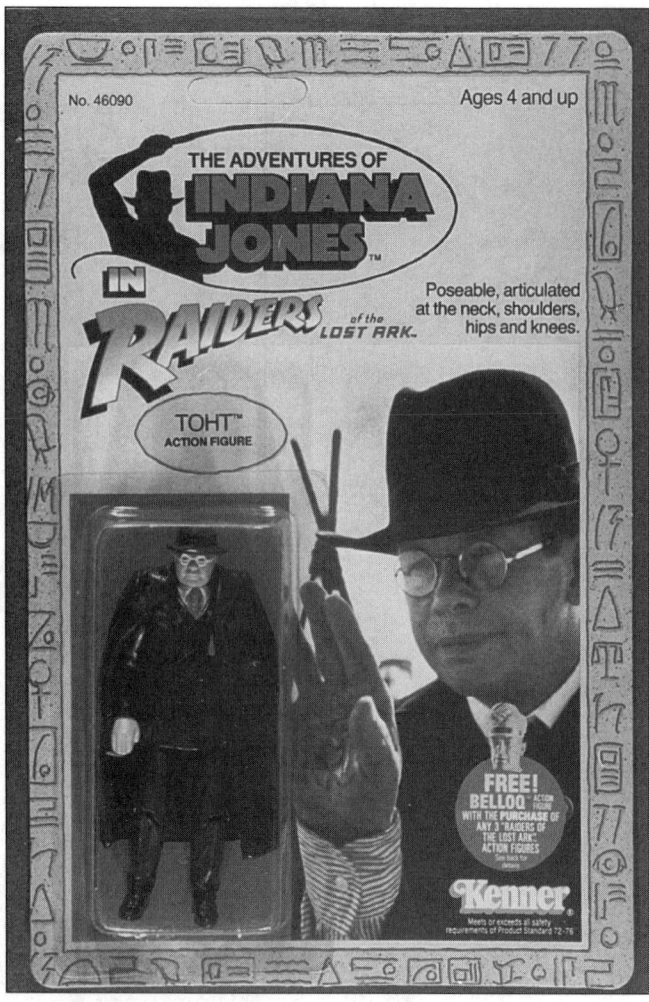

Toht, Adventures of Indiana Jones, $15

Gene Simmons, KISS, $260

JAMES BOND: MOONRAKER

	C8	C10
(Mego, 1979)		
12" Figures		
Drax	150	200
Holly	150	200
James Bond	125	150
James Bond, deluxe version	350	500
Jaws	400	500

JOHNNY WEST

	C8	C10
(Marx, 1975)		
Jeb Gibson	125	275
Johnny West w/Quick Draw	35	70
Sam Cobra w/Quick Draw	40	80
Sheriff Garrett	35	70
Thunderbolt, Western Ranch Horse	25	50

KISS

	C8	C10
(Mego, 1978)		
12" Boxed Figures		
Ace Frehley	100	260
Gene Simmons	110	260

Paul Stanley, KISS, $260

	C8	C10
Paul Stanley	100	260
Peter Criss	100	260

LAVERNE AND SHIRLEY

	C8	C10

(Mego, 1978)

12" Boxed Figures

	C8	C10
Laverne and Shirley	60	125
Lenny and Squiggy	90	175

LONE RANGER RIDES AGAIN

	C8	C10

(Gabriel, 1979)

Figures

	C8	C10
Dan Reid	25	50
Little Bear w/Hawk	25	50
Lone Ranger	20	40
Red Sleeves	25	50
Tonto	20	40

LONE RANGER, LEGEND OF

	C8	C10

(Gabriel, 1982)

Figures

	C8	C10
Buffalo Bill Cody	10	25
Butch Cavendish	10	20
General Custer	10	20
Lone Ranger	10	20
Lone Ranger w/Silver	20	50
Scout	10	20
Silver	15	30
Smoke	10	25
Tonto	7	15
Tonto w/Scout	25	50

LOVE BOAT

	C8	C10

(Mego, 1981)

4" Carded Figures

	C8	C10
Captain Stubing	10	20
Doc	10	20
Gopher	10	20
Isaac	10	20
Julie	10	25
Vicki	10	25

M*A*S*H

	C8	C10

(Tristar, 1982)

3-3/4" Figures and Vehicles

	C8	C10
B.J.	5	15
Colonel Potter	5	15
Father Mulcahy	5	15
Hawkeye	5	15
Hawkeye w/Ambulance	15	35
Hawkeye w/Helicopter	8	20
Hawkeye w/Jeep	10	25
Hot Lips	10	20
Klinger	5	15
Klinger in Drag	15	35
M*A*S*H Figures Collectors Set	26	65
Winchester	5	15

8" Carded Figures

	C8	C10
B.J.	15	35
Hawkeye	15	35
Hot Lips	12	30

MAD MONSTER SERIES

	C8	C10

(Mego, 1974)

8" Figures

	C8	C10
The Dreadful Dracula	80	160
The Horrible Mummy	50	100
The Human Wolfman	75	150
The Monster Frankenstein	45	90

Accessories

	C8	C10
Mad Monster Castle, vinyl	300	600

MAJOR MATT MASON

	C8	C10

(Mattel, 1967-70)

Figures

	C8	C10
Callisto, 6"	100	600
Captain Lazer, 12"	125	520
Doug Davis, 6"	100	300
Jeff Long, 6"	100	500
Major Matt Mason, 6"	75	225
Mission Team Four-Pack	175	625
Scorpio, 7"	500	2250
Sergeant Storm, 6"	100	400

Vehicles and Accessories

	C8	C10
Astro-Trak	35	75
Firebolt Space Cannon	35	80
Gamma Ray Guard	30	125

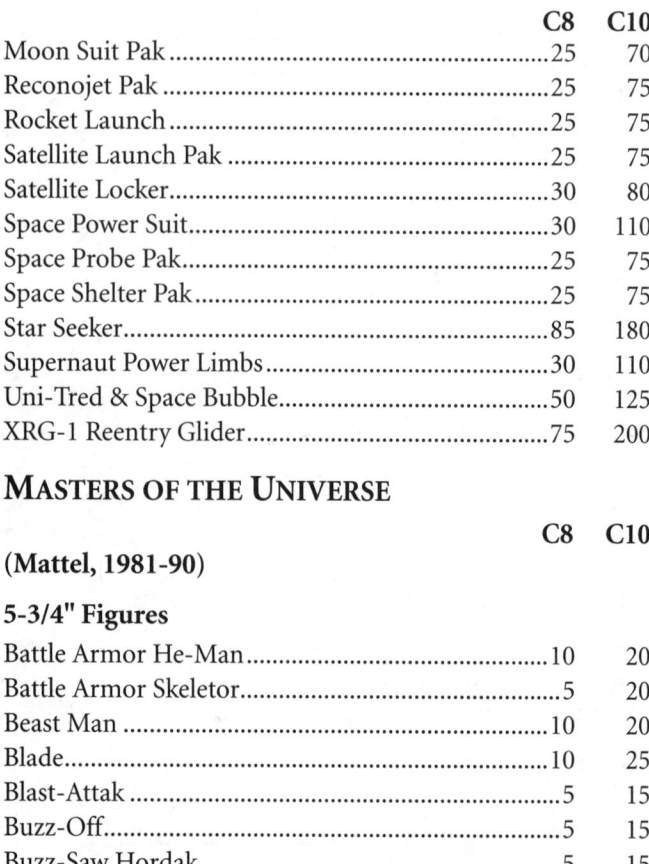

Space Probe Pak, Major Matt Mason, $75

King Randor, Masters of the Universe, $2

	C8	C10
Moon Suit Pak	25	70
Reconojet Pak	25	75
Rocket Launch	25	75
Satellite Launch Pak	25	75
Satellite Locker	30	80
Space Power Suit	30	110
Space Probe Pak	25	75
Space Shelter Pak	25	75
Star Seeker	85	180
Supernaut Power Limbs	30	110
Uni-Tred & Space Bubble	50	125
XRG-1 Reentry Glider	75	200

MASTERS OF THE UNIVERSE

(Mattel, 1981-90)

5-3/4" Figures

	C8	C10
Battle Armor He-Man	10	20
Battle Armor Skeletor	5	20
Beast Man	10	20
Blade	10	25
Blast-Attak	5	15
Buzz-Off	5	15
Buzz-Saw Hordak	5	15

	C8	C10
Clamp Champ	5	15
Clawful	10	20
Dragstor	5	15
Evil-Lyn	15	30
Extendar	5	15
Faker	15	40
Faker (reissue)	5	15
Fisto	5	15
Grizzlor	5	15
Gwildor	5	15
He-Man, original version	15	30
Hordak	5	15
Horde Trooper	5	15
Jitsu	10	20
King Hiss	5	15
King Randor	10	25
Kobra Khan	5	20
Leech	5	15
Man-At-Arms	10	20
Man-E-Faces	10	20
Mantenna	5	15
Mekaneck	5	15
Mer-Man	5	25
Modulok	5	20
Mosquitor	5	15
Moss Man	5	15
Multi-Bot	5	20

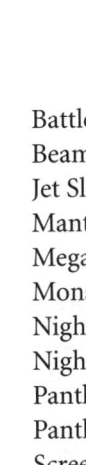

Dragon Walker, Masters of the Universe, $25

	C8	C10
Ninjor	5	20
Orko	5	20
Prince Adam	10	25
Ram Man	15	35
Rattlor	5	15
Rio Blast	5	15
Roboto	5	15
Rokkon	5	15
Rotar	5	15
Saurod	5	20
Scare Glow	15	35
Skeletor, original version	10	25
Snake Face	5	20
Snout Spout	5	15
Sorceress	10	25
Spikor	10	20
SSSqueeze	5	15
Stinkor	5	15
Stonedar	5	15
Stratos, blue wings	10	20
Stratos, red wings	10	20
Sy-Klone	5	15
Teela	10	25
Trap Jaw	10	25
Tri-Klops	10	20
Tung Lashor	5	15
Twistoid	5	15
Two-Bad	5	15
Webstor	5	15
Whiplash	5	15
Zodac	10	20

Accessories

	C8	C10
Battle Bones Carrying Case	5	10
Battle Cat	10	25

	C8	C10
Battle Cat w/He-Man, original version	20	40
Beam-Blaster and Artilleray	15	30
Jet Sled	5	15
Mantisaur	8	15
Megalaser	5	15
Monstroid Creature	15	30
Night Stalker	5	15
Night Stalker w/Jitsu	10	25
Panthor (evil cat)	10	25
Panthor w/Skeletor, original version	15	40
Screech	5	15
Screech w/Skeletor, original version	10	25
Stilt Stalkers	5	15
Stridor Armored Horse	5	15
Stridor w/Fisto	10	25
Weapons Pak	2	5
Zoar	5	15
Zoar w/Teela	15	30

Fifth Anniversary Figures

	C8	C10
Dragon Blaster Skeletor	10	25
Flying Fists He-Man	10	25
Hurricane Hordak	10	25
Terror Claws Skeletor	10	25
Thunder Punch He-Man	10	25

GraySkull Dinosaur Series

	C8	C10
Bionatops	10	25
Turbodaltyl	10	25
Tyrantisaurus Rex	10	25

Meteorbs

	C8	C10
Astro Lion	5	15
Comet Cat	5	15
Cometroid	5	15
Crocobite	5	15
Dinosorb	5	15
Gore-illa	5	15

Slime Pit, Masters of the Universe, $20

	C8	C10
Orbear	5	15
Rhinorb	5	15
Tuskor	5	15
Ty-Gyr	5	15

Play Sets

	C8	C10
Castle GraySkull	25	100
Eternia	100	200
Fright Zone	25	50
Slime Pit	10	20
Snake Mountain	25	50

Vehicles

	C8	C10
Attak Trak	10	25
Bashasaurus	10	40
Battle Ram	10	40
Blasterhawk	15	40
Dragon Walker	10	25
Fright Fighter	10	40
Land Shark	10	25
Laser Bolt	10	25
Point Dread	10	50
Road Ripper	10	25
Roton	10	30
Spydor	15	40
Wind Raider	10	40

MICRONAUTS

	C8	C10

(Mego, 1976-80)

Alien Invaders Carded

	C8	C10
Antron, 1979	15	30
Centaurus, 1980	35	70
Karrio, 1979	10	20
Kronos, 1980	35	70
Lobros, 1980	35	70
Membros, 1979	15	30
Repto, 1979	13	25

Alien Invaders Play Sets

	C8	C10
Rocket Tubes, 1978	23	50

Alien Invaders Vehicles

	C8	C10
Alphatron	5	10
Aquatron, 1977	10	20
Betatron	5	10
Gammatron	5	10
Hornetroid, 1979	20	40
Hydra, 1976	7	15
Mobile Exploration Lab, 1976	17	35
Solarion, 1978	15	30
Star Searcher, 1978	15	40
Taurion, 1978	11	22
Terraphant, 1979	20	40

Boxed Figures

	C8	C10
Andromeda, 1977	10	25
Baron Karza, 1977	15	30
Biotron, 1976	10	25
Force Commander, 1977	10	25
Giant Acroyear, 1977	10	25
Megas, 1981	10	25
Microtron, 1976	5	20
Nemesis Robot, 1978	7	15
Oberon, 1977	10	25
Phobos Robot, 1978	12	25

Carded Figures

	C8	C10
Acroyear II, 1977, red, blue, orange	7	15
Acroyear, 1976, red, blue, orange	10	20
Galactic Defender, 1978, white, yellow	7	15
Galactic Warriors, 1976, red, blue, orange	4	10
Pharoid w/Time Chamber, 1977, blue, red, gray	10	20
Space Glider, 1976, blue, green, orange	5	10
Time Traveler, 1976, clear plastic, yellow, orange	3	10
Time Traveler, 1976, solid plastic, yellow, orange	5	15

Micropolis Play Sets

	C8	C10
Galactic Command Center, 1978	20	40
Interplanetary Headquarters, 1978	20	40
Mega City, 1978	20	30
Microrail City, 1978	20	40

Play Sets

	C8	C10
Astro Station, 1976	10	20
Stratstation, 1976	15	30

Vehicles

	C8	C10
Battle Cruiser, 1977	30	60
Crater Cruncher w/figure, 1976	5	15
Galactic Cruiser, 1976	7	17
Hydro Copter, 1976	10	25
Neon Orbiter, 1977	6	20
Photon Sled w/figure, 1976	5	15
Rhodium Orbiter, 1977	6	20
Thorium Orbiter, 1977	6	20
Ultronic Scooter w/figure, 1976	5	15
Warp Racer w/figure, 1976	5	15

NOBLE KNIGHTS

	C8	C10

(Marx, 1968)

	C8	C10
Black Knight	75	190
Bravo Armor Horse	100	130
Gold Knight	60	120
Silver Knight	60	120
Valiant Armor Horse	100	130
Valor Armor Horse	100	130
Victor Armor Horse	100	130

ONE MILLION YEARS, B.C.

	C8	C10

(Mego,1976)

	C8	C10
Dimetrodon, 1976, boxed	75	150
Grok, 1976, carded	25	50
Hairy Rino, 1976, boxed	75	150
Mada, 1976, carded	25	50
Orm, 1976, carded	25	50
Trag, 1976, carded	25	50
Tribal Lair Gift Set (five figures), 1976	70	180
Tribal Lair, 1976	60	120
Tyrannosaur, 1976, boxed	75	150
Zon, 1976, carded	25	50

OUTER SPACE MEN

	C8	C10

(Colorforms, 1968)

Carded Figures

	C8	C10
Alpha 7 / Man from Mars	90	250
Astro-Nautilus / Man from Neptune	90	250
Colossus Rex / Man from Jupiter	100	300
Commander Comet / Man from Venus	90	250
Electron / Man from Pluto	90	250
Orbitron / Man from Uranus	90	250
Xodiac / Man from Saturn	90	250

PLANET OF THE APES

	C8	C10

(Mego, 1973-75)

8" Figures

	C8	C10
Astronaut Burke, 1975, boxed	50	130
Astronaut Burke, 1975, carded	50	100
Astronaut Verdon, 1975, boxed	50	140
Astronaut Verdon, 1975, carded	50	125
Astronaut, 1973, boxed	50	150
Astronaut, 1975, carded	50	100
Cornelius, 1973, boxed	40	140
Cornelius, 1975, carded	40	100
Dr. Zaius, 1973, boxed	40	150
Dr. Zaius, 1975, carded	40	100
Galen, 1975, boxed	40	140
Galen, 1975, carded	40	100
General Urko, 1975, boxed	50	130
General Urko, 1975, carded	50	100
General Ursus, 1975, boxed	50	120
General Ursus, 1975, carded	50	100
Soldier Ape, 1973, boxed	50	140
Soldier Ape, 1975, carded	50	100
Zira, 1973, boxed	30	150
Zira, 1975, carded	30	100

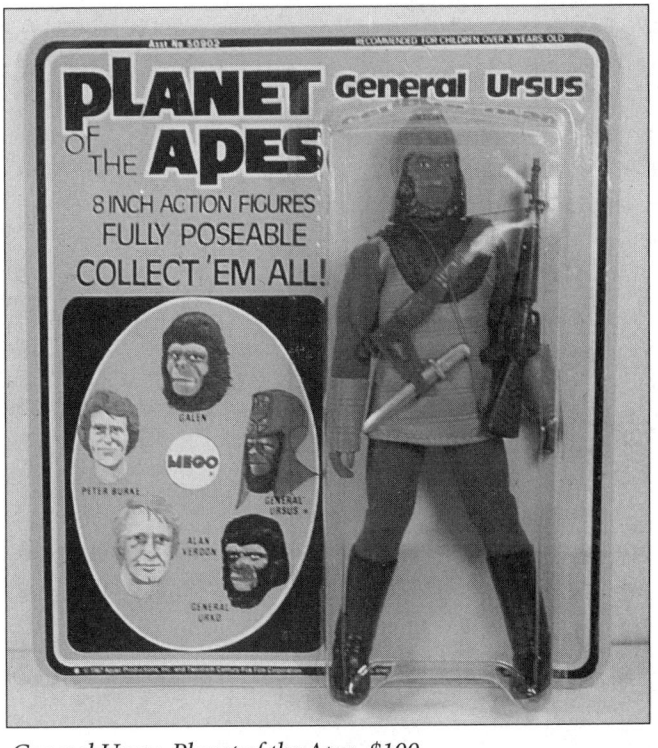

General Ursus, Planet of the Apes, $100

	C8	C10

Accessories

	C8	C10
Action Stallion, brown motorized, 1975, boxed	50	100
Battering Ram, 1975, boxed	20	40
Dr. Zaius' Throne, 1975, boxed	20	40
Jail, 1975, boxed	20	40

Play Sets

	C8	C10
Forbidden Zone Trap, 1975	65	150
Fortress, 1975	60	120
Treehouse, 1975	50	100
Village, 1975	60	130

Vehicles

	C8	C10
Catapult and Wagon, 1975, boxed	25	50

POCKET SUPER HEROES

	C8	C10

(Mego, 1976-79)

3-3/4" Figures

	C8	C10
Aquaman, 1976, white card	50	100
Batman, 1976, red card	20	40
Batman, 1976, white card	20	40
Captain America, 1976, white card	50	100
Captain Marvel, 1979, red card	20	40
General Zod, 1979, red card	5	15
Green Goblin, 1976, white card	50	100
Hulk, 1976, white card	15	40
Hulk, 1979, red card	15	30

	C8	C10
Joker, 1979, red card	20	40
Jor-El (Superman), 1979, red card	10	20
Lex Luthor (Superman), 1979, red card	10	20
Penguin, 1979, red card	20	40
Robin, 1976, white card	20	40
Robin, 1979, red card	20	40
Spider-Man, 1976, white card	15	40
Spider-Man, 1979, red card	15	30
Superman, 1976, white card	15	30
Superman, 1979, red card	15	30
Wonder Woman, 1979, white card	20	45

Accessories

Batcave, 1981	120	300

Vehicles

Batmachine, 1979	40	100
Batmobile, 1979, w/Batman	80	200
Invisible Jet, 1979	50	125
Spider-Car, 1979, w/Spider-Man	30	75
Spider-Machine, 1979	40	100

ROBIN HOOD AND HIS MERRY MEN

(Mego, 1974)

8" Figures

	C8	C10
Friar Tuck	25	75
Little John	45	100
Robin Hood	75	150
Will Scarlett	75	150

SHOGUN WARRIORS

(Mattel, 1979)

Figures

	C8	C10
Daimos	75	150
Dragun	75	175
Dragun (2nd figure)	75	150
Gaiking	75	150
Godzilla	100	200
Godzilla (2nd figure)	100	250
Mazinga	85	175
Mazinga (2nd figure)	75	150
Raydeen	75	150

SIX MILLION DOLLAR MAN

(Kenner, 1975-78)

Accessories

	C8	C10
Backpack Radio	10	20
Bionic Cycle	10	20

Bionic Bigfoot, Six Million Dollar Man, $120

	C8	C10
Bionic Mission Vehicle	25	55
Bionic Transport	10	30
Bionic Video Center	25	65
Critical Assignment Arms	15	30
Critical Assignment Legs	15	30
Dual Launch Drag Set	45	80
Flight Suit	15	30
Mission Control Center	25	50
Mission to Mars Space Suit	15	30
OSI Headquarters	30	70
OSI Undercover Blue Denims	15	30
Porta-Communicator	20	50
Tower & Cycle Set	25	50
Venus Space Probe	50	80

Figures

Bionic Bigfoot	75	120
Maskatron	40	100
Oscar Goldman	50	100
Steve Austin	50	100

SPACE: 1999

(Mattel, 1976)

Figures

	C8	C10
Commander Koenig	30	60
Dr. Russell	30	60
Professor Bergman	30	60

STAR TREK

(Mego, 1974-80)

12" Boxed Figures

	C8	C10
Arcturian, 1979	30	60

	C8	C10
Captain Kirk, 1979	25	55
Decker, 1979	45	115
Ilia, 1979	25	50
Klingon, 1979	40	85
Mr. Spock, 1979	30	60

3-3/4" Carded Figures

	C8	C10
Acturian, 1980	75	150
Betelgeusian, 1980	75	150
Captain Kirk, 1979	10	25
Decker, 1979	10	25
Dr. McCoy, 1979	10	25
Ilia, 1979	10	20
Klingon, 1980	75	150
Megarite, 1980	75	150
Mr. Spock, 1979	10	25
Rigellian, 1980	75	150
Scotty, 1979	10	25
Zatanite, 1980	75	150

8" Carded Figures

	C8	C10
Andorian, 1976	200	400

Betelgeusian, Star Trek, $150

Dr. McCoy, Star Trek, $75

	C8	C10
Captain Kirk, 1974	25	50
Cheron, 1975	75	150
Dr. McCoy, 1974	35	75
Gorn, 1975	80	180
Klingon, 1974	25	50
Lt. Uhura, 1974	50	135
Mr. Spock, 1974	25	50
Mugato, 1976	150	300
Neptunian, 1975	100	225
Romulan, 1976	300	600
Scotty, 1974	35	80
Talos, 1976	165	300
The Keeper, 1975	75	175

Play Sets

	C8	C10
Command Bridge (for 3-3/4" figures), 1980	45	105
Enterprise Bridge (for 8" figures), 1976	60	150
Enterprise Bridge w/Figures, 1976	95	250
Mission to Gamma VI (for 8" figures), 1976	200	500

STAR WARS

	C8	C10

Accessories

Droids

	C8	C10
Droids Lightsaber, 1985	55	200

Empire Strikes Back

	C8	C10
Darth Vader Carrying Case, 1982	10	35
Display Arena, 1980	25	105
Hoth Wompa, 1982	15	55
Laser Pistol, 1980	20	85
Lightsaber, red or green, 1980	20	55
Lightsaber, yellow, 1980	20	70
Mini Figure Case, 1980	10	30

	C8	C10
Tauntaun, solid belly, 1980 20		60
Tauntaun, split belly, 1982 19		60
Three-Position Laser Rifle, 1980 55		200

Ewoks

Ewoks Treehouse, 1985 18		45

Return of the Jedi

Biker Scout Laser Pistol, 1984..............................25		70
C-3PO Carrying Case, 1983....................................17		40
Chewbacca Bandolier Strap, 1983 6		15
Darth Vader Carrying Case w/three figures, 1983...11		210
Ewok Assault Catapult, 1983 11		25
Laser Rifle Carrying Case, 1984............................15		35
Lightsaber, red or green plastic.............................20		50
Rancor Monster, 1983 30		70
Tri-Pod Cannon, 1983...9		20
Vehicle Maintenance Energizer, 1983......................8		20

Star Wars

24-Figure Carrying Case 15		45
Action Figure Display Stand, Mail-In Premium, 1977.40		300
Han Solo's Laser Pistol 20		115
Inflatable Lightsaber, 1977.....................................35		150

Action Figures

	C8	C10

12" Figures

Ben (Obi-Wan) Kenobi, 1979..................................135		290

Jawa, Star Wars, $195

Kea Moll, Droids, $155

	C8	C10
Boba Fett, ESB box, 1979 160		390
Boba Fett, Star Wars box, 1979..............................160		450
C-3PO, 1979 55		150
Chewbacca...75		155
Darth Vader, 1978 85		200
Han Solo, 1979 210		500
IG-88, ESB box, 1980 230		650
Jawa, 1979 75		195
Luke Skywalker 140		300
Princess Leia Organa, 1977 110		240
R2-D2, 1979 55		140
Stormtrooper, 1979 115		250

Droids

A-Wing Pilot, 1985...45		155
Boba Fett, 1985..25		475
C-3PO, 1985 20		60
Jann Tosh, 1985 8		20
Jord Dusat, 1985 8		20
Kea Moll, 1985...8		20
Kez-Iban, 1985...8		20
R2-D2, 1985 25		50

	C8	C10
Sise Fromm, 1985	25	50
Thall Joben, 1985	8	20
Tig Fromm, 1985	18	50
Uncle Gundy, 1985	8	20

Empire Strikes Back

	C8	C10
2-1B, 1980	9	45
4-LOM	10	140
AT-AT Commander, 1980	8	40
AT-AT Driver, 1981	8	50
Bespin Security Guard, black, 1980	8	45
Bespin Security Guard, white, 1980	8	50
Bossk, bounty hunter, 1980	10	85
C-3PO, w/removable limbs, 1982	8	55
Cloud Car Pilot, 1982	14	50
Dengar, 1980	9	55
FX-7, 1980	8	55
Han Solo in Bespin outfit, 1981	14	95
Han Solo in Hoth outfit, 1980	12	75
Hoth Rebel Soldier, 1980	8	45
IG-88, 1980	12	80
Imperial Commander, 1981	9	40
Imperial TIE Fighter Pilot, 1982	12	75

Imperial Dignitary, Power of the Force, $85

	C8	C10
Lando Calrissian	10	55
Lobot, 1981	8	45
Luke Skywalker in Bespin outfit, 1980	20	140
Luke Skywalker in Hoth battle gear, 1982	14	70
Princess Leia in Bespin gown, 1980	19	120
Princess Leia in Hoth outfit, 1981	16	80
R2-D2 w/sensorscope	10	55
Rebel Commander, 1980	8	40
Snowtrooper, 1980	14	70
Ugnaught, 1981	10	40
Yoda, 1981	20	80
Zuckuss, 1982	11	70

Ewoks

	C8	C10
Dulok Scout, 1985	8	16
Dulok Shaman, 1985	8	16
King Gornesh, 1985	8	16
Logray, 1985	8	18
Urgah, 1985	8	17
Wicket, 1985	9	20

Mail-Away Figures

	C8	C10
Admiral Ackbar	9	18
Anakin Skywalker	30	40

A-Wing Pilot, Power of the Force, $100

Luke in Stormtrooper outfit, Power of the Force, $350

	C8	C10
AT-AT Commander	8	15
AT-ST Driver	10	15
C-3PO, removable limbs	8	15
Emperor	11	19
Han Solo in Hoth outfit	12	20
Han Solo in trench coat	14	20
Luke Skywalker in Hoth outfit	14	20
Nien Nunb	8	17
Pruneface	9	15
R2-D2 w/sensorscope	10	15

Power of the Force

	C8	C10
A-Wing Pilot, 1985	30	100
Amanaman, 1985	85	200
Anakin Skywalker, 1985	30	400
AT-AT Driver	8	500
AT-ST Driver	9	65
B-Wing Pilot, 1985	8	25
Barada, 1985	45	100
Ben (Obi-Wan) Kenobi, 1985	15	90
Biker Scout, 1985	11	75

	C8	C10
C-3PO, w/removable limbs	8	75
Chewbacca	11	175
Darth Vader	15	115
Emperor, 1985	11	95
EV-9D9, 1985	80	155
Gamorrean Guard	9	230
Han Solo in Carbonite outfit, 1985	110	240
Han Solo in Trench Coat	14	360
Imperial Dignitary, 1985	40	85
Imperial Gunner, 1985	75	130
Jawa, 1985	14	80
Lando Calrissian General Pilot, 1985	55	120
Luke in X-Wing Fighter Pilot Outfit, 1985	13	105
Luke in Battle Poncho	70	110
Luke in Jedi Outfit, green saber	35	190
Luke in Stormtrooper outfit, 1985	145	350
Lumat, 1985	14	70
Nikto	10	325
Paploo, 1985	17	45
R2-D2 w/pop-up Lightsaber, 1985	75	150
Romba, 1985	25	45
Stormtrooper	14	190
Teebo	10	165
Warok, 1985	25	50
Wicket, 1985	15	140
Yak Face, 1985	150	1350
Yoda	20	340

Return of the Jedi

	C8	C10
8D8, 1983	9	30
Admiral Ackbar, 1983	9	25
AT-AT Commander	9	25
AT-ST Driver	9	25
B-Wing Pilot	9	25
Bib Fortuna	10	30
Biker Scout, 1983	11	30
Chief Chirpa, 1983	10	20
Emperor, 1983	9	25
Emperor's Royal Guard	11	35
Gamorrean Guard, 1983	9	25
General Madine, 1983	8	25
Han Solo in trench coat, 1984	14	40
Klaatu, 1983	8	20
Klaatu in Skiff guard outfit, 1983	9	25
Lando Calrissian, 1983	12	35
Logray, 1983	9	25
Luke Skywalker in Jedi outfit, blue saber, 1983	50	160
Luke Skywalker in Jedi outfit, green saber, 1983	30	80
Lumat, 1983	14	30
Nien Nunb, 1983	8	30
Nikto, 1984	10	20
Paploo	17	35
Princess Leia in Boushh outfit, 1983	20	50

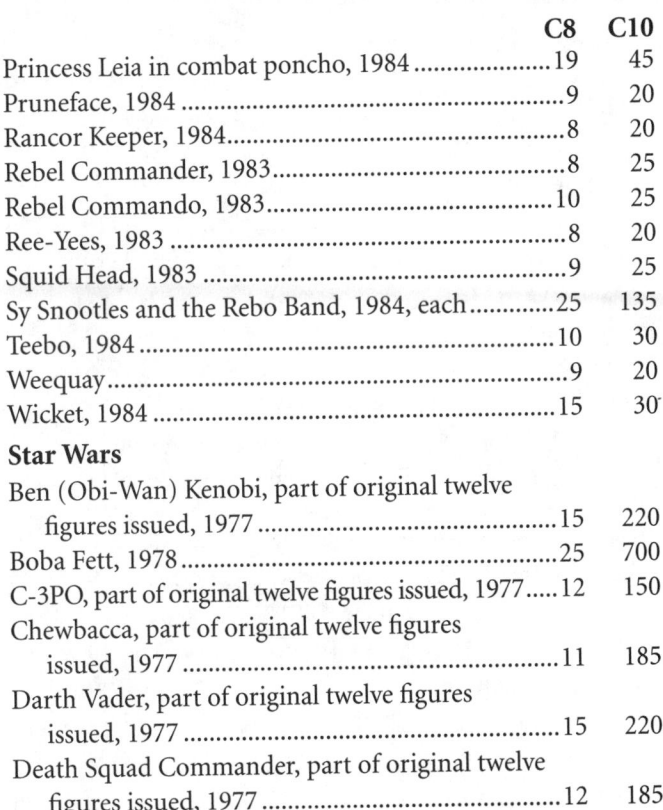

Princess Leia in Boushh outfit, Return of the Jedi, $50

Teebo, Return of the Jedi, $30

	C8	C10
Princess Leia in combat poncho, 1984	19	45
Pruneface, 1984	9	20
Rancor Keeper, 1984	8	20
Rebel Commander, 1983	8	25
Rebel Commando, 1983	10	25
Ree-Yees, 1983	8	20
Squid Head, 1983	9	25
Sy Snootles and the Rebo Band, 1984, each	25	135
Teebo, 1984	10	30
Weequay	9	20
Wicket, 1984	15	30

Star Wars

	C8	C10
Ben (Obi-Wan) Kenobi, part of original twelve figures issued, 1977	15	220
Boba Fett, 1978	25	700
C-3PO, part of original twelve figures issued, 1977	12	150
Chewbacca, part of original twelve figures issued, 1977	11	185
Darth Vader, part of original twelve figures issued, 1977	15	220
Death Squad Commander, part of original twelve figures issued, 1977	12	185

	C8	C10
Death Star Droid, 1978	12	125
Early Bird Figures, part of original twelve figures issued, 1977	220	520
Greedo, 1978	11	115
Hammerhead, 1978	11	115
Han Solo, large head, part of original twelve figures issued	25	550
Han Solo, small head, part of original twelve figures issued, 1977	30	510
Jawa, cloth cape, part of original twelve figures issued, 1977	14	165
Jawa, vinyl cape, part of original twelve figures issued, 1977	270	2610
Luke Skywalker, part of original twelve figures issued, 1977	30	330
Luke Skywalker X-Wing Pilot, 1978	13	130
Luke Skywalker, w/telescoping saber, part of original twelve figures issued, 1977	150	3230
Power Droid, 1978	9	115
Princess Leia Organa, part of original twelve figures issued, 1977	35	300
R2-D2, part of original twelve figures issued, 1977	13	160

Jawa, cloth cape, Star Wars, $165

Walrus Man, Star Wars, $115

	C8	C10
R5-D4, 1978...11		115
Snaggletooth, blue body (Sears Exclusive), 1978 165		250
Snaggletooth, red body, 1978....................10		115
Stormtrooper, part of original twelve figures issued, 1977 14		210
Tusken Raider, part of original twelve figures issued, 1977 16		210
Walrus Man, 1978 11		115

Micro Series

	C8	C10
Bespin Control Room, 1982 12		40
Bespin Freeze Chamber, 1982..................30		80
Bespin Gantry, 1982 12		35
Death Star Compactor, 1982 30		70
Death Star Escape, 1982 15		45
Death Star World, 1982..............................50		155
Hoth Generator Attack, 1982....................14		40
Hoth Ion Cannon, 1982..............................19		45
Hoth Turret Defense, 1982 15		40
Hoth Wampa Cave, 1982 14		40

	C8	C10
Hoth World, 1982.......................................60		155
Imperial TIE Fighter, 1982.......................20		60
Millennium Falcon, 1982..........................175		390
Snow Speeder, 1982...................................110		250
X-Wing Fighter, 1982.................................20		70

Mini Rigs

	C8	C10
AST-5, 1983 8		20
CAP-2 Captivator, 1982 9		25
Desert Sail Skiff, 1984 10		25
Endor Forest Ranger, 1984........................11		20
INT-4 Interceptor, 1982 9		25
ISP-6 Imperial Shuttle Pod, 1983 8		20
MLC-3 Mobile Laser Cannon, 1981............9		25
MTV-7 Multi-Terrain Vehicle, 1981............9		30
PDT-8 Personal Deployment Transport, 1981 9		30
Radar Laser Cannon, 1982..........................9		20
Security Scout...45		115
Tri-Pod Laser Cannon, 1982.......................9		20
Vehicle Maintenance Energizer, 1982.........9		20

Cloud City Play Set, Empire Strikes Back, $390

Cantina Adventure Set, Return of the Jedi, $570

Play Sets

	C8	C10
Empire Strikes Back		
Cloud City Play Set, Sears Exclusive, 1981	120	390
Dagobah, 1982	25	70
Darth Vader's Star Destroyer	50	160
Hoth Ice Planet, 1980	45	135
Imperial Attack Base, 1980	25	80
Rebel Command Center, 1980	65	220
Turret and Probot, 1980	45	110
Power of the Force		
Jabba's Dungeon, 1983	220	340
Return of the Jedi		
Ewok Village, 1983	35	75
Jabba's Dungeon, 1983	45	120

	C8	C10
Star Wars		
Cantina Adventure Set, Sears Exclusive, 1977	230	570
Creature Cantina, 1977	45	130
Death Star Space Station, 1977	90	270
Droid Factory, 1977	50	115
Land of the Jawas, 1977	45	135

Vehicles

	C8	C10
Die-Cast Vehicles		
Darth Vader's TIE Fighter, 1979	25	65
Land Speeder, 1979	25	70
Millennium Falcon, 1979	40	155
Slave I, 1979	25	85
Snowspeeder, 1979	30	90
Star Destroyer, 1979	45	175
TIE Bomber, 1979	290	830
TIE Fighter, 1979	20	60
Twin Pod Cloud Car, 1979	25	80
X-Wing, 1979	25	75
Y-Wing, 1979	45	160
Droids		
A-Wing Fighter, Droids Box, 1983	240	580
ATL Interceptor, 1985	20	60
Imperial Side Gunner, 1985	20	55
Empire Strikes Back		
AT-AT, 1980	105	260
Rebel Transport, 1980	40	100
Scout Walker, 1982	25	80
Slave I, 1980	45	150
Snowspeeder	40	95
Twin-Pod Cloud Car, 1980	30	85

Rebel Command Center, Empire Strikes Back, $220

Chopper, Starsky and Hutch, $45

	C8	C10
Ewoks		
Ewoks Fire Cart, 1985	10	25
Ewoks Woodland Wagon, 1985	10	25
Power of the Force		
Ewok Battle Wagon, 1985	45	135
Imperial Sniper Vehicle, 1985	50	85
One-Man Sand Skimmer, 1985	40	80
Security Scout Vehicle, 1985	55	120
Tatooine Skiff	270	670
Return of the Jedi		
B-Wing Fighter, 1984	65	130
Ewok Combat Glider, 1984	12	25
Imperial Shuttle, 1984	150	310
Speeder Bike, 1983	15	35
TIE Interceptor, 1984	60	115
Y-Wing Fighter, 1983	60	125
Star Wars		
Darth Vader's TIE Fighter, 1977	50	130
Imperial TIE Fighter, 1977	40	155
Jawa Sand Crawler, battery-operated, 1977	220	610
Land Speeder, battery-operated, 1977	20	70
Millennium Falcon, 1977	85	300
Sonic Land Speeder, J.C. Penney Exclusive, 1977	180	580
X-Wing Fighter, 1977	45	165

STARSKY AND HUTCH

	C8	C10
(Mego, 1976)		
8" Figures & Accessories		
Captain Dobey	25	50
Car	65	125
Chopper	25	45
Huggy Bear	25	50
Hutch	20	45
Starsky	20	45

SUPER HERO BENDABLES

	C8	C10
(Mego, 1972)		
5" Figures		
Aquaman	50	120
Batgirl	50	120
Batman	35	90
Captain America	35	90
Catwoman	70	175
Joker	60	150
Mr. Mxyzptlk	50	125
Penguin	60	150

Brainiac, Super Powers, $30

	C8	C10
Riddler	60	150
Roin	30	75
Shazam	50	125
Supergirl	70	175
Superman	30	75
Tarzan	25	60
Wonder Woman	40	100

SUPER POWERS

	C8	C10

(Kenner, 1984-86)

5" Figures

	C8	C10
Aquaman, 1984	15	35
Batman, 1984	25	55
Brainiac, 1984	15	30
Clark Kent, mail-in figure, 1986	100	150
Cyborg, 1986	75	200
Cyclotron, 1986	35	75
Darkseid, 1985	5	15
Desaad, 1985	10	30
Doctor Fate, 1985	25	50
Firestorm, 1985	15	35
Flash, 1984	10	20
Golden Pharoah, 1986	30	65
Green Arrow, 1985	25	55
Green Lantern, 1984	30	60
Hawkman, 1984	25	50
Joker, 1984	15	30
Kalibak, 1985	5	15
Lex Luthor, 1984	5	15
Mantis, 1985	10	30
Martian Manhunter, 1985	10	30

Darkseid, Super Powers, $15

Flash, Super Powers, $20

	C8	C10
Mr. Freeze, 1986	15	35
Mr. Miracle, 1986	75	200
Orion, 1986	20	40
Parademon, 1985	15	35
Penguin, 1984	20	40
Plastic Man, 1986	40	80
Red Tornado, 1985	25	55
Robin, 1984	25	50
Samurai, 1986	25	50
Shazam (Captain Marvel), 1986	20	40
Steppenwolf, in mail-in bag, 1985	15	0
Steppenwolf, on card, 1985	15	75
Superman, 1984	20	35
Tyr, 1986	25	50
Wonder Woman, 1984	10	20

Accessories

Collector's Case, 1984	10	20

Play Sets

Hall of Justice, 1984	30	100

Vehicles

Batcopter, 1986	40	75
Batmobile, 1984	40	75
Darkseid Destroyer, 1985	25	50
Delta Probe One, 1985	15	30

	C8	C10
Justice Jogger Wind-Up, 1986	10	20
Kalibak Boulder Bomber, 1985	10	25
Lex-Soar 7, 1984	10	20
Supermobile, 1984	15	30

TEEN TITANS

(Mego, 1976)

6-1/2" Carded Figures

	C8	C10
Aqualad	175	350
Kid Flash	175	300
Speedy	300	500
Wondergirl	200	450

VIKINGS

(Marx, 1960s)

	C8	C10
Eric the Viking	35	65
Mighty Viking Horse	30	60
Odin the Viking Chieftan	35	65

WALTONS

(Mego, 1975)

8" Figures

	C8	C10
Grandma and Grandpa	25	50
John Boy and Ellen	25	50
Mom and Pop	25	50

Accessories

	C8	C10
Barn	50	100
Country Store	50	100
Truck	40	80

Play Sets

	C8	C10
Farm House	50	100
Farm House w/Six Figures	0	200

WORLD'S GREATEST SUPER HEROES

(Mego, 1972-78)

12-1/2" Boxed Figures

	C8	C10
Amazing Spider-Man, 1978	35	75
Batman, 1978	60	125
Captain America, 1978	75	150
Hulk, 1978	30	60

8" Figures

	C8	C10
Aquaman, 1972, boxed	50	150
Aquaman, 1972, carded	50	150

	C8	C10
Batgirl, 1973, boxed	125	300
Batgirl, 1973, carded	125	250
Batman, fist fighting, 1975, boxed	150	350
Batman, painted mask, 1972, boxed	60	150
Batman, painted mask, 1972, carded	60	100
Batman, removable mask, 1972, boxed	200	350
Batman, removable mask, 1972, Kresge card only	200	450
Bruce Wayne, 1974, boxed, Montgomery Ward exclusive	400	500
Captain America, 1972, boxed	60	200
Captain America, 1972, carded	60	150
Catwoman, 1973, boxed	100	225
Catwoman, 1973, carded	100	225
Clark Kent, 1974, boxed, Montgomery Ward exclusive	400	500
Conan, 1975, boxed	120	300
Conan, 1975, carded	120	300
Dick Grayson, 1974, boxed, Montgomery Ward exclusive	400	500
Falcon, 1974, boxed	60	150
Falcon, 1974, carded	60	200
Green Arrow, 1973, boxed	100	250
Green Arrow, 1973, carded	100	400
Green Goblin, 1974, boxed	90	225

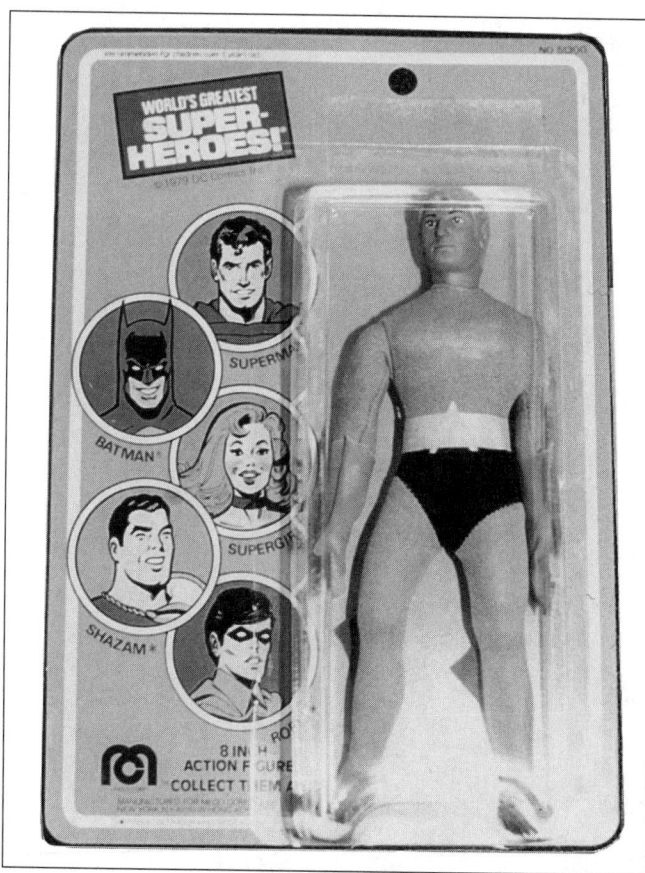

Aquaman, World's Greatest Super Heroes, $150

Falcon, World's Greatest Super Heroes, $150

Mr. Mxyzptlk, World's Greatest Super Heroes, $75

	C8	C10
Green Goblin, 1974, carded	90	300
Human Torch, Fantastic Four, 1975, boxed	25	90
Human Torch, Fantastic Four, 1975, card	25	50
Incredible Hulk, 1974, boxed	20	100
Incredible Hulk, 1974, carded	20	50
Invisible Girl, Fantastic Four, 1975, boxed	30	150
Invisible Girl, Fantastic Four, 1975, card	30	60

Isis, World's Greatest Super Heroes, $125

	C8	C10
Iron Man, 1974, boxed	75	125
Iron Man, 1974, carded	75	250
Isis, 1976, boxed	75	250
Isis, 1976, carded	75	125
Joker, 1973, boxed	60	150
Joker, 1973, carded	60	150
Joker, fist fighting, 1975, boxed	150	400
Lizard, 1974, boxed	75	200
Lizard, 1974, carded	75	250
Mr. Fantastic, Fantastic Four, 1975, boxed	30	140
Mr. Fantastic, Fantastic Four, 1975, carded	30	60
Mr. Mxyzptlk, open mouth, 1973, boxed	50	75
Mr. Mxyzptlk, open mouth, 1973, carded	50	150
Mr. Mxyzptlk, smirk, 1973, boxed	60	150
Penguin, 1973, boxed	60	150
Penguin, 1973, carded	60	125
Peter Parker, 1974, boxed, Montgomery Ward exclusive	400	500
Riddler, 1973, boxed	100	250
Riddler, 1973, carded	100	400
Riddler, fist fighting, 1975, boxed	150	400
Robin, fist fighting, 1975, boxed	125	350
Robin, painted mask, 1972, boxed	60	150
Robin, painted mask, 1972, carded	60	90
Robin, removable mask, 1972, boxed	250	400
Shazam, 1972, boxed	75	200
Shazam, 1972, carded	75	150
Spider-Man, 1972, boxed	20	100
Spider-Man, 1972, carded	20	40
Supergirl, 1973, boxed	300	450

	C8	C10
Supergirl, 1973, carded	300	450
Superman, 1972, boxed	50	125
Superman, 1972, carded	50	100
Tarzan, 1972, boxed	50	150
Tarzan, 1976, Kresge card only	60	225
Thing, Fantastic Four, 1975, boxed	40	150
Thing, Fantastic Four, 1975, carded	40	60
Thor, 1975, boxed	150	300
Thor, 1975, carded	150	300
Wonder Woman, boxed	100	250
Wonder Woman, Kresge card only	100	350
Wondergirl	100	240

Accessories

	C8	C10
Super Hero Carry Case, 1973	40	100
Supervator, 1974	60	120

Play Sets

	C8	C10
Aquaman vs. the Great White Shark, 1978	200	500
Batcave Play Set, 1974, vinyl	125	250
Batman's Wayne Foundation Penthouse, 1977, fiberboard	600	1200
Hall of Justice, 1976, vinyl	125	250

Superman Series

	C8	C10
General Zod, 1978	50	100
Jor-El, 1978	50	100
Lex Luthor, 1978	50	100
Superman Play Set, 1978	75	150
Superman, 1978	50	125

Vehicles

	C8	C10
Batcopter, 1974, boxed	75	150
Batcopter, 1974, carded	55	110
Batcycle, black, 1975, boxed	75	185
Batcycle, black, 1975, carded	60	150
Batcycle, blue, 1974, boxed	75	170
Batcycle, blue, 1974, carded	75	135
Batmobile and Batman	40	100
Batmobile, 1974, boxed	50	125
Batmobile, 1974, carded	50	120
Captain America, 1976	100	200
Green Arrowcar, 1976	175	350
Jokermobile, 1976	150	300

	C8	C10
Mobile Bat Lab, 1975	125	250
Spidercar, 1976	50	125

Wonder Woman Series

	C8	C10
Major Steve Trevor, 1978	26	65
Queen Hippolyte, 1978	40	100
Queen Nubia, 1978	40	100
Wonder Woman Play Set, 1978	50	100
Wonder Woman w/Diana Prince outfit, 1978	55	80

WORLD'S GREATEST SUPER KNIGHTS

(Mego, 1975)

8" Boxed Figures

	C8	C10
Black Knight	80	160
Ivanhoe	60	120
King Arthur	60	120
Sir Galahad	75	150
Sir Lancelot	75	150

Accessories

	C8	C10
Castle Play Set	80	160
Jousting Horse, battery operated	40	70

WORLD'S GREATEST SUPER PIRATES

(Mego, 1974)

8" Boxed Figures

	C8	C10
Blackbeard	70	150
Captain Patch	70	150
Jean LaFitte	80	160
Long John Silver	80	160

ZORRO

(Gabriel, 1982)

	C8	C10
Amigo	10	20
Captain Ramon	10	20
Picaro	15	35
Sergeant Gonzales	10	20
Tempest	10	25

Escape for the Deathstar Game, $50

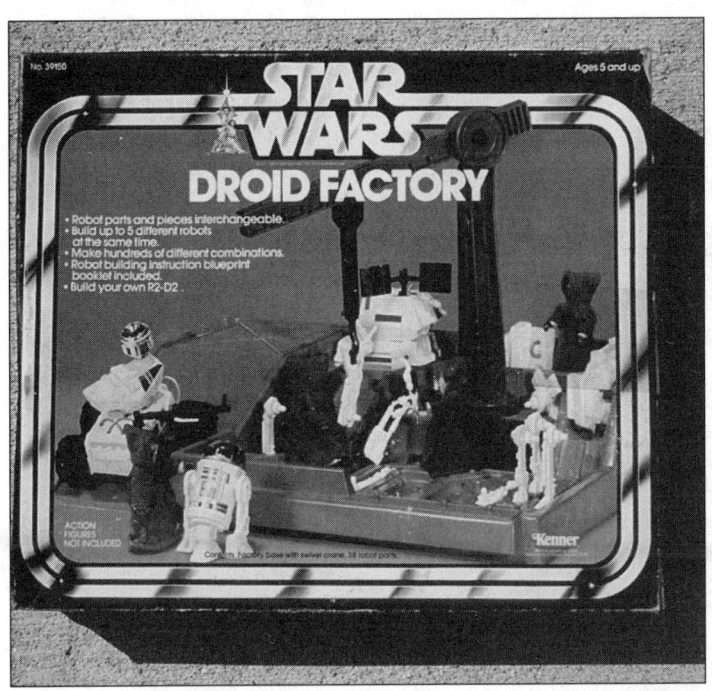

Droid Factory, $155

Top to Bottom: Imperial Attack Base, $80; Imperial TIE Fighter, $155

Note: Prices given for Star Wars figures are for items in C10 condition.
Items without their original boxes or cards can be worth much less.

Land of Jawas Play Set, $135

Top to Bottom: Ion Cannon Action Play Set, $45; Hoth World Action Play Set, $155

Left to right: Stromtrooper, Original Twelve, $210; Jawa with cloth cape, Original Twelve, $165; Tusken Raider, Original Twelve $210; Death Squad Commander, Original Twelve, $185

Note: Prices given for Star Wars figures are for items in C10 condition.
Items without their original boxes or cards can be worth much less.

Left to Right: Princess Leia, Original Twelve, $210; Luke Skywalker with retractable light saber, Original Twelve, $3,230; Ben (Obi-Wan) Kenobe with retractable light saber, Original Twelve, $220; Darth Vader, with retractable light saber, Original Twelve, $220

Left to Right: Chewbacca, Original Twelve, $185; R2-D2, Original Twelve, $160; C-3PO, Original Twelve, $150; Han Solo, large head, Original Twelve, $550

Left to Right: Death Star Droid, $128; Power Droid, $115; Boba Fett, $700; Luke Skywalker as X-Wing Pilot, $310

Note: Prices given for Star Wars figures are for items in C10 condition.
Items without their original boxes or cards can be worth much less.

Left to Right: Hammerhead, $115; Snaggletooth, red, 2-3/4", $115; Snaggletooth, Sears Exclusive, blue, 3-3/4", $250; Walrus Man, $115; Greedo, $115

Left to Right: Luke Skywalker in Hoth Gear, $70; Han Solo in Hoth Gear, $75; Rebel Commander, $40; Rebel Snow Soldier, $45

Left to Right: Dengar, $55; 4-Lom, $140; Zuckuss, $70; EV-9D9, $155; Bossk, $85

Note: Prices given for Star Wars figures are for items in C10 condition. Items without their original boxes or cards can be worth much less.

Left to Right: Princess Leia in Bespin Gown, $120; Han Solo in Bespin outfit, $95; Lando Calrissian, $55; C-3PO, with removable limbs, $55

Left to Right: 2-1B, $45; Princess Leia in Hoth Outfit, $80; FX-7, $55

Left to Right: Dagobah, $70; R2-D2, with sensorscope, $55; Yoda, 1981, $80

Note: Prices given for Star Wars figures are for items in C10 condition.
Items without their original boxes or cards can be worth much less.

Left to Right: Snowtrooper, $70; AT-AT Driver, $50; Imperial TIE-Fighter, $75; Imperial Commander, $40; AT-AT Commander, $40

Left to Right: Lobot, $45; Could Car Pilot, $50; bespin Security Guard, white, 450, Ugnaught, $40; Bespin Security Guard, black $45

Left to Right: B-Wing Pilot, $25; General Madine, $25; Admiral Ackbar, $25; Nien Nunb, $30

Note: Prices given for Star Wars figures are for items in C10 condition.
Items without their original boxes or cards can be worth much less.

Left to Right: Biker Scout, $30; Rebel Commando, $25; Princess Leia in Combo Poncho, $45

Left to Right: Klaatu ,$20; Klaatu Skiff Guard, $25; 8D8, $30;Nikton, $20

Left to Right: Wicket, $30; Chief Chirpa, $20; Logray, $25; Teebo, $30

Note: Prices given for Star Wars figures are for items in C10 condition. Items without their original boxes or cards can be worth much less.

Han Solo in Hoth Gear, $75; on Tauntaun with solid belly, $60

Millennium Falcon, $390; Han Slol with large head, Original Twelve, $550; Chewbacca, $185

Note: Prices given for Star Wars figures are for items in C10 condition.
Items without their original boxes or cards can be worth much less.

Snowspeeder, $90; Luke Skywalker as X-Wing Pilot, Original Twelve, $330

Darth Vader TIE Fighter, $130; Darth Vader, Original Twelve, $220

Note: Prices given for Star Wars figures are for items in C10 condition.
Items without their original boxes or cards can be worth much less.

TIE Fighter, $155; TIE Fighter Pilot, $75

X-Wing Fighter, $165; Luke as X-Wing Fighter Pilot, $130

Note: Prices given for Star Wars figures are for items in C10 condition. Items
without their original boxes or cards can be worth much less.

Land Speeder, battery-operated, $70; Luke, with retractable light saber, Original Twelve, $3,230

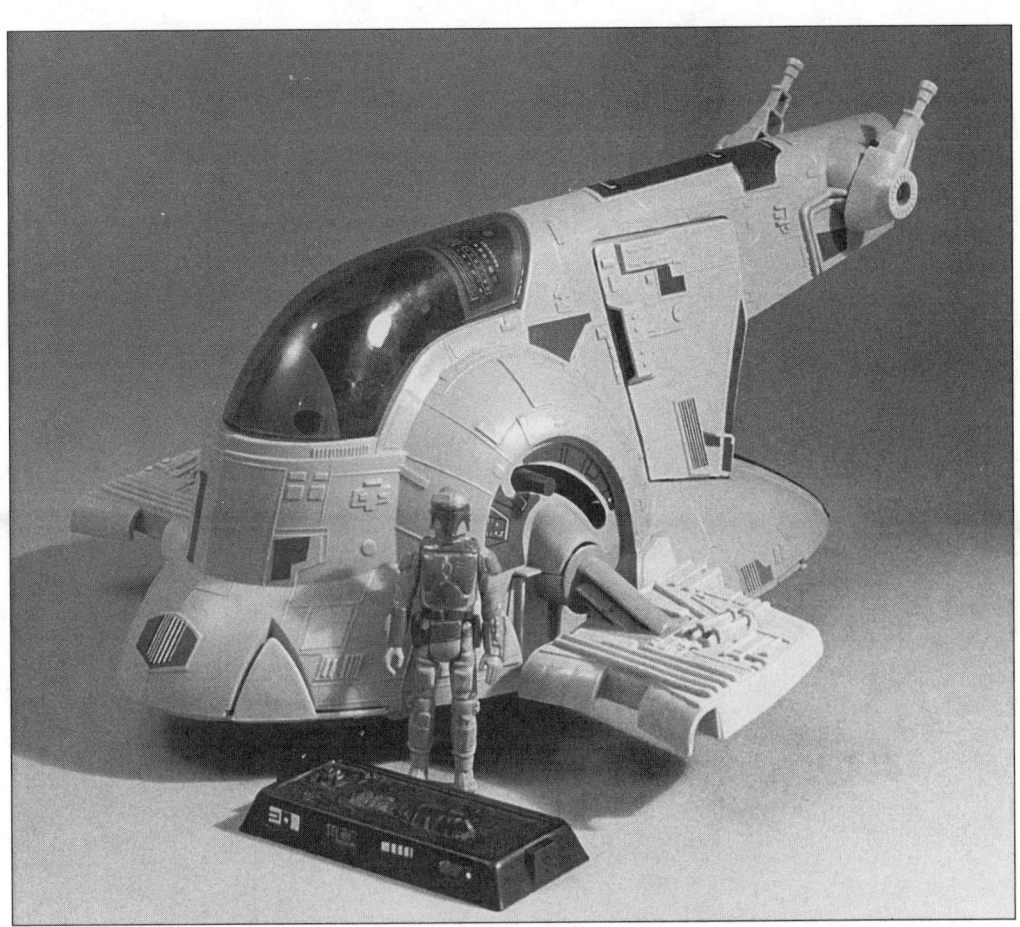

Slave I with Han Solo in Carbonite, $85; Boba Fett, $75

Note: Prices given for Star Wars figures are for items in C10 condition. Items without their original boxes or cards can be worth much less.

Imperial Troop Transport (figure not included), $100

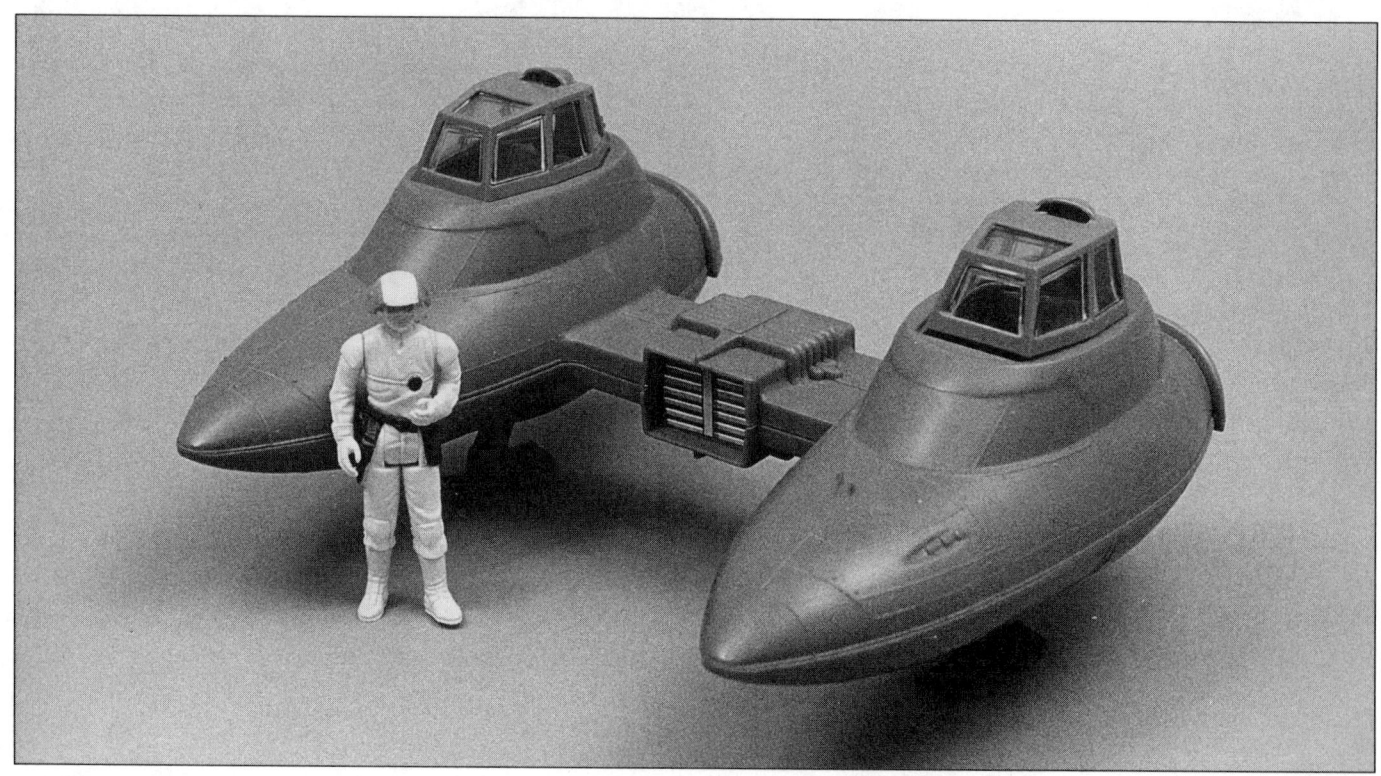

Twin Pod Cloud Car, $85; Cloud Car Pilot, $50

Note: Prices given for Star Wars figures are for items in C10 condition. Items without their original boxes or cards can be worth much less.

AT-ST. $80; Stromtrooper, $210

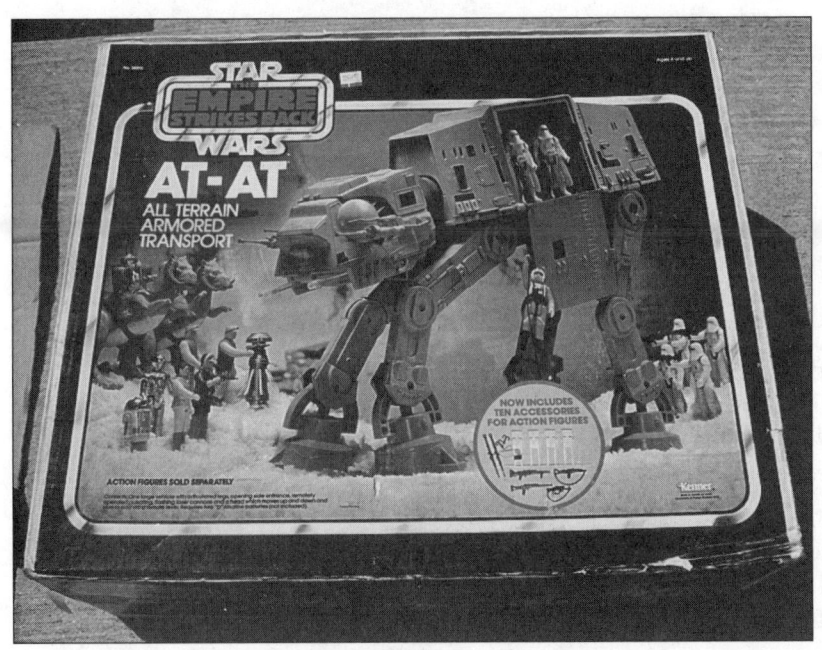

AT-AT, *Empire Strikes Back, 1980, $260*

Note: Prices given for Star Wars figures are for items in C10 condition. Items without their original boxes or cards can be worth much less.

AIRCRAFT

See also Tin Wind-Ups, Comic Characters, Premiums and Paper, and Vehicles

The airplane, until the last several years, was one aspect of toy collecting that attracted little interest and even less enthusiasm. Prices of toy airplanes generally reflected this lethargy.

As those of us born and raised during 1920-1940 (the golden age of aviation) acquired the time, the inclination and the means to obtain those objects on which our fantasies were transported during childhood, the scramble began, and demand and prices have been climbing steadily ever since.

Collecting toy aircraft and memorabilia has finally come into its own. As an investment, they seem a good risk, although I find few true collectors who get any joy from acquiring only objects that are guaranteed to appreciate in value. True value lies in the ability of an object to rekindle our memories or stir the imagination.

Those interested in collecting die-cast toy aircraft can choose from Hubley, Erie, Manoil, Barclay, Dinky, Mercury, S.R., Solido, Tekno, C.I.J., and a host of others. Cast iron was used by numerous companies before World War II, including Hubley, Arcade, Dent and Kilgore. Pressed steel seemed to be dominated by Wyandotte and Marx for the smaller types, and Keystone, Kingsbury and Steelcraft, among others, produced the larger types. Tin toy aircraft was made by many companies. The prewar types were made by Marx, Strauss, Chein, Kingsbury, Girard, American Flyer, and numerous European manufacturers. Japanese companies, although having produced some very desirable toys prior to World War II, joined the fray in the 1950s. Some of the later Japanese tin types were very accurate representations of actual aircraft, while others resembled real aircraft as much as Godzilla resembles Snow White.

Some of the nicest toy aircraft ever produced were the "Gnom" series made by Lehmann in the 1930s. These accurate small tin toys were based on two Heinkel aircraft and variations thereof. They are difficult to find and quite a nice display item.

In addition to the above, there are numerous examples of slush-cast items from Barclay, Kansas Toy and Novelty, Tommy Toy, Ralstoy, Lincoln White Metal, Best and perhaps the finest examples of the slush-cast toy industry from C.A. Wood. In addition to the above, some very unique planes were made by the Sun and Auburn rubber companies but well-preserved and undistorted rubber toy aircraft are very rare.

Some excellent plastic types were produced immediately after World War II and into the 1960s. Some items, such as the P-38, B-25, B-17 and P-40 by Renwal and the B-26 by Hubley, were faithful copies as well as those made by Relliable Plastics of Canada, while others, such as the P-39 by Ideal, are so out of proportion that they lack even the symbiotic charm that often accompanies grotesqueness. Other toy manufacturers of plastic toy aircraft were Thomas, Acme, Premier, Lido and Reliable.

If one collects toy aircraft, it follows that one wants to display toy aircraft, and they really look best on the numerous toy airports depicting structures of the same time period. In addition to airfields and hangars, there were numerous ground support personnel and vehicles.

Interest in aviation continues, and the flight of the Voyager, along with the development of the Stealth and numerous other record-setting craft, will have a dramatic effect on the interest in things related to flight. Consequently, prices will rise and availability will decrease in inverse proportion to interest.

Contributors: Capt. Perry R. Eichor, ASAF (retired) and Donna Eichor, 703 North Almond Drive, Simpsonville, SC, 29681. I.D. Planes—Richard L. MacNary, 4727 Alpine Dr., Lilburn, GA 30247. Captain Eichor has been collecting aircraft toys since he was a young officer in the Air Force, his twenty-one years as an Air Force officer only served to deepen his interest in

Arcadia Airport, Arcade, $1,400

Monocoupe, pull toy, Arcade, $3,200

the subject. Today when he is not collecting, researching or writing about aeronautical toys, he works as a crminal justice administrator as well as an appraiser and auctioneer.

ARCADE

	C6	C8	C10
Airplane No. 361, cast iron, twin engine, "United Boeing," 4-7/8" wingspan	50	90	150
Airplane No. 3620, cast iron, tri-motor, pressed steel props, 4" wingspan	50	75	120
Airplane No. 3630, cast-iron body, twin engine, pressed steel wing, 7" wingspan	175	265	350
Airplane No. 3640, cast-iron body, single engine, pressed steel wing, body resembles Corsair, red and yellow, or blue and yellow, 10" wingspan	230	345	500
Arcadia Airport	600	950	1400
Monocoupe No. 353, 4-1/2" long	150	200	300
Monocoupe No. 355, cast iron, steel wing, 8-1/2" wingspan	462	695	925
Monocoupe No. 357, pull toy, cast iron, 11" wingspan	1300	2100	3200
Monocoupe, 5-1/2" long	262	395	525

AUBURN RUBBER

	C6	C8	C10
Army Pursuit Plane, "US 1X2755" on wings, Curtiss P-37, No. 586	10	30	60
Boeing C-98 "Clipper," No. 1548, 8" wingspan	25	70	115
Consolidated A-11 light bomber, 4" wingspan	10	30	60
Douglas DC2 Transport	20	60	100
Jet 559	22	33	45
Jet, marked "XR577," 8"	35	52	70

BARCLAY

	C6	C8	C10
Dirigible, early to mid-1930s, 4-3/8"	20	30	40
Giant Zeppelin, No. 57	17	25	35

	C6	C8	C10
Lindy-type plane, No. 307, early to mid-1930s, 4-3/8" long wingspan	20	30	40
Monoplane, single engine, high wing, Crackerjack size, one-piece, sold w/Aeroplane Carrier and piggy-back on No. 195 Aeroplane	17	25	35
Monoplane, single engine, No. 307	48	72	95
Rocket Ship, No. 610	100	150	200
Rocket Ship, No. 611	100	150	200
The Atlantic Bremen, c. 1928	30	50	90

C.A.W. NOVELTY COMPANY

Charles A. Wood was known as the "Pioneer Birdman" in Clay Center, Kansas. Master aircraft mechanic, early pilot and aviation booster, his emphasis on aircraft in his toy line reflected his life-long love. Unfortunately his toys have been largely unavailable to collectors.

Wood's line was heavy with miniature airplanes. It was reported he flew his toys to Eastern markets: This could have been true under special circumstances only, for in its best years (over sixty employees and two million toys) the company output would have been too large to ship by air.

In comparing his toys and others, we see that Wood didn't take any shortcuts. He manufactured a Ford Trimotor with the landing gear and outboard motors on struts; pilots' heads showing through open cockpit windows; and a most realistic model of Ben Howard's famous stunt-plane with "Mr. Mulligan" prominently embossed. Wood's early production had metal disk wheels with painted black "tires." Later toys had rubber or plastic wheels. All aircraft had cast propellers, tapered and rounded wings except C.A.W. All of his pieces are more models than toys. His replicas of famous aircraft, local airliners, and mailplanes are miniature souvenirs of history.

Because Wood was such an activist a brief biography may be of interest. He was born about 1891, and went to work for Longren Aircraft Mfg. Co. in Topeka, Kansas in 1915. He opened the toy factory in Clay Center in 1925, and was influential in establishing a local airport in a wheat field in 1929. He received a pilot's license, bought a Waco F biplane, erected a Butler hangar, and opened a repair service in 1930. He was active in persuading Midland Air Express and Western Air Express lines to make route stops in Clay Center, which put this county seat on the air map.

In 1938, during National Airmail Week, Wood flew a commemorative from Morganville to Kansas City. One mail sack was delivered to the airfield by a Pony Express horseman. During the World War II war he was an instructor at a naval training center. Later, he owned a Rearwin plane, was a Piper Cub dealer, and in 1955, designed and built a monoplane dubbed "Little Monster." He continued to fly until 1976—a grand old man of early aviation.

Monoplane, low wing cabin-type, C.A.W., $100

	C6	C8	C10
Army Pursuit Plane No. 37, low wing marked "Seversky" P-37 Monoplane, under wings is Air Corps mark, "37" and "Made in USA," cowled radial engine, 2-7/8" x 3-1/2"	50	80	120
Boeing Bomber No. 36, low wing marked "Boeing," "NC 13361," and "Made in USA," bimotored, three bladed props, looks like a Boeing model 247 airliner, 2-5/8" x 3-1/2"	30	50	75
Champion high wing monoplane, cast iron, 5" long	90	135	180
Jr. Low Wing Monoplane No. 28, Lockheed or Northrop Cowled radial engine, six windows, pilot in open cockpit near tail	30	50	70
Monoplane, high wing, Ford model, V-12 engine, eight window, plus two restrooms, crew of two in open cockpit behind wing, tail wheel, 3-5/8" x 3-1/2"	30	40	60
Monoplane, high wing, Ford model, V-12 engine, eight window, plus two restrooms, closed cockpit ahead of wing, tail wheel, 3-5/8" x 3-1/2"	10	20	35
Monoplane, large, Amphibian, Douglas Dolphin, bimotored, 3-1/4" x 3-5/8"	40	70	100
Monoplane, large, high wing Lindy Ryan type, but V-8 engine, oversized propeller, five windows and door	20	40	60
Monoplane, low wing cabin or pursuit plane, cowled radial engine, forward cockpit, divided windshield, open windows w/pilot's head inside, 3-1/2" x 3-5/8"	40	60	100
Monoplane, No. 12, Ford Trimotor model 4, seven cylinder, radial engines, outboards and landing gear on struts, tail wheel, complex molding, 3-1/8" x 4-3/8"	60	90	125
Monoplane, small, Amphibian, Douglas Dolphin, bimotored, 2-1/4" x 2-1/2"	20	30	40
Monoplane, small, high wing Lindy-type, six cylinder radial engine, negative dihedral in wings, 2-3/8" x 2-1/8"	15	20	30
Monoplane, small, high wing racing type, V-8 engine, closed cockpit in front of wing, six windows, marked "C A W" and "Pat., appld. for," under tail plane, 2-5/8" x 2-1/2"	30	45	60
Mr. Mulligan Airplane No. 34, high wing, "Mr. Mulligan," "NR-273Y," cowled radial engine, two windows, two doors, c. 1936 production, 3" x 3-1/2"	40	80	120
Sr. Low Wing Monoplane No. 29 Lockheed or Northrop Cowled radial engine, six windows, pilot in open cockpit near tail	40	60	100

Monoplane, Ford tri-motor model, C.A.W., $125

Monoplane, small, Lindy-type, C.A.W., $30

Los Angeles Dirigible, cast iron, C.A.W., $1,700

DENT

	C6	C8	C10
Air Express, cast iron, 12" wingspan	750	1200	1500
Air Express, cast iron, trimotor, 11-1/2" wingspan	2500	4000	7000
Airline Monoplane, "?" on fuselage, cast aluminum, stripes on rudder, 12-1/2" wingspan	700	1050	1400
Airline Monoplane, "X5043" cast on rudder, cast iron, 12-1/2" wingspan	500	750	1000
Ford trimotor, cast iron, "1417" cast on rudder above "Ford," 12" wingspan	2000	3500	5750
Lindy, cast iron, 12-1/2" wingspan	1000	1700	2400
Los Angeles dirigible, c. 1932, 6-3/4" long	150	225	300
Los Angeles dirigible, cast iron, c. 1920s, 10-3/4" long	700	1200	1700
Los Angeles dirigible, cast iron, c. 1925, 13" long	1000	1500	2000
Los Angeles dirigible, cast iron, c. 1925, 8-1/2"	450	675	900
Lucky Boy, 4" wingspan	175	263	350
Lucky Boy cast iron, "X6043" cast on rudder, 12-1/2" wingspan	800	1200	1600
Lucky Boy Glider, cast iron, high wing, 6-1/2" wingspan	300	500	800
Lucky Boy trimotor, cast iron, 7" wingspan	550	800	1200
Question Mark trimotor, cast iron, "?" on fuselage, 12" wingspan	3000	6000	8000
Zep Zeppelin, aluminum, 5" long	65	198	130
Zep Zeppelin, cast iron, 5"	100	150	200
Zep Zeppelin, cast iron, 6-1/2" long	150	300	400

HUBLEY

	C6	C8	C10
302 DO-X, cast iron, high wing seaplane, six engine, 4" wingspan	70	100	250
Air Ford cast iron, two open cockpits, 4" long	150	225	300

	C6	C8	C10
Air Ford, 3-3/4" wingspan	85	125	170
Airplane, No. 467, die-cast, folding wings, retractable landing gear, plastic cockpit, resembles Brewster Buffalo, red and silver w/four-bladed prop in early version, later version was green and yellow w/two-blade prop, 8-5/8" wingspan	52	78	105
America, cast iron, largest cast-iron plane made, trimotor, open cockpit, pilot, copilot, 17" wingspan	1800	3700	6000
America, cast iron, single engine, wire spring drive, w/two pilots in open cockpit, 17" wingspan	3000	7500	12,000
American Eagle or Flying Circus, "No. 495" on wings, single engine, die-cast, folding wings, retractable landing gear, sliding plastic cockpit, 11-1/2" wingspan:			
Early—red and silver, four-bladed prop, no airscoop on top of engine cowl	50	75	125
Mid—two tone blue, red cowl, large airscoop atop engine cowl, 4-bladed prop	40	75	125
Late—orange and yellow, large airscoop, either four- or two-bladed prop	20	40	75
Attack Bomber, No. 326, plastic, retractable landing gear Martin B-26 Marauder copy, 7-7/8" wingspan	50	80	140
Bell Airacuda, XFM-1, die-cast, red and silver, folding landing gear, movable guns in front of twin pusher engines, three-bladed props, new in 1940	100	200	400
Bremen, aluminum, 6-1/2" wingspan	250	500	1000
Bremen, cast iron, 6-1/2" wingspan	600	1000	1450
Bremen, cast iron, 7" wingspan	500	1000	1500
Bremen, cast iron, marked "Junkers Bremen" on fuselage, open cockpit w/two pilots, prop turned by wheels, 10" wingspan	1000	5000	10,000
Crusader, No. 427, die-cast, twin engine, twinboom, marked, "TAT NC-31," 5-1/8" wingspan	35	75	110

Bremen, Hubley, $1,450

Friendship, seaplane, Hubley, $10,000

Lockheed Sirius, Hubley, $10,500

	C6	C8	C10
Delta wing jet, No. 751 folding, die-cast, retractable landing gear, red and silver plastic cockpit, 6-1/8" wingspan	30	60	100
DO-X cast iron, larger version of above, 5" wingspan	100	270	350
Friendship, cast-iron seaplane, marked "Fokker" embossed on fuselage, 13" wingspan	2500	6000	10,000
Giro plane, No. 304, cast iron w/nickel plate rotor, prop and engine	50	75	100
Hellcat, plastic, 9-1/4" wingspan	10	15	20
Jet, No. 430, die-cast, single engine, folding wings, retractable landing gear, cast cockpit, red and silver or blue and silver, 6" wingspan	30	50	70
Lindy Glider, cast iron, 6-1/4" long	300	700	1200
Lindy, cast iron, 10" wingspan	600	1000	1400
Lindy, cast iron, prop turns via gear attached to wheel, 10" wingspan	1000	1500	3000
Lindy, cast iron, w/"Spirit of St. Louis" decals, ratchet drive action noise-maker, has wing struts	1000	2000	3500
Lindy, No. 377, cast iron, single engine, 3-1/2" wingspan	75	100	150
Lockheed Sirius, marked "Lindy NR-211," 9" long	3000	7000	10,500
Monoplane, No. 303, cast iron, low wing single engine nickel plate wings and prop w/various colored body, 5" wingspan	50	80	120
Monoplane, No. 305, cast iron, low wing single engine monoplane, nickel plate wings and prop, 3-3/4" wingspan	30	50	75
Navy Blimp, 4-1/2" long	140	210	280
P-38, die-cast, red and silver, retractable landing gear, later versions are yellow and green camouflage, 12-5/8" wingspan	100	150	200

	C6	C8	C10
P-39, die-cast and tin, "U.S. Army" imprinted on rear horizon stabilizers, tin wings are 5-1/2"	30	50	75
P-40, die-cast, early version was silver and red w/three-bladed prop, later version orange and yellow w/two-bladed prop, 8" wingspan	68	100	135
Piper Club, No. 433, red, also in olive drab L-4 version, 7-7/8" wingspan	20	40	60
Question Mark trimotor, 12-1/2" wingspan	1500	2750	4250
Twin engine, No. 389, cast iron, painted and nickel plate, marked "TAT NC 431," 5-5/8" wingspan	40	70	100
Twin engine, silver and red or green, 3-3/8" wingspan	30	60	80
U.S. Army Plane, No. 431, die-cast, white rubber tires, enclosed in cast fairings, single engine, low wing monoplane, 5-1/2" wingspan	15	25	40
U.S. Army, die-cast, low wing, single engine Monoplane, folding wheels, silver and red (early versions had red wood hubs w/white rubber tires, cast cockpit may have openings or be cast or solid), introduced in 1939, 8" wingspan	65	100	130
U.S. Army, plastic, like above, folding wheels, "U.S. Army" embossed on horizontal stabilizer, 6" wingspan	25	45	75
U.S.N. 3-B-4, die-cast, twin engine, twin vertical stabilizer, retractable landing gear, 5-1/8" wingspan	60	80	110

I.D. PLANES

Black I.D. planes, as they are popularly known, were manufactured during World War II primarily as training aids for the United States, Navy and later the United States Army. There were also postwar I.D.s. The World War II airplanes covered in this section were all made in 1:72-scale and were usually marked on the bottom in raised lettering with the country of ownership/design (United States, Britain, Germany, etc.), the aircraft type (P-38, Spitfire, FW 189, etc.), and the date of model issue (7-42, 8-42, 5-42, etc.).

The program reportedly started the day after Pearl Harbor, but the earliest marking on any of the known models is May 1942. (The dates so marked on the planes are dates of model issue or copyright, not the date the actual plane became operational.) Some of the early World War II attempts at manufacturing these identification aircraft used materials such as reinforced plaster (too lumpy), papier-mâché (too little detail), a hard rubber-like material (too pliable for long sections like wings), metal, and even cast iron (too heavy for shipping and perhaps needed elsewhere).

The vast majority of I.D. aircraft were molded by the Cruver Company of Chicago. The master molds were made by either the Comet Engraving Company or H & H Specialty Company, also both of Chicago. A few models were molded by Design Center and Leominster.

Although they were manufactured for the U.S. Armed Forces, Polk's Hobbies of New York did sell some domestically under the Aristo-Craft name. Most of the surviving World War II types, though, were probably "midnight requisitioned" by pilot or gunner trainees. The quantity produced during the war was staggering. The February 1944 issue of *Flying* magazine states that Cruver had manufactured over 2,000,000 model aircraft since the spring of 1941 (they meant spring of 1942). Not many remain today.

The following listing of World War II model planes was taken from the most complete compilation known, however, it may not be totally inclusive nor may all of these planes have been made in quantity. The best history of I.D. aircraft made from different materials and in different scales, as well as those of the later Korean War vintage, was written by Robert C. Mikesh in the May/June 1984 issue of *Fine Scale Modeler* magazine.

You will note in the guide that not much distinction is made between the values for similar-size models. There is neither enough buying and selling nor enough large collections to accurately determine which plane is more rare than another. They could all be equally hard to find today.

As to grading, C10 means no scuffs, no warpage, no "prune-skin," no repainting or, in other words, a brand new 45-year-old airplane. C8 covers models that are very nice—planes should be complete with wheels or floats; free of serious defects like "prune-skin" or missing parts, and not repainted. The C6 grade covers everything else and probably includes the majority of the models still in existence. Each model is identified by type and date marked.

A special thanks is still due to master modeler Ray ".43 Magnum" Wheeler of Lilburn, Georgia, for his help in identifying some of the more obscure types listed.

*molded by Design Center
**molded by Leominster
All other molded by Cruver

United States

	C6	C8	C10
A-20 Havoc, 6-42	25	37	50
A-24 Dauntless, SBD - 3, 7-42	15	22	30
A-26 Invader, 2-44	25	37	50
A-29 Hudson (PBO-16), none	25	37	50
A-30 Baltimore, 2-43	25	37	50
A-31 Vengeance, 7-42	15	22	30
A-31 Vengeance, 7-44	15	22	30
A-35 Vengeance, 4-44	15	22	30
AT17 Bobcat*, 7-43	30	60	90
B-17 Flying Fortress, 7-42	100	150	200
B-24 Liberator, 7-42	100	150	200
B-25 Mitchell, 7-42	75	100	125
B-26 Marauder, 10-42	75	100	125
B-26 Marauder, none	75	100	125
B-29 Super Fortress, 3-44	100	150	200
B-29 Super Fortress, 9-44	100	75	100
B-29 Super Fortress, none	100	75	100
B-32 Dominator, 12-44	150	225	300
C-46 Commando, 3-43	50	75	100
C-47 Skytrain, 3-43	40	60	80
C-47 Skytrain**, 5-43	40	60	80
C-54 Skymaster, 3-43	60	90	120
C60A Lodestar, 3-43	25	38	50
C69 Constellation, 4-44	100	150	200
C78 Bobcat, 6-44	30	45	60
C87 Liberator, 3-44	100	150	200
CG-4A Waco Glider, 6-43	30	45	60
F4F-4 Wildcat, 5-43	15	22	30
F4U-1 Corsair, 3-43	15	22	30
F6F Hellcat, 4-43	15	22	30
GH-1 Nightingale*, 5-43	25	37	50
J2F-4 Duck, 12-42	60	75	90
JRF OA-09 Goose*, 7-43	60	75	90
JRS-1 (S43), 11-42	30	45	60
JR2S-1 (S44) Excalibur, 11-44	100	150	200
L-1 Vigilant, 3-43	25	37	50
L-2 Grasshopper, 7-44	25	37	50
L-4 Grasshopper, 2-43	25	37	50
L-5 Sentinel, 1-44	25	37	50
OS2U (on floats)*, 2-43	25	37	50
OS2U (on wheels)*, 2-43	25	37	50
OS2U-1 (on floats), 7-43	25	37	50
PBM-3 Mariner, 6-43	50	75	100
PBY-5 Catalina, 5-43	40	60	80
PB2Y-3 Coronado, 4-43	75	100	150
PV-1 (B-39) Ventura, 5-43	25	37	50
PV-2 Harpoon, 5-43	25	37	50
P-38 Lightning, 7-42	25	37	50
P-39 Airacobra, 6-42	15	22	30

	C6	C8	C10
P-40 Warhawk, 9-42	15	22	30
P-40 Warhawk, 4-44	15	22	30
P-43 Lancer, 5-43	15	22	30
P-47 Thunderbolt, 9-42	15	22	30
P-47 (D) Thunderbolt, 2-44	15	22	30
P-47 (N) Thunderbolt, 4-45	15	22	30
P-47 Thunderbolt*, none	15	22	30
P-51 Mustang, 6-42	15	22	30
P-51D Mustang, 4-45	15	22	30
P-61 Black Widow, 2-44	25	37	50
P-63 King Cobra, 5-44	15	22	30
P-80 Shooting Star, 4-45	20	30	40
SB2A-2 Buccaneer, 5-43	15	22	30
SB2C-1 Helldiver, 3-43	15	22	30
SB2C-2 Helldiver, 2-45	15	22	30
SB2C-2 Helldiver, (floats)*, 3-43	30	45	60
SB2C-2 Helldiver, (wheels)*, 3-43	25	37	50
SB2U-3 Vindicator, 6-43	15	22	30
SNJ-2 Texan, 7-42	15	22	30
SNJ-3 Texan, 7-42	15	22	30
S03C-1 Seagull (floats), 3-43	30	45	60
S03C-2 Seagull (wheels), 3-43	25	37	50
SR-10B Reliant, 10-42	25	37	50
TBD-1 Devastator, 5-43	15	22	30
TBF Avenger, 7-43	15	22	30

British

	C6	C8	C10
Albacore, 8-42	30	45	60
Albemarle, 9-44	25	37	50
Barracuda, 2-43	15	22	30
Beaufighter 1, 9-42	30	45	60
Beaufighter 2, 9-42	30	45	60
Beaufighter 6, 5-44	30	45	60
Beaufort, 9-42	25	37	50
Beaufort, none	25	37	50
Blenheim IV, 8-42	25	37	50
Boomerang (Aust.)*, none	15	22	30
Botha, 8-42	30	45	60
Defiant, 8-42	15	22	30
Firefly, 2-43	15	22	30
Fulmar, 8-42	15	22	30
Halifax, 9-42	75	100	125
Hampden, 8-42	25	37	50
Hastings, none	50	75	100
Horsa, 9-44	25	37	50
Hotspur, 6-43	15	22	30
Hurricane, 8-43	15	22	30
Lancaster, 4-43	75	100	150
Lerwick, 9-42	30	45	60
Lysander, 7-43	25	37	50
Manchester, 8-42	25	37	50
Maryland, 2-43	25	37	50

	C6	C8	C10
Mosquito, 3-43	30	45	60
Roc, 8-42	15	22	30
Skua, 8-42	15	22	30
Spitfire, 8-42	25	37	50
Spitfire, 1-44	25	37	50
Spitfire 9A, 10-44	25	37	50
Spitfire 9B, 10-44	25	37	50
Spitfire 22, 7-45	25	37	50
Stirling, 5-42	50	75	100
Sunderland, 9-42	90	120	150
Swordfish, 9-42	40	60	80
Tempest 2, 3-45	15	22	30
Tempest 5, 10-44	15	22	30
Typhoon, 6-43	20	30	40
Walrus, 4-44	25	37	50
Wellington 2, 9-42	30	45	60
Wellington 3, 9-42	30	45	65
Whirlwind, 8-43	25	37	50
Whitley, 9-42	25	37	50
York, 9-44	50	75	100

German

	C6	C8	C10
Arado Ar196, 12-43	25	37	50
Blohm & Voss BV138, 5-44	50	75	100
Blohm & Voss HA139, 11-42	100	150	200
Blohm & Voss BV222, 2-44	100	150	200
DFS 230, 8-43	15	22	30
Dornier DO 172, 9-42	25	37	50
Dornier DO 215, 9-42	25	37	50
Dornier DO 217E, 8-42	25	37	50
Fi 156 Storch, none	40	60	80
Focke Wulf FW 187, 8-42	25	37	50
Focke Wulf FW 189, 5-42	25	37	50
Focke Wulf FW 190, 7-42	15	22	30
Focke Wulf FW 190, 12-42	15	22	30
Focke Wulf 200, 3-44	100	150	200
Focke Wulf FW 200K, 9-42	100	150	200
Gotha Go 242, 7-42	25	37	50
Heinkel He 111, 9-42	25	37	50
Heinkel He 112, 7-42	20	30	40
Heinkel He 113, 5-42	20	30	40
Heinkel He 113, 9-42	20	30	40
Heinkel He 115K, 9-42	40	60	80
Henschel Hs 126, 10-42	25	37	50
Henschel Hs 129, 8-44	25	37	50
Junkers Ju 52, 8-42	60	90	120
Junkers Ju 86K, 9-42	25	37	50
Junkers Ju 87B, 8-42	15	22	30
Junkers Ju 88, 9-42	25	37	50
Junkers Ju 90, 9-42	50	75	100
Junkers Ju 188, 7-44	25	37	50
Messers. Me 109E, 7-42	20	30	40

	C6	C8	C10
Messers. Me 109F, 7-42	20	30	40
Messers. Me 110, 8-42	25	38	50
Messers. Me 210, 7-43	30	45	60

Italy

	C6	C8	C10
Cantiere Z. 506B, 9-42	100	150	200
Cantiere Z. 1007, 9-42	30	45	60
Caproni CA. 133, 9-42	75	100	125
Fiat BR. 20, 6-42	25	38	50
Fiat CR. 42, 9-42	40	60	80
Fiat CR. 42, 1-43	40	60	80
Fiat G. 50, 8-42	20	30	40
Macchi C. 200, 8-42	20	30	40
Macchi MC. 202, 3-43	20	30	40
Piaggio P. 32 BIS, 9-42	25	38	50
Reggiane Rc. 2000, 9-42	20	30	40
Reggiane Re. 2001, 3-43	20	30	40
Savoia Marchetti 79, 9-42	50	75	100
Savoia Marchetti 81, 9-42	100	150	200
Savoia Marchetti 82, 9-42	30	45	60
Savoia Marchetti 84, 4-43	30	45	60

Japan

Note: Japanese abbreviations below: Kawa.=Kawanishi; Mitsu.=Mitsubishi; Naka.=Nakajima

	C6	C8	C10
(Adam) Naka. 97, 11-42	30	45	60
(Ann) Mitsu. T-98, 7-42	30	45	60
(Babs) Mitsu. T-97, 6-42	40	60	80
Betty (G4M1), 9-43	50	75	100
Betty (G4M2), 4-45	50	75	100
(Claude) Mitsu. T-96, 6042	50	75	100
(Dave) Naka. T-95-NOB, 7-42	25	37	50
Dinah (Ki46), 8-44	30	45	60
Emily (H8K2), 3-45	40	60	80
Francis (PIY), 3-45	25	37	50
Frank (Ki84), 5-45	20	30	40
George (NIKI-J), 5-45	15	22	30
Hamp (T-00, Zeke 32), 7-43	15	22	30
Helen (Ki49)	30	45	60
(Ida) Mitsu. T-98 ALB, 6-42	30	45	60
Irving (J1N1), 5-45	30	45	60
Jack (J2M1), 12-44	25	37	50
Jake (E13A), 9-44	25	37	50
Jill (B6N), 5-45	15	22	30
Judy (D4Y), 3-45	30	30	40
(Kate) Naka. T-97, 6-42	15	45	60
Lily (Ki48), 9-43	20	30	40
(Mary) T-97 ALB, 6-42	30	45	60
(Mavis) Kawa., 11-42	100	150	200
Myrt (C6N), 3-45	15	22	30
(Nate) "97" Fighter, 9-42	25	37	50

	C6	C8	C10
(Nell) Mitsu. T-96, 6-42	25	37	50
Nell (G3M), 1-44	25	37	50
Nick (Ki45), 8-44	25	37	50
Oscar T-01 (Ki43), 9-43	20	30	40
Paul 14, Exp, 12-44	25	37	50
Pete (F1M2), 6-43	30	45	60
Rufe (A6M2-N), 8-43	40	60	80
(Sally) Mitsu. T-97, 6-42	25	38	50
(Sonia) Mitsu. T-99, 7-42	15	22	30
Tojo (Ki44), 6-44	15	22	30
Tojo (Ki44), 3-45	15	22	30
Tony (Ki61), 4-45	15	22	30
(Topsy) Mitsu. MC-20, 10-42	25	37	50
(Val) Aichi T-99, 6-42	40	60	80
Val T-99 MK2, 8-43	40	60	80
(Zeke) Mitsu. 00, 9-42	20	30	40
Zeke 52 (A6M5)*, 12-44	20	30	40

Netherlands

	C65	C8	C10
Fokker T8W, 11-42	50	75	100

Russia

	C65	C8	C10
DB-3F, 9-42	25	50	75
DB-3F, 4-44	25	50	75
I-16, none	15	22	30
IL-2, 9-42	15	22	30
IL-2, 12-43	15	22	30
MiG-3, 8-42	15	22	30
I-18 (MiG-3), 2-43	15	22	30
MiG-3, 2-44	15	22	30
Pe-2, 9-42	15	22	30
SB-3, 11-43	15	22	30
TB-7*, 4-44	15	22	30

KANSAS TOY & NOVELTY COMPANY

The years 1920-1940 were decisive for aviation—it was an era of ferment and growth, and was a time of barnstorming and record-breaking; Lindbergh and Earhart made headlines.

The state of Kansas played a large part in the development of airmail and airlines with its manufacturing centers at Topeka and Wichita (Beach, Boeing, Cessna, Laird, Stearman and others), but the toy industry reflected only dimly the excitement of the era.

Listed below are the aircraft said to have been made by Kansas Toy and Novelty from 1924 to about 1931, using metal disc or wire wheels. Reproductions from Best Toy and Ralstoy will be found with later wheels. Best Toys' later reproductions will have "Made in U.S.A." embossed and may have small white rubber wheels.

For a more detailed history of Kansas Toy & Novelty, see their section in the vehicles chapter.

Airliner, marked "KTN 47," Kansas Toy & Novelty Company, $75

	C6	C8	C10
Airliner, marked "45," Fokker?, high, oval, corrugated wing and tail, nine circular cabin windows, nine rectangular flightdeck windows, six cylinder, radial engine, large tin propeller, 2-1/2" x 2-1/2"	30	45	75
Airliner, marked "KTN 47," Fokker, sometimes called a "seaplane," 3-5/8" x 3-1/2"	30	50	75
Cabin Plane, large, "24," high wing, larger "U.S. Mail" version of above, dot-in-two-circles insignia, V-8 engine, cast propeller, white disc wheels w/painted black "tires," 5-5/8" x 4-3/8"	30	40	75
Cabin Plane, large, Lindy type, high negative dihedral wing w/large stars, six cylinder radial engine, wheels w/black tires, 5"	30	50	75
Cabin Plane, marked "6", high wing w/flaring positive dihedral, Army Air Corps star-in-circle insignia, six cylinder, radial engine, pilot head in open cockpit, eight oval windows, cast prop, lacquer finish, also unnumbered version with large tin propeller, 3-3/4" x 3"	20	35	50
Cabin Plane, small, marked "32," high, positive dihedral wing, Air Corps star insignia, six cylinder, radial engine, six oval windows, three metal "wire"			

Airliner, marked "45," Kansas Toy & Novelty Company, $75

TAT, largest Kilgore plane, $7,700

	C6	C8	C10
wheels, large tin or cast propeller, 2-3/8" x 2-1/8"	20	30	40
Cabin Plane, small, similar to above, w/o "windows" and diff. rudder, or wingtip, 2-3/8" x 2-1/8"	20	30	40
Glider, marked "56," high oval wing w/"GLIDER," pilot in front, flat lattice fuselage, 2-5/8" x 2-3/8"	15	25	40
Zeppelin, marked "44," front and rear cabins, three tail planes, mooring loop on nose, rear axle through rear cabin, 4-1/4"	50	75	100

KILGORE

	C6	C8	C10
Bullet open cockpit monoplane, cast iron, 4" long	100	175	275
Ford Trimotor, cast iron, "TAT," 13-1/2" wingspan	2000	3000	6000
Kilgore Comet cap-firing plane	25	38	50
Monocoupe, high wing, 5-1/2"	125	200	250
Monoplane high wing, 3-1/2" long	50	75	100
Monoplane, marked "N4," open cockpit cast iron, 4" long	125	188	250
Seagull, high wing, pusher prop, 4" wingspan	200	300	400
Seagull, high wing, pusher prop, 8-1/4" wingspan	625	938	1250
TAT, largest Kilgore plane	2500	4200	7700
TAT, No. 401," twin engine passenger monoplane, 4-1/2" long	150	250	325
Travel Air Mystery, double open cockpits, cast iron, 6" long	250	375	500

MARX

	C6	C8	C10
Air Mail Biplane, four-engine, 1930	300	450	600
Air Mail Monoplane, two-engine, 1930	165	248	330
Airplane, light fuselage, No. 90	100	150	200
Airplane, medium fuselage, No. 90	100	150	200
Airplane, U.S. Army two-engine, no guns, No. 6, 18" wingspan	163	245	325

P-35-type bomber, Marx, $210

Skycruiser Stratoliner 700, two engine, Marx, $100

	C6	C8	C10
American Airlines Flagship, 27-1/2" wingspan	155	230	310
Army Bomber, three-engine, c. 1935, No. 1025, 26" wingspan	75	150	250
Astrojet Airport Set, planes, helicopter, etc.	155	230	310
Bomber, four-engine, drops wooden bombs, 14-3/4" wingspan	80	125	250
Bomber, tin litho, sparkling mechanism, camouflaged, four engine, 18" wingspan	60	140	200
City Airport Set	300	500	750
Crop Duster Plane Set	75	125	200
Curtiss Transport, khaki, pressed steel, 9-1/2" wingspan	50	75	100

	C6	C8	C10
DC-3 Transport, pressed steel, c. 1939, 10" wingspan	60	80	120
DC-4 type, four-engine passenger, pressed steel, c. 1930s,	60	125	250
DC-6 Transport plane, plastic	75	120	150
Electric Lighted Radio Airport, 1930s, 5" x 2-1/2" x 3-1/2"	200	350	500
F84 Jet Fighter, remote control	68	100	135
Futuristic Airport	212	318	425
Gyroplane	50	80	120
Hangar, tin litho, c.1941	50	75	100
Little Lindy Aeroplane, 1930s, friction, 6" wingspan	100	150	200
Lockheed Prop Jet	125	188	250
Mainstream Airport, c. 1930s	110	165	220
Municipal Airport hangar, early, w/plane	400	600	800
P35, pressed steel, w/ and w/o wheel skirts, 13-1/2" wingspan	60	90	120
P35-type, two-engine bomber, 15-7/8" wingspan	105	158	210

Bomber, camouflaged, four engine, Marx, $200

Piggyback airplane set, Marx, $150

Skycruiser Stratoliner 700, four engine, Marx, $125

	C6	C8	C10
Pan American Super 7 clipper, also as American Airlines, 17-1/2" wingspan	160	240	320
Pan American, four-engine, propeller-driven, pressed steel, also as PAA, 1940, 27" wingspan	200	300	400
Piggyback Airplane Set	75	125	150
Pioneer Air Express, tin litho, high wing monoplane, 25-1/2" wingspan	100	125	250
Skycruiser, two-engine Transport Plane w/siren and whirling propellers, Stratoliner 700, rubber wheels, c. 1940s, 18" wingspan	180	300	450
Skycruiser Stratoliner 700, two-engine	50	75	100
Skycruiser Stratoliner 700, four-engine	45	75	125
Sparkling Rocket Fighter, No. 1425, tin litho	37	56	75
Swingtail Flying Tiger transport	300	450	600
Transport, friction-powered four-engine w/whirling propellers, tin litho	60	90	200
Trimotor Biplane, 9-1/2" wingspan	60	90	120
Universal Airport w/two metal planes, c. 1940s, 12" long	55	90	200
Zeppelin, "Akron" Marx, c. 1930s, 28" long	100	140	250

RALSTOY

Ralstoy issued new aircraft and reproduced popular Kansas Toy numbers issued during the 1920s. The late 1930s toy reflected the growing awareness of the war in Europe.

	C6	C8	C10
Cabin Plane, high wing, cowled radial engine, two doors, six windows, marked "Ralstoy" and "Made in USA," 3-5/8" x 3-1/2"	35	45	70
Cabin Plane, large, Lindy-type, high wing, six cylinder, radial engine, metal wheels	20	30	40
Cabin Plane, marked "NC414" and "Ralstoy," midwing, V-12 engine, tin propeller, 3-3/8" x 3-3/8"	30	40	60
Cabin Plane, slim midwing, cowled radial engine, pilot, tin propeller, underside marked "Scout" and "Made in USA," 3" x 3-3/4"	25	35	45
Cabin Plane, small, marked "32" and "Ralstoy," wings positive dihedral, 2-1/2" x 2-1/4"	20	30	40
Pursuit Plane, P40, Curtiss "U.S. Army," midwing, Air Corps star-in-circle insignia, V-12 engine, two machine guns, three-bladed propeller, marked "Made in USA" and "Ralstoy" in diamond, 3" x 3-1/4"	20	30	40

RENWAL

	C6	C8	C10
B-17, plastic, c. 1944, 9-1/4" wingspan	25	50	100
B-17, small	10	30	40

DC-4, Renwal, $60

Martin Mars, Renwal, $120

	C6	C8	C10
B-25, plastic, c. 1944, 6-3/4" wingspan 30	60	100
B-29, No. 29 30	60	100
C54 Transport, large, plastic 20	30	60
DC-4, 7" wingspan 20	30	60
Martin Mars No. 15 30	60	120
P38, plastic 20	40	100
P40, plastic 20	45	100
P47, plastic 20	40	100
PB2Y Flying Boat 20	40	100

STEELCRAFT

	C6	C8	C10
Akron blimp pull toy, 25" long 75	112	150
Army Scout Plane, single engine, high wing monoplane, c. 1920s, 22-1/2" wingspan 700	1100	1825
Army Scout Plane, trimotor, single high wing, c. 1920s 300	750	2200
Army Scout Plane, green and orange, 23" wingspan 100	300	500
Graf Zeppelin, pressed steel, pull toy, 30-1/2" 250	375	500
Graf Zeppelin, pull toy, 32" long 300	450	600
Lockheed Sirius, pull toy, 21-1/2" wingspan 650	1200	1740
Macon Zeppelin, 25" long 350	525	700

Graf Zeppelin, pull toy, $500

	C6	C8	C10
Monoplane, two open cockpits, c. 1930s, 16" wingspan 250	375	600
NX107, "Little Jim," 23" wingspan 550	825	1300
NX130 U.S. Mail Plane, one engine 388	580	775
NX130, blue eagles on wings, 23" wingspan 475	700	950
NX131, trimotor, U.S. Mail plane, pull toy, 26-1/2" wingspan 700	1200	1650
Pan Am airliner, 26" 135	200	300
Pedal Plane "Pursuit," 1940 1000	1700	3000
Pedal Plane, high wing Monoplane, No. 79, 32" wingspan, 48" long 1500	2500	4000

WYANDOTTE

	C6	C8	C10
Airacuda, pressed steel, twin vertical stabilizers, twin pusher engines, blue or red, 8-1/2" wingspan 45	70	90
Airliner, four engine, pressed steel, 12-3/4" wingspan 73	110	145
Airliner, two engine, wooden wheels, WWII-era 75	110	150

Army Scout Plane, single engine, Steelcraft, $1,825

Lockheed Sirius, pull toy, Steelcraft, $1,740

Mystery Plane, twin engine, Wyandotte, $100

Rockett Racer, Wyandotte, $150

	C6	C8	C10
Bomber, Army, pressed steel, two engine...... 90	135	180
China Clipper, No. 207, 13" wingspan 125	200	300
City Airport, American Airlines, two hangars, control tower, etc., lights up 150	250	375
Crusader, 9-3/4" wingspan........................... 35	55	85
Crusader, twelve-window version 40	75	100
Gyrocopter, twin engine passenger plane, c. 1930s, 12-1/2" wingspan 100	200	300
High Wing Passenger Monoplane, No. 2 Lockheed Vega, single engine, bullet nose, 18" wingspan 175	265	350
Military Air Transport, 13" wingspan 40	60	80
Mystery Plane, twin engine, wings trail backward, No. 101, 4-1/2" wingspan 30	50	100
Rocket Racer No. 319, c. 1935 70	120	150
Stratocruiser, 13" wingspan 75	120	150
Super Jet.. 80	120	160
U.S. Navy Seaplane, c. 1941, 14-1/2" wingspan 215	322	430

MISCELLANEOUS

	C6	C8	C10
Adam Bomb, c. 1946, wood and metal (also "Atom Bomb"), 11" wingspan........ 50	100	150
Aeroplane w/clip of bombs attached to it, No. 195.. 45	70	110
Aeroplane w/Monoplane piggy-backed on it, No. 195... 50	75	120
Aeroplane, "U.S. Army," single engine transport, No. 195, 3-3/4" wingspan...... 20	30	50
Aeroplane, marked "U.S. 256," Air Corps star insignia, Metal Cast, No. 321, 3-1/4" long................................. 15	20	25
Aeroplane, two engine, lead (some marked "Fred Greene"), c. 1940s, Metal Cast, No. 66, 4-1/2" wingspan 10	15	25
Air mail pedal plane, American National, 1926.. 3000	5000	9000
Air Mail, Kenton, wingspan approx. 8"..... 600	1000	1450

Airplane, tri-motor, Lincoln White Metal, $75

	C6	C8	C10
Airmail plane, pressed steel, marked "NX-265," Keystone, 24" wingspan 800	1500	2130
Airmail, "NC-263," Keystone 500	750	1000
Airplane and Pylon, Lionel No. 55 300	450	1100
Airplane Kit, "Schoenhut's Airplane Builder," wood...................................... 130	200	300
Airplane, early 1900s, single wing, prop behind tail, pilot, open fuselage 300	450	600
Airplane, streamlined, swallow-shaped, pilot, cowled radial engine, tin propeller, Lincoln White Metal, c. 4-1/2" x 3".. 50	80	140
Airplane, streamlined, swallow-shaped, pilot, cowled radial engine, tin propeller, Lincoln White Metal, c. 3" x 2-1/2" 40	75	110
Airplane, trimotored, Fokker F-11(?), tapered high wings w/wings symbol embossed, seven cylinder, radial engines, outboards mounted on landing gear struts, tin propellers, metal wheels, no windows, Lincoln White Metal, 3-1/4" x 4-1/2" 50	75	125
Airplane, trimotored, Fokker F-11(?), tapered high wings w/wings symbol embossed, seven cylinder, radial engines, outboards mounted in wings, unrealistic window patterns, metal wheels, Lincoln White Metal, 2-1/2" x 2-1/2" 30	50	75
Airplane, wood, ride-on 75	100	150
Airport mechanical tin litho airport w/early plastic planes that fly, control tower controls for stunts, crash truck pumps water, airport bus, gasoline truck, Set No. 88, T. Cohn Co., c. 1940s 75	125	250

	C6	C8	C10
Amphibian, two overhead engines, hand-painted, tin wind-up, Bing, 16" wingspan 1400	1400	2500	3400
Army Tank Transport Plane, two detachable tanks under wings, tanks have hum motor device, pressed steel, Buddy L., No. 959, 1941, 27" wingspan .. 460	460	690	925
Best: See Kansas Toy & Novelty			
Biplane, c. 1920s, Schieble, 15-1/2" long..... 300	300	450	600
Biplane, steel wind-up, cast-iron pilot, Kingsbury, 16" long...................... 350	350	525	700
Biplane, wooden, tin tail, aluminum propeller, pull plane, propeller spins, approx. 7-1/2" wingspan 40	40	70	200
Blimp, "U.S.N.," Savoye, 4" long 20	20	30	60
Boeing 247 twin engine "U.S. Army," Erie.... 25	25	45	70
Boeing B-17, Erie...................... 25	25	60	125
Bombing Plane No. 11-P, cast iron, double barrel, steel propeller, Big Bang, 13" long................. 350	350	600	800
Bombing Plane No. 11-P, cast iron, single barrel, die-cast propeller, Big Bang, 13" long................. 600	600	900	1500
Bonanza B-35, Manoil, No. 519 30	30	50	75
Build-A-Zep, builds twenty-one different 18" zeppelins, Metalcraft 242	242	365	485
Cargo Plane, Eldon, 11" long........ 20	20	30	40
Chicago" Dirigible, tin litho, Strauss, 10"... 125	125	188	250
Defiant, plastic, Thomas Toys, 4" long........ 20	20	30	40
Dirigible, slush lead, "USN," Tommy Toy1930s 25	25	38	50
Dual-Control Plane, Sun Rubber, No. 12010, 4-1/2" long................ 25	25	35	50
Electronic Fighter Jet, Ideal, c. 1959 135	135	200	270
Ercoupe, Manoil, No. 520 30	30	50	75
Erector Biplane, w/electric motor, A.C. Gilbert 150	150	260	600
F-80 Jet Action Rocket Launcher, Thomas Toys 20	20	30	40
Fighter, tin, c. 1940, single engine, four machine guns mounted on wing..... 20	20	30	60

	C6	C8	C10
Flagship America airplane, metal Ford trimotor, pressed steel, c. 1930s, 25" wingspan 175	175	300	600
Flying Airship, aluminum wind-up, Strauss 275	275	350	550
Flying Boxcar, Remco........ 50	50	75	100
Flying Plane, Liberty Playthings, early 1930s 150	150	225	300
Ford Trimotor, Metalcraft........ 112	112	162	225
Ford Trimotor, steel, Schieble, 29-1/2" long........ 500	500	900	1550
Futurmatic Airport, Automatic Toy Co...... 150	150	225	300
Giant Flyer Monoplane, Tip Top, c. 1920s, 23" long 200	200	350	500
Globemaster, Ideal........ 42	42	63	85
Graf Zeppelin, Strauss, 16" long........ 240	240	360	480
Helicopter, Army, tin litho, friction drive, spinning prop, 13" long 40	40	70	100
Helicopter, friction, Irwin, c. 1950, 15" long.. 30	30	45	60
Heliport City Play set, Ideal........ 70	70	105	140
High Wing Monoplane, marked "U.S.," single engine, open ironwork body, spool wheel works, prop, 8" wingspan 200	200	300	400
High wing monoplane, pressed steel, Girard, 10" wingspan........ 125	125	250	470
High wing monoplane, pressed steel, Girard, 18" wingspan........ 150	150	500	750
Hillclimber Biplane, c. 1917 225	225	338	450
Ikarus, tin and paper, Lehmann early, 18" wingspan........ 1200	1200	2000	3000
Jet, USAF, friction powered, tin litho, 5" wingspan 15	15	20	35
KD-1 Mak-a-plane, 4" long, all metal w/rubber wheels, mechanical, 1940s 40	40	50	70
Kennedy Airport, Remco 58	58	85	115
Lindy cast iron, nickel prop and wheels, 3-1/2" wingspan 105	105	158	210
Lindy-type plane, cast iron, North & Judd, 4-3/8" long 175	175	265	350
Lindy-type plane, lead, 2-1/4" wingspan 10	10	20	30
Lindy-type plane, small, No. 52 15	15	20	30
Lockheed F90, Manoil, No. 517........ 30	30	50	75
Los Angeles dirigible, Kenton, 8" long 500	500	750	1050
Luscombe Airplane, 4" long........ 30	30	45	60
Monoplane and Catapult Hanger, Buddy L, No. 2007, c. 1930-31 1200	1200	2200	3000
Monoplane, "A.F. Lines Air Service," American Flyer No. 560 c. 1929, 24" wingspan 350	350	525	700
Monoplane, high wing, open cockpit and pilot, red, yellow or blue, painted disc wheels, Dayton, No. 700, 13" wingspan 125	125	250	400

Blimp, "U.S.N.," Savoye, $60

	C6	C8	C10
Monoplane, high wing, trimotor, clockwork, Kingsbury, 15" wingspan...... 475	475	715	950
Monoplane, Liberty V-12 engine, cast propeller, eight oval and two round windows, ailerons and tail surfaces detailed and three disc wheels w/ those black painted "tires," 3-3/16" x 3-5/8" 25	25	40	70
Monoplane, Savoye, 3-1/2" wingspan 30	30	40	80
Monoplane, two pilots in open cockpit Liberty V-12 engine, cast propeller, eight oval and two round windows, two painted main gear disc wheels, Midwest, 3-1/8" x 3-5/8" 25	25	40	70
Navion, Manoil, No. 518.................. 30	30	50	75
Northrup Alpha Monoplane, marked "PURE the Pure Oil Company," Metalcraft, 17" wingspan 600	600	800	1400
Northrup Delta single engine passenger airliner, Erie.................. 30	30	60	125
NX-130, high wing monoplane, pressed steel, Boycraft, 22" wingspan... 350	350	525	850
The Pathfinder, trimotor monoplane, Katz Toys, 22" wingspan 350	350	600	900
Pedal Car, Biplane, two motor, 54" long ... 500	500	900	1800
Pedal Car, Pursuit Plane, 1941.................. 1800	1800	3100	4450
Pony Blimp, cast iron, Kenton, 6" long 125	125	200	400
Pursuit Ship, marked "25-P75," Sun Rubber, c. 1940-41, 4-1/4" wingspan 20	20	35	50
Pyro Jet, 6" long, plastic 10	10	15	25
The Red Arrow No. 137 single monoplane, Katz Toys, pull toy..................... 300	300	450	850
Ride 'Em Mail Plane, marked "NC-273," 1930s, Keystone, 23-1/2" wingspan.... 1200	1200	2000	3000
Riding plane, No. 293, marked "Ride 'Em" fighter, Keystone, 28" wingspan 400	400	600	850
Riding plane, seat over tail, steering bar over cabin, single wing, high, one engine, Keystone, 23-1/2" long............. 500	500	750	1000
Riding Rocket, Metalcraft, 24" long 100	100	150	200
Rocket and Space Ship No. 305, friction, tin litho w/rubber wheels, sparks, Automatic Toy Co., late 1930s, 9" long, 4-1/2" wide, 3" tall 30	30	50	75
Shenandoah Dirigible, Lehmann, 7-1/2" long.................................. 225	225	388	450
Silver Eagle, aluminum plane, wooden wheels, two engine, Automatic Toy Co., c. 1930s, 13" wingspan 75	75	125	200
Single high wing monoplane, Buddy L, No. 5000, c. 1929-31 400	400	600	800
Single seat open cockpit Northrup Gamma, Erie 50	50	80	135
Sky Cruiser, tin litho, two-motor transport, engines turn w/ friction mechanism, 18" wingspan......................... 40	40	75	100
Spirit of America pull toy aeroplane, steel and litho, 14" long 30	30	50	75
Spirit of America, c. 1928, American Flyer, 18" wingspan......................... 150	150	225	400
Spirit of Columbia, "555," pressed tin friction, American Flyer, wingspan 18"......................... 500	500	750	1000
Spirit of St. Louis, came as kit, Metalcraft, 9" long 118	118	175	235
Spirit of St. Louis, go around tower, two planes, pressed steel, electrical, United Electric......................... 800	800	1200	1600
Spirit of St. Louis, lead, marked "Pat. No. 74042" and "Ancient Art Metal Co., Brooklyn, N.Y.," c. 1927, 5-1/8" wingspan 40	40	70	125
Swallow high wing monoplane, American National, 24" wingspan 1200	1200	2000	3000
Theodore Hahn Aeroplane, lead alloy, No. 187, 1920s......................... 20	20	40	75
Thick-winged monoplane, w/oversized wheels, approx. 2-1/2" long 20	20	30	45
Tin Goose, tri-engine, Kingsbury, c. 1930s, 21" wingspan......................... 600	600	900	1500
Trans Atlantic Monoplane, painted pressed steel wind-up, Kingsbury, c. 1930, 11" long......................... 200	200	300	500
Transport Airplane (Ford), Buddy L, No. 603, c. 1946, 27" wingspan 300	300	450	600
Transport, Sun Rubber, No. 12009, 4" long 40	40	70	100
Trimotor, Keystone, 1920s 900	900	1400	2200
Triple Hangar and three planes (planes are monocoupes), Buddy L, No. 5010, c. 1931......................... 1700	1700	2700	3750
Turner High Wing Monoplane, one-engine, 1930s, 18-1/2" wingspan......................... 275	275	400	600

Monoplane, Savoye, $80

	C6	C8	C10
Turner High Wing Monoplane, pressed steel, 22-1/2" wingspan	300	450	700
Twin engine bomber, B-25?, Metal Cast, No. 43, 5-1/4" wingspan	10	15	20
Two-place open cockpit, "U.S. Army" on wings, Erie	30	50	75
U.S. Airmail biplane, steel wind-up, Kingsbury, 15" long	200	500	900
U.S. Navy Rescue Float Plane, plastic wind-up, Ideal, 10" wingspan	32	48	65
United Boeing twin engine, cast iron, Kenton	112	168	225
UX-166, Lindy-type plane, cast-iron nickeled engine and wheels, A.C. Williams, 5-3/4" wingspan	75	112	150
UX83, cast iron, A.C. Williams, 3-1/4" wingspan	100	150	200
UX-99, cast iron, A.C. Williams, 4-1/2" wingspan	112	170	225
Warhawk, plastic, Thomas Toys, 4" long	20	30	40
Watrous single engine biplane, pressed steel bell toy, c. 1915, 8-1/4" wingspan	200	400	700
Whirlybird Helicopter, Remco	20	30	40
Whiz Skyfighter biplane, Girard, early	100	200	300
WWI "Air Aces" Playset, Remco, 1965	138	205	275

	C6	C8	C10
Zeppelin, "EPL 1," Lehmann No. 651	400	800	1200
Zeppelin, "EPL 2," Lehmann No. 652, c. 1907	350	600	1000
Zeppelin, "Goodyear" decals, hatch opens, 25" long	125	225	350
Zeppelin, "Graf Zeppelin," aluminum, Strauss, 16" long	175	250	350
Zeppelin, "Graf Zeppelin," cast iron, A.C. Williams, 5" long,	50	75	125
Zeppelin, "Graf Zeppelin," cast iron, A.C. Williams, 5-1/2" long	100	150	200
Zeppelin, "Graf Zeppelin," cast iron, A.C. Williams, 8" long	100	175	275
Zeppelin, "Los Angeles," cast iron, 12" long	300	750	1500
Zeppelin, "Pony DE107," cast iron, 5-1/2" long	50	100	250
Zeppelin, "U.S. Akron," pot metal, c. 1932, 6" long	25	40	75
Zeppelin, "ZEP," cast iron, 4" long	80	120	160
Zeppelin, cast iron, approx. 3" long	40	60	80
Zeppelin, metal, 25" long	42	64	85
Zeppelin, pull toy, "Little Giant"	50	100	200
Zeppelin, pull toy, silver, c. 1920-30s, cast iron, 6" long	60	90	120

AMERICAN PAPER TOYS

Paper toys and dolls (also called cut-outs, punch-outs and press-outs) have been around since the mid-1600s when they were called Pantins. Dolls as well as forts, planes, and trains, have been produced in paper. Paper toys and dolls were extremely popular from the end of the last century to the period after World War II. Almost every type of toy can be found in a paper or cardboard version.

American companies began turning out paper toys by the thousands around 1900. The most popular manufacturer was the McLoughlin Bros. Company which started out with paper toys in 1857 in New York City. McLoughlin was eventually bought out by Milton Bradley and moved to Springfield, Massachusetts in 1920. McLoughlin/Milton Bradley products included beautifully lithographed covered boxed sets of cardboard figures on wooden stands and sheets of American and foreign soldiers.

During the years 1895 to 1905, almost every major newspaper in America had Sunday Art Supplements which were paper toys for the children. These sheets included a wide range of subjects including armies and navies of the world, historical panoramas, political figures, personalities of the day, and cut-out dolls of celebrities with vast wardrobes. Paper houses and villages were sold by several companies including McLoughlin Bros., Milton Bradley, Built-Rite and Megow . The World War II-era was the golden age of paper toys in the United States.

During the 1940s every conceivable type of toy was available in paper, usually with a patriotic wartime theme. The Major Paper doll publishers were Merrill and Saalfield, and they produced the paper doll books that children of the 1940s through 1960s played with.

There are now quite a few books on paper dolls and paper toys, including *Blair Witton: Paper Toys of the World*, Hobby House Press, 1986; *Paper soldiers* by Edward Ryan, *WWII-era Paper Toys* by John Matthews, *and Ann Tolstoi Wallach: Paper Dolls*, Van Nostrand 1982.

Contributor: Judith Izen, P.O Box 623, Lexington, MA 02173. Izen is a noted doll and paper doll authority whose paper doll articles have appeared in several publications and writes a monthly column for *Toy Shop* magazine. Her books include *Collectors Guide to Ideal Dolls and Collectors Encyclopedia of Vogue Dolls* (coauthored with Carol Stover).

Photos in this section by Jonathan Newman, and courtesy of Barbara and Jonathan Newman, and Judith Izen.

BUILT-RITE

Built-Rite began to produce cardboard construction toys in 1934. Judging by their catalogs, Built-Rite sold its last fort (25A) in 1954 and its last few construction sets in 1956, that is until 1963-64, when the No. 1033 Doll House and No. 1027 Stock Farm appeared. In 1978, Built-Rite added plastic play sets No. 6002 Fort Laredo and No. 6001 Starship Counterforce Action Playset. It dropped the Built-Rite name and became Warren in 1976, and they continue to make card games, games and puzzles under that name. Its greatest period of success was probably enjoyed prior to and during World War II.

	C6	C8	C10
No. 1 Toy Soldiers, WWI helmets, each	2	3	4
No. 2 Toy Trench	25	45	60
No. 7 Private Garage, brick	35	45	55
No. 7 Army Plane Hangar	48	60	70
No. 8 House, brick	65	80	90
No. 9 House, stucco and brick	65	80	90
No. 10 House, two-story, brick and shingle	65	80	90

	C6	C8	C10
No. 14 "Front Line" Trench and Soldier set, w/trench and six WWII soldiers	40	55	60
No. 15 Commercial Garage	65	80	90
No. 16 Fort, no ramp	70	90	125
No. 17 Service Station	65	80	90
No. 18 Airport	65	80	85
No. 19 Railroad Station	60	70	80
No. 20 Railroad Tunnel	12	22	27
No. 20 Army Battery set	90	125	145
No. 22 Army Outpost	45	65	75
No. 25 Fort, one ramp	90	120	130
No. 25A Twenty-six-piece fort and soldier set, same fort as No. 25, WWII soldiers, two sandbag foxholes and fiberboard pistol, sold through 1954	120	150	175
No. 26 United Airlines Airport Hangar	60	75	85
No. 27 Barn w/animals	30	45	55
No. 28 Garage and Super Service Station	70	85	95
No. 29 Three cart set	25	40	45
No. 33 Lokdwood Dolls, late 1940s, paper dolls	25	35	45
No. 33 House, Tudor type	65	80	90
No. 34 House, two-story	65	80	90

	C6	C8	C10
No. 35 Modern Doll House	65	80	90
No. 36 House	65	80	90
No. 36F Three-room furnished doll house	85	95	105
No. 37 Farm Machinery set	35	50	60
No. 45 Living Room Furniture	45	55	65
No. 46 Dining Room Furniture	45	55	65
No. 47 Bedroom Furniture	45	55	65
No. 48 Bathroom Furniture	45	55	65
No. 49 Kitchen Furniture	45	55	65
No. 50 Army Raiders' Victory Unit, twenty-eight pieces, truck, tank, AA gun, jeep, semi-track truck and twenty soldiers, WWII	75	90	100
No. 55 Five miniature cardboard houses	35	55	65
No. 56 Five miniature buildings, church, school, RR station, firehouse and drugstore	35	55	65
No. 57 M Eight-piece farm set	40	50	65
No. 60 Navy Battle Fleet and Coast Artillery Gun	35	60	75
No. 66 Three-piece kitchen	30	45	55
No. 75 Living Room Furniture	45	55	65
No. 76 Dining Room Furniture	45	55	65
No. 77 Bedroom Furniture	45	55	65
No. 77 American Ranger Fighters, eight vehicles, WWII soldiers	80	90	100
No. 78 Kitchen Furniture	45	55	65
No. 83 Weapons Carrier	15	20	30
No. 84 Armored Car	15	20	30
No. 100 A Fortress, w/two ramps, c. 1938	120	155	180
No. 105 Farm set w/twenty plastic animals	35	45	55
No. 111 Railroad Accessory set	25	30	40
No. 112 American Fighters, includes 100A fortress w/soldiers, cannons, etc., fifty-five pieces, no flag on tower	120	155	180
No. 115 Doll House, garage set w/car	65	80	90
No. 119 Farm set	45	65	75
No. 120 Five-room suburban doll house	65	85	90
No. 127 Large Barn w/animals	30	40	50
No. 128 Miniature Village and Scenery set	35	48	60
No. 148 Train Accessory set	30	40	50
No. 156 Miniature houses and buildings	55	65	70
No. 178 Train Accessory set	30	40	50
No. 201 Twenty-six-piece Guardsman set, two trenches, artillery base, cannon, pistol and WWII soldiers	70	90	120
No. 202 Train Scenery, twenty-eight pieces	45	65	75
No. 204F Furnished Country Estate	60	80	90
No. 210 Railroad Station and accessories	30	40	50

	C6	C8	C10
No. 212 Station and Railroad accessories	35	45	55
No. 245 Miniature Village	35	50	60
No. 252 Fort Set, twenty-six pieces, No. 25 fort, post-war	110	150	180
No. 298 Train Accessory set	30	40	50
No. 300 Stock and Grain Elevator	30	35	45
No. 375 Station and Railroad set	30	40	50
No. 415 House, boxed set w/19" house and garage, twenty-seven pieces of furniture, sedan, baby buggy, shrubbery, etc.,c. 1943, 13" x 20"	85	110	135
No. 459 Five rooms of toy furniture	45	55	65
No. 460 Pocket size series of miniatures paper doll set	15	20	24
No. 498 Train Accessory set	25	35	45
No. 566 Village	40	55	65
No. 1001 Modern Stock Farm	50	60	80
No. 1027 Stock Farm	50	60	80
No. 1033 Doll House	50	65	75
No. 1422 Fort and Soldiers, ninety-four pieces, two-ramp fort	110	145	175
No. 2050 Country Estate, house, bushes, dog, cat, baby buggy	70	90	100
Ranch, over 180 pieces	150	185	200

McLoughlin Bros.

McLoughlin Brothers was the largest American producer of paper soldiers and one of the earliest in the paper doll field. The Brooklyn, New York firm, founded in 1828, began producing paper dolls as early as 1857. Among the other paper toys it sold were dollhouse furniture, toy theaters with actors and scenery, and blocks. The company was sold in 1920 to Milton Bradley.

	C6	C8	C10
02 Series, c. 1904-1910, price per each			
British Highlanders	2	3	4
U.S. Zouaves	2	3	4
U.S. Continentals	2	3	4
U.S. Navy	2	3	4
U.S. Infantry in Campaign Uniforms (Spanish-American War)	2	3	4
American Indians, kneeling and standing	2	3	4
West Point Cadets	2	3	4
West Point Cadets (round base), c. 1915	2	3	4
100 Soldiers on Parade, first set, c. 1898	300	350	400
100 Soldiers on Parade, second set, c. 1898	300	350	400
260 Series, c. 1889-1895			
U.S. Regulars, spiked helmet, each	2	3	4
U.S. Infantry	2	3	4

	C6	C8	C10
West Point Cadets 2		3	4
U.S. Regulars 2		3	4
U.S. Infantry... 2		3	4
Bandsmen, various instruments, each..... 3		4	5
Navy - USS Boston 2		3	4
Grenadier Guards, each 2		3	4
Annapolis Cadets, each............................. 2		3	4
Boy Scouts, holding rifles across chests, c. 1915... 5		6	7
Brass Band, 1890, each 4		5	6
British Infantry Red Coats w/spiked helmets on small wooden blocks, c. 1898, 6" high, each 4		5	6
Complete set.. 150		200	250
Dutch Paper doll, boy of the Village of Vollendam, No. 0103 c. 1910, 10-1/2" x 10-1/2" sheet 18		25	30
Figures, horizontal sheet of ten figures, uncut, c. 1890 35		50	75
Grenadiers, 1890, each 3		4	5
Infantry Soldiers, printed 1857, each 3		4	5
Infantry, c. 1875, each 3		4	5
Landing party for USS Texas, printed 1898, sailor 5-1/4" high........................... 4		5	6
Mounted U.S. Cavalry, Hussar type, charging, several different poses, c. 1884, each 3		4	5
New Folding Doll House, cardboard w/litho paper, boxed set, 1897............. 400		500	575
New Pretty Village Church set, 1897 90		125	145
New Pretty Village School set, 1897 90		125	145

	C6	C8	C10
New Pretty Village, individual buildings 12		15	18
Series No. 4026, paper soldiers on sheet, seven soldiersplus officer in field uniform, includes Belgium, Italy, France and Britain, 10-1/2" x 10-1/2" c. 1916, each 20		30	40
U.S. Infantry, from Spanish-American War, c. 1898, approx. 6" high on wooden blocks, each 4		5	6
U.S. Regulars, glossy series of figures in full dress, c. 1898, 5" high 4		5	6
U.S. Zouaves, Civil War era, blue coats, red baggy trousers on small wooden blocks, c. 1898, 6" high 4		5	6
West Point Cadets, small glossy series, c. 1898, 4-1/2" high 4		5	6
Zouaves, 1884, each..................................... 3		4	5

MISCELLANEOUS

	C6	C8	C10
A Day With Diane, Saalfield No. 1770, by Laura Bischoff 25		35	45
Air-Hostess, Saalfield 2546, 1947 30		40	50
Alice in Wonderland, Whitman, 1976 5		10	15
Alice Faye, Merrill No. 4800, 1941 100		150	200
American Beauties Paper Dolls, Reuben Lilja & Co. No. 917, c. 1942 15		20	25

Individual building from The New Pretty Village, McLoughlin Bros., $18

Alice Faye Paper Dolls with costumes, Merril, 1941, $235

	C6	C8	C10
American Beauty Paper Dolls, w/dresses worn by White House First Ladies from 1789-1951, Merrill No. 154815, 1951 20	20	30	40
American Defense Battles Punch-out Book by George Trimmer, Merrill No. 3430, 1940...... 75	75	95	105
American Family Paper-Doll Book "Costumes for all the family from 1610 to now," Grinnel No. C1002 40	40	50	75
Amos & Andy cut-out, cardboard of just Andy, stand-up, 8-1/2" high 5	5	7	10
Animal Paper Dolls to Dress, includes bear, monkey, pig and kitten, Saalfield 2598, 1950 15	15	20	25
Animals to Paint, Saalfield, 1910 10	10	15	23
Ann Blythe, Merrill No. 2250-25, 1952....... 45	45	55	90
Army Air Forces Aircraft Identification Silhouette Model-Feb. 1943, 1:72-scale of Japanese fighter Najajima T-97, A.N.F., 7" x 11" envelope...... 16	16	20	27
Army Ambulance, Handi-Kraft, c. 1942 30	30	40	48
Army Cut-outs, Saalfield No. 245, 1937...... 55	55	65	80
Army Nurse and Doctor paper dolls, Merrill 3425, 1942...... 32	32	40	65
Around the World with Bob and Barbara, Children's Press No. 3000, 1946 15	15	20	30
Assemble Nine Model Warplanes, four Model Tanks, Fawcett Publications, Lowe, 1941...... 55	55	75	85
Ava Gardner, Whitman No. 119215, 1949, 1952 60	60	85	125
Baby Brother by Queen Holden, Whitman No. 920, 1929...... 55	55	85	110
Baby Brother Tender Love, Whitman, 1977 5	5	10	15
Baby First Step, (Mattel) Whitman No. 1997, 1965 10	10	15	24
Babyland Merrill No. 3642, 1955...... 20	20	35	45
Baby Pat, Whitman No. 2072, 1963...... 10	10	15	20
Babysitter paper dolls, Lowe No. 945 15	15	20	30
Barbara Britton Paper Dolls with Magic Stay-on costumes, boxed set, Saalfield No. 5190, 1954...... 50	50	65	75
Barbie and Ken, boxed set, Whitman No. 4797, 1962, 7" x 12"...... 25	25	35	55
Barbie and Skipper, yachting outfits, Whitman No. 1957, 1964...... 20	20	30	40
Barbie and Skipper Campsite at Lucky Lake, Whitman No. 1836, 1980...... 7	7	10	15
Barbie Boutique, Whitman No. 1954, 1973 10	10	15	25
Barbie Costume Dolls, Whitman No. 1976, 1964 25	25	35	55

	C6	C8	C10
Beautiful Paper Dolls by Betty Campbell, has some of same paper dolls as Little Miss America Paper Dolls, Saalfield No. 242, 1941 20	20	35	45
Belle of the Ball Paper Dolls, 1948, Saalfield No. 2702 20	20	35	45
Beth Ann, Whitman No. 1953, 1970 7	7	10	15
Betsy McCall Sheets from *McCalls* magazine *3*	*3*	*5*	*8*
Betsy McCall, Whitman No. 4744, 1971 25	25	35	45
Betsy McCall Around the World Paper dolls, c. 1962 20	20	30	40
Betsy McCall Dress 'n Play Paper Dolls, boxed set, Standard/Toycraft/McCall No. 802, 1963, 12" x 18"...... 25	25	40	50
Betsy Ross and Her Friends, boxed set, Platt and Munk No. 224B, 1963, 7" x 11" 7	7	10	15
Betty and Joan, Lois and Joan, Whitman No. 1015, 1941, 1945 20	20	30	40
Betty Bonnet Her Family and Friends, by Sheila Young, George W. Jacobs & Co., Phila., 1915Each series includes six sheets and folder. First series...... 125	125	150	180

Betty Bonnet, Her Family and Friends, second series, George W. Jacobs & Co., $175

Betty Grable Paper Dolls, Merrill, 1951, $110

	C6	C8	C10
Second series 100		145	175
Third series.. 100		145	175
Betty Grable, Merrill No. 1558, 1951 55		80	125
Betty Sue A Cut-out Doll No. 1010,			
c. 1940.. 15		25	35
The Beverly Hillbillies: Jed, Jethro,			
Granny and Elly May, Whitman			
No. 1955, 1964 35		55	75
Big-Girl Paper Dolls, McLoughlin Bros.			
(Milton Bradley), No. 707, 1940 20		30	40

Bild-A-Set Constructor Kit, $35

Bob Hope and Dorothy Lamour Cut-out Book, Whitman, 1942, $240

	C6	C8	C10
Big Invasion Punch-out Book, punch-out			
of beach landing, Whitman			
No. 1936, 1964 25		35	40
Bild-A-Set Constructor Kit, Erector-type			
set of cardboard, boxed, No. 85 22		30	35
Binson-Freeman Pre Flight Trainer,			
cockpit and how-to-fly course 75		113	150
Birthday Party Stand-up Cut-out Dolls,			
twenty boys and girls, National			
Syndicate Displays, Inc., 1944 20		35	45
Blue Bonnet Paper Dolls by Florence			
Salter, Merrill No. 3444, 1942.................. 20		35	45
Blue Feather and Silver Cloud,			
Native-American dolls, Abbott			
No. 1356, 1940s.. 25		40	55
Boarding School Dolls and Clothes,			
Merrill No. 3492, 1942............................. 25		40	55
Bob Hope and Dorothy Lamour,			
Whitman No. 976, 1942 100		150	250
Bobby Socks Cut-out Dolls designed by			
Doris Lane Butler, Whitman			
No. 988, 1945 20		30	40
Bombers by Schomburg, inlcudes B-17,			
B-25, B-24, Douglas A-20A, short			
"Stirling," Whitman No. 961, 1943 60		75	100
A Book of Airplanes, Whitman No. 923,			
1930 20		25	30
Book of Paper Doll Cut-outs, Saalfield			
No. 2051, 1927 40		55	65

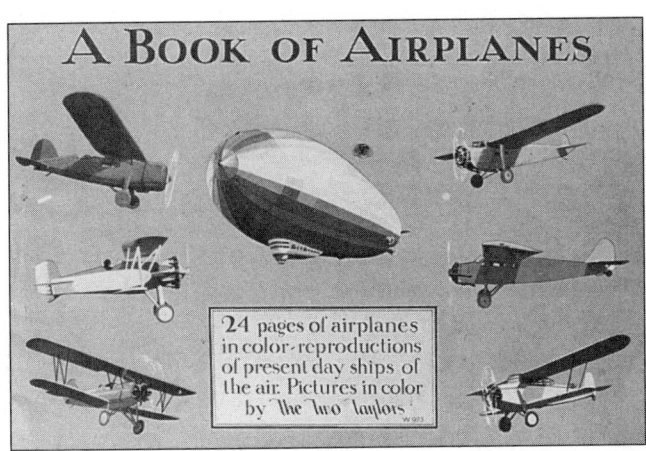

A Book of Airplanes, Whitman, 1930, $30

	C6	C8	C10
The Brady Bunch, includes toy phonograph and records, boxed set, Whitman No. 1976, 1973	35	60	75
Brenda Lee, De Journette No. 4360, 1964, 6-1/2" x 10"	45	55	85
Brenda Lee Teenage Celebrity, Lowe No. 2785, 1961	40	60	80
Bridal Doll Book, Watkins-Strathmor No. 1818, 1963	15	20	30

	C6	C8	C10
Bridal Doll Book, Whitman No. 1983, 1978	7	10	15
Bridal Party, set contains five dolls, Whitman No. 1187, 1950	20	30	40
Bridal Party Paper Dolls, Saalfield, 1963	15	25	35
Bride and Groom, Merrill No. 3443, 1949	25	35	50
Bride and Groom, Merrill No. 1555, 1949	25	35	50
Bride and Groom, Western box set, 1982	3	5	8
Bride and Groom, Whitman No. 1957, 1968	10	15	25
Bride and Groom Military Wedding Party, set includes sixteen dolls, Merrill No. 3411, 1941	40	60	80
Bride Doll Cut-out Book, Samuel Lowe No. 1043, 1940s	20	30	40
Brother and Sister Statuette Dolls, heavy cardboardWhitman No. 1182-15, 1950, 7-1/2" dolls	15	25	30
Buffy Paper Dolls (Family Affair), Whitman No. 1955, 1968	32	45	65
Buffy and Jody, (Family Affair), two magic dolls w/stay-on wardrobes, WhitmanNo. 4764, 1970	30	40	60
Camouflage Defense Force, heavy cardboard, airplanes,soldiers,			

Bridal Party Paper Dolls, Saalfield, 1963, $35

Cinderella, Saalfield, $45

	C6	C8	C10
anti-aircraftguns all hiddenwithin farm buildings, boxed, Jay Line Mfg. Co., No. 431, c. 1943 55	55	75	90
Career Girls Artcraft, No. 4471, 1960s 15	15	20	30
Career girls w/cloth-like clothes, Whitman No. 937, by Doris Lane Butler, 1944 20	20	30	40
Charmin' Chatty, Whitman No. 1959, 1964 20	20	30	45
Charming Paper Dolls, Saalfield No. 1357, c. 1960 10	10	15	25
Cheerleader-Teenage Doll, Mary and Elaine w/four pages of clothes, Stephens Publishing Co. No. 182, 1950? 10	10	15	20
Children From Other Lands, eight cut-out dolls w/native costumes, Whitman No. 2089, 1961 10	10	15	20
Children in the Shoe, Merrill No. 1562, 1949 20	20	30	40
Cinderella, Saalfield No. 1610, 1950 by Ethel Hays 25	25	35	45
Cinderella Steps Out, Lowe No. 1242 25	25	35	50
Circus Day, by Art Tanchon, animals, clown, circus cages and wagons, Stephens Printing Co. No. 135, 1946 18	18	22	28
Circus Paper Dolls, Saalfield No. 2610, 1952 10	10	15	20
Claire McCardell, designer of the American look, Whitman No. 2067, 1956 30	30	45	65
Claudette Colbert, Saalfield No. 2451, 1943 100	100	150	200

	C6	C8	C10
Cloth-Like Clothes for Three Cute Girls, Whitman No. 1178:15, flocked clothes, 1949 20	20	25	35
Clothes Make a Lady, Lowe No. 1029, 1941 20	20	30	40
The Coke Crowd, eight teens w/costumes, Merrill No. 3445, 1946 30	30	45	65
College Chums, Saalfield No. 719, 1950s 25	25	35	45
College Style Paper Dolls, Merrill No. 3400, 1941 30	30	45	65
Colonial Paperdolls, Saalfield No. 1353 25	25	40	50
Colorgraphic Statue-ettes, three-dimensional and stand-up paper dolls of Marine, Soldier, Sailor, Nurse, WAAC and WAVE, boxed, 1943 25	25	40	50
Comet Model Airplane Co. Die-Cut Glider, containing die-cut U.S. Army fighter, printed in 1942 by the Comet Model Airplane Co., 5-1/2" x 8" sheet 10	10	15	18
Commando Machine Gun, thin cardboard cut-out makes model over 25" long,1940s 18	18	22	28
Connie Francis, Whitman No. 1956, 1963 30	30	45	65
Coronation Cut-out Model Book 55	55	65	70
Coronation Glitter Model Book 25	25	40	50
Coronation Paper Dolls and Coloring Book, Queen Elizabeth, Prince Philip, young Prince Charles,and Princess Ann, Saalfield No. 4450, 1953, 10-1/2" x 15" book 50	50	75	100
Cowboy and Cowgirl Cut-outs, Merrill No. 3449, 1950 25	25	40	50
Cowboy Cutouts, Platt and Munk, c. 1930s 40Cowboys and Indians Cut-outs, Saalfield, 1937 30	30	40	55
Cowgirl Jill and Cowboy Joe, Merrill No. 3459 25	25	35	45

Circus Day Cut-out Book, Stephens Printing Co., 1946, $28

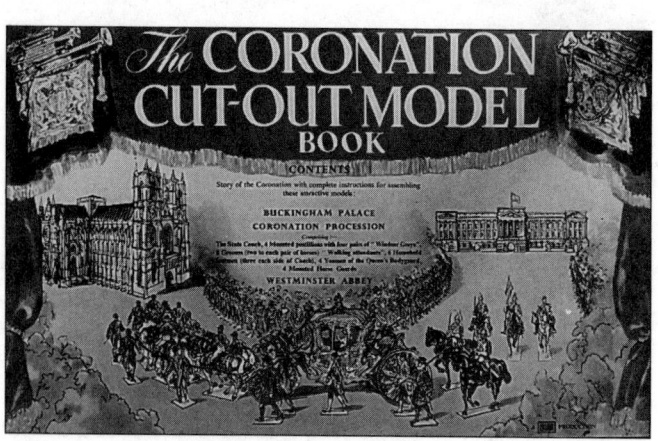

The Coronation Cut-out Model Book, $70

New Pretty Village Box

Coronation Glitter Model Book, $50

New Pretty Village Church Set, $145

Birthday Party National, Syndicate Displays, $45

College Style Paper Dolls, Merrill, $65

Gonw With the Wind Paper Dolls, Merrill No. 3405, (was re-issued in 1989 by The Turner Store), $400

Diana Lynn Paper Dolls, Saalfield, $65

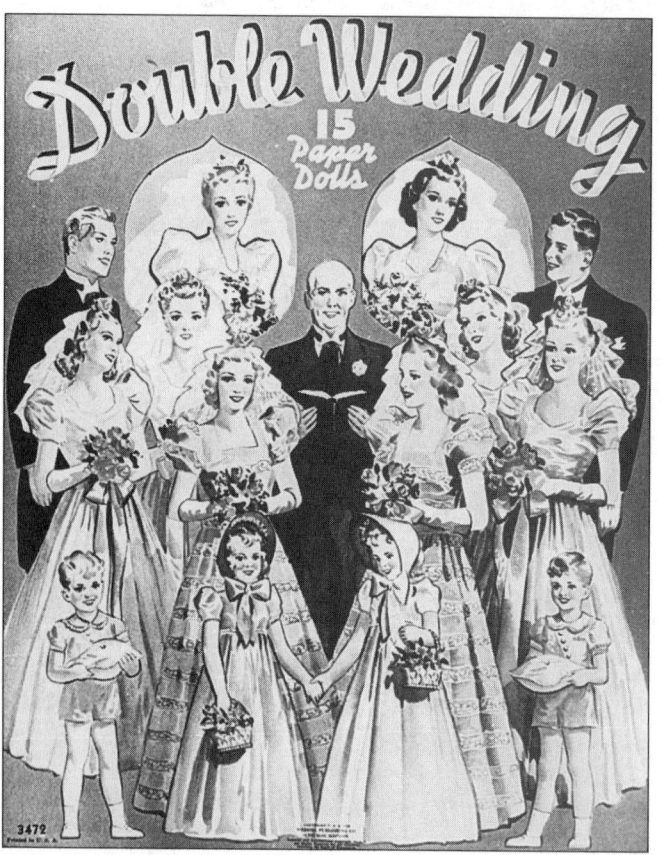

Double Wedding, Merrill, $85

Cut and Stick, our Army and Navy in Action, Merrill, 1942, $50

	C6	C8	C10
The Cradle Crowd, four doll babies w/ cloth-like clothes, Whitman No. 1173, 1948	25	35	50
Cut and Stick, Our Army and Navy in Action, Merrill No. 4835, 1942	35	45	50
Cut-Me-Out Paper Dolls, Abbott No. 1358, 1940s	20	30	35
Cut-out Dolls, Puppies and Kittens, Whitman No. 931, 1939	50	75	100
Cut-out Dolls w/paints and clothes to color, book w/four 17" children and sixteen pages of clothing and sheet of paints by Avis Mac, Whitman No. 983, c. 1930s, 11" x 18"	30	45	65
Cyd Charisse, Whitman No. 2084, 1956	50	75	100
Dancing Black Baby, Littauer & Bauer, 1895	75	100	150
Dancing Dolls w/famous costumes, ballet dancers, Merrill No. 3448, 1954	20	35	45
Date Time, Saalfield, half size book	4	6	8
Davy Crockett Punch Out Book, No. 1943, 1955	40	65	85
Deanna Durbin, Merrill No. 3480, 1940	50	100	165

Cut-out Dolls, Puppies and Kittens, Whitman, 1939, $125

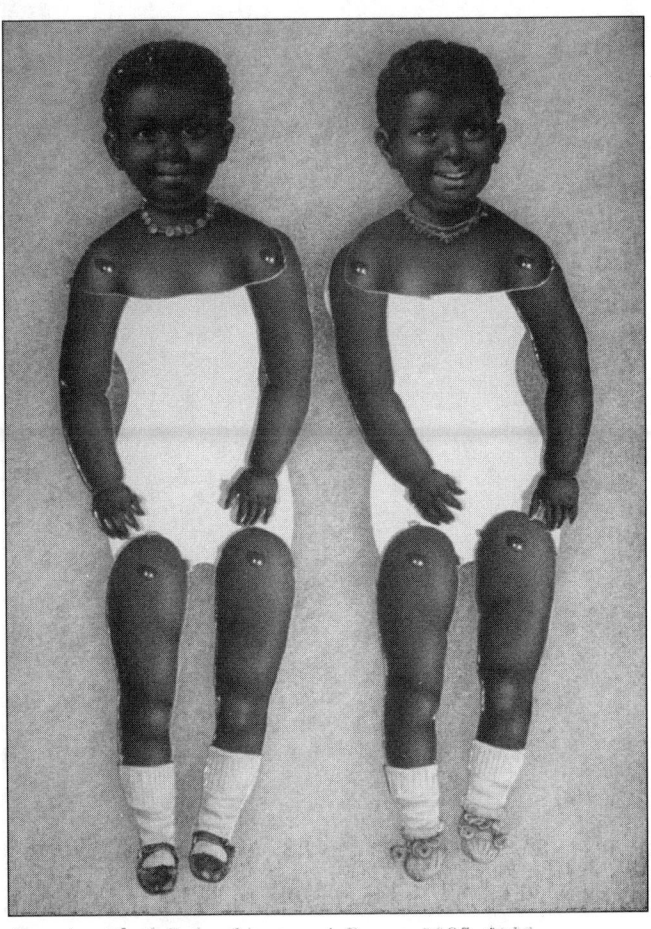

Dancing Black Baby, Littauer & Bauer, 1895, $150

	C6	C8	C10
Debs and Sub Debs Paper Doll Book, twenty punch-outs, Saalfield No. 2361, 1941 20	35	45
Decal sheet of soldiers, by Frank Krupp, meant to be attached to heavy cardboard backing, All-Nu, c. 1942 60	75	100
Decalco-Litho Co. Paper Dolls Sheets, 1) woman and girl and nine outfits; 2) woman and girl and ten outfits; 3) two women and seven outfits; c. 1920s, 8" x 10-1/2" sheets, price per sheet 12	18	25
Dennison's Crepe Paper Doll Outfit, No. 36 55	65	110
Dennison's Dolls and Dresses, No. 37, c. 1930 55	65	115
Diane and Daphne the Round About Dolls Book, large cut-outs by Campbell, McLoughlin Bros. No. 545,1937 30	55	65

	C6	C8	C10
Diana Lynn Paper Dolls, Saalfield No. 157910, 1953 30	45	65
Dick the Sailor, Samuel Lowe No. L1074, c. 1942 20	35	45
Disneyland Park Punch Out, No. 175, 1960 25	35	50
Dodie from "My Three Sons," Dodie and Dolly, Artcraft No. 5115, 1971 30	40	55
Dolls from Storyland by Vivian Robbins, Merrill No. 1554, 1948 25	40	50
Dolls that Walk, "They Walk-They Dance-They Play," two identical girls and two identical boys designed by Emily Sprague Wurl, Whitman No. 977, 1939 35	50	70
Donna Reed Paper Dolls, boxed set, Saalfield/Artcraft No. 5197, 1960, 9" x 12" 50	75	100
Doris Day, Whitman No. 210325, 1952 75	90	125
Dorothy Provine, Whitman No. 1964, 1962 35	45	65
Double Date Cut-out Dolls, by Elinee Fon Vaughan, Whitman No. 962, 1949 20	30	40
Double Wedding, Merrill No. 3472, 1939 ... 40	65	85
Down On The Farm, Lowe No. 1056, 1940s 15	20	30
Dr. Kildare and Nurse Susan, Lowe No. 2740, early 1960s 35	55	70
The Dress-Up Doll Book, Treasure Books No. T-167, 1953 8	14	20
Dress-Up For the New York World's Fair, by Judy and Barry Martin, Spertus No. 700, 1963 15	20	30
Dress-Up Paper Doll Cut-outs, Reuben Lilja & Co., 1947 10	15	25

Crepe Paper Doll Outfit, Dennison, $125

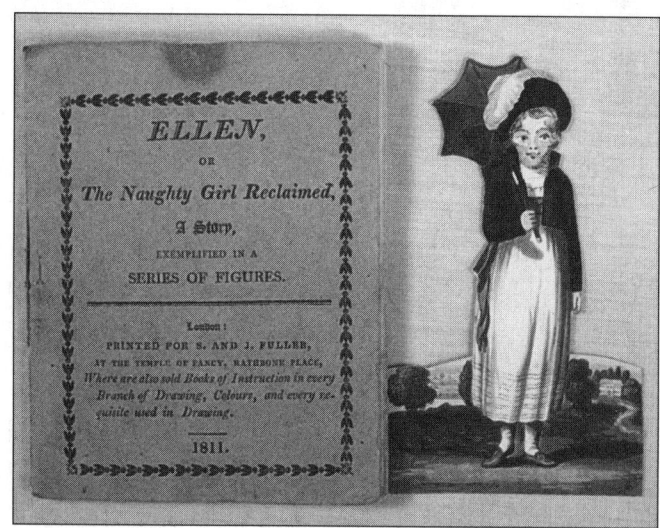

Ellen or Naughty Girl Reclaimed, S & J Fuller, 1811, $250

	C6	C8	C10
The 8 Ages of Judy, by Fern Bisel Peat, Judy as baby and ages one to seven, Lowe L1025, 1941	40	60	80
Ellen or the Naughty Girl Reclaimed, S & J Fuller, 1811	150	200	250
Elizabeth Taylor, Whitman No. 973-10, 1950	90	120	160
Eskimo Cut-outs by Milo Winter, Whitman No. 1054, 1939	20	35	45
Esther Williams, three dolls, Merrill No. 1563, 1950	55	75	110
Eve Arden Paper Dolls, Saalfield No. 158510, 1953	40	60	80
Evelyn Rudy—Little Star of Screen and Television, Saalfield No. 1745, 1958	25	40	50
Fabulous High Fashion Models, Bonnie Brooks/Child Craft No. 2776, 1958	10	15	20
Fairy Folk Cut-out Paper Dolls, by Margaret Carlson, Still & Edwards Co., Inc., 1920s	15	25	35
Family Princess Paper Dolls, Merrill No. 1548, 1958	25	40	55
Family Affair, Whitman No. 4767, 1968	25	40	55

Fiesta Paper Dolls, Saalfield, 1950s, $35

Fairy Folk Cut-out Dolls, Little Bo Peep, Still 7 Edwards Co., 1920s, $40

	C6	C8	C10
Family of Paper Dolls, Saalfield No. 2564, 1947	15	20	30
Family of Paper Dolls, by Queen Holden, mother, father, nurse and six kids, Whitman No. 991	55	75	110
Farm Cut-outs by Milo Winter, six pages of heavy paper cut-outs, Whitman No. 1054, 1938, 6-1/2" x 10-1/2"	5	25	35
The Fashion Book of the Round About Dolls, by Betty Campbell, eight stand-up dolls plus scissors and pack of paper dolls clothes in package, McLoughlin Bros., 1936	35	55	75
Fashion cut-outs w/Sturdibilt dolls, Lowe No. 1243, 1940s	15	20	30
Fashion Flatsy, Whitman No. 1992:69, 1971	15	20	30
Fiesta Paperdolls, Saalfield No. 2771, 1950s	15	25	35
Fifteen ABC Blocks to Play and Learn, book containing fifteen die-cut blocks to put together, each w/illustrations of nursery rhymes, alphabet letters, animals and numbers on each block , Whitman No. 976, 1933	20	30	40
Fire Fighters in Action, Saalfield, 1938	22	48	52

Esther Williams, Merrill, $110

Kiddieland Village, Whitman, $95

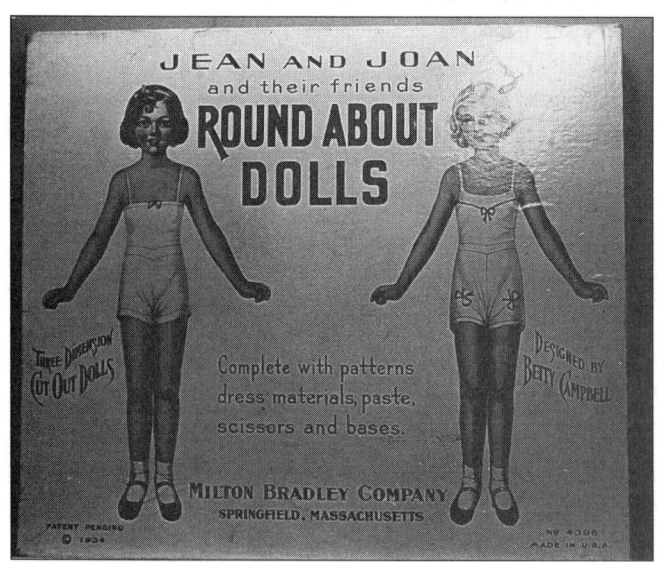

Jean and Joan and their Friends, Milton Bradley, $70

On Guard, Lowe, $50

	C6	C8	C10
Fire House P-18, brick firehouse, boxed set, Megow, 1945	35	48	58
Five Little Peppers, Little Women and Annie three-book set, Lauries, Lowe No. L1030, 1941	35	55	75
The Flying Nun, Artcraft No. 4417, 1968, 1969	25	40	50
Four Sisters Paper Dolls, Saalfield No. 269, 1943	15	20	30
Fourteen Dogs To Cut Out and Stand Up, twelve cardboard punch-out pages of dogs, Whitman No. 935, copyright 1930	25	35	48
Freckles & Sniffles Whitman 1977	3	5	8
French Infantry, cardboard figures, Milton Bradley, c. 1915, approx. 6" high	3	5	6
Frontier Fort, Merrill No. 257225, 1952	15	25	30
Fun Farm, Reed and Associates	8	15	18
Gene Autry Melody Ranch Cut-out dolls, Whitman No. 990-10, 1950	45	65	95
Gene Autry Ranch cut-out book, Merrill, 1940	65	80	90
Gene Autry Ranch cut-out book, 1953	50	70	80
Gigi Perreau Paper Dolls, Saalfield No. 1542, 1951	25	40	55
Gigi Perreau, Saalfield No. 2605, 1951	25	40	55

Glenn Miller, Marion Hutton Turnabout Doll Book, Lowe, 1942, $200

	C6	C8	C10
The Ginghams, Whitman box sets	3	5	10
Girl Friend-Boy Friend paper dolls, Saalfield No. 1605, 1955	15	20	30
Girl Friends paper dolls, Whitman No. 974, 1944	20	30	40
Girl Pilots of the Ferry Command, Merrill No. 4852, 1943	55	75	115
Girls in Uniform paper dolls book, No. L1048, c. 1942	35	65	95
Glamour Parade Cut-out Dolls, four models and four pages of clothes, Stephens Publishing Co., No. 184, 1950s?	10	15	25
Glenn Miller, Marion Hutton Turnabout Doll Book, Lowe No. 21041, 1942	100	150	200
Gloria Jean Paper Doll Cut-outs, Saalfield No. 1661, 1940	55	85	115
Gone With the Wind, includes eighteen dolls, Merrill No. 3404, 1940	200	300	400
Gone With the Wind, includes five dolls, Merrill No. 3405, 1940	200	300	400
Good Neighbor paper dolls, Saalfield No. 2487, 1944	10	15	25
Grace Kelly 2 Cut-out Dolls and Clothes, Whitman No. 2049, 1955	60	95	130

Girl Pilots of the Ferry Command, Merrill, 1943, $115

Grace Kelly 2 Cut-out Dolls and Clothes, Whitman, 1955, $95

	C6	C8	C10
Grace Kelly, Whitman No. 2069, 1956	65	95	130
Gulliver's Travels Cut-outs, Saalfield No. 1261, 1939	35	55	75
Hair-Do Dolls, by Queen Holden, Whitman No. 991, 1948	50	75	100
Harry the Soldier, Samuel Lowe No. L1074, 1941	45	65	75
Hayley Mills, "The Moonspinners," Whitman No. 1960, 1964	30	50	60
Heavy Cruiser, "This is the Navy," Skyline Mfg. Co., c. 1943	20	30	40
Hedy Lamarr Paper Dolls, Saalfield No. 1555	75	115	150
Hee Haw, Artcraft No. 5139, 1971	25	40	45
Heidi and Peter, Saalfield No. 1355, c. 1970	20		
Here Comes the Bride, Whitman No. 118915, 1952	25	35	45
Here's the Bride, Whitman No. 2109, 1953	25	35	45
High School Girls, Merrill No. 1551, 1948	40	45	55
Historical Dolls To Cut Out and Dress, includes mother, father and two children of heavycardboard, plus outfits, boxed set, Platt & Munk No. 226B, 1961, 7" x 11"	20	30	35

	C6	C8	C10
Holiday paper dolls, Saalfield No. 1742, 1950s	10	15	20
Hollywood Fashion Dolls, twelve male and female dolls plus clothes, Saalfield No. 397, 1939	30	45	60
Hollywood Fashions, Saalfield No. 1535, 1949	25	35	45
Hour of Charm paper dolls, women musicians, Saalfield No. 2481, 1943	55	80	110
House For Sale, Lowe No. 9042, 1962	35	45	50
House that Jack Built, Bliss, paper litho, house and story's characters w/stands, c. 1895	400	500	600
Howdy Doody Puppet Show Punchout Book, punch-out cardboard puppets may be controlled by strings, includes Howdy, Bluster, Inspector, Dilly Dally, Clarabell and Flubadub Whitman No. 211129, copyright 1952	40	65	80
Howdy Doody Sticker Fun, Whitman No. 219525, copyright 1951	25	35	40

House For Sale, Lowe, 1962, $50

	C6	C8	C10
Howdy Doody Sticker Fun, Whitman No. 215825, copyright 1953	25	35	40
Howdy Doody Sticker Fun Circus, Whitman No. 2165, copyright 1955	25	35	40
I Love Lucy, Lucille Ball and Desi Arnaz, Whitman No. 2101, 1953	55	75	110
It's A Date, Whitman No. 1976, 1956	10	15	20
Jack and Jill, six dolls and clothes from storyland, Merrill No. 1561, 1962	15	20	30
Jane Russell, Saalfield No. 2611, 1955	40	60	80
Janet Leigh Cut-outs and Coloring Book, Merrill No. 2554, 1953	40	55	85
Janet Leigh, Abbott No. 1805, 1958	30	55	75
Jaunty Juniors, No. 903, 1946	15	25	35
Jean and Joan and their Friends, Roundabout Dolls, designed by Betty Campbell, boxed set, Milton Bradley No. 4396, 1934	45	65	85
Jeanette MacDonald, Merrill No. 3640, 1941	100	150	200
Jimmy & Jane Visit Gene Autry at Melody Ranch, Whitman No. 118415, 1951	35	55	70

June Bride, Stephens Publishing Co., 1946, $42

	C6	C8	C10
Joan's Wedding by Florence Sarah Winship, clothes designed by Ruth M. Ruhman, Whitman No. 990, 1942	25	35	55
Judy Paper Doll, Saalfield No. 1713, 1960s	10	15	20
Judy and Jack, Peg and Bill Cut-out Dolls, by Pelagie Doane, Lowe No. L1024, 1940	35	45	70
Julia, includes Diahann Carroll, Julia, Corey, Marie and Earl J. Waggedorn, Artcraft No. 5140, 1968	25	40	50
Julia, includes Julia, Earl J. Waggedorn and Corey, Saalfield, 1969	25	35	50
June Allyson, Whitman No. 119015, 1950, 1952	50	65	85
June Allyson, Whitman No. 1173:15, 1953	55	65	85
June Bride, by Art Tanchon, Stephens No. 136, 1946	20	35	45
Junior Bombardier, Einson & Freeman Co. No. 202, 1953	25	35	50
Junior Prom, by Newman, Lowe 1042, 1942	20	35	45
Karen Goes to College!, Merrill No. 1564, 1955	20	30	40
Kiddieland Village, nine buildings and sixty-five cut-out figures, boxed set, Whitman No. 2004, c. 1935, 11-1/2" x 15"	65	80	95
Kitty goes to Kindergarten, Merrill No. 1548, 1956	15	25	35
Lazy Dazy, Whitman, 1973	3	5	10

Judy and Jack Cut-out Dolls, Lowe, 1940, $80

The Lettie Lane Paper Family, George W. Jacobs & Co., 1909, $180

Little Fairy Lightfoot, Brown, Taggard and Chase, $250.

	C6	C8	C10
Lennon Sisters, Whitman No. 1979, 1957	25	35	50
Lennon Sisters, Whitman No. 1983, 1961	25	35	50
Lettie Lane Paper Family, Third Series, original house folder and six sheets, George W. Jacobs & Co., 1909	130	155	180
Liberty Belles Paper Doll Book, Merrill No. 3477, 1943	25	35	50
Lilac Time, Saalfield No. 1362	20	30	40
Little Ballerina, Merrill No. 154215, 1953	20	35	45
Little Ballet Dancers, Saalfield No. 1743, 1950s?	10	15	20
Little Brothers and Sisters, includes Tim, Kay Ann and Pete, Whitman No. 971:10, 1953	10	15	25
Little Fairy Lightfoot, Chandler's Paper Dolls, Brown, Taggard & Chase No. 4	150	200	250
Little Folks' Friends, Saalfield No. 156, 1915	15	20	25
Little Friends, from History by Muriel Wilhoite, Rand McNally No. 186, 1936	25	40	50
Little Friends Paper Dolls, Saalfield No. 1746, 1950s	10	15	20

Little Friends from History, Saalfield, 1915, $22

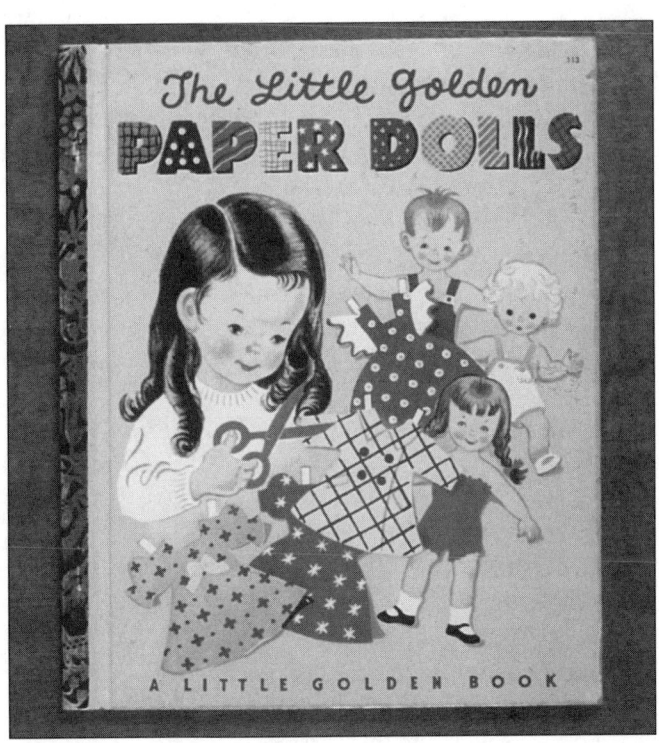

Little Golden Paper Dolls, Golden, 1950s, $45

Lots of Little Paper Dolls, Saalfield, 1949, $40

	C6	C8	C10
Little Golden Paper Dolls, Golden, 1950s, Hilda Miloche	25	35	45
Little Miss America Paper Doll Book, fifteen punch-outs by Campbell, Saalfield No. 2358, 1941	25	35	45
Little Nurse Cut-out Book, Reuben H. Lilja and Co., Inc., No. 909, early 1940s	20	30	40
The Little Red School House Kindergarten, by Margo Voight, includes two teachers and twenty-three children, McLoughlin Bros., 1940	30	45	55
Little Women, Artcraft No. 5127, c. 1970	15	25	35
Little Women, Saalfield, No. 1377	25	35	45
Lois and Joan Cut-out dolls, Whitman No. 1015, 1941, 1945	20	30	40
The Lone Ranger Rides Again punchout set, makes fences, figures of LR and Tonto, horses and campfire, DeJournette Mfg. Co.	35	45	55
Look-a-Like cut-out dolls, two mother and daughter pairs of dolls, Whitman No. 97210, 1952	15	20	30
Look Who I Am!, by Doris Stelberg, w/fifteen costumes, spiral bound, Hart Publishing Co., 1952, 18" doll	15	20	25
Lori Martin in National Velvet, Whitman No. 4612, 1962, 6" x 11-1/2", boxed set	35	45	55

	C6	C8	C10
Lost Horizon, Artcraft No. 5112, 1973	15	20	25
Lots of Little Paper Dolls by Angela Tuite Price, Saalfield No. 1537, 1949	15	25	35

Lucille Ball, Desi Arnaz Cut-out Dolls with Little Ricky, Whitman, 1953, $90

	C6	C8	C10
Lucille Ball, Desi Arnaz Cut-out Dolls with Little Ricky, Whitman No. 2116:25, 1953	86	100	125
Lucille Ball Paper Dolls, Saalfield No. 2475, 1944	55	75	110
Madame Hattie Fashions, Reuben Lilja No. 908, 1940s	35	45	48
Magic Mary, complete w/magnetic doll and strips to put on clothes, boxed set, Milton Bradley No. 4010-1, 1955, 10-1/2" x 10-1/2"	10	15	25
Magic Stay On Dresses, Whitman No. 4618	10	15	25
Make Your Own Battle Set Mechanized Force, Electric Corporation of America, 1942	45	50	55
Malibu Skipper, Whitman No. 1952, 1973	10	15	25
Margaret O'Brien Paper Dolls, Whitman No. 96410	100	135	165
Marge and Gower Champion, Whitman, 1959	50	75	100
Martha Hyer Paper Dolls, Saalfield No. 4423, 1958	30	45	60
Mary and Joan, Whitman No. 1015, 1941, 1945	20	30	40

	C6	C8	C10
Mary Belle Cut-out Doll, by Fern Bisel Peat, four separate sheets, w/three sheets of clothes, Saalfield No. 2100, 1934, 17" doll	45	55	70
Mary Jane, A Cut-out Doll by Florence Winship, w/suitcase for accessories, Whitman No. 1010, 1939, 1941	20	35	45
Mary Lee, A Cut-out Doll, Whitman No. 1010, c. 1939	20	35	45
Mary Martin, Saalfield No. 2427, 1942	115	160	225
Mary of the WACS, A Young American, by Hilda Miloche and Wilma Kane, Whitman No. 1012, 1943	30	40	60
Mary Poppins, Whitman No. 1977, 1973	20	35	45
Marybelle Mercer's Front and Back Dolls, w/wrap-around dresses, by Queen Holden No. 978	50	75	100
Me and Mimi, a Bonnie Story Book Doll, done in the style of the Little Golden Books, a Doll and her Dolly Story Book, plus dolls and their dresses, 6" x 8", 1957	15	25	35
Mexican Cut-outs, by Milo Winter, six pages of people, animals and houses, Whitman No. 1054, 1938	30	38	48
Mickey and Minnie paper dolls, two figures w/clothes, 1930s, 10"	100	135	175
Midge-Barbie's Best Friend, Whitman, 1963	30	45	60
Mini Mod PDs with London Fashions, Saalfield No. 1348, 1966	20	25	35

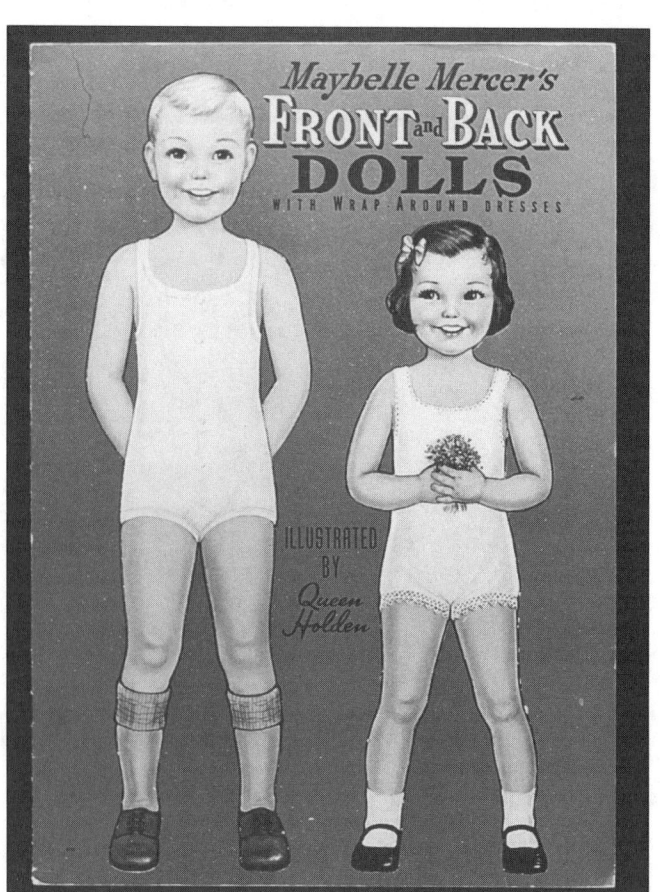

Maybelle Mercer's Front and Back Dolls, Queen Holden, $110

Model Tanks, Lowe, 1941, $75

	C6	C8	C10
Model Airplanes, WWII airplanes, International, Samuel Lowe No. 1069, 1941 50		65	75
Model Battleship, Reed, c. 1945, 7" x 10" 20		25	30
Model Flat-top, Reed, c. 1945 20		25	30
Model Tanks, Lowe No. 1065, 1941 50		65	75
Model Tanks Construction set, boxed set, Lowe No. 1267, 1942.................... 50		65	75
Model War Planes Construction set, 1942, Lowe No. 1266, boxed set 50		65	75
Modern Miss in Paper Dolls, by Van Swearingen, Saalfield No. 2397, 1942 30		40	45
Molly Bee, Whitman No. 2091, 1962 20		30	40
Mommy and Me, Whitman No. 977:10, 1954 15		20	30
Mother and Daughter, by Patrie Winston, includes mother and daughter doll w/two scotties,Grinnel Lithographic No. C-1005, 1940, 15" mother, 11" daughter...................... 20		35	45
Mouseketeer Cut-outs, Whitman No. 1974, 1957 25		35	45
Movie Starlets, includes Gail Russell, Diana Lynn, Olga San Juan, Marjorie Reynolds and Joan Caulfield, Whitman No. 960, 1946 35		55	75
Movie Starlets Paper Dolls, includes Miss Premier, Miss Stardust, Miss Hollywood and Miss Preview plus four pages of costumes, Stephens Publishing Co. No. 178, c. 1949 15		20	30
Mrs. Beasley Paper doll book (Family Affair), Whitman No. 1973, 1970 25		35	550
My Fair Lady, by Evon Hartman, Ottenheimer Publishers No. 2960-2, 1965 25		35	50
My Paper Doll's Sewing Kit, by Margot Voight, Grinnell C-1018, 1940 15		20	30
My Twin Babies with Older Brother and Sister, Whitman No. 970, 1940 20		30	45
My Very First Paper Doll Book, a Bonnie Book, Samuel Lowe No. 4732, 1957....... 10		15	20
Nancy and Her Dolls with 7 Busy Days of Fun, Saalfield No. 2478, 1944............ 15		25	35
Nanny and the Professor, Artfield No. 4283, 1971 25		35	45
Natalie Wood Paper Dolls, Whitman, 1958 70		100	130
National Velvet, Whitman No. 1958, 1961 30		40	60
Navy Scouts Paper Doll book, Merrill No. 3428, 1942 45		65	85

The New Shirley Temple in Paper Dolls, Saalfield, 1942, $150

	C6	C8	C10
The New Shirley Temple in Paper Dolls, Saalfield No. 2425, 1942 65		80	135
New York World's Fair Make a Model, by Ottenheimer, includes Unisphere, Swiss Ride, N.Y. Port Authority and Heliport, Spertus No. 600-50, 1963 25		30	35
Night Before Christmas, w/cut-outs, Whitman No. 948 10		15	25
Nineteen Farmyard Animals to Cut Out and Stand Up, twelve pages, Whitman No. 935, copyright 1930 35		40	45

Our Happy Family Cut-out Sheets, Sam'l Gabriel Sons Co., 1928, $90

	C6	C8	C10
Oklahoma with Shirley Jones and Gordon MacRae, Whitman No. 1954, 1956 45		60	90
On Guard, Lowe No. L535, 1942 40		45	50
One Hundred Soldiers Punch-out Book, Whitman No. 999, 1943 55		60	65
Our Happy Family Cut-out Sheets, Sam'l Gabriel Sons Co. No. D141, 1928 65		75	90
Our New Home, story by Susan S. Popper, pictures by Helen E. Ohrenschall, hardcover book w/six pages of rooms and six gummed pages of people, furniture, etc., Sam'l Gabriel Sons, 1930 80		100	125
Our Nurse Nancy, A Young American, by Hilda Miloche and Wilma Kane, cut-outs, Whitman No. 1012, 1943 25		40	55
Our Sailor Bob, doll w/uniforms, Whitman, c. 1943, 10" 25		40	50
Our Soldier Jim, designed by Hilda Milocheand Wilma Kane, standup			

Paper Doll Family and their Trailer, Merrill, 1938, $90

	C6	C8	C10
doll w/uniforms, Whitman No. 3980, 1943, 10-1/2" 25		40	50
Our Soldiers Cut-out Army Uniforms, by Nat Falk, four cut-out dolls and several uniforms, Dell, 1941 30		45	55
Our Wave Joan, A Young American, by Hilda Miloche and Wilma Kane, Whitman No. 1012, 1943 35		45	55
Outdoor Paper Dolls, fourteen dolls and four pages of clothes, Saalfield No. 1958, 1941 10		15	20

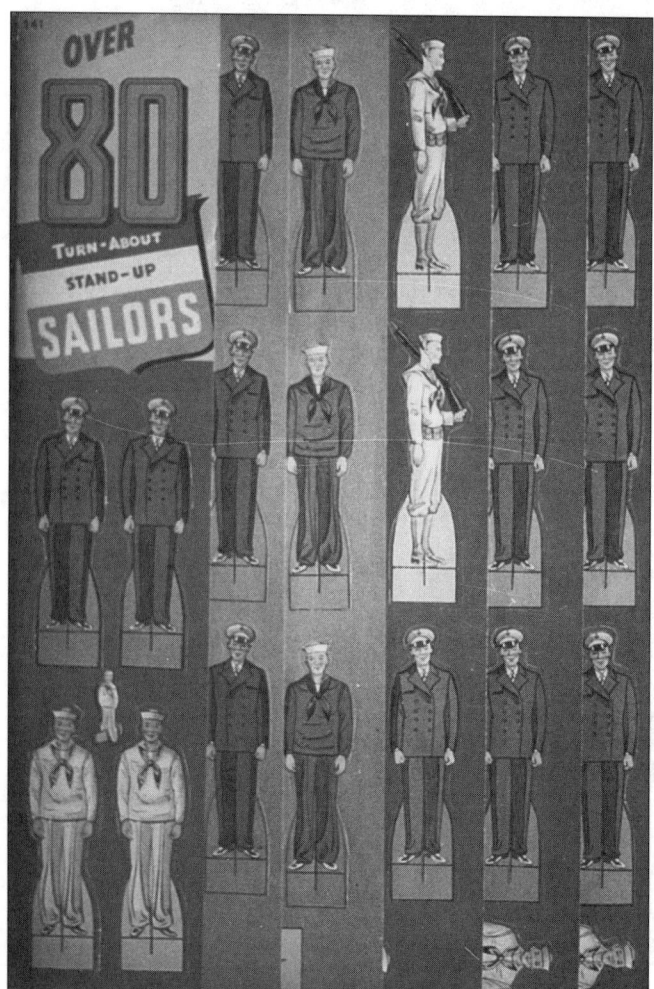

Over 80 Turn-about Stand-up Sailors, Lowe, 1943, $60

Paper Dolls Julie and Marie, Saalfield, 1958, $25

	C6	C8	C10
Over 80 Turn-About, Standup Sailors, Lowe No. 141, 1943	45	55	60
Over 80 Turn-About, Standup Sailors, Lowe No. 140, 1943	45	55	60
Paper Dolls and Their Dollies, Saalfield No. 1615, 1950s, by Mary Knight	20	30	40
Paper Doll Family and Their House, by Florence and Margaret Hoopes, Saalfield No. 4125, 1934	60	70	75
Paper Doll Family and Their Trailer, Merrill No. 3436, 1938	70	80	90
Paper Doll "Joan" and Paper Doll "Bobby," by Queen Holden, Whitman No. 907, 1928	70	85	100
Paper Doll Outfit, American Toy Works, No. 102, boxed set	50	65	80
Paper Doll Playmates, nurse and nineteen children, costumes, toys, Saalfield No. 154, 1940	25	35	50
Paper Dolls from Mother Goose, includes Mary, Bo-Peep, Boy Blue, Bobbie Shaftoe, Miss Muffet and Jack Horner, Saalfield No. 2758, 1957	15	20	30

Paper Dolls of All Nations, New York World's Fair, Saalfield, 1939, $60

	C6	C8	C10
Paper Dolls Julia and Marie, by Angela Tuite Price, Saalfield No. 1530, 1958	15	20	25
Paper Dolls of All Nations, New York World's Fair, Saalfield No. 227, 1939	40	50	60

Paper Dolls of All Nations, Saalfield, 1939, $65

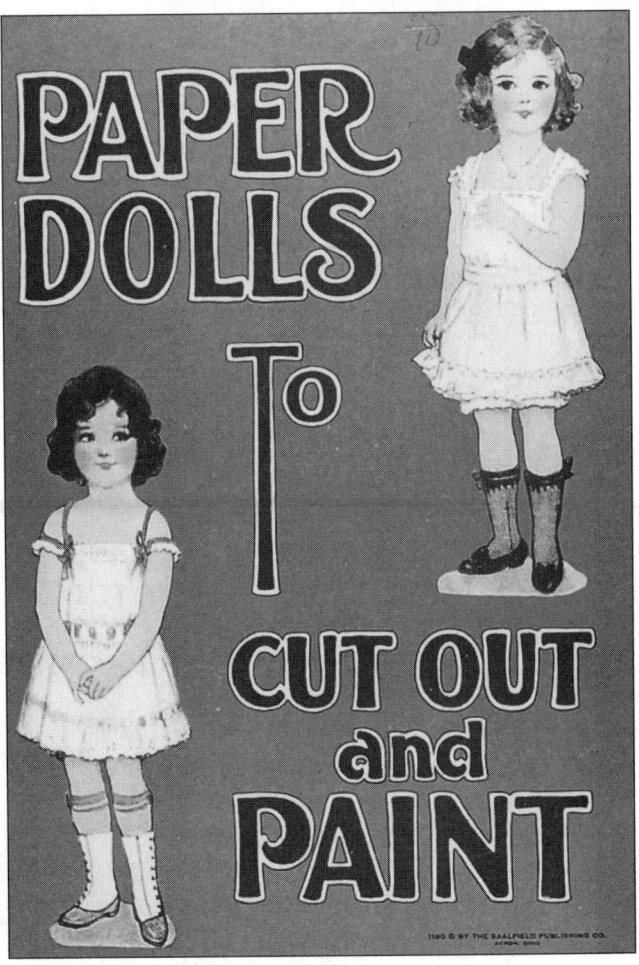

Paper Dolls to Cut Out and Paint, Saalfield, 1920s, $75

Paper Doll Outfit, American Toy Works, $80

Playhouse Paper Dolls, Lowe, 1941, $30

Pressed Board Dolls and their Dresses, Lowe, $45

Playhouse Paper Dolls, Saalfield, 1947, $30

	C6	C8	C10
Paper Dolls of Eve Arden, Saalfield No. 1706, 1956	45	65	85
Paper Dolls of the Latest Paris Fashions Brown, Taggard & Chase, 1800s	150	200	250
Paper Dolls Peter and Peggy, by Dixon, sixty-four pages w/very large punch-outs on front and back Whitman No. 965, 1935	45	50	55
Paper Dolls To Cut Out and Paint, Saalfield No. 1180, 1920s	55	65	75
Paper Dolls United We Stand, by Margot Voight, six children w/uniforms, Saalfield No. 113	60	65	75
The Partridge Family, Artcraft No. 5137, 1971	30	45	60
Partridge Family, Artcraft No. 5143, 1972	35	45	55
Pat Boone, Whitman No. 1968, 1959	25	35	45
Pat Crowley, Whitman No. 2050, 1955	25	35	45
Patience and Prudence, Lowe No. 2736, 1958	10	15	20
Patsy, includes Patsy, dog, doghouse, etc., Children's Press No. 30002, 1946	15	25	35
Patsy a Wooden Doll with Dresses, standup cardboard doll w/wood backing, Whitman No. 3037, c. 1938, 10"	20	30	40

	C6	C8	C10
Patsy Ann and Her Trunk full of Clothes, by Queen Holden, Whitman No. 992, 1939	65	85	110
Patti Page, book of paper dolls, 1958	60	70	80
Patty's Party Paper Dolls, Stephens Publishing Co. No. 175, c. 1950	15	20	30
Pert and Pretty, Merrill No. 1552, 1948	25	30	50
Peter and Peggy, 1950, Whitman No. 99210	15	20	25
Peter and Peggy, Jerry and Joan Paper Dolls, by Rachel Taft Dixon, Whitman No. 985, 1935	30	45	60
Photo Fashions, Whitman No. 973, 1953	10	15	25
Pig Tails, Merrill No. 344410, 1949	20	30	40
Pilot and Stewardess Airliner Paper Dolls, Merrill No. 3423, 1941	25	30	50
The Pink Wedding, Merrill No. 1559, 1952	45	55	65
Piper Laurie, Merrill No. 2551, 1953	55	65	75
Playhouse Dolls, four dolls and four pages of clothes, Stephens Publishing Co. No. 1965, 1949	10	15	25
Playhouse Paper Dolls, designed by Doris and Marion Henderson, Lowe No. 1028, 1941	20	30	40
Playhouse Paper Dolls, Saalfield No. 381, 1947	15	20	30
Playmates, Whitman No. 99510, 1952	15	20	25
Playthings To Cut Out and Stand Up, includes ventriloquist's dummy, floating ships, general's hat, lantern, animals and other moving toys, Whitman No. 934, c. 1935	32	36	45
Play Time, Whitman No. 210525, 1952	10	15	20
Playtime Pals, Lowe No. 1045, 1946	10	15	20
Polly Patchwork and Her Friends by Pelagie Doane, Lowe No. 1024, 1941	20	30	40
Pollyana Cut-out Dolls, Whitman No. 995, 1941	30	40	50
Popular Paper Dolls, Saalfield No. 1973, 1942	15	20	25
Portrait Girls, w/cloth-like clothes, designed by Hilda Miloche and Wilma Kane, Whitman No. 1170, 1947	35	40	45
Power Models Cut-out Dolls Book, six dolls, Whitman No. 981, 1942	65	90	110
Pressed Board Dolls and Their Dresses, boxed set, Lowe No. 1942	25	35	45
Pre-Teen Paper Dolls, Saalfield No. 1366, c. 1960s	10	15	20
Pretty As a Picture, Saalfield No. 2775, 1950s	20	30	40
Pretty Belles, Whitman No. 1966, 1965	7	10	15

Pilot and Stewardess Airliner Paper Dolls, Merrill, $52

	C6	C8	C10
Prince and Princess Paper Dolls, Saalfield No. 2706, 1949 20		25	35
Prom Time, Whitman No. 2084, two dolls and party clothes, 1962 10		15	20
Queen Holden! Betty and Bob, Whitman No. 99110, 1952, 12-1/2" 45		55	65
Queen Holden! Hair-Do Dolls, three dolls, clothes and thirty-one different hair-dos, Whitman No. 99110, 1948...... 55		65	75
Quiz Kids Paper Dolls, Saalfield No. 2430, 1942 100		120	140
Raggedy Ann and Andy, by Ethel Hays, Saalfield No. 2719, 1953.......................... 20		30	40
Raggedy Ann and Andy Paper Dolls, Saalfield No. 2719-15, 1944 35		45	55
Raggedy Ann and Andy Paper Dolls, by Ethel Hays, Saalfield No. 2741, 194435 45		55	
Raggedy Ann and Andy, Whitman No. 4740, 1968 7		10	15
Raggedy Ann and Andy, Whitman No. 1944, 1974 3		5	10
Rap-A-Jap, Woodburn Mfg. No. C1, c. 1943.. 55		65	72
Ready Cut Village, no mfg. Listed, 1930s.... 55		70	80
Really Truly Paper dolls, Saalfield No. 453 25		35	45
Ricky Nelson Paper Dolls, 1959................. 35		45	55
Riders of the West Paper Dolls, Saalfield No. 2716-15, 1950.................................. 10		15	25

	C6	C8	C10
Rigby's Book of Model Ships, 1953 75		85	90
Rigby's Easy to Build Models of Fighting Planes.. 85		95	115
Rigby's Easier to Build Models of Naval Craft, designed by Wallace Rigby, twenty-four models of warships, twenty-seven pages, includes Battleship North Carolina, aircraft carrier, cruiser and destroyer, 1944, 11-1/2" x 14" 95		120	135
Rigby Flying Models of Jet and Rocket Planes, includes ten planes, Garden City Books, 1949 70		80	90
Rigby's Model Book of Flying Clippers, designed by Wallace Rigby, includes two scale models of Douglas DC-Jet Clipper and Douglas DC-7C, 1947, 11"x14" book 60		70	80
Rigby's Model Sports Cars of the World, "Sportsracer," includes Chevette, Jaguar, Mercedes-Benz, etc., 1954, 18" 60		70	80
Robin Hood and Maid Marian paper dolls, Saalfield No. 1761, 1950s 25		35	45
Rock Hudson Paper Dolls, Whitman No. 2087, 1957 45		55	65
Rosemary Clooney, Samuel Lowe No. 1256 40		50	60
Rosemary Clooney, Samuel Lowe No. 2487, 1958 40		50	60
Rowan & Martin's Laugh-In Punch-Out Paper Doll Book, includes Rowan, Martin, Jo Ann Worley, Arte Johnson, Judy Carne and Goldie Hawn, Saalfield No. 1325, 1969 30		40	50

Really Truly Paper Dolls, Saalfield, $45

Royalty Cut-out Books: A Procession of the Knights of the Garter, $70

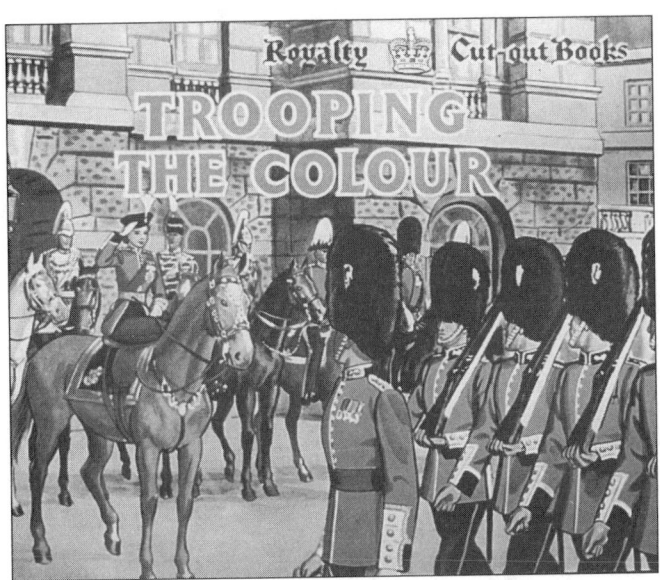

Royalty Cut-out Books: Trooping the Colour, $70

	C6	C8	C10
Royalty Cut-out Books: A Procession of the Knights of the Garter	55	65	70
Royalty Cut-out Books: Trooping the Colour	55	65	70
Rub-A-Dub Doly, Whitman No. 1941, 1977	10	15	20
Ruth Newton's Cut-out Dolls and Animals, includes over eighty pieces to cut out and play with, 1934, 11" x 17"	55	65	75
Sally Ann a Cut-out Doll, Whitman No. 1010, c. 1940	15	25	35
Sally's Silver Skates, Merrill No. 1549, 1956	25	35	45
Sally the Standing Doll, Lowe No. 1042, 1940s	20	30	40
Sandra and Sue Statuette Dolls and their Clothes, by Lee Lunzer, Whitman No. 1180, 1948	15	25	35
Sandra Dee, two dolls and thirty-four costume pieces, boxed, Saalfield No. 5511, 1959	45	55	65
Sandy and Sue, Whitman No. 1956, 1963	10	15	20

	C6	C8	C10
Roy Rogers and Dale Evans, Whitman No. 1186, 1950	55	65	75
Roy Rogers and Dale Evans, Whitman No. 1950, 1954	55	65	75
Roy Rogers Cut-out Dolls, Whitman No. 995, 1948	60	70	80
Roy Rogers Sticker Fun Book, No. 2161, 1953	22	30	36

Sally the Standing Doll, Lowe, 1940s, $48

Sheree North, Saalfield, 1957, $65

Box for Milton Bradley Co.'s Sharp-Shooters

	C6	C8	C10
School Girl Paper Dolls, Saalfield No. 2400, 1942 20		30	40
Schoolmates, Saalfield No. 1757, 1950s 5		7	10
Scissors Bird Paper Dolls, Stephens Publishing Co. No. 137, 1946 10		15	20
Service Kit of America's Armed Forces-On Land-On Sea-In the Air, Lowe No. 265, 1942 45		55	60
Sheree North, Saalfield No. 1728, 1957 45		55	65
Six Good Little Dolls, Stephens Publishing Co. No. 183 13		15	22
Six Movie Starlets, including Anne Nagel, Peggy Moran, Jane Frazee, Anne Gwynne, Helen Parrish and Ann Gillis, 1942 85		100	125
Sharp-Shooters, includes two sets of five cardboard soldiers and one officer on stands, boxed, Milton Bradley No. 4103, c. 1915 85		100	135

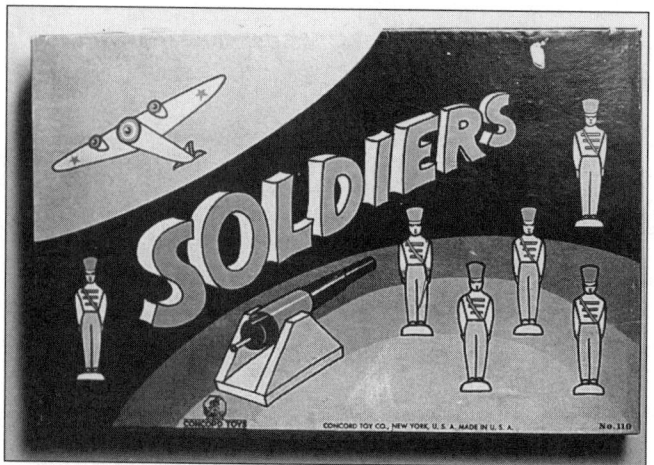

Soldiers, Concord Toy Co., c. 1940, $75

	C6	C8	C10
Skating Party Paper Doll Book, includes seventeen punch-outs, Saalfield No. 2328, 1941 20		30	40
Skating Stars, Whitman No. 2105, 1954 25		35	45
Smart Paper Dolls, Saalfield No. 1935, 1940 15		25	35
Smash the Axis, Electric Corp. of America, 1943 40		55	60
Snow White and the Seven Dwarfs, Whitman No. 970, 1938, 12" x 17" 100		125	150
Snow White and the Seven Dwarfs, Whitman No. 1998, c. 1970 15		20	30
Soldiers, on heavy cardboard, All-Nu, c. 1942-3, 5" high			
100 Officer marching w/sabre 4		5	7
101 Marching, slope arms, WWI helmet 4		5	7
102 Bugler, campaign cap 4		5	7
103 Signalman, WWI helmet 4		5	7
104 Officer kneeling w/binoculars 4		5	7
105 Kneeling firing rifle w/WWI helmet 4		5	7
106 Throwing grenade, WWI helmet 4		5	7
107 Fixed bayonet, WWI helmet 4		5	7
108 Charging w/gas mask, WWI helmet 4		5	7
Soldiers, on heavy cardboard, All-Nu, c. 1942-3, 5" high			
109 Charging w/rifle, port arms, WWI helmet 4		5	7
110 Seated machine gunner, WWI helmet 4		5	7
111 Flag-bearer, WWI helmet 4		5	7
112 General McArthur 12		14	16
113 Nurse 4		5	7
114 Two men carrying wounded soldier on stretcher, WWII helmets 4		5	7
115 Two men firing rifles from prone position, WWII helmets 4		5	7
116 Soldier on wireless radio 4		5	7
117 Three soldiers w/rifles leaving boat, WWII helmets 4		5	7
118 Two paratroopers, one w/tommy gun, WWII helmets 4		5	7
119 Ski trooper 4		5	7
120 Soldier advancing w/rifle, WWII helmet 4		5	7
150 Three men in jeep, WWI helmets 4		5	7
151 Five man team w/cannon, WWI helmets 4		5	7
152 Two men manning wheeled AA gun, WWI helmets 4		5	7

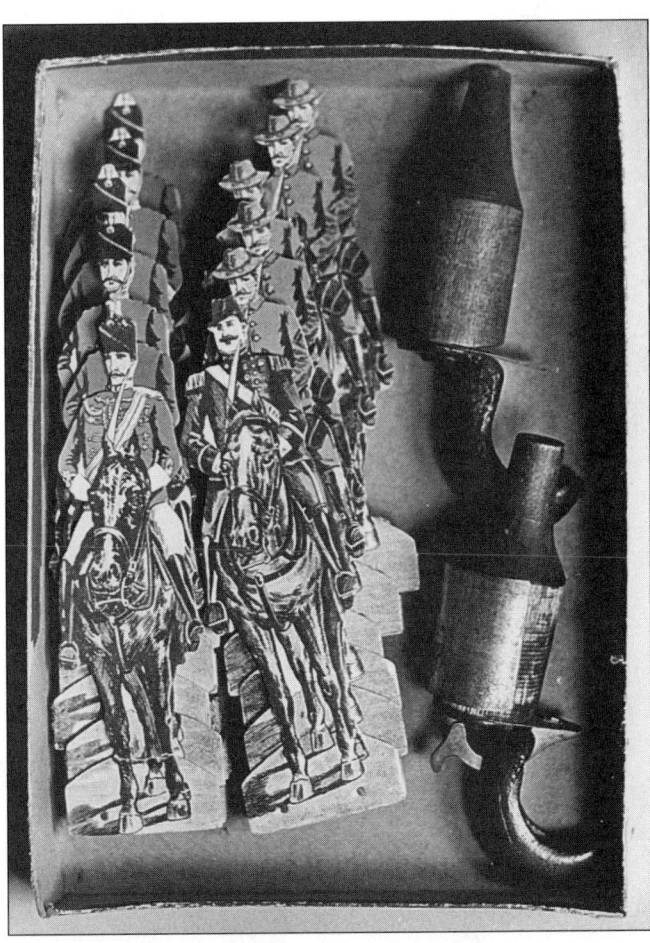

Sharpshooters, Milton Bradley, $135

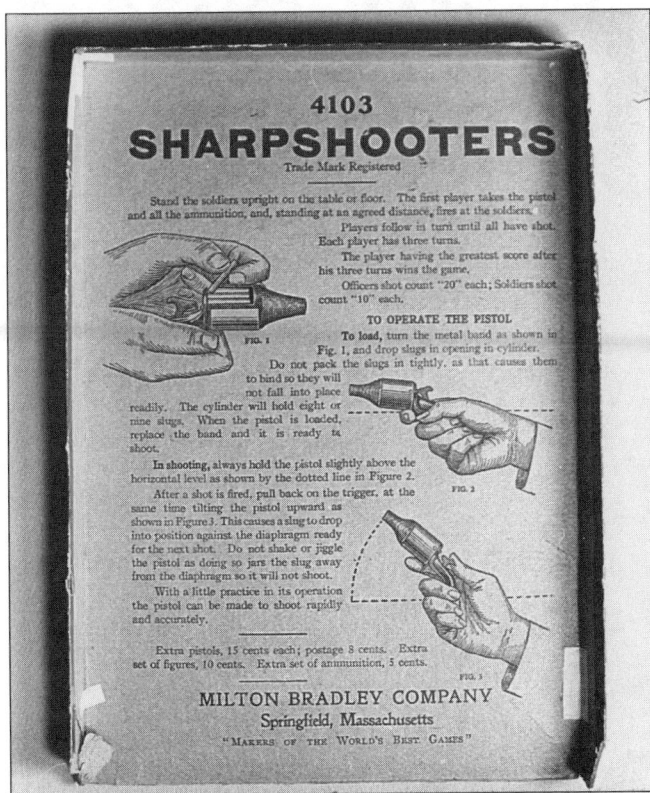

Inside cover of Sharpshooters box.

Stand-Up Dolls Honey and Bunny, Merrill, $70

Cinderella Paper Dolls, Whitman, 1965, $75

	C6	C8	C10
153 Tank w/three men	4	5	7
154 Ambulance	4	5	7
155 Truck w/soldiers in rear, WWII helmets	4	5	7
Soldiers, contains nine press-out soldiers, boxed set, wooden cannon and ammunition, Concord Toy Co., c. 1940, 3-1/2" each	50	60	75
Soldiers Set, contains five cardboard soldiers, and marbles by J. Pressman and Co., Inc., New York No. 1551, c. 1940, 4-1/2"each	35	50	60
Soldiers, cardboard, Navy, both officer and sailors on wooden blocks, c. 1920, approx. 6" high, each	3	4	5
Soldiers, cardboard, U.S. sailor on wooden blocks, approx. 6" high, each	3	4	5
Soldiers, cardboard, U.S. Infantry in campaignhats, mounted,, approx. 6" high, each	3	4	5
Soldiers, cardboard, West Point Cadets, approx. 6" high, each	4	5	6
Soldiers Five, 5 cardboard soldiers, pistol, boxed set, Milton Bradley No. 4395, c. 1920	80	100	125
Soldiers on Parade, set of ten, Milton BradleyNo. 4518	55	80	90
Spaceport, U.S.A., Whitman, 1953	15	20	22
Sports Time, Whitman No. 210525, 1952	5	10	15
Square Dance Paper Dolls, Saalfield No. 2717, 1950	15	20	25

	C6	C8	C10
Square Dance Paper Dolls, by J. Voelz, Lowe No. 968-10	15	20	25
Stage Door Canteen, Saalfield No. 2468, 1943	70	80	90
Stand-Up Dolls Honey and Bunny, Merrill No. 3403, 1936	50	60	70
Star Bright, Saalfield No. 2797, 1950s	20	30	40
Statuette Dolls, two women, Whitman No. 992, 1943	15	25	35
Statuette Dolls and their Clothes, Whitman No. 998, 1942	20	30	40
Statuette Dolls And Their Clothes, two girls and a boy, Whitman No. 986, 1946	15	25	35
Stencils Large and Small, by Roy Best, thirty animal punch outs and stencils, w/tiny box of crayons, (Whitman?) No. 954, c. 1935	15	22	28
Stock Farm set, 1200 die-cut pieces including house, barn, silo, chicken house and tractor, boxed, Concern No. 123, c. 1944	45	55	60
The Story of Cinderella, A Fold-A-Way Toy Book, designed by Will Pente, Reilly & Britton Co., c. 1925	30	45	48

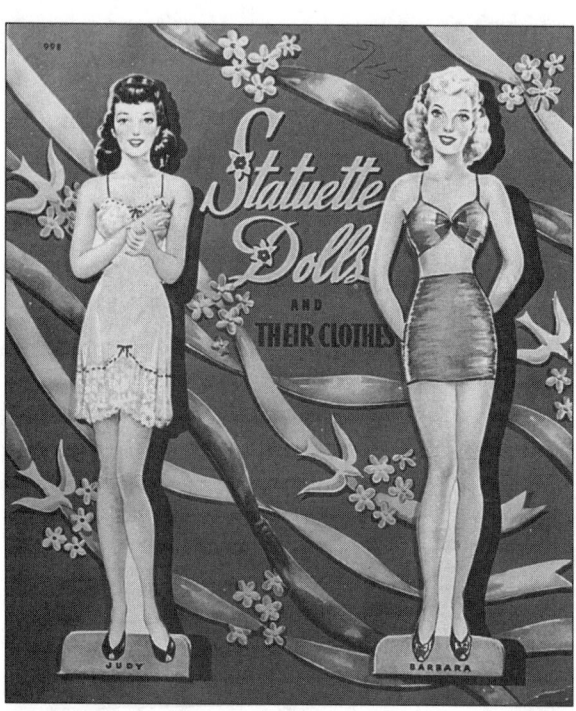

Statuette Dolls, Whitman, 1943, $40

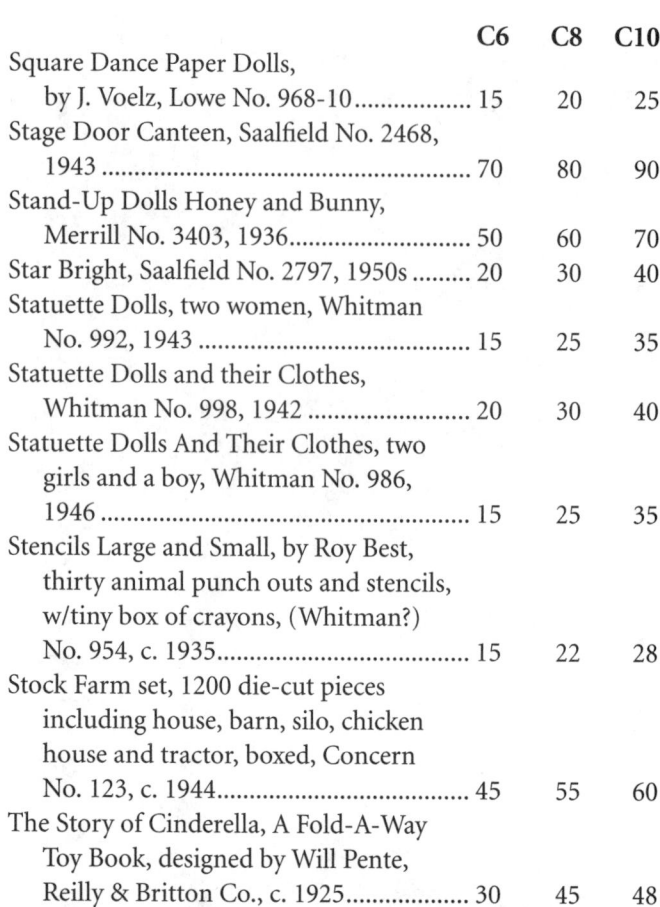

Story Princess-Alene Dalton, Saalfield, 1957, $50

Sunshine Cut-Outs Sports Series, Stroll & Edwards Co., $90

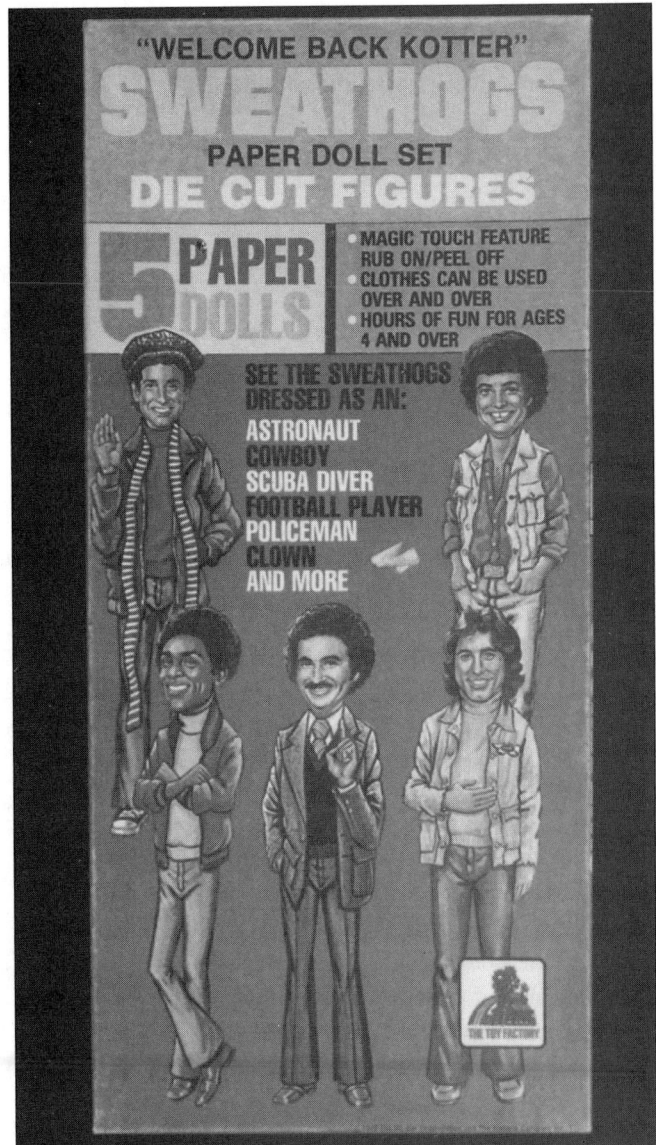

Sweathogs Paper Doll Set, The Toy Factory, 1977, $20

Brady Bunch Paper Dolls Cut-out Book, Whitman, 1976, $90

	C6	C8	C10
Story Princess-Alene Dalton, Saalfield No. 1727, 1957 30		40	50
Streamline Flyer, contains engine, station, crossing gates, crossing signal, baggage truck, baggage and people, boxed set, Concord Toy Co. No. 122, c. 1940, 10-3/4" x 13-1/2" 45		55	62
Style Shop Paper Dolls, Saalfield No. 1516, 1943 20		25	35
Sub-Deb Paper Dolls, by Irving Nurick, twelve teenage boy and girl dolls w/clothes, Merrill No. 3408, 1941 25		35	45
The Sue and Tom Cut-out Dolls Book, Lowe No. 149, 1946.................. 15		20	25
Sunbonnet Sue, Whitman No. 2062-29, 1951 15		20	25
Sunshine Cut-outs Sports Series - Spring, four-part foldout, by M. and F. Hoopes, Stroll & Edwards Co., 1926.................... 70		80	90
Susan Dey as Laurie (Partridge Family), Fashions by Kate Greenaway, Artcraft, 1972 25		35	45
Sweetheart Paper Dolls, Saalfield No. 2458, 1943 20		25	30
Sweetie Pie Twins, Jane and Jean, Stephens Publishing Co. No. 166, 1949 10		15	25
Swing-A-Plane, model of a Flying Tiger and on a string, by J.L. Schilling Co., 1944.................... 12		18	20
Tammy, includes paper dolls to cut out and dress, illustrated by Ada Salvi, A Little Golden Story Book, 1963 30		35	45
Tarzan of the Apes, figure set, 1933 40		50	55
Teen Gal Cut-out Dolls, by Hilda Miloche and William Kane, Whitman No. 980, 1943.................... 30		40	50
Teen Town, Merrill No. 3443, 1949 25		30	35
That Girl Marlo Thomas, Saalfield No. 1351, 1967 35		45	55
That Girl Marlo Thomas, Saalfield No. 1379, 1967 25		35	45
They Stand Up, by Avis Mac, includes five children, Whitman No. 932, 1939, 13" x 18".................... 40		50	60
Thirty Toy Soldiers, Whitman No. 2950, c. 1943.................... 40		50	60
This is Bunny, One of the Five Cut-out Dolly Sisters, Whitman, 1939.................. 20		30	40
This is Dotty, One of the Five Cut-out Dolly Sisters, Whitman, 1939.................. 20		30	40

	C6	C8	C10
This is Magic, One of the Five Cut-out Dolly Sisters, Whitman, 1939.............. 20		30	40
This is Patsy, One of the Five Cut-out Dolly Sisters, Whitman, 1939.............. 20		30	40
This is Peggy One of the Five Cut-out Dolly Sisters, Whitman No. 1002, 1939 20		30	40
This is the Navy, includes destroyer and PT boat, Skyline Mfg. No. 500A, c. 1942.............. 25		35	40
This is the Navy, heavy cruiser, Skyline Mfg. No. 501, c. 1942.................. 25		35	40
Three Bears Cut-out Book, includes Goldilocks and the three bears, Whitman No. 1020, copyright 1939 30		40	50
Three Flying Models of Famous Allied Fighting Planes, by Judd Reed, contains Hell Cat, Spitfire and Stormovik planes, included is "American Ace Spotter," w/turning dial of forty-eight three-view silhouettes of sixteen planes in little windows, 9"x12", 1944 30		40	50
Three Little Girls Who Grew and Grew and This is How They Grew, Whitman No. 99410, 1945 25		35	45

Toni Hair-do Cut-out Dolls, Lowe, 1950, $55

	C6	C8	C10
Three Little Girls Who Grew and Grew and This is How They Grew, w/cloth-like clothes, flocked, Whitman No. 1176, 1945 25	35	45	
Three Little Pigs Cut-out Book, includes pigs and Big Bad Wolf, Whitman No. 1020, copyright 1939 25	35	45	
Three Sweet Baby Dolls to Cut Out and Dress, Whitman No. 975, 1954 10	15	20	
Thrilltown Railroad, pullman passenger set, Reed, 1943 65	80	90	
Tina and Trudy, No. 1967, 1967, by Kathy Lawrence 20	25	30	
Tiny Chatty Twins Paper Dolls, Whitman No. 1985, 1963 30	35	40	
Toby Tyler Circus Playbook Punch-Out, No. 1936, 1959 35	45	55	
Tom Corbett Space Cadet Punch-Out Book, Saalfield No. 4304, 1952, 14" long, 10-1/2" wide 40	48	52	
Tom the Aviator, Samuel Lowe No. L1074, c. 1942 25	35	45	
Toni Hair-do Cut-out Dolls, Lowe No. 1284, 1950 35	45	55	
Toni Hair-Do Dress-Up Dolls, Lowe, No. 1251 40	50	60	
Top Notch Paper Dolls, Saalfield No. 1504, 1948 20	25	30	
Toy Models: Warplane and Tank Punch-out, Fawcett Publications, Lowe, 1941 45	50	65	
Toy Town, series of fifty different buildings, boxed set, American Color Type Co., 1916 75	100	125	
Transfer Pictures, includes 100 decals, Whitman No. 1085, copyright 1939 10	15	18	
Treasure Hour Puppet Book, The Rustlers of Rocky Ranch, a play of cowboys and Indians in five scenes, cut-out section makes model theater Murray Sales and Service No. 4, 1968 20	30	35	
Tricia, Artcraft No. 4248, 1969 190	225	245	
Tricia Paper Dolls White House Tour Game, White House stand-up doll of Tricia Nixon and costumes, Saalfield No. 1248, 1970 12	23	45	
Trudy Phillips and Her Crowd, Whitman No. 2104, 1954 15	20	25	
Tuesday Weld Paper dolls, two dolls and fifty-eight costume pieces, boxed, Saalfield No. 5112, 1960 40	50	60	
The Turnabouts Dolls Book, dolls printed front view on each side, Lowe No. 1048, 1940s 25	30	35	

	C6	C8	C10
TV Star Time Paper Dolls, Abbott No. 1367, c. 1950s 20	25	30	
TV Tap Stars Paper Dolls, Lowe No. 99010 6	12	25	
Twenty-two Animals To Cut Out and Stand Up, includes rabbits, bears, owls, and squirrels, Whitman No. 935, Copyright 1930 35	45	50	
Twiggy Paper Doll, w/Twiggy dress for small girls, Whitman No. 1999, 1967 35	45	55	
Two Little Charmers, Saalfield 3	5	10	
Tyrone Power & Linda Darnell, Merrill No. 3438, 1941 150	175	200	
Umbrella Girls, wrap-around dresses, Merrill No. 2562, 1956 30	40	45	
Uncle Sam's Little Helpers Paper Dolls, by Ann Kovach, Saalfield No. 2450, 1943 35	45	50	
United States Soldiers, Samuel Lowe No. L1063, 1942 50	55	60	
U.S. Commandos Book, Lowe No. 1089, 1943 45	55	60	

WACS and WAVES, Whitman, 1943, $75

	C6	C8	C10
U.S. Infantry-Spanish/American War, soldier on small wooden block, approx. 6" high	3	4	5
Victory Girls Arlene the Airline Hostess, Lowe, c. 1940s	35	45	55
Victory Punch-Out Tanks, Soldiers, Sailors, Planes, Lowe No. 848, c. 1943	50	55	60
Victory Volunteers, dolls w/uniforms by Merlin, Merrill No. 3424, 1942	55	65	75
Virginia Mayo, Saalfield No. 4422, 1957	50	60	70
WACS and WAVES, Whitman No. 985, 1943	55	65	75
Walking Paper Doll Family, Saalfield No. 1074, 1934	55	65	75
Walt Disney's Babes in Toyland, Golden Punch-Out Book No. 10363, 1961	40	45	50
Walt Disney's Jane and Michael from Mary Poppins, Watkins/Strathmore 1892-6, 1963	40	45	50
Walt Disney's Let's Build Disneyland, sets for Adventureland, Frontierland, Tomorrowland and Fantasyland, Whitman No. 1986, 1957	25	35	40
Walt Disney's Mary Poppins, Whitman No. 1982, 1964	40	45	50
Walt Disney Match and Patch Sticker Fun, includes Mickey Mouse, Donald Duck, Pluto, and Goofy, Whitman, 1953	15	18	20
Walt Disney Presents Hayley Mills in That Darn Cat, Whitman No. 1955, 1965	45	50	55
Walt Disney Sticker Fun Book, Whitman, 1951	10	12	15
Walt Disney Sticker Fun with Peter Pan, Whitman, 1952	12	15	18
War Between the States, Golden Press No. GF152, 1959	55	65	75
War Plane Cut-outs, heavy-stock, eight different scale models, 1943, 10" x 14"	35	40	45
Wedding Day, Saalfield/Artcraft No. 4458, 1968	20	25	30
Wedding Day, Saalfield No. 4246, 1970	15	20	25

	C6	C8	C10
Wedding Paper Dolls, Whitman No. 1970, 1970	10	15	20
We're a Family Cut-out Dolls, Whitman No. 1181, 1954	25	30	35
White House Party Dresses, Merrill No. 1550, 1961	25	30	35
Whitman little paper doll books, copyright 1939, No. 1146, 3-1/2" x 7-1/2"			
Nancy and Tommy	35	40	45
Ann and Arthur	35	40	45
Kitty and Billy	35	40	45
Muriel and David	35	40	45
Cynthia and Bobby	35	40	45
Judy and Dick	35	40	45
Whitman Paper Doll Book, four dolls and ten sheets of clothes in folder, No. 3059, 1933	35	40	45
Winnie's New Wardrobe, by Geraldine Cline, McLoughlin Bros. No. 555, 1939	30	32	36
Wispy Walker Whitman 1976	4	7	10
Young Patriot Invasion set, contains destroyer, amphibian tractor, tank, jeep, anti-tank gun, bomber and diver bomber, boxed set, Colorgraphic No. 500, c. 1944, 10-1/2" x 13"	75	80	95
Young Patriot Learn to Know Your Army, includes tank, howitzer, jeep, anti-tank gun, bomber, fighter and soldiers, w/shooting guns and dropping bombs, Colorgraphic No. 350, 1943	75	80	95
Young Patriot Learn to Know Your Navy, construction set includes battleship, destroyer, aircraft carrier, mosquito boat, submarine, planes and depth charges, w/moveable parts, Colorgraphic No. 360, 1943, 10" x 14"	75	80	95
Ziegield Girl Paper Dolls, No. 1, Merrill No. 3466, 1941	100	150	200
Zoo Cut-outs by Milo Winter, six pages of heavy cut-out animals, Whitman No. 1054, 1938	30	38	48

ANIMAL-DRAWN

In this category, the toys generally commanding the highest prices are horse-drawn cast-iron pieces. One reason for the eye-opening prices is that horse-drawn cast-iron toys have considerable value apart from their lure as toys—there is an air of genuine Americana about them, and they are likely to attract the interest of many who otherwise pay no attention to toys (decorators figure largely in this area).

Since prices are often so high, reproductions, whether honest or dishonest, can be a problem. Things to look for when a reproduction is suspected include a rougher surface than an old toy would have (recastings are invariably rougher), uneven fit of pieces, a blurring of details and "aging" that doesn't have the patina of age. Since at least one company, John Wright (formerly Grey Iron), is still manufacturing turn-of-the-century horse-drawn vehicles—some of them from the original molds—it is wise to become familiar with the field before investing heavily.

ALTHOF, BERGMANN

Althof, Bergmann began in 1867, when L. Althof teamed with the brothers Bergmann to form a jobbing firm (the brothers were already jobbers). In 1874 the New York company received two patents, one for a bell toy with three soldiers. In addition to bell and animal-drawn toys, they made (or jobbed out) toy furniture, banks and hoop and clockwork toys.

	C6	C8	C10
Fruits and vegetables, 17-1/2" long 5000		7500	10,000
Milk cart, "Pure Milk," c. 1880, 14" long .. 500		750	1000
Milk wagon, tin, 13" long........................... 600		900	1200
Pull toy, wagon, "Express" tin w/iron wheels, 26" 3000		5000	8000

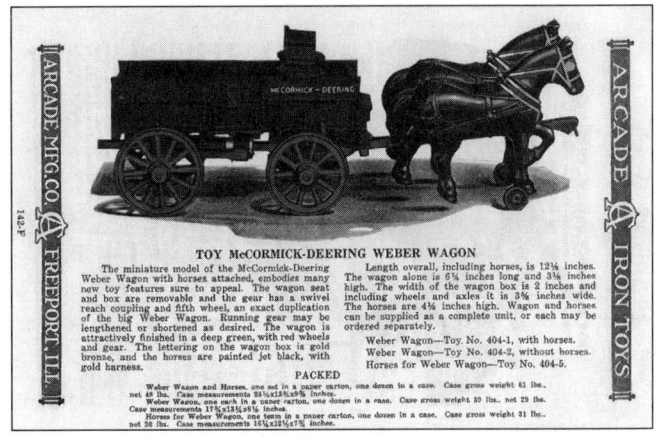

Page from Arcade Catalog featuring the McCormick-Deering Weber Wagon, $800

ARCADE

All Arcade toys are cast iron.

	C6	C8	C10
Bakery wagon, 13" long.............................. 300		450	600
Circus wagon, c. 1917 400		600	800
Cart, wicker, horse, driver, cast iron.......... 100		150	200
Coal car w/horse 150		225	300
Contractors dump wagon, w/horse team and driver, 14" long.............................. 250		375	500
Contractors dump wagon, w/two horses and driver, 1930s, 13-1/4"..................... 230		345	460
Farm wagon, w/two horses and driver, 10-3/4" long... 463		695	925
McCormick-Deering plow........................... 175		265	350
McCormick-Deering Weber wagon, w/two horses.. 400		600	800
McCormick-Deering manure spreader, w/team of horses, 14" long ... 375		560	750
Sulky plow, w/one horse, 10-1/2" 150		250	350
Wagon, "Big Six Circus & Wild West" Wagon, 14-1/2" long.............................. 425		638	850

Milk Wagon, Althof, Bergmann, $1,200

Pull Toy, wagon, "Express," Althof, Bergmann, $8,000

Fire Hook and Ladder, Bliss, $4,000

BLISS

Biss was founded about 1832 by Rufus Bliss, and by 1871 they were advertising their toys. Most were made of wood, and the range was wide, including dollhouses, trains, Noah's arks and ships. In 1883 Bliss made what might have been the first toy telephone set. The brilliant color lithography of Bliss's toys has made many of them prime collectibles.

	C6	C8	C10
Cinderella coach, 1890, paper litho on wood, w/two horses and two coachmen, lift off roof, blocks inside tell Cinderella story, 26" long	1000	3500	5500
Fire hook and ladder, w/two firemen and two horses, 29" long	2000	3000	4000
Fire hook and ladder, paper litho on wood, 30" long	1500	2500	4000
Pansy four-horse stagecoach, 1890, paper litho on wood, 31"	1000	1500	2500
Rough and Ready fire engine, w/two horses, 30" long	1600	2700	4000

Rough & Ready Fire Engine, Bliss, c. 1895 (missing rear fireman), $4,000

Fire Patrol, with two horses, Carpenter, 1885 (missing one figure), $1,900

CARPENTER

Carpenter (Francis W.) of Harrison and Port Chester, New York, was in business from 1844 to 1925. Malleable iron was its trademark because it was less fragile. Its two predominant lines were horse-drawn toys and trains.

	C6	C8	C10
Cart, animated, cast iron, c. 1902, 10-1/2" long	450	675	900
Cart, w/two horses, 12" long	635	950	1270
Cart, two-wheel, w/one horse and no driver, pat. 1882	250	400	500
Coal cart, iron	2000	3000	4000
Delivery wagon, pat. 1881, 12" long	200	300	400
Doctor's cart	400	600	800
Dump cart, w/one horse, 12"	400	600	800
Dump cart, w/two horses	350	600	800
Fire patrol, cast iron, w/two horses, one driver and three figures, 1885, 16-1/2" long	900	1400	1900
Fire wagon, w/one horse and one fireman	350	500	750
Hook and ladder, w/two horses, and two firemen in standard helmets, early	800	1200	1600
Hook and ladder, cast iron, w/two horses, one driver and rear man, ladders, c. 1883-1890, 26-1/2"	700	1050	1400
Horse and carriage, painted cast iron, 1880, 14" long	750	1000	1500

Left to Right: Cart, with two horses, Carpenter, $1,270; Dump cart, with one horse, Carpenter, $800

Tally-Ho, with four horses and seven riders, Carpenter, $12,000

	C6	C8	C10
Horse cart, cast iron, w/one horse and two men, c. 1880, 14-1/2" long	800	1200	1600
Ox cart, cast iron, w/two oxen, c. 1880-1903, 11" long	400	600	800
Pumper, w/two horses, No. 33, 18" long	1100	1850	2800
Tally-ho, cast iron, w/four horses and seven festive riders in coach, 27-1/2"	4000	9500	12,000
Wagon, w/two horses, 10" long	550	850	1300

DENT

	C6	C8	C10
Buckboard, w/rider, one horse, very early, primitive looking	125	190	250
Cart, w/horse and driver, 10" long	125	190	250
Cart, w/lady driver and horse, 11" long	150	225	300
Cart, mule, driver	250	375	500
Contractors dump wagon, w/two horses, 15" long	150	225	300
Coupe, w/one horse and driver, 9-3/4"	125	190	250
Dray, w/two horses and driver	550	980	1300
Dump cart, w/black man and mule	300	450	600
Fire engine pumper, silver w/two horses, 21" long	400	750	1000
Fire engine steam pumper, three horses, 21" long	1000	1700	2400

Hose Reel, with figures and three horses, Dent, $2,900

	C6	C8	C10
Fire hook and ladder, 27" long	1000	1700	2400
Fire patrol, w/three horses and firemen figures, 15-1/2" long	400	1000	2000
Fire patrol, w/three horses, cast iron, w/driver and six riders, c. 1905, 22" long	1200	2000	2800
Fire pumper, paint and nickel plate, w/three horses and driver, c. 1908, 15-1/2"	500	800	1100
Fire snorkle wagon, w/three horses and driver	500	750	1000
Hansom cab, cast iron, w/driver and lady passenger, c. 1905, 14" long	700	1150	1600
Hansom cab, No. 57, two-wheeled, w/one horse	175	260	350
Hook and ladder, w/three horses, extra large	500	1000	1500
Hook and ladder, painted cast iron, mechanized horses, 1915, 14" long	250	400	800
Hose reel, w/figures and three horses, figures, 24" long, 10" horse	1200	2000	2900
Horse and cart, tin	150	225	300
Horse and cart, cast iron, low sides	125	190	250
Ice wagon, w/two horses, 12" long	100	200	300
Ice wagon, w/one horse, 14" long	300	500	750
Ice wagon, cast iron, black horse pulling yellow and orange ice wagon, w/driver, c. 1910, 15-1/2"	675	1000	1350
Ladder wagon, 1890, w/four horses, 43-1/2" long	3000	4500	6500
Ox wagon, cast iron, w/driver and two oxen, 16" long	250	500	600
Ox cart, stake sides, w/one ox	125	190	250
Police patrol, w/driver, policeman and three horses, 21" long	800	1350	1875
Pony cart, No. 20, w/driver and team of horses, stake sides on cart	125	190	250
Pumper, painted cast iron, moving horses, 1915, 14-1/2" long	650	1000	1500
Road car, w/driver in top hat, two seats and one horse, 16" long	450	675	900
Sleigh, w/one horse, c. 1905, 16-1/4"	900	1500	2200
Small truck wagon, stake sides	200	300	400
Dent truck wagon, w/driver and one horse stake sides, 16" long	200	300	400
Sulky, w/jockey	150	225	300
Surrey, horse w/wheel attached to one leg	200	300	400
Transfer wagon, w/two horses, 21" long	450	750	1150
Transfer wagon, w/driver and two horses, 26" long	500	850	1200
Water tower, w/two horses, c. 1910, 31" long	900	1500	2200

JAMES FALLOWS

James Fallows was a foreman at the early American tin toy company Francis, Field and Francis. In 1874 he formed James Fallows & Company in Philadelphia. Most of Fallows' toys were tin, though often with cast-iron wheels many were marked "IXL." Papier-mâché was another primary material in a toy line that consisted of over 200 items.

	C6	C8	C10
Cart, tin, 12" long	500	750	1000
Cart and horse, painted tin, 1870, 8-1/2" long	100	200	400
Covered wagon, painted tin w/litho paper scenes on sides, 12"	800	1000	1500
Delivery wagon, "Fine Groceries," 7-1/2" long	1250	1875	2500
Dump wart, tin, w/one horse, c. 1890, 16" long	600	1000	1200
Fancy Goods and Toys, 21" long	1750	2625	3500
Fire pumper, w/two horses, very early, 18" long	5000	8500	10,000
Fire pumper, tin, very early, 24" long	5000	10,000	15,000
Horse and carriage, 1890, painted and stenciled tin, 12-1/2" long	500	750	1000
Streetcar, "4th Avenue," tin, w/one horse	500	800	1200
Streetcar, 9" long	400	600	900
Streetcar, w/two horses, 10" long	350	500	800
Wagon, "Pure Milk," painted and stenciled tin, 1895, 12-1/2"	800	1200	2000
Wagon, w/Donkey, cast iron, 10-1/2" long	175	260	350

GEORGE BROWN

In 1856 George W. Brown together with Chauncey Goodrich, founded George W. Brown and Company. Brown, an innovator, introduced the American clockwork toy (he'd spent eleven years in the clockmaking business). He invented many of his toys' mechanisms and may also have designed all or most of his toys. Brown worked primarily in tin, jobbing some of the work out to companies like Union Manufacturing Company in Clinton, Connecticut. Necessarily simple because of the material and manufacturing techniques employed, Brown's toys made up for it with brilliant hand-painted color and stenciling. Tops, rattles, flutes, wagons, fire engines, swords, trains and toy buckets were among the many items put out by the firm. The company merged with Stevens in 1868 and was dissolved in 1880.

	C6	C8	C10
Cab, w/driver and one horse, 8-1/2" long	560	840	1120
Cart, "Fine Groceries," w/horse	1250	1875	2500

Wagon, "Express," George Brown, $600

	C6	C8	C10
Cart and horse, painted and stenciled tin, 1880, 7-1/2" long	200	300	500
Delivery cart, 12"	1100	1800	2600
Doctor's buggy, tin and cast iron, 14" long	650	975	1300
Dog cart, c. 1870	400	700	1000
Dump cart, painted tin, 1885, 8-1/4" long	100	150	200
Dump cart, tin, back gate lifts out for dumping, 1880, 13"	200	300	400
Eagle chariot, painted tin, 1870, 11" long	500	1000	2500
Gig, tin, 9" long	300	450	600
Gig, tin, w/one horse, 10" long	150	225	300
Goat cart, 7" long	300	450	600
Grand Central Depot trolley, tin, w/two horses, 13-1/2" long	600	950	1350
Horse cart, 1870, tin, 11-1/2" long	125	190	250
Ox cart, 1880, painted tin, 9" long	500	1000	2000
Peddle wagon, tin, wheeled horses, driver andawning, c. 1880, 2 20" long	1000	2500	5000
Rockaway passenger cart, w/two horses, 13" long	1850	2500	4500
Sulky, 8-3/4" long	250	375	500
Sulky, clockwork, 13" long	3000	5500	9000
Yankee notions peddler wagon, 16-1/2" long	3000	7000	10,000
Wagon, "Express," tin w/iron wheels, 10-1/2" long	300	450	600

GIBBS

After manufacturing wooden barrels and tubs and metal plows since about 1830, Gibbs Manufacturing Company of Canton, Ohio, began turning out toys in 1896. The company's first toy was a political giveaway for William McKinley who was from Canton. The first toy was a spring-operated top, and variations of it remained in the firm's catalogs until 1969, when it stopped making toys. Most Gibbs toys were wood or tin, with much use made of lithographed paper for decoration. Many of Gibbs' playthings were of the push and pull variety.

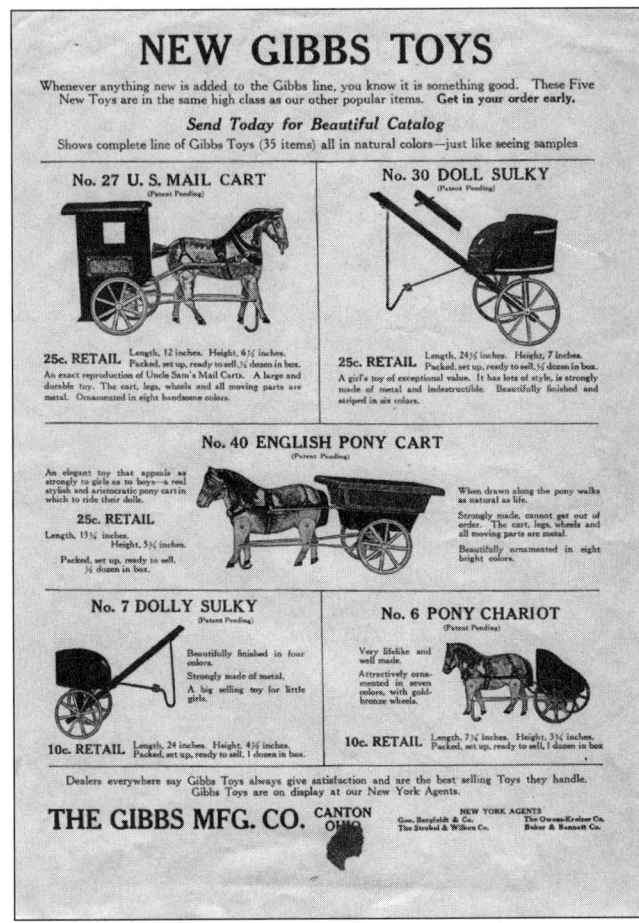

A Gibbs Advertisement from 1914

U.S. Mail Cart, Gibbs, $600

	C6	C8	C10
Cart and horse, paper litho on wood, 13" long	150	225	300
Cart, "Groceries The Great Atlantic and Pacific Tea Co.," mule-drawn, 12" long	350	500	1000
Delivery 14, No. 14	150	225	300
Dog cart, boy driver	375	560	750
English pony cart, No. 40	110	165	220
Gray beauty pacers, No. 50	150	225	300

	C6	C8	C10
Gypsy wagon, No. 57	250	375	500
Hay wagon, w/two horses, 19" long	100	150	200
Pacing Joe, No. 35	175	263	350
Pioneer wagon, No. 32	65	100	130
Pony chariot, No. 6	165	250	350
Pony circus wagon, No. 53	200	300	400
Pony pacer, No. 15, 7" long	115	170	230
Tea Co. mule cart	350	500	1000
U.S. Mail cart, No. 27	300	450	600
Yankee dump cart, No. 56	225	338	450

HARRIS

Harris Toy Company of Toledo, Ohio, seems to have begun production of cast-iron toys during the late 1880s. The firm, which also jobbed for Dent, Hubley and Wilkins, stopped making toys in 1913.

	C6	C8	C10
Brownie shell cart, cast iron, 1903	225	340	450
Cart, w/mule driver, 10" long	250	500	750
City truck, w/one horse and driver	1300	2000	3150
City truck, w/two horses and driver, 15" long	1200	1900	2700
Dog cart, cast iron, w/girl driver, 7" long	275	360	550
Fire patrol wagon, w/driver, three riders and two horses, 19" long	800	1400	1900
Goat cart, shell-type, cast iron, w/driver, 5" long	100	250	350
Goat cart, w/rider, 9-1/2" long	800	1425	1950
Goat cart, cast iron, w/driver and two goats,	1000	2500	3000
Hook and ladder, cast iron, w/three horses, 19" long	140	210	280
Transfer wagon, w/three horses, 1903, 18-1/2" long	400	650	850
Wagon, mule, 12" long	300	450	600

English Pony Cart, Gibbs, $220

Front to Back: Brake, two seat, Hubley, $7,500; Brake, three seat, $12,500

HUBLEY

	C6	C8	C10
Barrel wagon, "Dray," w/barrels and barrel ramp, w/driver and two horses, 23" long	1100	1750	2500
Brake, four-seat, w/four horses and eight articulated passengers, 28"	2000	3500	5625
Brake, cast iron, three-seat, w/two horses, 18" long	4000	7000	12,500
Brake, cast iron, three-seat, w/four horses, 18" long	4200	7300	13,000
Brake, cast iron, two-seat, w/driver and three women passengers, 16-1/2" long	2500	5000	7500
Brake, cast iron, two-seat, 16" long	1600	2700	4000
Brougham, cast iron w/nickeled, horse and driver, 16" long	300	1000	1500
Brougham, w/top-hatted driver and one horse, 17" long	550	850	1300
Cab, 14" long	300	500	700
Cane wagon, 15" long	600	900	1200
Cart, w/driver, 5-1/2" long	150	225	300
Cart, w/horse and driver, 8" long	155	232	310

Cab, Hubley, $700

Coal Wagon, with two horses, Hubley, $1,000

	C6	C8	C10
Cart, wood w/iron wheels and iron horse, 1910, 10-1/2" long	175	265	350
Chariot, cast iron, 8-3/4" long	500	750	1000
Chariot, w/driver and two horses, 9-1/2"	600	900	1200
Chariot cast iron, w/clown and three horses, early, 12-1/2" long	800	1200	1600
Chariot bank, elephant-drawn, 13" long	650	1100	1600
Chariot, Roman, cast iron, w/three small horses	425	637	850
Chariot, Roman, cast iron, w/three large horses	600	900	1200
Chariot, Roman, w/driver and three horses, 16" long	200	300	400
Coal wagon, w/mule, 9" long	300	450	600
Coal wagon, w/two horses, 16"	500	750	1000
Conestoga wagon, tin w/cloth canopy, w/two horses, 15" long	550	825	1350
Essex trap, 1890, cast iron, driver and horse, 13" long	500	1500	2500
Farm wagon, cast iron, w/one horse, c. 1915, 12-1/2" long	400	600	800
Fire patrol, cast iron, driver, w/four riders, all in standard helmets, 13" long	750	1200	1750
Fire pumper, cast iron, w/two horses and driver, c. 1910, 14" long	200	400	600
Fire patrol, cast iron, driver, w/four firemen and prancing horse team, 21" long	700	1100	1500
Fire pumper, cast iron, white-painted, w/two horses, c. 1906-1910, 19" long	500	775	1100

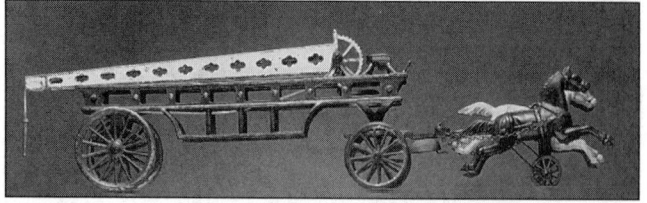

Hose Tower Wagon, Hubley, c. 1915, $1,800

	C6	C8	C10
Fire pumper, cast iron, w/two horses, driver and two firemen, 20" long 750	750	1125	1500
Fire pumper, cast iron, w/three horses and driver, c. 1906-1910, 20-1/2" long........ 800	800	1200	1600
Fire pumper, cast iron w/American Eagle, w/two horses, c. 1905-1910, 21" long... 500	500	1000	1500
Fire pumper, cast iron, w/three horses, 22" long................ 800	800	1400	2090
Gig, cast iron, horse-drawn w/lady driver, 15" long................ 350	350	650	950
Cab, cast iron w/driver cast in, w/one horse 300	300	500	750
Hook and ladder, cast iron, w/three horses, two firemen and two wooden ladders, c. 1906-1910, 27-3/4" long...... 550	550	850	1300
Hook and ladder, cast iron, w/two horses, 28" long 700	700	1200	1650
Hook and ladder, cast iron w/eagle on shield on side, w/three horses, 33" long................ 1000	1000	1700	2450
Hook and ladder, cast iron, "126," w/three horses, 33-1/2" long................ 438	438	657	875
Hose reel, cast iron, w/three horses and driver, c. 1906, 19" long 750	750	1200	1700
Hose reel, cast iron, w/one horse and three figures, 13" long 500	500	750	1000
Hose tower wagon, cast iron, c. 1915, 28" long................ 800	800	1300	1800
Ice wagon, cast iron, 8" long 100	100	150	200
Ice wagon, cast iron, 1920s, 9-1/2" 175	175	265	350
Ice wagon, cast iron and nickel plate, painted, w/driver and horse, 1910, 14"................ 400	400	850	1200
Ice wagon, cast iron, w/one horse, 15" 800	800	1300	2000
Ice wagon, cast iron, w/two horses, 15" long................ 500	500	800	1200
Ice wagon, cast iron, w/two black horses pulling green wagon and driver, c. 1906, 15-1/2" long 800	800	1300	2000
Ice wagon, cast iron, w/two horses and driver, 16-1/2" long 1000	1000	1650	2200
Landau carriage, cast iron, painted, 1905, 16-1/2" long................ 1400	1400	2100	2800

Police Patrol, Hubley, $2,200

	C6	C8	C10
Log wagon, cast iron, w/two oxen and driver,c. 1905, 15" long 500	500	750	1100
Log wagon, w/one horse, 19" long 400	400	600	800
Milk cart, cast iron, 12-1/2" long.............. 425	425	640	850
Milk wagon, 5" long 140	140	210	280
Phaeton, cast iron, w/one horse 1200	1200	2000	3000
Police patrol, cast iron, w/driver and three riders, early, 13" long................ 500	500	750	1000
Police patrol, cast iron, w/driver and riders, 17-1/2" long 600	600	950	1430
Police patrol, cast iron, w/driver and six cops, 21" long 1000	1000	1600	2200
Royal Circus, cast iron, w/animals, driver and two horses, 15" long............ 500	500	1000	1200
Royal Circus bandwagon, cast iron, w/four horses and seven riders, 22" ... 1000	1000	2000	3000
Royal Circus bandwagon, cast iron, w/two horses and seven riders, c. 1920, 22-1/2" 1800	1800	2900	4000
Royal Circus bandwagon, cast iron, w/eight musicians and driver, 1920, 30" 1500	1500	2250	3000
Royal Circus bear wagon, cast iron, 15" long 1500	1500	2250	3000
Royal Circus calliope, cast iron, 12-3/4" long................ 1400	1400	2400	3400
Royal Circus clown on trapeze van, cast iron, 1920, oval-mirrored sides, 16-1/2" 1600	1600	2700	4000

Ice Wagon, with one horse, Hubley, $2,000

Royal Circus Bandwagon, Hubley, $3,000

Royal Circus Bear Wagon, Hubley, $3,000

Santa Claus Sleigh, 1910, Hubley, $1,500

	C6	C8	C10
Royal Circus farmer van, cast iron, head revolves and disappears in top of wagon as toy pulled,1920, 16" long....	1700	1850	4250
Royal Circus giraffe cage, cast iron, w/large and small giraffes and driver, 1920, 27" long	3000	5500	9200
Royal Circus lion cage, cast iron, 9"	375	565	750
Royal Circus lion wagon, cast iron, w/rare gray horses and wagon, 15-3/4"	700	1100	1650
Royal Circus polar bear cage, cast iron, 1920s, 11-3/4" long	600	1000	1375
Royal Circus rhino wagon, 16" long	850	1700	2500
Royal Circus tiger wagon cage, cast iron, w/driver and two tigers, 1920, 16" long	500	750	1000
Santa Claus sleigh, cast iron, w/one reindeer, early, 15" long	1500	2500	4000
Santa Claus sleigh, cast iron, w/two reindeer, 1910, 16" long	600	1000	1500
Santa Claus sleigh, cast iron, early, 17" long	800	1300	2000

	C6	C8	C10
Shell cart and horse, cast iron, 1905, 7" long	250	375	500
Sleigh, cast iron, painted, w/one horse, 1910, 14-1/2" long	500	800	1200
Sleigh, cast iron, w/one horse and woman w/movable arms, early, 14-3/4" long	700	1200	1700
Sleigh, cast iron, nickel plated and painted, w/one horse, 1900, 15" long	250	375	500
Sleigh, cast iron, nickel plated and painted, w/two horses, 1910, 15" long	800	1300	2000
Spring wagon, cast iron, w/horse and driver	200	300	400
Stanhope gig, cast iron, 11-1/2"	200	300	400
Sulky, 8-1/2" long	187	280	375
Surrey, clockwork, cast iron w/brass works, 1894, 9" long	500	1000	1500
Surrey, cast iron, w/one horse and lady driver, 13-3/4" long	318	475	635
Surrey, cast iron, w/two horses, driver and rider,c. 1900, 12" long	240	360	480
Surrey, 2 horses, woman driver, 13-3/4" long	750	1125	1500
Surrey, cast iron, w/two horses and driver, 18"	400	600	800

Left to Right: Royal Circus Rhino Wagon, Hubley, $2,500;
Royal Circus tiger wagon, Hubley, $1,000

Stanhope Gig, Hubley, $400

	C6	C8	C10
Surrey, cast iron, two-seat w/driver, woman passenger and two horses, 13-3/4" long	600	900	1200
Trotter, cast iron, w/horse and driver, 1900, 8-3/4" long	200	300	400
Trotter gig, cast iron, w/lady driver, 11"	150	225	300
Van, Monkey Trapeze Circus Mirror Van, 12-1/2" long	500	800	1300
Wagon, expandable, cast iron w/wood bed, w/two horses and driver, 26"	750	1125	1500
Wagon, "Eagle Milk & Cream," 12" long	500	750	1000
Wagon, cast iron, w/horse, 12"	150	225	300

HULL & STAFFORD

Dump cart	700	1000	1600
Express wagon	350	550	750
Gig, w/china doll, c. 1885, 12" long	650	1150	1500
Prospect Park omnibus, w/two horses and driver, c. 1880, 16-1/2"	5000	10,000	15,000
Wagon, 9" long	800	1400	2000

IVES

Ives is one of the fabled companies in American toy history. Founded by Riley Ives as a metal stamping shop in the late 1850s in Bridgeport, Connecticut. It was around 1856

Ives advertisement from Playthings *magazine.*

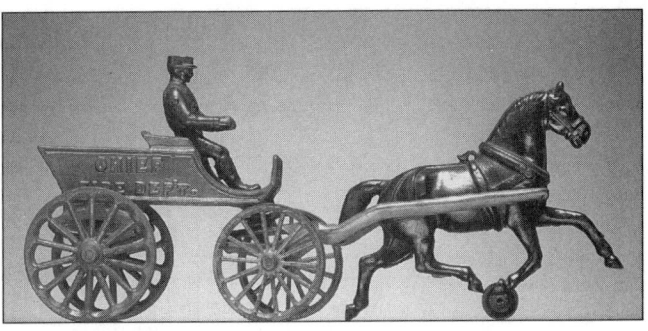

Chief Fire Dept. Wagon, Ives (incorrect driver shown), $1,000

when Ives began making tin whistles for New York Rubber's squeak toys. This led to Ives' first true toys—hot air playthings. These were toys put into motion by the hot air from stoves, lanterns, etc., and were first sold in 1868. Ives' son Edward joined the company around 1860, and his son, Harry, took the reins in 1895. Harry Ives was ousted in 1929, and the firm was dissolved in 1932.

During its heyday, which lasted about forty years, Ives put out a deluge of toys of every type, and quality was its watchword. Toy making was carried on in Bridgeport, Connecticut, from about 1870 until the end.

	C6	C8	C10
Adams express, w/two horses, 21"	750	1300	1800
Bandwagon, cast iron, w/nine passengers, 31-1/2" long	2500	4000	6000
Brewery Wagon, w/two horses, 18-1/2" long	1000	1700	2500
Caisson, w/driver, cannon, rider and two horses, 21" long	1700	3000	4000
Chief Fire Dept., 15-1/2" long	400	700	1000
Coal dump cart, w/donkey and black driver	363	545	725
Coal dump wagon, w/donkey and black driver	375	560	750
Doctor's cart, w/two wheels, 10-1/4"	400	600	1000
Dray wagon, stake sides, w/horse, 15" long	1100	2100	3000
Fast mail wagon, cast iron, w/walking horses, 17" long	750	2000	3500
Fire patrol, w/one horse, five riders and driver, c. 1890, 19" long	1200	1900	2700

Hansom Cab, Ives, $4,000

Hook and Ladder, with driver and two horses, Ives, $3,700

	C6	C8	C10
Fire patrol, cast iron, w/two horses, driver, and six firemen, c. 1880-1910, 20-1/2"	900	1400	2200
Fire pumper, w/two horses, 13" long	400	650	900
Gig, 1890s, driver w/top hat, 5-1/2" long	500	750	1000
Hansom cab, w/walking horse, 18" long	1500	2500	4000
Hook and ladder, Phoenix, c. 1890, 28" long	1500	2400	3600
Hook and ladder, No. 45, w/ladders and pails, c. 1885, 28" long	900	1500	2100
Hook and ladder, cast iron, w/two horses and two riders, c. 1890, 29" long	900	1400	2200
Hook and ladder, cast iron, w/driver and two horses, 34" long	1500	2400	3700
Horse cart, tin, 1870, 10" long	600	950	1400
Horse cart, 1883, w/two horses, 17-1/2"	750	1200	2500

Hose Reel Wagon, with one horse and driver, Ives, $1,300

Phoenix Pumper, with driver and two horses, Ives, $2,300

Stake Wagon, with two donkeys, Ives, $800

	C6	C8	C10
Hose reel wagon, w/driver, rider, and one horse, very low back platform	2000	4000	7000
Hose reel wagon, "Phoenix," cast iron, w/one horse and driver, c. 1880-1910, 15" long	1600	2400	3200
Hose reel wagon, w/one horse and driver 16" long	600	950	1300
Wagon, w/mules, 1896	600	950	1400
Ox Cart, w/two oxen	400	750	1150
Patrol fire wagon, 22" long	800	1350	2050
Phoenix pumper, cast iron, w/driver and two horses, 17-1/2" long	950	1600	2300
Phoenix pumper, c. 1890, cast iron clockwork, rarest of Ives pumpers, 19" long	900	1500	2200
Police patrol wagon, 1890s, w/six patrolmen and driver, 20-1/2" long	1000	2000	3000
Pull toy, walking horse, horse walks by means of wheel mechanism, pulls two-wheeled cart; late 19th century	1800	2800	4000
Pumper, 23" long	2000	3200	4500
Stake wagon, w/two donkeys, 15-1/2"	400	600	800
Steam pumper, w/two horses, 20-1/2"	4000	6000	8000

KENTON

Kenton Lock Manufacturing Co. was incorporated in May 1890, in Kenton, Ohio. In November of 1894 it became the Kenton Hardware Manufacturing Company, and around this period the company began producing toys. It ceased production of horse-drawn toys in the early 1920s (except for a 1930s beer wagon), but in 1939 introduced a completely new line of horse-drawn pieces. This line continued through 1954.

	C6	C8	C10
Aerial fire tower, w/three horses and driver, 30" long	800	1400	1900
Ambulance - 2nd Regiment, w/driver and one horse, 15" long	1200	2400	3600
Back to back trap, w/driver and woman rider, 12-1/2" long	1100	1900	2750

Advertisement for Kenton Hardware Company from a 1952 Playthings *magazine.*

	C6	C8	C10
Bakery wagon, 1941	325	500	650
Band wagon, w/musicians, driver and rider on horse	150	225	300
Beer wagon, cast iron, w/driver and two horses, 15" long	500	800	1200
Boar cart, c. 1910, cast iron, w/Egyptian driver, 8" long	350	500	750
Cement Mixer, w/driver and horse, 14" long	350	750	1000
Chariot, camel-drawn w/clown driver, 11" long	700	1200	1600
Chariot, cast iron, 6" long	150	225	300
Chariot, cast iron, w/comic driver, 1910, 7-1/2" long	250	375	500
Chariot, cast iron, w/three horses	600	900	1200
Chief wagon, w/horse and driver, 12-1/4" long	500	800	1500
Circus cage wagon, w/two horses, two riders, driver and animal in cage	350	700	1000
City Express wagon, w/driver and one horse, 17" long	500	750	1045
Coal Cart, w/donkey and black driver	365	550	725

	C6	C8	C10
Contractor's Wagon, w/black driver and two horses, 15-1/2" long	500	800	1200
Covered wagon, cast iron, w/two horses	130	195	260
Cupid in Slipper, cast iron, w/one-horse cart, 8-1/2" long	450	800	1100
Cupid in horse-drawn slipper, w/one horse, 10-1/2" long	550	950	1400
Delivery cart, cast iron, w/donkey	150	225	300
Delivery wagon, No. 5, w/driver and two horses, 15" long	250	375	500
Dog cart, greyhound pulling dog riding in cart, 7" long	250	375	500
Dray, cast iron, w/two black and white horses pulling green dray w/driver, 13-1/2"	300	450	600
Dray, No. 5, cast iron, painted, 1930, 14-1/2" long	175	265	350
Dray, cast iron, w/two horses pulling a green cart w/driver, late 1940s, 14-3/4" long	95	140	190
Dump wagon, w/two horses, lever releases bottom wagon	250	375	500
Dump wagon, "Sand and Gravel," w/driver and two horses, 10" long	180	270	360
Dump wagon, early 1900s, 10-1/4" long	150	225	300
Dump wagon, "Sand and Gravel," w/driver and two horses, 15" long	175	260	350
Egyptian cart, "Cairo Express," elephant drawn, 10" long	500	800	1100
Egyptian cart, elephant drawn	300	450	600
English trap, w/two horses, woman and dog, c. 1895, 14" long	1600	2700	4000
Express wagon, cast iron, w/horse and driver, 12" long	200	300	400
Farm Cart, mule, black driver, 10-1/2" long	375	562	750
Farm wagon, w/driver and one horse, 14" long	500	750	1100
Farm wagon, cast iron, w/two horses and figure, 14-1/2" long	500	750	1100
Farm wagon, w/driver and one horse, early, 15" long	300	450	600
Farm wagon, w/two horses and driver, 15" long	325	490	650
Fire ladder wagon, w/front driver only, 12" long	150	225	300
Fire ladder wagon, horse drawn, w/drivers front and rear, 17" long	135	200	270
Fire patrol wagon, w/driver and three riders, 12" long	360	535	714
Fire pumper, w/two horses and driver, 20" long	175	260	350
Fire pumper, cast iron, 26-1/2" long	600	1000	1400

Hook and Ladder Wagon, with two horses, driver and passenger, $3,700

Left to Right: Overland Circus Bandwagon, Kenton, $1,210; Overland Circus Bear Wagon, Kenton, $470

	C6	C8	C10
Fire wagon, nickel plated wagon, w/two horses, driver, equipment and bell, 23" long	200	300	400
Goat cart, figure w/large cars, 7" long	250	375	500
Gravel wagon, w/two horses, 13" long	150	225	300
Hansom cab, cast iron, w/top-hatted driver and lady rider	700	1050	1400
Hansom cab, w/top-hatted driver, 8" long	150	225	300
Hansom cab, w/one horse and top-hatted driver, 10" long	1000	1500	2000
Hansom cab, 12" long	500	750	1000
Hansom cab, w/figures and horse, 15-1/2" long	300	500	700
Hook and ladder, cast iron, w/three horses, 16" long	300	450	650
Hook and ladder, w/three horses, 17" long	250	375	500
Hook and ladder, cast iron, w/three horses, c. 1910, 19" long	150	225	300
Hook and ladder wagon, w/two horses and driver, 20" long	250	375	500
Hook and ladder, nickel-plated, w/two horses and driver, 20" long	200	300	400
Hook and ladder, cast iron, painted, w/ladders, 1915, 26" long	600	1000	1400
Hook and ladder, 30" long	1400	2200	3200
Hose reel, 1920, cast iron, painted, 13-1/2" long	500	750	1000

	C6	C8	C10
Hose reel, cast iron, w/two horses, c. 1905, 14-1/2" long	600	900	1200
Ice wagon, cast iron, w/two horses and driver,1920s, 15" long	250	375	500
Landau, cast iron, white horse pulling green carriage w/driver, c. 1910, 15" long	600	900	1200
Log wagon, w/one horse and driver, 14-1/2" long	425	640	850
Log wagon, cast iron, black man w/two oxen, early 1900s, 15" long	500	800	1100
Milk wagon, w/horse and driver, 12-1/2" long	280	420	540
Overland Circus bandwagon, w/six musicians and driver, 15-3/4"	500	800	1210
Overland Circus bear wagon, cast iron, w/two horses, driver and cage containing cast-iron bears, 1940s, 13"	235	350	470
Overland Circus calliope wagon, 14-1/2" long	300	500	700
Ox cart, cast iron, 5" long	100	150	200
Ox cart, 7" long	110	165	220
Ox cart, 12-1/2" long	385	575	770
Ox wagon, w/two oxen, 18" long	400	600	800
Patrol wagon, w/driver and rider, 12" long	275	415	550
Patrol, No. 526, w/two horses, driver and riders, 17" long	650	1100	1500

Milk Wagon, with horse and driver, Kenton, $540

Spider Phaeton, Kenton, $2,000

	C6	C8	C10
Plantation cart, 1910, black driver, mule,			
10" long... 500		800	1210
Police patrol, w/mule team, 16"................. 500		750	1000
Pumper, w/three horses, 18" long............. 400		600	800
Rabbit pulling two-wheeled cart, cast			
iron, 5" long... 200		300	500
Rhino cart, 8" long 100		200	300
Spider phaeton, cast iron, 11-1/2" long..... 850		1350	2000
Stake wagon, w/two horses and driver			
w/reins, 15" long	83	125	165
Sulky, driver cast to sulky, 6" long	75	112	150
Sulky, cast iron, w/driver, 7" long 250		375	500
Surrey, cast iron, w/two horses, driver			
and passenger, 12-1/2" 263		395	525
Surrey w/fringe top, w/driver, passenger			
and two horses, 1952, 13" long............. 145		220	290
Surrey, w/one horse, c. 1940, 16" long 150		225	300
Team of horses w/log and black driver...... 500		750	1000
Transfer wagon, w/two horses and driver 650		975	1300
Beer delivery wagon (3.2), cast iron,			
w/two horses, driver and ten wooden			
kegs, 1930s, 14-1/2" long 350		525	700
Victoria cab and horse, cast iron,			
w/driver and woman, 15-1/2" long 150		225	300
Wagon, No. 3, w/one-horse and driver,			
15" long.. 125		190	250
Wagon, No. 5, w/one horse, 15" 125		190	250
Wagon, w/two horses, 15" long...................	90	135	180
Wagon w/driver and two horses, 10-1/4".. 100		150	200
Water tower wagon, c. 1915, driver and			
two horses, 32" long............................... 440		660	880

KINGSBURY

	C6	C8	C10
Dray, cast iron, w/two horses,			
20-1/4" long.. 300		450	600
Hook and ladder, cast iron and pressed			
steel, w/three horses and two riders,			
rubber covers on wheels, 25-1/2" 400		600	800
Hook and ladder, w/two horses, driver			
and three ladders, 27" long................... 600		900	1200
Ladder truck, 1900, cast iron, tin and			
wood, 13" long 300		450	600

LANCASTER

	C6	C8	C10
Hook and ladder, cast iron, w/two			
horses, 25" long...................................... 150		225	300
Hook and ladder, cast iron, w/two			
horses and two drivers, 28" long 200		300	400
Hook and ladder, cast iron, w/three			
horses and two drivers, 28" long 250		375	500

Brake, four seat, Pratt & Letchworth, $11,000

	C6	C8	C10
Surrey, no driver, Hubley No. 58	75	115	150
Surrey, w/one seat, driver and horse,			
Hubley No. 174 150		225	300

PRATT & LETCHWORTH

Pratt & Letchworth of Buffalo, New York, was in operation from c. 1880 into the 1890s and sold its toys under the name Buffalo Toy Works. Iron and steel were its main materials, and all of its most prominent toys seem to have been horse-drawn.

	C6	C8	C10
Barouche, w/driver and two horses,			
17" long 750		1400	2000
Brake, four-seat, w/four horses, driver			
and seven passengers, 28" long........... 4000		7000	11,000
Cart, "Pratt & Letchworth," 10" long 150		225	300

Top to Bottom: Hansom Cab, Pratt & Letchworth, c. 1892, $1,800; Surrey, two seat, Pratt & Letchworth, c. 1890, $1,100

Pumper, with driver, rider and two horses, Pratt & Letchworth, $2,000

	C6	C8	C10
Chemical wagon, w/three horses and driver	3000	6000	9000
Chief's wagon	1100	1650	2200
City delivery wagon, w/driver, barrels and horse, c. 1885,	1100	1700	2500
Doctor's cart, w/one horse and driver, 11" long	650	1100	1550
Double surrey, 15" long	450	750	1100
Dray, cast iron and wood, w/one horse, 1890, 12" long	800	1450	2200
Fire chief's wagon, w/figure and horse, c. 1885, 12" long	700	1100	1500
Gig, cast iron and pressed steel, w/one horse and one rider, 10-1/2" long	400	600	800
Hansom cab, cast iron, c. 1892, 13" long	700	1200	1800
Hay cart, 10-1/2"	500	750	1000
Hose reel, w/one horse and driver in standard helmet	900	1350	1800
Hose reel, w/one horse, 14-1/4" long	900	1350	1800
Pony cart, 11" long	413	620	825
Pony phaeton, w/driver and one horse, c. 1892, 15-1/4" long	600	1000	1500
Pumper, w/driver, rider and two horses, 17" long	750	1400	2000
Sulky, 8-1/2" long	700	1200	1820
Sulky, 15" long	550	850	1300
Surrey, rear seat, w/one horse, c. 1890, 15-1/2" long	500	850	1100
Dray, w/one horse and driver, 14-1/2" long	500	850	1500

REED

	C6	C8	C10
Band chariot, w/fourteen bandsmen, 28-1/2" long	800	1200	2000
Mammoth Show Circus wagon, paper on wood, w/three animals and two trainers, c. 1890, 14" long	1100	1700	2500
Trolley, "Bowery & Central Park," paper on wood, w/two horses, 28" long	1500	2300	3500

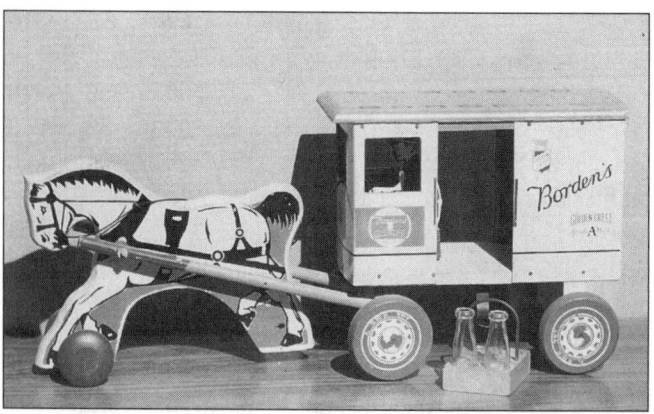

Dairy Cart, "Borden's Golden Crest," Rich Toys, $480

RICH TOYS

Rich Toys, founded by E.M. and M.E. in 1921, added toys to their line around 1923. Their first toys were manufactured in Morrison, Illinois, and then moved to Clinton, Illinois. In 1953, Rich moved to Tupelo, Mississippi, where, about 1962, a flood put an end to the business.

	C6	C8	C10
Dairy cart, "Borden's Golden Crest," wood, 18" long	240	360	480
Beer wagon, "Budweiser"	300	500	800
Wagon, "National Biscuit Company," w/one horse	400	600	800
Streetcar, No. 59, w/two horses, c. 1925, 20" long	600	900	1200
Wagon, "Sand and Gravel," cast iron, w/driver, 9-1/2" long	150	225	300
Wagon, "Sand and Gravel," cast iron, w/driver and two horses, 14-3/4" long	100	150	200
Wagon, "Sand and Gravel," cast iron, w/driverand two horses, cast iron, 15" long	150	225	300

Streetcar, No. 59, Rich Toys, c. 1925, $1,200

Choice Family Groceries Tea, Coffee & Spices, Shimer, $1,200

SHIMER

	C6	C8	C10
Choice Family Groceries Tea, Coffee & Spices, 12-1/2" long	500	800	1200
Ice wagon, cast iron, w/driver and two horses, 13" long	375	560	750
Lumber wagon, cast iron, w/two horses, 26" long	358	535	715
Patrol, cast iron, animated, w/black prisoner and five policemen, 21" long	3500	6500	9000
Surrey, woman driver	375	560	750

WILKINS TOY COMPANY

Wilkins Toy Company, founded by James S. Wilkins in Keene, New Hampshire, began as the Triumph Wringer Company. The tiny model Wilkins produced to promote his product proved so intriguing to prospective customers and their children that requests for the toys outnumbered the actual product. Wilkins quickly forgot his original idea and turned to toy making. Wilkins' toys were generally cast iron and steel. The firm was acquired by Kingsbury in 1894, and they are still in business as a tool and die maker.

	C6	C8	C10
Aerial fire wagon, cast iron, w/three horses and driver, 43" long	2000	3500	5150
Artillery, w/rider on caisson and two horses, seat top lifts off, cannon, c. 1895, 10" long	1000	1500	2000

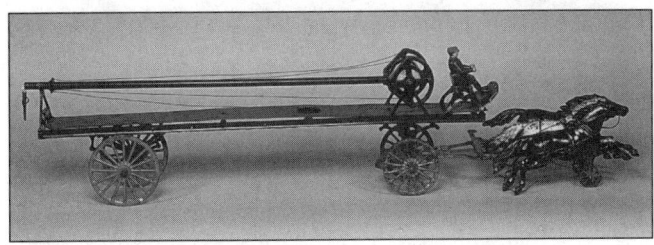

Aerial Fire Wagon, with three horses and driver, Wilkins, $5,150

	C6	C8	C10
Buckboard, cast iron	120	180	240
Caisson, horse-drawn, 18"	650	1000	1500
Cane wagon, w/mule and driver, 11" long	300	450	600
Carriage, w/driver in derby, passenger and one horse	1000	1500	2000
Cart, animated, 6" long	250	375	500
Cart and horse, 10" long	450	700	1000
Cart and horse, w/driver, 12"	750	1200	1600
Chariot, w/four horses, 7" long	180	270	360
Chariot, cast iron, woman driver w/three horses, 10-1/2" long	400	600	800
City truck, cast iron, w/two horses and driver	1000	1500	2000
Coal and wood wagon	750	1125	1500
Delivery wagon, w/driver and prancing horse team, 21" long	600	900	1200
Doctor's cart, c. 1900, 10-1/2" long	500	750	1100
Dog cart, cast iron, 1890, 7-1/2" long	150	225	300
Dog cart, cast iron, w/St. Bernard-type dog and rider in cap, c. 1890, 10-1/2" long	600	950	1400
Donkey cart, 11" long	237	355	475
Donkey cart, 13-1/4" long	350	525	700
Dray, cast iron, w/black driver, and one horse, 12" long	500	750	1100
Dray, cast iron, 15" long	300	450	600
Dray, cast iron, w/six horses, 16" long	325	500	700
Dray, w/driver and two mules, 17-1/2" long	600	900	1250
Dray, cast iron and tin, drawn by two horses, w/driver in derby hat, c. 1910, 20-1/2" long	900	1350	2200
Fire chief buggy, w/one horse and rider, 12" long	650	1050	1500
Fire chief engine pumper, w/two horses, 19" long	500	750	1000
Fire hose reel, 10-1/2" long	350	550	750
Fire ladder truck, cast iron, w/three horses and two firemen, c. 1910, 20"	415	620	830
Fire patrol, w/six firemen and three horses, 20" long	500	750	1050
Fire patrol wagon, w/firemen, 12" long	450	675	900
Fire patrol wagon, cast iron, w/two horses and two firemen, 20-1/2" long	550	825	1200
Fire pumper wagon, w/two horses, 18"	1700	2800	4000
Fire pumper wagon, horizontal chemical tank, w/two horses, 19-1/2" long	1700	2800	4000
Fire pumper wagon, w/driver and two horses, 20" long	600	900	1200

Ox Cart, Wilkins, $700

	C6	C8	C10
Fire pumper wagon, w/driver and three horses, 25" long	1800	3200	5000
Gentleman's cart, w/gentleman driver and white horse, 1900, 10"	300	450	600
Gig, fancy, w/driver, 10"	150	225	300
Goat cart, driver, c. 1900, 9-1/2" long	900	1350	2200
Groceries wagon, w/one horse, c. 1900, 13-1/2" long	200	300	400
Hansom cab, cast iron, 15" long	600	950	1400
Hook and ladder, 24" long	700	1100	1700
Hook and ladder, cast iron, w/prancing team, 27" long	600	925	1350
Hook and ladder, w/two horses, ladders and figures; horses sit on pegs	1000	1500	2000
Hook and ladder, w/two horses and two firemen, 19-1/2" long	385	575	770
Hose reel, w/two horses and two firemen in standard helmets, 16" long	1500	2500	3500
Hose reel, c. 1890, cast iron, w/one horse, 18" long	800	1300	1900
Huckster's wagon, w/two horses and driver	800	1450	1950
Ice wagon, horse, tin and cast iron, 10" long	150	225	300
Landau, cast iron, w/articulated horses, two coachmen and opening doors, 15-1/4" long	1200	2000	3100
Panama earth mover, w/driver and two horses, 1903, 20" long	400	600	800

	C6	C8	C10
Ox cart, cast iron	300	500	700
Phaeton, w/driver in top hat and gray pony	450	750	1100
Phaeton, w/woman driver, late 1800s, 16" long	1000	2500	4000
Plantation cart, cast iron and pressed steel, 1910, 11"	460	690	920
Plow, w/one horse and driver, 10-1/2"	1200	1900	2800
Police patrol, w/driver, two horses and six policemen, 1911, 20" long	1700	2700	3700
Pony cart, w/one horse and driver, 7-1/2" long	400	600	800
Pony cart, w/one horse and driver, 9-1/2" long	500	750	1075
Pumper, w/two horses and two firemen	1100	1650	2200
Spring wagon, w/driver and horses	300	450	600
Stake wagon, 1907	500	675	1000
Steam engine, w/two horses and driver, 17" long	600	900	1300
Street sweeper, "D.P.W," w/one horse, brush anddriver, 13" long	2000	3200	5700
Streetcar, "Broadway Car Line 75," horse-drawn	900	1600	2400
Streetcar, "Consolidated Street R.R. 712," cast iron, 14" long	1200	1900	2800
Streetcar, "World's Fair Street R.R. 372," cast iron, w/one horse and six passengers, 15"	900	1600	2400
Transfer wagon, tin and cast iron, 15" long	500	850	1200
Wagon, "Boys Express Co.," cast iron, w/two horses, 16-1/2" long	700	1200	1600
Wagon, w/driver and mule, 9" long	300	450	600

Streetcar, "Consolidated Street RR712," with one horse and six passengers, Wilkins, $2,800

Top to Bottom: Streetcar, "World's Fair Street R.R. 372," with one horse and six passengers, Wilkins, $2,400; Transfer Wagon, Wilkins, $1,200

Band Chariot, Reed, $2,000

Doctor's Cart, cast iron, $2,000

MISCELLANEOUS

	C6	C8	C10
Bakery wagon, cast iron, w/one horse, 13" long	100	200	300
Band chariot, paper on wood, w/fourteen band members, Reed, 28-1/2" long	800	1200	2000
Bread wagon, "Bread and Cakes" w/driver and tin horse, 12-1/2" long	350	525	700
Brewery wagon, cast iron and pressed steel, w/two horses and driver, 20-1/2"	350	525	700
Buckboard, cast iron, w/one horse and driver, 14" long	200	300	400
Buckboard, pressed steel, painted, w/one horse, Mason & Parker, 1910, 31"	500	750	1000
Buggy, pressed steel w/cast-iron wheels and horse	40	60	80
Buggy, cast iron, w/driver, 6-1/2"	70	100	140
Buggy, tin, w/horse, 7" long	175	265	350
Cab and horse, painted and stenciled tin, Merriam, 1880, 8-1/2" long	1300	2700	4000
Cart, painted pressed steel, w/horse, mechanical action from axle, Mason & Parker, 1910, 13" long	500	750	1000
Circus wagon, "Animal Cage" lead and tin, Barclay, c. 1930s, 9-7/8"	30	45	60
Coach, slush lead, Barclay, c. 1930s, approx. 10-1/4"	30	45	60
Covered wagon, "1849," w/oxen, Barclay 1930s, 7" long	30	40	55
Circus cage, "Barnum and Bailey," stained and litho wood, painted, elephant-drawn, 1930, 35" long	400	600	800
Carriage, metal and wood, w/horse, malleable iron horse w/articulated legs and tail	300	450	600
Cart, cast iron, two-wheeled cart pulled by bulls	100	150	200

	C6	C8	C10
Cart, cast iron, two-wheeled cart pulled by lions, 8" long	125	190	250
Cart, cast iron, w/one horse, 9" long	75	115	150
Cart, tin, w/one horse, 8" long	200	300	400
Cart, tin, painted, w/one horse, 1890, 15" long	250	500	750
Cart cast iron, w/driver and buffalo, 7-1/2" long	400	600	800
Cart, cast iron, w/woman and prancing horse, 10-1/4" long	500	750	1200
Cart, cast iron, 7" long	125	190	250
Cart, cast iron, stake sides, w/one horse, 7" long	150	225	300
Chariot, drawn by tin horse, 13-1/2" long	125	190	250
Chariot, cast iron, w/clown and camel	1000	1600	2400
Chief's wagon, "Chief," cast iron, w/one horse, c. 1915-1920, 12" long	150	225	300
Chief fire wagon, cast iron, w/one horse, 15-1/2" long	350	525	700
Circus wagon, iron and tin, w/two horses and lion cage, 9" long	200	300	400
Circus wagon, cast iron and wood, contains carved wood bear, 13" long	250	340	500
Coal wagon, cast iron, w/driver and coal shovel, 9-1/4"	137	200	275
Conestoga wagon, cast iron, w/cloth cover and two horses, 12-1/2" long	50	75	100
Conestoga wagon, litho, w/walking horses and iron wheels, 18" long	140	210	280
Covered wagon, cast iron w/cloth top, w/one horse and driver, 13" long	170	255	340
Covered wagon, tin, Indian head litho on side, w/driver and horse	40	60	80
Doctor's cart, cast iron, 11" long	850	1450	2000
Dog cart, tin, c. 1875, 10" long	400	600	800
Donkey cart, cast iron, w/driver	200	300	400
Donkey cart, tin w/iron star wheels, 8" long	300	450	600
Donkey cart, tin, 8-1/2" long	250	375	500
Dray, cast iron, w/one black horse pulling dray, 14" long	150	225	300

Dog Cart, tin, c. 1875, $800

	C6	C8	C10
Dray wagon, cast iron, w/driver and two horses, 18" long	250	375	500
Dump cart, "Hard and Soft Coal-Coke and Kindlings," tin, 19" long	500	750	1000
Dump truck, cast iron and tin, w/one horse	200	300	400
Farm wagon, "Whitewater," w/two horses, Vindex	1400	2400	3700
Farm wagon, John Deere, w/two horses, Vindex, 7-1/2" long	800	1300	1900
Farm wagon, cast iron, w/two horses, 10"	200	300	400
Farm wagon, cast iron, w/driver and two unusual horses, 14" long	250	375	500
Farm wagon, cast iron and wood, large heavy horses, 25-1/2" long	300	450	600
Farm wagon and team, Auburn Rubber	50	70	95
Fire hose reel, cast iron, horse-drawn, 6" long	150	225	300
Fire patrol, cast iron, wagon contains two firemen and driver, drawn by three horses, 17" long	900	1350	1800
Fire patrol cast iron, w/two horses, three firemen and driver, c. 1910, 19"	1250	1875	2500
Fire patrol, cast iron, w/two horses, three firemen and driver, c. 1890, 20-1/2" long	600	950	1300
Fire pumper, cast iron, 3 horses, 11-1/4"	500	750	1000
Fire pumper, cast iron, w/two horses and driver, 13" long	600	900	1200
Fire pumper, cast iron, w/three horses, 14-1/2"	650	1050	1500
Fire pumper, "Friendship 1774," cast iron, w/rubber hose, 16" long	375	565	750
Fire pumper, c. 1910, cast iron, w/three horses, 17-1/2" long	500	750	1000
Fire pumper, cast iron, w/three horses, w/driver, and fireman, c. 1910, 18-1/4" long	425	640	850
Fire pumper, cast iron, w/two horses and driver, 19-3/4" long	500	750	1000

	C6	C8	C10
Goat cart, iron goat and wheels w/tin cart, 7-1/2" long	100	150	200
Goat cart, tin, early, 10-1/2" long	150	225	300
Grass cutter, cast iron, two-wheeled cart w/two horses and driver	1000	1500	2000
Hansom cab w/driver, cast iron, 9-1/2"	120	188	250
Hansom cab, cast iron, w/one horse and driver, 10" long	285	425	570
Hansom cab, tin, movable legs on horse, 15-1/2" long	175	265	350
Hay wagon, cast iron, w/driver and one steer, Kyser & Rex, 11-1/2" long	550	850	1300
Hay wagon, cast iron, w/driver and two steers, Kyser & Rex, 13" long	700	1200	1700
Hook and ladder, pressed steel and iron, w/figures, ladders, unusual hanging horses	250	375	500
Hook and ladder, cast iron, tin and wood, w/two horses, driver and three ladders, 16-1/2" long	150	225	300
Hook and ladder, cast iron and tin, w/three horses, two firemen and ladders, 21"	175	265	350
Hook and ladder, cast iron, w/two horses, 22-3/4" long	1000	1650	2000
Hook and ladder, cast iron, w/three horses and driver, 25" long	500	750	1000
Hook and ladder, cast iron, w/three horses, 25-1/2" long	600	900	1200
Hook and ladder, w/three horses, driver, 27-1/2" long	750	1125	1500
Hook and ladder, wood ladder w/figurines and three horses, 29-1/2" long	750	1125	1500
Hook and Ladder, cast iron, w/three horses, two drivers and four ladders, c. 1910-1914, 31-1/4" long	1000	1500	2000
Horse and cart, litho paper on wooden horse, tin cart	150	225	300
Horse and cart, open carriage w/driver in top hat, tin, 5-1/2" long	150	225	300
Hose reel, cast iron, w/one horse and driver, 11" long	1000	1650	2500
Hose reel, cast iron, w/one horse and driver, 12" long	1000	1650	2500
Hose reel, cast iron, w/one horse and driver and cord fire hose, 12-1/2" long	500	750	1000
Hose reel, Welker & Crosby. 13-1/2"	800	1400	1900
Hose reel, cast iron, w/three horses, c. 1910, 19" long	600	900	1200
Hose reel, cast iron, w/driver, two horses and man standing on rear bumper, 21" long	750	1125	1500

	C6	C8	C10
Hose reel, cast iron, c. 1910-1914, w/three horses, one driver and fireman, 21"	1000	1500	2000
Hose wagon, cast iron, w/two firemen, three horses and bell, 21-1/2" long	750	1125	1500
Ice wagon, cast iron, w/one horse, 12"	500	750	1000
Ice wagon, cast iron, w/two horses, 12"	600	900	1200
Ice wagon, "The Klondike Ice Co., New York," tin, w/two horses, 17-1/2"	350	525	700
Ladder wagon, cast iron, w/two ladders and three galloping horses, 13-1/2"	150	225	300
Ladder wagon, cast iron, w/two horses andthree sections of ladder, w/bell, 25-1/2"	250	375	500
Ladder wagon, cast iron, w/two drivers and three horses, four sections of ladder, Dart type, 30-1/2" long	800	1400	2100
Log wagon, cast iron, w/driver and two oxen, 15-1/4" long	450	675	900
Mail cart, tin, horse-drawn	140	210	280
Mail wagon, tin, w/two horses, 17"	175	260	350
Mess cart, WWI-type, tin, painted, w/two horses	100	150	200
Milk wagon, tin, painted, goat-drawn, possibly George Brown, 6"	150	225	300
Milk wagon, w/driver and one horse, 12-3/4" long	200	300	400
Milk wagon, "Sheffield Farms Company," wood,horse w/articulated legs, 21" long	250	400	650
Milk wagon, "Golden Pasture Farm Products, Milk & Cream," wood, painted and stenciled, steering mechanism for child to ride, 1915, 30" long	500	750	100
Mower, cast iron, w/two horses and driver, 10" long	150	225	300
Omnibus, "People's," tin, w/two horses and driver, c. 1880s-1890s	4000	6000	8000
Ox Cart, w/two oxen and black driver, Welker & Crosby	600	900	1200
Pansy stage coach, w/four horses, driver and litho alphabet blocks, Reed, 28"	1000	1500	2000
Plow, cast iron, w/one horse, cast iron, 10-3/4" long	150	225	300
Police patrol wagon, cast iron, w/one horse, figures and driver, 11-1/2" long	100	150	200
Police Patrol, cast iron, w/one horse, 12"	150	225	300

Produce Wagon, with one horse, $700

	C6	C8	C10
Police Patrol wagon, cast iron, w/driver, five policemen and two horses, 15"	1700	2800	4000
Produce wagon, tin, painted, w/one horse, possibly George Brown, 12-1/2" long	350	525	700
Pull toy, cloth and wood, "Dry Goods," c. 1860, 26" long	400	600	800
Pull toy, "Dump Cart," horse pulling cart, 7-3/4" long	80	120	160
Pull toy, tin, horse and cart w/iron wheels, 11" long	250	375	500
Pull toy, tin, horse and covered delivery wagon, 5-1/4" long	150	225	300
Pull toy, tin, horse and two-wheeled wagon, 9-1/4" long	125	190	250
Pull toy, tin, horse-drawn carriage, 12"	150	225	300
Pull toy, tin w/iron wheels, horse pulling water wagon, 6-3/4" long	350	525	700
Pull toy, tin w/iron wheels, horse pulling water wagon, 7-1/4" long	125	190	250
Pull toy, wood, horse-drawn wagon w/articulated legs, "Borden's Farm Products,"	315	470	625
Pumper, driver part of casting, w/two horses, 15-1/2" long	200	300	400
Pumper, cast iron w/driver and two horses	125	188	250
Pumper, cast iron, w/three horses and figure, 13" long	300	450	600
Santa Claus and sleigh, wooden sleigh, composition Santa and plush reindeer, 25" long	1500	2250	3000
Santa Claus and sleigh, two reindeer pulling black-painted Santa in white sled containing black-painted Santa Claus	500	800	1200
Sheep, cast iron and tin, sheep pulling two-wheeled wagon, 8" long	125	200	300
Spring wagon, cast iron w/driver and horse, 11" long	150	225	300

	C6	C8	C10
Spring wagon, cast iron, w/driver and horse, 14-1/2" long	150	250	350
Spring wagon, cast iron, w/driver and two horses, 14-1/2" long	150	275	400
Spring wagon, cast iron, w/driver and two horses, plus miniature pick, shovel and sledgehammer, 14-1/4" long	600	900	1200
Spring wagon, cast iron, w/two horses, 15"	150	225	300
Stagecoach, cast iron, w/cowboy driver and two horses, 11" long	130	195	260
Stagecoach, cast iron, w/six horses, 27" long	60	90	120
Stake bed wagon, cast iron, w/one horse, 14-3/4" long	400	700	1000
Surrey, "Stanley," w/driver, lady passenger and two horses, 14-3/4" long	100	150	200
Steam pumper, cast iron, w/stationary driver andtwo horses, 9-1/4" long	100	150	250
Steam pumper, cast iron, w/stationary driver and three horses, 10-1/2" long	150	225	300
Steam pumper, cast iron, w/stationary driver, and two horses, 15" long	500	750	1000
Steam pumper, cast iron, w/driver and three horses, bell, 17-1/2" long	600	900	1200
Steam pumper, cast iron, w/two horses and w/driver, 18" long	600	1000	1500
Steam pumper, cast iron, w/driver and two horses, 20-1/2" long	800	1300	2000
Sulky, cast iron, w/horse and rider, cart mounted w/4 bells, 6-1/2" long	200	300	400
Sulky, cast iron, w/driver, 7-1/4" long	150	225	300
Sulky, cast iron, Williams, c. 1920, 8" long	150	225	300
Sulky, cast iron, w/driver, c. 1890s, 8-1/2" long	250	400	550
Sulky racer, plastic wind-up, Wolverine	55	80	110
Transfer wagon, cast iron, w/two horses, driver, 18" long	300	450	600
Transfer wagon, cast iron, w/three horses and driver, wagon bolted to team, 19"	325	488	650

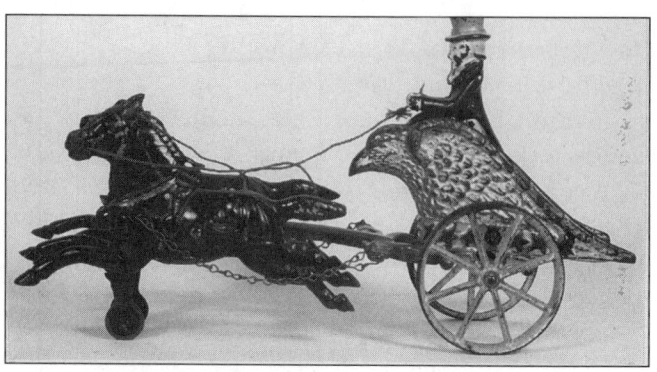

Uncle Sam Eagle Chariot, cast iron, Jones & Bixler, $8,000

	C6	C8	C10
Transfer wagon, cast iron, w/driver and two horses, 19-1/2" long	400	600	800
Trolley, "Bowery & Central Park," paper on wood, w/two horses, 28" long	1500	2300	3500
Trotter, w/jockey and horse, cast iron, 6" long	150	225	300
Uncle Sam Eagle Head Chariot, cast iron, w/two horses, Jones & Bixler	3000	5000	8000
Wagon, "Fine Groceries," tin, w/two horses, 14" long	400	600	800
Wagon, "National Express", tin litho, w/one horse, 15" long	250	375	500
Wagon, "United States Transfer Co. No. 7,"wood w/cast-iron wheels, w/two stuffed horses, 31" long	300	450	600
Wagon, cast iron, two-wheeled w/driver, 7-1/4" long	100	150	200
Wagon, cast iron, two-wheeled w/mule and driver, 9-1/2" long	300	450	600
Wagon, cast iron, two-seater, w/one horse	150	225	300
Wagon, "Delivery" wood seat, w/one horse, Converse, c. 1915	350	525	700
Wagon, "Dispatch," w/one horse, Chein, 11-1/2" long	90	135	180
Wagon, "Milk 16" Converse	70	1100	1700
Wagon, "U.S. Mail 17" Converse	700	1100	1700
Wagon and horse, tin, painted and stenciled, Merriam, 1890, 19-1/2" long	2500	3375	5000

Hook and Ladder, "126," Hubley, $875

Fire Pumper, three-horse, Hubley, 22" long, $2,090

Tally-Ho, Carpenter, 27-1/2" long, $12,000

Hose and Reel, one-horse, Hubley, 13" long, $1,000

Royal Circus Farmer Van, Hubley, $4,250

Royal Circus Lion Cage, Hubley, $750

Royal Circus Polar Bear Cage, Hubley, $1,375

Bandwagon, Ives, 31-1/2" long, $6,000

Coal Dump Wagon, Ives, $750

Dray Wagon, stake sides, Ives, 17" long, $3,000

Fire Patrol, Ives, 20-1/2" long, $2,200

Patrol Fire Wagon, Ives, 22" long, $2,050

Log Wagon, Kenton, 15" long, $1,100

BB Guns

Spring Air BB guns, sometimes referred to as air rifles, are simple in design and operation. They cannot be pumped up to high pressures and their muzzle velocity is usually in the neighborhood of 400 feet per second. Operation is simple: a one-stroke cocking action compresses a spring and draws a piston back through a cylindrical air chamber. Locked in this position, the BB gun is ready to fire. Meanwhile a BB has been placed in the breach, either manually or by an automatic feed mechanism. When the trigger is pulled the piston is driven forward, forcing the air in the cylinder out through the barrel, driving the BB ahead of this blast of air.

A BB gun is not a toy in the traditional sense. If improperly handled it can be dangerous and cause injury. Yet it was conceived, designed, manufactured and advertised for use by children. Common sense tells us that a BB gun should not be placed in the hands of a child too young to understand its dangers or who has not been properly instructed in its safe use.

Daisy and Markham/King both went into the BB gun business in the late 1880s. Located just across the railroad tracks from one another in Plymouth, Michigan, they were in vigorous competition for years. By the early 1930s, Daisy not only owned King but the King guns were being produced in the Daisy plant. During that period of about forty years, as many as thirty companies tried their hand at the BB gun business. Few made a great success of it; none have survived. By the 1930s, "Daisy" and "BB Gun" had become pretty much synonymous terms.

Daisy started life as the Iron Windmill Company in 1882. Iron windmills weren't great sellers, and when windmill designer C.J. Hamilton brought in a small prototype BB gun to be considered for manufacture, the board of directors was cool toward the idea. Eventually it was decided that the little gun would be made as a premium to be given to windmill purchasers. But as Cass Hough, grandson of one of Daisy's founders, said in his 1976 book *It's A Daisy*, "It didn't take long for the tail to begin to wag the dog." A few months later production started in earnest and the first Daisy was on the market.

The people who were running the Iron Windmill company didn't realize their BB gun was only the first of hundreds of models that would be produced over the next century. Neither that first Daisy nor the variations and new models that followed over the next few years were assigned a letter or number designation. Finally, in 1900 Daisy produced a variation with the designation "Model B." The designations such as "first model, second model," etc. are informal terms used by collectors. The BB guns are not so marked. The first Daisy was simply marked "DAISY MFD. BY IRON WIND MILL CO. PLYMOUTH MICH. PAT. APD. FOR." After that, Daisy produced BB guns with names, letters, numbers, or combinations of same. Their system, or more accurately, lack of system, is confusing to the average collector, and even the advanced collector cannot answer questions about the chronology of Daisy BB guns with absolute certainty every time. Daisy didn't know they were making "collectibles," or that anyone would care a hundred years later when a particular model was manufactured. Some guns have no special marking except a name, which may be shared with several models. Some have a single letter or number designation, still others may have a combination of letters and numbers. Many of Daisy's guns from the late 1930s, have a number and a model number such as "No. 111 Model 40," in addition to a name, in this case "Red Ryder." A classic case is the No. 50 Golden Eagle of 1936. This out of sequence number was used because the gun was made to commemorate Daisy's 50th anniversary.

To make it easy for the reader, the Daisy listings have been broken down into several sections. Name-only guns are in the first section. Those identified by a letter (alphabet guns) are next, followed by numbered guns. Guns with a combination of letters and numbers will be listed according to whichever appears first, the letter or the number.

With a few exceptions, the listing are limited to guns made between 1888 and early 1942. BB guns made after World War II have not yet aroused much collector interest. That is not to say that none of the postwar guns are collectible or that some collectors do not collect these later models, but most collector interest is focused on the prewar era. This eliminated most of the plastic-stocked guns from this chapter and most of the guns from Daisy's facility at Rogers, Arkansas. Daisy switched to plastic stocks around 1950 and moved to Rogers in 1958.

Like the prices of all collectibles, BB gun prices are somewhat subjective and actual prices paid can vary widely. Many factors have to be considered. Supply and demand, nostalgia, condition, how badly the buyer wants the item, and the thickness of the buyer's wallet are all important factors in the collectibles game. There is no infallible guide to BB gun values. The prices listed are based on collecting, buying and selling BB guns over the past few years and may not reflect prices in every area.

One last word on the listing method used in this book: The term C10 means a piece that is in exactly the condition it was in on the day it was made. In the case of many of the early BB guns, no such piece will ever be found. Just because it is the best example you have ever seen or heard of does not make it a C10.

There have been many contributors to this chapter, far too many to list here, but two deserve mention. Jim E. Thomas of Tulsa, Oklahoma, has long been my mentor in learning the intricacies of Daisy BB gun chronology. In addition, Bill and Lynn Johnson of Rosamond, California, have been a great assistance in sorting out the very early Daisys and Kings. Much of this early information is very obscure. Daisy did not bother to keep complete records of early model changes or production. Bill, who has studied the subject for many years and has a fine collection of old Daisy/King ads and other paper, was nice enough to go over the evaluations and lend his personal input prior to publication.

Two other important sources of information have been Arni Dunathan's 1971 book *The American BB Gun,* and *It's A Daisy,* by Cass S. Hough. Hough, grandson of one of Daisy's founders, was mainly responsible for developing the great Daisy character guns of the 1930s. The Buck Jones, Buzz Barton, and that most famous of all BB guns, the Daisy Red Ryder, were all Hough creations.

Abbreviations Used

LA: Lever Action

BA: Break Action

PA: Pump Action

SS: Single Shot

RPTR: Repeater

WDS: Wood Stock

PLAS: Plastic Stock

NIC: Nickel Finish

BLU: Blued Finish

PNTD: Painted Finish

Contributor: Jim Buskirk, c/o TGCA, 3009 Oleander Ave., San Marcos, CA 92069. A casual BB gun collector for years, Buskirk began collecting in earnest in 1985, and in 1989 he began publishing The Toy Gun Collectors of America Newsletter, a quarterly magazine for toy gun buffs. His collection of cap guns, BB guns and related items number several hundred pieces and consists of mostly of pre-WWII items, and its main focus is the 1930s era. The Daisy Red Ryder BB guns are of special interest, and his collection includes what is believed to be the first Red Ryder ever made—a factory prototype that was hand-built on a King Model 5536 frame.

DAISY

Daisy with Names

	C6	C8	C10
20th Century, 1899, marked "20th Century," BA, SS, WDS, NIC, w/cast-metal grip frame	180	210	300

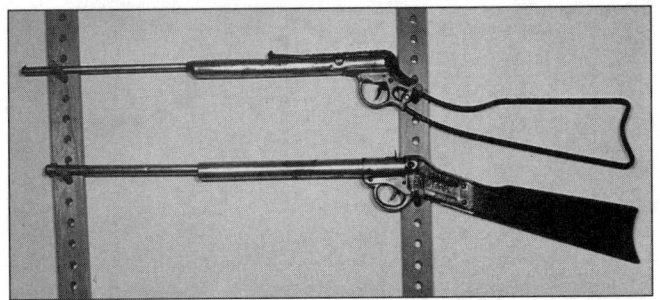

Top to Bottom: First model, 1890, Daisy, $600; 20th Century, 1899, Daisy, $300

	C6	C8	C10
500 Shot Daisy, 1905, marked "500 Shot Daisy" on top and/or side of frame, LA, RPTR, WDS, NIC	150	175	250

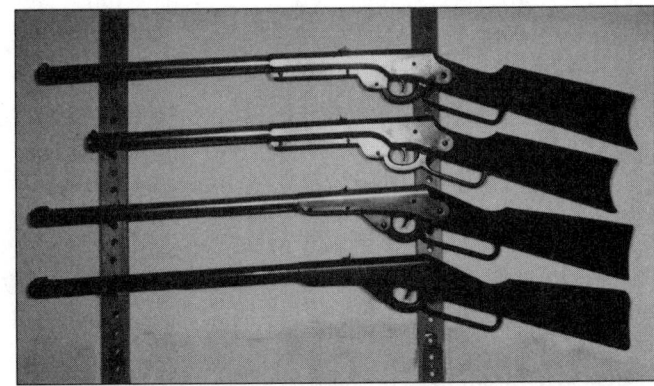

Top to Bottom: 1000 Shot Daisy, 1905, $250; 500 Shot Daisy, 1905, $500; two versions of the Model B by Daisy, 1909, $70-120

	C6	C8	C10
1000 Shot Daisy, 1903, marked "1000 Shot Daisy" on top and/or side of frame, LA, RPTR, WDS, NIC............ 150		175	250
Daisy, first model, 1889, marked "Daisy PatApd For" or "Daisy Pat Aug 13, 89," LA, SS, wire stock, NIC, cast-metal grip frame........................... 360		420	600
Daisy, second model, 1890, marked "Daisy Imp'd Pat May 6, 90," BA, SS, wire stock, NIC, cast-metal grip frame........ 300		350	500
Daisy, third model, 1891, marked "Daisy Pat May 6, 90," July 14, 91, BA, SS, stock may be wire or wood, NIC, cast-metal grip frame may have checkering, wire stock may have wood insert........................... 210		275	375
Daisy, 1901, BA, SS, WDS, NIC, marked "Daisy" in indented rectangle on side of grip frame, also marked "Pat. Aug 13, 1889, July 14, 91, Jan. 21, 92, March 26, 1901,"frame is all sheet metal, referred to by collectors as the "20th Century sheet metal," but not so marked........... 100		115	175
Daisy, 1901, repeater variation of above gun........................... 120		140	200
Sentinel, 1899, marked "Sentinel," BA, RPTR, WDS, NIC, repeater variation of the above gun................................... 100		115	175
Sentinel, 1899, marked "Sentinel," BA, SS, WDS, NIC, Daisy's first all sheet metal gun, somewhat streamlined in appearance compared to the earlier guns, semi pistol-grip stock and grip frame............................ 100		115	175

Daisys with Letter Designations

	C6	C8	C10
Model A, 1907, BA, RPTR, WDS, NIC, repeater variation of the above.............. 90		105	150
Model A, 1907, BA, SS, WDS, NIC 120		140	200
Model B, 1909, LA, RPTR, WDS, BLU (1000 shot) 35		50	75
Model B, 1909, LA, RPTR, WDS, BLU (500 shot) 40		50	70
Model B, 1909, LA, RPTR, WDS, NIC (1000 shot) 60		75	120
Model B, 1909, LA, RPTR, WDS, NIC (500 shot) 55		65	90
Model C, 1910, BA, SS, WDS, NIC 60		75	120
Model C, 1912, BA, RPTR, WDS, NIC, repeater variation of the above (350 shot) 60		75	120
Model H, 1913, LA, SS, WDS, BLU 55		65	90

	C6	C8	C10
Model H, 1913, LA, SS, WDS, NIC............. 75		90	125
Model H, 1914, LA, RPTR, WDS, BLU (350 or 500 shot) 55		65	90
Model H, 1914, LA, RPTR, WDS, NIC (350 or 500 shot) 75		90	125

Daisys with Number Designations

	C6	C8	C10
Model 21, 1968, double barrel, BA, RPTR, PLAS, PNTD 180		210	300
Model 1938, Red Ryder, 1972, LA, RPTR, WDS, PNTD, later variation, similar in appearance to the earlier variations, brand may be on left or right side of stock.................................... 25		45	80
Number 3B, 1914, LA, RPTR, WDS, Black Nickel finish, came in colorful lithographed box marked "Daisy Special" (1000 shot)................................ 90		105	150
Number 11, 1917, LA, RPTR, WDS, BLU, may also have model number (500 shot) 55		65	90
Number 11, 1917, LA, RPTR, WDS, NIC, may also have model number (500 shot) 75		90	125

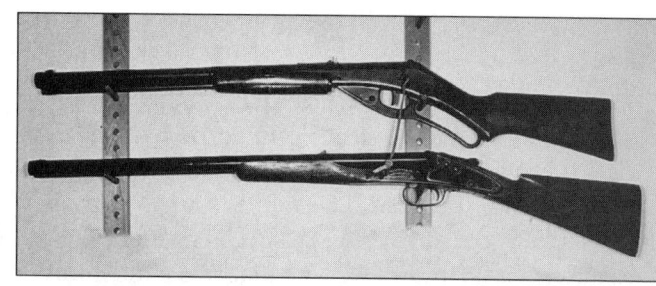

Top to Bottom: Number 111, Model 40 Red Ryder, Daisy, later version, $60; Model 21, double barrel, 1968, $300

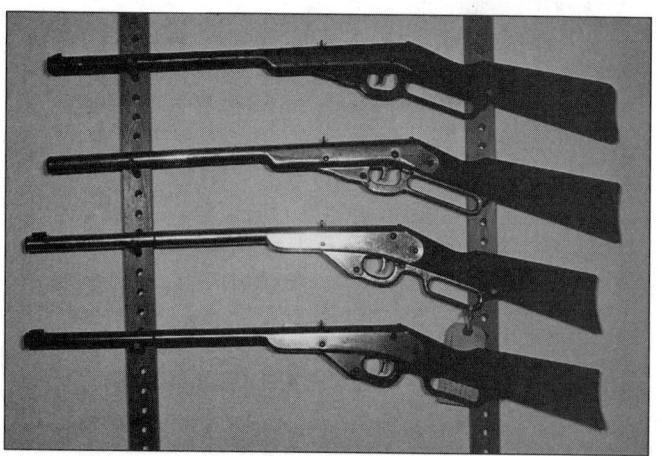

Top to Bottom: No. 101, Model 33, Daisy, 1933, $30; No. 102, Model 33, Daisy, 1933, $30; No. 12, Model 29, 1918, $125; No. 11, Model 29, Daisy, 1917, $90

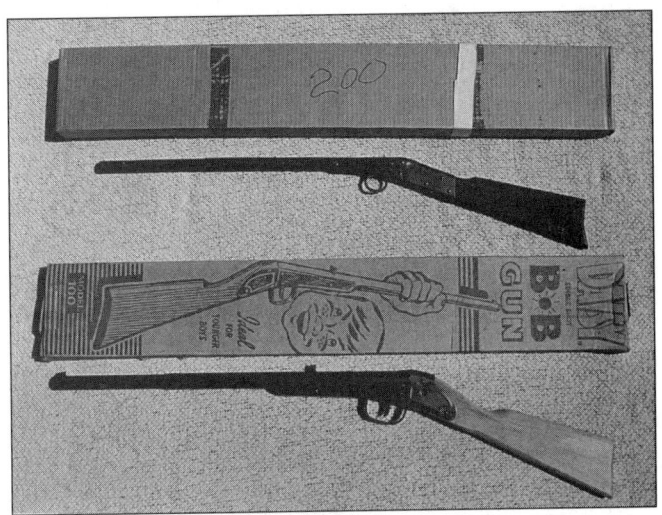

Top to Bottom: No. 20, Little Daisy, 1908, $90-125; No. 100, Model 38, $50

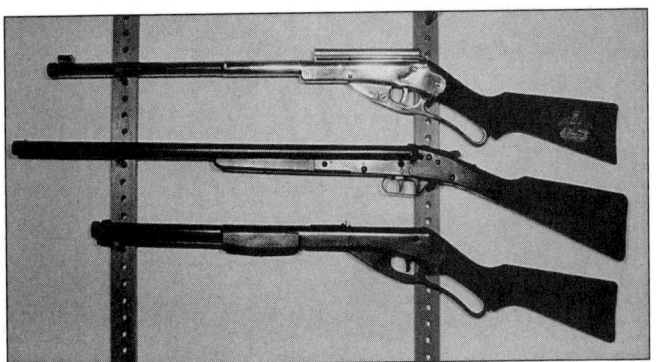

Top to Bottom: No. 50, Golden Eagle, Daisy, 1936, $125; No. 104, Daisy, 1938, $500; No. 108, Daisy, 1939, $75

	C6	C8	C10
Number 12, 1918, LA, SS, WDS, NIC, may also have model number	75	90	125
Number 12, 1918, LA, SS, WDS, BLU, may also have model number.................	55	65	90
Number 20, Little Daisy, 1908, BA, SS, WDS, NIC, w/no grip frame	75	90	125
Number 20, Little Daisy, 1912, BA, SS, WDS, NIC, two screws in grip frame.....	75	90	125
Number 20, Little Daisy, 1915, BA, SS, WDS, BLU, w/three rivets in grip frame and "ring" trigger.............	55	65	90
Number 20, Little Daisy, 1915, BA, SS, WDS, NIC, w/three rivets in grip frame and "ring" trigger	70	80	110
Number 25, BB Gun, 1986, Daisy's Centennial Commemorative Model, comes in colorful litho box, w/medallion in stock	40	50	75

	C6	C8	C10
Number 25, 1914, pump gun, PA, RPTR, WDS, BLU, w/straight stock.......	40	50	75
Number 25, 1925, pump gun, PA, RPTR, WDS, BLU, w/pistol grip stock	40	50	75
Number 25, 1936, pump gun, PA, RPTR, WDS, BLU, w/pistol grip stock and engraved frame	30	35	50
Number 30, 1925, LA, RPTR, WDS, BLU, may also have model number (500 shot)	34	38	40
Number 30, 1925, LA, RPTR, WDS, NIC, may also have model number (500 shot)	44	48	60
Number 40, 1916, LA, RPTR, WDS, BLU, Daisy's WWII military-styled gun, w/full-length wood stock, sling and bayonet	150	175	250
Number 50, Golden Eagle, 1936, LA, RPTR, WDS, entire gun is copper plated, stock painted black and w/special eagle decal, w/rear tube sight ..	75	90	125

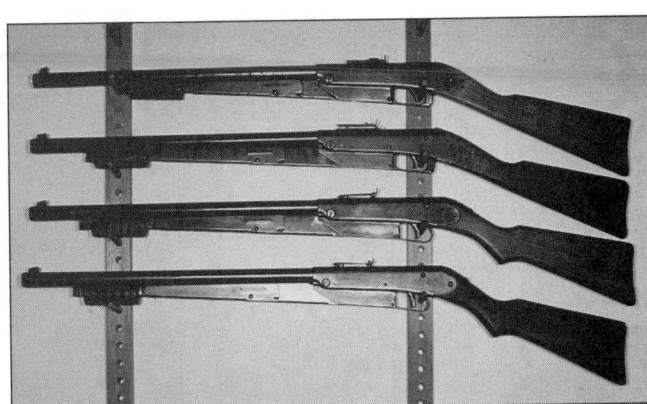

Four different versions of Daisy's No. 25, $50-75. Top to Bottom: Early version with short cocking lever and straight stock; long lever with straight stock; long lever with pistol grip stock; and long lever and pistol grip stock with hunting scene stamped on frame.

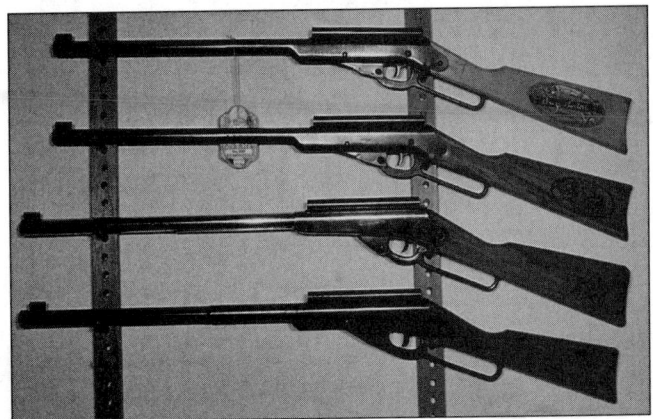

Top to Bottom: No. 195, Buzz Barton Special with Paper Buzz Barton label, Daisy, $100; No. 195, Buzz Barton brand on stock, Daisy, 1932, $125; No. 103, Model 33, "Buzz Barton," Daisy, 1934, $180; No. 195, Model 36, with oval brand, Daisy, 1936, $100

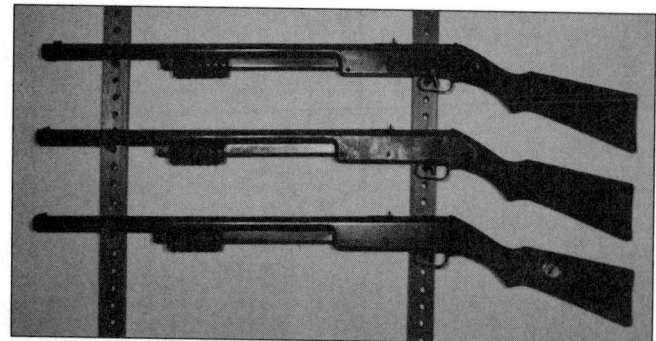

Top to Bottom: No. 5, Pump Gun, King, 1931, $150; No. 105, Junior Pump Gun, Daisy, 1932, $200; No. 107, Buck Jones Special, Daisy, 1934, $110

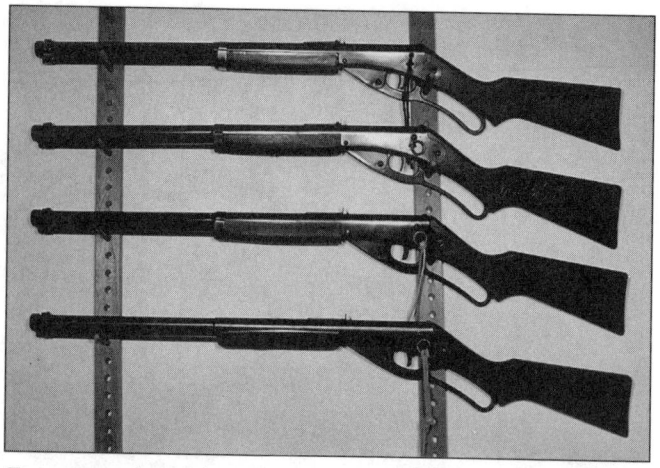

Four examples of the No. 111, Model 40 Red Ryder by Daisy, from top to bottom: two examples of the No. 111 with an iron lever, $90-125; aluminum lever, $75; plastic forestock, $60.

	C6	C8	C10
Number 94, Red Ryder, 1955, LA, RPTR, PLAS, PNTD (1000 shot) 28		32	40
Number 100, Model 38, 1938, BA, SS, WDS, BLU 30		35	50
Number 101, Model 33, 1933, LA, SS, WDS, BLU 18		20	30
Number 101, Model 36, 1936, LA, SS, WDS, BLU 18		20	30
Number 102, Model 33, 1933, LA, RPTR, WDS, BLU (500 shot) 18		20	30
Number 102, Model 36, 1936, LA, RPTR, WDS, BLU (500 shot) 18		20	30
Number 102, Model 36, 1936, LA, RPTR, WDS, NIC 28		32	40
Number 103, Model 33, 1933, LA, RPTR, WDS, NIC, w/rear tube sight 100		115	165
Number 103, Model 33, 1934, LA, RPTR, WDS, NIC, "Buzz Barton" variation of the above gun, w/star-shaped Buzz Barton brand on stock 110		120	180
Number 104, double barrel, 1938, BA, RPTR, WDS, BLU 300		350	500
Number 105, Junior Pump Gun, 1932, PA, RPTR, WDS, BLU 120		140	200
Number 107, Buck Jones Special, 1934, PA, RPTR, WDS, BLU, engraved frame, compass and sundial stock 70		80	110
Number 108, Model 39 Carbine, 1939, LA, RPTR, WDS, BLU 45		55	75
Number 111, Model 40 Red Ryder, 1940, LA, RPTR, WDS, BLU, w/cast-iron cocking lever and copper plated barrel bands 75		90	125
Number 111, Model 40 Red Ryder, 1941, LA, RPTR, WDS, BLU, w/cast-iron cocking lever 50		63	90

	C6	C8	C10
Number 111, Model 40 Red Ryder, 1947, LA, RPTR, WDS, BLU, w/aluminum cocking lever 40		50	75
Number 111, Model 40 Red Ryder, 1950, LA, RPTR, WDS, BLU, w/plastic forestock 40		50	75
Number 111, Model 40 Red Ryder, 1951, LA, RPTR, PLAS, BLU or PNTD, both stock and forestock are plastic 38		48	60
Number 140, Defender, 1941, LA, RPTR, WDS, BLU, w/long wooden forestock, dummy bolt and bolt handle and sling 120		140	200
Number 195, Buzz Barton Special, 1932, LA, RPTR, WDS, BLU, w/oval Buzz Barton brand on stock 70		90	125
Number 195, Model 36 Buzz Barton Special, 1936, LA, RPTR, WDS, BLU, w/oval Buzz Barton brand on stock 60		70	100

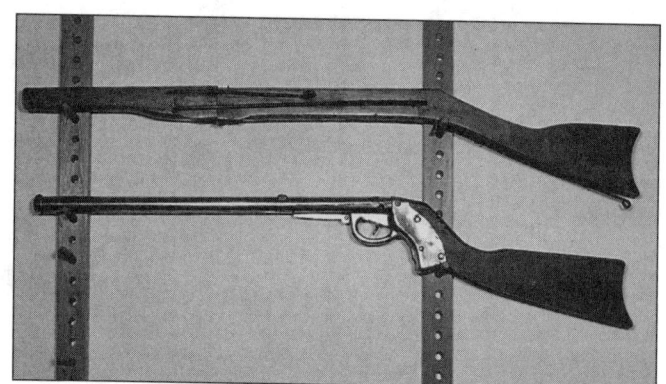

Top to Bottom: Chicago, Markham/King, 1888, $150; New King, 1895, $135

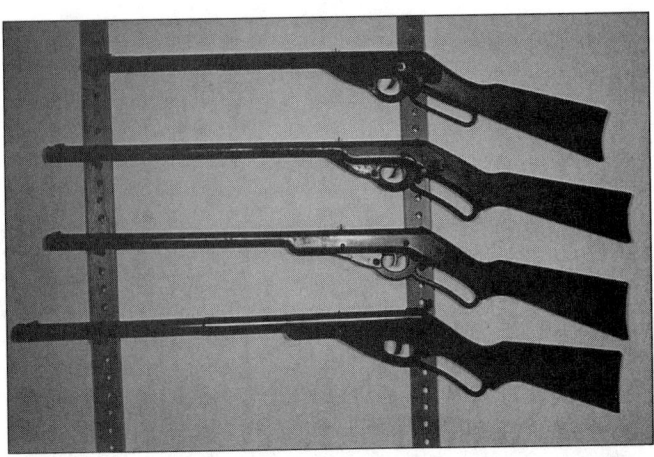

Top to Bottom: No. 21, 1916, Markham/King, $100; No. 55, 1921, Markham/King, $60; No. 5533, Markham/King, $60; No. 5536, Markham/King, $75

MARKHAM/KING BB GUNS

Markham/King All Wood Guns

	C6	C8	C10
Challenge, 1887, under-barrel cast-iron cocking lever, sheet metal trigger guard, single shot, may have no markings	225	265	375
Chicago, 1888, break action, single shot, outside cocking rods on both sides, oval Markham logo on stock	90	105	150

Markham/King Metal Guns with Names

	C6	C8	C10
Model C, 1905, repeater variation of the above gun	45	55	75
Model D, 1905, BA, SS, WDS, NIC, grip frame wraps around wrist of stock, streamlined shape without pistol grip stock	45	55	75
New King, 1895, BA, SS, WDS, NIC, stock stained red, pistol grip stock is stamped "New King Patent 483153" in oval logo	80	95	135
New King, 1896 (repeater), BA, RPTR, WDS, NIC, repeater variation of the above gun, w/small lever on muzzle cap used to allow a BB to drop into the shot tube	90	105	150

Number 2236, Markham/King, $30

Markham/King Guns with Number Designations

	C6	C8	C10
Junior No. 10, 1910, BA, SS, WDS, NIC	60	70	100
New Chicago No. 24, 1923, BA, SS, WDS, BLU	75	90	125
Number 1, 1910, same as "Model D" above, redesignated No. 1 in 1910	45	55	75
Number 2, 1910, same as "Model C" above, redesignated No. 2 in 1910	45	55	75
Number 4, 1908, LA, RPTR, WDS, NIC, frame w/octagon shape (500 shot)	100	115	175
Number 5, Pump Gun, 1931, PA, RPTR, WDS, BLU	75	100	150
Number 5, 1908, LA, RPTR, WDS, NIC, frame w/octagon shape (1000 shot)	100	115	175
Number 5B, 1910, LA, RPTR, WDS, BLU, a deluxe variation of the No. 5, came in a lithographed box	120	140	200
Number 17, 1917, BA, SS, WDS, BLU, w/outside cocking rods	65	80	115
Number 21, 1916, LA, SS, WDS, NIC	60	70	100
Number 22, 1916, LA, RPTR, WDS, BLU	60	70	100
Number 55, 1921, LA, RPTR, WDS, BLU, may have straight or curved lever (1000 shot)	38	42	60
Number 2136, 1936, LA, SS, WDS, BLU	18	21	30
Number 2236, 1936 LA, RPTR, WDS, BLU (500 shot)	18	21	30
Number 5533, 1933, LA, RPTR, WDS, BLU (1000 shot)	38	42	60
Number 5536, 1936 LA, RPTR, WDS, BLU (1000 shot)	45	55	75

BANKS

MECHANICAL BANKS

After trains, mechanical banks are perhaps the most avidly pursued of all the toys cataloged in this book. The most collectible remain those that were produced in cast iron from around 1870 to 1908—over three hundred different types were produced during that period. One factor that adds to their interest is that many were manufactured with an eye toward adults as well as children (the "Tammany" bank, for instance). As a result, prices are high—and they were high long before any of the other toys in this book were thought of as collector's items. Because their rarity, several of the banks listed have only auction prices, and these prices may seem astronomical. This was done to demonstrate how high mechanical banks can sell for, please keep in mind that not all mechanical banks will sell for such prices.

With such valuable items the problem of counterfeiting arises, and care is strongly urged in the purchase of any high-priced bank. Counterfeits tend to be rougher, to fit together less smoothly, and to lack the patina or "look" of age.

	C6	C8	C10
Acrobat Bank, 5" high	3000	6000	8800
Alligator in Trough, patented 1867	10,000	20,000	35,000
Always Did Despise A Mule, black jockey on mule, 1879, 10" long	600	1200	1800
Always Did Despise A Mule, black on bench being kicked by mule, 1897	550	1100	1700
American Bank sewing machine	3000	6000	10,000
Artillery Bank, Union Officer w/mortar, firing at fort, 1877	500	900	1400
Astronaut's Bank, gold moon w/rocket on stand, has rings showing orbit of space capsule, ring has astronauts' names—"Shepard, Grissom, Glenn, Carpenter, Schirra, Cooper," little plane up side of rocket shoots money into moon, pot metal, 11" high	25	38	50
Atlas Bank	1000	1750	3000
Bad Accident, mule and black on two-wheeled cart, 1887	1100	1900	3300
The Bank Teller, J&E Stevens Co., 1876, auctioned in 1998			96,000
Bear Hugging Tree	450	675	900
Bill E. Grin	500	1300	2100
Bird on Roof	1200	2400	3600

Book of Knowledge Reproduction of Original Banks, c. 1950—Artillery Bank; Bulldog Bank; Creedmore; Eagle and Eagles; Jonah & Whale; Magician; Man and Pig;

Top: Magician, 1882, $5,250. Bottom, left to right: Cat & Mouse Bank, Stevens, $3,500; Mason and Hod Carrier, 1887, $7,000

	C6	C8	C10
Man milking Cow; Teddy and the Bear; Trick Dog; Trick Pony, Tree Trunk and Buffalo; each	195	295	390

Note: The original markings are sometimes filed away from the bottom in an attempt to sell one of these items as an original.

	C6	C8	C10
Boy on Trapeze, J. Barton & Smith	1450	2900	4300
Boy Robbing Nest	850	2500	4000
Boy Scout	3100	4700	8250
Boy Stealing Watermelons	750	1500	2500
Bread Winner	7500	15,000	22,000
Bull & Bear, brass model	1000	1750	2500
Bulldog Savings Bank, Ives, Blakeslee & Wms	1400	2800	4200
Bulldog, c. 1887, Judd	600	1200	1800
Bulldog, Stevens	350	525	700
"Butting" Buffalo	2600	5200	7800
Butting Goat In Tree Stump, c. 1887, Judd	262	393	525
Calamity, three football players, pat. J&E Stevens Co., August 29, 1905	5000	10,000	15,750
Called Out, 3 known, auctioned in 1993			14,300

Left to Right: Jonah and the Whale, Jonah in Boat, $4,000; Chief Big Moon, 1899, $3,000

	C6	C8	C10
Cat and Mouse Bank, Stevens	750	2000	3500
Charlie McCarthy, sitting w/legs crossed on top of trunk, drop coin in back and mouth moves, pot metal, copyright 1938, 5-3/4" high	75	125	200
Chein Monkey, seated, tips hat when coin dropped in, tin litho, 5" high	70	105	140
Chief Big Moon, Indian in teepee, 1899	1000	2000	3000
Chimpanzee	1500	2200	3500
Chinese Reclining, 1882	2900	4300	8800
Circus Bank, auctioned in 1994			14,950
Circus Ticket Taker	500	1000	1500
Clown & Harlequin, auctioned in 1988			90,000
Clown on Bar, auctioned in 1993			70,000
Clown on Globe, 1873	1150	2400	3500
Columbus	300	450	600
Confectionary	3500	7000	12,000
Cow Kicking, cow kicks over boy	7500	15,000	25,000

The Circus Bank was auctioned in 1994 for $14,950

Darktown Battery, 1888, $5,200

	C6	C8	C10
Creedmore Bank, man firing into tree, Stevens, 1877, 10" long	390	585	785
Crowing Rooster	500	750	1000
Dapper Dan	200	400	600
Darktown Battery, black pitcher and catcher, 1888	1750	3500	5200
Darky Football, auctioned in			245,000
Darky and Cabin, 1885	500	750	1000
Darky and Watermelon (Foot Ball Bank), 1888, Stevens Co., auctioned in 1998			354,500
Dentist Bank, white dentist working on black patient, 1880	4500	9500	14,000
Dinah, bust of black woman, 6-1/2"	450	675	900
Ding Dong Bell, tin, 1888, auctioned in 1998			74,000
Dog Charges Boy, bronze finish	400	700	1000
Dog on Turntable, Judd Mfg. Co.	480	720	960
Dog Standing	150	350	500
Eagle and Eaglets, 1883	500	1000	1500
Elephant, late-cast iron, Hubley	100	175	250
Elephant, Three Star, cast iron, trunk flips up to catch coin, 5" high	50	75	100
Elephant and Clowns	900	1800	2700
Elephant Howdah, 1920	250	500	750
Elephant Howdah, c. 1934, Hubley	375	563	750
Ferris Wheel, Hubley/Bauer	1000	2000	3000
Fortune Teller, safe, complete w/roll of fortunes, pat. February 19, 1901	400	600	800
The Forty-Niner, donkey moves ear and tail	100	225	400
Fowler, sportsman shoots bird, Stevens	6500	14,000	20,000
Freedman, auctioned in 1998			321,500
Frog and Snake in Pond, tin litho, in the form of a snake striking at a frog which opens its mouth to receive the coin	3000	4500	6500

Girl Skipping Rope, $31,000

	C6	C8	C10
Frog, Goat and Old Man	1500	3500	6000
Frog on Arched Track, auctioned in 1988			35,000
Frog on Lattice, Stevens, 1870s	450	675	900
Frog on Rock, Kilgore Mfg. Co.	500	750	1000
Frog on Stump, 1872	435	650	870
Frogs, two, J&E Stevens	1200	2400	4000
Gem, Dog and Building	250	375	500
Giant, holding a club	10,000	15,000	20,000
Girl Skipping Rope, w/key	10,000	20,000	31,000
Globe Savings Fund Bank	250	375	500
Guessing Bank	1500	2500	3500
Hall's Excelsior Bank, monkey cashier	500	800	1100
Hall's Lilliput, 1875	500	750	1000
Hen and Chick, c. 1901, Stevens	1300	2600	3850
Hindu, 1882, Kyser & Rex	1000	1500	2000
Hold the Fort, five-hole, c. 1877	1200	2500	3500
Home building w/two pillars, teller at window, tin	230	345	460
Horse Race	6000	9000	15,000
Humpty Dumpty	800	1600	2400
Independence Hall	300	450	600
Indian Shooting Bear, 1888	1150	1725	2300
Initiating Bank First Degree	3500	6500	10,000
Jolly Nigger, bust	270	405	540
Jolly Nigger, high hat, 8" high	225	338	450
Jolly Nigger, moves ears	75	112	150
Jonah and the Whale, cast iron, Jonah in boat	1350	2700	4000

	C6	C8	C10
Jonah and Whale, Jonah emerges	20,000	30,000	45,000
Jumbo on Platform	850	1700	2500
"Keeping 'Em Flying" dime register, tin	25	37	50
Kick Inn, litho paper and wood, a mule standing in front of a small building, Presto	250	375	500
King Aqua, auctioned in 1988			95,000
Leap Frog Bank, two boys and tree, 1891	1300	2600	3900
Liberty Bell	200	300	500
Lighthouse Bank, 1891	750	1600	2300
Lion and Monkeys	650	1300	1950
Lion Hunter	2000	4000	6000
Little Jocko	500	1000	1500
Little Joe	122	185	245
Locomotive	300	600	900
Magic	540	1100	1625
Magician Bank, 1882	1750	3500	5250
Mama Katzenjammer and the Kids, 5-3/4"	3200	5000	6500
Mammy Feeding Child	3200	5000	6500
Mason and Hod Carrier, 1887	2300	4700	7000
Merry-Go-Round, Kyser & Rex	5300	11,000	16,000
Meyers No. 84, Jumbo Elephant	100	250	350
The Mikado Bank, 1880s, Kyser & Rex, auctioned in 1998			123,500

The Mikado Bank was auctioned in 1998 for $123,500

	C6	C8	C10
Money Box Bank, hand-carved on wood base, 10-1/4"	800	1200	1600
Monkey and Coconut	850	1700	2500
Mosque	550	1200	1750
Mule Bucking, black man riding a mule	500	750	1000
Mule Entering Barn	500	800	1200
National Bank	2500	5000	8000
Naughty Girl Bank, modern	25	50	75
New Creedmore, Meyer, No. 54	600	1200	2000
New Bank, cast iron, brass policeman in building, c. 1875, 4-1/2" long	170	255	340
North Pole, Eskimos and dog sled, J&E Stevens Co.	10,000	15,000	25,000
Novelty Bank, house-like bank, 1873	450	900	1500
Old Woman in the Shoe, W.S. Reed Co., auctioned in 1998			426,000
Organ Bank, monkey and revolving cat and dog, 7-1/4" high	500	750	1050
Organ Bank, monkey only	500	775	1070
Organ Boy and Girl, monkey flanked by boy and girl holding tambourine, pat. June 13, 1882	450	675	900
Organ Grinder And Bear	1400	2800	4200
Organ Grinder And Monkey, 1929	330	485	600
Owl, slot in book, cast iron	290	400	585
Owl, slot in head	150	300	500
Owl, turns head, cast iron	425	635	850
Paddy and His Pig	900	1800	3000
Panorama, building	3000	6000	10,000
Patronize the Blind Man and His Dog, J&E Stevens Co., pat. Feb. 19, 1878	2000	4500	7000
Pegleg Beggar	565	1200	1700
Pelican, cast iron, "Boy thumbs nose"	775	1550	2310
Perfection Registering	4500	7000	10,000
Piano, c. 1900, E.M. Roche	250	500	750
Picture Gallery, auctioned in 1998	20,700		
Pig, Bismarck	1500	3000	4500
Pig in High Chair	400	600	800
Preacher in Pulpit	30,000	40,000	50,000
Presto, shape of building	165	250	330
Presto-Mouse on Roof, litho paper on wood	7500	12,000	17,500
Professor Pug Frog's Great Bicycle Feat, auctioned in 1998			96,000
Pump, Bucket	300	700	1000
Punch & Judy, Shepherd Hardware, Buffalo, NY, c. 1890	1050	2100	3500
Rabbit, tall	600	1200	2000
Rabbit, small, circular base	275	415	550
Rabbit in Cabbage Patch	100	150	200
Red Riding Hood	15,000	20,000	35,000
Roller Skating	20,000	30,000	45,000
Rooster	445	670	890
Santa Claus at Chimney	675	1350	2260

	C6	C8	C10
See Him Frisk, auctioned in 1988			55,000
Shoot the Chute	12,500	17,500	25,000
Speaking Dog Bank, J&E Stevens, pat. 1885	630	945	2100
Springing Cat, lead alloy, sold in 1991			23,100
Squirrel and Tree Stump	1200	2400	3600
Standing Bear	100	165	220
Strato Bank, pot metal, rocket and planet, 1950s, 8" long	10	15	25
Stump Speaker, cast iron	1400	2800	4200
Tabby	150	350	600
Tammany Bank, 1875, 5-3/4" high	325	490	650
Tank and Cannon, 1916	325	490	650
Teddy and The Bear, man firing at bear in tree, 1907	900	1800	3000
Telephone	150	300	450
Three-Star Elephant, brass	150	300	450
Trick Dog, clown w/hoop, dog and barrel w/six-part base, 1888 version,	750	1500	2500
Trick Dog, clown w/hoop, dark dog and dark barrel, 1929	365	550	730
Trick Pony	535	1070	1600
Turtle Bank, auctioned in 1988			30,000
U.S. Building, c. 1878, boy and dog in windows, Stevens?	3100	4650	6200
U.S. and Spain	3000	4000	5000
Uncle Remus	2500	3500	5500
Uncle Sam, bust	300	450	600
Uncle Sam, w/umbrella in left hand, 1886, Shepard Hardware, auctioned in 1998			9200
Uncle Tom, w/lapels and one star	325	485	650
Uncle Tom, w/lapels, one star, brass base	600	900	1200
United States Bank, Stevens	650	975	1300

William Tell, 1896, $1,000

	C6	C8	C10
Watchdog Safe	270	405	540
Weeden's Plantation, tin	600	1250	1850
William Tell, 1896	500	750	1000
Wireless Bank, 1913	125	190	250
Woodpecker	1500	2800	4000
World's Fair	600	1200	1800
Zig Zag, cast iron, tin and papier-mâché, auctioned in 1998			189,500
Zoo	450	900	1400

STILL BANKS

The same companies that made mechanical banks often made still banks as less expensive alternatives. Several banks can be found in both still and mechanical versions. Companies such as Arcade, Ives, Kenton and Stevens are familiar to still and mechanical bank collectors alike.

Building-shaped banks are perhaps the single largest type of still banks, with others fashioned as animals, people and busts, and appliances like safes, clocks, mail boxes and globes.

One notable class of still banks is the registering bank. Often in the shape of a safe or cash register, these banks typically accept certain coins, such as dimes or nickels. They keep a running tally of deposits and pop open once the bank is filled, typically at $5 or $10. While their delayed reaction mechanism has earned them places in some mechanical collections, they are generally classified as still banks.

As in many other areas of collecting, restoration of banks is strongly discouraged in the marketplace. Unless undertaken by an experienced professional, the restoration of a bank can result in irreparable damage to its collector value.

	C8	C10
$100,000 Money Bag, silver gray finish, Unknown, 3-5/8" tall	300	650
1 Pounder Shell Bank, artillery shell, "1 Pounder Bank," Grey Iron Casting, 1918, 8"	25	95
1876 Bank, Large, building bank w/bronze/copper finish, H.L. Judd, 1895, 3-3/8" tall	75	250
1926 Sesquicentennial Bell, Grey Iron Casting, 1926, 3-3/4" x 3-7/8" diam.	75	200
A.A.O.S.M.S. Shriner's Fezm, red fez w/tassle and gold lettering, Allen Mfg., 1920s, 2-3/8"	250	650
Administration Building, unpainted, Magic Introduction, 1893, 5",	250	650
Air Mail Bank on Base, red, Dent, 1920, 6-3/8" tall	375	1000
Alamo, unpainted bronze finish, Alamo Iron Works, 1930s, 1-7/8" tall, 3-3/8" wide	200	450
Alphabet Bank, octagonal, Unknown, 3-1/2"	1200	3000
Amherst Buffalo, Unknown, 1930s, 5-1/4" tall, 8" long	150	350
Amish Boy, painted, John Wright, 1970, 5" tall	10	65
Amish Boy in White Shirt, blue coveralls, black hat, John Wright, 1971, 5" tall	10	65

	C8	C10
Amish Girl, painted, John Wright, 1970, 5" tall	10	65
Andy Gump, Andy sits reading a paper, painted, Arcade, 1928, 4-3/8" tall	500	950
Apollo 8, red, white and blue, John Wright, 1968, 4-1/4"	20	75
Apollo, Plain, unpainted, John Wright, 1968, 4-1/4"	20	65
Apple, painted apple on twig w/leaves, Kyser & Rex, 1882, 5-1/4" tall	600	1450
Arabian Safe, Kyser & Rex, 1882, 4-9/16" x 4-1/4"	100	300
Armoured Car, 6-3/4" long, red car on gold wheels, 3-3/4" tall, A.C. Williams, 1900s	650	2500
Art Deco Elephant, red, Unknown, 4-3/8" tall	100	225
Aunt Jemima, also called Mammy with Spoon, A.C. Williams, 1900s, 5-7/8"	125	325
Auto, black, red wheels, four passengers, A.C. Williams, 1910?, 5-3/4" long	500	1200
Baby in Cradle, rocking cradle, Unknown, 1890s, 3-1/4" tall	500	1400
Bank of Columbia, unpainted, "Bank of Columbia," Arcade, 1800s, 4-7/8"	150	375
Bank of England Safe, identical to Egyptian Safe except front is embossed Bank of England, Kyser & Rex, 1882	350	650
Barrel, H.L. Judd, 1873, 2-3/4" tall	100	225
Baseball on Three Bats, Hubley, 1914, 5-1/4"	350	1400
Baseball Player, gold, A.C. Williams, 1909, 5-3/4"	100	325
Baseball Player, several colors, A.C. Williams, 1910s, 5-3/4" tall	200	475
Basket Puzzle Bank, unpainted, Nicol, 2-3/4" tall, 3-1/2" wide,	300	650
Basket Registering Bank, Woven, Chas. A. Braun, 1902, 2-7/8" x 3-3/4"	50	125
Basset Hound, bronze finish, Unknown, 3-1/8"	650	1500
Battleship Maine, "Maine," Grey Iron Casting, 1800s, 5-1/4" tall, 6-5/8" long	650	3000
Battleship Maine, white, J & E. Stevens, 1901, 6" tall, 10-1/4" long	500	3500
Battleship Oregon, silver finish, J & E. Stevens, 1890s, 4-7/8" long,	200	450
Be Wise Owl, A.C. Williams, 1900s, 4-7/8" x 2-1/2"	150	375
Bean Pot, red cooking pot, nickel registering, Unknown, 3"	150	450
Bear Seated on Log, Unknown, 7"	400	950
Bear Stealing Pig, painted, Ober, 1913, 5-1/2" tall	400	1000
Bear with Honey Pot, painted, Hubley, 6-1/2" tall	75	175
Bear, Begging, bronze finish, A.C. Williams, 1900s, 5-3/8"	75	150
Beehive Bank, Kyser & Rex, 1882, 2-3/8"	250	500

	C8	C10
Beehive Registering Savings Bank, Unknown, 1891, 5-3/8" x 6-1/2"	200	425
Beehive with Brass Top, unpainted, W.M. Gobeille, 5-1/2" tall on base	350	750
Bethel College Administration Building, Service Foundry, 1935, 2-7/8" x 5-1/4"	175	350
Bicentennial Bell, Unknown, 1976, 4" x 4"	25	45
Billiken, on square base, bronze finish, red cap, A.C. Williams, 1909, 4-1/4" tall	55	125
Billiken on Throne, A.C. Williams, 1909, 6-1/2" tall	65	175
Billy Bounce, silver painted body, Hubley, 1900s, 4-11/16" tall	375	900
Billy Possum ("Possum & Taters"), on base "Billy Possum," J.M. Harper, 1909, 3" x 4-3/4"	1200	4500
Bird Bank Building, unpainted cupola building w/bird on top, "Bank New York," Unknown, 5-7/8"	650	2800
Bird Cage Bank, similar to Crystal Bank No. 926, but glass is replaced by open mesh, Arcade, 1900s, 3-7/8" tall	50	125
Bismark Bank, (Pig), "Bismark Bank," Unknown, 1883, 3-3/8"	100	300
Bismark Pig with Rider, bronze finish, Unknown, 1880s, 7-1/4" tall, 6-1/2" long	1000	3500

	C8	C10
Boss Tweed, Unknown, 1870s, 3-7/8" tall	1500	3500
Boston State House, painted, Smith & Egge, 1800s, 6-3/4" tall	3000	6000
Boxer Bulldog, seated, bronze finish, Hubley, 1900s, 4-1/2"	125	225
Boy Scout, brown finish, A.C. Williams, 1910s, 5-7/8" tall	50	125
Boy with Large Football, brown, Hubley, 1914, 5-1/8" tall	2000	3200
Buckeye (SBCCA), painted "Ohio The Buckeye State," "SBCC 1973," Filler, Lou, 1973, 3-1/2"	25	150
Buffalo Bank, gold, A.C. Williams, 1900s, 3-1/8" x 4-3/8"	50	175
Buffalo Nickel, Knerr, George, 1970s, 3-7/8"	35	100
Building with Belfry, in browns, Kenton, 8" tall	550	3500
Bull on Base, unpainted, Unknown, 4" tall	200	450
Bull with Long Horns, painted, Unknown, 3-11/16" tall	50	125
Bulldog, Large, painted, John Wright, 1960s, 6"	25	65
Bulldog, Seated, Hubley, 1928, 3-7/8"	200	400
Bulldog, Standing, painted, Arcade, 1900s, 2-1/4"	250	450
Bungalow Bank, white cottage w/green roof, Grey Iron Casting, 1900s, 3-3/4" x 3"	225	425
Bust of Man, Unknown, 5"	100	350
Buster Brown & Tige, A.C. Williams, 1900s, 5-1/2"	100	275
Cadet, blue uniform w/gold trim, Hubley, 1905, 5-3/4" tall	300	750
Camel, Kneeling, Kyser & Rex, 1889, 2-1/2" tall, 4-3/4" long	350	750
Camel, Large, A.C. Williams, 1900s, 7-1/4" x 6-1/4"	200	425
Camel, Small, Hubley, 1920s, 4-3/4" x 3-7/8"	100	225
Camera, Wrightsville Hardware, 1888	1000	5000
Camera Bank, bronze finish bellows camera on tripod, Wrightsville Hdw., 1800s, 4-5/16" tall	2500	5000
Campbell Kids, A.C. Williams, 1900s, 3-5/16" x 4-1/8"	150	350
Cannon, black cannon on red wheels, Hubley, 1914, 3" tall, 6-7/8" long	2500	5000
Capitalist, The (Everett True), painted, Ober, 1913, 5" tall	1200	1800
Capitol Bank, Riverside Foundry, 1981, 5-1/8"	25	50
Captain Kidd, Kidd stands by tree trunk w/shovel, base reads "Captain Kidd," Unknown, 1900s, 5-5/8" tall,	275	450
Carpenter Safe, J.M. Harper, 1907, 4-3/8"	2500	5000
Cash Register Savings Bank, unpainted, "Cash Register Savings Bank," Hubley, 1906, 4-3/4"	500	750

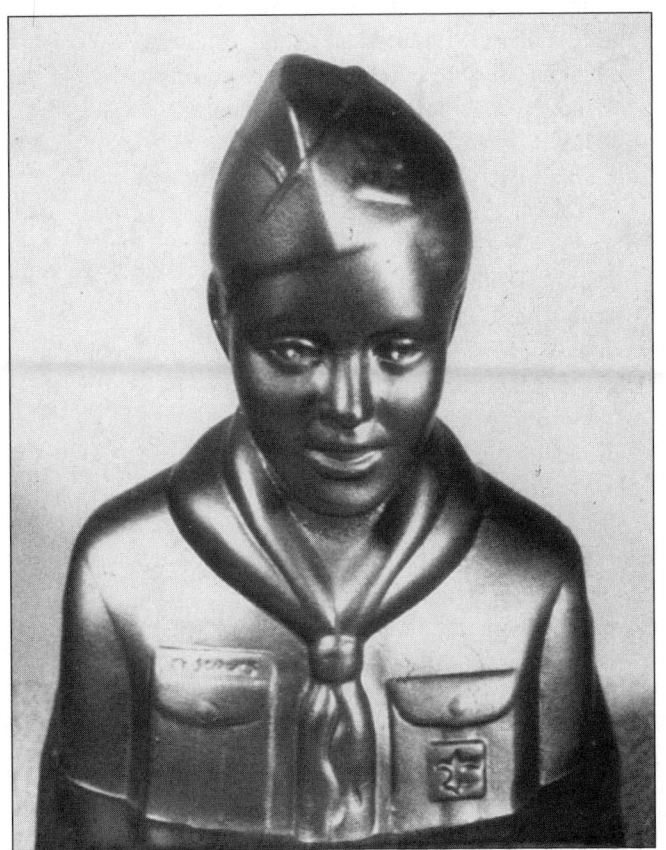

Boy Scout, A.C. Williams, $125

Century of Progress Building, Arcade, $1,800

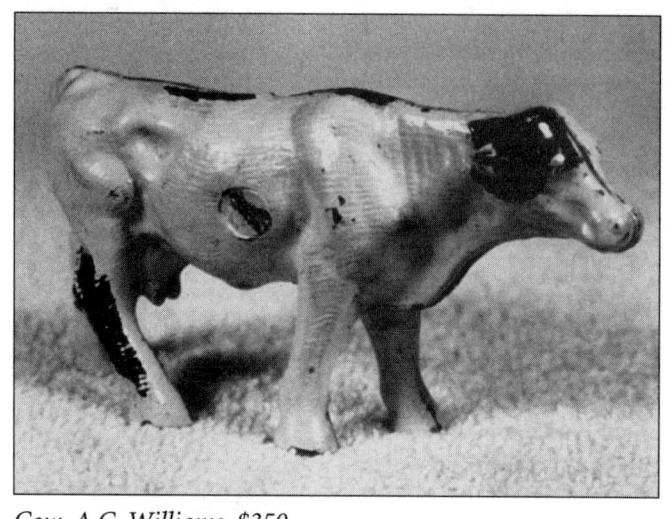

Cow, A.C. Williams, $350

	C8	C10
Cash Register Savings Bank, round face on three claw foot feet, "Cash Register Savings Bank," Unknown, 1880s, 5-5/8" tall	350	850
Cash Register with Mesh, red finish w/gold-bronze mesh, Arcade, 1900s, 3-3/4" tall	50	125
Castle Bank, Small, Kyser & Rex, 1882, 3" x 2-13/16"	200	450
Cat on Tub, bronze finish, A.C. Williams, 1920s, 4-1/8" tall	100	200
Cat with Ball, A.C. Williams, 1900s, 2-1/2" tall	200	375
Cat with Bow, Hubley, 1930s, 4-1/8"	275	575
Cat with Bow, Seated, brown finish, Grey Iron Casting, 1922, 4-3/8" tall	225	475
Cat with Bow, Seated, painted, white body, red bow, John Wright, 4-3/8" x 2 7/8"	25	50
Cat with Long Tail, Grey Iron Casting, 1910s, 4-3/8" tall, 6-3/4" long	375	875
Cat with Soft Hair, Seated, Arcade, 1900s, 4-1/4" x 2 7/8"	85	225
Century of Progress Building, white, "A Century Of Progress" building from Chicago World's Fair, Arcade, 1933, 4-1/2" x 7"	800	1800
Champion Heater, green and black, "Champion," Unknown, 4-1/8"	125	400
Chanticleer (Rooster), bronze finish, painted face and comb, Unknown, 1911, 4-5/8"	850	6000
Chicken Feed Bag, "Chicken Feed," Geaorge Knerr, 1973, 4-5/8"	35	300
Chipmunk with Nut, black, Unknown, 4-1/16"	300	950
Church Towers, Unknown, 6-3/4"	850	1900
Church Window Safe, Shimer Toy, 1890s, 3 1/16"	50	125
City Bank with Chimney, painted, Unknown, 1870s, 6-3/4" tall	650	2200
City Bank with Crown, painted w/red "crown" on roof, Unknown, 1870s, 5-1/2" tall	600	1800

	C8	C10
City Bank with Teller, bronze finish, H.L. Judd, 5-1/2"	400	700
Clown, gold and red w/tall curved hat, A.C. Williams, 1908, 6-1/4"	125	250
Clown Bust, painted, Knerr, George, 1973, 4-7/8"	100	350
Coca-Cola Bank, red and green w/logo, Unknown, 3-3/8" tall	600	1500
Coin Registering Bank, w/red doors and dome, Kyser & Rex, 1890, 6-3/4"	2500	6500
Colonial House with Porch, Large, white, A.C. Williams, 1900s, 4" tall	100	275
Colonial House with Porch, Small, brown finish w/red, green or gold roof, A.C. Williams, 1910s, 3 " tall	75	200
Columbia, silver finish building bank, Kenton, 4-1/2" tall	600	900
Columbia Bank, unpainted silver finish, Kenton, 1890s, 5-3/4" tall	300	700
Columbia Bank, 8-3/4" tall, bronze finish, Kenton, 1890s	600	1000
Columbia Magic Savings Bank, unpainted, "Columbia Magic Savings Bank," Magic Introduction, 1892, 5"	300	700
Columbia Tower, unpainted three-story tower, Grey Iron Casting, 1897, 6-7/8"	450	950
Covered Bridge, white w/red roof, John Wright, 1960s, 2-1/2" tall, 6-1/8" long	35	75
Covered Wagon, unpainted, Wilton Products, 6-5/8" long	10	25
Cow, brown or red finish, A.C. Williams, 1920, 3-3/8" x 5-1/4"	75	350
Crosley Radio, Large, green w/gold highlights, Kenton, 1930s, 5-1/8" tall	650	1500
Crosley Radio, Small, green, Kenton, 1930s, 4-5/16" tall	150	600

Dutch Girl, Grey Iron Casting, $850

	C8	C10
Cross, dark finish, "God Is Love" on base, Unknown, 9-1/4" tall	750	2200
Crown Bank on Legs, Small, painted, Unknown, 4-5/8"	600	850
Cupola Bank, painted building w/center roof cupola, Vermong Novelty Works, 1869, 5-1/2" tall	300	650
Cupola Bank, red and gray, J & E. Stevens, 1872, 4-1/4" x 3-3/8"	100	365
Cupola Bank, black, J & E. Stevens, 1870s, 3-1/4" tall	75	225
Cutie Dog, painted, Hubley, 1914, 3-7/8"	65	175
Daisy, red safe bank, Shimer Toy, 1899, 2-1/8" tall	50	175
Darkey Sharecropper, toes visible on one foot, A.C. Williams, 1900s, 5-1/2" tall	75	375
Decker's Iowana, (Pig), unpainted, Unknown, 2-5/16"	75	200
Derby, "Pass Around the Hat," Unknown, 2-5/16"	100	325
Dime Registering Coin Barrel, unpainted, Kyser & Rex, 1889, 4" x 2-1/2"	125	225

	C8	C10
Dime Savings, "Dime Savings," Shimer Toy, 1899, 2-1/2" safe	200	425
Dog on Tub, bronze finish, A.C. Williams, 1920s, 4-1/16" x 2" diam.	125	200
Dog Smoking Cigar, painted, white body, red bow tie, Hubley, 4-1/4"	450	850
Dolphin Boat Bank, sailor boy in boat holds anchor, Grey Iron Casting, 1900s, 4-1/2" tall	500	850
Domed Bank, A.C. Williams, 1899, 3" tall	20	95
Domed Mosque Bank, gold/bronze finish, Grey Iron Casting, 1900s, 4-1/4" tall	85	175
Domed Mosque Bank, bronze finish, Grey Iron Casting, 1900s, 3-1/8" tall	65	145
Donkey, black w/red yoke, Unknown, 3-1/4" tall	100	200
Donkey "I Made St. Louis Famous," gray finish, Arcade, 1903, 4-11/16" tall	800	1500
Donkey on Base, Unknown, 6-9/16" tall	250	650
Donkey with Blanket, painted, gray w/red blanket, Kenton, 1930s, 3-7/8" tall	450	950
Donkey, Large, painted, A.C. Williams, 1920s, 6-13/16" tall	150	275
Donkey, Small, blue, gold or gray finish, Arcade, 1910s, 4-1/2" tall	85	200
Dormer Bank, painted building bank w/red roof, Unknown, 4-3/4" tall	3500	6000
Double Door, building w/two doors, painted white w/gold highlights, A.C. Williams, 1900s, 5-7/16"	200	375
Doughboy, painted World War I soldier, Grey Iron Casting, 1919, 7" tall	350	850
Dry Sink, dark finish, John Wright, 1970, 3" x 2-3/4"	25	45
Duck, white painted body, Hubley, 1930s, 4-3/4"	150	275
Duck Bank, unpainted, A.C. Williams, 1900s, 4-7/8"	150	275
Duck on Tub "Save for a Rainy Day," Hubley, 1930s, 5-3/8"	95	450
Duck, Round, painted, yellow body, red beak and top of head, Kenton, 1930s, 4" tall	225	450
Dutch Boy, Grey Iron Casting, 6-3/4" tall	600	850
Dutch Boy, doorstop conversion, Unknown, 8-1/4" tall	150	275
Dutch Boy on Barrel, Hubley, 1930s, 5-5/8"	75	275
Dutch Girl, bronze finish, Grey Iron Casting, 6-1/2" tall	600	850
Dutch Girl Holding Flowers, painted, iron trap in base, Hubley, 1930s, 5-1/2" tall	100	275
Eagle Bank Building, painted building w/gold eagle on roof, Unknown, 9-3/4" tall	450	950
Eagle with Ball, Building, building w/eagle and ball on roof, Unknown, 10-3/4" tall	850	4500
Edison Bust, Blevins, Charlotte, 1972, 5-5/16"	35	65

	C8	C10
Eggman (Wm. Howard Taft), Arcade, 1910, 4-1/8" tall	850	2500
Egyptian Tomb, safe on base, decorated w/Sphinx and obelisk on front, sides show, pyramid, walled ruins and urn w/flowers, gold, Kyser & Rex, 1882, 6-1/4" square	450	750
Electric Railroad, Shimer Toy, 1893, 8-1/4" long	2500	6000
Elephant on Bench on Tub, A.C. Williams, 1920s, 3-7/8"	125	225
Elephant on Tub, in bronze finish, A.C. Williams, 1920s, 5-3/8"	100	185
Elephant on Tub, Decorated, painted version of No. 483, A.C. Williams, 1920s, 5-3/8"	125	200
Elephant on Wheels, unpainted, A.C. Williams, 1920s, 4" tall	150	300
Elephant Trumpeting, black finish, John Wright, 1971, 7-1/4" tall	15	35
Elephant with Bent Knee, tan finish, Kenton, 1904, 3-1/2"	200	375
Elephant with Chariot, Large, also made w/o chariot, Hubley, 1900s, 4-3/4" tall	2000	3000
Elephant with Chariot, Small, gray elephant, red chariot, yellow wheels, Hubley, 1906, 7" long	1400	2200
Elephant with Howdah, Large, gold, A.C. Williams, 1900s, 6-3/4"	85	150
Elephant with Howdah, Large, A.C. Williams, 1900s, 4-7/8" x 6-3/8"	65	125
Elephant with Howdah, Short Trunk, painted gray w/red belt, Hubley, 1910, 3-3/4" tall	125	275
Elephant with Howdah, Small, A.C. Williams, 1900s, 3-1/2" x 5"	65	125
Elephant with Raised Slot, gray body, gold blanket, Unknown, 4-1/2" tall	150	350

	C8	C10
Elephant with Swivel Trunk, black finish w/gold swivel trunk, Unknown, 2-1/2"	125	250
Elephant with Tin Chariot, red chariot, Wing, 1900s, 8" long	1000	1600
Elephant with Tucked Trunk, red or green, Arcade, 1900s, 2-3/4" x 4-5/8"	65	125
Elephant with Turned Trunk, Seated, unpainted, Unknown, 4-1/4"	450	950
Elephant, "GOP 1936," Hubley, 1936, 3-1/2" tall	750	1200
Elephant, Circus, painted, w/lavender pants and red dotted white shirt, Hubley, 1930s, 3-7/8"	150	350
Elf, painted, converted doorstop, Unknown, 10" tall	150	450
English Setter, black, John Wright, 1970, 8-1/2" tall	125	275
Fidelity Safe, Large, green w/gold trim, "Fidelity Safe," Kyser & Rex, 1880, 3-5/8" tall	150	300
Fidelity Trust Vault, Lord Fauntleroy, Barton Smith Co., 1890, 6-1/2" x 5-7/8"	300	650
Fido, painted, white body, black eyes and ears, red collar, Hubley, 1914, 5"	60	145
Fido on Pillow, painted, Hubley, 1920s, 7-3/8" long	100	200
Finial Bank, building bank w/single finial on roof, Kyser & Rex, 1887, 5-3/4" tall, 4-3/8" wide	275	850
Flags Bank (SBCCA), white pyramid w/color US flags, Littlestown Harware, 1976, 3-1/4" tall, 6" square	75	125
Flat Iron Building Bank, silver, Kenton, 1900s, 5-1/2" tall	135	350
Floral Safe (National Safe), J & E. Stevens, 1898, 4-5/8" x 4-1/8"	125	350
Football Player, bronze finish, A.C. Williams, 1910s, 5-7/8" tall	250	450
Foreman, painted, Grey Iron Casting, 1951, 4-1/2"	175	350
Fort, unpainted bronze finish, Unknown, 1910s, 4-1/8"	125	275
Fort Mt. Hope, Unknown, 2-7/8" tall	125	425
Four Tower, painted white building w/red roof, Ohio Foundry, 1949, 5-3/8"	35	85
Four Tower, unpainted w/gold highlights, J & E. Stevens, 5-3/4"	125	375
Foxy Grandpa, painted, Hubley, 1920s, 5-1/2" tall	150	375
Frog, deep green finish, Iron Art, 1973, 4-1/8"	75	125
Frowning Face, hanging bank, chin drops below surface level, Unknown, 5-5/8" tall	850	1750
G.E. Radio Bank, brown cabinet radio on four legs, Arcade, 1930s, 3-3/4" tall	125	325
G.E. Refrigerator, Small, blue, Hubley, 1930s, 3-3/4"	75	225

Elephant with Swivel Trunk, $250

	C8	C10
Gas Pump, red, Unknown, 5-3/4" tall	275	650
Gem Stove, brown finish, Abendroth Bros., 4-3/4"	75	175
General Butler, cast iron, Stevens, J.& E., 1880s	1800	3500
General Butler, J & E. Stevens, 1880s	1000	3500
General Butler, painted head on frog body, J & E. Stevens, 1884, 6-1/2" tall	1500	3500
General Pershing Bust, bronze finish, Grey Iron Casting, 1918, 7-3/4" tall	75	150
General Sheridan on Base, General seated on rearing horse, Arcade, 1910s, 6" tall	250	650
George Washington Bust on Safe, J.M. Harper, 1903, 5-7/8" tall	1000	2500
Gettysburg Bank, gray monument w/reclining soldier, Wilton Products, 1960, 4-3/4" x 7-1/4"	75	200
Give Me A Penny, Black figure in hat, painted, Hubley, 1900s, 5-1/2" tall	200	450
Globe Bank with Eagle, red w/eagle on globe, Enterprise Mfg., 1875, 5-3/4"	125	350
Globe on Arc, red, Grey Iron Casting, 1900s, 5-1/4" tall	100	300
Globe on Claw Feet, Kenton, 6"	175	375
Globe on Hand, bronze finish, Unknown, 1893, 4"	375	1275
Globe on Wire Arc, painted spinning globe, red continents, Arcade, 1900s, 4-5/8" tall	125	450
Globe Safe with Hinged Door, Kenton, 1900s, 5"	100	250
Globe Savings Fund Bank, painted "Globe Savings Fund 1888," Kyser & Rex, 1889, 7-1/8"	1800	3000
Gold Eagle, John Wright, 1970, 5-3/4"	5	20
Good Luck Horseshoe, Buster Brown & Tige w/horse inside horseshoe, Arcade, 1908, 4-1/4" tall	150	400
Goose Bank, unpainted, Arcade, 1920s, 3-3/4"	85	175
Graf Zeppelin, silver gray finish, A.C. Williams, 1920s, 6-5/8" long	85	375
Graf Zeppelin on Wheels, silver pulltoy bank, A.C. Williams, 1934, 7-3/4" long	150	475
Grandpa's Hat, top hat, Unknown, 2-1/4" tall, 3-7/8" wide	225	450
Grenade with Pin, Bartlett Mayward, 4-1/4"	85	175
Gunboat, blue hull, white top, twin masts, Kenton, 8-1/2" long	650	1800
Hall Clock, brown finish, paper face, Hubley, 1900s, 5-1/4" tall	275	475
Hall Clock, dark finish w/gold highlights, Arcade, 1923, 5-5/8" tall	300	700
Hall Clock with Cast Face, Hubley, 1920s, 5-3/26" tall	275	425
Hanging Mailbox, green, wall mount mailbox replica, gold lettering, A.C. Williams, 1920s, 5-1/8" tall	65	175
Hanging Mailbox on Platform, red box hangs on post in platform base, Unknown, 1800s, 7-1/4" tall	650	1500
Hard Hat, white w/red lettering, George Knerr, 1970s, 1-15/16" tall	100	250
Harleysville Bank, white w/gray roof, Unicast Foundry, 1959, 2-5/8" tall, 5-1/4" long	75	225
Hen on Nest, bronze finish w/red highlights, Unknown, 1900s, 3"	100	1750
High Rise Building, Kenton, 7" tall	200	550
High Rise, Tiered, Kenton, 5-3/4"	125	350
Hippo, bronze w/red highlights, Unknown, 2" tall, 5-3/16" long	3500	6000
Holstein Cow, black finish, Arcade, 1910s, 2-1/2" tall, 4-5/8" long	125	350
Home Bank, dark finish, H.L. Judd, 1890s, 4" x 3-1/2"	175	500
Home Bank with Crown, painted, "Home Bank," J & E. Stevens, 1872, 5-1/4"	475	1400
Home Savings Bank, "Property of Peoples Savings Bank, Grand Rapids, Mich.," Unknown, 10-1/2" painted	175	650
Home Savings Bank, painted, Shimer Toy, 1899, 5-7/8"	150	525
Home Savings Bank, painted, Unknown, 9-5/8" tall	175	650
Home Savings Bank with Dog Finial, J & E. Stevens, 1891, 5-3/4" tall	125	450
Home Savings Bank with Finial, mustard finish, J & E. Stevens, 1891, 3-1/2" tall	125	375
Honey Bear, silver finish unpainted bear sits eating honey, Unknown, 2-1/2"	675	1200
Hoover/Curtis Elephant "GOP," ivory finish, Hubley, 1928, 3-3/8"	675	1600
Horse on Tub, Decorated, A.C. Williams, 1920s, 5-5/6"	135	300
Horse on Wheels, deep red finish, A.C. Williams, 1920, 4-1/4"	150	450
Horse, "Beauty," black w/raised "Beauty" on side, Arcade, 1900s, 4-1/8" x 4-3/4"	85	175
Horse, Prancing, black w/gray hooves, Arcade, 1910s, 4-1/4" tall	55	150
Horse, Prancing with Belly Band, light bronze finish, Unknown, 4-1/2"	175	375
Horse, Prancing, Large, bronze finish, A.C. Williams, 1910s, 7-3/16" tall	75	165
Horse, Rearing on Oval Base, A.C. Williams, 1920s, 5-1/8" x 4-7/8"	95	250
Horse, Rearing on Pebbled Base, gold finish, Unknown, 7-1/4" x 6-1/2"	85	165
Horseshoe with Mesh, Horse head inside horseshoe that forms end of mesh coin cage, bronze finish, A.C. Williams	65	145

	C8	C10
Hot Point Electric Stove, white, on legs, Arcade, 1925, 6"	350	975
House with Basement, painted, Ohio Foundry Co., 1893, 4-5/8" square	850	1600
House with Bay Window, painted, Unknown, 1874, 5-5/8" tall	900	2200
House with Chimney Slot, painted, Unknown, 2-7/8" x 2-13/16"	275	850
House with Knight, unpainted "Savings Bank" w/knight figure on roof peak, Unknown, 7-1/4"	375	950
Hub, Magic Introduction, 1892, 5" x 5-1/4" x 1-5/8"	300	850
Humphrey-Muskie Donkey, pale silver finish, "Humphrey Muskie 68," Unknown, 1968, 4-1/2" tall	10	35
Humpty Dumpty, painted, white egg, red brick wall, Unknown, 1930s, 5-1/2" tall	375	850
Humpty Dumpty, Seated, painted, Edward K. Russell, 1974, 5-3/8" tall	75	25
Husky, Grey Iron Casting, 1910s, 5"	200	550
I Made Chicago Famous, Large Pig, J.M. Harper, 1902, 2-5/8" x 5-5/16"	250	550
I Made Chicago Famous, Small Pig, J.M. Harper, 1902, 2-1/8" x 4-1/8"	200	400

Indian with Tomahawk, Hubley, $550

	C8	C10
Ice Box, white, "Save For Ice," Arcade, 4-1/4" tall	175	650
Independence Hall, mustard building on base w/bell tower, Unknown, 1875, 8-1/8" tall, 15-1/2" long	1800	3500
Independence Hall, deep red/brown finish, Enterprise Mfg., 1875, 10" tall	450	1150
Independence Hall Tower, Enterprise Mfg., 1876, 9-1/2"	225	525
Indian Chief Bust, unpainted, Unknown, 1978, 4-7/8"	35	85
Indian Family, unpainted, J.M. Harper, 1905, 3-5/8" x 5-1/8"	850	2200
Indian Head Penny, Knerr, George, 1972, 3-1/4" diam.	35	75
Indian Seated on Log, unpainted, A. Ouve, 1970s, 3-5/8" tall	85	150
Indian with Tomahawk, Hubley, 1900s, 5-7/8"	175	550
Indiana Paddle Wheeler, black w/red trim, Unknown, 1896, 7-1/8" long	4000	8000
International Eagle on Globe, unpainted, Unknown, 8" x 8"	1200	2500
Ironmaster's House, unpainted, Kyser & Rex, 1884, 4-1/2"	600	1250
Japanese Safe, Kyser & Rex, 1882, 5-3/8" tall	100	300
Japanese Safe, painted, Kyser & Rex, 1883, 5-1/2" tall	125	375
Jarmulowsky Building, bronze finish building bank, J & E. Stevens, 7-3/4" tall	1200	2000
Jewel Safe, unpainted, J & E. Stevens, 1907, 5-3/8"	125	350
John Brown Fort, red w/white cupola, Unknown, 3" tall	85	135
Junior Cash Register, Small, elaborate cast w/slot at top, J & E. Stevens, 1920s, 5-1/4" x 4-5/8"	175	375
Kelvinator Bank, white w/grey trim replica refrigerator, Arcade, No. 832, 1930s, 4-1/2" tall	150	375
Key, silver finish skeleton key, W.J. Somerville, 1905, 5-1/2" long	250	650
Key, St. Louis World's Fair, dark finish, Unknown, 1904, 5-3/4" long	275	700
King Midas, painted, Hubley, 1930s, 4-1/2" tall	1250	2500
Kitty Bank, painted, white body w/blue bow, Hubley, 1930s, 4-3/4" tall	65	150
Klondyke, Unknown, 3-1/4" cube	650	1400
Kodak Bank, "Kodak Bank," J & E. Stevens, 1905, 4-1/4" tall, 5" wide	200	450
L'il Tot, Watkins, Bob, 1982, 5-7/8"	125	175
Labrador Retriever, black finish w/gold collar, Unknown, 4-1/2"	125	375
Lamb, painted white w/black highlights, John Wright, 1970, 3-1/4" tall	35	75

	C8	C10
Lamb, Small, painted white, Unknown, 3-3/16"	200	375
Laughing Pig, painted, Hubley, 2-1/2"	125	275
Liberty Bell, J.M. Harper, 1905, 3-3/4"	275	550
Liberty Bell with Yoke, Arcade, 1920s, 3-1/2"	25	65
Liberty Bell, Miniature, Penncraft, 3-1/2" x 1-3/4"	20	35
Lighthouse, "Light of the World," Lane Art, 1950s, 9-1/2" tall	125	250
Lighthouse, red tower rises from unpainted base, Unknown, 1891, 10-1/4" tall	1200	3000
Limousine, same as No. 1478, but w/steel wheels, Arcade, 1921	1200	2800
Limousine, black w/white rubber tires, Arcade, 1920s, 8-1/16" long	750	2500
Limousine Yellow Cab, repaint of No. 1478, Arcade, 1921	1400	2800
Lincoln High Hat, black finish, "Pass Around the Hat," Unknown, 1880s, 2-3/8" tall	125	225
Lion on Tub, Decorated, A.C. Williams, 1920s, 5-1/2" tall	125	225
Lion on Tub, Plain, bronze finish, A.C. Williams, 1920s, 7-1/2" tall	100	200
Lion on Tub, Small, brown or green finish, A.C. Williams, 1920s, 4-1/8" tall	85	175
Lion on Wheels, gold, A.C. Williams, 1920s, 4-1/2" x 5-1/2"	145	225
Lion, Ears Up, A.C. Williams, 1930s, 3-5/8" x 4-1/2"	75	125

	C8	C10
Lion, Small, A.C. Williams, 1934, 2-1/2" x 3-5/8"	85	150
Lion, Tail Between Legs, Unknown, 3" x 5-1/4"	85	145
Lion, Tail Left, bronze finish, Hubley, 1910s, 3-3/4" tall	100	175
Lion, Tail Right, bronze finish, A.C. Williams, 1900s, 5-1/4" tall	55	150
Lion, Tail Right, Arcade, 1900s, 4" tall	55	100
Lion, Tail Right, A.C. Williams, 1920s, 3-1/2" x 4-15/16"	55	100
Little Red Riding Hood Safe, painted, J.M. Harper, 1907, 5-1/16" tall	2000	4000
Log Cabin, painted, Kyser & Rex, 1882, 2-1/2" x 3-1/4"	175	425
Lost Dog, unpainted, Judd H.L., 1890s, 5-3/8"	275	850
Lucky Cabin, painted w/horseshoe over door, John Wright, 1970, 4-1/8" tall	35	65
Mailbox on Legs, Large, green street corner box replica, Hubley, 1920s, 5-1/2" tall	85	225
Mailbox on Legs, Small, green replica street corner mailbox, Hubley, 1928, 3-3/4" tall	35	100
Main Street Trolley with People, bronze finish, A.C. Williams, 1920s, 3" x 6-3/4"	175	475
Main Street Trolley without People, A.C. Williams, 1920s, 6-3/4" long	175	400
Majestic Radio Bank, mahogany finish replica of a floor standing radio on four legs, coin slot in back, w/key, Arcade, 1930s, 4-1/2" tall	125	200
Majestic Refrigerator Bank, in red, green or blue w/gold trim, replica of single door fridge on four legs, coin slot in back, w/key lock, Arcade, 1930s, 4-1/2" tall	375	600
Mammy, doorstop conversion, red dress, white apron, Unknown, 1970s, 8-1/4" tall	10	25
Mammy with Hands on Hips, red dress, white apron, Hubley, 1900s, 5-1/4" tall	85	400
Man in Barrel, painted, J & E. Stevens, 1890s, 3-3/4" tall	175	375
Man on Cotton Bale, painted darkie sits on hay bale, red scarf, yellow pants, US Hardware, 1898, 4-7/8" tall	1500	2500
Marietta Silo, gray finish, Unknown, 5-1/2"	275	650
Marshall Stove, red, Unknown, 3-7/8"	125	225
Mary & Little Lamb, painted white w/red trim, Unknown, 1901, 4-3/8" tall	350	1000
Mascot, boy stands on baseball, Hubley, 1914, 5-3/4" tall	850	1850
McKinley/Teddy Elephant, bronze finish, Unknown, 1900, 2-1/2" tall	350	650
Mean Standing Bear, Hubley, 5-1/2"	100	225
Mellow Furnace, brown finish, Liberty Toy, 3-9/16" x 3-1/8"	125	225

Mammy with Hands on Hips, Hubley, $400

	C8	C10
Mermaid Boat, companion piece to Dolphin, girl in boat holds fish, Grey Iron Casting, 1900s, 4-1/2" tall	350	850
Merry-Go-Round, unpainted, Grey Iron Casting, 1920s, 4-5/8" tall	175	550
Metropolitan Bank, "Metropolitan Bank," J & E. Stevens, 1872, 5-7/8"	125	275
Mickey Mouse, bookend bank, painted, John Wright, 1970s, 5" x 3-3/4"	85	150
Mickey Mouse, Hands on Hips, painted, Unknown, 9" tall	125	450
Middy with Clapper, brown finish, Unknown, 1887, 5-1/4"	150	350
Minuteman, painted, Hubley, 1905, 6" tall	200	525
Model T Ford, black, Arcade, 1920s, 4" tall	650	1250
Moody & Sankey, painted, two oval portraits on front, Smith & Egge, 1870, 5"	800	1850
Mosque, Large, Three-Story, A.C. Williams, 1920s, 3-1/2" tall	45	125
Mosque, Small, Two-Story, Unknown, 2-7/8" tall	35	115
Mother Hubbard Safe, J.M. Harper, 1907, 4-1/2" tall	1500	5000
Mulligan Policeman (Keystone Cop), painted, A.C. Williams, 1900s, 5-3/4"	175	400
Multiplying Bank, painted building, J & E. Stevens, 1883, 6-1/2"	700	2200
Mutt & Jeff, gold, A.C. Williams, 1900s, 4-1/4" x 3-1/2"	75	275
National Safe, unpainted, J & E. Stevens, 1800s, 3-3/8" tall	65	125
Nest Egg, bronze finish egg on side, "Horace," Smith & Egge, 1873, 3-3/8" tall on base	450	850
Nesting Doves Safe, bronze finish, J.M. Harper, 1907, 5-1/4"	1500	3500
New Heatrola Bank, green finish w/red trim, Kenton, 1920s, 4-1/2" tall	85	275
Newfoundland Dog, blue or green finish, Arcade, 1930s, 3-5/8" x 5-3/8"	100	225
Newfoundland Dog with Pack, Unknown, 4-11/16" tall	85	175
Nixe, silver boy in boat, "Nixe," Unknown, 4-1/2" tall	350	1450
Nixon Bust, Blevins, Charlotte, 1972, 5-5/16"	45	85
Nixon/Agnew Elephant, Unknown, 1968, 2-5/8"	15	35
North Pole Bank, unpainted, "Save Your Casting Money And Freeze It," Grey Iron, 1920s, 4-1/4"	375	775
Oak Stove, unpainted, Shimer Toy, 1899, 2-3/8" tall	125	475
Old Abe with Shield, Eagle, unpainted, Unknown, 1880, 3-7/8"	450	1300

	C8	C10
Old South Church, bronze finish, Unknown, 10" tall	2000	5000
One Car Garage, painted, A.C. Williams, 1920s, 2-1/2"	125	250
One Story House, Grey Iron Casting, 1900s, 3" tall	65	175
Oregon Gunboat, blue hull, gray guns, black and red stacks, "Oregon," Kenton, 11" long	850	1800
Organ Grinder, painted, Hubley, 6-3/16" x 2-1/8"	125	350
Oriental Boy on Pillow, painted, Hubley, 1920s, 5-1/2" tall	85	200
Oriental Camel, on rockers, Unknown, 3-3/4" tall	300	875
Ornate Hall Clock, tan finish, paper face, Hubley, 1900s, 5-7/8" tall	200	425
Osborn Pig, "You can bank on the Osborn…," Unknown, 2" x 4"	100	350
Oscar the Goat, black w/silver hooves and horns, Unknown, 7-3/4" tall	75	175
Owl, painted, Vindex Toys, 1930, 4-1/4"	75	325
Owl on Stump, red, Unknown, 3-5/8"	65	125
Ox, painted, Kenton, 4-3/8"	85	150
Palace, 8" wide, Ives, 1885, 7-1/2" tall	850	3000
Park Bank Building, Unknown, 4-3/8" painted	450	1450
Parlor Stove, gray and black, Unknown, 6-7/8"	275	425
Parrot on Stump, painted, Unknown, 6-1/4"	125	450
Pavillion, Kyser & Rex, 1880, 3-1/8" x 3"	225	500

Pavillion, Kyser & Rex, $500

	C8	C10
Pay Phone Bank, unpainted, J & E. Stevens, 1926, 7-3/16"	450	1800
Pearl Street Bank, unpainted, silver finish, Unknown, 4-1/4"	350	850
Peg Legged Pirate, unpainted, Unknown, 5-1/4"	25	85
Pelican, painted white, Hubley, 1930s, 4-3/4"	350	1000
Penny Register Pail, unpainted, Kyser & Rex, 1889, 2-3/4"	125	250
Penthouse Building, silver finish, A.C. Williams, 5-7/8" tall	350	850
Peters Weatherbird, Arcade, 4-1/4" tall	750	2500
Phoenix Dime Register Trunk, steamer trunk, Piaget, 1890, 3-3/4" x 5"	125	250
Pig, A Christmas Roast, Unknown, 3-1/4" x 7-1/8"	85	250
Pig, Seated, A.C. Williams, 1900s, 3" x 4-9/16"	35	125
Plymouth Rock 1620, "1620", Unknown, 3-7/8" long	650	1850
Polar Bear, Begging, white, Arcade, 1900s, 5-1/4"	275	450
Policeman Bank, blue w/aluminum finish on gloves and star, gold buttons, black shoes, flesh face and hands, Arcade, 1930s, 5-5/8" tall	250	1000
Policeman Safe, J.M. Harper, 1907, 5-1/4"	1250	4500
Polish Rooster, Unknown, 5-1/2"	850	2500
Polish Rooster, painted, Unknown, 5-1/2" tall	850	2200
Pooh Bank, Unknown, 5" x 4-7/8"	5	15
Possum, silver finish, Arcade, 1910s, 2-3/8" tall, 4-3/8" long	125	575
Postal Savings Mailbox, Nicol, 1920s, 6-3/4"	85	275
Pot Bellied Stove, flat black finish, Knerr, George, 1968, 5-3/4" tall	25	65
Potato, "Bank," Martin, Mary A., 1897, 5-1/4" long	850	1650
Presto Bank, silver finish w/gold dome, A.C. Williams, 1900s, 3-5/8" tall	85	175
Presto Bank, silver finish, "Bank," Unknown, 3-1/4" tall	65	150
Presto Bank, building, silver w/gold dome, Unknown, 4-1/4" tall	85	175
Presto Trick Bank, red doors and roof, Kyser & Rex, 1892, 4-1/2" tall	250	850
Professor Pug Frog Bank, A.C. Williams, 1900s, 3-1/4"	75	550
Pugdog, Seated, painted, Kyser & Rex, 1889, 3-1/2"	250	475
Puppo, painted bee on body, Hubley, 1920s, 4-7/8" tall	125	250
Puppo on Pillow, painted brown, cream, black, pink, Hubley, 1920s, 5-5/8" x 6"	150	275
Put Money in Thy Purse, change purse, black, Unknown, 1886, 2-3/4" tall	625	950

Rabbit Standing, large, A.C. Williams, $325

	C8	C10
Puzzle Try Me, safe, "Puzzle Try Me," Unknown, 1868, 2-11/16" tall	475	975
Quadrafoil House, Several Makers, 1900s, 3-1/8" tall	125	225
Queen Stove, "Queen" on oven door, John Wright, 1975, 3-3/4" to cook top	25	65
Quilted Lion, bronze finish, Unknown, 3-3/4" tall, 4-3/4" long	185	450
Rabbit Lying Down, unpainted, Unknown, 2-1/8" x 5-1/8"	175	575
Rabbit Standing, Large, brown metal finish, A.C. Williams, 1908, 6-1/4" tall	125	325
Rabbit with Carrot, painted white, orange and green carrot, George Knerr, 1972, 3-3/8"	85	200
Rabbit, Begging, A.C. Williams, 1900s, 5-1/8"	85	275
Rabbit, Large, Seated, painted white w/pink highlights, Hubley, 1900s, 4-5/8" tall	125	375
Rabbit, Small, Seated, Arcade, 1910s, 3-5/8" tall	125	325
Radio Bank, metallic blue, Hubley, 1928, 3-5/16" tall	100	375
Radio Bank with Three Dials, red, Kenton, 1920s, 3" tall, 4-5/8" long	100	350
Radio with Combination Door, metal sides and back, Kenton, 1930s, 4-1/2" red	125	375
Reclining Cow, black, Unknown, 2-1/8" tall, 4" long	100	400
Recording Bank, Unknown, 6-5/8" x 4-1/4"	200	575
Red Ball Safe, red ball on base, Unknown, 3"	175	425
Red Goose Shoes on Base, on pedestal w/base, Arcade, 1920s, 5-1/2"	300	750

	C8	C10
Red Goose Shoes on Pedestal, red goose on bronze base, Unknown, 4-7/16"	175	350
Red Goose Shoes, Squatty, red body, yellow feet, Arcade, 1920s, 4" tall	275	500
Reindeer on Base, John Wright, 1973, 10" x 8"	75	125
Reindeer, Large, bronze finish, A.C. Williams, 1900s, 9-1/2" tall	125	250
Reindeer, Small, bronze finish, A.C. Williams, 6-1/4" tall	75	150
Reliable Parlor Stove, Schneider & Trenkramp, 6-1/4"	425	850
Republic Pig, painted pig in business suit, Wilton Products, 1970s, 7" tall	35	85
Rhesus Monkey, converted doorstop, painted, Unknown, 8-1/2"	35	125
Rhino, gold, Arcade, 1910s, 2-5/8" tall, 5" long	225	650
Rochester Clock, w/working clock, Unknown, 5" tall	225	750
Rocking Chair, brown finish, Manning, C.J., 1898, 6-3/4" tall	1500	2750
Rocking Horse, white w/red saddle, "SBCC," George Knerr, 1975, 5-5/8"	350	550

	C8	C10
Roller Safe, Kyser & Rex, 1882, 3-11/16" x 2-7/8"	125	245
Roof Bank, J & E. Stevens, 1887, 5-1/4" x 3-3/4"	125	350
Roof Bank, Grey Iron Casting, 1900s, 5-1/4"	125	300
Rooster, brown finish w/red comb and wattle, Hubley/Williams, 1910s, 4-3/4"	125	300
Rooster, black w/red comb, Arcade, 1910s, 4-5/8"	125	350
Rooster, Large, unpainted except for red comb and wattle, Unknown, 1913, 6-3/4"	550	1250
Rumplestiltskin, Unknown, 1910s, 6" x 2-1/4"	200	500
Saddle Horse, Grey Iron Casting, 1928, 4-3/8" tall	375	650
Safe Deposit, "Safe Deposit", Shimer Toy, 1899, 3-5/8"	85	150
Safety Locomotive, gray, Unknown, 1887, 3-1/4" tall	1250	2200
Sailor, Medium, Hubley, 1910s, 5-1/4" tall	225	475
San Gabriel Mission, painted, musical building, Unknown, 4-5/8" x 3-3/4"	2000	7500
Santa Claus, painted w/arms folded in front, Hubley, 1900s, 5-3/4"	450	950
Santa Claus with Tree, w/arms folded in front, tree at back, painted, Hubley, 1910s, 5-3/4"	450	950

Sailor, Medium, Hubley, $475

Santa Claus with Tree, Hubley, $950

	C8	C10
Santa with Wire Tree, w/removable ornate tree, Ives, 1890s, 7-1/4" tall	875	1500
Scottie, Seated, black finish, red collar, Hubley, 1930s, 4-7/8" x 6"	125,	00
Scrollwork Safe, Unknown, 1900s, 2-3/4" tall	85	225
Seal on Rock, black, Arcade, 1900s, 3-1/2"	175	500
Security Safe, red door, Unknown, 1894, 4-1/2" tall	125	275
Security Safe Deposit, Unknown, 1881, 3-7/8" tall	95	150
Shell Out, conch shell on base, off white, J & E. Stevens, 1882, 4-3/4" long	225	700
Show Horse, Lane Chair, 1973, 5-7/8" tall	75	150
Six Sided Building, two story, Unknown, 3-3/8" tall	100	275
Six-Sided Building, unpainted, Unknown, 2-3/8" tall	225	650
Skyscraper Bank, silver building, four gold posts, A.C. Williams, 1900s, 5-1/2" tall	85	150
Skyscraper Bank, silver building, four gold posts, A.C. Williams, 1900s, 4-3/8" tall	85	125
Skyscraper with Six Posts, silver building, gold posts, A.C. Williams, 1900s, 6-1/2" tall	125	450
Songbird on Stump, bronze finish, A.C. Williams, 1900s, 4-3/4"	300	800
Sace Heater with Bird, English, Chamberlain & Hill, 1890s, 6-1/2" tall	175	375
Space Heater with Flowers, English, Far East motif, red finish, Unknown, 1890s, 6-1/2" tall	175	375
Spaniel, Large, painted, John Wright, 1960s, 10-1/2" long	65	125
Spitz, bronze finish, Grey Iron Casting, 1928, 4-1/4"	225	575
Squirrel with Nut, Unknown, 4-1/8"	425	1250
St. Bernard with Pack, Large, A.C. Williams, 1900s, 5-1/2" x 7-3/4"	125	225
St. Bernard with Pack, Small, A.C. Williams, 1900s, 3-3/4" x 5-1/2"	85	175
Star Safe, Kyser & Rex, 1882, 2-5/8" tall	150	450
State Bank, unpainted building bank, Kenton, 1890s, 3" tall	95	200
State Bank, Kenton, 1900, 8" x 7"	550	1200
State Bank, bronze building bank, Kyser & Rex, 1890s, 5-1/2" tall	125	325
State Bank, bronze finish, Arcade, 1910s, 4-1/8" tall	85	175
Statue of Liberty, A.C. Williams, 6-3/8" tall	85	125
Statue of Liberty, Kenton, 1900s, 6-1/16" tall	85	125
Statue of Liberty, silver finish w/gold highlights, Kenton, 1900s, 6-3/8" tall	100	175
Statue of Liberty, Large, silver gray finish, gold highlights, Kenton, 1900s, 9-1/2" tall	350	1200

	C8	C10
Steamboat, brown finish, A.C. Williams, 190s, 7-5/8" long	125	375
Steamboat with Small Wheels, silver finish, Kenton, 7-7/16" long	175	425
Stop Sign, green w/red and gold highlights, Dent, 1920, 5-5/8" tall	325	850
Stork Safe, J.M. Harper, 1907, 5-1/2"	850	1750
Street Car, painted, Grey Iron Casting, 1891, 4-1/2" long	250	650
Sun Dial, Arcade, 1900s, 4-5/16" tall	650	2000
Sunbonnet Sue, painted, Unknown, 1970, 7-1/2"	65	165
Tabernacle Savings, unpainted, Keyless Lock Co., 2-1/4" x 5"	850	1250
Taft-Sherman Bust, one side Smiling Jim, other side Peaceful Bill, J.M. Harper, 1908, 4" tall	1000	1850
Tank Bank 1918, Large, gold finish, A.C. Williams, 1920s, 3" tall x 3-11/16" long	100	200
Tank Bank 1918, Small, gold finish, A.C. Williams, 1920s, 2-3/8" long	65	150
Tank Bank 1919, silver finish, "1919," Unknown, 3" x 5-1/2"	125	350
Tank Savings Bank, "Tank Savings Bank," Ferrosteel, 1919, 9-1/2" long	175	525
Teddy Bear, Arcade, 1900, 2-1/2" x 3-7/8"	125	350
Teddy Roosevelt Bust, A.C. Williams, 1919, 5" tall	175	450
Templetone Radio, red, Arcade, 1930s, 4-1/2"	275	575

Tower Bank, J.M. Harper, $375

	C8	C10
Thoroughbred, bronze finish, Hubley, 1946, 5-1/4"	75	150
Three Wise Monkeys, A.C. Williams, 1900s, 3-1/4" tall, 3-1/2" wide	225	550
Time Is Money Clock Bank, alarm clock shaped, gold finish, "Time Is Money," A.C. Williams, 1910s, 3-1/2" tall	125	200
Time Safe, unpainted, Roche, E.M. Co., 7" tall, 3-3/4" wide	375	750
Tower, unpainted, Kenton, 1915, 4-1/8"	175	375
Tower Bank, unpainted, brown finish, J.M. Harper, 1900s, 9-1/4" tall	175	375
Tower Bank, building w/tower rising from roof, "Tower Bank 1890," Kyser & Rex, 1890, 6-7/8"	1200	2200
Town Hall Bank, red, "Town Hall Bank," Kyser & Rex, 1882, 4-5/8"	375	950
Toy Soldier, painted, "SBCCA," Laverne A. Worley, 1982, 7-1/2" tall	15	65
Treasure Chest, smaller version is No. 928, John Wright,1970, 2-3/4" x 4"	60	35
Triangular Building, "Bank," Hubley, 1914, 6" tall	325	675
Trick Buffalo, black, Unknown, 5-1/2" tall	750	1500
Trolley Car, painted silver, Kenton, 1900s, 5-1/4" long	225	650
Trunk on Dolly, Piaget, 1890, 2-5/8" x 3-9/16"	175	350
Trust Bank, J & E. Stevens, 1800s, 7-1/4"	1800	3000
Tug Boat, red, pulltoy, Unknown, 5-1/2" long	4500	7500
Turkey, Large, painted wattle, A.C. Williams, 1900s, 4-1/4" x 4"	250	550
Turkey, Small, red head and wattle, A.C. Williams, 1900s, 3-3/8" tall	150	275
Turtle Bank, Unknown, 1" tall, 3-7/16" long	2000	3500
Two Car Garage, painted, A.C. Williams, 1920s, 2-1/2"	125	350
Two Goats Butting, two goats on tree stump, "Two Kids" on base, J.M. Harper, 4-1/2"	950	2000
Two Story House, brown finish w/red roof, A.C. Williams, 1930s, 3-1/16" tall	75	150
Two-Faced Black Boy, Large, A.C. Williams, 1900s, 4-1/8" tall	125	350
Two-Faced Black Boy, Small, A.C. Williams, 1900s, 3-1/8" x 2-3/4"	85	300
Two-Faced Devil, deep red, A.C. Williams, 1004,4-1/4" tall	550	1250
Two-Faced Indian, bronze finish w/painted highlights, A.C. Williams, 1900s, 4-5/16" tall	1500	2750
U.S. Bank, Eagle Finial, x green w/gold trim, Unknown, 1890s, 4-5/16" tall	850	1500
U.S. Mail, silver gray w/red lettering, Kenton, 1900s, 4-3/4" tall	100	375
U.S. Mail Bank with Combination Lock, silver gray w/red lettering, Fish, O.B., 1903, 6-7/8" tall	225	775
U.S. Mail with Eagle, Kenton, 1930s, 4-1/8" x 3-1/2"	85	175
U.S. Mail with Eagle, Hubley, 1906, 4" x 4"	175	325
U.S. Mail, Small, silver or green mail box w/red lettering, Kenton, 1900s, 3-5/8" x 2-3/4"	75	150
U.S. Navy Akron Zeppelin, silver finish, "US Navy Akron," A.C. Williams, 1930, 6-5/8" long	175	500
U.S. Treasury Bank, painted, Grey Iron Casting, 1920s, 3-1/4"	250	475
Ulysses S. Grant Bust, Unknown, 1976, 5-1/2" tall	125	250
Ulysses S. Grant Bust on Safe, J.M. Harper, 1903, 5-5/8" tall	1750	3000
Uncle Sam Hat, red, white and blue, George Knerr, George, 2" x 3"	125	350
United Banking and Trust, Building Bank, 3" tall, bronze finish, A.C. Williams	225	450
Victorian House, unpainted deep gray finish, J & E. Stevens, 1892, 4-1/2"	175	375
Victorian House, gray metallic finish, Unknown, 3-1/4" tall	150	275
Villa, unpainted except for red finial, Kyser & Rex, 1894, 5-9/16"	375	850
Villa Bank, "1882," Kyser & Rex, 1882, 3-7/8" x 3-3/8"	375	700
Vindex Bulldog, painted, "Vindex Toys," Vindex Toys, 1931, 5-1/4" tall	125	275
Washington Bell with Yoke, red, Grey Iron Casting, 1932, 2-3/4"	125	325
Washington Monument, A.C. Williams, 1900s, 6" tall	150	325
Washington, George, Bust, bronze finish, Grey Iron Casting, 1920s, 8" tall	850	1450
Watch Dog Safe, w/brass handle, dog stands guard on front, Unknown, 5-1/8"	1850	4000
Water Spaniel with Pack (I Hear A Call), J.M. Harper, 1900, 5-3/8" x 7-7/8"	225	450
Weaver Hen, white w/red comb and wattle, "Weaver," Unknown, 1970s, 6"	20	50
Westside Presbyterian Church, silver finish, Unknown, 1916, 3-3/4" x 3-5/8"	350	950
Whale of a Bank, "A Whale of a Bank," George Knerr, 1975, 2-3/4" x 5-3/16"	85	200
Whippet on Base, gold finish, Unknown, 3-1/2" tall	75	125
White City Barrel No. 1 on Cart, unpainted, "White City Puzzle Savings Bank, A Barrel of Money," Nicol, 1894, 5" long	275	475

World's Fair Administration Building, 1893, $2,250

Uncle Remus, $5,000

Yellow Cab, Arcade $2,400

	C8	C10
White City Barrel, Large, silver finish barrel, Nicol, 1893, 5-1/8" tall	175	275
White City Pail, silver finish pail w/handle, Nicol, 1893, 2-5/8" tall	125	225
White City Puzzle Safe No. 10, unpainted, Nicol, 1893, 4-5/8"	125	225
White City Puzzle Safe No. 12, unpainted, Nicol, 1893, 4-7/8"	150	325
White Horse on Base, Knerr, George, 1973, 9-1/2" tall	125	225
Wirehaired Terrier, painted, Hubley, 1920s, 4-5/8"	125	275
Wisconsin Beggar Boy, "Help the Crippled Children of Wisconsin," Unknown, 6-7/8" tall	525	900
Wisconsin War Eagle, Unknown, 1880, 2-7/8"	675	1500
The Wise Pig, painted off-white pig holding plaque, Hubley, 1930s, 6-5/8" tall	85	225
Woolworth Building, Kenton, 1915, 5-3/4" x 1-1/4"	85	150
Woolworth Building, bronze finish, Kenton, 1915, 7-7/8" tall	100	225

	C8	C10
Work Horse on Base, painted white, Unknown, 9" tall	75	125
Work Horse with Flynet, Arcade, 1910s, 4" tall	300	800
World's Fair Administration Building, painted, Unknown, 1893, 6" x 6"	1400	2250
Yellow Cab, orange and black, rubber tires, Arcade, 1921, 7-7/8" long	1500	2400
York Stove, unpainted, "York Stove," Abendroth Bros., 4" tall	225	525
Young America, Kyser & Rex, 1882, 4-3/8" x 3-1/8" safe	125	275

Boy Scout, $8,250

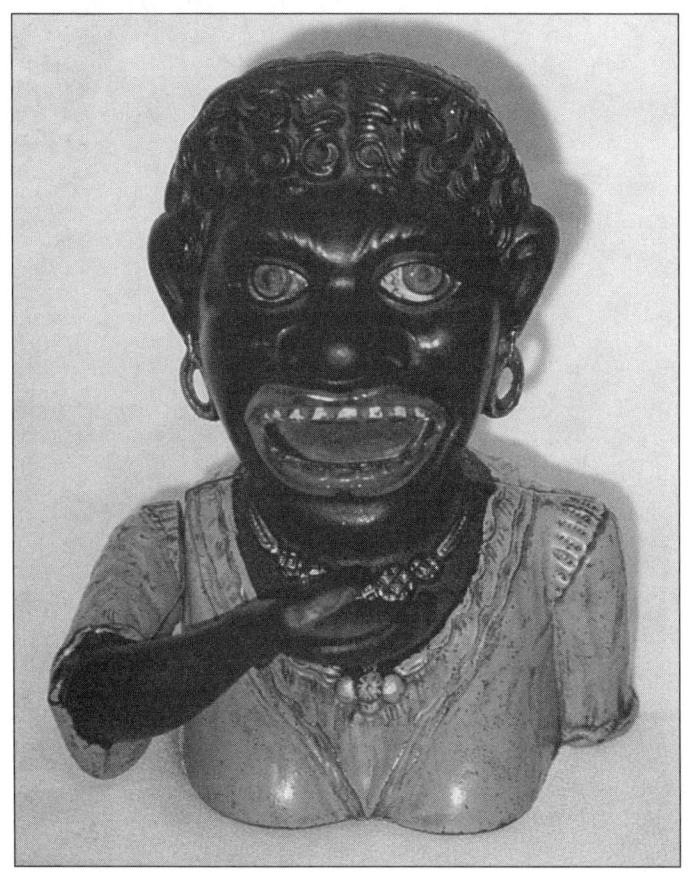

Dinah, 5-1/2" high, $900

Jolly Nigger, bust, $540

Hall's Lilliput, $1,000

Leap frog Bank, $3,900

Trick Dog, 1888, $2,500

Professor Pug Frog's Great Bicycle Feat, auctioned in 1998 for $96,000

Left to Right: Speaking Dog Bank, $2,100; Clown on Globe, $3,500

BATTERY-OPERATED TOYS

Made in Japan are the words toy collectors look for in their pursuit of high-quality mechanical tin toys.

Before World War II, these same words were synonymous with cheap, poor-quality, drab-looking toys made from recycled materials and ideas. Most of the toys were people and animal-oriented with less emphasis on vehicle, nautical, or aircraft-type toys. They were powered either by a spring or a flywheel and didn't last very long or do very much as far as play-value goes. These inexpensive, poor-quality toys kept Japan a third-rate toy manufacturing nation until after the second World War, when Japan's surrender resulted in economic chaos for this industrial nation.

In their quest for economic recovery and to compete in a toy market already dominated by Germany and America, the Japanese knew they had to come up with a new, different and exciting type of toy that would be more desirable than those produced by their competitors.

The Japanese toy designers concentrated their technology on a different type of toy operation. Not satisfied with the limited action and short duration of spring-driven or flywheel-propelled toys, the toy engineers developed a small electric motor powered by flashlight batteries. This mini-motor took up less room than other mechanisms, had a longer-running duration and enabled the toy to perform more functions. This development opened up an entirely new dimension in toy design—it introduced the concept of the battery-operated toy.

The toy designers integrated this new concept into hundreds of automaton-like toys, capable of as many as eight different types of actions in one cycle. These unique toys were an instant hit with the foreign market, especially the United States. These clever, unusual and high-quality toys made Japan the dominant toy producer and exporter for the next twenty to thirty years.

It should be noted that Japan flooded the market with these ingenious, well-made toys while quality control remained a high priority. These merits were not only apparent in their figural toys, but also in their vehicle line. The Japanese toy makers concentrated on very fine detail and quality, especially in their scale-model passenger cars. Their ultimate goal was to produce toys that looked like the real thing. They succeeded. Their workmanship carried over into their other vehicle lines—motorcycles; emergency and construction vehicles; and novelty (silly) and comic character cars; trucks; and space toys.

No other nation was able to equal (much less surpass) the impetus and determination of the Japanese toy makers until Japan relinquished its domination by redirecting its economy.

Now that they are approaching middle age, it is no wonder that these fine toys remain in great demand today and often command a very high price.

The value of a battery-operated toy depends not only on its desirability, rarity and complexity, but very much on its condition. A toy in Mint condition is generally worth twice as much as a toy in Good condition. A toy in Very Good condition will be priced about halfway between good and mint.

C-10: Mint. A Mint toy is in the condition in which it was originally issued (perfect) regardless of age. It will also be in perfect mechanical condition, complete with all accessory parts when applicable, and will look brand new. The cloth or fur (plush) covering on some battery toys may reveal some discoloration (yellowing) due to age, but this should not affect its value as a Mint toy as long as it is clean. All toys in this category must be in perfect working condition. The original box in Mint condition will significantly enhance the value.

C-8: Very Good. A battery toy that has seen some use and is starting to show its age is described as Very Good. It will still be in perfect working order and have all its accessory parts when applicable. It will have some age soiling, but will have no rust or corrosion. Overall, it will have an appearance of freshness and still be highly desirable to the fussy collector.

C-6: Good. The term Good applies to a battery toy that has seen considerable use, wear and tear, and some age-soiling, but is still in perfect working condition with no missing parts or accessories. The wet toys may show some slight surface rust that can be easily removed. A toy in Good condition is still a welcome addition to any toy collection, but will be targeted for upgrading by a piece in better condition.

Any battery toy below the condition of Good will reflect a drastic reduction in value. Toys in good shape, but missing accessory parts, will not lose as much value as those that are severely rusted, corroded, painted over, have parts broken off, or are totally inoperable. These toys in Poor condition are usually collected for their scrap value by the toy repairer and seldom are they worth more than $10.

The key to grading is to use common sense and avoid wishful thinking. Grading the condition of a toy may be difficult at times, and consulting with an expert in the field can help dispel doubts about your judgment or your purchase.

To keep it in Excellent condition, your prized battery toy needs some tender loving care. If it stops working, you could have frustration, if not a disaster, on your hands. The following suggestions should be of some help in avoiding this.

Battery toys, like other mechanical toys, should be operated periodically to keep them loosened up. A light-weight spray lubrication now and then will help considerably if the mechanism is accessible. Do not over lubricate as the excess may stain any cloth or fur covering on the toy.

A quality car wax or polish will keep the lithographed and bare metal parts looking like new, especially on the "wet" toys. Always test an obscure lithographed area to make sure the polish doesn't soften or dissolve the paint. Care should be exercised when polishing metal parts adjoining any cloth or plush covering, as the cleaning substance may stain the coverings. Light surface rust usually disappears with a careful polishing. Nothing can be done for deep rust or corrosion without further ruining the value of the toy. Repainting will only further reduce the value and is not recommended.

Should your battery toy fail to operate, the following steps might be helpful.

1. Make sure it is not gunked-up and that no moving parts are binding.
2. Make sure the battery contacts are not dirty or corroded. If they are, clean them with crocus cloth. Always use fresh batteries!
3. Lightly tap the toy with your finger or lightly nudge one of the moving parts while the switch is in the on position.

If none of the above steps work, then your toy needs major surgery. This means the toy must be completely torn down, repaired and reassembled. Most battery toys are repairable as long as they have not been destructively tampered with and no parts are missing or corroded beyond repair. This job is best left to an expert in toy repair and should never be attempted by one who doesn't know what he or she is doing. Expert repairs will not affect the value of a battery toy as long as the repair is undetectable and the toy looks and functions exactly as it did before the repair. Such repairs are acceptable in toy collecting circles. Expert repairs are expensive but well worth the investment if it means the difference between a highly-prized Mint toy and one below the grade of Good. An inoperable toy is practically worthless, regardless of condition.

Contributer: Leo Rishty, Toydoc, 2563 Jardin Lane, Weston, FL 33327, toydoc@aol.com. Rishty has been collecting and repairing toys for over 20 years.

	C6	C8	C10
A-B-C Fairy Train, M-T Co., 1950s, 14-1/2" long; one piece, four actions	80	95	160
Accordion Bear, "Y" Co., 1950s, 10-1/2" tall; six actions	220	330	440
Accordion Bear, MST Co. 1950s, (Flare Toy), 9-1/4" high, five actions	150	225	300
Accordion Player Bunny, Alps Co., 1950s, 12" tall, 9" long; six actions	200	325	450
Accordion Player Hobo with Baby Monkey Playing Cymbals, Alps Co., 1950s; six actions	275	425	525
Acrobat Clown, Y-M Co., 1960s, 9" tall; minor toy	60	90	120
Acro Chimp Porter, Y-M Co., 1960s, 8-1/2" tall; minor toy	50	75	100
Acrobat Robot, S-H Co., 1970s, 4-1/2" tall; three actions	225	338	450
Air Cargo Prop-Jet Airplane, Seaboard World Airlines, Marx Co., 1960s, 12" long, 14-1/2" wingspan; five actions	150	300	425

	C6	C8	C10
Air Control Tower, Bandai Co., includes detachable airplane and helicopter, 1960s, 11" high, 37" span extended; four actions	210	315	450
Air Defense Pom-Pom Gun, Linemar Co., 1950s, 14" long, five actions	115	175	260
Air Taxi Helicopter, Haji Co., 1960s; three actions	50	75	100
Aircraft Carrier, Marx Co., 1950s, 20" long; six actions	275	450	625
Aircraft Carrier Forrestal, Linemar, includes detachable plastic airplane, 1950s, 13-3/4" long; three actions	200	300	400
Aircraft Carrier, Marx Co., 1950s, 20" long; eight actions	200	300	400
Airport Saucer, MT Co., 1960s, 8" diameter; four actions	100	150	200
Airport Saucer, 1960s, S-T Co., 9" diameter; four actions	100	150	200
All Stars Mr. Baseball Jr., K Co., includes eight plastic balls, 1950s; three actions, rare	500	750	1000

	C6	C8	C10
Alley, the Exciting New Roaring Stalking Alligator, Marx Co., 1960s, 17-1/2" long; five actions	150	225	300
American Airlines 4 Prop Airliner, Waco Co., 12" long, 1960s, 16-1/2" wingspan; four actions	120	180	240
American Airlines DC-7, w/automatic turnover propellers, Linemar, c. 1950s, 19" wingspan; seven actions	200	300	400
American Airlines Airliner DC-7 Multiaction, Yonezawa Co., 1960s, 21" long, 23-1/2" wingspan; seven actions	195	285	380
American Airlines Airliner DC-7, Linemar Co., 1960s, 17-1/2" long, 19" wingspan; seven actions	200	325	450
American Airlines Electra, Linemar Co., 1950s, 18" long, 19-1/2" wingspan	175	300	450
American Airlines Flagship Caroline, Linemar Co., 1950s, 18" long, 19-1/2" wingspan; three actions	175	300	400
American Circus Television Truck, Exelo Co., includes detachable metal antenna, 1950s, 9-1/4" long; six actions, rare	600	900	1200
Amphibian Navy Patrol Plane with flashing lights, Alps Co., 1950s, 13" long, 15" wingspan; five actions, rare	900	1350	1800
Amtrak Locomotive, ST Co., 1960s, 16" long; minor toy	60	90	120

	C6	C8	C10
Andy Gard Brink's Armored Car-Bank, General Molds & Plastics Corp., 1950s, 6-3/4 long; minor toy	40	60	80
Andy Gard Combat Knight No. 143, includes lance, stanchion, three plastic rings, and helmet plume, General Molds & Plastics Corp., 1960s, 10-1/4" high; three actions	50	75	100
Animated Santa on Rotating Globe, HTC Co., 1950s, 15" high; five actions	400	600	800
Animated Squirrel, S&E Co., 1950s, 8-1/2" tall; eight actions, rare	100	150	200
Answer Game Machine robot, educational toy, Ichida Co., 1960s, 14-1/2" tall; eight actions	400	600	800
Anti-Aircraft Jeep, K Co., 1950s, 9-1/2" long; five actions	100	150	200
Anti-Aircraft Jeep, includes detachable tin radar antenna, T-N Co., 1950s, 11" long; six actions	250	375	500
Anti-Aircraft Unit No. 1, Linemar Co., 1950s, 12-1/2" long; three electrical actions and three manual actions	150	225	300
Antique Gooney Car, Alps Co., 1960s, 9" long; four actions	100	125	150
Apollo II-American Eagle Lunar Module, includes detachable plastic antenna, DSK Co., 1960s, 10" high; seven actions	200	300	400

Amphibian Navy Patrol Plane, Alps Co., 1950s, $1,800

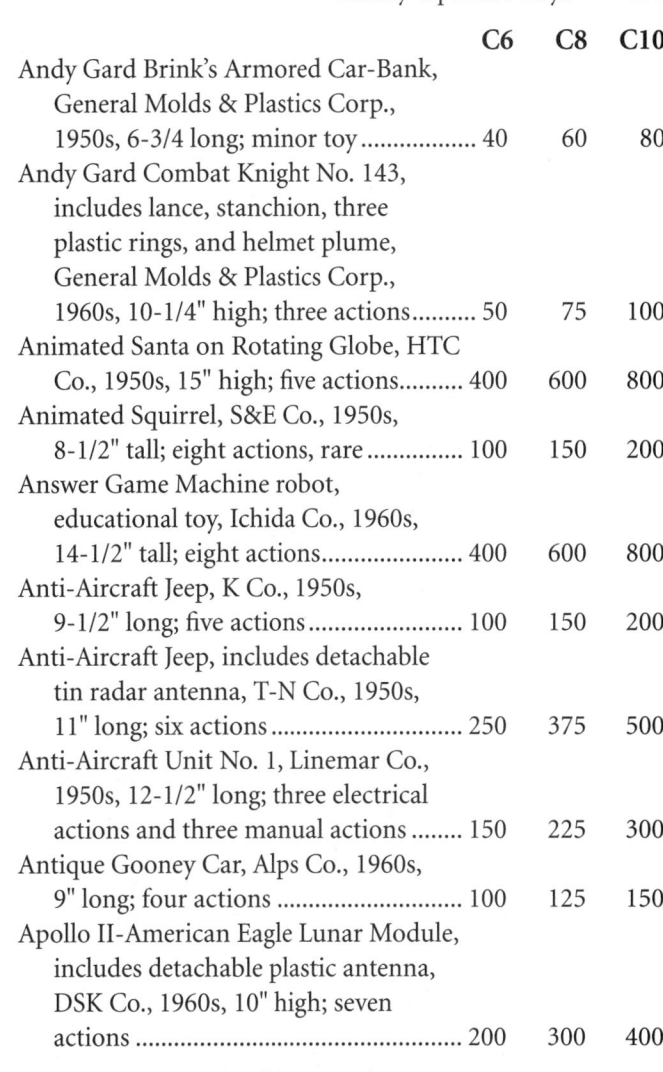

Atom Rocket 7, M-T Co., 1950s, $240

	C6	C8	C10
Apollo Lunar Module, DSK Co., 1970s, mostly plastic, 6" high; four actions.....	170	205	240
Apollo Spacecraft, M-T Co., includes detachable astronaut, 1960s, 10" long; four actions	200	300	400
Apollo Space Ship USA NASA, M-T Co., 1960s, 9" long; four actions	100	125	150
Apollo Super Space Capsule, S-H Co., 1960s, 9" high; five actions	100	150	200
Apollo-X Moon challenger rocket, T-N Co., 1960s, 16" long; six actions ...	150	225	300
Armored Attack Set, includes fifteen 2" plastic figures, Marx Co., 1960s, jeep 6-1/4" long and tank 5-1/4" long.........	150	225	300
Army Radio Jeep J1490, Linemar Co, 1950s, 7-1/4" long; four actions	75	125	165
Army Helicopter, Huey by Bell, T-N Co., 1960s, 10-1/2" long; six actions	90	135	180
Arthur A-Go-Go, 1960s, Alps Co., includes detachable cymbals and drum set, 10" high; six actions	130	200	295
Astro Captain, Daiya Co., 1960s, 6-1/2" tall; three actions, rare	300	450	600
Astro Dog, (looks like Snoopy), "Y" Co., 1960s, 11" high; two cycles; five actions.........	100	150	200
Astro Dog, Y-M Co., 1960s, 11" tall; three actions.........	90	135	180
Astrobase, motorized, Ideal Co., 1960s, 20" high; six actions	140	210	280
Atom Motorcycle, M-T Co., 1950s, 11-3/4" long; five actions	500	750	1000
Atom Rocket 7 vehicle with fins, M-T Co., 1950s, 9-1/2" long; four actions	120	180	240
Atomic Boat, Famus Co., 1950s, 15" long; minor toy.........	150	225	300
Atomic Fighter robot, S-H Co., 1950s, 11" tall; five actions	100	150	200
Atomic Rocket X-1800, M-T Co., 1960s, 9" long; three actions	150	225	300
Attacking Martian Robot, S-H Co., 1950s, 11-1/2" tall; seven actions, two cycles ..	150	200	250
Auto-Top Ferrari Convertible, Bandai Co., 1960s, 11" long; three actions	450	675	900
Automated Santa, Santa Creations Co., c. 1960s, 10-1/4" tall; three actions	100	150	200
Automatic Toll Gate, Sears, includes 8 tin Valiant, 1955, 16" x 17" base; six actions	150	225	300
B-58 Hustler Jet, Marx Co., 1950s, 21" long, 12" wingspan; four actions ...	425	650	925

	C6	C8	C10
Baby Carriage, includes plastic baby bottle to activate switch, 1950s, T-N Co., 11-3/4" long, 7" high; minor toy	60	90	120
Ball Blowing Clown, w/ball, T-N Co., 1950s, 11" tall; three actions.........	200	300	400
Ball Playing Bear, includes five celluloid balls and one umbrella, no marking, 1940s, 10-1/2" tall; six actions, rare	200	300	400
Ball Playing Dog, Linemar Co., 1950s, 9" high; three actions.........	125	200	250
Balloon Blowing Monkey, Alps Co., 1950s, 11-1/8" tall; five actions w/balloon	100	150	200
Balloon Blowing Teddy Bear, Alps Co., 1950s, 11-1/8" tall; six actions w/balloon	100	150	200
Balloon Vendor, includes four plastic balloons and tin tray, "Y" Co., 1960s, 12" tall; four actions	130	195	260
Baragon (Godzilla), Bullmark Co., 1960s, 10" tall; three actions.........	290	435	580
Barber Bear, T-N Co. (Linemar), 1950s, 9-1/2" tall; five actions	175	300	400
Barking Boxer Dog, Marx, 1950s, 7" long; minor toy.........	45	65	85

Barber Bear, T-N Co. (Linemar), 1950s, $400

	C6	C8	C10
Barking Dog, STS Co., 1950s, 7" long, 7" high; four actions, two cycles	50	75	100
Barking Spaniel Dog, Marx, 1950s, 7" long; minor toy	50	75	100
Barney Bear Drummer, Alps Co., 1950s, 11" tall; five actions, resembles Steiff bear	130	195	260
Barnyard Rooster, Marx, 1950s, 10" high; five actions	100	150	200
Bartender, T-N Co., 1960s, 11-1/2" tall; six actions	50	75	100
Batmobile, 1972 National Periodical Publications, ASC Co., 12" long; three actions	200	300	400
Battery Locomotive No. 123, T-N Co., 1950s, 10" long; three actions	30	45	60
Bear Chef (Cutey Cook), includes chef hat and tin litho egg, "Y" Co., 1960s, 9-1/2" tall; five actions	175	250	325
Bear Target Game, includes gun, rubber-tipped darts, detachable drum M-T Co., 1950s, 8-3/4" high and 4" x 5" base; four actions	180	280	375
Bear the Cashier, M-T Co., 1950s, 7-1/2" high; five actions	200	300	400
Bear the Magician, MTS Co., 1950s, 12-1/2" tall; nine actions, rare	1000	1500	2000
Beauty Parlor Bear, S&E Co., 1950s, 9-1/2" high; seven actions, rare	600	900	1200
Begging Puppy, "Y" Co., 1960s, 9" long; six actions	40	60	80
Bengali the Exciting New Growling, Prowling Tiger, Marx Co., 1961, Linemar Div., 18-1/2" long from nose to end of tail; three actions, two cycles	100	150	200

Beauty Parlor Bear, S&E Co., 1950s, $1,200.

	C6	C8	C10
Betty Bruin Cashier, Linemar, 1950s, 9" tall; six actions: See Super Susie			
Big Dipper, includes three tin cars, Technofix Co., 1960s, 21" long, 11" high; minor toy	100	150	200
Big Hunter Automatic Gun, Tada Co., 1950s, 21" long extended; three actions	50	75	100
Big John, Alps Co., 1960s, 12" high; three actions	60	90	120
Big John the Indian Chief, T-N Co., c. 1960s, 12-1/2" tall; five actions	100	150	200
Big Loo Your Friend from the Moon, includes ball, darts, compass, etc., Marx Co., 1960s, 38" tall; twelve actions	950	1500	2200
Big Max Robot, Remco Co., 1958, 8" long, 7" tall; four actions	80	125	175
The Big Parade, includes detachable gun and baton, Marx Co., 1963, 11-1/2" tall, 15" wide; four actions	120	180	240
Big Ring Circus Truck, M-T Co., 1950s, 13" long; three actions	140	210	280
Big Shot Cadillac, T-N Co., 1950s, 10" long; four actions, rare	200	300	400
Big Wheel Coca Cola Truck, Taiyo Co., 1970s; three actions	80	120	160
Big Wheel Family Camper, 1970s, 10" long; three actions	60	90	120
Big Wheel Ice Cream Truck, 1970s, 10" long; three actions	60	90	120
Biller Train No. 573, includes rubber cable track and two hopper cars, T-N Co., 1950s, 13" long; a minor toy, rare	70	105	140
Billy Blastoff Space Scout, Eldon Co., 1960s, 16" long; four actions	90	135	180
Billy the Kid Sheriff, "Y" Co., 1950s, 10-1/2" tall; four actions, two cycles	200	300	400
Bimbo the Clown, Alps Co., includes detachable hat, 1950s, 9-1/4" tall; three actions	190	325	400
Bingo Clown, T-N Co., 1950s, 13" tall; three actions	200	300	400
Blacksmith Bear, A-1 Co., 1950s, 9-1/2" tall; six actions	200	300	400
Black Smithy Bear, T-N Co., 1950s, 9" high; four actions, rare	150	200	250
Blink-A-Gear-Robot, S-H Co., 1960s, 14-1/2" tall; five actions	400	600	800
Blinky-the-Clown, includes multicolor paper hat, no marking, 1950s, 10-1/2" tall; five actions	300	450	600

	C6	C8	C10
Blow-Up-Ball Locomotive, includes celluloid ball, M-T Co., 1950s, 9-1/2" long; minor toy	80	120	160
Blushing Willie, "Y" Co., 1960s, 10" tall; four actions	65	85	110
Bobby Drinking Bear, "Y" Co., 1950s, 10" tall; six actions	200	300	400
Bobby the Drumming Bear, Alps Co., 1950s, 10" tall; four actions	175	275	380
Boeing 727 Jet Liner, "Y" Co., 1960s, 17-1/2" long, 16-1/4" wingspan; three actions	140	210	280
Boeing 727 Jet Plane, M-T Co., 1960s, 12-1/2" long, 10-3/8" wingspan; three actions	150	225	300
Bomber Pilot, K-O Co., 1960s, 10-1/2" long, 9" wingspan; six actions	190	285	380
Bongo, Drumming Monkey, includes plastic hat, Alps Co., 1960s, 9-1/2" high; three actions	80	120	160
Bongo Player, Alps Co., 1960s, 10" tall; four actions	80	120	160
Bowling Bank, M.B. Daniel & Co., 1960s, 10" long; three actions	100	150	200
Brave Eagle, T-N Co., 1950s, five actions; 11" tall	100	150	200
Breakfast Chef, includes plastic egg and coffee maker, K Co., 1960s, 8-1/4" tall; minor toy	70	105	140
Brewster the Rooster, Marx Co., 1950s, 9-1/2" high; five actions	150	200	250
Bristol Bulldog Airplane, T-360, S&E Co., 12" long,14-1/2" wingspan; four actions (lights, prop spins and stop and go, noise)	160	240	320
Broadway Trolley, M-T Co., 1950s, 10-1/2" long; four actions, two cycles: See Tinkling Trolley			
Bruno the Accordion Bear, "Y" Co., 1950s, 10-1/2" tall; five actions	150	225	300
Bubble Blowing Bear, M-T Co., 1950s, 9-1/2" high, 4" x 5" base; four actions	150	225	300
Bubble Blowing Boil Over Car, M-T Co., 1950s, 10" long; three actions	100	150	200
Bubble Blowing Boy, "Y" Co., 1950s, 7" high; four actions	100	200	300
Bubble Blowing Bunny, "Y" Co., 1950s, 7" high; four actions	100	150	200
Bubble Blowing Dog, "Y" Co., 1950s, 8" high; three actions	100	150	200
Bubble Blowing Kangaroo, M-T Co., 1950s, 9" high (base to tip of ears); three actions, rare	200	300	400

	C6	C8	C10
Bubble Blowing Lion, M-T Co., 1950s, 7-1/2" high, 3-1/2" x 7" base; four actions	100	150	200
Bubble Blowing Musician, "Y" Co., 1950s, 11" tall; three actions	250	350	450
Bubble Blowing Monkey, includes plastic bowl for bubble solution, Alps Co., 1950s, 10" tall; four actions	125	150	225
Bubble Blowing Popeye, Linemar Co., 1950s, 11-3/4" tall; five actions	750	1200	2500
Bubble Blowing Washing Bear, includes plastic washtub, "Y" Co., 1950s, 8" high; three actions	200	275	350
Bubbling Bull, Linemar Co., w/plastic bowl, 1950s, 6-1/2" long, 8" high; five actions	100	150	200
Bulldozer, T-N Co., 1950s, 7-1/2" long; five actions	60	80	120
Bulldozer, M-T Co., 1950s, 11" long; six actions	70	105	140
Bunny the Cashier, M-T Co., 1950s, 7-1/2" high; five actions	150	225	300
Bunny the Magician, includes card-ribbon apparatus for card trick, Alps Co., 1950s, 14-1/2" tall; five actions	300	400	500
Burger Chef, includes chef's hat and tin-litho hamburger, "Y" Co., 1950s, 9" tall; eight actions	150	225	325
Busy Bizzy Friendly Bug, M-T Co., 1950s, 6-1/4" long; three actions	60	90	120
The Busy Housekeeper, Alps Co., 1950s, 8-1/2" tall; four actions	175	300	375
The Busy Housekeeper (bunny), Alps Co., 1950s, 10" tall; four actions	175	250	325
Busy Cart Robot, includes plastic wheelbarrow, S-H Co., c. 1960s, 11" high; four actions	200	300	400
Busy Secretary, Linemar Co., 1950s, 7-1/2" high, 7-1/4" long; seven actions	125	200	300
Busy Shoe Shining Bear, Alps Co., 1950s, 10" high; five actions	110	175	240
Butt Stompin' Ashtray, includes tin manhole cover, ashtray insert and 4-1/2" high plastic shoe, Poynter Prod., 1977, 7-1/4" high; four actions	40	60	80
Buttons, Puppy with a Brain, also called Buttons the Push Button Pup, Marx, 1960s, 12" high; eight actions	200	300	400
B-Z Porter Baggage truck, includes three pieces of luggage M-T Co.,1950s, 7-1/2" long, 6-1/2" high; minor toy	140	210	280

	C6	C8	C10
B-Z Rabbit, M-T Co., c. 1950s, 7" long; four actions	60	90	120
B-Z Vendor, ice cream cart, M-T Co., 1950s, 7-1/2" long; three actions, rare	450	675	900
Cabin Cruiser, SGK Co., c. 1950s, 21-1/2" long; three actions	150	225	300
Cabin Cruiser with Outboard Motor, Linemar Co., 1950s, 12" long; minor toy	100	135	200
Cable Train, T-N Co., 1940s, 12" long; four-piece set; minor toy	80	120	160
Cadillac car, Ashai Toy Co., 1949, 10" long; three actions	150	225	300
Calypso Joe, Linemar, 1950s, 11" tall; four actions, rare	190	310	400
Camera Shooting Bear, includes plastic worms, Linemar Co., 1950s, 11" tall; five actions also called Cine-Bear	350	475	700
Candy Vending Machine Bank, Wonderful Toy Co., 1950s, 9" high; five actions, rare	600	900	1200
Capitol Airlines Viscount 321, Linemar, 1950s, 11" long, 14" wingspan; four actions	160	240	320
Cappy the Baggage Porter Dog, Alps Co., 1960s, 12" high, 11" long; four actions	100	150	200
Captain Blushwell, "Y" Co., 1960s, 11" tall; six actions	80	120	160
Captain Hook, includes tin sword and felt hat, Marusan Co., 1950s, 10-3/4" high; three actions, rare	800	1200	1600
Caterpillar, Alps Co., 1950s, 16" long; three actions	90	135	180
Caterpillar Tank M-1, M-T Co., 1950s, 8-1/2" long, 11" long with barrel extended; five actions	150	225	300
Central Choo Choo, M-T Co., 1960s, 15" long; three actions	40	60	80
Champion Weight Lifter, Y-M Co., 1960s, 10" tall; five actions	100	150	200
Chaparral 2F car, Alps Co., 1960s, 11" long; five actions	80	120	160
Charlie the Drumming Clown, includes detachable drum and cymbals, Alps Co., 1950s, 9-1/2" tall; six actions	150	225	300
Charlie Weaver, T-N Co., 1962, 12" tall; six actions	75	100	125
Change Man Robot, astronaut, S-H Co., 1960s, 13-1/4" tall; four actions, rare	4000	6000	8000
Charm the Cobra, Alps Co., 1960s, 6" high; three actions	90	130	175

	C6	C8	C10
Chee Chee Chihuahua, Mego Co., 1960s, 8" high; five actions	50	75	100
Chef Cook, includes tin litho egg and hat, "Y" Co., 1960s, 11-1/2" tall w/hat; five actions	100	225	300
Chemical Fire Engine, HTC Co., 1950s, 10" long; four actions	100	150	200
Chief Robotman, K.O. Co., 1950s, 12" tall; four actions	450	675	900
Chimp and Pup Rail Car, T-N Co., 1950s, 8" high; four actions	90	135	180
Chimp with Xylophone, includes four records and hammer, "Y" Co., 1970s, 12" long, 8" high; minor toy	100	150	200
Chimpee the One-Man Drummer, includes detachable drum and cymbals, Alps Co., 1950s, 9" high; six actions	70	105	140
Chippy the Chipmunk, Alps Co., 1950s, 12" long (nosetip to tail tip); four actions	75	120	155
Christmas Time, Marusan Co., 1950s, 10" high, 7" base diameter; three actions, rare	400	600	800
Cindy the Meowing Cat, Tomiyama Co., 1950s, 12" high (nosetip to tail tip); four actions, two cycles	50	75	100
Cine Bear: See Camera Shooting Bear			
Circus Elephant with Blowing Ball and Parasol, includes celluloid ball and tin litho umbrella, T-N Co., 1950s, 9-3/4" high; three actions, rare	200	275	350
Circus Fire Engine, M-T Co., 1960s, 11" long; four actions	110	175	235
Circus Jet, T-N Co., 1950s, 9" high assembled, jet 6-1/4" long; three actions	90	135	180
Circus Lion, includes whip and flannel carpet w/levers Rock Valley Toy Co. (Via), 1950s, 11" high; four actions, two cycles	300	450	600
Clancy the Great, includes plastic hat and test coin, Ideal Toy Co., 1960s, 19-1/2" tall without hat; three actions	85	135	200
Climbing Donald Duck On His Friction Fire Engine, Linemar Co., 1950s, 12" long; four actions	300	525	700
Climbing Fireman, includes three tin ladder sections, T.P.S. Co., 1950s, 24" high assembled; five actions	200	300	400
Climbing Linesman, includes three tin pole sections, T.P.S. Co., 1950s, 24" high when assembled; three actions, rare	250	375	500

	C6	C8	C10
Clown Circus Car, M-T Co., 1960s, 8-1/2" long, 9" high; five actions	100	175	235
Clown and Lion, M-T Co., 1960s, 11-3/4" high from base to top of tree; four actions	250	375	500
Clown on Unicycle, M-T Co., 1960s, 10-1/2" high; three actions	180	280	375
Clown with Lion, includes spiral apparatus, T-N Co., 1950s, 12" high; four actions	200	300	400
The Clowns Bank, all plastic, unmarked, 1940s, 10" high; minor toy	80	120	160
Clown the Magician No. 40244, includes card-ribbon apparatus for card trick, Alps Co., 1950s, 12" tall; six actions	200	300	400
Coca-Cola Dispenser Bank, includes four plastic Coke glasses and rubber stopper, Linemar Co., 1950s, 9-1/2" tall; minor toy	450	675	900
Cock-A-Doodle-Doo Rooster, Mikuni Co., 1950s, 8" high; four actions	80	120	160
Colonel Hap Hazard Robot, Marx Co., 1968, 11-1/4" tall; four actions	300	440	600
Combi-O-Mixer, Excelo Co., mixer-blender, 1950s, 9" long, 9" high; minor toy	30	45	60
Comic Hungry Bug, VW auto, Tora (S-T) Co., 1970s, 7-3/4" long; five actions	40	60	80
Comic Musical Car, T-N Co., 1960s, 6" long, 8-1/2" tall; four actions	70	105	140

	C6	C8	C10
Comic Road Grader, Bandai Co., 1950s, 9" long; four actions	70	105	140
Comic Road Roller, Bandai Co., 1960s, 9" long; four actions	70	105	140
Coney Island Penny Machine, includes plastic prizes, Remco Co., 1950s, 13" high; minor toy	90	130	300
Coney Island Rocket Ride, Alps Co., 1950s, 13-1/2" high; four actions	300	450	600
Continental Blue Locomotive, M-T Co., 1960s, 12-1/2" long; four actions	30	45	60
Corvair Bertone, Bandai Co., 1970s, 12" long; four actions	50	75	100
Cowboy Riding Horse, T-N Co., 1950s, 7" high; three actions	70	105	140
Cragstan Astronaut, Daiya Co., 1950s, 14" tall; four actions	400	600	800
Cragstan Beep Beep Greyhound Bus, Cragstan Co., 1950s, 20" long; three actions	100	150	220
Cragstan Biplane, 7F7, U.S. Navy, T-N Co., 1950s, 9-1/2" long, 11-1/2" wingspan; four actions	200	300	400
Cragstan Biplane 7F18, T-N Co., 1950s, 12" long, 14-3/8" wingspan; five actions	220	330	440
Cragstan Crapshooter, includes pair of small dice, "Y" Co., 1950s, 9-1/2" tall; four actions	100	150	200

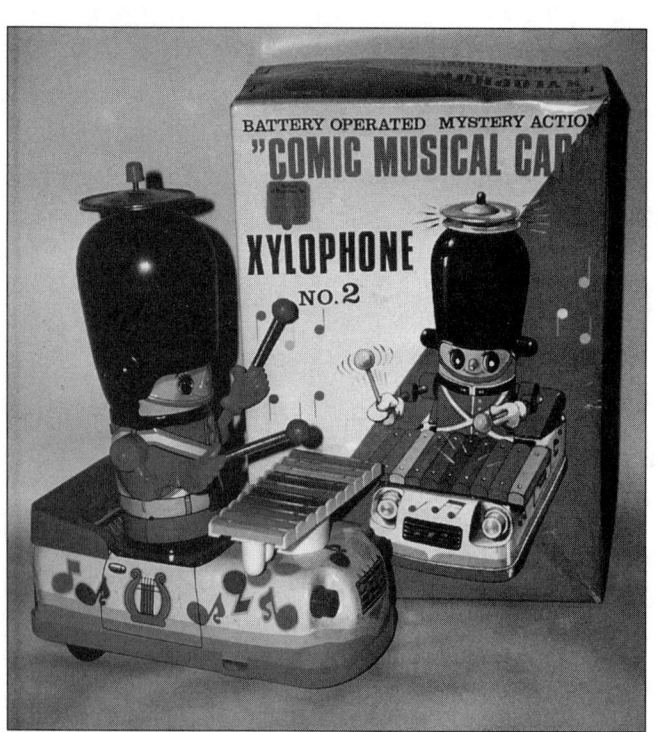

Comic Musical Car, T-N Co., 1960s, $140

Cragstan Mother Goose, "Y" Co., 1960s, $165

	C6	C8	C10
Cragstan Crapshooting Monkey, includes pair of small dice, Alps Co., 1950s, 9" tall; three actions	100	150	200
Cragstan Dishwasher Automatic, includes twenty-four-piece dish set, two dish baskets and metal tray, Alps Co., 1960s, 9" high; minor toy	50	75	100
Cragstan Firebird III, Alps Co., 1950s, 11-1/2" long; three actions	400	600	800
Cragstan Flying Plane with Pylon Tower, 1950s, plane 8" long, 9-1/2" wingspan, tower 26" high; minor toy	120	180	240
Cragstan Great Astronaut, Alps Co., 1960s, 14" tall; five actions	500	750	1000
Cragstan Mr. Robot, "Y" Co., 1960s, 10-1/2" tall; four actions	350	525	700
Cragstan Mother Goose, "Y" Co., 1960s, 8-1/4" high; six actions	100	150	200
Cragstan One-Arm Bandit, "Y" Co., 1960s, 6-1/4" high; three actions, includes 3" x 3-1/4" sign	100	150	200
Cragstan Peanut Vendor, includes felt hat, T-N Co., 1950s, 8" tall; five actions	180	270	360
Cragstan Playboy, Cragstan Co., 1960s, 13" high; five actions	75	150	200
Cragstan Roulette, A Gambling Man, includes steel ball, chips, tin table, game sheet, "Y" Co., 1960s, 9" tall; five actions	150	225	300
Cragstan Satellite, Cragstan Co., 1950s, 8" diameter, 5-1/2" high	90	135	180
Cragstan Smoking Jet Plane - U.S.A.F. T-N Co., 1950s, 11-1/2" long, 7-1/2" wingspan; four actions	120	180	240
Cragstan Talking Robot, "Y" Co., 1960s, 10-1/2" tall; three actions	400	550	800
Cragstan Telly Bear, S&E Co., 1950s, 8" high; six actions	240	360	480
Cragstan Tootin'-Chugging Locomotive, longest single-piece battery toy made, 1950s, Cragstan Co., 24" long; three actions	70	105	140
Cragstan Two Gun Sheriff, includes tin hat, "Y" Co., 1950s, 9-1/2" tall; five actions	175	225	300
Cragstan Tugboat, San Co., 1950s, 12-3/4" long; three actions	140	210	280
Cragstan Vertol 1107 Helicopter, includes rotors, T-N Co., 1950s, 13-1/2" long; four actions	120	180	240
Cragstan Western Locomotive, Cragstan Co., 1950s, 12" long; four actions	60	90	120

	C6	C8	C10
Crane Tractor, SKK Co., 1950s, 7-1/2" long, 11-1/2" high extended	70	105	140
Crawling Baby, Linemar Co., 1940s, 11" long, 8-1/2" high; minor toy	50	75	100
Crazy Car, Marusan Co., 1950s, 9" long; five actions	60	90	120
Cycling Daddy, Bandai Co., 1960s, 10" high; four actions	125	175	225
Cyclist Clown, K Co., 1950s, 7" high; seven actions	200	300	400
Cyclist Clown, M-T Co., 1950s, 6-1/2" high; six actions	200	300	400
Cyclist Clown, Alps Co., 1950s, 9" high; five actions	200	300	400
Cymbal Playing Turnover Monkey, T-N Co., 1960s, 8" tall; three actions	50	75	100
Daisy the Jolly Drumming Duck, includes detachable drum and cymbals, Alps Co., 1950s, 9" high; seven actions, rare	150	200	275
Dalmatian One-Man Band No. 90262, includes cymbals and stand, Alps Co., 1950s, 9" high; six actions	120	180	240
Dancing Merry Chimp, Kuramochi Co. (C-K), 1960s, 11" tall; five actions	100	150	200
Dancing Sweethearts, T-N Co., 1950s, 7" tall; minor toy	90	135	180
Dandy the Happy Drumming Pup, includes detachable drum and cymbals, Alps Co., 1950s, 8-1/2" high; six actions	85	150	200
Dapper Jigger Dancer, Haji Co., 1950s, 12" tall; minor toy	150	225	300
Dennis the Menace (Playing London Bridge), includes xylophone Rosko, 1950s, 9" high; three actions	120	180	240
Dentist Bear, includes detachable head, S&E Co., 1950s, 9-1/2" tall, 6-3/4" x 4-1/4" base; seven actions	300	450	600
Desert Patrol Jeep, includes turret gunner, M-T Co., 1960s, 11" long; four actions	90	135	180
Destroyer 206 boat, includes detachable antenna and five depth charges, "Y" Co., 1950s, 14" long; six actions	110	165	220
Diesel Locomotive, Cragstan Co., 1950s, 16-1/2" long; minor toy	30	45	60
Dino Robot, S-H Co., 1960s, 11" tall; five actions	500	750	1000
Disney Acrobats (Mickey, Donald and Pluto), Linemar Co., 1950s, 9" high; minor toys	300	625	800

	C6	C8	C10
Disney Fire Engine, Linemar Co., 1950s, 11" long; four actions 425		660	880
Disneyland Fire Engine, Linemar Co., 1950s, 18" long; five actions.................. 350		550	750
Docking Rocket, includes plastic radar antenna, Daiya Co., 1960s, 16" long; 24" extended; six actions.................... 100		150	200
Dog Family, Alps Co., 1960s, 11" long; four actions 50		75	100
Dog Sled, 1950s, T-N Co., 14" long; four actions, rare 300		450	600
Dolly Dressmaker, includes cloth sample, Dolly Seamstress on box, T-N Co., 1950s, 7" high; ten actions, rare 175		250	325
Donald Duck, Linemar Co., 1960s, 8" tall; four actions.................................. 200		300	400
Donald Duck Locomotive, M-T Co., 1970s, 9" long; three actions................. 150		225	300
Donald Duck Trolley, M-T Co., 1960s, 11" high; three actions 160		240	320
Douglas C-124 Globe Master, Yonezawa Co., c. 1950s, 20-1/2" wingspan, 18" long; eight actions...................... 300		450	600
Douglas DC-9TWA Jet Plane, T-N Co., 1960s, 14" long, 17" wingspan; four actions... 100		150	200
Doxie the Dog, Linemar Co., 1950s, 9" long; five actions 20		25	45
Dozo the Steaming Clown, T-N Co., 1960s, Rosko toys, 10" tall; five actions.. 200		300	400
Dream Boat Hot Rod, T-N Co., c. 1950s, 7" long; four actions............................. 140		210	280
Drill, includes attachments, Linemar Co., 1950s, 6" long; minor toy................ 20		30	40
Drinker's Savings Bank, Illfelder Co., 1960s, 9" high; minor toy 90		135	180
Drinking Bear, Alps Co., c. 1970s, 12" high; six actions 75		125	150
Drinking Captain, S&E Co., 1960s, 12" tall; six actions 100		150	200
Drinking Dog, "Y" Co., 1950s; four actions... 90		135	180
Drinking Licking Cat, T-N Co., 1950s, 10" high, 4" x 4" base; six actions 120		180	240
Drum Bear, Alps Co., c. 1950s, 7-3/4" tall; five actions (walks, lights, beats drum, noise) 150		225	300
Drum Monkey, Yada Co., 1970s, 8" high; three actions 40		60	80
Drummer Bear, Alps Co., 1950s, 10" tall; six actions 140		210	280

	C6	C8	C10
Drumming Mickey Mouse, Linemar, 1950s, 10" tall; four actions, rare.......... 800		1000	1600
Drumming Polar Bear, Alps Co., 1960s, 12" tall; three actions 75		120	165
Ducky Duckling, Alps Co., 1960s, 8" high; four actions 35		55	85
Dump Truck No. 7343, T-N Co., 1960s, 10-1/4" long; seven actions..................... 60		90	120
Dynamic Fighter Robot, Junior Toy Co., 1960s, 10" tall; five actions..................... 70		105	140
Earthman-Astronaut, T-N Co., 1950s, 9-1/2" tall; five actions, rare.................. 900		1300	1800
El Toro-Cragstan Bullfighter, includes detachable tin matador, T-N Co., 1950s, 9-1/2" long; four actions 90		145	200
Electric Powered TV and Radio Station, Marx, 1950s, 30" long; three actions...... 80		120	160
Electric Remote Control Robot, M-T Co., 1950s, 7-1/2" tall; four actions, rare..... 500		750	1000
Electric Robot, Marx, 1950s, 14-1/2" tall; five actions.. 300		450	600
Electric School Bus, M-T Co., 1950s, 9-1/2" long; minor toy 70		105	140
Electric Vibraphone, T-N Co., 1950s, 7-1/2" long, 5-1/2" high; three actions... 70		105	140
Electro Special Racer, Yonezawa Co., 1950s, 10" long; three actions............... 500		750	1000
Electro Train Transcontinental, M Co., 1950s, 20-1/2" long, three pieces; three actions.. 90		135	180
Electronic Countdown, Ideal Toy Co., 1959, 24" long; six actions 60		90	120
Electronic Fighter Jet 4800, 1950s, 19" long; eleven actions 120		180	240
Electronic Fire House, Banner Co., includes plastic fire engine, 1940s, 7" square; minor toy 70		105	140
Electronic Periscope (Nautilus) Firing Range, Cragstan, 1950s, 11" high on tripod; three actions 100		150	200
Eectronic Twin Train Set #372, includes two three-piece trains, Woodhaven Metal Stamping Co., 1950s, 28" long, 11" wide; minor toy 100		150	200
Engine Robot, S-H Co., 1960s, 9-1/2" tall; four actions......................... 100		150	200
Excavator Robot, S-H Co., 1960s, 10" tall; four actions............................. 200		300	400
Expert Motor Cyclist, MT Co., 1950s, 12" long; five actions, rare 600		900	1200
F-14-A Navy Jet Fighter, T-N Co., 1960s, 13" long, 13" wingspan; six actions...... 200		300	400

	C6	C8	C10
F-101A Voodoo Fighter, K-O Co., minor toy, 15" long, 14" wingspan; 1960s	100	150	200
FS-059 Fighter Plane, jet w/prop, T-N Co., 1950s, 11" long, 13" wingspan; five actions	170	255	340
Fairyland Loco, locomotive, Daiya Co., 1950s, 9" long; four actions	60	90	120
Farm Truck, Alps Co., 1960s, 11" long; three actions	120	180	240
Farm Truck, T-N Co., 1950s, 9" long; five actions	120	180	240
F.D. Fire Engine, Y-M Co., 1960s, 10" long, 12" high when ladder is extended; four actions	110	165	220
Feeding Bird Watcher, includes detachable tin branch and bird, Linemar, 1950s, 9" high; five action, rare	300	350	600
Ferris Wheel Truck, Linemar Co., c. 1950s, 11" long; four actions	400	600	800
Fido the Xylophone Player, includes detachable xylophone, Alps Co., c. 1950s, 8-3/4" high; six actions (body sways, head turns, arms activate lights and sound)	115	170	240
Fighter (airplane), K-O Co., 1960s, 10-1/2" long, 9" wingspan; six actions	160	240	320
Fighter Airplane, Marx Co., c. 1960s, 7" wingspan; four actions	60	90	120
Fighter Jet, Marx Co., c. 1960s, 7" wingspan; four actions	60	90	120
Fighting Bull, Alps Co., 1960s, 9-1/2" long; five actions	100	125	150

	C6	C8	C10
Fighting Bull, Rock Valley Tech Co., 1970s, 12" long nose to tail tip; four actions, two cycles	100	150	200
Fighting Robot, all plastic, S-H Co., 1970s, 10" tall; four actions	70	105	140
Fighting Spaceman, S-H Co., 1960s, 12" tall; five actions	150	225	300
Fire Boat, M-T Co., 1950s, 15" long; five actions	150	225	300
Fire Chief No. 8 Car, "Y" Co., 1960s, 11-1/4" long; three actions	90	135	180
Fire Chief Mystery Action Car, T-N Co., 1960s, 9-3/4" long; four actions	130	195	260
Fire Command Car, T-N Co., 1950s; five actions	170	255	340
Fire Engine, Marusan Co., 1950s, 9" long; four actions	120	180	240
Fire Engine, T-N Co. (Electro Toy), 1950s, 9" long, ladder extends 13"; three actions	150	225	300
Fire Engine, "Y" Co., 1950s, 12" long, ladder extends 16"; six actions	100	150	200
Fire Engine, S-H Co., c. 1950s, 8" long; three actions	100	150	200
Fire Patrol Boat, KKS Co., 1950s, 12" long; three actions	110	165	220
Firebird Racer, Tomiyama Co., 1950s, 14-1/4" long; four actions	300	450	600
Fire Tricycle, T-N Co., 1950s, 9-1/2" long; four actions	180	270	360
Fishing Bear (also Fishing Panda Bear, Polar Bear, Forest Bear), includes detachable pond, tin fish, Alps Co., 1950s, 10" high; six actions	200	300	400
Fishing Bears Bank, Wonderful Toy Co., 1950s, 9-1/2" tall; six actions, rare	500	750	1000
Flashing Jet-FC-657 Airplane-U.S.A.F. 7452, Marx Co., 1950s, 7" long, 6" wingspan; four actions	100	150	200
Flashy Jim, S.N.K. Co. (Ace), 1950s, 7-3/4" tall; minor toy, rare	1100	1650	2200
Flashy Ray Space Gun, T-N Co., 1950s, 18-1/2" long; minor toy	50	75	100
Flintstone Yacht, Remco Co., 1961, 17" long	90	145	200
The Floating Satellite Target Game, includes tin gun, rubber-tipped darts and celluloid ball, 1960s, 8-1/2" high	100	150	200
Flutter Birds, Alps Co., includes detachable pulley assembly, 1950s, 26-1/2" high when assembled; six actions, rare	300	450	600

Left to Right: Fighting Spaceman, S-H Co., 1960s, $300; Turn Signal Robot, T-N Co., 1960s, $320

	C6	C8	C10
Flying Dutchman-PH-KLM Airliner, T-N Co., 1950s, 11" long, 14" wingspan; five actions	100	150	200
Flying Jet Plane-Boeing 747P, J Toy Co., 1960s, 13" long, 12" wingspan; five actions	90	135	180
Flying Platform, Cragstan Co., includes detachable tin soldier, 1950s, 5-1/2" diameter, 9" high; four actions, rare	200	300	400
Flying Tiger Airplane, Marx Co., 1960s, 7" long, 7" wingspan; four actions w/remote control	60	90	120
Ford Model T, includes detachable tin roof, Nihonkogei Co., 1950s, 10-1/4" long; four actions	60	90	120
Ford Mustang 2 x 2, Wenmac-AMF Co., 1960s, 16" long; four actions	60	90	120
Ford Skyliner, T-N Co., 1950s, 9" long; four actions	100	150	200
4 Prop Airplane, Waco Co., 1960s, 17" long, 16-1/4" wingspan; four actions	140	210	280

Go-Go Girl, Poytner Prod. Co., 1969, $80

	C6	C8	C10
Fork Lift Truck, M-T Co., 1960s, 10-1/4" high; minor toy	80	120	160
Foto Finish, racehorse, M-T Co., 1950s, 12" long; minor toy	120	180	240
Frankenstein, tin, Marx Co. (Japan), 1950s, 12" tall; w/five actions, remote control	600	900	1200
Frankenstein Monster, T-N Co., 1960s, 14" tall; six actions	125	175	225
Frankie the Rollerskating Monkey, Alps Co., 1950s, 12" tall	150	225	300
Fred Flintstone on Dino, Marx Co. (Japan), 1961, 22" long; eight actions	400	600	800
Fred Flintstone Bedrock Band, Alps Co., 1962, 9-1/2" high; four actions	500	650	1000
Friendly Jocko, includes detachable cymbals, plastic cup; My Favorite Pet, Alps Co., 1950s, 8" high; five actions	110	175	245
Fruit Juice Counter, includes plastic barrel, lid, glasses and tin tray, K Co., 1960s, 8" long, 8" high; three actions	90	135	180
Funland Cup Ride, Sonsco Co., includes six umbrellas, 1960s, 7" tall, 6" x 6" base; three actions	100	150	200
Galloping Cowboy Savings Bank, "Y" Co. (Cragstan), 1950s, 8" high, 6-1/2" long; minor toy, rare	450	675	900
Gama Mercedes-Benz 220 SE Sedan, Mignon Co., 1960s, 9" long; three actions	150	225	300
Gear Robot, "Y" Co., 1960s, 10" tall; four actions	250	375	500
Gino the Neapolitan Balloon Blower, includes bubble solution plastic tray Tomiyama Co. (Rosko), 1960s, 10" tall; five actions	100	150	200
Girl with Baby Carriage, T-N Co., 1960s, 8" high; three actions	100	150	200
Go-Go Girl (bar toy), Poynter Prod. Co., 1969, 15-1/4" tall; minor toy, risqué toy, PG-rated	40	60	80
Go-Kart, M-T Co., includes control wire w/steering key, 1960s, 6-1/2" long; minor toy	90	135	180
Go-Kart, Rosko Co., includes detachable head, 1950s, 10" long; three actions	90	135	180
Godzilla, Bullmark Co., 1960s, 10-1/2" tall; five actions	300	450	600
Godzilla Monster, Marusan Co., 1970s; 11-1/2" tall; three actions	150	200	300
Golden Locomotive, Nihonkogei Co., 1950s, 10-1/2" long; minor toy	40	60	80

Gypsy Fortune Teller, Ichida Co., 1950s, $2,200.

	C6	C8	C10
Golden Gear Robot, S-H Co., 1960s, 9" tall; five actions	300	450	600
Golden Roto Robot, S-H Co., 1960s, 8-1/2" tall; five actions	100	150	200
Gomora Monster, includes plastic missiles, Bullmark Co., 1960s, 8" tall; four actions	150	225	300
Gorilla, T-N Co., white or brown, 1950s, 9-1/4" tall; five actions	200	300	400
Go-Stop Benz Racer, Marusan Co., 1950s, 11" long; three actions	150	225	300
Good Time Charlie, M-T Co., 1960s, 12" tall; seven actions	100	150	200
Grace Ocean Liner, M-T Co., 1950s, 15" long; three actions	250	375	500
Grandpa Bear, including rocking chair, Alps Co., 1950s, 9" tall; five actions	175	250	325
Grand-Pa Car, "Y" Co., 1950s, 9" long; four actions	75	100	125
Grandpa Panda Bear, M-T Co., 1950s, 9" tall; five actions	100	175	245
The Great Garloo, includes chain and medallion, Marx Co., 1960s, 23" tall; seven actions	300	450	600
Green Caterpillar, Daiva Co., 1950s, 19-1/2" long; three actions	150	250	350
Greyhound Bus, KKK. Co., 1950s, 7-1/4" long; minor toy	90	135	180
Greyhound Bus Scenicruiser, I.Y. Metal Toy Co., 1950s, 16" long; three actions	90	135	180
Greyhound Bus with Headlights, Linemar Co., 1950s, 10-1/4" long; three actions	100	150	200

	C6	C8	C10
Grumman F9F Navy Jet, Cougar, K Co., 1950s, 11-1/2" long, 10-1/4" wingspan; three actions	150	225	300
Guided Missile Launcher, includes plastic missiles, Irco Co., 1950s, 8" long, 3" tall, 5" wide; three actions	110	165	220
Gypsy Fortune Teller, includes twenty fortune cards, Ichida Co., 1950s, 12" high w/hat, 5-3/4" x 7" base; five actions, rare	1100	1700	2200
H-O Gauge Electric Train set with Real Smoke, seventeen-piece set, Amico Co., 1960s, 23" long	70	105	140
Hamburger Chef, includes tin frying pan, hamburger, plastic bottles, K Co., 1960s, 8" long, 8" high; three actions	125	200	275
Handy Hank Mystery Tractor, T-N Co., 1950s, 9" long; four actions	75	100	125
Happy Band Trios, M-T Co., 1970s, 12" high; seven actions, rare	400	600	800
Happy Clown Car, "Y" Co., 1960s, 6-1/2" long; three actions	100	150	200
Happy Clown Theater, w/Pinocchio-like puppet, "Y" Co., 1950s, 10" tall; three actions	200	300	400
The Happy Fiddler Clown, includes tin litho violin, Alps Co., 1950s, 9-1/2" high; four actions	200	300	425

Haunted House Bank, Brumberger Co., 1960s, $500.

	C6	C8	C10
Happy Miner, Bandai Co., 1960s, 11" tall; three actions	110	165	220
Happy Naughty Chimp, Daishin Co., 1960s, 9-1/2" high assembled; four actions	75	100	150
Happy 'N' Sad Face Cymbal Clown, "Y" Co., 10" tall, 1960s; five actions	120	180	200
Happy'n Sad Magic Face Clown, "Y" Co., 1960s, 10" tall; five actions	150	225	300
Happy Plane, TPS Co., 1960s, 9" long, 10-1/2" wingspan; three actions	100	150	200
Happy Santa, Z Co., 1960s, 11" tall; three actions	100	150	200
Happy Santa (walking), Alps Co., 1950s, 11" tall; five actions	150	225	300
Happy Santa One-Man Band, includes cymbals and stand Alps Co., 1950s, 9" high; six actions	100	185	245
Happy Singing Bird, M-T Co., 1950s, 9" high, bird 3" long, 5-5/8" diameter base; three actions	60	90	120
Happy the Clown Puppet Show (w/Pinocchio-like puppet), "Y" Co., 1960s, 10" tall; three actions	190	285	380
Happy Tractor, Daiya Co., 1960s, 8" long; four actions	40	60	80
Harbor Queen Boat, M-T Co., 1950s, 12" long; minor toy	150	225	300
Hasty Chimp, "Y" Co., 1960s, 9" high; four actions	50	75	100
Haunted House Mystery Bank (Disneyland promotion), Brumberger Co., 1960s, 7-5/8" high; four actions	300	425	550
Heavy Machine Gun, (includes detachable tripod and plastic ammo belt), T-N Co., 1950s, 24" long, 13" high on tripod; four actions	100	150	200
Hi Bouncer Moon Scout robot, includes five plastic balls, Marx Co., 1968, 11-1/4" tall; five actions, rare	450	675	900
High Jinks of the Circus, T-N Co., 1950s, 14" high, extends to 29"; six actions	250	350	450
Highway Drive, (includes tin magnetic car), T-N Co., 1950s, 15-1/2" long; three actions	70	105	140
Highway Patrol Police Special, "Y" Co., 1960s, 11-1/2" long; five actions	100	150	200
Highway Patrol Jeep, Daiya Co., 1950s, 10" long; four actions	70	105	140
Highway Skill Driving, K Co., 1960s, 13" long; three actions	70	105	140

	C6	C8	C10
Hiller Hornet Helicopter, Alps Co., 1950s, 12-1/4" long, 15" two-piece metal rotor; four actions	120	180	240
Hippo Chef (Cuty Cook), includes chef hat and tin litho egg, "Y" Co., 1960s, 10" tall; five actions	100	160	600
Hobo Clown with Accordion (w/cymbal-playing monkey), Alps Co., 1950s, 10-1/2" high; six actions	275	425	525
Hole-in-One Bank, includes marked test coin and golfer, no marking, 1960s, 8-1/2" long x 3-1/2" wide; minor toy	70	105	140
Holiday Sink-Stove Combination, includes three-piece pan set, T-N Co., 1950s, 9" high; minor toy	40	60	80
Hoop Zing Girl, Linemar Co., 1950s, 11-1/2" tall; minor toy	115	185	245
Hoopy the Fishing Duck, includes magnetic fish and detachable pond, Alps Co., 1950s, 10" high; seven actions	275	375	525
Hootin' Hollow Haunted House, 1960s, Marx, 11" high; eight actions	500	750	1000

The Hysterical Robot, S-H Co., 1060s, $300

	C6	C8	C10
Hooty the Happy Owl, Alps Co., 1960s, 9" tall; six actions	65	100	145
Hot Rod Car, T-N Co., 1950s, 10" long; minor toy	160	240	320
Hot Rod Custom 'T' Ford, Alps Co., 1960s, 10-1/2" long; four actions	180	270	360
Hot Rod Limousine, Alps Co., 1960s, 10-1/2" long; four actions	180	270	360
Hungry Baby Bear, "Y" Co., 1950s, 9-1/2" tall; six actions	200	300	400
Hungry Cat, Linemar Co., includes tin tray and plastic fish, 1960s, 9" high; seven actions	250	450	700
Hungry Hound Dog, "Y" Co., 1950s, 9-1/2" high; six actions	150	275	300
Hungry Sheep, M-T Co., 1950s, 9" long; three actions, two cycles	100	150	200
Hy Que Monkey, T-N Co., 1960s, 17" tall; six actions	150	225	300
The Hysterical Robot, (a.k.a. Hysterical Harry and Happy Harry), S-H Co., 1960s, 13-1/2" tall; seven actions	150	225	300
Ice Cream Baby Bear, M-T Co., 1950s, 9-1/2" high; three actions, rare	200	300	400
Ice Cream Truck, Bandai Co., 10-1/2" long, 1960s; five actions	100	150	200
Indian Joe, Alps Co., 12" tall, 1960s; four actions	75	110	150
Indian Signal Choo Choo, Kanto Toys Co., 1960s, 9-1/2" long; four actions	80	120	160
Interceptor, target game, S&E Co., 1950s, 13" high, 16" wingspan; four actions	150	225	300
Interplanetary Rocket, "Y" Co., 1960s, 14-3/4" tall; five actions	120	180	240
JDN 7673 Sedan-4-door, Distler Co., 1920s, 14" long; minor toy and one of the earliest battery-operated toys, rare	400	600	800
James Bond's Aston-Martin: See 007 Aston-Martin			
James Bond 007 Car M101, includes ejectable driver, Daiya Co., 1960s, 11" long; seven actions: See M101 Aston Martin			
Jeep USA, TKK Co., 1950s, 12-1/2" long; minor toy	70	105	140
Jeep No. 10560, Cragstan, 1950s, 5-1/2" long; minor toy	70	105	140
Jet Airport with 4 Jet Airplanes, Turnpike Lines (Sears), 1960s, 12-1/2" long; seven actions	200	275	350
Jet Plane Base, includes crank, "Y" Co., 1950s, 7-1/4" x 11" base, plane 9" long, 7" wingspan; seven actions, rare	450	675	900

	C6	C8	C10
Jig-Saw-Matic, Z Co., 1950s, 7-1/4" high, 4-1/2" x 8-1/2"; minor toy	40	60	80
Jo-Jo the Flipping Monkey, T-N Co. (Illfelder), 1970s, 10" high; minor toy	35	75	80
Jocko the Drinking Monkey, includes top hat, Linemar, 1950s, 11" tall; four actions	100	150	200
John's Farm Truck, T-N Co., 1950s, 9" long; seven actions	100	150	200
Jolly Bambino, includes candy pieces, Alps Co., 1950s, 9" high; five actions	200	300	400
The Jolly Bear Peanut Vendor, includes felt hat, T-N Co., 1950s, 8" high; five actions	250	285	500
Jolly Bear the Drummer Boy, K Co., 1950s, 7" tall; five actions	100	150	200
Jolly Bear with Robin, M-T Co., 1950s, 10" high; three actions, rare	400	600	800
Jolly Daddy, Marusan Co., 1950s, 8-3/4" tall; four actions	160	240	350
Jolly Drummer Chimpy, includes cymbals and stand, Alps Co., 1950s, 9" high; six actions	100	125	150
Jolly Drumming Bear, T-N Co., 1950s, 7" tall; four actions	100	125	150
Jolly Penguin, T-N Co., 1950s, 7" tall; five actions	100	150	200
Jolly Pianist, Marusan Co., 1950s, 8" high; five actions	100	150	200
Jolly Santa on Snow, includes tin skis, Alps Co., 1950s, 12-1/2" tall; four actions, two cycles	150	225	300

Jolly Penguin, T-N Co., 1950s, $200

	C6	C8	C10
Josie the Walking Cow, Daiya Co., 1950s, 14" long, 8-1/2" high; seven actions, two cycles	125	175	225
Journey Pup, S&E Co., c. 1950s, 7-1/2" long; four actions, remote control	75	100	125
Jumbo the Bubble-Blowing Elephant, includes plastic bowl for bubble solution, "Y" Co., 7-1/4" high, 1950s; three actions	55	85	115
Jungle Jumbo, B.C. Co., 1950s, 10" high; six actions, two cycles, hunter resembles Teddy Roosevelt	200	300	400
Jungle Trio, includes tin litho whistle, Linemar, 1950s, 8" high; eight actions	400	600	800
Jupiter Robot, Yonezawa Co., 1950s, 12-3/4" tall; four actions	150	225	300
Jupiter Rocket Launching Pad, T-N Co., 1960s, 8-1/2" long, 7" high	190	285	380
K-55 Electric Tractor, M-T Co., c. 1950s, 7" long; three actions	70	105	140
King Flying Saucer, K.O. Co., 1960s, 7-1/2" diameter; three actions	70	105	140
King Size Fire Engine, Bandai Co., 1960s, 12-1/2" long; three actions	150	225	300
Kissing Couple, Ichida Co., 1950s, 10-3/4" long; five actions	150	200	300
Kitchen-ette Stove and Sink, no marking, 1940s, 6-1/2" long x 6-3/4" high; minor toy, includes kitchen utensils and side tray and stoppers	50	75	100
Knight in Armor, M-T Co., 1950s, 10" tall; five actions, rare	1100	1650	2200
Knight in Armor Target Game, includes crossbow and rubber tipped darts, M-T Co., 1950s, 12" tall; three actions	200	300	400

	C6	C8	C10
Knitting Grandma, T-N Co., 1950s, 8-1/2" tall; three actions	175	250	350
Kooky-Spooky Whistling Tree, w/two color schemes, Marx Co., 1950s, 14-1/4" tall; six actions	450	760	1600
Ladder Fire Engine, Linemar Co., 1950s, 13" long; five actions	170	255	340
Lady Pup Tending Her Garden, Cragstan Co., 1950s, 8" high; five actions	200	275	400
Lambo with Magnetic Trunk and Light, includes two tin logs and trailer, Alps Co., 1950s, 16" long w/trailer; seven actions, rare	250	375	500
The Laughing Clown, S-H Co., 1960s, 14" tall; seven actions	160	240	320
Lectric Revolver, Daisy Mfg. Co., 1950s, 11-1/2" long; three actions	40	60	80
Leo the Growling Pet Lion with Magic Face Change, Toyiyama Co., 1970s, 9" long; three actions, two cycles	100	150	200
Light House, includes detachable spin-ball tower, Alps Co., 1950s, 8-1/2" high, 6-3/4" x 6-3/4" base; five actions, rare	600	900	1200
Lighted Freight Train, five pieces w/eight-section track, "Y" Co., 1950s, 25-1/2" long; four actions	70	105	140
Lighted Space Vehicle with Floating Satellite, includes celluloid ball, M-T Co., 1960s, 8-1/2" long; three actions	150	225	300
Linda Lee Laundromat, washing machine, T-N Co., 1940s, 6-1/2" high; minor toy	30	45	60
Linemar Music Hall, Linemar Co., 1950s, 8" high, 7-3/4" x 5-1/2" base; four actions	100	120	200
Lion, Linemar, 1950s, 9" long; four actions	100	150	200

Jungle Jumbo, B.C. Co., 1950s, $400.

Linemar Music Hall, Linemar Co., 1950s, $200

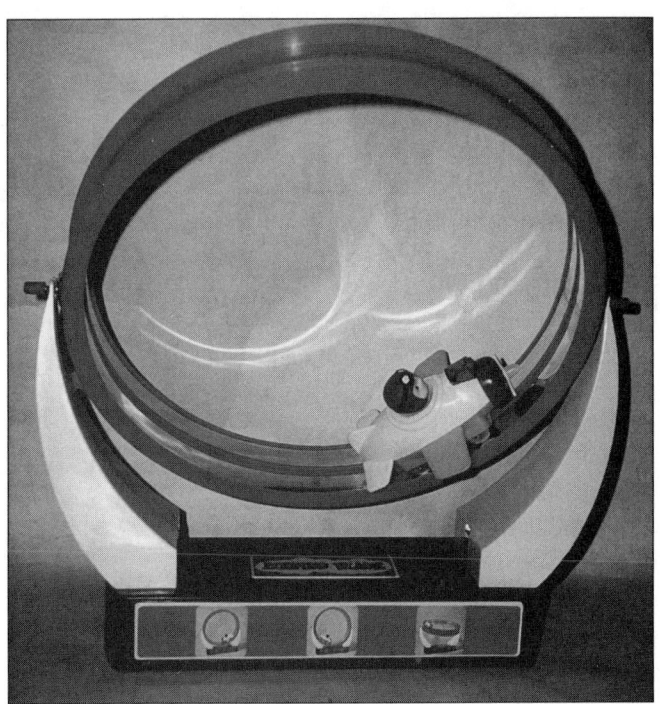

Looping Airplane, "Y" Co., c. 1960s, $80

	C6	C8	C10
Lion Target Game, includes dart gun and darts, M-T Co., 1950s, 7-1/2" high; four actions	120	180	240
Locomotive Continental Blue, M-T Co., 1970s, 13" long; four actions	40	60	80
Loop the Loop Clown, T-N Co., 1960s, 10" high; minor toy	60	120	175
Looping Airplane, "Y" Co., Sears (distributor), c. 1960s, 14-1/2" high, airplane 5" long; minor toy	40	60	80
Looping Space Tank, Daiya Co., 1960s, 8" long; five actions	300	450	600
Los Walky-Son, includes detachable rifles and baton, Geyper Co., 1960s, 11-1/2" high, 15" wide	120	180	240
The Loser (Bar Toy), Poynter Prod. Co., c. 1971, 13" high; three actions	40	60	80
Lost in Space Robot, Remco Co., 1966, 13" tall; three actions	200	300	400
Love-Beetle-Volks, K.O. Co., 1960s, 10" long; three actions	60	90	120
Lucky Crane, includes tin prizes, M-T Co., 1950s, 8-1/2" high; five actions, rare	400	600	800
Lucky Locomotive, Marusan Co., 1950s, 8" long; four actions	40	60	80
Lucky Seven Dice-Throwing Monkey, includes plastic straw hat, five dice, two game sheets, twenty chips, Alps Co., 1960s, 11-1/2" tall; five actions	50	75	100

	C6	C8	C10
Lufthansa Jet Airplane, GAMA Co., 1960s, 19-1/2" long, 18-1/2" wingspan; three actions	110	165	220
Lunar Captain, T-N Co., 1960s, 13-1/2" long extended; five actions	110	165	220
Lunar Loop/Swing and Orbiting Action, Daiya Co., 1960s, 14" high, 12" diameterhoop; three actions	100	150	200
M-101 Aston-Martin Secret Ejector Car, includes ejectable passenger, Daiya Co., 1960s, 11" long; six actions	200	300	400
Mac the Turtle, "Y" Co., 1960s, 8" high; five actions	85	135	185
Magic Action Bulldozer, T-N Co., 1950s, 9-1/2" long; three actions	100	150	200
Magic Color Moon Express, S-H Co., 1960s, 13" long; four actions	100	150	200
Magic Man Clown, Marusan Co., 1950s, 11" tall; five actions	260	385	525
Magic Snowman, includes detachable tin broom, plastic pipe, and styro ball, M-T Co. (Santa Creations), 1950s, 11-1/4" tall; four actions	125	190	265
Magnet Rail Moon Orbiter, "Y" Co., 1960s, 14" high, 12" diameter; minor toy	70	105	140
Main Street, Linemar Co., 1950s, 19-1/2" long; three actions, rare	600	1000	2000
Major Tooty, includes drum and hat, Alps Co. (R.F.), 1960s, 14" tall; three actions	85	130	175
Make Up Bear, M-T Co., 1960s, 9" high; four actions, rare	500	750	1000
Mambo the Jolly Drumming Elephant, includes cymbals and stand, Alps Co., 1950s, 9-1/2" high; six actions	90	150	200

Mac the Turtle, "Y" Co., 1960s, $185

	C6	C8	C10
Man in Space Astronaut, Alps Co., 1960s, 6" tall; minor toy	100	150	200
Mars Explorer, robot, S-H Co., 1950s, 9-1/2" tall; seven actions	200	300	400
Mars Explorer, astronaut, S-H Co., 1960s, 10" tall; six actions	250	375	500
Mars King Robot No. 12101, S-H Co., 1960s, 9-1/2" tall; four actions	210	315	420
Marshal Wild Bill, includes tin cowboy hat, "Y" Co., 1950s, 10-1/2" tall; four actions, two cycles	180	280	375
Martian Robot, SJM Co., 1970s, 12" tall; four actions	75	100	125
Marvelous Car, T-Bird, T-N Co., 1956, 11" long; three actions	250	375	500
Marvelous Fire Engine, "Y" Co., 1960s, 11" long; four actions	100	150	200
Marvelous Mike, Saunders Co., 1950s, 17" long; four actions	100	175	245
Maxwell Coffee-Loving Bear, T-N Co., 1960s, 10" tall; five actions	100	150	200
McGregor, T-N Co., 1960s, 12" tall when standing; six actions	125	175	225
Mechanic Robot, S-T Co., 1960s, 12" tall; five actions	150	225	300
The Mechanized Robot (Robby), T-N Co., 1950s, 13-1/2" tall; four actions, rare	600	900	1200
Mercury Explorer, T.P.S. Co., 1960s, 8" long; five actions	120	180	240
Mercury X-1 Space Saucer, "Y" Co., 1960s, 8" diameter; four actions	70	105	140
Merry Christmas Santa In His Rockin' Chair, includes detachable tree and stocking, 1950s, Alps Co., 21" tall assembled; three actions, rare	500	750	1000
Merry Ice Cream Truck, Bandai Co., 1960s, 10-1/2" long; five actions	90	135	180
Mexicali Pete-Drum Player, Alps Co., 1960s, 10-1/2" high; three actions	60	90	120
Mickey Mouse and Donald Duck Fire Engine, M-T Co., 1960s, 16" long; three actions	300	450	600
Mickey Mouse Locomotive, M-T Co., 1960s, 9" long; six actions	200	300	400
Mickey Mouse Melody Railroad, includes four circular rails w/ xylophone bars, Frankonia Co., 1960s, handcar 6-3/4" long; minor toy, rare	800	1200	1600
Mickey Mouse on Handcar, M-T Co., 1960s, 9-3/4" long, 7-3/4" high; three actions	350	500	650
Mickey Mouse Sand Buggy, M-T Co., 1960s, 11" long; four actions	150	225	300
Mickey Mouse Trolley, M-T Co., 1960s, 11" high; three actions	150	225	300
Mickey the Magician, includes tin rabbit, Linemar, 1960s, 10" tall; four actions	785	1200	2500
Mighty Mike the Barbell Lifter Bear, K Co., 1950s, 10-1/2" tall; four actions	150	225	300
Mighty Kong, Marx, 1950s, 11" tall; five actions	250	375	500
Mighty Robot, K-O Co., 1960s, 11-1/2" tall; four actions	900	1350	1800
Military Air Defense Truck, Linemar Co., 1950s, 15-1/4" long; four actions	100	150	200
Military Command Car, T-N Co., 1950s, 11" long; five actions	150	225	300
Military Jet Plane, Marx Co., 1960s, 16" long, 14" wingspan; three actions	100	150	200
Military Police Car, Linemar, 1950s, 8-1/2" long; six actions	100	150	200
Million Bus, KKK Co., 1950s, 12" long; three actions, rare	1250	1875	2500
Mimi Poodle with Bone, includes plastic bone, T-N Co., 1950s, 11" long, 10" high; five actions, two cycles	50	75	100
Mischievous Monkey, M-T Co., includes tree and monkey, 1950s, 18" tall; six actions	200	300	400
Mischievous Monkey with Bulldog, T-N Co., 1950s, 12" high; four actions	220	330	440
Miss Friday the Typist, w/removable head, T-N Co., 1950s, 8" tall; six actions	150	225	300
Missile Robot Mr. 45, M-T Co., 17-1/2" tall; five actions	100	150	200
Mr. Atom the Electronic Walking Robot, 1950s, Advance Doll & Toy Co., 17" tall; six actions	400	600	800
Mr. Atomic, robot, Cragstan, 1950s, 11" tall; three actions, rare	2500	3750	5000
Mr. Baseball Jr., w/game box, T-N Co., 1950s, 7" high; three actions	500	750	1000
Mr. Chief Robot, K-O Co., 1950s, 12" tall; four actions	450	675	900
Mr. Fox, the Magician with the Magical Disappearing Rabbit, includes plastic rabbit, "Y" Co., 1960s, 9" tall; five actions	400	600	800
Mr. Hustler Robot, Taiyo Co., 1960s, 11" tall; six actions	200	300	400

Mr. MacPooch, SAN Co., 1950s, $280

Mr. Mercury, Marx Co., 1960s, Type I (left) and Type II (right), $800, each

	C6	C8	C10
Mr. MacPooch Taking a Walk and Smoking His Pipe, SAN Co., 1950s, 8" tall; four actions	150	200	300
Mr. Magoo Car, includes cloth roof top, Hubley Co., 1961, 9" long; five actions	175	260	350
Mr. Mercury Type I, all tin, Marx Co., 1960s, 13" tall; seven actions	400	600	800
Mr. Mercury Type II (lighted), Marx Co., 1960s; seven actions	400	600	800
Mr. Robot the Mechanical Brain, Alps Co., 1950s, 8" tall; three actions, rare	600	900	1200
Mr. Strong Pup Weight-Lifting Dog, K Co., 1950s, 9" tall; five actions	130	195	260
Mr. Traffic Policeman, A-I Co., 1950s, 14" tall, 6" x 6" base; four actions	175	270	365
Mr. Zerox, S-H Co., 9-1/2" tall, 1960s; four actions	150	225	300
Mix-ette Mixer, KDP Co., includes mixer stand and bowl 1940s, 9" high when assembled; minor toy	30	45	60
Mobile Satellite Tracking Station, includes detachable antenna, "Y" Co., 1960s, 9" long; six actions	400	600	800

	C6	C8	C10
Mobile Space TV Unit with Trailer, T-N Co., 1960s; six actions, rare	500	750	1000
Mod Monster Blushing Frankenstein, T-N Co., 1960s, 13-1/4" tall; five actions	150	225	300
Modern Robot, Yoshiya Co., 1950s, 12" tall; four actions, rare	450	675	900
Monkee Mobile, ASC Co. (Aoshin Co.), 1967, 12" long; minor toy	300	450	600
Monkey Handcar, T-N Co., 1950s, 7" high; three actions	70	105	140
Monkey on a Picnic, Alps Co., 1950s, 9-1/2" high; seven actions	150	225	300
Monorail Rocket Ship, Linemar Co., 1950s, 10" long w/supports and rail rods; minor toy	140	210	280
Monster Robot, S-H Co., 1970s, 10" tall; three actions	100	125	150
Moon Astronaut, Daiya Co., 1950s, 9" tall; four actions	500	750	1000
Moon Explorer Robot, Bandai Co., 1960s, 17-1/2" tall (feet to antenna top); five actions, rare	600	900	1200
Moon Explorer Vehicle, Gakken Co., 1960s, 11" long; five actions	150	225	300
Moon Express, Magic Color, TPS Co., 1950s, 12" long; three actions	120	180	240
Moon Globe Orbiter, rocket orbits globe, noise, lights, "Y" Co. (Mego), c. 1960s, 10-1/2" high; three actions	100	150	200
Moon Orbiter, includes six sections of track and trestles, "Y" Co., 1960s, 4" long; minor toy	120	180	240
Moon Patrol Space Rover, Gakken Toy Co., 1960s, 11-1/2" long; five actions	140	210	280

	C6	C8	C10
Moon Rocket, "Y" Co., 1950s, 15-1/4" long; three actions, rare	400	600	800
Moon Traveler Apollo Z, T-N Co., 1960s, 12" long, 15" extended; five actions	120	180	240
Mother Bear Sitting and Knitting in Her Old Rocking Chair, M-T Co., 1950s, 9-1/2" high; four actions	170	255	340
Motorcycle Cop, Daiya Co., 1950s, 10-1/2" long, 8-1/4" high; five actions	350	500	650
Mountain Cable Car, includes cable, Cragstan Co., 1950s, 9" long; minor toy	60	90	120
Movieland Drive-In Theater, includes six small cars, ad cards, filmstrips, Remco Co., 1959, 14" long; minor toy	60	90	120
Multi Action Electra Jet KLM Royal Dutch Airlines PH-DSF, T-N Co., 1960s, 14" long, 17" wingspan; three actions	110	165	220
Mumbo Jumbo, Hawaiian drummer, Alps Co., 1960s, 9-3/4" high; three actions	85	120	160
Musical Bank Organ Grinder & Monkey, includes test coin and detachable celluloid monkey, HTC Co., 1950s, 8" tall; four actions, rare	500	750	1000
Musical Bear (Drum and cymbals), includes detachable tin horn, Linemar Co., 1950s, 10" tall; six actions	200	300	400
Musical Bulldog Playing Piano, 1950s, SAN Co., 8-1/2" tall, 6" x 9" base; four actions	600	900	1200

	C6	C8	C10
Musical Cadillac Car, Irco Co., 1950s, 9" long; minor toy	200	300	400
Musical Clown (New Adventures of Clown), T-N Co., 1960s, 9" tall; three actions	150	225	300
Musical Comic Jumping Jeep, Alps Co., 1970s, 12" long; six actions	70	105	140
Musical Drummer Robot, T-N Co., 1950s, 8-1/4" tall; three actions, rare	4000	6000	8000
Musical Jackal, Linemar Co., 10" tall, 1950s; six actions, rare	150	225	600
Musical Jolly Chimp, C-K Co., 1960s, 10-1/2" high; five actions, two cycles	75	100	125
Musical Marching Bear, includes detachable tin horn, Alps Co., 1950s, 11" tall; four actions	115	170	600
Musical Showboat, Gakken Toy Co., includes two detachable smokestacks, 1960s, 13" long; minor toy	100	150	200
My Fair Dancer, Haji Co., 1950s, 10-1/2" tall; minor toy	100	150	200
Mystery Fire Chief Car No. 81, Sanshin Co., 1950s, 9-1/4" long; three actions	100	150	200
Mystery Plane, T-N Co., 1950s, 10" long, 10-1/2" wingspan; four actions	120	180	240
Mystery Police Car, T-N Co., 1960s, 9-3/4" long, 6" wide, 4" high; three actions	100	150	200
NAR Television Truck, includes six film stripinserts, Linemar Co., 1950s, 12" long; four actions	300	450	600
NBC Television Truck, Linemar Co., 1950s, 9" long; five actions	300	450	600
Neptune Tugboat, M-T Co., 1950s, 15" long, 7" high; four actions	90	135	180
New Astronaut Robot, S-H Co., 1970s; 9-1/2" tall; six actions	80	120	160
New Bell Ringer Choo Choo, locomotive, M-T Co., 1960s, 10" long; three actions	50	75	100
New Space Capsule, S-H Co., 1960s, 9" long; six actions	120	180	240
News Service Car, T.P.S. Co., 1960s, 10" long; four actions	150	225	300
Non-Stop Robot, M-T Co., 1960s, 15" tall; three actions, rare	600	900	1200
Nutty Mad Indian, Marx, 1960s, 12" tall; four actions	100	150	200
Nutty Mads Car (Drincar), Marx Co., 1960s, 9-1/4" long; three actions	175	250	325

Movieland Drive-In Theater, Remco Co., 1959, $120

	C6	C8	C10
Nutty Nibs, includes litho bowl of nuts and steel ball, Linemar, 1950s, 11-1/2" tall; minor toy, rare	700	850	1400
007 Aston-Martin, includes ejectable passenger, Gilbert Co., 1966, 11-1/2" long; eight actions	210	315	420
007 Secret Agent's Car (Impala), Spesco Co. (Joy Toy), 1960s, 15" long; five actions	170	255	340
Ol' MacDonald's Farm Truck, includes plastic pig, cow and chicken, Frankonia, 1960s; four actions	100	150	200
Ol' Sleepy Head RIP, "Y" Co., 1950s, 9" long; seven actions	150	250	320
Old Fashioned Fire Engine, M-T Co., 1950s, 12-1/2" long; four actions	120	180	240
Old Fashioned Car, S-H Co., 1950s, 10" long; four actions	50	75	100
Old Fashioned Telephone Bear (?), M-T Co., 1950s, 9-1/2" high; four actions	125	175	225
Old Ford Touring Car, 1950s, Z Co., 10" long; four actions	40	60	80
Old Time Automobile, includes detachable tin litho driver and steering wheel, "Y" Co., 1950s, 8-3/4" long; three actions	80	120	160
Old Timer, Car, Cragstan Co., 1950s, 9" long; three actions	100	150	200
Oldtimer Automoball, includes celluloid ball, M-T Co., 1950s, 10" long; three actions	90	135	180
Oldtimer Sunday Driver, Daiya Co., 1960s, 9" long; four actions	70	105	140
Overland Choo Choo Express locomotive, M-T Co., 1950s, 14" long; minor toy	30	45	60
Overland Stage Coach, Ichida Co., 1960s, 18" long; four actions	100	150	200
P-51 Mustang Shooting Fighter Plane, T-N Co., 1950s, 9" long, 9" wingspan; minor toy	90	135	180
Pacific Piping Express Locomotive, Kanto Toy Co., 1960s, 14" long; four actions	40	60	80
Pan Am Sky Taxi Helicopter, Haji Co., 1960s, 11" long; three actions	70	105	140
Pan American World Airways 'Seven Seas' DC-7, T-N Co., 1950s, 15" long, 19" wingspan; five actions	140	210	280
Panda Bear, mostly plastic, M-T Co. (Masudaya Co.), 1970s, 10" long; four actions	30	45	65

	C6	C8	C10
Papa Bear Reading & Drinking in His Old Rocking Chair, M-T Co., 1950s, 10" high; four actions	150	225	300
Passenger Bus, "Y" Co., 1950s, 16" long; four actions	230	345	460
Pat O'Neill, standing, T-N Co., 1960s, 12" tall; six actions	150	225	300
Pat the Dog, NGS Co., 1950s, 9-1/2" long; five actions, two cycles	30	45	60
Pat the Roaring Elephant, w/attached baby elephant, "Y" Co., 1950s, 9" long; four actions	100	160	225
Patrol Auto Tricycle, T-N Co., 1960s, 19" long, 7-1/2" high; four actions	200	300	400
Patrol Helicopter No. 7, Bandai Co., 1960s, 11" long; four actions	70	105	140
P.D. No. 5 Police Patrol Car (Buick), Asakusa Toy Co., 1960s, 11-1/2" long three actions	80	120	160
Penguin on Tricycle, T-N Co., 1950s, 6-1/2" high; three actions	100	150	200
Pepi Tumbling Monkey, Yanoman Toy Co., 1960s, 9-1/2" high; minor toy	40	60	80
Peppermint Twist Doll, Haji Co., 1950s, 12" tall; minor toy	150	225	300
Peppy Puppy, includes tin litho bone, "Y" Co., 1950s, 8" long, 6-1/2" high; seven actions, two cycles	50	75	100
Pet Turtle, Alps Co., 1960s, 7" long; four actions, two cycles	70	105	140
Pete the Space Man (Walking Mate Series), Bandai Co., 1960s, 5" tall; minor action	60	90	120
Peter the Drumming Rabbit (VIA-Cragstan), Alps Co., 1950s, 13" tall; five actions	150	225	300
Phillips '66' Power Yacht, includes plastic parts for yacht and dock, unmarked, 1950s, 18" long; minor toy	70	105	140
Pick-Up Truck, T-N Co., 10" long; four actions	100	150	200
Picnic Bear, w/Coke, Pepsi and generic logo, Alps Co., 1950s, 10" high; five actions	100	150	200
Picnic Bunny, Alps Co., 1950s, 10" tall; four actions	100	150	200
Picnic Monkey, Alps Co., 1950s, 10" high; four actions	100	150	200
Picnic Poodle, STS Co., 1950s, 7" long, 7" high; four actions, two cycles	40	60	80
Pierrot Monkey Cycle, M-T Co., 1950s, 8" long, 10-1/2" high; five actions	325	460	650

	C6	C8	C10
Piggy Barbecue, includes chef's hat and tin litho fried egg, "Y" Co., 1950s, 9-1/2" tall; five actions 150	150	225	300
Piggy Cook, includes chef's hat and tin litho fried egg, "Y" Co., 1950s, 9-1/2" tall, 4" x 6" base; five actions 150	150	225	300
Pinkee the Farmer, M-T Co., 1950s, 9-1/2" long; seven actions 90	90	100	180
Pinky the Clown, includes tin litho propeller, ball on nose, Rock Valley Toy Co. (Via), 1950s, 10-1/4" tall; five actions, rare 200	200	300	400
Pinocchio Playing London Bridge, includes xylophone, T-N Co. (Rosko), 1962, 10" tall; three actions.................. 150	150	225	300
Pioneer Covered Wagon, includes detachable canopy and driver, Ichida Co., 1960s, 14-1/2" long; four actions.. 120	120	180	240
Pipie the Whale, Alps Co., 1950s, 12" long; minor toy 250	250	270	500
Pistol Pete, includes tin hat, Marusan Co., 1950s, 10-1/4" high; five actions... 250	250	270	500
Piston Action Bulldozer, Linemar Co., 7-1/2" long, 1960s; two cycles................ 90	90	135	180
Piston Action Robot, resembles Robbie, T-N Co., 1950s, 8-1/4" tall; three actions 900	900	1350	1800
Piston Head Robot, S-H Co., 1960s, 10" tall; three actions 150	150	225	300
Piston Robot, S-H Co., 1960s, 10-1/2" tall; four actions 110	110	165	220
Planet Explorer, S-H Co., 1950s, 9" long; four actions 150	150	225	300
Planet Rover, wheeled tank, J Co., 1960s, 9" long, 6-1/2" high; six actions 140	140	210	280
Planet 'Y' Space Station, T-N Co., 1960s, 9" diameter; three actions..................... 140	140	210	280

Playful Pup in Shoe, "Y" Co., 1960s, $80

	C6	C8	C10
Playful Pup in Shoe, "Y" Co., 1960s, 10" long; three actions 40	40	60	80
Playful Puppy, M-T Co., 1950s, 7-3/8" long, 5" high; four actions......... 100	100	150	200
The Playing Monkey, includes detachable hat and tin yo-yo, S&E Co. (Ahi Brand), 1950s, 10" tall; six actions...................................... 200	200	300	400
Pluto, Linemar Co., 1960s, 10" long; five actions.. 300	300	450	600
Polar Bear, Alps Co., 1970s, 8" long; three actions... 50	50	75	100
Police Auto Cycle, motorcycle w/plastic driver and remote control, Bandai Co., 1960s; five actions 150	150	225	300
Police Motorcycle, M-T Co., 1950s, 11-3/4" long; seven actions.................. 200	200	300	400

Piston Action Robot, T-N Co., 1950s, $1,800

Popcorn Eating Bear, M-T Co., 1950s, $200

	C6	C8	C10
Police No. 5 Police Car, T-N Co., 1950s, 9-1/2" long; four actions	90	135	180
Police Patrol Jeep, T-N Co., 1960s, 9-1/4" long; four actions (lights, bump and go, noise and smoke)	100	150	200
Pom Pom Tank, S&E Co., 1950s, 12" long; five actions	160	240	320
Popcorn Eating Bear, M-T Co., 1950s, 9" high; five actions	100	150	200
Popcorn Vendor, No. 4035, includes litho umbrella, S&E Co., 1960s, 8" high, 7" long; six actions	200	300	400
Popcorn Vendor Truck, T-N Co., 1960s, 9" long, three actions	150	225	300
Popeye and Rowboat with Moving Oars, Linemar Co., 1950s, 10" long; three actions, rare	5000	7500	10,000
Porsche with Visible Engine, Bandai Co., 1964, 10" long; three actions	90	135	180
Poverty Pup, bank, Poynter Products Co., 1966, 6" long, 4-1/4" high; three actions	60	90	120
Power Shovel, Alps Co., 1950s, 15" long extended; six actions	90	135	180
Pretty Peggy Parrot, T-N Co., 1950s, 11" long; six actions	250	375	500
Princess the French Poodle, no markings, 1950s, 9" long, 8" high; five actions	40	60	80
Professor Owl, includes two discs, E-T Co., 1950s, 8" high; five actions	200	300	400
Project Yankee Doodle, includes plastic missiles, rockets and accessories, Remco Co., 1959, 15" long; six actions	60	90	120
Puffy Morris, "Y" Co., 1960s, 10" tall; five actions, uses real cigarette	125	175	225
Puzzled Puppy, M-T Co., 1950s, 7-1/2" long, 5" high; five actions	100	150	200
Queen of the Sea, includes detachable antenna and flag, M-T Co., 1950s, 21-1/2" long; four actions	300	450	600
RCA NBC Mobile Color TV Truck, Yonezawa Co., 1950s, 9" long; four actions	300	450	600
R.R. Line Locomotive, Marx, 1950s, 6-1/2" long; four actions	40	60	80
R-35 Robot, M-T Co., 1950s, 7-1/2" tall; five actions	300	450	600
The Rabbits and Carriage, S&E Co., 1950s, 10" tall; four actions	150	225	300
Racecar #25, Alps Co., 1950s, 9" long; three actions, rare	800	1200	1600
Radar Jeep, T-N Co., 1950s, 11" long; four actions	150	225	300
Radar Robot, remote robot w/face control box, T-N Co., 1960s, 9" tall; three actions	600	900	1200
Radar Robot, S-H Co., 1970s, 12" tall; five actions	70	105	140
Radar Scope Space Scout, S-H Co., 1960s, 9-1/4" tall; three actions	140	210	280
Radio Rex, includes celluloid dog, Elmwood Button Co., 1920s, 5" x 7" dog house; minor toy	100	150	200
Railroad Hand Car, includes rubber track, KDP Co., 8" long, 1950s; minor toy	90	135	180
Railway Yard Shuttle Train, , includes locomotive boxcar and track; ATC Co., 1950s, 8" long, 28" long track; three actions	100	150	200
Ranger Robot, Daiya Co., 1950s, 11" tall; six actions	400	600	800
Ray Gun, machine gun, includes tripod, T-N Co., 1950s, 17-1/2" long; three actions	50	75	100
Reading Bear, Alps Co., 1950s, 9" tall; five actions	100	175	225
Rembrandt Monkey Artist, Alps Co., 1950s, 8" high; five actions	170	240	365
Reversible Diesel Electric Tractor, Marx Co., 1950s; minor toy	50	75	100
Ricki the Begging Poodle, Rock Valley Toys (VIA), 1950s, 9" long, 8" high; five actions	30	45	60
Riverboat, includes detachable tin smokestack, Marusan Co., 1950s, 12-3/4" long; three actions	130	195	260
River Queen Sidewheeler, M-T Co., 1950s, 13-1/2" long; three actions	140	210	280
Road Construction Roller, Daiya Co., 1950s, 8-1/2" long; four actions	60	90	120
Road Grader, T-N Co., 1960s, 12" long; three actions	50	75	100
Road Roller, M-T Co., 1950s, 9" long; four actions	60	90	120
Roaring Gorilla (white gorilla), T-N Co., 1950s, 9-1/4" tall; five actions: See Gorilla			
Roaring Gorilla Shooting Gallery, includes fold-outtarget box, tin gun, plastic darts, M-T Co., 1950s, 9-1/2" tall; three actions	200	300	400
Roarin' Jungle Lion, Marx Co., 1950s, 16" long nose to tail tip; four actions, two cycles	175	250	325

	C6	C8	C10
Robbie Robot, Yonezawa Co., 1950s, 13" tall; five actions: See Mechanized Robot			
Robby Space Patrol, T-N Co., 1950s, 12-1/2" long; five actions, rare	2000	3000	4000
Robert the Robot, Ideal Toy Co., 1950s, 14" tall; three actions	120	180	240
Robert the Robot Mechanical Bulldozer, Ideal Toy Co., 1950s, 9" long; four actions, rare	300	450	600
Robot, "Y" Co., 1950s, 6" tall; minor toy, rare	600	900	1200
Robot, "Y" Co., 1960s, 10-1/2" tall; three actions	400	600	800
Robot 2500, Durham Industries, 1970s, 10-1/2" tall; four actions	60	90	120
Robotank TR-2, T-N Co., 1960s, 5" high; four actions	140	210	280
Robotank Z Space Robot, T-N Co., 1960s, 10-1/4" high; five actions	300	450	600
Rock 'N' Roll Hotrod (Dreamboat), T-N Co., 1950s, 7" long; three actions	150	225	300
Rock 'N' Roll Monkey (three variations), includes plastic hat, Rosko Co., 1950s, 13" tall; five actions	140	200	280
Rocket Express Rocket Ship Monorail, twenty-piece rail and girder set, Linemar Co., 1950s, 10" long; three actions	100	150	200
Rocket Launching Pad, includes tin litho satellite and rocket, "Y" Co., 8-1/2" high, 1950s; five actions	160	240	320
Rocking Chair Bear, M-T Co., 1950s, 10" high; five actions	125	175	200
Rocking Santa, Alps Co., 1950s, 10" high; four actions, rare	300	450	600
Roller Skater, Alps Co., 1950s, 12" tall; minor toy	100	150	200
Rollerskating Clown, T.P.S. Co., 1950s, 6" tall; minor toy, rare	500	750	1000
Romance Car M-841, M Co., 1950s, 8" long; three actions	90	135	180
Rootbeer Counter, includes plastic barrel, glasses, and tin tray, K Co., 1960s, 8" long, 8" high; three actions	100	160	230
Rosko Robot, Rosko Co., 1950s, 13" tall; five actions	500	750	1000
Rotate-O-Matic Super Astronaut, S-H Co., 1960s, 11-1/2" tall; six actions, two cycles	100	150	200
Rover the Poodle Bell Ringer, Alps Co., 1960s, 10-1/2" tall; three actions, two cycles	60	90	120

	C6	C8	C10
Roy Rogers Western Telephone, Ideal Co., 1950s; 9" high; three actions	90	135	180
Royal Cub In Buggy, pushed by Mama Bear, S&E Co., 1940s, 8" long, 8" high; six actions	140	210	280
Rudy the Robot, Remco Co., 1968, 16-1/4" tall; four actions	110	165	220
SSN-571 Submarine Nautilus, Marusan Co., 1950s, 16" long w/rudder extended; minor toy	120	180	240
SSN-571 Submarine, Skate, Marusan Co., 1950s, 16" long w/rudder extended; minor toy	120	180	240
Sam the Shaving Man, includes metal mirror, Plaything Toy Co., 1960s, 11-1/2" tall; seven actions	140	200	285
Sammy Wong the Tea Totaler, T-N Co., 1950s, 10" tall; four actions	100	140	200
Santa Bank, HTC Co. (Trim a Tree), 1960, 11" high; four actions	150	225	300
Santa Claus Bellringer, Santa Creations Co., 1950s, 13" tall; five actions	100	150	200
Santa Claus, No. M-750 (Sitting on House), H.T.C. Co., 1950s, 8" high; four actions	125	175	225

Santa the Bellringer, Chase Import Co., 1950s, $200

	C6	C8	C10
Santa Claus on Handcar, M-T Co., 1960s, 10" high; three actions	100	140	200
Santa Claus on Scooter, M-T Co., 1960s, 10" high; four actions	100	140	180
Santa Claus Stands & Sits, T-N Co., 1960s, 10" tall; six actions	150	225	300
Santa Copter, M-T Co., 1960s, 8-1/2" long; three actions	100	150	200
Santa in Rocker, includes detachable tree and stocking, Alps Co., 1950s, 21" high from base to tree top; four actions rare: See Merry Christmas			
Santa Claus Phone Bank, includes remote 4-3/4" high pay phone, S&E Co., 1950s, 8" high; seven actions	400	600	800
Santa Sled, T-N Co., 1950s, 14" long; four actions, rare	300	450	600
Santa the Bellringer, electromagnet activated and Blinker bulb, Chase Import Co., 1950s, 7" high; minor toy	100	150	200
Santa Fe Diesel Battery Cable Train with Headlight (two-piece hookup), T-N Co., 1950s, 13-1/2" long; minor toy	80	120	160
Satellite Interceptor, two-piece target set w/two darts and styro ball, Linemar Co., 1950s, 6-1/2" long gun-telescope, 5" high blower; minor toy	200	300	400
Satellite Target Game, includes celluloid ball and special gun, S-H Co., 1960s, 8" high, 10-1/2" wide; minor toy	100	150	200
Saxophone Playing Monkey, Alps Co., 1950s, 9-1/2" high; four actions	200	300	400
School Bus, 1950s, Cragstan, 20-1/2" long; minor toy	70	105	140
Sea Bear #7 Racing Boat, Bandai Co., 1950s, 10" long; minor toy	60	90	120
Seascape Tugboat, Marx Co., 1950s, 6-1/2" long; three actions	50	75	100
Secret Service Action Car (Green Hornet motif), 1960s, ASC Co., 11" long; four actions, rare	400	600	800
Serpent Charmer, Linemar Co., 1950s, 7" high; four actions	175	300	425
Shaggy the Friendly Pup, Alps Co., 1960s, 8" long; three actions	35	45	65
Shaking Classic Car, T-N Co., 1960s, 7" long; four actions	50	75	100

	C6	C8	C10
Shaking Old-Timer Car No. 2511-1, includes plastic driver, T-N Co., 1960s, 9" long; four actions	60	90	120
Shark-U-Control Racing Car, all plastic, Remco Ind. Inc., 1961, 19" long; minor toy	80	120	160
Sheriff Car, T-N Co., 1950s, 10" long; four actions	80	120	160
Shoe Maker Bear, T-N Co., 1960s, 8-1/2" high; three actions	125	200	250
Shoe-Shaking Dog, M-T Co., 1950s, 8" long, 6" tall; five actions	40	60	80
Shoe Shine Bear, T-N Co., 1950s, 9" tall; five actions	150	225	300
Shoe Shine Joe, Alps Co., 1950s, 11" high; six actions	150	225	300
Shoe Shine Monkey, T-N Co., 1950s, 9" high; five actions	150	225	300
Shooting Bear, SAN Co., 1950s, 10" tall; six actions	160	240	320
Shooting Gorilla, includes tin gun and darts, M-T Co., 1950s, 12" high; four actions	200	300	400
Shutterbug, photographer, T-N Co., 1950s, 9" tall; five actions	500	700	900

Shoe Maker Bear, T-N Co., 1960s, $225

	C6	C8	C10
Shuttling Freight Train, includes locomotive, lumber car, four pieces of track, platform and logs, Cragstan Co., 1950s, 51" long assembled; six actions	150	200	250
Shuttling Train and Freight Yard, includes locomotive, baggage car, two platforms and litho luggage, Alps Co., 1950s, 11" long, track 51" long; four actions	120	180	240
Sight Seeing Bus, Bandai Co., 1960s, 14-1/2" long; four actions	100	150	200
Sight Seeing Bus, Yonezawa Co., 1950s, 9" long; minor toy	140	210	280
Sikorsky Rescue Army Helicopter, Alps Co., 1950s, 11" long; four actions	90	135	180
Silver Bell Choo Choo, Kanto Co., 1950s, 12" long; three actions	40	60	80
Silver Mountain Express Locomotive, M-T Co., 1960s, 15-3/4" long; four actions	50	75	100

Skipping Monkey, T-N Co., 1960s, $80

	C6	C8	C10
Silver Mountain Locomotive, M-T Co., 1950s, 16" long; three actions	50	75	100
Silver Ray Secret Weapon Space Scout, S-H Co., 1960s, 9" tall; six actions, rare	750	1075	1500
Silver Streak Locomotive No. 6682, M-T Co., 1950s, 16" long; four actions	50	75	100
Singing Bird In Cage, T-N Co., 1950s, 9" high, 4" x 6" rectangular base; four actions	100	150	200
Siren Fire Car, M-T Co., 1950s, 9" long; four actions	130	195	260
Siren Patrol Car, M-T Co., 1960s, 12-1/2" long; four actions	90	135	180
Siren Patrol Motorcycle, M-T Co., 1960s, 12" long; three actions	250	350	450
Skating Circus Clown, T.P.S. Co., 1950s, 6" tall; minor toy, rare	450	595	800
Skiing Santa, includes tin skis, M-T Co., 1960s, 12" tall; four actions	150	225	300
Skipping Monkey, T-N Co., 1960s, 9-1/2" tall; minor toy	40	60	80
Sky Patrol Flying Saucer, includes detachable antenna, K-O Co., 1950s, 7-1/2" diameter; seven actions	100	150	200
Sky Patrol Space Cruiser, T-N Co., 1950s, 13" long; five actions	150	225	300
Sky Taxi-Panam-Boeing Vertol 107, includes two detachable rotors Haji Co., 1970s, 12-3/4" long; three actions	120	180	240
Slalom Game, includes plastic skier, T-N Co., 1960s, 15-1/4" long; minor toy	100	160	225
Sleeping Baby Bear, includes detachable alarm clock, Linemar, 1950s, 9" long; six actions	195	285	400
Sleeping Pup, Alps Co., 1960s, 9" long; five actions	45	75	100
Slurpy Pup, T-N Co., 1960s, 6-1/2" long, 4" high; four actions	50	75	100
Smilex Deluxe Coffee Set, includes four sets of cups, saucers and spoons, plastic, "Y" Co., 1950s, 12" high assembled; minor toy	60	90	120
Smoky Bear, includes detachable tin hat, SAN Co., 1950s, 9" tall; four actions	250	300	500
Smoky Bill on Old-Fashioned Car, T-N Co., 1960s, 9" long; four actions	120	180	240
Smokey the Bear Jeep, M-T Co., 1950s, 10" long; four actions	220	330	440

Smoking Bunny, SAN Co., 1950s, $185

Smoking Elephant, Marusan Co., 1950s, $225

	C6	C8	C10
Smoking Bulldozer, WKC Co., 1960s, 9" long; four actions	90	135	180
Smoking Bunny, SAN Co., 1950s, 10-1/2" tall; four actions	125	150	200
Smoking Elephant, Marusan Co., 1950s, 8-3/4" tall; four actions	115	165	225
Smoking Grandpa, (in Rocking Chair), Type I—eyes open, SAN Co., 8" tall, 1950s; four actions	175	250	325
Smoking Grandpa, (in Rocking Chair), Type II—eyes closed, 1950s, SAN Co., 8" tall; four actions	200	300	400
Smoking Jet Plane, T-N Co., 1950s, 12" long, 11" wingspan; four actions	150	225	300
Smoking Pop Locomotive: The General, SAN Co., 1950s, 10-1/4" long; four actions	70	105	140
Smoking Popeye, Linemar, 1950s, 9" tall; five actions, rare	800	1200	1600
Smoking Robot, all plastic, M-T Co., 1960s, 10" tall; four actions	90	135	180
Smoking Spaceman, Linemar Co., 1950s, 12" tall; six actions	750	1200	1600

	C6	C8	C10
Smoking U.S.A.F. Jet, T-N Co., 1950s, 13" long, 12" wingspan; four actions	150	225	300
Smoking Volkswagen, Aoshin Co., 1960s, 10-1/2" long; four actions	60	90	120
Smoking PaPa Bear, SAN Co., 1950s, 8" tall; four actions	150	200	250
Smoky Joe Fancy Mobile, T-N Co., 1960s, 9" long; four actions (smokes, lights, bump and go and noise)	100	150	200
Snake Charmer (and Casey the Trained Cobra), Linemar Co., 1950s, 8" high; four actions	250	375	500
Snappy the Dragon, T-N Co., 1960s, 30" long; six actions, rare	2000	3000	4000
Sneezing Bear, Linemar Co., 1950s, 9" high; five actions	200	300	400
Snoopie the Non-Fall Dog, Amico Co., 1960s, 8" long; three actions	50	75	100
Snoopy Sniffer, M-T Co., 1960s, 8" long; four actions	40	60	80
Somersaulting Pup with Bark, T-N Co., 1960s, 9" long; four actions, two cycles	50	75	100
Sonicon Space Rocket, M-T Co., 1960s, 13" long; minor toy	250	375	500
Space Capsule, includes styrofoam saucer and astronaut, M-T Co., 1960s, 10" long; four actions	100	150	200

Snake Charmer, Linemar Co., 1950s, $500

	C6	C8	C10
Space Capsule-5, M-T Co., 1960s, 10-1/2" long; four actions	150	225	300
Space Commando Spaceman, M-T Co., 1960s, 7-3/4" tall; four actions	500	750	1000
Space Commando Space Station, T-N Co., 1960s, 10" diameter; four actions	150	225	300
Space Explorer #1041, Yonezawa Co., 1960s, 7-3/4" high, extends to 11-1/2" high; six actions, rare	600	900	1200
Space Explorer Ship, M-T Co., 1950s, 11" diameter (saucer); six actions	100	150	200
Space Fighter, robot, S-H Co., 1970s, 9" tall; six actions	70	105	140
Space Frontier Saturn 5 Rocket, K-Y Co. (Yoskino Toy Co.), 1960s, 18" long; six actions	100	150	200
Space Patrol Car, T-N Co., 1950s, 9-1/2" long; four actions	300	450	600
Space Patrol Car, w/lighting guns, 1950s, Linemar Co., 9" long; three actions	450	675	900
Space Patrol Robot, S-H Co., 1950s, 11" tall; six actions	140	210	280
Space Patrol Rocket, M-T Co., 1970s, 11" long; three actions	70	105	140
Space Patrol Snoopy, M-T Co., 11" long, 1960s; four actions	100	150	200
Space Patrol Tank, includes detachable tin jet plane, Cragstan Co., 1950s, 9" long; five actions	150	225	300

	C6	C8	C10
Space Patrol 3 Saucer, K-O Co., 1950s, 7-1/2" diameter; five actions	100	150	200
Space Patrol Vehicle, K Co., 1950s, 9" long; four actions	130	195	260
Space Patrol Vehicle, M-T Co., 1960s, 9-1/2" long; three actions	100	150	200
Space Pioneer Vehicle, M-T Co., 1960s, 12" long; three actions	100	200	300
Space Robot Trooper, K-O Co., 1950s, 7-1/2" tall; three actions, rare	500	750	1000
Space Robot (X-70), T-N Co., 1960s, 12" tall; five actions	500	750	1000
Space Robot Car, Yonezawa Co., 1950s, 9-1/4" long; six actions, rare	1000	1500	2000
Space Rocket Blue Eagle, Masuya Toy Co., 1950s, 15" long from tail to probe tip	150	200	250
Space Rocket Solar X, T-N Co., 1960s, 15-1/2" tall; five actions	150	225	300
Space Scooter, M-T Co., 1960s, 10-1/2" high, 8" long; three actions	100	150	200
Space Scooter, Snoopy or Astro-Dog, M-T Co., 1960s, 8" long; three actions	80	120	160
Space Ship, I.Y. Co., 1950s, 9-1/2" diameter; four actions	180	270	360
Space Ship, M-T Co., 1970s, 9" long; three actions	90	135	180

Space Fighter, S-H Co., 1970s, $140

	C6	C8	C10
Space Ship X-5, M-T Co., 1970s, 8" diameter; four actions	60	90	120
Space Ship X-8, Tada Co., 1960s, 8" long; four actions	100	150	200
Space Station, T-N Co., 1950s, 9" diameter; four actions	100	150	200
Space Station, S-H Co., 1950s, 11-3/4" diameter; five actions	500	750	1000
Space Tank, K-O Co., Robbie Type, 1960s, 6" long; four actions	2000	3000	4000
Space Tank, Daiya Co., 1950s, 8" long; four actions	120	180	240
Space Tank-M41, includes detachable plastic antenna, M-T Co., 1950s, 9" long; four actions	100	150	200
Spaceman, Robot, Linemar, 1950s, 7-1/2" tall; three actions	350	525	700
Spaceman, Robot, T-N Co., 1950s, 9-1/4" tall; four actions	400	600	800
Spad XIII S-7 Stunt Biplane, T.P.S. Co. 1960s, 9" long, 10-3/8" wingspan; three actions	130	195	260
Spanking Bear, Linemar Co., 1950s, 9" high; six actions	160	200	320
Sparking Burp Gun, Mark Co., 1950s, 24" long; three actions	40	60	80
Sparkling Mike the Robot, Ace Co., 1950s, 7-1/2" tall; three actions, rare	1000	1500	2000
Sparky Savings Bank, electromagnet action, includes 4" long composition dog, Byron Co., 1930s, 4" long, 4-1/2" high doghouse; minor toy	60	90	120
Sparky the Seal, includes celluloid ball, M-T Co., 1950s, 6" high, 7" long, four actions; two cycles	100	150	200
Spirit of 1776, locomotive No. 4406, 1976, M-T Co., 15-3/4" long; five actions	40	60	80
Sports Car Race Set, T.P.S. Co., includes four plastic race cars, 1960s, 8" x 14" base; minor toy	80	120	160
Star Strider Robot, S-H Co., 1980s, 12" tall; six actions	110	165	220
Steam Roller (Road Roller), T-N Co. (Rosko), 1950s, 12" long w/trailer; four actions	90	135	180
Steam Roller, includes tin trailer, "Y" Co., 1950s, 8" long; four actions	100	150	200
Steerable Tank, Linemar Co., 1950s, 9" long; five actions	60	90	120
Strange Explorer, DSK Co., 1960s, 7-1/2" long; four actions	300	450	600
Strato Jet U.S.A.F., T-N Co., 1950s, 13" long, 14" wingspan; three actions	120	180	240

	C6	C8	C10
Strutting My Fair Dancer (Dancing Sailor Girl), Haji Co., 1950s, 12" tall; two pieces, minor toy	100	150	200
Struttin' Sam, Haji Co., 1950s, 10-1/2" tall; minor toy	250	350	450
Sunbeam Jeep No. 1, Marusan Co., 1940s, 10" long; three actions	100	150	200
Sunday Driver, includes detachable driver, M-T Co., 10" long, 1950s; four actions	55	90	125
Super Astronaut, Robot, S-H Co., 1960s, 11-1/2" tall; five actions, two cycles	110	165	220
Super Astronaut Robot, SJM Co., 1960s, 12" tall; four actions	150	225	300
Super Giant Robot, S-H Co., 1960s, 15-1/2" tall; six actions	200	300	400
Super Jet, T-N Co., 1950s, 12" long, 8" wingspan; three actions	250	375	500
Super Space Capsule, S-H Co., 1960s, 9" high; four actions	100	150	200
Super Space Commander, S-H Co., 1960s, 10" tall; three actions	70	105	140
Super Susie, Linemar Co., 1950s, 9" high; six actions	350	625	700
Superman Tank, Linemar Co., 1950s, 10-1/4" long; three actions, rare	600	900	1200

Suzette the Eating Monkey, Linemar Co., 1950s, $625

	C6	C8	C10
Surrey Jeep, T-N Co., 1960s, 11" long; three actions	90	135	180
Suzy-Q Automatic Ironer, GW Co., 1950s, 7" high; four actions	90	135	180
Suzette the Eating Monkey, includes tin litho steak, Linemar Co., 1950s, 8-3/4" high, 7" x 5" base; five actions, rare	300	450	625
Swingtail Airplane Flying Tigers, Marx Co., 1960s, 19-1/2" long, 21" wingspan; seven actions	300	450	600
Sing Tail Cargo Plane Flying Tiger, T-N Co., 1960s, 14" long, 14" wingspan; five actions	300	450	600
Switchboard Operator, Linemar, 1950s, 7-1/2" high; four actions, rare	250	380	800
Swivel-O-Matic Astronaut robot, 1960s, S-H Co., 11-1/2" tall; five actions, two cycles	80	120	160
T 360 Monoplane, S&E Co., 1950s, 12" long, 14-1/2" wingspan; four actions: See Bristol Bulldog Airplane			
Talking Parrot (called Pete), 1950s, T-N Co., 18" high; six actions	250	350	450
Talking Police Car Mystery Action, "Y" Co., 1960s, 14" long; three actions	70	105	140
Talking Robot, Yonezawa Co., 1960s, 10-3/4" tall; three actions, rare	600	900	1200
Tank M-4 Combat Tank, Taiyo Co., 1960s, 11-1/2" long, 13" w/gun barrel extended; five actions	100	150	200

	C6	C8	C10
Tank M-35, HTC Co., 1950s, 8" long; three actions	100	150	200
Tank M-41, J Co., 1970s, 8-1/4" long; four actions	100	150	200
Tank M-48-T, T-N Co., 1960s, 8-1/4" long; four actions	100	150	200
Tank M-56, M-T Co., 1940s, 7-1/2" long; wheel drive, seven actions	100	150	200
Tank M-81, M-T Co., 1960s, 8-1/2" long; seven actions	100	150	200
Tank M-103, M-T Co., 1950s, 7" long; three actions	100	150	200
Tank M-107 U.S. Army, includes four missiles, "Y" Co., 1950s, 6" long; four actions	120	180	240
Tank M-X, T-N Co., 1950s, 8-1/2" long; five actions	70	105	140
Tank T-5, includes detachable radar antenna, T-N Co., 1950s, 8-1/2" long; three actions	110	165	220
Tank 392 U.S. Tank Division, Marx Co., 1950s, 9-1/2" long; three actions	100	125	150
Tank X-3 (explorer defense), includes six cartridge shells, Cragstan Co., 1950s, 7-3/4" long; five actions	130	195	260
Tank X-75, includes tin gun and darts, M-T Co., 9" long, 1950s; three actions	110	165	220
Tank Daisymatic No. 64 Rapid Fire Tank, Daisy Mfg. Co., 1960s, 8" long; four actions	120	180	240
Tank Daisy-Matic No. 80, includes darts, Daisy Mfg. Co., 1965, 8-1/2" long; five actions	100	150	200
Tank Robot, S-H Co., 1960s, 10" tall; five actions	300	450	600
Tarzan, Marusan Co. (Banner), 1966, 13" tall; four actions	500	765	1000
Taxi, yellow cab, Linemar Co., 1950s, 7-1/2" long; five actions	100	150	200
Taxi Cab, "Y" Co., 1950s, 8-1/2" long; five actions	90	135	180
Taxi Cab, "Y" Co., 1960s, 9" long; four actions	90	135	180
Teddy Bear Circus Acrobat, includes detachable bear flyer, Tomiyana Co., 1950s, 15" high; three actions, rare	500	750	1000
Teddy Bear Swing, includes four wire supports and tin sign, T-N Co., 1950s, 17" high; three actions, two cycles	300	380	600
Teddy-Go-Kart, Alps Co., 1960s, 10-1/2" long; four actions	75	125	160

Swivel-O-Matic Astronaut, S-H Co., 1960s, $160

	C6	C8	C10
Teddy the Artist, includes removable tray and nine patterns, "Y" Co., 1950s, 8-1/2" high, 5-1/4" x 7" base; three actions	300	450	600
Teddy the Boxing Bear, "Y" Co., 1950s, 9" tall; five actions	115	190	240
Teddy the Rhythmical Drummer, Alps Co., 1960s, 11" tall; three actions	100	150	200
Telephone Bear, Linemar, 1950s, 7-1/2" high; six actions	200	300	400
Telephone Bear Ringing and Talking In His Old Rocking Chair, M-T Co., 1950s, 10" high; four actions	250	350	450
Telephone Bunny Ringing and Talking In His Old Rocking Chair, M-T Co., 1950s, 10" high; four actions	170	255	340
Television Spaceman, Alps Co., 1960s, 14-1/2" high to tip of antenna; six actions	400	600	825
Television Truck, Linemar Co., 1950s, 11" long; three actions	250	375	500
Thunder Jet Boat, Bandai Co., 9-3/4" long, 1950s; three actions	130	195	260
Tin Man, robot, all plastic, Remco Industries, Inc., 1960s, 21" tall; four actions	100	150	200

Twist Dancer, 1960s, $200

Tin Man, Remco Industries, 1960s, $200

	C6	C8	C10
Tinkling Trolley, includes two plastic cowcatchers, M-T Co., 1950s, 10-1/2" long; four actions, two cycles	150	200	250
Tiny Jeep, WACO Co., 1950s, 4-1/4" long; minor action	30	45	60
Tiny Tank, WACO Co., 1950s, 4-1/4" long; minor action	30	45	60
Tom and Jerry Car, Rico Co. (Spain), 1960s, 13" long; three actions, rare	400	600	800
Tom and Jerry Choo Choo, M-T Co., 1960s, 10-1/4" long; five actions	125	185	255
Tom and Jerry Handcar, Jerry, M-T Co., 1960s, 7-3/4" high, 7-3/4" long; three actions	150	225	300
Tom and Jerry Handcar, Tom, M-T Co., 1960s, 9-3/4" high, 7-3/4" long; three actions	150	225	300
Tom and Jerry Helicopter, 1960s, M-T Co., 9-1/2" long; three actions	125	175	250
Tom and Jerry Highway Patrol, M-T Co., 1960s, 8" long; three actions	120	180	240

	C6	C8	C10
Tom and Jerry Jumping Jeep, M-T Co., 1960s, 9" long; three actions	120	180	240
Tom-Tom Indian, "Y" Co., 1961, 10-1/2" tall; four actions	80	120	160
Topo Gigio Playing the Xylophone, T-N Co., 1960s; three actions	265	440	525
Torpedo Boat-PT 107, Linemar, 1950s, 11-1/2" long; three actions	110	165	220
Tractor, Showa Co., includes litho tin driver, 1950s, 7-1/2" long; four actions	60	90	120
Tractor, "Y" Co., 1960s, 6" long; three actions	50	75	100
Tractor On Platform, T-N Co., 1950s, 9" long tractor w/7" trailer long; minor toy	80	120	160
Train Robot, M-T Co., 1950s, 15-1/2" tall; four actions, rare	1500	2250	3000
Traveler Bear, Linemar Co., 1950s, 8" high; three actions	100	150	200
Treasure Chest Bank, Illfelder Co., 1960s, 11" tall; five actions, two cycles, risqué toy, PG-rated	90	135	180
Tric-cycling Clown, M-T Co., 1960s, 12" high; five actions	300	450	600
Tricky Dog House, No. 673, "Y" Co., 1960s, 6-3/4" high, 7-1/4" long, 6-3/4" wide; four actions	60	90	120
Trumpet Playing Bunny, Alps Co., 1950s, 10" high; four actions	150	225	300
Trumpet Playing Monkey, includes tin horn, Alps Co., 1950s, 9" high; four actions	150	225	300
Tubby the Turtle, "Y" Co., 7" long, 1950s; three actions	50	75	100
Tugboat, Marx, 6-1/2" long, 1950s; minor toy	50	75	100
Tugboat, Marusan Co., 1950s, 13-1/2" long; three actions	110	165	220
Tumbles the Bear, includes porter's hat, Y-M Co. (Yanoman), 1960s, 8-1/2" tall; minor toy	100	150	200
Turn Signal Robot, Auto Accessory, T-N Co., 1960s, 11" tall; five actions	160	240	320
Turn-O-Matic Gun Jeep, T-N Co., 1960s, 10" long; five actions	100	150	200
Turntable Xylophone Melody Train, 1960s, Cragstan Co., 29-1/2" long assembled; three actions	50	75	100
TWA Multiaction DC-7C Airliner, 1960s, Yonezawa Co., 22-1/2" long, 23-1/4" wingspan; seven actions	200	300	400
Twin Coupled Tram Cars, two cars, K Co., 1950s, 11-1/2" long; minor toy	100	150	200

	C6	C8	C10
Twin Racing Cars, Alps Co., 1950s, 7" long, 10" long w/coupling rod; three actions	400	600	800
Twirly Whirly, Alps Co., 1950s, 13-1/2" high; four actions	290	450	600
Twist Dancer (Let's Twist), includes two plastic-rubber rockets, no mfr. mark, 1960s, 15" high; minor toy	100	150	200
Two Stage Rocket Launching Pad, T-N Co., 1950s, 7" long, 4" wide, 8" high; three actions	250	375	500
UFO-X05, M-T Co., 1970s, 7-1/2" diameter; three actions	50	75	100
Union Mountain Cable Lines, Monorail set, T-N Co., 1950s, 8" long car w/22" x 32" 16-piece oval track; minor toy	80	120	160
United DC7 Mainliner, Yonezawa Co., 1950s, 14" wingspan; five actions	200	300	400
United Mainliner Stratocruiser, Linemar, 1950s, 19-1/2" long, 13" wingspan; four actions	190	285	380
United States Ocean Liner, Linemar Co., 1950s, 14" long; three actions	200	300	400
United States Ocean Liner, "Y" Co., 1950s, 18-1/2" long; three actions	300	450	600
Universal Machine Gun, T-N Co., 1950s, 14-3/4" long; three actions	70	105	140
USA NASA Apollo Space Ship, M-T Co., 1960s, 9" long; four actions	150	225	300
USA NASA Gemini Space Capsule, includes detachable astronaut, M-T Co., 1960s, 9" long; four actions	120	180	240
U.S. Army Machine Gunner, unmarked, 1960s, 10" long; four actions	100	150	200
U.S. Air Force Military Airlift Command Jet, T-N Co., 1960s, 14" wingspan; four actions	130	195	260
U.S. Air Force Smoking Jet No. 75029, T-N Co., 1950s, 12" wingspan; three actions (smokes, engine noise and bump and go), rare	200	300	400
U.S. Navy Pom Pom Gun, Remco Co., 1950s, 20" long; four actions	80	120	160
U.S. Royal Tire Mechanical Toy (Ferris wheel), includes plastic figures, souvenir for 1964-65 N.Y. World's Fair, Ideal, minor toy; 10" high	100	150	200
Video Robot, S-H Co., 1960s, 10" tall; three actions	150	175	225
V.I.P. the Busy Boss, S&E Co., 8" high, 1950s; six actions	225	325	425

U.S. Royal Tire Mechanical Toy, souvenir from 1964-65 N.Y. World's Fair, Ideal, $200

Walking Bear with Xylophone, Linemar Co., 1950s, $365

	C6	C8	C10
Visible Ford Mustang, Bandai Co., 10" long, 1960s; four actions	80	120	160
Vision Robot, S-H Co., 1960s, 11-3/4" tall; five actions	150	225	300
Voice Control Astronaut Base, includes plastic missiles and phonograph records, Remco Co., 1969, 19" long; four actions	90	135	180
Volkswagen Convertible, T-N Co., 1950s, 9-3/4" long; three actions	250	375	500
Volkswagen-Elektrik, Mignon Co., 1950s, 8-1/2" long; three actions	70	105	140
Volkswagen No. 7653, Bandai Co., 1960s, 10" long; three actions	90	135	180
Volkswagen with Visible Engine, K.O. Co., 1960s, 7" long; three actions	80	120	160
Volkswagen with Visible Engine No. 4049, Bandai Co., 1960s, 8" long; three actions	90	135	180
Wagon Master, M-T Co., 1960s, 18" long; four actions	120	180	240
Walking Bear with Xylophone, Linemar Co., 1950s, 10" high; seven actions	175	270	365
Walking Elephant, Linemar Co., 1950s, 8-1/2" long; three actions	100	150	200
Walking 'Esso' Tiger, Marx Co., 1950s, 11-1/2" tall; four actions	250	350	450
Walking Itchy Dog, Alps Co., 1950s, 9" long; five actions	45	75	100

	C6	C8	C10
Walky-Son (Los), includes detachable guns and baton, Geyper Co., 1960s; four actions, 11-1/2" high; rare: See Los Walky-Son			
Warpath Indian, Alps Co., 1950s, 12" tall; three actions	100	150	200
Wash-O-Matic washing machine, includes lid, T-N Co., 1940s, 5-3/4" high, 4-1/4" diameter; minor toy	30	45	60
Water Spouting Whale with Flopping Tail, KKS Co., 1950s, 13" long; minor toy	100	150	200
Western Badman Red Gulch Bar, includes three plastic bottles and two plastic glasses, M-T Co., 1960s, 9-3/4" high; eight actions	300	450	600
Western Express, Locomotive, Kanto Toy Co., 1960s, 14" long; four actions	50	75	100
Western Locomotive, M-T Co., 10-1/2" long, 1950s; four actions	45	65	80
Western Special Locomotive, M-T Co., 1950s, 12" long; five actions	50	75	100
Wheel-A-Gear Robot, Taiyo Co., 1960s, 14" tall; five actions	250	375	500
WHOH Skyway Patrol Helicopter, M-T Co., 1950s, 18" long; four actions	100	150	200
Whirlybird Helicopter, Remco Co., 1960s, 25" long; three actions	80	120	160
Whistling Showboat, M-T Co., 1950s, 14" long; three actions	120	180	240

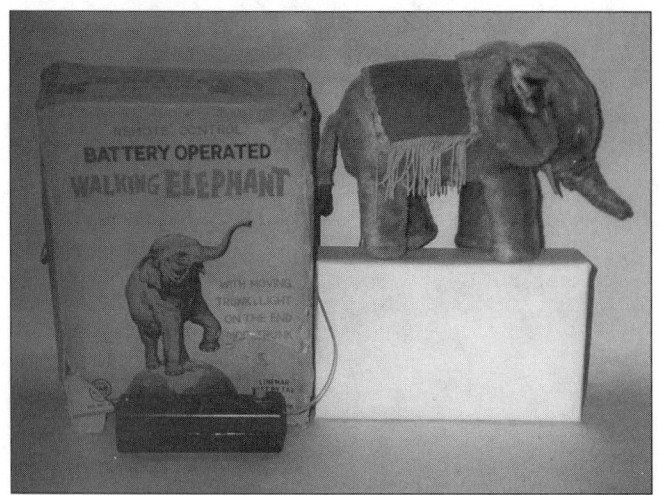

Walking Elephant, Linemar Co., 1950s, $155

X-70 Robot, T-N Co., 1960s, $1,000

	C6	C8	C10
Wild West Rodeo, includes plastic bowl for bubble solution, Linemar, 6-1/2" long, 8" high, 1950s; five actions	100	150	200
Windy the Elephant, includes celluloid ball and tin litho umbrella, T-N Co., 1950s, 9-3/4" high; three actions	150	200	250
Winner 23, Rocket, includes rubber track, KDP Co. (Excelo), 1950s, 5-1/2" long; minor action	150	225	300
Winner of the West Overland Stagecoach with Four Galloping Horses, Alps Co., 1950s; 18" long; four actions	200	300	400
Winston the Barking Bulldog, Tomiyama Co., 1950s, 10" long; threeactions, two cycles	70	105	140
Worried Mother Duck and Baby, T-N Co., 1950s, 11" long, 7" high; three actions	100	150	200
X-7 Space Explorer Ship, M-T Co., 1960s, 7" diameter; four actions	90	135	180
X-70 Robot, T-N Co., 1960s, 12-1/4" tall; five actions, rare	500	750	1000
X-1800 Space Vehicle, includes detachable plastic antenna, M-T Co., 1960s, 9" long; five actions	140	210	280
X-F 160 Jet Airplane, K-O Co., 1960s, 8" wingspan	80	120	160
Yeti the Abominable Snowman, Marx, 1960s, 12" tall; four actions	250	335	500

	C6	C8	C10
Yo-Yo Clown, includes plastic yo-yo, Alps Co., 1960s, 9" high; three actions	150	190	300
Yo-Yo Monkey, includes plastic yo-yo, Alps Co., 1960s, 9" tall; three actions	100	185	245
Yo-Yo Monkey, Y-M Co., 1960s, 12" tall, spring extension to 32"; minor toy	85	135	180
Yummy Yum Kitty, Alps Co., 1950s, 9-1/2" high; five actions	170	270	325
Zero Fighter Plane, Bandai Co., 1950s, 12-1/2" long, 15" wingspan; three actions	150	230	300
Zoom Motorboat, K Co., 1950s, 12" long; three actions	100	150	200
Zoomer the Robot, T-N Co., 1950s, 8" tall; three actions	250	375	500

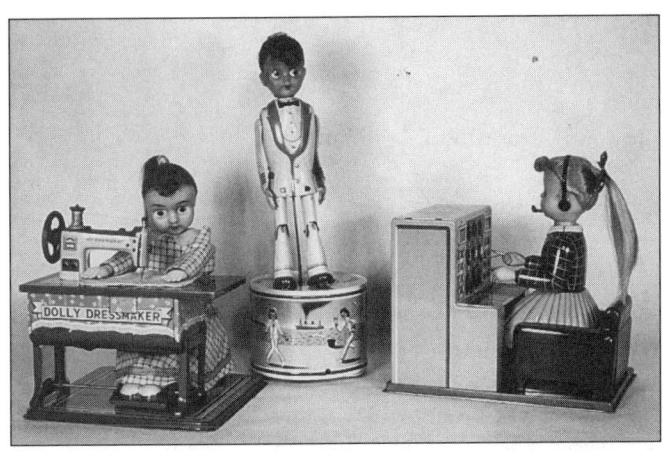

Left to Right; Dennis the Menace, Rosko, $240; Chimp with Xylophone, "Y" Co., $200

Left to Right: Dolly Dressmaker, T-N Co., 1950s, $325; Strutting My Fair Dancer, Haji Co., 1950s, $200; Switchboard Operator, Linemar, 1950s, $800

Dentist Bear, S&E Co., $600

BELL TOYS

	C6	C8	C10
Acrobats holding bells, Gong Bell Co. No. 54	310	465	620
Alligator ridden by Black Boy, N.N. Hill, 1910, cast iron, 5-1/2" long	1000	1700	2300
Alligator snapping at teasing boy, cast iron, 9-1/4" long	1500	2400	3500
Althof Bergmann, tin, "Chime & Design Patd. May 19th 1874," three soldiers, one w/flag, two w/rifles	1600	2400	3200
Are You a Buffalo, Gong Bell Co.	800	1200	1600
Bear on tricycle, 4" long	150	225	300
Bear, iron, bounces in air	800	1100	1600
Billy Goat, Gong Bell Co., No. 51, cast iron, goat mechanically butts bell, 1900, 7-1/2" long	750	1125	1500
Bird and bell, tin and iron, 6" long	600	900	1200

	C6	C8	C10
Boy and Goat, Althof Bergmann, tin, 9" long	600	900	1200
Boy Scouts, iron, rest pressed steel, heart-shaped tin wheels, 13-1/2" long	750	1125	1500
Boys eating Bananas, cast iron	700	1050	1400
Camel with Rider, tin, Althof Bergmann, c. 1874, 9" long	1200	2000	2800
Cat and Dog, Gong Bell Co.	2000	3200	4500
Cinderella Chariot, 9-1/4" long	425	638	850
Clown and Black man on see-saw, c. 1905, six color, Watrous, cast iron, 6-1/2" long	600	900	1200
Clown and Pig, 1900	325	488	650
Clown bell-ringers riding back to back on a mule	1000	1500	2000
Clown, Gong Bell Co., 5-3/4" long	262	393	525
Comic Characters, two, pressed steel and iron, three bells, pierced heart wheels	700	1125	1400
Daisy, Gong Bell Co., 9" long	600	1000	1400
Darky Fishing, Stevens, 8" long	440	660	880
Ding Dong Bell, Pussy's Not in The Well, cast iron, c. 1880, Gong Bell Co., 9-1/2" long	600	925	1235
Dog on Platform, Fallows	400	650	900
Eagle, c. 1906, Gong Bell Co., cast iron, 5-1/4" long	550	850	1200
Elephant & Rider in Howdah, driver on elephant's head, 4-1/2" long, cast iron	700	1100	1500

Are You a Buffalo, Gong Bell Co., $1,600

Cat and Dog, Gong Bell Co., $4,500

Daisy, Gong Bell Co., 9" long, $1,400

Hello, Hello Telephone Chimes with Monkey, Gong Bell Co., $4,000

	C6	C8	C10
Elephant on Platform, Fallows, 6-3/4" long	425	638	850
Elephant w/ bell in trunk, N.N. Hill, c. 1905	700	1050	1400
Eskimo & Bear, pressed steel body, iron figures	750	1125	1500
Evening News Baby Quieter, cast iron, man reading paper to baby, 1890s, Stevens, 8" long	1100	1700	2450
Goat, Lamb and Girl on platform, George Brown, tin, early, 11" long	550	850	1200
Goat, painted tin, Fallows, 1880, 14"	1100	1650	2200
Goat, tin, c. 1890, small woman at left leg of goat, either Althof Bergmann or Ives, 7-1/2" high	500	750	1000
Goats, two, butting, Gong Bell Co.	1200	2000	3000
Hello, Hello Telephone Chimes w/monkey, Gong Bell Co.	2000	3000	4000
Horse and Rider, heart-shaped wheels, tin, 9" long	750	1125	1500
Hunter and Rabbit, cast-iron rabbit pops out, N.N. Hill, 1900	750	1125	1500
Jack and Jill on seesaw, cast iron and tin, Watrous, 7-1/2" long	440	660	880
Jockey on Horse, early, 7-1/2" long	200	300	400

Monkey and Coconut, N.N. Hill, $700

	C6	C8	C10
Jonah and Whale, Hill, 5" long	800	1400	2000
Landing of Columbus, 7" long	492	740	985
Liberty Bell Centennial, Gong Bell Co., 8" long	800	1200	1600
Mary and Her Little Lamb, Gong Bell Co., 8" long	600	900	1250
Monkey and Coconut, N.N. Hill, "Monkey Mobile," 6" long	350	525	700
Monkey and Dog, heart wheels, cast iron and tin, 7" long	500	750	1000
Monkey and Horse, Gong Bell Co., cast iron and tin, "No. 23"	1500	2250	3000
Monkey on a Log, cast iron, Gong Bell Co. Mfg. Co., c. 1900	750	1125	1500

Ding Dong Bell, Pussy's Not in The Well, Gong Bell Co., 9-1/2" long, $1,235

Landing of Columbus, 7" long, $985

Trick Elephant, Gong Bell Co., 7-3/4" long, $1,600

Poodle Dog Bell Ringer with Clown, Gong Bell Co., $4,200

	C6	C8	C10
Monkey on a Velocipede, cast iron, 8" high	1500	2400	3800
Monkey riding Elephant, tin, clockwork, Fallows, 10" long	1400	2100	2800
Oriental Clown & Poodle, No. 44, painted cast iron, 1900, cloth in hoop, poodle jumps through hoop and back, 13" long	1250	1875	2500
Pig with Clown Rider, Gong Bell Co., 6" long	418	625	835
Poodle Dog Bell Ringer w/Clown, Gong Bell Co.	1200	2800	4200
Rough Rider, Watrous, early, 6-1/2" long	123	185	245
Saw the Watermelon, Gong Bell Co., 8-1/2" long	1100	1700	2800
Steeplechase, two jockeys on horses, Hubley	600	900	1200

	C6	C8	C10
Tramp, cast iron, Gong Bell Co., 6" long	438	655	875
Trick Elephant, Gong Bell Co., 7-3/4" long	800	1200	1600
Trick Pony, cast iron "39," Gong Bell Co., 1893, 8" long	600	1000	1350
Uncle Sam and The Don, Gong Bell Co.	2250	3375	4500
Victory in a shell-form Chariot, cast iron, mounted w/bell and eagle	1500	2250	3000
Watermelon, N.N. Hill Brass Co., c. 1905, 8-1/2" long	600	900	1200
White horse pulling heart-shaped wheels, Ives, c. 1896, 9-1/2" long	1000	1500	2000
Wild Mule Jack, cast iron	750	1125	1500
Young America, cast iron, Gong Bell Co., c. 1880, 6" long	450	675	900

CATALOGS

	C6	C8	C10
A.C. Williams, 1908	220	330	440
A.C. Williams, c. 1930, c. 1934, each	45	68	90
A.C. Williams, c. 1934	45	68	90
Aldens Christmas, 1946	40	60	80
Arcade, 1889	100	150	200
Arcade, 1899	105	158	210
Arcade, 1900	115	172	230
Arcade, 1901	375	562	750
Arcade, 1902-03	85	128	170
Arcade, 1917	500	750	1000
Arcade, 1924	150	225	300
Arcade, 1931	125	188	250
Arcade, 1940	100	150	200
Auburn Rubber, pre-WWII	50	75	100
Aurora, 1960	27	41	55

	C6	C8	C10
Aurora, 1963, 1964, each	50	75	100
Aurora, 1965, 1967, each	55	82	110
Aurora, 1971, 1972, each	17	26	35
Aurora, 1973	27	41	55
Aurora, 1975	25	38	50
Aurora, 1977	22	33	45
Baltimore Price Reducer, 1928, illustrated w/toys, games, etc.	15	22	30
Barclay, pre-WWII	200	300	400
Bilt E-Z, 1924	5	8	10
Buddy L, 1926 flier	175	263	350
Buddy L, 1929	275	352	550
Buddy L Jr., 1930	150	225	300
Buddy L, 1932 Robotoy flier	125	188	250
Buddy L, 1935	175	262	350
Buddy L, 1940	125	188	250
Buddy L, 1941	135	202	270
Buddy L, 1952, 1953, 1956, 1957, 1959, each	7	11	15
Buddy L, 1961	22	33	45
Buffalo Toy, 1939	75	112	150
Butler Bros. 1889, tin toys, squeak toys, etc.	30	45	60
Butler Bros. 1891, illustrated w/mechanical banks, toys, dolls, etc.	30	45	60
Butler Bros., Nov. 1899	40	60	80
Butler Bros., June 1917	70	105	140
Butler Bros., Christmas 1930	35	52	70
Butler Bros., Christmas 1931	35	52	70
Butler Bros., 1935, 1936, each	40	60	80
Butler Bros., Spring, 1941	60	90	120
Carpenter, Francis, 1880s	900	1350	1800
Champion, four pages and cover	150	225	300
Chein, 1956, 1960, each	50	75	100
Corgi, 1966, 1967, each	10	15	20
Daisy, 1975	22	33	45
Dayton, 1929	150	225	300
Dent Hardware Co., 1900, forty pages	40	60	80
Dent Hardware Co., 1905	37	56	75
Dent Hardware Co., c. 1910	37	56	75
Dent Hardware Co., Fullerton, Pa., undated	30	45	60
Dent Hardware Co., Fullerton, Pa., iron toys, 1930	32	48	65
Dinky, 1950s	27	41	55
"Dunham," Buckley & Co., New York, 1895, toys, etc.	40	60	80

FIFTY-FIRST EDITION

The
A. C. WILLIAMS CO.

TOYS

House Furnishing Specialties
and
HARDWARE

RAVENNA, OHIO
U. S. A.

This Catalog Supercedes All Other Catalogs
WRITE FOR PRICES.

A.C. Williams, c. 1934, $90

Fisher-Price, 1966, $50

	C6	C8	C10
Durable Toy & Novelty, c. 1920s	10	15	20
Ehrich Bros., New York, 1892, illustrations of banks, toys, dolls, etc.	40	60	80
Eldon, 1961, autos	6	9	12
Eldon, 1961, boats	6	9	12
Erector Set, 1938, 38 pp.	15	22	30
Ertl, 1974	3	5	6
Eureka Trick & Novelty Co., c. 1875, thirty-two pages	20	30	40
A.J. Fisher, New York, 1877, illustrating cap pistols, etc.	18	27	36
Fisher-Price, 1954	6	9	12
Fisher-Price, 1966	25	38	50
Garton pedal cars, 1940	100	150	200
Gendron, 1927	600	900	1200
Gilbert, 1966	27	41	55
Gould, L., 1922, Christmas	125	188	250
Gould, L., 1940	55	83	110
Grey Iron, c. 1920s, No. 24	115	172	230
Hasbro, 1975	27	41	55
Hasbro, 1987, 1989	20	30	40
Howdy Doody Merchandise, 1955	27	41	55
Hubley 1914-15	55	83	110
Hubley, 1939	60	90	120
Hubley, 1966	16	24	32

	C6	C8	C10
Hubley, 1969	11	16	22
Hubley, 1974	22	33	45
Ideal, 1973	12	18	25
Ideal, 1976	12	18	25
Ives, Blakeslee & Williams, two-sided broadside, c. 1890, 18" x 24"	70	105	140
Ives Yachts, Ships and Shipping, c. 1915, 24 pages	50	75	100
Illustrated brochure of cap pistols and animated cap pistols by Ives and Williams	20	30	40
JCPenney, Christmas, 1963, 1964, 1965, each	68	102	135
JCPenney, Christmas, 1966 through 1970, each	50	75	100
JCPenney, Christmas, 1971 through 1975 each	35	52	70
JCPenney, Christmas, 1975 through 1980, each	27	41	55
Jones & Bixler, 1912	100	150	200
Kenton Hardware Co., No. 16, 1920s, 112 pages	70	105	140
Kenton Hardware Co., 1934; illus. in color	50	75	100
Kilgore 1977-78	22	33	45
Kingsbury, 1919	55	82	110
Kingsbury, c. 1920, c. 1925, each	32	48	65
Kingsbury, c. 1930s, small-size, 128 pp.	100	150	200
Kingsbury Toys, Motor Driven, 1936, 16 pages	40	60	80
Knapp Electric Toys No. 35	10	15	20
Knickerbocker, 1961	8	12	17
Manoil, c. 1935-1939	100	150	200
Marx, 1930s, 36 pp.	225	338	450
Marx, 1964	125	188	250
Marx, 1966	100	150	200

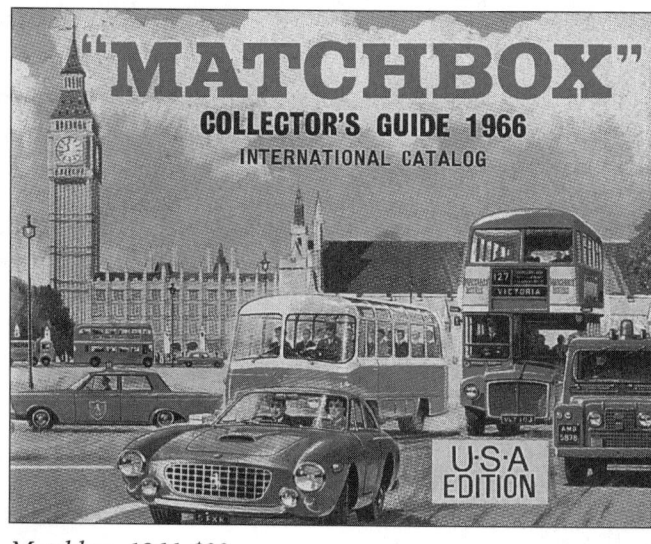

Matchbox, 1966, $30

Matchbox, 1968, $15

	C6	C8	C10
Marx, 1969	110	165	220
Marx, 1976	12	18	25
Matchbox, 1964	25	38	50
Matchbox, 1965	22	33	45
Matchbox, 1966	15	22	30
Matchbox, 1968	7	11	15
Matchbox, 1969	6	9	12
Matchbox, 1970	4	6	8
Matchbox, 1973	11	16	22
Matchbox, 1978	13	19	26
Mattel, 1967	150	225	300
McCadden & Bros. Philadelphia, illustrated iron and tin toys, banks, mechanical toys, dolls, games, etc.	50	75	100
Mego, 1967-69, each	50	75	100
Mickey Mouse Merchandise Catalog, 1935, by Kay Kamen Co., 80 pages, hundreds of illustrations of Mickey Mouse items	300	450	600

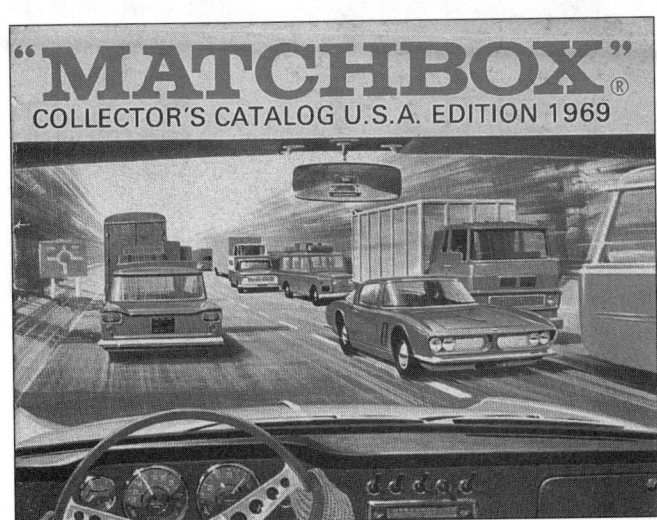

Matchbox, 1969, $12

	C6	C8	C10
Montgomery Ward, Christmas, 1934 through 1940, each	82	123	165
Montgomery Ward, Christmas, 1941 through 1965, each	68	102	135
Montgomery Ward, Christmas, 1966 throug 1970, each	50	75	100
Montgomery Ward, Christmas, 1971 through 1975, each	35	52	70
Montgomery Ward, Christmas, 1976 through 1980	27	41	55
Montgomery Ward, Christmas, 1981 through 1985	20	30	40
Nicol & Co. 1895, illustrating banks, etc.	27	41	55
Ohio Art, 1961	8	12	17
Popsicle Pete Radio News and Premium catalog, early	40	60	80
Popsicle Pete's 1949 four-page gift list	10	15	20
Pyro, 1966, 1967, each	19	28	38
Pyro, 1970	9	13	18
Rel Toy Boats foldout, 1958	20	30	40
Revell, 1957-58	37	56	75
Revell, 1958-59	25	38	50
Revell, 1969	10	15	20
Schoenhut , 1903	100	150	200
Schoenhut Circus, 1918	112	168	225

Mattel, 1967, $300.

Woolworth's Christmas, 1954, $30

Woolworth's Christmas, 1952, $30

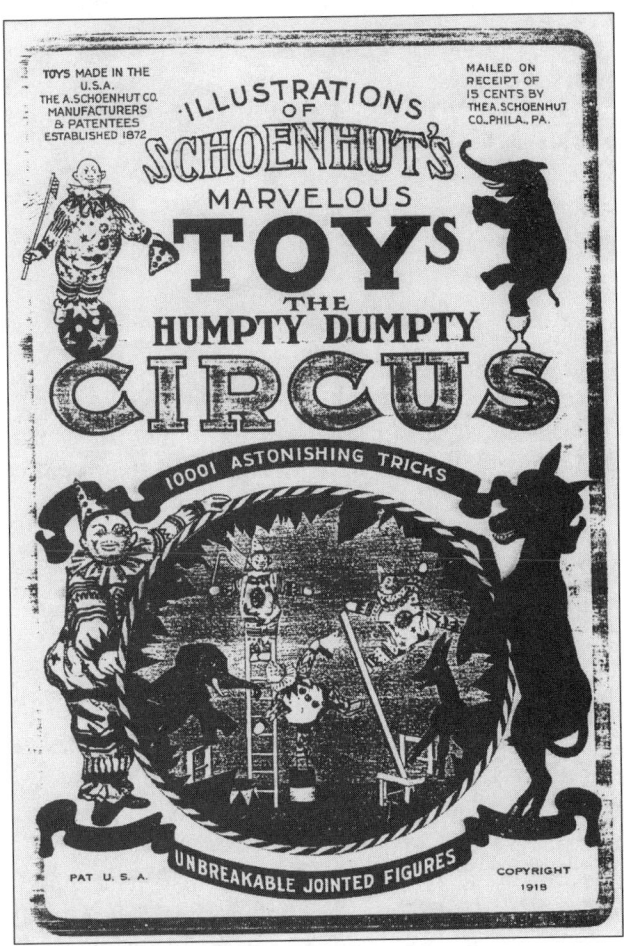

Schoenhut, 1918, $225

	C6	C8	C10
Schoenhut Circus, 1928	100	150	200
Schoenhut Humpty Dumpty Circus (other toys as well), c. 1915, many illustrations	100	165	220
Sears, 1919, Fall-Winter	30	45	60
Sears Christmas 1926	67	100	135
Sears Christmas 1933	60	90	120
Sears Christmas 1936 through 1940, each	82	123	165
Sears Christmas 1941 through 1945, each	82	123	165
Sears Christmas 1946 through 1950, each	82	123	165
Sears Christmas 1951 through 1955, each	82	123	165
Sears Christmas 1956 through 1960, each	82	123	165
Sears Christmas 1961 through 1965, each	82	123	165
Sears Christmas 1966 through 1970, each	60	90	120
Sears Christmas 1971 through 1975, each	45	68	90
Sears Christmas 1976 through 1980, each	30	45	60
Selchow & Righter, 1894-5, games and toys, illustrated trains, boats, bell toys, mechanical banks, etc.	120	180	240

	C6	C8	C10
Selchow & Righter, 1908-1909, 108 pages	80	120	160
Selchow & Righter, 1921	32	48	65
Shure, N. 1940	85	128	170
Smith-Miller, 1954	40	60	80
Spiegel, Christmas, 1941 through 1965, each	68	102	135
Spiegel, Christmas, 1966 through 1970, each	50	75	100
Spiegel, Christmas, 1971 through 1975, each	35	52	70
Spiegel, Christmas, 1976 through 1980, each	27	41	55
Spiegel, Christmas, 1981 through 1985, each	20	30	40
Spiegel, Christmas, 1986 through 1990, each	15	22	30
State, Adams & Dearborn Sts., Chicago, illustrated	10	15	20
Steelcraft, 1934, 44 pp.	300	450	600
Steelcraft, 1936	350	525	700
Stern, Carl P., illustrating cap pistols, etc.	15	22	30
Stevens, J.E. Co., 1906, illustrations of iron toys and mechanical banks	40	60	80
Stevens, J.E. Co., No. 51, Export	40	60	80
Strauss, c. 1926, tiny, 32 pp.	37	56	75
Structo Toys, 1931, 8 pages	10	15	20
Supplee-Biddle of Philadelphia, 1930, 174 pages, many toys	90	135	180
Thorsen & Cassady, 1894, guns, etc.	20	30	40
Tinkertoy, 1926	6	9	12
Tom Mix, 1936 Premium Catalog	30	45	60
Toy Yearbook, 1952-53, 1956-57, 1957-58, 1958-59, each	12	18	25
Transogram, 1949	15	22	30
Vindex, c. 1932	275	365	550
Walt Disney Character Merchandise, 1930s	250	375	500
Walt Disney Character Merchandise, 1940-41	250	375	500
Western Auto, 1960 through 1969, each	32	48	65
Williams, Charles, 1928	22	33	45
Woolworth's Christmas Catalogs, pre-WWII	30	45	60
Woolworth's Christmas, 1951	30	45	60
Woolworth's Christmas, 1952	15	22	30
Woolworth's Christmas, 1954	15	22	30

COMIC CHARACTERS

See also Battery-Operated, Mechanical Banks, Paper, Premiums, Movies, Ramp Walkers,
Vehicles - Tootsietoy, Wood & Composition Toys

We stand at the gateway to a new era in collecting. It is an exciting time to be a collector, and it is only going to get more better as we count down the days until the year 2000 and then the end of the century. When the century concludes on December 31, 2000 and the new millennium begins, we will see for the first time in the twentieth century as a complete unit. No one is better prepared to see the combined forces of history and nostalgia than is the collector.

Toys, particularly the highest desirable block we call comic character collectibles, represent an amazing faction of collectors who can rightly be proud of their achievements in recent years. Collectors, researchers and other enthusiasts have worked exhausting hours tracking down information on older toys and documenting the release of newer ones.

Part of the puzzle was, of course, the question that stuck in the minds of many collectors: What exactly qualifies as a toy? What separates, for instance, a die-cast truck from a poster or a premium from a store-bought item? *Webster's New World Dictionary,* 3rd College Edition defines a toy as any article to play with, especially playthings for children. That is a very open, inclusive definition to be sure, but it is also very appropriate since we all know toys can certainly not be limited to Barbies, Matchbox cars and Lincoln Logs.

The record prices realized in recent years for high grade items, particularly those in their original packaging, is not a fluke. The attention to items from our past is growing and it is going to keep growing as more pieces of the puzzle are fit together. Unlike fads that explode onto the scene, fade out, return, and fade out again, the interest in both nostalgia and history is going to expand for the foreseeable future. Those who suggest that nostalgia itself is a fad simply aren't dealing with the facts.

History has never been more accessible. Whether you want the factual history of people, dates and events, or the parallel pop culture history, it is now generally at your fingertips. Turning the page in a book such as this, clicking a computer mouse or a TV remote control now opens the world of the past to us instantly.

The History Channel, A&E, The Learning Channel, Nickelodeon's Nick at Nite and TV Land, ESPN's Classic Sports, Discovery's Discovery Channel and Animal Planet are functioning from the same basic impulse: We want to know more. When we get to know more, we want even more. As a society we seem bent on documenting everything, and as we document we understand. As we understand, we tend to see items we overlooked or passed by in a different light. What was just there, is now intriguing or even cool.

And it is not just limited to collectors recapturing their own childhood either. The demographics of those cable channels, the expanding use of the Internet and the proliferation of books on collecting suggest just the opposite. The link collectibles provide to the past is a tangible, hold-it-in-your-hands understanding of what was going on way back when. Those who think that this type of nostalgia is anything but here to stay have missed the boat (and beware, many of them will spend a lot of time trying to convince you they're right when they're looking to buy your collection.)

If you still think nostalgia for a particular period is limited to those who lived through it, how would you explain the revival of swing music? For that matter, have Beethoven's manuscripts lost value since all of his peers passed away? How about Van Gogh's artwork or Civil War-era coins?

No reasonable person would suggest that a small collection of toys could put your child through college, but high-grade character collectibles represent one of the best investments you could have made in the past few years. Like anything else, though, the market varies based on region and a number of other factors, including the ability of a salesman to sell his product. Many times the marketplace is misunderstood by would-be sellers who are not adequately informed about what they have, what they need to do to sell it, and what they should expect to get out of it. This isn't surprising considering how new our hobby is.

The process of breaking down, identifying, recording and researching these vast areas of collectibles began less than 30 years ago, and it is only in the last decade that we've really accelerated the process, if you consider the huge amount of information that was missing when we started getting organized as collectors.

Certainly the documentation efforts aren't going to end with the end of the century, and neither is the interest in these items. A new term to go with our outlook does seem in order, though.

"Twentieth century collectibles" is a name which spans and includes such sub-groups as toys, Jazz Age Trinkets and Art Deco design. While those and other similar terms are at least somewhat subjective, the time frame twentieth century is not.

Contributor: John K. Snyder, Jr., Diamond International Galleries, 1966 Greenspring Drive, Suite 401, Timonium, MD 21093. Snyder is President of Diamond International Galleries and is a leading expert on comic character collectibles. He serves as a pricing advisor to *The Overstreet Comic Book Price Guide*, *The Overstreet Toy Ring Price Guide*, *Hake's Price Guide to Character Toys*, *Collecting Figures* magazine, *Tomart's Radio Premiums Price Guide*, Krause Publication's *Radio Premiums Price Guide and Toys & Prices*, and the *Original Comic Art Price Guide*.

ALPHONSE

	C6	C8	C10
Nodder, cast iron, movable arms and hands, two goats pulling wagon, Hubley, early 1900s, 13-3/4" long, 7-1/2" high	200	300	500
Nodder, cast iron, mule pulling wagon, Hubley, 7" long	250	450	750
Nodder, cast iron, movable arms and hands in a goat-pulled cart, Hubley, early 1900s, 13-3/4" long, 7-1/2" high	550	450	750
Nodder, in horse-drawn carriage, nodder toy, c. 1910, 10-1/2" long	500	825	1200

Alphonse Nodder, cast-iron, Hubley, $750

BARNEY GOOGLE

	C6	C8	C10
Barney Google and Sparkplug Pull Toy, tin litho, Sparkplug in barn	1500	2250	3500
Barney Google and Sparkplug Scooter Race, pull toy, Nifty Toy Co., 1920s, 8" long	3000	4800	7000
Barney Google and Sparkplug, tin wind-up, Nifty	650	975	1300
Barney Google Candy Container, glass	150	282	375
Barney Google Doll, wood w/composition head and movable arms and legs, 9" high	175	325	450
Barney Google Hand Puppet, Gund	45	72	150
Barney Google Riding Sparkplug Paperweight, metal, 3"	75	150	200
Barney Google Wind-up, tin, c. 1923	350	750	1000

BATMAN

	C6	C8	C10
Bat Grenade, 1966	50	65	75
Bat Ray, Remco, 1977	25	38	60
Batchute, 1966, in box add $200	30	63	100
Batmobile, Corgi, No. 267	55	83	125
Batmobile-Batman Driver, Marx, 1966	65	98	175
Batmobile-Robin Driver, Marx, 4" long	65	98	150
Bullhorn, plastic, Bayshore Ind., 1966	25	45	75
Escape Gun, Lincoln, c. 1966	42	63	125
Flying Batman, inflatable, Ideal, 1966, 12"	10	15	30
Glasses, 1966	4	10	20
Hand Puppet, cloth body	27	41	75
Hand Puppet, vinyl, Ideal, 1965	27	41	75
Helmet and Cape, helmet fits over whole head, Ideal, 1966	145	218	350
Hot Line Batphone, Marx	250	375	600
Pay Set, Ideal, 1973	25	50	75
Picture Pistol, Marx, 1966	225	338	500
Soaky	30	40	65
Thingmaker Set, on original card, 1960s	35	75	155

	C6	C8	C10
Utility Belt Set, Remco, 1979	50	75	100
Utility Belt, w/belt-radio buckle, on original card, 1960s	50	75	125

BUCK ROGERS

	C6	C8	C10
Atomic Pistol, 1946, U-235, Daisy	150	250	350
Battle Cruiser, two grooved wheels on topto run on string, Tootsietoy, 1937	100	150	225
Casting Set, Junior Caster, Rapaport Bros, 1930s	325	488	650
Chemical Laboratory, large set, Gropper Toys, 1937	800	1200	1500
Chemical Laboratory, small set, Gropper Toys, 1937	600	950	1250
Disintegrator Pistol, Daisy, 1936, w/box $300	200	275	375
Figure, Tootsietoy, 1-3/4" high	38	56	75
Flash Blast Attack Ship, two grooved wheels on top to run string, Tootsietoy, 1937, 4-1/2" long	225	338	450
Flying Saucer, paper, 1940s	75	112	150
Helmet, leather, Daisy, 1933	300	500	750

	C6	C8	C10
Liquid Helium water pistol, Daisy, 1936, w/box add $1,000	450	600	800
Pop Pistol, 1930s	112	168	225
Rocket Pistol, XZ-31, Daisy, 1934, 9-1/2" long, w/box add $300	132	210	300
Rocket Police Patrol, wind-up, Marx, 1939	800	1300	1800
Rocket Ship, wind-up, Marx, 1934, 12" long,	358	535	715
Rubber Band Gun, 1940, 5" x 10"	50	75	100
Sonic Ray Gun, yellow plastic, 1952	65	100	150
Strato Kite, 1946	37	56	75
Super Sonic Glasses (binoculars), 1953	70	105	140
Super Sonic Ray Gun w/box	150	200	300
Super-Scope, 1952, w/adjustable plastic telescope, Norton-Honer Mfg. Co., 8-1/2" long	92	138	185
U-238 Atomic Pistol and Holster set, 1948, w/box add $300	400	600	850

Buck Rogers Atomic Pistol U-235, Daisy, 1946, $350

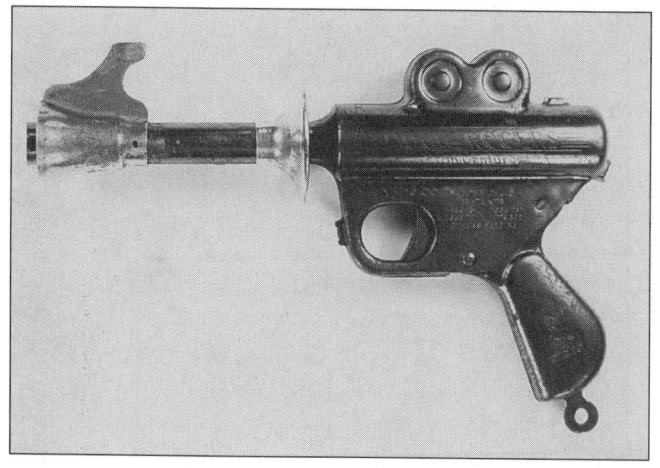

Buck Rogers Rocket Pistol XZ-31, Daisy, 1934, $300

Buster Brown and Tige wind-up tin with Streetlamp and bell, c. early 1900s, $5,500

	C6	C8	C10
U-238 Atomic Pistol and Holster set, adventure book and coupon, w/box, Daisy, 1946	800	950	1250
USN Los Angeles, Tootsietoy, 5" long	117	175	235
Venus Duo Destroyer, two grooved wheels on top to run on string, Tootsietoy, 1937	170	255	340
Walkie Talkie, 1950s	110	165	220
Wilma pistol and holster set, small version of Buck Rogers "Pop" pistol, 1930s	200	300	400

BUSTER BROWN AND TIGE

	C6	C8	C10
Buster Brown and Tige Paper Dolls, w/envelope, dolls, Tige, four suits and hats, and hat for Tige, J. Ottman Lith. Co., N.Y.	150	200	300
Buster Brown and Tige Ring, brass, 1930s	35	50	75
Buster Brown and Tige, cast iron, Buster in cart pulled by Tige, 7-1/2" long	500	750	900
Buster Brown and Tige Wind-up, tin, w/street lamp and bell, c. early 1900s	2000	3500	5500
Buster Brown Doll, 1920s, 23" high	200	300	400
Buster Brown Figure, lead	20	35	50
Buster Brown Secret Agent Periscope, c. 1950, 20" long	25	40	60

CAPTAIN MARVEL

	C6	C8	C10
Flying Captain Marvel, paper, Reed, 1944-47, 7" x 10"	15	20	30

Captain Marvel tin wind-up race cars range from $275-$300 individually; the complete Mint-in-Box set with keys is valued at $1,500.

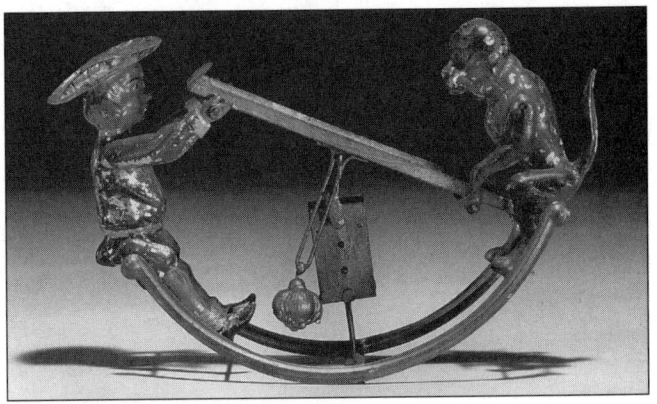

Captian Marvel Buzz Bomb, $40

	C6	C8	C10
Buzz Bomb	20	30	40
Comic Hero Punch-Outs, includes two Captain Marvels, Capt. Marvel Jr., Bulletman, Bulletgirl, Spy Smasher, Ibis, two Golden Arrows, Minute Man, Freddy Freeman, Mr. Scarlet, Commando Yank, Pinky, Bulletdog; Samuel Lowe, 1942	150	200	250
Gun, movie gun w/film	175	263	350
Magic Eyes, Reed, c. 1945	15	30	40

Captain Marvel Comic Hero Punch-Outs, 1942, $250

	C6	C8	C10
Magic Flute, copyright picture of Captain Marvel on side, 1946, on original card	100	150	175
Magic Picture, Reed, c. 1944	50	70	90
Porsche Car, Corgi, 1979, No. 262	37	56	75
Race Car No. 1, tin wind-up, 1947, 4" long	175	250	300
Race Car No. 2, tin wind-up, 1947, 4" long	175	225	275
Race Car No. 3, tin wind-up, 1947, 4" long	125	188	275
Race Car No. 4, tin wind-up, 1947, 4" long	125	188	275
Rocket Raider, Reed, c. 1944-47	15	30	40
Toss Bag	50	60	80

DICK TRACY

	C6	C8	C10
Air Detective Wings, c. late 1930s	65	75	90
Automatic, w/picture of Eagles, Hubley	90	125	175
Click Pistol, Marx No. 36	105	160	250
Click Pistol, No. 78, Marx, aluminum	45	68	90
Copmobile, plastic, Ideal, 1963	35	52	70
Crime Stoppers Lab, Porter Chem Co., 1940s, 10" x 12" box	150	225	350
Crimestoppers Set, includes badge, handcuffs, billy club, John Henry	45	68	90
Detective Badge with secret compartment, large, metal, leather pouch on back, late 1930s	50	75	150
Detective Fingerprint Set, 1933	100	150	200
Dick Tracy and B.O. Plenty w/Crimestopper whistle and clue detector	40	60	80
Doll, painted composition, mouth moves, 13-1/2" high	275	500	600
Double Target Game, 1941, 9-1/2" square w/8" tin gun and darts	150	200	300
Electronic Wrist Radio, Remco	35	52	70

Dick Tracy Police Station with tin automatic siren car, 1950s, $400

Dick Tracy Riot Car, Marx, c. 1946, $250

	C6	C8	C10
G-Man gun, wind-up, Marx	150	200	250
Hand Puppet, Ideal, 1961	37	56	75
Handcuffs for Junior, No. 700, John Henry Products, c. 1946	50	75	100
Hingee Paper Pigures, 1940s, set of six	20	30	40
Inspector General badge	600	800	950
Pen-Lite, 1939	75	85	110
Police Car, tin wind-up, 1949, 7" long	175	275	375
Police Station, w/7" long automatic siren car, 1950s, w/box add $250	200	300	400
Power Jet Squad Gun, Mattel, 1962, 28" long	72	108	145
Riot Car, heavy tin or sheet metal litho w/friction motor, Marx, c. 1946, 7-1/2" long	125	200	250
Shootin' Shell Snubnose .38 pistol and holster	125	175	250
Siren Police Whistle, tin, Marx, No. 64	40	60	80
Siren pistol, red w/blue siren, c. late 1930s	40	65	85
Space Coupe, 1966, Aurora	375	563	800
Sparkling Pop Pistol, tin litho, Marx No. 96	125	175	250

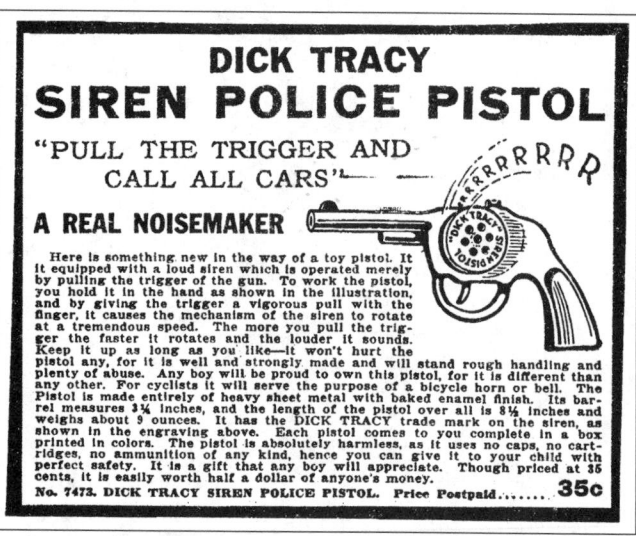

A newspaper ad for the Dick Tracy Siren Pistol, Marx, c. late 1930s. The pistol is valued at $85.

Dick Tracy Squad Car No. 1, Marx, 6-3/4" long, $225

Dick Tracy Squad Car No. 1, Marx, 11" long, $350

	C6	C8	C10
Squad Car, convertible, heavy tin or sheet metal, friction motor w/siren and battery-powered flashing light, Dick Tracy and Sam Catchum in plastic, Marx, c. 1948, 20" long	250	375	500
Squad Car, friction, No. 1, Marx, 11" long	200	275	350
Squad Car, friction, No. 1, Marx, 6-3/4" long,	110	175	225
Sub-Machine Gun, "Raider," 1946	150	200	250
Target Game, Marx, G25	150	200	250
Target Game, Marx, G34	150	200	250
Telephone, Marx, 1967	37	56	75
Water Pistol, plastic, 1955	50	75	100

FELIX THE CAT

	C6	C8	C10
China Set	75	125	150

Felix the Cat on Scooter, Nifty, $1,450

Left to Right: Felix the Cat tin wind-up walker, German, $700; Felix the Cat pull toy, $1,200

	C6	C8	C10
Doll, stuffed, Gund, hands molded rubber, the rest cloth, c. 1950, 15" high	80	120	175
Felix the Cat on scooter, Nifty	600	950	1450
Figure, cast iron, Dent, 1923, 2" high	180	270	360
Figure, cast iron, w/tin umbrella, 2-1/2" high	200	300	450
Figure, composition, c. 1930s, 13" high	275	400	600
Figure, lead, 2-1/2" high	188	285	375

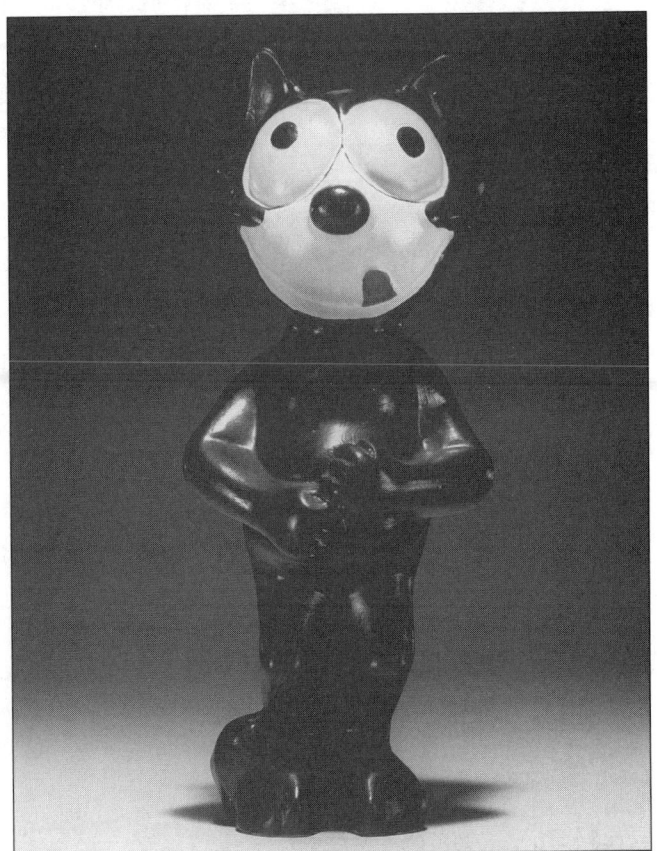

Composition Felix the Cat Figure, c. 1930s, $600

	C6	C8	C10
Figure, wood, 12" high	300	450	650
Figure, wood, jointed w/rubber head, 1940s, 9" high	100	150	250
Nodder, pot-metal, copyright Pat Sullivan on bottom of feet, 2" high	100	150	250
Pull Toy, Felix chases mice	525	850	1200
Pull Car, Borgfeldt, 1925, 12" long	300	450	600
Pull Toy, Felix on tricycle, Gong Bell	220	330	475
Pull Toy, Felix on fire truck, Gon Bell	110	165	220
Soaky	35	52	70
Speedy Felix, in car	1000	1600	2500
Squeeze Toy, rubber, Eastern Moulded Products, 6-1/2"	75	100	150
Walker, tin wind-up, German	325	490	700

FLASH GORDON

	C6	C8	C10
Air Ray pistol, shoots blast of air using rubber diaphragm, 10"	125	188	280
Arresting Ray, picture of Flash on handle, Marx, 1952,	133	200	300
Automatic Disintegrator, Hubley	200	300	450
Belt, large plastic buckle showing rocket ship flight, 1950s	70	105	140
Casting Set, Home Foundry, 1934, w/original box	800	1000	1200
Click Ray Pistol, Marx, 1950s, 10" long, w/original box	400	600	750
Jet-propelled Kite	27	41	55
Play Set, die-cast, Tootsietoy, No. 1793, 1978, w/original box	27	41	55
Play Set, Mego	58	87	115
Radio Repeater clicker pistol, Marx, No. 58, 1950s, 10" long	205	308	425
Rocket Fighter, wind-up, Marx, 1939, 12" long	265	400	600
Signal Pistol, tin litho, Marx, No. 74, 1940s	600	900	1200
Solar Commando, three plastic space men and one ship, 1950s	80	90	150
Space Cruiser, 1952	50	75	120
Space Outfit, Esquire Novelty, 1952	90	135	180
Space Target, metal, standup, Alex Raymond illustration, 12" x 14"	100	160	200
Sparkling Battle Rocket, 1969	40	60	80
Strat-O-Wagon, Wyandotte, 9" long	100	150	200
Two-Way Telephone, Marx, c. 1940	100	150	250
Water Gun, plastic, 1950s, Marx, 7" long, w/original box add $150	175	300	400

FOXY GRANDPA

	C6	C8	C10
Bell Toy, cast iron, vehicle pulled by two boys, 7" long	425	638	900
Doll, cloth and composition, 17" high	450	675	950
Figure, clockwork, tin, German, 8-1/4" high	300	450	650
Jack-in-the-Box, papier-mâché and paper litho on wood, 1900, 4" square	200	300	400
Nodder, cast iron, in donkey cart, Harris, 7-1/4" long	225	338	500
Nodder, cast iron, large-headed Grandpa in cart pulled by donkey, Hubley, c. 1910, 6-1/2"	500	750	1100
Nodder, papier-mâché, 1900, 6" tall	150	200	300
Pull Toy, composition, Grandpa rides donkey, 9" long platform	450	675	900

HAPPY HOOLIGAN

	C6	C8	C10
Candy Container, Happy on rabbit, composition, 7-1/2"	1000	1500	2000
Cymbals player	300	450	650
Donkey Cart, c. 1925, 10" long	240	360	500
Figure, 9-1/2" high, bisque face, dressed as clown	700	1000	1500
Hand Puppet, cast iron and cloth, 9-1/4"	50	70	100
Happy Hooligan in car, Cast iron, Hill Brass, c. 1903, 5-3/4"	1800	2900	4000
Happy Hooligan in Cart, cast iron, Kenton, horse-pulled and head nods, early 1900s, 10-1/4" long, 7-1/2" high	600	1000	1500
Happy Hooligan in Donkey Cart, wind-up, Ingap Co., 1930s, 6-3/8" long,	575	950	1350

Cast-iron Happy Hooligan in Car, Hill Brass, c. 1903, $4,000

Felix the Cat an Mickey Mouse Hoop toy, tin hoop with papier-maché figures, Spain, $1,700

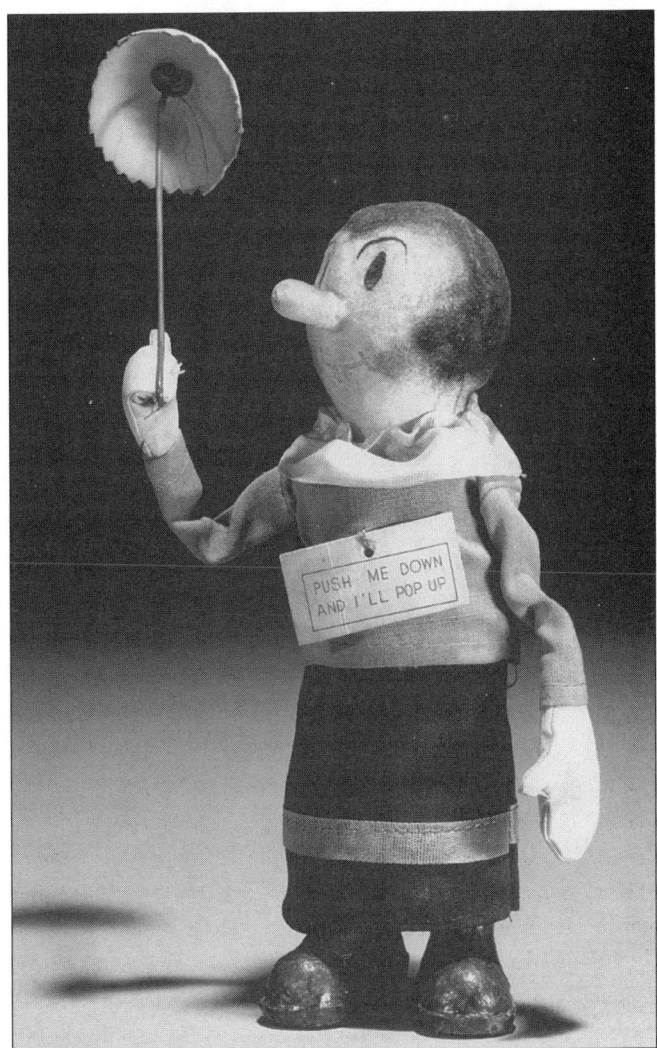

Olive Oyl Squeaker Pop-up Toy, composition and cloth, Linemar, 7" high, $200

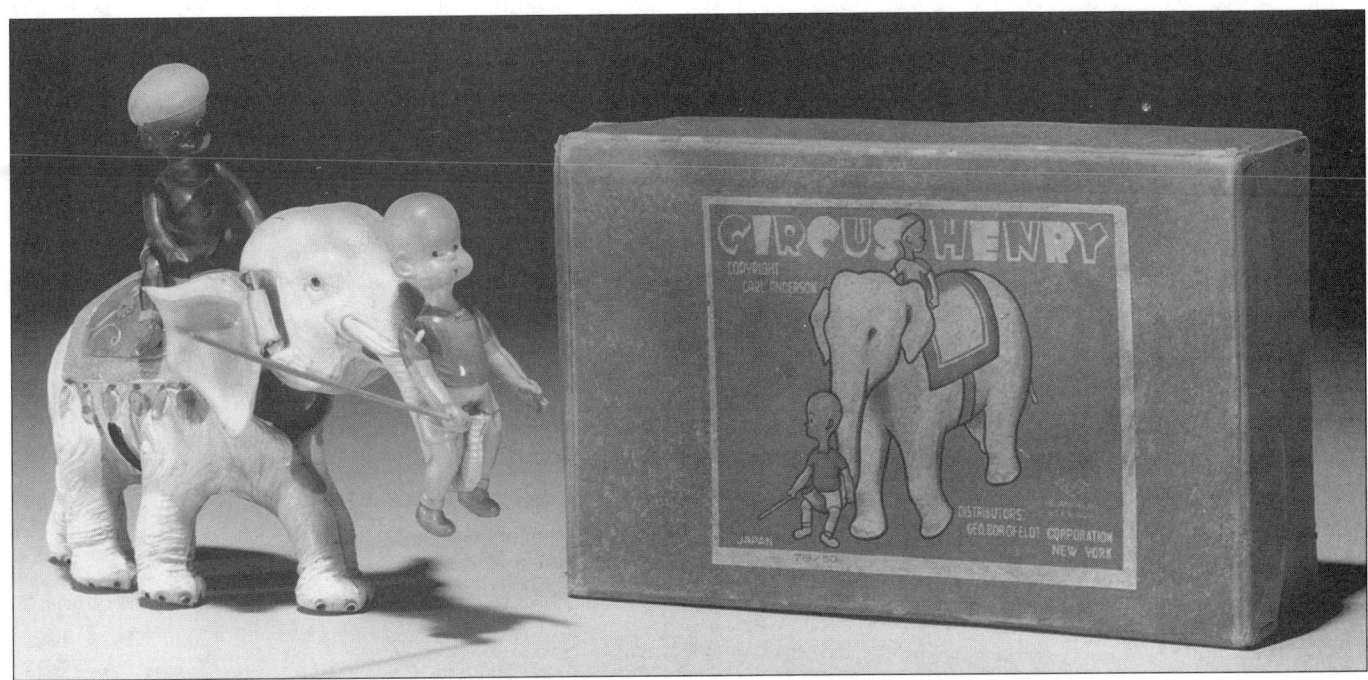

Circus Henry Wind-up, celluloid, Japan, c. 1934, $2,000

Happy Hooligan Clown Doll with bisque face, $1,500

Cast-iron Happy Hooligan, Kenton, $3,000

	C6	C8	C10
Police Patrol, Happy hit by cop as Gloomy Gus drives, Kenton	1200	2000	3000
Roly-Poly	75	100	150

HENRY

	C6	C8	C10
Henry and his Brother Wind-ups, celluloid, on wheels Japanese	700	1100	1600
Henry and his Swan, celluloid mechanical	1900	3200	4500
Henry Eating Candy, Linemar, 1950s	500	750	950
Henry on Elephant wind-up, celluloid and tin, Henry sits on elephant's trunk, w/Mahout, Japanese	700	1100	1600
Henry on Trapeze Wind-up, celluloid	365	525	700
Henry Rubber Squeeze Toy, 1950s, 9-1/2" high	30	50	75
Henry Trapeze Wind-up, part celluloid, Henry, brother and Mahout, Japan	900	1400	1850
Henry's Mahout on Donkey	450	625	800

	C6	C8	C10
Happy Hooligan in Goat Cart, cast iron, 7-1/2" long,	200	350	500
Happy Hooligan in Horse Cart, cast iron, Wilkins, 17" long	500	850	1100
Happy Hooligan in Horse-drawn Wagon, cast iron, w/Gloomy Gus and driver, Harris, c. 1905	1800	2800	3650
Happy Hooligan Jigger, Kiddies' Metal Toys Co., tin litho, dressed as clown, tap dances on drum, wind-up, 9"	750	1050	1350
Happy Hooligan Jigger, w/crank action, Kiddee Metal Toys, 1920s, 10" tall	900	1300	1650
Happy Hooligan on a ladder	300	400	550
Happy Hooligan on donkey, celluloid	325	425	550
Happy Hooligan walking toy, wind-up, Chein, 1932, 6" high	400	600	800

Cast-iron Happy Hooligan, Gloomy Gus and driver in horse-drawn wagon, Harris, c. 1905, $3,650

Left to Right: Henry and His Brother Wind-up, Japanese, $1,600; Henry's Mahout on donkey, $800; Henry on Trapeze Wind-up, $700

	C6	C8	C10
Jeep (Popeye) Doll, wood-jointed, 1930s, 14"	800	1400	2000
Jeep (Popeye) Doll, wood-jointed, 1930s, 7-1/4"	350	525	700
Jeep (Popeye) Doll, wood-jointed, 1930s, 8", rare	750	1000	1500
Jeep (Popeye) Doll, wood-jointed, 1930s,6" (rare)	425	638	850

JOE PALOOKA

	C6	C8	C10
Championship Belt Buckle, heavy gold-plated brass buckle shows Palooka w/hands raised in victory, early 1950s	75	100	125
Doll, wood-jointed, 5-1/2" high	60	85	150
Doll, wood-jointed, 4" high	45	60	80
Filmatic, twelve different comic strips	30	45	60
Punching Bag, c. 1950	30	45	60

LI'L ABNER

	C6	C8	C10
Dogpatch Family Doll, c. 1950s	110	165	220
Flyin' Saucer, Brian Specialties, 1962	42	63	85
Li'l Abner and His Dogpatch Band wind-up, 1945, Unique	350	525	700
Li'l Abner Hand Puppet, Baby Barry, 1957	42	63	85
Li'l Abner Stringless Marionette, National Mask & Puppet Corp., 1940s,	40	60	80

Little Lulu Doll, felt, $200

LITTLE LULU

	C6	C8	C10
Doll, felt, 10" high	100	150	200
Doll, stuffed, Georgene Novelties, 14" high	365	545	750
Doll, w/mask face, M.H. Buell, 1944, 14" high	55	83	110
Shape Book, Whitman No. 1970, 1971	10	15	25

LITTLE ORPHAN ANNIE

	C6	C8	C10
Commandos, Saalfield No. 299, 1943	50	75	100

Little Lulu Doll, Georgene Novelties, $750

Sandy's Dog House, Marx, $650

Little Orphan Annie Stove, $150

	C6	C8	C10
Doll, oilcloth, c. 1920s, 16-1/4" 150	200	275
Doll, printed fabric, 1930s, 9-1/2" 100	150	200
Doll, wood jointed, Jaymar, 5" high 65	100	150
Hingees, Annie, Sandy,			
Daddy, Punjab, 1944, price per set 20	30	40
Little Orphan Annie and Sandy Figures,			
celluloid 450	675	900
Little Orphan Annie and Sandy pull			
Toy, wood, 1930s, 8" 130	195	260
Little Orphan Annie and Sandy Wind-up,			
tin wind-up, two-piece set, Marx,			
1930s, 4-1/2" long 450	675	950
Little Orphan Annie Skipping Rope			
Wind-up, tin, 1930s, Marx, 5" high 425	638	850
Sandy's Dog House, w/wheeled Sandy,			
Marx 300	450	650
Soaky 14	21	35
Stove, 4-3/8" high 62	93	150
Stove, Marx, c. 1930s, 8" high 80	120	175
Water Pistol... 90	150	175

POPEYE

	C6	C8	C10
Bluto Dippy Dumper Truck,			
celluloid and tin, 9-1/2" 500	750	1200
Bluto on Horse Cart, celluloid and tin			
wind-up, 7-1/2" 400	600	850
Brutus Mask, cardboard mask, 1940s 40	60	80
Olive Oyl Ballet Dancer, tin mechanical,			
Linemar 250	375	550

Bluto Dippy Dumper, $1,200

	C6	C8	C10
Olive Oyl and Swee' Pea handcar, Marx,			
1930s... 240	360	525
Olive Oyl Doll, jointed wood, Jaymar,			
c. 1940s, 5" high, ... 92	137	185
Olive Oyl Figure, cast iron, 2-1/2" high 175	263	350
Olive Oyl Hand Puppet, Gund, c. 1938 60	90	120
Olive Oyl Hingees paper punch-outs,			
Reed & Associates, No. 102 12	18	24
Olive Oyl Marionette, Gund, 11" 37	56	75
Olive Oyl Mask, cardboard, 1940s 20	30	40

Popeye Dippy Dumper, Marx, $1,400

Left to Right: Popeye and Olive Oyl Jiggers, Marx, $2,200; Popeye Express, Marx, 1935, $1,200

Popeye and Olive Oyl Ball Toss, Linemar, c. 1959, $1,500

	C6	C8	C10
Olive Oyl Wind-up, riding tricycle, Linemar, 4"	1400	2100	3000
Olive Oyl Squeeze Toy, rubber 1950s	90	135	180
Popeye "Bifbat" Paddle Toy, 1929	46	85	150
Popeye "Bo Lo Paddle," 1929	20	50	75
Popeye "Dippy Dumper" Truck, Marx	550	1000	1400
Popeye "Eccentric Plane," wind-up, Marx 1940, 8" long	375	565	800
Popeye "Sparkling Popeye," Chein, 1959, 5" long	173	260	345
Popeye "Spinach Patrol" Hubley	1400	2500	3800
Popeye "Tumbling Popeye," wind-up, Linemar, 5" high	450	675	1000
Popeye and Mean Man Mechanical Fighters, Linemar Co., 1950s, 6" long, rare	6000	9000	12,000
Popeye and Olive Oyl Ball Toss, tin wind-up, Linemar, c. 1950, 19" long	600	1000	1500
Popeye and Olive Oyl Handcar, composition, 6" long	700	1050	1500
Popeye and Olive Oyl Jiggers, Popeye dancing on roof, Olive Oyl Playing Concertina, Marx	900	1500	2200
Popeye and Olive Oyl Sand Toy, tin litho, T. Cohn, 8-1/4" high	450	700	1000
Popeye and Olive Oyl Slinky Handcar Pull Toy, Linemar, 1950s	500	850	1200
Popeye Acrobat, Marx, tin wind-up	2700	4050	5600
Popeye Basketball Player, tin wind-up, Linemar	700	950	1400
Popeye Doll, "Cameo" hard rubber, jointed at neck, hips and shoulders, 14" high	115	172	250

	C6	C8	C10
Popeye Doll, Chein, c. 1935, 11" high	293	440	600
Popeye Doll, composition, "Popeye 1935 King Features Syn," 14" high	300	450	625
Popeye Doll, composition, Popeye is rolling up sleeve, 15" high	100	150	210
Popeye Doll, jointed wood body, w/composition head, 8" high	90	135	180
Popeye Doll, stuffed body w/rubber arms and head, Gund, c. 1950s, 20" high	70	105	140
Popeye Doll, stuffed cloth, Knickerbocker, 1930s, 17" high	187	250	385
Popeye Doll, wood and composition, jointed arms and legs, "1935," 14" high	200	300	410
Popeye Doll, wood jointed, c. 1935, 11" high	300	450	625
Popeye Doll, wood-jointed, c. 1932, 10-1/4" high	225	338	580
Popeye Doorstop, cast iron, 10" high, Hubley	1500	2300	3400

Popeye Acrobat Wind-up, marx, $5,600

Popeye Doll, composition, $625

Popeye in Barrel Wind-up, Japan, $1,600

	C6	C8	C10
Popeye Jack-in-the-Box, tin mechanical, Popeye pops out of spinach can, Mattel	45	75	100

	C6	C8	C10
Popeye Drummer, 7-1/8" high, Chein	550	1000	1400
Popeye Express, wind-up, Popeye pushing box w/parrot, Marx, 1935	500	800	1200
Popeye Express, overhead airplane flies over train, Marx, 1935	500	800	1200
Popeye Figure, cast iron, c. 1930, 3-1/2" high	175	300	400
Popeye Figure, hollow rubber, dated "1935" on back, 7" high	90	135	180
Popeye Figure, jointed wood, Jaymar, 5" high	68	125	150
Popeye Figure, solid celluloid, 1930s, 4" high	90	150	175
Popeye Hand Puppet, Gund	20	30	50
Popeye Heavy Hitter, tin wind-up, Chein, 11-1/2"	2500	4000	6250
Popeye Hingee paper Figures, Reed No. 102, 1945	50	80	100
Popeye in a Barrel, celluloid wind-up walker, Japan, 5-1/2" high	700	1100	1600
Popeye in a Barrel, Chein, 7" high	350	525	800
Popeye in a Horsecart, celluloid and tin, Marx, c. 1935, 7-1/2"	1500	2500	3650
Popeye in a Rowboat, Hoge, 1935	2500	4200	5800

Popeye Express Wind-up, Popeye pushing wheelbarrow, Marx, 1935, $1,200

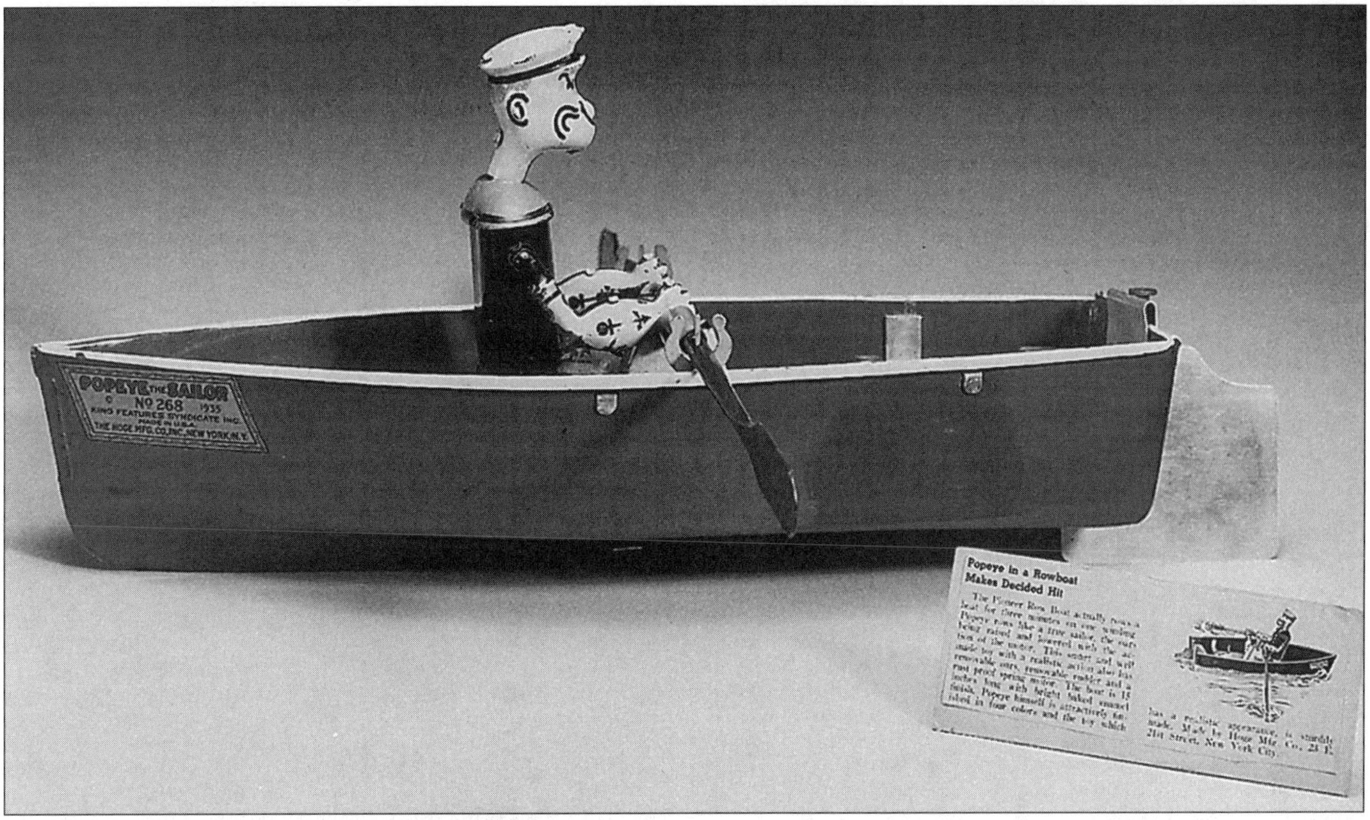

Popeye the Sailor Tin Wind-up, Hoge Mfg. Co., c. 1935, 15-1/2" long, $6,000

Make Your Own Funnies Set, contains wooden jointed figures of Popeye, Chinaman, Komical Kop, Orphan Annie, Sandy, Kayo, Funny frog, Comical Mouse, and Moon Mullins, $1,300 for the set

Superman Figure, composition, Syrocco, 6" high, $1,500

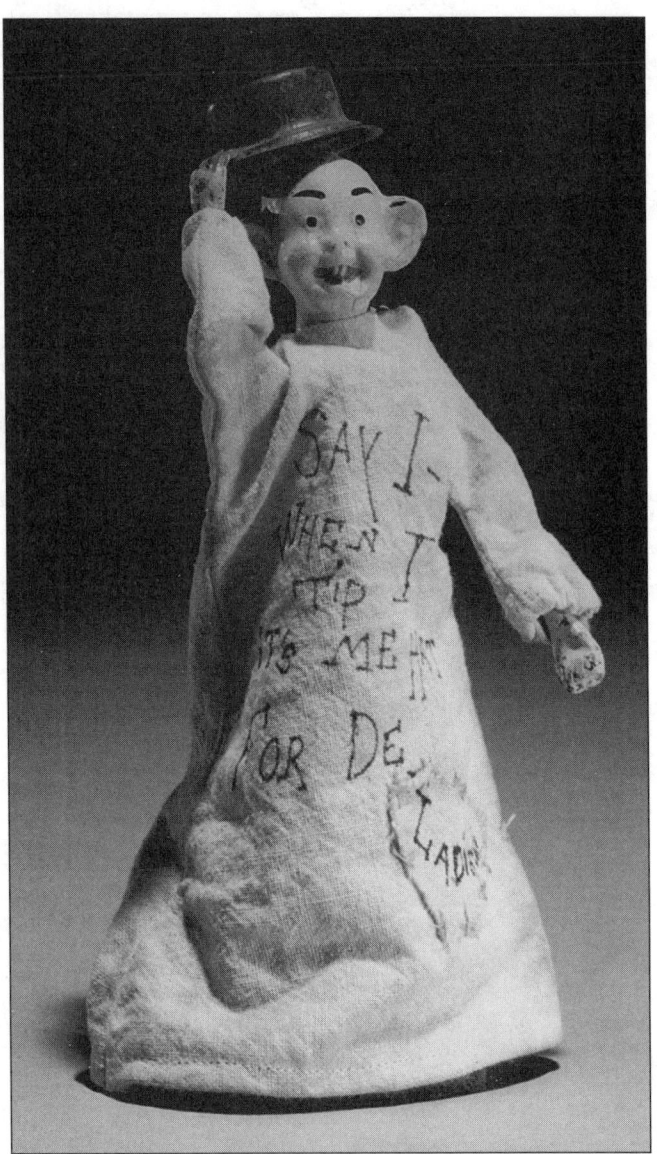

Yellow Kid Figure, papier-maché and wood, early 1900s, $1,000

Superman Tank, tin, battery opeated, Linemar, 1958, 10-1/4" long, $2,000

Popeye in Barrel, Chein, $800

	C6	C8	C10
Popeye Jigger, wind-up, Marx, 9-1/2" high	500	850	1200
Popeye Knockout Bank, Straits Mfg. Co., 1935	1000	1500	2200
Popeye Lantern Toy, Linemar, 1950s, 7-1/2" high	400	600	750
Popeye Mask, cardboard, 1940s	30	45	60
Popeye Moving Van, tin friction, Linemar	400	600	850
Popeye on a Tricycle, metal and celluloid, Linemar	370	555	800
Popeye On A Unicycle, wind-up, Linemar, 1950s	600	1000	1350
Popeye One-Man Band, pole with drum and cymbals, rubber Popeye head on top, 1950s, 69" high,	100	150	200
Popeye Patrol, Hubley, 8-1/2" long	2500	4500	6000
Popeye Pirate, click pistol, Marx, No. 68	175	300	400
Popeye Puncher, tin and celluloid w/floor bag, Chein, 1930,	800	1450	1900
Popeye Puncher, overhead bag, Chein	1600	3000	3800
Popeye Rollerskating, Linemar	550	825	1300
Popeye Roly Poly Target Game, Knickerbocker, 1958	95	143	200

	C6	C8	C10
Popeye Roly-Poly, celluloid, Japan, 3-1/2"	150	200	300
Popeye Sand Toy, teeter-totter, tin litho, w/Popeye, Swee' Pea, Olive Oyl and Jeep	500	750	1200
Popeye Shadow Boxer, Chein, 1930s, 7" tall	700	1150	1800
Popeye Soaky	22	33	55
Popeye Spinach Wagon	1000	1600	2450
Popeye Spinning Olive Oyl in a Chair, Linemar, 1950s, 9" high	800	1300	1800
Popeye Strength Tester, Holgate, 14"	65	98	150
Popeye the Champ, Marx	1100	1900	2800
Popeye the Pilot, later version, 8" long	490	800	1150
Popeye the Pilot, wind-up, early version, Marx, 1930, 8" long	500	800	1200
Popeye Transit Co. Truck, tin trailer, Linemar	650	1050	1650
Popeye Turnover Tank, Linemar, tin wind-up, 1950s, 6" long	360	540	820
Popeye Walker, Popeye pushing wheelbarrow, plastic walker, Marx, c. 1950s	50	75	100
Popeye Walker, wind-up, tin, Chein, 6-1/2" high	340	525	700
Popeye Whistle Pipe, cardboard bowl w/illus. of Popeye characters, metal stem w/whistle at base, Northwest Products of St. Louis, 3-1/2" long	70	105	150

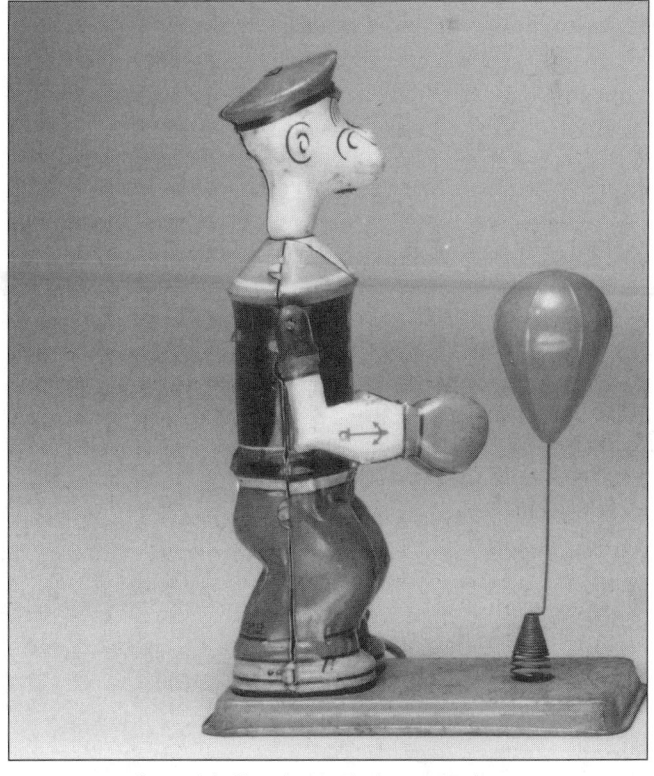

Popeye puncher with floor bag, Chein, 1930, $1,900

Popeye the Champ, Marx, $2,800

	C6	C8	C10
Popeye Wind-up celluloid wind-up, neck goes up and down, c. 1930, 9" high	475	700	950
Popeye Wind-up, Popeye carrying parrots in cages, Marx, 1935, 7-3/4" high	268	450	600
Popeye Xylophone Player, 1957, American Preschool Co., 9" long	263	395	600
Popeye Yazoo Pipe, Northwestern Productions, St. Louis, Mo., 1934	80	120	180
Swee' Pea Hingees paper punch-outs, Reed, No. 102, 1944	20	30	40
Swee' Pea mask, cardboard, 1940s	10	15	20
Wimpy Dippy Dumper	500	800	1100
Wimpy Figure, cast iron, Hubley, 3-1/8" high	175	263	375
Wimpy Figure, hard plastic, 1960s, 3"	12	18	24
Wimpy Figure, jointed wood, "by K.F.S.," 4" high	100	150	225
Wimpy Figure, jointed wood, Jaymar, 5" high	100	150	225
Wimpy Hand Puppet, Gund	29	44	65
Wimpy Mask, cardboard, 1940s	20	30	50
Wimpy Motorcyclist, Linemar	400	650	900

	C6	C8	C10
Wimpy Squeeze Toy, rubber, 8" high	60	90	150
Wimpy Tricyclist, Linemar	500	800	1100

SUPERMAN

	C6	C8	C10
"2 in 1" Hand Puppet, one side Superman, other Clark, early 1950s	200	300	500
Bendee, Mego, 1973, 5" high	22	33	45
City of Metropolis Adventure Set, Corgi, 1979	65	100	150
Colorforms, 1964	25	40	65
Cut-outs, Saalfield, No. 177, 1940	25	1500	2000
Figure, wood and composition, Ideal, 1940, 13" high	600	1000	1400
Flying Toy, Transogram, 1954	68	102	150
Hand Puppet, Ideal, 1965	32	48	64
Krypto-Ray Gun, w/seven filmstrips and box, Daisy No. 94, 1939	600	1000	150
Krypton Rockets, c. 1939	150	225	300
Kryptonite Rock, 1978	10	15	20
Movie Viewer w/film, Acme, 1947	95	142	250
Movie Viewer, Acme, 1940	333	500	665
Movie Viewer, Acme, 1965	30	45	60
Movie Viewer, w/film, Acme, 1955	60	90	150
Play Set, Ideal, 1973	34	51	68
Rollover Airplane, blue version, Marx, 1940s, 6-1/2" long	1000	1500	2200

Superman Krypto Raygun with Filmstrips, Daisy, 1939, $1,500

Left to Right: Superman Rollover Airplanes, Marx, 1940s—blue, $2,200; red, $2,100; bronze-tone, $1,650

	C6	C8	C10
Rollover Airplane, bronze-tone version, 1940s, Marx, 6-1/2" long	700	1100	1650
Rollover Airplane, red version, Marx Co., 1940s, 6-1/2" long	950	1600	2100
Rollover Tank, Japan, 1940s, 4" long	290	435	580
Rollover Tank, silver version, Marx, 1940s, 4" long	550	850	1300
Soaky	27	41	75
Superman holding airplane, wind-up, Marx, 1940	900	1600	2200
Tricky Trapeze, 1966, Kohner	75	100	150
Water Pistol, in the shape of Superman flying, c. 1950s	35	75	100

TARZAN

	C6	C8	C10
Dart Board Game, Tarzan in the Jungle, large, 1935	130	195	260
Gift Set, Figures and truck w/cage trailer, Corgi, No. 36	40	60	80
Mask of Akut the Ape, paper, Northern Paper Mills, 1933	60	80	100
Mask of Numa the Lion, paper, Northern Paper Mills, 1933	60	80	100
Mask of Tarzan, paper, Northern Paper Mills, 1933	70	105	140
Target Game, Tarzan in the Jungle, battery operated, 1935	140	210	280
Thingmaker Kit, Mattel, 1966	44	66	88

YELLOW KID

	C6	C8	C10
Cap Bomb, cast iron, 1-1/2" high	100	150	200
Doll, papier-mâché and wood, early 1900s, 11" high	500	750	1000

Left to Right: Cast-iron Yellow Kid Figure, $1,100; Cast-iron Yellow Kid in cart being pulled by mule, Kenton, 1900s, $2,000

	C6	C8	C10
Figure, cast iron, burlap gown, movable arms, 6-1/2" high	600	850	1100
Figure, "Design copyrighted 1894 and 1896," Arnold Printworks, 8" high	250	450	550
Ladder Toy, 16-1/2" high	700	1100	1400
Yellow Kid in cart, cast iron, he is being pulled by mule, Kenton, early 1900s, 10" long, 6" high,	900	1400	2000
Yellow Kid in goat cart, painted cast iron, Kenton, 1890, 7-1/2" long	500	750	1000

MISCELLANEOUS

	C6	C8	C10
Albert Alligator Figure(Pogo), plastic, 1969, approx. 5" high ("Duz")	5	11	20
Alfred E. Neumann Figure, vinyl, Effanbee, 1960	75	188	250

Andy Gump Roadster, Arcade, $3,000

Buster Brown and Tige wind-up tin seesaw, German, $1500

	C6	C8	C10
Andy Gump Dancing Doll, Doll, wooden w/tin legs, 9" high	125	188	275
Andy Gump Roadster, "348," Arcade, deluxe version	2000	3500	6500
Andy Gump Roadster, "348," Arcade, 7" long	750	1900	3000
Archie and Veronica Jalopy, tin wind-up w/illustration on side, Spanish, 7"	145	218	350
Archie Hand Puppet, vinyl, Ideal, 1973	25	38	50
B.O. Plenty holding Sparkle Plenty, tin wind-up, Marx, mid-1940s	150	270	375
Baby Snookums (The Newlyweds) Doll, fabric, 5-1/2" high	100	225	400
Baby Sparkle Plenty Paper Dolls, Saalfield, No. 1510	35	75	100
Beauregard Figure (Pogo), plastic, 1969	7	11	15
Beetle Bailey Figure, vinyl, 3"	8	12	16
Beetle Bailey Hand Puppet, Gund	45	68	90
Beetle Bailey, "Pop Up Beetle Bailey," tin lithoLinemar	180	270	360
Beetle Bailey's Camp Swampy Playset, MPC	115	172	230
Billy Batson Magic Box (Capt. Marvel)	75	100	150
Blondie Hingees Set, 1944	20	30	40
Blondie Paper Cut-Outs, Whitman 967, 1947	37	56	75
Blondie Paper Cut-Outs, Whitman 982, 1940	60	100	150
Blondie, "Blondie's Jalopy," 16" long	1200	2000	2800
Boob McNutt Wind-up, tin, Strauss	450	675	900
Boots and Her Buddies Paper Dolls, Saalfield, No. 2460, 1943	35	50	65
Bringing Up Father, Hingees, 1944	17	26	35
Broom Hilda Figure, Knickerbocker, c. 1970, 14" high	38	53	75

	C6	C8	C10
Buster Brown Seesaw, tin wind-up, w/Buster and Tige, German, 9-1/2"	600	1000	1500
Buster Brown Wind-up, tin, drives horseless carriage, Lehmann	500	800	1200
Buttercup & Spareribs, Buttercup beats Spareribs with broom, Nifty, 1920s, 7-1/2" long	700	1200	1600
Buttercup Doll (Toots and Casper), stuffed cloth, jointed head, arms, legs, c. 1924, 18" high	250	375	500
Buttercup Doll, cloth, 14"	450	700	1000
Buttercup Wind-up, tin, crawls, German, 4-1/4"	650	1100	1750
Captain America Hand Puppet, 1966	30	50	75
Captain America Jailhouse Lock Set, Larami, 1974	10	15	20
Captain America Utility Set, Remco, 1977	16	25	33
Charlie Brown Bobbing Head, composition, possibly first Peanuts toy,1950s,	80	100	150
Charlie Brown Figure, plastic jointed, marked "1952"	14	21	28
Chester Gump Cart w/Horse, open two-wheel cart w/Chester driving, Arcade, 1920s	280	420	600
Chester Gump Doll, oilcloth, Live Long Toys, c. 1920s, 13" high	150	175	300
Churchy (Pogo) Figure, plastic, 1969, 4-1/2" high	14	21	28
Comic Strip Rings, includes Phantom, Blondie and Barney Google, King Features, 1953	15	22	30

Buttercup and Spareribs, Nifty, 1920s, $1600

Humpty Dumpty Doll, cloth, Steiff, 10" high, $2,000

Mutt and Cicero Tin Wind-up, Günthermann, 5-1/2" long, $2,500

Porky Pig and Petuna Pig Dolls, cloth, each with pie-cut eyes, c. 1935, 11" tall, $500 for the pair

Dagwood the Driver Crazy Car, Marx, 1935, $1,050

Hi-Way Henry Wind-up, 1920s, $3,900

	C6	C8	C10
Comics Paper Doll Cut-Out Book, page each of Popeye, Katzenjammers, Just Kids, Blondie, Dumb Dora, Annie Rooney, Polly and Her Pals, Saalfield, 1935	175	263	350
Dagwood Aeroplane, 1935, Marx, "Dagwood's Solo Flight"	350	525	750
Dagwood Marionette, wood body w/plastic head, hands, feet and life-like hair, marked "Hazelle's," 1940s, 15"	60	90	
120Dagwood the Driver Crazy Car, Marx, 1935, 8" long	500	750	1050

	C6	C8	C10
Daisy Mae and Li'l Abner paper Dolls, Saalfield, No. 280, 1942	75	100	150
Daisy Mae and Li'l Abner paper Dolls, w/Mammy and Pappy Yokum, Saalfield, 1941, No. 2360	75	100	150
Daisy Mae Dogpatch Family Doll, c. 1950s	125	188	250
Daisy Mae stringless marionette, 1940s, National Mask & Puppet Corp.	70	105	140
Dan Dunn Det. Corps Secret Operative 28 Tin Badge, c. 1930s	50	75	100
Dennis the Menace Squirt Gun Figure, plastic, 1954, 5-1/2" high	40	60	80
Dennis the Menace Figure, Hall, 197, 7" high	42	63	85
Don Winslow Flashlight gun	70	105	140
Dr. Pimm (Little Nemo) Rolly Dolly, Schoenhut, 11-1/2" high	2500	4000	5000

Flip (Little Nemo) Bell Toy, cast-iron, $850

Cast-iron Gloomy Gus in Horse Cart, Harris, $3,500

Humphrey Mobile (Joe Palooka) Wind-up, tin, Wyandotte, mid-1940s, $650

	C6	C8	C10
Ella Cinders Doll, cloth and composition, 1925, 17" high	125	175	225
Elmer Fudd Hand Puppet, 1950s	35	52	70
Elmer Fudd Soaky, 1960s, 10" high	18	25	40
Famous Komics Film Viewer, w/three boxes of films, Acme, 1940	200	300	400
Favorite Funnies Rubber Print Set, Dick Tracy, Orphan Annie, etc., fourteen stamps, pad, booklet, large size	45	75	125
Flip (Little Nemo) Bell Toy, cast iron, 6-1/2" long	400	600	850
Gasoline Alley Garage and Auto Racer, tin litho, garage and "Bearcat Racer" car, Girard, 1924	400	750	1000
Gloomy Gus (Happy Hooligan's brother) Figure, cast iron, Harris Toy Co., 1903, 5" tall	150	225	400
Gloomy Gus in Goat Cart, cast iron, 14" long	400	700	900
Gloomy Gus in Horse Cart, cast iron, Harris, 14" long	1600	2600	3500
Gloomy Gus in Mule Cart, cast iron, Harris	300	450	600
Harold Teen Ukulele, wood, 1930s, 21"	125	200	250
Herby Doll, oilcloth, 10"	30	40	60
Herman (Harvey Comics character) Nodder, Linemar, 1950s, 4-1/2" high, rare	350	500	650
Hi-Way Henry Wind-up, jalopy w/man, woman, laundry above roof, 1920s	1500	2800	3900
Hoppy the Flying Marvel Bunny, paper c. 1944-47, Reed,	10	15	20
Howland Owl (Pogo), 1969, plastic, 4-1/2" high	8	10	15
Humphrey Doll, cloth and composition, Ideal, 14-1/2" high	225	300	450

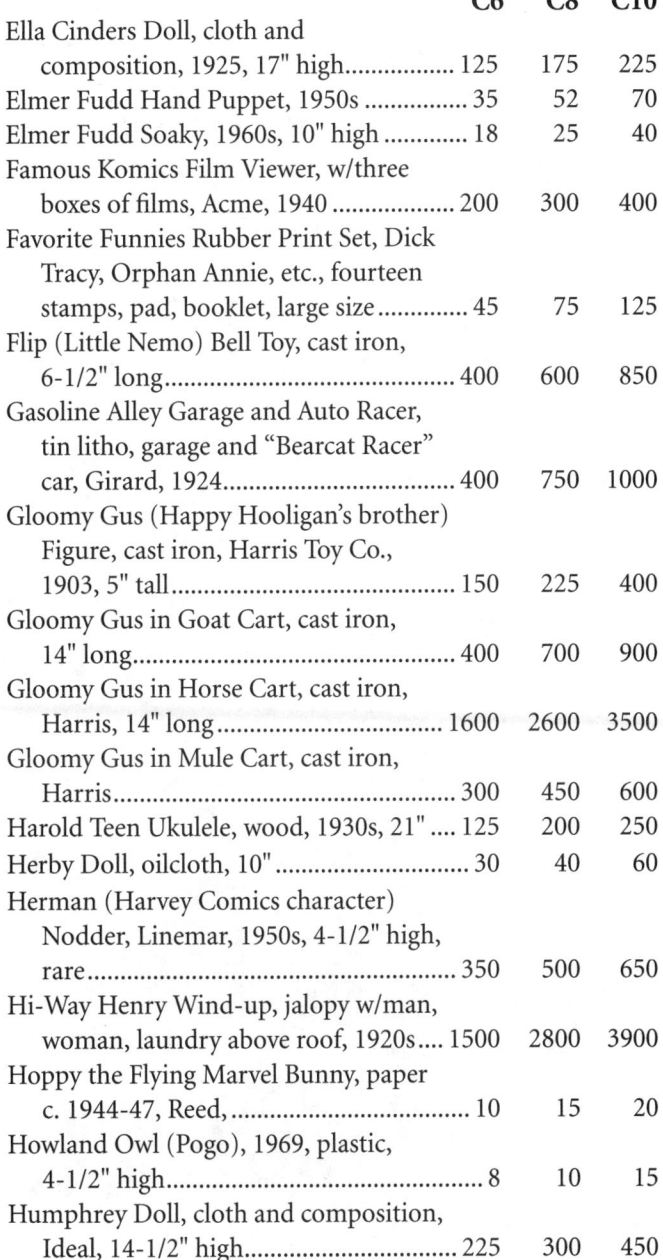

Ignatz (Krazy Kat) Figure, $300

	C6	C8	C10
Humphrey Mobile Wind-up (Joe Palooka), tin, c. mid-1940s, Wyandotte, 7-1/2" high w/smokestack	350	525	650
Ignatz Figure (Krazy Kat), 6" high	150	200	300
Jane Arden Paper Dolls, Saalfield, No. 2408, 1942	45	65	85
Jeff Figure, bendable, 1946	120	180	240
Jeff Stick puppet, 12" high	40	60	80
Jiggs Doll, hard plastic, 1960s, 3" high	6	9	12
Jiggs Doll, wood-jointed, Jaymar, 5"	80	120	160
Jiggs Jazz Car, wind-up, Nifty, 1920s, 6-1/2" long	1100	3000	5500
Jiggs Stick Puppet, 12" high	80	120	160
Katzenjammer Kids Hingees, 1945	16	24	32
Katzenjammer Kids See-Saw Bell Toy, Kenton	900	1350	1850
Katzenjammer Kids, Mama spanking kid, other kid standing, as sailor drives mule cart, Kenton, 1911, 12" long	1050	1700	3300
Kayo (Moon Mullins) Doll, wood jointed, Jaymar, 5" high	56	84	112
Kayo Doll, oilcloth, 9-3/4"	100	150	200
Kayo Figure, head swivels, Sun Rubber, c. 1937, 10" high	200	300	450
Komic Kamera, all metal viewer, w/set of five filmstrips, c. mid-1930s,	80	120	160
Komic Kamera, w/o filmstrips	24	36	48

Jiggs Jazz Car Wind-up, Nifty, 1920s, $5,500

	C6	C8	C10
Little Max Speshul (Joe Palooka) wind-up, tin	3500	5250	7000
Little Nemo and Mr. Flip Bell Toy	435	650	870
Lonesome Polecat (Li'l Abner) rubber squeak toy, Reinert, 1950s	50	75	100
Lucy Doll, plastic, jointed, "1952"	14	21	28
Lucy Squeeze Toy, high, 1950s, 7-3/4"	12	18	24
Lucy Squeeze Toy, vinyl, 1950s, 8-3/4" high	15	22	30
Maggie and Jiggs Squeeze Toy, tin litho, German, c. 1925, 8"	400	600	850
Maggie and Jiggs Wind-up, Strauss, 1924, 7-1/4" long	800	1200	1750
Maggie and Jiggs, seated on four-wheeled platform, Nifty, 1920s, 8" long	750	1100	1500
Maggie Doll, hard plastic, 1960s, 3" high	6	9	12
Mammy Yokum Hand Puppet, Baby Barry Co, 1957	42	75	100
Mammy Yokum, Dogpatch Family Doll, 1957, Baby Barry Co.	30	60	75
Mandrake the Magician Magic Kit, Transogram, 1949	75	100	150
Mighty Mouse Doll, rubber head w/oilcloth body, 1942, 12" high	400	600	800
Mighty Mouse Doll, vinyl, 1950	125	150	175
Mighty Mouse Soaky	25	35	50
Moon Maid's Daughter Doll (Dick Tracy), w/space helmet, Ideal, 1965, 16-1/2"	92	140	200

	C6	C8	C10
Krazy Kat Platform Toy, tin wind-up, Nifty, 1920s, 7-1/2" long	600	1000	1500
Krazy Kat Teacup and Saucer, Chein, 1930s	30	40	60
Little Beaver Archery Set, 1951	30	45	60
Little King Pull Toy, wood, Jay-Mar, 1938, 4" high	70	105	150
Little Mary Mixup and Her Friend Peggy paper Dolls, Saalfield, No. 294, 1922	60	75	100

Maggie and Jiggs Squeeze Toy, tin, German, c. 1925, $850

Porky Pig Wind-up cowboy, Marx, 1949, $750

Sandy with Suitcase in Mouth wind-up, $450

	C6	C8	C10
Moon Mullins and Kayo on Handcar, tin wind-up, Marx, 1930s, 6" long 395	600	850
Moon Mullins and Mamie Face masks, 1933, each 20	30	50
Moon Mullins Doll, stuffed, Famous Artists Synd., 1930s, 11-1/2" high 50	75	125
Moon Mullins Doll, wood jointed, Jaymar, 5" high 55	83	125
Movie Komics, reels of film for toy viewers, c. 1940s 14	21	40
Mrs. Blossom Doll (Gasoline Alley), oilcloth, Live Long Toys, 17" high, ... 120	180	275
Mutt dancing Doll, wooden 40	60	80
Mutt Doll, composition w/ball joints, felt clothes, 8" high 188	300	450
Mutt Figure, bendable, 1946 140	210	280
Nancy Doll, stuffed, Georgene Novelties, 14" high 90	150	250
Pal Doll (Gasoline Alley), oilcloth, cotton-stuffed, Live Long Toys, 1923 90	135	180

Porky Pig Wind-up, Marx, 1939, $550

Roosevelt Bear on Bicycle, c. 1920, $450

	C6	C8	C10
Pappy Yokum Doll, Dogpatch Family Doll, 1957, Baby Barry Co. 100	150	200
Pappy Yokum Hand Puppet, Baby Barry, 1957 42	63	85
Peanuts Figures: Charlie Brown, Lucy, Linus, Schroeder, Snoopy, Avon, each ... 10	15	20
Peter Rabbit Chickmobile 312	468	675
Pogo Figure, plastic, 1969, 4" high 7	11	16
Pogo Pogomobile 200	300	450
Porky (Pogo) Figure, plastic, 1969 7	11	14
Porky Pig Cowboy w/lariat, tin wind-up, Marx, 1949, 9" high 325	550	750
Porky Pig Hand Puppet, 1950s, 8" high 30	45	60
Porky Pig Soaky, 9" high, 1960s 20	30	40
Porky Pig Squeeze Toy, hollow w/squeaker, has hands behind back, Sun Rubber, c. 1940, 6" high, ... 68	125	175
Porky Pig Wind-up, tin litho, holding umbrella, Marx, 1939, 8-1/2" high 250	375	550
Porky Pig Wind-up, tin litho, holds umbrella, raises hat, Marx, 1939, 8" 500	750	1100
Prince Valiant Castle Fort, boxed set w/knights, Marx 225	340	450
Prince Valiant Crossbow Pistol Game 22	33	45
Prince Valiant Shield, tin litho 30	45	60
Prince Valiant Sword and Scabbard, tin, 1950s, Mattel 29	45	58
Rachel Doll (Gasoline Alley), cotton-stuffed oilcloth Live Long Toys, 1923 150	200	300
Red Ryder Molding Set, 1948 40	60	100

	C6	C8	C10
Red Ryder Target Game, 1939, w/box add $150	34	100	150
Robin Hand Puppet, Ideal, 1966	70	105	140
Robin Soaky	40	60	150
Roosevelt Bear on Bicycle, tin litho, c. 1920, 9" long	225	338	450
Rudy the Ostrich (Barney Google), tin, Nifty, 1924	448	730	975
Sad Sack Doll, vinyl w/cloth uniform, Sterling Doll Co., c. 1952, 20" high	70	105	140
Sad Sack Doll, vinyl, 1950, 15-1/2"	105	158	210
Sandy Dog w/Magic Tail, Marx, 1930s, 7" long	162	245	350
Sandy Doll, oilcloth, c. 1920s, Live Long Toys, 10-1/2" long	140	210	280
Sandy w/Suitcase in Mouth, tin wind-up	215	325	450
Schroeder (Peanuts) Squeeze Toy, rubber, c. 1960	10	15	30
Secret Agent X-9 Gun and Billy Club	25	40	50
Sergeant Snorkel (Beetle Bailey) Hand Puppet	37	56	75
Shmoo (Li'l Abner) Doll, vinyl inflatable, 1940s, 15" high	60	90	150
Sight Seeing Auto 899, cast iron, w/Mama Katzenjammer, Uncle Heine, Alphonse, Gloomy Gus, Happy Hooligan, Kenton, c. 1910, 10-1/2" long	2500	5000	6500
Skeezix Doll, cotton-stuffed oilcloth, (as boy) Live Long Toys, 1924	125	175	250
Skeezix Doll, cotton-stuffed oilcloth, (Baby Skeezix), Live Long Toys, 1924	100	150	225
Skeezix Radio Toy, tin litho, c. 1924, 5" high	1000	1500	2200
Skippy Figure, celluloid, 5-1/2" high	150	225	375
Skippy Figure, oilcloth w/hat, 12" high	75	100	150
Smitty Doll, oilcloth, 9-3/4" high	125	175	225

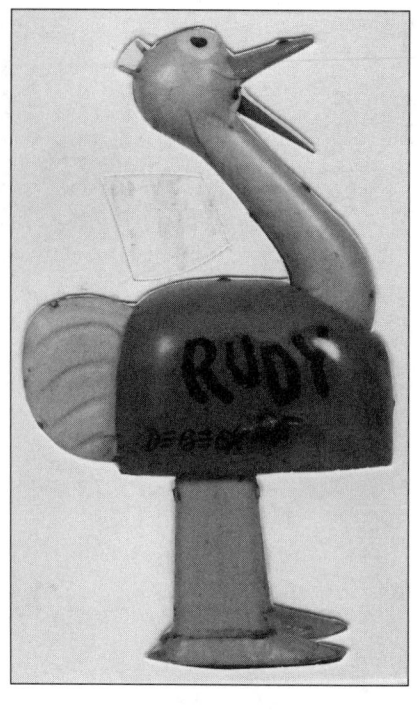

Rudy the Ostrich (Barney Google), Nifty, 1924, $975

	C6	C8	C10
Smitty on a Scooter, tin wind-up, Marx, c. 1930, 8" high	1100	1700	2000
Smokey Stover Figure, hard plastic, 1960s, 3" high	12	18	35
Smokey Stover, Hingees, 1944	8	13	17
Snoopy Astronaut Doll, vinyl, 9-1/2" high, 1969	30	45	60
Snoopy Bus, tin litho, 1960s	16	24	32
Snoopy Squeeze Toy, rubber, 1958	25	38	50
Snowflakes and Swipes Platform Toy, tin litho, c. 1929, 7-1/2" long	800	1350	1850
Snuffy Smith Hand Puppet, cloth w/rubber head, "King Features," Gund	35	52	75
Sparkle Plenty Paper Doll Set, Saalfield No. 5160, 1948	35	50	75

Cast-iron Sight Seeing Auto 899 with Mama Katzenjammer, Kenton, c. 1910, $6,500

Smitty on a Scooter Wind-up, Marx, c. 1930, $2,000

Snowflake and Swipes Platform Toy, c. 1929, $1,850

Uncle Wiggily Crazy Car, Distler, c. 1922, $5,500

	C6	C8	C10
Sparkle Plenty Washing Machine, tin litho, w/crank action, Kalon Radio Corp., c. 1947, 13" tall	100	150	250
Sparkplug (Barney Google), on wheels, 3-1/4" high	225	338	475
Sparkplug Candy Container	145	218	290
Sparkplug Doll, stuffed cloth	125	188	300
Sparkplug Wa-Gee walker, wind-up, cloth, felt and metal, 9" long	295	445	690
Spider-Man Hand Puppet, Ideal, 1966	42	63	85
Spider-Man Walker, wind-up, Marx, 1966	125	188	250
Spider-Man Webmaker, Chemtoy, 1977	16	25	33
Steve Canyon Glider Bomb Truck, Ideal	88	132	175
Steve Canyon Jet Helmet, 1959	50	75	100
Steve Canyon Space Goggles, Rock Industries, c. 1950s	25	38	50

Left to Right: Wind-up of The Powerful Katrinka from the Tonerville Trolley pushing Jimmy in a wheelbarrow, Lehman, 1925, $3,250; Wind-up of The Powerful Katrinka holding Jimmy, Nifty, 1925, $2,200

	C6	C8	C10
Sunshine X Riding Sparkplug Platform Toy (Gasoline Alley), 9" long	1400	2300	3300
Terry and the Pirates Hingees, set includes Terry, Flip Corkin, Pat Ryan, Burma, Taffy Tucker, 1944	22	33	45
Thimble Theatre Mystery Playhouse, composition figures w/wooden shuffle feet, "Starring Popeye with Wimpy and Olive Oyl," copyright 1939, Harding Products, Philadelphia, 12" x 10" x 3"; individual figures sell for $350 in Mint condition	1500	2200	3000
Three Flying Marvels (Captain, Jr., Mary), paper, Reed, c. 1944-47	15	20	30
Toonerville Candy Container, glass, 3-1/4" long	250	375	500
Toonerville Trolley Wind-up, Strauss, 1921, rare	425	638	500
Toonerville Trolley Wind-up, tin, boy in wheelbarrow, "Powerful Katrinka," 6-1/2" long, Lehmann, 1925	1300	2300	3250
Toonerville Trolley Wind-up, tin, marked "Copyright 1922 by Fontaine Fox," 7-1/2" high, Skipper driving, Nifty	500	750	1050
Toonerville Trolley Wind-up, tin, raises and lowers Jimmy in her hand, "The Powerful Katrinka," Nifty, 1925, 6-3/4" high	900	1400	2200
Toonerville Trolley, 1-7/8" high	275	410	575
Toonerville Trolley, aluminum, Dent	357	562	750
Toonerville Trolley, cast iron, Dent	450	675	900
Toonerville Trolley, lead, c. 1923	100	150	200
Toonerville Trolley, wood, includes six people, 7" long	125	188	250
Tweety Bird Soaky	15	22	30
Tweety Bird Squeeze Toy, rubber, 1950s	15	22	30
Uncle Walt (Gasoline Alley) Doll, oilcloth, Live Long Toys, 26" high	80	120	160

Mama Katzenjammer Doll, felt, Steiff, c. 1908,
$2,000

Left to Right: Toonerville Trolley Wind-up Tin, c. 1922, 7-1/2" high, $1,050; Toonerville Trolley, cast iron, Dent, $900; Pair of Toonerville Trolleys, lead, c. 1923, $200 each

Left to Right: Cast-iron Yellow Kid Figure, $1,100; Cast-iron Yellow Kid in cart being pulled by mule, Kenton, 1900s, $2,000.

	C6	C8	C10
Uncle Wiggily Crazy Car, Distler (Germany), c. 1922, 9-1/2" long	2200	4000	5500
Uncle Wiggily Crazy Car, Marx	438	660	900
Walter Lantz Ink Stamp Character Set, includestwelve different rubber stamps	12	18	24
Western Thrills w/Billy The Kid, character from Funny Animals Comics, paper, Reed, c. 1944-47	12	18	24
Willie The Worm and Sammy Fish-n Fun	10	15	20
Willie The Worm and Sammy Flying Machine	12	18	25

	C6	C8	C10
Willie The Worm and Sammy in Car Trouble, paper, Fawcett Comics characters, Reed, c. 1944-47	10	15	20
Wonder Woman String Puppet, Madison, 1977	37	56	75
Woody Woodpecker Figure, rubber, "Walter Lantz," 6-1/2" high	10	15	20
Woody Woodpecker Hand Puppet, rubber head, cloth body, "W. Lantz," Mattel, 1962	20	30	40
Woody Woodpecker Soaky	20	25	35
Zero (Beetle Bailey) Hand Puppet, vinyl and cloth, Gund, 1960s	30	45	65

Uncle Wiggly, Marx, $900

DISNEY

See also Ideal Dolls, Paper, Premiums, Fisher-Price

Walt Disney was involved in animation as early as 1920, but his first truly notable character was Oswald the Rabbit, introduced in 1927. Disney did not own the rights to Oswald, however, and they eventually fell into the hands of another animator, Walter Lantz.

Although Mickey Mouse first appeared in the 1928 short "Plane Crazy," the third Mickey cartoon, "Steamboat Willie," seems to have been the first released (on November 18, 1928). Mickey was a success from then on. Minnie Mouse also appeared in "Steamboat Willie," and Pluto emerged in 1930 but was not known by that name until 1931. Goofy debuted in 1932 and Donald Duck came along in 1934. Mickey Mouse toys were first produced in 1930 and since then the stream of Disneyana (apparently all of it deemed collectible) has been endless.

BABES IN TOYLAND

	C6	C8	C10
Soldier, tin wind-up, Linemar, 1950s, 6-1/2" tall ...	175	263	350
Wood Officer on horseback, wheeled, Jaymar ...	175	263	350
Wood Soldier w/cannon, Jaymar ...	210	315	420
Wood Soldier w/rifle, Jaymar, 9" high ...	60	90	120
Wind-up, tin litho, Indian on rollerskates, Linemar, 1950s, 6-1/2" tall ...	100	150	200
Thumper Doll, Gund, 1950s, 14" high ...	38	57	76
Thumper Doll, Gund, early 1940s, 17" high ...	80	120	160
Thumper soaky ...	11	16	22
Thumper Squeeze Toy, rubber, Sun Rubber, 7" high ...	30	45	60

Babes in Toyland Soldier, Linemar, 1950s, $350

	C6	C8	C10
Thumper, friction, Marx, 1950s, 6" high ..	100	150	200
Thumper, tin friction, Linemar, 1950s, 3" long ...	70	105	140

BAMBI

	C6	C8	C10
Bambi Soaky ...	15	22	30
Bambi, "Jumping Bambi," trigger action, Linemar, 1950s, 6" high ...	250	375	500
Flower, tin friction, Linemar, 1950s, 3" long ...	115	172	230

CINDERELLA

	C6	C8	C10
Hand Puppet, "1957" ...	22	33	45
Handcar, Jaq and Gus, 8" long ...	383	575	775
Soaky, w/movable arms, 1960s ...	15	22	30
Wind-up, Cinderella and Prince Dancing, plastic, Irwin Co., No. 7000, 1950s, 5" high ...	65	98	130
Wind-up, umbrella, spins and dances, Irwin, 4-3/4" high ...	62	93	125

DAVY CROCKETT

	C6	C8	C10
Alamo Play Set, Marx ...	250	375	500
Auto-Magic Picture Gun ...	42	63	85
Badge, "Frontier Marshal," 1950s ...	27	41	55
Coonskin Hat ...	22	33	45
Doll, Fortune Toy, 1950s, 8" high ...	60	90	120
Doll, vinyl, 20" high, Gund ...	60	90	120

Davy Crockett Powder Horn, Daisy, $40

	C6	C8	C10
Flying Arrows, balsa wood figures to be made into flying arrows, copyright 1955	25	38	50
Handgun, pop-action, tin litho, 1950s	40	60	80
Play Knife, 1950s	22	33	44
Powder Horn, Daisy	20	30	40
Prairie Wagon, 5" long	26	39	52
Wagon Train, plastic, 1950s, Marx, 14" long	150	225	300
Frontierland Davy Crockett Outfit, gun, coonskin hat, etc.	70	105	140

DISNEYLAND

	C6	C8	C10
Concert Xylophone, Tudor, 18" long	30	45	60
Ferris Wheel, tin wind-up, Chein, c. late 1956, 17" high	350	525	700
Happy Birthday Carousel, Ross Co., 1950s, 6" high	80	120	160
Jeep, push toy, Marx, 1960s, 10" long	100	150	200

Disneyland Ferris Wheel, Chein, late 1956, $700

	C6	C8	C10
Melody Player extra paper rolls, different songs, 1950s, for Melody Player, each	10	15	20
Melody Player, w/four rolls, 1950s, Chein, 7"	95	142	190
Play Set, Marx	425	638	850
Roller Coaster, two tin cars, Chein, 10" high, 1950s	250	375	500

Disneyland Happy Birthday Carousel, 1950s, $160

Disneyland Roller Coaster, Chein, 1950s, $500

Donald Duck Climbing Fireman, Linemar, 1950s, $600

DONALD DUCK

	C6	C8	C10
Acrobat, Linemar, 1950s, 8-1/2" high........	325	490	650
Captain, wood and plastic, push puppet, Kohner, 1950s..........................	100	150	200
Convertible, tin, friction, Linemar, 1950s, 5" long..........................	263	395	525
Climbing Fireman, wind-up, Linemar, 1950s, 13-1/2".......................	300	450	600

Donald Duck Doll in Russian costume, $2000

Donald Duck and His Nephews, pull-string action, Linemar, $800

	C6	C8	C10
Crawler, celluloid wind-up, 9-3/4" long....	650	1100	1500
Delivery Tricycle, tin and plastic, Marx, 5"................................	450	675	900
Dipsy Car, tin car w/plastic Mickey or Donald, Marx, 1950s, 5-1/4" long........	385	575	770
Disney Flivver, Linemar, 1950s, 5-1/2" long..............................	300	450	600
Doctor Kit......................................	60	90	120
Doll, composition and cloth, long-billed, in Russian costume, 9" high	1000	1500	2000
Doll, Gund, c. 1949, 13-1/2" high	110	165	220
Doll, long-billed, 1930s, 16" high...............	75	112	150
Doll, long-billed, composition, Knickerbocker, 1930s, 9" high.............	250	375	500
Doll, stuffed, long-billed, Knickerbocker, 1930s, 13" high...........	150	225	300
Donald Duck and His Nephews, plastic wind-up, Marx, 1950s, 11" long..........	225	338	450
Donald and His Nephews, pull-string action, Linemar, 1950s, 5-1/2" high.....	400	600	800
Donald Duck and Huey w/Voice, string pull toy, 1950s, Linemar, 7" long	500	750	1000
Donald Duck and Pluto in Roadster, Sun Rubber, 1930s, 6-1/2" long	80	120	160
Donald Duck in His Convertible, friction, Linemar, 1950s, 6" long	275	415	550
Donald Duck Duet, tin wind-up, small Donald w/large Goofy, Marx, c. 1945..	440	660	880
Donald Duck Jigger, wind-up, papier-mâché, 11" high	800	1200	1600
Donald Duck Mouseketeers Hat	15	22	30
Donald Duck on Pluto, celluloid wind-up..............................	1400	2200	3200
Donald Duck on Rocking Horse, celluloid tin, wind-up, Japan, 3-3/8" long...........................	3000	4500	6000
Donald Duck on Tractor, friction, plastic, Marx, 1950s, 3-1/2" long..........	120	180	240

Donald duck on Rocking Horse, wind-up, Japan, $6,000

Donald Duck Riding Mule, celluloid wind-up, $1,700

Donald Duck Duet Wind-up Tin, Marx, c. 1945, $880

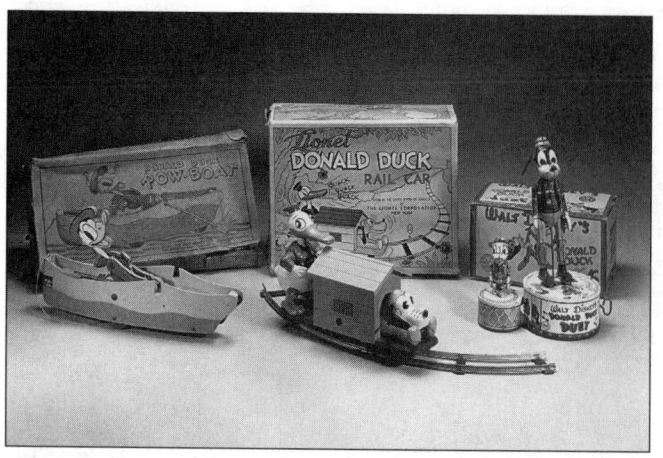

Left to Right: Donald Duck Rowboat, Chad Valley, $600; Donald Duck Rail Car with Pluto and Doghouse, Lionel, 1930s, $600; Donald Duck Duet, Marx, c. 1945, $880

	C6	C8	C10
Donald Duck on Trapeze, Borgfeldt, 1930s, 9" high 275		362	550
Donald Duck pulled by Pluto, long billed Donald, celluloid w/tin cart, Japan, 1930s 1750		2625	3500
Donald Duck Riding Mule, long billed, celluloid wind-up, 7-3/4" 850		1275	1700
Donald Duck Skier, Linemar 300		450	600
Donald Duck Skier, plastic, Marx, 1940s .. 375		565	750
Donald Duck Swimmer, celluloid wind-up, 6-1/2" 650		1000	1500
Donald Duck Tricycle, w/twirling parasol, M-T Co. (Japan) 1950s, 7-1/2" high 200		300	400
Donald Duck Tricycle, wind-up, Linemar, 1950s, 3-1/2" long 285		430	570
Donald Duck w/Whirling Tail, plastic wind-up, Marx, 1950s, 6-1/2" high 92		135	185
Donald Duck w/Whirling Tail, tin wind-up, Linemar, 1950s, 5-1/4" high 300		450	600
Donald Duck Zylophone, Tudor, 10" long.. 55		83	110
Donald Race Car, celluloid wind-up, Occupied Japan 225		338	450
Donald the Driver, friction car, Linemar, 1950s, 6-1/2" long 225		338	450
Donald the Drummer, wind-up, Marx, 1950s, 9" tall 275		363	550
Drummer, wind-up rocker, 1950s, Linemar, 6" high 250		375	500
Drummer, wind-up walker, Linemar, 1950s, 6" high 265		400	530
Dump Truck, Linemar, 1950s, 5" long 300		450	600
Figure, celluloid, 1940s, 13" high 135		198	270
Figure, long-billed, 1930s, Seiberling Rubber, 6" high 150		225	300

	C6	C8	C10
Figure, long-billed, celluloid, 1930s, Borgfeldt (Japan), 5" high 262		395	525
Figure, Sun Rubber, 10" high 21		32	42
Fire Chief Crazy Car, wind-up, tin litho w/rubber hat, Linemar, extremely rare 700		1250	1700
Rail Car, w/Pluto and doghouse, Lionel No. 1107, 1930s, 10" long 413		625	825
Roly-Poly, 3-3/4", 1940s 187		280	375
Rowboat, wood and paper litho, Chad Valley (England), 12-1/4" long... 300		450	600
Rubber Boat, Sun Rubber Co., c. 1940s 40		60	80
Soaky 11		16	23
Straight Shooter, plastic wind-up, 1960s, 6-1/2" high 187		280	375
Teapot, Ohio Art 30		45	60
Tractor, Sun Rubber 112		188	225
Waddler, "K" Co., 1930s, 3-1/2" tall 600		900	1200
Waddler, long-billed, tin and celluloid, "K" Co. (Japan), 1930s, 3-1/4" high 600		900	1200
Walker, wind-up, celluloid, Japan, 3-1/2" high 400		600	800
Washing Machine, M-T Co. (Japan), 1950s, 7-1/2" high 400		600	800
Wind-up, German, "984," Schuco, 6" high 158		235	315
Wind-up, hard plastic, Marx, 1960s, 7" high 30		45	60
Wind-up, tin, w/umbrella, Linemar, 4" high 300		450	600

FERDINAND THE BULL

	C6	C8	C10
Doll, jointed, wood, 9" 125		188	250
Figure, late 1930s, hard rubber, Seiberling, 6" long, 3-1/2" high 102		153	205
Hand Puppet, Crown, 1938 55		82	110
Pull Toy, Hill, 8-3/4" long 170		255	340
Wind-up, Ferdinand and Matador, tin, Marx, 1938 600		900	1200

Ferdinand and Matador, Marx, 1938, $1200

Ferdinand the Bull, Marx, 1938, $425

Jiminy Cricket, Linemar, 1950s, $600

	C6	C8	C10
Wind-up, tail whirls, body shakes, Marx, copyright 1938	212	320	425

GOOFY

	C6	C8	C10
Figure, tin, 1930	400	600	800
Soaky	20	30	40
Wind-up, Goofy Tricycle, Linemar, 1950s, 4" tall	650	975	1300
Wind-up, Goofy the Walking Gardener, tin, Marx	482	625	965
Wind-up, Goofy on a Unicycle, tin, Linemar, 5-1/2" high	500	750	1000
Wind-up, Goofy w/Whirling Tail, Linemar, 1950s, 5" tall	300	450	600
Wind-up, Goofy w/Whirling Tail, plastic wind-up, 1950s, Marx, 8" high	92	140	185
Wind-up, Goofy's Disneyland Stock Car, Linemar, 1950s, 6" long	200	300	400
Wind-up, Goofy's Stock Car, Linemar, 1950s, 6" long	200	300	400

Goofy the Walking Gardner, Marx, $965

JIMINY CRICKET

	C6	C8	C10
Doll, cloth body w/rubber head and wooden feet, Gund, 12"	22	33	45
Doll, felt and cloth, 15-1/2" high, Crown Toy	150	225	300
Doll, felt and cloth, Crown Toy, 14" high	150	225	300
Doll, Knickerbocker, 10" high, c. 1940	300	450	600
Doll, latex head, hands and feet w/cloth body, 13" high	60	90	120
Doll, wood jointed, Ideal, 9" high, 1940	225	368	450
Facemask, Gillette, 1939	25	38	50
Hand Puppet, vinyl and cloth, Gund	32	48	65
Soaky	10	15	20
Walkie, Jiminy Cricket Pushing Bass Fiddle, Marx	15	22	30
Wind-up, tin litho, Linemar, 1950s, 5-1/2" tall	300	450	600

MICKEY AND MINNIE MOUSE

	C6	C8	C10
Acrobats, Borgfeldt, 1934, 11" high	500	750	1000
Bell Toy, wood and metal, Gong Bell, c. 1933, 10-3/4" long	1050	1575	2100
Mickey and Minnie Mouse Playland, celluloid, Japan	3000	5500	10,000
Swing Toy, celluloid w/red and green flag, 11-1/2" tall	420	630	840
Tea Set, thirteen pieces, c. 1935	140	210	280
Wind-up, Mickey and Minnie Mouse on Motorcycle, tin litho	8000	14,000	20,000

MICKEY MOUSE

	C6	C8	C10
Acrobat, clockwork trapeze w/celluloid Mickey, Japan, 1930s, 9" high	243	365	485
Acrobat, wood, Strombecker, 1950s	45	68	90
Banjo, 1930s, 17" long	140	210	280

Mickey Mouse Acrobat, Japan, 1930s, $485

Mickey Mouse Doll, cloth, Geo. Borgfeldt, $675

	C6	C8	C10
Bubble Buster Gun, cast iron, Mickey standing at gun sight, Kilgore, 6" long...	75	112	150
Circus Train Set, engine, tender, containing Mickey, three carriage cars, dining car, Mickey Mouse Circus, Mickey Mouse Band, composition Mickey and track, Lionel No. 1536	1300	2200	3500
Circus, two wood figures revolving on swinging mechanism, Geo. Borgfeldt 6/3785, 1931, 11" long	500	850	1200
Clicker, tin litho, Mickey showing teeth while playing violin, c. 1930	90	135	180
Dipsy Car, tin car w/plastic Mickey Marx, 1950s, 5-1/4" long	318	475	635

	C6	C8	C10
Dipsy Car, tin, Linemar, 1950s, 5-1/4" long..........	300	450	600
Doll, Borgfeldt, 12" high	625	938	1250
Doll, cloth, marked "Walt Disney Mickey Mouse Geo. E. Borgfeldt & Company New York" on bottom of one foot, 11" high	337	505	675
Doll, Cowboy Mickey, Knickerbocker, c. 1935, 19-1/2" high	1400	2100	2800
Doll, Cowboy Mickey, Knickerbocker, 1936, 12" high	2000	4000	6200
Doll, felt, Character Co., c. 1939-40, 18" high..........	70	105	140

Mickey Mouse Doll with Cowboy Outfit, Knickerbocker, c. 1935, $2800

Mickey Mouse Bandleader, Knickerbocker, 1935, $1500

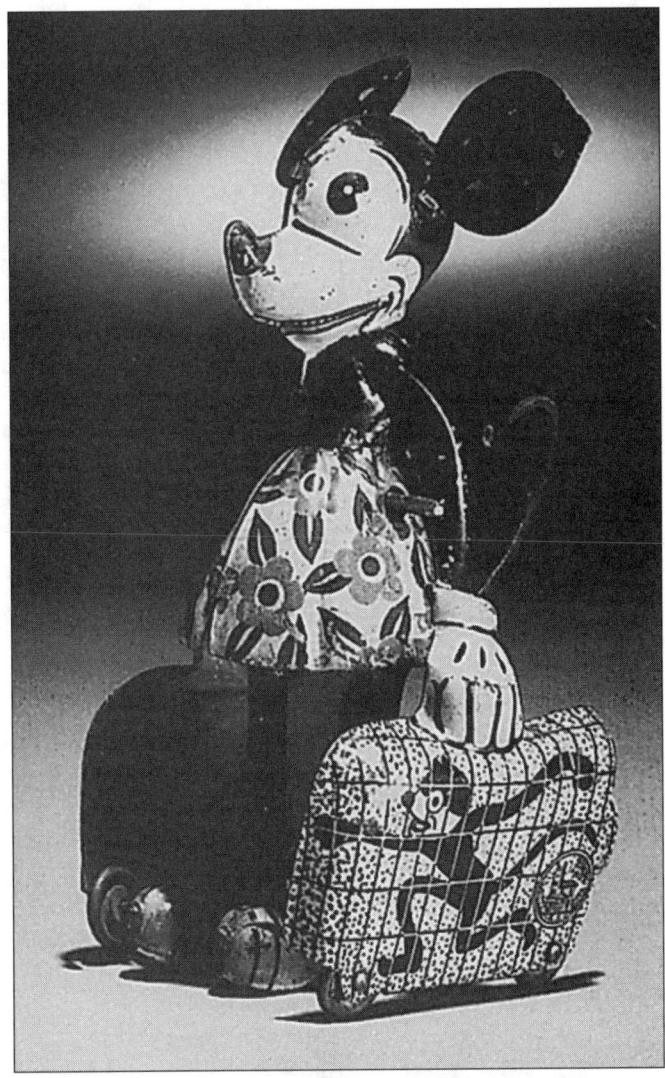

Minnie Mouse Wind-up Tin, lithographed, depicts Minnie carrying two Felix the Cat suitcases, Spain, c. 1928, $9,000

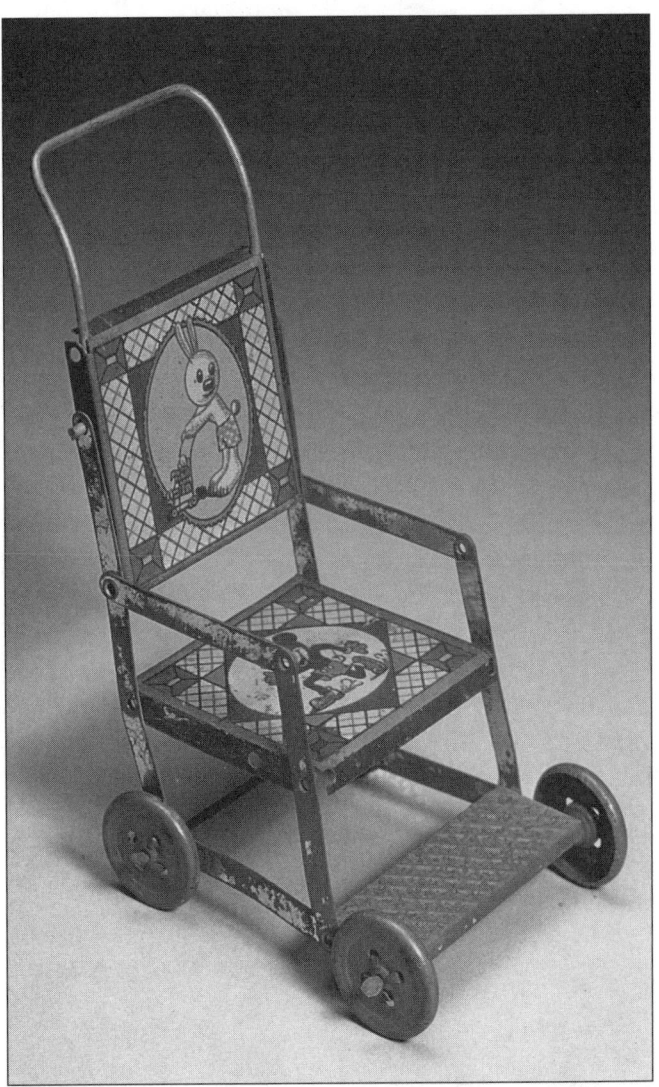

Mickey Mouse and Oswald Stroller, lithographed tin, Spain, $1,200

Mickey and Minnie Mouse Dolls, cloth, Knickerbocker, c. 1930, 15" high, $2,500 for the pair

Mickey Mounse Drummer Wind-up Tin, lithographed, Linemar, c. 1955, $1,000

Back: Mickey and Minnie Mouse Dolls, cloth, Charlotte Clark, c. 1930s, 9" high, $300 for the pair; Front: Mickey Mouse on Scooter Wind-up Tin, Linemar, c. 1955, $1,500

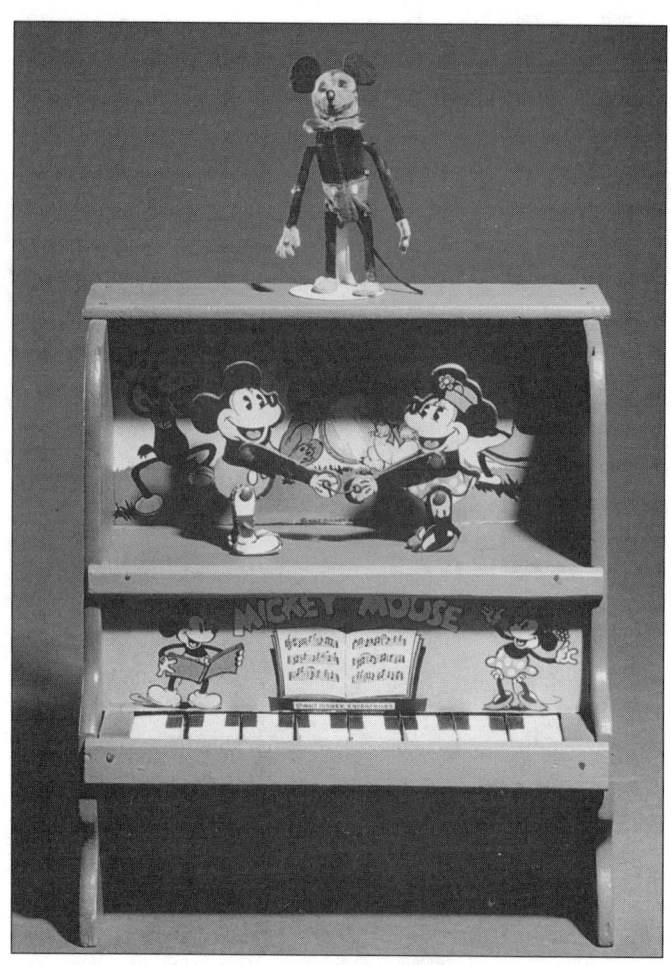

Mickey Mouse Tumbler, Schuco, 4" high, $400

Mickey Mouse Bank, cast iron, France, c. 1931, 9" high, $900

Mickey Mouse Waddle Book, Blue Ribbon Book, Inc., 1934, unused, $6,000

Mickey Mouse Drum, tin, Ohio Art, $260

Mickey Mouse Figure, Fun-E-Flex, $500

	C6	C8	C10
Doll, felt, dressed in black jacket w/yellow buttons, red pants, bells on toes of yellow shoes, storage space in back, 1950s, 31" high	120	180	240
Doll, felt, Steiff, early 1930s, 12" high	600	950	1280
Doll, Knickerbocker, 1930s, 12" high	325	488	650
Doll, Knickerbocker, 1935, 22" high	500	750	1000
Doll, Mickey Mouse Bandleader, Knickerbocker, 1935, 12" high	650	1100	1500
Doll, stuffed, (Dean Rag?), 13-3/4" high	400	600	800
Doll, wooden w/jointed hands, arms, legs and wire tail, leather ears, first toy made by Borgfeldt of NY, 1930, marked "Copyright 1928-1930 by Walter E. Disney"	550	825	1100
Drum, tin, Ohio Art, 6" diameter	130	195	260
Drum Set, tin and cardboard, shows Minnie watching Mickey juggle c. 1940	240	360	480

	C6	C8	C10
Figure, cast iron, depicts Mickey holding flag, 1930s	140	210	280
Figure, celluloid Mickey on wood hobby horse, c. 1935, 4-1/2"	1050	1700	2300
Figure, celluloid, w/fat head, 5" high	150	225	300
Figure, Fun-E-Flex, 1930s, 3-1/2" high	150	225	300
Figure, lead, Allied Toys, 1933, 2-1/2" high	70	105	140
Figure, rubber, Dell, 9-1/2" high	50	75	100
Figure, rubber, Lakeside Mfg. Co.	80	120	160
Figure, rubber, Seiberling, 1930s, 3-1/2" high	90	135	180
Figure, rubber, Seiberling, c. 1935, 6" high	168	250	335
Figure, rubber, Sun Rubber, 1940s, 10" high	30	45	60
Figure, Sun Rubber, 8" high	65	98	130
Figure, wood, Fun-E-Flex, 7-1/2" high	325	490	650
Figure, wood jointed, Borgfeldt, early, 7" high	300	450	600

Mickey Mouse Figure, jointed, Geo. Borgeldt, $600

Mickey Mouse Handcar with Santa Lionel, 1935, $1800

Mickey Mouse Handcar with Minnie, orange housing, Lionel, 1930s, $1700

	C6	C8	C10
Figure, wood w/leather ears, Fun-E-Flex, 5" high	250	375	500
Figure, wood w/jointed arms and legs, c. 1933, 8" high	600	900	1200
Flute, tin	40	60	80
Handcar, "Santa Car with Mickey Mouse and His Gift Pack," Lionel No. 1105, 1935	900	1350	1800
Handcar, w/Minnie, orange housing, Lionel Co., 1930s, 7" long	650	1100	1700
Hingees, 1944	25	38	50
Jazz Drummer, finger-activated tin toy, Nifty, 4-3/4" high	1500	2700	4100
Kaleidoscope, 1950s	32	48	65
Marionette, felt body stuffed w/cotton, c. 1930, 9-1/2" high	112	158	225
Marionette, Peter Puppet Playthings Co., 1952, 14" tall	55	83	110
Mask, cardboard, c. 1935	60	90	120
Mickey Mouse and Donald Duck handcar, wind-up plastic, Marx, 1948	200	300	400
Mickey Mouse and Donald in fire truck, Sun Rubber, late 1930s, 6-1/2" long	75	112	150
Mickey Mouse and Donald on Boat, celluloid	1050	1650	2300

	C6	C8	C10
Mickey Mouse and Donald Walker, plastic, both on back of alligator, Marx, 1950s	60	90	120
Mickey Mouse Club Auto-Magic Picture Gun, projects films, 1946	35	52	70
Mickey Mouse Club Bow and Arrow Set, c. 1955	20	30	40
Mickey Mouse Club Newsreel Projector	68	102	135
Mickey Mouse Club Snap-on Ears, plastic, 1950s	10	15	20
Mickey Mouse Motorcycle, tin friction, Linemar, 1950s, 3" long	200	300	400
Mickey Mouse Motorcycle, tin friction, Linemar, 1950s, 3-1/2" long	150	225	300
Mickey Mouse Organ Grinder, depicts Minnie Mouse dancing on organ pushed by Mickey, German	1200	1800	2400
Mickey Mouse Pirate Ship, Ideal	138	210	275
Mickey Mouse Trapeze, celluloid, Borgfeldt, 1930s	500	750	1000
Mickey Mouse Trapeze, wood, c. 1930s	34	51	68
Mickey Mouse Tricycle, Linemar, 1950s, 4" tall	500	775	1100
Mickey Mouse Tumbling, Marks Bros., 8" high, 1947	42	63	85
Mickey the Driver, friction, Marx (Japan), 6-1/2" long, 1950s	400	600	800
Mickey, Minnie and Goofy sand pail, tin litho, Ohio Art, 1938	112	168	225
Mickey's Service Truck, plastic friction, Marx, 1950s, 3-1/2" long	50	75	100
Mickey's Tractor, Mickey's head turns, Sun Rubber, 1930s, 4-1/2" long	65	98	130
Mickey-in-the-Box, 7" high	260	390	520
Mickey the Magician, battery-operated, Linemar, 10"	500	800	1200

Mickey Mouse and Donald Duck Handcar, Marx, 1948, $400

Mickey Mouse Bus Lines - Walt Disney Stars, riding toy, Gong Bell, c. 1960, $300

Mickey the Magician, battery-operated, Linemar, $200

	C6	C8	C10
Movie Fun Optical Toy, Mastercraft, 1950s, 7" x 7" x 5"	150	225	300
Movie Projector, Keystone No. E-18, 1930s, 10" high	125	188	250
Movie-Jector, 1935	135	200	270
Newsreel, 1950s, includes three records and five films, Mattel, 9-1/2" high	110	165	225
Piano, Marks Bros., c. 1935, 10"	1250	1875	2500
Piano, wooden, grand piano w/decal showing Mickey playing, Minnie listening, c. 1935	200	300	400
Pocket Knife, 1935	40	60	80
Puppet, cloth body w/composition head, hands and feet and cloth ears, early 1940s style	175	263	350
Puppet, Gund, 10" high	11	16	22
Puppet, rubber legs and arms, wood body, Pelham, 24" high	40	60	80
Push Puppet, Gabriel, 1977	10	15	20
Push Puppet, Mickey Mouse Drummer, Kohner,1950s	100	150	200
Race Car, T.M. Co., 1930s, 3" long	300	450	600
Riding Toy, Mickey Mouse Bus Lines - Walt Disney Stars, Gong Bell, c. 1960, 19-1/2" long	150	225	300
Roly-Poly, celluloid, early, 4" high	187	280	375
Rower, wooden, Fun-E-Flex, 10-3/4"	1700	2550	3400
Saxophone Player, 1930s	800	1300	2000

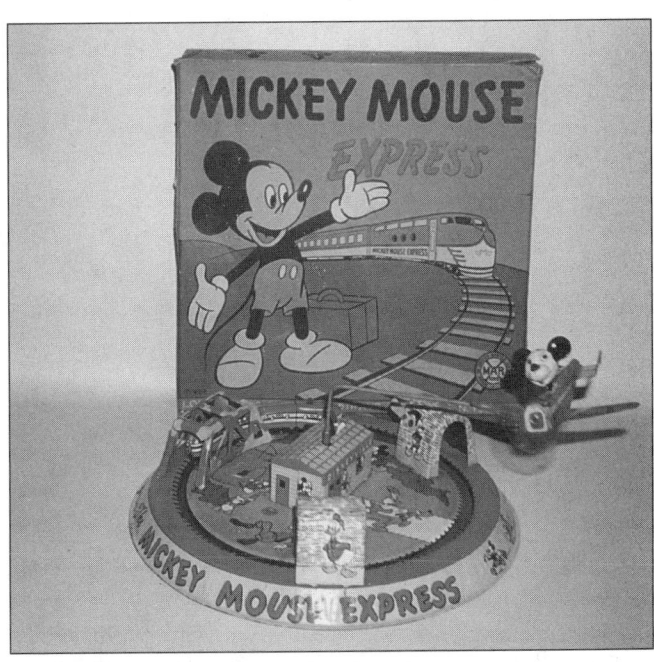

Mickey Mouse Express, Marx, 1950s, $850

	C6	C8	C10
Snow Shovel, Mickey and Pluto, shows them building a snowman, 26" long	90	135	180
Soaky	20	30	40
Soda Jerk Hat, felt, shows Mickey from shoulders up saying "have one on me," c. 1930, 5" x 11"	60	90	120
Soldier Set, cardboard soldiers, gun	500	850	1200
Sparkler Toy, Nifty, 1930s, 5-1/2" tall	325	490	650
Squeeze Toy, rubber, large size w/clothes, Sun Rubber, 1950	30	45	60
Squeeze Toy, w/red shirt and yellow pants, Sun Rubber, 1950	34	51	68
Tambourine, heavy paper head, depicts Mickey juggling while Minnie watches, Noble & Cooley Co., 1936, 9"	310	465	620
Tea Service, tin, twenty-four pieces, Chein, 1930s	120	180	240
Tool Chest, Hamilton Metal, 1935, complete	170	255	340
Tumbler, pie-eyed, Schuco, 1930s, 4" long	150	225	300
Tumbler, Schuco, 4" high	200	300	400

Mickey Mouse Rower, Fun-E-Flex, $3400

Mickey Mouse Racing Car, 1930s, $800

Mickey Mouse Xylophone Player, Linemar, 1950s, $665

	C6	C8	C10
Viewer, w/film of "Brave Little Tailor," 1946	60	90	120
Walker, Borgfeldt, 1934	3000	5000	8000
Washboard Set, tin, c. 1935, complete	80	120	160
Washing Machine, tin litho, shows two scenes w/Mickey, Minnie, Pluto, Ohio Art Co., 1932 or 1933, 7" high	100	150	200
Wind-up, "Running Mickey on Pluto," celluloid, 1940s, M-T Co., 5-1/2" long	2000	3500	6500
Wind-up, Mickey Mouse Express, Mickey in airplane, Marx, 1950s, 9" diameter	425	638	850
Wind-up, Mickey Mouse Express, tin litho train set, Marx, 1950s, 14" long, base 21" x 13"	700	1100	1700
Wind-up, Mickey Mouse Meteor Five-Car Train, tin litho, Marx, 43" long	800	1000	1500
Wind-up, Mickey Mouse on Handcar, Japan, 8" long, basket on back	138	208	275
Wind-up, Mickey Mouse on Tricycle, tin litho w/celluloid Mickey, 1940s, 3-1/2" long	450	675	900
Wind-up, Mickey Mouse Racing Car, red lithographed tin wind-up w/Mickey at the wheel, 1930s, 4" long	400	600	800
Wind-up, Mickey Mouse Rollerskater, Linemar, 1950s, 6" high	450	750	1130
Wind-up, Mickey Mouse w/Twirling Tail, Linemar, 1950s, 5-1/2" high	130	195	260
Wind-up, Mickey Mouse Xylophone Player, tin, Linemar, 1950s, 6" high	333	500	665
Wind-up, Mickey Mouse, plastic, "Scooter Jockey," Mavco Co., 1950s, 6" high	400	600	800

	C6	C8	C10
Wind-up, Mickey on Scooter, tin, Linemar, 4-1/2" high, 1950s, rare	350	525	700
Wind-up, Mickey on Unicycle, Linemar, 1950s, 5" high	650	975	1300
Wind-up, Mickey Race Car, celluloid, Occupied Japan	250	375	500
Wind-up, Mickey the Musician - I Play the Xylophone, wind-up, Marx, 1950s, 10" high	312	465	625
Wind-up, Mickey's Delivery, tin litho, Pluto on tricycle cart, celluloid head on Pluto, Linemar, 1950s, 5-1/2" long	375	565	750
Wind-up, Mickey's Mousekemovers, Linemar, 1950s, 13" long	500	750	1025
Wind-up, Rocking Mickey Mouse on Pluto, Linemar	800	1400	2000
Wind-up, tin, vibrates, Linemar, 1950s 5-1/2" high	300	450	600

MINNIE MOUSE

	C6	C8	C10
Doll, cloth, early 1930s, 16" high	650	975	1300
Doll, Minnie Mouse Cowgirl, Knickerbocker, 1936, 18" high	470	705	940
Doll, wearing dress and high heels, 1930, 12" high	225	338	450
Figure, celluloid, string tail, 6" high, 1930s	425	638	850
Figure, cloth, dressed in a red and white polka dot skirt, wearing composition high-heeled shoes, 14-1/2" high	300	450	600
Figure, Fun-E-Flex, 7" high	300	450	600
Figure, lead, Allied Toys, 1933, 2-1/2" high	70	105	140
Figure, Sun Rubber, 1940s, 10-1/2" high	85	125	170

Minnie Mouse Doll, cloth, early 1930s, $1,300

Minnie Mouse Knitter, Linemar, 1950s, $750

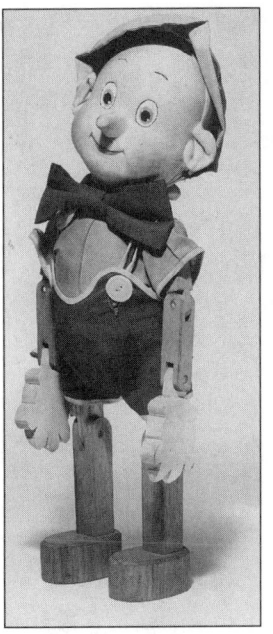

Pinocchio Figure, jointed wood and cloth, Kreuger, $320

	C6	C8	C10
Figure, w/fat head, celluloid, 1930s, 5" high	225	338	450
Figure, wooden, 1930s, 5-1/2" high	187	286	375
Figure, wooden, Fun-E-Flex, 4" high	140	210	280
Figure, wooden, jointed, 3" high, 1940s	200	300	400
Hand Puppet, Peter Puppet Playthings, c. 1952	100	150	200
Marionette, felt body stuffed w/cotton, c. 1930, 9-1/2" high	112	168	225
Marionette, wood and composition, 1950s, 13"	150	225	300
Mask, cardboard, c. 1935	40	60	80
Puppet, wood body w/rubber legs and arms, Pelham, 24" high	195	292	390
Roly-Poly, celluloid, 4"	60	90	120
Tricycle, Linemar, 1950s, 4"	450	675	900
Walker, plastic	20	30	40
Washing Machine, Precision Specialties, Inc., 1950	100	150	200
Wind-up, hard plastic, 1960s, Marx, 7" high	70	105	140
Wind-up, Minnie Mouse Knitter, tin litho, Linemar, 1950s, 7" high	375	562	750

PETER PAN

Captain Hook Hand Puppet, Gund, 1950	17	26	35
Captain Hook Marionette, Peter Puppet Playthings	95	143	190
Peter Pan Figure, Sun Rubber, 9-3/4" high, c. 1952	30	45	60
Peter Pan Jolly Roger Pirate Ship	17	26	35
Peter Pan Marionette, Peter Puppet Playthings, c. 1952	70	105	40
Peter Pan Tea Set, twenty-three pieces, c. 1953,	275	363	550
Peter Pan Train Car, 1977	22	33	45
Tinkerbell Hand Puppet, Gund	32	48	65
Wendy (Peter Pan) Hand Puppet, Gund	14	21	28
Wendy marionette, 1950s	75	112	150

PINOCCHIO

	C6	C8	C10
Cleo Facemask, Gillette, 1939	20	30	40
Cleo the Goldfish squeeze toy, Sun Rubber	23	35	47
Donkey Doll, stuffed, Knickerbocker	95	142	190
Donkey Figure, rubber, Seiberling Rubber, 1940	70	105	140
Figaro, tin friction toy, Linemar, 1950s, 3" long	70	105	140
Figaro Mask, paper, Gillette, 1939	25	38	50
Gepetto Facemask, Gillette, 1939	22	33	45
Gepetto Figure, wood, holding his chin, Multi Products, 1940, 5-1/2"	70	105	140
Pinocchio Delivery, Marx	250	375	500

Pinocchio Doll, wood and composition, Ideal, $500

Walking Pinocchio, plastic, Marx, 1950s, $80

	C6	C8	C10
Pinocchio Doll, jointed wood and composition, Ideal, 12" high 300	450	600
Pinocchio Doll, jointed, 19-3/4" high, c. 1940.. 400	600	800
Pinocchio Doll, jointed, c. 1940, 11" high 200	300	400
Pinocchio Doll, jointed, Ideal, circa 1940, 7-1/2" high.................................... 150	225	300
Pinocchio Doll, soft cloth, c. 1940s, 18" high 125	188	250
Pinocchio Doll, stuffed, Knickerbocker, 15" high 92	138	185
Pinocchio Doll, wood and composition, jointed, Ideal, 10-1/2" high.................... 250	375	500
Pinocchio Figure, cloth and jointed wood figure, Kreuger 160	240	320
Pinocchio Figure, molded wood fiber, Multi Products, 1940, 5" high 100	150	200

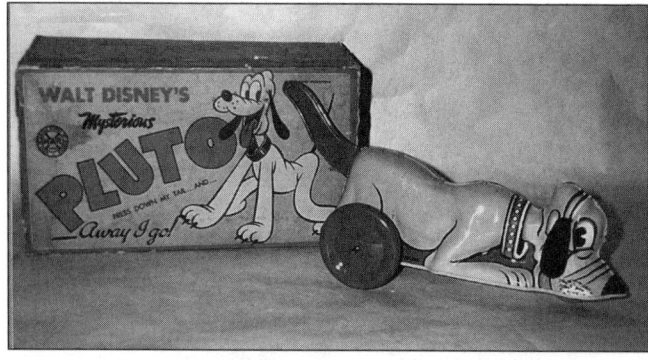

"Mysterious Pluto," Marx, $300

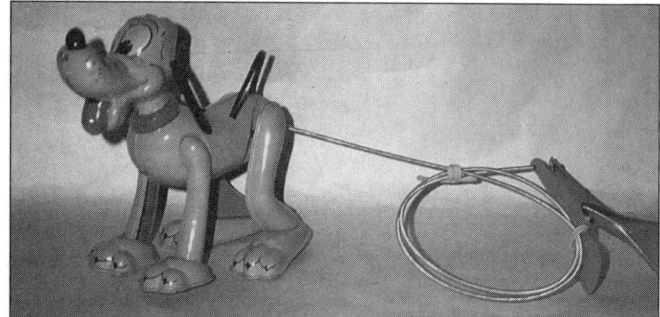

Pluto Squeeze-Action Toy, Marx, 1950s, $150

	C6	C8	C10
Pinocchio Figure, molded wood fiber, Multi Products, 1940, 2-1/2" high 100	150	200
Pinocchio Figure, rubber, Seiberling, 5-1/2" high 27	41	55
Pinocchio Hand Puppet, Gund, 1950s........ 10	15	21
Pinocchio Mask, paper, Gillette, 1939......... 20	30	40
Pinocchio Soaky 12	18	25
Pinocchio the Acrobat, tin wind-up, "Watch Him Go!" Marx, 1939 385	575	770
Pinocchio, "Walking Pinocchio," plastic, Marx, 1950s... 40	60	80
Pinocchio, Ideal, 8" high 132	198	264
Pinocchio, tin litho wind-up, Linemar Co., 1950s, 5-1/2" tall...................... 350	525	700
Pinocchio, tin wind-up w/litho eyes, Marx, c. 1940, 8-1/2" high.................... 300	450	600
Pinocchio, tin wind-up w/moving eyes, Marx, 1939, 8-1/2" high...................... 312	470	625
Pinocchio, wood and papier-mâché wind-up, George Borgfeldt, 1940, 10-1/2" high 318	475	635

PLUTO

	C6	C8	C10
Figure, lead, Allied toys, 2-1/2" high, 1933 60	90	120
Figure, Seiberling, 7-1/2" 65	98	130
Figure, Seiberling, c. 1935, 4" 60	90	120
Figure, wood jointed, 9".............................. 250	375	500
Figure, wood, Borgfeldt, 6" 175	263	350
Figure, wooden w/bendable legs, c. 1934, 3"... 140	210	280
Hand Puppet, Gund, 1950s 15	22	30
Musical Pluto, plastic, Marx, 1960s, 8" x 8" base 400	600	800
Mysterious Pluto, Marx 150	225	300
Pluto in His Sports Car, plastic friction drive, 1950s, 4" long,.............................. 50	75	100
Pluto Motorcycle, tin friction, 1950s, Linemar, 3-1/2" long............................ 300	450	600

"Drum Major," tin, Linemar, 1950s, $450

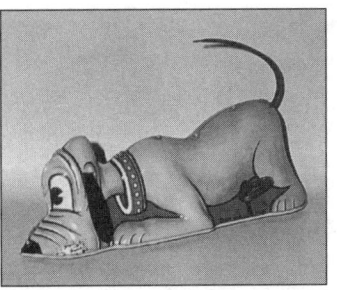

"Wise Pluto," Marx, 1939, $425

	C6	C8	C10
Wind-up, Pluto, "Begging Rollover Pluto," Linemar, 1950s, 6-1/2" long	100	150	200
Wind-up, Watch Me Roll Over, Marx, 1939	130	195	260
Wind-up, Wise Pluto, Marx, 1939, 8" long	212	318	425

	C6	C8	C10
Pluto on Rockers, wooden, c. 1930s	150	225	300
Pluto Pulling Cart, Linemar friction, 1950s, 8-1/2" long	392	588	785
Pluto Tricycle, Linemar, 1950s, 4" tall	278	415	555
Soaky	11	16	22
Squeeze Action Toy w/Cable, tin litho, Linemar, 1950s, 4-1/4" tall	200	300	400
Squeeze Toy, rubber, in sitting position, 1960s	20	30	40
Squeeze Toy, rubber, Sun Rubber No. 11520, 1930s	30	45	60
Wind-up, "Drum Major," tin litho wind-up, Linemar, 1950s, 6-1/2" tall	225	338	450
Wind-up, Playful Pluto & Goofy, two-piece set, Linemar, 1950s	800	1300	2000
Wind-up, Pluto w/Whirling Tail, wind-up, 1950s, Linemar, 4" high	235	350	470

SNOW WHITE AND THE SEVEN DWARFS

	C6	C8	C10
Bashful Doll, stuffed	60	90	120
Bashful Doll, Ideal, 7" high	125	188	250
Bashful Doll, Ideal, 1938, 12" high	80	120	160
Bashful Figure, lead, Britains, 1-1/2"	40	60	80
Bashful Figure, Seiberling, 5-3/4" high	90	135	180
Bashful Party Mask, 1937	20	30	40
Doc Doll, composition w/velvet clothes, Knickerbocker, 9" high	100	150	200
Doc Doll, Ideal, approx. 7" high	125	188	250
Doc Doll, Ideal, 1938, 12" high	82	123	165
Doc Figure, lead, Britains, 1-1/2" high	60	90	120
Doc Party Mask, 1937	14	21	28
Doc Figure, Seiberling, 1938	50	75	100
Dopey Doll, composition w/velvet clothes, Knickerbocker, 9" high	175	263	350
Dopey Doll, Ideal, 7" high	125	188	250

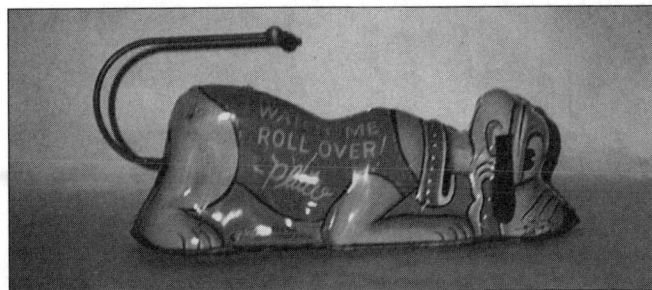

"Watch me Roll Over" Pluto, Linemar, 1950s, $260

"Playful Pluto & Goofy," Linemar, 1950s, $2,000

Doc Doll, Ideal, 1938, $165

A complete set of Ideal's Snow White and the Seven Dwarfs Dolls with original boxes is valued at $2,000

Seven Dwarfs, puppet-marionettes, Pelham, $3,000 for the set

Bashfull Doll, Ideal, 1938, $160

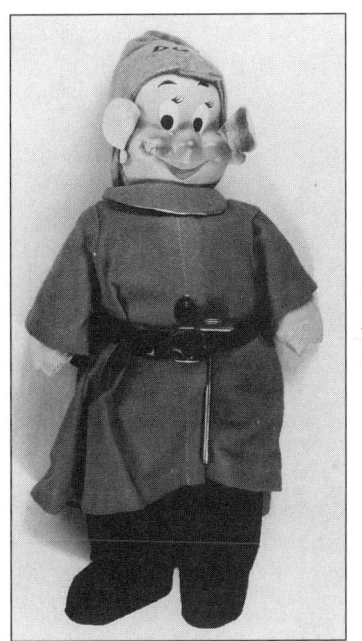

Dopey Doll, Ideal, 1938, $300

	C6	C8	C10
Dopey Doll, Ideal, 1938, 12" high.............. 150	150	225	300
Dopey Doll, Ideal, 7" high.......................... 125	125	188	250
Dopey Figure, lead, Britains, 1-1/2" 40	40	60	80
Dopey Hand Puppet, composition w/bell and buckling belt, 1938, Crown Toys..... 90	90	135	180
Dopey Hand Puppet, Gund, 1950s.............. 12	12	18	25
Dopey Marionette, Peter Puppet Playthings, c. 1952 80	80	120	160
Dopey Party Mask, 1937 20	20	30	40
Dopey soaky 17	17	25	34
Dopey squeeze toy, rubber, 1950s, 10" high 10	10	15	20

	C6	C8	C10
Dopey, Doc Pull Toy, 14" long 200	200	300	400
Dopey, tin wind-up, Marx, 1938 263	263	395	525
Grumpy Doll, composition w/velvet clothes, Knickerbocker, 9" high............ 100	100	150	200
Grumpy Doll, Ideal, 1938, 11" high 80	80	120	160
Grumpy Figure, Ideal, 7" high, ... 140	140	210	280
Grumpy Figure, lead, Britains, 1-1/2" high 40	40	60	80
Grumpy Par-T Mask, 1937 7	7	11	15
Grumpy Squeeze Toy, rubber, 1950s 10	10	15	20
Grumpy, stuffed w/molded oilcloth face, Ideal, 11-1/2" high 90	90	135	180
Happy Doll, Ideal, 1938, 12" high 110	110	165	220
Happy Doll, Ideal, 7" high 130	130	195	260
Happy Figure, lead, Britains, 1-1/2" 30	30	45	60
Happy Figure, Seiberling Rubber, 3-1/4" high, 1938................................... 60	60	90	120
Happy Marionette, Madame Alexander, 1938, 9-1/2" high................................... 110	110	155	220
Happy Party Mask, 1937 40	40	60	80
Happy Squeeze Toy, rubber, 1950s 10	10	15	20

Grumpy Doll, Ideal, 1938, $160

Seven Dwarfs Dolls, Seiberling, 1938, the set $700

Happy Doll, Ideal, 1938, $220

Sneezy Doll, Ideal, 1938, $240

	C6	C8	C10
Horace Horsecollar Hand Puppet, Gund, c. 1960	17	25	34
Seven Dwarfs Dolls, Seiberling, 1938, 5-1/2" high, the set	350	525	700
Seven Dwarfs Puppet-Marionettes, Pelham, the set	1500	2250	3000
Seven Dwarfs Squeeze Toy, vinyl, 1950s, approx. 8", each	30	45	60
Sleepy Doll, Ideal, 1938, 12" high	120	180	240
Sleepy Doll, Ideal, 7" high	125	188	250
Sleepy Figure, lead, Britains, 1-1/2" high	45	68	90

	C6	C8	C10
Sleepy Party Mask, 1937	20	30	40
Sneezy Doll, Ideal, 1938, 12" high	120	180	240
Sneezy Doll, Ideal, 7" high	125	188	250
Sneezy Figure, lead, Britains, 1-1/2" high	45	68	90
Sneezy Figure, Seiberling, 1938, 3-1/4" high	60	90	120
Sneezy Party Mask, 1937	20	30	40
Sneezy Squeeze Toy, rubber, 1950s	10	15	20
Snow White Doll, Knickerbocker, 1940s, 12" high	187	280	375
Snow White Doll, Madame Alexander, 1938, 13" high	120	180	240

Sleepy Doll, Ideal, 1938, $240

Snow White Doll, Ideal, 1938, $300

	C6	C8	C10
Snow White Doll, Ideal, 1938, 15" high.....	150	225	300
Snow White Doll, Seiberling......................	250	375	500
Snow White Figure, lead, Britains, 2-1/2" ...	45	68	90
Snow White Kitchen Set, Wolverine...........	60	90	120
Snow White Party Mask	20	30	40
Snow White Sink and Stove, Wolverine	40	60	80
Snow White Soaky	17	26	35
Snow White Washing Machine, Revell Plastics, c. 1950, 7-1/2" high w/wringer	80	120	160
Snow White and the Seven Dwarfs blocks, set of eighteen w/box.............................	175	263	350
Snow White and the Seven Dwarfs dining Set, includes dishes, china, with cups, creamer, sugar bowl, plates, 4-1/2" dishes, 6" plate	210	315	420
Snow White and the Seven Dwarfs Drum, tin litho, 1930s...................................	125	188	250
Snow White and the Seven Dwarfs figures, Britains No. 1654, each..............	20	60	90
Snow White and the Seven Dwarfs figures, lead, by Lincoln Logs, set.........	500	750	1000
Snow White and the Seven Dwarfs musical top, Chein, 6-1/2" across.........	110	165	220
Snow White and the Seven Dwarfs sewing Set, Hasbro	20	30	40
Witch Party Mask	20	30	40

THREE LITTLE PIGS

	C6	C8	C10
Big Bad Wolf and The Three Little Pigs, four-piece set, Linemar, 1950s, 4-1/4" tall	750	1125	1500
Big Bad Wolf Halloween costume, 4" high..	60	90	120
Big Bad Wolf pinback, celluloid, 1-1/4".......	38	53	75
Big Bad Wolf stuffed toy in tux, w/carnation, glass eyes, 20" tall	450	675	900
Three Little Pigs Acrobats, celluloid, Japan	312	465	625
Three Little Pigs Clothes washer, Chein....	102	153	205
Three Little Pigs Drummer, Schuco, 1930s, 4-1/2" tall....................................	175	263	350
Three Little Pigs Figures, wood w/fiber arms and legs, Borgfeldt, c. 1933, 3-1/4" high	120	180	240
Three Little Pigs Flutist, Schuco, 1930s, 4-1/2" tall	175	263	350
Three Little Pigs Par-T-Mask, 1933	40	60	80
Three Little Pigs Sand Bucket, 3" tall...........	30	45	60
Three Little Pigs Violinist, Schuco, 1930s, 4-1/2" tall....................................	212	318	425
Three Little Pigs Walkers, tin wind-up, Linemar, each	130	195	260

Disneykins, Marx, $210

WALT DISNEY

	C6	C8	C10
Character Carousel, Linemar Co., 1950s, 7" high w/3" characters..............	300	450	600
Character T.V. Set, Automatic Toy Co., 1950s, 5" cubic	150	225	300
Stars Bus, 19" long, Gong Bell	450	675	900
Television Car, Marx, 1950s, 7-1/2" long ..	275	365	550
Friction Delivery Wagon, features Mickey, Donald, Pluto, etc., Linemar, 1950s, 6" long	450	675	900
Friction Go-Mobile, features Mickey, Pluto, Donald, etc., 1960s, Marx, 6" long..	150	225	300
Mechanical Tricycle, features Pluto, Mickey, Donald, etc., 1950s, Linemar, 4" high..	200	300	400
Television Playhouse, w/thirty-nine characters, Marx Play set	232	348	465

ZORRO

	C6	C8	C10
Flintlock Pistol, Marx..................................	35	52	70
Hand Puppet, Gund	50	75	100
Hat, hideaway mask and gloves, 1950s........	46	69	92
Play Set, Marx...	400	600	800
Ring, black top w/"Z" and "Zorro" name...	22	33	44

	C6	C8	C10
Sword, 1960s, 24" long 5	8	10
Zorro on Rearing Horse, Marx 160	240	320

MISCELLANEOUS

	C6	C8	C10
1001 Dalmatians, set of six wooden nodders, 1959 125	188	250
Alice in Wonderland Marionette, Peter Puppet 85	128	170
Casey Jr. Disneyland Express, tin and plastic, locomotive, three cars, Marx 73	110	145
Disney Show Boat, plastic, Playworld Toys,1981 4	6	8
Disney Showboat, large, 1960 62	93	125
Disneykins, Marx 105	158	210
Dumbo Hand Puppet, Gund, c. 1955, 10".. 25	38	50
Dumbo Squeeze Doll, vinyl, 1960s, 9" 22	33	45
Dumbo, tin wind-up, Dumbo flips over, Marx, 1941, 4" high.............................. 300	450	600
Eeyore Squeeze Doll, vinyl, 1960s 37	56	75
Elmer Elephant Figure, celluloid and string, 1930s, 5" 120	180	240
Elmer Elephant, rubber, w/moveable head, Seiberling................................ 162	243	325
Frontierland Logs, Halsam No. 915 45	68	90
Gym Toys Acrobats, includes Mickey, Donald, Minnie, Linemar, 1950s, 8-1/2" high, each 200	300	400
Huey - Louie - Dewey Locomotive, plastic friction, Marx, 1950s, 3-1/2" long... 50	75	100

Dumbo, Marx, 1941, $600

	C6	C8	C10
Johnny Tremain flintlock cap pistol, Marx 60	90	120
Jungle Book Dancing Bear, plastic wind-up, Marx.................................. 80	120	160
Ludwig Von Drake Go-Cart, friction, Marx, 1961 158	235	315
Ludwig Von Drake squeeze toy, rubber, Dell, c. 1960, 7" 58	90	115
Ludwig Von Drake Talking Doll 50	75	100
Ludwig Von Drake, tin litho wind-up, Linemar, 1950s, 6" tall 290	435	580
Mad Hatter (Alice in Wonderland) Puppet 85	130	170
Mad Hatter Doll, Gund 200	300	400
Mad Hatter's Taxi, Linemar, 1950s, 5" long 300	450	600
Mousketeer Electric TV Story Teller, tin litho, includes TV, record player, records and film reels, T. Cohn, late 1950s... 160	240	320
Mousketeer Hat, wool and rayon, Benay-Albee, 1950s............................ 5	8	10
Mousketeer Play Outfit 75	112	150
Mousketeer Soaky 17	26	35
Nautilus Submarine (20,000 Leagues Under the Sea) 155	235	310
Oswald the Rabbit, crib toy, celluloid c. 1927, 6-1/2" long.............................. 250	375	500
Parade Roadster, tin litho wind-up, convertible car decorated w/Mickey and other Disney characters, Donald is at the wheel w/Pluto,Mickey and Minnie as passengers, Marx, 1950s, 11-1/4" long... 350	525	700
Pecos Bill, wind-up, plastic, Marx, 1950s 200	300	400
Piglet squeeze Doll, vinyl, 1960s................ 9	14	17
Practical Pig Doll, Gund 112	168	225

Elmer Elephant, Seiberling, $325

	C6	C8	C10
Practical Pig, tin litho wind-up, Linemar	260	390	520
Professor Von Drake Go Mobile, 1950s, 6" long, Linemar, wind-up	150	225	300
Si-Am (Lady and the Tramp) Doll, stuffed w/vinyl face, 16" high, Gund, c. 1955	40	60	80
Sleeping Beauty Hand Puppet, Gund, 1950s	31	47	62
Sleeping Beauty Squeeze Toy, sitting w/animals, 6-1/2"	44	66	88
Tigger Squeeze Doll, 1960s, 9"	9	13	18

	C6	C8	C10
Timothy Mouse (Dumbo) Doll, stuffed, Character Novelty, 1942, 17" high	150	225	300
Tramp Hand Puppet, Gund	35	52	70
Tramp the Dog, Linemar friction, 1960s, 4" high	90	135	180
Uncle Scrooge Hand Puppet, wearing high hat, 1960s	20	30	40
Uncle Scrooge Limousine, w/"$" on back fender	110	165	220
Uncle Scrooge Squeeze Toy Bank, vinyl, c. 1960, 7" high	40	60	80

DOLLHOUSES AND MINATURE FURNITURE

As World War II ended, consumers had a huge pent-up demand for goods which had been scarce during the war. The peacetime economy boomed as American industry became the supplier to the rest of the war ravaged world. Unlike the Depression years, which had immediately preceded the Second World War, employment surged, as did disposable family income. Newly affluent parents were able to provide their children with much more than the bare necessities. The American toy industry, with excess capacity built to serve the war effort and utilizing materials developed during the war, answered the demands of the Baby Boomers and their parents by making low cost toys available through five-and-dime stores and through the catalogs of Sears and Montgomery Wards.

Dollhouses and the miniature furniture and accessories to fit them were originally made, not as toys, but to assist in the education of refined young women of the Victorian era. As "pictures of the times" they were designed to be looked at, not played with. They were often made by German toymakers, for the English market. Following the pattern established in the early part of the twentieth century by companies like Converse, Bliss and Schoenhut, postwar toy manufacturers utilized mass production techniques to produce toys with play value. Prewar houses were often made of heavy printed cardboard or of wood covered with brightly and highly-detailed lithographed paper. Furniture was usually made of wood by companies like Strombecker or of cast-metal by companies like Tootsietoy.

World War II had shown the utility of plastic materials, and industries had honed their thermoplastic molding and sheet-metal stamping skills. Plastic toys could be made in high-speed processes with minimal need for hand finishing. Toys could be produced in any color of the rainbow as well as in combinations of colors. They were hygienic, and could be formed with amazing details. Dollhouse furniture and accessories could be produced to resemble their real life counterparts. Couches could be made with wood-toned bases and brightly colored upholstery. Swings could be made to hold and move little family members. Sewing machines had moving parts as did trash cans, lawn mowers and ironing boards. The toys were aimed at little homemakers eager to be just like their parents.

Companies like Renwal, Ideal and Plasco made a wide range of furniture, while manufacturers like Acme Thomas, Irwin and Commonwealth produced numerous accessories that complemented the furniture lines. During the mid-fifties the Marx Toy Company began to dominate the market for dollhouses and furniture. Marx furniture was molded in one color and generally did not have moving parts. The furniture was packaged and sold with Marx dollhouse play sets. Later, manufacturers like Superior and Wolverine produced one-piece molded furniture usually from polyethylene, a soft flexible plastic, also for inclusion with their dollhouse play sets.

As suburbia grew so did the types of miniature dollhouses to hold the plastic furniture and accessories. The postwar dollhouses generally were produced from two different materials—fiberboard and sheet steel. The more expensive fiberboard houses, first actually produced before the War, were most often silk screened in four colors. The number of colors and the screening method limited the interior and exterior detail. The flat sides and roofs were screwed together, forming sturdy houses capable of withstanding a lot of play. Windows frames of plastic or metal were sometimes inserted in the exterior walls. Hinged wooden doors generally opened and closed, and a few of the houses contained staircases and closets. The houses were roughly 3/4-inch to one foot in scale, making it easy for little hands to rearrange dolls and furniture inside the four-to-six-room houses. Rich Toys, Keystone and Jayline Toys are the best known of the fiberboard manufactures. Many of these durable homes survive today.

Sheet metal provided toy manufacturers with a more flexible material with which to design houses, copying the styles of the day. The metal walls, floors and roofs, prior to being stamped from large sheets of the thin metal, were lithographed with the designs of the interiors and exteriors of the houses. As time progressed the detail became quite elaborate as the manufacturers moved beyond four-color lithography to use six, eight or more colors. Perhaps the first of the postwar steel houses, were the two houses produced by National Can Company and marketed under the Playsteel name. In 1948, T. Cohn introduced a now well-recognized house with a red tiled roof. The house had five rooms and an upstairs patio. Each of these earlier houses was 3/4-inch to one foot in scale and well matched the furniture of

Renwal, Ideal and Plasco. Soon thereafter, Meritoy of Boston introduced an interesting two-story Cape.

In 1949, the market changed dramatically when Marx Toys first introduced a dollhouse packaged with its own furniture, car and play yard selling for $3.95. Although Marx produced large and well-detailed dollhouses in its 3/4-inch-scale deluxe and "Marxie Mansion" lines, the majority of its houses were 1/2-inch to one foot in scale. They ranged in style from two-story colonials with or without attached family room to L-shaped ranches and split-levels. Interior lithography changed from time to time, reflecting "modern" decorating trends. The smaller 1/2-inch-scale caught on and dominated the market in the 1950s and sixties as companies like T. Cohn and Wolverine introduced 1/2-inch-scale houses, following the Marx example.

There are still many examples of Baby Boomer miniature furniture and houses to be found at antique shops, flea markets and through online markets. Prices have continued to rise, as toys in good to excellent condition become scarce. Condition and rarity continue to be the factors that determine price. A piece of unscratched, unbroken or repaired plastic toy without melt marks will command a higher price than a well played with piece. Toys with moving parts and opening drawers and cabinet doors are generally priced higher than one-piece toys. Collectors will find many paths to follow in assembling their collections. Besides the better known companies like Renwal, Ideal and Marx, manufacturers such as Kleeware of Great Britain, Reliable of Canada, Jaydon, Allied, Best and Mattel all produced miniature furniture and accessories which continue to be fun to play with fifty years later.

Contributor: Marcie Tubbs, 6405 Mitchell Hollow Rd., Charlotte, NC 28277, e-mail: CARDAD@aol.com. Tubbs began collecting an eclectic assortment of baby boomer dollhouses, dollhouse furniture and figures after purchasing a furnished T. Cohn dollhouse at the Brimfield, Mass. antique shows a number of years ago; she has been hooked ever since. Tubbs not only enjoys collecting, but also researching the history of the subject. She and her husband, Bob, have written several articles on dollhouses and their inhabitants. She is always interested in adding unusual examples to her ever-growing collection and enjoys hearing from others about the hobby.

Photos in this section by Marcie Tubbs.

ACME/THOMAS TOY

Acme Plastics Manufacturing Co., originally founded in 1935, merged with and became the marketing arm of Thomas Toy Company in 1945. Acme/Thomas never attempted to produce a line of dollhouse furniture with the breadth of Renwal, Ideal Plasco or Marx, but instead focused on toys with high play value. These pieces were brightly colored nursery and outdoor toys in 3/4-inch-scale that complemented the toys of the other manufacturers. Acme/Thomas also produced a number of dollhouse dolls from the rubber-like Vinylite, which are often found with Baby Boomer plastics. Unfortunately, the chemicals from the Vinylite causes melt marks when the dolls come in contact with hard polystyrene toys. The hard plastic pieces are generally marked either Acme or Thomas along with one or more mold numbers.

Various Acme/Thomas Toy playground and nursery pieces, clockwise left to right: Baby Carriage ($7); Hammock ($20); Horsehead Stroller ($10); Slide ($15); Single Swing ($15); Dogsled with harness and dog ($40); Express wagon ($12); Horsehead Seesaw ($10); Tommy Horse ($15)

No.	Description	C10
I-139	Baby Carriage	7
I-144	Express Wagon	12
I-154	Single Swing	15
I-154	Double Swing	30
I-154	Triple Swing	50
I-154	Horsehead Swing	70
I-156	Horsehead Stroller	10
I-159	Horsehead Seesaw	10
I-163	Ferris Wheel	40
I-166	Hammock	20
I-171	Slide	15
I-179	Tommy Horse	15
I-184	Dogsled w/harness and dog	40

COMMONWEALTH

Commonwealth Plastics Corporation of Leominster, Mass. started as a manufacturer of buttons and costume jewelry. It branched into the production of a small line of party favors and dollhouse accessories that are quite collectible today. The reel-type electric motor makes a "motor" sound as it is rolled along, and the lovebird cage on a stand complements the furniture of the larger toy manufacturers.

Birdcage, Commonwealth, $30

Description	C10
Lawn Mower	15
Birdcage	30
Watering Can and Garden tools	15
Wheelbarrow	10
Lamppost w/mailbox	18

IDEAL

Established in 1903 the Ideal Toy and Novelty Company—the originator of the "Teddy Bear"—was the largest of the postwar American toy and doll manufacturers. They introduced four different lines of dollhouse furniture for Baby Boomers. In 1947 they introduced a line of beautifully detailed 3/4-inch-scale furniture from brightly colored hard plastic. The toys generally are marked with the Ideal trademark and one or more mold numbers. Early boxed sets included room box walls or an outdoor setting. In later boxed sets, the furniture could be seen through cellophane panels. The nursery and outdoor pieces tend to bring higher prices today than the more common living, dining and bedroom pieces. Two different kitchen lines were sold during this period, a standard and the more desirable deluxe version. The slightly larger and more detailed deluxe line also included a dishwasher, a front opening washing machine and a mangle with a rotating drum. The 3/4-inch-scale furniture was produced until 1952.

In 1950 and 1951, Ideal produced a set of furniture known as Young Decorator. The Young Decorator furniture was almost 1-1/2-inch to on foot in scale making it easy to rearrange and play with on a blueprint-styled playmat included in each box.

In 1964 the Ideal Toy Corporation (the name having been changed in 1951) introduced another line of doll-

This plastic Garden Furniture from Ideal, valued at $700-750, is the most highly sought-after Ideal boxed set. The set includes: Patio Umbrella, Plastic Pole, Lawn Bench, Doghouse, Black Scottie Dog, Pool, Birdbath, Circular Lawn Table, Lawn Chair, Picnic Table, Trellis and Lawn Chair.

house furniture in 3/4-inch to one-foot scale. The Petite Princess Fantasy Furniture with real cloth upholstery had glass and metal details and accessories to highlight the plastic furniture. The furniture was too expensive to appeal to the mass toy market, and in 1965 the line was reintroduced as Princess Patti furniture. The materials used to decorate the Princess Patti furniture were not as expensive as the Petite Princess line. With some nod to reality, the Princess Patti line included the now rare kitchen, bathroom and TV set. Much of this Fantasy furniture is found individually packaged in boxes today.

No.	Description	C10
I-1003	Circular Lawn Table	20
	Pastic Pole	5
I-1004	Patio Umbrella	20
I-1016	Doghouse	40
	Black Scottie Dog	90
I-1008	Lawn Bench	20
I-1012	Trellis	100
	Birdbath	20
I-1060	Pool	100
I-1000	Picninc Table	35
I-1115	Lawn Lounge Chair	20
I-1018	Lawn Chair	15
I-980	Chinese Modern Red Dining Table	25

No.	Description	C10
I-948	Red Dining Chair w/arms	12
I-948	Red Dining Chair w/o arms	10
I-983	Red Buffet	15
I-979	Red Breakfront	20
I-942	Sofa	15
	Coffee Table	8
I-959	Bed	20
I-1559	Vaccum Cleaner	25
I-1563	Carpet Sweeper	20
I-1315	Lawn Mower	35
I-1084	Well Pump	40
I-1329	Seesaw	60
I-1312	Octagonal Sanbox w/Pole and Umbrella	100
I-2040	Young Decorator Dining Table	15
I-2045	Young Decorator Dining Chair	8
I-2034	Young Decorator Buffet	15
I-2036	Young Decorator China Cabinet	20
I-2100	Young Decorator Kitchen Table	20
I-2098	Young Decorator Kitchen Chair	12
I-2052	Young Decorator Range	30
I-2048	Young Decorator Refrigerator	25
I-2062	Young Decorator Sink	60
I-2172	Young Decorator Bathtub	20
I-2164	Young Decorator Sink	20
I-2168	Young Decorator Toilet	40
I-2170	Young Decorator Diaper Pail/Waste Can	20
I-2098	Young Decorator Blue Bathroom Chair	15
I-2077	Young Decorator Living Room Sofa End Section	15
I-2079	Young Decorator Living Room Sofa Center Curved Section	15
I-2078	Young Decorator Living Room Sofa Center Square Section	15
I-2089	Young Decorator Coffee Table	10
I-2090	Young Decorator Television Set	40
I-2081	Young Decorator Torchiere Lamp	30
I-2057	Young Decorator Bed	15
I-2076	Young Decorator Nightstand	10
I-2084	Young Decorator Wardrobe	15
I-2086	Young Decorator Vanity	15
I-2060	Young Decorator Vanity Stool	8
I-2082	Young Decorator Bathinette	40
I-2109	Young Decorator Crib	25
I-2179	Young Decorator High Chair	25
I-2108	Young Decorator Playpen	25
	Young Decorator Tricycle w/Bell	30
4416-4	Petite Princess, Little Princess Royal Bed, MIB	30
4417-2	Petite Princess, Royal Dressing Table and Stool, MIB	30
4420-6	Petitie Princess, Palace Chest w/Picture, MIB	15

Two-story lithographed masonite house with six rooms, fireplace, stairs and closet, 3/4-inch-scale, Keystone, $175

No.	Description	C10
4426-3	Petite Princess, Lyre Table w/Lamp and Painting, MIB	20
44081	Petite Princess, Boudoir Chaise Lounge, MIB	15

KEYSTONE

Among the nicest of the postwar fiberboard homes, were those made by Keystone Manufacturing Company of Boston, Mass. between 1940 and the early 1950s. In the forties, Keystone shipped their dollhouses already assembled, a big plus for harried parents on Christmas Eve. The Keystone fiberboards generally have three distinct features—a curving staircase, a fireplace and an upstairs closet. The interior walls often have silk-screened wallpaper and floor designs. The windows are either metal or plastic framed, depending on the age of the house. Unique to Keystone were three "Put-A-Way" houses with one or two extensions that folded back into the house when play was finished. The dollhouses were often marketed with 3/4-inch-scale plastic furniture. Many of the Keystone houses are marked with the company name, and some have a turntable attached to the bottom. The fiberboard houses often cost two to three times the price of a tin counterpart and manufacturing of these well-constructed toys ceased before the end of the Baby Boomer era.

Scale	Description	C10
3/4"-scale	Two-story lithographed masonite w/six rooms, fireplace, stairs and closet	175
	Two-story lithographed masonite w/six room, single wing "Put-A-Way"	200
	Two-story lithographed masonite w/eight rooms, double wing "Put-A-Way"	250

MARX TOYS

The Louis P. Marx Company became a dominant manufacturer of toys during the postwar era. Originally formed in 1917, Louis Marx applied modern mass production methods to the making of toys. The efficiencies he achieved both in manufacturing and marketing made affordable toys with great play value available to all. In 1949 Marx, attempting to fill up his manufacturing facilities, introduced a two-story brightly lithographed tin dollhouse filled with six rooms of hard plastic dollhouse furniture. The house and furniture was produced in 1/2-inch-scale. While the detail of the lithography was enhanced by the use of ten-color lithography, the furniture was of a single color, one-piece construction with no moving parts. During the twenty-five years that the Marx Company marketed dollhouses, approximately fifteen different styles were produced, although there are many decorating and packaging variations of each style as Marx constantly sought appropriate price points for each distribution channel. While the majority of the houses were 1/2-inch-scale, the houses in the 3/4-inch-scale deluxe and Marxie Mansion lines have some of the best of the Baby Boomer-era dollhouses. The large-scale mansions came in six and seven room versions, electrified and non-electrified, with and without cloth curtains, cornices, awnings, shutters and doorbells.

As the Marx dollhouses changed over time, so did the furniture packaged with them. The early hard polystyrene pieces were replaced with softer, less breakable polyethylene. Styles for the 1/2-inch-scale furniture included "overstuffed" traditional, French Provincial and contemporary. Furniture was made for the primary living areas of the houses as well as for laundry rooms, family rooms, patios, gardens and swimming pools. The hard plastic pieces are often marked with the Marx logo, but the matching soft plastic pieces sometimes are not. In 1964 Marx introduced a beautiful line of all plastic furniture known in the United States as Marx Little Hostess and in Canada as Little Miss Deb. The furniture was often multi-colored or had gilt detailing and was accompanied by plastic or metal accessories. In 1976, after the sale of Marx, the line was reintroduced in England as Amanda Ann.

Scale	Description	C10
1/2"-scale	Circular Couch, hard plastic	10
	Coffee Table, hard plastic	5
	Piano, hard plastic	10
	Piano Bench, hard plastic	5
	Juke Box, hard plastic	20
	Ping-Pong Table, hard plastic	25
	Milk Bar, hard plastic	20
	Stool, hard plastic	20
	Round Table, hard plastic	5
	Captain's Chair, hard plastic	5

Kitchen appliances by Marx, $3-5, each

Scale	Description	C10
	Other common hard plastic furniture, each	3-5
	Soft plastic furniture	1
3/4"-scale	Kitchen, hard plastic	8
	Kitchen Chair, hard plastic	5
	Sink, hard plastic	5
	Stove, hard plastic	5
	Refrigerator, hard plastic	5
	Common items, soft plastic, each	3-5
	Kitchen appliances, pots and pans, each	3-5

Marx Little Hostess

Description	C10
Tub/Shower	30
Sink/Vanity Combination	30
Bench	15
Toilet	15
Hamper and Mirror	20
Medicine Cabinet	25
Folding Screen	20

Marx Houses

Scale	Description	C10
	L-shaped ranch w/TV antennae, cupola, chimney and room divider	125

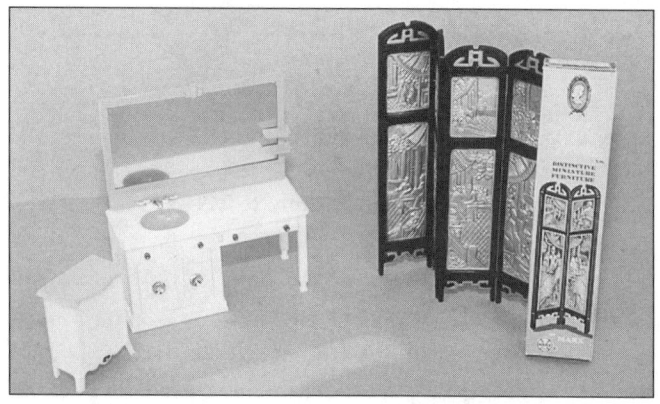

Left to Right: Sink/Vanity Combination, Marx Little Hostess, $30; Hamper and Mirror, Marx Little Hostess, $20; Folding Screen, Marx Little Hostess, $2

Dollhouse Family, Ideal, rare, $100

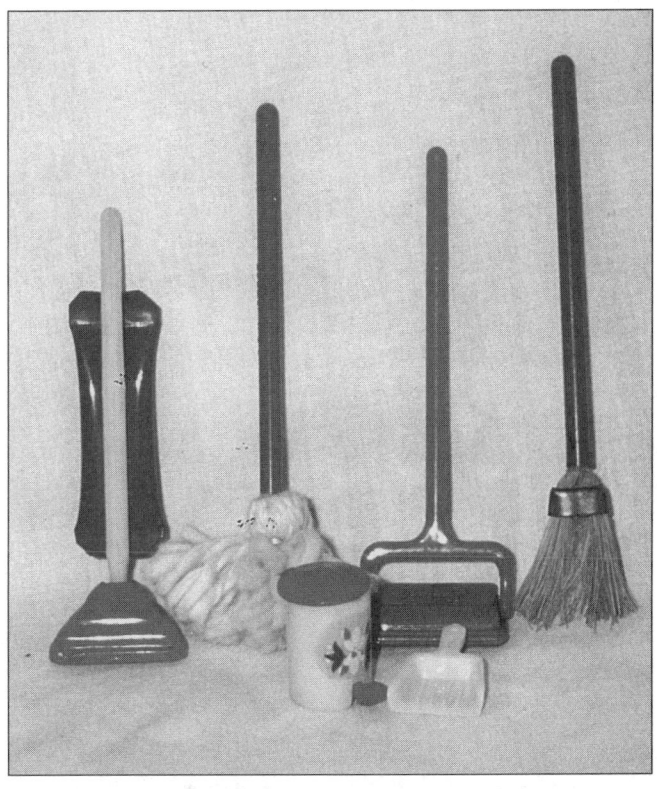

Left to Right: Renwal accessories without the original cards—Vacuum, Mop, Trash Can with Flip-top Lid, Dustpan, Carpet Sweeper with Rollers, and Broom

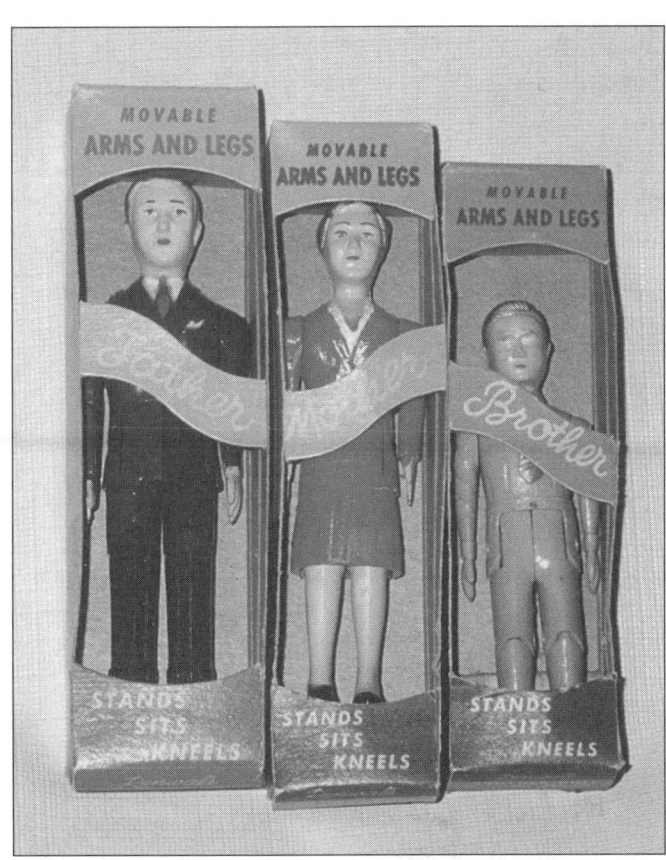

Left to right: Father, Mother and Brother, Renwal, $30 each

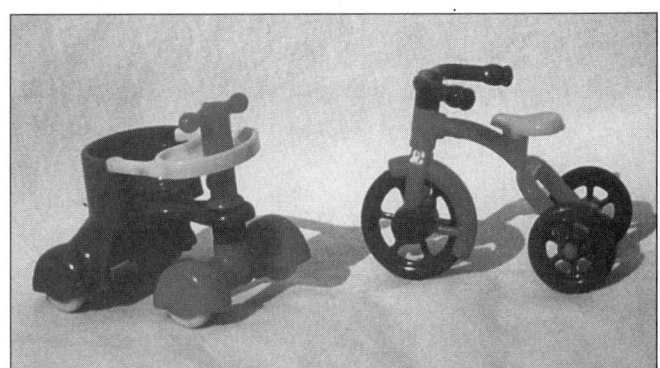

Left to Right: Kiddie Car, Renwal $35; Tricycle, Renwal, $17

Left to Right: Sewing Machine, Renwal, $25; Sewing Machine, Ideal, $25

Colonial mansion with Florida room, 3/4-inch-scale, Marx, $175

Two-story house with attached breezeway and rumpus room, 1/2-inch-scale, Marx, $140

Scale	Description	C10
	Split level w/front and back steps, railings, fireplace and chimney	125
1/2"-scale	Two-story w/tin soldier nursery	50
	Two-story w/Disney nursery and garage	125
	Two-story w/attached breezeway and rumpus room	140
3/4"-scale	Colonial mansion w/Florida room	175

MERITOY

Two-story Cape Cod, 1/2-inch-scale, Meritoy, $150

Among the first of the postwar tin dollhouses is an easily recognized Cape Cod with three dormers produced by Meritoy Corporation of Boston. The six-room house was close to 1/2-inch to foot in scale, and the furnished versions were sold with either Allied or Kleeware half-scale, hard plastic furniture. The windows were made of a silk-screened sheet of plastic and are difficult to find intact today.

Scale	Description	C10
1/2"scale	Two-Story Cape Cod	150

PLASTIC ART TOY CORPORATION OF AMERICA (PLASCO)

The Plastic Art Toy Corporation of America produced the Little Homemaker line of dollhouse furniture from 1947 until nearly the end of the Baby Boomer era. The 3/4-inch-scale furniture owed much of it popularity to its affordable price and broad product line. The inside covers of early boxed sets included room-like settings. As time progressed Plasco was sold in cellophane window boxes and on blister packs. Later versions of the furniture were cheaply produced and marketed without bases, legs or headboards. This later furniture is not as highly valued as the older, more detailed pieces. As with many lines of dollhouse furniture, the nursery pieces are among the most prized. Plasco made three dollhouses, all of which are hard to find today. The two ranch houses were made primarily of plastic and the round, futuristic "Open House" was made of fiberboard.

Description	C10
Sofa	10
Club Chair	7
Wing Chair	7
Coffee Table	5
Television Set	30

Left to Right: Television Set, Plasco, $30; Grandfather Clock, Plasco, $15

Description	C10
Fireplace	15
Grandfather Clock	15
Bathinette	30
Crib	25
Highboy	10
Nightstand	5
Vanity Chair	3

PLAYSTEEL

Playsteel was the toy division of National Can Company. Immediately after World War II they introduced two five-room tin dollhouses, a two-story red roofed, brick and clapboard Colonial, and a two-story "Buck's County farmhouse" with a fieldstone exterior and blue slate roof. The houses were originally packed in boxes that were meant to unfold to serve as landscaped yards. The interiors of the two homes were identical. The panes of the windows were cut from the steel and the front door of the Buck's County house opened. The farmhouse was also packaged with two window boxes that attached to the second-story windows. The 3/4-inch-scale was perfect for the furniture of Renwal, Ideal and Plasco, and mail-order catalogues and dimestores often featured the homes packaged with Renwal.

Scale	Description	C10
3/4"-scale	Two-story "Bucks County" w/blue roof	150
	Two-story Colonial w/red roof	150

RELIABLE

The needs of Canadian Baby Boomers were met nicely by the Reliable Plastics Company, Limited of Toronto. Reliable produced a wide range of hard plastic dollhouse toys. Many of the well-detailed pieces appear to be made from Ideal molds or molds made from Ideal toys, but many of the toys are quite individual in their styling. Most of the toys are hallmarked and fit the then common 3/4-inch scale.

Description	C10
Vanity Stool	8
Vanity Dresser w/Mirror	17

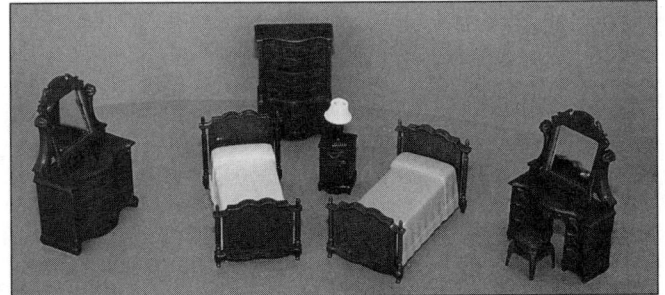

Left to Right: Reliable Bedroom set—Dresser with mirror ($17); Highboy ($15); Twin Bed ($18, each); Nightstand ($10); Table Lamp ($20); Vanity Dresser with Mirror ($17); Vanity Stool ($8)

Description	C10
Twin Bed	18
Nightstand	10
Dresser w/Mirror	17
Highboy	15
Table Lamp	20

RENWAL

Founded in 1939, Renwal is one of the best recognized of the Postwar manufacturers. Besides cars, trucks and other "boys toys," Renwal produced a wide selection of dollhouse furniture, accessories and dolls. The toys, made from the hard plastic polystyrene, were approximately 3/4 inch to one foot in scale. Almost all the pieces were hallmarked with the Renwal name and bear an item number. Introduced in 1945, early Renwal boxed sets contained a cardboard room box for displaying the furniture. Later versions of the furniture had opening drawers and doors. These, together with the later stenciled versions of the toys, bring higher prices today. Renwal stopped producing the furniture in 1956, and eventually the molds were sold. The more common pieces of furniture reappeared in the 1980s marked as made in Hong Kong.

No.	Description	C10
	Dustpan	15
#7	Tricycle	17
#10	Scale	12
#12	Stool	11
#37	Vaccuum Cleaner	22
#41-44	Family Members, each	25
#64	Trash Can w/Flip-Top Lid	12
#89	Sewing Machine	25
#116	Carpet Sweeper w/Rollers	95
#117	Mop	50
#121	Broom	125
B23	Dresser w/opening drawer	12
B23	Dresser w/o opening drawer	9

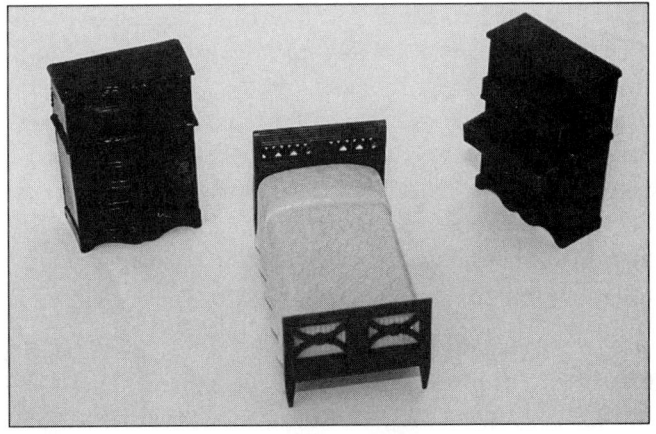

Left to Right: Dresser without opening drawers, Renwal, $??; Twin Bed, Renwal No. B23, $10; Dresser with opening drawers, Renwal No. B23, $9

Left to Right: Renwal accessories—Stool ($11); Trash can with Flip-top Lid ($12); Dustpan ($15); Scale ($12); Vacuum Cleaner ($22); Broom ($125); Mop ($50); and the Carpet Sweeper with Rollers ($95)

Three-room Ranch, 3/4-inch-scale, T. Cohn/Superior, $45

No.	Description	C10
B81	Twin Bed	10
B82	Vanity w/elaborate filigree	16
B82	Vanity w/o elaborate filigree	10
B84	Night Stand	5
B85	Highboy	8
L73	Pedestal End Table	8
L75	Vanity Bench	3
L78	Sofa	12
T95	Bathtub	10
T96	Sink	5
T97	Toilet	10
T98	Hamper	5

RICH

Rich Toy Manufacturing Co. enjoyed a prominent position among toy manufacturers for a period between 1935 to the early 1960s. Originally designed to match the one-inch-scale wooden furniture of companies like Strombecker, these fiberboard homes, when made in 3/4-inch-scale, worked perfectly with the plastic furniture introduced in 1946. Rich houses can be found in many different styles ranging from two-room cottages to a curved Art-Deco style. Exteriors were generally applied with four-color silk screens. Early models had metal window frames that were replaced by plastic in later models. Interiors were sparsely decorated. Larger houses occasionally had staircases and the most elaborate had rudimentary lighting and doorbells. Rich rarely marked its houses, although they can often be identified by the pine tree design found on the window shutters.

No.	Description	C10
3/4"-scale	Two-story lithographed fiberboard w/four rooms, front stoop w/benches	100
1"-scale	Two-story lithographed fiberboard w/six rooms, interior staircase	175

No.	Description	C10
	Two-story lithographed fiberboard w/six rooms, Arts and Crafts-style bungalow	250

T. COHN/SUPERIOR

The single patio Spanish-styled dollhouse with red tiled roof is among the most recognizable of the Baby Boomer dollhouses. Produced by T. Cohn of Brooklyn, New York, it was introduced in time for the 1948 Christmas season. The house was sold both furnished with furniture made by Plasco or Renwal and in an unfurnished version. The scale matched nicely with the furniture of Renwal and Ideal and the dollhouse is often found with an eclectic mix of the postwar furniture. The windows were made of metal and opened, casement style. T. Cohn continued to market a slightly smaller scaled Superior line through the 1960s,

Spanish-style house with single patio, 1/2-inch-scale, T. Cohn/Superior, $45

introducing several additional house styles. Houses produced before about 1957 were packaged with hard-plastic, one-color furniture marked Superior. After that time, the houses were sold with inferior 1/2-inch-scale soft plastic furniture, reportedly made for Superior by Marx.

Description	C10
Soft plastic furniture	1
Hard plastic furniture	5
Tin swimming pool	50
Patio Bench	50

T. Cohn Houses

Description		C10
1/2"-scale	Spanish style w/double patio	125
	Three-room Ranch	45
	Modern style pastel w/single patio	60
3/4"-scale	Spanish style w/single patio	150

ERECTOR SETS

Erector Set collecting has recently come to the forefront as people tire of modern toys. Very few modern toys stimulate the imagination as the toys of old. Imagine the questions posed by a chemistry set, an Erector set or a microscope set. If you think Nintendo can supply the mental stimulation that these toys of yesteryear could, well . . . you're just not in the right gear!

A.C. Gilbert, the inventor of Erector sets, was a medical doctor (1908 graduate of Yale University) as well as the winner of the gold medal for the pole vault at the 1908 World Olympics in London. In addition to his many other skills, A.C. Gilbert was an accomplished professional magician and an outgoing, gregarious individual. With this background and a taste for hard work he acquired overcoming boyhood deficiencies, there was no question of the outcome of his venture.

Erector went through three development stages. From 1913 to 1923 (Stage I) the sets featured plenty of large, strong girders. Ads showed boys sitting on the bridges built with Erector sets—and it was no exaggeration. After the trauma of World War I and the consequent inflation in the United States (and worse in Europe), Erector was redesigned and slimmed down. Girders were smaller, narrower and lighter, but Gilbert also introduced countless other shapes to make the Erector system more versatile and more capable of building unique and beautiful models. Thus in 1924 Stage II was born, and continued on until the advent of Stage III in 1963, which really signaled the end of the Gilbert company. Although true collectors are interested in the total history of the once great company, most are more familiar with, and desire, the products of Stage II (1924 to 1962). One may call this the shining hour of the most successful scientific toy company in the United States.

A.C. Gilbert ceased to be a major toy producer after 1962. The decline was somewhat agonizing, ending with the purchase of the rights to the famous name "Erector" by Meccano, SA of France, which also acquired Gilbert's old competitor in England.

Before launching into a discussion on value, consider some common sense rules. Of about 45 million Erector sets produced, ninety percent probably went to people who didn't take very good care of them. That leaves about 4.5 million fairly nice sets in a good state of preservation, but you should figure that about half of these were thrown out or otherwise disposed of. Now we have about 2.25 million pretty nice Erector sets left. Where are they?

Most of us are inclined toward flea markets and garage sales, but this is probably not your best source. You may get lucky, but in most cases this represents the low end of the market. Many sets from these sources are what we in the business call "mixed trash." Whether intentional or not, a set may be only fractionally complete and usually will contain a variety of parts from different years mixed together. If you are looking for fine quality sets in the C10 category, carefully watch for estate auctions, look for high-quality dealers, or buy from established collectors who are continually refining their collections.

Estate auctions are listed in your local newspaper. Many avid collectors are members of the A.C. Gilbert Heritage Society (1440 Whalley, Suite 252, New Haven, CT 06515) or the Southern California Meccano and Erector Club (Box 7653, Porter Ranch Sta., Northridge, CA 91327), or both. The former is the larger of the two; together they represent 500 of the largest collections in the world. Some members have over 1,000 Erector sets, and many have several hundred.

Keep in mind that unless a set was carefully preserved in a dry climate, there is little chance of acquiring a set that is in truly Mint condition (meaning in the same condition as it left the factory). Standard grading categories are listed below.

C10: 100 percent complete. All parts pinned with the original T clips; all cardboards present; no rust or white rust; manual present, near perfect, labels near perfect; only the lightest of scratches, parts may show very light cloudy oxidation (dingy).

C8: 98 to 100 percent complete. Some or all cardboards present but may not be all correctly pinned; manual present (may have folded corners); motor must be present and working; less than five percent of the parts may show the very slightest real rust (like in corners, the type that auto chrome polish can easily remove).

C6: 90 to 95 percent complete. Probably no cardboard; motor there and working; acceptable manual, labels may show serious wear; considerable scratching on bottom, some on top; minor dents in metal box, some signs of rust on five to ten percent of parts.

Since most of what you will come across in flea markets is well below C6 condition, a new category has been introduced—C4. You will need a great deal of help, skill and new parts to restore these sets.

C4: 50 to 75 percent complete. Considerable rust; parts from other sets or brands; possibly a working motor or tattered manual; dents, scratches and torn labels needing total restoration.

Contributors: W.S. (Bill) Harrison III 223 Boa Vista Street, Punta Gorda, FL 33983-5644; Paul Piontkowski, Pandy's Collectibles (successor to Marion's Designs), 16 Palmer Street, Medford, MA 02155; Francis Usinski, 11612 Ketchum Road, Lawtons, NY 14091. Harrison boasts of an engineering background that spans more than forty years. He has engineered and designed machinery and special equipment in aerospace, executed project management assignments with Monsanto and was chief engineer in metal forging and rubber molding companies. Harrison also has a love of Erector sets. In the past he restored and sold over 1,000 Erector sets before selling his company, Marion Designs, to Pandy's Collectibles in 1996. He has now permanently retired to Florida.

NA: means prices not applicable
WB: wood box

Type I: 1913 to 1923 (the era of girders 1-1/8" wide)

Most of the more valuable sets came in oak boxes with jointed corners. Smaller sets in cardboard boxes are not often seen, but can be quite valuable if discovered. Sets from 1913, the first year, have a unique motor and girder and are the most valuable.

1913

	C4	C6	C8	C10
Mysto Erector, #1, cardboard	150	300	500	700
Mysto #4, w/motor, wood box	125	225	350	500
Mysto #8, largest, 3 layer, WB	650	1000	2200	5000

1914-16

	C4	C6	C8	C10
Mysto Erector, #1, cardboard	75	125	200	325
Mysto #4, w/motor, wood box	65	90	125	180
Mysto #8, largest, three layer, WB	800	1000	1800	4000

1917-23

	C4	C6	C8	C10
Now called Gilbert Erector, #1	60	100	150	275
Erector #4, w/motor, WB	80	150	250	400
Erector #4, w/motor, WB, metal cover	80	175	300	525
Erector #7, '23 WB, metal cover	175	275	400	700
Erector #8, three layer WB sets	500	750	900	2500
Erector #8, two layer WB sets	150	225	500	1000
Erector #10, three layer WB sets	900	1500	2300	5000

Type II: 1924 to 1962 (the era of girders 5/8" wide)

These sets have a greater variety of parts and are capable of building more complex models. Sets from No. 4 up continued in wooden boxes (four with cardboard cover) until 1933, when metal boxes were introduced to the larger sets (except the Hudson, which went metal in 1934). Half numbers were introduced, confusing some collectors.

1924-26

	C4	C6	C8	C10
Erector #00 (25¢ original)	NA	50	75	125
Erector #0 (50¢ original)	NA	60	95	170
Erector #1	NA	40	60	100
Erector #4, w/motor, WB	75	120	160	300
Erector #8	300	500	1100	2500
Erector #10, multi-drawer	500	1200	2500	5000
Erector #7, '26 Steam Shovel, brown box	125	200	350	500
Erector #7-1/2 '26 White Trk., brown box	150	300	500	750

1927-28

	C4	C6	C8	C10
Erector #7-1/2, White Trk., red WB	125	200	300	550
Erector #7, Steam Shovel, red WB	70	130	180	320
Erector "B" giant red ferris wheel	300	500	750	1000
Erector #10, multi-drawer, WB	1500	2700	4000	6500

1929-30

	C4	C6	C8	C10
Same as above except for #9 Mech. Wonders Set	600	1200	2400	3500
2nd Zepplin Set	600	1200	2500	2600

1931-32

	C4	C6	C8	C10
Erector White Trk. rec. lid w/picture	175	300	400	650
Erector Hudson Loco. "A" engine only	600	1100	1600	2000
Erector Hudson #8 engine only w/7 pts	700	1250	1800	2300
Erector Hudson #8-1/2 engine and Tend+WT	800	1200	2500	4000
Erector #10 "Climax," largest set ever made, 150 lbs	NA	500	10,000	20,000
Erector #9 Zeppelin Set	600	1200	1800	2600

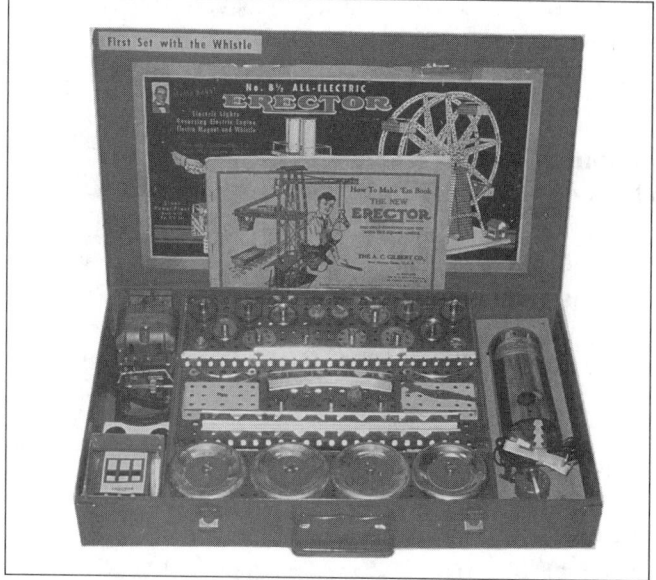

The 1939 #8-1/2 , Classic Ferris Wheel set. This was the first set with a whistle; it was dropped after 1941. Valued at $400 in C10 condition. Restoration by William S. Harrison III.

1933

	C4	C6	C8	C10
Erector Hudson #8-1/2, in WB....	1000	1500	2600	6000
Erector Super 6, w/P56G, 110V motor...	90	175	275	500
Erector Sensa. 7, automotive parts..	125	250	400	600

1934

	C4	C6	C8	C10
Erector Super 6 as above, green box	90	175	275	500

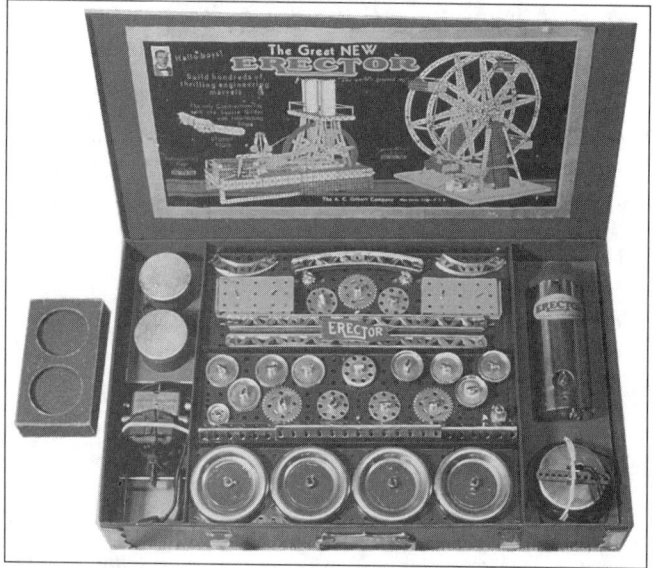

The 1937 #8-1/2, Classic Ferris Wheel set. Introduced in 1936, the 1937 is valued at $400 in C10 condition. Restored by William S. Harrison III.

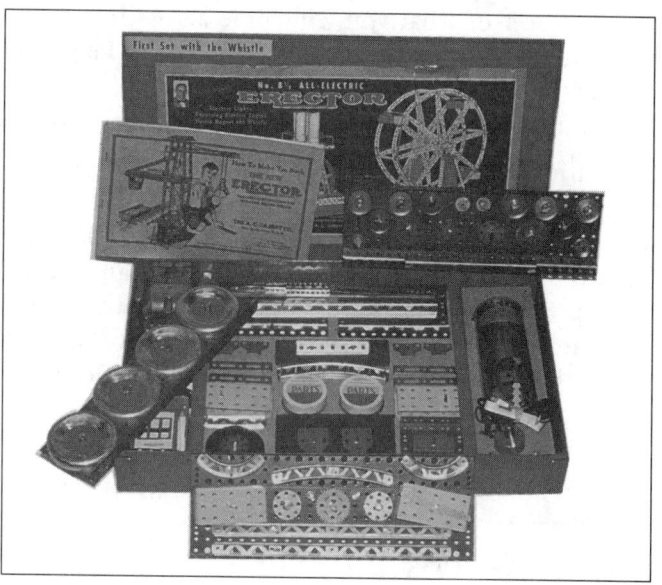

The contents of the 1939 #8-1/2. It should have a large nickel-plated magnet.

	C4	C6	C8	C10
Erector Sensa. 7, no automotive parts, red box...................................	100	200	350	550
Erector #7-1/2 Automotive Set......	125	250	450	650
Erector #8 Hudson and Tend., blue met....................................	1000	1200	2500	4000

1935

Sets this year only featured architectural panels. If present, sets are more valuable. Many new parts were introduced.

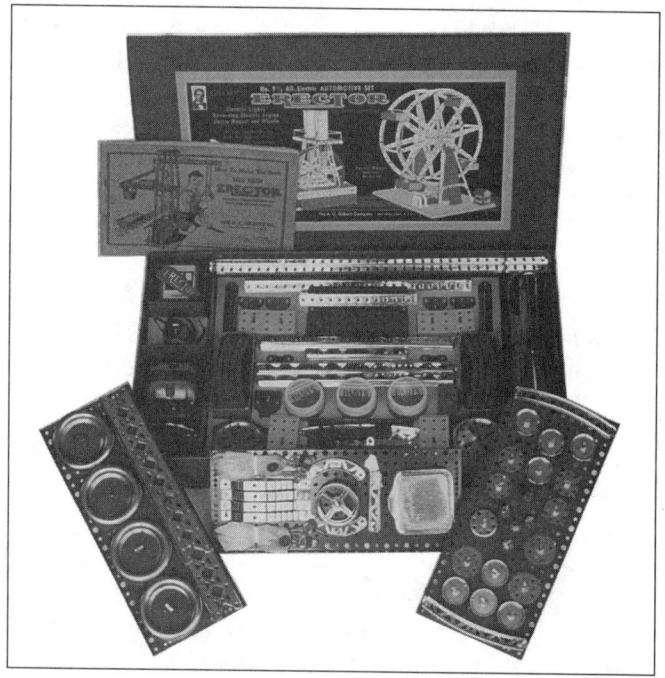

The 1948 #9-1/2 Automotive Set makes the manual contol P-jump but not the Merry-go-round. In C10 condition the 9-1/2 is valued at $675. Restored by William S. Harrison.

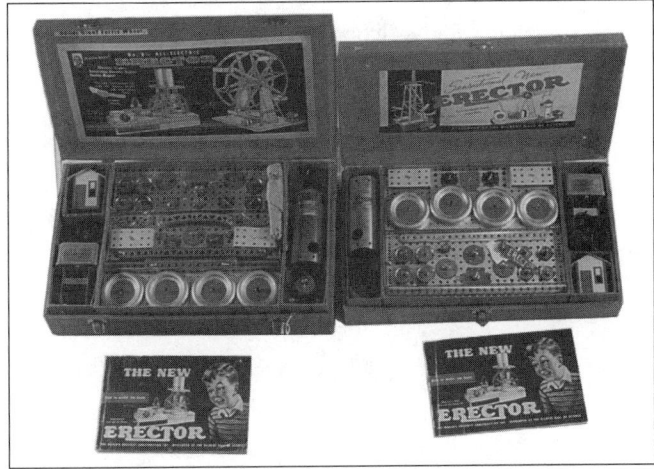

Erector's #8-1/2 (left) and #7-1/2 (right) from 1950 show the heavy cardboard boxes an aluminum baseplates used during the Korean War era. In C10 condition the 8-1/2 is valued at $00 and the 7-1/2 and $600. Restored by William S. Harrison III.

	C4	C6	C8	C10
Erector Super 6-1/2, P51 motor, boiler	NA	225	300	550
Erector 7-1/2, Classic Ferris Wheel	125	275	400	600
Erector 8-1/2, Automotive Set	150	300	475	700
Erector 9-1/2, Hudson Set	1000	1900	3600	6500

1936

	C4	C6	C8	C10
Erector 5-1/2, w/A52 110V motor	100	200	275	425
Erector 8-1/2, Classic Ferris Wheel	80	83	220	400
Erector 9-1/2, Automotive Set	175	335	500	675
Erector 10-1/2, Hudson Set	1000	1500	2900	5800

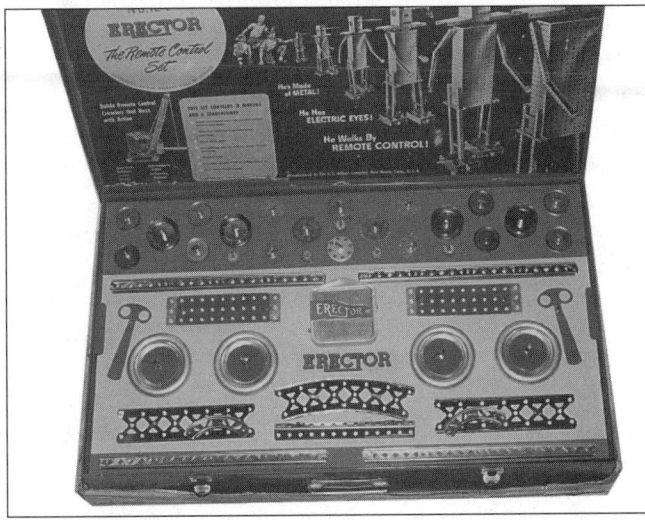

The late 1948 #12-1/2 does not make the Merry-go-round or the continuous running parachute jump. In C10 condition the #12-1/2 is valued at $1,500. Restored by William S. Harrison III.

1938

	C4	C6	C8	C10
Erector 10-1/2 became Electric Train Set w/American Flyer engine and track, plus NN, NM, NP	750	1000	1500	3300

1948

	C4	C6	C8	C10
Erector 10-1/2 becomes the 12-1/2, remote control/robot set w/P55 motor, full tray, A-48 and A-49	350	500	900	1500

1949

	C4	C6	C8	C10
10-1/2 intro in 9-1/2 box w/Merry-Go-Round capability and continuos parachute jump	150	300	500	800

1957

Two momentous changes occurred in 1957—metal boxes up through 8-1/2 had lithographed covers with pictures of the featured model, and the set numbers became a five-digit computer code. Unfortunately, the gauge of metal in the boxes was thinned out and these do not survive as well. The small plastic DC-3 motor of inadequate power was also a 1957 creation.

	C4	C6	C8	C10
10041 Erector 5-1/2 "Motorized" (DC-3)	20	40	75	125
10051 Erector 6-1/2 "Electric Engine"	25	55	85	130
10061 Erector 7-1/2 "Engineer's"	35	70	110	190
10071 Erector 8-1/2 "All Electric" Ferris Wheel	60	150	225	350
10080 Erector 10-1/2 "Amusement Park"	100	200	350	600
10091 12-1/2 "Master Builder"	250	475	900	1350

1958

This year saw the introduction of the famous "musical parts." They are very fragile, hence very valuable and scarce! The record alone brings $100. In the same order as preceding. Note the "name" changes.

	C4	C6	C8	C10
10041 "Power Model," same as 5-1/2	20	40	75	125
10052 "Rocket Launcher," same as 6-1/2	25	55	85	135
10062 "Steam Engine"	35	70	110	190
10072 "Musical Ferris Wheel," w/music	NA	150	225	400

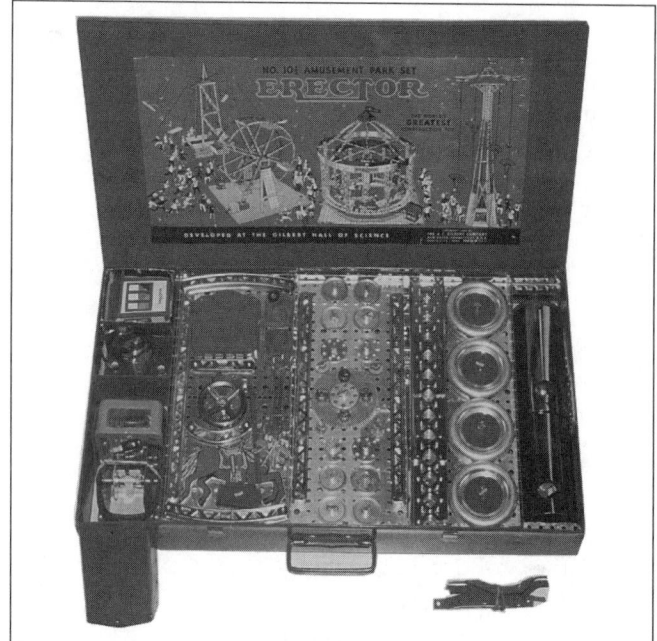

The 1950-51 #10-1/2 Amusement Park set. The Aluminum baseplates and A-47 motor are, once again, due to the Korean War. The #10-1/2 is valued at $800 in C10 condition. Restored by William S. Harrison.

	C4	C6	C8	C10
10082 "Amusement Park," w/music	NA	250	475	750
10092 "Master Builder," w/music	NA	650	900	1500

1959

	C4	C6	C8	C10
10042 "Automatic RadarScope," same as 10041	20	40	75	125
10053 "Rocket Launcher," same as 10051 $30 premium if gold labelintact	25	55	85	135
10063 "Automatic Conveyor," same as 10062, premium $20 if one belt present	35	70	110	190
10073 "Musical Ferris Wheel," same as 10072, w/music, $20 premium if one belt present	NA	150	225	400
10083 "Amusement Park," same as 10082, w/music, $20 premium if one belt present	NA	250	475	750
10093 "Master Builder," same as 10092, w/music, $20 premium if one belt present	NA	650	900	1500

1960

Musical parts were dropped and Styrofoam packing introduced this year. Amusement Park and Master Builder used metal boxes made by joining two smaller boxes. Sets retained earlier prices due to scarcity. Production and sales fell sharply in 1960.

	C2	C4	C6	C8
10042 "Automatic Radar Scope"	20	40	75	125
10053 "Rocket Launcher"	25	55	85	135
10063 "Automatic Conveyor"	35	70	110	190
10074 "Ferris Wheel"	80	150	250	350
10084 "Amusement Park," same as 10083, double box	NA	250	475	750
10094 "Master Builder," same as 10093, double box	NA	650	900	1500

1962

This year saw the demise of the "classic" Erector set with trussed girders.

	C4	C6	C8	C10
10181 "Action Helicopter," same as 10042	20	40	75	125
10201 "Rocket Launcher," same as 10053	25	55	85	135
10211 "Cape Canaveral," same as 10063	35	70	110	190
10221 "Lunar Drilling Rig," same as 10074	80	150	250	350
10231 "Astronaut," same as 10084, double box	NA	250	475	750
10094 "Master Builder," double box	NA	650	900	1500

Type III: 1963

In 1962 the Gilbert Company was in receivership and production and sales continued to drop. Tooling was worn out, with little money to replace it. The system was redesigned, eliminating the truss configuration. This easily cut the cost of new tooling in half, as any tool engineer can tell you. Thus was born Type III Erector, a bit flimsier and not as realistic but still challenging to the young mind. At present, sets from this era are not much in demand compared to the classic sets of Type I and II. This could change as more collectors dry up the supply. Most of the smaller sets were presented in containers not given to survival such as corrugated boxes, tubes, etc.

The following sets were in metal boxes with a sliding plastic cover. An overcover of cardboard was included with colorful scenes of the models in action on the moon or somewhere in space. The C10 prices include these covers, which did not survive well. If really nice, add twenty persent to C10 prices. All three sizes had foam inserts to hold the parts, and these are impossible to duplicate. The next two years, 1964 and 1965, saw a continuation of these three sets. After 1965 the company was sold to Gabriel Industries, hence Type III sets are many times referred to as Gabriel Era trash.

	C4	C6	C8	C10
10127 "Lunar Vehicle Set"	30	60	90	150
10128 "Planetary Probe Set"	50	80	150	200
10129 "Master Power Set"	100	150	225	500

Vital Parts and Accessory Sets

	C10
1E Square Girder Kit, 20-"C," 8-"B," 14-7/8" sc and nt	85
A-48 Mechanical Motor w/Key, check for spring slip	40
A-49 Motor and Gearbox, 115 volt AC, running, EXC	40
A-52 Motor, 115 volt AC, running	85
Illumination Kit	150
Musical Parts-comp. reproducer, record, mechanism	200

	C10
P-51 Motor and Gearbox, 115 volt AC, running	110
P-55 Motor and remote control, 12 volt AC/DC, runs	150
P-56G Motor, 115 volt AC, tapered ends, running	125
P-58 Motor, "Joe Long" rebuild	50
P-58 Motor, 6-12 volt AC/DC, "basket case," not running	10
Smoke and Choo-Choo Kit, 7-15 volt AC	125
Whistle Kit, 7-15 volt AC	100

FIGURE KITS

In the 1960s—the golden age of figure kits—Aurora lead the way in diversity of product and demand. Their line of original and glow Universal Studios monsters are today's most sought-after figure kits.

Rating the condition of a figure kit can be difficult because value can be drastically affected by factors such as assembled parts, painted parts, missing pieces, missing instructions, box condition and country of origin.

MIB SEALED. Mint in Box with original factory shrink wrap. Collectors may pay a premium over the MIB price if the box is not damaged. Beware of resealed kits.

MIB. A complete, unused kit with an excellent box and instructions and no glue or paint on pieces. Most collectors insist that plastic trees that held pieces be present with pieces still attached. Prices listed in the chapter are based on kits in Mint-in-Box condition.

PARTIAL ASSEMBLY. A partially-built kit with Excellent box/instructions and no paint is worth eighty-five percent of the MIB price. The more assembly, the more the price decreases. Old styrene glues actually melted pieces together, and white glues (Elmers) do not decrease value as much as Styrene glues because they can be removed.

PARTIAL PAINTING. A complete, partially-painted kit with Excellent box/instructions and no glue is worth eighty-five percent of the MIB price. Painting is not as serious as gluing because most experienced modelers know how to strip paint. Again, the more painting, the more price decreases because stripping takes time and is not always completely successful.

PARTIAL ASSEMBLY/PAINTING. Together these two factors can make pricing very difficult. A general value guideline would be seventy percent of the MIB price with Excellent box/instructions.

BUILT-UP. A fully assembled, complete kit with no box/instructions has a value of fifteen to forty-five percent of the MIB price. The more desirable the MIB kit, the more desirable the built-up. If a kit was issued several times, built-up value decreases. For example, Aurora's design of Frankenstein was issued four times—Aurora 1961, 1969, 1972, and Monogram 1983. Thus its value is about fifteen of the MIB kit. Vehicles such as Batmobiles and UFOs go toward low percentages because of low visual appeal. Without instructions a novice kit builder will find it virtually impossible to determine if a built-up is complete. Except for very high-priced kits incomplete built-ups have little value.

MISSING PIECES. One missing piece from a kit will result in a large decrease in value regardless of all other combined factors. Even a kit missing one piece is worth only eighty percent of a complete MIB kit. Simply put, many collectors will not buy a kit missing a piece.

INSTRUCTIONS. Missing instructions reduce the MIB price by five to ten percent. Instruction sheets from the sell in the $5-$10 range. Sheets for rare, expensive kits such as Aurora's Gigantic Frankenstein can bring over $35!

BOXES. The market for empty figure kit boxes is almost exclusive to Aurora boxes. A box in Excellent condition box has no split corners, tape, paint, glue, punctures, severe creases or scuffs. Excellent boxes alone have maximum value of forty percent of a kit in MIB condition. Aforementioned box defects decrease value on MIB kits by twenty percent or more.

FOREIGN ISSUE. This factor is an issue primarily with Aurora kits. Because Aurora had branches in Canada, England and Holland they sometimes issued boxes and instructions with wording in other languages and plastic parts in colors other than what American issues had. Ninety percent of the kits you'll ever see will not be foreign issue, but just in case, some collectors devalue MIB foreign issue kits to about seventy-five percent of American MIB prices.

If you're more confused about how to price a kit now than you were before, don't feel bad! Even experienced dealers have a difficult time pricing kits when faced with missing pieces, painted parts, box wear, etc. These guidelines are just that—guidelines.

It should be noted that kit values vary widely due to the geographic region and local collector demand. There is strong interest in American kits in Europe and Japan. The values listed here are conservative, mid-range prices that are indicative of what most collectors would be willing to pay. Obviously, some collectors will pay more and some will pay less.

Special thanks to Greg Roccaro of Staten Island, New York. Some kit numbers and dates were taken from *Science*

Fiction and Figure Kits by John Burns of Edmond, Oklahoma. Though not a price guide, it serves as an excellent reference regarding all known kits of this genre.

Contributor: David Welch, P.O. Box 714, Murphysboro, IL 62966. Welch is a nationally known dealer in cartoon, comic, and TV character items. He has been collecting and/or dealing since the age of 13. He has contributed information for various price guides including *Tomart's Disneyana* (condensed edition), *Tomart's Space Adventure Collectibles*, and *Overstreet's Comic Book Price Guide*.

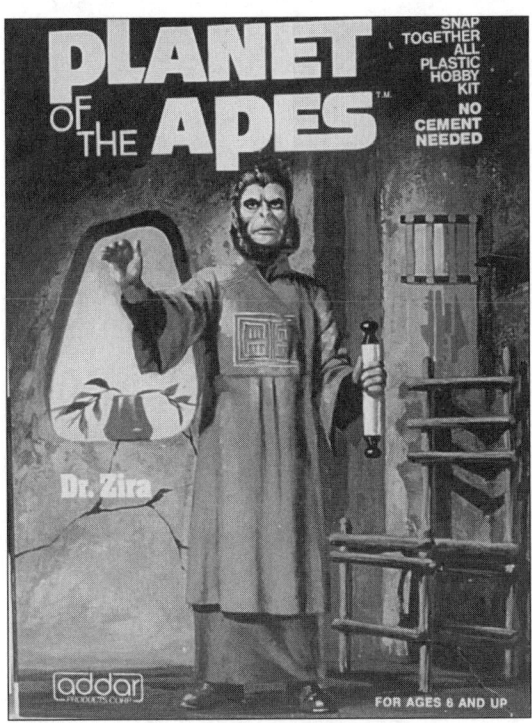

Dr. Zira, Planet of the Apes, AMT, $160

ADDAR

Founded by former Aurora employees in 1973, Addar was acquired the license to produce Planet of the Apes figural kits. Although they were known for their Planet of the Apes kits, Addar also issued Super Scenes—dioramas that looked like they were built in a bottle. They also made kits based another popular 1970s character—Evel Knievel.

The popularity of Planet of the Apes wore off sooner than the people of Addar assumed or wanted, and they closed their doors in 1977.

	MIB
Caesar, Planet of the Apes, No. 106, 1974	60
Cornelius, Planet of the Apes, No. 101, 1973	60
Cornfield Roundup, Super Scenes, No. 216, 1975	60
Dr. Zaius, Planet of the Apes, No. 102, 1973	60
Dr. Zira, Planet of the Apes, No. 105, 1974	60
General Aldo, Planet of the Apes, No. 104, 1974	60
General Ursus, Planet of the Apes, No. 103, 1974	60
Jail Wagon, Super Scenes, No. 217, 1975	60
Soldier on Stallion, Planet of the Apes, No. 107, 1975	75
Spirit in a Bottle, Super Scenes, No. 227, 1975	60
Tree House, Super Scenes, No. 215, 1975	60

AMT

Celebrating their fiftieth anniversary in 1998, AMT is known for their vehicle model kits. In the 1960s they began producing Star Trek-related models. Over the years they have expanded their line of figure kits to include Bigfoot and Leonard DaVinci's Invention series.

AMT was purchased by Matchbox in 1978 and again by Ertl in 1984. Currently AMT/Ertl produces only a handful of figural kits.

	MIB
Bigfoot, No. 7701	25
Dragula, Munsters TV car, No. 905, 1964	250
Exploration Set, No. 958, 1974	75
Fred Flintstone's Family Sedan, No. 496, 1974	45
Fred Flintstone's Rock Cruncher, No. 497, 1974	60
Fred Flintstone's Sports Car, No. 495, 1974	60
Galileo 7, No. 959, 1974	45
Klingon Cruiser, No. 922, 1967	120
Klingon Cruiser, No. 952	65
Klingon Cruiser, No. 971, 1979	28
Klingon Cruiser, No. 6682, 1985	13
K-7 Space Station, No. 955, 1975	40
Mr. Spock with Snake, No. 956, 1975	60
Mr. Spock without Snake, No. 973, 1979	30
Munsters Koach, Munsters TV car, 1964	200
Romulan Ship, No. 957, 1975	45
Spaceship Set, No. 953, 1975	60
Spaceship Set, No. 6677, 1984	28
USS Enterprise with Lights, No. 931, 1967	175
USS Enterprise without Lights, No. 951, 1976	50
USS Enterprise, No. 970, 1979	28

Munsters Koach, AMT $200

	MIB
USS Enterprise, No. 6676, 1983	18
USS Enterprise, No. 6675, 1985	18
USS Enterprise Bridge, No. 950, 1975	28
Vulcan Shuttle, No. 5112, 1979	24
Vulcan Shuttle, No. 972, 1980	24
Vulcan Shuttle, No. 6679, 1985	15

AURORA

Aurora Plastics Corporation began in 1950 when Abe Shikes made a plastic bow and arrow from a faulty plastic hanger. It was in 1952 that Aurora intoduced their first model kit, The gumann Panther F9F Jet Fighter.

It wasn't until 1955 that Aurora made figure kits. They made a series titled Guys and Gals of All Nations. They were highly-detailed 1:8-scale figure kits designed to draw girls into the world of model kits. Although the series was a success, it did not attract many girls model building. Aurora's marketing shifted back to boys and young men. Aurora's monster figure kits were introduced in 1960 and established Aurora as a pop culture icon of the sixties.

Aurora was purchased in 1971 by Nabisco. Wanting to avoid any controversy, only "cute" toys were produced under Nabisco. Kits were not completely abandoned, but gone were the days of monster figures.

Nabisco closed Aurora in 1977. Aurora's molds were purchased at auction by Monogram.

For the Aurora line in general, it is the kit name and kit number that are most relevant, dates listed may vary a year either way. Please note that different kits carried identical numbers (i.e., King Kong Glow, 465 and Frankenstein's Flivver, 465).

Some clarification may be needed on the Aurora Frankenstein listing. Frankenstein was first issued in 1961 in a long, rectangular box. The 1969 Frightening Lightning issue was the same kit with optional duplicate glow parts. The box was the same shape, and a lightning bolt was added to the artwork. In 1969 and 1972 the optional glow format continued and square boxes with altered artwork were introduced. The 1969 glow boxes are thicker and sturdier than the 1972 glows. In many cases, the color of the plastic of the original was different from the color of the glow issues. The plastic kit itself will always carry the date of its original issue. The Monster Scenes and Monsters of the Movies Frankensteins are completely different kits from the 1961, 1969 and 1972 issues.

Many of these rare and valuable kits are being reissued in beautifully done boxes. Listed below are Aurora kits being reissued by other manufacturers. How can you tell a reissue from an original? Look carefully at the box. Current issues are marked with a UPC code, a 1990s copyright date and a company name other than Aurora. None of these kits were produced to deceive; however, some people have attempted to sell them as originals.

Aurora Reissues

Monogram	Polar Lights
Frankenstein	Bride of Frankentstein
Dracula	Creature from the Black Lagoon
Wolfman	King Kong Thronster
Mummy	Addams Family Haunted House
Creature	The Munsters Living Room Scene
Godzilla	Wolfman's Wagon
	Mummy's Chariot
Cinemodels	Lost in Space No. 420
Prisoner	Lost in Space No. 419
Phantom of	Lost in Space Robot
the Opera	Undertakers Dragster

	MIB
Addams Family House, No. 805, 1965	750
Alfred E. Neumann, No. 802, 1965	200
Allosaurus, No. 736, 1972	125
American Astronaut, No. 409, 1967	80
Ankylosourus, No. 744, 1974	125
Apache Warrior, No. 401, 1961	300
Aramis, No. K10, 1958	100
Archie's Car, No. 582, 1969	85
Athos, No. K8, 1958	100
Babe Ruth, No. 862, 1965	250
Banana Splits Buggy, No. 832, 1969	350
Batboat, No. 811	500
Batcycle, No. 810, 1967	500
Batman, No. 467, 1964	250
Batman Comic Scenes, No. 187, 1974	85
Batmobile, No. 486, 1966	300
Batplane, No. 487, 1966	200
Black Beauty, (Green Hornet), No. 489, 1967	500
Black Knight, No. various issues	15
Blackbeard, No. 463, 1965	125
Blue Knight, various issues	12
Bride of Frankenstein, No. 482, 1964	800
Captain Action, No. 480, 1966	300
Captain America, No. 476, 1966	300
Captain America Comic Scenes, No. 192, 1974	80
Captain Kidd, No. 464,1965	125
Cave, No. 732,1972	50
Cave Bear, No. 738, 1972	65
Chinese Girl, No. 416, 1957	35
Chinese Mandarin, No. 415, 1957	35
Chitty Chitty Bang Bang, No. 828, 1968	80
Confederate Raider, No. 402, 1959	350
Crusader, No. K7, 1959	100
Creature from the Black Lagoon, No. 426, 1963	350
Creature from the Black Lagoon, Glow, No. 483, 1969/1972	150

Aurora Model Kits—top row, Left to right: Land of the Giants, $400; Frankenstein instruction sheet; Godzilla, $500; Gigantic Frankenstein, $1,500; King Kong, $500.

Middle Row, Left to Right: Witch, $350; King Kong's Thronester, $1,500; The Bride of Frankenstein, $800; Frankenstein's Flivver, $400; Dracula's Dragster, $425; Wolfman's Wagon, $550; Mummy's Chariot, $550.

Bottom row, Left to Right: Lost in Space, $1,000; Mummy, $250; Phantom of the Opera, $275; Dracula, $300; Hunchbank, $250; Wolfman, $300; Dr. Jekyll, $325; The Creature, $450; Robot, Lost in Space, $700.

Athos, Aurora, $100

Dutch Boy, Aurora, $35

	MIB
Creature from the Black Lagoon, Monsters of the Movies, No. 654, 1975	150
Cro Magnon Man, No. 730, 1971	50
Cro Magnon Woman, No. 731, 1971	50
Customizing Monster Kit No. 1, No. 463, 1963	175
Customizing Monster Kit No. 2, No. 464, 1963	175
D'Artagnan, No. 410, 1966	90
Dempsey vs. Firpo, No. 861, 1965	100
Dick Tracy, No. 818, 1968	165
Dick Tracy Space Coupe, No. 819, 1968	135
Dimetrodon, No. 745, 1974	125
Dr. Deadly's Daughter, (The Victim), Monster Scenes, No. 632, 1971	90
Dr. Deadly, Monster Scenes, No. 631, 1971	120
Dr. Jekyll, No. 460, 1965	325
Dr. Jekyll, Glow, No. 482, 1969/1972	100
Dr. Jekyll, Monsters of the Movies, No. 654, 1975	75
Dracula, No. 424, 1962	300
Dracula's Dragster, No. 466, 1966	425
Dracula, Frightening Lightning, No. 424/454, 1969	350
Dracula, Glow, No. 454, 1969/1972	100
Dracula, Monsters of the Movies, No. 656, 1975	165
Dutch Boy, No. 413, 1957	35
Dutch Girl, No. 414, 1957	35
Flying Reptile, No. 734, 1974	100

	MIB
Flying Saucer, No. 256, 1975	95
Flying Sub, No. 254, 1975	100
Flying Sub, No. 817, 1968	175
Forgotten Prisoner, No. 422, 1966 (repros say "1992 Tomy")	450
Forgotten Prisoner, Frightening Lightning, No. 422/453, 1969	500
Forgotten Prisoner, Glow, No. 453, 1969/1972	135
Frankenstein, No. 423, 1961	295
Frankenstein, Frightening Lightning, No. 423/449, 1969	325
Frankenstein, Glow, No. 449, 1969	135
Frankenstein, Glow, 1972	80
Frankenstein, Monster Scenes, No. 633, 1971	175
Frankenstein, Monsters of the Movies, No. 651, 1975	175
Frankenstein's Flivver, No. 465, 1964	400
Frog, The No. 451, 1966	225
George Washington, No. 852, 1965	100
Ghidrah, Monsters of the Movies, No. 658, 1975	325
Giant Bird, No. 739, 1972	75
Giant Woolly Mammoth, No. 743, 1972	100
Gigantic Frankenstein ("Big Frankie"), No. 470, 1964, w/three bottles paint and brush	1500
Gladiator, No. 405, 1959, w/sword	175
Gladiator, No. 406, 1959, w/trident	175
Godzilla, No. 469, 1964	500
Godzilla, Glow, No. 466, 1969/1972	150

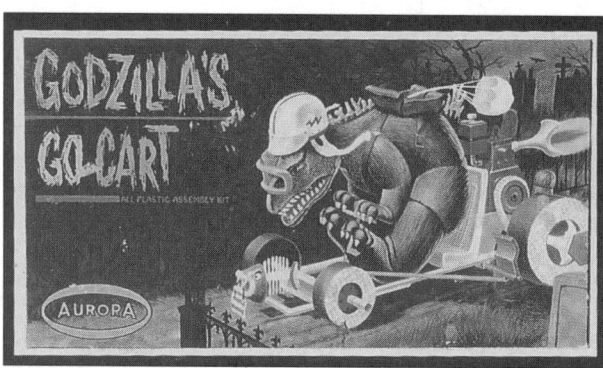

Godzilla's Go-Cart, Aurora, $1,500

Jesse James, Aurora, $200

MIB

Godzilla's Go-Cart, No. 485, 1966 1500
Gold Knight on Horseback, K5, No. 1957/475, 1965 200
Green Beret, No. 413, 1966 100
Gruesome Goodies, Monster Scenes, No. 634, 1971 100
Guillotine, No. 800, 1964 500
Hanging Cage, Monster Scenes, No. 637, 1971 100
Hercules, No. 481, 1965 175
Horned Dinosaur, No. 741, 1972 100
Hulk, No. 421, 1966 250
Hulk, Comic Scenes No. 184, 1974 75
Hunchback, No. 461, 1964 250
Hunchback of Notre Dame, No. 481, 1969/1972 100
Illya Kuryakin, No. 412, 1966 200
Indian Chief, No. 417, 1957 75
Indian Squaw, No. 418, 1957 75
James Bond, No. 414, 1966 300
Jerry West, No. 865, 1965 110
Jesse James, No. 408, 1966 200
Jimmy Brown, No. 863, 1965 90
John F. Kennedy, No. 851, 1964 150
Johnny Unitas, No. 864, 1965 90
Jungle Swamp, No. 740, 1972 100
King Kong, No. 468, 1964 500
King Kong's Thronester, No. 484, 1966 1500
King Kong, Glow, No. 465, 1969/1972 100
Land of the Giants, Snake Scene, No. 816,1968 400
Land of the Giants Spaceship, No. 830, 1968 400
Lone Ranger, No. 808, 1967 125
Lone Ranger, Comic Scenes, No. 188, 1974 35
Lost in Space, No. 419, 1966 750
Lost in Space, No. 420, 1966 1000
Mad Barber, No. 455 1000
Mexican Caballero, No. 421,1957 75

Mod Squad Woodie, Aurora, $100

MIB

Mexican Senorita, No. 422, 1957 75
Mod Squad Woodie, No. 583, 1970 100
Moon Bus, 2001: A Space Odyssey, No. 829, 1968 210
Mr. Hyde, Monsters of the Movies, No. 655, 1975 75
Mummy, No. 427, 1963 250
Mummy's Chariot, No. 459, 1965 550
Mummy, Frightening Lightning, No. 427/452, 1969 400
Mummy, Glow, No. 452, 1969 100
Mummy, Glow, 1972 65
Munsters Family, No. 804, 1965 950
Napoleon Solo, No. 411, 1966 175
Neanderthal Man, No. 729, 1972 50
Nutty Nose Nipper, No. 806, 1965 175
Odd Job, No. 415, 1966 375
Orion, No. 252, 1975 95
Pain Parlor, No. 635, 1971 125
Pan Am Space Clipper, 2001: A Space Odyssey,
     No. 148, 1968 150
Pendulum, The, Monster Scenes, No. 636, 1971 120
Penguin, No. 416, 1967 550
Phantom of the Opera, No. 428, 1963 275

Mummy, Glow, Aurora, $65-100

Mummy's Chariot, Aurora, $550

Gold Knight, Aurora, $200

Hunchback, Aurora, $250

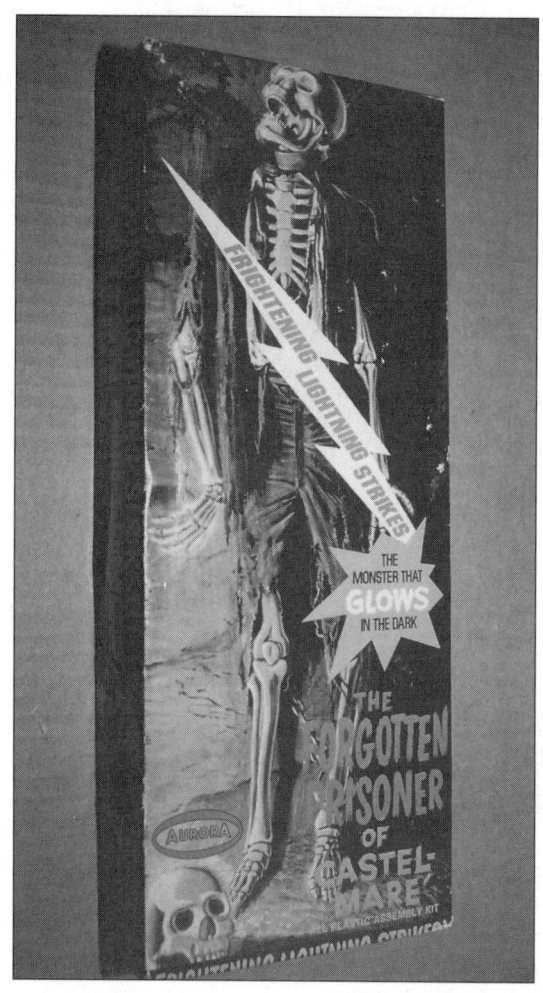

Forgotten Prisoners, Glow, Wurora, $135

Odd Job, Aurora, $375

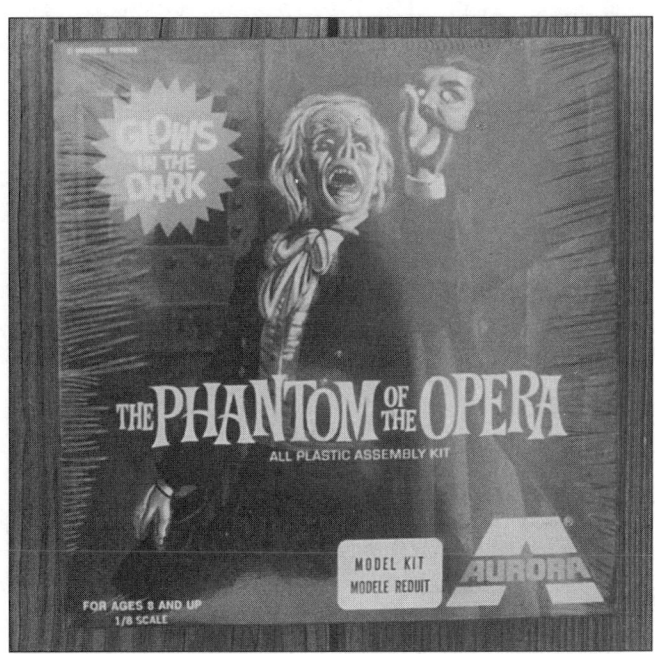

Phantom of the Opera, Aurora, 1969, $100

	MIB
Phantom of the Opera, No. 451, 1969	100
Phantom of the Opera, 1972	65
Phantom of the Opera, Frightening Lightning, No. 428/451, 1969	350
Porthos, No. K9, 1958	100
Pushmi-Pullyu, Dr. Doolittle, No. 814, 1968	100
Rat Patrol Diorama, No. 340, 1967	100
Red Knight, various issues	30
Robin, No. 488, 1966	100
Robin, Comic Scenes, No. 193, 1974	75
Robot, Lost in Space, No. 418, 1968	700
Rodan, Monsters of the Movies, No. 657, 1975	325
Sabre Tooth Tiger, No. 722, 1972	90
Scotch Lad, No. 419, 1957	40
Scotch Lassie, No. 420, 1957	40
Seaview, No. 707, 1966	250
Seaview, No. 253, 1975	100
Silver Knight, various issues	15
Spartacus, No. 405, 1965	180
Spider-Man, No. 477, 1966	325
Spider-Man, Comic Scenes, No. 182, 1974	100
Spiked Dinosaur, No. 742, 1972	90
Spindrift, No. 255, 1975	100
Steve Canyon, No. 404, 1966	125
Superboy, No. 478, 1965	300
Superboy, Comic Scenes, No. 186, 1974	95

	MIB
Superman, No. 562, 1963	300
Superman, Comic Scenes, No. 185, 1974	65
Tar Pit, No. 735, 1971	100
Tarzan, No. 820, 1967	175
Tarzan, Comic Scenes, No. 181, 1974	24
Tonto, No. 809, 1967	135
Tonto, Comic Scenes, No. 183, 1974	20
Tyrannosaurus Rex, No. 746, 1974	400
U.S. Infantryman, 1956	75
U.S. Marine, No. 412, 1956	75
U.S. Marshall, No. 408, 1959	100
U.S. Sailor, No. 410, 1958	75
U.F.O., No. 813, 1968	200
Undertakers Dragster, No. 570	200

Robin, Comic Scenes, Aurora, $75

Superboy, Comic Scenes, 1974, $95

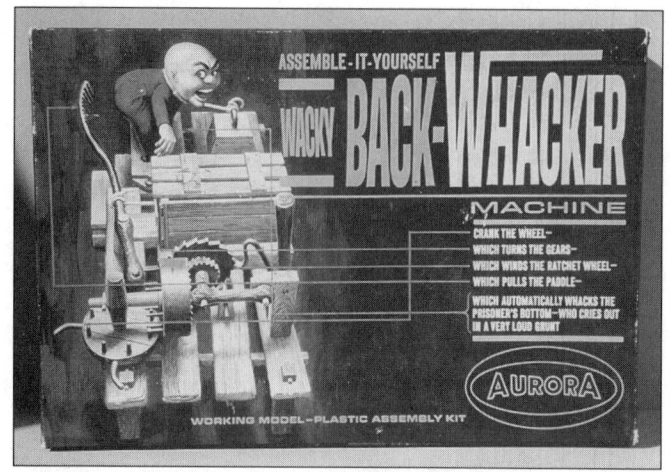

Wacky Back-Whacker, Aurora, $200

	MIB
Vampire, No. 452, 1966	250
Vampirella, Monster Scenes, No. 638, 1971	175
Viking, No. K6, 1959	120
Voyager, Fantastic Voyage, No. 831, 1969	500
Wacky Back Whacker, No. 807, 1965	200
Willie Mays, No. 860, 1965	200
Witch, Glow, No. 470, 1969/1972	120
Witch, No. 483, 1965	350
Wolfman, No. 425, 1962	300
Wolfman's Wagon, No. 458, 1965	550
Wolfman, Frightening Lightning, No. 425/450, 1969	400
Wolfman, Glow, No. 450, 1969	100
Wolfman, Glow, 1972	65

Sling Rave Curvette, Hawk, $25

	MIB
Wolfman, Monster of the Movies, No. 652, 1975	175
Wonder Woman, No. 479, 1965	550
Zorro, No. 801, 1965	200

HAWK

Beach Bunny Catchin' Rays, No. 542, 1964	65
Daddy the Swingin Suburbanite, No. 532, 1963	65
Davey the Psycho Cyclist, No. 531, 1963	65
Digger the Way Out Dragster, No. 530, 1963	65
Drag Hag, No. 536, 1963	65
Endsville Eddy, No. 537, 1963	65
Francis the Foul, No. 535, 1963	30
Frantic Banana Punishing Skins, No. 548, 1965	75
Frantic Cats, No. 549, 1965	75
Freddie Flameout, No. 533, 1963	75
Hodad Making the Scene, No. 543, 1964	75
Hot Dogger Hangin Ten, No. 541, 1964	75

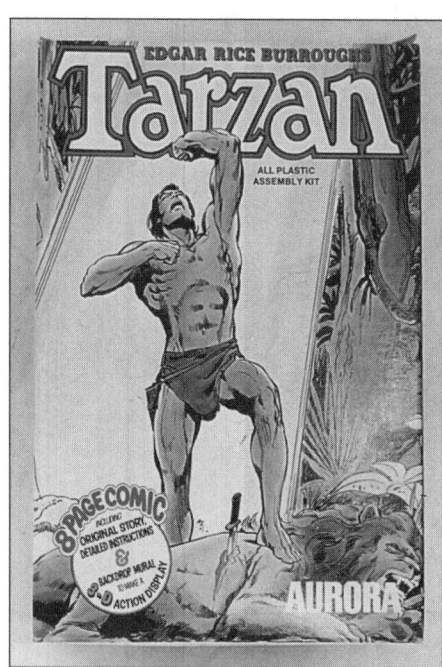

Tarzan, Comic Scenes, Aurora, 1974, $24

King Kong, Aurora, $500

Penguin, aurora, $550

	MIB
Hot Dogger Hangin Ten, Glow, No. 164, 1970	45
Huey's Hut Rod, No. 538, 1963	75
Huey's Hut Rod, Glow, No. 163, 1969	45
Killer McBash, No. 539, 1963	75
Leaky Boat Louie, No. 534, 1963	75
Riding Tandem, No. 544, 1965	75
Sling Rave Curvette, No. 637, 1964	25
Steel Pluckers Havin' a Bash, No. 547, 1965	75
Totally Fab, No. 550, 1965	75
Wade A. Minit, No. 636, 1964	75
Weirdsville Customizing Kit, No. 301, 1964	300
Woodie on a Surfari, No. 540, 1964	75
Woodie on a Surfari, No. 165, 1970	40

LINDBERG

Founded in 1933, Lindberg is one of the oldest model kit companies in the United States, although they are best known for a series of kits made in the 1906s—Lindy Looneys. These were creepy hot rod models made to cash in on the 1960s weird character craze.

	MIB
Big Wheeler, 277, 1965	100
Blurp, 280, 1964	45
Creeping Crusher, 273, 1965	100
Glob, 281, 1964	45
Green Ghoul, 274, 1965	100
Krimson Terror, 272, 1965	150
Mad Maestro, 284, 1965	175
Mad Mangler, 275, 1965	100
Road Hog, 276, 1965	100
Satan's Crate, 279, 1965	250
Scuttle Bucket, 278, 1965	100
Voop, 283, 1964	45
Zopp, 282, 1964	45

MONOGRAM

Monogram's first models were balsa wood ships from 1945, and nine years later the company produced their first plastic kits. As modelers know, they expanded their line to include vehicles and figures in the subsequent years.

When Aurora ceased production, Monogram acquired their molds, and they reissued a number of Aurora's kits.

Revell and Monogram—two of the largest manufacturers of plastic model kits—merged in 1986. Revell-Monogram continues to produce figural model kits, including models made from the Aurora molds.

	MIB
Dracula, No. 6008, 1983, reissue of Aurora kit	25
Flip Out, Fred Flypogger, No. 105, 1965	200
Frankenstein, No. 6007, Aurora reissue	25
Godzilla, No. 6300, 1978, Aurora reissue	40
Mummy, No. 6010, 1983, Aurora reissue	25

	MIB
Speed Shift, Fred Flypogger, No. 106, 1965	200
Super Fuzz, Fred Flypogger, No. 104, 1965	200
Superman, No. 6301, 1978, Aurora reissue	15
Wolfman, No. 6009, 1983, Aurora reissue	25

MPC

MPC produced some of the best non-Aurora kits during the 1960s. Like many kit manufacturers, MPC started with vehicles and later moved into figures. Their early figure kits include Stroker McGurk and Hot Curl. Cashing in on the popularity of the sixties TV show *Dark Shadows,* MPC released two model kits based on characters from the show, Barnabas and the Werewolf.

MPC continued to produce kits into the 1970s, including *Star Wars* and *Alien* kits.

	MIB
Alien, No. 1961, movie, 1979	95
Barnabas Collins, Dark Shadows, No. 1550, 1969	250
Barnabas Vampire Van, Dark Shadows, No. 1626, 1969	195
Batman, No. 1702, 1984, Aurora reissue	20
C3PO, Star Wars, No. 1913, 1978-1980	15
C3PO, Star Wars, No. 1935, 1983	10
Condemned to Chains, Disney Pirates of Caribbean, No. 5003, 1973	100
Curl's Gurl, No. 103, 1965	75
Curl's Gurl with Hot Shot, No. 103, 1965	75
Darth Vader, No. 1916, 1978/1980	20
Dead Man's Raft, Pirates of Caribbean, No. 5005, 1973	125
Dead Men Tell No Tales, Disney Pirates of Caribbean, No. 5001, 1973	100
Escape from the Crypt, Disney Haunted Mansion, No. 5053, 1974	100
Fate of the Mutineer, Disney Pirates of Caribbean, No. 5004, 1974	100
Freed in the Nick of Time, Pirates of Caribbean, No. 5007, 1973	100

Barnabas Vampire Van, MPC, $195

	MIB
Ghost of America with Stroker McGurk, No. 104, 1964	110
Ghost of the Treasure, Pirates of Caribbean, 5006, 1973	80
Grave Robbers Reward, Disney Haunted Mansion, No. 5050, 1974	100
Hoist High the Jolly Roger, Pirates of Caribbean, No. 5002, 1973	100
Hot Curl, No. 101, 1965	75
Hot Shot with Hot Dog, No. 103, 1965	75
Incredible Hulk, No. 1932, 1979	20
Play It Again Sam, Disney Haunted Mansion, No. 5052, 1974	125
Raiders Coach, Paul Revere & Raiders, No. 1969, 0622	225
R2-D2, Star Wars, No. 1912, 1978-1980	20
R2-D2, Star Wars, No. 1934, 1983	10
Spider-Man, 1931, No. 1978	20
Stroker McGurk and Surf Rod, No. 100, 1964	65
Superman, No. 1701, 1985, Aurora reissue	20
Tall T with Stroker McGurk, No. 102, 1964	65
Vampire Midnight Madness, Disney Haunted Mansion, No. 5051, 1974	100
Werewolf, Dark Shadows, No. 1552, 1969	250
Yellow Submarine, Beatles, No. 617, 1968	275

MULTIPLE

Multiple Products, Inc., a division of Loral Corporation, was known for their toys—the Fireball XL-5 Space City and Daniel Boone toys to name a few. The few kits they did produce were of exceptional quality.

Their original figure kit series was the Crazy Invention line. It included such kits as A Simple Way to Feed a Baby and A Painless Tooth Extractor, they were based on ideas created by comic-strip great Rube Goldberg.

Other Multiple series included Ripley Believe it or Not and World's Greatest Stage Illusions.

	MIB
Automatic Baby Feeder, No. 955, 1965	50
Back Scrubber and Hat Remover, No. 958, 1965	50
Disappearing Lady, No. 1257, 1966	100
Floating on Air, No. 1256, 1966	100
Iron Maiden, No. 981, 1966	200
Painless Tooth Extractor, No. 956, 1965	50
Saw the Lady in Half, No. 1258, 1966	100
Signal for Shipwrecked Sailor, No. 957, 1965	50
Torture Chair, No. 980, 1966	200
Torture Wheel, No. 979, 1966	200

PYRO

Beginning in the early fifties, Pyro produced both vehicle and figure kits. Some of their best-known figure kits include Ghost Rider, Li'L Corporal, Surf's Up and Wyatt Earp.

Pyro's molds were acquired by Life-Like in the 1970s, and Lindberg reissued many of Pyro's molds in the early 1980s.

	MIB
The Curler, No. 177, 1970	50
Der Baron, No. 166, 1970	50
Ghost Rider, No. 167, 1970	50
The Gladiator, No. 175, 1970	50
Lil Corporal, No. 168, 1970	50
Rawhide, No. 276, 1958	60
Restless Gun, No. 277, 1958	60
Surf's Up, No. 176, 1970	40
Wyatt Earp, No. 278, 1958	60

REMCO

Remco produced Flintstone kits while the TV show was at the height of popularity. Easily classified as half-toy half-model, these kits were comprised of numerous gears and mechanical parts.

	MIB
Flintstones Sports Car, No. 450, 1961	175
Flintstones Yacht, No. 451, 1961	175
Flintstones Paddy Wagon, No. 452, 1961	175

REVELL

Revell has been involved in the production of model kits since the Forties, and behind Aurora, Revell is probably the most-recognized name in the model kit industry.

Revell was noticed when they introduced an all-plastic model of the 1910 Maxwell, the car driven by comedian Jack Benny. During the 1960s Revell ventured into he area of figure kits with models of The Beatles and the now-

Wyat Earp, Pyro, $60

famous Ed "Big Daddy" Roth Rat Fink series. Revell merged with Monogram in 1986.

Many of the Rat Fink kits were reissued by Revell from 1993-1995, depressing the values of the original issues.

	MIB
Angel Fink, No. 1307, 1965	150
Beatnik Bandit, Ed Roth, No. 1279, 1963	100
Birthday Bird, No. 2051, 1960 (Dr. Seuss)	300
Bonanza, No. 1931, 1966	175
Brother Rat Fink, No. 1304, 1964	75
Busby the Afghan Yak, No. 2006, 1959 (Dr. Seuss)	300

Left to Right: George Harrison, Revell, $200; John Lennon, Revell, $200

The box from Revell's Brother Rat Fink. The Mint-in-Box kit is valued at $75.

Angel Fink, Revell, $150

Mother's Worry by Revell. The Mint-in-Box kit is valued at $100.

	MIB
Cat in the Hat, No. 2000, 1958 (Dr. Seuss)	300
Cat in the Hat with Thing 1 & 2, No. 2050, 1960 (Dr. Seuss)	300
Dragnut, Ed Roth, No. 1303, 1963	95
Fink Eliminator, Ed Roth, No. 1310, 1965	200
Flash Gordon and Martian, No. 1450, 1965	120
Flipper and Sandy, No. 1930, 1965	90
Game of the Yertle, No. 2100, 1960 (Dr. Seuss)	250

Norval the Bashful Blinket, Revell, $300

Rat Fink, Revell, $40

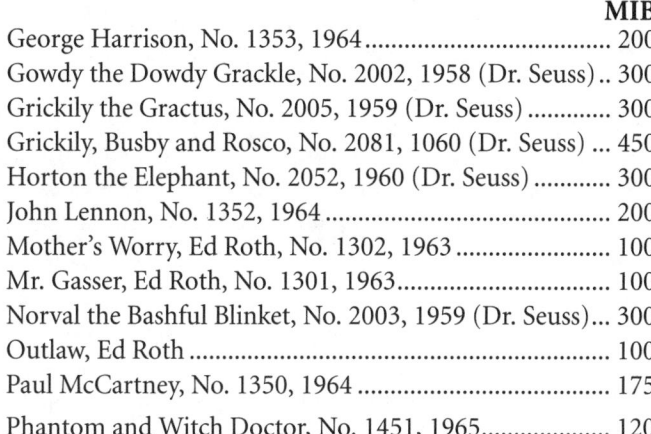

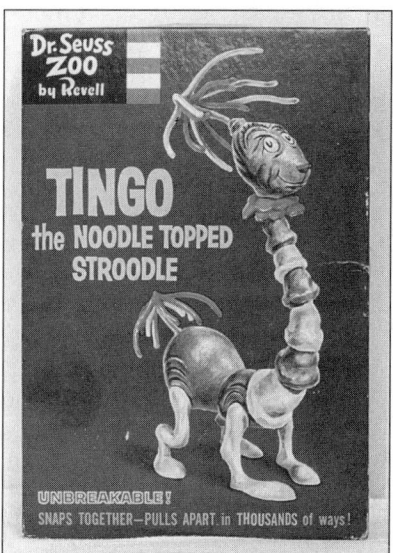

Tingo the Noodle Topped Stroodle, Revell, $300

	MIB
George Harrison, No. 1353, 1964	200
Gowdy the Dowdy Grackle, No. 2002, 1958 (Dr. Seuss)	300
Grickily the Gractus, No. 2005, 1959 (Dr. Seuss)	300
Grickily, Busby and Rosco, No. 2081, 1060 (Dr. Seuss)	450
Horton the Elephant, No. 2052, 1960 (Dr. Seuss)	300
John Lennon, No. 1352, 1964	200
Mother's Worry, Ed Roth, No. 1302, 1963	100
Mr. Gasser, Ed Roth, No. 1301, 1963	100
Norval the Bashful Blinket, No. 2003, 1959 (Dr. Seuss)	300
Outlaw, Ed Roth	100
Paul McCartney, No. 1350, 1964	175
Phantom and Witch Doctor, No. 1451, 1965	120

	MIB
Rat Fink, No. 1305, 1963	40
Ringo Starr, No. 1351, 1964	200
Robin Hood Fink, Ed Roth, No. 1270, 1965	300
Roscoe the Many Footed Lion, 2004, No. 1959 (Dr. Seuss)	300
Scuz Fink, No. 1308, 1964	300
Superfink, No. 1308, 1964	300
Surfink, No. 1306, 1965	100
Tingo the Noodle Topped Stroodle, 2001, No. 1958 (Dr. Seuss)	300
Tingo, Gowdy, and Norval, 2080, No. 1960 (Dr. Seuss)	450
Tweedy Pie with Boss Fink, Ed Roth, No. 1271, 1965	300

FISHER-PRICE

On October 1, 1930, in East Aurora, New York, the Fisher-Price Toy Company began operation. Located on a small side street of a small town, it would eventually be considered one of the major manufacturers of toys.

Herman Fisher and Irving Price shared their names to develop a name for their new company. Herman Fisher, a past employee of the FairChild Company (a manufacturer of games), and Irving Price, who had sound experience with the Woolworth Company, formed the guidelines by which they would run their new company.

The first manufacturing facility was located on Church Street in East Aurora. It would be considered small for any type of manufacturing today, but it served as the only facility for Fisher-Price toys for the company's first twenty years. It still exists, but was sold by Fisher-Price in the 1970s due to lack of use.

The most important factor in constructing this new company was to create a work force that could contribute their efforts towards a smooth, profitable venture. Among the most important employees were Helen M. Schelle and Margaret Evans Price.

Helen M. Schelle was the first secretary and treasurer of Fisher-Price toys. She developed her skills in the retail management field in the Walker Toy Shop in Binghamton, New York. Given the opportunity to manage the company's early activities, Schelle proved to be a great asset to the advancement of Fisher-Price toys.

Margaret Evans Price was the company's first artist and designer for their new line of toys. She developed her skills as a writer and illustrator for Rand McNally and Harper & Brothers, and as a creator of children's art for Strecher Lithography Company of Rochester, New York. Much of Price's artwork can still be found on early postcards, Valentines and children's books. These early paper collectibles are most often marked "M.E.P." Price created the early artwork for the reproduction of color lithography for the toys. She was also talented in drawing, produced designs for early toys, and contributed to the development of her concepts for Fisher-Price's early line of toys.

The Roycroft Printers contributed their skills to produce the sales catalogs that prospective retailers would use to choose the toys that they would market.

The company began to build a labor force to construct the new toy line, to be sold to the public in 1931. The initial work force was approximately twenty-five employees. Typical of any small town, most employees were neighbors, friends and relatives who took great pride in the product that they made, since many of the operations were done by hand. Many of the early operations—band sawing, drilling, nailing, and painting—were shared by these early employees.

As Fisher-Price began making toys, numbers were assigned to each toy. This number system started at Number 5 and went up into the thousands. To add to the confusion for collectors today, many of the numbers have been used more than once on various toys.

Because pine was abundant and easy to work with, it was the main wood used in construction of Fisher-Price toys. During the 1930s another material was used—heavy cardboard with inserted brass eyelets used prevent wear from spinning axles.

Creating action from child power was of great importance. The use of bellows was common to produce sound and, as time passed, the introduction of bells was added to create sound and action.

Because of the immense amount of time required to assemble various toys, cottage-type industries were set up by employees, families and residents of East Aurora. Toys such as the Pop-up Kritter were completely hand assembled in area homes. This would prove to be a quick and efficient method of assembly.

As the demand for Fisher-Price toys rose, the company began to use the skills of freelance designer Edward Savage. A mechanical engineer from the University of Minnesota, Savage created some of Fisher-Price's most successful toys. In his home in Rochester, New York, Savage created such toys as the Pop-Up Kritters, Snoopy Sniffer—one of the most popular toys he created—and many of the wind-up toys.

After almost two decades of growth in the 1930s and 1940s, Fisher-Price faced the challenge of limited production. When the United States entered World War II, Fisher-Price, like many companies, turned to different type of manufacturing. Fisher-Price was set up to create and produce wood products, and this dictated which essential goods they produced for the war. Ship fenders, first-aid kits, cots, bomb crates, and glider ailerons were among the items produced from 1943-1946.

The toys from this period were made from scraps of wood, with bells and some metal parts painted instead of plated. Parts from similar toys were used, this resulted in odd and sometimes unusual variations.

As World War II came to an end, normal production began to resume. Well into the 1950s, Ponderosa pine, with its proven durability, was the main source of material in Fisher-Price toys. As wood became more difficult to obtain, the experimentation with plastics began. The first toy to use this new material successfully was the Busy Bee. Because of the ease of molding, durability and bright colors, plastic was more prevalent in toys of the 1950s.

In 1951, Fisher-Price moved to its new manufacturing facility on Girard Avenue in East Aurora. This facility handled most operations for most of the 1950s. In 1957, Tri Mold, a plastics manufacturer of Kenmore, New York, became a subsidiary and main molding facility of Fisher-Price. As the demand for plastics grew, a new molding facility was built in Holland, New York, in July 1962. The Holland Plant produced many of the plastic parts used in the construction of a more plastic-dominated toy line, and as the 1960s advanced, plastic eventually took over as the main material used to produce toys.

In 1966, Herman Fisher had resigned as president of the company; although, he was chairman of the board until the Quaker Oats acquired Fisher-Price three years later. Quaker expanded the company by building a new plant in Medina, New York and numerous other plants and facilities were created both nationally and internationally.

Considered one of the oldest and largest manufacturers of toys, Fisher-Price still has its main offices at the Girard Avenue address in East Aurora, New York.

ToyTown USA has created a large following with their limited edition (under 5,000) toys manufactured for the Toyfest celebration held in East Aurora each year. This event attracts collectors of toys from all over the North America and Europe. The toys manufactured for this event are as follows:

#6550 Buzzy Bee, 1987
#6558 Little Snoopy, 1988
#6575 Toot Toot Engine, 1989
#6590 Prancing Horses, 1990
#6592 Teddy Bear Parade, 1991
#6599 Molly Bell, 1992
#6145 Jingle Elephant, 1993
#6464 Gran'pa Frog, 1994

#76593 Squeeky the Clown, 1995
#76594 Woodsy-Wee Zoo, 1996
#76880 Raggedy Ann and Andy, 1997, also made in 200 numbered special limited edition
#980750 Space Blazer, 1998, also made in 200 numbered special limited edition
#990705 Popeye Cowboy, 1999, also made in 200 numbered special limited edition

The second year toy has sold for well over $500 MIB, and others are moving upwards in value because of the limited availability.

The Fisher-Price Collectors Club is a great opportunity for fellow collectors to advance their knowledge, buy, sell and communicate with other collectors. Collectors are encouraged to join the club, as information on new and old Fisher-Price toys is plentiful in the newsletter. For information, contact the Fisher-Price Collector's Club, Attn: Jeanne Kennedy, 1442 North Ogden, Meza, AZ 85205.

Many factors may contribute to the value of a Fisher-Price toy. The most important factor to consider is the paper lithography. Most Fisher-Price toys found have edge wear. Most toys found with edge wear may also be called normal-wear toys. Toys in this condition often fall in a value class of Good/Very Good. When determining condition of a toy, other areas of importance to the lithography would include the amount of soil on the artwork and the extent to which it has faded and/or lost its color. These areas may be considered less important, unless there is more than slight soiling or discoloration. When a Fisher-Price toy has advanced wear, soiling or missing lithography, the toy is considered to be in Poor condition.

Paint is also important when determining a toy's value. Toys with slight paint wear on wheels, bases and handles fall into the Good/Very Good condition category. Any parts missing—especially lithography parts—also affects the value of the toy. Once the lithography is gone, there is no means of replacement. Missing wheels and axles also lessen the value of a toy.

A toy that is in Mint condition has absolutely no wear or damage. Lithography, paint, wheels, etc. are complete. Boxes—depending on its condition, of course—for older Fisher-Price toys may add up to twenty percent to the value of a Mint toy. Because of their age and scarcity, boxes from the 1930s are of the highest value.

Comic character toys and toys displaying other companies' names demand higher prices. Just because a toy features Disney characters, Popeye or other comic figures does not necessarily mean that it is a rare toy. Rarity is based on the amount of toys produced over a given period of time and the amount still in existence.

Toys that had accessories or figures that were often misplaced will also bring higher values. Often these accessories and/or figures are difficult to locate separately from the toy itself. If a toy is found mint in the box with accessories, it most certainly will demand a higher price. The Fisher-Price toy prices listed in this guide were established by averaging toy prices taken from toy shows, flea markets, dealers, and collectors.

Contributors: John J. Murray, Box 29, Eden, NY 14057. Murray, orginally from Buffalo, New York, presently lives in Eden, New York with his wife Mary and daughter Amanda. Currently employed at Fisher-Price, Murray is part of the Research and Devlopment Art Production Department where he is responsible for creating new color development and decoration for photo and TV models. Murray also serves as Chairman of the Board and CEO of the ToyTown USA Foundation which oversees the ToyTown USA Museum and ToyFest, the largest toy gathering in the United States.

Murray was a pioneer in the area of Fisher-Price documentation. Murray along with co-author and Fisher-Price Senior Sales Representative Bruce R. Fox are presently compiling a comprehensive guide to Fisher-Price toys.

	C6	C8	C10
Allie Gator, No. 653	85	120	150
American Airlines Flagship, w/original propellers, No. 170	600	900	1200
Baby Chick Tandem Cart, No. 50	85	125	170
Barky Dog, No. 462	85	125	175
Big Bill Pelican, w/cardboard fish-add $25, No. 794	65	85	120
Big Performing Circus, w/all accessories, No. 900	375	500	700
Blackie Drummer, No. 785	500	600	1000
Boom-Boom Popeye, No. 491	450	800	110
Bossy Bell, No. 656	40	60	80
Bouncing Bunny Cart, No. 307	45	60	90
Bouncy Racer, No. 8	40	60	80
Bucky Burro, No. 166	115	175	230
Buddy Bullfrog, No. 728	85	100	125
Bunny & Cart, No. 406	45	60	90
Bunny Basket Cart, No. 301	40	60	80
Bunny Basket Cart, No. 303	95	140	190
Bunny Bell Drummer, No. 508	85	125	160
Bunny Cart, No. 10	95	135	180
Bunny Cart, No. 401	200	300	400
Bunny Cart, No. 487	225	325	450
Bunny Egg Cart, No. 28	85	150	170
Butch the Pup, No. 333	85	125	170
Buzzy Bee, No. 325	15	25	35

Cicrus Wagon, $800

	C6	C8	C10
Cackling Hen, red, No. 123	40	65	80
Cackling Hen, white, No. 120	40	65	60
Cement Mixer, No. 926	260	325	485
Chatter Monk, No. 798	85	125	160
Chick & Cart, No. 407	40	60	80
Chick Basket Cart, No. 302	40	60	80
Chug Chug, w/two cars, No. 168	30	45	60
Chuggy Pop-Up, No. 616	85	125	170

Boom-Boom Popeye, $1,100

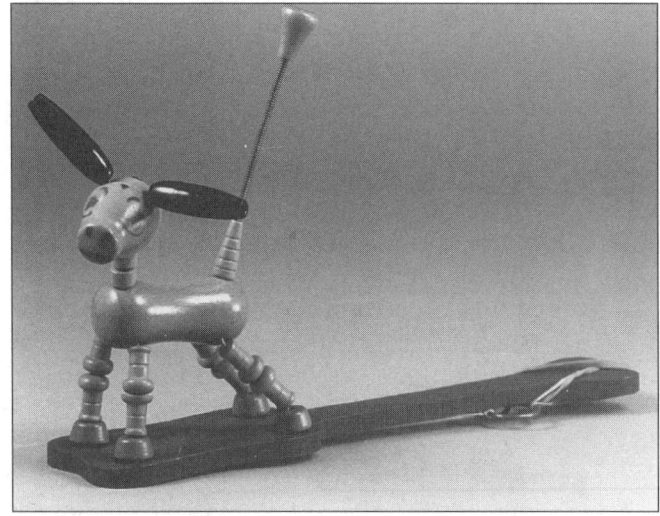

Dizzy Donkey, $155

Donald Duck Drum Major, $270

	C6	C8	C10
Circus Wagon, No. 156	425	600	800
Cookie Pig, No. 476	40	50	60
Dandy Dobbin, No. 765	200	275	400
Dashing Dobbin, No. 742	450	650	850
Dizzy Donkey, No. 433	75	115	155
Doc & Dopey Dwarfs, No. 770	750	1000	1500
Donald Choo-Choo, No. 450	185	275	370

Donald Duck Drummer, $450

Ferdinand the Bull, $1,200

	C6	C8	C10
Donald Duck & Nephews, w/two nephews, No. 479	400	500	600
Donald Duck Cart, No. 544	225	325	425
Donald Duck Drum Major, No. 400	135	200	270
Donald Duck Drummer, No. 454	225	325	450
Donald Duck Xylophone, No. 177	180	270	360
Donald Duck Xylophone, No. 185	400	600	800
Dr. Doodle, No. 132	170	255	340
Dr. Doodle, No. 477	225	350	450
Ducky Cart, No. 11	85	125	170
Ducky Cart, No. 16	85	125	170
Dumbo Circus Racer, original arms, No. 738	800	1100	1600
Elsie's Dairy Truck w/two milk bottles, add $50 for each bottle, No. 745	475	600	800
Ferdinand the Bull, No. 434	600	900	1200
Fido Zilo, No. 707	85	110	150
Fisher-Price General Hauling, No. 733	225	250	330
Fuzzy Fido, No. 444	225	325	450

Fuzzy Fido, $450

Bucky Burro, $230

Teddy Bear Zilo, $160

Donald Duck Xylophone, No. 177, $360

Super-Jet, $220

Hot Dog Wagon, No. 445, $400

Katy Kackler, $240

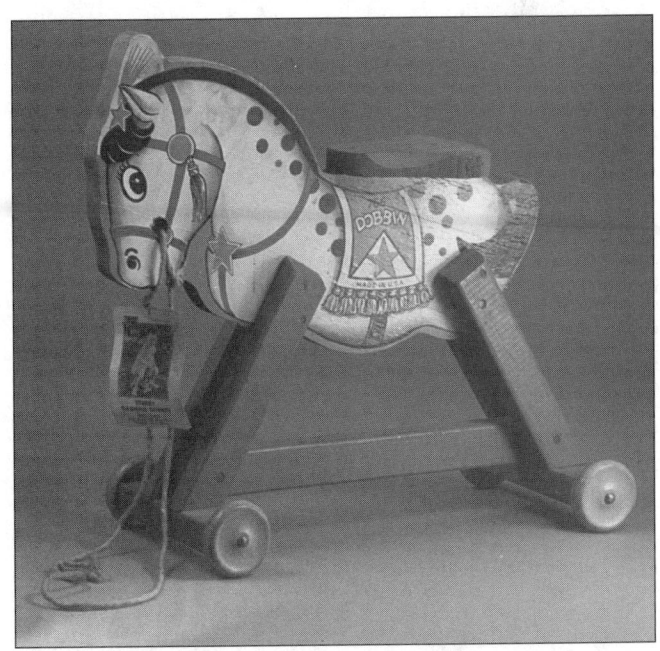

Dandy Dobbin, $400

Gold Star Stage Coach, $375

Leo the Drummer, $375

	C6	C8	C10
Gabby Goofies, No. 775	40	60	80
Gabby Goofies, No. 776	40	60	80
Go'n Back Mule, w/original ears, No. 350	700	1100	1400
Gold Star Stage Coach, w/baggage, No. 175	190	285	375
Golden Gulch Express, No. 191	85	125	170
Goofy Gertie, No. 440	300	425	575
Happy Helicopter, No. 498	225	285	375
Happy Hippo, No. 151	85	150	170
Hot Dog Wagon, No. 445	225	300	400
Hot Dog Wagon, No. 750	400	600	800
Huffy Puffy Train, w/four cars, No. 999	110	150	225
Humpty-Dumpty, No. 755	160	240	325
Jingle Giraffe, No. 472	225	300	375
Jolly Jumper, No. 450	85	125	170
Juggling Jumbo, No. 735	225	300	400
Jumbo Rollo, No. 755	225	300	400
Katy Kackler, No. 140	120	180	240
Kriss Kricket, No. 678	100	150	200
Lady Bug, No. 658	45	60	80

	C6	C8	C10
Leo the Drummer, No. 480	225	280	375
Looky Chug-Chug, No. 220	95	125	170
Looky Chug-Chug, w/tender, No. 161	90	135	180
Looky Fire Truck, No. 7	85	125	125
Looky Push Car w/steering wheel push stick, No. 875	95	125	165
Lop-Ear Looie, No. 415	225	335	450
Merry Mousewife, No. 662	40	60	80
Merry Mutt, No. 473	85	125	150
Mickey Mouse Choo-Choo, early version, No. 432	650	975	1300
Mickey Mouse Choo-Choo, No. 485	95	140	175
Mickey Mouse Drummer, No. 476	275	350	475
Mickey Mouse Puddle Jumper, No. 310	90	150	190
Mickey Mouse Safety Patrol, No. 733	250	375	500
Mickey Mouse Xylophone, No. 798	300	600	975

Mickey Mouse Choo-Choo, $175

Lop-Ear Looie, $450

The cover of the 1969 Fisher-Price catalog.

The cover of the 1949-1950 Fisher-Price catalog.

Popeye the Sailor, $1,600

	C6	C8	C10
Molly Moo-Moo, No. 190	225	275	350
Moo-oo Cow, No. 155	85	105	140
Mother Goose, No. 164	65	95	135
Musical Duck, No. 795	85	125	165
Musical Elephant, w/original ears, No. 145	250	375	500
Musical Sweeper, No. 100	160	225	240
Musical Sweeper, No. 225	85	125	185
Musical Sweeper, No. 230	85	125	170
Nifty Station Wagon, w/roof and four figures, No. 234	350	450	650

	C6	C8	C10
Nosey Pup, No. 445	75	120	145
Perky Pot, No. 686	85	110	140
Peter Bunny Cart, No. 472	250	325	400
Peter Bunny Engine, No. 721	225	325	450
Pinky Pig, No. 695	85	110	140
Pinocchio Express, No. 720	650	850	1150
Playful Puppy, No. 625	45	55	65
Playful Puppy, No. 626	45	55	65
Playland Express, No. 192	85	125	170
Plucky Pinocchio, No. 494	450	600	800
Pluto Pop-Up, No. 440	90	135	185
Pluto the Pup, No. 210	400	525	625
Pony Chime, No. 137	40	60	80
Pony Chime, No. 138	30	40	50
Pony Chime, No. 758	165	250	335
Poodle Zilo, No. 739	85	120	180
Popeye Spinach Eater, No. 488	650	950	1200
Popeye the Sailor, No. 703	800	1200	1600
Pudgy Pig, No. 478	40	60	80
Puffy Engine, No. 444	45	70	95
Quacky Family, No. 799	65	90	120
Queen Buzzy Bee, No. 314	40	65	85
Racing Rowboat, No. 730	225	260	300
Riding Horse w/original tail, No. 237	600	900	1200
Roller Chimes, w/push stick, No. 123	85	120	155
Safety School Bus, w/ all figures, No. 984	225	350	550
Safety School Bus, w/all figures, No. 983	500	750	1000
Shaggy Zilo, No. 738	85	120	180
Sleep Sue, No. 495	45	55	70
Smokie Engine, No. 642	40	60	75
Snoopy Sniffer, No. 180	70	105	140
Snorky Fire Engine, w/all figures, No. 168	85	125	170
Snorky Fire Engine, w/all figures, No. 169	85	125	170
Space Blazer, No. 750	265	400	530
Sports Car, No. 674	85	125	150
Squeaky the Clown, No. 777	160	250	325
Stoopy Storky, w/original cardboard feet, No. 410	275	375	550

Queen Buzzy Bee, $85

Shaggy Zilo, $180

	C6	C8	C10
Streamliner Express, No. 215	900	1300	1800
Super-Jet, No. 415	110	165	220
Suzie Seal, ball, No. 621	40	50	60
Suzie Seal, umbrella, No. 623	40	50	60
Tailspin Tabby Pop-Up, No. 600	225	275	325
Tailspin Tabby, No. 455	85	125	170
Tailspin Tabby, No. 610	70	105	140
Tailspin Tabby, original pull loops, No. 400	90	135	180
Talking Donald Duck, No. 76	70	105	140
Talky Parrot, No. 698	95	140	165
Tawny Tiger, No. 654	85	100	125
Teddy Bear Parade, No. 195	600	900	1200
Teddy Bear Zilo, No. 777	85	125	160
Teddy Tooter, No. 712	225	250	300
Teddy Xylophone, No. 752	160	240	320

	C6	C8	C10
Thumper Bunny, No. 533	425	575	800
Timber Toter, No. 810	85	110	150
Timmy Turtle, No. 150	85	135	180
Tiny Teddy, No. 634	40	65	85
Tiny Teddy, No. 635	30	45	65
Tiny Teddy, No. 636	60	90	120
Toy Wagon, No. 131	225	325	450
Tuggy Turtle, No. 139	85	125	160
Uncle Timmy Turtle, w/glasses, 125	85	120	150
Walking Duck Cart, No. 305	45	60	90
Walt Disney's Elmer the Elephant, No. 211	400	525	625
Whistling Engine, No. 617	95	140	175
Wiggily Woofer, No. 640	85	120	145
Winky Blinky Fire Truck, No. 200	85	120	150

GUNS

See also Premiums, Comic Characters

It can be argued that guns have changed and shaped the course of history in the United States. Throughout every conflict, beginning with the Revolutionary War, guns played a major role in the outcome of battles, both here and abroad. Important in a historical context, guns are a vital and important category of toy collecting. When toys began to be mass-produced after the Civil War, toy guns were among the first to appear on the market. Their success was instantaneous, and toy guns remained among the most popular selling toys through the 1960s.

Although toy guns were patented in the 1850s, they were not manufactured in any quantity until a decade later due to the wartime shortages. These early toy guns were, for the most part, pea shooters and cork poppers and were usually made of wood with metal hardware, although iron and lead types may occasionally be found among them. These early examples are hard to find today and most are known only through their patent drawings. By 1870, inventors, trying to add realism to these toy guns, began using paper caps. This invention had been developed just prior to the Civil War and was known as the Maynard Tape Primer. The tape primer was originally intended to detonate muzzle-loading arms and closely resembled a roll of modern paper caps. For the first time, toy guns could make a loud noise, yet still be relatively safe and harmless. Naturally this spurred the demand for these new toys and designers worked overtime to create new and appealing guns. Their output was prolific, and today the period from 1870 to 1900 is regarded as the "golden age" of the toy gun—especially the toy cap pistol.

By 1880 the cast-iron cap pistol had become the most popular type of toy gun by far, and the various toy makers—primarily J. & E. Stevens and Ives—were competing among themselves to see who could produce the most unique and appealing designs. A glance at any collection of these early toy pistols will show that realism was secondary to artistic imagination. Many pistols from this period were covered with ornamentation and, in some cases, any resemblance to a real gun was purely coincidental. Leaf-and-scroll designs were the most popular, but pistols can also be found with numerous other designs, including two- and three-dimensional figures, and animated figures. Guns with moving figures, though not as rare as some, are worth much more to a collector than an ordinary-looking pistol from the same period.

A variety of classic Hubley die-cast pistols from the 1950s, the lock in is a pistol, too.

Another very desirable pistol from the same era is known as the head pistol. It featured a head, either animal or human, placed at the breech end of the barrel with the mouth open to receive the cap. Over two dozen varieties of head and animated pistols are known to exist, but are so much in demand that they are seldom offered for sale.

The most popular material used to make these early toy pistols was cast iron, which continued to be used heavily into the twentieth century, until the demands of World War II cut off the supply. Many varieties of old toy guns were, however, made from such diverse materials as paper, wood, steel, tin, lead, rubber, zinc, glass and even wax. During World War II toy guns were even made of molded sawdust mixed with glue. After the war, a few cast-iron pistols were produced and assembled, using both new and old parts, but the cost proved to be prohibitive, and makers soon turned to less expensive metals such as steel and die-cast zinc. By 1950 most toy pistols were being made of die-cast material and plastic, both of which continue to be used today.

From almost the very beginning, toy gun makers have felt the need to personalize their products; hundreds of different names can be found embossed on these little guns. Some examples that come to mind are Excelsior, Victor, American Bulldog, Acorn, Sun, Boom, Darb, Ace, Daisy, Cowboy King, Polo, Triumph and Terror. Many names were used only once on one particular gun and then dropped, while others have reappeared time and again on different models over the years. This custom of naming toy guns still goes on today; a visit to any toy store will turn up names such as Cowhand, Top Gun Jr. and 007. Many of these names seem to reflect current events or personalities, but the meanings of others have become obscure.

Collectors of toy guns can choose from a large array of models and styles, and because of the tremendous historical popularity of these toys, collectors have the opportunity to acquire interesting and unusual examples at an affordable price. Guns from as far back as the 1920s and 1930s can still be found at flea markets, garage sales and second-hand stores, often at a price that is only a fraction of what other toys from these same years will sell for.

Contributor: Charles W. Best, 11523 Pine Valley Dr., Franktown, CO 80116. Best is a leading authority on toy weapons and has been collecting them in earnest since 1966. His collection is regarded as one of the finest and most comprehensive in existence and has won many awards at various gun shows. In addition to writing a number of articles on the subject in such magazines as *Gun Report and Antique Toy World,* he is also the author of *Cast-Iron Toy Pistols* and co-author, with Sam Logan, *of Cast-Iron Toy Guns and Capshooters,* both of which are now out of print.

Note: Measurements given, in general, are from one end of the gun to the other, rather than on a diagonal from grip to muzzle. Dates of manufacturers can vary within five years, though most of the later dates are considerably more accurate.

	C6	C8	C10
2 in 1 cap pistol, cast iron, 9-1/4"	85	125	175
2 Monkeys animated cap pistol, cast iron, maker unknown, 1882; monkey hits head against coconut held by another monkey, 4-1/2"	500	750	1000
5-Star steel dart pistol, Wyandotte	15	22	30
6-Shot cap pistol, cast iron, "Pat. U.S.A., Jan. 22, 1895," Stevens, 1895, 6-3/4"	275	365	550
6-Shot Rapid Load cap pistol, cast iron, "Made in U.S.A.," Stevens, 1932, 6-1/2"	50	65	85
6-Shot, Stevens, 1932, 6-1/4"	45	60	80
25 Jr. cap automatic, cast iron, "Made in U.S.A., Patented," Stevens, 1930, 4-1/8"	30	45	60
25-50 cap automatic, cast iron, "Made in U.S.A.; Pat, Appld. For," Stevens, 1935, 4-1/2"	22	33	45

	C6	C8	C10
25-50 cap automatic, cast iron, "Oil Moving Parts; Made in U.S.A., Patented," Stevens, 1935, 4-1/2"	25	38	50
25-50 cap automatic, cast iron, "Oil Moving Parts; Made in U.S.A., Patented," Stevens, 1935; can be fired rapidly w/crank, hole near muzzle holds removable crank	60	80	110
25-50 cap automatic, cast iron, "Pat. Appl'd. For, Made in U.S.A.," Stevens, 1928, 4-1/2"	30	45	60

25-50 cast-iron cap automatic pistol, Stevens, 1935, $110

6 Shot cast-iron pistol, Stevens, 1895, $550

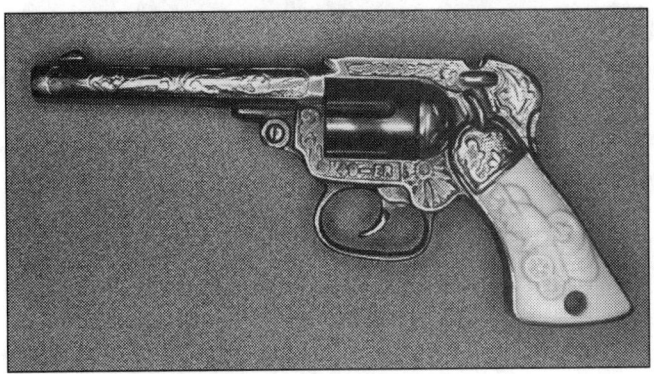

49-ER cast-iron pistol, Kilgore, 1935, $285

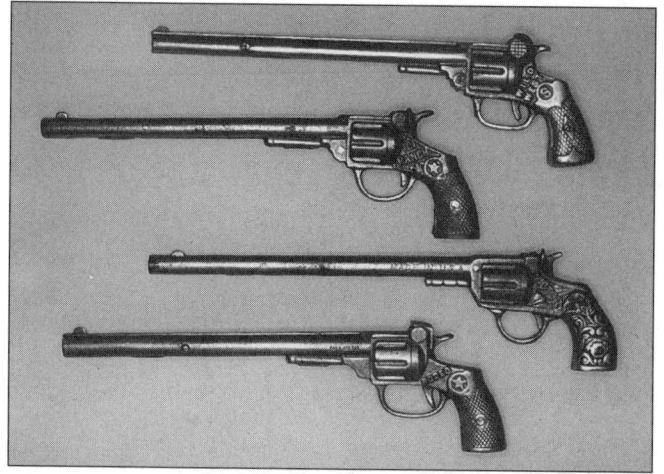

Top to Bottom: Wild West cast-iron cap pistol, Kenton, 1926, $225; 101 Ranch cast-iron cap pistol, Hubley, 1930, $250; Victor cast-iron cap pistol, Stevens, 1924, $250; Rodeo cast-iron cap pistol, Hubley, 1924, $200

	C6	C8	C10
25-50 Target automatic, w/silencer-type barrel, "Oil Moving Parts; Made in U.S.A., Patented" Stevens, 1935	150	200	300
.45 Smoker, c. 1946; blows cap smoke	30	45	60
49-ER cap pistol, cast iron, Stevens, 1940, 9"	142	215	285
101 Ranch cast iron pistol, Hubley, 1930, 11-1/2"	150	200	250
1776-1876 cap pistol, cast iron, produced for America's centennial, Stevens, 1876, 5-1/4"	150	225	300
Ace cap pistol, cast iron, "Made in U.S.A.," Stevens, 1930, 5" long	27	41	55
Ace cap pistol, cast iron, Kilgore, 5" long, 1935	22	33	45
Acme automatic, steel cap, repeater, c. 1930	12	18	25
Acorn pistol, cast iron	75	100	150
Admiral Dewey cap bomb, cast iron	125	150	200
Aeromatic Glider Gun, steel automatic, c. 1940; shoots balsa airplanes	50	75	100

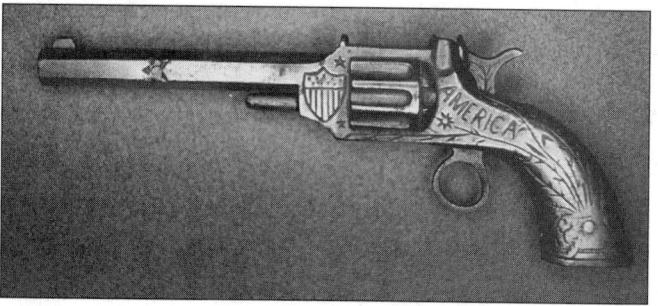

America pistol, Stevens, 1880, $275

	C6	C8	C10
The Agitator, cap and torpedo shooter, cast iron, John Fox, 1908, 8-1/4"	125	188	250
Aim To Save, c. 1909	150	225	300
Air Blaster, Wham-O, plastic; shoots burst of air	40	60	80
Air Raid Warning Signal pistol	40	60	100
America cap pistol w/shield, pat. 1873	150	225	300
America, Stevens, 1880, 8-3/4"	135	200	275
American Bulldog .22 blank shooter, cast iron, Kenton, 1920, 4-1/2" long; second trigger tips barrel to load, handle curves inward	55	75	100
American Bulldog .22 cal. blank shooter, cast iron, Kenton, 1910, 4-1/2" long; second trigger tips barrel to load, handle projects outward	50	70	95

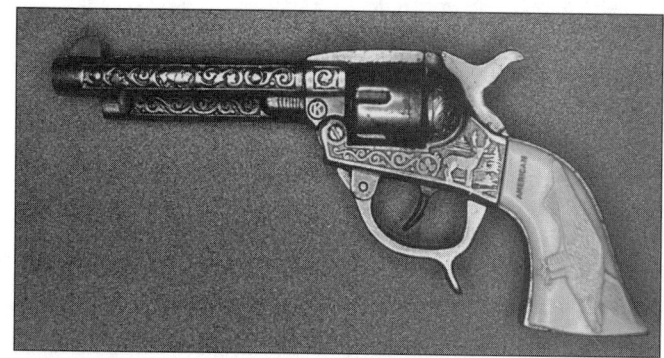

American cast-iron pistol, Kilgore, 1940, $550

Ace cast-iron cap pistol, Kilgore, 1935, $45

Army 45 cast-iron cap automatic cover, Hubley, 1940, $160

	C6	C8	C10
American cap pistol, cast iron, Kilgore, 1940, 9-5/8"	275	365	550
Army 45 cap automatic, cast iron, Hubley, 1940, "Made in U.S.A." 6-5/8"	80	120	160
Army 45 cap automatic, die-cast zinc, plastic grips, "Made in U.S.A.," Hubley, 1940, 6-1/2" long	45	68	90
Army cap pistol, cast iron, 1910	40	60	80
Army pistol w/revolving cylinder, tin litho, Marx No. 625	20	30	45
Army Sparkling Pop Gun, Marx No. 197	20	30	45
Astro Ray Signal-Dart gun, plastic, Ohio Art, 1960s, 10"	50	75	100
Atomic Disintegrator cap pistol, Hubley	175	260	350
Atomic Flash Space Gun, Chein	35	50	70
Auto Magic Picture Gun, w/film and instructions, 1936; projects film onto wall	75	100	125
Auto Repeating Cap Exploder	45	68	90
Automatic cap pistol, die-cast, Hubley No. 290, 6-1/2"	25	50	70
Automatic Repeater Paper Pop Pistol, aluminum, Marx No. 74	20	25	30
Automatic Repeater, pressed steel, Wyandotte No. 40, 1920s, 7" long	20	25	30
Bang cap pistol, cast iron, "Made in U.S.A.," Kilgore, 6" long	25	38	50
Bang-O cap pistol, cast iron, "Made in U.S.A.," Stevens, 1938, 7" long	42	63	85
Banner, blank-shooting pistol, cast iron, Ives, 5"	150	175	250
Bell Pistol, Wyandotte	15	23	31
Benjamin Pump early BB gun, before 1910	75	112	150
Biff cap automatic, cast iron, "Made in U.S.A. Pat. Apld. For," Kenton, 1935, 4-1/2"	42	63	85
Biff Jr. cap automatic, cast iron, "Made in U.S.A. Pat. Apld. For," Kenton, 1935, 4-1/8" long	30	45	60
Big Bang pistol, No. 6P, 7-7/8" long	150	225	300
Big Bang rifle, No. 21-60, 21-3/16" long	750	2000	3500
Big Bill cap pistol, cast iron, large hammer, "Made in U.S.A.," Kilgore, 1935, 4-7/8"	30	45	60
Big Bill cap pistol, cast iron, large hammer, "Made in U.S.A.," Kilgore, 1930, 5-3/4"	25	35	45
Big Bill cap pistol, Kilgore, 1925, 5-1/2" long	25	35	45
Big Buster cap automatic, cast iron, w/two-piece trigger, "Patd Jul 2 1907, Made in U.S.A.," Kilgore, 1915, 5"	75	112	150

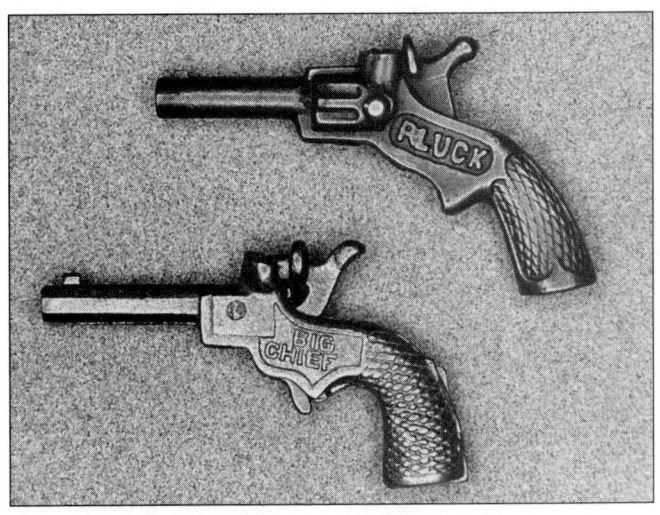

Top to Bottom: Big Chief cast-iron cap pistol, Dent Hardware, 1930, $35; Pluck cast-iron cap pistol, Stevens, 1930, $25

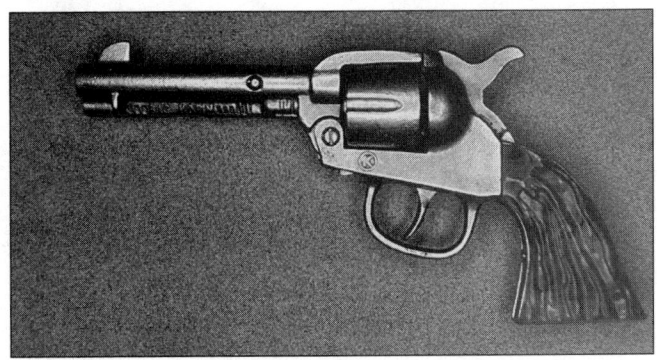

Big Horn cast-iron cap pistol, Kilgore, 1930, $365

	C6	C8	C10
Big Chief cap pistol, cast iron, "Made in U.S.A.," Dent, 1930, 3-1/2"	22	25	35
Big Chief cap pistol, cast iron, marked w/star and "K," Kilgore, 1935, 6"	22	33	45
Big Chief cap pistol, cast iron, Kilgore, 1935, 6" long	20	30	45
Big Clip cap pistol, cast iron, "Made in U.S.A.," Stevens, 1930, 6-3/4"	25	38	50
Big Horn cap pistol, cast iron, revolving cylinder, Kilgore, 1939, 8-3/8"	175	275	365

Bigger Bang cast-iron cap pistol, Kilgore, 1930, $65

	C6	C8	C10
Big Injun, hammerless	150	225	300
The Big Noise, c. 1922	45	68	90
Big Scout, 1935	30	45	60
Big Scout, engraved, 1940	30	45	60
Bigger Bang cap pistol, cast iron, large hammer, Kilgore, 1930, 6" long	32	48	65
Billy The Kid cap pistol, cast iron, Stevens, 1938, 6-3/4"	75	112	150
Black Jack cap pistol, cast iron, long barrel, "Pat. Sept. 11-23," Kenton, 1930, 11"	125	188	250
Blaze Away Dart Pistol, Marx No. G23	15	22	30
Bob cap pistol, cast iron, Kilgore, 1930, 5" long	25	38	50
Bobcat cap pistol, die-cast, Kilgore, 1950s, 4-1/4"	15	20	35
Border Patrol cap automatic, cast iron, Kilgore, 1930, 4-1/4" long	30	40	50
Border Patrol cap automatic, cast iron, "Pat. Apld. For, Made in U.S.A.," Kilgore, 1935, 4-1/2" long	30	40	50
Border Patrol, 1940	35	52	70
Boss mammoth cap pistol, cast iron Kenton, 1925, 6-1/4"	30	45	60
Boy's Delight cap pistol, cast iron, pat. June 1891	150	225	300
Boy's Police Automatic pop gun, cardboard, c. 1940s, 8"	8	12	15
Brat cap pistol, cast iron	30	45	60
Brevet Depose	300	450	600
Bronc cap pistol, cast iron, "Kenton Madein U.S.A.," Kenton, 1935, 6"	30	45	60
Buc-A-Roo cap pistol, cast iron, Kilgore, 1940, 7-3/4"	50	75	100
Buccaneer flintlock pistol, Nichols, 1958, 3-1/2"; fires plastic bullets	37	56	75
Buck pistol, cast iron, Hubley, 1930, 3-1/4"	40	60	90
Buckle Gun, w/bullets, Mattel	48	72	95
Buddy, 1930	25	38	50
Buddy, 1935	25	38	50
Buffalo Bill cap pistol, cast iron, "Made in U.S.A.," Stevens, 1940, 7-3/4" long	72	110	145
Buffalo Bill cap pistol, cast iron, long barreled, "Pat. Sept. 11-23," Kenton, 1925, 11-3/8"	150	225	300
Buffalo Bill cap pistol, cast iron, long barreled, "Pat. Sept. 11-23," Kenton, 1930, 13-1/2"	150	225	300
Buffalo Bill, cast iron, single shot, Stevens, 1890	200	300	400
Buffalo cap rifle, Hubley	82	125	165

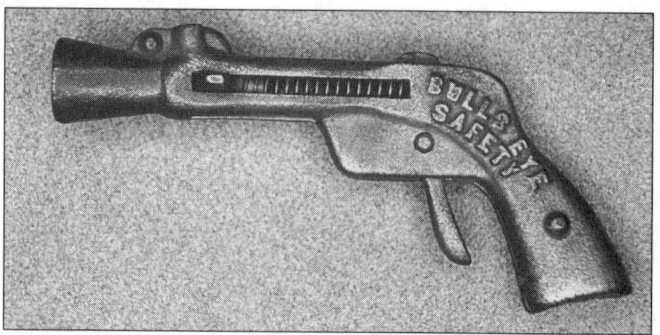

Bulls Eye Safety pistol, Stevens, 1910, $150

	C6	C8	C10
Bull cap pistol, cast iron, "Pat Appld. for Pat. Mch. 25, '24," Hubley, 1940, 6-1/4"	25	38	50
Bull Dog cap pistol, cast iron, "Pat. 1,488,046," Hubley, 1935, 6-1/4" long	25	35	45
Bulls Eye Safety pistol, cast iron flare barrel w/spring, Stevens, 1910, 5-1/2"	75	112	150
Bulldog cap pistol, cast iron, Kenton, 1923, 5-1/2"	37	56	75
Bulldozer cap pistol, six-shooter, cast iron, July 1874	150	225	300
Bunker Hill cap pistol, cast iron, National, 1925, 5-1/4" long	30	45	60
Burp Gun, aluminum, die-cast and plastic Mattel, 1956, 13" long,	45	68	90
"Buster," maker unknown, "Pat. May 28 1901," 6"	195	250	325
Buster cap automatic, cast iron, Kilgore, 1910, 5-1/2"	45	68	90
Butting Match mechanical pistol, cast iron	300	400	600
Cannon animated cap pistol	250	375	500
Cap bomb, cast iron, head shape	75	112	150
Cap bomb, dog's head	100	150	200
Cap bomb, double-faced, cast iron	75	120	175
Cap pistol, cast iron, revolving cylinder, 1887	100	150	200

Buster pistol, maker unknown, 1901, $325

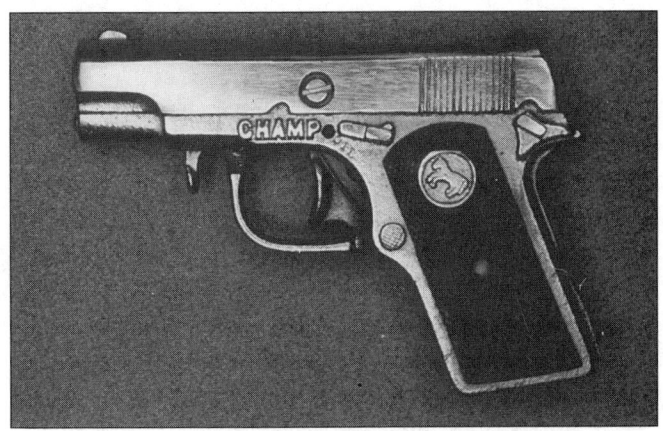

Champ die-cast automatic pistol, Hubley, 1940, $110

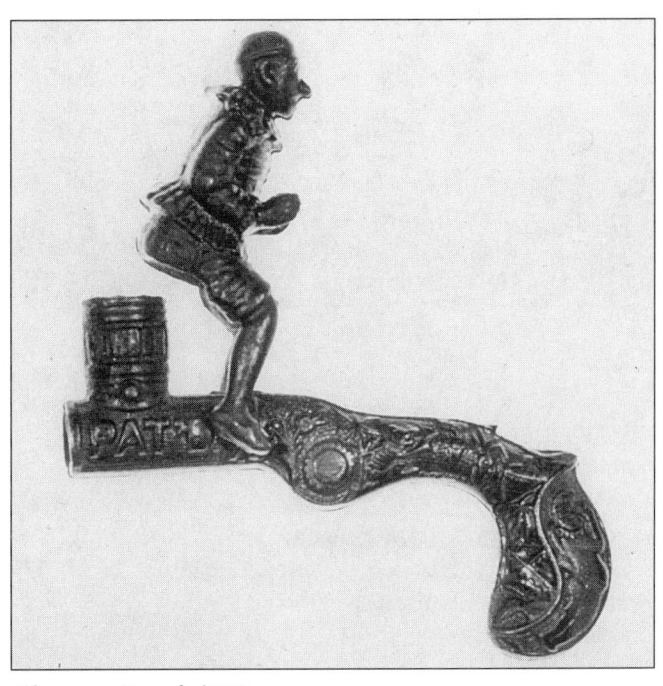

Clown on Barrel, $800

	C6	C8	C10
Cap pistol, cast iron, hammerless w/four revolving triggers, "Pat. Appl'd For," Stevens, 1892, 7-1/4"	150	225	300
Cap pistol, cast iron, ornate, 1878	50	75	125
Cap pistol, cast iron, six-shot, dated 1895	125	175	250
Cap pistol, double-barrel, cast iron, dated 1880	125	188	250
Cap pistol, nickel-plated cast iron, marked w/W on one side, S on other, normal size barrel	25	30	35
Cap pistol, steel, repeating, red, Wyandotte, 8" long	15	22	30
Captain cap automatic, cast iron, Kilgore, 1940, 4-1/4" long	30	40	50
Cavalier cap automatic, cast iron, "Pat. Appld. For, Made in U.S.A.," Kilgore, 1935, 4-1/2"	35	52	70
Challenge, 1890	150	225	300
Champ automatic, die-cast metal, Hubley, 1940, 5"	55	82	110
Chief, 1900-1910	35	45	55
Chief cap pistol, aluminum, single shot, Hubley	30	45	60
Chief cap pistol, cast iron, "Pat 1,488,046," Hubley, 1930, 6-1/8"	25	38	50

	C6	C8	C10
Chief cast iron .22 cal. blank shooter, Kenton, 1915, 6" long; second trigger tips up barrel to load	50	75	100
Chieftain cap pistol, cast iron, National, 1920, 11" long	75	112	150
Chinese Must Go cap pistol, mechanical	350	450	700
Click Pistol, pressed steel, Marx, approx. 7-3/4" long	15	22	30
Click Pistol, tin litho, Marx No. 36	15	22	30
Clicker Pistol, plain black, late 1930s-early 1940s	15	22	30
Clip 50, Bakelite and cast iron, Kilgore, 1940, 4-1/4"	60	90	120
Clip Jr. cap pistol, cast iron, Stevens, 1935, 5-1/4"	25	38	50
Clipper cap automatic, cast iron, Kilgore, 1935, 4-1/8"	48	72	95
Clown on a barrel	400	605	800
Clown and mule pistol, animated	600	800	1500
Colt .45, die-cast metal, Hubley	85	130	170

Click Pistol, pressed steel, Marx, $30

Columbia cast-iron cap pistol, Stevens, 1890, $400

Corporal, maker unknown, 1900, $125

	C6	C8	C10
Colt cap pistol, cast iron, "Patented June 17, 1890, Made in U.S.A.," Stevens, 1920, 5-1/2"	50	75	100
Colt cap pistol, cast iron, Stevens, 1935, 6-1/2"	27	41	55
Columbia cap pistol, cast iron, Stevens, 1890, 8-3/4"	200	300	400
Columbia cap pistol, cast iron, pat. June 1891	200	300	400
Columbia cap pistol, cast iron, 1885	200	300	400
Columbian Junior, early BB gun	250	375	500
Comet, Stevens, 1885, 5-1/2"	150	225	300
Comet, Stevens, 1925, 7-1/8"	40	60	80
Cop cap pistol, cast iron, "Pat 1,488,046" or "Pat. Mch. 25 '24," Hubley, 1930, 5"	25	38	50
Cork gun-rifle, double-barrel, Marx No. 232	50	75	100
Cork-popper pistol, spur trigger, Wyandotte	15	20	30
Cork-shooting rifle, Marx No. 206	15	20	30
Corn Shooter cap pistol	55	82	110
Corporal, maker unknown, 1900, 8-7/8"	62	93	125
Cowboy cap pistol, cast iron, "Made in U.S.A.," Stevens, 1935, 3-1/2"	15	22	30
Cowboy cap pistol, cast iron, "Made in U.S.A.," Hubley, 1940, 8"	55	83	110
Cowboy cap pistol, cast iron, Ives, 1890, 7-5/8"	125	188	250
Cowboy cap pistol, cast iron, long barrel, "Made in U.S.A.," Stevens, 1930	175	263	350

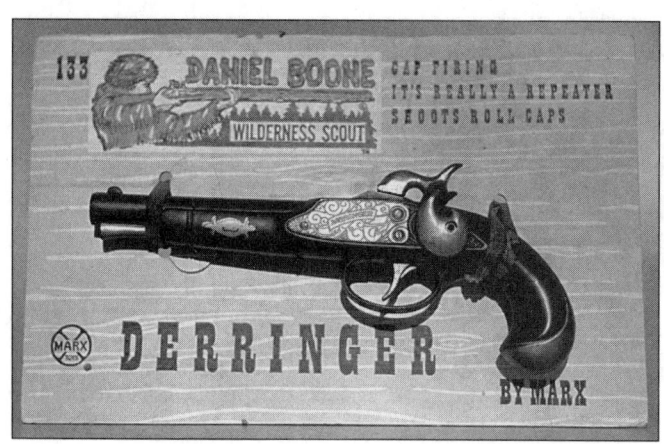

Daniel Boone Wilderness Scout Derringer, Mark, $50

	C6	C8	C10
Cowboy King, 1940	138	205	275
Coyote, die-cast, Hubley	30	45	65
Crack, 1925, Stevens, 5"	40	60	80
Cupid, 1900, 5-1/4"	62	93	125
Dagger Derringer, die-cast, Hubley, 1955	35	52	70
Dandy cast iron cap pistol, w/a variety of markings, Hubley, 1935, 5-3/4"	35	52	70
Daniel Boone Wilderness Scout Derringer, Marx	25	38	50
Darb cap pistol, cast iron, "Pat. Sept. 11-23," Kenton, 1930, 5-1/2" long	30	45	60
Dart pistol, colorful w/fancy lithographing, Wyandotte	11	16	22
Dart pistol, Wyandotte, 1950s	27	41	55
Dead Shot, Stevens, 8-3/4"	125	188	250
Defence, 1896	75	112	150
Derby cap pistol, cast iron, Hubley, 1930, 7"	30	45	60
Desert Patrol Luger & Silencer, Marx, 1960s, 10"	20	25	35
Detroit cap pistol, cast iron, 1910, 6-5/8" long	65	98	130
Dick cap automatic, cast iron, Hubley, 1940, "Made in U.S.A.," 4-1/8"	30	45	60

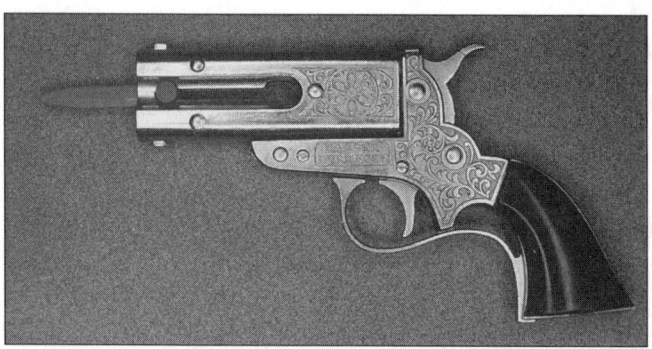

Dagger Derringer die-cast pistol, Hubley, 1955, $70

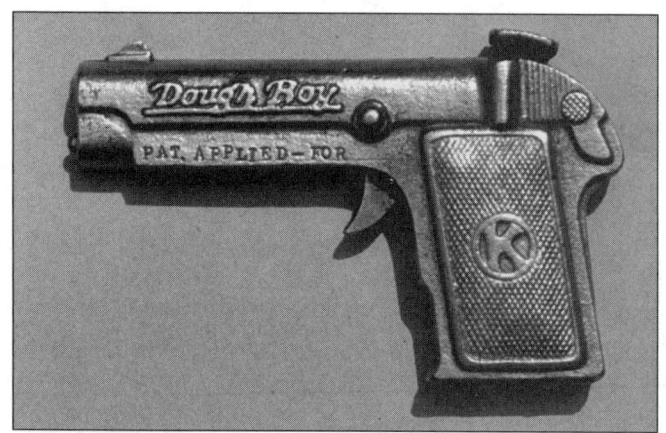

Doughboy cast-iron automatic pistol, Kilgore, 1920, $90

Dragnet Detective Repeating Revolver Cap Gun, c. 1955, $55

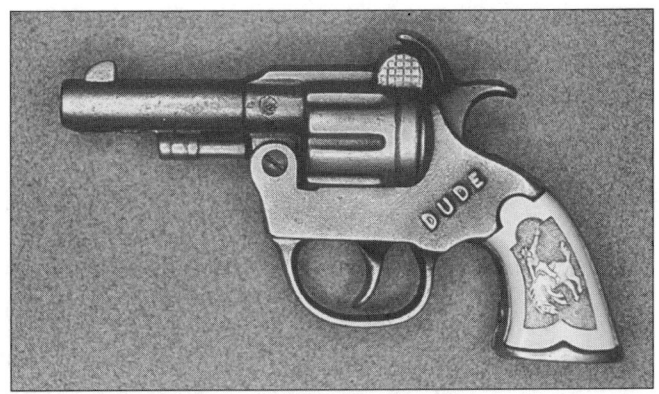

Dude cast-iron cap pistol with plastic grips, Kenton, 1941, $80

	C6	C8	C10
Dick cap automatic, die-cast, 4-1/4"	20	25	30
Dick cap pistol, cast iron, Hubley, 1930, 6"	30	45	60
DIK cap pistol, cast iron, "Pat. Sept. 11-23," Kenton, 1935, 4-3/4"	27	41	55
Dixie (1888-1890)	75	112	150
Dixie cap pistol, cast iron, "Made in U.S.A. Pat. Appld. For," Kenton, 1935, 6-1/4"	42	63	85
Doc cap pistol, cast iron, "Pat. Sept. 11-23," Kenton, 1926, 4-1/2"	40	50	60
Dolphin cap pistol, animated	400	600	800
Double barrel shotgun, steel and wood, Wyandotte, c. 1935, 25"	52	78	105
Doughboy cap automatic, cast iron, "Made in U.S.A.,"Kilgore, 1920, 5"	45	68	90
Dragnet Detective Special Repeating Revolver Cap Gun, c. 1955	27	41	55
Duck cap pistol, animated, cast iron, 1884, 3-3/4" long	2500	3000	5000
Dude cap pistol, cast iron w/plastic grips, Kenton, 1941, 6-1/2"	40	60	80
Dude pistol, cast iron, "Pat. Mar. 22 '87," Stevens, 1887, 3-1/2"	75	112	150

	C6	C8	C10
Eagle cap pistol, cast iron, "Pat. June 17, 1890," Stevens, 1995, 7-1/2"	82	123	165
Eagle, c. 1940	40	60	80
Echo cap pistol, cast iron, six-shooter, 1881	425	638	850
Echo cap pistol, cast iron, Stevens, 1920, 4-1/4"	30	40	50
Echo cap pistol, cast iron, Stevens, 1930, "Made in U.S.A.," 4-1/2"	30	40	50
Electronic Space Gun, plastic w/flashlight gun, Remco	37	56	75
Excelsior cap pistol, cast iron, "Pat'd Apr. 22, '73," Stevens, 1875, 5-1/4"	125	188	250
Federal cap automatic, cast iron w/removable clip to hold caps, Kilgore, 1940, 4-7/8"	37	56	75
Federal cap pistol, cast iron, "Pat. Dec. 14; Made in U.S.A.," Kilgore, 1920	37	56	75
Federal cap pistol, cast iron, Kilgore, 1920, 5-1/2"	25	38	50
Federal No. 2 cap pistol, cast iron, Kilgore, 1925, 6-3/8"	60	90	120
Federal-Kilgore No.1 cap pistol, cast iron, Kilgore, 1925, 5-1/4"	25	38	50
Fido, 1910, 4"	50	60	70

Duck animated cast-iron cap pistol, 1884, $5000

Federal-Kilgore No. 1 cast-iron cap pistol, Kilgore, 1925, $50

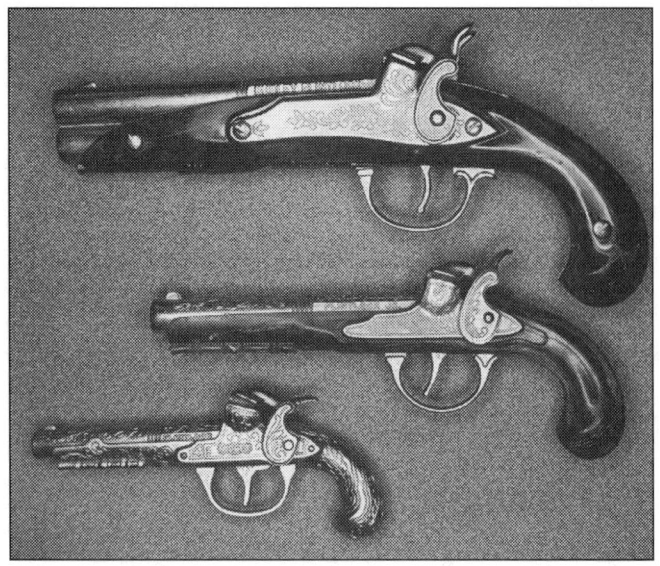

Top to Bottom: Flintlock die-cast pistol, Hubley, $70; Flintlock Jr. die-cast pistol, Hubley, $35; Flintlock Midget die-cast pistol, Hubley, $30

	C6	C8	C10
Firecracker pistol, cast iron w/filigree handle	100	150	200
Firecracker pistol, five-barrel, iron and brass, 1877	500	800	1200
First No. 1, 1920, 6-3/4"	135	190	270
Flash cap pistol, cast iron, "Pat'd," Hubley, 1934, 6-1/4"	45	55	75
Flintlock Junior, die-cast, Hubley	17	26	35
Flintlock Midget, die-cast, Hubley	15	22	30
Flintlock, die-cast metal, Hubley No. 280, 9-1/4"	35	52	70
Flying Saucer Gun, Auburn Rubber, 1964	12	18	25
The Forty Five cap pistol, cast iron, "Made in U.S.A.,"unusual shape, National, 1928, 11-1/8"	75	100	125
Four Way cap pistol, cast iron, "Pat. Appld. For," Kenton, 1930; shoots pea or dart, rubber band and cap	150	225	300
Fox cap pistol, cast iron, Hubley, 1935, 4-1/2"	30	40	50

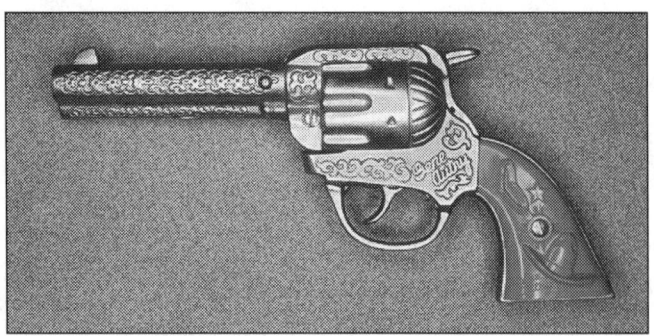

Gene Autry cast-iron cap pistol, Kenton, 1939, $175

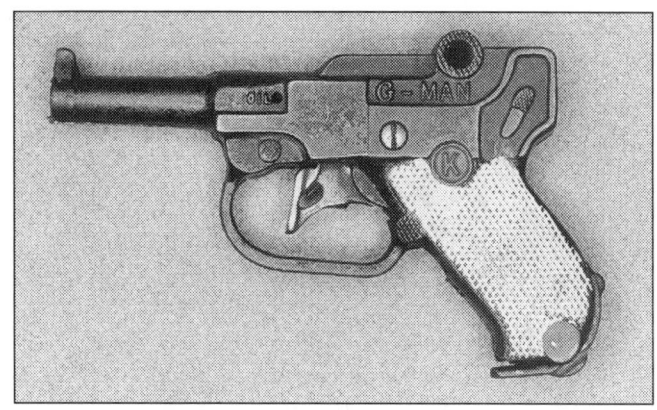

G-Man cast-iron automatic, Kilgore, $200

	C6	C8	C10
Frontier cap pistol, cast iron, dog's head atopthe barrel facing hammer, "Pat. June 21, 1887 and June 17, 1890," Ives, 1890	200	300	400
Gang Busters Crusade Against Crime Sub-Machine Gun, Marx	125	188	250
Gem pistol, cast iron, Stevens, 1900, 3"	27	41	55
Gene Autry bull's eye cap pistol, cast iron, "Gene Autry" signature on grips, Kenton, 1950s, 6-1/2"	125	188	250
Gene Autry cap pistol, cast iron Kenton, 1939, 8-3/8"	88	130	175
Gene Autry cap pistol, cast iron, "Made in U.S.A. Pat. Appl'd For," Kenton, 1939, 6-1/2"	75	112	150
Gene Autry cap pistol, cast iron, "Made in U.S.A.," Kenton, 1940, red grips, 6-1/2"	75	112	150
Gene Autry cap pistol, cast iron, Kenton, 1940, "Made in U.S.A.," 6-1/2"	90	135	180
Gip, 1900	25	38	50
G-Man Automatic Sparkling Pistol, aluminum, Marx No. 43	58	90	115
G-Man Automatic Sparkling Pistol, tin, Marx No. 44	58	90	115
G-Man cap automatic, cast iron, Kilgore, 1935, 6"; looks like German Luger, removable magazine holds caps	100	150	200
G-Man clicker pistol, tin, black	25	35	45
G-Man gun, Marx No. 707	37	56	75
G-Man silent alarm pistol, Marx No. 54, tin	25	35	45
G-Man sparkling Sub-Machine Gun, tin, Marx, 26" long	75	100	150
G-Man Sparkling Tommy Gun, tin litho w/wood stock, Marx, 1936	165	250	330
G-Man Wind-Up Machine Gun, tin, miniature, 1940s	20	30	40
G-Man wind-up spark pistol, steel w/painted finish	60	100	125

	C6	C8	C10
G-Man wind-up spark pistol, steel w/nickel finish and jewels on grip 60	100	125
G-Man, Bakelite-framed cap automatic, Kilgore, 1940, 6" 50	75	100
Go Bang 100	150	200
Guard cap pistol, cast iron, Kilgore, "Made in U.S.A.,"1935, 6-1/4" 30	45	60
Hanson-Lindsborg K.S. firecracker pistol, cast iron, "Pat. Appl'd For," Hanson, 1905; fires firecracker, 6-3/8" ... 65	98	130
Hawk automatic cap pistol, die-cast, Hubley No. 2343, 5-3/4" 32	48	65
H-Bar-O cap pistol, cast iron, Kilgore, 1925, "Made in U.S.A." 7-1/2" 60	75	125
Hero Auto cap automatic, cast iron, Stevens, 1920, 4-3/4" 45	65	85
Hero cap pistol, cast iron, Stevens, 1937, 5-1/4" 30	45	60
Hi-Ho cap pistol, cast iron, "Made in U.S.A.," Stevens, 1940, 7" 37	56	75
Hi-Ho cap pistol, cast iron, "Pat. Sept. 11-23," Kenton, 1940, 5-1/8" 37	56	75
Hi-Ho cap pistol, cast iron, Kilgore, 1940, 6-1/2" 37	56	75
Hi-Ho cap pistol, cast iron, Stevens, 1940, "Made in U.S.A.," 7" 37	56	75
Hi-Ranger cap pistol, cast iron, Stevens, 1940, 7-3/4" 50	70	90
Hopalong Cassidy Revolver, "Hopalong" on both sides of handle, Wyandotte, 1950s, 9" 180	270	360
Hopalong Cassidy Revolver, with bust of Hopalong, Schmidt, 1950s, 10" 135	200	270
Hub cap pistol, cast iron, Hubley, 1940, 6-1/4" 25	38	50
Hustler pistol, cast iron 55	82	110
Ibex, Stevens, 1895, 4-1/2" 60	90	120
Imperial cap pistol, cast iron, Kilgore, 1935, 5-1/4" 60	80	110

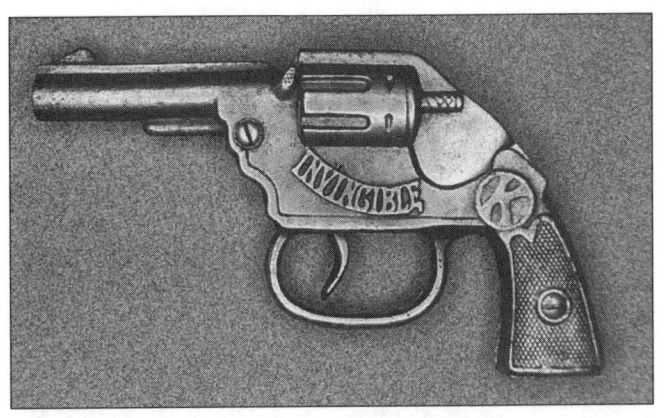
Invincible cast-iron cap pistol, Kilgore, 1935, $60

	C6	C8	C10
Indian cap pistol, cast iron, Kenton, 1931, 8-1/8" 60	90	120
Invincible cap pistol, cast iron, Kilgore, 1935, "Pat. Dec. 14," 5-1/4" 30	45	60
Invincible New 50 Shot, 1930 30	45	60
Jack Armstrong airplane gun, Daisy, 1936.. 45	60	100
Jax cap pistol, cast iron, "Pat. Sept. 11-23," Kenton, 1930, 4" 22	33	45
Jet Jr. space cap gun, die-cast, Stevens, 1949, 6-1/2" 110	165	220
Johnnie's Little Gun 700	1100	1700
Jr. Police Chief cap automatic, cast iron, Kenton, 1938, "Made in U.S.A.," 3-7/8" 30	45	60
Jr. Ranger .32 cal., 1925 25	38	50
Jumbo cap pistol, cast iron, "Pat. June 17, 1890: Made in U.S.A.," Stevens, 1895, 9-1/2" 110	165	220
Junior Police .32 cap pistol, cast iron, "Hubley; Pat'd. 2088891," Hubley, 1940, 5-1/4" 30	45	60
Junior Six-Shooter cap pistol, cast iron, Kilgore, 1935, 5-1/2" 30	45	60
Just Out animated cap pistol, cast iron, 1880s.. 2000	3500	6200
Kido cap pistol, cast iron, "Kenton Made in U.S.A.," Kenton, 1936, 5-3/8" 25	38	50
Kilgore cap pistol, cast iron, Kilgore, 1910, 5" 42	63	85
Kilgore cap pistol, cast iron, Kilgore, 1912, 5-1/4" 42	63	85
King cap pistol, cast iron, Pat. Aug. 1879.. 100	150	200
King cap pistol, "Made in U.S.A.," Stevens, 1925, 4-3/4" 50	60	75
Kit Carson cap pistol, cast iron, "Pat. Sept.11-23," Kenton, 1928, 9" 50	75	100
Las cap pistol, cast iron 80	120	160
Lasso 'Em Bill cap gun, cast iron, red rubies in handle w/turning cylinder, 1930, 9" 145	220	290

Hopalong Cassidy Revolver, Wyandotte, 1950s, $360

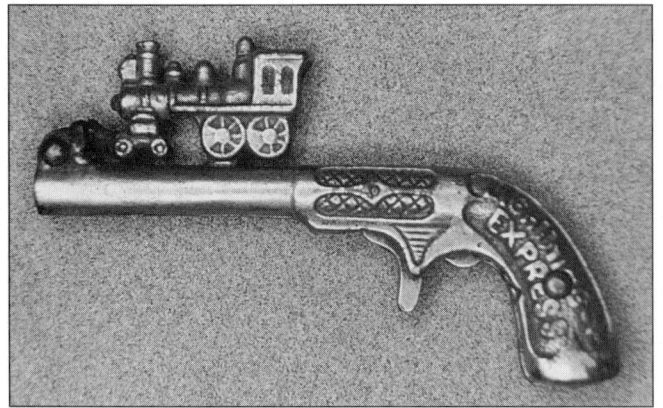

Lightning Express mechanical cap pistol, 1913, $600

	C6	C8	C10
Lawmaker cap pistol, cast iron, Kenton, 1941, 8-3/8"	100	150	200
Liberty, 1875	162	243	325
Liberty, tin, ornate, c. 1912	35	52	70
Lightning Express mechanical cap pistol, Arcade or Kenton, 1913, 5"; train slides forward along barrel to explode cap at end	300	450	600
Lion head cap pistol, cast iron, Pat. 1890, Stevens 5-1/4"	200	300	400
Lion, Ives, 1887, 3-3/4"	300	450	600
Lion, Stevens, 1890, 5-1/4"	200	300	400
Little Bill cap pistol, cast iron, Kilgore, 1925, 5"	25	35	50
Little Chief Firefighter water squirt gun	10	15	20
Lone Eagle cap pistol, cast iron, Kilgore, 1929, 5-1/4"	60	85	125
Lone Ranger .45 Flasher Flashlight Pistol, Marx	35	50	70
Lone Ranger cap pistol, cast iron, Kilgore, 1938, 8-1/2"	170	255	340
Lone Ranger Click Pistol, Marx, 9"	55	82	110
Lone Ranger Pop Gun, tin w/picture of Lone Ranger on handles, 1950s,	40	50	70
Lone Ranger Sparkling Pop Pistol, tin litho, Marx No. 096	40	55	80

Top to Bottom: Lone Eagle cast-iron cap pistol, 1929, $125; Patrol cast-iron cap pistol, Hubley, 1939, $55

	C6	C8	C10
Lone Ranger Western Gun Collection, six miniature guns mounted on a card w/history of guns on back, c. 1939	75	100	150
Long Boy cap pistol, cast iron, "Made in U.S.A.," Kilgore, 1922, 11"	80	120	160
Long Tom cap pistol, cast iron, Kilgore, 1939, 10-3/8"	250	375	500
Look Out cap pistol, dogs head, cast iron	300	450	600
Luger water pistol, plastic, Park Plastics, 7", 1960s	10	15	20
M&L water pistol, die-cast, w/rubber ball	10	15	20
Machine Gun, cast iron cap automatic w/crank, "Ra-Ta-Ta-Tat," Kilgore, 1938, 5"; caps fired rapidly when the crank is turned	195	300	390

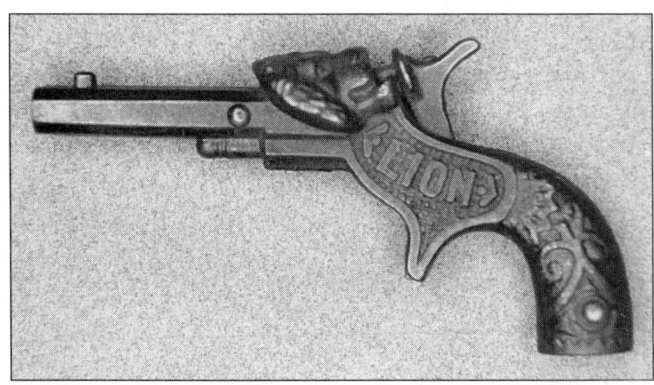

Lion, Ives, 1887, $600

Lone Ranger cast-iron cap pistol, Kilgore, 1938, $340

	C6	C8	C10
Magic.22 cal. blank pistol, cast iron, ornate, has second trigger to open barrel for loading, "Pat'd Oct. 17, '99,"Kenton, 1900, 6-1/4"	85	130	170
Man from U.N.C.L.E. cap gun, Ideal, c. 1965	35	52	70
Marx miniatures of Famous Guns: Civil War Revolver, Mare's Leg, Tommy Gun, Saddle Rifle, each	30	55	75
Mascot cap automatic, cast iron, Kilgore, 1936, 3-7/8"	27	41	55
Master cap automatic, cast iron, Kilgore, 1922, 4-5/8"	27	41	55

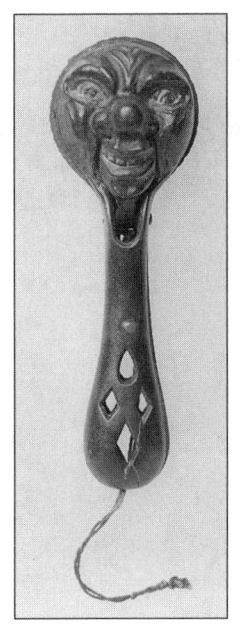

Moonface capshooter, Stevens, c. 1880, $1000

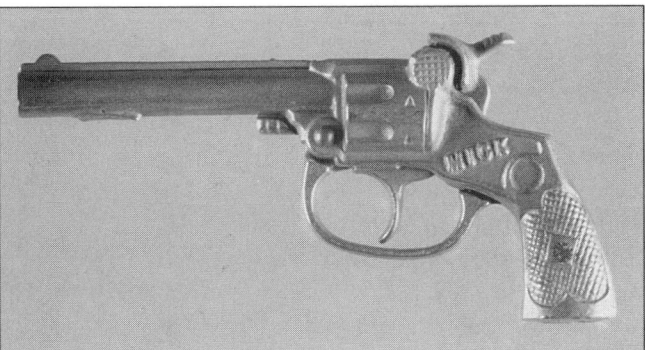

Mick, 1930, $65

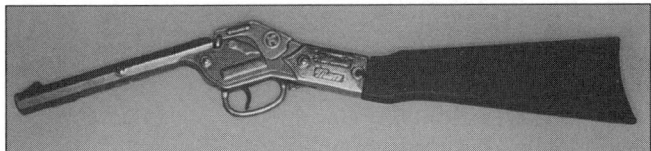

Minute Man cast-iron cap rifle, Kilgore, 1936, $350

Monkey and Coconut animated cap pistol, 1870s-1880s, $750

	C6	C8	C10
Master cap automatic, cast iron, Kilgore, 1930, 4-5/8"	60	90	120
Match-shooting pistol, double-trigger, cast iron, large, Stephens PA, 1873	125	188	250
The Mauser, maker unknown, 1915, 6-3/4"	250	375	500
Me and My Buddy animated pistol, steel w/figure, Wyandotte	55	82	110
Medrick Repeater	75	112	150
Mick, 1930	32	48	65
Minute Man cap rifle, cast iron, "Pat. Appl'd For, Made in U.S.A.," Kilgore, 1936, 20"	175	250	350
Monkey and Coconut animated cap pistol, 1870s-1880s, 4-1/4"	400	550	750
Monkeys animated cap pistol, Lockwood, 1882, 4-1/4"	550	825	1100
Moonface capshooter, Stevens, c. 1880	500	750	1000
Mordt cap pistol, cast iron, maker unknown, 1930, 8"	60	90	120

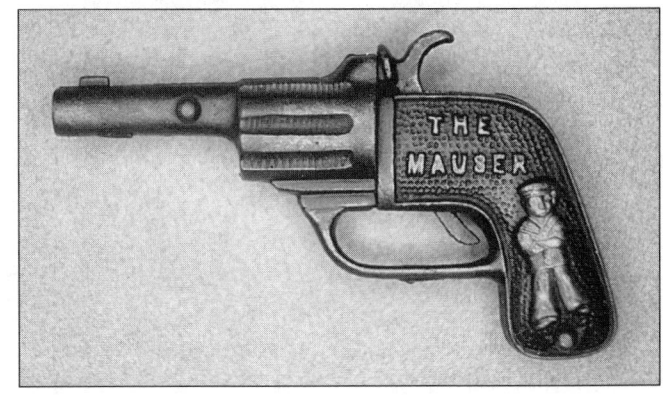

The Mauser, maker unknown, 1915, $500

Mordt cast-iron cap pistol, Stevens, c. 1880, $120

	C6	C8	C10
Mountie cap automatic, die-cast, Kilgore No. 6, 6", 1950	20	30	40
National cap automatic, cast iron, National, 1915, 3-3/4"	35	50	65
National cap automatic, cast iron, National, 1925, 4-1/4"	40	60	80
National cap automatic, cast iron, "Made in U.S.A.,"National, 1925, 5-1/4"	42	50	60
National cap pistol, cast iron, National, 1909, 4-7/8"	35	50	65
National cap pistol, cast iron, National, 1911, 5"	35	50	65

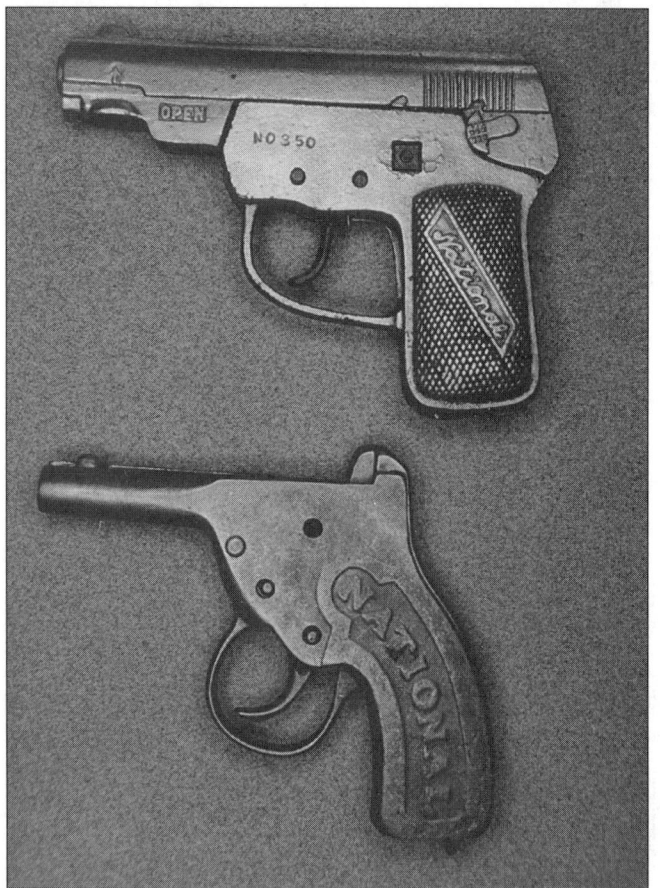

Top to Bottom: National No. 350 cast-iron cap pistol, National, 1928, $80; National cast-iron cap pistol, National, 1911, $65

National Liquid Pistol, Parker/Stearns, 1900, $110

	C6	C8	C10
National cap pistol, cast iron, Stevens, 1920, 3-5/8"	35	55	65
National Liquid Pistol, Parker/Stearns, 1900, 4-7/8"	55	82	110
National No. 350 cap automatic, cast iron, National, 1928, 5-1/2"	45	60	80
National No. 380 cap pistol, cast iron, National, 1930s, 7"	40	55	70
Navy cap pistol, cast iron, "Pat. Sept. 11-23," Kenton, 1930, 5-1/2"	37	56	75
Navy double-barrel cap pistol	150	225	300
Navy, 1878	125	188	250
Navy, 1907	75	112	150
Navy, 1925	35	52	60
Nemo cap pistol, cast iron, maker unknown, 1910, 6-5/8"	45	68	90
New 50-Shot Invincible cap pistol, cast iron, Kilgore, 1930, 5-1/2"	35	50	65
Nigger Head cap pistol, cast iron, Ives, 1887, 4-1/2"	400	500	600
No. 500 (like Luger), 1935	55	82	110

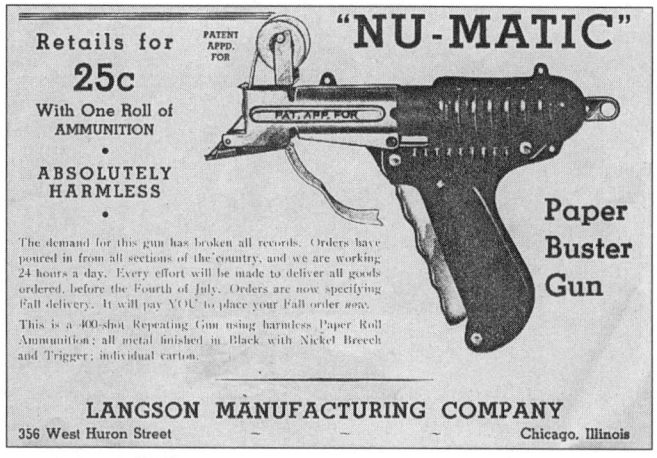

Ad for Langson Manufacturing's Nu-Matic Paper Buster Gun; currently valued at $45, the Nu-Matic originally retailed for 25 cents.

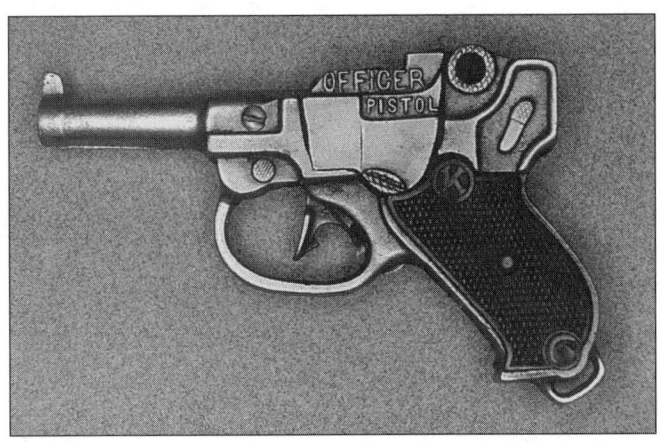

Official Pistol cast-iron cap automatic, Kilgore, 1940, $125

Hubley's Pirate in it's original holster, $120-125

	C6	C8	C10
Novelty cap pistol, cast iron, "Pat. Appl'd For," Stevens, 1885, 5"	150	225	300
Nu-Matic Paper Buster Gun, Langson Manufacturing Co., 7"	22	33	45
Officer Pistol cap automatic, cast iron, Kilgore, 1940, 6"; modeled after German Luger	62	93	125
Official Detective-Type Sub-Machine Gun, Marx No. 2146	50	75	100
Oh Boy automatic cap, "Made in U.S.A.; Pat'd., Aug. 8, 1933," Kilgore, 1933, 4-1/8"; works both as automatic and crank-operated rapid-fire gun	85	128	170
Oh Boy cap pistol, cast iron, National, 1922, 5-1/2"	35	52	70
Oh Boy cap pistol, iron, "Pat. Sept. 11-23," Kenton,1930, 5-1/8"	25	38	50
OK cap automatic, cast iron, maker unknown, 1935, 3-3/4"	35	52	70
Old Ironsides cap pistol, cast iron, 10-3/4"	65	98	130
Our Army Forever	175	263	350
P-38 steel clicker pistol, c. 1945	20	30	40
Padlock cup pistol, w/key, Hubley, 4-1/4" ...	92	140	185
Pal cap automatic, cast iron, Kilgore, 1930, 4"	25	35	50
Pal cap pistol, cast iron, Kilgore, 1930, 4" ...	20	30	45

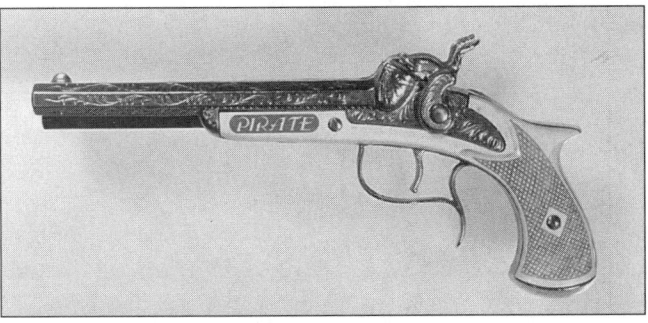

Patrol cast-iron cap pistol, Hubley, 1941, $125

	C6	C8	C10
Pat pistol, cast iron, Kenton, 1935, "Pat. Sept. 11-23," 6-1/8"	25	35	45
Patrol cap pistol, cast iron, "Made in U.S.A.," Hubley, 1939, 6"	35	45	55
Pawnee Bill, c. 1940	100	150	200
Pea Matic pea-shooting repeater, steel	15	22	30
Pea Shooter, pewter, highly embossed handle	35	52	70
Peacemaker cap pistol, cast iron, "Made in U.S.A.," Stevens, 1940, 8-1/2"	68	100	135
Peerless, 1905, 5-1/2"	70	105	140
Persuader cap pistol, cast iron, "Made in U.S.A., Pat. Appld. For," Kenton, 1939, 6-3/8"	70	105	140
Pet, die-cast, Hubley, 4-1/4"	10	15	20
Ping-Pong rifle	20	25	30
Pioneer, die-cast, Hubley	60	90	120
Pirate cap pistol, die-cast zinc w/cast-iron hammers and trigger, two-barrel, two hammers that cock, Hubley, 1941, 9-3/8"	45	75	125
Pirate cap pistol, die-cast zinc, nonfiring, Hubley, 1950	60	90	120
Pistol Packin' Mama, wood w/cardboard sides, four revolving triggers, shoots wooden pegs, c. 1944, 8-1/2"	30	40	50
Pluck cap pistol, cast iron, "Made in U.S.A.," Stevens, 1930, 3-1/2"	15	20	25
Pluck cap pistol, cast iron, 1895	62	93	125
Police automatic cap pistol, steel, 8"	20	30	40
Police automatic, 1935	40	60	80
Police cap automatic, Bakelite-framed Kilgore, 1940, 5-1/4"	55	83	110
Police Chief gun and leather shoulder holster set, Wyandotte, c. late 1940s	35	45	65
Police Chief, Kenton, 1938, 4-5/8"	40	50	65
Polo, Ives, 1878, 6"	75	90	125
Pono cap pistol, cast iron, "Pat. Sept. 11-23," Kenton, 1936, 5-1/8"	30	45	60
Pop gun-rifle, double-barrel, Marx No. 230	50	75	100

Presto cast-iron cap automatic pistol, Kilgore, 1940, $60

	C6	C8	C10
Powder keg cap bomb, cast iron	85	128	170
Premier Safety, 1914	37	56	75
President, cap pistol, cast iron, Kilgore, 1925, 8-3/4"	40	60	80
Presto cap automatic, cast iron, Kilgore, 1940, 5-1/8"	30	45	60
Private Eye cap pistol, Kilgore, 6-1/2"	12	18	25
Punch and Judy animated cap pistol, cast iron, Punch explodes cap w/nose on Judy's back, Ives, 1880, 5"	450	600	750
Ranger cap pistol, cast iron, Kilgore, 1940, 8-1/2"	35	52	70
Ranger cap pistol, cast iron, Kilgore, 1939, 8-1/2"	85	130	175
Ranger cap pistol, cast iron, Kilgore, 1920, 5-3/8"	50	60	75
Ranger, 1890-1900	80	120	160
Red Ranger clicker pistol, steel, Wyandotte, c. 1939, black, red "jewel," 8"	40	60	80

Punch and Judy animated cap pistol, 1880, $750

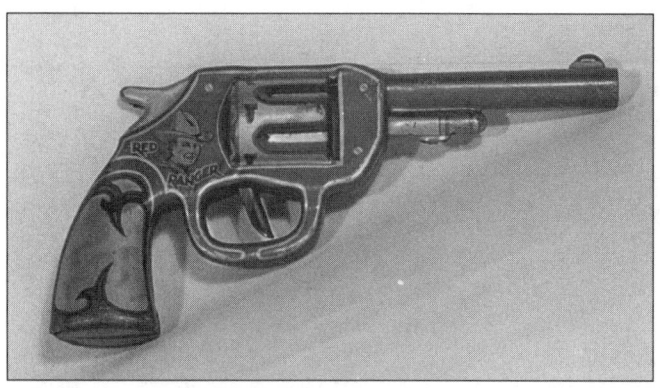

Red Ranger steel clicker pistol, Wyandotte, c. 1941, $60

	C6	C8	C10
Red Ranger clicker pistol, steel, Wyandotte, c. 1941, 8"	30	45	60
Red Ranger rifle, plastic, Wyandotte	30	50	65
Red Ranger six-shooter repeater, steel w/plastic handles and revolving cylinder, Wyandotte	37	56	75
Remington .36, die-cast, Hubley	50	70	95
Repeater cap pistol, cast iron, "Mammoth Cap; Made in U.S.A.," Stevens, 1930, 6-1/4"	70	105	140
Repeater Space Gun, Wyandotte, 1930s	35	52	70
Repeating Cap Pistol, die-cast, Marx No. G375	20	30	40
Rex cap automatic, cast iron, Dent, 1914, 4-1/8"	30	45	60
Rex cap automatic, cast iron, Kilgore, 1939, 3-7/8"	35	52	70
Rex Mars Planet Patrol X-92 Gun	100	150	200
Rifleman Flip Special cap rifle, die-cast plastic, Hubley, 32-1/2"	82	125	165
RIP, c. 1909	75	100	125
Rob Roy, c. 1875	150	225	300
Rocket Ship Space Pistol, Irwin, late 1940s	30	45	60

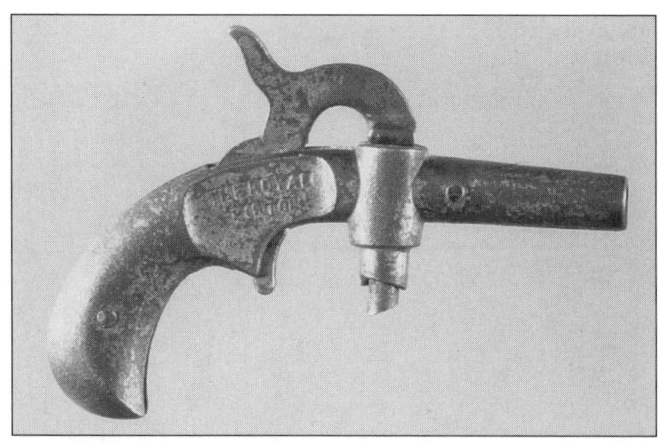

The Royal Pistol cast-iron mechanical cap pistol, Iver Johnson, 1938, $800

	C6	C8	C10
Rodeo cap pistol, cast iron, Hubley, 1938, 7"	35	55	75
Rodeo cap pistol, cast iron, Hubley, 11-1/4"	125	165	200
Rotor Fifty cap pistol, cast iron, Kilgore, 1930, 6-1/8"	50	70	95
Roy Rogers cap pistol, cast iron, Hubley, 1940, 8-1/4"	250	375	500
Roy Rogers cap pistol, cast iron, Kilgore, 1940, 10-1/4"	300	450	600
The Royal Pistol, mechanical cap, cast iron, "Pat. Apr. 23, '78," Iver Johnson 1878, approx. 5"; fires spring-loaded top that is attached to bottom of the barrel	400	600	800
S & W cap gun, cast iron, 6"	20	25	30
Safety cap pistol, cast iron, "Pat. Mch. 25, '24," Hubley, 1924, 5"	30	45	60
Safety First cap automatic, cast iron, "Safe," maker unknown, 1920, 3-3/8"	30	45	60
Sambo cap pistol, cast iron, "Pat. June 21, 1887," Ives, 1887, 4-3/8"; hammer hits head	175	263	350
Say I bomb, cast iron	100	130	175
Scout cap pistol, cast iron, "Made in U.S.A.," Stevens, 1935, 6-3/4"	35	50	65
Scout cap pistol, cast iron, "Pat. June 17, 1890," Stevens, 1890, 7"	40	60	80
Scout cap pistol, cast iron, Stevens, 1940, 6-1/8"	35	50	65
Scout cap pistol, tin, automatic, 1914	30	40	50
Scout Jr. cap pistol, cast iron, "Made in U.S.A.," Stevens, 1935, 6"	35	50	65
Scoutmaster, Dent, 6-3/4"	65	98	130
Senator cap pistol, cast iron, marked w/star and "K," Kilgore, 1925, 7"	50	75	100
Sharpshooter cap rifle, Hubley, 37"	75	112	150
The Sheriff cap pistol, cast iron, Stevens, 1940, 8-1/2"	75	112	150
Shoo Fly cap pistol, cast iron	90	135	180
Shoot the Hat mechanical cap pistol, cast iron	475	715	950
Shootin' Shell Buckle Gun, Mattel, 1959	42	63	85
Shotgun, double-barreled, steel, wooden stock, 28"; both barrels break down, cock and shoot	35	52	70
Siren Signal Pistol, hard plastic, Marx, 1950s,	20	30	40
Siren Signal Pistol, tin, Marx, 1940s	20	30	40
Siren Sparkling Airplane Pistol, tin litho, Marx No. 182	50	75	100
Siren Sparkling Pistol, tin litho, Marx No. 164	45	68	90

	C6	C8	C10
Six Shooter Automatic cap pistol (not an automatic), cast iron, Kilgore, 1934, 6-1/2"	65	85	110
Six Shooter cap pistol, cast iron w/plastic grips, "Made in U.S.A." on hammer, Kilgore, 1938, 6-1/2"	60	80	100
Six Shooter cap pistol, cast iron w/plastic grips, Kilgore, 1935, 6-1/2"	60	80	100
Six Shooter cap pistol, cast iron, Kilgore, 1930, 7"	40	60	80
Six Shooter cap pistol, cast iron, Kilgore, 1935, 6-1/2"	40	60	80
Six Shooter cap pistol, cast iron, "Made in U.S.A." on hammer, Kilgore, 1938, 6-1/2"	40	60	80
Sliko cap pistol, cast iron, "Pat. Sept. 11-23," Kenton, 1930, 6-1/4"	30	45	55
Snappy Jack, English, c. 1935	45	60	75
Snappy, Dent, 1930, 5"	35	45	60
Space Gun, Remco	25	38	50
Space Rocket Gun, plastic, M&L, 9"; fires two Space Rocket Spheres	62	93	125
Sparkling Atom Buster, die-cast, Marx No. 46	30	45	60
Sparkling Pop Gun, Marx No. 198	25	38	50
Sparkling Space Gun, Marx	45	68	90
Sparkling Sure Shot	20	30	40
Spitfire cap automatic, cast iron, Stevens, 1940, "Made in U.S.A.," 4-5/8"	40	50	60
Sport cap pistol, cast iron, "Made in U.S.A.," Kilgore, 1930, 7-1/2"	35	50	65
Sport, Ives, 1875, 4"	175	263	350
Spud Gun, die-cast, B.J. Cossman, Hollywood, Calif., No. 504	30	45	60
Spud Gun, tin, automatic, c. 1940	25	35	45
Spy cap pistol, cast iron, "Made in U.S.A.," Kilgore, 1936, 4-1/4"	30	45	60
Star cap pistol, cast iron, Stevens, 1910, 6-1/4"	35	52	70

Sport, Ives, 1874, $350

	C6	C8	C10
Star cap pistol, pot metal, steer on handle 5		8	10
Stephans, Pat., 1873, 5" 120		180	240
Streamline Siren Sparkling Pistol, tin litho, Marx No. 155 35		52	50
Sun cap pistol, cast iron 125		150	175
Super cap pistol, cast iron, "Pat. Sept. 11-23," Kenton, 1930, 8-3/4" 45		60	75
Super Nu-Matic Paper Buster Gun 20		30	40
Sure Shot cap automatic, cast iron, Hubley, 1940, 4-1/4" 35		45	60
Sure Shot, 1870-1880 125		150	175
Target cap pistol, cast iron, "Pat.1,488,046,"Hubley, 1935, 8" 50		75	100
Targeteer pistol, Daisy 45		68	90
Teddy cap pistol, cast iron, Hubley, 1938, 5-5/8" 25		38	50
Terror cap automatic, cast iron, "Pat. Jan 16 '15," Dent, 1915, 4-1/4" 40		60	80
Terror cap pistol, cast iron w/people embossed, 1882 175		260	350
Terror, 1888 250		375	500
Terror, 1925 30		45	60
Texan cap pistol, cast iron, "Made in U.S.A.," Hubley, 1940, 9-1/4" 100		150	200
Texan Jr. cap pistol, cast iron, Hubley, 1941, "Made in U.S.A.," 8-1/8" 88		132	175
Texas cap pistol, cast iron, "Pat. No. 1993916," Kenton, 1936, 5-3/4" 60		90	125
Texas cap pistol, cast iron, "Pat. Sept. 11-23," Kenton, 1930, 6-5/8" 45		68	90
Texas Centennial, 1936, 11" 225		338	450
Texas Jack, Ives, 1886, 9-3/8" 150		225	300
Thunder-Burp machine gun, Mattel, 1960s 40		60	80
Thundergun rifle, Marx, 36" long 100		150	200
Tiger cap pistol, cast iron, Hubley, 1935, 6-7/8" 27		41	55
Tiger cap pistol, cast iron, Stevens, 1915, 6-3/4" 32		48	65

Texan cast-iron cap pistol, Hubley, 1940, $200

	C6	C8	C10
Tin Tin Gun, Woodhaven Metal Stamping Co., 3 x 5"; turn crank and it makes noise 15		22	30
Tip Top cap pistol, cast iron, 1880, Stevens, 3-1/2" 125		150	175
Trapper cap automatic, cast iron, Kilgore, 1935, 4-1/2"; fires only single shot, but roll of caps can be carried in the grip 45		68	90
Triumph, 1878, 5-1/8" 125		175	225
Trooper cap pistol, cast iron Hubley, 1938, 5-1/8" 20		30	40
Trooper Safety cap pistol, cast iron Kilgore, 1930, 10""Pat. Pend; Made in U.S.A.," operates either as straight cap pistol or can be fired w/crank 85		128	170
Trooper Safety cap pistol, cast iron, Kilgore, 1925, 10-1/4" 75		112	150
Trooper Safety, 1925 35		52	70
Trooper, die-cast, Hubley 6-1/2" 25		38	50
Two Time pistol, cast iron cap and rubber band, "Pat. Appld. For," Kenton, 1930, 9-1/4" 85		125	175
U.S. Navy, 1885, 6-1/2" 65		98	130
U.S.A. Liquid Pistol water pistol, cast iron Parker-Stearns, 1896, "Pat. June 30, 1896," 4-3/4" 65		90	125
Victor pistol, cast iron 125		150	175
Victor pistol, cast iron, Stevens, 1924, 12" 150		200	250
Villa cap pistol, cast iron, "Made in U.S.A.," Dent, 1934, 4-3/4" 40		50	60
Volunteer cap pistol, cast iron, "Pat. April 22, '73" Stevens, 1873 125		188	250
War cap pistol, cast iron, "Pat. Sept. 11-23," Kenton, 1930, 4-1/4" 35		50	65
Warrior cap pistol, cast iron, "Pat. Appld. For, 1926,"maker unknown, 1926, 9"..... 75		112	150
Water Pistol, unmarked, Wyandotte 30		45	60
Water Pistol, Wyandotte No. 41 30		45	60
Western cap pistol, cast iron w/plastic grips,Kenton, 1931, 7-1/4" 65		98	130
Western cap pistol, cast iron, "Pat. Sept. 11-23," Kenton, 1935, 7"............... 35		48	65
Western cap pistol, cast iron, Kenton, 1939, "Made in U.S.A.," 7-1/2" 30		45	60
Westo cap pistol, cast iron, "Kenton," Kenton, 1936, 7" 30		45	60
Westo pistol, cast iron, Kenton, "Kenton," 1938, 7" 35		45	55
Whoopie cap pistol, cast iron, Kenton, 1932, 5-7/8".. 35		45	60

	C6	C8	C10
Wild West cap pistol, cast iron, "Made in U.S.A.," National, 1930, 6-1/2"	35	52	70
Wild West cap pistol, cast iron, Kenton, 1926, 11-1/2"	125	175	225
Wild West cap rifle, w/sight, Marx, 30"	48	72	95
Winner cap automatic, cast iron, Hubley, 1940, 4-3/8"	35	45	60
Woodsman cap automatic, cast iron, "Patented; Made in U.S.A.," Stevens, 1938, 5-1/4"	60	85	110
Xtra pistol, cast iron, "Made in U.S.A.," Kenton, 1936, 5"	30	45	55

	C6	C8	C10
Yank cap pistol, cast iron, 1880	125	175	225
Yankee cap pistol, cast iron, Stevens, 1895, 5-1/2"	125	175	225
York cap pistol, cast iron, "Pat. Sept. 11-23," Kenton, 1930, 7"	40	55	75
Young Sportsman, wood, c. 1868	75	112	150
Zip cap pistol, cast iron, Hubley, 1930, 5"	30	45	55
Zip cap pistol, cast iron, Hubley, 1938, 6"	30	45	55
Zulu cap pistol, cast iron w/decoration of African warrior with spear pursuing bird, maker unknown, 1890, 6-5/8"	150	225	300

IDEAL DOLLS

Ideal Toy Corporation, one of America's largest and oldest manufacturers of dolls and toys, produced high quality dolls for over eighty years. Each decade of this century saw a wildly popular Ideal doll. Doll collectors depending on their age may remember playing with such Ideal dolls as Flossie Flirt (1920s), Shirley Temple and Betsy Wetsy (1930s), Toni (1940s), Miss Revlon (1950s), Patti Playpal and Tammy (1960s) or Crissy (1970s). Many of the Ideal dolls are now very desirable to doll collectors and, since they were mass-produced, affordable.

Always an innovator, Ideal used new technology to produce their dolls. Ideal dolls come in materials ranging from cloth, celluloid, composition, hard rubber, latex "magic skin" rubber, hard plastic, injection-molded vinyl, rotation-molded vinyl and blow-molded vinyl. Ideal is responsible for many of the technological breakthroughs in doll manufacturing and holds dozens of patents for innovations such as flirty eyes (eyes that roll from side to side), "ma-ma" voices, "magic skin" latex rubber and blow-molded vinyl dolls (example Patti Playpal).

Ideal was also a forerunner in licensing—tying in with comic-strip characters, merchandisers and movie stars in promoting their dolls. The company started when Morris Michtom named a stuffed bear after President Theodore Roosevelt and called it the Teddy Bear. Ideal was the first American dollmaker to tie-in with a cartoon character—the 1907 comic Yellow Kid. Their first tie-in with a merchandiser was the Uneeda Kid of the National Biscuit Company in 1914. Ideal was the first to strike it big licensing a movie star when they obtained the rights to produce a Shirley Temple doll in 1934. Ideal was a family business owned by the Michtoms until the 1980s when it was sold to C.B.S, which subsequently sold it to View-Master who sold it to Tyco in 1989. The trademark is currently held by the Mattel Toy Corporation.

Contributor: Judith Izen, P.O. Box 623, Lexington, MA 02173. Izen is a noted doll and paper doll authority whose paper doll articles have appeared in several publications. Her books include *Collectors Guide to Ideal Dolls* and *Collectors Encyclopedia of Vogue Dolls* (coauthored with Carol Photos).

Photos courtesy Judy Izen unless otherwise noted.

	C10
Abbott & Costello, 1984, each	60
The Addams Family Puppets, 1964	65
Angel Babies, 1982	15
Archie Bunker's Grandson, 1976	40
Baby Baby—A Handful of Love, 1976	15
Baby Beautiful, 1938	175
Baby Big Eyes, 1954	80
Baby Coos, 1948	100
Baby Crissy, 1973	65
Baby Doll, vinyl head and limbs, cloth body, 1950s	80
Baby Dreams, 1975	45
Baby Giggles, 1968	50
Baby Jesus, 1958	85
Baby Kiss-a-Boo, 1981	30
Baby Pebbles, 1963	130
Baby Snooks, 1938	200
Bam-Bam, 12", 1964	120
Bam-Bam, 16", 1964	160
Bam-Bam, 16", 1964	160
Bat Girl, 1967	600
Bat Man Puppet, 1965	150
Belly Button Baby, 1971	40
Betsy McCall, 1953	250

Baby Doll, vinyl head and body, 1950, $80

Belly Button Baby, 1971, $40

Bride, 1939, $200. Photo courtesy Marge Beisinger

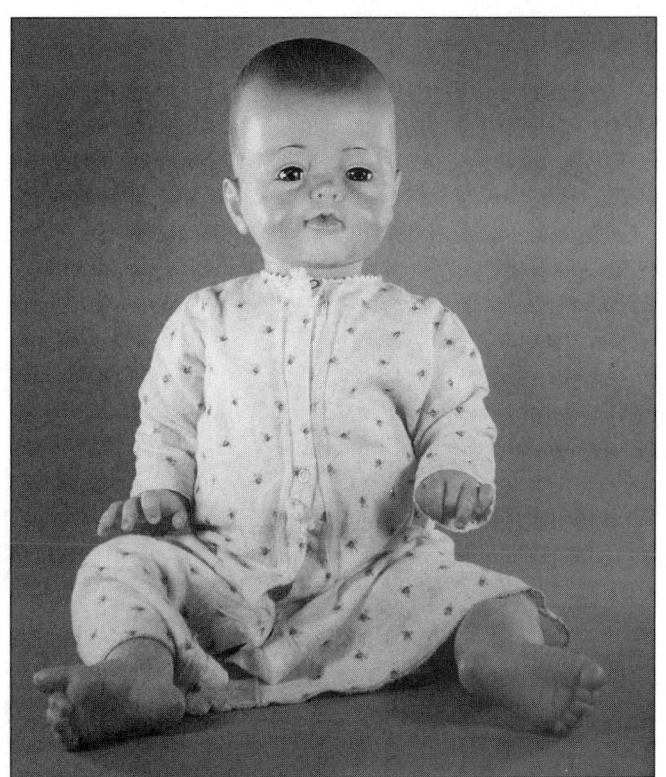

Bye-Bye Baby, 1960, $325

Cinderella, 1938, $250. Photo courtesy Marge Meisinger

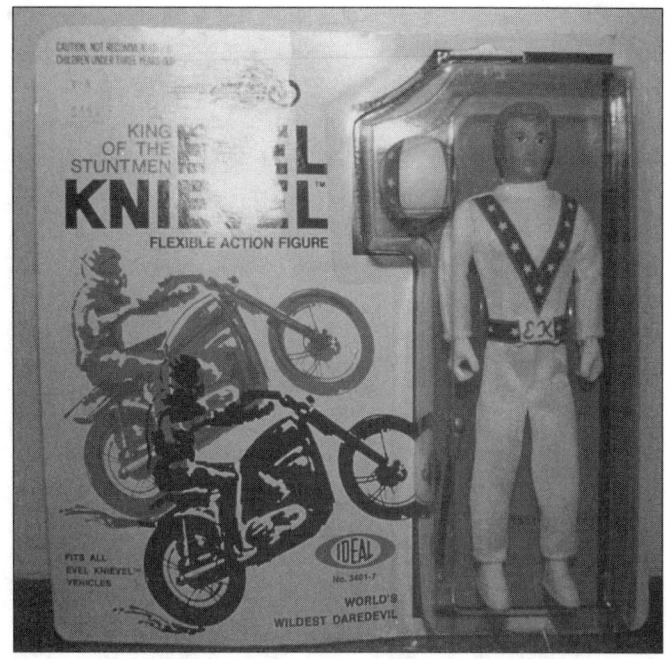

Evel Knievel, 1974, $30

Honey Moon, 1965, $60

Miss Ideal, 1961, $325

Pepper, 1963, $35

Sara Stimson, 1980, $40

	C10
Peter Playpal, 1960	850
Pinocchio, 1939	225
Plassie, 1942	125
Play 'N Jane, 1971	40
Playtex Dryper Baby, 1960	150
Pos'n Pete, 1965	45

	C10
Pos'n Salty, 1965	45
Posie, hard plastic, 1954	150
Posie, bendable vinyl, 1969	50
Princess Beatrix, 1938	250
Princess Mary, 1955	175
Queen of the Ice, 1938	150
Raggedy Ann and Andy, 1983, the set	100
Rub-A-Dub Dolly, 1974	35
Ruth, 1953	100
SallyKins, 1934	175
Samantha the Bewitching Doll, 1965	350
Sara Ann, 15", 1951	175
Sara Ann, 21"	250
Sara Stimson, 1980	40
Saralee, 1951	200
Saucy Walker, hard plastic, 1953	225
Saucy Walker, vinyl, 1960	250
Seven Dwarfs, 1938, each	175
Shirley Temple, 12", 1982	60
Shirley Temple, composition, 11", 1939	650
Shirley Temple, composition, 13", 1939	600
Shirley Temple, composition, 15", 1939	625
Shirley Temple, composition, 17", 1939	650
Shirley Temple, composition, 22", 1939	800
Shirley Temple, composition, 25", 1939	825

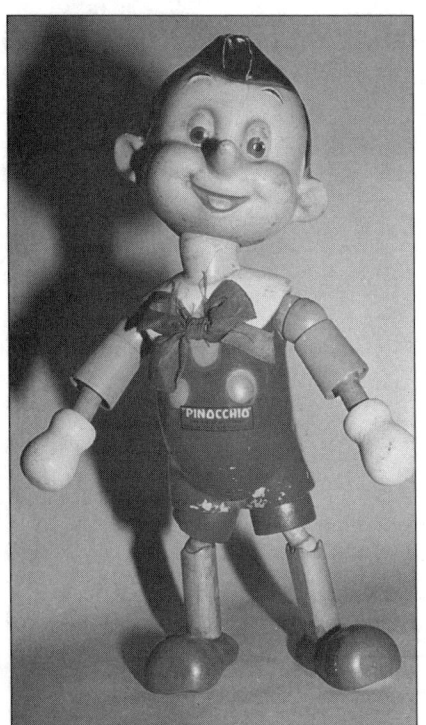

Pinocchio, 1939, $225

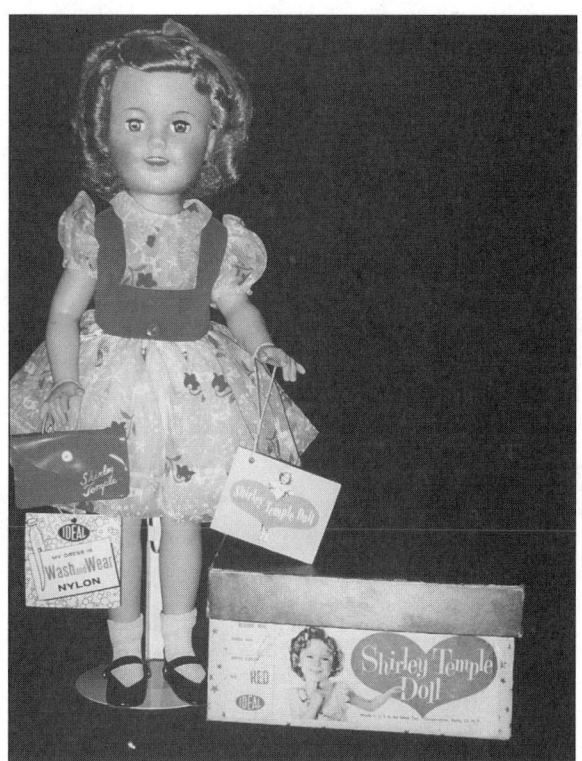

Shirley Temple, 17", 1957-61, $195

Tickletoes, 1931, $150

	C10
Shirley Temple, composition, 27", 1939	900
Shirley Temple, porcelain, 1984	200
Shirley Temple, vinyl, 12", 1957-61	175
Shirley Temple, vinyl, 17", 1957-61	195
Shirley Temple, vinyl, 19", 1957-61	225
Shirley Temple, vinyl, 1974	80
Shirley Temple, vinyl, 8", 1982	40
Shirley Temple, vinyl, 1984	50

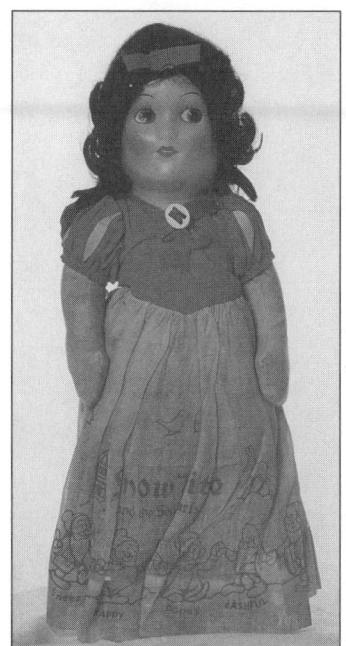

Snow White, 1938, $200.
Photo courtesy Marge
Meisinger

	C10
Shirley Temple, vinyl, 36", 1960	1200
Shirley Temple Baby, 1935	600+
Smokey the Bear, 1953	85
Snoozie, 1933	150
Snow White, 1938	200
Snuggles, 1978	30
Soldier, 1940s	150
Soozie Smiles, 1923	125
Sparkle Plenty, 1947	150
Storybook Dolls, 1938	100
Stretchie, 1973	25
Suntan Dodi, 1977	30
Suntan Eric, 1977	40
Suntan Tuesday Taylor, 1977	35
SuperGirl, 1967	600
Superman Puppet, 1965	150
Suzette, 1936	150
Suzy, 1936	150
Suzy Play Pal, 1959	350
Tabatha, 1966	400
Talkytot, 1950	90
Tammy, 1962	40
Tammy's Dad, 1963	55
Tammy's Mom, 1963	55
Tara, 1976	75
Tearie Dearie, 1963	30
Ted, 1963	40

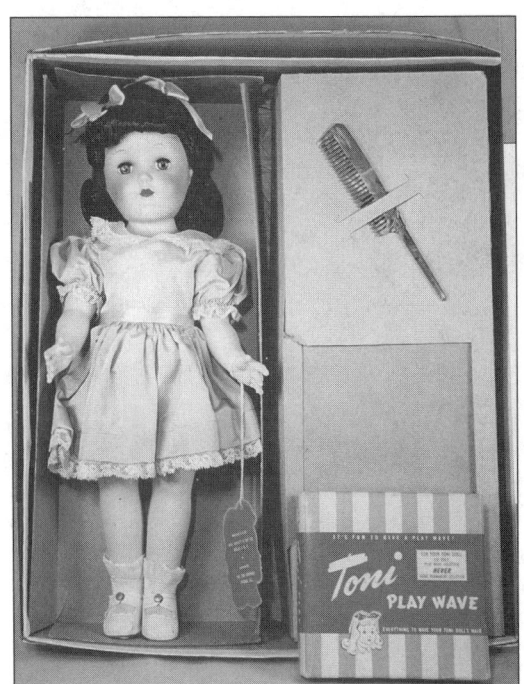

Toni, 1949, $200-600

	C10
Teddy Bear, cloth, 1907	900
Teddy Bear, porcelain, 1984	80
Terry Twist, 1962	150
Three Stooges hand Puppets, 1960	300
Thumbelina, 1961	150
Tickletoes, 1931	150

	C10
Tiffany Taylor, 1974	65
Timmy Tumbles, 1977	40
Tiny Tears, vinyl 1984	35
Tiny Tears, porcelain 1984	60
Tippy Tumbles, 1977	40
Toni, 14", 1949	200
Toni, 22", 1949	600
Toni Walker, 14", 1954	200
Toni Walker, 21", 1954	300
Tressy, 1970	70
Trilby, 1951	100
Tubsy, 1967	50
Tuesday Taylor, 1976	45
Twinkle Eyes, 1957	60
Uneeda Kid, 1914	250
Upsy Dazy, 1973	35
Vampy, 1966	65
Velvet, 1974	40
Victorian Ladies, 8", 1984	25
Victorian Ladies, 12", 1984	30
Vinyl Doll, all vinyl body, 1955	80
Wake-Up Thumbelina, 1976	35
Whoopsie, 1978	45
Wizard of Oz Series, 1984	45
Wolfie, 1966	65
Wonder Woman, 1967	600
Yellow Kid, 1907	500
Zu-Zu Kid, 1916	275

JAPANESE TIN AIRPLANES

Starting with the birth of aviation, toy manufacturers began making toy replicas of anything that flew—old pusher planes through the Spirit of St. Louis, World War I biplanes, World War II fighters and bombers, commercial and military jets and the Concord. Manufacturers stopped using tin in the late 1960s and early 1970s and switched to plastic.

Contributor: Ron Smith, 33005 Arlesford, Solon, OH, 44139. Smith has always loved toy cars and planes, he can still show you his first Dinky Toy his aunt bought him at Fred Harvey's Toy Store in Cleveland's Terminal Tower Building. Smith has collected die-cast cars, trucks and planes, cast-iron toys and plastic promotional cars, but for the past fifteen years he has specialized in tin-plate cars and planes. Smith lives in Ohio with his wife Joan and their two cats, T-2 and Bogart.

	C6	C8	C10
1930s German, wind-up, Tipp, 16" wingspan	700	1500	3200
American Airlines Boeing 727, battery, "Y" Co., 16" wingspan	125	175	225
American Airlines DC-7, battery, Japan, 24" wingspan	200	300	500

	C6	C8	C10
American Airlines Electra, battery, Linemar, 20" wingspan	200	400	500
B-29, friction, "Y" Co., 19" wingspan	150	300	475
B-36, friction, "Y" Co., 26" wingspan	300	600	1200
B-45 Tornado, friction, Bandai, 16" wingspan	100	150	250
B-47 USAF, friction, Daiya, 12" wingspan	150	225	325
B-50 Superfortress, friction, TCP, 15" wingspan	200	300	400
B-50 USAF, battery, "Y" Co., 19" wingspan	200	300	400
B50, friction, Bandai, 7-1/2" wingspan	40	60	125
Bluebird Seaplane, friction, S&E, 13" wingspan	50	80	175
Boeing 707, battery, Japan, 18" wingspan	200	300	400
Boeing Stratocruiser, friction, T.N., 20" wingspan	300	400	600
Bristol Bulldog, friction, S&E, 14-1/2" wingspan	80	150	350
C-120 Pack Plane, friction, Japan, 16" wingspan	250	500	850
C-124 Globemaster, friction, "Y" Co., 20" wingspan	250	600	850

1930s German Wind-up, Tipp, $3,200

Bristol Bulldog, friction, S&E, $350

Cessna, friction, T.N., $450

Jenny Biplane, friction, S&E, $225

	C6	C8	C10
Cessna, friction, T.N. 25" wingspan	100	200	450
Cessna, friction, West German, 12" wingspan	50	150	300
Comet Jetliner, friction, "Y" Co., 19" wingspan	100	200	300
Constellation, friction, Ingap, 15" wingspan	100	200	400
Construction, England, 22" wingspan	125	175	400
De Havilland Comet, wind-up, Rico, 13" wingspan	100	200	400
Disney Comic Plane, friction, Linemar, 10" wingspan	100	150	400
Eastern Constellation, friction, Hadson, 12" wingspan	200	350	500
Eastern Constellation, friction, MSK, 7-1/2" wingspan	100	150	250
Eastern DC-7, friction, Bandai, 17-1/2" wingspan	300	400	600
F-102 USAF, friction, HTS, 11" wingspan	125	150	225

	C6	C8	C10
F-104 Lockheed, friction, "Y" Co., 16" wingspan	125	150	175
F3F Biplane, battery, Cragstan, 11-1/2" wingspan	150	300	600
F-80, friction, Bandai, 7-1/2" wingspan	40	70	100
F-84 Airforce, battery, Linemar, 13" wingspan	100	150	200
F-86 Airforce friction, "J" Co., 10" wingspan	75	125	175
F-94C Starfire, friction, "Y" Co., 18" wingspan	150	300	450
Farman, friction, Japan, 10" wingspan	400	600	1200
Fiat CR-42, wind-up, Ingap, 10" wingspan	500	700	1500
Ford, friction, T.N., 15" wingspan	60	150	300
German Biplane, Bar/wind-up, Tipp, 20" wingspan	500	1000	3000
Hein, friction, Banda, 14" wingspan	200	350	500
Hospital Plane, Tekno, 14" wingspan	400	800	1600
Jenny Biplane, friction, Haji, 11-1/2" wingspan	30	50	100
Jenny Biplane, friction, S&E, 14-1/2" wingspan	75	125	225

Hospital Plane, Tekno, $1,600

Ford, friction, T.N., $300

P-47 Thunderbolt, friction, HTC, $300

P-51 Mustang, friction, HTC, $300

WWII Fighter, friction, Japan, $250

	C6	C8	C10
Lockheed Sirus, friction, Japan, 13" wingspan	400	800	1000
Northwest DC-7, friction, "Y" Co., 10" wingspan	100	150	225
Northwest DC-7, friction, Asahi, 19" wingspan	300	600	950
Northwest Orient, battery, "Y" Co., 24" wingspan	300	500	650
P-47 Thunderbolt, friction, HTC, 10" wingspan	100	200	300
P-51 Mustang, friction, HTC, 10" wingspan	100	200	300
Pan Am DC-7, friction, T.N., 17" wingspan	300	600	800
Pan Am Jet Clipper, battery, Linemar, 18" wingspan	200	300	425
Pan Am Stato Clipper, friction, Japan, 14" wingspan	225	300	450
Presidents Plane, battery, Japan, 20" wingspan	275	350	500
Ryan Spirit of St. Louis, friction, HTC, 12" wingspan	100	200	400

	C6	C8	C10
Sky Bird "Spirit of St. Louis," friction, Bandai, 9" wingspan	50	80	150
Spitfire, friction, HTC, 10" wingspan	80	150	250
Stuka, Dux, 12" wingspan	200	400	800
TWA Constellation, friction, "Y" Co., 12" wingspan	200	300	450
TWA DC-2, wind-up, Japan, 10" wingspan	175	300	425
TWA DC-4, friction, Linemar, 19" wingspan	150	350	475
U.N. Hospital Plane, friction, HTC, 12" wingspan	70	150	250
United DC-7 Mainliner, battery, T.N., 19" wingspan	150	275	350
United DC-7, friction, Japan, 23" wingspan	125	250	400
WWII Fighter, friction, Japan, 14-1/2" wingspan	80	150	250
WWII Fighter, wind-up, Spain, 8-1/2" wingspan	100	200	400
WWII Tri-Motor, wind-up, Spain, 9" wingspan	100	200	400
Zero, friction, new issue, Japan, 15-1/2" wingspan			250
Zero, friction, Nomura, 14" wingspan	150	275	350

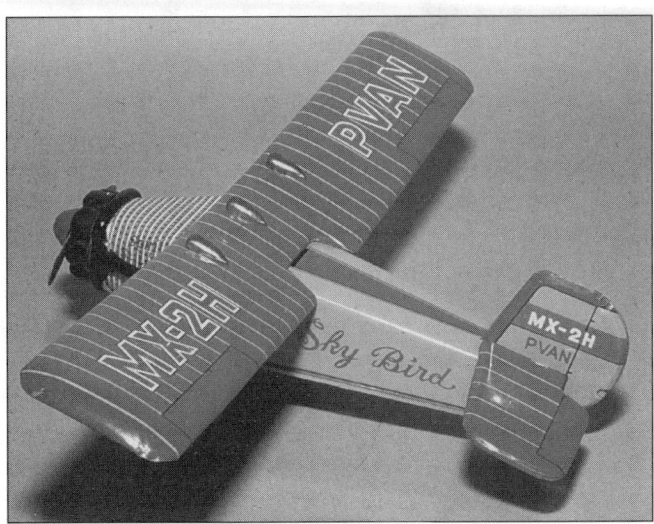

Sky Bird "Spirit of St. Louis," friction, Bandai, $150

WWII Tri-Motor, wind-up, Spain, $400

JAPANESE TIN CARS

Tin toy cars have been manufactured since the first horseless carriages roamed the streets of the United States and Europe. They ranged in size and price from the tiny one-inch penny toy to the twenty-eight-inch Eldorado that sold for ten dollars. Although there are German, Spanish and French toy cars listed here, this chapter concentrates on the 1950s—the Golden Era of Japanese tin toy cars. These examples are popular today and prices continue to raise.

Contributor: Ron Smith, 33005 Arlesford, Solon, OH, 44139. Smith has always loved toy cars and planes, he can still show you his first Dinky Toy his aunt bought him at Fred Harvey's Toy Store in Cleveland's Terminal Tower Building. Smith has collected die-cast cars, trucks and planes, cast-iron toys and plastic promotional cars, but for the past fifteen years he has specialized in tin-plate cars and planes. Smith lives in Ohio with his wife Joan and their two cats, T-2 and Bogart.

	C6	C8	C10
Agajanian Racer No. 98, friction, "Y" Co., 1950s, 18"	500	1000	3000
Aston-Martin DB5 (James Bond), friction, Gilbert, 1960s, 11-1/2"	75	150	350
Aston-Martin DB6, friction, Asahi Toy Co., 1960s, 11"	200	500	850
Atom Car, friction, Yonezawa, 1950s, 17"	200	400	800
Atom Jet Car, friction, "Y" Co., 1950s, 30"	300	500	1100

	C6	C8	C10
Austin Healey 100 Six Convertible, 1959, Bandai friction, 8"	50	100	200
Austin Healey 100 Six Coupe, friction, Bandai1959, 8"	50	100	200
BMW 600 Isetta, friction, Bandai, 1950, 9"	150	300	500
BMW Isetta (three wheels), friction, Bandai, 1950, 6-1/2"	75	125	150
Buick Century, Bandai, friction, 1958, 8"	80	110	130
Buick Century, Yonezawa, friction, 1958, 12"	400	600	1200
Buick Emergency Car, T.N., friction, 1961, 14"	50	95	125
Buick Futuristic LeSabre, friction, Yonezawa, 1950s, 7-1/2"	200	300	600
Buick LeSabre, friction, Asahi Toy Co., 1966, 19"	100	150	300
Buick Roadmaster, Yoshiya, friction, 1955, 11"	125	175	400
Buick Sportswagon, friction, Asakusa, 1968, 15"	150	200	300
Buick Station Wagon, unknown, battery-op, 1954, 8"	75	150	200

Agajanian Racer No. 98, friction, "Y" Co., 1950s, $3,000

Aston-Martin DB5 (James Bond), friction, Gilbert, 1960s, $350

Cadillac Sedan, friction, Bandai, 1959, $175

Buick, battery-op/friction, Ichko, 1959, $350

Chevrolet Corvair, friction, Bandai, 1963, $125

	C6	C8	C10
Buick Wildcat, friction, Ichiko, 1963, 15"	200	400	800
Buick, friction, Marusan, 1953, 7"	50	100	200
Buick, battery-op/friction, Ichiko, 1959, 12"	100	275	350
Buick, Ichiko, friction, 1960, 17-1/2"	150	300	800
Buick, T.N., friction, 1959, 11"	90	150	300
Buick, T.N., friction, 1961, 11"	100	150	250
Cadillac 60, friction, unknown, 1961, 9"	95	125	150
Cadillac Convertible, friction, Bandai, 1959, 12"	50	100	175
Cadillac El Dorado, friction, Ichiko, 1967, 28"	200	400	800
Cadillac Fleetwood, friction, SSS, 1961, 17-1/2"	100	200	350
Cadillac Sedan, friction, Bandai, 1959, 12"	50	100	175
Cadillac, battery-op, Joustra, 1954, 12"	100	200	450
Cadillac, battery-op, Marusan, 1950, 11"	400	800	1200
Cadillac, battery-op, T.N., 1952, 13"	100	250	500
Cadillac, friction, Alps, 1952, 11-1/2"	250	400	800
Cadillac, friction, Asahi Toy Co., 1965, 17"	125	250	425
Cadillac, friction, Bandai, 1960s, 17"	125	175	375
Cadillac, friction, Bandai, 1963, 17"	100	200	350
Cadillac, friction, Gama, 1954, 12"	100	200	450
Cadillac, friction, Ichiko, 1965, 22"	300	400	600
Cadillac, friction, K.O., 1967, 10-1/2"	100	150	250
Cadillac, friction, Marusan, 1950, 11"	300	500	750
Cadillac, friction, unknown, 1967, 10-3/4"	75	100	125
Cadillac, friction, Yonezawa, 1960, 18"	100	150	300
Cadillac, friction, Yonezawa, 1962, 22"	100	250	350
Champion Racer No. 15, friction, German, 1950, 18"	500	750	1200
Champion Racer No. 42, friction, Gem, 1950, 18"	500	750	1200
Champion Racer No. 98, friction, "Y" Co., 1950s, 18"	500	800	1200
Chevrolet Camaro Rusher, Taiyo, battery-op, 1971, 9-1/2"	10	20	30

	C6	C8	C10
Chevrolet Camaro, friction, Taiyo, 1967, 9-1/2"	10	20	30
Chevrolet Camaro, Modern Toys, friction, 1967, 11"	25	50	75
Chevrolet Camaro, battery-op, T.N., 1967, 14"	150	250	400
Chevrolet Convertible, friction, Bandai, 1956, 9-1/2"	100	150	225
Chevrolet Convertible, friction, Bandai, 1958, 8"	60	90	125
Chevrolet Corvair, friction, Bandai, 1963, 8"	50	65	125
Chevrolet Corvair, friction, Bandai, 1960s, 8"	30	50	80
Chevrolet Corvette, battery-op, Ichida, 1964, 12"	150	225	350
Chevrolet Corvette, battery-op, Taiyo, 1968, 9-1/2"	20	40	80
Chevrolet Corvette, friction, Bandai, 1953, 7"	100	200	300
Chevrolet Corvette, friction, Bandai, 1962, 8"	50	75	100
Chevrolet Corvette, friction, Bandai, 1965, 8"	50	75	100

Chevrolet Camaro, battery-op, T.N., 1967, $400

	C6	C8	C10
Chevrolet Corvette, friction, Yonezawa, 1958, 9-1/2" 200		300	600
Chevrolet Impala Convertible, friction, Bandai, 1961, 11" 100		200	400
Chevrolet Impala Sedan, friction, Bandai, 1961, 11" 100		250	500
Chevrolet Impala, friction, unknown, 1963, 18" 200		300	400
Chevrolet Pickup Truck, friction, Bandai, 1958, 8" 50		65	90
Chevrolet Pickup, friction, Bandai, 1956, 9-1/2" 75		125	175
Chevrolet Red Cross Ambulance, friction, Bandai, 1958, 8" 20		30	50
Chevrolet Secret Agent, battery-op, unknown, 1962, 14" 50		75	125
Chevrolet Sedan, friction, Bandai, 1958, 8" 75		100	125
Chevrolet Sedan/Convertible/Wagon, friction, SY, 1959, 11-1/2" 200		300	600
Chevrolet Station Wagon, friction, Bandai, 1956, 9-1/2" 60		120	160
Chevrolet Station Wagon, friction, Bandai, 1958, 8" 50		60	85
Chevrolet, battery-op, Marusan, 1955, 10-3/4" 300		600	1000
Chevrolet, friction, Marusan, 1954, 11" 300		600	900
Chevrolet, friction, Marusan 1960, 11-1/2" 200		300	600
Chevrolet, friction, unknown, 1962, 11"... 125		250	350
Chrysler Imperial Convertible, friction, Bandai, 1959, 8" 50		100	175
Chrysler Imperial Sedan, friction, Bandai, 1959, 8" 50		100	175
Chrysler Imperial, friction, Asahi Toy Co., 1962, 16" 600		1200	2500
Chrysler New Yorker, friction, Alps, 1957, 14" 500		700	1200
Chrysler Valiant, friction, Bandai, 1960, 8" 20		30	50

Chrysler, friction, Yonezawa, 1953, $350

	C6	C8	C10
Chrysler, battery-op, unknown, 1958, 13" 300		400	800
Chrysler, friction, Guntherman, 1950, 11" 100		200	500
Chrysler, friction, Yonezawa, 1953, 10"..... 100		225	350
Chrysler, friction, Yonezawa, 1955, 8"....... 100		200	300
Citroen 2 CV, friction, Daiya, 1960, 8"...... 100		150	250
Citroen DS 19 Convertible, friction, Bandai, 1960, 12" 300		600	900
Citroen DS 19 Sedan, friction, Bandai, 1960, 12" 300		600	900
Citroen DS 19 Station Wagon, friction, Bandai, 1960, 12" 300		600	900
Corvair Bertone, battery-op, Bandai, 1963, 12" 75		150	200
Daihatsu Auto Tricycle, friction, Nomura, 1950s, 11" 100		150	300
Daihatsu Midget, friction, Kokyu Shokai, 1950, 5" 75		100	200
Daihatsu Midget, friction, Yonezawa, 1950s, 7" 75		100	200
Datsun Bluebird 1200, friction, Bandai, 1960s, 8" 60		75	125

Chrysler Imperial Convertible, friction, Bandai, 1959, $175

Citroen 2 CV, friction, Daiya, 1960, $250

Dodge Sedan, friction, T.N., 1958, $800

Ford Panel Truck, friction, Bandai, 1955, $600

	C6	C8	C10
DeSoto, friction, Masudaya, 1930s, 8"	300	400	800
Divco Dugans Bakery Truck, friction, unknown, Japan, 1950s, 7-1/2"	200	400	500
DKW 1000 Convertible, friction, Bandai, 1960, 8"	90	125	200
Dodge Pickup, friction, unknown, 1959, 18-1/2"	350	500	1000
Dodge Sedan, friction, T.N., 1958, 11"	300	400	800
Dodge Truck, friction, unknown, 1959, 24"	350	500	1000
Dodge Yellow Cab, friction, T.N., 1968, 12"	100	200	500
Dream Car Buick Phantom, friction, Tipp & Co., 1950s, 12"	300	400	800
Dream Car Firebird III, friction, Alps, 1960s, 11"	100	200	400
Dream Car, friction, "Y" Co., 17"	600	800	1500
Edsel Ambulance, friction, Haji, 1958, 11"	200	250	400
Edsel Convertible/Sedan, friction, Haji, 1958, 10-1/2"	300	500	1000
Edsel Hardtop, friction, Asahi, 1958, 10-3/4"	300	400	600
Edsel Station Wagon, friction, T.N., 1958, 11"	150	200	300
Edsel Wagon, friction, Haji, 1958, 10-1/2"	200	300	600

Edsel Hardtop, friction, Asahi, 1958, $600

	C6	C8	C10
Edsel, friction, Yonezawa, 1958, 10-1/2"	300	400	600
Edsel, Hardtop, friction, Toy Nomura, 1958, 8-1/2"	100	150	250
Electrospecial #21, battery-op, "Y" Co., 10"	300	500	1000
Ferrari 250 G. Convertible, friction, A.T.C., 1957, 9-1/2"	150	300	750
Ferrari Super America Convertible, friction, Bandai, 1960s, 12"	100	200	350
Ferrari Super America Coupe, friction, Bandai, 1960, 12"	100	200	350
Ferrari, battery-op, Bandai, 1958, 11"	90	150	350
Fiat 600 Sedan, friction, Bandai, 1960s, 8"	50	70	100
Ford Ambulance, friction, Bandai, 1955, 12"	150	250	300
Ford Convertible, friction, Haji, 1956, 11-1/2"	400	600	900
Ford Convertible, friction, Rico, 1964, 17"	200	400	600
Ford Convertible. friction, Bandai, 1955, 12"	200	400	700
Ford Country Sedan, friction, Asahi, 1962, 12"	200	350	700
Ford Country Sedan, friction, Bandai, 1961, 10-1/2"	125	150	250
Ford Country Squire Station Wagon, friction, Bandai, 1958, 8"	60	80	125
Ford Fairlane Hardtop/Convertible, friction, Sankei Gangu, 1958, 9"	90	115	125
Ford Fairlane Hardtop/Convertible, friction, Bandai, 1958, 8"	60	80	125
Ford Fairlane Sedan, friction, Ichiko, 1957, 10"	100	200	300
Ford Fairlane Skyliner, friction, Sankei Gangu, 1959, 9"	90	115	125
Ford Falcon, friction, Bandai, 1960s, 8"	20	30	50
Ford Galaxie Hardtop, friction, MT, 1965, 11"	125	150	250
Ford Good Humor Ice Cream Truck, friction, KTS, Japan, 1950, 10-3/4"	100	300	600

	C6	C8	C10
Ford GT, battery-op, Bandai, 1960s, 10"..... 65	85	125
Ford Gyron, battery-op, Ichida, 1960, 11" .. 75	100	200
Ford Hardtop, friciton, Ichiko, 1964, 13".. 200	450	700
Ford Hardtop, friction, Rico, 1964, 17"..... 200	400	600
Ford Hardtop, friction, T.N., 1957, 12"..... 100	200	300
Ford Hardtop, friction, Yonezawa, 1956, 12"................................. 300	500	950
Ford Mustang (FBI), friction, Bandai, 1965, 11"................................... 100	175	375
Ford Mustang Convertible, battery, Yonezawa, 1965, 13-1/2" 90	125	200
Ford Mustang F.B., friction, Bandai, 1965, 11"................................. 45	65	90
Ford Mustang F.B., friction, T.N., 1966, 17"................................... 120	200	325
Ford Mustang Hardtop/Convertible, friction/battery-op, Bandai, 1965, 11" ... 75	125	150
Ford Mustang, battery-op, Bandai, 1967, 13"................................... 45	65	100
Ford Panel Truck, "Flowers," friction, Bandai, 1955, 12" 200	400	600
Ford Pickup, friction, Bandai, 1955, 12"... 150	250	300
Ford Retractable Top, friction, K. Japan, 1958, 10"................................. 80	100	165
Ford Retractable Top, battery-op, T.N., 1958, 11"................................. 80	100	165
Ford Retractable, friction, T.N., 1959, 11" .. 80	100	165
Ford Sedan, friction, Marusan, 1956, 13"..... 500	800	1500
Ford Sedan, wind-up, Guntherman, 1949, 11"................................... 150	300	400
Ford Sedan, wind-up, Guntherman, 1951, 11"................................... 150	300	400
Ford Sedan/Convertible/Wagon/Pickup, Bandai, 1957, 12" 200	250	300
Ford Sedan/Convertible/Wagon/Pickup, friction, Joustra, 1957, 12" 200	250	300
Ford Station Wagon, friction, Nomura, 1957, 7-1/2" 60	80	100

	C6	C8	C10
Ford Station Wagon, friction, Bandai, 1955, 12" 150	250	300
Ford Station Wagon, friction, T.N., 1959, 12".. 100	150	200
Ford Taunus 17M, friction, Bandai, 1960s, 8" 40	60	80
Ford Thunderbird Convertible, friction, Asahi, 1964, 12-1/2" 150	200	400
Ford Thunderbird Convertible, friction, Bandai, 1959, 8" 50	80	125
Ford Thunderbird Hardtop Clear Top, friction, T.N., 1956, 11" 200	300	400
Ford Thunderbird Hardtop, friction, Asahi, 1964, 12"................................... 150	200	400
Ford Thunderbird Hardtop, friction, Bandai, 1965, 10-3/4" 60	90	175
Ford Thunderbird Retractable, battery-op, Yonezawa, 1961, 11".......................... 80	150	200
Ford Thunderbird Retractable, battery-op, Yonezawa, 1962, 11".......................... 80	150	200
Ford Thunderbird Retractable, battery-op, Yonezawa, 1963, 11".......................... 80	150	200
Ford Thunderbird Sedan, friction, Bandai, 1959, 8" 50	80	125
Ford Thunderbird, battery-op, T.N., 1956,11"................................... 200	300	400
Ford Thunderbird, friction, Bandai, 1955, 7" 100	150	200
Ford Thunderbird, friction, Ichiko, 1964, 16"................................... 100	200	400
Ford Thunderbird, friction, T.N., 1956, 11" 200	300	400
Ford Torino, friction, S.T., 1968, 16"......... 175	250	475
Ford Wagon, friction, Nomura, 1956, 10-1/2".................................... 100	150	300
Ford, friction, Haji, 1960, 11".................... 125	200	350
GM's Gas Turbine Powered Firebird II, friction, Asahi, 1956, 8-1/2" 100	200	200
International Cement Mixer, friction, SSS, 1950s, 19" 300	600	1000

Ford Taunus 17M, friction, Bandai, 1960s, $80

Ford Thunderbird, friction, Bandai, 1955, $200

	C6	C8	C10
International Grain Hauler, friction, SSS, 1950s, 23"..........	300	600	1000
Jaguar 3.4 Convertible, friction, Bandai, 1960s, 8"........	50	60	135
Jaguar 3.4 Sedan, friction, Bandai, 1960s, 8"........	50	60	135
Jaguar XK 140, friction, Bandai, 1960s, 9-1/2"........	40	60	80
Jaguar XK150 Hardtop Convertible, friction, Bandai, 1960, 9-1/2"........	75	125	225
Jaguar XKE Convertible, friction, T.T., 1960s, 10-1/2"........	75	100	200
Jaguar XKE Coupe, friction, Lendolet Auto, 1960s, 10-1/2"........	75	100	125
Jaguar XKE, battery-op, Bandai, 1960s, 10"........	90	125	200
Jaguar XKE120, friction, Alps, 1965, 6-1/2"........	90	150	350
Land Rover "88" Station Wagon, friction, Bandai, 1960s, 8"........	30	40	80
Lincoln Continental Mark II, friction, Linemar, 1956, 12"........	400	600	1500
Lincoln Continental Mark III Convertible, friction, Bandai, 1959, 12"........	90	125	175
Lincoln Continental Mark III Sedan, friction, Bandai, 1959, 12"........	90	125	175
Lincoln Hardtop/Convertible friction, Yonezawa, 1960, 11"........	100	150	300
Lincoln Sedan, friction, Yonezawa, 1955, 12"........	250	325	500
Lincoln, friction, Ichiko, 1956, 16-1/2".....	150	250	375
Lincoln, friction, unknown, 1954, 12"......	175	275	375
Lincoln, friction, unknown, 1964, 10-1/2".....	90	175	275
Lotus Elite, friction, Bandai, 1950s, 8-1/2".....	25	35	60
Mazda Auto Tricycle K360, friction, Bandai, 1950s, 6"........	75	100	200
Mazda Auto Tricycle, friction, Bandai, 1950s, 8"........	75	100	200
Mercedes Limousine friction, Tipp & Co., 1950s, 14"........	500	800	1000

Lincoln, friction, 1964, $275

Mercedes-Benz 219 Sedan, friction, Bandai, 1960s, $120

	C6	C8	C10
Mercedes, friction, Ichiko, 1960s, 12-1/2"....	100	150	175
Mercedes-Benz 219 Convertible friction, Bandai, 1960s, 8"........	50	80	120
Mercedes-Benz 219 Sedan, friction, Bandai, 1960s, 8"........	50	80	120
Mercedes-Benz 230 SL, battery-op, Modern Toys, 1960s, 15"........	175	210	250
Mercedes-Benz 230 SL, battery-op, Yanoman, 1960s, 14-1/2"........	125	155	185
Mercedes-Benz 230 SL, bettery, Alps, 1960s, 10"........	65	75	95
Mercedes-Benz 250 S, friction, Daiya, 1960s, 14"........	110	155	175
Mercedes-Benz 250 SE, battery-op, Ichiko, 1960s, 13"........	110	140	185
Mercedes-Benz 300 SL, battery-op, Dist. Cragstan, 1950s, 9"........	65	95	125
Mercedes-Benz 300 SL, battery-op, KS, 1950s, 7"........	45	65	85
Mercedes-Benz 300 SL, battery-op, T.N., 1950s,11"........	125	150	200
Mercedes-Benz 300 SL, friction, Bandai, 1950s, 8"........	65	95	150
Mercedes-Benz 300 SL, friction, Marusan, 1957, 8-1/2"........	200	300	400
Mercedes-Benz 600, friction, unknown, 1960s, 10"........	95	125	175
Mercedes-Benz Racer W196, battery-op, Marusan, 1950s, 10"........	150	200	300
Mercedes-Benz Racer, friction, Line Mar, 1950s, 9-1/2"........	95	150	185
Mercedes-Benz Taxi, battery-op, Bandai, 1960s, 10"........	75	100	125
Mercedes-Benz, battery-op, SSS, 1962, 12"........	150	200	300
Mercedes-Benz, friction, Ichiko, 1970, 24"........	125	150	200
Mercury Cougar Hardtop, friction, Asakusa Toys, 1967, 15"........	200	400	800
Mercury Cougar Hardtop, battery-op, Taiyo, 1967, 10"........	25	45	90

	C6	C8	C10
Mercury Hardtop, battery-op, Rock Valley Toys, 1954, 9-1/2"	100	150	250
Mercury Hardtop, friction, Alps, 1956, 9-1/2"	600	800	1400
Mercury Hardtop, friction, Yonezawa, 1958, 11-1/2"	250	325	400
Mercury Station Wagon, friction, Bandai, 1958, 8"	60	80	100
Messerschmitt 4 Wheels Convertible, friction, Bandai, 1960s, 8"	200	250	350
Messerschmitt 4 Wheels Sedan, friction, Bandai, 1960s, 8"	200	250	350
MG Magnette Mark III Convertible, friction, Bandai, 1960s, 8"	95	125	165
MG Magnette Mark III Sedan, friction, Bandai, 1960s 8"	95	125	165
MG TD, friction, SSS, 1954, 6-1/2"	35	65	80
MG TF, friction, Bandai, 1955, 8"	95	125	150
MG TF, friction, unknown, 1952, 8-1/2"	50	75	100
MGA, frictin, A.T.C., 1957, 10"	175	250	500
Midget Special #6, friction, "Y" Co., 7"	300	500	1000
Mitsubishi Auto Tricycle Leo, friction, Bandai, 1950s, 5"	75	100	200
Mitsubishi Auto Tricycle, friction, Bandai, 1950s, 11"	100	150	300
Nash Ambassador, friction, Sankei Gangu, 1956, 8"	100	125	150
Nash, battery-op, MSK, 1950s, 8"	40	70	90
Oldsmobile Convertible, frictino, Yonezawa, 1961, 12"	75	125	200
Oldsmobile Sedan, friction, A.T.C., 1958, 12"	200	300	400
Oldsmobile Sedan, friction, Ichiko, 1959, 12-1/2"	75	125	175
Oldsmobile Sedan, friction, Ichiko/Kanto, 1956, 10-1/2"	200	400	600
Oldsmobile Sedan, friction, "Y" Co., 1958, 16"	300	400	700

Plymouth Hardtop, friction, A.T.C., 1959, $600

	C6	C8	C10
Oldsmobile Super 88 Sedan, friction, A.T.C., 1958, 13"	250	325	425
Oldsmobile Super 88 Sedan, friction, Masudaya, 1956, 16"	300	400	600
Oldsmobile Toronado, battery-op, Bandai, 1966, 11"	65	110	150
Oldsmobile Toronado, friction, Ichiko, 1968, 17-1/2"	300	400	500
Oldsmobile, friction, "Y" Co., 1952, 11"	150	350	500
Opel Sedan, battery-op, Yonezawa, 1950s, 11-1/2"	70	90	150
Orient Auto Tricycle, friction, Yonezawa, 1950s, 9"	75	100	200
Packard Convertible/Sedan, friction, Alps, 1953, 16"	500	800	1600
Packard Hawk Convertible, battery-op, Schuco, 1957, 10-3/4"	300	400	800
Plymouth Convertible, friction, A.T.C., 1959, 10-1/2"	250	400	600
Plymouth Fury Hardtop, friction, Kusama, 1964, 10"	30	60	90
Plymouth Fury Hardtop, friction, "Y" Co., 1957, 11-1/2"	300	400	600
Plymouth Fury, friction, Bandai, 1958, 8"	75	90	165
Plymouth Hardtop, friction, unknown, 1956, 8-1/2"	150	200	400
Plymouth Hardtop, battery-op, Alps, 1956, 12"	300	400	600
Plymouth Hardtop, friction, A.T.C., 1959, 10-1/2"	200	400	600

Plymouth T.V. Car, battery-op, Ichiko, 1961, $350

Pontiac Firebird, friction, Bandai, 1967, $75

Renault, friction, Bandai, 1960, $200

Volkswagen Karmann-Ghia, friction, Bandai, 1960, $300

	C6	C8	C10
Plymouth Sedan, friction, Ichiko, 1961, 12"	150	300	550
Plymouth Station Wagon, friction, Ichiko,1961, 12"	150	250	500
Plymouth T.V. Car, battery-op, Ichiko, 1961, 12"	125	175	350
Pontiac Dream Car, friction, Mitsubishi, 1950s, 10"	100	200	600
Pontiac Firebird w/wipers, battery-op, Bandai, 1967, 9-1/2"	40	55	75
Pontiac Firebird, friction, Akasura, 1967, 15-1/2"	200	400	900
Pontiac Firebird, friction, Bandai, 1967, 10"	30	55	75
Pontiac Star Chief, friction, Asahi, 1954, 11"	250	350	700
Pontiac, Minister, friction, India, 1954, 11"	10	20	30
Porsche 911, battery-op, Bandai, 1960, 10"	65	95	125
Porsche Speedster, battery-op, Distler, 1950s, 10-1/2"	200	300	500
Rambler Rebel Station Wagon, friction, Bandai, 1960s, 12"	60	90	150
Record Racer NSU, friction, Bandai, 1950s, 18"	100	150	300
Renault, friction, Bandai, 1960, 7-1/2"	95	150	200
Rolls Royce "Silver Coupe" Convertible, friction, Bandai, 1960, 12"	100	150	300
Rolls Royce "Silver Coupe" Sedan, friction, Bandai, 1960s, 12"	100	150	250
Rolls Royce w/electric lights, battery-op, Bandai, 1960s, 12"	150	300	600
Rolls Royce, friction, T.N., 1960, 10-1/2"	200	300	500
Saab 93B, friction, Bandai, 1960s, 7"	50	70	90
Studebaker Avanti, friction, Bandai, 1960s, 8"	125	175	350
Studebaker, friction, Yoshiva, 1954, 9"	150	200	375
Subaru 360, friction, Bandai, 1960s, 7"	75	100	150

	C6	C8	C10
Toyopet Crown, friction, Bandai, 1960s, 9"	80	150	225
Toyota 2000 GT, friction, A.T.C., 1967, 15"	125	250	350
Toyota, friction, Ichiko, 1960s, 16"	150	275	325
Triumph TR-3 Convertible, friction, Bandai, 1960s, 8"	50	80	175
Triumph TR-3 Coupe, friction, Bandai, 1960s, 8"	50	80	175
Vespa, friction, Bandai, 1960s, 9"	80	125	200
Volkswagen Bus, battery-op, Tipp & Co, 1950s, 9"	250	375	450
Volkswagen Bus, battery-op/friction, Bandai, 1960s, 9-1/2"	75	125	200
Volkswagen Bus, friction, A.T.C., 1960s, 12"	125	175	350
Volkswagen Bus, friction, Bandai, 1960s, 8"	50	60	100
Volkswagen Convertible, battery-op, Bandai, 1960s, 7-1/2"	40	60	80
Volkswagen Convertible, battery-op, Bandai, 1960s, 11"	110	145	200
Volkswagen Convertible, battery-op, Taiyo, 1960s, 10-1/2"	25	40	80
Volkswagen Convertible, friction, T.N., 1950, 9-1/2"	100	150	225
Volkswagen Karmann-Ghia, friction, Bandai, 1960, 7"	100	150	300
Volkswagen Pickup Truck, friction, Bandai, 1960s, 8"	50	60	100
Volkswagen w/ or w/o Sun Roof, friction, Bandai, 1960s, 15"	60	90	125
Volkswagen, battery-op, Bandai, 1960s, 10-1/2"	25	50	75
Volkswagen, battery-op, Bandai, 1960s, 11"	25	50	75
Volkswagen, friction, Bandai, 1960s, 8"	25	45	60
Volvo, wind-up, Sweden, 1950s, 11"	600	700	1800
Willys Jeep FC-150 Pickup, friction, T.N. Toy Nomura, 1960s, 11"	50	75	95
Zuendapp Janus, friction, Bandai1950s, 8"	200	400	600

MOVIES, RADIO & TELEVISION

See also Action Figures, Banks, Comic Character, Paper, Premiums, Figure Kits Marx Play sets,
Miscellaneous, Ramp Walkers and Wood & Composition Toys

AMOS AND ANDY

	C6	C8	C10
Amos Sparkler	500	750	1050
Amos and Andy in Car, glass, Victory Glass Co., 4-1/2" long	218	327	438
Amos Wind-up, tin, w/moving eyes, Marx, 1930,12" high	493	740	985
Amos Wind-up, tin, w/out moving eyes, Marx, 1930, 12" high	450	675	900
Andy Panda, plush, Ideal, 14" high, copyright 1960	60	90	120
Andy Wind-up, tin, w/moving eyes, Marx, 1930s, 12" high	485	725	970
Andy, Wind-up, tin, w/out moving eyes, Marx, 1930s, 12" high	450	675	900
Fresh-Air Taxi, cast iron, Dent, 6" long	600	950	1300
Fresh-Air Taxi, tin wind-up, Marx, 1930s, 8" long	500	800	1185
Dolls, wood jointed Jaymar, 6" high, pair	300	450	600

BEANY & CECIL

	C6	C8	C10
Beany Doll, non-talking, Mattel, 1960, 15" high	45	68	90
Beany Doll, talking, Mattel, 1960, 17" high	62	93	125
Beany Halloween costume, Ben Cooper	35	52	70
Beany hat w/two propellers	35	52	70
Cecil Doll, non-talking, Mattel, 1960, 24" high	30	45	60
Cecil Doll, talking, Mattel, 1960, 29" high	90	135	180

	C6	C8	C10
Cecil Halloween costume, Ben Cooper	37	56	75
Cecil hand puppet, talking, Mattel, 1961	32	48	65
Cecil music box, metal, plays show's theme song and Cecil pops up, Mattel, 1961	85	128	170
Cecil Soaky, 8" high, 1950	30	45	60
Colorforms Set, 1961, w/box	60	90	125
Dishonest John hand puppet, talks, Mattel, 1961	63	95	125
Ge-tar, Cecil's eyes move, Mattel, 1961	78	115	155
Leakin' Lena plastic toy boat, Irwin Toy, 1962	75	112	150

Leakin' Lena plastic toy boat, Irwin Toy, 1962, $150

Amos & Andy Fresh Air Taxi, Marx, 1930s, $1,185

Leakin' Lena Pound-N-Pull, Pressman, 1961, $95

Left to Right: Betty Boop Doll, jointed wood and composition, c. 1930, $1,300; Betty Boop figure, celuloid, Japanese, $1,200

	C6	C8	C10
Leakin' Lena Pound-N- Pull, wooden, Pressman, 1961	48	72	95
Leakin' Lena Ship, wood, Pressman, 1960s	138	205	275
Tea Set, six-place settings, 1960, Worcester	36	54	72

BETTY BOOP

	C6	C8	C10
Acrobat, wind-up, celluloid and metal, Japanese, 1930s	700	1100	1550
Betty Boop and Bunny Mechanical Toy	150	225	300
Doll, jointed, 1930s, 9-1/2" tall	240	360	480
Doll, wood and composition, jointed, c. 1930, 12" high	550	800	1300
Doll, wood-jointed, marked "1931," Jaymar, 3-3/4" high	90	135	180
Figure, celluloid, head shakes, Japanese, 7" high	600	900	1200

BOZO THE CLOWN

	C6	C8	C10
Bendee, Lakeside, 6" high	10	15	20
Bendem Doll, Knickerbocker, 9" high	11	16	23
Doll, stuffed, Gund, 1970, 14" high	75	112	150
Doll, talking type, Mattel	45	68	90
Doll, Terrytoons, 1961, 15" high	80	120	160
Flexie, Wham-O	8	12	17
Hand Puppet, Capital, 1962	15	22	30
Jumpkin, Kohner, 1960	25	38	50
Periscope, Lido, 1960s	8	12	16

	C6	C8	C10
Soaky	14	21	29
Soaky, 11" high	22	33	44
Squeeze Toy, 9"	60	90	120

CASPER THE FRIENDLY GHOST

	C6	C8	C10
Casper the Talking Ghost, Mattel, 14"	65	98	130
Doll, stuffed w/beanbag body, 1960s, 11"	35	52	70
Hopper, Linemar, 1950s, 5" high	200	300	400
Soaky	16	24	33
Squeak Toy, 8" high	48	72	95
Turnover Tank, tin wind-up, Linemar	150	225	300
Video Spaceport Play Set, Superior	250	375	500

CHARLIE CHAPLIN

	C6	C8	C10
Dancing Charlie, cardboard	87	131	175
Bell Toy, cast iron, c. 1912, 9-3/4"	300	450	600
Bicycle Rider String Toy, c. 1920s	350	525	700
Cymbal Player, tin litho, squeeze action, German, 6-3/4"	700	1050	1400
Doll, "Charlie's Back," Milton Bradley, 1971	35	52	70
Doll, composition and cloth, Louis Amberg, 14" high, c. 1915	75	113	150
Doll, steel, lead and cloth, ball-jointed w/movable arms, legs and feet, Boucher, 7-1/2" high	250	375	500
Figure, celluloid, 4" high	900	1350	1800
Figure, composition, marked "CHAS. CHAPLIN" on base Mark Hampton Company, 9" high	350	525	700

Left to Right: Charlie Chaplin Cymbal Player, tin, German, $1,400; Charlie Chaplin Wind-up Walker, composition and tin, French, $900; Charlie Chaplin Figure, composition, Mark Hampton Company, $700; Charlie Chaplin Squeeze Toy, tin, Spanish, c. 1925, $1,800; Charlie Chaplin Wind-up Walker, composition, cloth and metal, $1,000; Charlie Chaplin Bell Toy, cast iron, c. 1912, $600; Charlie Chaplin Wind-up, composition, Ferguson Novelty Co., $2,200.

Charlie McCarthy and Mortimer Snerd Private Car, Marx, $2,265

	C6	C8	C10
Squeeze Toy, tin litho, Spanish, c. 1925, 7-3/4" high	900	1350	1800
Squeeze Toy, tin litho metal bell, German, 7-1/4"	900	1350	1800
Tricycle Rider, tin wind-up, c. 1930, 3-1/2"	900	1350	1800
Walker, wind-up, composition, cloth and metal, 11-1/2" high	500	750	1000
Walker, wind-up, composition, tin and cloth, French, 7" high	450	675	900
Whistler Toy, wood, whistles "How Dry I Am," c. 1920, 13-1/4" high	1250	1875	2500
Wind-up, composition, cloth and metal walker, Ferguson Novelty Co., 9" high	1100	1650	2200
Wind-up, flat tin litho, tips hat when string is pulled	110	165	220

	C6	C8	C10
Wind-up, tin and cloth, Boucher, 8-1/4" high	1000	1500	2000
Wind-up, tin, driving three-wheel vehicle, Paya	1100	1650	2200
Wind-up, tin, Schuco, 1920s	285	428	570
Wind-up, tin, w/spinning cane, 6-3/4" high	900	1350	1800
Wind-up, tips hat, CKO No. 256, pre-war Germany	150	225	300

CHARLIE MCCARTHY

	C6	C8	C10
Charlie McCarthy and Mortimer Snerd Private Car, Marx	1000	1700	2265
Charlie McCarthy in his Benzine Buggy, Marx	463	695	925
Doll, composition w/moving mouth, 13" high, 1930s	238	357	475
Doll, rubber, Effanbee	45	68	90
Doll, w/moving mouth and summer suit, Effanbee, 20" high	400	600	800

Charlie McCarthy Doll Wearing Tweed Jacket, Effanbee, $850

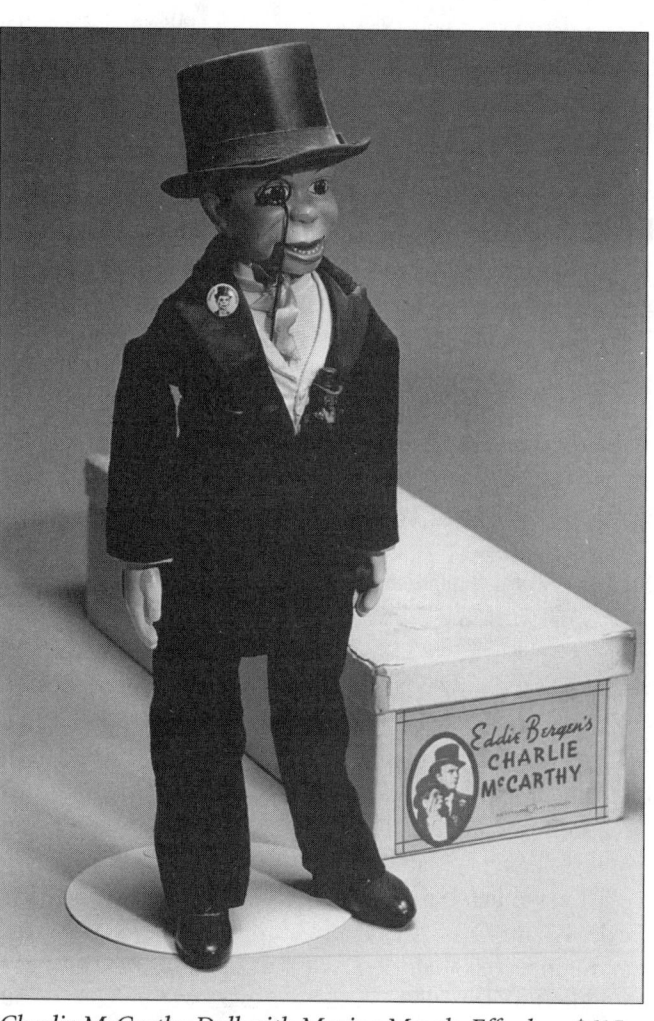

Charlie McCarthy Doll with Moving Mouth, Effanbee, $615

Charlie McCarthy Drummer Boy, Marx, 1938, $1,000

Charlie McCarthy Wind-up, c. 1938, $370

	C6	C8	C10
Doll, w/moving mouth and tweed jacket, 20" high, Effanbee	425	638	850
Doll, w/moving mouth, Effanbee, 20" high	308	462	615
Drummer boy, tin wind-up, Marx, 1938, 8" high	500	750	1000
Facemask, molded gauze, w/separate monocle	50	75	100
Figure, celluloid, 7-1/2" high	337	455	675
Hand Puppet, composition head, c. 1939	75	112	150
Paper Money	3	4	5
Puppet, 1950s, cardboard, 20" high	45	68	90
Tap Dancer, Marks Bros., 1938	125	188	250

Charlie McCarthy Paper Money, front (top), back (below), $5

	C6	C8	C10
Ventriloquist Doll, composition w/cloth body, ring pull in back of head activates lower jaw, 14-1/2" tall	600	900	1200
Ventriloquist Doll, Puppet Maker K&S, 33" tall	500	750	1000
Wind-up, tin, marked "Charlie McCarthy" on top hat, c. 1938, 8" high	185	278	370

DANIEL BOONE

	C6	C8	C10
Cannon, Remco, 1964	80	120	160
Canoe, vinyl, 18" long	15	22	30
Crime Lab, includes flashlight, signal gun, badge, handcuffs, and fingerprint kit, 1955	90	135	180
Doll, Remco	40	60	80
Los Angeles Police badge, No. 714	10	15	20
Play Set, Grant exclusive, w/box	80	120	160
Police Set, includes gun, handcuffs and badge	35	52	70
Shoulder Holster and Pistol, 1950s	62	93	125
Talking Police Car, Ideal Toys, c. 1954	105	158	210
Water Pistol, c. 1955, No. 714 badge emblazoned on handle	25	38	50
Whistle, black plastic	6	9	12

FLINTSTONES

	C6	C8	C10
Bamm-Bamm Soaky	15	22	30
Bamm-Bamm, Ideal, 12-1/2" high	39	60	78
Barney Rubble, vinyl doll, 1960, 10" high	36	48	72
Choo Choo Train, "Bedrock Express," tin wind-up, Marx, 1950s, 13" long	188	280	375
Dino On Tricycle, Linemar, 1962, 4" high	500	750	1000

Flinstone Pals Wind-up, Linemar; Fred (left), $385; Barney (right), $520

Left to Right: Harold Lloyd Bell Toy, German, $600; Harold Lloyd "Funny Face" Walker, Marx, 1929, $800; Harold Lloyd Sparkler, German, $750

	C6	C8	C10
Dino the Dinosaur, Linemar, 1961, 9" long	188	280	375
Flintstone Friction Cars, includes Fred, Barney, Wilma, etc., 1962, Linemar, 4" long, each	123	185	245
Flintstone Pals, wind-up, Barney on Dino, Linemar, 1962, 8" long	193	290	385
Flintstone Pals, wind-up, Fred on Dino, Linemar, 1962, 8" long	260	390	520
Flintstone Flivver, friction type, 1962, Marx, 6-3/4" long	308	460	615
Fred Flintstone figure, hollow vinyl, 5-3/4" high	37	56	75
Hopping Barney Rubble, wind-up, 1962, Marx, 4" high	200	300	400
Hopping Dino, Linemar, 1962, 4" high	240	360	480
Hopping Fred Flintstone, Linemar, 4" high	200	300	400
Mechanical Shooting Gallery, Marx, 1962, 13" long	48	72	95
Motorized Yacht	375	562	750
Paddy Wagon, Remco, 1961	100	150	200
Pebbles doll, jointed, 7" high	60	90	120
Play Set, Marx	205	308	410
The Flintsones Bedrock Express Handcar, wind-up play set, Marx, 1962, 22" x 26"	225	338	450
Tinykins, Marx	25	38	50
Tricycle, Wilma rider, Marx	240	360	480
Turnover Tank, tin wind-up, Linemar, 1950s, 4" long	310	465	620

GREEN HORNET

	C6	C8	C10
Bendee, Lakeside, 1967	50	75	100
Car, die-cast, Corgi	192	280	385

Harold Lloyd Donkey Cart, Spanish, c. 1929, $4,500

	C6	C8	C10
Hand Puppet, Ideal	200	300	400
Hat w/flipdown mask, Arlington Hat Co.	65	98	130
Raft	175	263	350
Signal Ray, Colorforms, 1966	300	450	600
Walkie Talkies, Remco	200	300	400

HAROLD LLOYD

	C6	C8	C10
Bell Toy, German, 6-1/2" high	300	450	600
Donkey Cart, tin litho, Spanish, c. 1929, 9-1/4" long	2200	3300	4500
Funny Face walker, wind-up, Marx, 1929	400	600	800
Policeman wind-up, tin, 12" high	375	562	750
Sparkler, tin litho, German	375	562	750

HOPALONG CASSIDY

	C6	C8	C10
Automatic Television Set, 1950s, Automatic Toy Co., 5" square	150	225	300

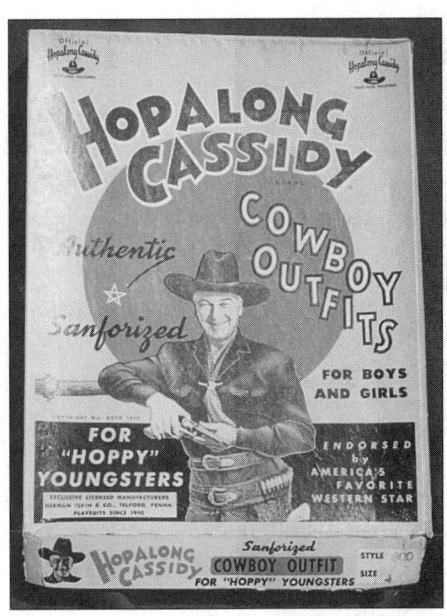

Hopalong Cassiy Cowboy Outfit, $40

	C6	C8	C10
Badge, tin w/insert photo	27	41	55
Binoculars, c. 1950, plastic	78	115	155
Compass	105	158	210
Cowboy Outfit	200	300	400
Cowgirl Outfit	125	188	250
Dart Board, depicts stagecoach holdup and target practice, Toy Ent., 1950, 14" x 17"	110	165	220
Doll, 1930s-40s, 28" high	175	263	350
Field Glasses, metal, 1940	85	128	170
Flashlight gun, plastic, marked w/Hoppy's name on side, 8" long	30	45	60
Hand Puppet, 1940s	200	300	400
Knife, c. mid-1940s, 3-1/2" long	80	120	160
Photo Ring, c. late 1940s	35	52	70
Picture Gun and Theater, Stephens Co., 1939, 12" x 8"	200	300	400
Rocking Horse, Topper	188	282	375
Shooting Gallery, Automatic Toy Co., 1950s, 18" long	170	255	340
Signet Ring, all metal, late 1940s	30	45	60
Spurs, leather and metal	110	165	220
Western Frontier set, w/figures, stagecoach and buildings	300	450	600
Wind-up, tin, "Hop-A-Long Cassidy," on "Range Rider" rocker base, Marx, 9-1/2" high	315	472	630
Zoomerang Gun, shoots paper, Tigrett Enterprises, Chicago, 1950, 9" long	100	150	200

HOWDY DOODY

	C6	C8	C10
Acrobat, Arnold, 1950s	205	308	410

	C6	C8	C10
Air-O-Doodle Circus Train, Kagran, 1950s, wind-up, 16" long	90	135	180
Airplane Squeeze Toy, Stahlwood	230	345	460
Clarabelle Clown wind-up, 1950s, Linemar, 5" high, Kagran Corp.	225	338	450
Clarabelle Clown Squeeze Action Cable, 1950s, Linemar, 6-1/2" high	188	280	375
Clarabelle Hurdy Gurdy, FBA Industries, 1950s, Kagran, 8" long	200	300	400
Clarabelle marionette, Peter Puppet, Playthings, 1950s	140	210	280
Clarabelle playsuit, Wonderland Costumes	145	220	290
Clarabelle's horn 1950s	50	75	100
Dilly-Dally marionette, Peter Puppet, Playthings, 1950s	260	390	520
Doll, 1950s, w/plastic cloth clothes, eyes close and mouth opens, 7-1/2" high	312	468	625
Doll, Ideal, 1950s, 21" high	225	338	450
Doll, w/moveable jaws, Goldberger Dolls, 12" high	85	130	170
Doll, wood-jointed, 13" high	175	263	350
Doll, wood-jointed, holding NBC microphone, 5-1/2" high	200	300	400
Flub-A-Dub Figure, plastic, 3-1/2" high	65	98	130
Flub-A-Dub marionette, early 1950s	225	338	450
Flub-A-Dub Push Puppet, felt and wood, 5" high	50	75	100
Hand Puppets, rubber heads w/cloth bodies	25	38	50
Jeep, wind-up, Marx	200	300	400
Life Preserver, plastic, shows Howdy, Mr. Bluster, etc., 1950s	21	31	42
Marionette, composition head w/hands and feet, hand-painted features, 16" high, 1950s	145	220	290
Marionette, composition head w/wooden arms and legs, 17" high	120	180	240
Mask, rubber	12	18	24
Princess SummerFall WinterSpring marionette, Peter Puppet	125	188	250

Howdy Doody Flub-A-Dub Push Puppet, $100

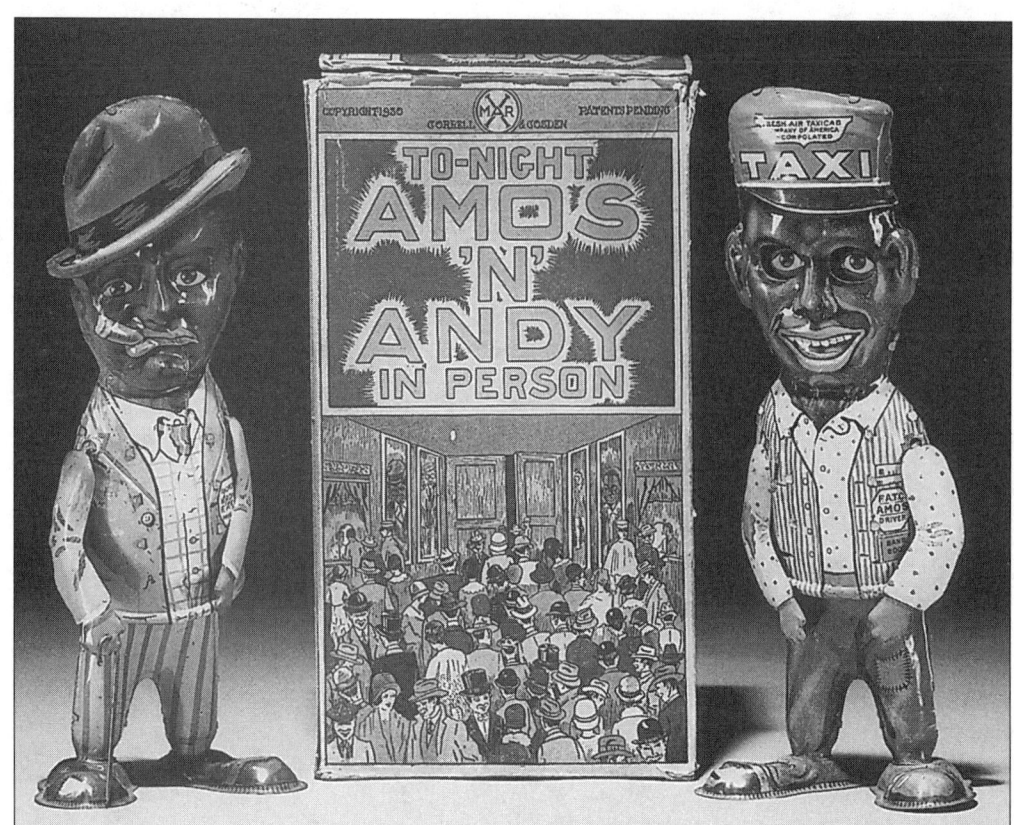

Amos & Andy Tin Wind-ups, with moving eyes, Marx, with one original box $1,995 for the pair

Left to Right: Amos & Andy Fresh Air Taxi, cast-iron, Dent, $1,300; Amos & Andy Tin Wind-ups, without moving eyes, $1,800 for the pair; Amos & Andy Fresh Air Taxi, Tin Wind-up, Marx $1,185; Amos & Andy Figure, cast-iron, 4-1/4" high, $300; Amos & Andy Figures, chalkware, c. 1930, $800 for the pair.

Howdy Doody tin wind-up, Marx, c. 1950, $1,100

	C6	C8	C10
Puppet Set, plastic w/levers in back of head to move mouths, includes Howdy, Bluster, Clarabelle, Princess, Dilly Dally, Tee-Vee Toys, No. 549, the set	70	105	140
Push Puppet, plastic, w/NBC mike, Kohner, 4" high	85	128	170
Put-In-Head, similar to Mr. Potato Head, but w/Howdy characters: Howdy, Bluster, Clarabelle, Princess, the set	50	75	100
Sand Forms, molds of Howdy, Bluster, Flub-A-Dub, Clarabelle, w/shovel, 1952	43	65	85
Squeeze Toy, 7" high	75	112	150
TV Set, w/paper filmstrips, Lego, 1950s	42	63	85
Ukulele, plastic, Emenee, 1950s	55	82	110
Ventriloquist Dummy, 26" high	75	112	150
Wall Walker Doll, 6" high	27	41	55
Wind-up, tin, Howdy Doody and Bob Smith at the piano, Unique	680	1020	1360
Wind-up, tin, Howdy does jig and Bob Smith sits at piano, Marx, c. 1950, 5-1/2" high	550	825	1100
Wind-up, tin, Howdy plays banjo and moves head, c. 1950, Marx, 5" high	240	360	480
Zippy the Chimp Marionette, 1950s, Peter Puppet Playthings	550	800	1200

HUCKLEBERRY HOUND

	C6	C8	C10
Aeroplane, "Huckleberry Hound Yogi Bear," tin friction, Linemar	425	638	850

Huckleberry Hound Aeroplane, tin friction, Linemar, $850

	C6	C8	C10
Doll, stuffed, Knickerbocker, 1959, 18" high	27	41	55
Fireman Squeeze Toy, rubber, fireman, 1960s, 9" high	100	150	200
Hand Puppet, Knickerbocker, 1959	14	21	28
Squeeze Toy, rubber, w/top hat, Dell, 1960s, 6" high	22	33	44
Wind-up, "Huckleberry Hound Car," tin, Marx, 1962, 4" long	130	195	260
Wind-up, "Huckleberry Hound Hopper," tin, Linemar, 1962, 4-1/2" high	200	300	400
Wind-up, "Huckleberry Hound Tricycle," 1961, Linemar, 4" high	400	600	800

JAMES BOND

	C6	C8	C10
007 attache case, includes code book, rifle, bullets, Code-O-Matic, billfold w/money, James Bond business cards and instructions, c. 1965, 11"	263	395	525
100 Shot Repeater Cap Pistol w/Silencer, from *Goldfinger, 9" long, 1961, Lone Star Co.*	*88*	*132*	*175*
Aston Martin, die-cast, No. 270, Corgi	98	150	195
Aston Martin, die-cast, No. 271, Corgi	105	158	210
Camera	138	205	275
Hand Puppet, A.C. Gilbert, 1965	140	210	280
Moonraker Shuttlecraft	38	57	75

JETSONS

	C6	C8	C10
George Jetson squeeze action cable, Marx, 1963, 4" high	150	225	300

Jetson Express Choo Choo Train, Marx, 1960s, $500

	C6	C8	C10
Jetson Express Choo Choo Train, wind-up, Marx, 1960s, 13" long 250		375	500
Turnover Tank, tin wind-up, Linemar 205		308	410
Wind-up, "Astro - the Jetsons' Dog," tin, 1963, Marx, 5" high 212		318	425
Wind-up, George Jetson, tin, Marx, c. 1965, 4" high 190		275	380

LONE RANGER

	C6	C8	C10
Bendy, Lakeside, No. 8705, 1967, 6" high.... 16		24	32
Chuck Wagon Lantern 75		112	150
Deputy Badge, 1950s 9		13	18
Doll, composition, Dollcraft, 1938, 20" high 300		450	600
Double Target set, includes two-sided target, gun, two darts, Marx, 1939 125		188	250
Flashlight.. 80		120	160
Hand Puppet, "Stringless Marionette," cloth and vinyl 120		180	240
Hand Puppet, Ideal, 1966 25		38	50
Hand Puppet, vinyl head, c. 1956 80		120	160
Harmonica, Magnus, 1950 40		60	80
Hat, 1930s 65		98	130
Hat, white felt w/red trim, marked "Lone Ranger Hi! Yo! Silver!," 1940s 22		33	45
Lone Ranger and Silver Figure, composition, 4-1/2" high 88		132	175
Lone Ranger Official Outfit, M.A. Henry Co., 1942 70		105	140
Movie Viewer, Lone Ranger Rides Again, 1939 113		170	225
Moviescope Set, includes four films—No. 1 Superman, No. 2 Lone Ranger, No. 3 Lone Ranger, No. 4 Lone Ranger, w/pop-up box, Acme, 1948 72		108	145

Left to Right: Lone Ranger Doll, composition, Dollcraft, 1938, $600; Tonto Doll, composition, Dollcraft, 1938, $1,000

Left to Right: Lone Ranger Wind-up, lithographed tin, Marx, 1938, $385; Lone Ranger Wind-up, chromed tin, Marx, 1938, $360

	C6	C8	C10
Official First-Aid Kit, tin litho, w/contents, 1938 105		158	210
Official Outfit, includes mask, jail keys, badge, silver bullet, glow belt, and Lone Ranger buckle, shows Lee Powell and Chief Thundercloud on belt, 1939 62		93	125
Picture Printing set, includes eight rubber stamps, 1939 75		112	150
Play Set, Ranch Set, series 500, Marx 250		375	500
Push Toy, w/wood base, Kohner, 1950s....... 42		63	85
Rodeo Play Set, w/metal bldgs., plastic figures, etc., Marx, 1950s, No. 9392 200		300	400
Signal Siren, w/silver bullet secret code, United States Electric Mfg. Co., 1950s... 65		98	130
Silver Bullet Knife, 3" long closed................ 92		138	185
Strongbox (coin bank), 1938 100		150	200
Target Game, Marx, 1938 52		78	105
Wind-up, on "Range Rider" rocker base, Marx, 1938, 10-1/2" high...................... 350		525	700
Wind-up, on "Range Rider" rocker, chrome version, Marx, 1938, 8-1/2" high from top of lariat.............. 180		270	360
Wind-up, on "Range Rider" rocker, litho version, Marx, 1938, 8-1/2" high from top of lariat 193		290	385

MORTIMER SNERD

	C6	C8	C10
Doll, composition and wire, Ideal, 13" high 338		505	675
Figure, celluloid, 5" high 200		300	400
Hand Puppet 75		112	150
Jack-in-the-Box, c. 1930s, 8" high 100		150	200

Mortimer Snerd Doll, composition and wire, Ideal, $675

Oliver Hardy Sparkler, Isla, Spanish, $2,000

	C6	C8	C10
Teeth, plastic teeth w/dental wax, c. 1950	15	22	30
Tricky Auto, Marx, 1939	370	555	740
Wind-up, "Home Town Band," tin, Marx, 1935	450	675	900
Wind-up, tin, Mortimer's hat tips as he walks, Marx, c. 1939	300	450	600

OLIVER HARDY

	C6	C8	C10
Bendy Doll, 1960, Knickerbocker, 9" high	27	41	55
Hand Puppet, Knickerbocker	25	38	50
Roly-Poly, plastic, 10-1/2" high	22	33	44
Sparkler, Isla, Spanish	1000	1500	2000
Wind-up, Lakeside, 1960s, 5" high	35	52	70

ROY ROGERS

	C6	C8	C10
Bandanna, large	48	72	95
Bobbin' Head Doll, 6" high, 1962	90	135	180
Branding Iron Set	40	60	80
Double R Bar Ranch, tin litho ranch house, Marx, 1950s	175	263	350
Mineral City, tin, town inlcudes hotel, music hall, cafe, bank, barber shop, and trade goods	185	278	370

Mortimer Snerd Home Town Bank, Marx, 1935, $900

Roy Rogers Chuck Wagon, Ideal, 1950s, $245

Roy Rogers Stage Coach Wagon Train, Marx, 1950s, $160

	C6	C8	C10
Nellie Belle Jeep, metal	30	45	60
Pocket Flashlight	37	56	75
Quickshooter Hat w/Secret Gun	90	135	180
Ranch Lantern, hurricane-type w/plastic chimney, No. 90, 1950s, 7-3/4" tall	78	115	155
Rodeo Ranch Play Set, Marx	125	188	250
Roy Rogers and Bullet Hobby Horse, 1950s, N.N. Hill Brass Co. No. 812, 19" long	200	300	400
Roy Rogers and Trigger pocket knife	75	112	150
Roy Rogers Buckboard, Ideal, 1950s, 16" long	65	98	130
Roy Rogers Chuck Wagon, Ideal, 1950s, 13" long	123	185	245
Roy Rogers Fix-it Stagecoach, Ideal, 1950s, 13" long	90	135	180

Roy Rogers Signal Flashlight, $190

	C6	C8	C10
Roy Rogers Horse Trailer and Jeep, Ideal, 1950s, 15" long	180	270	360
Roy Rogers Stage Coach Wagon Train, wind-up, plastic, 14" long, 1950s	80	120	160
Signal Flashlight	95	140	190
Telescope	40	60	80
Wagon Train, Marx	150	225	300
Western Town Play Set, Marx	125	188	250

TOM CORBETT

	C6	C8	C10
Cosmic Vision Space Helmet, one-way vision, plastic, early 1950s	207	310	415
Official Outfit, Yankiboy	92	138	185
Polaris Rocket Ship, wind-up, depicts Tom, Astro and Rogers looking out of cockpit, Marx, 1952, 12" long	300	450	600
Space Academy Set, Marx No. 7000	238	355	475
Space Cadet 2-Way Space Phone, Zimmerman	80	120	160
Space Cadet Field Glasses, three power, Herald, 5-1/2" long	60	90	120
Space Cadet Flashlight w/built-in signal siren, 7" long, metal, U.S. Alite Corp	90	135	180
Space Cadet Molding and Coloring Set, Model Craft	55	82	110
Space Cadet Official Space Pistol, Marx No. 105	180	270	360
Space Cadet Rifle, Marx No. 0239	140	210	280
Space Hat, Lee	40	60	80
Space Station	325	490	650
Spurs, metal and leather, 1934	150	225	300
Tom Corbett Space Cadet Atomic Rifle, Marx, 1950s, 24" long	150	225	300
Tom Corbett Space Cadet Official Space Pistol, 1950s, Rockhill, 9-1/2" long	105	158	210

YOGI BEAR

	C6	C8	C10
Doll, stuffed, Knickerbocker, 1973, 7-1/2" high	45	68	90
Friction car, Marx, 1962	100	150	200
Go-Cart, Linemar	138	205	275
Hand Puppet, 1959	12	18	24
Jellystone National Park Play Set, Marx	350	525	700
Tricky Trapeze, 1967, 5" high	17	25	34
Yogi Bear Car, Marx, 1962, 4" long	100	150	200
Yogi Bear Hopper, wind-up, Linemar, 1962, 4" high	300	450	600

MISCELLANEOUS

	C6	C8	C10
Alvin Chipmunk Soaky	10	15	20

Left to Right: Amos tin wind-up, Marx, without box.

Beverly Hillbillies Wind-up Car, Ideal, 1960s, $540

	C6	C8	C10
Augie Doggie Soaky	27	41	55
Babalooie Soaky	15	22	30
Babalooie, vinyl face, Knickerbocker, 14" high	30	45	60
Baby Huey Hand Puppet, Gund, late 1950s	24	36	48
Baby Sandy Pull Toy, Sandy & Goose, Gong Bell, 12-1/2" long	150	225	300
Bat Masterson Gun and Holster Set, w/cane and vest, Carnell, 1958	138	205	275
Beatles Figures, vinyl, Ringo, John, Paul, George, Remco, 1964, 5" high, each	45	68	90
Beatles Soakies, each	62	93	125
Ben Casey Doll, 1962, 12" high	85	127	170
Ben Casey Play Hospital Set, Transogram	60	90	120
Ben Hur Sword, scabbard and shield, Marx, 1959	142	213	285
Beverly Hillbillies car, wind-up, Ideal, 1960s	270	405	540
Bob Burns Bazooka, brass kazoo-like toy, metal sliding tube, M.M. Pochapia Toys, 1930s, 13" long not extended	20	30	40
Bob Hope Hand Puppet, c. 1940	32	48	65

	C6	C8	C10
Bojangles Dances Again, tin litho and wood, tap button on base and he dances, 1930s	200	300	400
Buck Jones Rangers chaps	90	135	180
Buffalo Bill Jr. Belt and Buckle, 1950s	25	38	50
Bugs Bunny & Porky Pig Talking Toy, 1940s	95	143	190
Bugs Bunny Hand Puppet, early 1950s	22	33	45
Bugs Bunny Soaky, 10" high	12	18	25
Bullet (Roy Rogers' dog) Doll, stuffed, c. 1955	40	60	80
Buster Keaton Sparkler, tin litho, w/moving arms and legs, Spanish, c. 1925, 7" high	1650	2475	3300
Captain Gallant Foreign Legion holster outfit	80	120	160
Captain Gallant Play Set, Marx	400	600	800
Captain Kangaroo Badge, tin shield, 1960s	20	30	40

The Box for Bat Masterson Gun and Holster Set. The complete set, by Carnell, is valued at $275.

Buster Keaton Sparkler with Moving Arms and Legs, Spanish, c. 1925, $3,300

	C6	C8	C10
Captain Kangaroo Doll, talking type, Mattel, 1967, 20" high	21	32	42
Captain Kangaroo Hand Puppet, 1960s	22	33	45
Charlie Weaver Nodder	112	188	225
Cheyenne Target Game, Mettoy, 1961	62	93	125
Chitty Chitty Bang Bang, Corgi	125	188	250
Cisco Kid Broomstick Horse, 1950s	35	53	70
Cisco Kid Neckerchief, w/nickel sombrero slide	50	75	100
Cisco Kid Western Outfit, 1950s	98	145	195
Clyde Beatty Hingees Set, 1944	25	38	50
Cowardly Lion Facemask (Wizard Of Oz), molded gauze	40	60	80
Creature Soaky	55	83	110
Danny O'Day (Jimmy Nelson) Ventriloquist Doll	40	60	80
Deputy Dawg Doll, stuffed, Ideal, 1961, 14" high	37	56	75
Deputy Dawg Soaky	15	22	30
Dick Van Dyke Doll, talking type, from Chitty Chitty Bang Bang, Mattel, 1967	125	188	250
Doggie Daddie Doll, vinyl head, Knickerbocker	100	150	200
Dorothy and Toto (Wizard of Oz) Figure, Mego	19	28	38
Dr. Dolittle Hand Puppet, talking type, Mattel, 1967	32	48	65
Dr. Dolittle Music Box, Gee-Tar, Mattel, 1967	40	60	80
Dr. Dolittle Pushmi Pullyu, 1965	43	65	87
Ed Wynn Fire Chief, jointed wood w/ax in hand	80	120	160
Emerald City Play Set (Wizard of Oz), Mego	80	120	160
Fanny Brice (Baby Snooks) Doll, composition and wire, Ideal, 12" high	125	188	250
Farfel (Jimmy Nelson) Hand Puppet, Juro	85	127	170
Farmer Alfalfa (Terrytoons) Doll, stuffed body w/vinyl head and hands, c. 1950, 17-1/2" high	30	45	60
Flip Wilson Geraldine Doll, talking type, Shindana, 1970	25	38	50
Flying Nun Flying Toy, Rayline, 1970	25	38	50
Flying Nun, Hasbro, 1960s, 4-3/4"	25	38	50
Frankenstein Soaky	55	83	110
Froggie the Gremlin Squeeze Toy, 10-3/4" high	170	255	340
Froggie the Gremlin Squeeze Toy, 6-1/2" high	34	51	68
Froggie the Gremlin Squeeze Toy, 9-1/4" high	40	60	80

	C6	C8	C10
Froggie the Gremlin Squeeze Toy, hollow rubber, Rempel, 1950s, 5" high	62	93	125
Gabby Doll (Gulliver's Travels), wood-jointed, Ideal, 10-1/2" high	300	450	600
Gangbusters Target Game, Marx	55	83	110
Gene Autry Marionette, 18" high, 1940s	140	210	280
Gene Autry spurs	60	90	120
General Figure (Wizard of Oz), Mego	45	68	90
Get Smart Spy Purse Kit, Miner Ind., 7" long	30	45	60
Gilligan's Island Floating Island Play Set	88	132	175
Glinda Figure (Wizard of Oz), Mego, 1972, 8" high	19	28	38
Gomez Hand Puppet (Addams Family)	70	105	142
Groucho Marx "Ventriloquist Play Pal," Goldberger	40	60	80
Gulliver's Travels Boat, wooden, Paramount	110	165	220
Gulliver's Travels Drum, tin, Chein, 1939	25	38	50
Gulliver's Travels Musical top, Chein	30	45	60
Gulliver's Travels Sandpail, tin, Chein	45	68	90
Gumby, Bendee Figure	11	16	23
Gumby, Hand Puppet, Lakeside, 1965	17	26	35
Gumby, Wind-up, vinyl, dated 1966, 4" high	50	75	100
Gumby's Jeep, metal, 1960s, 12"	125	188	250
Gunsmoke Handcuffs and Badge, c. 1952	42	63	85
Henry Fonda Texas Ranger Sheriff Badge, The Deputy, 1951	17	26	35
Herman Munster Doll, Mattel	88	132	175
Herman Munster Hand Puppet, vinyl, 1960s	95	140	190
Herman Munster Puppet, talking-type	200	300	400
Highway Patrol Pistol Outfit, includes gun, holster, badge, handcuffs, ID, whistle, etc., Halco, 1956	125	188	250
Highway Patrol, "Highway Patrol Car," Broderick Crawford, 8" long	75	112	150

Jackie Coogan Wind-up Walker, German, $1,600

Jackie Gleason "Away We Go" Bus, $900

	C6	C8	C10
Hoot Gibson Cowboy Outfit, Wornova Clothes, 1935	70	105	140
Hoot Gibson Lariat	40	60	80
Hoot Gibson Outfit, "Squaw style," Wornova Clothes, 1930s	60	90	120
Hugh O'Brian-Wyatt Earp, Dodge City Western Town, Marx, 1950s	450	675	900
I Spy target set	17	26	35
J. Fred Muggs Hand Puppet (Today show), 1954	41	62	82
J. Fred Muggs pull toy, Gong Bell	90	135	180
Jackie Coogan ("The Kid") Walker, tin wind-up, German, 7" high	800	1200	1600
Jackie Coogan Candy Container, glass, 5" high	800	1200	1600
Jackie Coogan Figure, celluloid, 5-1/2" high, 1920s	130	195	260
Jackie Gleason Bus, "Away We Go," 13" high	450	675	900
Jackie Gleason Climbing toy	62	93	125
Jackie Gleason Doll, 1950s, 30" high	200	300	400
Jackie Gleason, "Story Stage Theatre," Utopia Enterprises, copyright 1955	123	185	245
Jerry Lewis/Dean Martin Hand Puppet, two-sided	150	225	300

Joe Penner tin wind-up, Marx, c. 1930s, $700

	C6	C8	C10
Jerry Mahoney Ventriloquist dummy	115	173	230
Joe Penner, tin wind-up, tips hat, walks, marked "Wanna Buy a Duck?," Marx, c. 1930s, 8" high	350	525	700
Jungle Jim Play Set, Marx	500	800	1100
King Little (Gulliver's Travels), jointed composition, Ideal, 12"	325	488	650
Kukla & Ollie Puppet theatre, cardboard, 1962	50	75	100
Lambchop Shari Lewis Hand Puppet	18	27	36
Lion (Wizard of Oz) Figure, Mego, 1972, 15" long	15	22	30
Lucy ("Peanuts") Squeeze Doll, vinyl, 1950s	15	22	30
Lurch (Addams Family), Remco	100	150	200
Magilla Gorilla Doll, Ideal, 1960s, 19" high	90	135	180
Magilla Gorilla Doll, Ideal, 8" high	62	93	125
Magilla Gorilla Hand Puppet, Ideal, 1960s.	24	36	48
Man from U.N.C.L.E. Secret print putty, c. 1965	25	38	50
Mary Poppins Hand Puppet, Gund	48	72	95
Matt Dillon (Gunsmoke) badge, U.S. Marshall	9	30	38
Mayor Munchkin (Wizard of Oz) Figure, Mego	45	68	90
Men Into Space Space Helmet, retractable visor, space mike, made of fortiflex	65	98	130
Milton Berle Car, w/two large and two small wheels, "What the Hey," written on car, Marx, 1950s	215	323	430
Morticia (Addams Family), Remco, 1964	93	140	195
Mr. Ed Hand Puppet, Mattel, 1962	48	72	95
Mr. Magoo Doll, Ideal, 15" high	45	68	90
Mr. Magoo Hand Puppet, vinyl, 1962	32	48	65
Mr. Magoo Soaky, 11" high	20	30	40
Mummy Soaky	60	90	120
Munchkinland Play Set (Wizard of Oz)	65	98	130
Munchkins (Wizard of Oz) Figures, Mego, total of four, each	48	72	95
Munster, Herman: See Herman Munster			
Munsters, Grandpa Hand Puppet, vinyl, 1960s	93	140	185
Munsters, Lily Munster hand puppet, 1960s	95	140	190
My Favorite Martian, "Martian Magic Tricks," magic set, Gilbert, 1964	115	175	230
Pink Panther Hand Puppet, cloth body, early, Gund	20	30	40
Pinky Lee Doll, vinyl, squeeze and his head pops up, 1950	90	135	180
Pinky Lee pull toy, Gong Bell	100	150	200
Poky (Gumby) Bendee Figure	14	22	29

	C6	C8	C10
Poky Hand Puppet, Lakeside, 1965 24	36	47
Poky Jack-in-the-Box, Lakeside, 1965 16	24	32
Poky Wind-up, vinyl, dated 1966, 4" high .. 37	56	75
Quick Draw McGraw "Quick Draw McGraw Hopper," Linemar, 1962, 4-1/2" high 200	300	400
Quick Draw McGraw Squeeze Toy, Dell, 9-1/2" high 100	150	200
Quick Draw McGraw, "Animal Airplane," Linemar, 1960s, 8-1/2" long w/9-1/2" wingspan 400	600	800
Quick Draw McGraw, Knickerbocker, 17-1/2" high..................... 105	158	210
Ramar of the Jungle Play Set..................... 217	325	435
Rat Patrol Giant Action Battle Set 250	375	500
Rat Patrol Jeep, Marx..................... 200	300	400
Ricochet Rabbit, Ideal..................... 52	78	105
Rifleman (TV) Ranch, Marx..................... 600	1000	1500
Rin Tin Tin and Rusty knife, 1950s 60	90	120
Rin Tin Tin Bugle, w/banner 37	56	75
Rin Tin Tin Doll, stuffed, Ideal..................... 37	56	75
Rin Tin Tin, Fort Apache Stockade, Marx No. 3628, 1950s 190	285	380
Robin Hood Bow and Arrow Set, Richard Greene, 1956..................... 6	9	12
Robin Hood Money Pouch, w/fifteen foreign coins 20	30	40
Robin Hood money pouch, w/six foreign coins, 1953-54 20	30	40
Robin Hood Shield. Badge, w/embossed Robin Hood and gem stone, c. 1956...... 25	38	50
Rocky the Flying Squirrel Bendee Figure, 1960s, Wham-O 10	15	21
Rocky the Flying Squirrel Hand Puppet 25	38	50
Rocky the Flying Squirrel Soaky..................... 20	30	40
Rookies (TV) Official Police Car, Fleetwood, 1975 15	22	30
Rootie Kazootie Doll, Effanbee, 19" high.... 62	93	125
Rootie Kazootie Marionette, rubber head and hands, wooden shoes, 14" high 90	135	180
Scarecrow Facemask (Wizard of Oz), molded gauze 60	90	120
Scarecrow Figure (Wizard of Oz), Mego, 1972, 8" high..................... 14	21	28
Scrappy & Margie pull toy, wooden, 13-1/2" long..................... 165	248	330
Scrappy Doll (Columbia Pictures), cloth and composition, E.D. & T.C. Co., c. 1935, 14-1/2" high 320	480	640
Secret Squirrel Soaky..................... 37	56	75
Sgt. Bilko Holster Set, from CBS TV series "You'll Never Get Rich," contains leather holster and belt w/die-cast		

	C6	C8	C10
Army, arm patch and Sgt. Bilko hat w/Badge, Halco Brand, 1956 100	150	200
Shadow Crimefighter Detection Belt, w/pistol and handcuffs, Madison, Ltd., 1978 15	22	30
Shadow Felt Hat, early 1940s..................... 187	280	375
Shirley Temple playhouse 120	180	240
Simon Chipmunk Soaky..................... 11	16	23
Sneak Facemask (Gulliver's Travels), molded gauze 1939 50	75	100
Soupy Sales Doll, Sunshine Doll Co., 1965, 5" high 90	135	180
Soupy Sales Marionette, Knickerbocker, 1966 37	56	75
Stan Laurel Bendem Doll, Knickerbocker, 1960, 9" high 22	33	45
Stan Laurel Doll, Dean..................... 400	600	800
Stan Laurel Hand Puppet, Knickerbocker..................... 24	36	48
Stan Laurel, wind-up, Lakeside, 5" high, 1960s..................... 35	52	70
Star Trek, Mr. Spock Vulcan Ears, 1976 7	11	15
Sylvester Hand Puppet, early 1950s............. 50	75	100
Sylvester Soaky 16	24	32
Sylvester, cloth, 1971, 15" high 30	45	60
Tales of the Texas Rangers Deputy Badge ... 12	18	24
Tarzan Bendy, Mego, 1972 25	38	50
Tennessee Tuxedo Soaky..................... 17	26	35
Theodore (Chipmunk) Soaky 10	15	20
Three Stooges as part of Jolly Theatre, 1930s..................... 125	188	250
Three Stooges Hand Puppet, includes Moe, Curley, and Larry, 1959, 9-1/2" high, each 90	135	180
Tim Holt Litho Target, w/dart gun 70	105	140
Tinman Facemask (Wizard of Oz), molded gauze 60	90	120
Tinman Figure (Wizard of Oz), Mego, 1972, 8" high 15	22	30
Tom Mix on Tony, Arcor Rubber, 1930s 85	128	170
Tom Mix Rocking Horse, wooden 1930s.. 175	263	350
Tom Mix Rodeo Rope, 1928, w/box and instructions 100	150	200
Tonto (Lone Ranger) Doll, composition head,hands, feet, Dollcraft, 20" high, 1938 500	750	1000
Tonto Hand Puppet, Ideal, 1966 21	31	42
Tonto Hand Puppet, vinyl head, mid 1950s..................... 48	72	95
Topo Gigio (Ed Sullivan Show) nodder...... 75	112	150
Topo Gigio airplane, friction 75	112	150
Umbriago (Jimmy Durante) Hand Puppet, American Merchandise, 1945................ 45	68	90

W.C. Fields Doll with Movable Mouth, Effanbee, $850

	C6	C8	C10
Untouchables Detective set, includes gun, holster, etc., Marx	112	168	225
Untouchables Tommy Gun, Marx, 1950s, 23" long	48	72	96
W.C. Fields Doll, w/movable mouth, Effanbee, 19" high	425	638	850
Wagon Train Play Set, Marx	213	320	425
Waterfront "Cheryl Ann" Tugboat (TV series), 1950s, 21"	100	150	200
Wicked Witch Figure (Wizard of Oz), Mego, 1972, 8" high	20	30	40
Wild Bill Hickok and Jingles Holster Set	50	75	100
Wild Bill Hickok Marshal Star Badge, w/picture of Hickok and Jingles in center	42	63	85
Wile E. Coyote, Dakin, 1970s	12	18	25
Witch's Castle (Wizard of Oz), Mego	175	262	350
Wizard (Wizard of Oz) Figure, Mego, 8" high	8	12	17
Wizard of Oz masks, Einson-Freement Co., Inc., 1939, set of five	138	205	275
Wizard of Oz, four-headed hand puppet, talks, Mattel, c. 1967	105	158	210
Wolfman Soaky	60	90	120
Wyatt Earp Play Set, Marx	275	415	550
Wyatt Earp U.S. Marshall Badge, 20th century, 1950s	14	21	28
Wyatt Earp U.S. Marshall Badge, L one Star	18	27	36
Yellow Submarine, Corgi	180	270	360
Yosemite Sam Squeak Toy, Dakin, 1970, 4" high	16	24	33

	C6	C8	C10
Uncle Fester Hand Puppet, vinyl, 1960s	65	98	130
Underdog Doll, large	62	93	125
Underdog Doll, medium	50	75	100
Underdog Doll, small	40	60	80

PEZ

PEZ candy dispensers first became available in the United States around 1950, although the candy was produced in Austria as far back as the 1930s. It wasn't until the late 1940s that the "box" or dispenser became available with the candy. The very first dispenser had no head (the aspect most of us associate with PEZ), making it resemble a cigarette lighter. Soon thereafter, a Spacegun, a full-bodied Santa, a full-bodied Robot and many more dispensers appeared. Who can forget the fun of favorite cartoon friends tilting their heads back to offer a piece of PEZ candy?

Over the years PEZ dispensers have been manufactured in Austria, Yugoslavia, Hong Kong and the United States. Dispensers are usually marked with one of these five patent numbers—2,620,061; 3,410,455; 3,845,882; 3,942,683; or 4,966,305, which appears on items dated from 1992 to the present. It is virtually impossible to date a dispenser with any certainty, although the patent number can sometimes be a vague indicator. Neither the country of origin, the patent number, nor the age are necessarily tied to value. The bottom line on value is which head is on the dispenser.

Since their introduction in the United States, PEZ dispensers have been continuously available. As of late 1998, there are approximately 350 different PEZ dispensers known. This figure excludes color variation and other minor differences occurring on individual dispensers. Only the more valuable dispensers are are found in these listings. Other companies—Totems, Yummies and Smarties—have copied the dispenser with head concept, but none have approached the universal acceptance of PEZ.

The years 1997 and 1998 were big years for PEZ collectors. It was not unusual to see prices rise 100 percent over the 1996 figures. The influence of the Internet, the large American market and increased foreign collector interest made PEZ one of the blue-chip collectibles of the late 1990s.

Prices given are for dispensers in Excellent to Mint condition. Defects such as missing pieces, melt marks, scuffs, excessive dirt and cracks decrease the value by a minimum of twenty percent. The condition of the stem that holds the candy does not affect value as much as the condition of the head. Exceptions to this rule apply in the cases of Regulars, Die-Cuts, Guns, Zorro A, Psychedelics and other dispensers in which the stem itself is an important part of the identity or appearance. Missing head pieces and facial melt marks can render most dispensers valueless. However, the heads alone are sometimes of value on the most expensive dispensers.

Contributor: David Welch, P.O. Box 714, Murphysboro, IL 62966. Welch is convinced he has spent more money on PEZ items than any other two people combined. He also claims the finest collection of PEZ-related advertising in the world. Welch has authored several books on PEZ dispensers and Pez collecting—*Pictorial Guide to Plastic Candy Dispensers featuring PEZ* and *Collecting PEZ*.

	C10
Alpine, 1972 Olympics	1200
Arithmetic	650
Astronaut	
White helmet	150
Blue helmet	175
Clear helmet	150
Clear helmet w/"Cocoa Marsh" on side	200
Small helmet, silver or white	600
Baseball Glove w/ball	225
Baseball Glove w/home plate/bat	600
Batman w/cape	125
Betsy Ross	150
Bozo	175
Bozo Die-Cut w/"Bozo/Butch" on side	225
Bride w/white veil	1500
Brutus (from Popeye)	225

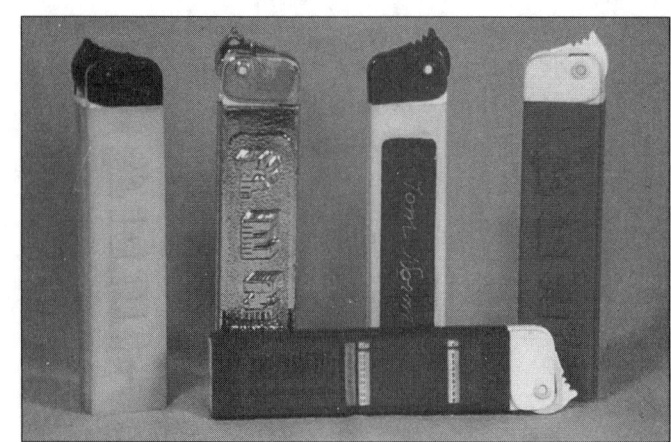

Left to Right: Regular, no markings, $150; Regular, Golden Glow with gold shiny finish, $300; Regular, personalized with paper label on side, $300; Regular, no markings. Bottom: Arithmetic, $650

Left to Right: Little Orphan Annie, $145; Bullwinkle, $275; Brutus, $225; Olive Oyl, $250; Popeye, $150

	C10
Bullwinkle	275
Camel Whistle	50
Captain	150
Captain Hook	150
Casper	225
Casper Die-Cut ("Casper" on side)	300
Chick in Egg w/o hat	85
Cow w/large nose and circular ears	100
Cowboy	275
Creature from the Black Lagoon	
Green cartridge/head	300
Darker green head/orange cartridge	175
Black head	200
Crocodile	100
Dalmatian Pup, foreign issue	50
Daniel Boone w/coonskin cap	175
Doctor	65
Dog	40
Donald Duck Die-Cut, w/three duck nephews on side	175
Dopey	225
Easter Bunny with thin/straight ears	225

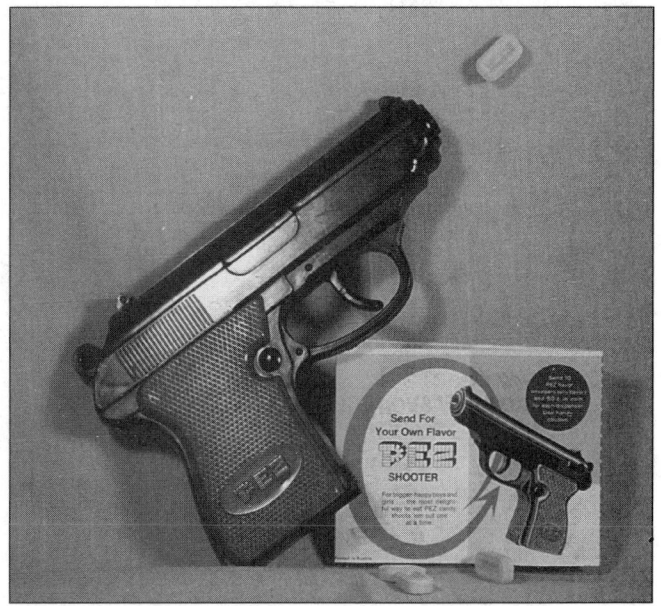

Pez Handgun, $125

	C10
Easter Bunny Die-Cut w/bunny w/eggs on side	600
Football Player	150
Frankenstein	250
Giraffe	175
Green Hornet	225
Groom w/black top hat and hat band	500
Gun	
Space, 1950s	400
Handgun, mail-order premium	125
Space, 1980s	85
Indian Brave	200
Indian Chief	125
Indian Squaw	120
Joker (from Batman), soft head	150
Knight	300

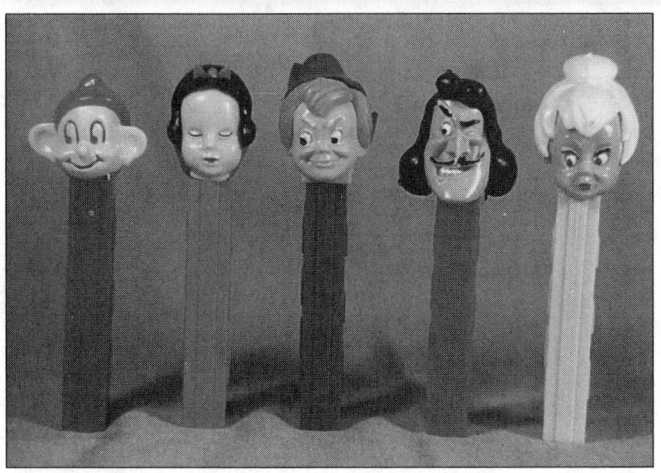

Left to Right: Dopey, 225; Snow White, 175; Peter Pan, $150; Captain Hook, $150; Tinkerbell, $250

Left to Right: Uncle Sam, $175; Wounded Soldier, $135; Betsy Ross, $150; Captain, $150; Daniel Boone with Coonskin Cap, $175

Left to Right: Astronaut with white helmet, $150; Astronaut with clear helmet, $150; Astronaut with small helmet, $600; Tobot, $400

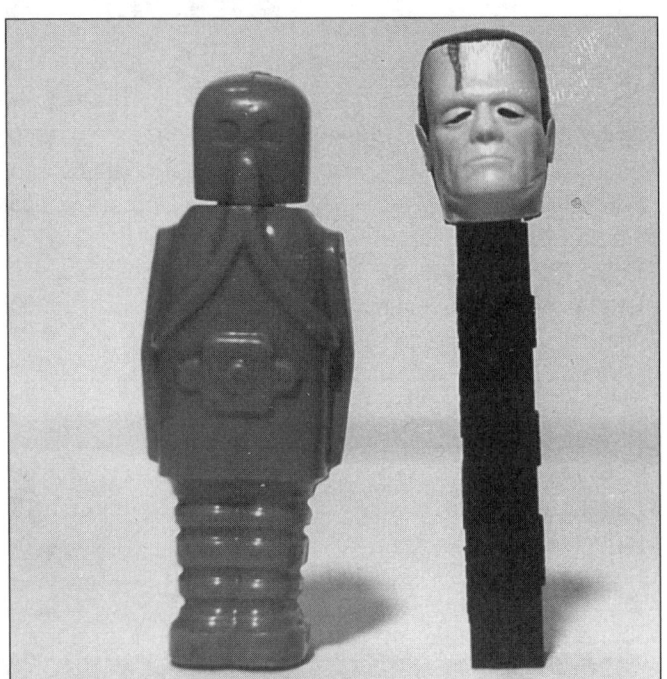

Left to Right: Robot, $400; Frankenstein, $250

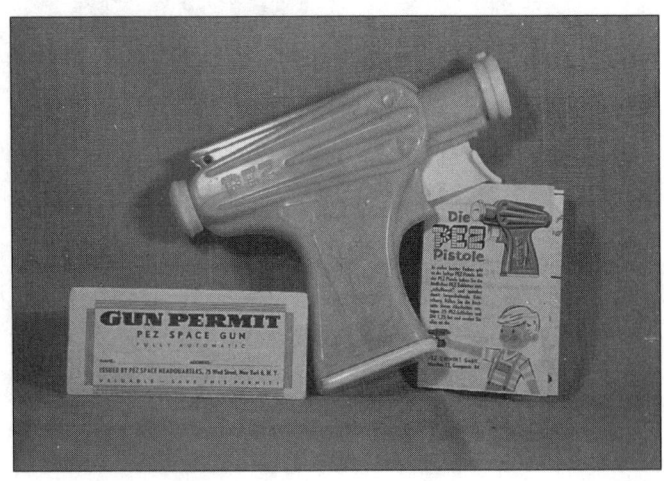

Space Gun, 1950s, $400

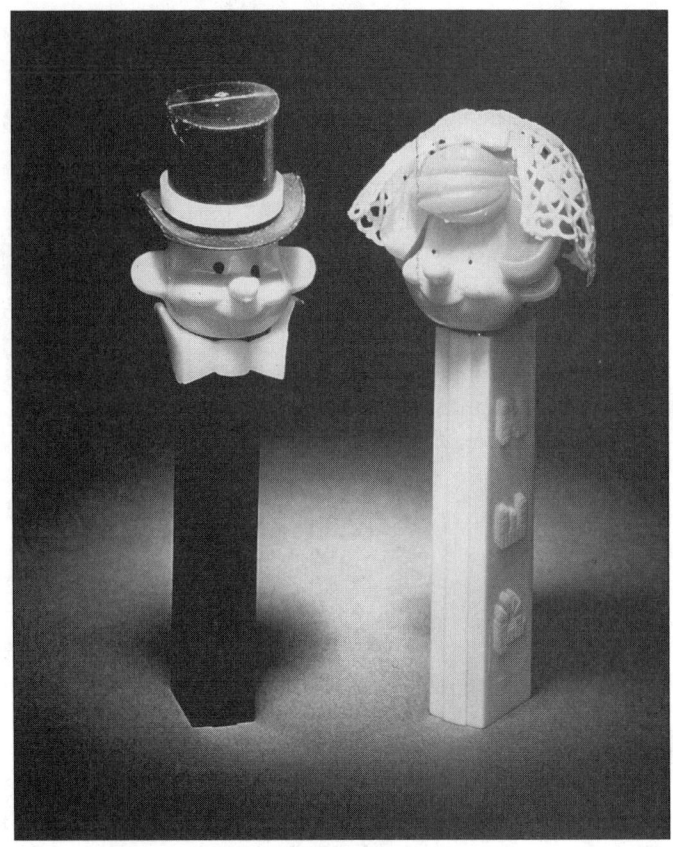

Left to Right: Groom, $500; Bride, $1,500

Left to Right: Wolfman, $275; Creature from the Black Lagoon, green cartridge/head, $300; Frankenstein, $250

Left to Right: Pear, $1,000; Pineapple with Sunglasses, $1,700+; Orange, 200

C10

Koala whistle.. 20
Lion's Club Lion, 1962, stem inscribed .... 2500+
Little Orphan Annie 145
Make-A-Face, similar to Mr. Potato Head w/seventeen
    face pieces, loose .... 2500+
    Same as above, mint on card................................ 3000+
Mary Poppins 750
Mickey Mouse Die-Cut, w/"Minnie" on side 175
Monsters, soft heads, six varieties, each 175
Olive Oyl.. 250
Orange 200
Panther, blue head 165
Pear w/visor 1000
Penguin (from Batman), soft head.................................. 165
Peter Pan 150
Pilgrim 135
Pineapple w/sunglasses .... 1700+

C10

Pinocchio (old version), has eyes looking up, feather
    is part of hat 200
Popeye (old version), hat cannot be removed 150
Psychedelic Eye, hand holding eyeball (versions
    marked "© 1967" or "1968" are 1998 reissues)............500
Psychedelic Flower, eyeball in flower 600
Regular (no heads)
    Personalized w/paper label on side...............................300
    Witch w/pictures of witches on side........................ 2000+
    Golden Glow w/gold shiny finish 150
    U.S. Zone Germany marking...200
    No markings 150
Rhino Whistle..25
Robot, full body, three colors 400
Sailor, full white beard w/blue hat...................................150
Santa, full body...225
Santa, face and beard same color 125
Santa, small head w/flesh face and white beard...............125
Snow White 175
Snowman w/Arms, 1976 Olympics..................................475
Stewardess...175
Thor, helmet w/wings 300
Tinkerbell...250
Uncle Sam..175
Witch, w/one-piece orange head 300
Wolf, 1984 Olympics
    Ski hat...700
    Bobsled hat 700
    No hat 700
Wolfman 275
Wounded Soldier...135
Zorro
    Marked "Zorro" on side...65
    Not marked "Zorro" on side...40

Left to Right: Santa, face and beard same color, $125; Santa, full body, $225; Santa, flesh face and white beard, $125

Left to Right: Mickey Mouse Die-Cut, $175, Donald Duck Die-Cut, $175; East Bunny Die-Cut, $600; Casper Die-Cut, $300; Bozo Die-Cut, $225

PLASTICVILLE

Bachman Bros., the producer of Plasticville buildings and accessories, dates back to 1833 when they manufactured ivory cane handles and combs, and by 1907 they were producing plastic eyeglass frames.

After WWII, the growth in the toy train market led Bachmann to create plastic picket fences to enclose toy train platforms. This evolved into building kits, the first of which was the Log Cabin. Production of HO- and N-scale accessories continued into the late 1960s, although in recent years Bachmann has reintroduced some of the old O/S scale buildings. During its heyday the Plasticville line boasted over 100 items.

	C6	C8	C10
Airport Admin Bldg	15	35	50
Airport Hangar	8	26	35
Apartment House	15	35	45
Apartment Add-a-Floor	8	18	25
Autumn Trees	15	35	50
Bank	8	21	28
Barn	8	18	25
Barbecue	1	2	2
Barnyard Animal Set	15	35	45
Billboard	1	2	3
Birdbath, Fence Section, Trellis	6	10	15
Bungalow	7	15	20
Cape Cod House Kit	8	26	35
Cathedral	20	48	65

Barnyard Animal Set, $45

Birdbath, Fence Section, Trellis, $15

Barn, $25

Left to Right: Outhouse, $12; Telephone Booth, $10; Well, $10; Barbecue, $2; Pump, $5

Cape Cod House Kit, $35

Diner Kit, $55

Fence and Gate, $6

Frosty Bar, $40

	C6	C8	C10
Cattle Loading Pen	8	11	15
Church/Parish Church	8	22	30
Coaling Station	8	10	12

	C6	C8	C10
Colonial Church	8	22	30
Colonial Mansion	8	26	35
Corner Store	7	18	25
Country Church	4	8	10
Covered Bridge	5	11	14
Dairy Barn	8	22	30
Diner Kit	18	42	55
Factory	25	58	75
Fence and Gate, twelve pieces	3	5	6
Fire House Kit	6	15	20
5 & 10	11	17	36
Freight Station	12	28	38
Frosty Bar	12	30	40
Gas Station, small	9	22	30
Greenhouse	19	27	62

Fire House Kit, $20

5 & 10, $36

Log Cabin, Rustic Fence and Tree, $25

Hobo Shacks, $50

Mobile Home, $50

	C6	C8	C10
Hobo Shacks, two buildings	15	38	50
Hospital w/furniture	20	48	65
House under Construction	30	75	100
Log Cabin, Rustic Fence and Tree	7	18	25
Mobile Home	15	38	50
Motel	6	15	20
New England Ranch House	10	24	32
Outhouse	4	9	12
Passenger Station	11	29	38
Pharmacy/Hardware	12	30	40
Plasticville Citizens	15	25	35
Police Dept., HO-scale	6	15	20
Police Dept., O-scale	14	34	45

Plasticville Citizens, $35

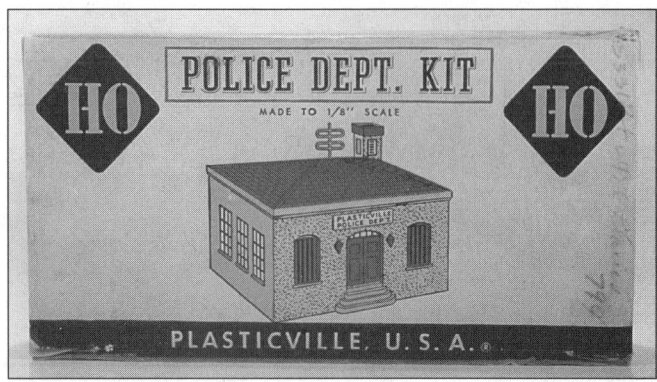

Police Dept., HO-scale, $20

Police Dept., O-scale, $45

	C6	C8	C10
Post Office	8	21	28
Pump	3	4	5
Railroad Accessories	12	30	40
Railroad Signal Bridge	4	8	11
Railroad Work Car	15	38	50
Ranch House	6	12	17
Road Signs	14	33	45
Roadside Stand	6	15	20
Schoolhouse	6	15	19

Supermarket, $16

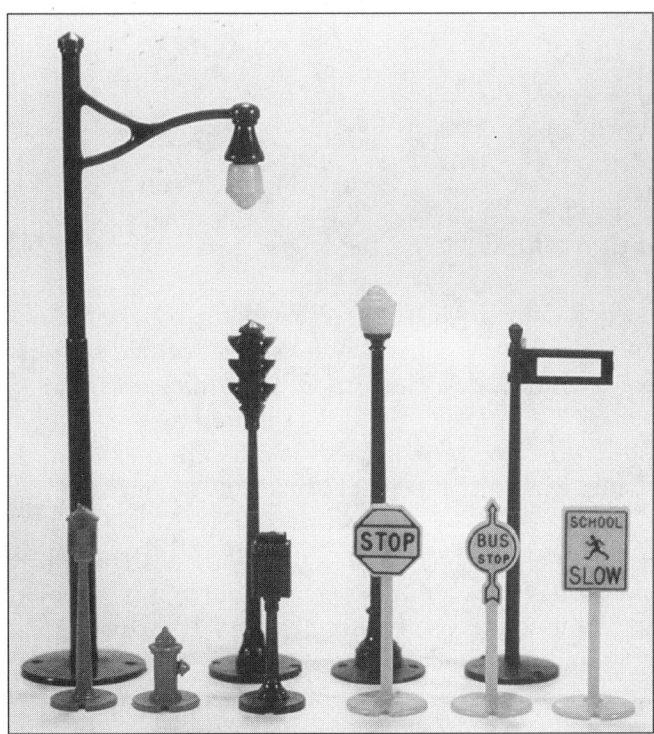

Street Accessories Unit, fifteen pieces, $45

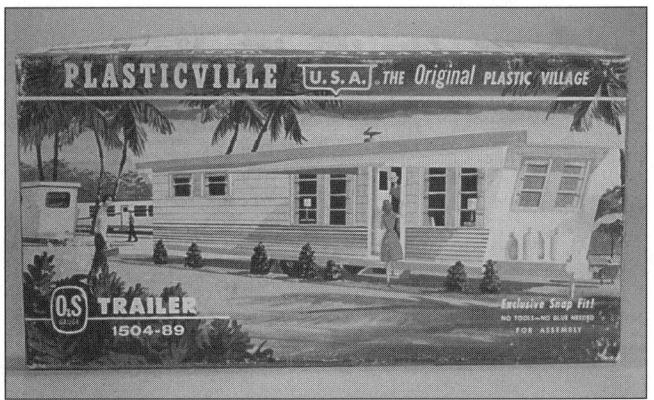

Trailer, $35

	C6	C8	C10
Split Level House	11	25	35
Street Accessories Unit, fifteen pieces	22	33	45
Suburban Station	3	7	9
Supermarket, large	10	26	35
Supermarket, small	5	12	16
Switch Tower (Railroad)	5	11	15
Telephone Booth	3	8	10
Town Hall	8	18	25
Trailer	11	26	35
Turnpike Interchange	15	38	50
TV Station	5	12	16
Union Station	14	33	45
Water Tank (Railroad)	3	8	10
Well	3	8	10
Windmill	18	45	60

Roadrace Accessories

	C6	C8	C10
Grandstand	12	30	40
Officials' Stand	8	18	25
Pit Stop	12	30	40
Sitting People	9	22	30

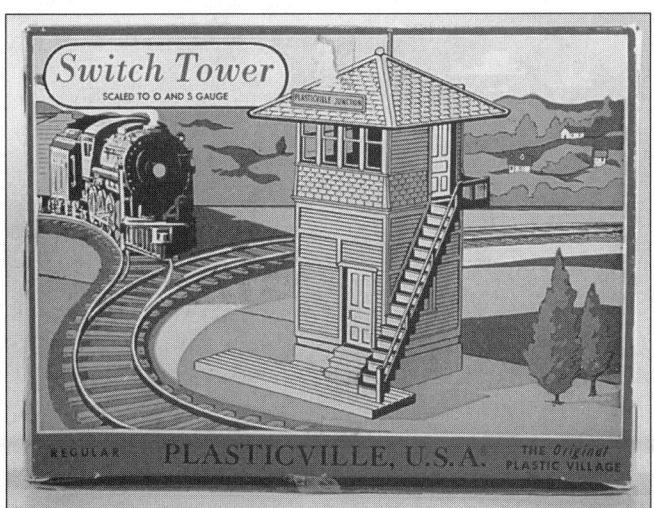

Switch, $15

Suburban Station, $9

Water Tank (Railroad), $10

PREMIUMS

Many radio premiums were nearly as free as the wonderful radio shows that advertised them.

We did have to pay the electric bill (or our folks did) to run the radio, and to get the offered toys we did have to send in a box-top from the sponsor's product.

Sometimes it was only that, a proof of purchase. Orphan Annie and Captain Midnight were particularly generous in responding with gifts for inner labels or inner seals from Ovaltine drink mix. Other times, usually only a dime was required "to handle the cost of handling and mailing." (That's really all it did do—the cost of the premium itself came from the advertising budget.)

The lure of the premium for kids then and for grown-up kids who are now collectors is difficult to explain to those who never lived through the era themselves. The ring or badge was more than the toy itself; it was our tangible link to those magical friends on the other side of the speaker cloth.

Those voices were wonderful out there: The rumbling bass of Brace Beemer as the Lone Ranger; the slightly "country" sound of Curley Bradley as Tom Mix; Bret Morrison, whom we recognized even as children was "sophisticated" as Lamont Cranston (alias The Shadow). But they were bodiless and yes, a bit remote. It was the premium they offered, the same as the one they were using in the story, that put us in touch with them.

There were historic precedents for radio premiums. There were pictures of famous actresses in cigarette packages around the turn of the century, and early radio personalities, such as bandleader Vincent Lopez, offered their autographed pictures. Such footnotes to history aside, radio premiums began with Little Orphan Annie in 1931. The plucky little waif from the Sunday comics first gave away sheet music of her theme song ("Who's that little chatterbox with the pretty auburn locks?") and her own photo, but very shortly, she offered a drinking mug that could be used to shake up Ovaltine powder with milk to make something resembling a soda fountain milk shake. The first significant radio premium, it was the only successful one that encouraged further use of the sponsor's product.

Many different models of the shake-up mug were offered by Annie and later by Captain Midnight (on both radio and TV). So successful were the offers, shake-up mugs are not rare or high in value. (The most sought after is the orange and blue, embossed—not decaled—Midnight mug.)

It was two years after Annie came to radio that the fledgling medium developed its classic adventure heroes. In 1933 there appeared the Lone Ranger, Tom Mix and Jack Armstrong. Unlike Annie, the two Westerners and the All-American Boy were still around until the 1950s, when television began driving out radio drama. In those nearly twenty years, the shows offered hundreds of give-away toys, which inspired similar premiums on dozens of other shows.

Any small toy that could be manufactured inexpensively might turn up as a premium. Those concerned with the great outdoors were popular. We had compasses, pedometers, telescopes, flashlights, pocket knives, signal mirrors, and portable telegraph sets.

Secret decoders and manuals of every size and description had special emblems and tokens. It is these and other paper items that have the greatest dollar value. They were the most easily lost or used up in the rush to adulthood. A Captain Midnight Secret Manual is worth more than the metallic decoder it accompanied.

The rarest paper item is the Lone Ranger Frontier Town, offered about 1947. To complete this model of a Western village, one had to get four different envelopes by mail, then augment this by buying several packages of Cheerios to cut out the model buildings from the packs. The complete set has been known to sell for hundreds of dollars and today might bring $4,000 for a Mint set.

Perhaps the most popular single type of premium was the ring. Rings let the listener show loyalty to the fraternity of his or her favorite hero, but in a less officious and more "grown-up" way than the badge (although they were also highly popular). Besides…the rings looked neat, and many of them could do things—some of them pretty incredible things.

As with radio premiums in general, the Tom Mix show (and Ralston cereal's premium manufacturer, the Robbins Company) blazed the trail with ingenious ring designs. In 1937, Tom Mix Straight Shooters could get a Signet Ring with their own initial on it. (Years later, Captain Midnight would offer a ring that would ink-stamp your initial.) By 1938, Tom had a ring that let you look in a peep-hole and see a magnified picture of himself and his horse, Tony. (Technology had progressed so much that by the fifties, Straight Arrow offered a similar ring that put your own photo, if supplied, alongside radio's great Indian hero.)

After World War II and the ease in metal rationing, Tom Mix offered a Magnet Ring. His spinning siren whistle ring was neat (but admittedly borrowed in design from Jack Armstrong's 1937 Egyptian Whistle Ring). Tom's Sliding Whistle Ring, which played different musical notes (about 1948), was unique, however. His Look-Around Ring concealed an inner mirror that let you see behind you (sort of), a design rustled for a later Tennessee Jed ring.

The final Tom Mix ring looked attractive, sporting a glowing cat's-eye, but the 1949 Tiger-Eye Ring was only lightweight plastic, a far cry from the well-crafted metal rings of a decade earlier. But then, the decade was nearly over, and so was the era, fading in the light of another glowing eye in the living room.

The Shadow's own Glow-in-the-Dark Ring (1939) had a band composed of two sculpted Shadow figures holding up a jagged blue stone—a proxy lump of his sponsor's product, Blue Coal. One of the very few Shadow premiums and the best-looking, this ring has sold for $950.

The identical mold for one glowing plastic ring was used for several different radio shows. The band had two crocodiles holding a setting in their mouths. The "stone" was black when it was Jack Armstrong's Dragon Eye Ring in 1940. It was green for "Terry and the Pirates" in the mid-1940s, but it was black for Carey Salt's Shadow ring in 1947 (not the rare Blue Coal model). The setting was red for Buck Roger's Ring of Saturn in 1945. It is black again in the slightly lumpy counterfeit being manufactured today. This ring is one of the handful of premiums of simple enough design to be faked for profit. The best way to authenticate these rings is by the accompanying paper instruction sheets naming the famous character whose prize it is.

These rings are worth whatever you will pay to possess them, as are all radio premiums. A fair average price is $60, with $300 a top price for very rare, complex and fragile items. Of course, many items are priced much higher. But anybody who is not familiar with the whole field should not pay more, even though $500 or more may be easier to come by today than a dime and a box-top were in those days of yesteryear.

Since 1992 there has been a radical change in the prices of radio and early TV premiums (and associated toys). For nearly twenty years there had been no appreciable rise in premium prices. In fact, premium prices had not even kept up with inflation. You could have bought a Tom Mix Magnet Ring for $35 in 1967 and bought the Magnet Ring for the same $35 in 1987. But now there has come a radical change in premium pricing, especially for rings. The Magnet Ring generally brought $150 in 1998.

Part of the reason is the unnatural influence of "investor" types who have manipulated the market, much as they did the old comic book market. The results have been mixed. Prices have risen, but the number of premium collectors and the number of premium objects is far smaller than their counterparts in the comic book field. As a result, most premiums have virtually disappeared from the market. Now is the time to buy, if premiums can be found. They may never be cheaper, and they may never be seen again.

Despite rarity, condition is still very important. No matter how rare, a premium that is battered, defaced or broken is virtually worthless. It may bring a token price of $5.

Stores of premiums newly found in attics no longer seem to be turning up, but older collectors are retiring from their occupations and, sadly, selling their collections for needed money. Some die, and survivors sell. These collectors and families know the value of collectibles and sell for top market value. The number of these "retiring" collectors is still fairly small and does not greatly affect the general state of rarity of premiums.

The items connected to once well-known characters (and those still famous) such as the Lone Ranger, Tom Mix, Buck Rogers, Buck Jones, and Gene Autry, have the highest prices. These prices are still on the rise. Even minor and nearly forgotten characters such as Scoop Ward and Speed Gibson are not being given away. Such once well-known characters will generally prevent a button from selling for less than $15, a badge for less than $25 or a ring for under $30.

Rings have a great appeal to many, and are the hottest ticket in the premium market. The rare ones are going up and up. The Shadow Blue Coal Ring, Green Hornet Seal Ring, and Captain Midnight Mystic Sun God have gone into the thousands of dollars.

Cereal boxes of the sponsors who offered the premiums, especially ones with premium offers on the boxes, have become valuable. Near the top of the line are complete boxes of the nine Lone Ranger Frontier Town Cheerios packs (about $200 each; the backs off the boxes with unassembled model buildings can go for $35). Tom Mix Ralston boxes from the late 1940s-1950s go for up to $400.

A few new authentic premiums have appeared in recent years. Boraxo offered a 20 Mule Team model in 1980 (similar to the Death Valley Days original of the 1930s, 1940s, and 1950s); Cheerios offered a Lone Ranger Deputy Kit in 1981 styled after the movie of that year but similar to earlier offers with mask, badge, etc.

In 1982, Ralston began a limited Tom Mix revival. Premiums offered included a set of four Mix Ralston cereal bowls, a wind-up wrist watch, a Straight Shooters membership kit, a Tom Mix photo, a Mix in-box miniature comic and a LP recording with old Mix radio episodes and one 1983 episode featuring Curley Bradley. In 1993-94, Ralston again showcased Tom Mix on their boxes, but offered only a chance for the customer to write in their memories of Tom. A full-color box came in 1996.

In 1987, Ovaltine resurrected their original formula in jars and instituted new premiums of their character, Captain Midnight of the Secret Squadron. The 1987 premium was a tee-shirt, in 1988 a Midnight digital watch was offered, and in 1989 an arm patch was available (apparently the last of the current revival). Dick Tracy premiums, such as the Quaker wrist radio, came with the new movie in 1990. Superman continued his fifty-year-plus association with Kellogg's cereals in 1994, appearing on the box and inside, with a mini-comic book for Kellogg's Cinnamon Mini-Buns.

Prices on these are already comparable to older premiums, topped by the Tom Mix watch at $300. The biggest premium news of the early 1990s was the sale of a Superman comic book premium ring for a record $18,000 and its resale for $43,000. But this event was really a part of the world of incredibly-priced Golden Age comic books. In effect, the ring was treated as another rare old comic book, not as the premium ring it was. This astonishing sale only raised the value of a real radio premium, the Superman Crusaders Club ring, from $65 to a less than overwhelming $250. Real radio and TV premiums from broadcast series have broken the $1,000 barrier, with the complete Lone Ranger Frontier Town and rings—Captain Midnight Mystic Sun God, Green Hornet Seal, Shadow Blue Coal and many others in a new and much changed market.

	C6	C8	C10
Admiral Television Studio Giveaway, paper punch-out TV studio and characters, features Sky King, Flight to Mars, Walt Disney's Peter Pan and Three Little Pigs, 1953, 15" x 16"	65	131	262
Amos & Andy Pepsodent Giveaway, Amos' Wedding	48	72	95
Amos & Andy Puzzle	55	83	110
Archie Comics Club Button	5	8	10
Aunt Jemima Breakfast Club Badge, metal	12	18	30
Barney Baxter Junior Birdmen of America Wings, metal, c. late 1930s	12	18	25
Bendix Radio, WW II military figures, c. 1944, 5-1/2"; color photos w/stands—a.) Navy Lt. (jg); b.) Marine 1st Lt. (dress uniform), c.) Coast Guard Commander, d.) Army Air Force officer w/parachute harness, e.) 2nd Lt. w/modern Mae West, f) Flier w/flying suit; g.) Army Air Force Capt., h.) Air officer w/fur-lined jacket and helmet; each	4	6	10
Betty Boop Face Mask, theatre premium, 1931	27	41	63
Betty Boop Pin, "Roxy Theatre, New York," large	20	30	50
Westinghouse, 1940	10	15	20
Bobby Benson Code Rule, cardboard decoder, Hecker H-O, 1935	32	65	130
Bobby Benson's Game Circus, 1934	50	97	195
Buck Jones Club Ring	50	100	200
Buck Jones Horseshoe Pin	25	50	100
Buck Jones Jr. Sheriff Badge	25	50	100
Buck Rogers Badge, enameled	83	125	165
Buck Rogers Chief Explorer Badge	45	90	180

	C6	C8	C10
Buck Rogers Lead Figures, solid, inlcudes Cocomalt, Buck, Wilma, Killer Kane, each	30	60	120
Buck Rogers Flight Commander Whistle Badge	90	175	350
Buck Rogers Girl's Charm Bracelet	83	125	180
Buck Rogers Helmet	193	290	385
Buck Rogers Knife	83	125	165
Buck Rogers Morton Salt Punch-O-Bag, 1930s	42	63	85
Buck Rogers Morton Salt Spaceship, came in envelope	83	125	165
Buck Rogers Pendant	42	63	100
Buck Rogers Pinback Button, "Buck Rogers in the 25th Century," Whitehead and Hoag, c. 1935	42	63	100
Buck Rogers Repeller Ray Ring, seal ring	750	1500	3000
Buck Rogers Ring of Saturn, glows in the dark, w/red stone	250	375	575
Buck Rogers Ring of Saturn Instruction Sheet	63	125	250
Buck Rogers Solar Scouts Badge, all brass color	55	83	110
Buck Rogers Solar Scouts Spaceship Commander Badge, 1936 Cream of Wheat premium	55	83	110
Buck Rogers Solar Scout Sweater Emblem	1000	2000	4000
Buck Rogers Space Ranger Kit, Sylvania	70	125	250
Buck Rogers Telescope	70	105	140
Buck Rogers items given away for Cream of Wheat green triangle (also sold in stores)Buck Rogers Films for Projector	10	15	20
Buck Rogers Interplanetary Game	83	125	165

Buck Rogers Space Ranger Kit, $250

	C6	C8	C10
Buck Rogers Lead Figures, hollow lead, Buck, Wilma, Huer, Robot, Kane, Ardala, average price per each, Britains	200	300	400
Buck Rogers Lite Blaster Flashlight	30	60	100
Buck Rogers Movie Projector	110	200	400
Buck Rogers Printing Set, twelve rubber stamps	48	72	150
Buck Rogers Super Dreadnaught, balsa wood	310	625	1250
Buck Rogers Uniform	400	800	1600
Buffalo Bill Bamby Bread Horseshoe Badge, late 1930s	12	18	30
Buffalo Bill Jr. Brass Ring, Buffalo in relief on top, TV premium	20	40	80
Buster Brown Gang (Smilin' Ed) Ring	40	75	150
Buster Brown Gang Tab Pins, assorted, each	10	15	25
Butter-Nut Bread Premium, "Sail-Me" glider, 4-1/2" wingspan, c. 1930	6	10	25
Captain America Sentinel of Liberty Badge	190	375	750
Captain Franks Air Hawks Ring	60	125	250
Captain Franks Air Hawks Wings, c. late 1930s, Post's 40% Bran Flakes premium	35	50	75
Captain Gallant Medal, w/an animal, c. 1950 dated 1939-1945	17	26	35
Captain Gallant Medal, cross w/GRI, 1950s	17	26	35
Captain Hawk Sky Patrol Propeller Badge, c. late 1930s	15	30	65
Captain Marvel Club Button, five styles	35	70	140
Captain Marvel's Magic Whistle, full-color picture of Captain Marvel			

	C6	C8	C10
on both sides, American Seed Co. ad on the inside, c. 1943, American Seed Co.	27	41	55
Captain Midnight Aerial Torpedo Bomber, 1941	65	98	130
Captain Midnight American Flag Loyalty Badge, 1940	75	150	300
Captain Midnight Flight Patrol Wings Badge, 1941	48	72	95
Captain Midnight Flight Patrol Wings Badge, 1942	48	72	95
Captain Midnight Code-O-Graph Decoder Pin, eagle on top, 1941	50	100	200
Captain Midnight Code-O-Graph Badge, w/photo of Captain Midnight, 1942	60	140	275
Captain Midnight Code-O-Graph, magnifier, 1945	83	125	165
Captain Midnight Code-O-Graph, Mirrormatic, 1946	110	165	220
Captain Midnight Code-O-Graph, works as a whistle, 1947	50	100	200
Captain Midnight Code-O-Graph, round, w/mirror, 1948	50	100	200
Captain Midnight Code-O-Graph, Key-O-Matic, w/key, 1949	100	125	250
Captain Midnight Detect-O-Scope, 1941	55	85	150
Captain Midnight Flight Commander Commission, 1956	35	50	100
Captain Midnight Flight Commander Flying Cross, 1942	50	100	200
Captain Midnight Flight Commander Ring, 1941	150	225	450
Captain Midnight Flight Commander Signet Ring, 1957	500	1000	2000
Captain Midnight Jumping Bean Target, 1939	75	150	300
Captain Midnight MJC-10 Plane Detector, 1942, distance-finder	300	600	1200
Captain Midnight Magic Blackout Lite-Ups, 1942	125	250	500
Captain Midnight 1941 Manual for Decoder	50	100	200
Captain Midnight 1942 Manual for Decoder	75	150	300
Captain Midnight 1945 Manual for Code-O-Graph	55	83	125
Captain Midnight Manual for Code-O-Graph, 1946	55	83	125
Captain Midnight Manual for Code-O-Graph, 1947	52	63	100
Captain Midnight Manual for Code-O-Graph, 1948	52	63	100

	C6	C8	C10
Captain Midnight Manual for Code-O-Graph, 1949 50		100	200
Captain Midnight Manual for Decoder Badge, 1956 115		225	450
Captain Midnight Manual for Silver Dart Decoder, 1957 100		200	300
Captain Midnight Marine Corps Ring, 1942 175		250	500
Captain Midnight Medal, brass, pictures of cast, secret word, spinner, 1940 15		23	30
Captain Midnight Mystic Eye Detector Ring, 1942 125		188	250
Captain Midnight Mystic Sun God Ring, 1946 1125		2250	4000
Captain Midnight Printing Ring, 1948 80		160	325
Captain Midnight Secret Squadron Decoder Badge, gold, 1956 110		165	250
Captain Midnight Secret Squadron Decoder Badge, silver, 1957 85		100	250
Captain Midnight Secret Squadron Insignia Transfer, 1949 20		30	40
Captain Midnight Service Ribbon Pin, 1944 60		115	225
Captain Midnight Spy Scope, 1947 53		80	105
Captain Midnight Surprise Package, 1942 27		41	55
Captain Midnight 3-Way Mystic Dog Whistle, 1942 25		50	100
Captain Midnight Trick and Riddle Book, Skelly Oil premium, 1939, 64 pages 15		35	70
Captain Midnight Weather Wings, 1940, predicts weather 42		63	85
Captain Midnight Whirlwind Whistling Ring, 1941 140		275	550
Capt. Tim Ivory Club Pin, Ivory Soap, c. 1936 9		13	25
Captain Video Flying Saucer Ring 375		750	1500
Captain Video Rite-O-Lite 50		100	200
Captain Video Rocket Launcher and Ships, 1950s 110		165	220
Captain Video Secret Seal Ring, 1950s 150		300	600
Captain Video Space Fleet Ray Gun, TV premium, Powerhouse, 1952 138		210	275
Captain Video X-9 Rocket Balloon, 1950s .. 30		45	60
Chandu the Magician Galloping Coin Trick, 1930s 30		45	60
Chandu the Magician Hindu Cones, 1930s 30		45	60
Chandu Boxed Set of Tricks 375		565	750
Charlie McCarthy Puppet Doll, cardboard, Chase & Sanborn mailer, 21" high 25		50	100

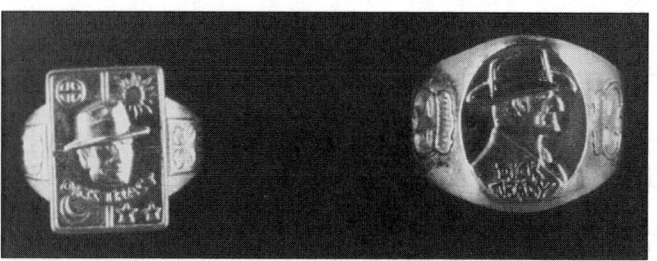

Left to Right: Dick Tracy Secret Compartment Ring, $40; Dick Tracy Portrait Ring, $300

	C6	C8	C10
Charlie McCarthy Radio Party Game, giveaway by Standard Brands, twenty-one cardboard figures, 1938 25		50	100
Cinnamon Bear Silver Star, annual Christmas show, c. 1940s) 35		50	100
Cisco Kid Badge, western hat on chain, 1950s 17		26	35
Cisco Kid Cardboard Gun, Harvest Bread giveaway, clicker sounds when handle squeezed, 7" long 20		50	100
Cisco Kid and Pancho Face Masks, 1953, each 25		38	50
Cisco Kid Triple S Club Kit 25		38	50
Cisco Kid Picture Ring, 1950s 35		63	125
Cisco Kid Secret Compartment Ring 200		400	800
Coco Wheats Radio Club Badge, shape of microphone 22		33	45
David Harding Counterspy, Junior Agent Badge 37		56	75
Davy Crockett Goldplated Ring 10		15	20
Dick Tracy Air Detective Ring 125		350	700
Dick Tracy Badge, "Captain" 90		175	350
Dick Tracy Badge, "Crime Stoppers" 12		18	25
Dick Tracy Badge, "Detective," picture of Tracy and Junior 17		25	50
Dick Tracy Badge, "Inspector General" 200		410	825
Dick Tracy Badge, "Lieutenant" 50		100	200
Dick Tracy Badge, Republic Pictures 50		100	200
Dick Tracy Badge, "Sergeant" 40		80	160
Dick Tracy Decoder, green, 1948 22		33	45
Dick Tracy Decoder, red, 1948 22		33	45
Dick Tracy Detective Club Badge, secret money pouch in rear 38		75	150
Dick Tracy Glider Airplane, 1938 38		75	150

Dick Tracy Badge, "Crime Stoppers"

Dick Tracy Badges, top row, left to right: Lieutenant, $200; "Captain," $350; bottom row, left to right: "Sergeant," $160; "Inspector General," $825

	C6	C8	C10
Dick Tracy Portrait Ring, enameled	60	180	300
Dick Tracy Secret Compartment Ring	10	20	40
Dick Tracy Secret Service Patrol Member Pinback, early 1940s	50	100	200
Dick Tracy Secret Service, second year member pin	50	100	200
Dick Tracy's Secret Detective Methods & Magic Tricks, 1939 Quaker Oats, sixty-eight pages	30	60	120
Dionne Quints "All Aboard for Shut-Eye Town" Paper Dolls, Palmolive Soap	17	26	35
Don Winslow Decoder Torpedo	875	1750	3500
Don Winslow Honor Badge	75	125	250
Don Winslow Magic Slate Secret Code Book	35	75	150
Don Winslow Ring	340	675	1350
Don Winslow USN Secret Code Book, sixteen-pages, Oxydol giveaway, 1935, 7-3/4" x 4"	40	75	150
Donald Duck Punch-out Figure, Donald Duck bread, c. late 1940s	50	100	200
Donald Duck Playboard, comics giveaway, 1946, 9" high	50	100	200
Elsie The Cow, set of four figural buttons on color illustrated card, Borden, 1949	11	16	35
Fighting Devil Dogs Ring, w/bulldog headon top, Republic Pictures serial ring, 1938	100	200	400

	C6	C8	C10
Flash Gordon Ring, Post Toasties Corn Flakes, 1949	27	41	55
Fort Apache (Rin Tin Tin) Plastic Ring, 1950s, TV premium	15	22	30
Frank Buck Explorer's Sun Watch, post-WWII, offered by Jack Armstrong	53	80	105
Frank Buck Leopard Ring	800	1600	3200
G.E. Punch-out Circus, sixty-five pieces	65	98	130
G.E. Rodeo Punch-out, sixty-five pieces	65	98	130
G-Man Badge	10	15	20
G-Man Official Signet Ring, metal, radio program premium, 1933-35	32	65	125
Gabby Hayes Antique Cars, 1950s, price for set	40	80	160
Gabby Hayes Quaker Cannon Ring, 1950s	75	150	300
Gabby Hayes Western Gun Collection, six weapons, six pistols, six rifles, solid non-working, 1950s	37	56	75
Gabby Scoops Junior Press Club Card, Crackajack Comics, 1945	9	13	25
Gabby Scoops Press Card, Crackajack Comics, 1940-41	9	13	25
Gangbusters Pin	25	38	50
Goofy Playboard, 1946, 9" high, comics giveaway	17	25	35
Green Hornet Secret Compartment Ring, Hornet seal, glows in dark	440	875	1750
Gun, cardboard, giveaway from Theatorium in Lykens, Penn., Pat'd Dec. 1914 by Spots Spec. Co., Lexington, Ky.	6	9	13
H.C.B. Club Kit, contains badge, etc., early Cream of Wheat	22	33	45
Hop Harrigan Para-Plane, cardboard plane from Grape Nut Flakes plus two code signal blinders, small parachute w/water container in tail of plane	240	475	950
Hop Harrigan Sun Dial Ring, unmarked	30	45	60
Hopalong Cassidy Bar 20 Compass Ring	63	125	250
Hopalong Cassidy Face Ring	45	90	175
Hopalong Cassidy Tin Badge, Post Raisin Bran giveaway, c. 1950s	17	26	35
Howdy Doody Climber, cardboard, w/string, Welch's Premium, 1950s	37	56	75
Howdy Doody Face Flashlight Ring, 1950s	60	120	240
Howdy Doody Flicker Key Chain, three-dimensional picture of Howdy Doody flicks to Poll Parrot (Poll Parrot Shoes), 1950s	15	30	60

	C6	C8	C10
Howdy Doody Flicker Ring, flicks from Howdy to Poll Parrot, Poll Parrot premium 15	15	30	60
Howdy Doody, flexible cardboard figure, Wonder Bread, 8" 32	32	48	65
Howdy Doody Puppet, cardboard, Mars Candy, 1950s, 15" high 37	37	56	75
Howdy Doody Princess Dancing Puppet, moveable joints, Snickers premium, 1950s, 13" 17	17	26	35
Howdy Doody, Princess WinterSpring SummerFall, cardboard figure, 14" 17	17	26	35
I Am A Spy Smasher Button, 1940, Fawcett Comics 25	25	38	100
Indian Chief Tin Badge, Post Raisin Bran, c. 1950s 4	4	7	9
Indian Gum Chief's Head Ring, Goudey Gum card premium, silver, 1930s 10	10	15	20
Jack Armstrong Crocodile Ring, glows inthe dark, green stone 200	200	400	800
Jack Armstrong Big 10 Football Game 45	45	68	90
Jack Armstrong Explorer's Telescope 17	17	25	50
Jack Armstrong Flashlight 15	15	30	60
Jack Armstrong Hike-O-Meter 25	25	50	100
Jack Armstrong Magic Answer Box 37	37	75	150
Jack Armstrong Ped-O-Meter, blue or silver models 25	25	50	100
Jack Armstrong, Secret Norden Bomb Sight, w/three bombs, paper target ships, c. WWII 150	150	300	600
Jack Armstrong paper airplane models, many different, price per each 17	17	25	35
Jack Armstrong paper airplane models, many different, reprints, price per each ... 5	5	8	10
Jack Armstrong Secret Whistle Code Card for Secret Egyptian Coder Siren Ring 15	15	20	45
Jack Armstrong Secret Egyptian Coder Siren Ring, Wheaties, late 1930s 62	62	93	125
Jack Armstrong 3-D Viewer, filmstrip 63	63	125	250
Jeff Paper Mask, Shell Oil, 1933 10	10	15	20
Jimmie Allen Colonial Gasoline Flying Cadet Wings, bronze, late 1930s 17	17	26	35
Jimmie Allen High-Speed Gasoline Flying Cadet Wings, bronze, late 1930s 20	20	30	40
Jimmie Allen Richfield Hi-Octane Flying Cadet Wings, c. 1930s 20	20	30	40
Jimmie Allen Richfield Hi-Octane Pilot's Identification Bracelet, all metal, late 1930s 21	21	32	42
Jimmie Allen Skelly Oil Die-Cut Airplane Cadet Wings, late 1930s 15	15	23	30
Jimmie Allen Skelly Oil Flying Cadet Wings, bronze, late 1930s 15	15	23	30

	C6	C8	C10
Joe E. Brown Pin 10	10	15	20
Junior G-Men Membership Kit, c. mid-1930s 50	50	100	200
Junior G-Men of America, gold-plated tin badge, late 1930s 22	22	33	45
Junior Texas Ranger Badge, 1936 17	17	26	35
Kellogg's Frogmen, add baking soda and they swim underwater, 1950s 10	10	15	35
Kellogg's Krumbles Around-the-World Paper Dolls; each cutout from box contains boy and girl; includes Italy, Mexico, France and Czechoslovakia, each 4	4	7	9
Kellogg's Nautilus Nuclear Submarine, 1950s 20	20	40	75
Kellogg's Pep Airplane Carrier, cut-out sheet w/airplane carrier and five planesw/3/4" wingspan, carrier 6-1/2" x 10" 37	37	56	75
Kellogg's Pep Warplanes, balsa, w/Superman ad on envelope, c. 1945 10	10	17	35
Kellogg's Pep Warplanes, cardboard, c. 1944, each 7	7	11	20
The Liberty Gun For Young America - McGrath's Big Store, w/photos of Charlie Chaplin, 7" cardboard 20	20	30	40
Little Orphan Annie Necklace, metal enamel figure of Annie on metal chain,c. 1936 63	63	125	250
Little Orphan Annie Pinback Button, Little Orphan Annie, Member Funny Frosty's Club, mid-1930s 21	21	32	42
Lone Ranger, A Republic Serial, brass star badge 88	88	175	350
Lone Ranger Atom Bomb Ring 75	75	112	150
Lone Ranger Blackout Kit, Kix cereal glow-in-the-dark material (two pieces), glow-in-the-dark pledge to flag, glow-in-the-dark Lone Ranger Volunteers armband, plus instructions, 1942 52	52	78	105
Lone Ranger Bond Bread Safety Club Badge, 1938 22	22	33	45
Lone Ranger Chief Scout Badge, Silvercup Bread, early 1940s 75	75	112	150
Lone Ranger Clicker Pistol, black, movie giveaway, Lone Ranger on one side and ruby on other, non-moveable silver cylinder, 1939 83	83	125	200
Lone Ranger Deputy Shield, brass w/secret compartment 37	37	56	90
Lone Ranger Flashlight Ring 42	42	63	95
Lone Ranger Frontier Town, full set 1000	1000	2000	4000

Lone Ranger Movie Film Ring, $150

	C6	C8	C10
Lone Ranger Glow-in-the-Dark Belt, 1941	83	125	165
Lone Ranger Hi-Yo Silver Pin, 1938	15	30	60
Lone Ranger Kix Air Base w/cereal box cut-outs, plus map, precursor of Frontier Town	125	250	500
Lone Ranger Lucky Piece, advertises seventeenth anniversary 1933-50	50	100	200
Lone Ranger Mask, back of black mask promotes a personal appearance by "The Lone Ranger and Silver!," one of the last radio premiums, c. 1953 or 1954	20	35	75
Lone Ranger Movie Film Ring, Cheerios, late 1949-50	75	112	150
Lone Ranger Pedometer, Cheerios, 1948	15	23	30
Lone Ranger Rubber Band Gun and six different targets, 1938 Morton Salt giveaway, cardboard	100	225	450
Lone Ranger Secret Compartment Ring, w/picture of Lone Ranger and Silver	125	188	250
Lone Ranger Silver Bullet, secret compartment compass	35	50	100
Lone Ranger Silver Saddle Film Ring, Cheerios, late 1940s,	75	112	150
Lone Ranger Safety Scout Badge, Silvercup Bread, 1935	22	33	65
Lone Ranger Silvercup Bread Safety Patrol, metal, silver and blue	22	33	65
Lone Ranger Six-Shooter Ring, gun ring w/plastic and metal gun attached to top, turn wheel and flint sparks	125	188	250
Lone Ranger Victory Corps Badge, Kix Cereal, 1942	32	48	65
Lone Ranger Weather Ring, color square stone on top w/litmus paper, no markings to identify as Lone Ranger	38	57	75
Magic Show Kit, General Mills, 1946	14	21	35
Magician's Book of Cigarette Tricks, Camel Cigarettes, 1933	9	13	30

	C6	C8	C10
Major Bowes Home Microphone	30	50	100
Maltex Health Club Pinback Button	4	7	9
Melvin Purvis Junior G-Man Corps Badge, late 1930s	25	35	75
Melvin Purvis Junior G-Man Corps Roving Operative Badge, late 1930s	25	35	75
Melvin Purvis Law and Order Ring	50	100	200
Melvin Purvis Law and Order Patrol Lieutenant's Secret Operator Badge, mid-1930s	37	56	75
Melvin Purvis Law and Order Patrol Secret Operator Badge, late 1930s	37	56	75
Melvin Purvis Secret Operator, Girl's Division	30	45	60
Mickey and Donald's Race to Treasure Island, Standard Oil giveaway, 1939, 12" x 25"	98	148	195
Mickey and Donald's Race to Treasure Island, map of U.S. in full color, Calco Gasoline giveaway, w/stamps, 1939, 20" x 27"	330	495	660
Mickey Mouse Club Pinback Button, "Copyright 1928-30 by W.E. Disney," 1-1/4"	55	83	110
Mickey Mouse Globe Trotters Map, NBC Bread, 1937, 28" x 20"	355	525	715
Mickey Mouse Globe Trotters Map, NBC Bread, w/all pictures pasted on, 28" x 22"	355	525	715
Mickey Mouse Globe Trotters Map, Pevely Milk premium, 1930s	355	525	715
Mickey Mouse Official Money, Mickey Mouse Cones dollar bills, one dollar denomination, 1930s, each	12	18	25
Mickey Mouse Playboard, comics giveaway, 1946 9" high	27	41	55
Morton Salt "Bat-O-Ball," features The Shadow (cartoon), 1939	62	93	125
My-T-Fine Grocery Store, folds into a full-color grocery store w/period products on the shelves, shoppers and workers, dated 1930, 8" x 3"	30	60	125
Nabisco Finger Puppet Rings, Slim Chants, horse Humbolt, gun, Prairie Mary, Tagalong Boswell, Cold Deck Charlie, Sam Spiel, each	2	3	5
Nabisco Santa Fe Twin Unit Diesel Train, includes engine, train, tracks, ground, background, 1956	12	18	25
Nabisco Sound-Jet Glider	10	15	20
Nabisco Trailblazers of America cards, six cards make up horse-drawn van and open van, 1956	5	8	10

	C6	C8	C10
Nabisco Shredded Wheat Nabisco Flying Circus, designed by Wallace Rigby, series of 24, 1948, 4" x 7" cards, price per each 5		8	10
The Nebbs - Detroit Times series No. 27544 (comic strip) 7		11	15
New York World's Fair Children's World G-Man Badge, giveaway, three-color brass badge 25		38	50
Newsboy Brand Soups and Vegetables Official Booster Badge, late 1930s 4		7	9
Pep Pins, Dick Tracy 15		22	30
Pep Pins, Little Orphan Annie 7		11	15
Pep Pins, Flash Gordon 15		22	30
Pep Pins, Felix the Cat 5		8	10
Pep Pins, The Phantom 7		11	15
Pep Pins, Popeye and Olive Oyl, each 7		11	15
Pep Pins, Superman 20		30	40
Pep Pins, Others; includes Smitty, Harold Teen, Skeezix, Corky, Pop Jenks, Goofy, Spud, Andy Gump, Gravel Gertie, Punjab, Hans, Kayo, Smilin' Jack, Dagwood, B.O. Plenty, Mr. Bailey, Shadow, Moon Mullins, Flattop, Rip Winkle, Uncle Willie, Emma, Inspector, Chief Brandon, Vitamin Flintheart, Sandy, Uncle Bim, Sundown, Lillums, Tilda, Uncle Walt, Perry Winkle, Judy, Min Gump, Wilmer, Smoky Stover, Daisy, Ma Winkle, Tess Trueheart, Herbie, Mamie, Breezie, Pat Patton, Maggie, Barney Google, Fat Stuff, Chief Brandon, Toots, Nina, etc., average 7		11	20
Pep Rings, Jack Kramer, Dennis O'Keefe, Burt Lancaster, Sitting Bull, Pocahontas, Pan American Clipper, Douglas F-3D Sky Knight, Republic XF91 Thundercepter, each 10		15	20
Pepsodent's Moving Picture Machine shows Mickey Mouse, Donald Duck, Snow White and Seven Dwarfs, in color 325		490	650
Pillsbury-Farina Complete Tel-A-Phone Set, two holders, mouthpieces, ear phones and fifty feet of line, 1938 25		38	50
Pinocchio Playboard, Disney Comics subscription giveaway, 1946 25		38	50
Popeye The Sailor Man Button, copyright 1935, theatre giveaway, 3/4" 15		22	30
Popsicle Movie Star Coins, aluminum coins, includes Irene Dunne, Clark Gable, Marion Davies, Fredric March, Marie Dressler, Gary Cooper, c. 1930s 5		8	15

	C6	C8	C10
Porcelain Enamel & Mfg. Co. West Point Cadet on card w/Pemco ad on back, 6" figure, 3" x 6" card 2		3	5
Post Grape Nuts Flakes Playing-Filling Station, c. 1950s 5		8	10
Post Toasties Walt Disney cut-out figures on box, Mickey the Traffic Cop, two types of Pinocchio, 1939, each 27		41	60
Post Toasties Corn Flakes Comic Rings, Fritz, Hans, Tillie the Toiler, Toots and Casper, 1949 17		26	35
Post's Cereal Junior Detective Club Sergeant Badge, late 1930s 10		15	35
Post's Explorer Ring, includes compass, sun watch, sunset predictor and star finder, plastic dome, 1947 25		38	50
Post Cereal Rings, Perry Winkle, Winnie Winkle, Harold Teen, Skeezix, Lillums, Herbie andSmoky Stover, 1948 17		26	35
Post Cereal Rings, Dick Tracy, 1948 17		26	35
Post Grape Nuts Tin Rings, Little King, Phantom, Skeezix, Lillums, Harold Teen 17		26	35
Post Raisin Bran Sheriff Badge 10		15	20
Radio Orphan Annie, Annie and Joe Corntassel button, 1931 150		300	600
Radio Orphan Annie, Associated Membership Pin, 1934 10		25	50
Radio Orphan Annie Bandanna, 1934 20		40	80
Radio Orphan Annie Birthstone Ring, 1935 100		200	400
Radio Orphan Annie Capt. Sparks Aviation Trainer 250		375	500
Radio Orphan Annie Circus Cut-Outs, 1935 150		250	500
Radio Orphan Annie Code Captain Belt and Buckle, 1940 75		150	300
Radio Orphan Annie Code Captain Pin, 1939 25		50	100
Radio Orphan Annie Manual, 1934 62		93	125
Radio Orphan Annie Decoder Manual, 1935 62		93	125
Radio Orphan Annie Decoder Manual, 1936 62		93	125
Radio Orphan Annie Decoder Manual, 1937 62		93	125
Radio Orphan Annie Decoder Manual, 1938 62		93	125
Radio Orphan Annie Decoder Manual, 1939 62		93	125
Radio Orphan Annie Decoder Manual, 1940 83		125	165
Radio Orphan Annie Decoder Manual, w/Cardboard Decoder, 1942 198		300	385

Front to Back: Radio Orphan Annie Decoder Manual, 1937, $125; Decoder Badge, 1937, $100

	C6	C8	C10
Radio Orphan Annie Magic Transfer Pictures, 1935	20	40	85
Radio Orphan Annie Magic Transfer Picture, 1937	20	40	85
Radio Orphan Annie Mask, 1933	50	75	100
Radio Orphan Annie Mystic Eye Ring, 1939	125	250	500
Radio Orphan Annie Package, includes Whirl-O-Matic Decoder, Whistle Badge, booklet, and order blanks, 1942	100	250	500
Radio Orphan Annie Pin, 1937	17	26	50
Radio Orphan Annie Portrait Ring, ring has head of Annie embossed on top, 1934	48	72	95
Radio Orphan Annie Punch-Outs	120	180	240
Radio Orphan Annie Ring, 1934	48	72	95
Radio Orphan Annie Ring, 1935	48	72	95
Radio Orphan Annie Roller Skates, 1938	50	100	200
Radio Orphan Annie Secret Egyptian Compass and Sundial, 1938	48	72	95
Radio Orphan Annie Signet Ring, 1937	63	125	250
Radio Orphan Annie Silver Star Pin, 1934	48	72	95
Radio Orphan Annie Silver Star Pin, 1935	48	72	95

	C6	C8	C10
Radio Orphan Annie Altascope Ring, fewer than fifteen known to exist			24,000
Radio Orphan Annie Decoder Pin, 1935	25	38	50
Radio Orphan Annie Decoder Badge, 1936	25	38	50
Radio Orphan Annie Decoder Badge, 1937	25	38	100
Radio Orphan Annie Decoder Badge, 1938	30	60	120
Radio Orphan Annie Decoder Badge, 1939	30	60	120
Radio Orphan Annie Decoder Badge, 1940	30	60	120
Radio Orphan Annie Foreign Coins, 1937	25	38	50
Radio Orphan Annie Goofy Circus, 1939	188	375	750
Radio Orphan Annie Identification Bracelet, 1934	25	50	100
Radio Orphan Annie Identification Bracelet, 1935	25	50	100
Radio Orphan Annie Identification Tag, 1939	20	35	75

Radio Orphan Annie Decoder Manual, 1938, $125

	C6	C8	C10
Radio Orphan Annie Secret Society Silver Star Ring, 1936	94	188	375
Radio Orphan Annie Silver Star Ring, 1937	94	188	375
Radio Orphan Annie Silver Star Ring, 1938	94	188	375
Radio Orphan Annie School Pin, 1939	20	40	75
Radio Orphan Annie Secret Guard Clicker, 1942	25	50	100
Radio Orphan Annie Shake-Up Game, 1931	25	50	100
Radio Orphan Annie 3-Way Dog Whistle, 1940	25	50	100
Radio Orphan Annie Treasure Hunt Game, 1933	75	150	300
Radio Orphan Annie Treasure Hunt Game, 1935	75	150	300
Range Rider & Dick West Button, Peter Pan bread, 1950s	37	56	75

	C6	C8	C10
Red Ryder Lucky Coin	7	11	15
Renfrew of Mounted Pinback	10	15	20
Rin Tin Tin "Ball-in-the-Hole" Games, sealed coin-size games of Rinty, Rip Masters, Fort Apache, etc., each	9	13	18
Rin Tin Tin Ring, plastic, 1950s	17	26	35
Rin Tin Tin Set of Plastic Dinosaurs, radio-TV, 1954	62	93	125
Rin Tin Tin Wonderscope, Telescope-Microscope-Compass w/"Rin Tin Tin" on face, radio-TV, 1954	30	45	100
Rip Masters (Rin Tin Tin) Plastic Rings, 1950s	20	30	40
Rocky Lane's Explorer's Sun Watch, 1951, Carnation Milk	20	40	75
Roy Rogers Branding Iron Ring	75	125	250
Roy Rogers Deputy Badge	10	15	20
Roy Rogers Microscope Ring, 1947, Quaker Oats	62	93	125
Roy Rogers Paint Set, 1950s	12	18	25
Roy Rogers Signal Badge, w/mirror, secret compartment and whistle	40	88	175
Roy Rogers Silver Hat Ring	20	400	800
Roy Rogers Trigger's Lucky Horseshoe, full size, black rubber	12	18	35
Roy Rogers Tuck-A-Way Gun	12	18	35
Scoop Ward News of Youth Official Reporter Badge, late 1930s, Ward's Soft Bun Bread giveaway	10	15	20
Secret Three Badge, w/manual of secret codes	10	15	20
Sgt. Preston Distance Finder	42	63	85
Sgt. Preston Firefighting Set	42	63	85
Sgt. Preston Flashlight, signals has two filters	25	50	100

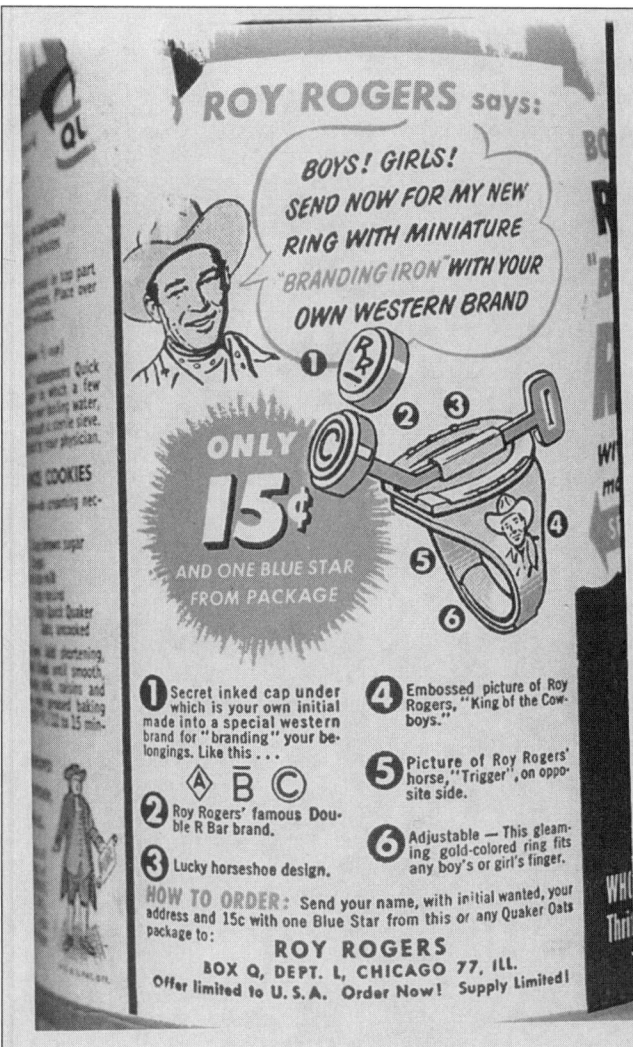

Ad for Roy Rogers Branding Iron Ring on Quaker Oats Box, value for ring in C10 condition is $250

Roy Roger Deputy Badge, $20

	C6	C8	C10
Sgt. Preston Klondike Land Pouch 25		38	50
Sgt. Preston Klondike Movie Film Viewer .. 52		100	200
Sgt. Preston Pedometer 15		30	65
Sgt. Preston Police Whistle, nylon cord,			
brass, 1950.. 27		41	55
Sgt. Preston Skinning Knife 125		250	300
Sgt. Preston Totem Pole Set 55		100	200
Sgt. Preston Trail Kit, the most complex			
of all premiums, rare............................ 300		450	600
Sgt. Preston Yukon Village 300		450	600
Shadow Ring, Glow in Dark, "blue coal"			
jewel on white ring.............................. 475		715	950
Shadow "Carey Salt" Ring, same as			
J. Armstrong Crocodile ring w/black			
stone, (this ring has been counterfeited;			
original is smoothly circular w/clean-cut			
design, requires identifying papers			
for C10 price) 250		500	1050
Shield G-Man Club Badge, lithographed			
celluloid pinback, Pep Comics			
premium, 1942..................................... 35		75	125
Skippy S.S.S.S. Captain, pinback button,			
all celluloid, 1930s............................... 12		18	25
Skippy Compass, 1930s? 10		15	20
Sky Birds Propeller Ring, brass and silver,			
Goudey Gum premium, 1930s............... 12		18	25
Sky King Aztec Indian Ring 250		500	1000
Sky King Detecto Microscope..................... 53		78	105
Sky King Detecto Writer 70		105	140
Sky King Electronic Television Ring........... 100		150	200
Sky King Magni-Glo Ring 100		150	200
Sky King Mystery Picture Ring.................... 55		83	110
Sky King Navajo Indian Ring...................... 125		190	250
Sky King Small Plastic Statues, of Sky			
King, Penny, Sky King's horse, Sky			
King's plane, The Songbird, Nabisco			
giveaways in Wheat Honey and Rice			
Honey, 1950s, each.............................. 15		22	30
Sky King Signal Scope 70		105	140
Sky King Stamp Kit 48		72	95
Sky King Teleblinker Ring.......................... 125		190	250
Snow White Game, Tek Toothbrush 35		75	150
Space Patrol Binoculars, c. 1950s............. 110		165	220
Space Patrol Diplomatic Pouch, contains			
money, stamps, etc............................... 138		210	275
Space Patrol Goggles 53		78	105
Space Patrol Jet Glow Code Belt, 1951 138		210	275
Space Patrol Ring, w/secret powder			
compartment, c. early 1950s 138		210	275
Space Patrol Smoke Gun, 1950s 150		225	300
Space Patrol Space Helmet, c. 1950s......... 180		270	360
Space Patrol Space-O-Phone, 1952 98		150	195
Space Patrol Space Ship, c. 1950s............. 88		132	175

	C6	C8	C10
Speed Gibson's Flying Police Badge,			
Dreikorn's Bread 12		18	25
Straight Arrow Face Ring, c. early 1950s..... 52		80	105
Straight Arrow Magic Cave Ring,			
w/original art, 1949 100		140	275
Straight Arrow Puppets and Props,			
Nabisco radio premium, 1949............... 30		45	60
Straight Arrow Target Game, lithographed			
tin target board, National Biscuit			
Company copyright on the edge,			
10" x 14" 37		56	75
Straight Arrow Tom-Tom, c. early 1950s 25		50	75
Straight Arrow Wrist Bracelet, w/secret			
compartment, c. early 1950s 35		75	150
Sunbrite "Junior Nurse Corps" Brass			
Badge 4		7	9
Sunbrite "Junior Nurse Corps" Pinback			
Button, pictures of Dorothy Hart 3		5	7
Superman Crusader Ring 125		188	250
Superman Kellogg's Gy Rocket.................... 50		100	200
Superman Kellogg's Silver Jet Airplane			
Ring, plane flies off 75		125	250
Superman Kellogg's Walkie-Talkie 37		56	75
Superman Pin, "Read Superman Action			
Comics Magazine," 1940s....................... 20		35	75
Superman Planes from Pep Cereal, set of			
eight, 1948 30		45	60
Superman Premium Club Set, certificate,			
button and decoder 188		375	750
Superman Tim Club Ring........................ 3750		7500	15,000
Superman's Secret Code, c. 1939 24		36	63
Supermen of America Button, pinback			
button, 1939 version, 1-3/8".................. 20		40	75
Tarzan Gift Statues, Foulds, Tarzan, Jane,			
Kala, etc., 1930s, price per set.............. 300		600	1100

Mail-in form for Tarzan Gift Statues, price for set $1,100

	C6	C8	C10
Tarzan Jungle Map and Treasure Hunt Weston Biscuit, 1933	250	300	600
Tennessee Jed Lariat	37	56	75
Tennessee Jed Look Around Ring, 1940s	125	250	500
Tennessee Jed Paper Gun, c. 1940s	21	32	42
Terry And The Pirates Glow-in-the-Dark Ring, crocodiles on sides	37	56	75
Terry And The Pirates Gold Detector Ring	62	93	125
Texas Longhorn Tin Badge, Post Raisin Bran, c. 1950s	4	7	9
Tom Corbett Space Cadet Badge, early 1950s	35	75	150
Tom Corbett Space Cadet Belt Buckle Decoder, early 1950s	75	150	300
Tom Corbett Decoder, cardboard, 1950s	35	52	70
Tom Corbett Rings, Kellogg's, 1950-55; twelve different rings, including—Space Cruiser, Rocket Scout, Space Academy, Space Suit, Space Helmet, Corbett-Space Cadet, Cadet Dress Uniform, Girl's SpaceUniform, Parallo-Ray Gun, Strate-Telescope, Sound Ray Gun, per each	17	26	35
Tom Mix Airplane and Parachute	100	150	200
Tom Mix Arm Patch, Tom Mix bar on checkerboard design, 1933, predominantly blue; 1947, predominantly red; 1983, predominantly black	20	35	75
Tom Mix Badge Ranch Boss	130	263	525
Tom Mix Bag of Marbles	20	30	40
Tom Mix Bandanna, has Tom Mix brand	50	100	200
Tom Mix Baseball	25	38	50
Tom Mix Baseball Bat	25	38	50
Tom Mix Baseball Cap	27	41	55
Tom Mix Belt Buckle w/Secret Compartment, belt glows in the dark, offered only on cereal boxes after radio show ended	75	125	250
Tom Mix Blowdart Game	250	300	600
Tom Mix Branding Iron, w/Tom Mix brand	52	78	105
Tom Mix Bullet Flashlight	52	78	105
Tom Mix Bullet Telescope, w/bird-call device, 4" long	35	52	105
Tom Mix Catalog of Straight Shooter Premiums, black and white sheet w/order form on reverse, descriptions and small pictures of premiums on the front, includes sheepskin vest, rodeo rope, leather cuffs, wood gun, lucky spinner, etc., 8-1/2" x 11"	20	30	60

	C6	C8	C10
Tom Mix Charm Bracelet, charm steer head, gun, horseman, w/Tom Mix brand	50	100	200
Tom Mix Coloring Book, Ralston, c. 1949	20	30	40
Tom Mix Compass Magnifying Glass, silver color, 1947 (originals have "Japan" written on the back; imitations have the words "Comet-Japan" on the back)	45	68	90
Tom Mix Compass Magnifying Glass, brass, 1939	50	100	200
Tom Mix Compass Magnifying Glass, plastic, glows in the dark, c. 1948	75	125	150
Tom Mix Cowboy Shirt	75	150	300
Tom Mix Cowboy Vest	82	125	165
Tom Mix Cowgirl Skirt	150	225	300
Tom Mix Decoder Badge, moveable six-shooter points to symbols, 1940	100	150	250
Tom Mix Decoder Buttons Instruction Sheet, Ralston, 1946	15	25	45
Tom Mix Decoder Pins, Tony, Jane, Sheriff, Wash, each	15	25	45
Tom Mix Decoder Pin, "Curley Bradley"	15	30	60
Tom Mix Deputy Ring, chewing gum premium, 1934	1500	3000	6000
Tom Mix Glow-in-the-Dark Arrowhead, has compass and magnifying glass, 1946	75	125	150
Tom Mix Gold Ore Badge	25	50	100
Tom Mix Ore Charm, Ralston, contains genuine gold ore under plastic dome, 1940	42	63	85
Tom Mix "Good Luck" Spinner	27	41	55
Tom Mix Horseshoe Nail Ring, 1933 (rounded point identifies original)	25	50	75
Tom Mix Identification Bracelet	42	63	85
Tom Mix Initial Ring, 1935	100	150	200
Tom Mix Look-Around Ring, c. 1945	62	93	125
Tom Mix Lucky Wrist Band, metal, w/leather strap and buckle, Tom Mix brand, Ralston premium, 1936	50	100	200
Tom Mix Magnet Gun and Signal Arrowhead Bracelet, gun and arrowhead glow in the dark	50	80	165
Tom Mix Magnet Ring, 1945	50	75	150
Tom Mix Makeup Kit, two grease-paint model, plus five grease-paint model	300	450	600
Tom Mix Manual, 1941	50	80	160
Tom Mix Manual, 1944	50	80	140
Tom Mix Manual, 1946	40	60	115
Tom Mix Mask, cardboard	385	580	770
Tom Mix Mystery Picture Ring, w/"look-in" picture of Tom Mix and Tony, viewed through one side of the ring, 1939	163	245	325

Tom Mix Western Movie Viewer, $250

	C6	C8	C10
Tom Mix Parachute, Ralston premium, 1936	75	125	250
Tom Mix Periscope	75	125	250
Tom Mix Postal Telegraph Set, metal clicker, blue, 1938	45	75	150
Tom Mix Premium Enclosures and Correspondence, many picture postcards, letters on Straight Shooter stationery, etc.; sent out to listeners who wrote to the radio show; these and various coupons, instruction sheets, contest entries are offered by dealers and collectors	20	30	40
Tom Mix Telegraph Set, red, uses batteries, 1940	133	200	265
Tom Mix Ralston Straight Shooters Pocket Knife, 1940	40	80	175
Tom Mix RCA TV Set, shows photographs or comic strips, brown or reddish model	25	50	75
Tom Mix RCA TV Set, shows photographs or comic strips, gold	75	150	300
Tom Mix Secret Code Manual	25	50	100

	C6	C8	C10
Tom Mix Sharpshooters Medal, glows in the dark	83	125	165
Tom Mix Sheriff of Dobie County Siren Badge, Ralston, 1946	48	72	115
Tom Mix Signal Arrowhead, w/magnifying glass and "whizzer" flute-type whistle, made of lucite, 1949	40	75	150
Tom Mix Signal Flashlight	40	75	150
Tom Mix Signature Ring, pre-WWII	125	188	250
Tom Mix Siren Ring, 1945	62	93	125
Tom Mix Six-Shooter, wooden, barrel breaks and cartridge drum spins, 1933	60	180	320
Tom Mix Six-Shooter, wooden, barrel spins, 1936	75	150	300
Tom Mix Six-Shooter, wooden, no moving parts, 1939	80	140	275
Tom Mix Spinning Rope, Ralston, hemp w/wood handle, 1936	53	78	105
Tom Mix Spurs, metal, w/plastic glow-in-the-dark rowels	50	100	200
Tom Mix "Square and Fair" Spinner	37	56	75
Tom Mix Straight Shooters Campaign Medal, gold	42	63	85
Tom Mix Straight Shooters Campaign Medal, silver	42	63	85
Tom Mix Sundial Watch	45	75	150
Tom Mix Telephone Set	45	75	150
Tom Mix Telescope, Tom Mix brand on side	45	75	150
Tom Mix Tiger Eye Ring, Ralston, 1949	150	225	300
Tom Mix TM Brand Ring, c. 1933	75	112	150
Tom Mix Western Movie Viewer, shows scenes from Tom Mix films, 1935	75	125	250
Tom Mix Whistle Ring, 1945	63	95	125
Tom Mix Wrangler Badge, Ralston, 1936	40	80	175
Toonerville Trolley Cardboard Village, put out by Coca-Cola	88	132	175
Trigger Button, 7/8", Post Grape Nut Flakes	12	18	25
Welch's Grape Juice Train, paper engine, box car, passenger car, caboose, each	3	5	7
Complete set	12	18	25
Wheaties Jogometer, 1960s	12	18	25
Wheaties Pedometer, c. late 1940s	10	15	20
Wild Bill Hickok Bunkhouse Set, cut-out pin-ups of Bill, Jingles, guns, ropes, etc.	15	25	50
Wild Bill Hickok Treasure Map and Guide, Kellogg's, 1952	48	72	95

RAMP WALKERS

Ramp walkers—those funny looking characters that waddle down slanted surfaces—are fondly remembered by many aging Baby Boomers. While popular from the thirties to the sixties, one of the earliest ramp walkers dates back to the late 1900s. In 1873, Ives patented two versions of a cast-iron elephant walker—one had a pivoting trunk while the other had a fixed trunk with lead feet. While many were manufactured in the United States, wood, cardboard and composition walkers also came from such exotic locations as Czechoslovakia, Argentina and Germany.

Louis Marx Co. was the primary manufacturer of plastic walkers during the early 1950s and mid 1960s. By far, the majority were produced in Hong Kong, while a few were made in the United States and sold under either the Marx logo or the Charmore Co., a subsidiary of the Marx Co. Colorful tin lithographed ramps were available for some of the Marx plastic walkers, but most relied on homemade ramps or a weighted string that hung over the end of a table and pulled the toy along. In addition to the United States and Hong Kong, plastic walkers were manufactured in England, Germany and Argentina.

Other manufacturers include, Fun World, Dolls, Inc., Ohio Art, Educational Toys, a subsidiary of Topper Corp. and Gantry of England.

The most popular walkers—Wilson Walkies—were made by John Wilson of Watsontown. Sold nationwide, most of the two-legged Walkies consisted of an empty cardboard thread body and stood approximately 2-1/4-inches tall. Walkers produced between 1940 and 1950 are marked with the U.S. Patent number 2140275 on the bottom of one foot, while earlier versions were marked "Made in U.S.A. Pat. Pending" or "Made in U.S.A. Pat'd 12-18-40."

There is a new series of approximately 30 smaller ramp walkers being manufactured in China; they are currently selling between $1-$5.

There are three common sizes of ramp walkers—(a) small, approx. 1-1/2" x 2"; (b) medium, approx. 2-3/4" x 3"; and (c) large, approx. 4" x 5". Most smaller walkers were unpainted, while the medium and larger sizes were either hand-painted or spray painted.

Backing card from the Charmore Co.

There were some quite interesting variations on the use of walkers. A few are listed below:

The Minnesota Electronics Corp. took the generic pig made by Marx and glued a small magnet in the back end. This was boxed with a plastic children's ring which had a small magnet glued to the top. When the ring was placed near the pig's back end, the like opposing forces of the magnets forced the pig to walk along a flat surface. The toy was named Maggie the Magnetic Pig.

Ohio Art produced a plastic farm set named the Walker Farm. This included a bard and a ramp along the seven ramp-walking people and animals pushing interchangeable parts such as a lawnmower, lawn roller, wheelbarrow and spreader.

The Comical Action Target Game by Marx includes a long lithographed tin ramp, a plastic bear ramp walker, a small working plastic rifle and five wooden bullets. The box was placed behind the ramp as a backdrop. The child would shoot at the bear as it waddled down the ramp.

In 1971, Educational toys made a Sesame Street walking letter set, Big Birds Blunder Proof Walking Letter Set. This set included six ramp-walking letters, twelve word keys and a plastic ramp.

A word key with a picture on it was inserted into the base of the ramp, the child would then attempt to spell the word for the picture on the key.

The letters would march up and down the ramp, and if the word was spelled correctly, Big Bird would pop up with a sign that read "OK!" If the word was spelled incorrectly, all the letters would fall down. Additional letters and a ramp extension were available separately.

In 1995, Milton Bradley began marketing a children's game named Penguin Shuffle. The game includes two sets of like-colored penguins and two ramps which lead down to a slow turning battery-operated wheel. The wheel has five openings into which the penguins will fit. Two children each play with one set of penguins. The object is to get all three of the same colored penguins into the wheel, the first one to do so wins. If the penguin does not waddle down the ramp and walk into the opening on the wheel at just the right moment, it falls down a slide and the child must try again.

Because the value of a walker is significantly reduced when the paint is scratched or when there are cracks and breaks, only prices for walkers in Mint condition are listed.

Contributor: Randy Welch, Raven 'Tiques, 27965 Peach Orchard Dr., Easton, MD 21601-5441. Welch began collecting ramp walkers after the purchase of a Huckleberry Hound and Yogi Bear walker at a flea market rekindled childhood memories of marching walkers down his wooden school desk. After discovering there wasn't any reference material available on ramp walkers, Welch began compiling a list and photo collection of over 300 known walkers. His other areas of interest include tin wind-ups and tin lithographed sparklers. Welch welcomes correspondence from other collectors.

Disney (Plastic)

	C10
Big Bad Wolf and Mason Pig, Marx	50
Big Bad Wolf and Three Little Pigs, Marx	150
Donald pushing a wheelbarrow, Marx	25
Donald pulling three nephews in a wagon, Marx	35
Donald and Goofy riding a go-cart, Marx	40
Fiddler and Fifer Pigs, Marx	45
Goofy riding a hippo, Marx	45
Jiminy Cricket w/cello, Marx	30
Mad Hatter and March Hare, Marx	50
Mickey and Minnie carrying a basket of food, Marx	40
Mickey pushing lawn roller, Marx	35
Minnie pushing baby stroller, Marx	35
Mickey and Donald riding on an alligator, Marx	40
Mickey w/Pluto hunting, Marx	40
Pluto, Marx	20

Hanna-Barbera and King Features (Plastic)

	C10
Astro, Marx	150

Donald and Goofy riding a go-cart, Marx, $40

Big Bad Wolf and Three Little Pigs, Marx, $150

Mickey with Pluto hunting, Marx, $40

Fred Flinstone riding on green Dino, Marx, $75

Top Cat and Benny, Marx, $65

	C10
Astro and Rosey, Marx	95
Astro and George Jetson, Marx	90
Fred Flintstone and Barney, Marx	40
Fred and Wilma Flintstone riding on dinosaur, Marx	60
Fred Flinstone riding on green Dino, Marx	75
Little King and guard	70

Astro and Rosey, Marx, $95

Yogi Bear and Huckleberry Hound, Marx, $50

	C10
Pebbles riding on purple Dino, Marx	75
Popeye pushing spinach can wheelbarrow, Marx	25
Top Cat and Benny, Marx	65
Yogi Bear and Huckleberry Hound, Marx	50

Marx Animals with Riders Series (Plastic)

	C10
Ankylosaurus w/clown	35
Bison w/native	35
Brontosaurus w/monkey	35
Hippo w/native	35
Lion w/clown	35
Stegosaurus w/black caveman	35
Triceratops w/native	35
Zebra w/native	35

Fred Flinstone and Barney, Marx, $40

Bunny with carrot on back of dog, Marx, $60

Left to Right: Frontiersman with dog, Marx, $95; Indian woman pulling baby on travois, Marx, $95

Other (Plastic)

	C10
Baseball player w/bat and ball, Marx	40
Bear, Marx	20
Boy and girl dancing, Marx	45
Bull, Marx	20
Bunnies carrying large carrot	35
Bunny pushing cart, Marx	60
Bunny w/carrot on back of dog, Marx	60
Camel w/two humps, head bobs up and down	20
Chicks carrying large Easter egg	35
Chilly Willy penguin on sled pulled by parent, Marx	25
Chinamen carrying a duck in a basket, Marx	30
Chipmunks in marching band playing drum and horn, Marx	35
Chipmunks carrying acorns, Marx	35
Dachshund dog, Marx	20
Dairy Cow, Marx	20
Duck Mama w/three ducklings, Marx	35
Duck, Marx	20
Dutch boy and girl, Marx	40

	C10
Elephant, Marx	20
Farmer pushing wheelbarrow, Marx	30
Figaro the Cat w/ball, Marx	30
Firemen, Marx	35
Frontiersman w/dog, Marx	95
Goat	20
Hap and Hop soldiers, Marx	25
Horse circus style, Marx	20
Indian woman pulling baby on travois, Marx	95
Kangaroo w/baby in pouch, Marx	25
Marty's Market lady pushing shopping cart, Marx	65
Monkeys carrying bananas, Marx	60
Mother Goose w/goose, Marx	60
Nurse maid pushing baby stroller, Marx	20
Pig, Marx	20
Pigs, two carrying third in basket, Marx	40
Poodle, Gantoy, England	40
Pumpkin head man and woman, faces on both sides, Fun World	100
Reindeer, Marx	45
Sailors S.S. Shoreleave, Marx	25

Figaro the Cat with ball, Marx, $30

Monkey carrying bananas, Marx, $60

An advertisement for Marx ramp walkers.

Pumpkin head man and woman, Fun World, $100

Popeye and Wimpy, Marx, $65

	C10
Santa w/white sack, Marx	40
Santa w/yellow sack, Marx	40
Santa w/gold open sack, Marx	45
Santa and Mrs. Claus (faces on both sides), Fun World	45
Santa and Snowman (faces on both sides), Fun World	45
Sheriff facing outlaw, Marx	65
Spark Plug the horse, Marx	200
Tin Man robot pushing a cart, Marx	150

Long John Silver Premium (Plastic)

1989 - with plastic coin weight

	C10
Capt. Flint parrot, green, LJS	15
Flash turtle, green and yellow, LJS	15
Quinn penguin, black and white, LJS	15
Sylvia dinosaur, lavender and pink, LJS	15
Sydney dinosaur, yellow and purple, LJS	15

Funny Face Kool-Aid Premium (Plastic)

All with plastic coin weight

	C10
Choo-Choo Cherry, Pillsbury	60
Goofy Grape, Pillsbury	60
Jolly Ollie Orange, Pillsbury	60
Root'n Toot'n Raspberry, Pillsbury	60

Small Plastic with Metal Legs

	C10
Cow, head up, Marx	20
Cow, head down, Marx	20
Cowboy on horse	30
Donald Duck pushing wheelbarrow, Marx	40
Dog (brown Pluto-like), Marx	20

	C10
Elephant	30
Mexican cowboy on horse	30
Mickey and Minnie Mouse, Marx	40
Pluto, Marx	35

Large Plastic

	C10
Baby Walk-a-Way baby, Marx	40
Baby Teeny Toddler walking girl, Dolls, Inc.	40
Baby Walking baby w/moving eyes, cloth dress, Marx	40
Baby Walking baby in Canadian Mountie uniform, Marx	50
Baby Walking baby in Pirate clothes, Marx	50
Cow Milking cow, Marx	40
Cow Wiz Walking Milking Cow Charmore, Marx	40
Double Walking Doll (boy behind girl), Hong Kong	60
Horse w/English rider, Marx	50
Horse, Marx	30
Horse w/rubber ears and string tail, Marx	30
Popeye and Wimpy w/heads on springs, Marx	65

Argentina (Plastic)

	C10
Horse cream color w/pink legs (similar to Marx)	25
Pig blue (similar to Marx only smaller)	25
Cow blue (same size as pig)	25

Argentina (Bakelite Cone and Legs)

	C10
Penguin (very similar in size and shape to Wilson)	75

Argentina (Paper Cone and Wood Legs)

	C10
Gaucho (cowboy)	75
China (Gaucho's wife), versions red, blue and green	75

Various Argentinean Walkers. Front row, left to right: Penguin, Bakelite, $75; Chinese man pushing tin cart, $90; Gaucho with elephant head pushing tin cart, $90; Clown with elephant head, $90; Gaucho with pig head pushing tin cart, $90; Clown pushing tin cart, $90. Back row, left to right: School boy, $75; Musketeer, $75; Gaucho, $75; Policeman, $75; China (Gaucho's wife), in green, red and blue, $75.

	C10
Policeman	75
Musketeer	75
School boy	75
Gaucho w/elephant head pushing tin cart	90
Gaucho w/pig head pushing tin cart	90
Clown pushing tin cart	90
Clown w/elephant head pushing tin cart	90
Chinese man pushing tin cart	90

Erwin (Celluloid)

	C10
Popeye, 5-3/4" tall	60

Ives (Cast Iron)

	C10
Elephant Pat. 1873, w/iron feet and swivel trunk	125
Elephant Pat. 1873 w/lead feet and fixed trunk	125

Wilson Walkies. Left to right: Indian Chief, $70; Black Mammy, $40; Soldier, $30

Wilson Walkies. Left to right: Little Red Riding Hood, $40; Clown, $40; Nurse, $30

Wilson Walkies (Wood and Composition)

	C10
Black Mammy	40
Clown	40
Donald Duck	175
Elephant on four legs	30
Eskimo	75
Indian Chief	70
Little Red Riding Hood	40
Nurse	30
Olive Oyl	175
Penguin	25
Pig	40
Pinocchio	200
Popeye	200
Rabbit	60
Sailor	30
Santa Claus	90
Santa Claus w/box	150

Wilson Walkies: Left to right: Penguin,, $25; Elephant with four legs, $30; Pig, $40

Left to Right: Santa with box, $150; Santa, $90

	C10
Soldier	30
Wimpy	175

Czechoslovakia (Wood and Composition)

	C10
Dog on four legs	30
Donald Duck w/wood ramp, walks w/front-to-back motion	90
Man with carved wooden hat	35
Monkey	35
Pig	20
Policeman	60

Germany (Wood and Composition)

	C10
Goat	60

Donald Duck with wood ramp, Czechoslovakia, $90

Left to Right: Pig, Zebra and Goat, wood, $60 each

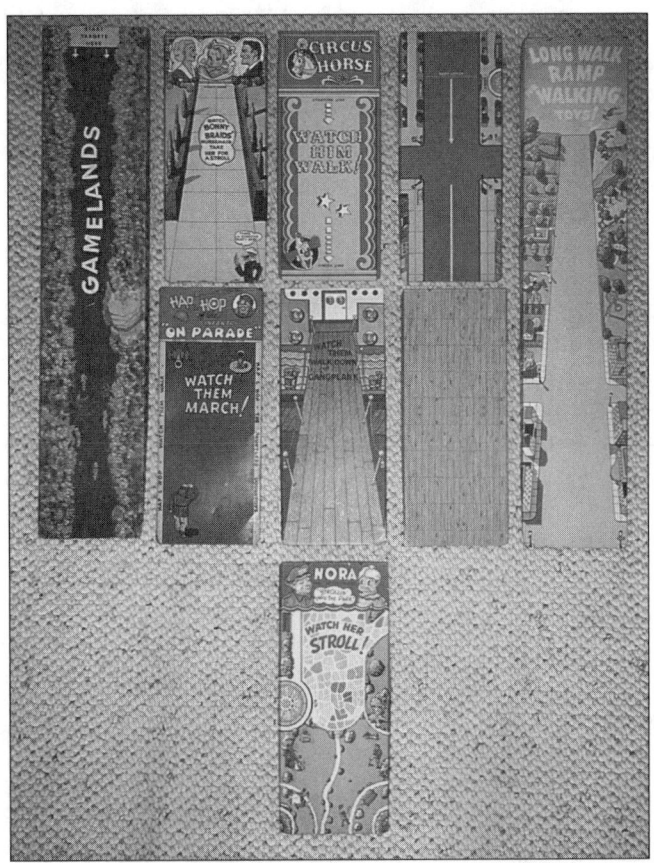

Top Row: Comical Action Bear, Marx, $150; Dick Tracy's Nursemaid, Marx, $125; Circus Horse, Marx, $65; Street Scene (generic), Charmore, $75; Disney long ramp with street scene, Marx, $200. Bottom Row: Hap and Hop, Marx, $50; S.S. Shoreleave, Marx, $75; Plank ramp, Marx, $50; Nora the Nursemaid, Marx, $75.

	C10
Pig	60
Zebra	60

Ramps in Box

	C10
Circus Horse, Marx	65
Comical Action Bear w/long ramp, including gun and bullets, Marx	150

Dog with wood ramp, made in Japan for Shackman of New York, $75.

C10

Dick Tracy's Nursemaid takes Bonny Braids for stroll,
Marx 125

Disney long ramp w/generic street scene, Marx 200

Dog, wood w/wood ramp, made in Japan for Shackman
of New York 75

Felix wood ramp w/wood walker 1,400

Hap and Hop the Dauntless Doughboys, Marx 80

C10

"I Like Ike" elephant, Marx 125

Nora the Nursemaid, Marx 75

Plank ramp (generic) for cow, pig, ducks, bear, etc.,
Marx 50

S.S. Shoreleave sailors, Marx 75

Street scene (generic) short ramp for farmer pushing
wheelbarrow, etc., Charmore 75

G.I. Joe Action Pilot Series Official Space Capsule Set,
(Action Figures), Hasbro, 1966, No. 8020, $350

Hartland Sgt.
Lance O'Rourke,
(Action Figures),
No. 804, $400

Army Bomber, (Aircraft), three-engine, c. 1935,
No. 1025, $250

Whitman Charmin, Chatty Cut Outs, (American Paper
Toys), No. 1959, 1964, $45. Photo courtesy Judith Izen

Saalfield Little Women Paper Dolls, (American Paper Toys), No. 1377, $45. Photo courtesy Judith Izen

Hubley Landau Carriage, (Animal-Drawn), cast iron, painted, 1905, 16-1/2" long, $2,800

Hubley Royal Circus Lion Wagon, (Animal-Drawn), cast iron, with rare gray horses and wagon, 15-3/4", $1,650

Hull Prospect Park Omnibus, (Animal-Drawn), with two horses and driver, c. 1880, 16-1/2", $15,000

Reed Trolley, "Bowery &
Central Park," (Animal-Drawn),
paper on wood, with two
horses, 28" long, $3,500

Kenton Overland Circus
Calliope Wagon, (Animal-
Drawn), 14-1/2" long, $700

Three mechanical banks—Back row: Dentist Bank, white dentist
working on black patient, 1880, $14,000; Front row, left to right:
Calamity, three football players, pat. J&E Stevens Co., August 29,
1905, $15,750; Clown on Globe, 1873, $3,500

The Mechanized Robot, (Battery-Operated Toys), T-N
Co., 1950s, 13-1/2" tall, $1,200

Tootsietoy Flash Blast Attack Ship, (Comic Characters), 1937, 4-1/2" long, $450

Distler Uncle Wiggily Crazy Car, (Comic Characters), c. 1922, $5,500

Left to Right: Sofa, Ideal No. I-942, (Dollhouse and miniature furniture) $15 with Ideal Coffee table, $8; Sofa, Renwal No. L78, $12 with Pedestal end table, Renwal No. L73, $8

Left to Right: Young Decorator Television Set, (Dollhouse and miniature furniture), $40; Young Decorator Coffee Table, $10; Young Decorator Torchiere Lamp, $30; and Young Decorator Sectional Sofa, individual pieces, $15 each

Revell Mr. Gasser, (Figure Kits), Ed Roth, No. 1301, 1963, $100

Revell Rat Fink, (Figure Kits), No. 1305, 1963, $40

Hard plastic doll house furniture from Marx, Left to Right: Milk Bar ($20); Stool ($20, each); Round Table ($5); Chair ($3-5); Ping-Pong Table ($25); Piano ($10); Piano Bench ($5); Juke Box ($20); Coffee Table ($5); Circular Couch ($10)

(Dollhouse and Miniature Furniture) Two-story lithographed fiberboard house with four rooms, front stoop and benches, 3/4-inch-scale, Rich, (Dollhouse and Miniature Furniture), $100

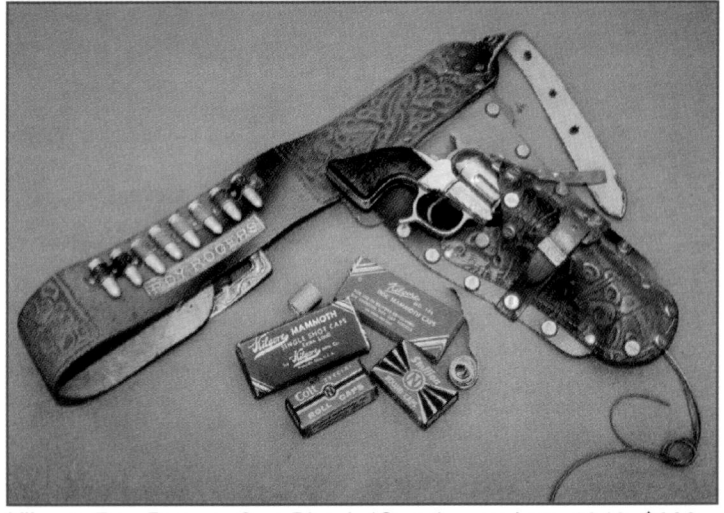

Kilgore Roy Rogers Cap Pistol, (Guns), cast iron, 1940, $600

Fisher-Price Katy Kackler, (Fisher-Price), No. 140, $240

Fisher-Price Mickey Mouse Xylophone, No. 798, (Fisher-Price) $975

Marx Flintstone Flivver (left) and Rumble Wreck (right), (Movies, Radio & Television), friction type, 1962, $615, each

Gumby's Jeep, (Movies, Radio & Television), metal, 1960s, 12", $250

Wolverine Sandy Andy Ferry, (Ships), tin litho, 13-1/2" long, $150

Plasticville Supermarket, large, $35

Left to Right: Subway Express, (Tin Wind-ups), with plastic tunnel, Marx 1950s, $180; Chein Ski Boy, No. 157, 1940s, $310CS

Plasticville Log Cabin, Rustic Fence and Tree, $25

Peacock, (Tin Wind-ups), with bellows, Orober, $900

Marx Merrymakers, (Tin Wind-ups), four mice, three in band and one dancer, without marquee, has conductor with baton, $1,175

Left to Right: Marx Let the Drummer Boy Play, (Tin Wind-ups), 1930s, $875; Marx Tidy Tim Streetcleaner, pushing wagon, 1933, $700

Marx Honeymoon Express, (Tin Wind-ups), streamlined train on circular track, 1947, $175

Marx Ring-A-Ling Circus, (Tin Wind-ups), early ringmaster and circus animals, $1,280

Ohio Art Giant Ride Ferris Wheel, (Tin Wind-ups), 1950s, 16" high, $500

Strauss Knock-Out Prize Fighters, (Tin Wind-ups), c. 1910, No. 52, $500

Reed Circus, (Wood & Composition Toys), $2,000

Noah's Ark, (Wood & Composition Toys), wood with painted figures, top opens to hold animals, late 1800s-early 1900s, $750+

A.C Williams Sedan, (Vehicles), c. 1931, cast iron, interchangeable body, 6-3/4" long, $700

Wolverine Zilotone, (Tin Wind-ups), 1930s, $645

Hot Wheels Maserati Mistral, (Vehicles), assorted, Mattel, 6277, 1969, $125

Hot Wheels Mutt Mobile, (Vehicles), assorted, Mattel, 5185, 1971, $175

Hot Wheels T-4-2, (Vehicles), assorted, Mattel, 6177, 1971, $165

Marx Merchants Transfer Truck, (Vehicles), tin wind-up, 1929, $700

Marx Mechanical Coupe, (Vehicles), tin wind-up, 1933, $575

Strauss Knock-Out Prize Fighters, (Tin Wind-ups), c. 1910, No. 52, $500

Reed Circus, (Wood & Composition Toys), $2,000

Noah's Ark, (Wood & Composition Toys), wood with painted figures, top opens to hold animals, late 1800s-early 1900s, $750+

A.C Williams Sedan, (Vehicles), c. 1931, cast iron, inter-changeable body, 6-3/4" long, $700

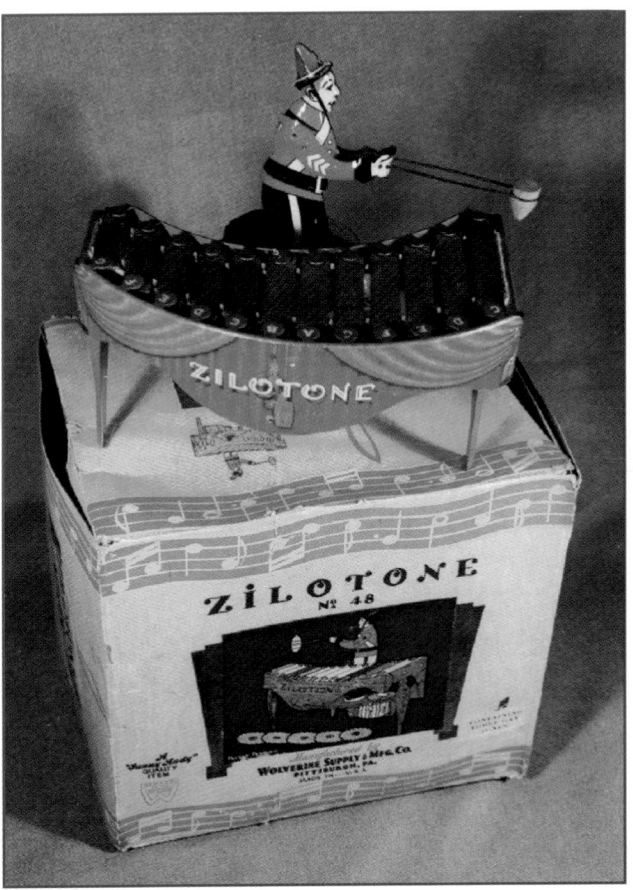

Wolverine Zilotone, (Tin Wind-ups), 1930s, $645

Banner American Express Truck, (Vehicles), tin, 10" long, $350

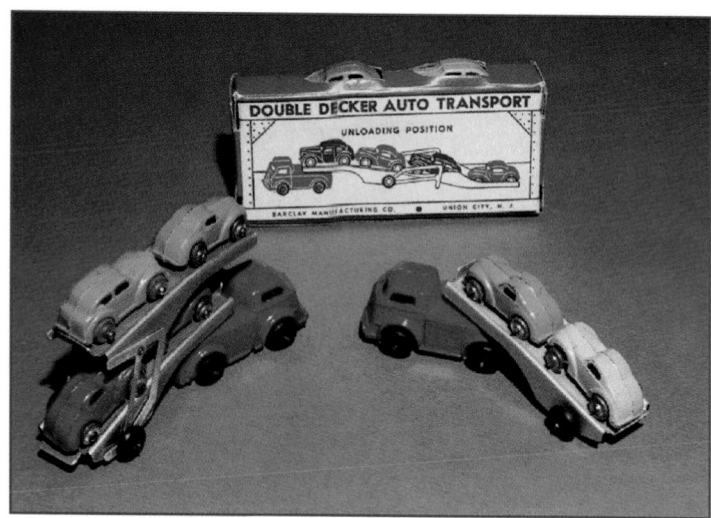

Left to Right: Double Transport Set, (Vehicles), Banner, No. 440, 1960s, $145; Auto Transport Set, Banner, No. 330, $73

Arcade Mack Bus, (Vehicles), 1929, No. 318, 13-1/4" long, $3,000

Four variations of Barclay's Oil Truck, (Vehicles), c. 1960s, $18, each

Two versions of Arcade's Yellow Cab Bank, (Vehicles), 1927, "Flat Top," $4,000

Left to Right: Banner Dump Truck, (Vehicles), plastic, $20; Banner Side Dump Truck, plastic, 1950s, $30

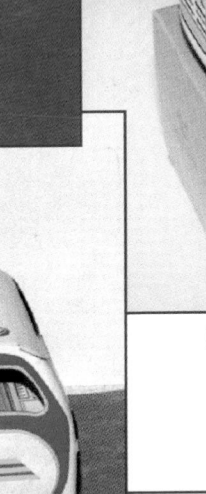

Banner Grocery Service Truck, (Vehicles), $300

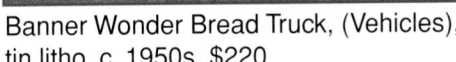

Banner Wonder Bread Truck, (Vehicles), tin litho, c. 1950s, $220

Buddy "L" Merry-Go-Round Truck, (Vehicles), No. 5429, $250

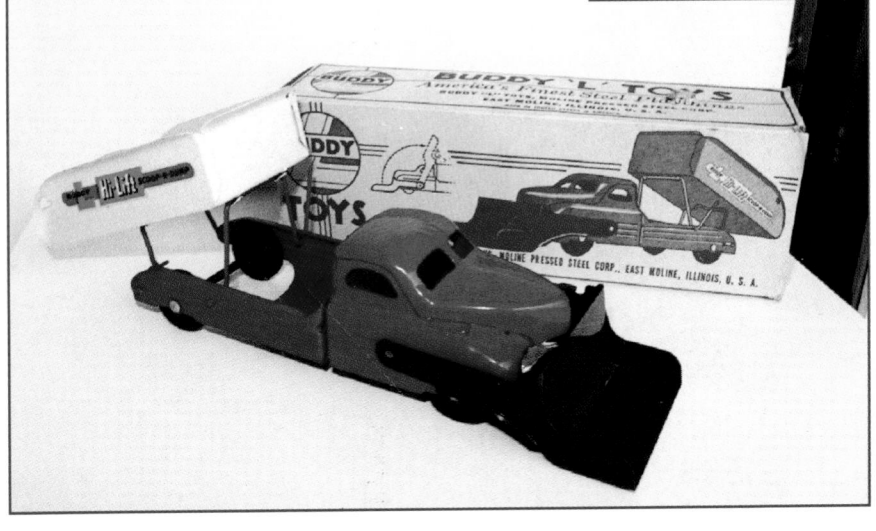

Buddy "L" Hi-Lift Scoop-A-Dump, (Vehicles), $150

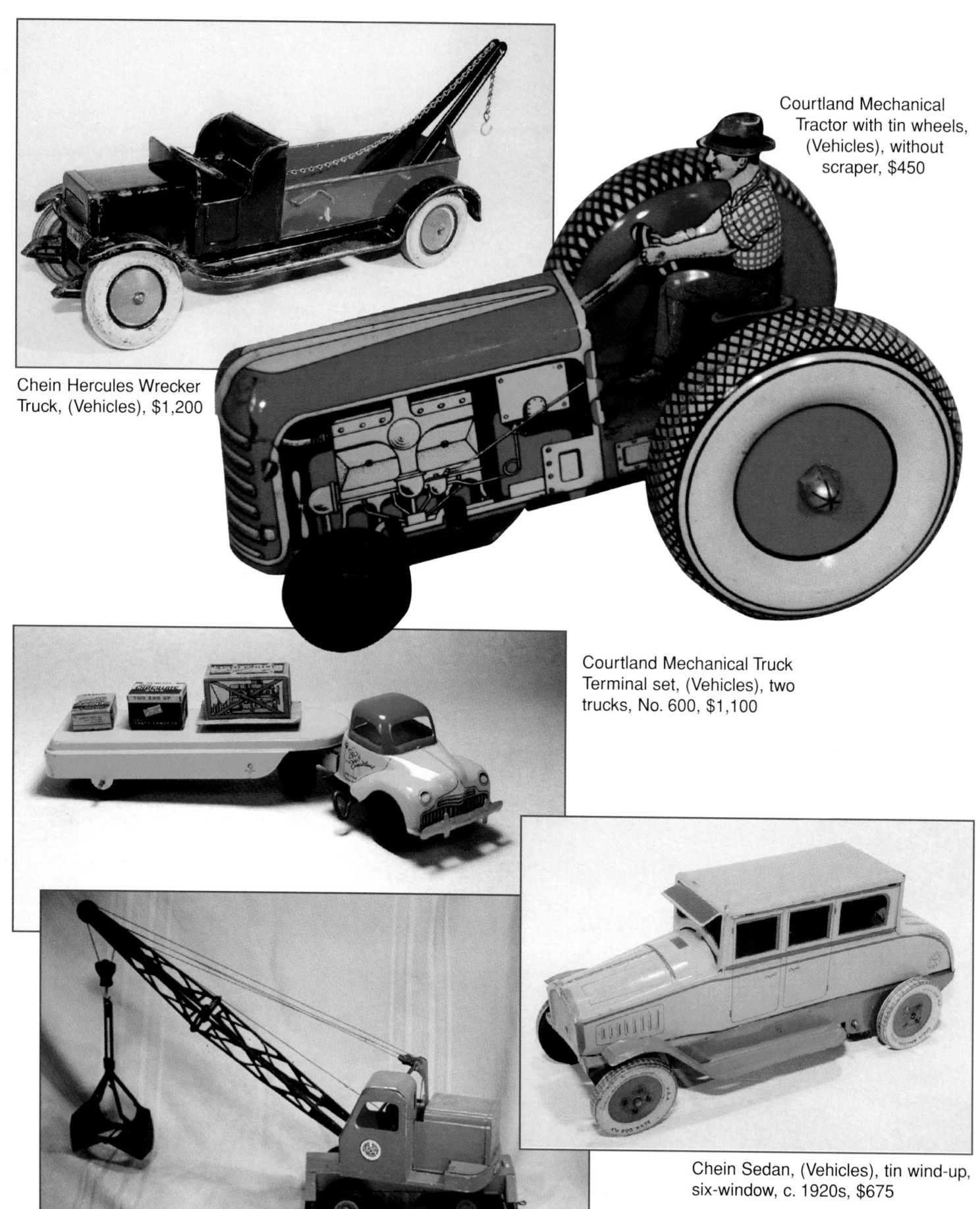

Chein Hercules Wrecker
Truck, (Vehicles), $1,200

Courtland Mechanical
Tractor with tin wheels,
(Vehicles), without
scraper, $450

Courtland Mechanical Truck
Terminal set, (Vehicles), two
trucks, No. 600, $1,100

Chein Sedan, (Vehicles), tin wind-up,
six-window, c. 1920s, $675

Doepke No. 2007 Unit Mobile Crane, (Vehicles), 11-1/2" long, $310

1972-4 Amerada Hess Tanker Truck,
(Vehicles), $325

1983-85 "First Hess Truck" bank,
(Vehicles), $65

1989 Hess
Ladder Fire
Truck, (Vehi-
cles), white,
$35

Hot Wheels Custom Mustang,
(Vehicles), assorted, Mattel,
6206, 1968, $425

Hot Wheels King Kuda, (Vehicles), chrome,
Club Kit, Mattel, 6411, 1970, $120

Hot Wheels Maserati Mistral, (Vehicles), assorted, Mattel, 6277, 1969, $125

Hot Wheels Mutt Mobile, (Vehicles), assorted, Mattel, 5185, 1971, $175

Hot Wheels T-4-2, (Vehicles), assorted, Mattel, 6177, 1971, $165

Marx Merchants Transfer Truck, (Vehicles), tin wind-up, 1929, $700

Marx Mechanical Coupe, (Vehicles), tin wind-up, 1933, $575

Tootsietoy Midget Series/Cracker Jacks, (Vehicles), No. 510 Boxed Set (eight-piece), 1936, 1" vehicles, $150

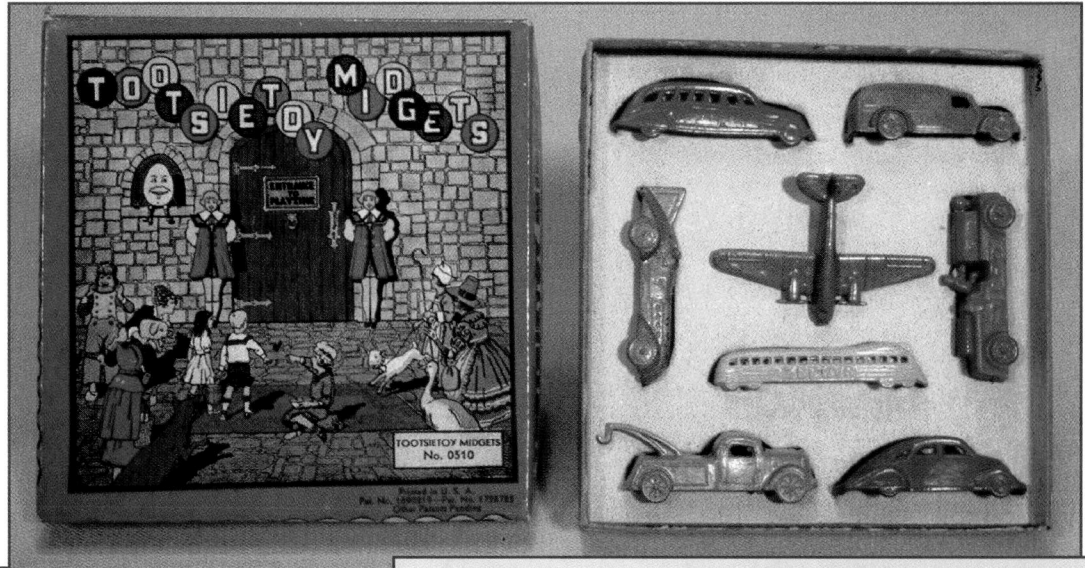

Metalcraft Waldorf Lager, (Vehicles), white, $900

Tootsietoy Federal Delivery Van Series, (Vehicles), Grocery, No. 4630, 192, $85

Tonka No. 120 Tractor and Carry-All Trailer with No. 50 Steam Shovel, (Vehicles), $350

Tootsietoy USN Los Angeles Dirigible, (Vehicles), No. 1030, 1937, $125

Baldwin Coast
Defense Gun,
(Miscellaneous),
No. 830, wood
and metal, $78

Tootsietoy P-39 Fighter,
(Vehicles), 1947, $150

Tootsietoy Dive-
Bomber Waco
Biplane, (Vehicles),
1937, $140

This Old Mammy
Washing Clothes
(Miscellaneous)
clockwork toy by Ives
was auctioned in
1993 for $13,800.

SCHOENHUT

The A. Schoenhut Company had a long history of toy manufacturing. Many items were produced, including animals, figures, moving pictures, Palmer Cox Brownies, children's musical instruments and dolls. This section covers some of the items in the Humpty Dumpty Circus.

The Humpty Dumpty items covered in this section span the years of 1903 to 1935. Glass-eyed animals and two-part head personnel, along with other rare examples, are priced higher than painted-eye animals and pressed-head figures produced later. Delavan items are generally priced lower than reduced-size figures.

In the past few years, the toys' popularity among toy collectors and folk art collectors has driven prices up. Particular interest in Teddy Roosevelt's Adventures in Africa series (produced from 1909 to 1911) has led the price increase.

Although this history is not all inclusive, it should help the collector identify age for some animals/figures.

1872	Produced the first toy pianos
1903	Began producing Humpty Dumpty Circus items
	Began producing glass eyes animals, molded/two-part head personnel
1909/11	Produced Teddy Roosevelt figures
1910	Produced bisque head ring master, lady circus rider, lion tamer, lad gent acrobats
1918	Produced painted eyes animals, wooden-head personnel
1923	Began producing reduced-size circus
1927	Produced miniature set (donkey, elephant, clown)
1935	Company closed
1950	Nelson Delavan purchased manufacturing rights and produced several figures and animals

There are a few rules to keep in mind while collecting Schoenhut toys.

Condition determines price.

Mint condition Schoenhut toys are virtually nonexistent. Mint condition means the toy was never played with and demand higher prices. Boxes increase value, and Mint in Box items commands a sizable premium.

Glass-eyed animals, early figures with plaster faces, and rare animals demand high prices.

Bisque-headed figures and molded/two-part head figures generally demand a higher price than carved-face figures.

Condition on the majority of animals and figures found today is between C4 and C7.

Skillful restoration can increase value. Anyone selling an animal or figure with restored sections should indicate where restoration has occurred.

Prices in this guide have not been established for every style of animal and figure.

Because of the importance of condition and classification for the Schoenhut category of toys, the existing definitions of Schoenhut categories need to be explained.

A magazine ad for the "New additions to Schoenhut's Humpty Dumpty Circus Toys." The original sets were sold for between 50-cents and $25, depending on the number of figures in the set.

Rating	Definition
C1	Bits and pieces of Schoenhut toys.
C2	Poor quality with no paint or with a "child's" effort to repaint, or missing a major part. Definitely needs repair.
C3	Fair with no missing major parts but with little paint; moisture/moth/animal damage and soiling. Needs repair.
C4	Good with play wear; soiled/worn clothing, damaged paint/chips, missing leather and/or other attachable parts.
C5	Very good with restored paint, clothes, and/or leather.

C6	Fine with good paint, new or worn leather and minor restorations. Could also have some soiling/wear/color loss and missing minor attached parts.
C7	Very fine with minor wear/color loss and fractional restoration.
C8	Almost perfect with no restoration but may have slight color loss.
C9	Perfect, meaning no damage or color loss of any kind. Almost new.
C10	Mint, meaning never played with and stored under ideal conditions. Factory new.

Note: Restringing is not considered restoration. If the restringing effort is not done properly, however, wood damage can occur and reduce the value of the piece. Additional information on Schoenhut figures or dolls can be obtained by joining the Schoenhut Collectors Club. For a membership application, please contact Pat Girbach, 103 West Huron Street, Ann Arbor, MI 48103.

Contributors: Jim and Patsy Carlson, 7939 Caberfare Trail, Clarkston, MI 48348-3708. The Carlson's purchased a partial Schoenhut circus in 1988 as a remembrance to a deceased parent. That remembrance has grown to include several specialized Schoenhut pieces. They are active members of the Schoenhut Collectors Club and Antique Toy Collectors of America. In addition to Schoenhut toys, they collect platform animals, American rocking horses, early squeak toys, folk art and American primitive folk art.

Circus Animals: Glass-Eyed and Painted-Eyed (Regular Size)

Prices below are for the animals that are most frequently seen; not all animals have been included. Glass-eyed animals were made from 1903, when A. Schoenhut Company began to produce Circus animals and performers, to about 1918. Painted-eyed animals were produced from about 1918 to 1933, when the A. Schoenhut company closed.

	C2	C4	C6	C8
Alligator, glass eyes	100	175	350	475
Alligator, painted eyes	75	125	250	385
Brown Bear, glass eyes	175	325	425	600
Brown Bear, painted eyes	75	120	250	375
Bulldog, glass eyes, carved mane	200	350	850	1250
Bulldog, painted eyes	100	150	250	425
Buffalo, glass eyes, cloth	100	200	325	500
Buffalo, glass eyes, curved	200	400	750	1050
Buffalo, painted eyes	100	200	300	450
Burro, painted eyes	100	175	275	400
Camel, one hump, glass eyes	100	150	300	425
Camel, one hump, painted eyes	95	120	250	375

	C2	C4	C6	C8
Camel, two hump, glass eyes	200	475	950	1400
Camel, two hump, painted eyes	95	135	275	400

Left to Right: Camel with one hump (Arabian), glass eyes and open mouth, C8 condition, $425; Camel with two humps (Bactrian), glass eyes, carved head and neck showing tool marks, C8 condition, $1,400.

Brown Bear with glass eyes in C6 condition, $425

Elephant with glass eyes, blanket and triangular-shaped head-dress, the most sought-after of all elephants; C7 condition, $450-700

Left to Right: Monkey with black face, one-piece molded head, C6 condition, $400; Monkey with white face, C5 condition, $225-500

	C2	C4	C6	C8
Cat, glass eyes	500	1000	1600	2400
Cat, painted eyes	200	360	725	1100
Cow, painted eyes	50	125	250	385
Deer, glass eyes	200	300	575	875
Deer, painted eyes	175	325	425	600
Donkey, glass eyes	30	60	120	175
Donkey, painted eyes	20	30	50	75
Elephant, glass eyes	40	70	135	200
Elephant, glass eyes w/blanket	125	325	450	700
Elephant, painted eyes	30	50	100	150

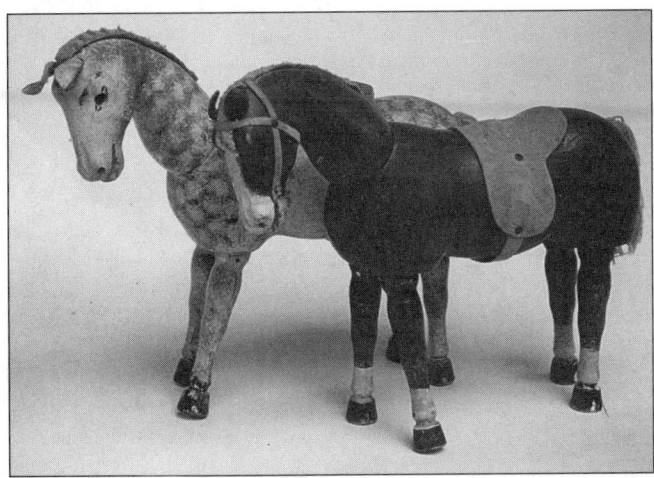

Left to Right: White horse with glass eyes, referred to as "Educated Horse," C8 condition, $275; Brown horse with glass eyes, leather saddle and bridle, C8 condition, $250

	C2	C4	C6	C8
Gazelle, glass eyes	400	1000	1600	2400
Gazelle, painted eyes	300	400	775	1200
Giraffe, glass eyes	100	175	350	500
Giraffe, painted eyes	75	120	250	350
Goat, glass eyes	75	200	275	350
Goat, painted eyes	50	150	225	300
Goose, painted eyes	75	150	350	475
Gorilla, molded ears	1000	1300	1600	2400
Gorilla, leather ears	1000	1700	2300	3000
Hippopotamus, glass eyes	100	275	550	800
Hippopotamus, painted eyes	75	120	250	375
Horse, brown, glass eyes	75	100	160	250
Horse, brown, painted eyes	30	50	100	150
Horse, white, glass eyes	85	120	175	275
Horse, white, painted eyes	40	75	125	190
Hyena, glass eyes	1400	1600	2200	3200
Hyena, painted eyes	400	500	950	1400
Kangaroo, glass eyes	400	500	2100	3000
Kangaroo, painted eyes	200	350	700	1000
Leopard, glass eyes	100	275	550	825
Leopard, painted eyes	75	150	300	450
Lion, glass eyes, carved mane	300	475	1050	1500
Lion, glass eyes, cloth mane	100	200	400	700
Lion, painted eyes	95	175	375	525

Giraffe with glass eyes and open mouth, C6 condition, $350; Flexible Cage, C6 condition, $525

Tiger, with glass eyes, full ball-jointed neck and leather ears, C8 condition, $925

	C2	C4	C6	C8
Monkey, black face	100	200	400	600
Monkey, white face	120	225	500	750
Ostrich, glass eyes	200	300	600	900
Ostrich, painted eyes	100	225	300	550
Pig, glass eyes	125	275	550	825
Pig, painted eyes	100	175	300	450
Polar Bear, glass eyes	300	475	850	1275
Polar Bear, painted eyes	250	350	575	875
Poodle, glass eyes, carved mane	100	225	400	675
Poodle, painted eyes	40	70	135	200
Rhinoceros, glass eyes	175	375	600	950
Rhinoceros, painted eyes	125	300	400	600
Sea Lion, glass eyes	200	400	625	900
Sea Lion, painted eyes	125	225	450	700
Sheep, glass eyes	100	175	385	550
Sheep, painted eyes	75	135	275	400
Tiger, glass eyes	100	275	650	925

Zebra with glass eyes, closed mouth, head and neck in two sections leather strip mane and cord tail, C7 condition, $1,200

	C2	C4	C6	C8
Tiger, painted eyes	75	150	300	450
Wolf, glass eyes	1000	1300	1600	2400
Wolf, painted eyes	300	400	775	1200
Zebra, glass eyes	175	425	725	1200
Zebra, painted eyes	150	325	425	600
Zebu, glass eyes	1200	1400	2100	3000
Zebu, painted eyes	400	500	950	1400

Circus Accessories (Regular and Reduced Size)

These items are most commonly found in "play wear" condition of C4 to C7 category. Not all accessories have been included.

	C2	C4	C6	C8
Ball	10	20	40	50
Ball, reduced	10	15	30	40
Barrel	2	4	6	10
Chair	2	4	6	10
Flexible Cage	75	175	525	675
Goblet	3	5	8	12
Hoop	10	15	25	40
Horizontal Bar	75	175	375	500
Ladder	2	4	6	10
Pedestal, short	10	20	30	45
Pedestal, tall	15	25	40	60
Table	15	25	40	65
Tent, 24" x 16" (small)	200	400	500	750
Tent, 24" x 36" (large)	700	1100	1400	2200
Tent, litho w/panels	2000	3000	6000	9000
Tub	10	20	35	50
Weights, 50/100/200 lbs.	75	150	200	325
Whip, 4-1/2" shaft	10	20	30	45
Whip, 5-1/2" shaft	15	25	40	65
Wild Animal Cage Wagon	300	400	775	1200

Left to Right: Tall pedestal, Short pedestal and Tub, all are painted wood with applied printed paper bands; all in C7 condition valued at $40-60, $30-45 and $35-50, respectively

	C2	C4	C6	C8
Lady Rider	30	65	125	225
Negro Dude	65	140	370	500
Ring Master	30	60	120	200

Animals, Reduced

	C2	C4	C6	C8
Brown Bear	75	120	275	400
Buffalo	65	140	225	350
Camel, two humps	75	120	275	375
Donkey	20	30	40	50
Elephant	25	45	95	125
Giraffe	75	120	275	400
Hippopotamus	100	240	325	500
Horse, brown	30	50	100	135
Horse, white	30	50	100	135
Leopard	75	120	275	375
Lion	75	120	275	375
Ostrich	85	150	300	425
Pig	100	250	400	425
Poodle	75	120	275	400
Rhinoceros	85	150	300	425
Tiger	75	120	275	375
Zebra	150	325	450	600

Chinaman with two-part head, C6 condition, $325

Performers Wooden/Pressed One-Part Head (Regular Size)

The manufacturing sequence for figures was plaster face two-part head/faces, bisque heads, and finally wooden/pressed one-part head. Not all figures have been included.

	C2	C4	C6	C8
Chinaman	100	200	325	450
Clown	20	65	100	125
Hobo	45	145	250	325
Lady Acrobat	65	150	275	375
Lady Rider	45	145	250	325
Lion Tamer	45	145	250	325
Negro Dude	100	200	325	450
Ring Master	65	150	275	375

Reduced-Size Figures and Animals

Reduced-size figures and animals were first produced around 1927 by the A. Schoenhut Company to appeal to another market and as a last-ditch effort to save the company. Unfortunately, the company closed in 1933. Not all figures and animals have been included.

Circus Figures, Reduced

	C2	C4	C6	C8
Clown	15	40	65	100
Hobo	55	130	280	410

Clown with two-part head, Dresden "footprint" glued to front of suit and star collar, rare, C7 condition, $100-125

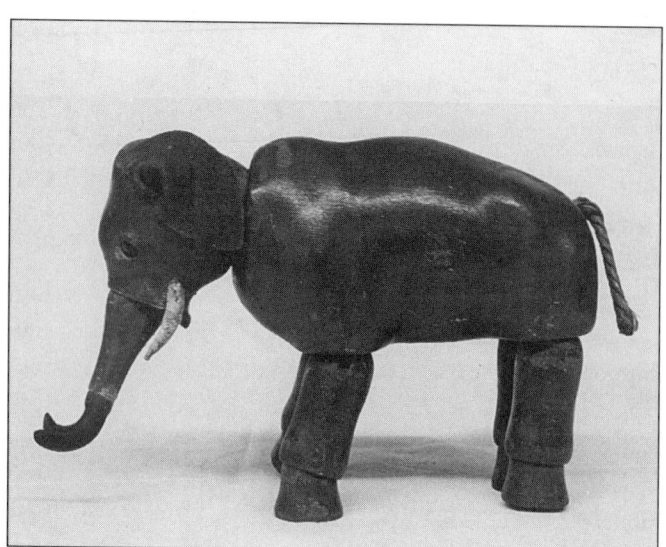

Lady Rider, C4 condition $145

Elephant, with glass eyes, C8 condition $200

A group of Schoenhut Humpty Dumpty Circus figures and accessories, $2,000-3,000

Teddy Roosevelt's Adventures in Africa

These figures were produced in low volume from 1909 to 1911 and represent "rare" or "scarce" toys. Some of the animals were used in circus play toys produced with glass eyes until 1918.

Teddy Roosevelt Figures

	C2	C4	C6	C8
Teddy Roosevelt	750	1000	1300	2000
Photographer (Kermit)	850	1300	1700	2450
African Native	950	1400	2200	3200
African Drummer	950	1400	2400	3500
African Chief	650	900	1500	2200
Arab Chief	950	1400	1800	2700
Doctor	950	1400	1800	2700
Naturalist	950	1400	2200	3500

Teddy Roosevelt Animals

	C2	C4	C6	C8
Alligator, glass eyes	100	175	350	475
Camel, glass eyes, one hump, closed mouth	100	150	300	425
Deer, glass eyes	200	300	575	875
Elephant, glass eyes	40	70	135	200
Gazelle, glass eyes	400	1000	1600	2400
Giraffe, glass eyes, closed mouth	175	350	475	650
Gorilla, leather ear	1000	1700	2300	3000
Hippopotamus, glass eyes	100	275	550	800
Hyena, glass eyes	1400	1600	2200	3200
Lion, glass eyes, carved mane	300	475	850	1500
Rhinoceros, glass eyes	175	375	600	950
Zebra, glass eyes, closed mouth	175	375	625	950
Zebu, glass eyes	1200	1400	2100	3000

Miscellaneous

	C2	C4	C6	C8
Doll House, small	100	150	250	375

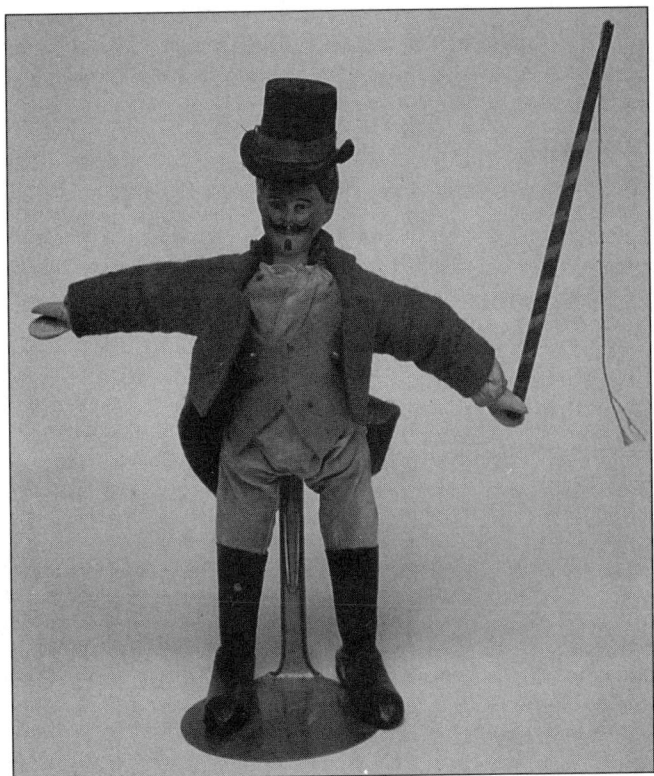

Close-up of bisque-head Ringmaster

	C2	C4	C6	C8
Doll House, medium	125	175	375	425
Doll House, large	150	225	500	750
Golfer, Girl	125	200	375	475
Golfer, Man	125	175	350	425
Milk Wagon, horses and driver	1250	2400	3000	4000
Piano, 14" x 10"	30	60	120	175
Railroad Station, large	125	175	350	475
Roly Poly, Black Clown	200	300	600	850

Left to Right: bisque-head performers—Lion Tamer, C6 condition, $250; Lady Rider, C6 condition, $250; Lady Acrobat, C6 condition, $275; Ringmaster, C6 condition, $275

Left to Right: Variations of Clowns with two-part heads— Clown with Dresden "footprint"; sunburst with cat, pig and moons; multicolored with hearts, clubs, spades, diamonds, stars and moons; diamond patterns; white polka-dot on pink field with Dresden "footprint"

*Gorilla with two-part head and leather ears, C7 condition,
$2,300-3,000*

Comic Character

	C2	C4	C6	C8
Barney Google and Sparkplug	300	360	725	1100
Bonzo	300	360	725	1100
Boob McNutt	250	575	1050	1500
Felix, 4"	30	60	120	175
Felix, 6"	100	275	550	800
Felix, 8"	95	135	275	400
Happy Hooligan	250	575	1050	1500
Koko the Clown, rare	4000			
Maggie/Jiggs, rolling pin and bucket	200	400	775	1200
Mary and Her Lamb	325	450	600	900
Max and Moritz, pair, early model	275	675	1100	1600
Rolly Dolly				
Dutch Girl	65	150	275	375
Foxy Grandpa, large	100	275	550	800
Santa, medium	225	475	975	1350
Santa, large	500	1000	1600	2400

SHIPS

See also Tin Wind-Ups, Paper

LIBERTY PLAYTHINGS

Liberty Playthings was in business in the late 1920s and early 1930s in Niagara Falls, New York. All its toys, which were made of wood and metal, had names related to the word "Liberty," and all to have nautical themes. Those advertised in 1929 were No. 2 Tug and Scow, No. 5 Freighter, No. 6 Airplane Carrier, No. 7 Fireboat, No. 8 Destroyer, and No. 22 Seaplane. The Carrier, which in the ad was called "Liberator," sold for $10. The "Libertania" Aircraft Carrier seems to be the same ship, or a slight variation.

	C6	C8	C10
Cruiser or Battleship	225	338	450
Destroyer No. 8	225	338	450
Fire Boat, 23"	200	300	400
Aircraft Carrier, "Libertania," wood and tin litho w/lead planes, 27-3/4" long	250	375	500
Runabout, wind-up	155	233	310

ORKIN

Orkin, of Cambridge, Massachusetts, was founded by Samuel Orkin about the end of World War I. His metal ships were modeled after the real thing. They were big, ranging from about fifteen to thirty-five inches, but relatively inexpensive.

Orkin Battleships. Top, left to right: "New Jersey," $1,400; "Nevada," $1,100. Middle, left to right: "Pennsylvania," $1,700; "New Mexico," $1,000. Bottom row: "Constitution," $1,000.

	C6	C8	C10
Battleship B2, pressed steel, 36" long	3000	5000	8000
Battleship "Constitution," steel keywind, c. 1914, 25" long	500	750	1000
Battleship "Marcella," 18" long	600	900	1350
Battleship "Nevada," steel keywind, c. 1914, 22" long	550	825	1100
Battleship "New Jersey" tin and wood, c. 1920, 35" long	600	900	1400
Battleship "New Mexico," steel keywind, c. 1914, 25" long	500	750	1000
Battleship "Pennsylvania," steel keywind, c. 1914, 30" long	700	1100	1700
Battleship "Texas," steel keywind, 30" long	1000	1800	3800

ORKIN CRAFT

Orkin Craft was owned by the president of the Waterman Pen Company. Manufacturing was done by Calwis Industries Ltd. of Beverly Hills, California. The pleasure boats sold by the firm were too expensive for the era (the price was in the $15-$20 range), which is probably why they failed about 1935 or 1936. All the boats were motor-driven. Some were all metal, and some had wooden decks.

	C6	C8	C10
Cabin Cruiser, 30" long	700	1200	1700
Speedboat, clockwork, 29" long	600	1000	1450

MISCELLANEOUS

	C6	C8	C10
49 LST, includes tank, Buddy L, 12" long	50	75	100
Action Submarine, Keystone	50	75	100
Adirondack Sidewheeler, cast iron, 13" long	500	750	1000
Adirondack, cast iron, Dent, 15" long	1000	1700	2300
Admiral Dewey Flagship, paper litho on wood, c. 1900, 30" long	300	450	600
Admiral Dewey's Flagship from the White Fleet, wood and paper, 6" long	100	150	200
Admiral gunboat, gun shoots, Bliss, 20"	260	390	520
Aeroplane Carrier, Barclay 372	25	38	50

Action Submarine, Keystone, $100

	C6	C8	C10
Aircraft Carrier "65," tin litho, large, c. 1950s	50	75	100
Aircraft Carrier "Mighty Matilda" plastic, complete w/all accessories, Remco, 35" long	83	125	165
Aircraft Carrier, Eldon, 22" long	55	83	110
Aircraft Carrier, friction, Cragstan, 8-1/2" long	60	90	120
Aircraft Carrier, plastic, Saunders, 12" long	32	48	65
Aircraft Carrier, plastic, Thomas Toys, 5-1/2" long	12	18	25
Aircraft Carrier, steel, w/ three jet planes that fire rockets, shell or drop bombs, Argo, 6" planes, 36" long	68	102	135
Aircraft Carrier, wooden, Keystone 12" long	50	75	100
Aircraft Carrier, Wyandotte	55	82	110
Amazon Sidewheeler, plastic and metal, Atwood Motors, California c. 1950s	125	188	250
Atomic Submarine, Hasbro	32	48	65
Barracuda Submarine, twenty-three man crew, Remco	75	112	150

49 LST, Buddy L, $100

Aircraft Carrier, Keystone, $100

	C6	C8	C10
Battle Fleet, Tillicum No. 115, Milton Bradley, c. late 1920s	31	46	62
Battleship "Admiral," paper litho, 1890, 20" long	600	900	1200
Battleship "Fighting Lady," Remco No. 710, 31" long	115	172	230
Battleship "Indiana," litho on wood, c. 1900, Converse, 32" long	650	1100	1600
Battleship "New York," c. 1900, Dent, largest cast-iron boat made at 21"	2000	3200	4350
Battleship "New York," cast iron, c. 1920s, 20"	375	565	750
Battleship "Oregon," tin litho and wood, Converse, c. 1900	500	750	1000
Battleship "Philadelphia," paper litho on wood, Reed, 30" long	440	660	880
Battleship "Rover," paper litho and wood, 20" long	600	900	1200
Battleship, pressed steel, Hillclimber, 15" long	200	300	400
Battleship Missouri, all wood and metal, radio control, w/ three electric motors, Sterling "56" scale model	350	525	700

Battle Fleet, Tillicum, $62

Battleship, Hillclimber, $400

Destroyer, Ideal, $35

	C6	C8	C10
Battleship New York, paper litho and stained wood, 1890, Bliss, 36" x 22" 450	450	675	900
Battleship Oregon, paper litho and wood, 25" long 700	700	1050	1400
Battleship, Auburn Rubber, No. 1582, c. 1940,8-1/4" long 22	22	33	45
Battleship, Barclay 373 27	27	41	55
Battleship, cast iron, 14-1/2" long 400	400	600	800
Battleship, cast iron, Wilkins 800	800	1400	2000
Battleship, clockwork, Markli, 28" long .. 2500	2500	4500	9000
Battleship, Fleischmann 2000	2000	3000	4000
Battleship, friction, c. 1920, Dayton, 16" long.. 200	200	300	400
Battleship, friction, painted pressed steel, Ohio, 16" long 140	140	210	280
Battleship, glass, candy container, approx. 3" long...................................... 60	60	90	120
Battleship, Keystone, early 1940s, under 2' length 64	64	96	128
Battleship, litho and wood, Bliss, 36" 1800	1800	3000	4300
Battleship, plastic, Banner, 4" long 15	15	22	30
Battleship, plastic, Thomas Toys, 5-1/2" long 12	12	18	25
Battleship, tin clockwork, Bing, 16" 800	800	1300	1800
Battleship, tin friction, c. 1920s, 9-1/2" long.. 200	200	300	400
Battleship, unpowered, c. 1927, Schiebel.. 1000	1000	1500	2000

Battleship, Bliss, $4,300

	C6	C8	C10
Battleship, wood stacks and large wood guns and turrets, friction motor, Schiebel, c. 1920 1250	1250	1875	2500
Battleship, wooden, airplanes take off from a spring on deck of ship, Keystone, 2' long w/guns 130	130	195	260
B-LO Submarine, metal, pat. no. 1318048 75	75	113	150
Boat, cast iron, Freidag, c. 1920s 225	225	338	450
Boat, Hot Air, tin with driver, 9" long 100	100	150	200
Boat, Kingsbury, 10" long 100	100	150	200
Boat, pull motor, metal 100	100	150	200
Boat, tin friction, lithographed 100	100	150	200
Boat, tin friction, painted, early 100	100	150	200
Boat, tin friction, painted, early 150	150	225	300
Boat, tin friction, two smokestacks, four lifeboats, 13" long 90	90	135	180
Boat, wood and brass, wind-up motor concealed withinthe rudder, controlled from the wheel in the circular cockpit w/a start-stop lever, marked "C.C. JR," 14-1/2" long.. 90	90	135	180
Bremen, tin keywind, c. 1920, Falk, 18" long 1300	1300	2100	3000
Canoe, wood, 6" long.................................... 15	15	22	30
Cargo Ship, Renwal No. 139, 4" long 4	4	6	8
Carrier, Mighty Magee Carrier, Remco 80	80	120	160
Clipper Ship, c. 1887, wood and paper litho, Reed, 36" long.............................. 550	550	800	1200
Columbia side paddlewheeler, paper litho on wood, c. 1890, Bradley, 24" long..... 400	400	600	800
Conqueror, paper litho on wood, Bliss, 20" long 900	900	1400	2000
Convoy Set, c. 1940s, two destroyers, three freight boats, three ocean liners, two patrol boats, painted wood, Tillicum, Milton Bradley, destroyers 5-1/2" long, others about 4-1/2" long.. 350	350	525	700
Cruiser, Wannatoys 25	25	38	50
Destroyer, cast iron w/wheels, 12" long .. 1000	1000	1500	2000
Destroyer, plastic, Ideal, 15" long 17	17	28	35

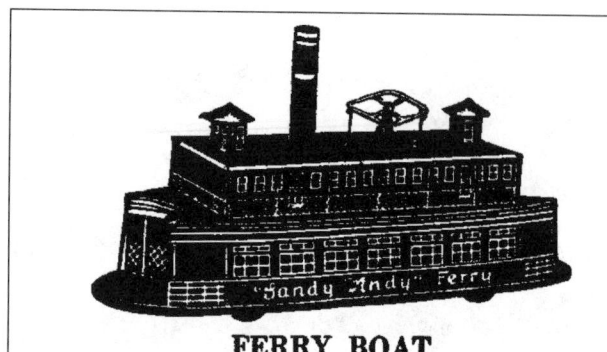

FERRY BOAT

No. 170—Boat travels rapidly along floor until either end strikes any solid object, then reverses automatically and travels in opposite direction. Has long running clockwork 13½ inches long ..**$3.50**

Ferry "Sandy Andy Ferry," Wolverine, $150

	C6	C8	C10
Destroyer, tin clockwork, Bing, 22-1/2" long	1500	2400	3500
Diving Submarine, Wolverine, 13" long	105	158	210
Drawbridge Set, w/bridge, twelve cars and boats, Renwal	50	75	100
Dreadnaught, Auburn Rubber, 1941, extremely rare, 9-1/8" long	30	50	70
Ferry "Ferry Go" w/twin paddlewheels, pull toy, tin litho, 14" long	125	185	250
Ferry "Sandy Andy Ferry," tin litho, Wolverine, 13-1/2" long	75	113	150
Ferry and Cars, plastic, Pyro, 7" long	25	38	50
Ferry No. 140, Renwal, 4" long	4	6	8
Ferry w/sailboat, nine cars, plastic, Thomas Toys No. 481	12	18	25
Ferry, clockwork, Bing, 16" long	800	1300	1800
Ferry, Sandy Andy "Ferrygo," tin and wood, Wolverine, 11" long	150	225	300
Ferry, wooden, w/two cars and trucks, c. 1930s, Keystone, 14" long	40	60	80
Fighting Fire Boat, 1950s, Knickerbocker 13" long	40	60	80
Fireboat, Pumping w/ siren, plastic, 1955, Ideal	60	90	120
Fishing Boat, wooden, c. 1940s, Keystone, 12" long	37	56	75
Freighter, Auburn Rubber, 1941, 9-1/4" long	22	33	45
Freighter, Eldon, 20" long	40	60	80
Freighter, plastic, Thomas Toys, 5-1/2" long	12	18	25
Freighter, Wannatoys	25	38	50
French Warships, includes Richelieu, Algiers, Fantasque and others, Authenticast, each	17	26	35

	C6	C8	C10
Frieghter Ocean Wave, paper litho on wood, w/cargo, Reed, c. 1883, 35" long	650	1100	1500
Gee Whiz speedboat, painted sheet metal, heavy clockwork motor, bronze propeller, Boucher, 25" long	550	825	1000
German Warships, scale models including Narvik, Galster and others, Authenticast, each	22	33	44
Gunboat "Kearsage," cast iron, 13-3/4" long	700	1150	1700
Gunboat, friction, 19" long	400	600	800
Gunboat, hand-painted tin, Bing, 29" long	1800	3000	5500
Gunboat, tin friction, rocks back and forth on wheels, 10" long	250	375	500
Gunboat, two guns, two small stacks, two stories above deck, wheeled, friction, 1920s or earlier	300	450	600
Harbor Set, Tillicum, Milton Bradley	20	30	40
Hill Climber, pressed steel battleship, 18" long	300	450	600
Houseboat, Ideal, 5" long	12	18	25
Japanese Warships, incl. Fuso, Kaga, Mogani and others, Authenticast, each	17	26	35

Ferry, with sailboat and nine cars, Thomas Toys, $25

Liner, "Columbus," Marklin, $16,500

	C6	C8	C10
L.C.T. Landing Craft, Eldon, 10" long	17	26	35
Launch, steam-driven, Weeden, 18" long	350	525	700
Life Boat, steel, simple design, c. late 1930s, 11" long x 5-1/4" wide	20	30	40
Liner "Columbus," tin, electrified, Marklin, 42" long	4000	8000	16,500
Luxury liner, "Caribbean," friction, sparkling, Marx, 15" long, 3-1/2" tall	42	63	85
Marguerite Sailing Schooner, Bliss, 22" long	350	525	700
Merchant Marine Ship, tin keywind, Ives, 13" long	450	675	900
Motorboat "Sea Wolf," Fleetline, 16" long	112	168	225
Motorboat, "Sea Horse," cast-iron, Hubley	1750	2625	3500
Motorboat, Slo Motion VI, wind-up motorboat, Ideal, 13" long	60	90	120
Motorboat, wind-up, Irwin	25	38	50
National Defense Set, Tillicum, Milton Bradley	40	60	80
Naval Base Play set, Cohn, No. 888	180	270	360

Racing Boat, "Baby," $120

	C6	C8	C10
Navy Gun Boat cast iron, Big Bang, No. 9B, 8-1/4" long	125	200	250
Navy Ship "Tirpitz," Comet, 19" long	75	112	150
Ocean Liner, "New York," Ives, 13" long	500	800	1100
Ocean Liner, Fleischmann, 15-1/2" long	1000	1600	2250
Ocean Liner, Fleischmann, 7-1/2 long	80	120	160
Ocean Liner, painted tin clockwork, 1930, Fleischmann, 20-1/2" long	700	1350	1800
Ocean Liner, Renwal	30	45	60
Ocean Liner, tin keywind, c. 1925, Bing, 13-1/2" long	400	650	900
Ocean Liner, tin keywind, c. 1930, Arnold, 11-1/2" long	400	650	900
Ocean Liner, Wolverine	125	188	250
Oil Tanker, "Esso," Fleischmann, 20" long	600	1000	1350
Panama Canal, Renwal No. 273, c. 1957, 29" x 11"	108	162	215
Passenger liner "St. Lous," paper litho on wood, Reed? 31" long	800	1300	1800
Patrol Boat w/radar mast and accessories, Multiple Products	27	41	55

Panama Canal, Renwal, $215

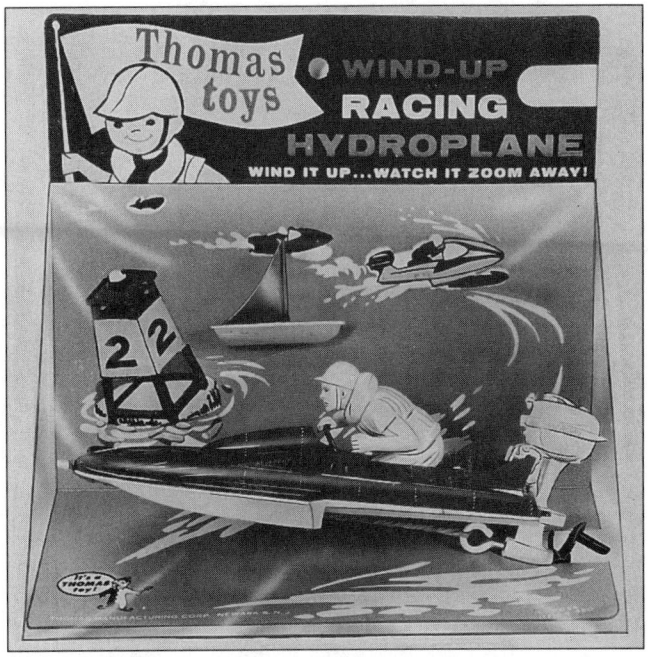

Racing Hydroplane, Thomas Toys, $25

	C6	C8	C10
Phantom Raider, Ideal	60	90	120
Pike steam launch, Buckman	2500	3800	5500
Pirate Ship, plastic w/pirates, Multiple Products	60	90	125
Pirate Ship, plastic, w/six pirates, Ideal, 1953	75	112	150
Pocket Battleship, tin litho, wheeled, Wyandotte, 7" long	70	105	140
Police boat, Harbor Police, Ideal	30	45	60
PT Boat, Ideal	50	75	100
PT107	30	45	60
Pull For The Shore, litho paper on wood, W.S. Reed	3500	8000	12,000
Pull Toy Boat, wood with some metal parts, oarsmen row in unison, Hustilar Toy Corp.	75	112	150
Putt Putt Boat, Mosquito Fleet, Marx	55	83	110
Queen Mary, plastic, Thomas Toys, 5-1/2" long	15	22	30
Racing Boat, "Baby," cast-iron, wheeled, Hubley?, c. 1930, 4-1/2" long	60	90	120
Racing Hydroplane, plastic, Thomas Toys No. 480	12	18	25
Racing Sailboat, wood, Keystone	30	45	60
Radar Rocket Ship, Keystone	75	112	150
Riverboat "Atlantic," sidewheel, painted and stenciled tin, George Brown, 14" long	2250	3375	4500
Riverboat "City of New York," Wilkins, 15" long	800	1400	2035
Riverboat "Jumbo" w/sidewheel, painted tin, mechanical walking beam, Fallows, 1880, 14" long	1000	1500	2000

	C6	C8	C10
Riverboat "Ocean Queen" Riverboat, litho on wood, Reed, 23" long	750	1300	1800
Riverboat "Pacific," Althof-Bergmann, 14" long, auctioned in 1995	3,850		
Riverboat "Pilgrim," paper litho, Reed, 28-1/2" long	1000	1500	2000
Riverboat "Puritan," Wilkins, 10-1/2" long	600	1000	1400
Riverboat, "Priscilla," Marklin, 30" long, auctioned in 1995			17,600
Riverboat, cast iron, c. 1910, Wilkins, 7-1/2" long	250	375	500
Riverboat, cast iron, Wilkins, 10-1/2" long	450	675	900
Riverboat, paper and tin litho and wood, working walking beam, "Columbia," c. 1890, 2' long	700	1100	1650
Riverboat, Wilkins, 5-3/4" long	135	205	270
Roman Warship "Big Caesar," w/figures, Remco, 29" long	175	265	350
Roman Warship, Gallant Gladiator, Remco, 17" long	60	90	120
Rover Torpedo Boat, paper litho on wood, Bliss, c. 1896, 20" long	850	1375	1900
Rowboat, cast iron, w/four men and oars, mechanical, 9" long	1250	1875	2500
Rowboat, tin, rubber band driver w/man rowing, 9" long	40	60	80
Rowers, cast iron big-wheeled boat, four-man crew and coxswain, Wilkins, c. 1890, 10" long	1250	1875	2500
Rowers, eight-man crew and coxswain, cast iron, large wheels, U.S. Hardware, c. 1890, 14-1/2" long	1800	3000	4200
Rowers, four-man crew and coxswain, cast iron, large wheels, U.S. Hardware, c. 1890	2000	3500	5200
S.S. America, moves on metal wheels, 1930s, Wyandotte, 7" long	50	75	100

Riverboat, "Priscilla," Marklin, auctioned in 1995 for $17,600

Scull, Varsity racing, Ideal, $4,000

IF3114—
"Show Boat,"
11¼ x 3¼ x 3⅞,
white enameled
body, red deck,
green hull, red
letters, gilt trim,
iron wheels,
balloon shape
tires, cord, an-
chor, bell rings
when boat is
pulled.

⅓ doz. in box.....................Doz $13.50

Showboat, Arcade, $1,050

	C6	C8	C10
Sailboat, Hercules "Peggy Jane," Chein, 23" long	252	375	505
Sailboat, wheeled, Chein	112	168	225
Scull, nin-man crew, wheeled, U.S. Hardware, 14" long	1600	2400	3200
Scull, Varsity Racing, cast iron, eight rowers w/moving oars, coxswain, Ideal, c. 1890,14" long	2000	3000	4000
Sea Raider, Payton, 34" long	20	30	40
Shore Patrol, battery operated, tin boat, 9" long	10	15	20
Showboat Theater, Remco	75	112	150
Showboat, cast iron, 11" long	1000	1500	2000
Showboat, cast iron, Arcade, 1929, 10-3/4" long	500	750	1050
Sidewheeler "America," painted tin, Althof-Bergmann c. 1874, 20" long	7000	11,000	18,000
Sidewheeler "Constitution" Fallows, 10" long	2000	3000	4000
Sidewheeler "New York," cast iron, 15" long	500	750	1000
Sidewheeler "New York," tin and cast iron, w/five lead figures, Marklin, 19-1/2" long, auctioned in 1994			47,000
Sidewheeler "New Orleans," cast iron, 11" long	600	950	1400

	C6	C8	C10
Sidewheeler "Priscilla," cast iron, Dent or Wilkins, approx. 10" long	500	750	1000
Sidewheeler "Priscilla," paper litho on wood, 37" long	2000	3500	5800
Sidewheeler "Puritan," cast iron, 10-1/2" long	480	720	960
Sidewheeler "River Queen," litho on wood, Reed, c. 1895, 25" long	440	660	880
Sidewheeler Boat "The Star," tin, height w/stand, 21", length 14-1/2"	3500	5200	7000
Sidewheeler, cast iron, 10-1/2" long	150	225	300
Sidewheeler, cast iron, 8" long	188	275	375
Sidewheeler, cast iron, approx. 5-1/2" long	100	150	200
Sidewheeler, marked "Betsy," Buffalo Toys, 26" long	350	525	700
Sidewheeler, tin clockwork, 11" long	90	135	180
Sidewheeler, tin, Bramwell-Smith, pat. 1872	2000	3500	5000
Sinking Battleship, rubber band torpedo strikes die on ship and sinks it, Walbert Mfg.	250	375	500
Speed Boat, A.C. Williams, cast iron w/rider, 4-3/4" long	120	180	240
Speed Boat, A.C. Williams, cast iron, 4" long	45	68	90
Speed Boat, A.C. Williams, cast iron, 5-1/4" long	60	90	120
Speed boat, Blue Speed Boat, cast iron, A.C. Williams, 4-3/4" long	120	180	240
Speedboat, "Miss Liberty," steam-powered, Ives, 13-1/2" long	750	1125	1500
Speedboat, "Baby," cast iron, Hubley	60	90	120
Speedboat, "Johnson's Sea Horse," cast iron, w/figure, 10-1/2" long	1750	2625	3500
Speedboat, "Peggy Jane" Speedboat, Chein, 14-1/2" long	115	175	235
Speedboat, "Vim," Ives, 10-1/2" long	650	975	1300

Sidewheeler, "New York," Marklin, $300

Sidewheeler, "River Queen," Reed, $880

Steamboat, Buckman, $3,000

Torpedo Boat, Bing, $6,500

	C6	C8	C10
Speedboat, "Vixen," Ives, 12" long	650	975	1300
Speedboat, cast iron, Kenton	90	135	180
Speedboat, Renwal No. 141, 4" long	4	6	8
Speedboat, wind-up Lionel Craft, No. 43	290	435	580
Speedboat, wind-up, Lionel Craft, No. 44	750	1100	1700
Speedboat, wood, rubber band propelled	40	60	80
SS United States, tin friction, 6-1/2" long	50	75	100
St. Louis, litho on wood liner, c. 1895, Bliss, 34-1/2" long	800	1300	1800
Steamboat "Dewey," Weeden, c. 1900, 15-1/2" long	500	750	1000
Steamboat Buckman No. 55, c. 1870, 19" long	1500	2500	3500
Steamboat, Buckman, c. 1872, 11" long	1300	2000	3000
Steamboat, live steam, Weeden, 15" long	300	450	600
Steamboat, tin, self-propelled, 17" long	150	225	300
Steamboat, twin sidewheeler, steam engine, marked "Patented May 7, 1872," Buckman, 11" long	2000	3500	5000
Steamer, litho paper on wood, 39" long, 22-1/2" high	450	675	900
Steamship, alcohol burner, c. 1885, 19" long	200	300	400
Submarine and Dreadnought Naval War Toy, torpedo explodes ship, Schoenhut, Pat. 4/6/15	70	105	140
Submarine, Auburn Rubber, c. 1941, 6-1/2" long	20	30	40
Submarine, dives, c. 1910, tin keywind, Ives, 10" long	400	600	800
Submarine, fires torpedo, Thomas Toys, 11-1/2" long,	12	18	25
Submarine, lead alloy, Manoil No. 79	15	22	30
Submarine, plastic, w/torpedoes, Ideal, 1950s	20	30	40
Submarine, steel, 6" long	40	60	80
Submarine, tin litho, remote control, Automatic	40	60	80
Submarine, tin litho, remote controlled, "575," c. 1960	40	60	80
Submarine, tin, clockwork, Marklin, 9-1/2" long	288	430	575
Swamp Buggy, motorized, plastic, Thomas Toys No. 487	12	18	25
Tanker, Texaco	80	120	160
Torpedo Boat, Bing, 27-1/2" long	2000	3500	6500
Torpedo Boat, Sparking, plastic, wind-up, Ideal, 12" long	50	75	100
Treasure Hunter, plastic, Ideal	75	112	150
Tugboat, 1929-30, Buddy L, No. 3000, 28" long	5000	8500	13,500
Tugboat, plastic, Auburn Rubber	37	56	75
Tugboat, Renwal No. 142, 4" long	4	6	8
Tugboat, Thomas Toys, 8-1/4" long	15	22	30
Tugboat, wood, c. WWII?, Cass, 15" long	37	56	75
Turbo Boat, pressed tin, 10-1/2" long	40	60	80
U.S. Coast Guard Patrol Boat, w/figures, Eldon, 22",	37	56	75
U.S. Merchant Marine Boat, painted pressed tin clockwork, Ives, 10-1/2" long	250	375	500
U.S. Naval Base, Superior	60	90	120
U.S. scale model warships, WWII including Iowa, Enterprise, Sims and Farragut and submarine Sarge, Authenticast, each	17	26	35
U.S. Submarine, painted wood, fires torpedo for target set, 13" long	20	30	40

Yacht, Chris-Craft, Kilgore, $6,000

Viking Ship, Renwal, $110

	C6	C8	C10
U.S. Wasp, carrier, wood storage under deck for planes, 27" long	50	75	100
U.S.S. Enterprise, Wyandotte	80	120	160
U.S.S. Maine paper litho on wood, Reed?	600	900	1200
U.S.S. Narwahl, submarine, lead, mfg. unknown, 1930s, 7-1/2" long	20	30	40

	C6	C8	C10
U.S.S. New Mexico, battleship, lead, manufacturer unknown, 1930s	20	30	40
Union ferry, sidewheel, c. 1900, Bliss?, 24" long	225	375	450
Vesuvius gunboat, paper litho on wood, Bliss, 25-1/2" long	1200	2000	2800
Viking Ship, Renwal No. 245, 1955, 17" long	55	83	110
Volunteer IXL, Fallows, 16" long	1800	2700	3600
Warship "Oregon," tin	400	600	800
Warship, clockwork, Bing, c. 1915, 19" long	500	800	1100
Weekend Cruise Set, w/boat trailer Thomas Toys No. 339, 4-1/4" car, 4-1/2" boat	22	33	45
Yacht, Chris-Craft Commuter Yacht, cast iron, Kilgore, c. 1930, 11" long	2000	3500	6000
Yacht, steam, "Priscilla," tin, Marklin 20-1/2" long	2000	3500	6000
Yacht, wood, c. WWII?, Cass, 15" long	37	56	75
Yacht-type ship, spring wind motor, either Ives or Bing, 28" long	2000	3000	4000

SOLDIERS

The price of a toy soldier depends not only on its desirability, but on its condition. Mint condition means the item is in the condition in which it was originally issued—perfect, regardless of age, not the slightest blemish. Needless to say this is a fairly rare state of affairs, but enough soldiers exist in Mint condition to make it an employable term. Many people, hoping to dispose of toys, are tempted to term them Mint when they are really Near Mint, Very Good, or sometimes even just Good. Inevitably this can result in unhappiness all around and, not infrequently, in a canceled sale.

Very Good condition indicates a soldier that has obviously seen use. It has signs of wear and aging, but most of its paint remains and, in general, it has a freshness to its appearance that makes it seem attractive and collectible to all but the most discriminating.

Good condition signals a soldier that has seen considerable wear, but has at least one-half to one-third of its original paint, and is basically sound. Collectors will collect it, but they will often not be wholly satisfied with it as an example of their collection, and thus the price is well below that of the same item in Mint condition.

A condition below Good results in another drastic drop in price. Figures with missing parts, although otherwise in Excellent condition, will usually fall into this lower-priced category. At present, a Barclay soldier minus its tin helmet (signaled by a large round hole in the top of its head) is worth about half of what it would otherwise bring. On the cast-iron soldiers, even small spots of rust can seriously lower their price, as can repainting of any of the soldiers. Near Mint, Fine, Very Fine and similar terms denote conditions between Mint and Very Good, and are priced accordingly.

The key to grading is to avoid wishful thinking. Grading can sometimes be a problem for the uninitiated, but common sense will usually prevail, and when possible, a consultation with an expert in the field can often clear up lingering doubts. A toy in its original box is worth up to ten to twenty percent more if the box is in Mint condition, with the price dropping as condition lessens.

AMERICAN METAL TOYS

Until recently, these 3-1/4-inch dime-store soldiers were attributed to Chicago toy soldier maker J. Edward Jones. Though Jones did make many other figures, research has established that the following were produced by American Metal Toys, Inc. of Chicago. The president of the firm was Royce Reyff (1898-1986) and his equal partner was C. Raymond Pierson. Although the company was formally incorporated on October 24, 1939, they began in 1937 and went out of business in April 1942, when its supply of metal was cut off by the demands of World War II. The sculpting and diemaking were done by Henry Kasselowski.

	C6	C8	C10
Ammunition Carrier	200	300	400
Bugler	78	117	155
Charging, port arms	125	188	250
Cook w/chef's hat, frying pan	75	112	150
Cowboy kneeling	30	45	60
Cowboy on rearing horse, firing backward	130	195	260
Cowboy shooting (on foot)	15	22	30
Doctor w/bag	40	60	80
Farmer	6	9	13
Farmer's Wife	7	10	14
Firing machine gun on stump	40	60	80

	C6	C8	C10
Firing machine gun on stump, No. 1 on pocket	100	150	200
Flagbearer	120	180	240
German, charging w/rifle	107	160	215
German, kneeling w/rifle	95	142	190
German, kneeling w/short rifle	110	165	220
German, prone machine gunner	71	106	143
Grenade thrower, no weapons	67	100	135
Indian kneeling, shooting	27	42	55
Indian on rearing horse	50	75	100
Kneeling w/AA Gun	45	68	91
Kneeling w/searchlight	62	93	125
Kneeling w/searchlight, "27," "Made in USA" on sides of stanchion	55	82	110
Kneeling, firing anti-tank gun w/barrel brace, "23" on wheel	50	75	100
Kneeling, firing anti-tank gun	52	78	105
Kneeling, firing rifle, no stand	60	90	120
Kneeling, firing shorter rifle, no stand	75	112	150
Knight w/pennant, flat underbase	64	95	128
Marching w/rifle	57	85	115
Motorcyclist w/machine gun mounted on motorcycle	70	105	140
Nurse w/bag	45	68	90

	C6	C8	C10
Observer w/binoculars and rifle	41	61	82
Officer in greatcoat, pointing, holding pistol	110	165	220
Prone w/rifle, trunk upraised	70	105	140
Prone, body arched, firing machine gun	60	90	120
Prone, firing double-barreled machine gun	78	117	155
Seated w/phone	55	83	110
Seated w/rifle	40	60	80
Soldier w/gas mask, plunging rifle down, slightly smaller in size	107	160	215
Soldier w/rifle, gassed or shot in neck	170	255	340
Standing, firing rifle	49	73	98
Stretcher-bearer	50	75	100
Tramp	7	11	15
Wire-cutter, prone	225	338	450
Wounded supine	42	63	85

AUBURN RUBBER

Auburn (also Aub-Rub'r) was founded in 1913 in Auburn, Indiana, as the Double Fabric Tire Corporation to make auto tubes and tires for Model T Fords. They produced five soldiers in 1935—their first toys. The prototype was a Palace Guard that Auburn president and chief stockholder A.L. Murray obtained in England. The model was taken to a local pattern maker where original molds were made from lead. Sample toys were made and taken to an artist and decorated per Murray's instructions. They immediately caught on when presented to buyers.

The soldiers were molded in twenty-four-inch rubber presses, each containing forty to sixty soldiers. Once trimmed, the soldiers were dipped in a base lacquer and sent down a decorating conveyor where as many as twenty-four women, using small camel-hair brushes, added the finishing touches—painting the faces, shoes, belts, buttons, medals, and finally eyes. After drying, each toy was individually wrapped in waxed paper and packed three dozen to a chipboard carton and twelve dozen to a corrugated carton for shipment. Design of the soldiers was credited to freelance artist Edward McCandlish.

	C6	C8	C10
200 U.S. Infantry Private	7	11	14
202 Bugler, U.S. Infantry	9	14	19
204 U.S. Infantry Officer	9	14	18
216 Observer w/Binoculars	8	12	17
238 Charging Soldier, w/tommy gun	8	12	17
230 Machine Gunner	10	15	21
206 Stretcher Bearer	18	27	36
208 Wounded Soldier	19	29	39
224 Red Cross Doctor	17	25	34
234 Bomb Thrower	15	22	30
232 Officer on Horse	17	25	34

	C6	C8	C10
226 Red Cross Nurse, white or khaki uniform	19	29	39
242 Anti-Aircraft Gun	17	25	34
222 Sniper, crawling, rifle over shoulder	25	38	50
264 Center, football player	16	24	32
252 Batter	20	30	41
268 Carrier, football player	17	25	34
260 Lineman, football player	19	28	38
256 Fielder or Baseman	21	31	42
266 Passer, football player	19	28	38
262 Backfieldman, football player	20	30	40
240 Motorcycle Soldiers, w/sidecar	25	38	50
272 Plane Shooter	18	27	36
258 Baserunner	24	36	48
250 Pitcher	26	39	52
296 Trench Mortar	16	24	33
236 Signalman	30	45	60
254 Catcher	27	41	55
214 & 218 Foreign Legion Private	12	18	24
1200 Infantry Private	8	12	17
1202 Infantry Bugler	10	15	20
1238 Charging Soldier	23	35	47
1546 Motorcycle Cop, blue or khaki as soldier	30	45	60
Aircraft Defender	15	22	30
Color Bearer	22	33	44
Cowboy, large, on wheeled horse	42	63	85
Ethiopian w/rifle and shield, in robes, only one known	75	112	150
Ethiopian w/shield and rifle	60	90	120
Firing Soldier	22	33	44
Foreign Legion, also White Guard officer, No. 220	12	18	24
Marching Soldier	12	18	25
Motor Scout	24	36	48
Motorcycle Cop, large, 5" high	25	38	50
Officer, early	10	15	20
Searchlight	20	30	40
Signalman, early smaller size, only three known	100	150	200
Sound Detector	15	22	31
Tank Defender	24	36	48
Tank Soldier, running w/box	19	29	39

BARCLAY

Barclay Mfg. Co. was the largest manufacturer of toy soldiers in the United States prior to World War II, selling millions of figures annually. The company, named after Barclay Street in West Hoboken, New Jersey, began in 1924 or late 1923, and was owned by Leon Donze (1865-1950) and by Michael Levy (c. 1895-1964). Around 1929, Levy took over the company, and he turned it into a major manufacturer. It grew from five employees in 1924 to a pre-war peak of 400 workers and moved several times to increasingly larger quarters.

Barclay's soldiers came in four styles prior to World War II. Soldiers from the first group, probably produced almost from Barclay's beginning, were small with moving arms on the mounted figures. The second group, approximately 3-1/4-inches high, seems to have debuted in 1935. These were designed and sculpted by Barclay employee Frank Krupp and had a separate tin helmet, which was subcontracted. These figures are rather stiff and are known by collectors as "short stride" because the marching figures' feet are close together. The third style, again by Krupp, also had a separate tin helmet, was more realistic and is known as "long stride." These were on sale as early as 1936. In 1937 or 1938, a clip was designed to hold on the tin helmets, as the formerly glued-on helmets frequently came off, drawing complaints from the chain stores, such as Woolworth's, that sold Barclay toys. The fourth style was introduced about 1939-1940 when Barclay moved from slush-casting to die-casting its soldiers. It was by freelance artist Olive Kooken (1904-1964) and is known as "cast helmet," as the soldiers featured helmets that were an integral part of the figure.

Barclay's soldiers were made of antimonial lead, consisting of about thirteen percent antimony and the rest lead. When slush-molding was done, only one mold was made of each figure. The lead would be poured into the mold, rocked, and immediately poured out, providing a hollow figure. Later, the die-cast molds produced a number of the same figure at the same time.

During World War II, Barclay laid off all but four of its employees and did subcontract work. The company was never as successful after the war and finally closed down in 1971. Although Barclay assigned numbers to its figures from the beginning for its own records, many of the soldiers themselves bore no numbers. Figures listed with a question mark after the number are based on the memory of longtime Barclay employee George Fall, whose memory, judged against known Barclay numbers, is accurate, but not infallible.

Pre-1934

	C6	C8	C10
87 Officer on Horse, smaller size, c. 1931	125	188	250
87? Mounted Officer, moving arm holding pistol, on cantering horse	32	48	65
87? Mounted Officer, moving arm holding sword, on rearing horse	26	39	52
87? Mounted Officer, moving arm holding bugle, on rearing horse	27	41	55
186? Cavalryman mounted, 2-3/4" high, no moving parts, modeled on French toy soldier, c. late 1920s-early 1930s	12	18	25
90? Mounted Cowboy w/moving arm, holding rifle	35	53	70

	C6	C8	C10
89? Mounted Indian, moving arm holding rifle or pistol	40	60	80
90? Mounted Cowboy w/pistol	40	60	80
200 Jockey on Horse	17	25	35
486 Cavalryman, approx. 2-1/4" high, c. early 1930s, no moving parts	10	15	21
Baseball batter, c. 1920s	42	63	85
Baseball fielder, approx. 1-7/8" high, c. 1920s	42	63	85
Baseball pitcher, c. 1920s	42	63	85
Mounted Indian on rearing horse	18	27	36

1934 and After

	C6	C8	C10
45 Machine Gunner and Driver	28	42	56
87 Officer on Horse, in cap, khaki or grey, larger black, grey or brown horse	15	22	30
87? Mounted in colored jacket and cap, may be Chinese or Japanese	24	36	48
87? Mounted, in grey cap, intermediate size	35	52	70
89 Indian on Horse	14	21	28
89 Indian on Horse	23	35	46
89 Indian on Horse, Indian's head turned to right	22	33	44
89 Indian on Horse, two feathers	26	39	52
90 Cowboy on Horse	15	22	30
90 Cowboy on Horse	22	33	45
90 Cowboy on Horse, variation, no bullets in gunbelt	50	75	100
90 Cowboy on Horse, variation, thinner bullets in gunbelt, saddle not as long	12	18	24
100 Masked Rider on Horse	350	525	700
100? Masked Rider w/Lasso, horse's tail up	18	27	36
100? Masked Rider w/Lasso, horse's tail down	25	38	50
310 Army Motorcyclist	18	27	36
310 Army Motorcyclist, post-war, dot eyes or none at all, larger, motor variation	25	38	50
310 Cop on Motorcycle	25	38	50
310 Cop on Motorcycle, head lower	20	30	40
310 Cop on Motorcycle, post-war, dot eyes or none at all, larger, motor variation	22	33	45
310 Motorcyclist, head higher	25	38	50
310 Motorcyclist, larger, markings on cycle, like B93A and B93B but cruder	25	38	50
374 Army Motorcycle, w/sidecar	32	48	65
495 Man on Skis	12	18	24
496 Girl on Skis	12	18	24
497 Man on Sled	9	13	19
498 Girl on Sled	9	13	18
499 Santa Claus on Sled	20	30	40
500 Santa Claus on Skis	26	39	52

	C6	C8	C10
500 Santa Claus on Skis, no skis or poles and no holes for them	27	41	55
510 One Horse Open Sleigh, includes sleigh, horse, seated man and woman	44	66	88
530 Man Pulling Children on Sled	23	35	47
535 Young Man Putting Skates on Girl Sitting on Bench	50	75	100
610 Woman Passenger, w/dog	8	12	16
611 Man Passenger, overcoat over arm	7	11	15
612 Conductor	8	12	16
613 Porter, w/whisk broom	8	12	16
614 Man in Red Cap, w/bags	9	14	19
615 Engineer	8	12	16
616 Boy	7	11	14
617 Girl	7	11	14
618 Elderly Woman	7	11	14
619 Old Man	8	12	16
620 Minister walking	27	41	55
621 Minister holding hat	9	14	18
621 Newsboy	7	11	15
622 Shoeshine boy	15	22	30
623 Detective w/pistol	65	98	130
624 Burglar	60	90	120
625 Bride	8	12	17
626 Groom	10	15	20
627 Girl in Rocker	10	15	20
628 Boy Skater	6	9	12
629 Girl Skater	6	9	12
630-1/2 Man and Woman on Park Bench	15	22	30
635 Man Speed Skater	8	12	16
636 Girl Figure Skater	7	11	15
701 Flagbearer, cast helmet	11	16	22
701 Flagbearer, tin helmet, long stride	11	16	22
701 Flagbearer, tin helmet, short stride	13	19	26
701 Machine-Gunner, kneeling, short stride	8	12	16
702 Machine-Gunner, kneeling, cast helmet	11	16	23
702 Machine-Gunner, kneeling, long stride	10	15	21
703 Sniper, kneeling, firing, long stride, tin helmet	11	16	23
703 Sniper, kneeling, firing, short stride	10	15	21
703 Sniper, kneeling, firing, short stride, shorter rifle, fat portion of gun and thin portion of barrel about equal length	10	15	20
704 Soldier on Parade, shoulder arms, long stride, tin helmet	9	14	19
704 Soldier on Parade, shoulder arms, short stride	9	14	19
705 Soldier at Attention (actually port arms)	11	16	22

	C6	C8	C10
705 Soldier at Attention (actually port arms), cast helmet	11	16	22
706 Soldier, charging, cast helmet	14	21	28
706 Soldier, charging, short stride w/shorter rifle, sling around hand, two known	425	638	850
706 Soldier, charging, short stride	11	16	23
706 Soldier, charging, tin helmet, long stride	55	82	110
706 Tall, tin helmet, solid puttees	300	450	600
707 At Attention, cast helmet	11	16	22
707 Sharpshooter, standing, firing, short stride	10	15	21
708 Marine Officer w/sword, cast helmet	35	52	70
708 Officer w/sword, cast helmet	30	45	60
708 Officer w/sword, short stride	12	18	24
708 Officer w/sword, tin helmet, long stride, no chest strap	60	90	120
708 Officer, w/sword, tin helmet, long stride	9	13	18
709 Bugler, long stride, tin helmet	10	15	21
709 Bugler, short stride	12	18	24
710 Drummer, long stride, tin helmet	13	19	26
710 Drummer, short stride	12	18	24
711 Drum Major, long stride, tin helmet	11	16	23
711 Drum Major, short stride	12	18	25
712 Knight, w/shield	7	11	15
713 Knight, w/pennant	9	14	19
714 Pirate	7	11	14
715 Cowboy, w/tin hat brim	10	15	20
716 Indian Chief	7	11	15
717 Indian Brave, rifle across waist	8	12	16
718 West Point Cadet, long stride	8	12	16
718 West Point Cadet, w/rifle, short stride	10	15	20
719 Sailor in White Uniform, in puttees	8	12	16
719 Sailor White Uniform, long stride, bell bottoms	9	13	19
719 Sailor White Uniform, marching, short stride	8	12	17
720 Sailor Blue Uniform, in puttees	10	15	20
720 Sailor Blue Uniform, marching, short stride	10	15	21
720 Sailor in Blue Uniform, long stride, bell bottoms	11	16	23
721 Naval Officer in blue, short stride, tin top to cap	50	75	100
721 Naval Officer, long stride	11	16	23
721 Naval Officer, short stride	12	18	24
721 Naval Officer, short stride, tin top to cap	45	68	90
722 Marine, long stride	12	18	25
722 Marine, long stride, white cap (probably post-war)	22	33	45

	C6	C8	C10
722 Marine, short stride................ 10	15	20
722 Marine, short stride, tin top to cap 50	75	100
723 Marine Officer w/sword, short stride... 16	24	32
723 Marine Officer w/sword, tin helmet, long stride, no chest strap, in blue 60	90	120
723 Marine Officer, w/sword, tin helmet, long stride.............. 19	28	38
724 Ethiopian Soldier, c. 1935-36 100	150	205
725 Ethiopian Officer, c. 1935-36 125	188	250
726 Italian Soldier, c. 1935-36 100	150	200
727 Italian Officer, c. 1935-36................ 75	112	150
728 Machine Gunner Lying Flat 9	14	19
728 Machine Gunner Lying Flat, cast helmet............. 10	15	20
728 Machine Gunner Lying Flat, cast helmet, lip of base extends under gun barrel........... 11	16	22
729 Soldier w/Binoculars, long binoculars............ 13	19	26
729 Soldier w/Binoculars, short binoculars............ 45	68	90
730 Soldier Signal Man w/Flag 13	19	26
731 Soldier Pigeon Dispatcher................. 15	22	30
732 Soldier Telephone Operator............. 9	14	19
733 Soldier Bullet Feeder 9	13	18
734 Soldier Ammunition Carrier 11	16	22
735 Soldier Range Finder................. 10	15	21
736 Soldier Sentry 11	16	23
737 Soldier Charging Machine Gunner, cast helmet............ 17	26	35
737 Soldier Charging Machine Gunner, tin helmet............ 9	14	18
738 Soldier Bomb Thrower............ 11	16	23
738 Soldier Bomb Thrower, rifle off ground, cast helmet........... 18	27	36
738 Soldier Bomb Thrower, rifle off ground, tin helmet............ 15	22	31
738 Soldier Bomb Thrower, tall, tin helmet, solid puttees 300	450	600
739 Soldier Fifer 12	18	25
740 Soldier French Horn............ 11	16	23
741 Aviator............ 9	14	19
743 West Point Officer, short stride............ 8	12	17
744 Nurse in blue, hand on hip 50	75	100
744 Nurse, hand on hip............ 10	15	21
745 Navy Doctor, in white, flat underbase 11	16	23
746 Army Doctor, in brown, flat underbase 11	16	23
746 Doctor, as above, inverted base............ 8	12	17
747 Sharpshooter, standing, firing, cast helmet............ 10	15	20

	C6	C8	C10
747 Sharpshooter, standing, firing, long stride 10	15	20
748 Soldier Running, w/rifle, cast helmet... 13	20	27
748 Soldier Running, w/rifle, tin helmet 11	16	22
749 Soldier Gas Mask, charging w/rifle....... 10	15	20
749 Soldier Gas Mask, charging w/rifle cast helmet............ 13	20	27
750 Soldier Crawling............ 11	16	22
751 Soldier Sharpshooter, prone position .. 11	16	22
752 Cowboy w/Lasso............ 9	14	19
752 Cowboy w/Lasso, post-WWII version, lasso goes directly through hands 9	14	18
752 Masked Cowboy w/Lasso............ 8	12	16
753 Cowboy w/Two Guns, pointing one....... 8	12	16
754 Indian Chief, tomahawk and shield 7	11	14
755 Indian w/Bow and Arrow 9	13	18
756 Bayoneting, same as above, no bayonet, cast helmet............ 80	120	160
756 Indian Chief, long headdress, may only have been produced post-WWII ... 40	60	81
756 Sailor Flagbearer, long stride 15	22	30
757 Indian Brave, standing w/bow and arrow, may only have been produced post-WWII............ 15	22	31
757 Sailor w/Signal Flags 13	19	26
757 Sailor w/Signal Flags, flat underbase, minor variations in cap 13	19	27
758 Camera Man, kneeling, tin helmet....... 17	25	34
759 Soldier Stretcher Bearer, closed hand... 10	15	20
759 Soldier Stretcher Bearer, open hand..... 36	54	72
760 Soldier Sitting Position 15	22	31
760 Surgeon, w/stethoscope 11	16	23
761 Lying wounded, tin helmet............ 9	13	18
762 Wounded, sitting, arm in sling............ 12	18	24
763 Raiding, in crouch, in helmet............ 12	18	25
765 Bayoneting, although no bayonet, thrusting w/gun muzzle, tin helmet 28	42	56
766 Clubbing w/rifle, cast helmet............ 47	70	95
766 Clubbing w/rifle, tin helmet 22	33	45
767 Advance, raised rifle, tin helmet............ 13	19	26
767 Nurse, kneeling............ 13	19	26
769 Cook, egg-timer 35	52	70
769 Cook, holding roast............ 16	24	32
770 At Mess, typist alone, apparently meant to sit at mess table 7	11	15
771 Peeling Potatoes............ 15	22	30
774 Soldier w/AA Gun, cast helmet 9	14	19
774 Soldier w/AA Gun, tin helmet............ 10	15	21
775 Wounded on crutches............ 13	20	27
776 Officer Reading Orders 10	15	21
776 Standing at searchlight, high seat, no rivets in front of left foot............ 16	24	32

	C6	C8	C10
776 Standing at searchlight, high seat, two rivets in front of left foot	18	27	37
776 Standing at searchlight, low seat, not connected to searchlight	14	21	29
776 Standing at searchlight, smooth lens, elevation wheel	50	75	100
776 Standing at searchlight, smooth lens, no elevation wheel	55	82	110
776 Standing at searchlight, ridges along base (this and following have ridged lenses)	16	24	32
776 Standing at searchlight, smooth base connected to searchlight, no elevation wheel	16	24	32
777 Marching w/pack, cast helmet	10	15	21
777 Marching w/pack, tin helmet	13	19	26
778 Officer w/gas mask, cast helmet	13	19	26
779 Firing from behind wall, cast helmet	33	50	67
780 Falling w/rifle, cast helmet	19	29	39
781 Digging, cast helmet	26	39	53
782 Leaning out, w/field phone, antenna, cast helmet	33	50	66
783 Crouching w/binoculars, cast helmet	18	27	37
784 Parachutist landing	12	18	25
785 Skier in brown, no skis	26	39	52
785 Skier in white, cast helmet, 1940, w/separate metal skis, meant to be Finn, no left breast pocket	23	35	47
785 Skier in white, no skis	13	19	26
787 Diver w/axe	350	525	700
788 Soldier Marching w/Gun Slung Behind Back, cast helmet	10	15	21
789 Soldier Shooting Triple-Barreled Gun, cast helmet, sitting	12	18	25
790 Soldier Shooting Anti-Tank Gun, cast helmet	12	18	25
791 Soldiers w/Mortar	14	21	29
792 Airplane Mechanic, prop spins, brace on back of engine bulges	24	36	49
793 Soldiers In Boat, cast helmets	32	48	65
801 Boy Scout Hiking	20	30	40
802 Boy Scout Saluting	14	21	28
803 Boy Scout Signaling	17	26	35
804 Boy Scout Cooking	26	39	52
850 Policeman, arm raised	9	14	18
850 Policeman, figure eight base	9	14	19
851 Fireman, w/axe	12	18	25
852 Fireman, w/hose	14	21	28
853 Postman	8	12	16
951 Soldier Wireless Operator	18	27	36
952 Soldier Dispatcher w/Dog	25	38	50
953 American Legionnaire in overseas cap, tall, made for 1937 Legion convention in New York	145	218	290
954? American Legionnaire flagbearer, tall, cloth flag, made in 1937, as above, five known	300	450	600
960 Surgeon and Soldier	46	69	92
961 At Typewriter, w/typewriter and table	38	58	77
Chinese or Mongolian Officer in steel helmet, c. 1937	125	188	250
Chinese or Mongolian Rifleman, c. 1937, pronounced right breast pocket	80	120	160
Fireman, w/axe, flat underbase	13	20	27
Japanese Officer, c. 1937, this is the original Ethiopian officer, painted as a Japanese	82	123	165
Japanese, charging w/rifle, c. 1937	60	90	120
Machine Gunner, seated, cast helmet, bandage-type puttees	17	25	34
Paint Your Own Army Set No. 2003, c. 1934, boxed	120	180	240
Same as above, narrower face, faint right breast pocket	82	123	165
Santa Claus seated, bag of toys at side, made to ride in sleigh	100	150	200
Santa Claus w/holly sprig	35	52	70
Seated man and woman in winter coats	15	22	31
Soldier eating	20	30	40
West Point Cadet, w/rifle, short stride, w/line-and-dot eyes, white pants, white gloves	10	15	20
West Point Cadet, w/rifle, short stride, but painted as wooden soldier, only four known	300	450	600

Post-WWII

	C6	C8	C10
701 Flagbearer, pot helmet	12	18	24
720 Blue Sailor	22	33	45
703? Kneeling, firing rifle	26	39	52
705 Port Arms	12	18	25
707 Order Arms	11	16	23
708 Officer w/Sword	11	16	22
728 Prone Machine Gunner	10	15	20
737 Tommy Gunner	11	16	22
747 Standing Firing Rifle	10	15	21
774 AA Gunner	13	19	26
777 Marching at Slope	10	15	21
788 Marching, rifle slung	10	15	21
789 AA gunner	12	18	25
Cowboy, two pistols, one in air	22	33	45
Drum Major	32	48	64
Drummer	27	41	54
Bugler	27	41	54
Bugler, buttons run down front of uniform	28	42	56

	C6	C8	C10
Clarinetist	28	42	57
Tubist	28	42	56
Sailor, white	20	30	41

Barclay Podfoot Series

Made from c. 1950s to 1971, most podfoot soldiers came in khaki and later green. Add fifty percent to the price for a green example.

	C6	C8	C10
81 Two Soldier Crew at Radar Equipment	15	22	30
82 Three Soldier Crew at Range Finder	17	25	34
83 Two Soldier Crew at Searchlight	14	21	29
84 Two Soldier Crew at Mobile Cannon	13	19	26
85 Two Soldier Crew at AA Gun	13	20	27
187 Officer on Horse, w/pot helmet	42	63	85
188 Cowboy on Horse, w/lasso	14	21	29
189 Indian on Horse	12	18	25
190 Cowboy w/Pistol on Horse	15	22	30
800 Black Knight w/Sword and Shield	12	18	24
801 Knight w/Red and Blue Shield and Sword	14	21	28
802 Knight w/Orange and Black Shield and Sword	8	12	17
803 Knight w/Red and Green Shield and Sword	8	12	17
901 Soldier Flag Bearer	7	11	14
903 Soldier Sniper, in red	45	68	90
903 Soldier Sniper, kneeling	5	8	11
906 Soldier Charging	6	9	13
906 Soldier Charging, in red	52	78	105
908 Soldier Officer	6	9	12
908 Soldier Officer, in blue	32	48	64
908 Soldier Officer, in red	60	90	120
909 Soldier Bugler	7	11	15
909 Soldier Bugler, in red	52	78	105
919 Sailor White Uniform	7	11	15
920 Sailor Blue Uniform	9	13	18
922 Marine	8	12	16
928 Soldier Machine Gunner Lying Flat	7	11	14

	C6	C8	C10
928 Soldier Machine Gunner Lying Flat, in red	45	68	90
929 Soldier w/Pistol Crawling	14	21	28
929 Soldier w/Pistol Crawling, in red	55	82	110
937 Soldier, Charging Machine Gunner, holding tommy gun	7	10	14
937 Soldier, Charging Machine Gunner, in red	50	75	100
938 Soldier Bomb Thrower	7	11	15
938 Soldier Bomb Thrower, in red	62	93	125
941 Aviator	7	11	14
941 Aviator, in red	62	93	125
947 Soldier Marksman	6	9	12
947 Soldier Marksman, in red	52	78	105
948 Soldier Running	6	9	13
948 Soldier Running, in red	52	78	105
950 Cowboy w/Pistol Shooting	18	27	36
951 Cowboy w/Rifle	8	12	16
952 Cowboy w/Lasso	8	12	16
953 Cowboy w/Pistol (upraised)	8	12	16
954 Indian w/Shield and Tomahawk	6	9	13
955 Indian w/Rifle	7	11	14
956 Indian w/Knife and Spear	6	9	13
957 Indian w/Bow and Arrow	7	11	14
960 Soldier, Wounded w/Crutches	15	22	31
960 Soldier, Wounded w/Crutches, in red	62	93	125
961 Soldier, Wounded Head and Arm	14	21	28
961 Soldier, Wounded Head and Arm, in red	62	93	125
962 Nurse	17	25	34
974 Soldier, Anti-Aircraft Gunner	7	10	14
974 Soldier, Anti-Aircraft Gunner, in red	52	78	105
977 Soldier Under Marching Orders, in red	45	68	90
977 Soldier Under Marching Orders, marching	5	8	11
988 Soldier, Marching w/Gun on Back, gun slung over shoulder	6	9	12
988 Soldier, Marching w/Gun on Back, gun slung over shoulder, in red	50	75	100
990 Soldier w/Bazooka	7	11	15
990 Soldier w/Bazooka, in red	52	78	105
991 Soldier Flame Thrower	7	11	14
991 Soldier Flame Thrower, in red	50	75	100

Barclay Podfoots in red. Some collectors believe they were meant to represent the Korean War enemy.

"Midi" Size (Smaller Than Podfoot)

	C6	C8	C10
200 Flame Thrower	47	70	95
350 Policeman	5	8	11
351 Man	5	8	11
352 Woman	5	8	11
353 Conductor	5	8	11
354 Red cap	5	8	11

	C6	C8	C10
355 Oiler	5	8	11
356 Brakeman	5	8	11
357 Engineer	5	8	11
358 Porter	5	8	11
359 Dining Steward	5	8	11
360 Hobo	5	8	11
361 Newsboy	5	8	11
362 Mailman	5	8	11
363 Fireman	5	8	11
366 Peg Legged Gateman	6	9	13
369 Woman Carrying Baby	5	8	11
370 Little Boy	5	8	11
371 Little Girl	5	8	11
372 Bride	10	15	20
373 Groom	8	12	17
Advancing w/Rifle	30	45	60
Bugler	32	48	65
Cowboy w/Pistol	25	38	50
Cowboy w/Rifle	25	38	50
Firing Bazooka	30	45	60
Firing Tommy Gun	30	45	60
Indian w/Hatchet	25	38	50
Indian w/Rifle	25	38	50
Marching, slung rifle	37	56	75
Officer w/binoculars	40	60	80
Talking on Field Phone	31	46	62
Walking Forward, rifle at side, pointing down	30	45	60

GREY IRON

Founded as the Brady Machine Shop in Mount Joy, Pennsylvania in 1840, Grey Iron made the only 3-1/4-inch cast-iron soldiers. In 1881, the company was organized as the Grey Iron Casting Company, Ltd., and as early as 1903 it was manufacturing toy banks and stoves, cap pistols, wheeled toys and trains, as well as a number of non-toy items.

On August 14, 1917, the company was granted two patents for their 40mm solid cast-iron Grey Klip Armies, which they manufactured through 1941. The last of this series was made in 1938 as "Uncle Sam's Defenders" which were painted khaki rather than nickel-plated. The soldiers were not successful at first, but with the advent of a new distributor, the company was swamped with orders, and in January 1933, introduced a new line of thirty-five different cast-iron soldiers that were approximately three inches tall. Four Revolutionary War soldiers—an infantryman, a foot officer, a flagbearer, and a mounted officer—may have been introduced earlier, as they are numbered lower, but were not part of the 1933 announcement.

The figures tended to be slight and, while apparently successful, were superseded in July 1936 by Grey Iron's "Iron Men" series, slightly larger, more robust models that continued to be sold until World War II.

There were at least two designers for the soldiers—Edward Musser and Samuel S. Schmidt. The soldiers were hand-poured and then painted on an assembly-line basis, and were initially sold for a dime, while their competitors charged a nickel.

Grey Iron is still in business today as the John Wright division of Donsco, and has recently been producing, on an erratic basis, some unpainted soldiers from its old molds.

	C6	C8	C10
1 Colonial Soldier	14	21	28
1A Colonial Foot Officer	14	21	28
1B Colonial Color-Bearer	175	263	350
1B Colonial Color-Bearer, 1950s version, w/rifle barrel drilled out for flag	25	38	50
1MA Colonial Mounted Officer	24	36	48
2 Cadet, early version	10	15	21
2 Cadet	14	21	28
2A Cadet Officer, early	11	16	22
2A Cadet Officer	14	21	29
3 U.S. Infantry, Shoulder Arms, early	9	14	19
3 U.S. Infantry, Shoulder Arms	7	11	15
3/1 U.S. Infantry, Port Arms	10	15	21
3A U.S. Infantry Officer, early	9	13	18
3A U.S. Infantry Officer	9	13	18
4 U.S. Infantry, Port Arms, early	10	15	20
4A U.S. Doughboy Officer w/Field Glasses	15	22	30
4/1 U.S. Doughboy Signaling	15	22	30
4/2 U.S. Doughboy Combat Trooper	13	20	27
4/3 U.S. Doughboy w/Range Finder	38	57	76
4/4 U.S. Doughboy Ammunition Carrier	42	63	85
4/5 U.S. Doughboy Sharpshooter	13	20	27
4/6 U.S. Doughboy w/Bayonet	13	19	26
5 U.S. Infantry Charging, early	7	11	15
6 U.S. Doughboy, Port Arms, early	9	14	19
6 U.S. Doughboy, Shoulder Arms	8	12	16
6A U.S. Doughboy Officer, early	10	15	21
6A U.S. Doughboy Officer	9	14	19
6AF Foreign Legion Officer	19	29	38
6F Foreign Legion Shoulder Arms	17	25	34
6/1 U.S. Doughboy, Charging	9	14	18
6/1F Foreign Legion, Charging	17	25	34
6/2 U.S. Doughboy Sentry	11	16	23
6/3 Foreign Legion Bomber	40	60	80
6/3 U.S. Doughboy Bomber, crawling	12	18	24
6/4 U.S. Doughboy Grenade Thrower	17	26	35
7 U.S. Doughboy Charging, early	10	15	21
8A/F Foreign Legion Cavalry Officer	31	46	63
8/F Foreign Legion Cavalryman	34	51	68
8M U.S. Cavalryman, early	18	27	36
8M U.S. Cavalryman	18	27	36
8MA U.S. Cavalry Officer, early	20	30	40
8MA U.S. Cavalry Officer	21	31	42
9 U.S. Marine, early	9	14	19

	C6	C8	C10
9 U.S. Marine	13	20	26
10 Royal Canadian Police, early	12	18	24
10 Royal Canadian Police	16	24	33
11 Indian, w/hatchet, early	8	12	16
11 Indian Chief, w/knife	9	14	19
11/1 Indian Brave, shielding eyes	14	21	28
11/2 Chief Attacking, upraised tomahawk	50	75	100
11M Indian Mounted, early	18	27	37
11M Indian Mounted, lying on horse	37	56	75
11/1M Indian Scout Mounted, firing pistol backwards	112	168	225
12 Cowboy, early	10	15	20
12 Cowboy	9	14	18
12/1 Hold-Up Man	11	16	23
12/2 Cowboy w/Lasso	23	36	55
12/3 Bandit, surrendering	54	81	108
12M Cowboy Mounted, early	20	30	41
12M Cowboy Mounted	28	42	56
12/1M Masked Cowboy Mounted	162	243	325
13 U.S. Machine Gunner, early	10	15	21
13 U.S. Machine Gunner	8	12	17
13/1 U.S. Machine Gunner	9	14	19
13F Foreign Legion Machine Gunner	17	26	35
14 U.S. Sailor, in blue, early	10	15	20
14 U.S. Sailor, in white, early	10	15	20
14 U.S. Sailor, in blue	9	14	19
14W U.S. Sailor, in white	9	14	19
14A U.S. Naval Officer, early, in blue	9	14	19
14AW U.S. Naval Officer, early, in white	10	15	20
14A U.S. Naval Officer, in blue	10	15	21
14AW U.S. Naval Officer, in white	9	14	19
14/1W U.S. Sailor Signalman	15	22	31
15/1 Boy Scout Saluting, early	11	16	23
15/2 Boy Scout Walking, early	11	16	22
16/1 Pirate Boy	14	21	28
16/2 Pirate Chief	12	18	25
16/3 Pirate w/Dagger	12	18	24
16/4 Pirate w/Hook	11	16	23
16/5 Pirate w/Sword	12	18	24
17/1 Legion Drum Major, early	25	38	50
17/1 Legion Drum Major	11	16	22
17/2 Legion Bugler, early	11	16	22
17/2 Legion Bugler	9	14	19
17/3 Legion Drummer, early	11	16	23
17/3 Legion Drummer	10	15	21
17/4 Legion Color Bearer	10	15	20
18/1 Ethiopian Tribesman, c. 1936	27	41	54
18/2 Ethiopian Chief	37	55	74
18/3 Ethiopian Soldier, Shoulder Arms	32	48	64
18/3A Ethiopian Officer	35	52	69
18/5 Ethiopian Soldier Charging	36	54	72
19 Knight in Armor	10	15	20
20 Red Cross Doctor	16	24	32

	C6	C8	C10
21 Stretcher Bearer	20	30	40
22 Stretcher w/Patient	15	22	30
22/1/Wounded Sitting	45	68	90
22/2 Wounded on Crutches	23	35	47
23 Red Cross Nurse	10	15	20
25 Aviator (24 is non-soldier)	22	33	44
D26 Nurse and Wounded Soldier	100	150	200
D27 Doughboy Supporting Wounded Soldier	130	195	260
75 Radio Set, Operator and Aerial	155	232	310
75 Radio Set, Operator Only	49	74	98
Italian or English Desert Infantryman	115	172	230
Italian or English Desert Officer	75	112	150
Ski Trooper, c. 1940	12	18	25
Greek Evzone	55	82	110
U.S. Cavalryman, earliest version	70	105	140
U.S. Cavalry Officer, earliest version	70	105	140

American Family Series

All American Family figures are approximately 2-1/4-inch high

The American Family Travels

	C6	C8	C10
Boy in traveling suit	6	9	12
Conductor	6	9	12
Engineer	7	10	14
Girl in traveling suit	7	10	14
Man in traveling suit	6	9	12
Newsboy	9	14	18
Old Colored Man, sitting	10	15	20
Policeman	7	11	15
Porter	8	12	16
Postman	6	9	13
Preacher	8	12	16
Seat	5	8	10
Woman in traveling costume	6	9	12

The American Family on the Farm

	C6	C8	C10
Calf	5	8	10
Cow	5	8	10
Dog	4	6	9
Farmer	5	8	11
Farmer's Wife	6	9	13
Fence	8	12	16
Gate w/Post	10	15	20
Girl	7	10	14
Goat	4	6	9
Goose	4	6	9
Hired Man digging	6	9	12
Horse	4	6	9
Pig	4	6	9
Sheep	4	6	9

The American Family at Home

	C6	C8	C10
Boy flying kite	10	15	20
Colored Cook	11	16	22
Colored Man, digging	18	27	37
Delivery Boy	7	11	15
Dog	4	6	9
Garageman	8	12	16
Girl skipping rope	12	18	24
Lawn Seat	5	8	10
Man w/watering can	7	11	14
Milkman	7	11	15
Old Man, sitting	5	8	10
Old woman, sitting	5	8	10
Woman w/basket	8	12	16

The American Family on the Beach

	C6	C8	C10
Bench	4	6	8
Boy in summer suit	6	9	12
Boy w/Ball	10	15	21
Boy w/Life Preserver	10	15	21
Girl Catching Ball	10	15	21
Girl in slacks	9	14	18
Girl w/Sand Pail	10	15	21
Life Boat	14	21	28
Life Guard	13	19	26
Life Guard's Chair	14	21	28
Man in bathing suit	13	19	26
Old Man Sitting	3	5	7
Woman in bathing suit	13	19	26

The American Family on the Ranch

	C6	C8	C10
Boy in Cowboy Suit	8	12	16
Bucking Bronco	10	15	20
Burro	7	11	15
Calf	5	8	11

	C6	C8	C10
Colt	6	9	12
Cowboy Rider	19	28	38
Cowboy squatting	8	12	17
Cowboy w/lasso	12	18	24
Cowgirl Rider	11	16	22
Girl in Riding Suit	9	14	18
Rooster and Chickens	4	6	8
Stallion	8	12	17
Three Ducks	5	8	10

Greyklip Armies

	C6	C8	C10
Set 1/Company A, at attention, consists of bugler, officer, flagbearer, drummer, rifleman, price per each	2	3	4
Set 2/Company B, marching, consists of bugler, officer, flagbearer, drummer, rifleman, price per each	3	4	5
Set 3/Company C, charging, consists of bugler, officer, flagbearer, drummer, rifleman, price per each	3	4	5
Set 4/Troop D, consists of four mounted troopers, one mounted officer, troopers all look alike, price per each	4	6	7
Set 5/Battery E, 2-piece set, led by officer from Troop D, second piece is a gun limber w/four horses, several attached soldiers, price for second piece	7	11	14
Set 6/Battery F, consists of shell stack, loader bending, loader standing, gunner, cannon, price per each, shells double	5	7	9
Set 5/Aviator Corps, consists of pilot (two of the same figure in set) and plane w/detachable wing, price for set	70	105	142
Uncle Sam's Defenders, consists of charging rifleman, machine gunner, charging officer, rifleman at attention, flagbearer, officer saluting, price per each (double the price on saluting officer and flagbearer)	3	5	6

MANOIL

Manoil began production of toy soldiers in 1935. It was in business as early as 1927 under the name Jack Manoil. The company changed its name to Man-O-Lamp Corporation on July 11, 1928 and was owned by Maurice Manoil (1893-1974) and Jack Manoil (1902-1955), two brothers who had emigrated from Romania in the early 1900s. The final name change to Manoil Manufacturing Co., Inc. took place on July 7, 1934.

Manoil advanced into toy making in 1934 manufacturing seven vehicles. The company moved to other addresses

This Grey Iron American Family at Home set is one of only two known.

as it grew, leaving Manhattan in 1937 for Brooklyn, and moving to Waverly, New York in June 1940 and employed 225 people at its peak.

With the onset of World War II, Manoil shut down, but resumed production of soldiers in a fine-grained composition (employing sulfur) in January 1944. The pieces were brittle and ultimately unsuccessful, and their manufacture stopped by the end of the year.

After the war the company introduced several new lines of soldiers, but they were no longer distributed as widely.

In 1953, the firm moved to a smaller location in Waverly, changing its name to Jack Manoil Specialty Company, but went out of business shortly after his death. Jack Manoil and sculptor Walter Baetz were both keenly interested in the company's soldiers and would work late into the night as they collaborated on ideas for them. One of Baetz's continuing concerns was to design the molds so that there was no structural weakness in the soldiers as a result of air bubbles. For this reason many of Manoil's soldiers were redesigned a number of times with sometimes subtle, and sometimes broad, variations.

Manoil's soldiers have a distinctive jauntiness to them, at times veering on caricature, the latter trait becoming more pronounced as the years wore on.

A page from a 1939 Manoil catalog.

	C6	C8	C10
7 Flag Bearer	13	19	26
7 Flag Bearer, hollow base version	45	68	90
7 Flag Bearer, second version	13	19	26
8 Parade, campaign cap straight on head	21	31	43
8 Parade, fifth version	10	15	20
8 Parade, hollow base version	21	31	42
8 Parade, number on back	32	48	64
8 Parade, stocky version	10	15	20
9 Officer, hollow base version	38	57	76
9 Officer, second version	11	16	22
10 Bugler, hollow base version	40	60	80
10 Bugler, second version	11	16	22
11 Drummer, hollow base version	38	57	75
11 Drummer, stocky version	13	20	27
11 Drummer, vertical drum	23	35	46
12 Machine Gunner (Prone), flat base, no grass	14	21	28
12 Machine Gunner (Prone), grass on base	13	20	26
12 Machine Gunner (Prone), no aperture between hands and gun	11	16	23
12 Machine Gunner (Prone), no aperture, pack on back	12	18	25
12 Machine Gunner (Prone), spaces under body	30	45	60
13 Cadet, hollow base, no buckle on belt	26	39	52
13 Cadet, second version	12	18	25
14 Sailor, hollow base	27	41	55
14 Sailor, in blue	30	45	60

	C6	C8	C10
15 Marine, hollow base	33	50	66
15 Marine, second version	10	15	21
16 Ensign	12	18	24
16 Ensign, hollow base	30	45	60
17 Signal Man, hollow base version	23	35	46
17 Signal Man, second version	21	32	43
18 Cowboy, hollow base version	21	32	42
18 Cowboy, second version	10	15	21
18A Cowboy w/Hands Up	12	18	24
18A Cowboy w/Hands Up, subtle variation	12	18	24
20 Doctor, but in white	12	18	25
20K Doctor, khaki	18	27	36
21 Nurse	10	15	21
21 Nurse, no hem in skirt, shorter	14	21	28
22 Indian, w/knives	11	16	22
22 Indian, w/knives, right toes off base	10	15	21
23 Machine Gunner Sitting, markings under base	13	19	26
23 Machine Gunner Sitting, seated on four pillows, bullets feed from ammo box	13	20	27
24 Cannon Loader	9	14	19
25 Sniper (kneeling), short thin rifle	16	25	33
25 Sniper (kneeling), folding rifle	165	248	330
25 Sniper (kneeling), hollow base, not Manoil, probably Paul Paragine	40	60	80
25 Sniper (kneeling), longer, thicker rifle	11	16	23
26 Sniper	10	15	21
26 Sniper, folding rifle	188	282	375

	C6	C8	C10
26 Sniper, shorter rifle, angle different on underside of rifle	11	16	22
27 Tommy Gunner, bloated version	21	31	42
27 Tommy Gunner, second version	10	15	21
28 Observer	12	18	24
29 Wounded Soldier (Walking)	12	18	25
30 Wounded Soldier (Lying)	10	15	21
30 Wounded Soldier (Lying), number on back, shorter head	11	16	22
31 Bomb Thrower, three grenades in pouch	14	21	28
31 Bomb Thrower, two grenades in pouch	14	21	28
32 Stretcher Carrier, medical kit	12	18	25
32 Stretcher Carrier, medical kit, number on back, buttons on uniform, different pockets and collar from above	50	75	100
32 Stretcher Carrier, no medical kit	11	16	23
33 Sitting Soldier	20	30	40
34 Aviator	16	24	32
35 Hostess, in Khaki	150	225	300
35 Hostess, in green	32	48	65
35 Hostess, in white	55	83	110
36 Soldier w/Bayonet Charging	21	31	42
37 Soldier w/Gun Charging	24	36	38
38 Soldier w/Gun Butting	27	41	55
39 Soldier w/Bayonet Jabbing	26	39	53
40 Soldier (Kneeling w/Bayonet)	30	45	60
41 Soldier (Crouching w/Hand Grenade)	27	41	54
42 Field Doctor (Crawling)	30	45	60
43 Officer (Lying Down, Shooting Revolver)	27	41	55
44 Crawling Scout w/Gun, left leg high when right leg on ground, only three known	90	135	180
44 Crawling Scout w/Gun, left leg lower	26	39	52
45 Observer (w/Periscope)	17	26	35
46 Anti-Aircraft Gunner, barrel of gun drops below arm	11	16	23
46 Anti-Aircraft Gunner, barrel of gun ends at arm	12	18	24
47 Anti-Aircraft Searchlight	13	19	26
47 Anti-Aircraft Searchlight, w/tin lens	55	83	110
47 like M75, number on back, helmet looks as if it was adapted to look like WWII helmet	19	28	39
48 Navy Gunner	13	20	27
49 Policeman	10	15	21
49 Policeman, slightly larger	9	13	19
50 Bicycle Dispatch Rider	17	25	34
51 Motorized Machine Gunner	33	50	66
52 Motorcycle Rider	20	30	40
52 Motorcycle Rider, number over rear wheel, grass base	21	31	42

	C6	C8	C10
53 Sitting Soldier w/o Gun	20	30	40
54 Sitting Soldier Eating	25	38	50
55 Sitting Soldier at Table w/Phone and Map	16	24	32
56 Paymaster	85	128	170
57 Camouflage Sharpshooter Lying Down	14	21	29
58 Parachute Jumper	15	22	31
59 Soldier Writing Letter	35	52	70
59 Soldier Writing Letter, foot not curled up, pencil is flat, helmet rounder, fuller	37	56	75
60 Cook's Helper w/Ladle, helmet looks as if it was adapted to look like WWII helmet	60	90	120
60 Cook's Helper w/Ladle, normal helmet	23	35	46
61 Soldier w/Camera	36	54	73
62 Soldier w/Gas Mask & Gun	13	20	27
63 Soldier w/Gas Mask w/Flare Pistol	13	20	27
64 Soldier Playing Banjo	55	82	110
65 Deep Sea Diver w/"65" on chest	12	18	25
65 Deep Sea Diver	12	18	25
65 Deep Sea Diver, painted gray	13	19	26
66 Soldier w/Gun on Parade w/Overseas Cap	32	48	65
67 Soldier w/Gun and Pack Marching	10	15	20
68 Soldier Boxing	42	63	85
77 Lineman and Telephone Pole, pole comes w/two different-shaped bases, oval or diagonal	50	75	100
78 Anti-Tank Gun, round shield, four variations based on Vickers 2.95 mountain gun	16	24	33
78 Anti-Tank Gun, squared shield	18	27	36
78 Anti-Tank Gun, wooden wheels	27	41	55
79 Soldier marching w/gun slung at angle	87	130	175
80 Anti-Aircraft Machine Gunner	11	16	23
81 Machine Gunner and Helper, aperture between hand and machine gun	17	25	34
81 Machine Gunner and Helper, no aperture	16	24	32
82 Anti-Aircraft w/Range Finder	14	21	28
83 Soldier Trench Mortar	15	22	31
84 Soldier w/Shell	17	26	35
85 Aviator Holding Bomb	14	21	29
86 Aviator Mechanic w/Propeller, away from head	250	375	500
86 Aviator Mechanic w/Propeller, orange prop, flat lower hand	52	78	105
86 Orange prop, curved lower hand	44	66	88
86 Silver prop	60	90	120
87 Aviator carrying bomb sight	22	33	45
88 Radio Operator Standing	35	52	70

	C6	C8	C10
89 Radio Operator (Lying Down)	17	26	35
90 Soldier Digging Trench	34	51	68
91 Soldier w/Barbed Wire	18	27	37
91 Soldier w/Barbed Wire, wide-faced version	21	31	42
92 Fire Fighter, in gray	90	135	180
92 Fire Fighter, in white	50	75	100
93 Soldier on Guard Duty	42	63	85
94 Soldier Running w/Cannon, marked "Manoil USA," "1," cannon slants to right when looked at from above	23	35	46
94 Soldier Running w/Cannon, no markings, cannon straight from above, face narrower	19	28	38
94 Soldier Running w/Cannon, wooden wheels, thin face	31	46	62
99 Finn w/Skis	35	52	71
100 Finn Machine Gunner	27	41	55
101 Soldier Jumping w/Chute	52	77	105
102 Soldier Jumping w/Machine Gun	46	69	92
Aviator Holding Bomb, hand variation	15	22	30
Indian, w/hatchet	75	112	150
Machine Gunner Sitting, squarer-looking, markings near right leg	12	18	25
Sailor, second version	11	16	22
Soldier w/Camera, thinner arm	33	49	66

Happy Farm Series

	C6	C8	C10
41/1 Bench	5	8	10
41/2 Girl	5	8	10
41/3 Young Man	5	8	10
41/4 Man Carrying Sack on Back	13	19	26
41/5 Farmer Pitching Sheaves	13	19	26
41/6 Farmer Sharpening Scythe	11	16	23
41/7 Blacksmith Making Horseshoes	13	20	27
41/8 Farmer Cutting w/Scythe	13	19	26
41/9 Farmer Cutting Corn	13	19	26
41/10 Farmer Sowing Grain	11	16	23
41/11 Man Carrying Sheaves Under Arm	12	18	24
41/12 Scarecrow w/Top Hat	13	20	27
41/13 Farmer Carrying Pumpkin	13	19	26
41/12 Darky Eating Watermelon	82	63	84
41/15 Scarecrow w/Straw Hat	12	18	24
41/16 Watchman Blowing Out Lantern	12	18	25
41/17 Hod Carrier w/Bricks	16	24	33
41/18 Man Chopping Wood	12	18	25
41/19 Mason Laying Bricks	20	30	41
41/20 Man Dumping Wheel Barrow	14	21	28
41/21 Old Man Fixing Shoe	16	24	32
41/22 Blacksmith w/Wheel	13	20	27
41/23 Carpenter Carrying Door	20	30	40
41/24 Hound	12	18	24

	C6	C8	C10
41/25 Carpenter Sawing Lumber	13	20	27
41/26 Carpenter w/Square	32	48	64
41/27 Shepherd w/Flute	31	46	62
41/28 Lady w/Pie	15	22	30
41/29 Lady w/Child	16	24	32
41/30 School Teacher	22	33	45
41/31 Girl Watering Flowers	12	18	25
41/32 Woman Lifting Hen From Nest	14	21	29
41/33 Woman w/Butter Churn	13	19	26
41/34 Woman Laying Out Wash on Grass	14	21	28
41/35 Woman Sweeping w/Broom	13	20	27
41/36 Man Juggling Barrel	27	41	55
41/36 Man Juggling Barrel, in khaki	24	36	48
41/37 Man Planting Tree	20	30	40
41/38 Girl Picking Berries	23	35	47
41/39 Farmer at Water Pump	13	20	26
41/40 Boy Carrying Wood	14	21	28
41/41 Stacks of Sheaves	11	16	22
Boxed Happy Farm Set, no standard contents, ten pieces	188	282	375

Manoil Composition

	C6	C8	C10
Firing camouflaged AA Gun	24	36	48
Motorcyclist	26	39	53
Motorcyclist, minor variation of above	26	39	53
Prone machine-gunner	26	39	53
Seated machine-gunner	24	36	48

Post-War

The following were the first new post-World War II series, and were produced only for a limited time. On a trial basis, early production was also sold unpainted.

	C6	C8	C10
45/10 At Attention, present arms	16	24	32
45/11 Sniper	19	28	38
45/12 Tommy Gunner	15	22	30
45/13 Soldier w/Bazooka Cannon, some marked "45/18"	18	27	37
45/14 Soldier w/Shell for Bazooka, some marked "46/14"	17	25	35
45/15 General, some "46/15"	78	117	155
45/16 Mine Detector, some "46/16"	22	33	45
45/6 Parade, thin, c. late 1945	14	21	28
45/7 Flag Bearer	20	30	40
45/8 Parade	10	15	21
45/9 Combat	14	21	29
46-A Parade, thin, c. late 1945	18	27	36
521 Flag Bearer, all 500s, c. 1950	19	29	39
522 Parade	14	21	28
523 Soldier in poncho	19	28	38
524 Combat	15	23	31
525 Aviator Holding Bomb	17	25	34

	C6	C8	C10
526 Observer	19	28	38
527 Aircraft Spotter	19	28	38
528 Soldier w/bazooka	14	21	28
529 Motorcycle rider	28	42	56
530 Machine gunner, lying	17	26	35
531 Machine gunner, sitting	17	26	35
532 Sniper, kneeling	18	27	36
533 Soldier w/gas mask w/flare pistol	19	29	38
534 Sniper	19	29	38
535 Soldier throwing hand grenade	24	36	48
536 Anti-Aircraft gunner	19	29	39
537 Soldier w/tommy gun	20	30	41
538 Soldier firing up	19	29	39
539 Stretcher bearer	55	83	110
540 Wounded Soldier, lying	57	86	115
Flag Bearer, thin, c. late 1945	14	21	29
Machine Gunner Lying, thin, c. late 1945	50	75	100
Machine Gunner Sitting, thin, c. late 1945	36	54	72
Sniper, thin, c. late 1945	27	41	55
Tommy Gunner, thin, c. late 1945	16	24	32

My Ranch Corral Series

	C6	C8	C10
C1 Fence	6	9	10
C2 Ranch fence, gate	33	50	67
C12 Blanket over Fence Section	24	36	48
C14 Brahma Bull	9	14	19
C18 Small Calf	7	11	15
C19 Cow feeding	8	12	16
C20 Bull, head turned	9	14	18
C22 Horse for Mounted Cowboy	15	22	30
C22 Horse for Mounted Cowgirl	15	22	30
C23 Cowboy Rider	7	11	15
C24 Cowgirl Rider	7	11	15
C25 Small Horse	11	16	23
C26 Large Cactus	13	20	26
C28 Short Cactus	9	14	18
C29 Mounted Cowboy	28	42	57
C30 Mounted Cowboy Shooting	27	41	55
Large Gate	14	21	28
Small Gate	15	22	30

TIN WIND-UPS

Today's toys may be durable, but most are made of plastic, which just doesn't hold the charm and nostalgia of yesterday's tin creations. Those tin toys, made in large numbers mainly before World War II, are among the priciest collectible toys today.

Metal toys produced before World War I are considered true works of art, especially since tin toys were often painstakingly hand painted.

But the advent of chromolithography changed the way most toys were produced. Chromolithography was actually developed late in the nineteenth century. The technique allowed multicolor illustrations to be printed on flat tin plates which were molded tin toys.

Starting in the 1920s, lithographed tin toys began to dramatically change toy production. American manufacturers could produce these colorful toys more inexpensively than the classic European toys that had dominated the toy market until this time.

With mass production came mass appeal. New tin mechanical toys were based on the characters and celebrities that were popular at the time. Newspaper comic strips and Walt Disney movies provided already popular subject matter for toy marketers.

Among the most well-known makers of mechanical tin toys were Marx, Chein, Lehmann and Strauss. Others include Courtland, Girard, Ohio Art, Schuco, Unique Art and Wolverine.

Many of these manufacturers had business relationships with each other. Over the years, some would be found working together, producing toys for others, distributing others' toys or being absorbed by other companies. There even appeared to be some pilfering and reproducing others' ideas.

One of the advantages of lithography was that it allowed old toys to be recycled in many ways. When a character's public appeal began to wane, a new image could be printed on the same body to produce a new toy. Or when a toy company was absorbed by another, older models could be dusted off and dressed up with new lithography. Many of the mechanical tin wind-up toys show up in surprisingly similar versions with other manufacturer's name on them.

Remember, the better the condition, the better the value, especially with tin. Those with the original box are true treasures. Tin robots have virtually become an endangered species. Those that are on the market generally command premium prices.

Contributor: Leo E. Rishty, ToyDoc, 2563 Jardin Lane, Weston, FL 33327-1510, e-mail: toy1doc@aol.com. Rishty has been reparing and collecting toys for over twenty years.

ANIMATE TOY CO.

In 1918 this firm was located at East 17th Street in New York City, and its president was L.T. Savage. By 1931 it had moved to 30 North 15th Street in East Orange, New Jersey and employed ten men and forty women. In 1934 the president-vice president was George V. Turnbull and the secretary-treasurer was George H. Webb. Five men and eleven women made up the work force.

	C6	C8	C10
Climbing Tractor, 1929, 9" long	100	150	200
U.S. Baby Tank, pat. 6/20/16, 1918, 2-1/2" long	40	60	80

AUTOMATIC TOY CO.

	C6	C8	C10
Alpine Express	75	112	150
Auto Speedway, c. 1930	125	175	225
Cross-Over Trolley Set	90	135	180

	C6	C8	C10
Dizzy Liz, No. 180, 1940s, 5" long	100	150	200
Jungle Pete, No. 175, 15" long	90	135	180
Magic Crossroads Track, w/two wind-up cars, c. 1950	130	195	260
Mystery Alpine Express, 1940s, 20" long, 14" wide, 2" high	100	150	200

Auto Speedway, Automatic Toy Co., $225

	C6	C8	C10
Operation Airlift, two plastic planes, 1950s	80	120	160
Rocket Space Ship, sparks, No. 305, 1940s, 8-1/2" long	100	150	200
Space Shooting Range, 1950s, 15" long	150	225	300
Speedway, w/two race cars and garage, 1930s	175	262	350

CHEIN

Chein (pronounced "Chain") was founded in 1903 by Julius Chein. The New Jersey company specialized in lithographed metal toys, the majority of them mechanical. In 1918 they were located at 310 Passaic Avenue, Harrison, New Jersey, with 250 employees. Chein made toys until 1979 and is still in business in Burlington, New Jersey.

	C6	C8	C10
Alligator w/native on its back	175	250	350
Army Drummer, 1930s, plunger-activated, 7" high	130	195	260
Barnacle Bill in a Barrel, 1930s, 7" high	275	400	550
Barnacle Bill the Sailor, punching a bag, 7-1/2"	212	319	425
Barnacle Bill, 1930s	250	350	500
Bass Drummer	150	225	300

	C6	C8	C10
Bear w/hat, pants, shirt, bow tie, c. 1938	65	90	115
Cabin Cruiser, 1940s, 9" long	65	98	130
Chick, brightly colored clothes and polka dot bow tie, 4" high	50	75	100
Chicken pulling wheelbarrow, 1930s, 6" x 3-1/2"	50	75	100
Clown in Barrel, 1930s, 8" high	300	375	575
Clown Puncher	375	562	750
Clown w/umbrella	125	200	275
Dan-Dee Dump Truck	200	300	400
Doughboy, 1920s, 6" high	175	262	350
Drum Major, 8-1/2" high	210	315	420
Drummer Boy, w/shako, c. 1930s, 9" high	100	150	200
Duck, long-beaked, in orange sailor suit, not Donald Duck, but similar, waddles, 6" high	110	160	210
Duck, waddles, 1930, 4" high	75	90	110
Ferris Wheel, six compartments, ringing bell, 1930s, 16-1/2" high	275	400	525
Greyhound Bus, 9" long	85	130	175
Handstand Clown, 1940s, 6" high	65	100	125
Indian in Headdress, 1930s, 5-1/2" high	110	175	225
Jumping Rabbit, 1925, 5" long	120	180	240

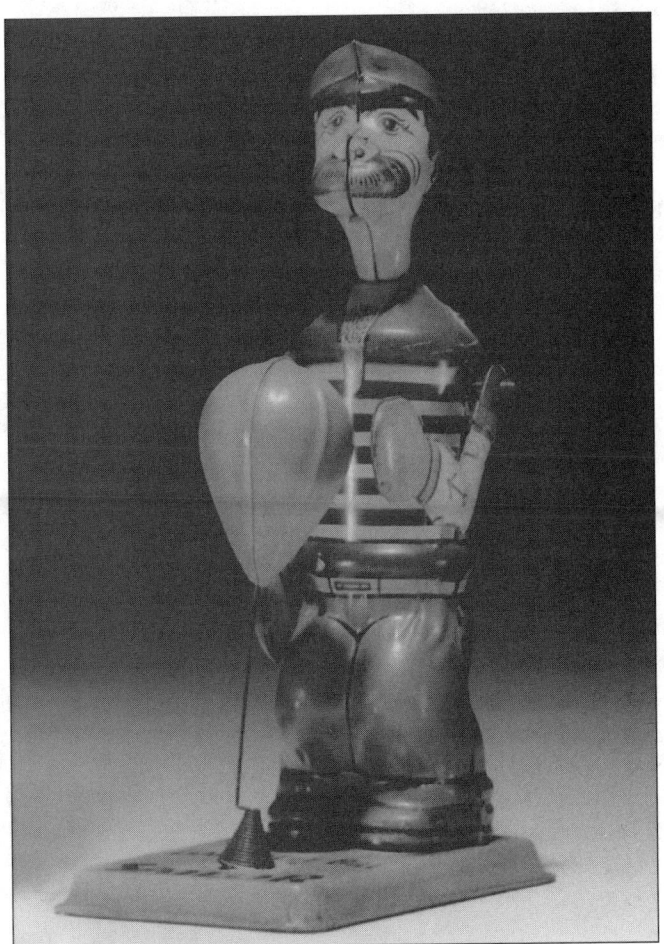

Barnacle Bill the Sailor, Chein, $425

Ferris Wheel, Chein, $525

Indian in Headdress, Chein, $225

Pig, Chein, $100

	C6	C8	C10
Marine, hand on belt, 1950s, 6" high 120		180	240
Mark I Cabin Cruiser, 1957, 8-1/2" long..... 33		50	65
Mechanical Aquaplane, No. 39, boat-like pontoons, 1932, no insignia, 8-1/2" long, 7-1/2" wingspan................ 200		300	400
Mechanical Aquaplane, post-WWII insignia 188		280	375
Mechanical Aquaplane, pre-WWII insignia 113		170	225
Mechanical Fish, 1940s, 11" 40		60	80
Mechanical Frog Man, 1950s, 11" long 100		150	200
Mechanical Rocket Ride, No. 400, 1950s, 18" high 600		900	1200
Melody Player, No. 135, 1930s, 4 rolls, 6-3/4" high... 100		150	200

Playland Merry-Go-Round, Chein, $800

	C6	C8	C10
Musical Aero Swing, 1940s, 10" high 283		425	565
Navy Frog Man, No. 122, 1950s, 12" long.... 100		150	200
Pan-Am Clipper, 1930s, pontoons, 11" wingspan... 388		582	775
Peggy Jane Boat, 13" long 62		93	125
Penguin in tuxedo type jacket, c. 1940........ 75		100	125
Pig, 1940s, 4-1/2" high 50		75	100
Playland Merry-Go-Round, 1930s, 9-1/2" high 400		600	800
Playland Whip, four bump cars, driver's head wobbles No. 340...................... 450		675	900
Rabbit in shirt and pants, c. 1938............... 53		78	105
Rabbit pulling cart 48		72	95
Rabbit w/wheelbarrow................................. 75		112	150
Race Car No. 52, 1930s, 6-1/2" long............ 80		120	160
Racer #3, 1920s, 6-1/2" long 150		225	300
Ride-A-Rocket 300		450	600
Rocket Ride No. 400, four rockets, 18" high, 11" diameter base.................. 455		685	910
Roller Coaster, w/two cars 1950s............... 200		300	400
Roller Coaster, w/two cars c. 1938............. 250		375	500
Santa Elf, 1920s, 6" high............................ 220		330	440
Ski Boy, No. 157, 1940s, 7-3/4" long, 5-1/4" tall.. 150		235	310
Skin Driver, No. 122, 1950s, 12" long.......... 55		83	110
Ski-Ride, No. 320, 19" long........................ 215		335	460
Space Ride No. 205, 1950s, 10" high 500		750	1000

Ride-A-Rocket, Chein $600

Galop Zebra Cart, Lehmann, $325

Rocket Fighter, Marx, c. 1950, $475

Wee Scottie, Marx, $175

Rollover Cat, Marx, $130

Old Jalopy, Marx, $300

	C6	C8	C10
Space Ride, lever action, 1940s, 9" high 425	638	850	
Spirit of St. Louis Airplane, 1930s,			
8" long, 8" wingspan 250	375	500	
Taxi, 1920s, 7" long 200	300	400	
Toy Town Helicopter, 1950s, 13" long 65	98	130	
Turtle w/native on back 250	375	525	
U.S. Army Sergeant No. 153, 1950s,			
5-1/2" high 105	158	210	
Walking Pelican, 1930s, 5" high 100	150	200	

COURTLAND MFG. CO.

Walter Reach, owner of Courtland, had a burning desire to be known as the second Louis Marx. He began production in 1944 with two die-cut cardboard toys of his own design—a rabbit and cart and horse and cart. Reach turned to tin litho toys after the war, a number of them non-wind-ups. At their height, Courtland, located first in Camden, New Jersey and later in Philadelphia, had 600 workers, and in 1947 its sales exceeded 1.5 million dollars. But success was short-lived—the firm lasted just seven years.

	C6	C8	C10
Checker Cab Car, green and white,			
No. 4000, 7-1/4" long, 3-1/4" wide,			
2-3/4" high 200	225	350	
Checker Cab Car, green and yellow,			
No. 4000, 7-1/4" long, 3-1/4" wide,			
2-3/4" high 200	225	350	
Circus Elephant & "African Lions" Cart,			
No. 400, 11-5/8" long, 3" wide,			
3-1/2" high 250	450	700	
Circus Elephant & "Circus Band" Cart,			
No. 500, 11-5/8" long, 3" wide,			
3-1/2" high 350	550	850	
Circus Elephant & "Monkeys" Cart,			
No. 300, 11-5/8" long, 3" wide,			
3-1/2" high 250	450	700	
City Meat Market Delivery Sedan,			
No. 4000, 7-1/4" long, 3-1/4" wide,			
2-3/4" high 75	125	150	

Checker Cab Car, green and yellow, Courtland Mfg. Co., $350

Fire Chief Car, red and white, Courtland Mfg. Co., $150

	C6	C8	C10
Country Produce Pickup, No. 4500,			
7-1/4" long, 3-1/4" wide, 2-3/4" high 75	100	125	
Easter Rabbit and Trailer, No. 200,			
11-5/8" long, 3" wide, 3-1/2" high 75	125	200	
Express Service Pickup, No. 4500,			
7-1/4" long, 3-1/4" wide, 2-3/4" high 75	100	125	
Fire Chief Car, red and white, No. 4000,			
7-1/4" long, 3-1/4" wide, 2-3/4" high ... 100	125	150	
Fire Chief Car, red, No. 4000, 7-1/4" long,			
3-1/4" wide, 2-3/4" high 100	125	150	
Mechanical "Automatic Ladder" Fire			
Truck, No. 1400, 9" long, 3" wide,			
2-3/4" high 175	250	350	
Mechanical "Black Diamond"			
Coal Truck, No. 5100, 10-1/2" wide,			
3" wide, 3-3/8" high 150	225	300	
Mechanical "ESSO" Gasoline			
Tractor-Trailer, No. 2000, 13" long,			
3" wide, 3-1/4" high 250	350	450	
Mechanical "Rocking R Ranch" See-Saw,			
No. 8000, 17-3/4" long, 2-1/8" wide,			
6" high 125	175	225	

Mechanical Caterpillar Tractor, No. 6100, Courtland Mfg. Co., $450

	C6	C8	C10
Mechanical Caterpillar Tractor, No. 6100, w/rubber treads, 6" long, 3" wide, 4-1/2" high............ 250	250	350	450
Mechanical Chromed Trimmed Tow Truck, No. 8500, tow boom is solid color, 8" long, 3-1/4" wide, 3-1/2" high.......... 225	225	350	450
Mechanical Chromed Trimmed Tow Truck, No. 8500, tow boom shows detail, 8" long, 3-1/4" wide, 3-1/2" high......... 125	125	200	275
Mechanical Combination Steam Shovel carried by low-boy tractor-trailer, No. 5300, 15-1/2" long, 3-7/8" wide, 10-1/2" high............ 350	350	550	775
Mechanical Dump Truck, No. 1600, 7" long, 3" wide, 2-3/4" high............ 100	100	150	200
Mechanical Dump Truck, No. 3100, 7" long, 3" wide, 3-1/4" high............ 100	100	125	150
Mechanical Emergency Rescue Squad Tractor-Trailer, 13" long, 3" wide, 3-1/4" high............ 150	150	200	250
Mechanical Express and Hauling Truck, No. 1300, 9" long, 3" wide, 2-3/4" high.... 125	125	200	275
Mechanical Farm Tractor, No. 6000, w/scraper, rear tires are large rubber and front are small rubber tires, 8-3/4" long, 4-3/4" wide, 4-1/2" high... 100	100	150	200
Mechanical Farm Tractor, No. 6050, w/o scraper, rear tires are large rubber and front are small rubber tires, 7-1/2"long, 4-3/4" wide, 4-1/2" high............ 75	75	100	150
Mechanical Farm Tractor, No. 6075, w/o scraper, rear tires are large tin litho while the front are small rubber tires, 7-1/2" long, 4-3/4" wide, 4-1/2" high... 250	250	350	450
Mechanical Fire Chief Car, No. 7000, w/siren, 7-1/4" long, 3-1/4" wide, 2-3/4" high............ 150	150	200	250
Mechanical Fire Patrol No. 2 Truck, No. 1300, 9" long, 3" wide, 2-3/4" high............ 125	125	200	275
Mechanical Freight Haulers Tractor-Trailer, No. 2600, 13" long, 3" high, 3-1/4" wide 200	200	300	375
Mechanical Gasoline Tractor-Trailer, No. 2000, 13" long, 3" wide, 3-1/4" high............ 250	250	350	450
Mechanical Heavy Duty Sand and Gravel Tractor-Trailer, No. 2375, 13" long, 3" wide, 3-1/4" high 200	200	250	300
Mechanical Hook and Ladder Tractor-Trailer, No. 2100, 13" long, 3" wide, 3-1/4" high 100	100	150	200

Mechanical Ice Cream Truck, No. 1300, Courtland Mfg. Co., $250

	C6	C8	C10
Mechanical Ice Cream Scooter, No. 6500, 6-1/2" long, 3" wide, 4-1/2" high 200	200	300	400
Mechanical Ice Cream Truck, No. 1300, 9" long, 3" wide, 2-3/4" high 150	150	200	250
Mechanical Lawn Mower, No. 15, 8-1/4" wide, 24" high, 3" wheels............ 50	50	75	100
Mechanical Lawn Mower, No. 20, 11-1/4" wide, 29" high, 5" wheels........... 65	65	85	110
Mechanical Lawn Mower, No. 21, 12" wide, 29" high, 5" wheels................. 65	65	85	110
Mechanical Logging Tractor-Trailer, No. 2200, 13" long, 3" wide, 3-1/4" high 150	150	200	250
Mechanical Milk Tractor-Trailer, No. 2050, "American Dairies," 13" long, 3" wide, 3-1/4" high 350	350	575	800
Mechanical Moving & Storage Truck, w/No. 130 litho on the sides of the truck bed 175	175	250	375
Mechanical Moving & Storage Truck, No. 1300, 9" long, 3" wide, 2-3/4" high 175	175	250	375
Mechanical No. 51 Steam Shovel, No. 5200, 15-1/2" long, 3-3/4" wide, 9-1/2" high 150	150	200	250
Mechanical Open Van Tractor-Trailer, No. 2300, 13" long, 3" wide, 3-1/4" high 125	125	175	225
Mechanical Open Van Tractor-Trailer, No. 2350, 13" long, 3" wide, 3-1/4" high 150	150	200	250
Mechanical Operation No. 51, Crane Truck, No. 5000, 13" long, 3-5/8" wide, 5" high 225	225	325	400
Mechanical Parking Meter and Bank, No. 7500, base 6" x 6", 24-1/2" high..... 150	150	225	300
Mechanical Power Lawn Mower, No. 25, 12" wide, 29" high, 5-3/4" wheels........... 75	75	100	125
Mechanical Road Roller Truck, No. 1500, 9" long, 3" wide, 3-1/4" high 250	250	350	450

	C6	C8	C10
Mechanical Road Roller Truck, No. 3000, 9" long, 3" wide, 3-1/4" high	250	350	450
Mechanical Side Tipper Tractor-Trailer, No. 2700, 13" long, 3" high, 3-1/4" wide	200	300	375
Mechanical Side Tipper Tractor-Trailer, No. 3900, "Black Diamond Coal Company-340," 13" long, 3" high, 3-1/4" wide	300	400	500
Mechanical Stake Bed Truck, No. 3200, 7" long, 3" wide, 3-1/4" high	125	150	175
Mechanical State Police Car, No. 7500, w/siren, 7-1/4" long, 3-1/4" wide, 2-3/4" high	165	225	275
Mechanical Trailer Tow Truck, No. 2400, 13" long, 3" wide, 3-1/4" high	225	325	400
Mechanical Trailer-Truck, No. 1200, 13" long, 3" wide, 3-1/4" high	200	250	375
Modern Bakery Delivery Sedan, No. 4000, 7-1/4" long, 3-1/4" wide, 2-3/4" high	100	150	175
Modern Decorators Pickup, No. 4500, 7-1/4" long, 3-1/4" wide, 2-3/4" high	100	125	150

GIRARD

C.G. Wood founded Girard Model Works in Girard, Pennsylvania, in 1906 and his son Frank joined the firm a few years after its inception. Originally the company made patterns, models and special machinery, but in 1918 they began making toys for an unidentified large firm in New York. It was in 1920 that they began making toys under the name Wood's Mechanical Toys. By 1931 Louis Marx was associated with Girard, and during the Depression Marx took over the firm. The last Girard toys seem to have been produced in 1975, though the firm remained in business until 1980. Many of Marx's and Girard's toys are interchangeable.

	C6	C8	C10
Air Mail Biplane, three-engine	600	900	1200
Airways Express plane, 13" wingspan	175	263	350
Bi-Wing Monoplane, 1918, 12" long, 14" wingspan (Wood's)	150	225	300
Bus w/driver, 12-1/2" long	200	300	400
Coolie & Pushcart	140	210	280
Farm Boy Walking, w/shovel and rake, 1920 (Wood's), 6"	450	675	900
Fire Chief Siren Coupe, 1930s, 14" long	288	430	575
Flasho the Mechanical Grinder, 1920s	235	350	475
Goble the Gobbling Goose	120	180	240
Man pushing wheelbarrow, 5-1/2"	200	300	400
Monoplane, high wing, one-engine, 1921-22, 13" long	350	525	700
Monoplane, high wing, one-engine, pilot, 9" long	275	395	550

	C6	C8	C10
Pierce-Arrow Coupe, green, orange and cream, c. 1932, 14" long	225	338	450
Race Car No. 2, 8" long	300	450	600
Railroad Handcar	200	300	400
Spirit of St. Louis, 9" long	400	600	800
Tri-Motor Air Lines, 1920s	175	263	350
Whiz Sky Fighter, biplane, 7" wingspan	313	470	625

KINGSBURY

	C6	C8	C10
Ambulance, 7" long	500	750	1000
Artillery Launcher	100	150	200
Biplane, single engine, rubber wheels, c. 1925, 16" long	450	700	950
Bi-Wing Airplane, w/cast-iron pilot 1918, 16" long, 17" wingspan	400	600	800
Borden's Milk Truck	250	375	500
Convertible w/rumble seat, electric headlamps, hard rubber wheels, 12-1/2" long	180	270	360
Fireman's Ladder Truck, hard rubber wheels, driver, 23-1/2" long	200	300	400
Monoplane, high wing, single engine, windup wheels and spins prop via rubber band, 1930s, 11" long	300	450	600
Roadster, electric headlamps, 12-1/2" long	250	375	500
Station Wagon, 1920s	150	225	300
Streetcar, 1930s, No. 782, 9" long	200	300	400
Transatlantic Air-Go-Round	250	375	500

LEHMANN

	C6	C8	C10
Adam the Porter, 1920s, 9" high	880	1320	1760
Aha Delivery Van, 1920s, 5-1/2" long	500	750	1000
Ajax Warrior w/two clubs	650	1000	1425
Alabama Coon Jigger	350	500	700

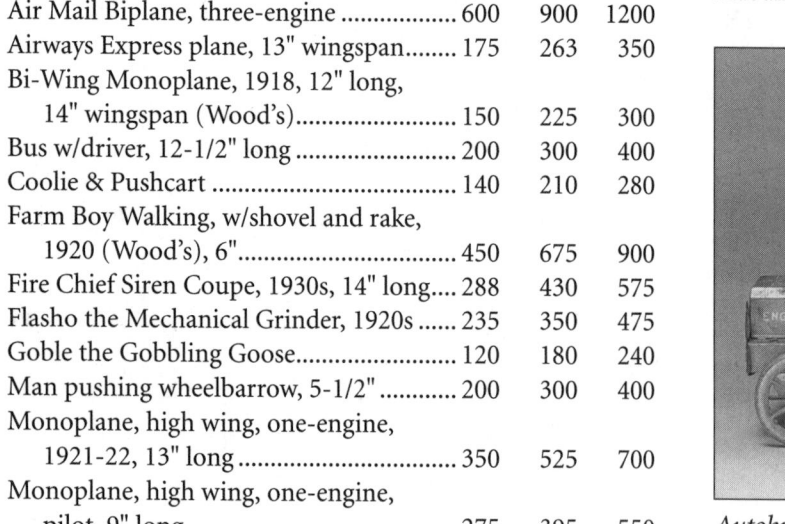

Autobus, Lehmann, $2,000

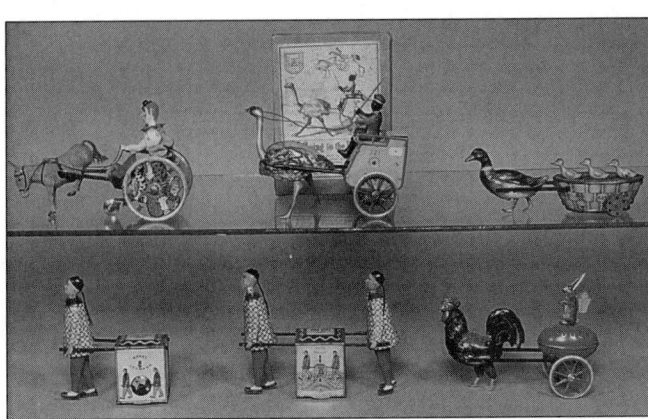

Left to Right, Top: Balky Mule, Lehmann, $475; Zulu, Lehmann, $1,130; Paak-Paak, Lehmann, $630. Bottom: Nu-Nu, Lehmann, $1,400; Kadi, Lehmann, $1,400; Duo, Lehmann, $1,540.

	C6	C8	C10
Am Pol, Amundsen driving, figure behind w/umbrella, map of North Pole	1800	2700	3750
Anxious Bride, chauffeur on tricycle, woman in car	800	1300	1965
Autobus	700	1300	2000
Autohutte Garage, No. 771, 6" long	450	675	900
Baker & Sweep	1500	2600	4260
Baldur Limousine, 10" long	700	1100	1800
Balky Mule, 1930s, 7-1/2" long	250	350	475
Berolina Car	1500	2400	3500
Bucking Bronco, Wild West, 6-1/2" long	415	622	830
Climbing Miller, cardboard blades	340	510	680
Crawling Beetle, The, 1900s, 4" long	140	210	280
Crocodile, c. 1905	200	300	400
Dancing Sailor, 1920s, 7-1/2" high	400	600	800
Daredevil Zebra Cart	400	600	800
Duo, rooster pulling rabbit	750	1100	1540
Echo Motorcycle No. 725, 1907, 8-3/4" long	1000	1500	2500
EHE & Co., open bed	320	480	640
EPL I dirigible	400	600	800
EPL II dirigible	500	700	1000
Express, porter pulling cart, c. 1927, 6" long	300	400	500
Galop Racer, w/garage, No. 1	800	1200	1600
Galop Zebra Cart	175	250	325
Going to the Fair	800	1300	1800
Heavy Swell, dude-it-up man	850	1400	1975
Ito Sedan, 1920s, 6-1/2"	468	700	935
Kadi, two Chinese carrying chest	600	950	1400
Lana Auto	1200	2000	2800
Lehmann's Autobus 590	1000	1800	2400
Li La, early car w/two excited women passengers, driver in top hat and dog w/turning head, 5-1/2"	1000	1850	2500

	C6	C8	C10
Lo Li, clown and ring master	5000	8000	12,000
Lo Lo, early car, driver	500	750	1100
Lu-Lu bird	100	150	200
Lu-Lu delivery truck, 7-1/4" long	1500	2500	4000
Mandarin, two coolies carrying Chinese in sedan chair	1500	2500	3700
Mars Cycle	450	675	900
Masuyama, coolie pulling rickshaw	800	1400	2000
Mensa Delivery Van	1400	2300	3500
Mikado Family, 1920s, 6-1/2" long	650	1100	1500
Mixtum	800	1350	1960
Motor Car Kutsche, 1897, 5-1/2" long	270	405	540
Motor Coach, 1920s, 5-1/2" long	339	510	675
Na-Ob, man driving horse cart, wheels marked w/elf, 6" long	200	300	400
Naughty Boy	800	1300	1870
New Century Cycle, 1907, 5" long	370	555	740
Nu-Nu, rickshaw w/puller and rider, No. 733, c. 1913, 4-1/2" long	600	950	1400
Oh My, 10" high	350	525	700
OHO, patented 1903	270	405	540
Onkel	375	562	750
Paak-Paak, ducklings in cart pulled by duck	315	472	630
Paddy Pig, c. 1912, 6" long	650	1000	1400
Pao Pao peacock, 10" long	250	375	500
Performing Sea Lion, The, 1900s, 7" long	75	112	150

Dancing Sailor, Lehmann, $800

	C6	C8	C10
Peter, three-wheeled car 1200	1900	2700
Power Carriage 360	540	720
Quack-Quack, mother duck pulling cart			
w/three small ducks 300	450	600
Rad-Cycle, c. 1927, 5" long 650	1180	1575
Rollo Chair................................ 1000	1700	2400
Sedan, No. 765, 5-1/2" long 275	403	550
Skirolf, skier 1300	2300	3050
Stubborn Donkey, clown in donkey cart,			
7-1/2" long 375	525	675
Taka Battleship 450	675	900
Tap Tap, man pushing wheelbarrow 150	225	300
Terra 550	950	1385
Tom, climbing monkey, 8" long............ 50	75	100
Tut-Tut, man in car w/horn, 6-3/4" long .. 500	900	1300
Tyras Walking Dog, 6" long 350	525	700
Uhu amphibious car 800	1400	2050
Walking down Broadway, strolling			
couple 2000	3000	4200
Walking Sailor, 7-1/2" high 525	775	1050
Wild West.................................. 350	525	700
Zig Zag patented 1903, 5" long 750	1125	1500
Zikra, No. 752, 1920s, 7" long...... 800	1300	1800
Zulu, black man in cart pulled by ostrich 500	780	1130

LINDSTROM

	C6	C8	C10
American Railway Express Truck &			
Trailer, 16" long.......................... 363	545	725
Baby Wee speedboat, 10-1/2" long 38	56	75
Betty, 1930s, shako walker, 8" tall 175	263	350
Bird.. 95	140	190
Bumper Car, 6-1/2" long................ 112	168	225
Dancing Dutch Boy, 1930s, 8" high 125	188	250
Dancing Lassie, shako, 1930s, 8" tall 100	150	200
Delfine 7 Motorboat, c. 1930 175	263	350
Ferry Boat, litho, approx. 8-1/4"................ 100	150	200
Flyer, 14" 100	150	200
Johnny the Dancing Clown, No. 122,			
1930s, 8" tall 200	300	400
Katrinka, 1930s, 8" tall 100	150	200
Mammy, 1930s, shako walker, 8" tall......... 300	450	600
Miss America speedboat 120	180	240
Parcel Post No. 2 Truck 200	300	400
Racing Car, 1930s, 6".................... 175	263	350
Skeeter Bug, bumper car, 1930s, 9" long... 100	150	200
Speedboat, 7" long.......................... 50	75	100
Speedboat, c. 1950, 18-1/2" long 163	245	325
Sweeping Betty 120	180	240
Sweeping Mammy, No. 1750, 1930s,			
shako walker while sweeping, 8" tall 212	318	425

LOUIS MARX TOY CO.

By the 1950s Louis Marx was the largest manufacturer of toys in the world; his empire included six large factories in the United States and ownership of interest in factories in seven other countries. Marx, born in Brooklyn in 1896, worked for "Toy King" Ferdinand Strauss during his teens, and by the age of twenty his energy and enterprise had made him a director of that company. A falling out with Strauss persuaded Marx to go into business for himself, and in 1921 he and his brother began making their own toys, including some adaptations of items by the now-defunct Strauss.

Marx's watchword seems to have been quality at the lowest possible price, and he was such a favorite with toy buyers that he had no need for salesmen or advertising.

Although Marx made almost every type of toy (with the exception of dolls), his tin wind-up toys are probably the most favored by toy collectors.

In April 1972, Marx sold his company to the Quaker Oats Company, who in 1976 sold it to Europe's largest toy manufacturer, Dunbee-Combex-Marx. The company went into bankruptcy in 1980. Louis Marx died in 1982 at the age of 85. In 1982 American Plastics bought much of the Marx assets and in 1990 began producing toys from the original molds. In the first Marx break-up, certain rights and molds were retained in Mexico, and these continue.

	C6	C8	C10
1st Batt. F.D. Chief's Car, siren, battery			
headlights, 16"........................ 300	450	600
Acrobatic Marvel, 1930s, monkey on			
13" spring and 7-1/2" rocking base 118	175	235

Acrobatic Marvel, Marx, $235

Balky Mule, Marx, $200

	C6	C8	C10
Alligator	75	110	150
Ambulance w/siren, 1930s, 14-1/2"	350	525	700
Ambulance, "M.D. War Dept.," 1930s	450	675	900
American Tractor w/implements, 1920s, 10" long	200	300	400
Armored Trucking Co.	150	225	300
Army Dive Bomber No. 482	137	205	275
Army Staff Car, 1930s, litho steel	250	375	500
Army Staff Car, w/flasher and siren, W-601158, 1940s, 11" long	135	200	300

Beat It The Komical Kop, Marx, $920

	C6	C8	C10
Army Truck, cloth cover, 1930s, 10"	300	450	600
Automatic Car Wash, w/wind-up car, 6"	200	300	400
Automatic Fire House, 1950s, Fire Chief Car, 7-1/2" long, Volunteer Fire Dept. Garage, 19" long	200	300	400
Automatic Reversing Road Roller, 1925, 9" long	200	300	400
Balky Mule, 1950s, 8" long	100	150	200
Balky Mule, pre-war	125	165	250
Be Bop-The Jivin' Jigger, 1948, 10"	210	325	425
Bear Cyclist, 1930s, 6" long	163	245	325
Beat It The Komikal Kop, 1930s	460	690	920
Big Lizzie Car, early 1930s, 7-1/4"	150	225	300
Big Parade, w/moving vehicles, soldiers, tin airplane, etc., 1929, 24" long	313	470	625
Big Silver, Mack Dump Truck	250	375	500
Big Three Aerial Acrobats, 1920	200	300	400
Boy on Trapeze	100	150	200
Bulldozer Climbing Tractor, caterpillar type, c. 1950s, 10-1/2" long	150	225	300
Bumper Auto, streamlined, c. 1939, large bumpers, front and rear	150	225	300
Busy Bridge, vehicles on bridge, 1935	350	525	700
Busy Delivery (Black Pinocchio), 1930s, 9" long, 8" high	675	1015	1350
Busy Miners, 1930s, includes 2-1/4" tin litho miner's car, 16-1/2" long	150	225	300
Busy Parking Station, 1930s, 17" long w/2" tin race car	200	300	400
Butter & Egg Man, 1930s, 8" high	525	775	1000
Cadillac Coupe, 1931	500	750	1150
Cadillac Roadster, trunk w/tools on luggage carrier, 1930, 13" long	250	375	500
Car Carrier, three racers, 22-3/4" long	1000	1600	2200
Careful Johnnie, 1950s, 5-1/2" long	100	150	200
Cat w/ball in front and two wheels in back, c. 1938: see "Roll Over Cat"			
Caterpillar Climbing Tractor, c. 1950s, 10" long	100	150	200
Charleston Trio, one black adult, black child dancer and dog, 1921	500	750	1000
Chicken Snatcher, black holding chicken, dog biting at the seat of his pants, c. 1927	650	950	1250
Climbing Tractor, sparkling, 1960s, 8-1/2" long	112	168	225
Climbing, Fighting Tank	125	188	250
Coast Defense, circular, w/three cannon, revolving airplane, 1929	450	685	925
Coast to Coast Greyhound Bus, 1930s	500	850	1200
Coke Coal City Coal Co. Truck	500	800	1150
Construction Tractor	300	450	600
Coo Coo Car, 1920s, 7-1/2" long	300	425	550

	C6	C8	C10
Cowboy Rider, cowboy w/lariat on dapple or black horse, c. 1941 157		235	315
Crazy Dora nodder head (also "Dan")...... 100		150	200
Cross-Country Flyer, Zeppelin and Airplane fly around 18" hangar tower, 1920 400		600	800
Dan Dipsy Car, 1950s, (plastic nodder), 5-1/2" long 200		300	400
Dapper Dan Coon Jigger, 1910 600		900	1300
Dare Devil Flyer, new in 1928 400		600	800
Daredevil Motor Drome, w/2" wind-up car, 1930s, 5-1/2" high, 9" diameter 100		150	200
Deluxe Delivery Truck, 1950s, 11" 100		150	200
Deluxe Tractor, six wheels, four in treads 250		375	500
Dipsy Doodle Bug Dodgem cars (Dan or Dora), 6" high (pair) 262		395	525
Donkey pulling cart, w/rider, 1950s, 10" long 110		165	220
Dora Dipsy Car, 1950s, (plastic nodder), 5-1/2" long 100		150	200
Dottie the Driver, 1950s, 6-1/2" 100		150	200
Doughboy Tank, no side turrets 118		175	235
Doughboy Tank, two side turrets, w/top turret, 1930, soldier w/gun pops out, 9-1/4" long 175		250	325
Driver Training Car, 1950s, 6" long 75		110	150
Drive-UR-Self Car, 1950s, 11" long 325		488	650
Dump Truck, 13" long 425		638	850
Fire Dept. Chief, c. 1950s, 11" long 150		200	250
Firemen Joe, 1930s, 8" tall 125		188	250
Firewater Boat, 1920, 9" long 350		525	700
Flipo the Jumping Dog, See Me Jump, on hind legs, c. 1940, 3-1/2" x 4" 125		175	225
Flying Fortress 2095 sparkling aeroplane, 1940s 225		338	450

	C6	C8	C10
Funny Face, new in 1928 500		750	1000
Funny Flivver, c. 1925 325		490	650
George the Drummer Boy, w/stationary eyes, No. 881, 1930s, 9" tall 125		175	225
George the Drummer Boy, w/moving eyes, 1930s, 9" tall 150		225	300
Ghee Whiz Auto Racer, 1930s, four 2" long tin cars, 13" diameter 450		700	1000
Giant King Racer, c. 1930s, marked "711" 150		225	300
Giant Reversing Tractor Truck w/tools, "Hauling," c. 1950s, 14" long 140		210	280
G-Man Pursuit Car, 1930s 355		525	710
Golden Pecking Goose, hops along pecking at ground, dated July 8, 1924, 9-1/2" long 100		150	200
Hauling Tractor Truck, six-wheel 200		300	400
Hee-Haw balky mule, 1929, six-color litho, goes backward, forward and rears, farmer and his dog on seat and five milk cans in cart, 10-3/4" long 200		300	400
Helicopter Skyport, 1950s, two plastic copters, 9" x 11" 100		150	200
Highboy Climbing Tractor, c. 1950s, 10-1/2" long 75		112	150
Highboy Tractor, sparkles, c. 1950s, 10" long 100		150	200
Honeymoon Cottage 125		188	250
Honeymoon Express, c. 1940, circling train and plane, 9-3/8" diameter 125		200	250
Honeymoon Express, c. late 1930s 100		150	200
Honeymoon Express, streamlined train on circular track, 1947, 9-3/8" 85		125	175
Hoppo the Waltzing Monkey w/Cymbals, 1930s, 9-1/2" high 200		300	400
Ice Man 300		450	600
Jalopy Pickup Truck, 7" 80		120	160
Jazzbo Jim, 1920s, 9" high 275		400	550
Jolly Joe Jeep, 1940s, plastic helmet, 6" long 188		293	375
Joy-Rider 1929, College Boy driver w/bag, wording on car "goes backward, forward, circles and rears" head moves, 8" long 310		475	625
Jumpin' Jeep, c. WWII, 6" 135		210	275
King Racer, 1930s, 8-1/2" long 325		490	650
Let the Drummer Boy Play, 1930s, 8-1/2" high 438		658	875
Light Duty Climbing Tractor, 1930s 162		243	325
Limping Lizzie Car 200		300	400
Looping Plane, No. 182 200		300	400
Looping Plane, No. 382 200		300	400
Lucky Stunt Flyer 200		300	400
Mack Dump Truck, 1930s, (City Coal Co.), 13" long 350		525	700

Doughboy Tank, no side turrets, Marx, $235

Piggy, Marx, $100

	C6	C8	C10
Main Street, moving vehicles, traffic cop, etc., 1929	350	525	700
Mammy's Boy, 1930s, 11" tall	500	750	1000
Mechanical Airplane	200	300	400
Mechanical Roadster, 1950s, 11"	100	150	200
Mechanical Speed Racer, 1930s, 9" long	100	150	200
Mechanical Speedway Racer	75	110	150
Mechanical Station Wagon	125	188	250
Mechanical Taxi Cab, 1950s, 11"	80	120	160
Mechanical Tractor w/Earth Grader, c. 1950s, 21-1/2" long	107	160	215
Mechanical Tractor, c. 1930s, 6"	110	165	220
Merrymakers, four mice, three in band andone dancer, 1929, w/marquee	750	1250	1725
Merrymakers, four mice, three in band and one dancer, 1929, w/o marquee, has conductor with baton	500	825	1175
Merrymakers, four mice, three in band andone dancer, 1929, w/o marquee, has violinist	600	950	1300
Midget Climbing Fighting Tank, c. 1935, Pat. No. 1334539, 5-1/2" long	65	98	130
Midget Climbing Tractor, c. 1950, 5-1/2" long	70	105	140
Midget Racer, 1950s, plastic, 6"	50	75	100
Midget Special, race car driver in old headgear and goggles, No. 2 racer, 1930s, 5" long	75	110	150

	C6	C8	C10
Midget Special, race car driver in old headgear and goggles, No. 7 racer, 1930s, 5" long	75	110	150
Monkey Cyclist, 1930s	100	150	200
Moon Creature, 1950s, (Japan) 5-1/2" high	90	135	180
Motor Squad, sidecar	240	360	480
Motorcycle Trooper, 1935	212	318	425
Mountain Climber, 1960s (Japan), 32" long, 4" car	80	120	160
Mysterious Kitty Kat, 1950s, 8"	90	135	180
Mystery Police Cycle, 1930s, 4-1/2"	125	175	250
Mystery Tunnel	60	90	120
Mystic Motorcycle, c. 1930s	150	225	300
New Flivver, 1920s, 7" long	200	300	400
New Rocket Racer, 1930s, 16"	200	300	400
New York, circular, w/train, new in 1928, tin airplane, 9-1/2" diameter	600	900	1200
Nodding Goose	75	120	150
North American Van Lines Inc. Long Distance Moving Truck	125	188	250
Old Jalopy, college boys, post-WWII	150	225	300
Old Jalopy, small, 1950s, Linemar	150	210	300
P.D. Motorcyclist, Pat. No. 2001625, 4" long	165	240	325
P.D. Police motorcycle w/sidecar, wood wheels, on-off lever, 1930s, 3-1/2" long	165	240	325
Parade Drummer, 1930s, marked "Let the Drummer Boy Play While You Swing and Sway"	400	600	800
Parcel Post U.S. Mail, early, 8-1/2" long	225	338	450
Peter Rabbit, eccentric car	300	450	600
Piggy, 4" high	50	75	100
Pike's Peak Mountain Climber, 1930s, 3-1/2" tin car, 30" long	300	450	600
Pinched Roadster, motorcycle cop in circular track, c. 1927, 9-1/2" x 9-1/2"	325	488	650
Play-Away-Piano, 1930s, w/songbook, 9" x 9"	60	90	120
Police Patrol, motorcycle w/sidecar, 1935	300	450	600
Police Precinct Police Patrol armored truck, c. early 1930s, 10-1/2"	1800	2800	3800
Police Siren Motorcycle, 1930s, 8" long	200	300	400
Police Squad, motorcycle cop w/sidecar, 8-1/2" long	275	400	550
Power Snap Caterpillar Climbing Tractor, 1950s, 8" long	112	168	225
Prone WW I Soldier, 1925, 8" long	100	150	200
Racer No. 2, 1930s, 5" long	75	110	150
Racer No. 3, 1930s, 5" long	75	110	150

Ride 'em Cowboy, Marx, $240

	C6	C8	C10
Racer No. 4, 1930s, 5" long	75	110	150
Racer No. 5, 1930s, 5" long	75	110	150
Racer No. 7, 1930s, 5" long	75	110	150
Racing Car, "27," plastic driver, litho, c. 1950	100	150	200
Racing Car, c. 1940, two-man team, litho, 12"	110	165	220
Racing Car, c. 1950, plastic driver, litho, 16" long	125	188	250
Range Rider, 1940s, 10-1/2" high on rocker base	200	300	400
Range Rider, 1940s, 8-1/2" high	150	225	300
Red Cap Porter	350	550	750
Red Devil Stunt Auto, 1930s, 12" long ramp w/2-1/2" tin racer	150	225	300
Reversible Coupe, marked "The Marvel Car,"c. 1938, 16-3/4" long	248	372	495
Reversing Road Roller	135	202	270
Reversing Tank, 1930s	65	98	130
Reversing Tractor	275	412	550
Rex Mars Planet Patrol, 1950s, pastel colors, 9-1/2" long	250	375	500
Rex Race Car, 1920s	162	243	325
Ride 'Em Cowboy	120	180	240
Ring-A-Ling Circus, early ringmaster and circus animals, green base	550	825	1280
Ring-A-Ling Circus, early ringmaster and circus animals, pink base	550	850	1300
Road Roller, w/driver, c. 1930, 8-1/2" long	375	562	750
Rocket Fighter, c. 1950s, complete w/tail fin and sparking mechanism	225	350	475

	C6	C8	C10
Rocket Racer, 1930, 16-1/2" long	225	350	475
Rodeo Joe, 1933	200	300	400
Roll Over Cat	65	98	130
Roll Over Plane, c. 1920s	138	205	275
Rollover Plane, c. 1940	112	168	225
Rollover Tank	55	83	110
Rookie Cop w/siren, 1930s, 8-1/2"	233	350	465
Rookie Pilot, No. 77, c. 1940, 7" long	295	445	590
Rooster Pulling Wagon, 1930s	60	90	120
Royal Bus Line, 10" long	275	410	550
Royal Coupe, 1920s, 9" long	350	525	700
Royal Van Co., marked "We Haul Anywhere," 9" long	375	562	750
Running Scottie, 1940s, 5-1/2" long	115	172	230
Safe Driving School: See Driver Training Car			
Sam, the Gardner, includes six plastic tools, 1950s, 8" tall,	125	175	235
Sand and Gravel Truck-Builders Supply Co., 1920	100	150	200
Scenic Express Train Set, c. 1950s	90	135	180
Sheriff Sam & His Whoopee Car, 1960s, 6" long	200	300	400
Single Track Speedway, 1938, eight track sections, 4" long wind-up car	70	105	140
Sky Hawk Airport Tower, No. 333, two planes, tower 7-1/2" high	175	263	350
Skybird Flyer, new c. 1927	187	280	375
Skyscraper Go-Round, 1930s, monoplane, Zeppelin, 13-1/2" high	400	600	800
Smoky Joe, The Climbing Fireman, 1930s	178	270	355
Smoky Sam, The Wild Fireman	138	210	275
Snoopy and Gus Hook and Ladder, 8" x 7-1/4"	700	1100	1550
Soap Box Derby Racer, marked "#3," 5-1/2" long	100	150	200
Soldier, prone, firing rifle, WWI helmet	90	135	180
Space Mobile, 1960s (Japan), 32" long, 4" long car	120	180	240
Space Satellite w/Launching Station, 1950s, 9" x 12" base and plastic accessories	70	105	140
Sparkling Climbing Bulldozer Tractor, later	187	280	375
Sparkling Climbing Fighting Tank, cannon recoils	125	188	250
Sparkling Climbing Tank, 1939	85	128	170
Sparkling Climbing Tractor and Trailer, c. 1950s, 16" long	130	195	260
Sparkling Climbing Tractor, 1940s	93	140	185
Sparkling Climbing Tractor, c. 1950s, 8-1/2" long	88	135	175
Sparkling Heavy Duty Bulldog Tractor w/Road Scraper, c. 1950s, 11"	115	162	230
Sparkling Luxury Liner, 1950s, 14" long	85	128	170

Tom Tom Jungle Boy, Marx, $200

	C6	C8	C10
Sparkling Mountain Climber Train Set, 1950s, tin loco and car, 9" long	100	150	200
Sparkling Rocket Fighter Ship	425	638	850
Sparkling Soldier Motorcycle, c. 1940	350	500	675
Sparkling Soldier, crawls, 7-3/4" long	150	225	300
Sparkling Space Tank	187	280	375
Sparkling Super Power Tank, c. 1950s, 9-1/2" long	115	172	230
Sparkling Tank, 4" long	95	142	190
Sparkling Tractor and Trailer Set "Marbrook Farms," c. 1950s, 21" long	100	150	200
Sparkling Tractor, tractor w/plow blade, 1939	140	210	280
Sparkling Turn Over Tank	50	75	100
Sparkling Warship (same as U.S.S. Washington), 14" long	90	135	180
Speed Boy Delivery motorcycle delivery, battery-operated lights, 1930s, 9-3/4" long	350	475	600
Speed Boy Delivery motorcycle delivery, no lights, 1930s, 9-3/4" long,	300	400	550
Speed King Racer, 1930s, 16" long	425	638	850
Speedway Coupe, battery to be inserted for headlights, 8" long	312	468	625
Spic and Span, the Hams What Am, drummer and dancer, 1924	1000	1600	2250
Spic Coon Drummer, 1924, 8-1/2" high	900	1400	2000
Streamline Speedway, tin figure-eight track, two wind-up cars), 1938, 31" long	118	175	235
Streamlined Coupe	225	338	450

	C6	C8	C10
Subway Express w/plastic tunnel 1950s, 9-3/8" diameter	90	135	180
Super Streamline Racer, 1950s, 17" long	138	207	275
Tidy Tim Streetcleaner, pushing wagon, 1933, 7-1/2" high, 8-1/2" long	350	500	700
Tom Tom Jungle Boy	100	150	200
Toto Acrobat	100	150	200
Tower Aeroplane, 1940s, two 3" tin airplanes, 7-1/2" high	200	300	400
Toy Town Dairy, horsedrawn cart, 1930s, 10-1/2" long	150	225	300
Toyland Farm Products, milk wagon, 1930s, 10-1/2" long	295	450	590
Tractor and Trailer, c. 1950s, 16-1/2" long	150	225	300
Tractor, early 1940s	105	158	210
Trans-Atlantic Zeppelin, 1930s, rear propeller, 10" long	250	375	500
Tricky Fire Chief, 1925, 4" car on 6" x 10" base	200	300	400
Tricky Motorcycle, 1930s, non-fail action, 4-1/4" long	150	225	300
Tricky Taxi On A Busy Street	175	262	350
Tricky Taxi, 1940s, 4-1/2" long	100	140	200

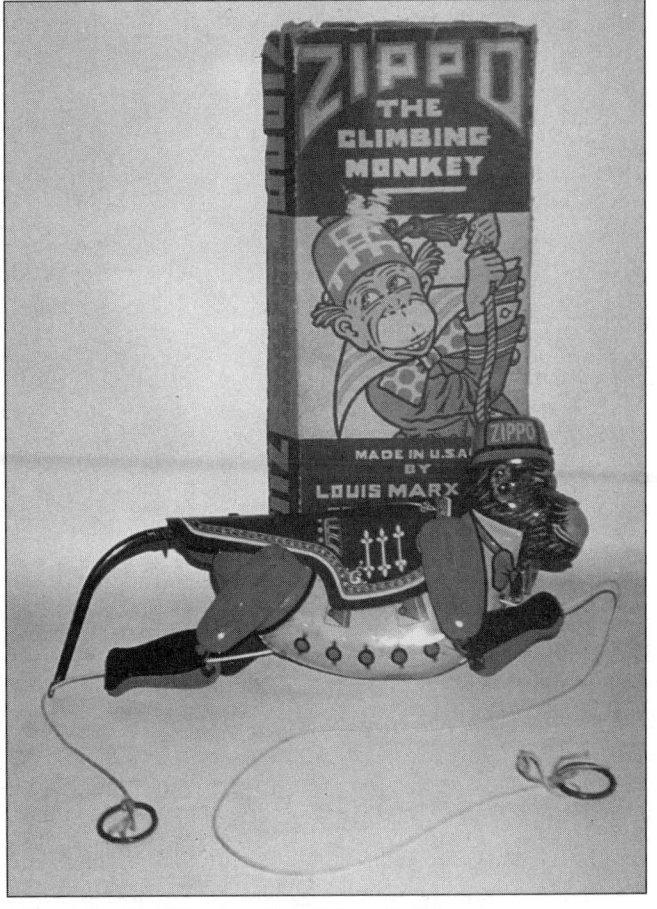

Zippo the Climbing Monkey, Marx, $175

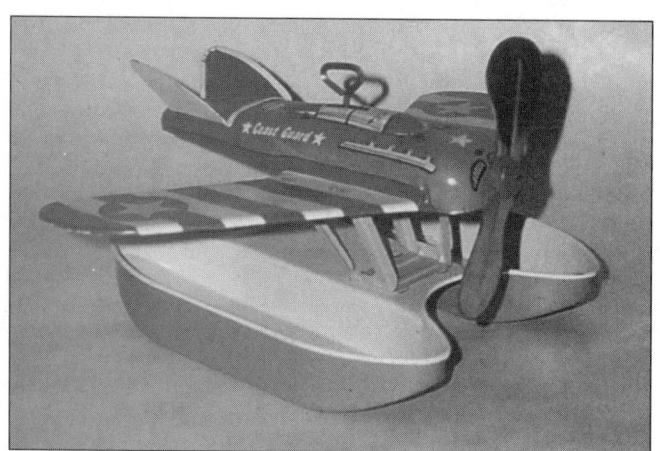

Coast Guard Seaplane, Ohio Art, $145

	C6	C8	C10
Trolley, headlight, bell, 9" long 170		255	340
Tumbling Monkey on Trapeze, 1920s, 6" high 100		150	200
Tumbling Monkey, 1930s, on two chairs, 5" high 110		165	220
Turn Over Tank No. 3 105		158	210
TWA-U.S. Mail-990, c. 1941, 5" 120		180	240
U.S. Army bomber, two-engine, post-war, 1940s 162		243	325
U.S. Army Fighter Plane, 1940, 8" wingspan 185		280	370
U.S. Mail Truck, 9-1/2" long 450		680	975
U.S. Mail-TWA Biplane, 1930s, 15" long, 18" wingspan 400		600	800
U.S.S. Washington Battleship 65		98	130
Vacationland Express 75		100	125
Wacky Taxi 110		165	220
Walking Clancy 400		600	800
Walking Drummer Boy, marked "Let The Drummer Boy Play While You Swing and Sway," c. 1939 350		525	700
Wee Scottie, 5" long 88		130	175
Whoopee Car w/Flappers, 7-1/2" long 250		375	500
Whoopee Car, "Yale-Princeton" pennants on wheels 350		525	700
Whoopee Car, laughing cows on wheels, driver looks like cowboy, 1929 200		300	400
Wonder Cyclist, 1930s, 9" high 170		255	340
Xylophonist, 5" 100		150	200
Yellow Cab-LMN 52, 1940s, 6-1/2" long... 150		225	300
Zeppelin TransAtlantic, 10" long 162		243	325
Zeppelin, 10" long 162		243	325
Zeppelin, 1930s, 27" long 200		300	400
Zeppelin, propeller on front, 1925, 11" long 175		263	350
Zippo, The Climbing Monkey, 1930s, 9-1/2" long 100		135	175

Giant Ride Ferris Wheel, Marx, $500

OHIO ART

	C6	C8	C10
Automatic Airport, 1940s, 9" high 90		135	180
Boat, 14" long 80		120	160
Cabin Cruiser, 15" long 58		88	115
Circus Shooting Gallery, 1950s, 12" high, 17" long 60		90	120
Coast Guard Seaplane, 1950s, 10" wingspan 72		108	145
Commando Joe, 1950s, 8" long 118		175	235
Giant Ride Ferris Wheel, 1950s, 16" high..... 275		375	500
Hot Job Floatplane 92		138	185
Injun Chief, 1950s, 8" long 80		120	160
Jungle Eyes Shooting Gallery, 1950s, 18" long, 14" high 90		135	180
Mechanical Sea Plane 100		150	200
Musical Sail Away Ride 200		300	400
Sea Patrol Seaplane, 10" wingspan 90		135	180
Switch and Dump Train, 1950s, 28" long..... 100		150	200
Traffic Control, 1950s, tin wind-up cars, 3-1/2" long, base 19" x 13" 60		90	120

Examico 4001, Schuco, $150

SCHUCO

Schuco was founded in 1912 by Heinrich Muller and Herr Schreyer as Schreyer and Co. They later adopted the name "Schuco" as its trademark. Schuco toys were produced from the 1930s to the 1950s and were marked either "Germany" or "U.S. Zone-Germany." Toys with other markings are reissues.

	C6	C8	C10
Akustico 2002, 1940s, 5-1/2" long	87	130	175
Anno 2000, 1940s, 5-1/2" long	80	120	160
Beer Drinker, 1950s, 5-1/2" high	100	150	200
Buick, No. 5311, 9" long	200	300	400
Cadillac DeVille Convertible 5505, plastic, 1960s, 11" long	90	135	180
Charly 1005, 1950s, motorcycle w/driver, 3-1/2" long	400	550	700
Clown Juggler, No. 965, 1950s, 5" high	300	450	600
Combination 4003, 1950s, w/wind-up horn, 7-1/2" long	175	263	350
Commando Auto No. 2000, 1950s, 5-3/4" long, responds to whistle	150	225	300
Curvo 1000, 1950s, 5" long	138	200	275
Dalli 1011 1950s, tin car w/plastic driver, 6-1/2" long	162	243	325
Disneyland Alweg Monorail, play set, 1950s	300	450	600
Electro Ingenico, play set No. 5311/61, 1950s, 8-1/2" long car	600	900	1200
Electro Submarine No. 5552, 1950s, 13" long	90	135	180
Elektro Ingenico 5311, remote control, 1950s, 8-1/2" long	180	270	360

Micro Racer 1040, Schuco, $150

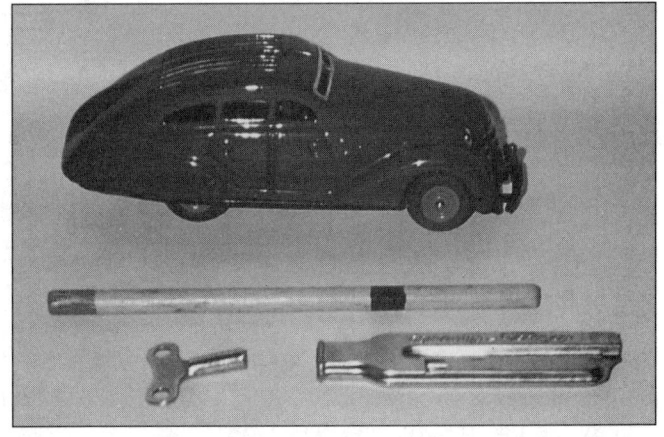

Magico Auto 2008, Schuco, $600

	C6	C8	C10
Examico 4001, 1950s, five-speed BMW, 6" long	75	110	150
Fernlenk Auto, No. 3000, part of playset, 1950s, 4-1/4" long,	160	240	320
Fex 1111, 1950s, 6" long	100	150	200
Fire Engine, w/remote control, 1950s, 11-1/8" long,	1000	1500	2000
Fox and Goose, No. 969, 1950s, 4-1/4" high	800	1200	1600
Gas Station 3054, 1950s, 8" long	60	90	120
Grand Prix Racer 1070, 1950s, 6"	100	150	200
Hegi-Fipsi 110, glider airplane kit, 1950	70	105	140
Hopsa, 1950s, 4" high	120	180	240
Ingenico 5311/56-MK, part of play set 1950, 8-1/4" long car	500	750	1000
Ingenico 5335 MK, play set, 1950s, 8" long car	700	1050	1400
Jaguar 1250, 1940s, 5-1/2" long	160	240	320
Kommando Anno 2000, 1940s, 5-1/2" long	100	150	200
Latso 3042, 1950s, truck, 4-1/2"	60	90	120
Magico Alpha Romeo No. 2010, 1950s, 9-1/2" long	600	900	1200
Magico Auto 2008, 1950s, responds to blowing, 5-1/2" long	300	450	600
Magico Car and Garage, 1950s, 6"	120	180	240
Mercedes 190SL, 2095, 1950s, 8"	225	338	450
Mercedes TYP SSK 1928, 1950s, 4" long	100	150	200
Mercer Auto 1225, 1950s, 7-1/2"	100	150	200
Micro Racer '57 Ford 1045, 1950s, 4" long	100	150	200
Micro Racer 101, 1950s, Porsche style, 3-1/2" long	100	150	200
Micro Racer 102, Indy style, 1950s, 3-1/2" long	100	150	200
Micro Racer 1036, 1950s, 4-1/2"	100	150	200
Micro Racer 1040, 1950s, 4" long	75	112	150
Micro Racer 1041, 1950s, 4" long	75	110	150

	C6	C8	C10
Micro Racer 1042, 1950s, 4" long 100	150	200
Micro Racer 1043, 1950s, 4" long 100	150	200
Micro Racer Apha Romeo 1048, 1950s, 4" long..................................... 100	150	200
Micro Racer Go Kart 1035, 1950s, 4" long..................................... 100	150	200
Micro Racer Hot Rod 1036, 1950s, 4" long.................................... 90	135	180
Micro Racer Mercedes Benz 1044, 1950s, 4" long..................................... 110	165	220
Micro Racer Mercedes-Benz 1038, 1950s, 4" long..................................... 100	150	200
Micro Racer Mercer 1036/1, 1950s, 4" long..................................... 100	150	200
Micro Racer Porsche 1047, 1950s, 4" long..................................... 110	165	220
Micro Racer Rally 1034, eight three-lane tracks,1950s, 10'6" long 60	90	120
Micro Racer Stake Truck 1049, 1950s, 4" long..................................... 100	150	200
Micro Racer Volkswagen 1046, 1950s, 4" long..................................... 100	150	200
Micro Racer Volkswagen Polizei 1039, 1950s, 4" long 100	150	200
Micro-Jet 1030 Thunderjet, 1950s, 5" wingspan, 5-1/2" long 80	120	160
Micro-Jet 1031 Magister 170R, 1950s, 5" wingspan, 5-1/2" long 80	120	160
Micro-Jet 1032 Super Sabre F 100, 1950s, 5" wingspan, 5-1/2" long............. 90	135	180
Micro-Jet 1033 Douglas F4 D-1, 1950s, 5" wingspan, 5-1/2" long 80	120	160
Mikifex 922, non-fall action mouse, 1950s, 3-1/2" long 40	60	80
Mirakocar 1001, 1950s, non-fall action, 4-1/2" long................................ 75	100	125

Synchromatic 5700, Schuco, $1,000

	C6	C8	C10
Mirakomot 1012, 1950s, non-fall action, 5-1/4" long............................... 300	450	600
Mirako-Peter, No. 1013, 1950s, 5" long, rare... 1000	1500	2000
Monkey Car, 1930s, orange-black, smiling monkey, 6" long 1400	2100	2800
Motodrill 1006, 1950s, circular action, 5" long 300	450	600
Motodrill Clown 1007, 1950s, motorcycle, composition head, 5" long, rare......... 1000	1500	2000
Mystery Car 1010, non-fall action, 1950s, 5-1/2" long 100	150	200
PanAm Clipper, 533S, 19" wingspan......... 300	450	600
Patent Motorcar, 1950s, 4-1/2" long........... 100	150	200
Pick-Pick, No. 905, 1950s, 4-1/2" long...... 100	150	200
Porsche Formel II-1037, 1950s, 4-1/2" long............................... 80	120	160
Racing Boat 1015, non-fall action, 1950s, 5" long 90	135	180
Radio 4012, musical car, 1950s, 6" 200	300	400
Sonny 2005, mouse w/balloon in BMW, 1950s, 5-1/4" long 300	450	600
Spirit of St. Louis plane, Lindbergh figure, 1920s, 4" long, rare 800	1200	1600
Station Car 3118, 1950s, 4-1/2" long........... 60	90	120
Studio Racer 1050, includes tools, 1950s, 5-1/2" long 125	188	250
Submarine 3007, tin and plastic, 1950s, 12" long 113	170	225
Synchromatic 5700, resembles Packard Hawk, 1950s, 11" long 500	750	1000
Telesteering 3000 Limo, 1950s, 4" long....... 75	100	125
Tippy, No. 990, Scotty, 1950s, 4" long......... 80	120	160
Trip-Trap, dog, 1950s, 7" long 400	600	800
Turn Miki Clown, 1950s, 3-3/4" high 200	300	400
Varianto 3010 Super, service station, 1950s, w/two 4-1/2" cars...................... 170	225	340
Varianto 3010, two-car play set, 1950s, cars are 4-1/2" long, ... 100	150	200
Varianto 3010/0, truck and garage, 1950s, 4-1/2" long............................... 75	100	125
Varianto 3041 Limo, 1950s, 4" long 100	150	200

Motodrill Clown 1007, Schuco, $2,000

Merrymakers with Marquee, Marx, $1,725

Jazzbo Jim the Dancer on the Roof, Strauss, 1910, $725

Climbing Fireman, Marx, 1950s, $350

	C6	C8	C10
Varianto 3064, all plastic, 1950s, 8" long.....	30	45	60
Varianto Box 3010/30, includes tin garage and 3041 Limo, 1950s, 4-1/2" long	135	200	250
Varianto Bus 3044, 1950s, 4" long	70	105	140
Varianto Electro 3112, truck, 1950s, 4" long....	75	100	125
Varianto Electro 3112u, truck, 1950s, 4-1/2" long....	75	100	125
Varianto Lasto, No. 3042, truck 1950s, 4-1/4" long....	80	120	160

STRAUSS

Ferdinand Strauss emigrated to the United States from Alsace, France. He worked as a toy importer in the early 1900s and by 1914 had four New York toy shops. When World War I disrupted imports, he began to manufacture toys himself. In 1918 his company was located in East Rutherford, New Jersey, and was staffed by fifty employees. Eventually Strauss was known as "The Founder of the Mechanical Toy Industry in America." Evidently Strauss was wholly or partially out of business in the late 1920s, but later resumed production of wind-ups and other toys until at least 1941-42. He is also famous for having employed the very young Louis Marx.

	C6	C8	C10
Air Devil monoplane....	300	450	600
Alabama Coon Jigger, 9-3/4"	400	575	750
Alabama Coon Jigger-Tombo, 1918, 10-1/2" high, 3" x 5" base....	425	600	775
Aluminum Flying Airship LA 1017, 1930s, 9" long	275	362	550
Big Show Circus Truck, 9-1/2" long	600	950	1400
Big Trixo, climbing monkey, 10" long	150	225	300
Billiards Player....	300	450	600
Black Porter pulling wheelbarrow, 6-1/4"	150	225	300
Bus Deluxe, 1920s, 12" long....	550	825	1250
Check-A-Cab, 8-1/2" long....	500	750	1025

Ham and Sam the Minstrel Team, Strauss, $1,250

	C6	C8	C10
Chicago Zeppelin, 1930s, 9" long	400	600	800
Circus Wagon, containing lion and tamer, no engine compartment, 8-1/2" long ..	420	630	840
Circus Wagon, w/engine compartment, 10" long	1100	1700	2500
Dandy Jim, copyright 1921....	500	750	1100
Dizzie Lizzie....	250	375	500
Flying Airship dirigible	200	300	400
Ham and Sam The Minstrel Team, piano player and banjoist, 1921, 6-1/2" long .	600	850	1250
Haul Away Truck, No. 22, dump body......	240	360	480
Hooligans Hack....	300	450	600
Interstate Double Decker Bus, 1920, 10-1/2" long....	500	750	1000
Jackee The Hornpipe Dancer, No. 51, 8-1/2" long....	500	800	1150
Jazzbo Jim The Dancer on the Roof, 1910, 10" high	375	550	725
Jenny the Balky Mule, six-color litho, goes backward, forward and rears, farmer holding extended tin grain pail from his seat in front of mule's face to keep him moving, vegetables in cart, No. 55, 10" long....	200	300	400
Jitney Bus, 9-1/4" long	213	320	425
Jocko the Golfer....	218	327	435
Knock-Out Prize Fighters, c. 1910, No. 52, 7" high	250	375	500
Kraka Jack Car, 1920s, 5-1/2" long	150	225	300
Leaping Lena	300	450	600
Long Haulage Truck....	350	525	700
Lux-A-Cab, 8-1/2" long....	500	800	1200
Mailplane....	225	338	450
Miami Sea Sled, 1920s, w/4" dinghy attached, 10" long	238	360	475
Monkey driving three-wheel cart pulled by bulldog, 1930s, 4-1/2" high	280	420	560
Old Jalopy, The, w/four college kids	100	150	200
Play Golf, 1920s, 7" x 12" base w/5" high golfer....	275	412	550
Red Star Van	400	600	800
Red-Cap Porter, porter pushing a large trunk....	300	450	600
Rollo Chair, black man pushing boardwalk chair, marked "Stock, DRGM, December 6, 1921"	500	800	1100
Santee Claus, in sleigh w/two reindeer, 1921, 6" high	950	1425	1900
Speedwagon....	200	300	400
Standard Oil, Truck, "73"	325	488	650
Tip Top Dump Truck	500	750	1050
Tip Top man w/wheelbarrow	80	120	160

	C6	C8	C10
Tip Top Porter, No. 40, 1920s, 6" long	275	400	525
Tippy Canoe	167	250	335
Tom Twist, 1920s, 8-1/2" tall.....................	450	675	900
Travel Chiks, chickens on railroad car	362	543	725
Trikauto, No. 53..	185	278	370
Water Sprinkle Truck	450	675	900
What's It? Car, No. 53, 1925, 9-1/2" long ..	600	900	1200
Yell-O Taxi, 8-1/2" long.............................	405	610	810

TECHNOFIX

The Technofix Co., founded in Nuremberg, Germany, by Gebruder Einfalt, was engaged in German military technology during World War II. After the war, Technofix diverted its expertise to toy manufacturing. Among their toys were impressively large, three-dimensional, platform toys. These colorful items were made from stamped tin blanks and highlighted with delicate relief features that duplicated realistic outdoor-recreational themes. In the late 1950s vacuform plastic took the place of tin, and, as a result, quality declined and sales dropped. Later many Technofix toys carried the Ohio Art trademark.

	C6	C8	C10
Alpine Express #300, 1950s, (Ohio Art #614), 6-1/2" x 32" long extended, two 3" tin cars........................	120	180	240
Cable Car #303, 1950s, 7-3/4" x 18-1/2" long, two 1-3/4" long tin cars	220	330	440
Coney Island #290, 1950s, 14" x 21" long, two 3" long tin cars	115	172	230
Grand Prix, 1950s, 14" x 21" long, three 3" tin cars	140	210	280
Holiday Camp #304, 1950s, 9" x 28-1/2" long, two 3-1/2" cars	400	600	800
International Airways #309, 1950s, 9" x 28" base, 5" long plastic jet airplane...	300	450	600
Lift Garage #308, 1950s, 10-1/2" x 15" long base, three 1-3/4" tin cars	100	200	300
Motorcycle & Sidecar #225, 1950s, 7" long, 4-3/4" high..............................	200	300	400
Mystic Station #306, 1950s, 17" x 8" base..	100	125	150
Rallye, plastic base and four tin cars, 1950s, 15" x 18"	300	450	600
Rocket Express, includes two tin cars, 1950s, 14-3/4" long	220	330	440
Silver Mine Express, 1950s, 23" x 6" base, w/3" long tin car.....................................	90	135	180
Toboggan #290, 1950s, 14" x 21" long base, two 3-1/2" tin cars........................	150	225	300
Touchdown Chimp, 1950s, 3-1/2" high	140	210	280
Traffic Control, 1950s, 13" x 19" long base, three 3-1/2" tin cars	50	75	100

	C6	C8	C10
Traffic Crossing w/Police Control, 1950s, two 3" tin cars	100	150	200
Trick Motorcycle, 1950s, 7" long	300	450	600

T.P.S.

T.P.S. is the trademark of Toplay, Ltd., founded in 1956 and noted for its most unusual and unique mechanical toys. More T.P.S. toys are listed in Battery Operated section.

	C6	C8	C10
Animal Barber Shop, 1950s, 5" high	200	300	400
Animals Playland, 1950s, 9-1/4"................	120	180	240
Ball Playing Giraffe, 1950s, 8-1/2" tall.......	100	150	200
Bear Golfer, 1950s, assembled 7-1/2" long...	150	225	300
Bear Playing Ball, 1950s, 19" long, 4" high....	200	300	400
Big League Hockey Player, 1950s, 6" tall.....	150	225	300
Bo Bo the Strongman, 1950s, 6"...............	200	350	600
Bobo the Mechanical Juggling Clown, flips ball, 1950s, 6" tall	300	450	600
Bouncing Ball Dolly, 1950s, 5-1/4" tall	100	150	200
Bunny Family Parade, 1950s, 13"	50	75	100
Busy Choo Choo, 1950s, 5-1/2" x 9-1/4" base, w/2-1/4" tin locomotive	90	135	180
Busy Mouse, 1950s, 6" x 9" base, w/3-1/4" tin mouse	90	135	180
Calypso Joe, 1950s, 6" tall	300	450	600
Candy Loving Canine, 1950s, 5-1/2" high ..	90	135	180
Champ On Ice-Bear Skater Trio, rare, 9" long	400	600	800
Circus Acrobatic Seal and Ball, 5" high	80	120	160
Circus Bugler, w/trombone, 1950s, 7" tall.....	300	450	600
Circus Clown and Monkey, 1950s, 5" high	150	225	300
Circus Clown on Ball, 1950s, 5-1/2" high	150	225	300
Circus Cyclist, 1950s, 6-1/2" tall	150	225	300
Circus Parade, 1950s, 11-1/2" long............	200	300	400
Circus Parade-Juggling Duck and Friends, 1950s, 9" long..........................	150	225	300
Circus Seal, w/plastic ball on nose, 1950s, 6-1/2" high	70	105	140

Bobo the Mechanical Juggling Clown, T.P.S., $600

Champ on Ice Bear Skater Trio, T.P.S., $800

	C6	C8	C10
Cleo Clown-The Dogs, 1950s, 4-1/2" high	200	300	400
Climbing Panda, 1970s, all plastic, 6" high	40	60	80
Climbing Pirate, string climber, 1950s, 6" long	120	180	240
Climbo the Climbing Clown, string climber, 1950s, 6" long	150	225	300
Clown Jalopy Cycle, friction, 1950s, 9" long	200	300	400
Clown Juggler w/Monkey, 1950s, 9-1/2" tall	600	900	1200
Clown Juggler, 1950s, 6" tall	200	300	400
Clown Making The Lion Jump Thru The Flaming Hoop, 1950s, 4-1/2"	180	270	360
Clown on Rollerskates, 1950s, 5-3/4" tall	200	300	400
Clown Trainer and His Acrobatic Dog, 1950s, 4-1/2" high	150	225	300
Cock-A-Doodle, 1960s, 8" long	50	75	100
Combat Tank On Battle Front, 1950s, 6-1/4" x 15" base, w/2-1/4" tank	120	180	240
Comical Clara, 1950s, 5-1/2" tall	350	525	700
Coney Island Scooter, 1950s, 10" square w/2-1/2" bumper car	100	150	200
Dancing Couple, 1950s, 5-1/2" tall	100	150	200
Dreamland Airport, 1950s, 6-1/2" x 12" base w/3-1/2" tin helicopter	90	135	180
Drive Tester, 1950s, 7" x 10-1/2" base and two 2" cars	100	150	200
Duck Amphibious Taxi, 1950s, 6-1/2" long, 4-3/8" high	140	210	280
Duck Family Parade, 1950s, 12" long	70	110	140
Duck the Mailman, Turn-N-Go action, 1950s, 4-1/2" high	300	450	600
Educational Pet Pooch, 1950s, 4" high	100	150	200
Elephant Circus Parade, 1950s, 11-1/2" long, (similar to "Circus Parade")	200	300	400
Fairyland Taxi, 1950s, 11" long, (similar to "Wagon Fantasyland")	140	210	280

	C6	C8	C10
Family Giraffe Loco, locomotive w/three cars called "Kiddy," "Mammy," and "Pappy," 1950s, 11" long	150	225	300
Fishing Bear, 1950s, 7-1/2" high	100	150	200
Fishing Monkey on Whale, 1950s, 9" long	400	600	800
Flying Birds w/voice, includes two birds, 1950s, 4" diameter base	200	300	400
Gay 90s Cyclist, 1950s, 7" high	150	225	300
Girl Skipping Rope, 1950s, 12" long, 6" high	150	225	300
Girl w/Chickens, 1950s, 6" tall, 5" long	100	150	200
Happy Caterpillar, 1950s, 13" long	80	120	160
Happy Hippo, 1950s, 5-1/2" long	350	525	700
Happy Skaters, bears, 1950s, 6-1/2" tall	250	375	500
Happy Skaters, monkey, 1950s, 5-1/2" tall	250	375	500
Happy Skaters, rabbit, 1950s, 5-1/2" tall	250	375	500
Happy the Violinist, 1950s, 9" tall	150	225	300
Hockey Player, 1950s, 6" tall	150	225	300
Hungry Whale, 1950s, w/3" long small whale or fish, 5" long	50	75	100
Joe The Acrobat, 1950s, 6" tall	300	450	600
Joe The Acrobat, clown, 1950s, 5-1/2" high	150	225	300
Joe The Xylophone Player, 1950s, 5" tall	200	300	400
Jolly Wiggling Snake, 1950s, 7-1/2" long	90	135	180
Juggling Clown, 1950s, 8-1/2" tall	200	300	400
Juggling Popeye and Olive Oyl, 1950s, 9-1/2" high (marked "Linemar")	1000	1500	2000
Ladder Truck, 1950s, 2" tin fire engine on 5-1/2" x 9-1/4" base	80	120	160
Lady Bug & Tortoise with Babies, 1950s, 7" long	60	90	120
Lady Bug Family Parade, 1950s, 12" long	80	120	160
Lucky Monkey Playing Billiards, includes plastic balls, 1950s, 6" long	150	225	300
Magic Choo Choo, 1950s, 5-1/2" x 9-1/4" base w/2-1/4" tin locomotive	90	135	180
Magic Circus, 1960s, includes tin seal and monkey, 6" high	80	120	160
Magic Cross Road, 1950s, 5-1/2" x 9-1/4" base w/2-1/4" tin locomotive	90	135	180
Magic Tunnel, 1950s, 6" x 9" base w/2" tin "Dreamland Bus"	90	135	180
Mailman with Geese, 1950s, 6" tall	150	225	300
Mama Kangaroo with Playful Baby In Her Pouch, 1950s, 6" tall	100	150	200
Midget Lady Bug, 1950s, 7-1/2" tall	60	90	120
Missile Robot, 1960s, 6" high	80	120	160
Monkey Basketball Player, 1950s, 7" high	150	225	300
Monkey Golfer, 1950s, assembled 7-1/2" long	150	225	300

	C6	C8	C10
Monkey on Whale, 1950s, 4" long, 3-3/4" high	300	450	600
Mountain Climber, 1950s, (string climber), 6-1/2" long	120	180	240
Mounted Cavalryman w/Cannon, 1960s, 5-1/2" high, w/2-1/2" long tin cannon....	300	450	600
Mouse Race Cat, 1950s, 10" x 10"	90	135	180
Mr. Caterpillar, 1950s, 12" long	50	75	100
Oscar the Seal, w/four-bladed plastic propeller on nose, 1950s, 6-1/2" high ..	125	200	280
Pango Pango, 1950s, 6" tall	120	180	240
Performing Seal and Monkey w/Fish, 1950s, 4-1/2" tall	300	450	600
Plane the Loop Pilot, w/remote control, 1950s, 6" high	150	225	300
Playland Scooter, 1950s, 6" x 9" base w/2" tin car	90	135	180
Police Patrol," 1950s, 5-1/2" x 9-1/2" base and 2" tin police car	80	120	160
Pop Eye Pete, 1950s, 5-1/2" tall	350	525	700
Pussy Cat Chasing Butterfly, 1950s, 4-1/2" high	110	165	220
Rabbit and Bear Playing Ball, 1950s, 19" long, 5" high	200	300	400
Samson the Strongman, 1950s, 6" tall	250	375	500
Satellite Fleet, 1960s, 12" long	150	225	300
Seal and Monkey with Fish, 1950s, rare, 5" high, 4" long	250	375	500
Shuttle Zoo Train, 1950s, 5-1/2" x 9-1/4" base and two-piece tin train	100	150	200
Skating Chef (black), 1950s, 6"	250	375	500
Skating Chef, 1950s, 6" tall	150	225	300
Skip Rope Animals, 1950s, 8" long	110	165	220
Skippy the Tricky Cyclist, 1950s, 6" tall	150	225	300
Slim the Seal and Friends, w/four-bladed propeller on nose, 1950s, 10" long	300	450	600
Sports Car Race, w/four plastic racers 1960s, 8" x 14" base	100	150	200

	C6	C8	C10
Susie the Ostrich, 1950s, rare, 5-1/2" high	300	450	600
Suzy Bouncing Ball, 1950s, 5-1/2" tall	90	135	180
Take-off Airport, 1950s, 5-1/2" x 9-1/2" base w/3" tin airplane	80	120	160
Tippy Toy Train, 1960s, gravity action, 6" diameter, 4" high	60	90	120
Touchdown Pete, 1950s, 5" tall	170	235	340
Tricycle Tot, 1960s, 5-1/2" long	70	105	140
Trombone Player, 1950s, 5-1/4" tall	150	225	300
Tumbling Chimp, 1950s, 4-1/2"	150	225	300
Two Gun Tex, 1960s, 11" long	110	165	220
Violin Player, 1950s, 5-1/4" tall	200	300	400
Wagon Fantasyland, 1950s, 11" long	150	225	300
World Champion Auto Racer, 1950s, 5-1/2" x 9-1/2" base, 2-1/4" tin car	70	105	140

Unique Art Mfg. Co.

Unique Art Mfg. Co. began producing toys in 1916 when it introduced its Merry Juggler and Charlie Chaplin. In 1931 it was located at Waverly and Peshine Avenues in Newark, New Jersey. Its president was Wm. Marbe. In a 1946-47 directory the address was 200 Waverly Avenue in Newark, and the president was Samuel Burger.

	C6	C8	C10
Artie the Clown in his Crazy Car	300	450	600
Bombo the Monk, two-piece, tree 9-1/2" high, monkey 5-1/2" long, 1930s	100	150	200

Touchdown Pete, T.P.S., $340

Bombo the Monk, Unique Art Mfg. Co., $600

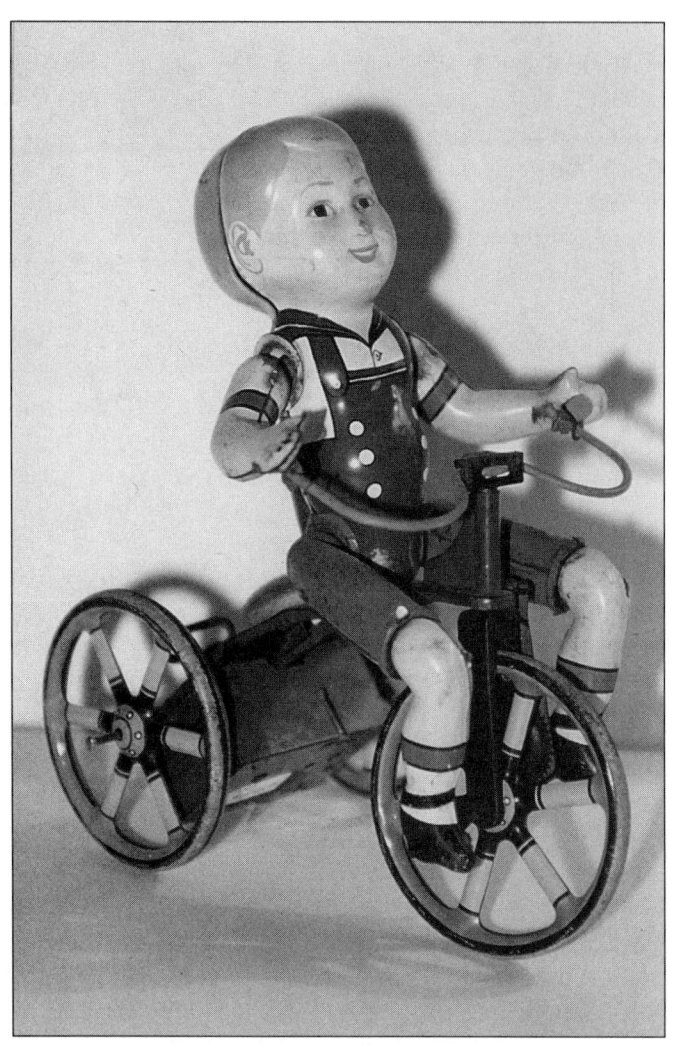

Kiddy Cyclist, Unique Art, $400

Man on the Flying Trapeze, Wyandotte, $200

LincolnTunnel, Unique Art, 1935

Daredevil Motor Cop, Unique Art Mfg Co., $600

	C6	C8	C10
Capitol Hill Racer, 1930s, 17-1/2" long, w/2" tin racing car	100	150	200
Casey the Cop, early	500	800	1200
Dandy Jim Dancer, 1921	500	750	1000
Daredevil Motor Cop, 1940s, 8-1/2" long	300	450	600
Finnegan, 1930s, w/cardboard luggage, 14" long	200	300	400
Flying Circus, elephant supports flying plane and flying clown	450	675	900
G.I. Joe and His Jouncing Jeep, post-WWII, 7"	200	275	400
G.I. Joe and the K-9 Pups, c. 1941, 9" high	150	225	300
Gertie the Galloping Goose, 1930s, 9-1/2" long	145	220	290

Jazzbo Jim The Dancer on the Roof, Unique Art Mfg Co., $500

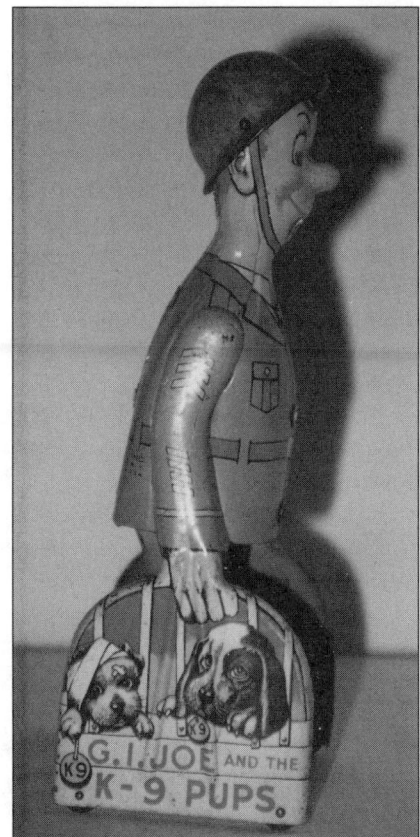

G.I. Joe and the K-9 Pups, Unique Art Mfg. Co., $300

	C6	C8	C10
Hee Haw donkey pulling milk cart, 10" long	150	225	300
Hillbilly Express, three pieces, 1930s, 3-1/4"tin locomotive, 18" long	100	150	200
Hobo Train, dog biting pants of hobo atop train, 1920s, 8-1/2"	300	450	600
Hott an' Tott musical band, 1920s	500	800	1200
Jazzbo Jim-The Dancer on the Roof, 1920s, 10" high, base 5" x 3" x 3"	250	375	500
Kiddy Cyclist, 1930s, steers figure-eight pattern and rings bell, 8-3/4" tall	200	300	400
Kid-Go-Round plastic horsemen and boat	150	225	300
Krazy Kar, new in 1921	300	450	600
Lincoln Tunnel, moving vehicles, cop, 1935, 24" long	200	300	400
Motorcycle Cop, 1930s, 9" long	300	400	500
Musical Sail-Way Carousel w/three kids in spinning plastic boats, 9" tall	170	255	340
Pecking Goose, Witch and Cat	350	525	700
Rap & Tap, boxers in ring, 1921	500	750	1000
Rodeo Joe Crazy Car	150	225	300
Rollover Motorcycle Cop, 1935	300	400	500
Sky Rangers plane and Zeppelin revolving from tower, 1933	200	300	400

Merry-Go-Round, Wolverine, $525

Carnival, Wyandotte, $850

WOLVERINE

	C6	C8	C10
Acrobat	110	165	220
Acrobatic Monkeys, No. 810, 1930s, 10" diameter base	200	300	400
Autolift, 1930s, includes 2-1/2" tin car w/four sections of track, 10-1/4" high.....	205	308	410
Drum Major, No. 27, pat. 1892546, 1930s, 13-5/8" tall on rectangular 4-1/2" x 6-1/2" base.............................	200	300	400
Drum Major, No. 27, patent 1892546, 1930s, 13-1/4" tall on circular 4-1/4" base	175	250	325
Drummer Boy, 14" high	150	250	300
Farm Wagon, 1950s, plastic, 10" long	25	38	50
Jet Roller Coaster and small car, 21" long extended	155	233	310
Loop-A-Loop, 1930s, includes small car No. 30, 19"....................................	175	262	350
Luxury Liner	100	150	200
Mechanical Man on the Flying Trapeze, 1930s, 8-1/2" high	120	180	240
Merry-Go-Round, includes four tin-litho flags, 1930s, No. 31, 11" diameter, 12" high...........................	275	400	525
Neck & Neck, 1940s, horse-racing game, 36" long	70	105	140
Pontiac Mystery Car	100	150	200
S.S. Wolverine, 14-1/2" long	100	150	200
Sandy Andy Caterpillar Tractor, Trailer, 21" long............................	500	750	1000
Sandy Andy Circus, dancing toy.................	150	225	300
Sandy Andy Tank, 14" long...........................	90	135	180
Zilotone, w/six interchangeable records, 1930s........................	323	490	645

WOODHAVEN

Research has established that in the 1930s Herman Joerger bought Animate Toy and Ranger Toys. He sold the business to his son, Herman, Jr., who in turn sold it to his son, Kurt. The firm made toys until at least 1939. It was located in Woodhaven, New York, and is now called Woodhaven Telesis Corporation, making sheet metal parts to order.

	C6	C8	C10
Robot Bus w/the Mechanical Brain, 1940s, 13-1/2" long	78	115	155
Tractor, marked "1916"	65	100	130

WYANDOTTE

	C6	C8	C10
Acrobatic Monkeys.....................................	200	300	400
Carnival, 16" x 11".....................................	425	638	850
Carousel, 5-1/4" high	150	225	300
Chicken pulling Chick in Cart, 7-1/2" long......................................	75	100	125
Duck pulling tin Easter cart, litho, wooden wheels, 15" long	50	75	100
Ducky Ducklings.....................................	90	135	180
Hoky-Poky, handcar w/two clowns...........	150	200	275
Man On The Flying Trapeze, 1930s, 9" high.......................................	100	150	200
Mechanical Handcar, 1935, 6-1/2" long....	200	300	400
Red Ranger Ride 'Em Cowboy," No. 515, 6-1/2" high	140	210	280

YONE

Yone was a Japanese manufacturer of tin wind-up and friction toys in the early to mid-1960s.

	C6	C8	C10
Bears Seesaw	130	195	260
Chef, Japanese, c. 1960s	90	135	180
Pirate, Japanese, c. 1960s	115	172	230
Soldier, Japanese, c. 1960s...........................	90	135	180

TRAINS, LIONEL

Lionel is unquestionably the greatest name in the history of toy trains. Founded in 1902 by Joshua Lionel Cowen (born August 25, 1877), it was incorporated as the Lionel Manufacturing Company on March 13.

In his teens Cowen had worked for New York's Acme Electric Lamp Company as a battery-lamp assembler, and he enjoyed experimenting in his spare time. In 1901 Cowen developed what was to become the first Lionel train—a battery-powered "Electric Express." It was originally designed to be used as a showpiece in a shop window. Customers were curious about the Electric Express, and eventually twelve of the showpieces eventually were sold. Cowen was on his way.

In 1902 Cowen added an trolley car, manufactured for him by Massachusetts' Morton E. Converse. At the same time he began adding six barrels to his Electric Express. Other accessories in first 1902 Lionel catalog included a suspension bridge, a track with a switch, a crossover track that allowed a figure-eight layout and a bumper for the end of a track. The Electric Express, like the trolley, could now be powered by batteries or electricity.

By 1909 Lionel was advertising its trains as "The Standard of the World." Cowen had a knack for advertising. Much of Lionel's early success can be attributed to the companies colorful and punchy ad campaigns and catalogs.

The next twenty years saw tremendous growth for Lionel. In 1915 O gauge cars were introduced. It eventually became the most popular scale of train. By the 1920s electricity was found in more homes, and no toy benefited more from electricity than the train. In 1927, Lionel's profits were almost a half-million dollars.

In 1930, the first full year of the Depression, Lionel's profits were down to $82,000, and in 1931 they lost $207,000. The firm temporarily went into receivership in 1934.

That same year the Streamlined Union Pacific diesel M10000 is released. Lionel orchestrates a major publicity campaign timed to coincide with the M10000's release; sales soared. It was in the fall of this year that Lionel developed the Mickey and Minnie Mouse handcar. It sold more than a quarter million units, and it is very likely the thing that saved the company from bankruptcy. By the next year his company was in the black by $154,000.

Standard Gauge was discontinued in 1940 and with the interruption of World War II, Lionel's only war years toy was a cardboard train set as it fulfilled government contracts.

Lionel's postwar line, known by many as the golden years of Lionel train, was introduced by a sixteen-page catalog contained in the November 23, 1946 issue of *Liberty* magazine. Though competition with American Flyer soon became fierce, Lionel was able to stay ahead. Bakelite and other plastics became prominent, along with such innovations as knuckle couplers, smoke units, a battery-operated diesel horn (1948) and "Mangnetraction" (Magnetized wheels and axles, which gave stronger pulling power) in the 1950s.

However, by the mid 1950s Lionel began to teeter. In 1957 Lionel introduced HO-scale trains, but that year was the last profitable one for the company. Ever sagacious, Cowen retired the next year and sold all of his Lionel stock the following year.

Cowen died at the age of 85 on September 8, 1965

No.	Year	Description	C6	C8	C10
—	1906	Half Section Straight Track, standard, (1/2S)	—	1	2
—	1906	Half Section Curved, standard, (1/2C)	—	1	2
—	1906	Straight Track, standard, (S)	—	1	2
—	1906	Curved Track, standard, (C)	—	1	2
—	1912	Racing Car Curved Track, standard, (O) thirty-six-inch diameter	28	42	55
—	1912	Racing Car Curved Track, standard, (I) thirty-inch diameter	25	38	50

No.	Year	Description	C6	C8	C10
—	1914	Transformer, (K) 150 watt	40	60	80
—	1914	Transformer, (L) seventy-five watt	10	15	20
—	1915	Curved Track, O, (O-CC) w/batteryconnections	1	2	3
—	1915	Curved Track, standard, (CC) w/battery connections	1	2	3
—	1915	Curved Track, O, (O-C)	—	—	1
—	1915	Transformer, (S) fifty watt	10	15	20
—	1915	Transformer, (Q) fifty watt	10	15	20
—	1915	Transformer, (T) seventy-five watt	10	15	20
—	1915	Racing Car Curved Track,			

No.	Year	Description	C6	C8	C10
		standard, (L) thirty-six-inch diameter	28	42	55
—	1915	Straight Track, O, (O-S)	—	—	1
—	1915	Straight Track, standard, (SC) w/battery connections	1	2	3
—	1915	Straight Track, O, (O-SC) w/battery connections	1	2	3
—	1916	Transformer, (A) forty watt	20	30	40
—	1917	Transformer, (B) fifty watt	13	23	45
—	1921	Lockton, O, (O-TC)	—	—	1
—	1921	Lockton, standard, (STC)	—	—	1
—	1922	Transformer, (C) seventy-five watt	15	25	50
—	1923	Transformer, (B) seventy-five watt	13	23	45
—	1926	Straight Track, standard, (SS) w/insulated rails	1	2	3
—	1926	Straight Track, O, (O-SS) w/insulated rails	—	—	1
—	1926	Curved Track, O, (O-CS) w/insulated rails	—	—	1
—	1930	Transformer, (F) sixty watt	10	15	20
—	1933	Curved Track, (MWC) mechanical	—	—	1
—	1933	Transformer, (U) fifty watt	10	15	20
—	1933	Straight Track, (MS) mechanical	—	—	1
—	1933	Transformer, (W) sevetny-five watt	5	8	10
—	1933	Curved Track, (MC) mechanical	—	—	1
—	1934	Square mechanical Key, (K-2) mechanical	3	5	10
—	1935	Insulated Curved Track, (SCS) mechanical	—	—	1
—	1935	Curved Track, (SMC) mechanical	—	—	1
—	1937	Track Clip, standard, (CS-1)	—	—	1
—	1937	Track Clip, O, (CO-1)	—	—	1
—	1937	Steel Pins, O/standard, (O-C-18) dozen	1	—	2
—	1937	Lockton, (UTC) universal	—	—	1
—	1938	Remote Control Track, O, (RCS)	3	4	5
—	1938	Transformer, (H) seventy-five watt	10	15	20
—	1939	Transformer, (Q) seventy-five watt	7	11	14
—	1939	Transformer, (Z) 250 watt	80	120	160
—	1939	Transformer, (V) 150 watt	55	83	110
—	1939	Transformer, (R) 100 watt	25	38	50
—	1939	Transformer, (Q-90) seventy-five watt	7	11	14
—	1939	Bulb, (Q-90) eight volt, clear	—	—	1
—	1942	Transformer, (N) fifty watt	10	15	20

No.	Year	Description	C6	C8	C10
—	1946	Electronic Control, (EUC-50) instruction booklet	5	10	15
—	1946	Electronic Control Unit, (EUC-1)	40	60	80
—	1947	Lockton, O, (CTC)	—	—	1
—	1947	Transformer, (A) ninety watt	13	23	45
—	1948	Transformer, (ZW) 250 watt	118	177	235
—	1948	Transformer, (RW) 110 watt	38	56	75
—	1948	Transformer, (VW) 150 watt	40	68	135
—	1949	Remote Control Uncoupling Track, O, (UCS)	4	6	8
—	1950	Lockton, O27, (LTC) w/light	10	15	20
—	1950	Transformer, (KW) 190 watt	80	120	160
—	1953	Transformer, (TW) 115 watt	27	45	90
—	1953	Transformer, (ZW) 275 watt	72	120	240
—	1956	Transformer, (LW) 125 watt	29	48	95
—	1961	Transformer, (SW) 130 watt	55	82	110
—	1962	Fiber Pins, O, (T-011-43) dozen	—	—	1
—	1962	Curved Track, O, (TOC)	—	—	1
—	1962	Steel Pins, O, (TOC-51) dozen	—	—	1
—	1962	Straight Track, O, (TOS)	—	—	1
—	1962	90 degrees Crossing, O, (T-020)	4	6	8
—	1962	Remote Control Switches, O, (T-022)	35	53	70
—	1966	Half Section Curved Track, O, (TOC-1/2)	—	—	1
—	1966	Half Section Straight Track, O, (TOS-1/2)	—	—	1

00-1

No.	Year	Description	C6	C8	C10
	1938-42	Loco, OO, steam, 4-6-4 Hudson full scale three-rail w/either 001T tender w/o whistle or 001W w/whistle	120	200	400

00-2

| | 1938-1942 | Loco, OO, steam, 4-6-4 Hudson, semi-scale three-rail w/either OO2T Tender w/o whistle or OO2W | 105 | 175 | 350 |

002W

| | | Tender, w/whistle | 120 | 200 | 400 |

00-3

| | 1938-1942 | Loco, OO, steam, 4-6-4 Hudson semi-scale three-rail w/either 002T Tender w/o whistle or 002W w/whistle | 120 | 200 | 400 |

00-4

| | 1938-1942 | Loco, OO, steam, 4-6-4 Hudson semi-scale two-rail | | | |

No.	Year	Description	C6	C8	C10
		w/either 004T Tender w/o whistle or 004W w/whistle	120	200	400
00-14					
	1938	Box, OO, yellow, Tuscan	24	40	80
00-15					
	1938	Tank, OO	27	45	90
00-16					
	1938	Hopper, OO	66	110	220
00-17					
	1938	Caboose, OO	25	41	82
00-24					
	1939	Box, OO	20	32	65
00-25					
	1939	Tank, OO	30	50	100
00-27					
	1939	Caboose, OO	21	35	70
00-31					
	1939	Curved Track, OO, two-rail	3	5	6
00-32					
	1939	Straight Track, OO, two-rail	5	10	15
00-34					
	1939	Curved Track Connection, OO	3	4	5
00-44					
	1939	Box, OO	25	42	85
00-44K					
	1939	Kit, OO, original box	110	165	220
00-45					
	1939	Tank, OO	21	85	70
00-45K					
	1939	Tank Kit, OO	100	150	200
00-46					
	1939	Hopper, OO	25	41	82
00-46K					
	1939	Hopper Kit, OO	100	150	200
00-47					
	1939	Caboose, OO	24	40	80
00-47K					
	1939	Caboose Kit, OO	100	150	200
00-51					
	1939	Curved Track, OO, three-rail	1	2	2
00-52					
	1939	Straight Track, OO, three-rail	6	8	10
00-54					
	1939	Curved Track Connect, OO	1	2	2
00-61					
	1938	Curved Track, OO, three-rail	3	5	6
00-62					
	1939	Straight Track, OO, three-rail	3	5	6

No.	Year	Description	C6	C8	C10
00-63					
	1939	Half Curve Track, OO, three-rail	3	5	6
00-64					
	1939	Curved Track Connection, three-rail	5	8	10
00-65					
	1939	Half Straight Track, OO, three-rail	1	2	2
00-66					
	1939	Straight Track, OO, three-rail	1	2	2
00-70					
	1939	90 Degree Crossing, OO, three-rail	8	11	15
00-72					
	1939	Switches, OO, electric, three rail, price per pair	150	225	300
00-72-70					
	1939	Bulb, O, twelve volt, yellow	—	—	1
00-74					
	1939	Box, OO, two-rail	22	38	75
00-75					
	1939	Tank, OO, two-rail	21	35	70
00-77					
	1939	Caboose, OO, two-rail	28	48	95
00-81					
	1938	KW Kit, Loco and Tender, OO, three-rail	600	900	1200
00-83					
	1939-1942	W Loco and Tender, OO, three-rail	180	300	600
00-91					
	1939	W Loco nad Tender, OO, two-rail	180	300	600
0-11					
	1933	Switches, O, electric, nonderailing, price per pair	50	75	100
0-11-11					
	1937	Fiber Pins, O	—	—	1
0-12					
	1927	Switches, O, electric	30	50	100
0-13					
	1929	Switches, O, panel board set	25	38	50
0-20					
	1915	90 Degrees Crossing, O	6	9	12
0-209					
	1934-1942	Barrels, O, wooden, set of six	17	26	35
0-20X					
	1915	45 Degrees Crossing, O	10	15	20
0-21					
	1915	Switch, O, w/light	12	18	25

No.	Year	Description	C6	C8	C10
0-22					
	1946-1949	Switches, O, Electric	26	39	52
0-23					
	1915	Bumper, O	4	6	8
0-25					
	1928	Bumper, O	17	25	35
0-27-C1					
	1949	Track Clip, O27	2	2	3
0-30					
	1931	Curved Rubber Roadbed	3	4	5
0-31					
	1931	Straight Rubber Roadbed, O	3	4	5
0-32					
	1931	Rubber Roadbed, O, ninety degree crossing	3	4	5
0-33					
	1931	Rubber Roadbed, standard O, forty-five degree crossing	3	4	5
0-33					
	1931	Rubber Roadbed, standard O, forty-five degree crossing	3	4	5
0-34					
	1931	Rubber Roadbed Switch, O	3	4	5
0-42					
	1938	Switch, O, manual, single	12	18	25
0-43					
	1929	Bild-A-Motor Gear Set, O	32	48	64
0-60					
	1929	Telegraph Pole, O, set of six	24	40	80
0-68					
	1926-1942	Warning Signal, O	7	11	14
0-69					
	1921-1935	Warning Bell, O	25	38	50
0-71					
	1929	Telegraph Poles, O, set of six	63	105	210
0-72		T-Rail, curved track, per section	2	2	3
0-77					
	1923-1939	Automatic Crossing Gate, O	20	30	40
0-78					
	1924	Train Control Block Signal, O, red or orange base	45	68	90
0-80					
	1926-1935	Semaphore, O	50	75	100
0-82					
	1927-1935	Train Control Semaphore, O	60	90	120
0-84					
	1928-1932	Semaphore, O	60	90	120
0-97					
	1934	Telegraph Pole Set, O	25	38	50
0-99					
	1930	Train Control Block, O	75	112	150
0440					
	1932	Signal Bridge, standard	235	350	470
1					
	1906-1910	Trolley, standard, motor car, four wheel, powered, "No. 1 Electric-Rapid Transit No. 1," cream body, blue roof	1260	2100	4200
1					
	1906-1910	Trolley, standard, motor car, four wheel, powered, "No. 1 Electric-Rapid Transit No. 1," white body, blue roof	1110	1850	3700
1					
	1906-1910	Trolley, standard, motor car, four wheel, powered, "No. 1 Electric-Rapid Transit No. 1," cream body, blue roof	750	1250	2500
1					
	1906-1910	Trolley, standard, motor car, four wheel, powered, "No. 1 Electric-Rapid Transit No. 1," blue body, blue roof	1050	1750	3500
1					
	1907	Trolley, standard, trailer, non-powered, cream body and blue roof	1050	1750	3500
1					
	1907	Trolley, standard, trailer, non-powered, white body and blue roof	1050	1750	3500
1					
	1928	Bild-A-Motor, O	150	225	300
1					
	1928	Bild-A-Motor, small	75	113	150
2					
	1906-1915	Trolley, standard four wheel, motor car, powered, No. 2 and doors	1050	1750	3500
2					
	1906-1915	Trolley, standard four-wheel, motor car, powered, No. 2 Electric-Rapid Transit No. 2 red body, cream windows and doors	1050	1750	3500
2					
	1906-1915	Trolley, standard, trailer, non-powered, cream body, red windows and doors	750	1250	2500
2					
	1906-1915	Trolley, standard, trailer,			

No.	Year	Description	C6	C8	C10
		non-powered, red body, cream windows and doors	750	1250	2500
2	1928	Bild-A-Motor, O, large	200	300	400
3	1906-1909	Trolley, standard, eight-wheel, motor car, powered No. 3 Electric-Rapid Transit No. 3, dark green body and roof	1350	2250	4500
3	1906-1909	Trolley, standard, eight-wheel, motor car, powered, No. 3 Electric-Rapid Transit No. 3, cream body, orange roof	1200	2000	4000
3	1906-1909	Trolley, standard, eight-wheel, motor car, powered, No. 3 Electric-Rapid Transit No. 3, light orange body, dark orange roof	1200	2000	4000
3	1906-1909	Trolley, standard, eight-wheel, trailer, non-powered, light orange body, dark orange roof	1200	2000	4000
4	1908-1910	Trolley, standard, eight-wheel, motor car, powered, double motor, No. 4 Electric-Rapid Transit No. 4, cream body and green roof	2700	4500	9000
4	1908-1910	Trolley, standard, eight-wheel, motor car, powered, double motor, No. 4 Electric-Rapid Transit No. 4, green body and roof	2700	4500	9000
4	1928-1932	Loco, O, electric 0-4-0, gray	300	500	1000
4	1928-1932	Loco, O, electric 0-4-0, orange	270	450	900
4U	1928	Loco, O, electric 0-4-0 "You build it," orange only, unassembled and complete w/instructions in original box	850	1275	1700
5	1906-1910	Trolley, standard, four-wheel, motor car, powered, No. 1			

No.	Year	Description	C6	C8	C10
		Electric-Rapid Transit No. 1, cream body, orange roof	1200	2000	4000
5	1906-1926	Loco, standard, steam 0-4-0, no tender, black cab and boiler, red window trim, "B&ORR"	360	600	1200
5	1906-1926	Loco, standard, steam 0-4-0, no tender, black cab and boiler, red window trim, "Pennsylvania"	900	1500	3000
5	1906-1926	Loco, standard, steam 0-4-0, no tender, black cab and boiler, red window trim, "NYC&HRRR"	780	1300	2600
5	1910-1911	Special Loco, standard, steam no tender, 0-4-0, black cab and boiler, red window trim w/tender	450	750	1500
5C		Test Set	1500	2500	4000
5D		Repair Station	800	1400	1900
6	1906-1923	Loco, standard, steam w/tender, 4-4-0 black cab and boiler, red window trim, "NYC&HRRR"	300	500	1000
6	1906-1923	Loco, standard, steam w/tender, 4-4-0 black cab and boiler, red window trim, "B&ORR"	630	1050	2100
6	1906-1923	Loco, standard, steam, w/tender, 4-4-0 black cab and boiler, red window trim, "Pennsylvania"	705	1175	2350
6	1908-1909	Loco, standard, special, steam 4-4-0 w/tender, black cab and boiler, red window trim, non-lettered	450	750	1500

No. 6 Loco. standard, 1906-1923, $1,000

No. 7 Loco, Standard, 1910-1923, $350

No.	Year	Description	C6	C8	C10
7					
	1910-1923	Loco, standard, steam 4-4-0, brass boiler, nickel cab and tender	1050	1750	3500
8					
	1908-1909	Trolley, standard eight wheel, motor car, powered, No. 8, "Pay as you enter No. 8," cream or dark green	1170	1950	3900
8					
	1925-1932	Loco, standard, electric 0-4-0, maroon	30	50	100
8					
	1925-1932	Loco, standard, electric 0-4-0, Mojave	60	100	200
8					
	1925-1932	Loco, standard, electric 0-4-0, olive	45	75	150

No.	Year	Description	C6	C8	C10
8					
	1925-1932	Loco, standard, electric 0-4-0, peacock	75	125	250
8					
	1925-1932	Loco, standard, electric 0-4-0, red	45	75	150
8E					
	1926-1932	Loco, standard, electric 0-4-0, Mojave	95	162	325
8E					
	1926-1932	Loco, standard, electric 0-4-0, olive	60	100	200
8E					
	1926-1932	Loco, standard, electric 0-4-0, pea green, cream stripe, Macy's	150	250	500
8E					
	1926-1932	Loco, standard, electric 0-4-0, peacock	110	180	360
8E					
	1926-1932	Loco, standard, electric 0-4-0, red	80	135	270
9					
	1909	Trolley, standard eight wheel, motor car, powered, No. 9, "Pay as you enter No. 9," cream or dark green	2100	3500	7000

Top, left to right: No. 341 Observation Car, standard, $300; No. 339 Pullman, standard, $90. Bottom, left to right: No. 10E Loco, standard, $280; No. 332 Railway Mail Car, $95

No.	Year	Description	C6	C8	C10
9					
	1929	Loco, standard, electric, dark green	600	1000	2000
9E					
	1928	Loco, standard, electric 0-4-0, 242, two-tone green	472	785	1575
9E					
	1931	Loco, standard, electric 2-4-2, gray	420	700	1400
9U					
	1928	Loco, standard, electric, orange, assembled	450	750	1500
9U					
	1929	Special Loco, standard, kit form w/original box, orange, unassembled	1200	1800	2400
10					
	1910	Interurban, standard, motor car, powered, "Interurban" and "New York Central Lines," lettered, "10 WB&B&A 10" and "Interurban"	1500	2500	5000
10					
	1910	Interurban, standard, motor car, powered, "Interurban" and "New York Central Lines," maroon	600	1000	2000
10					
	1925-1929	Loco, standard, electric 0-4-0, peacock blue, Mojave, gray	85	140	280
10					
	1930	Macy Loco, standard, electric, 0-4-0, red	180	300	600
10E					
	1926-1930	Loco, standard, electric, 0-4-0, brown, green frame	90	135	275
10E					
	1926-1930	Loco, standard, electric, 0-4-0, peacock or gray	74	122	245
10E					
	1926-1930	Loco, standard, electric, 0-4-0, peacock or red, w/Bild-a-Loco Motor	158	260	525
10E					
	1930	Macy Loco, standard, electric, 0-4-0, peacock w/orange stripe, uncataloged	85	140	280
11					
	1906-1926	Flat, standard	33	55	110
12					
	1906	Gondola, standard	30	50	100
13					
	1906	Cattle, standard	45	75	150
14					
	1906-1926	Box, standard	60	100	200
14					
	1920	Harmony Boxcar Creamery Special, standard, uncataloged	120	200	400
15					
	1906-1926	Oil, standard	48	80	160
16					
	1906-1926	Ballast, standard, dark green	65	108	215
17					
	1906-1926	Caboose, standard	105	175	350
18					
	1906-1910	Pullman, standard, dark olive, eighteen-inch, "New York Central Lines"	360	600	1200
18					
	1916-1917	Pullman, standard, light orange, eighteen-inch, "New York Central Lines"	360	600	1200
18					
	1918-1923	Pullman, standard, dark olive, "Parlor Car" and "New York Central Lines"	210	350	700
19					
	1906-1927	Combine, standard	180	300	600
19					
	1906-1927	Combine, standard	300	500	1000
19					
	1906-1927	Combine, standard	300	500	1000
20					
	1906	Direct, current shunt resistor	2	4	6
20					
	1909	90 Degrees Crossing, standard	6	9	12
21					
	1906	Crossing, standard	4	6	8
21					
	1915	Switch, standard, w/light	12	18	25
23					
	1906	Bumper, standard, red or black	9	13	18
24					
	1906	Station, standard	350	525	700
24					
	1915	Bulb, eight volt	—	—	1
25					
	1906	Station, standard	375	562	750
25					
	1911	Bulb, 3-1/2 volt, DC	—	—	1
25					
	1924	Bulb, pear shaped	—	—	5
25					
	1928	Bumper, standard, cream or black	20	30	40

No.	Year	Description	C6	C8	C10
26	1906	Passenger Foot Bridge, standard	100	150	200
26	1911	Bulb, fourteen volt AC	—	—	1
26	1948	Bumper, O, gray	65	98	130
26	1948	Bumper, O, red	32	48	65
27	1909	Station, standard	250	375	500
27	1911	Lighting, standard, set for cars	37	52	75
27	1927	Bulb, twelve volt, red, green or clear	—	—	1
27-6	1940	Bulb, twelve volt, clear	—	—	1
28	1927	Bulb, eighteen volt, red, green, amber or clear	—	—	1
28-3	1939	Bulb, eighteen volt, clear	—	—	1
28-6	1939	Bulb, eighteen volt, red	—	—	1
29	1909	Day Coach, standard, dark olive	112	188	375
29	1909	Day Coach, standard, maroon	180	300	375
29	1915	Bulb, 3-1/2 volt	—	—	1
29-3	1932	Bulb, eighteen volt, yellow	—	—	1
30	1915	Bulb, fourteen volt	—	—	1
30	1931	Curved Rubber Roadbed, standard	3	4	5
30	1947-1950	Water Tank, black support structure	42	70	140
30	1947-1950	Water Tank, gray support structure	39	65	130
31	1921	Combine, standard, orange, green, maroon	48	80	160
31	1931	Straight Rubber Roadbed, standard	3	4	5
31	1957	Curved Track, Super O	—	2	4
32	1910	Miniature Figures, standard, set of twelve	150	225	300
32	1921	Baggage, standard, maroon, dark olive, brown, orange	67	112	225
32	1931	Rubber Roadbed, standard, ninety degree crossing	3	4	5
32	1931	Straight Track, Super O	5	10	15
33	1913	Loco, electric, 0-6-0, engine only, dark green	240	400	800
33	1913-1924	Loco, standard, electric 0-4-0, dark olive or black	50	82	165
33	1913-1924	Loco, standard, electric 0-4-0, in gray	60	100	200
33	1913-1924	Loco, standard, electric 0-4-0, in peacock	75	125	250
33	1913-1924	Loco, standard, electric, 0-4-0, in maroon	120	200	400
33	1913-1924	Loco, standard, electric, 0-4-0, in red	150	250	500
33	1931	Rubber Roadbed, standard O, 45 degree crossing	3	4	5
33	1957	Half Curve Track, Super O	—	4	4
34	1912	Loco, standard, electric 0-6-0, dark green	150	250	500

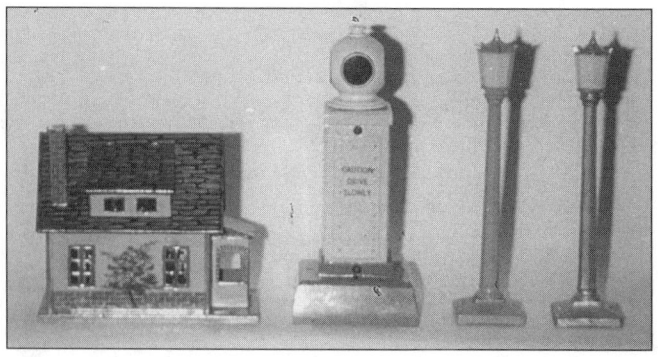

Left to Right: No. 184 Bungalow, 1923, $90; No. 78 Train Block Control Signal, standard, 1924, $80; No. 35 Lamp Post in silver and gray, $50, each

No.	Year	Description	C6	C8	C10
34					
	1913	Loco, standard, electric 0-4-0, dark green, uncataloged....... 120		200	400
34					
	1913	Rubber Roadbed Switch, standard 3		4	5
34					
	1957	Half Straight Track, Super O.....—		2	4
35					
	1915	Pullman, standard, dark olive, maroon or brown 21		34	68
35					
	1915	Pullman, standard, orange 49		65	130
35					
	1940	Lamp Post, gray or silver 15		25	50
36					
	1912	Observation, standard, dark olive, maroon or brown 21		35	70
36					
	1912	Observation, standard, orange 60		100	200
36RM					
	1937	Controller, standard .... —		2	3
37					
	1957	Uncoupling Track, Super O ......—		2	4
38					
	1913-1924	Loco, standard, electric 0-4-0, black or gray 75		125	250
38					
	1913-1924	Loco, standard, electric 0-4-0, in brown..................... 120		200	400
38					
	1913-1924	Loco, standard, electric 0-4-0, in pea green.................. 96		160	320
38					
	1913-1924	Loco, standard, electric 0-4-0, in red 150		250	500
38					
	1946-1947	Water Tower, brown roof 75		112	150
38					
	1946-1947	Water Tower, red roof.............. 225		338	450
38					
	1957	Accessory Adapter, Super O ......—		1	2
39					
	1927	Bulb, twelve volt, frosted ....—		—	1
39-25					
	1960	Operating and Upcoupling, Super O 3		4	5
39-3					
	1939	Bulb, twelve volt, frosted .... —		—	1
39-5					
	1957	Operating Unit, Super O, set 3		4	5

No. 42 Loco, standard, 1912, $1,500

No.	Year	Description	C6	C8	C10
40					
	1927	Bulb, thirteen volt .... —		—	1
40-25					
	1950	Four Conductor Cable and Reel.................. —		1	2
40-3					
	1939	Bulb, eight volt .... —		—	1
40-50					
	1960	Three Conductor Cable and Reel.................. —		1	2
41					
	1936	Accessory Contactor .... —		1	2
41					
	1955	Loco, O27, army switcher, black shell small motorized unit 39		65	130
42					
	1912	Loco, standard, electric, square body, 0-4-4-0, dark green 450		750	1500
42					
	1913-1923	Loco, standard, electric peacock........................ 825		1375	2750
42					
	1913-1923	Loco, standard, electric, dark green, gray black.......... 142		237	475
42					
	1913-1923	Loco, standard, electric, maroon................................ 240		400	800
42					
	1913-1923	Loco, standard, electric, Mojave.............................. 173		288	575
42					
	1957	Loco, O27, Picatinny Arsenal switcher, olive shell, small motorized unit 135		225	450
43					
	1929	Bild-A-Motor, standard, gear set..................................... 75		108	150
43					
	1933-1941	Pleasure Boat, cream, red and white.............................. 400		600	800
43					
	1957	Power Track, Super O ....—		1	2

No.	Year	Description	C6	C8	C10
44					
	1935-1936	Race Boat, green, white and dark brown	450	675	900
44					
	1959	Loco, Super O, US Army Missile Launcher	72	120	240
44-80					
	1959-1962	Four Missiles, Super O	2	3	4
45					
	1960-1962	Loco, O, U.S. Marine Missile Launcher, olive shell w/white missiles	97	162	325
46					
	1936	Bulb, eight volt	—	—	1
46					
	1939-1942	Single Arm Crossing, cream and green base, lantern ontip of gate	45	75	150
47					
	1916	Bulb, six volt	—	—	1
47					
	1937-1942	Double Arm Crossing Gates, w/two crossing gates on each side	70	105	140
47-40					
	1937	Bulb, eighteen volt, red	—	—	1
47-73					
	1942	Bulb, twelve volt	—	—	1
48					
	1936	Bulb, twenty-one volt	—	—	1
48					
	1958	Insulated Straight Track, Super O	—	2	4
48W					
	1937-1942	Whistle Station, lithographed building, red base housing whistle	10	18	36
49					
	1937-1939	Lionel Airport, printed cardboard base w/airplane and controls	1000	1250	1500
49					
	1958	Insulated Curved Track, Super O	2	3	4
50					
	1924	Loco, standard, electric gray, 0-4-0	90	150	300
50					
	1924	Loco, standard, electric, dark green	105	175	350
50					
	1924	Loco, standard, electric, maroon	105	175	350
50					
	1924	Loco, standard, electric, Mojave	105	175	350

No. 52, Fire Fighting Car, O27, 1958-1961, $220

No.	Year	Description	C6	C8	C10
50					
	1936	Airplane	400	600	800
50					
	1943	Paper Train Set, uncataloged	90	157	315
50					
	1954	Gang Car, O27	17	29	58
51					
	1912-1923	Loco, standard, steam, "5 Special," 0-4-0	380	650	1300
51					
	1936-1939	Airport, printed cardboard base for center control and airplane	300	450	600
51					
	1956-1957	Loco, O27, Navy switcher, blue shell small motorized unit	54	90	180
52					
	1933	Lamp Post, aluminum	35	52	70
52					
	1958-1961	Fire Fighting Car, O27, red shell w/man	66	110	220

Left to Right: No. 57 Lamp Post, "Broadway & Main Street," 1924-42, $85; No. 56 Lamp Post, 1925-1949, $65; No. 53 Lamp Post, 1931, $75; No. 61 Lamp Post, 1914-1936, $50; No. 57 Lamp Post, "Broadway & 42nd Street," 1924-1942, $100

No.	Year	Description	C6	C8	C10
53					
	1912-1914	Loco, standard, electric 0-4-0,Mojave, maroon, dark olive	360	600	1200
53					
	1920	Loco, standard, electric 0-4-0, Mojave, maroon, dark olive	150	250	500
53					
	1931	Lamp Post, gray, aluminum, Mojave	37	56	75
53					
	1957	Snow Plow, O27, DRG, Rio Grande, black and yellow, "A" in Grande correct	125	217	425
53					
	1957	Snow Plow, O27, DRG, Rio Grande, black and yellow, "A" in Grande backwards	97	162	325
53-8					
	1932	Bulb, eighteen volt	—	—	1
54					
	1912	Loco, standard, electric, square body, brass, 0-4-4-0	1050	1750	3500
54					
	1913-1923	Loco, standard, electric, 0-4-4-0, brass	750	1250	2500
54					
	1929	Lamp Post, double light, dark green	35	52	70
54					
	1957	Ballast Tamper, O27, yellow shell, small motorized unit, w/track trips	57	90	180
55					
	1924	Bulb, fourteen volt	—	—	1
55					
	1937-1939	Airplane, red and silver w/control	250	375	500
55					
	1957-1961	Tie Ejector, O27, red shell w/wooden track ties, small motorized unit and track trips	72	122	245
55-150					
	1957	Ties, O27, set of twenty-four	—	—	3
56					
	1925-1949	Lamp Post, gray, green, Mojave	32	48	65
56					
	1958	Loco, O27, M&StL Mining, red shell, small motorized unit	174	290	580

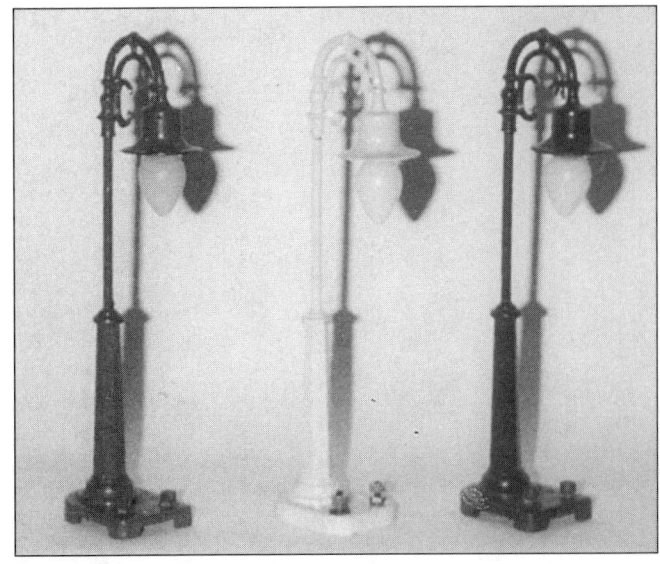

No. 58 Lamp Post in (left to right) green, cream and maroon, $48, each.

No.	Year	Description	C6	C8	C10
57					
	1924-1942	Lamp Post, orange "Broadway & 42nd Street"	30	50	100
57					
	1924-1942	Lamp Post, orange "Broadway & Fifth Ave."	24	40	80
57					
	1924-1942	Lamp Post, orange "Broadway & Main"	25	42	85
57					
	1924-1942	Lamp Post, yellow "Broadway & Main"	30	50	100
57					
	1959-1960	Loco, O27, A.E.C. Switcher, cream-red shell, small motorized unit	162	270	540
58					
	1922-1950	Lamp Post, green, maroon, cream	14	24	48
59					
	1920-1936	Lamp Post, green	15	25	50
59					
	1920-1936	Lamp Post, olive	22	37	75
59					
	1963	Loco, O27, U.S. Air Force Switcher, Minute Man, white shell 1962	172	288	575
59					
		Loco, U.S. Air Force switcher, white cab	150	250	500
60					
	1906	Automatic Trip Reverse, standard	3	5	6
60					
	1913	Loco, standard, Electric,			

No.	Year	Description	C6	C8	C10
		F.A.O. Schwarz Special, 0-4-0, uncataloged	360	600	1200
60					
	1920	Telegraph Pole, standard, set of six	66	110	220
60					
	1955-1958	Trolley, O27, black lettering	90	150	300
60					
	1955-1958	Trolley, O27, moving silhouettes, motor man in front w/direction of movement	135	225	450
60					
	1955-1958	Trolley, O27, red lettering, extremely rare	900	1500	3000
60					
	1955-1958	Trolley, O27, yellow w/red roof, blue lettering	54	90	180
61					
	1913	Loco, standard, electric, F.A.O. Schwarz Special, 0-4-4-0, uncataloged	450	750	1500
61					
	1914-1936	Lamp Post, dark green, maroon, Mojave, olive	15	25	50
61					
	1957	Ground Lockon, Super O	—	2	4
62					
	1913	Loco, standard, electric, F.A.O. Schwarz Special, 0-4-0, uncataloged	360	600	1200
62					
	1914	Automatic Reversing Trip, standard	3	4	5
62					
	1920-1932	Semaphore	12	20	40
63					
	1915-1921	Semaphore	30	45	60
63					
	1933-1942	Lamp Post, double globe, silver	81	135	270
63-10					
	1933	Opal Globe	3	4	5
63-11					
	1935	Bulb, eighteen volt, opal	—	—	1
64					
	1915-1921	Semaphore	21	35	70
64					
	1940-1942	Lamp Post, green	14	24	48
64-15					
	1940	Bulb, twelve volt, clear	—	—	5
64-26					
	1941	Bulb, twelve volt, opal	—	—	5
65					
	1915-1926	Semaphore	30	45	60

No.	Year	Description	C6	C8	C10
65					
	1915-1926	Semaphore	35	52	70
65					
	1935	Whistle Controller	6	9	12
65					
	1962	Motorized Hand Car, O27, yellow, two rubber men, small motorized unit it yellow or dark yellow	135	225	450
66					
	1936	Whistle and Reversing Controller	3	5	6
67					
	1915-1926	Lamp Post	30	50	100
67					
	1936	Whistle and Reversing Controller	4	5	7
68					
	1926-1939	Warning Signal, standard, non-operative	7	11	14
68					
	1958-1961	Executive Inspection Car, red DeSoto, small motorized unit	90	150	300
69					
	1921-1935	Warning Bell, standard	20	34	68
69					
	1960-1962	Motorized Maintenance Car, O27, gray platform, black frame, w/blue man and red danger sign	67	112	225
69-7					
	1933	Fiber Track Pins	—	—	1
69N					
	1936-1942	Warning Bell, standard/O	25	38	50
70					
	1921	Accessory Set, consists of two #62, one #68 and one #59	75	112	150
70					
	1949-1950	Lamp Post, yard light	17	29	58
71					
	1921	Telegraph Pole Set, set of six	54	90	180
71					
	1949-1959	Lamp Post, crackle gray	5	7	14
75					
	1921	Low Bridge Sign	35	52	70
75					
	1924	Bulb, twelve volt	—	—	1
75					
	1961-1969	Lamp Set, two, black plastic	17	26	35
76					
	1923	Block Signal, standard	25	42	85
76					
	1939-1942	Warning Bell and Shant, red base, orange roof, black	95	143	190

Top Row: No. 408E, Loco, 1927, standard, green, $3,600. Second Row: No. 381E, Loco, 1928 standard, $4,200. Third Row, left to right: No. 413, Pullman, 1929, standard, Colorado State Car, $2,200; No. 412, Pullman, 1929, standard, California State Car, $2,200. Bottom Row, left to right: No. 416, Observation, 1929, standard, New York State Car, $1,065; No. 414, State Car, 1930, Illinois, $2,000

No.	Year	Description	C6	C8	C10
76					
	1959-1969	Boulevard Lights, green plastic, set of three	10	15	20
77					
	1923-1939	Automatic Crossing Gate, standard	35	52	70
77N					
	1936-1939	Automatic Crossing Gate, standard/O	25	38	50
78					
	1924	Train Control Block Signal, standard, red base, orange base	40	60	80
79					
	1928-1942	Flashing Signal, cream or aluminum	60	90	120
79-23					
	1939	Bulb, Bulb, twelve volt, red	—	—	1
80					
	1926-1935	Semaphore, standard	75	112	150
80/81					
	1912-1916	Race Car Set, set consists of car, driver, eight sections of curve track	750	1125	1500
80N					
		Semaphore	62	93	125
81					
	1927	Rheostat	7	11	15
82					
	1927-1935	Train Control Semaphore, standard, yellow and green	55	82	110
82N					
	1936-1942	Train Control Semaphore, standard/O	92	138	185
83					
		Traffic Crossing Signal, red base 35-42	155	225	310
83					
		Traffic Crossing Signal, tan base 27-34	155	225	310
84					
	1912	Racing Cars	2000	3000	4000
84					
	1927-1932	Semaphore, standard	60	90	120
85					
	1912	Racing Cars	2000	3000	4000
85					
	1929-1942	Telegraph Pole, standard, orange	15	22	30
86					
	1932	Telegraph Poles, standard, setof six, including original box	82	138	185
87					
	1927	Crossing Signal, orange or green base	105	158	210
88					
	1915	Battery Rheostat	7	11	15
88					
	1933	Direction Controller	3	4	5
89					
	1923-1934	Flagstaff and Flag	50	75	100
89					
	1956-1958	Flag Pole	22	33	45
90					
	1927-1942	Flagstaff and Flag, w/round grass plot	25	38	50
90-93					
	1939	W Loco, OO, tender, two rail	180	300	600
91					
	1930-1942	Automatic Circuit, breaker, brown w/red light bulb	38	56	75
91					
	1957-1960	Circuit Breaker, brown w/red light	8	11	15
92					
	1931	Floodlight Tower, red, silver	92	138	185
92					
	1931	Floodlight Tower, terra cotta, green	90	135	180
92					
	1959	Circuit Breaker, w/controller	11	16	23
93					
	1932	Water Tower, O, green	20	30	40
93					
	1932	Water Tower, O, silver	47	71	95
94					
	1932	High Tension Tower, gray, terra cotta, silver and red	200	300	400
95					
	1934	Rheostat	12	18	25
96					
	1938-1940	Coal Elevator, manual control	95	132	190
97					
	1938-1942	Coal Elevator, electric	125	188	250
99					
	1932	Train Control Block Signal, standard, red or black base	85	128	170
99N					
	1936	Train Control Block Signal, standard/O, red or black base	85	128	170
109					
	1913	Tunnel, standard	50	75	100
109					
	1920	Five Section Bridge, O	40	60	80

No.	Year	Description	C6	C8	C10
100	1901	Loco, 2-7/8", No. 5 auctioned in 1995 in Excellent condition			4300
100	1910	Trolley, standard, motor car, blue or red, "100 Electric Rapid Transit 100"	600	1000	2000
100	1920	Bridge Approaches, standard	20	30	40
101	1910	Summer Trolley, standard, motor car, "101 Electric Rapid Transit 101," blue or red	600	1000	2000
101	1920	Three Section Bridge, standard, cream and green	55	82	110
102	1920	Four Section Bridge, standard	35	52	70
103	1913	Five Section Bridge, standard	90	135	180
104	1909-1914	Tunnel, standard	50	75	100
104	1920	Bridge, standard, center span	15	22	30
105	1911	Five Section Bridge, standard	40	60	80
105	1913	Three Section Bridge, standard	25	38	50
105	1920	Bridge Approaches, O	7	11	15
106	1911	AC Current Reducer, 110 or 120 volts	3	4	5
106	1920	Three Section Bridge, O, uncataloged	25	38	50
107	1911	DC Current Reducer, 110 volts	10	15	20
107	1911	DC Current Reducer, 220 volts	10	15	20
108	1912	Battery Rheostat	3	4	5
110	1920	Bridge, O, center span	15	22	30
110	1955-1969	Trestle Set, O, twenty-four pieces	10	15	20
111	1910	Trolley, standard, trailer	600	1000	2000
111	1920	Light Bulb Set	10	15	20
111	1956-1969	Trestle Set, O, ten pieces	9	13	18
111-100	1960-1963	Two Piers, O, two pieces	10	15	20
112	1910	Gondola, standard	135	225	450
112	1913	Gondola, standard	24	40	80
112	1931-1935	Station, standard, cream	162	243	325
112	1957-1960	Switch, Super O, w/controls, pair	42	63	85
113	1912-1926	Cattle Car, standard	33	55	110
113	1931-1934	Station, standard, cream	275	362	550
114	1912	Box, standard	36	60	120
114	1931-1934	Station, standard, cream	750	1125	1500
114	1957-1959	Newstand, O, w/horn	52	78	105
115	1935	Station, cream, red or green trim	215	322	450
115	1949	Station, cream, red or green trim	90	135	180
116	1910	Ballast, standard	54	90	180
116	1935	Station, cream, double station	600	900	1200

No. 115 Station, 1935, $450

No. 116 Station, 1935, $1,200

No. Year	Description	C6	C8	C10
117				
1912-1926	Caboose, standard	27	45	90
117				
1936-1942	Station	175	262	350
117				
1936-1942	Station, no outside lights	175	262	350
118				
1915-1920	Tunnel, O	45	68	90
118				
1958	Newstand, O, w/whistle	42	63	85
118L				
1927	Tunnel, O, lighted	40	60	80
119				
1915	Tunnel, standard/O	40	60	80
119				
1957	Tunnel, O	40	60	80
119L				
1927	Tunnel, standard/O, lighted	50	75	100
120				
1915	Tunnel, standard/O	62	93	125
120				
1957	Ninety Degree Crossing, Super O	8	12	16
120L				
1927	Tunnel, standard/O, lighted	67	100	135
121				
1909	Special Station, standard	300	450	600
121				
1959-1966	Tunnel, O	20	30	40
121x				
1917	Station, standard, w/lights	300	450	600
122				
1920	Station, standard	62	93	125
123				
1920	Station, standard	125	188	250

No. Year	Description	C6	C8	C10
123				
1933	Curved Tunnel, O	90	135	180
124				
1920	Station, standard	250	375	500
124				
1933	Station, standard	137	207	275
125				
1923	Station, standard	30	45	60
125				
1938	Track Template	5	8	10
125				
1950-1955	Whistle Station, gray or green base	22	33	45
126				
1923-1936	Station, standard	135	202	270
127				
1923-1936	Station	117	175	235
128				
1920	Tunnel, O, lighted	55	83	110
128				
1957-1960	Animated Newsstand	85	127	170
129				
1920	Tunnel, standard/O, lighted	70	105	140
129				
1928	Terrace, standard	900	1350	1800
129				
1929-1940	Station and Terrace, standard	800	1200	1600
130				
1920	Tunnel, O	150	225	300
130				
1957	60 Degrees Crossing, O	10	15	20
1301				
1925	Trailer Truck, standard, 200 series w/lights	4	6	12
130L				
1927	Tunnel, O, lighted	125	188	250
131				
1924-1928	Corner Elevation	350	525	700
131				
1959-1966	Curved Tunnel, O	35	53	70
132				
1924-1928	Corner Grass Plot	200	300	400
132				
1949-1955	Station, O	35	52	70
133				
1924-1928	Heart Shape Grass Plot	200	300	400
133				
1957-1966	Station, O	30	45	60
134				
1924-1928	Oval Grass Plot, large	200	300	400
134				
1937-1942	Stop Station, brown w/red roof	175	263	350

No.	Year	Description	C6	C8	C10
135					
	1924-1928	Oval Grass Plot, small 200		300	400
136					
	1937-1942	Stop Station, lighted 150		225	300
137					
	1937-1942	Stop Station, lighted 112		168	225
138					
	1953-1957	Water Tank, operating...............62		93	125
140					
	1954-1966	Banjo Signal, O 25		38	50
1400					
	1925	Trailer Truck, standard, 418 series.................5		8	16
1401					
	1925	Trailer Truck, standard, 418 series w/lights...........5		8	16
140L					
	1927-1932	Tunnel, standard, lighted 400		600	800
142					
	1957	Switches, Super O, manual, price per pair 15		23	30
145					
	1950-1966	Automatic Gateman, O 20		30	40
145C					
	1950	Contactor, O 6		9	12
147					
	1961	Whistle Controller, O 3		4	5
148					
	1957	Dwarf Signal, O 30		45	60
148-100					
	1957	Double Pole Switch....................4		6	8
150					
	1918-1925	Loco, O, electric, 0-4-0, dark green 60		100	200
150					
	1947-1950	Telegraph Poles, O, set of six 19		29	38
151					
	1947-1969	Semaphore, O 20		30	40
151-51					
	1950	Bulb, fourteen volt, clear ....—		—	1
152					
	1917-1927	Loco, O, electric, dark gray or dark green 75		125	250
152					
	1917-1927	Loco, O, light gray 113		187	375
152					
	1917-1927	Loco, O, peacock or Mojave....135		225	450
152					
	1945-1948	Crossing Gate, O.......................21		32	42
152-33					
	1940	Bulb, O, twelve volt, red ....—		—	1
153					
	1924	Loco, O, dark green 60		100	200
153					
	1924	Loco, O, electric, Mojave 75		125	250
153					
	1924	Loco, O, gray 60		100	200
153					
	1945-1969	Block Signal, O..........................22		34	45
153-23					
	1940	Bulb, six volt, red ....—		—	1
153-24					
	1940	Bulb, six volt, green ....—		—	1
153-48					
	1940	Bulb, fourteen volt green ....—		—	1
153-50					
	1940	Bulb, fourteen volt, red............—		—	1
153C					
	1940	Contactor, O.................................5		8	10
154					
	1917-1923	Loco, O, electric, 0-4-0, dark green 75		125	250
154					
	1940-1942	Highway Signal, O 19		27	38
154-18					
	1942	Bulb, twelve volt, red................—		—	1
154C					
	1940	Contactor, O.................................4		5	7
155					
	1930-1942	Freight Shed, yellow base maroon roof...........220		330	440
155					
	1930-1942	Freight Shed, ivory base roof, gray roof.......175		263	350
155					
	1955-1957	Signal Light, W.M. Bell.............50		75	100
156					
	1917-1923	Loco, O, electric, 4-4-4, gray, olive, maroon 225		425	850
156					
	1939-1940	Station Platform, O...................52		78	105
156-13					
	1939	Bulb, eighteen volt, clear...........—		—	1
156X					
	1923-1924	Loco, O, electric, same as 156, but w/o pilot trucks 300		500	1000
157					
	1930-1932	Hand Truck, standard, red 15		25	50
157					
	1952-1959	Station Platform, O...................37		56	75
158					
	1919-1923	Loco, O, electric, 0-4-0, black 135		225	450
158					
	1919-1923	Loco, O, electric, 0-4-0, gray.........120		200	400

No.	Year	Description	C6	C8	C10
158					
	1940-1942	Platform Set, lighted, two 156 platforms and one 136 station, w/original box	165	275	550
159C					
	1940	Block Signal contractor	4	5	7
160					
	1938	Unloading Bin	—	1	2
161					
	1930-1932	Baggage Truck, standard, green	30	50	100
161					
	1961-1963	Mail Pickup Set, O	35	52	70
162					
	1930-1932	Dump Truck, standard, red or gray	28	48	95
163					
	1930	Freight Accessory, includes two #157 handtrack, one #161 baggage cart one dump bin, w/original box	145	217	290
163					
	1961-1963	Block Signal, O, single target	15	22	30
164					
	1940-1950	Lumber Loader	102	170	340
164-64					
	1952	Set of Five Logs	—	—	5
165					
	1940-1942	Magnetic Crane	75	125	250
165-53					
	1940	Bulb, eighteen volt, red	—	—	1
165C					
	1940	Controller	32	48	65
166					
	1938	Controller, three button	3	4	5
167					
	1945	Whistle and Reverse Controller, O	5	8	10
167X					
	1940	Whistle Controller, OO	3	4	5
168					
	1940	Controller	3	4	5
170					
	1914	DC Current Reducer, 220 volts	5	8	10
171					
	1936	Inverter, DC to AC	5	8	10
172					
	1937	Inverter, DC to AC, 220 volts	5	8	10
175					
	1958-1960	Rocket Launcher, O	75	125	250
180					
	1911	Pullman, standard, maroon, brown, orange	50	85	170
180					
	1915	Trailer Truck, standard	600	1000	2000
181					
	1911	Combine, standard, maroon, brown, orange	60	100	200
182					
	1911	Observation, standard, maroon, brown, orange	66	110	220
182					
	1946-1949	Magnet Crane, w/165C controller	75	125	250
184					
	1923	Bungalow, lighted	45	68	90
185					
	1923	Bungalow, no lights	40	60	80
186					
	1923	Bungalow Set, set of five	300	450	600
186					
	1940	Log Loading Outfit, log loader, car, bin, uncoupler	120	200	400
187					
	1923	Bungalow Set, set of five	300	450	600
188					
	1938	Coal Elevator Outfit	120	200	400
189					
	1923	Villa, lighted	162	243	325
190					
	1907-1927	Observation, standard	180	300	600
190					
	1907-1927	Observation, standard	300	500	1000
190					
	1907-1927	Observation, standard	300	500	1000
191					
	1923	Villa, lighted	145	217	290
192					
	1959-1960	Railroad Control Tower	90	135	180
193					
	1927-1929	Automatic Accessory Set, O, includes one #69, one #76, one #78, one #77, one #80	175	263	350
193					
	1953-1955	Water Tower	62	93	125
194					
	1927-1929	Automatic Accessory Set, standard, includes one #69, one #76, one #78, one #77, one #80	175	263	350
195					
	1927	Terrace, standard, includes one #191 villa, one #189 villa, one #184 bungalow, one #90 flagpole, two #56 lamp posts	600	900	1200
195-75					
	1957	Spare Tower Head, add			

No.	Year	Description	C6	C8	C10
		lights and holder for #195 floodlight tower	5	8	10
196	1927	Accessory Set, standard/O, Includes #127 station, six #60 telegraph poles, #62 semaphore, #68 warning signal, two #58 lamp posts, w/original box	150	225	300
196	1946	Smoke Pellets, 100 pellets in bottle/package (price for complete package)	—	—	20
197	1957-1959	Radar Antenna, O, gray, gray base	30	53	105
197-75	1958	Replacement Radar Head	9	15	30
199	1924	Scenic Railway Set, standard	120	200	400
199	1958-1959	Microwave Tower	37	56	75
200	1910	Trolley, standard, trailer, non-powered	1200	2000	4000
200	1928	Turntable, standard, green and tan	175	263	350
200		Gondola, 2-7/8", motorized, actioned in 1994 in Good to Very Good condition			3100
201	1940	Loco, O, steam switcher 0-6-0, w/2201 B belltender	280	475	950
201	1940	Loco, O, steam, switcher 0-6-0, w/2201 T no bell tender	210	350	700
202	1910	Summer Trolley, standard, motor car, "202 Electric Rapid Transit 202"	900	1500	3000
202	1957	Loco, O27, UP Alco A diesel, orange w/black lettering	30	50	100
203	1917	Loco, O, Armored, 0-4-0, cannon, only prewar war, oriented locomotive	690	1150	2300
203	1940	Loco, O, steam, switcher, 0-6-0, no bell similar to 201	225	375	750
204	1940-1941	Loco, O, steam, 2-4-2, black, uncataloged	43	72	145
204	1940-1941	Loco, O, steam, 2-4-2, gun metal gray, uncataloged	67	113	225
204	1957	Loco, O27, A.T.S.F. Alco AA, diesel	36	60	120
205	1930-1938	L.C.L. Merchandise Containers, standard, dark green, price per each	75	112	150
205	1957	Loco, O27, M.P. Alco AA, diesel	50	75	150
208	1934-1942	Tool Set, gray box, includes tools, sledge hammer, pick, rake, shovel, ax	60	90	120
208	1934-1942	Tool Set, silver box, includes tools, sledge hammer, pick, rake, shovel, ax	50	75	100
208	1958	Loco, O27, A.T.S.F. Alco diesel AA	48	80	160
209	1934-1942	Barrels, standard, wooden, set of four	10	15	20
209	1958	Loco, O27, N.H. Alco AA, diesel, two units	270	450	900
210	1926	Switch, standard, automatic, pair	15	22	30
210	1958	Loco, O27, Texas Spec. Alco diesel AA	82	137	275
211	1926-1940	Flat, standard, w/wooden load	34	57	115
211	1962	Loco, O27, Texas Spec. Alco AA, diesel	54	90	180
212	1926-1940	Gondola, standard, gray	60	100	200
212	1926-1940	Gondola, standard, green, maroon	45	75	150
212	1958	Loco, O27, Alco diesel A, Marine	90	150	300
212	1964	Loco, O27, A.T.S.F. Alco diesel AA	30	50	100
213	1926-1940	Cattle Car, standard, cream body, maroon roof	300	450	600

No.	Year	Description	C6	C8	C10
213					
	1926-1940	Cattle Car, standard, Mojave body, maroon roof	200	300	400
213					
	1926-1940	Cattle Car, standard, terra-cotta, orange body, pea green roof	100	200	300
213					
	1964	Loco, O27, M&StL Alco AA, diesel	60	90	120
214					
	1926-1940	Box Car, standard, cream body, orange roof	100	200	300
214					
	1926-1940	Box Car, standard, terra-cotta, orange body, green roof	200	300	400
214					
	1926-1940	Box Car, standard, yellow body, brown roof	300	400	500
214					
	1953-1969	Girder Bridge, HO, light or dark gray	10	20	30
214R					
	1929-1940	Refrigerator Car, standard, ivory body, peacock roof	300	400	500
214R					
	1929-1940	Refrigerator Car, standard, white body, light blue roof	500	750	1000
215					
	1926-1940	Tank Car, standard, ivory, Sunoco decal	100	200	300
215					
	1926-1940	Tank Car, standard, pea green	75	125	150
215					
	1926-1940	Tank Car, standard, silver, Sunco decal	200	350	500
216					
	1926-1940	Hopper Car, standard, dark green	100	200	300
216					
	1958	Loco, O27, Burlington Alco A, diesel	100	200	300
216					
		Loco, O27, Minneapolis & St. Louis, Alco diesel A	75	100	125
217					
	1914	Lighting Set, standard, for cars, eight volts	30	50	100
217					
	1926-1940	Caboose, standard, orange and maroon	90	150	300
217					
	1926-1940	Caboose, standard, red, peacock	69	115	230

No. 217 Caboose, standard, 1926-1940, $300

No.	Year	Description	C6	C8	C10
217					
	1959	Loco, O27, B&M Alco AB, diesel	93	155	310
218					
	1926-1940	Dump, standard, Mojave	78	130	260
218					
	1959	Loco, O27, A.T.S.F. Alco AA, diesel	45	75	150
218					
	1961	Loco, O27, A.T.S.F. Alco AB, diesel	45	75	150
218C					
	1961	Loco, O27, A.T.S.F. Alco B, diesel	12	20	40
219					
	1926	Crane, standard, peacock cab	72	120	240
219					
	1926	Crane, standard, white, ivory cab	135	225	450
219					
	1926	Crane, standard, yellow cab	115	192	385
220					
	1931	Floodlight, standard, green base	120	200	400
220					
	1931	Floodlight, standard, terra cotta base	75	125	250
220					
	1961	Loco, O27, A.T.S.F. Alco A, diesel	30	50	100
221					
	1946	Loco, O27, steam, gray	48	80	160
221					
	1946	Loco, steam, black	60	100	200
221					
	1963	Loco, O27, A.T.S.F. Alco A, diesel, uncataloged	27	45	90

No.	Year	Description	C6	C8	C10
221					
	1963	Loco, O27, Alco A, diesel, Marine, uncataloged 124		207	415
221					
	1963	Loco, O27, D&RGW Alco A, diesel 36		60	120
222					
	1926	Switches, standard, price per pair 30		45	60
223					
	1932	Switches, standard, Non-derailing, price per pair 46		78	155
223-50					
	1963	Loco, O27, A.B.A.T.S.F. Alco, diesel 36		60	120
224					
	1943	Loco, steam, paper train, uncataloged, complete, w/original box...................... 100		150	200
224					
	1960	Loco, O27, Alco AB, diesel, Navy 60		100	200
224					
		Paper Train Set, Includes #224 loco, #2224 tender, #2812 red gondola, #61100 yellow box w/brown roof, #47618 red caboose, crossing signal, crossing gate, three figures, baggage, paper track 300		450	600
224/224E					
	1938-1942	Loco, steam 2-6-2, black w/2224 die-cast tender 54		90	180
224/224E					
	1938-1942	Loco, steam 2-6-2, black w/plastic tender 43		72	145
224/224E					
	1938-1942	Loco, steam 2-6-2, gunmetal gray w/2224 die-cast tender 110		183	365
224/224E					
	1938-1942	Loco, steam 2-6-2, gunmetal gray w/2689 sheetmetal tender 66		110	220
225					
	1960	Loco, O27, C&O Alco A, diesel 36		60	120
225/225 E					
	1939-1940	Loco, O, steam, 2-6-2, in gunmetal gray 105		175	350
225/225 E					
	1939-1940	Loco, O, steam, 2-6-2, w/2235, 2265, 2225, 2245 tenders, black 114		190	380

No.	Year	Description	C6	C8	C10
2257					
		Caboose, Non-illuminated 105		175	350
226E					
	1938-1941	Loco, O, steam, 2-6-4, w/2226 tender 150		250	500
227					
	1939	Loco, O, steam, 0-6-0 switcher scale, w/tender 2227T, "8976" under cab window, no bell ... 375		625	1250
227					
	1939	Loco, O, w/tender 2227B bell 378		630	1260
227					
	1960	Loco, O27, C.N.Alco A, diesel, Canadian market distribution, uncataloged 45		75	150
228					
	1939	Loco, O, steam, 0-6-0, switcher scale, similar to 227, w/228T tender, no bell.......... 318		530	1060
228					
	1939	Loco, O, steam, 0-6-0, tender 2228B, bell.................... 480		800	1600
228					
	1961	Loco, O27, C.N. Alco A, diesel, Canadian market distribution, uncataloged 45		75	150
229					
	1961	Loco, O27, M&StL Alco A, diesel 42		70	140
229/229E					
	1939	Loco, O, steam, 2-4-2, black 48		80	160
229/229E					
	1939	Loco, O, steam, gunmetal gray 30		50	100
229C					
	1962	Loco, O27, M&StL Alco B, diesel 27		45	90
229P					
	1962	Loco, O27, M&StL Alco A, diesel................................... 30		50	100
230					
	1939	Loco, steam, 0-6-0, switcher scale 600		1000	2000
230					
	1961	Loco, O27, C&O Alco A, diesel.. 30		50	100
231					
	1939	Loco, O, steam, 0-6-0, switcher scale 600		1000	2000
231					
	1961	Loco, O27, R.I. Alco A, diesel.. 24		40	80
232					
	1940	Loco, O, steam, 0-6-0, switcher scale 465		775	1550

No.	Year	Description	C6	C8	C10
232					
	1962	Loco, O27, N.H. Alco A, diesel	39	65	130
233					
	1940	Loco, O, steam, 0-6-0, switcher scale	600	1000	2000
233					
	1961	Loco, O27, steam, 2-4-2 w/233W tender	18	30	60
235					
	1962	Loco, steam O27, uncataloged 2-4-2	18	30	60
236					
	1961	Loco, O27, steam, 2-4-2	18	30	60
237					
	1963	Loco, O27, steam	18	30	60
238 or E					
	1936-1940	Loco, O, P.R.R., steam, w/222T, 2225W or 265W tender, black or gunmetal gray, torpedo type	113	188	375
238					
	1963	Loco, O27, steam 2-4-2	18	30	60
239					
	1965	Loco, O27, steam, 2-4-2	18	30	60
241					
	1963	Loco, O27, steam, 2-4-2, uncataloged	18	30	60
242					
	1962	Loco, O27, steam, 2-4-2	9	15	30
243					
	1960	Loco, O27, steam, 2-4-2	13	23	45
244					
	1960	Loco, O27, steam, 2-4-2	9	15	30
245					
	1959	Loco, O27, steam, 2-4-2	9	15	30
246					
	1959	Loco, O27, steam, 2-4-2	9	15	30
247					
	1959	Loco, O27, B&O, steam, 2-4-2	15	25	50
248					
	1926-1932	Loco, O, electric, red, orange, dark green, olive	49	83	165
249 or E					
	1936	Loco, O, steam, black	120	200	400
249 or E					
	1936	Loco, O, steam, gunmetal gray	80	133	265
249					
	1958	Loco, O27, P.R.R., steam, 2-4-2	15	25	50
250					
	1926	Loco, O, N.Y.C., electric,			

No. 250E Loco, O, 1935, $1,500

No.	Year	Description	C6	C8	C10
		0-4-0, dark green, peacock, orange	90	150	300
250					
	1934	Loco, O, Electric, 0-4-0, orange, terra cotta, uncataloged	60	100	200
250					
	1957	Loco, O27, P.R.R., steam, 2-4-2	21	35	70
250E					
	1935	Loco, O, Hiawatha, steam, w/tenders 250W, 250WX, 2250W	450	750	1500
251					
	1925	Loco, O, NYC, electric 0-4-0, box cab, gray or red cabs	100	168	335
251E					
	1927	Loco, O, NYC, electric 0-4-0, box cab, gray or red cabs	100	168	335
252					
	1926	Loco, O, NYC, electric 0-4-0, peacock, olive, dark green	60	100	200
252					
	1926	Loco, O, NYC, electric 0-4-0, terra cotta, orange	75	125	250
252					
	1926	Loco, O, NYC, Electric, 0-4-0, maroon, Macy's Special	120	200	400
252					
	1950-1962	Crossing Gate, O	20	30	40
252E					
	1933-1935	Loco, O, electric, 0-4-0, terra cotta or orange	84	140	280
253					
	1924	Loco, O, electric, 0-4-0, maroon	150	250	500
253					
	1924	Loco, O, electric, 0-4-0, peacock, Mojave, dark green	60	100	200
253					
	1924	Loco, O, electric, 0-4-0, red	135	225	450
253					
	1924	Loco, O, electric, 0-4-0, terra cotta	120	200	400

No.	Year	Description	C6	C8	C10
253					
	1956	Automatic Block Sign Signal, O	30	45	60
254					
	1924	Loco, O, electric, 0-4-0, apple green	120	200	400
254					
	1924	Loco, O, electric, 0-4-0, Mojave, olive, dark, pea green	83	138	275
254					
	1924	Loco, O, electric, 0-4-0, red	150	250	500
256					
	1924-1930	Loco, O, electric, orange, "Lionel" rubber stamped	150	250	500
256					
	1924-1930	Loco, O, electric, orange, "Lionel"	210	350	700
256					
	1950-1953	Freight Shed	27	41	55
257					
	1930	Loco, O, steam, 0-4-0, w/257T or 259T tender	90	150	300
257					
	1956-1957	Freight Station, w/horn	20	30	40
258					
	1930	Loco, O, steam, 2-4-0	75	125	250
258					
	1941	Loco, O, steam, 2-4-2, w/1689T tender, uncataloged	48	80	160
259					
	1932	Loco, O, steam, 2-4-2	54	90	180
259E					
	1933	Loco, O, steam, black	34	73	115
259E					
	1933	Loco, O, steam, gunmetal gray	48	80	160
260					
	1952	Bumper, O	9	13	17
260E					
	1930	Loco, O, steam, black, w/260T tender	150	250	500
260E					
	1930	Loco, O, steam, gunmetal gray, w/263 tender	180	300	600
261					
	1931	Loco, O, steam, 2-4-2, w/257T tender	75	125	250
262					
	1931	Loco, O, steam, 2-4-2, w/262T tender	90	150	300
262					
	1962	Crossing Gate, O	21	32	42
264					
		Operating Forklift Platform Assembly	85	142	285
270					
	1915	Lighting Set, standard, for two cars, 3-1/2 volt	40	60	80
270					
	1931	Bridge, O, maroon or red	52	78	105
271					
	1931	Bridge, O, two span	30	45	60
272					
	1931	Bridge, O, three span	60	90	120
280					
	1931	Bridge, standard	45	68	90
281					
	1931	Bridge, standard, two span	45	68	90
282					
	1931	Bridge, standard, three span	50	75	100
282					
	1954	Gantry Crane, O	72	120	240
289E					
	1937	Loco, O, steam 2-4-2, streamlined, 1689 tender, black	52	88	175
299					
	1961-1963	Code Transmitter Set	50	75	100
300					
	1901	Trolley, standard, "City Hall Park 175"	2100	3500	7000
300					
	1910	Trolley, standard, trailer, powered	1080	1800	3600
300					
	1928	Bridge, standard/O, "Hellgate," ivory, green, orange base	925	1390	1850
300					
	1928	Bridge, standard/O, "Hellgate," white, silver and red base, largest single span bridge Lionel ever made	810	1350	2700
303					
	1910	Summer Trolley, standard, motorcar, "303 Electric Rapid Transit 303"	1230	2050	4100
308					
	1945-1949	Metal Sign Set, O, five piece	10	15	20
309					
	1926	Pullman, standard, blue, apple green, pea green maroon, light brown, Mojave	43	73	145
309					
	1950-1959	Plastic Sign Set, nine piece	12	19	25
310					
	1903	Track, standard	5	8	10
310					
	1924-1929	Baggage, standard, blue, apple			

No.	Year	Description	C6	C8	C10
		green, pea green maroon, light brown, Mojave	40	68	135
310					
	1926	Baggage, standard, blue, apple green, pea green maroon, light brown, Mojave	54	70	140
310					
	1950-1968	Billboard Set, O, billboard and five different inserts	15	22	30
310R					
	1963	Billboard, O, racing maroon, light brown, Mojave	15	22	30
312					
	1926	Observation, standard, blue, apple green, pea green	54	70	140
313					
	1940-1942	Bascule Bridge, O, gray	312	468	625
313					
	1946-1949	Bascule Bridge, silver	120	212	425
314					
	1946-1950	Girder Bridge, O, gray	23	34	45
315					
	1946-1947	Trestle, O, bridge, illuminated silver	20	30	40
315-20					
	1940	Bulb, twelve volt, clear	—	—	1
317					
		Trestle Bridge, gray	35	52	70
318					
	1924	Loco, standard, electric 0-4-0, Mojave, pea green, gray	110	185	370
318					
	1924	Loco, standard, electric 0-4-0, state brown	140	238	475
318E					
	1926	Loco, standard, electric, 0-4-0, black	240	400	800
318E					
	1926	Loco, standard, electric, 0-4-0, pea green, Mojave, gray	100	170	340
318E					
	1926	Loco, standard, electric, 0-4-0, state brown	180	300	600
319					
	1924	Pullman, standard	54	85	170
320					
	1903	Switch, standard	20	30	40
320					
	1925	Baggage, standard	60	100	200
321					
	1958	Trestle Bridge, O	15	22	30
322					
	1924	Observation, standard	57	95	190
330					
	1903	90 Degrees Crossing, standard	10	15	20
332					
	1926	Baggage, standard, beige body, maroon roof	90	150	300
332					
	1926	Baggage, standard, gray, red, peacock, olive	28	48	95
332					
	1930	Macy Baggage, standard, uncataloged	60	100	200
332					
	1959-1966	Arch Bridge, O, gray	20	30	40
334					
	1957-1960	Operating Dispatching Board, O	75	125	250
337					
	1925	Pullman, standard, pea green, olive, red, Mojave	40	65	130
337					
	1930	Macy Pullman, standard, red, uncataloged	60	100	200
338					
	1925	Observation, standard, pea green, olive, red, Mojave	33	55	110
338					
	1930	Macy Observation, standard, uncataloged	60	100	200
339					
	1925	Pullman, standard, beige body, maroon roof	90	150	300
339					
	1925	Pullman, standard, peacock, brown, gray	27	45	90
339					
	1930	Macy Pullman, standard, red, uncataloged	60	100	200
340					
	1903	Bridge, standard	175	262	350
341					
	1925	Observation, standard, beige body, maroon roof	90	150	300
341					
	1925	Observation, standard, peacock, brown, gray	27	45	90
341					
	1930	Macy Observation, standard, red, uncataloged	60	100	200
342					
	1956-1958	Culvert Loader, O	57	85	190
345					
	1957	Automatic Culvert Unloader, O	105	175	350

No. 515, Tank, 1927, standard, Sunoco logo, $180

No. 384E, Loco, standard, with 384T tender, $585

No. 514, Box, 1929, standard, yellow/brown, $70

No.	Year	Description	C6	C8	C10
350					
	1903	Bumper, standard 25	38	50
350					
	1957-1960	Transfer Table, O 100	165	330
350-50					
	1957-1960	Transfer Table Extension, O 53	88	175
352					
	1955-1957	Ice Depot, O, red or brown base..............................75	125	250
352-55					
	1955	Ice Blocks, O, set of seven..........10	15	20
353					
	1960-1961	Trackside Signal, O 8	12	16
356					
	1952-1957	Freight Station, O, w/green and orange carts 50	75	100
362					
	1952-1957	Barrel Loader, O 39	65	130
362-78					
	1952	Barrels, O, set of six 7	11	15
364					
	1948-1967	Lumber Loader, O, Smooth gray or crackle gray 36	60	120
364C					
	1959	On-Off Switch.............................—	—	15
365					
	1958-1959	Dispatching Station, O 70	105	140
375					
	1962-1964	Turntable, O, motorized..........112	168	225
380					
	1903	Elevated Pillars, standard, price per each..........................30	45	60
380					
	1923	Loco, standard, electric, 0-4-0, maroon.......................192	320	640
380					
	1923	Loco, standard, electric, 0-4-0, Mojave, dark green....180	300	600
380E					
	1926	Loco, standard, electric, 0-4-0, maroon.......................180	300	600

No. 381E Loco, standard, 1928, $4,200

No.	Year	Description	C6	C8	C10
380E					
	1926	Loco, standard, electric, 0-4-0, Mojave or dark green............180	300	600
381					
	1928	Loco, standard, electric, 4-4-4, green body................1200	2000	4000
381E					
	1928	Loco, standard, electric, 4-4-4, green body and frame 1260	2100	4200
381U					
	1928	Loco, standard, electric, kit includes tools, track and original box 2300	3450	4600
384					
	1930	Loco, standard, steam, 2-4-0 w/384T tender.............180	300	600
384E					
	1930	Loco, standard, steam, 2-4-0 w/384T tender.............175	293	585
385E					
	1933	Loco, standard, steam, 2-4-2 w/384T, 385T, 385TW 295	490	980
390					
	1929	Loco, standard, steam, 2-4-2 w/390T, black 250	420	840
390C					
	1960	Control Switch, O 3	4	5
390E					
		Loco, two-tone green 540	900	1800
390E					
	1929	Loco, standard, steam, black, w/tender 390T 300	500	1000

No. 380E. Loco, standard, 1926, $600

No. 390E Loco, standard, 1929, w/390T Tender, $1,000

Top, left to right: No. 512 Gondola, standard, 1927, $120; No. 517 Caboose, standard, 1927, $80. Middle: Two No. 511 Flat Cars, 1927, $100-115. Bottom: No. 385E Loco, standard, 1933, w/No. 385TW tender, $980.

No.	Year	Description	C6	C8	C10
390E					
	1930	Loco, standard, two-tone blue, w/tender	420	700	1400
392E					
	1932	Loco, standard, steam, 4-4-2, black	380	630	1260
392E					
	1932	Loco, standard, steam, 4-4-2, gunmetal gray	495	825	1650
394					
	1949-1953	Rotary Beacon, aluminum, red or green tower frame	22	33	45
394-10					
	1951	Bulb, fourteen volt, clear	—	—	1
394-37					
	1953	Beacon Cap	—	—	5
395					
	1949-1956	Floodlight Tower, four lights, green tower	32	48	65
395					
	1949-1956	Floodlight Tower, four lights, red tower	50	75	100
395					
	1949-1956	Floodlight Tower, four lights, silver tower	24	36	48
395					
	1949-1956	Floodlight Tower, four lights, yellow tower	48	80	160
397					
	1948-1957	Diesel Type Coal Loader, later model, blue diesel motor cover	45	75	150
397					
	1948-1957	Diesel Type Coal Loader, yellow diesel motor cover	120	200	400
400					
	1901	Gondola, 2-7/8", trailer	720	1200	2400
400					
	1956-1958	Budd RDC Car, O, powered	80	135	270

No. 400E Loco, standard, blue, $2850

No.	Year	Description	C6	C8	C10
400E		Loco, standard, steam, 4-4-4 w/400T tender, black	675	1125	2250
400E		Loco, standard, steam, 4-4-4 w/400T tender, blue	855	1425	2850
400E		Loco, standard, steam, 4-4-4 w/400T tender, gunmetal gray	900	1500	3000
402	1923	Loco, standard, electric, 0-4-4-0, Mojave	200	330	660
402E	1926	Loco, standard, electric, 0-4-4-0, Mojave	180	300	600

No.	Year	Description	C6	C8	C10
404	1910	Summer Trolley, standard, motor car	1500	2500	5000
404	1957-1958	Budd RDC Baggage Car, O, powered	110	185	370
408E	1927	Loco, standard, electric, 0-4-4-0, apple green or Mojave	385	640	1280
408E	1927	Loco, standard, electric, 0-4-4-0, green	1080	1800	3600
408E	1927	Loco, standard, electric, 0-4-4-0, state brown	660	1100	2200
410	1956-1958	Billboard Blinker	20	30	40
412	1929	Pullman, standard, California, State Car, light brown	660	1100	2200
412	1929	Pullman, standard, California, State Car, light green	600	1000	2000
413	1929	Pullman, standard, Colorado, State Car, light brown	660	1100	2200

No. 402E Loco, standard, 1926, $600

No. 408E Loco, standard, 1927, $1,280

No. 414 State Car, light green, 1930, $2,000

No.	Year	Description	C6	C8	C10
413					
	1929	Pullman, standard, Colorado, State Car, light green	600	1000	2000
413					
	1962	Countdown Control Panel	20	30	40
414					
	1930	State Car, Illinois, light green	600	1000	2000
414					
	1930	State Car, light brown	660	1100	2200
415					
	1955-1967	Diesel Fueling Station	100	150	200
416					
	1929	Observation, standard, light brown	310	515	1030
416					
	1929	Observation, standard, New York State Car, light green	320	533	1065
418					
	1923	Pullman, standard, apple green	105	173	345

No.	Year	Description	C6	C8	C10
418					
	1923	Pullman, standard, Mojave	63	105	210
419					
	1923	Combine, standard, Mojave	60	100	200
419					
	1928-1932	Combine, standard, apple green	110	180	360
419					
	1962	Heliport, control tower	125	188	250
420					
	1930	Pullman, standard, "Faye," light blue body, dark blue roof, Blue Comet car	245	410	820
421					
	1930	Pullman, standard, "Westphal," Blue Comet car, light blue body, dark blue roof	245	410	820
422					
	1930	Observation, standard, "Tempel," Blue Comet car, light blue body, dark blue roof	245	410	820
424					
	1931	Pullman, standard, "Liberty Bell," Stephen Girard set, light green	155	258	515
425					
	1932	Pullman, standard, Stephen Girard set, light green	150	272	515
426					
	1931	Observation, standard, "Coral			

Top, left to right: No. 490 Observation, standard, 1923, $250; No. 431 Dining Car, 1927, $600. Bottom, left to right: No. 419 Combine, standard, 1923, $200; No. 418 Pullman Car, standard, 1923, $345

No.	Year	Description	C6	C8	C10
		Isle," Stephen Girard set, light green	150	272	515
428	1926	Pullman, standard, dark green	90	150	300
428	1926	Pullman, standard, orange	150	250	500
429	1926	Combine, standard, dark green	135	225	450
429	1926	Combine, standard, orange	105	175	350
430	1926	Observation, standard, dark green	90	150	300
430	1926	Observation, standard, orange	105	175	350
431	1927	Diner, standard, Mojave	180	300	600
431	1928-1929	Diner, apple green, orange, dark green	190	317	635
435	1926	Power Station	83	138	275
436	1926	Power Station	95	155	310
437	1926	Signal Tower, green roof	150	255	510
437	1926	Signal Tower, orange roof	180	300	600
437	1926	Signal Tower, peacock roof	125	212	425
438	1927	Signal Tower, orange, red	200	300	400
438	1927	Signal Tower, white, red	235	350	470
439	1928	Panel Board, maroon	90	135	180
439	1928	Panel Board, red	100	150	200
439	1928	Panel Board, silver, rare	150	225	300
441	1932-1936	Weighing Scale Platform, standard, green base, cream building	300	500	1000
442	1938	Diner	120	180	240
443	1960-1962	Missile Launching Platform	30	45	60
444	1932-1935	Roundhouse Section, standard	1700	2550	3400

No. 444 Roundhouse Section, standard, 1932-1935, $3,400

No.	Year	Description	C6	C8	C10
445	1952-1957	Operating Switch Tower	42	63	85
448	1961-1963	Missile Firing Range Set	62	93	125
440C		Panel Board	62	93	125
440N	1936	Signal Bridge, O/standard	175	262	350
450	1930	Macy Special Loco, O, electric, 0-4-0 red w/black frame, uncataloged	300	500	1000
450	1952-1958	Signal Bridge, gray or tan base	35	52	70
450L	1952	Signal Light Head	20	25	35
452	1961-1963	Gantry Signal	48	72	95
455	1932-1933	Electric Range	700	1100	1500
455	1950-1954	Oil Derrick, green base	90	135	180
455	1950-1954	Oil Derrick, red base	110	165	220
456	1950-1955	Coal Ramp and Hopper Car	75	125	250
460	1955-1957	Piggyback Terminal	75	112	150
460-150	1956	Two Trailers	12	18	25
461	1957	Piggyback, w/truck and trailers, most include, "Midge Toy Tractor," red	300	450	600

No.	Year	Description	C6	C8	C10
462					
	1961-1962	Derrick Platform Set	75	112	150
464					
	1956-1960	Lumber Mill	87	130	175
464-150					
	1956	Boards, set of six	1	3	6
465					
	1956-1957	Sound Dispatching Station	75	112	150
470					
	1959-1962	IRBM Missile Launch	55	83	110
480-25					
	1950	Conversion Coupler	—	—	4
490					
	1923	Observation, standard, apple green	109	180	360
490					
	1923	Observation, standard, Mojave	75	125	250
494					
	1954	Rotary Beacon, silver, red	25	38	50
497					
	1953-1958	Coaling Station	100	150	200
511					
	1927	Flat, standard, dark green	34	58	115
511					
	1927	Flat, standard, medium green	30	50	100
512					
	1927	Gondola, standard, bright green	36	60	120
512					
	1927	Gondola, standard, peacock	22	38	75
513					
	1927	Cattle, standard	39	65	130
513					
	1927	Cattle, standard, nickel trim	150	250	500
514					
	1927	Refrigerator, standard, Lionel ventilated refrigerator	52	88	175
514					
	1929	Box, standard, ivory/brown	57	95	190
514					
	1929	Box, standard, yellow/brown	50	85	170
514R					
	1929	Refrigerator, standard, ivory body, peacock roof	60	100	200
514R					
	1929	Refrigerator, standard, nickel trim	123	208	415
515					
	1927	Tank, standard, Shell, orange	240	400	800
515					
	1927	Tank, standard, Sunoco logo, terra cotta, ivory and silver	54	90	180
516					
	1928	Hopper, standard	72	120	240
517					
	1927	Caboose, standard, pea green	24	40	80
517					
	1927	Caboose, standard, red and black, coal train, nickel trim	90	150	300
517					
	1927	Caboose, standard, red, nickel trim	30	50	100
520					
	1931	Search Light, standard, green platform	75	128	255
520					
	1931	Search Light, standard, terra cotta platform	50	85	170
520					
	1956	Loco, O27, diesel, eighty ton, original pantograph must not be broken	60	100	200
529					
	1926	Pullman, O, olive green or terra cotta	13	21	42
530					
	1926	Observation, O, olive green or terra cotta	10	17	35
550					
	1932	Miniature Figures, set of six, includes original box	125	188	250
551					
	1932	Miniature Figure, engineer	15	22	30
552					
	1932	Miniature Figure, conductor	15	22	30
553					
	1932	Miniature Figure, porter	15	22	30
554					
	1932	Miniature Figure, male passenger	15	22	30
555					
	1932	Miniature Figure, female, passenger	15	22	30
556					
	1932	Miniature Figure, red cap	15	22	30
600					
	1915	Pullman, O, four wheel, maroon, dark green, brown	18	30	60
600					
	1933	Pullman, O, eight wheel, red w/red roof	54	90	180
600					
	1933	Pullman, O, gray w/red roof	45	75	150

No.	Year	Description	C6	C8	C10
600					
	1933	Pullman, O, light blue w/silver roof	18	30	60
600					
	1955	Loco, O27, diesel SW2, MKT	54	90	180
601					
	1915	Pullman, O, seven, dark green	25	42	85
601					
	1933	Observation, O, gray w/red roof	40	65	130
601					
	1933	Observation, O, light blue w/silver roof	18	30	60
601					
	1933	Observation, O, red w/red roof	45	75	150
601					
	1956	Loco, O27, diesel, Seaboard	60	100	200
602					
	1915	Baggage, O, dark green	21	35	70
602					
	1933	Baggage, gray w/red roof	37	63	125
602					
	1933	Baggage, light blue w/silver roof	54	90	180
602					
	1933	Baggage, red w/red roof	63	108	215
602					
	1957	Loco, O27, diesel SW2, Seaboard	62	105	210
603					
	1920	Pullman, O, later, orange	19	32	64
603					
	1921	Pullman, O, orange, uncataloged	21	35	70
603					
	1931	Pullman, O, late, red, green, orange, maroon	30	50	100
604					
	1920	Observation, O, later, orange	24	40	80
604					
	1931	Observation, O, late, red, green, orange, maroon	25	43	85
605					
	1925	Pullman, O, gray	30	50	100
605					
	1925	Pullman, O, olive	48	80	160
605					
	1925	Pullman, O, orange	48	80	160
605					
	1925	Pullman, O, red	48	80	160
606					
	1925	Observation, O, gray	48	80	160
606					
	1925	Observation, O, olive	48	80	160
606					
	1925	Observation, O, orange	48	80	160
606					
	1925	Observation, O, red	48	80	160
606					
	1930	Observation, O, Macy's, uncataloged	48	80	160
607					
	1926	Pullman, O	25	43	85
607					
	1931	Pullman, O, Macy's, uncataloged	80	135	270
608					
	1926	Observation, O	25	44	88
608					
	1931	Observation, O, Macy's, uncataloged	90	150	300
609					
	1937	Pullman, O, uncataloged	27	45	90
610					
	1915	Pullman, O, early	45	78	155
610					
	1926	Pullman, O, late	21	35	70
610					
	1926	Pullman, O, Macy's, uncataloged	24	40	80
610					
	1955	Loco, O27, diesel SW2, Erie	42	70	140
611					
	1937	Observation, O, uncataloged	18	30	60
611					
	1957	Loco, O27, diesel SW2, CNJ	66	110	220
612					
	1915	Observation, O, early	40	68	135
612					
	1926	Observation, O, late	21	35	70
612					
	1926	Observation, O, Macy	21	35	70
613					
	1931	Pullman, O, blue, Blue Comet set	180	338	675
613					
	1931	Pullman, O, red, aluminum roof	60	100	200
613					
	1931	Pullman, O, terra cotta	85	140	280
613					
	1958	Loco, O27, diesel SW2 UP	81	135	270
614					
	1931	Observation, O, blue, Blue Comet set	66	112	225

No.	Year	Description	C6	C8	C10
614					
	1931	Observation, O, red, aluminum roof	60	100	200
614					
	1931	Observation, O, terra cotta	63	105	210
614					
	1959-1960	Loco, O27, diesel SW2, Alaska, blue, yellow structure on roof	65	110	220
615					
	1933	Baggage, O, blue, Blue Comet set	60	100	200
615					
	1933	Baggage, O, red, aluminum roof	75	125	250
615					
	1933	Baggage, O, terra cotta	75	125	250
616					
	1935	E or W Diesel Type Power Car, O, Streamliner, Flying Yankee, black cast frame, chrome shells	60	105	210
616					
	1961	Loco, O27, diesel SW2, ATSF	66	110	220
616-13					
	1935	Bulb, twelve volt, clear	—	—	1
616T					
	1935	Vestibule, O	12	20	40
617					
	1935	Coach, O, blue and white, Blue Streak	36	60	120
617					
	1935	Coach, O, Streamliner, black and chrome	24	39	78
617					
	1963	Loco, O, diesel SW2, ATSF, black	90	150	300
618					
	1935	Observation, O, blue and white, Blue Streak	45	75	150
618					
	1935	Observation, O, Streamliner, black and chrome	25	43	85
619					
	1935	Combine, O, Streamliner, blue and white, Blue Streak	90	150	300
620					
	1937	Floodlight, O	30	45	60
621					
	1956	Loco, O27, diesel SW2, CNJ	37	62	125
622					
	1949	Loco, diesel SW2, Santa Fe, black	80	135	270
623					
	1952	Loco, O, diesel SW2, ATSF, black	73	123	245
624					
	1952	Loco, O, diesel SW2, C&O, blue, yellow stripe	78	130	260
625					
	1957	Loco, O27, diesel, forty-four ton, LV	42	70	140
626					
	1957	Loco, O27, diesel, forty-four ton, B&O	135	225	450
627					
	1956	Loco, O27, diesel, forty-four ton, LV, red body, white stripe	39	65	130
628					
	1956	Loco, O27, diesel, forty-four ton, NP, black w/yellow stripe	50	83	165
629					
	1924	Pullman, O, four wheel	20	32	65
629					
	1934	Pullman, O, eight wheel, uncataloged	39	65	130
629					
	1956	Loco, O27, diesel, forty-four ton, Burlington, silver, red stripe	105	175	350
630					
	1924	Observation, O, four wheel	16	28	55
630					
	1931	Macy Observation, O, four wheel, uncataloged	24	40	80
630					
	1934	Observation, O, eight wheel, uncataloged	27	45	90
633					
	1962	Loco, O, diesel SW2, Santa Fe	40	68	135
634					
	1962	Loco, O, diesel SW2, Santa Fe, blue body	18	30	60
636-13					
	1936	Bulb, eight volt, clear	—	—	1
6362					
	1955	Rail Truck Car, O, orange frame w/three sets of trucks	15	25	50
636W					
	1936	Diesel Type Power Car, O, Streamliner, yellow and brown, Union Pacific's, "City of Denver"	42	70	140
637					
	1936	Coach, O, Streamliner, "City of Denver"	30	50	100
637					
	1959	Loco, Super O, steam, 2-6-4, 2046W tender or 2040W tender	52	88	175

No.	Year	Description	C6	C8	C10
638					
	1936	Observation, O, Streamliner, "City of Denver," yellow and brown	30	50	100
645					
	1963	Loco, O27, diesel SW2, Union Pacific, yellow body	41	68	135
646					
	1954	Loco, O, steam, 4-6-4, 2046W tender	88	148	295
651					
	1935	Flat, O	15	25	50
652					
	1935	Gondola, O	16	28	55
653					
	1934	Hopper, O	19	33	65
654					
	1934	Tank, O, silver, orange	15	25	50
655					
	1934	Box, O	16	28	55
656					
	1935	Cattle, O	30	50	100
657					
	1934	Caboose, O	10	18	35
659					
	1935	Dump, O	24	40	80
665					
	1954	Loco, O, steam, 4-6-4, 6026W or 2046W tender	60	100	200
671					
	1946	Loco, O, steam, 6-8-6, 671W tender	70	115	230
671					
	1946	Loco, O, steam, 6-8-6, w/2671 tender	90	150	300
671					
	1952	R&R Loco, O, steam, 671W tender	75	125	250
671-75					
	1946	Smoke Bulb, fourteen volt	—	—	10
675					
	1947	Loco, O, steam, 2-6-2, 2466W, 2466WX or 6466WX tender	70	115	230
681					
	1950	Loco, O, steam, 6-8-6, 2671W tender	78	130	260
682					
	1954	Loco, O, steam, 6-8-6, 2046W 50 tender	140	233	465
685					
	1953	Loco, O, steam, 4-6-4, 6026W tender	85	142	285
700					
	1913-1916	Loco, O, electric, 0-4-0, dark green NYC Lines	225	375	750
700E					
	1937	Loco, steam and tender 072, 4-6-4, black, 700/700W, twelve wheel cast tender	750	1250	2500
700E250					
	1938	Display Stand and Track, w/Lionel ID plate	810	1350	2700
700EWX					
	1937	Loco, O72, steam and whistle tender, black 700/700W, twelve wheel cast tender	1200	2000	4000
700K					
	1939	Loco, O72, steam kit, 4-6-4, gray, kit form, six kits all original boxes	2800	4200	5600
701					
	1913-1916	Loco, electric, 0-4-0, dark green	270	450	900
703					
	1913-1916	Loco, O, electric, 4-4-4, dark green	660	1100	2200
703-10					
	1946	Smoke Bulb, O	—	—	10
706					
	1913-1916	Loco, O, electric, 0-4-0, dark green	420	700	1400
708					
	1939	Loco, O72, steam, scale switcher, 0-6-0, 8976 cast in boiler front	900	1500	3000
710					
	1924	Pullman, O, green, orange	75	125	250
710					
	1924	Pullman, O, red	60	100	200
710					
	1924	Pullman, O, two-tone blue	67	112	225
711					
	1935	Switches, O72, electric, pair	75	112	150
712					
	1924	Observation, O, green, orange	72	120	240
712					
	1924	Observation, O, red	60	100	200
712					
	1924	Observation, O, two-tone blue	66	110	220
714					
	1940	Box, O72	120	200	400
714K					
	1940	Boxcar, O72, kit, new only	—	—	1000
715					
	1940	Tank, O72	120	200	400

No.	Year	Description	C6	C8	C10
715K					
	1940	Tank, O72, kit, new only ....—	—	1000
716					
	1940	Hopper, O72 97	163	325
716K					
	1940	Hopper, O72, kit, new only.......—	—	1000
717					
	1940	Caboose, O72..........................165	275	550
717-54					
	1940	Bulb, eighteen volt, clear ....—	—	1
717K					
	1940	Caboose, O72, kit, new only .....—	—	500
720					
	1935	90 Degrees Crossing, O 7	22	58
721					
	1935	Switches, O72, non-electric, pair 42	70	140
726					
	1946	Loco, O, steam, 2-8-4, 2046W tender 108	180	360
726					
	1946	Loco, O, steam, 2-8-4, 2426W tender 200	330	660
730					
	1935	90 Degrees Crossing T-Rail, O72 15	22	30
731					
	1935	Switches, O72, electric, T-rail, pair 175	263	350
736					
	1950	Loco, O, steam, 2-8-4, 2046W tender 110	183	365
746					
	1957	Loco, O, steam, 4-8-4, "Norfolk & Western," 746W tender w/short stripe 330	550	1110
746					
	1957	Loco, O, steam, 4-8-4, w/long stripe.........................450	750	1500
752-9					
	1934	Bulb, eighteen volt, clear ....—	—	1
752E or W					
	1934	Streamliner Power Car, O 140	235	470
753					
	1934	Streamliner Coach, O 42	70	140
754					
	1934	Streamliner Observation, O......42	70	140
760					
	1935	Pack of Curved Track, sixteen sections.......................16	24	32
761					
	1934	Curved Track, O72 ....—	1	2
762					
	1934	Straight Track, O72..................—	1	2
762S					
	1934	Insulated Straight Track, O72, w/lock-on ....—	2	3
763E					
	1937	Loco, O, steam, 4-6-4, gunmetal gray 2226W or 2226WX tender....................720	1200	2400
763E					
	1937	Loco, O, steam, 4-6-4, semi-scale Hudson, black, 2226WX tender, or gunmetal gray 263 or 2263W tender....555	925	1850
771					
	1935	Curved Track, O72, T-rail ....—	2	3
772					
	1935	Straight Track, O72, T-rail........—	2	3
772S					
	1940	Insulated Straight Track, O72, T-rail..3	4	5
773					
	1936	Fish Plate Set, O72, 100 bolts, 100 nuts, fifty fishplates and wrench.....................................25	38	50
773					
	1950	Loco, O, steam, 4-6-4 Hudson 2426W tender.......................450	765	1530
773					
	1964	Loco, 4-6-4 Hudson, 2046W tender 240	400	800
782					
	1935	Streamliner Front Coach, O72, "The Milwaukee Road," part of articulated Hiawatha set, gray roof, orange sides and maroon underframe.............150	250	500
783					
	1935	Streamliner Coach, O72, "The Milwaukee Road," part of articulated Hiawatha set, gray roof orange sides and maroon underframe......150	250	500
784					
	1935	Streamliner Observation, O72, "The Milwaukee Road," part of articulated Hiawatha set, gray roof, orange sides and maroon underframe......150	250	500
793					
	1937	Streamliner Coach, O72, part of Rail Chief set, "793 Lionel Lines 793" 150	250	500
794					
	1937	Streamliner Observation, O72, part of Rail Chief set, "794		

No.	Year	Description	C6	C8	C10
		Lionel Lines 794," maroon roof, red sides, red underframe 150	250	500
800					
	1915	Box, O 33	55	110
801					
	1915	Caboose, O 19	33	65
802					
	1915	Stock, O 21	35	70
803					
	1923	Hopper, O, dark green 15	25	50
803					
	1923	Hopper, O, peacock 25	43	85
803					
	1929	Hopper, O 15	25	50
804					
	1923	Tank, O, early, dark gray 20	33	65
804					
	1923	Tank, O, Sunoco, silver 21	35	70
804					
	1923	Tank, O, terra cotta 20	33	65
804					
	1929	Tank, O 21	35	70
805					
	1927	Box, O, orange, maroon 15	25	50
805					
	1927	Box, O, pea green, orange 23	38	75
806					
	1927	Cattle, O 30	50	100
807					
	1927	Caboose, O 14	23	45
809					
	1931	Dump, O 18	30	60
810					
	1930-1940	Crane, O 60	100	200
811					
	1926	Flat, O, maroon 13	21	42
811					
	1926	Flat, O, silver 40	68	135
812					
	1926	Gondola, O 24	40	80
812T					
	1937	Tool Set, O 16	24	32
813					
	1926	Cattle, O 36	60	120
814					
	1926	Box, O, nickel plate 66	110	220
814					
	1926	Box, O, orange body, brown roof 30	50	100
814R					
	1929	Refrigerator, O, w/rubber-stamped lettering 360	600	1200

No.	Year	Description	C6	C8	C10
814R					
	1929	Refrigerator, O, white body, brown roof 85	143	285
815					
	1926	Tank, O, aluminum, silver 57	95	190
815					
	1926	Tank, O, Shell, orange 40	68	135
816					
	1927	Hopper, O, black 75	125	250
816					
	1927	Hopper, O, red, olive green 37	63	125
817					
	1926	Caboose, O 28	48	95
817					
	1926	Caboose, O, flat red, brown roof, rubber-stamped lettering 60	100	200
820					
	1915	Box, O, dark olive, rubber stamped ATSF and 48522 60	100	200
820					
	1915	Box, O, orange or maroon 27	45	90
820					
	1931	Floodlight, O, green base 68	113	225
820					
	1931	Floodlight, O, terra cotta base 45	75	150
821					
	1915	Cattle, O 27	45	90
822					
	1915	Caboose, O 22	38	75
831					
	1927	Flat, O 18	30	60
876					
	1965	Helios 21 Spaceship 12	20	40
900 or B					
	1939	Catalog, O, number for 230 and tender, 0-6-0, similar to loco 227 450	750	1500
900					
	1904	Express Trail Car, 2-7/8", auctioned in 1994 4500		
900					
	1917	Box, O, ammunition, part of armored train set 150	250	500
901					
	1919	Gondola, O, gray or maroon 20	33	65
902					
	1927	Gondola, O, apple green 8	13	25
902					
	1927	Gondola, O, peacock 8	13	25
902-5					
	1958	Rocks .... —	—	3

No.	Year	Description	C6	C8	C10
909					
	1957	Smoke Fluid, full bottle	—	—	5
910					
	1932	Grove, eleven trees	150	225	300
911					
	1932	Country Estate, 191 villa, shrubbery and trees	450	675	900
912					
	1932	Suburban Home, 189 villa, shrubbery and trees	375	525	750
913					
	1932	Bungalow, w/garden, flowers and trees	250	375	500
914					
	1932	Formal Garden Park, two grass plots, centerpiece, flowering bushes, cream base	175	268	350
915					
	1932	Curved Tunnel Mountain, O, large	200	300	400
916					
	1932	Curved Tunnel, O	175	263	350
917					
	1932	Mountain, medium	200	300	400
918					
	1932	Mountain, small	175	263	350
919					
	1932	Park Grass, eight ounces	9	14	18
920					
	1932	Scenic Park, small	2000	3000	4000
920					
	1957	Scenic Display Set	37	56	75
920-2					
	1958	Tunnel Portals	15	23	30
920-8					
	1958	Lichen	—	—	3
921					
	1932	Scenic Park, large	1400	2100	2800
921C					
	1932	Scenic Park, center section	400	600	800
922					
	1932	Lamp Terrace	175	263	350
923					
	1933	Tunnel, standard	200	300	400
924					
	1935	Curved Tunnel, O72	150	225	300
926					
	1955	Tube of Lubrication, full tube	—	—	3
927					
	1937-1942	Flag Plot	40	60	80
927					
	1950-1953	Lubrication and Maintenance, kit	10	17	33
927-3					
	1955	Can of Liquid Track Cleaner	—	—	5
928					
	1960-1963	Maintenance Kit	8	11	15
950					
	1958-1966	Railroad Map	25	38	50
951					
	1958	Farm Set, plastic, thirteen pieces	8	11	15
952					
	1958	Figure Set, plastic, thirty pieces	8	11	15
953					
	1959	Figure Set, plastic, thirty-two pieces	8	11	15
954					
	1959	Swimming Pool and Playground Set, plastic, thirty pieces	10	15	20
955					
	1958	Highway Set, plastic, twenty-two pieces	10	15	20
956					
	1959	Stockyard, plastic, eighteen pieces	10	15	20
957					
	1958	Farm Building and Animal Set, plastic, thirty-five pieces	10	15	20
958					
	1958	Vehicles, plastic, twenty-four pieces	10	15	20
959					
	1958	Barn Set, plastic, twenty-three pieces	6	9	12
960					
	1959	Barn Yard Set, plastic, twenty-nine pieces	6	9	12
961					
	1959	School Set, plastic, thirty-six pieces	10	15	20
962					
	1958	Turnpike Set, plastic, twenty-four pieces	10	15	20
963					
	1959	Frontier Set, plastic, eighteen pieces	10	15	20
964					
	1959	Factory, plastic, twenty-two pieces	10	15	20
965					
	1959	Farm Set, plastic, thirty-six pieces	13	19	26

No. Year	Description	C6	C8	C10
966				
1958	Firehouse, plastic, forty-five pieces 13		19	26
967				
1958	Post Office, plastic, twenty-five pieces 10		15	20
968				
1958	TV Transmitter, plastic, twenty-eight pieces 10		15	20
969				
1960	Construction Set, plastic, twenty-three pieces 10		15	20
970				
1958-1960	Ticket Booth, cardboard 65		98	130
971				
1959	Box of Lichen .... —		—	5
972				
1959	Trees .... —		—	5
973				
1959	Landscaping Set 7		11	14
974				
1962	Scenery Set 11		17	22
97C				
1938	Contactor 5		8	10
980				
1960	Ranch Set, plastic, fourteen pieces 10		15	20
981				
1960	Freight Yard Set, plastic, ten pieces 10		15	20
982				
1960	Surburban House, plastic, eighteen pieces 10		15	20
983				
1960	Farm Set, plastic, seven pieces 10		15	20
984				
1961	Railroad Set, plastic, twenty-two pieces 10		15	20
985				
1961	Freight Area Set, plastic, thirty-two pieces 13		19	26
986				
1962	Farm Set, plastic, twenty pieces 10		15	20
987				
1962	Town Set, plastic, twenty-four pieces 10		15	20
988				
1962	Railroad Structure, sixteen pieces 10		15	20
1000				
1910	Trailer Truck, standard, 100 series 840		1400	2800

No. Year	Description	C6	C8	C10
1000				
1910	Trolley, standard, trailer 840		1400	2800
1001				
1948	Loco, O27, steam, 2-4-2, w/1001T tender 15		25	50
1002				
1948	Gondola, O27 4		7	14
1004				
1948	Box, O27 7		11	22
1005				
1948	Tank, O27 4		7	13
1007				
1936	Platform and Background, O27 30		45	60
1007				
1948	Caboose, O27 3		4	8
1008				
1957	Uncoupling Track, O27, price per each .... —		1	2
1008-50				
1961	Automatic Uncoupling Track, O27, price per each..... —		1	2
1009				
1948	Manumatic Uncoupling Track Set, O27 5		7	9
1010				
1910	Interurban Trolley, standard................................ 1750		2625	3500
1010				
1931	Winner Loco, O27, electric, 0-4-0 30		50	100
1010				
1961	Transformer, thirty-five watt 4		6	8
1011				
1910	Interurban Trolley, standard, motor car 1050		1750	3500
1011				
1931	Winner Pullman, O27 9		15	30
1011				
1961	Transformer, fifteen watt 5		8	10
1012				
1910	Interurban Trolley, standard................................ 1050		1750	3500
1012				
1931	Winner Station Transformer 22		33	45
1012				
1950	Transformer, thirty-five watt 5		7	9
1013				
1934	Curved Track, O27 .... —		—	1
1013				
1968	Half Section Curved Track, O27 .... —		—	1

No. Year	Description	C6	C8	C10
1013-17				
1938	Track Pins, O27, steel, price per dozen	—	1	2
1014				
1931	Lockton, O27	—	1	2
1014				
1955	Transformer, forty watt	10	15	20
1015				
1931	Winner Loco, O27, steam, w/1016 tender, black, 0-4-0	30	50	100
1015				
1956	Transformer, forty-five watt	8	11	15
1016				
	Winner Loco, w/tender, black	30	50	100
1016				
1959	Transformer, thirty-five watt	3	4	5
1017				
1931	Winner Transformer Station	22	34	45
1017				
1933	Lionel-Ives Transformer Station	22	34	45
1018				
1934	Straight Track, O27	—	—	1
1018				
1968	Half Section Straight Track, O27	—	—	1
1019				
1931	Winner Observation, O27	7	13	25
1019				
1938	Remote Control Track Set, O27	5	8	10
1020				
1931	Winner Baggage, O27	7	13	25
1020				
1955	90 Degrees Crossing, O27	1	2	3
1021				
1933	90 Degrees Crossing, O27	1	2	3
1022				
1935	Curced Tunnel, O27	20	30	40
1022				
1955	Switch, O27, manual, price per pair	8	12	25
1023				
1934	Straight Tunnel, O27	18	27	35
1023				
1955	45 Degrees Crossing, O27, price per each	1	2	3
1024				
1935	Manual Switches, O27, price per pair	5	8	11
1025				
1946	Bumper, O27	4	6	8
1025				
1961	Transformer, forty-five watt	3	4	5
1026				
1963	Transformer, twenty-five watt	4	5	7
1028				
1935	Transformer, twenty-five watt	3	4	5
1029				
1936	Transformer, twenty-five watt	3	4	5
1030				
1932	Winner Loco, O27, electric, 0-4-0, orange w/green roof	30	50	100
1030				
1936	Transformer, forty watt	4	6	12
1032				
1948	Transformer, ninety watt	22	33	45
1033				
1948	Transformer, ninety watt	28	42	55
1034				
1948	Transformer, seventy-five watt	30	45	60
1035				
1932	Winner Loco, O27, steam, 0-4-0, w/1016 tender	30	50	100
1035				
1947	Transformer, sixty watt	12	18	25
1037				
1941	Transformer, forty watt	10	15	20
1039				
1938	Transformer, thirty-five watt	10	15	20
1040				
1938	Transformer and Whistle Controller, sixty watt	12	18	25
1041				
1940	Transformer, sixty watt	12	18	25
1042				
1942	Transformer, seventy-five watt	12	18	25
1043				
	Transformer, fifty watt	10	15	20
1043				
1953	Transformer, sixty watt	10	15	20
1043-500FX				
1957	Girls Train Transformer, sixty watt, ivory case	40	60	80
1044				
1957	Transformer, ninety watt	12	18	25
1045				
1938	Operating Watchman, nickle or brass sign	25	38	50
1045C				
1938	Contactor	—	—	1
1046				
1936	Mechanical Gateman and Crossing	45	68	90

No.	Year	Description	C6	C8	C10
1047					
	1959-1961	Switchman, w/flat 33	55	110	
1053					
	1956	Transformer, sixty watt.............30	45	60	
1055					
	1960	Loco, O, Alco A diesel, Texas Special, uncataloged 20	32	65	
1060					
	1960	Loco, O27, Scout team, 2-4-2, w/1050T tender 5	9	18	
1061					
	1969	Loco, O27, steam, 2-4-2, w/1061T tender 6	10	20	
1062					
	1963	Loco and Tender, O27, 2-4-2, w/1062T tender 12	19	38	
1063					
	1961	Transformer, seventy-five watt..22	33	45	
1065					
		Loco, O, Alco A unit only, diesel, Union Pacific, uncataloged..............................21	35	70	
1066					
		Loco, O, Alco A unit only, diesel, Union Pacific, uncataloged..............................21	35	70	
1073					
	1961	Transformer, sixty watt................5	8	10	
1100					
	1911	Summer Trolley, standard 1050	1750	3500	
1100					
	1924	Trailer Trucks, standard, thirty-five series.......................3	5	10	
1100					
	1935	Mickey Mouse Handcar, green base 225	375	750	
1100					
	1935	Mickey Mouse Handcar, mechanical, wind-up, orange base 300	500	1000	
1100					
	1935	Mickey Mouse Handcar, red base 180	300	600	
1101					
		Loco, 2-4-2 15	25	50	
1101					
	1924	Trailer Trucks, standard, w/lights, thirty-five series.........3	5	10	
1103					
	1935	Peter Rabbit Handcar, floor operation 210	350	700	
1103					
	1935	Peter Rabbit Handcar,			

No.	Year	Description	C6	C8	C10
		mechanical, wind-up, track operation 210	358	715	
1105					
	1935	Santa Claus Handcar, mechanical, Red base...........480	800	1600	
1105					
	1935	Santa Claus Handcar, mechanical, wind-up, green base..............................540	900	1800	
1107					
	1936	Donald Duck Rail Car, mechanical, wind-up, green roof...270	450	900	
1107					
	1936	Donald Duck Rail Car, red roof....................................270	450	900	
1110					
	1949	Loco, O27, Scout steam, 2-4-2 14	23	45	
1120					
	1950	Loco, O27, Scout steam, 2-4-2 15	25	50	
1121					
	1937	Switches, O27, electric, remote control, pair...............12	18	25	
1122					
	1952	Switches, O27, remote control 17	26	35	
1122-100					
	1957	Switch Control, O27 3	4	5	
1122-234					
	1957	Insulating Pins, O27 .... —	—	1	
1122-520					
	1957	Adapter Kit, O2 7	5	810	
1130					
	1953	Loco, O27, steam, 2-4-2, w/1130T tender.......................8	13	25	
1144					
	1968	Transformer, seventy-five watt..22	33	45	
1200					
	1923	Trailer Truck, standard, ten series...................................4	6	12	
1201					
	1923	Trailer Truck, standard, ten series w/lights.....................4	6	12	
1229					
	1938	Transformer, 220 volts 50	75	100	
1230					
	1938	Transformer, 220 volts 50	75	100	
1239					
	1941	Transformer, 220 volts 50	75	100	
1241					
	1941	Transformer, 220 volts 50	75	100	

No. Year	Description	C6	C8	C10
1300				
1925	Trailer Truck, standard, 200 series	4	6	12
1506				
1933	L.I. Loco, steam, mechanical	36	60	120
1506				
1935	Loco Outfit, mechanical, w/1509T Tender, 1515 tank and 1517 caboose	75	125	250
1506-8				
1935	Bulb, 1-1/2 volt, clear	—	—	1
1506L				
1933	Loco Outfit, mechanical, w/1502T tender	36	60	120
1508				
1935	Loco and Tender Outfit, mechanical, 0-4-0 Vanderbilt type, w/1509T tender	81	135	270
1511				
1936-1937	Loco and Tender Outfit, mechanical, 0-4-0 Commodore Vanderbilt type, black, w/1516 tender	45	75	150
1511				
1936-1937	Loco and Tender Outfit, mechanical, 0-4-0, red, w/1516 tender	54	90	180
1512				
1931	Winner Gondola, O27	18	30	60
1512				
1933	L.I. Gondola, O27	18	30	60
1512				
1936	Gondola, O27	18	30	60
1514				
1932	Winner Box, O27	9	15	30
1514				
1933	L.I. Box, O27	7	11	22
1514				
1934	Box, O27	12	21	42
1515				
1933	L.I. Tank, O27	11	19	38
1515				
1934	Tank, O27	19	32	64
1516T				
1936	Tender, O27	12	21	42
1517				
1931	Winner Caboose, O27	7	11	22
1517				
1931-1937	Caboose, O27	11	18	36
1517				
1933	L.I. Caboose, O27	9	15	30
1520				
1935	Animal	60	100	200
1521				
1937	Loco and Tender Outfit, mechanical, w/1516T tender	180	300	600
1550				
1933	Switches-mechanical, remote control, price per pair	20	30	40
1551				
1936	90 Degrees Crossing, mechanical	2	3	4
1555				
1933	Crossing 90 Degrees, mechanical	3	5	5
1560				
1933	Station, mechanical	15	22	30
1572				
1934	L. Jr. Telegraph Posts, mechanical	11	18	36
1573				
1934	L. Jr. Warning Signal, mechanical	8	12	16
1574				
1934	L. Jr. Clock, mechanical	5	8	16
1588				
1936	Loco and Tender Outfit, mechanical, w/1588 or 1516 tender, 0-4-0, torpedo type	66	110	220
1615				
1955	Loco, O27, 0-4-0, w/1615T tender, switcher	54	90	180
1615E				
1933	L.I. Loco, O27, electric, 0-4-0, red cab, brown roof	75	125	250
1625				
1958	Loco, O27, steam, 0-4-0, switcher, w/1625 tender	75	125	250
1630				
1938	Pullman, O27, blue sides, aluminum roof	20	33	65
1630				
1938	Pullman, O27, blue sides, gray roof	20	33	65
1631				
1938	Observation, O27, blue sides, aluminum roof	23	39	78
1640-100				
1960	Presidential Kit	22	33	45
1654				
1946	Loco, O27, steam, 2-4-2, w/1654W tender	30	50	100
1655				
1945	Loco, O27, steam, 2-4-2, w/6654W tender	45	75	150

No.	Year	Description	C6	C8	C10
1656					
	1948	Loco, O27, steam, 0-4-0 switcher, w/6403 tender 110		185	370
1661E					
	1933	L.I. Loco, O27, steam, 2-4-0, w/1661 Tender, gloss black 39		65	130
1662					
	1940	Loco, O27, steam, 0-4-0 switcher, w/2203 tender 125		205	410
1663					
	1940	Loco, O27, steam, 0-4-0 switcher, 2201 tender 138		230	460
1664 or E					
	1938	Loco and Tender Outfit, O27, 2-4-2, w/1689T, 1689W, 2666T or 2666W tender, black or gunmetal gray 60		103	205
1665					
	1946	Loco, O27, steam, 0-4-0, switcher w/2403B tender 125		210	420
1666 or E					
	1938	Loco and Tender Outfit, O27, 2-4-2 black w/2666T 39		65	130
1666 or E					
	1938	Loco and Tender Outfit, O27, 2-4-2, gunmetal gray 36		60	120
1668 or E					
	1937	Loco, O27, steam, 2-6-2, gunmetal gray 42		70	140
1668 or E					
	1937	Loco, O27, steam, 2-6-2, w/1689T or 1689W tender, black 40		68	135
1673					
	1936	Coach, streamliner, mechanical, red 14		23	45
1674					
	1936	Pullman, streamliner, mechanical.............................. 14		23	45
1675					
	1936	Observation, streamliner, mechanical.............................. 14		23	45
1677					
	1933	L.I. Gondola, O27 12		20	40
1677					
	1934	Gondola, O27 12		20	40
1679					
	1933	L.I. Box, O27 12		20	40
1679					
	1934	Box, O27.. 8		13	25
1680					
	1933	L.I. Tank, O27 12		20	40
1680					
	1934	Tank, O27................................. 13		21	42
1681 or E					
	1934	L.Jr. Loco, O27, steam, 2-4-0 black 42		70	140
1681 or E					
	1934	L.Jr. Loco, O27, steam, 2-4-0, red... 48		80	160
1682					
	1933	L.I. Caboose, O27 9		15	30
1682					
	1934	Caboose, O27 6		10	20
1684					
	1942	Loco, O27, steam, 2-4-2, gunmetal gray 29		48	95
1684					
	1942	Loco, O27, steam, 2-4-2, w/1689T, 1688T, 2689T or 2689W tender, black 45		78	155
1685					
	1933	Pullman, O, gray body, maroon roof, six-wheel trucks, uncataloged 135		225	450
1685					
	1933	Pullman, O, Ives transitional car, blue body, silver roof, four-wheel trucks, uncataloged 120		200	400
1685					
	1933	Pullman, O, red body, maroon roof, four-wheel trucks, uncataloged 90		150	300
1686					
	1933	Baggage, O, gray body, maroon roof, six-wheel trucks, uncataloged 135		225	450
1686					
	1933	Baggage, O, Ives transitional car, blue body, silver roof, four-wheel trucks, uncataloged 120		200	400
1686					
	1933	Baggage, O, red body, maroon roof, four-wheel trucks, uncataloged 90		150	300
1687					
	1933	Observation, O, gray body, maroon roof, six-wheel trucks, uncataloged 135		225	450
1687					
	1933	Observation, O, Ives transitional car, blue body, silver roof, four-wheel trucks, uncataloged 120		200	400
1687					
	1933	Observation, O, red body, maroon roof, four-wheel trucks, uncataloged 90		150	300

No. Year	Description	C6	C8	C10
1688 or E				
1936	Loco, O27, steam, 2-4-2, gunmetal gray 60		100	200
1688 or E				
1936	Loco, O27, steam, 2-4-2, w/1689T tender, black 36		90	120
1689E				
1936	Loco, O27, steam, 2-4-2, gunmetal gray 39		65	130
1689E				
1936	Loco, O27, steam, 2-4-2, w/1689T tender, black 35		55	110
169				
1940	Uncoupling and Reversing Controller ....—		2	3
1690				
1933	L.I. Pullman, O27, red w/red or brown roof.............. 15		25	50
1690				
1934	Pullman, O27, red, w/red or brown roof 12		20	40
1691				
1933	L.I. Observation, O27, red w/red or brown roof.............. 12		20	40
1691				
1934	Observation, O27, red w/red or brown roof 12		20	40
1692				
1937	Pullman, O27, peacock body and roof, uncataloged 12		20	40
1693				
1937	Observation, O27, peacock body and roof, uncataloged ... 12		20	40
1697				
1937	Loco,Tender and Transformer Outfit, O27..............................45		75	150
1698E				
1936	Loco, Tender and Transformer Outfit, O27..........................60		100	200
1699E				
1936	Loco, Tender and Transformer Outfit, O27..........................60		100	200
1700 or E				
1935	Power Car, O27, diesel, streamliner, "Lionel Jr.," aluminum and red.................66		110	220
1701				
1935	Coach, O27, streamliner, aluminum and red or chrome 36		60	120
1702				
1935	Observation, O27, streamliner, aluminum and red or chrome 36		60	120
1703				
1935	Front Coach, O27, w/drawbar, streamliner 12		20	40
1717				
1933	Gondola, O, orange and tan or yellow and green, uncataloged.............................15		25	50
1719				
1933	Box, O, peacock w/blue roof, orange doors, yellow and brown, uncataloged 13		23	45
1722				
1933	Caboose, O, orange body or red body, uncataloged........18		30	60
175-50				
1958	Extra Rockets, O..........................4		6	8
1766				
1934	Pullman, standard.....................85		142	285
1767				
1934	Baggage, standard 90		150	300
1768				
1934	Observation, standard 105		175	350
1811				
1933	L.I. Pullman, O27......................22		36	72
1811				
1934	Pullman, O27 22		36	72
1812				
1933	L.I. Observation, O27 22		36	72
1812				
1934	Observation, O27.......................22		36	72
1813				
1933	L.I. Baggage, O27 18		30	60
1813				
1934	Baggage, O27 18		30	60
1816 or W				
1935	Power Car, streamliner, mechanical, diesel wind-up, "Silver Streak"..................42		70	140
1817				
1935	Coach, streamliner, mechanical, chrome and orange.................10		16	32
1818				
1935	Observation, streamliner, mechanical, chrome and orange......................................10		16	32
1835E				
1934	Loco, standard, steam, 2-4-2, w/1835T, 1835TW or 1835W tender........................230		380	760
1862				
1959	Loco, O27, steam, 4-4-0, civil war, w/1862T tender, "General" 36		60	120
1865				
1959	Coach, O27, Western & Atlantic...................................20		34	68

No.	Year	Description	C6	C8	C10
1866					
	1959	Baggage Car, O27, Western & Atlantic	30	50	100
1872					
	1959	Loco, Super O, steam, 4-4-0, w/1872W tender, civil war, "General"	90	150	300
1875					
	1959	Coach, Super O, Western & Atlantic	55	112	225
1875W					
	1959	Coach, Super O, Western & Atlantic, w/whistle	60	100	200
1876					
	1959	Baggage, Super O, Western & Atlantic	36	60	120
1877					
	1959	Flat, O27, part of General set, six horses	22	36	72
1882					
	1959	Loco, Super O, steam, Sears Production, Civil War	150	250	500
1885					
	1959	Coach, Super O, Sears production, Western & Atlantic, uncataloged	75	125	250
1887					
	1959	Flat, O27, Sears Production, six horses, uncataloged	54	90	180
1903					
	1903	Ewing Merkle Catalog	21	35	70
1903					
	1903	Lionel Catalog	21	35	70
1904					
	1904	Lionel Catalog	21	35	70
1905					
	1905	Lionel Catalog	21	35	70
1906					
	1906	Lionel Catalog	21	35	70
1907					
	1907	Lionel Catalog	21	35	70
1908					
	1908	Lionel Catalog	21	35	70
1909					
	1909	Lionel Catalog	21	35	70
1910					
	1910	Lionel Catalog	21	35	70
1910					
	1910	Loco, standard, electric, 0-6-0, dark olive green, "New York, New Haven and Hartford"	600	1000	2000
1910					
	1910	Pullman, standard, dark olive green, maroon doors,			

No.	Year	Description	C6	C8	C10
		"1910 Pullman 1910," uncataloged	540	900	1800
1911					
	1910	Loco, standard, electric, 0-4-0, dark olive	330	550	1100
1911					
	1910	Loco, standard, electric, 0-4-0, maroon	300	500	1000
1911					
	1911	Lionel Catalog	21	35	70
1911					
	1911	Special Loco, standard, electric, 0-4-4-0, maroon either, "New York, New Haven and Hartford" or "New York Central Lines"	420	700	1400
1912					
	1910	Loco, standard, Electric, 0-4-4-0, "New York, New Haven and Hartford"	720	1200	2400
1912					
	1910	Loco, standard, Electric, 0-4-4-0, dark olive green	660	1100	2200
1912					
	1911	Special Loco, standard, electric, 0-4-4-0, all brass engine, polished	1500	2500	5000
1912					
	1912	Lionel Catalog	21	35	70
1913					
	1913	Lionel Catalog	21	35	70
1913					
	1913	Lionel Catalog, small	15	25	50
1914					
	1914	Lionel Catalog	21	35	70
1914					
	1914	Lionel Catalog, small	15	25	50
1915					
	1915	Lionel Catalog	21	35	70
1916					
	1916	Lionel Catalog	21	35	70
1917					
	1917	Lionel Catalog	21	35	70
1917					
	1917	Lionel Folder	8	13	25
1918					
	1918	Lionel Folder	8	13	25
1919					
	1919	Lionel Apology Folder	13	23	45
1919					
	1919	Lionel Folder	8	13	25
1920					
	1920	Lionel Catalog	21	35	70
1920					
	1920	Lionel Folder	8	13	25

No. Year	Description	C6	C8	C10
1921				
1921	Lionel Folder......................8	13	25	
1922				
1922	Lionel Catalog....................21	35	70	
1923				
1923	Lionel Catalog....................15	25	50	
1924				
1924	Lionel Catalog....................21	35	70	
1925				
1925	Lionel Catalog....................21	35	70	
1926				
1926	Lionel Catalog....................18	30	60	
1926-3				
1933	Lionel-Ives Bulb, six volt............1	0	0	
1927				
1927	Lionel Catalog....................22	38	75	
1928				
1928	Lionel Catalog....................22	38	75	
1928				
	Dealer Display, large cardboard background showing power station, roundhouses, etc.....210	350	700	
1929				
1929	Lionel Catalog....................21	35	70	
1930				
1930	Lionel Catalog....................21	35	70	
1930				
1930	Winner Folder....................11	21	35	
1931				
1931	Lionel Catalog....................21	35	70	
1931				
1931	Winner Folder....................11	21	35	
1932				
1932	Lionel Catalog....................22	38	75	
1932				
1932	Winner Folder....................11	21	35	
1933				
1933	Lionel Catalog....................16	28	55	
1934				
1934	Lionel Catalog....................15	24	48	
1935				
1935	Lionel Catalog....................17	28	55	
1936				
1936	Lionel Catalog....................15	24	48	
1937				
1937	Lionel Catalog....................11	18	35	
1938				
1938	Lionel Catalog....................14	23	45	
1939				
1939	Lionel Catalog....................11	18	35	
1940				
1940	Lionel Catalog....................12	20	40	
1941				
1941	Lionel Catalog....................14	23	45	
1942				
1942	Lionel Catalog....................14	23	45	
1945				
1945	Lionel Catalog....................5	8	16	
1946				
1946	Lionel Folder....................12	20	40	
1947				
1947	Lionel Catalog....................9	14	28	
1948				
1948	Lionel Catalog....................9	15	30	
1949				
1949	Lionel Catalog....................21	35	70	
1950				
1957-1969	Floodlight Tower....................30	45	60	
1950				
1950	Lionel Catalog....................12	20	40	
1951				
1951	Lionel Catalog....................8	13	26	
1952				
1952	Lionel Catalog....................9	15	30	
1953				
1953	Lionel Catalog....................7	12	24	
1954				
1954	Lionel Catalog....................5	9	17	
1955				
1955	Lionel Catalog....................5	9	17	
1956				
1956	Lionel Catalog....................5	8	16	
1957				
1957	Lionel Catalog....................3	6	11	
1958				
1958	Lionel Catalog....................4	6	12	
1959				
1959	Lionel Catalog....................4	7	13	
1960				
1960	Lionel Catalog....................3	5	10	
1961				
1961	Lionel Catalog....................4	6	12	
1962				
1962	Lionel Catalog....................3	6	11	
1963				
1963	Lionel Catalog....................2	3	5	
1964				
1964	Lionel Catalog....................2	3	5	
1965				
1965	Lionel Catalog....................1	2	4	
1966-1967				
1966	Lionel Catalog....................1	2	4	
1968				
1968	Lionel Catalog....................1	2	4	
1969				
1969	Lionel Catalog....................1	2	4	

No.	Year	Description	C6	C8	C10
1027					
	1934	Transformer Station	20	30	40
2016					
	1955	Loco, O27, steam, 2-6-4, w/6026W tender	60	100	200
2018					
	1956	Loco, O27, steam, 2-6-4, w/6026W tender	30	53	105
2020					
	1946	Loco, O27, steam, 6-8-6, w/2020W, 2466WX or 6020W tender	63	105	210
2023					
	1950	Loco, O27, UP Alco AA, diesel, yellow body, gray roof, or silver body w/gray roof	90	155	310
2023					
		Loco, O27, UP Alco AA, diesel Color Variation, yellow body, gray roof and gray nose	900	1500	3000
2024					
	1969	Loco, O27, Alco A, diesel, C&O	20	32	65
2025					
	1947	Loco, O27, steam, 2-6-2, w/6466WX or 6466W tender	53	88	175
2026					
	1948	Loco, O27, steam, 2-6-2, w/6466WX or 6466W tender	40	68	135
2026-58					
	1950	Bulb, eighteen volt, clear	—	—	1
2028					
	1955	Loco, O27, diesel, GP-7 PRR, Tuscan brown	135	225	450
2029					
	1964	Loco, O, steam, 2-6-4, w/ 243W tender	36	60	120
2031					
	1952	Loco, O27, R.I. Alco AA, diesel, black body, red middle stripe	125	205	410
2032					
	1952	Loco, O27, Erie Alco AA, diesel, black body, yellow middle stripe	82	138	275
2033					
	1952	Loco, O27, U.P. Alco AA, diesel, silver body	93	158	315
2034					
	1952	Loco, O27, steam, 2-4-2	36	60	120
2035					
	1950	Loco, O27, steam, 2-6-4, w/2466W tender	57	95	190
2036					
	1950	Loco, O27, steam, 2-6-4, w/6466W tender	33	55	110
2037					
	1953	Loco, O27, steam, 2-6-4, w/6026W or 6026T tender	33	55	110
2037-500					
	1957	Loco, O27, steam, 2-6-4, girl's set, pink	360	600	1200
2041					
	1969	Loco, O27, R.I., Alco AA, diesel, black body, white stripe	36	60	120
2046					
	1950	Loco, O27, steam, 4-6-4, w/2046W tender	80	135	270
2055					
	1953	Loco, O27, steam, 4-6-4, w/1025W or 2046W tender	66	110	220
2056					
	1952	Loco, O27, steam, 4-6-4, w/2046W tender	58	98	195
2065					
	1954	Loco, O27, steam, 4-6-4, 2046W or 6026W tender	63	105	210
2200					
	1910	Summer Trolley, standard, trailer, non-powered, "2200 Rapid Transit 2200"	1050	1750	3500
2240					
	1956	Loco, O27, Wabash F-3 AB, diesel, gray and blue shell, single motor	225	375	750
2242					
	1958	Loco, O27, New Haven F-3 AB, diesel, checkerboard scheme, silver and black, single motor	321	538	1075
2243					
	1955	Loco, O27, Santa Fe F-3 AB, diesel, silver shell, red nose, single motor	115	190	380
2245					
	1954	Loco, O27, Texas Special F-3 AB, diesel red shell, single motor	210	350	700
2321					
	1954	Loco, O, Lackawanna, diesel, double motor, gray	330	275	550
2321					
	1954	Loco, O, Lackawanna, diesel, gray w/maroon roof	200	338	675
2322					
	1965	Loco, O, Virginian, diesel,			

No. 517, Caboose, 1927, standard, red, $300

Two examples of Lionel's No. 2033 Loco, 1952, Loco, O27, U.P. Alco AA, diesel, silver body, $315

No. 2423, Observation, 1952, O27, silver roof, no stripe, $60

No.	Year	Description	C6	C8	C10
		double motor, yellow, blue roof...............190		318	635
2328					
	1955	Loco, O27, Burlington, diesel, silver shell 130		218	435
2329					
	1958	Loco, O, Virginian, electric, blue shell, yellow striping.....173		288	575
2330					
	1950	Loco, O, New Brunswick Green, GG-I, electric, five gold stripes, double motor...293		488	975
2331					
	1955	Loco, O, Virginian, diesel, double motor, yellow shell, black stripe, gold lettering ...285		475	950
2331					
	1955	Loco, Virginian, diesel, yellow, black roof.................450		750	1500
2331					
	1955	Loco, Virginian, diesel, yellow shell, blue stripe, yellow lettering..................240		400	800
2332					
	1947	Loco, GG-I, electric, five silver stripes 750		1250	2500
2332					
	1947	Loco, GG-I, electric, satin black, five gold stripes or silver stripes 510		850	1700
2332					
	1947	Loco, New Brunswick GG-I, electric, single motor, green, five gold stripes.....................265		440	880
2333					
	1948	Loco, O, NYC F-3 AA, diesel...300		500	1000
2333					
	1948	Loco, O, NYC F-3 AA, diesel, gray 240		400	800
2333					
	1948	Loco, O, Santa Fe or NYC F-3 AA, diesel, silver, red nose 210		350	700
2337					
	1958	Loco, O27, Wabash, GP-7, diesel, blue and gray body, white striping.........................78		130	260
2338					
	1955	Loco, O27, Milwaukee			

No. 2333 Loco, O, Santa Fe, 1948, engine only, $700

No.	Year	Description	C6	C8	C10
		Rd. GP-7, diesel, black and orange 78		130	260
2339					
	1957	Loco, O, Wabash GP-7, diesel, blue and gray w/white striping.....................93		155	310
2340-1					
	1955	Loco, O, GG-1, electric, maroon, double motor, Tuscan brown, five stripes....390		650	1300
2340-25					
	1955	Loco, O, New Brunswick, GG-1, electric, green, double motor, five stripes 375		625	1250
2341					
	1956	Loco, O, Jersey Central, diesel, double motor, orange body, blue stripe 480		800	1600
2343					
	1950	Loco, O, Santa Fe AA, F-3, diesel, double motor, silver w/red nose 175		290	580
2343C					
	1950	Loco, O, Santa FeB, diesel..........89		148	295
2344					
	1950	Loco, O, NYC F-3 AA, diesel, double motor, gray 187		313	625
2344C					
	1950	Loco, O, NYC F-3 B, diesel 93		155	310
2345					
	1952	Loco, O, Western Pacific F-3 AA, diesel, double diesel, louvered roof 500		840	1680
2346					
	1965	Loco, O27, Boston and Maine GP-7, diesel, blue shell, black cab, white trim.....96		160	320
2347					
	1962	Loco, O27, C&O GP-7, diesel, Sears, blue shell, yellow lettering, uncataloged.........1350		2250	4500
2348					
	1958	Loco, diesel, GP-9, M.St.L., O27 red shell, blue roof........120		200	400
2349					
	1959	Loco, O, diesel, GP-O, Northern Pacific, black shell, red striping, gold lettering 100		170	340
2350					
	1956	Loco, O, Electric, New Haven, black shell, orange and white striping.................155		258	515
2351					
	1957	Loco, O, Electric, Milwaukee			

No.	Year	Description	C6	C8	C10
		Rd., yellow shell, black roof, red stripe 123		205	410
2352					
	1958	Loco, O, diesel, PRR, Tuscan brown 185		308	615
2353					
	1953	Loco, O, diesel AA, F-3, Santa Fe, double motor, silver, red nose 192		320	640
2353C					
	1954	Loco, O, diesel, F-3, Santa Fe .. 120		200	400
2354					
	1953	Loco, O, diesel, AA, F-3, NYC, double motor, gray 215		360	720
2354C					
	1954	Loco, O, diesel, B, F-3, NYC 80		133	265
2355					
	1953	Loco, O, diesel, AA, F-3, Western Pacific, double motor, silver and orange 435		725	1450
2356					
	1954	Loco, O, diesel, AA, F-3, Southern RY, double motor, green 315		525	1050
2356C					
	1954	Loco, O, diesel, B, F-3, Southern Ry 150		250	500
2357					
	1948	Caboose, O 12		20	40
2358					
	1959	Loco, O, Great Northern, electric, orange and green 360		600	1200
2359					
	1961	Loco, O27, B&M GP-9, diesel, blue shell, black cab, shell, yellow stripes white trim 90		150	300
2360-1					
	1961	Loco, GG-1, electric, heavy heat stamped letters and numbers 225		373	745
2360-1					
	1961	Loco, GG-1, electric, light pressed letters and numbers, rubber stamped stripe 600		1000	2000
2360-1					
	1961	Loco, GG-1, electric, single stripe, double motor, Tuscan brown, decal letters and numbers rubber stamped stripe 350		583	1165
2360-10					
	1956	Loco, O, GG-1, electric, five stripes, Tuscan brown, double motor, heat-stamped letter			
		and number, five rubber stamped stripes 750		1250	2500
2360-25					
	1956	Loco, O, New Brunswick GG-1, Electric, green, green, heat stamped letters and numbers, double motor, five rubber stamped stripes 360		600	1200
2363					
	1955	Loco, O, Illinois Central F-3 AB, diesel, double motor, brown shell, orange stripe, yellow trim 300		500	1000
2365					
	1962	Loco, O27, C&O GP-7, diesel, blue shell 117		195	390
2367					
	1955	Loco, O, Wabash F-3 AB, diesel, double motor, gray and blue shell, white stripe and trim 260		433	865
2368					
	1956	Loco, O, B&O F-3 AB, diesel, blue shell w/black, white and yellow trim, double motor 277		463	925
2373					
	1957	Loco, Super O, Canadian Pacific AA F-3, diesel, double motor, gray and maroon, yellow trim 520		865	1730
2378					
	1956	Loco, O, Milwaukee Rd. F-3 AB, diesel, double motor, gray w/orange stripe 690		1150	2300
2379					
	1957	Loco, Super O, Rio Grande AB F-3, diesel, double motor, yellow body, silver roof and stripe 240		400	800
2383					
	1958	Loco, Super O, Santa Fe AA, F-3, diesel, silver, red nose, double motor 152		270	540
2400					
	1948	Pullman, O27, Maplewood, green shell, gray roof, yellow trim 37		63	125
2401					
	1948	Observation, O27, Hillside 34		58	115
2402					
	1948	Pullman, O27, Chatham 38		63	125
2404					
	1964	Vista Dome, O27, Santa Fe, aluminum, blue lettering 21		35	70

No. Year	Description	C6	C8	C10
2405				
1964	Pullman, O27, Santa Fe, aluminum, blue lettering	21	35	70
2406				
1964	Observation, Santa Fe, aluminum, blue lettering	21	35	70
2408				
1964	Vista Dome, O27, Santa Fe, aluminum, blue lettering	18	30	60
2409				
1964	Pullman, O27, Santa Fe, aluminum, blue lettering	18	30	60
2410				
1964	Observation, Santa Fe, aluminum, blue lettering	20	32	65
2411				
1946	Flat, O27, w/load of pipes, gray metal frame	23	38	75
2412				
1959	Vista Dome, O27, silver, blue stripe through windows, illuminated	35	58	115
2414				
1959	Pullman, O27, silver, blue stripe through windows, illuminated	35	58	115
2416				
1959	Observation, O27, silver, blue stripe through windows, illuminated	27	45	90
2419				
1946	Wrecker Caboose, O27, DL&W, gray metal frame, gray cab	27	45	90
2420				
1946	Wrecker Caboose, O, DL&W, w/light, gray metal frame, gray cab	28	48	95
2420-20				
1946	Bulb, fourteen volt, clear	—	—	1
2421				
1950	Pullman, O27, aluminum, gray roof, black stripe	28	48	95
2421				
1950	Pullman, O27, silver roof, no stripe	18	30	60
2422				
1950	Pullman, O27, aluminum, gray roof, black stripe	28	48	95
2422				
1950	Pullman, O27, silver roof, no stripe	18	30	60
2423				
1950	Observation, O27, aluminum, gray roof, black stripe	30	50	100
2423				
1950	Observation, O27, silver roof, no stripe	18	30	60
2426				
1946	WX Tender, O	87	145	290
2429				
1952	Pullman, O27, aluminum, gray roof, black stripe	18	30	60
2429				
1952	Pullman, O27, silver roof, no stripe	18	30	60
2430				
1946	Pullman, O27, blue, silver roof, sheet metal	7	12	24
2431				
1946	Observation, O27, blue, silver roof, sheet metal	7	12	24
2432				
1954	Vista Dome, O27, "Clifton," silver, red lettering	24	40	80
2434				
1954	Pullman, O27, "Newark," silver, red lettering	24	40	80
2435				
1954	Pullman, O27, "Elizabeth," silver, red lettering	21	35	70
2436				
1954	Observation, O27, "Mooseheart"	25	42	85
2436				
1954	Observation, O27, "Summit," silver, red lettering	25	42	85
2440				
1946	Pullman, O27, blue, silver roof	21	35	70
2440				
1946	Pullman, O27, green, dark green roof	21	35	70
2441				
1946	Observation, O27, blue, silver roof	21	35	70
2441				
1946	Observation, O27, green, dark green roof	21	35	70
2442				
1946	Pullman, O27, brown sheet metal	36	60	120
2442				
1956	Vista Dome, O27, "Clifton," aluminum, red window stripe	25	42	85
2443				
1956	Observation, O, brown sheet metal	27	45	90

No. Year	Description	C6	C8	C10
2444				
1956	Pullman, O, aluminum, red window stripe...................42		70	140
2452				
1945	Gondola, O27, "Pennsylvania"........................8		12	25
2452X				
1946	Gondola, O27, "Pennyslvania".......................11		19	38
2454				
1946	Box, O27, "Baby Ruth"...............9		15	30
2454				
1946	Box, O27, "Pennsylvania" 48		80	160
2456				
1948	Hopper, O, Lehigh Valley 8		14	27
2457				
1945	Caboose, O, N5 type, "Pennsylvania"........................15		25	50
2458				
1945	Box, O, automatic, "Pennsylvania," double door.........................20		33	65
2460				
1946	Operating Crane, O, Bucyrus Erie 25		43	85
2461				
1947	Transformer Car, O27, gray metal frame.....................36		60	120
2465				
1946	Tank, O27, double dome, Sunoco logo 5		8	15
2472				
1946	Caboose, O27, N5 type "Pennsylvania"........................10		18	35
2481				
1950	Pullman, O27, illuminated, yellow, red stripes, gray roof, Anniversary Set..............75		125	250
2482				
1950	Pullman, O27, illuminated, yellow, red stripes, gray roof, Anniversary Set..............75		125	250
2483				
1950	Observation, O27, illuminated yellow, red stripes, gray roof, Anniversary Set..............60		100	200
2521				
1962	Observation, Super O, "Pres. McKinley," illuminated, extruded aluminum shell, gold stripe 40		68	135
2522				
1962	Vista Dome, Super O, "Pres. Harrison," extruded aluminum shell, illuminated, gold stripe 52		88	175
2523				
1962	Pullman, Super O, "Pres. Garfield," illuminated, extruded aluminum shell, gold stripe 55		93	185
2530				
1956	Baggage, O, Railway Express Agency, extruded aluminum shell, large door.....................150		250	500
2530				
1956	Baggage, O, small doors.............68		113	225
2531				
1952	Observation, O, "Silver Dawn," extruded aluminum shell, illuminated 30		50	100
2532				
1952	Vista Dome, O, "Silver Range" 35		58	115
2533				
1952	Pullman, O, "Silver Cloud" 30		50	100
2534				
1952	Pullman, O, "Silver Bluff" 32		53	105
253E				
1931	Loco, O, electric, 0-4-0, green 125		213	425
253E				
1931	Loco, O, electric, 0-4-0, terra cotta 120		200	400
2541				
1955	Observation, O, Penn., "Alexander Hamilton," extruded aluminum, brown stripes, illuminated 75		123	245
2542				
1955	Vista Dome, O, Penn., "Betsy Ross,"...........................75		123	245
2543				
1955	Pullman, O, Penn., "William Penn," 120		200	400
2544				
1955	Pullman, O, Penn., "Molly Pitcher" 120		200	400
254E				
1927	Loco, O, electric, 0-4-0, apple green 90		150	300
254E				
1927	Loco, O, electric, 0-4-0, olive green 60		100	200
2550				
1957	Budd R.D.C. Mail Baggage Trailer, O, Baltimore and Ohio dummy to match motorized Budd 404, silver shell, blue lettering......173		288	575
2551				
1957	Observation, Super O,			

No. 2422, Pullman, 1950, O27, silver roof, no stripe, $60

No. 1684, Loco, 1942, O27, with tender, black, $155

No. 1682, 1934, Caboose, O27, $20

No.	Year	Description	C6	C8	C10
		"Banff Park," extruded aluminum shell, two brown stripes, top Canadian Pacific, bottom, name of car, illuminated	80	133	265
2552	1957	Vista Dome, Super O, "Skyline 500"	133	138	375
2553	1957	Pullman, Super O, "Blair Manor"	150	250	500
2554	1957	Pullman, Super O, "Graig Manor"	98	163	325
2555	1945	Tank-One-Dome, O	17	28	55
2559	1957	Budd Car Coach, O, Baltimore & Ohio, silver shell, blue lettering, dummy to match motorized 400 Budd	105	175	350
255E	1935	Loco, O, steam, 2-4-2, gunmetal gray w/263W tender	300	525	1050
2560	1946	Crane, O27, "Lionel Lines"	30	50	100
2561	1959	Observation, O, "Santa Fe Set, Vista Valley," extruded aluminum shell	78	130	260
2562	1959	Vista Dome, O, "Royal Pass"	78	130	260
2563	1959	Pullman, O, "Indian Falls"	78	130	260
2600	1938	Pullman, O, red body and roof	60	100	200
2601	1938	Observation, O, red body and roof	60	100	200
2602	1938	Baggage, O, red body and roof	60	100	200
2613	1938	Pullman, O, blue Comet, two-tone blue	81	135	270
2613	1938	Pullman, O, green	84	140	280
2614	1938	Observation, O, blue Comet, two-tone blue	81	135	270
2614	1938	Observation, O, green	84	140	280

No.	Year	Description	C6	C8	C10
2615	1938	Baggage, O, Blue Comet, two-tone blue	81	135	270
2615	1938	Baggage, O, green	120	200	400
261E	1935	Loco, O, steam, w/261T tender	84	140	280
2620	1938	Floodlight, O, red frame on searchlight	23	38	75
2623	1941	Pullman, O, Irvington, Tuscan brown Bakelite	150	250	500
2623	1941	Pullman, O, Manhattan, Tuscan brown Bakelite, uncataloged	80	133	265
2624	1941	Pullman, O, Manhattan, Tuscan brown Bakelite, uncataloged	240	400	800
2625	1946	Pullman, O, Irvington, Tuscan brown Bakelite	66	110	220
2625	1946	Pullman, O, Madison	75	125	250
2625	1946	Pullman, O, Manhattan	112	188	375
2627	1946	Pullman, O, Madison, Tuscan brown Bakelite	66	110	220
2628	1946	Pullman, O, Manhattan, Tuscan brown Bakelite	74	123	245
262E	1933	Loco, O, steam 2-4-2, w/262T or 265T tender	84	140	280
2630	1938	Pullman, O, light blue and silver or gray roof	30	50	100
2631	1938	Observation, O, light blue and silver or gray roof	30	50	100
263E	1936	Loco, O, steam 2-4-2, blue, Blue Comet	240	400	800
263E	1936	Loco, O, steam 2-4-2, gunmetal gray	255	425	850
2640	1938	Pullman, O, green and dark green roof	20	33	65
2640	1938	Pullman, O, light blue and silver roof	20	33	65

No.	Year	Description	C6	C8	C10
2641					
	1938	Observation, O, green and dark green roof	21	35	70
2641					
	1938	Observation, O, light blue and silver roof	24	40	80
264-150					
	1957	Boards, set of twelve	4	6	8
2642					
	1941	Pullman, O, light blue and silver or gray roof	24	40	80
2643					
	1941	Observation, O, light blue and silver or gray roof	15	25	50
264E					
	1935	Loco, O, steam 2-4-2, streamlined, black	120	200	400
264E					
	1935	Loco, O, steam 2-4-2, streamlined, red, Red Comet	225	375	750
2651					
	1938	Flat, O, bright green w/lumber load	15	25	50
2652					
	1938	Gondola, O, brown	18	30	60
2652					
	1938	Gondola, O, yellow	18	30	60
2653					
	1938	Hopper, O, black	38	62	125
2653					
	1938	Hopper, O, light green	15	25	50
2654					
	1938	Tank, O, "Shell"	21	35	70
2654					
	1938	Tank, O, aluminum, "Sunoco"	20	33	65
2654					
	1938	Tank, O, light gray, "Sunoco"	18	30	60
2655					
	1938	Box, O, cream body, maroon roof	18	30	60
2655					
	1938	Box, O, cream body, Tuscan brown roof	20	34	68
2656					
	1938	Cattle, O, light gray body, red roof	38	63	125
2657					
	1938	Caboose, O, red body and brown roof	9	15	30
2657					
	1938	Caboose, O, red body and red roof	12	20	40
2659					
	1938	Dump, O, green, black frame	12	23	45
265E					
	1935	Loco, O, steam 2-4-2, streamlined, black	87	145	290
265E					
	1935	Loco, O, steam 2-4-2, streamlined, blue, Blue Streak	180	300	600
265E					
	1935	Loco, O, steam 2-4-2, streamlined, gunmetal gray	105	175	350
2660					
	1938	Crane, O, red roof, green boom	27	45	90
2672					
	1942	Caboose, O27, Pennsylvania N5 type, Tuscan brown	12	20	40
2677					
	1940	Gondola, O27, red w/black frame	11	18	36
2679					
	1938	Box, O27, yellow, blue roof	9	15	30
2679					
	1938	Box, O27, yellow, maroon roof	9	15	30
2680					
	1938	Tank, O27, aluminum, "Sunoco"	8	12	25
2680					
	1938	Tank, O27, gray, "Sunoco"	8	12	25
2680					
	1938	Tank, O27, orange, "Shell"	8	12	25
2682					
	1938	Caboose, O27, brown w/brown roof	7	12	23
2682					
	1938	Caboose, O27, red w/red roof	7	12	23
2717					
	1938	Gondola, O, orange and tan, uncataloged	37	63	125
2719					
	1938	Box, O, peacock and blue roof, uncataloged	37	63	125
2722					
	1938	Caboose, O, red w/maroon roof, uncataloged	37	63	125
27-3					
	1950	Bulb, fourteen volt, clear	—	—	1
2755					
	1941	Tank, O, gray, "Sunoco"	45	75	150

No. Year	Description	C6	C8	C10
2757				
1941	Caboose, O, PRR-N5 type, Tuscan brown 12		20	40
2758				
1941	Box, O, automobile, "Pennsylvania," Tuscan body 21		35	70
2810				
1938	Crane, O, yellow cab and red roof 74		123	245
2811				
1938	Flat, O, aluminum w/eight logs 36		60	120
2812				
1938	Gondola, O, bright green 21		35	70
2812				
1938	Gondola, O, dark green 21		35	70
2813				
11938	Cattle, O, cream body, maroon roof..........................60		100	200
2814				
1938	Box, O, light yellow body, maroon roof 50		83	165
2814				
1938	Box, O, orange body, brown roof 120		200	400
2814R				
1938	Refrigerator, O, white body, brown roof..................185		325	650
2815				
1938	Tank, O, orange, Shell...............75		125	250
2815				
1938	Tank, O, silver, Sunoco 54		90	180
2816				
1938	Hopper, O, black, white rubber-stamped lettering.......54		90	180
2816				
1938	Hopper, O, red 60		100	200
2817				
1938	Caboose, O, light red body and roof 31		53	105
2817				
1938	Caboose, O, red, Tuscan roof, white rubber-stamped lettering....................29		48	95
2820				
1938	Floodlight, O, green base, cast lights 90		150	300
2820				
1938	Floodlight, O, two searchlights, green base, plate-stamped lights..................................54		88	175
2855				
1946	Tank, O, gray...........................59		98	195

No. Year	Description	C6	C8	C10
2855				
1946	Tank, O, one-dome, black S.U.N.X....................................62		103	205
289E				
1937	Loco, O, steam 2-4-2, streamlined, 1689 tender, gunmetal gray 45		75	150
2954				
1940	Box, O47, Tuscan brown, "Pennsylvania" 105		175	350
2955				
1940	Tank, O72, black, "S.U.N.X.".....78		130	260
2956				
1940	Hopper, O72, black, B&O 83		138	275
2957				
1940	Caboose, O72, NYC, Tuscan brown..........................93		155	310
3300				
1910	Summer Trolley, standard, trailer, gold rubber-stamped, 3300 Electric Rapid Transit, 3300, non-powered.............1200		2000	4000
3330				
1960	Flat, O, w/submarine 24		40	80
3330-100				
1960	Operating Submarine Kit 100		150	200
3349				
1960	Turbo Missile Firing Car, O.......17		28	55
3356				
1956	Operating Horse Car, O, w/horses and corral 40		68	135
3356-100				
1956	Set of Nine Horses, O, black horses..............................6		10	20
3356-150				
1956	Horse Corral, O, white fencing, corral only 12		20	40
3356-2				
1956	Operating Horse Car, O, green, car alone 18		30	60
3357				
1962	Operating Cop and Hobo Car, O, blue box car w/hydraulic lift and figures 30		50	100
3359				
1955	Operating Dump Car, O, two gray dump bins 17		28	55
3360				
1956	Operating Burro Crane, O, yellow cab and boom, motorized, including track trips 69		115	230
3361				
1955	Operating Lumber, O 17		28	55

No.	Year	Description	C6	C8	C10
3362					
	1961	Operating Helium Tank Car, green frame	20	32	64
3364					
	1966	Operating Log Dump Car, O, green frame	18	33	65
3366					
	1959	Operating Circus Car, O, white stock car, nine horses, white, and corral	66	110	220
3366-100					
	1959	White Horses, O, set of nine	9	15	30
3370					
	1961	Operating Sheriff and Outlaw Car, O, green stock car	25	43	85
3376					
	1960	Operating Giraffe Car, O, blue stock car, including track trips, w/teletails and poles	17	28	55
3376					
	1960	Operating Giraffe Car, O, green stock car	36	63	125
3410					
	1961	Operating Helicopter Launching Car, O, blue flat w/helicopter	45	75	150
3413-150					
	1961	Mercury Capsule Launching Car, O, red flat, gray platform	50	88	175
3419					
	1959	Operating Helicopter Launching Car, O, blue flat w/helicopter	21	35	70
3424					
	1956	Operating Brakeman Car Set, O, blue box car, set of track trips and teletails w/poles	21	35	70
3424-100					
	1956	Two Low Bridge Warning Poles, O, w/track clips	10	15	20
3428					
	1959	Operating Mail Car, O, red white and blue box car, man dumps mail bag	48	80	160
3429					
	1960	U.S.M.C. Helicopter Car, O, olive frame	75	125	250
3434					
	1959	Chicken Sweeper Car, O, brown stock car, man at door sweeps back and forth	30	53	105
3435					
	1959	Operating Aquarium Car, O, green box gold letters marked "Tank 1" and "Tank 2"	240	400	800
3435					
	1959	Operating Aquarium Car, O, green box w/four clear windows, fish move around on two spindles	36	60	120
3444					
	1957	Animated Hobo Gondola, O, "Erie," red gondola, cop chases hobo around freight load	24	40	80
3451					
	1946	Operating Lumber, O, black die-cast base, black platform w/log stacks	14	23	45
3454					
	1946	Operating Merchandise, O, silver box car, discharges five brown cubes	25	43	85
3456					
	1950	Operating Hopper Car, O, black, "N&W," drops ore	17	28	55
3459					
	1946	Operating Dump, O, die-cast frame, black	24	40	80
3459					
	1946	Operating Dump, O, green	25	43	85
3459					
	1946	Operating Dump, O, silver	93	155	310
3460					
	1955	Piggyback Flat, O, red flat w/two trailer containers	14	23	45
3461					
	1949	Operating Lumber, O, black die-cast frame	11	18	35
3461					
	1949	Operating Lumber, O, green frame	17	28	55
3462					
	1947	Milk Car Set, O, white box car, platform, green base, five cans, man discharges cans onto platform	17	28	55
3462-70					
	1952	Milk Cans, set of five	3	4	5
3462P					
	1952	Milk Car Platform, O	8	13	25
3464					
	1949	Operating Box, O, Santa Fe, orange shell, black doors, plunger mechanism opens door w/man	12	20	40

No.	Year	Description	C6	C8	C10
3464					
	1952	Operating Box, O, NYC, brown shell, black doors, plunger mechanism opens door w/man	11	18	35
3469					
	1949	Operating Dump, O, black die-cast frame	18	30	60
3470					
	1962	Aerial Target Launching Car, O, blue flatcar, white top shell, blue balloon carriage, batter operation inflates balloons	23	38	75
3472					
	1949	Operating Milk Car Set, O27, white box car, five cans, man discharges cans onto platform, green base	18	30	60
3474					
	1952	Operating Box, O27, W.P., silver box, yellow feather, plunger mechanism	27	45	90
348					
	1966	Manual Culvert Unloader, O	45	75	150
3482					
	1954	Operating Milk Car Set, O, white box car, man discharges cans onto platform, green base, five cans	24	40	80
3484					
	1953	Operating Box, O, Pennsylvania, Tuscan brown, plunger mechanism	18	30	60
3484-25					
	1954	Operating Box, O, Santa Fe, orange shell, orange doors, plunger mechanism	33	55	110
3494					
	1955	Operating Box, O, NYC Pacemaker, red and gray, red doors, plunger mechanism	33	55	110
3494-150					
	1956	Operating Box, O, MP, blue and gray, plunger mechanism	32	53	105
3494-275					
	1956	Operating Box, O, B.A.R., State of Maine, red, white and blue, plunger mechanism	24	40	80
3494-550					
	1957	Operating Box, O, Monon, maroon shell w/white stripe, plunger mechanism	115	193	385
3494-615					
	1957	Operating Box, O, Soo Line, Tuscan brown, plunger mechanism	120	200	400
3509					
	1959	Operating Satellite Car, O, green flat, black and silver satellite, yellow radar scope, manually operated	12	20	40
3510					
	1959	Operating Satellite Car, O, red flat	45	75	150
3512					
	1959	Fireman and Ladder Car, O, red frame and structure, black ladders	40	65	130
3512					
	1959	Fireman and Ladder Car, O, silver ladders	83	138	275
3519					
	1961	Automatic Satellite Car, O, remote track operated	16	28	55
3520					
	1952	Searchlight, O, gray die-cast frame, orange generator	15	25	50
3530					
	1956	G, M, Generator Car, O, blue box car w/white markings, transformer pole, remote searchlight	66	110	220
3535					
	1960	AEC Security Car, O, red shell, white lettering, gray gun and gray rotating searchlight, one man	29	48	95
3540					
	1959	Operating Radar Scanning Car, O, red flat, gray structure, yellow radar scope and silver radar antenna, revolving	39	65	130
3545					
	1961	Operating TV Monitor Car, O, black base, blue structure, yellow camera and screen, two men	53	88	175
3559					
	1946	Operating Ore Dump, O, black die-cast frame	14	23	45
3562					
	1954	Operating Barrel Car, O, black, six wood barrels	54	90	180
3562-25					
	1954	Operating Barrel Car, O, gray, blue lettering	25	38	50
3562-25					
	1954	Operating Barrel Car, O, red lettering	150	250	500

No.	Year	Description	C6	C8	C10
356-25					
	1952	Baggage Truck, O, set of two	9	14	18
3562-50					
	1955	Operating Barrel Car, O, yellow	25	43	85
3562-75					
	1958	Operating Barrel Car, O, orange	28	46	92
3619					
	1962	Reconnaissance Helicopter Car, O, yellow shell, black double door, w/helicopter	38	63	125
3620					
	1954	Searchlight, O, gray die-cast frame, orange generator	14	23	45
3650					
	1956	Searchlight Extension Car, O, gray die-cast frame	24	40	80
3651					
	1939	Operating Lumber, O, black frame, nickel stakes, w/logs and bin	13	20	40
3652					
	1939	Operating Gondola, O, yellow	25	42	85
3656					
	1950	Operating Cattle Car, O, "Armour," orange stock car, set includes car, cattle and corral, white lettering	25	42	85
3656					
	1950	Operating Cattle Car, O, black lettering	120	200	400
3656-150					
	1952	Cattle Car Platform, O, green base, ivory fencing	13	23	45
3656-34					
	1952	Cattle Set, O, black, set of nine	10	15	20
3657					
	1939	Dump Car, silver w/brown bin	120	200	400
3659					
	1939	Operating Dump, O, black frame, red hopper	20	33	65
3662					
	1955	Operating Milk, O, white shell, brown roof, includes five cans and platform	21	35	70
3662-79					
	1955	Milk Cans, O, set of five	6	9	12
3665					
	1961	Operating Minuteman Missile Car, O, white shell, blue double door roof, w/missile	35	58	115
3666					
	1960	Operating Marine Missile Car, O, Sears, white shell, blue double door roof, w/missile	160	268	535
3672					
	1959	Operating Bosco Box, O, yellow shell and brown roof, set includes seven Bosco cans and brown and yellow platform	105	175	350
3672-79					
	1959	Bosco Cans, O, brown and yellow, set of seven	12	20	40
3811					
	1939	Operating Flat, O, black frame w/lumber	18	30	60
3814					
	1939	Operating Merchandise, O, Tuscan body and roof, discharges five cubes	48	80	160
3820					
	1960	Operating Submarine Car, O, Olive, "U.S.M.C.," gray	120	200	400
3830					
	1960	Operating Submarine Car, O, blue, "Lionel," gray submarine	29	48	95
3854					
	1946	Operating Merchandise, O, Tuscan brown, doors open and eject five merchandise cubes	180	300	600
3859					
	1938	Operating Dump, O, black	25	41	82
3927					
	1956	Track Cleaner Car, O, orange shell, motor-operated cleaning disk, includes two gray washol containers	36	60	120
3927-50					
	1956	Track Cleaner Pads, O, package of twenty-five	5	10	25
3927-75					
	1956	Can of Liquid Track Cleaner, full	—	—	35
4357					
	1948	Caboose, O, electronic, green and white, "Electronic Control," decal, red metal Pennsylvania N5 type	68	112	225
4400					
	1910	Summer Trolley, standard, trailer	1200	2000	4000
4452					
	1946	Gondola, O, electronic, black, Pennsylvania	42	70	140

No. 1679, Box, 1934, O27, $25

No. 1680, Tank, 1934, O27, $42

No. 1688 or E, Loco, 1936, O27, gunmetal gray, with tender, $200

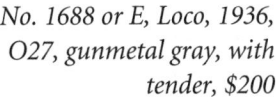

No. Year	Description	C6	C8	C10
4454				
1946	Box, electronic, Baby Ruth, P.R.R., orange w/brown doors	90	150	300
4457				
1946	Caboose, O, electronic	42	70	140
4671				
1946	Loco, O, steam, electronic, 6-8-0, 4671W tender	90	150	300
47618				
1943	Caboose, paper train, uncataloged	25	38	50
5100				
1963	Straight Roadway, O	—	—	1
5101				
1963	Straight Roadway, O	—	—	1
5102				
1963	Railroad and Roadway Crossway, O	—	—	1
5103				
1963	Straight Roadway, O, w/power connection	—	—	1
5104				
1963	Lane Change Over, O	—	—	1
5105				
1963	Roadway Intersection, O	—	—	1
5106				
1963	Inner Curved Roadway, O	—	—	1
5107				
1963	Inner Curved Roadway, O	—	—	1
5108				
1963	Outer Curved Roadway, O	—	—	1
5109				
1963	Outer Curved Roadway, O	—	—	1
5150				
1963	Banking Set	5	8	15
5151				
1963	Trestle Set, O	5	8	15
5152				
1963	Guard Rail and Flag Set, O	5	8	15
5154				
1963	Electric Lap Counter, O	5	8	15
5155				
1963	Pacesetter Timer, O	5	8	15
5156-24				
1963	Rail Clips, O	2	3	4
5157-34				
1963	Roadway Clips, O	2	3	4
5158				
1963	Barrels	2	3	4
5159				
1963	Lubrication Kit	3	4	5
5159-50				
1968	Lubrication Kit	3	4	5
5160				
1963	Official Viewing Stand	10	15	20
5163				
1965	Maintenance Kit	3	4	6
5200				
1963	Ferrari Racing Car, O	6	9	12
5201				
1963	"D" Jaguar Racing Car, O	6	9	12
5202				
1963	Corvette Racing Car, O	6	9	12
5210				
1963	Cooper Racing Car, O	6	9	12
5211				
1963	B.R.M. Racing Car, O	6	9	12
5222				
1964	Cooper Racing Car, O	6	9	12
5223				
1964	Corvette Racing Car, O	6	9	12
5230				
1964	Ferrari Racing Car, O	6	9	12
5231				
1964	B.R.M. Racing Car, O	6	9	12
5232				
1964	"D" Jaguar Racing Car, O	6	9	12
5233				
1964	Ford Racing Car, O	6	9	12
5234				
1964	Buick Racing Car, O	6	9	12
5235				
1964	Jaguar XKE Racing Car, O	6	9	12
5236				
1964	Buick Riviera Racing Car, O	6	9	12
5237				
1964	Buick Riviera Racing Car, O	6	9	12
5238				
1964	Ford Racing Car, O	6	9	12
5239				
1964	Ford Convertible Racing Car, O	7	11	15
5240				
1964	Ford Police Racing Car, O	7	11	15
5242				
1966	Conversion Kit	5	9	18
5300				
1963	Racemaster Power Pack	7	11	15
5302				
1965	Racemaster Power Pack	7	11	15
5304				
1965	HO Control Transformer	5	9	18
5310				
1963	Touch-A-Matic Speed Control	3	6	9

No. Year	Description	C6	C8	C10
5320				
1963	Touch-A-Matic Speed Control ...3		6	9
5321				
1965	Touch-A-Matic Speed Control ...3		6	9
5322				
1965	Touch-A-Matic Speed Control ...3		6	9
5400				
1963	Straight Roadway, HO..............—		—	1
5401				
1963	Straight Roadway, HO, w/power connector................—		—	1
5402				
1963	Railroad and Roadway Crossing, HO ....—		1	2
5403				
1963	Roadway Intersection, HO........—		1	2
5404				
1963	Lane Change Over, HO ....—		1	2
5405				
1963	Curved Roadway, HO...............—		—	1
5406				
1963	Curved Roadway, HO, forty-five degree ....—		—	1
5407				
1963	Inner Curved Roadway, HO, ninety degree ....—		—	1
5408				
1963	Outer Curved Roadway, HO, forty-five degree ....—		—	1
5409				
1963	Inner Curved Roadway, HO, forty-five degree ....—		—	1
5410				
1963	Straight Roadway, HO...............—		—	1
5411				
1963	Straight Roadway, HO...............—		—	1
5412				
1963	Straight Roadway, HO...............—		—	1
5415				
1963	Straight Roadway, HO, w/power connection...............—		—	1
5421				
1965	Touch-A-Matic Speed Controller, HO 5		8	10
5422				
1965	Touch-A-Matic Speed Controller, HO 5		8	10
5425				
1960	Loop-the-Loop Kit, HO 10		15	20
5430				
1966	Universal Roadway Kit, HO 9		14	18
5431				
1966	Mystery Route Selector, HO........5		10	15
5433				
1965	Car Lane Controller, HO.............6		9	13
5434				
1965	Car Lane Controller, HO.............6		9	13
5450				
1963	Trestle Set, HO 4		6	8
5455				
1966	Car Lane Controller, HO.............6		9	13
5457				
1966	Relay Kit, HO 10		15	20
5459				
1948	Operating Dump, O, electronic, black, "Lionel Lines"................36		60	120
5478				
1966	Guard Rail and Flag Set, HO.....10		15	20
5511				
1958-1961	Tie-Jector, O 51		85	170
5531				
1965	Buick Riviera Racing Car, HO.....3		5	10
5532				
1965	Buick Patrol Racing Car, HO 3		5	10
5533				
1965	Ford Hardtop Racing Car, HO....3		5	10
5534				
1965	Ford Convertible Racing Car, HO 3		5	10
5535				
1965	Ford Police Racing Car, HO 3		5	10
5537				
1965	Rolls Royce Racing Car, HO 3		5	10
5538				
1965	Bentley Racing Car, HO 3		5	10
5539				
1965	Jaguar XKE Racing Car, HO........3		5	10
5540				
1965	Car Lane Control Car, HO, Thunderbird 4		6	12
5541				
1965	Car Lane Control Car, HO, Jaguar, XKE 4		6	12
5542				
1965	Car Lane Control Car, HO, Thunderbird 4		6	12
5767-15				
1961	Valise Carrying Pack, HO 8		13	25
6002				
1949	Gondola, O27, NYC....................5		9	18
6004				
1950	Box, O27, Baby Ruth, P.R.R........4		7	13
6007				
1950	Caboose, O27, Lionel Lines, SP type 3		5	10
6009				
1953	Remote Control Track, O27 3		5	6

No.	Year	Description	C6	C8	C10
6012					
	1955	Gondola, O27, black, Lionel 3		4	8
6014					
	1951	Box, O27, Air Ex., blue 15		25	50
6014					
	1951	Box, O27, Air Ex., red............... 21		38	75
6014					
	1955	Box, O27, Baby Ruth, P.R.R. 5		8	10
6014					
	1957	Box, O27, Frisco 4		6	8
6014					
	1958	Box, O27, Bosco, P.R.R. 15		25	50
6014					
		WIX, cream white..................... 50		88	175
6014-325					
	1963	Frisco Savings Bank Car, O27 7		11	22
6014-325					
	1964	Box, O27, Frisco 7		11	22
6014-335					
	1965	Box, O27, Frisco 7		11	22
6014-410					
	1969	Box, O27, Frisco 7		11	22
6014-85					
	1969	Box, O27, Frisco 7		11	22
6015					
	1954	Tank, O27, Sunoco, silver, one dome 5		8	15
6017					
	1951	Caboose, O27, Lionel, brown 3		5	10
6017-100					
	1959	Caboose, B&M, dark blue 240		400	800
6017-100					
	1959	Caboose, B&M, light blue 15		25	50
6017-185					
	1959	Caboose, O27, ATSF, gray 9		15	30
6017-200					
	1960	Caboose, O27, Navy, dark blue 24		40	80
6017-225					
	1961	Caboose, O27, ATSF................. 18		30	60
6017-50					
	1958	Caboose, O27, Marine, dark blue 13		23	45
6019					
	1948	Remote Control Track................. 3		5	10
6024					
	1957	Box, O27, Nabisco 6		10	20
6024					
	1957	Box, O27, RCA-Whirlpool, red, uncataloged 15		25	50
6025					
	1956	Tank, O27, black 5		8	15
6025					
	1956	Tank, O27, gray....................... 11		18	36

No.	Year	Description	C6	C8	C10
6025					
	1956	Tank, O27, Gulf, orange 9		15	29
6029					
	1955	Uncoupling Track Set 3		5	6
6032					
	1952	Gondola, O27, "Lionel," black 2		3	5
6034					
	1953	Box, O27, Baby Ruth, P.R.R........ 8		14	28
6035					
	1950	Tank, O27, gray, single dome 2		3	5
6037					
	1952	Caboose, O27, brown, "Lionel Lines" 12		20	40
6042					
		Gondola, "Lionel," uncataloged 2		4	7
6044					
		Box, O27, Airex, light blue, uncataloged 12		20	40
6045					
		Tank Car, green, Cities Service 11		18	35
6047					
	1962	Caboose, O27, "Lionel Lines" 2		4	7
6050					
	1961	Savings Bank Car, O27, Libby Tomato Juice, Libby promotional car, uncataloged 15		25	50
6050					
	1961	Savings Bank Car, O27, white and green......................... 6		10	20
6050-100					
	1963	Savings Bank Car, O27, Swift's, red 22		38	75
6050-110					
	1962	Savings Bank Car, O27, Swift's, red 22		38	75
6057					
	1959	Caboose, O27, Lionel Lines, red................................... 3		4	8
6057-50					
	1962	Caboose, O27, H.H., orange 4		7	13
6058					
	1961	Caboose, O27, C&O, yellow 12		20	40
6059-50					
	1961	Caboose, O27, M&StL, maroon.................................... 8		13	25
6059-60					
	1969	Caboose, O27, M&StL, shiny or flat red 5		8	15
6062					
	1959	Gondola, O27, glossy black 3		5	9
6076					
	1959	Hopper, O27, A.T.S.F., gray 5		9	15

No. Year	Description	C6	C8	C10
6076-100				
1963	Hopper, O27, Lionel.................. 6		10	20
6076-75				
1963	Hopper, O27, LV, gray or black or red 6		10	20
6110				
1951	Loco, O27, steam, 2-4-2 15		25	50
61100				
1943	Box, paper train, uncataloged... 25		38	50
6111				
1955	Flat, O27, w/logs or pipes........... 8		13	25
6112				
1956	Gondola, O27, w/canisters, "Lionel," blue 3		5	9
6112				
1956	Gondola, O27, w/canisters, white........................... 15		25	50
6112-25				
1956	Set of Four Canisters, O27, white or red..................... 0		4	0
6119				
1955	Work Caboose, O27.................. 14		23	45
6119-100				
1963	Work Caboose, O27, DL&W 8		24	28
6119-110				
1964	Work Caboose, O27, DL&W 5		8	16
6119-25				
1957	Work Caboose, O27, DL&W 8		13	25
6121				
1956	Flat, O27, w/pipes....................... 5		8	16
6130				
1965	Work Caboose, O27, Santa Fe... 10		17	34
6139				
1963	Remote Control Uncoupling Track, O27 4		6	8
6142				
1963	Gondola, O27, w/canisters.......... 1		2	4
6142-100				
1964	Gondola, O27, w/canisters.......... 3		5	10
6142-125				
1964	Gondola, O27 3		5	10
6142-150				
1964	Gondola, O27 3		5	10
6142-75				
1963	Gondola, O27, w/canisters.......... 3		5	10
6149				
1964	Remote Control Uncoupling Track, O27 3		5	10
6151				
	Range Patrol...................... 31		53	105
6157				
	Caboose, O27, brown, uncataloged.......................... 3		5	10
6162				
1963	Gondola, O27, w/canisters, NYC, red................... 17		28	55
6162-100				
1964	Gondola, O27, w/canisters, NYC..................... 4		6	12
6162-110				
1965	Gondola, O27, w/canisters, NYC..................... 4		6	12
6162-25				
1959	Gondola, O27, w/canisters, blue..................... 4		6	12
6162-50				
1959	Gondola, O27, w/canisters, Alaska, yellow..................... 30		50	100
6167				
1963	Caboose, O27, Lionel.................. 4		6	12
6167-100				
1964	Caboose, O27, Lionel.................. 3		4	5
6167-125				
1964	Caboose, O27, unlettered 3		4	5
6167-50				
1963	Caboose, O27, D.R.W. 3		4	5
6167-85				
1969	Caboose, O27, U.P. 3		4	5
6175				
1958	Rocket Car, O27, red and white rocket, red or black frame........................... 15		25	50
6176				
1964	Hopper, O27, yellow 4		6	12
6176-50				
1964	Hopper, O27, L.V., yellow............ 3		5	9
6176-75				
1964	Hopper, O27, L.V., gray 3		5	9
6219				
1960	Work Caboose, O27, C&O, blue cab........................ 15		25	50
6220				
1949	Loco, O27, SW2 diesel, NYC or Santa Fe, black, similar to 622, w/bell............ 108		180	360
6250				
1954	Loco, O27, SW2 diesel Seaboard, blue and orange..... 40		158	315
6257				
1948	Caboose, O27 4		6	12
6257-100				
1964	Caboose, O27 2		3	5
6257-25				
	Caboose, O27, uncataloged......... 4		7	13
6257-50				
	Caboose, O27, uncataloged......... 3		5	9

No.	Year	Description	C6	C8	C10
6262					
	1956	Wheel Car, O, black or red frame w/eight set of wheels	11	18	35
6264					
		Forklift Accessory Flatcar, red frame, brown lumber rack	15	25	50
6311					
	1955	Flat, O, brown, no load	23	38	75
6315					
	1956	Tank Car, O, "Gulf," orange, three dome	22	36	72
6315-60					
	1963	Chemical Car, O, orange, single dome tank, "Lionel Lines"	11	19	37
6342					
	1957	Culvert Car, O, red gondola, w/inclined rake for culvert pipes	11	18	36
6343					
	1961	Barrel Ramp Car, O, red, gray ramp	14	24	47
6346					
	1956	Covered Hopper, O, Alcoa, silver	17	28	55
6352					
	1955	Refrigerator Car, O, for ice depot, Pacific Fruit Express, orange shell, door on roof for deposit of ice blocks, side door discharges	32	53	105
6356					
	1954	Stock, O, NYC, yellow	16	27	53
6357					
	1948	Caboose, O27, maroon, red, Tuscan brown	7	11	23
6361					
	1960	Timber Flat, O, green frame w/three lumber branches	25	42	83
6376					
	1956	Circus Car, O, white stock car	24	40	80
6401					
	1965	Flat, O, w/two vans	15	25	50
6402-50					
	1964	Flat, O, w/cable reels, gray frame w/orange reels	22	38	75
6405					
	1961	Flat, O, w/piggyback van, brown frame w/two trailer vans	11	18	35
6407					
	1963	Flat, O, w/rocket, red frame, gray supports w/red and white rocket, blue nose, actually a pencil sharpener	33	55	110
6408					
	1963	Flat, O, w/pipes	9	15	30
6409-25					
	1963	Flat, O, w/pipes	9	15	30
6411					
	1948	Flat, O27, w/logs, gray die-cast frame, five logs	11	18	35
6413					
	1962	Mercury Capsule Car, O, blue frame w/two gray Mercury capsules	38	63	125
6414					
	1955	Evans Loader Car, O, red frame, black metal car rack w/four cars	29	48	95
6414-25					
	1955	Set of Four Autos, O	18	27	36
6415					
	1953	Tank, O, Sunoco, silver, three dome	9	15	30
6415-60					
	1969	Tank, O, Sunoco	9	15	30
6416					
	1961	Four Boat Loader, O, red frame, black metal boat rack	54	85	170
6417					
	1953	Caboose, O, P.R.R., 536417, N5C type, Tuscan brown	12	20	40
6417					
	1953	Caboose, O, P.R.R., Lehigh Valley gray	39	65	130
6417					
	1953	Caboose, O, P.R.R., Tuscan	600	1000	2000
6418					
	1955	Depressed Center Girder Flat, O, gray die-cast frame w/two orange girder sections, four sets of trucks	30	50	100
6419					
	1948	Wrecker Caboose, O27, DL&W, gray cab	14	23	45
6419-100					
	1954	Wrecker Caboose, O27, N&W, light gray cab, 576419	30	50	100
6420					
	1949	Wrecker Caboose, O, DL&W, dark gray, die-cast frame w/searchlight	20	32	65
6424					
	1956	Twin Auto Car, O, black frame, two autos	14	23	45
6425					
	1956	Tank, O, Gulf, silver, three dome	15	25	50

No. Year	Description	C6	C8	C10
6427				
1954	Caboose, O, 64273, Tuscan brown, N5C type 14		23	45
6427-500				
1957	Caboose, O, girl's train, 57, 6427, blue shell, white lettering 83		138	275
6427-60				
1958	Caboose, O, Virginian, 6427, blue shell, yellow lettering, N5C type 120		200	400
6428				
1960	Box, O, U.S. Mail, red, white and blue 14		23	45
6429				
1963	Wrecker Caboose, O, gray die-cast frame, gray cab 30		50	100
6430				
1956	Flat, O, w/piggyback van, red frame w/two trailer vans 18		30	60
6434				
1958	Poultry Car, O, red stock car, gray doors, illuminated 24		40	80
6436				
1955	Hopper, O, N&W, red 12		20	40
6436-1				
1956	Hopper, O, L.V., black 15		25	50
6436-100				
1957	Hopper, O. L.V. 14		24	48
6436-110				
1963	Hopper, O, L.V. 23		38	75
6436-25				
1956	Hopper, O, L.V., maroon 15		25	50
6436-57				
1957	Hopper, O, L.V., lilac, maroon lettering, girl's set 54		70	140
6437				
1961	Caboose, O, Pennsylvania, N5C, Tuscan brown 13		23	45
6440				
1948	Pullman, O27, green sheet metal body, dark green roof 13		23	45
6441				
1948	Observation, O27, green sheetmetal body, dark green roof 13		23	45
6442				
1949	Pullman, O27, brown sheetmetal body and roof 20		33	65
6443				
1949	Observation, O27, brown sheetmetal body and roof 24		40	80

No. Year	Description	C6	C8	C10
6445				
1961	Fort Knox Gold Car, O, silver w/four clear windows, showing gold bullion 36		60	120
6446-25				
1956	Covered Hopper, O, N&W, gray 23		38	75
6446-54				
1954	Covered Cement, O, N&W, black 17		28	55
6446-54				
1954	Covered Cement, O, N&W, gray 30		50	100
6447				
1963	Caboose, O, Tuscan brown, N5C type 90		150	300
6448				
1961	Expolding Target Range Car, O, red shell, white lettering 11		18	35
6454				
1948	Box, O27, P.R.R., Tuscan brown 12		20	40
6454				
1949	Box, O27, NYC, brown 12		20	40
6454				
1950	Box, O27, Erie, brown 17		28	55
6454				
1950	Box, O27, Erie, SP 17		28	55
6456				
1948	Hopper, O, maroon, black, gray 6		10	20
6456				
1948	Hopper, O, shiny red, yellow letters 48		80	160
6456				
1948	Hopper, O, white letters 150		250	500
6457				
1949	Caboose, O, brown or maroon, SP type 8		14	28
6460				
1952	Crane, O, black cab 23		38	75
6460				
1952	Crane, O, gray cab 23		38	75
6461				
1949	Transformer Car, O27, gray die-cast frame, black transformer 32		53	105
6462-25				
1954	Gondola, O, NYC, black, bright red, green 5		8	15
6462-500				
1957	Gondola, O, girl's train, "NYC," pink 39		65	130
6462C				
1949	Gondola, O, NYC 4		6	12

This pamphlet from Lionel shows many new releases for the year of 1956. Top Row: No. 2350, Loco, O, 1956, New Haven, black shell, orange and white striping, $515. Second Row, left to right: No. 3530, GM Generator Car, 1956, O, includes transformer pole, remote searchlight, $220; No. 3424, Operating Brakeman (Tell-Tale) Car Set, 1956, O, blue box car, set of track trips and tell-tales w/poles, $70. Third Row, left to right: No. 3927, Track Cleaner Car, 1956, O, $120; No. 50, Gang Car, 1957, O27, $58; No. 3360, Operating Burro Crane, 1956, O, $230. Bottom Row: No. 400, Budd RDC Car, 1956, O, $270.

No. Year	Description	C6	C8	C10
6463				
1962	Rocket Fuel Tank Car, O, white shell, two dome, red lettering	23	38	75
6464-1				
1953	Box, O, W.P., silver	26	44	88
6464-100				
1954	Box, W.P., orange w/blue feather	300	500	1000
6464-100				
1954	Box, W.P., silver w/yellow feather	38	63	125
6464-125				
1954	Box, O, "Pacemaker," red and gray	39	65	130
6464-150				
1954	Box, O, M.P., blue and gray	39	65	130
6464-175				
1954	Box, O, R.I., silver	30	50	100
6464-200				
1954	Box, O, P.R.R., Tuscan brown	39	65	130
6464-225				
1954	Box, O, S.P., black	40	67	135
6464-25				
1953	Box, O, G.N., orange	23	38	75
6464-250				
1966	Box, O, W.P., orange w/blue feather	68	112	225
6464-275				
1955	Box, O, "State of Maine," red, white and blue	21	35	70
6464-300				
1955	Box, O, Rutland, green and yellow	37	63	125
6464-325				
1956	Box, O, B&O, "Sentinel," silver and aqua	96	160	320
6464-350				
1956	Box, O, M.K.T., maroon	60	100	200
6464-375				
1956	Box, O, C.G., maroon and silver	33	55	110
6464-400				
1956	Box, O, B&O, "timesaver," blue and orange	42	70	140
6464-425				
1956	Box, O, N.H., black	18	30	60
6464-450				
1956	Box, O, G.N., olive and orange	39	65	130
6464-475				
1957	Box, O, B&M, blue	18	30	60

No. Year	Description	C6	C8	C10
6464-50				
1953	Box, O, M&StL, maroon	23	38	75
6464-500				
1957	Box, O, Timken, yellow and white	39	65	130
6464-510				
1957	Box, O, Girls train, NYC, lilac	153	255	510
6464-515				
1957	Box, O, Girls train, M, K, T, yellow	180	300	600
6464-525				
1957	Box, O, M&StL, red	23	39	77
6464-650				
1957	Box, O, D.R.G.W., yellow and silver	33	55	110
6464-700				
1961	Box, O, Santa Fe, red	36	60	120
6464-725				
1962	Box, O, New Haven, black	15	25	50
6464-75				
1953	Box, O, R.I., green	21	34	68
6464-825				
1959	Box, O, Alaska, blue and yellow	111	185	370
6464-900				
1960	Box, O, NYC, light green	28	48	95
6465				
1948	Tank, O27, silver, "Sunoco," two dome	12	20	40
6465				
1958	Tank, O27, black, Lionel Lines, two dome	4	6	12
6465				
1958	Tank, O27, Gulf, black, two dome	12	20	40
6465				
1958	Tank, O27, orange, Lionel Lines, two dome	4	7	14
6465				
1960	Tank, O27, green Cities Service, two dome	6	11	21
6466T W or				
1948	Tender, O27	30	50	100
6468				
1953	Automobile, O, B&O, blue, double door	18	30	60
6468				
1953	Automobile, O, B&O, brown	75	125	250
6468-25				
1956	Automobile, O, N.H., orange, double door	22	36	72
6469				
1963	Liquefied Gas Tank Car, O, red frame, white cylinder	75	125	150

No.	Year	Description	C6	C8	C10
6470					
	1959	Exploding Box, O, red w/white lettering, spring mechanism 8		14	28
6472					
	950	Refrigerator, O, white box car.....................................9		15	30
6473					
	1963	Horse Transport Car, yellow, two horse heads bob in and out.......................................9		15	30
6475					
		Pickles Car...................................21		35	70
6475					
	1960	Pineapple Car, O, Libby, uncataloged.................36		63	125
6476					
	1957	Hopper, O, red, white letters.......4		7	14
6476-25					
	1963	Hopper, O, L.V., gray, black letters.............................3		5	10
6476-75					
	1963	Hopper, O, L.V., red, white letters...3		5	10
6477					
	1957	Pipe Car, O, same as 6467 but w/sidestakes......................24		40	80
6500					
	1962	Beechcraft Bonanza Transport Car, O, black frame w/red and white plane 245		425	850
6501					
	1962	Flat, O, w/motor boat, red frame w/white and brown boat..............................30		50	100
6502					
	1962	Flat, O, w/girder, blue flat w/orange bridge.........................7		13	25
6511					
	1953	Pipe Car, O, brown or red flat w/three aluminum colored pipes...15		25	50
6512					
	1962	Cherry Picker Car, O, black or blue frame, gray ladder support, black ladder w/man 23		38	75
6517					
	1955	Caboose, O, bay window, red, "Lionel Lines" 21		35	70
6517					
		Caboose, O, Erie, bay window, red, uncataloged 90		150	300
6518					
	1956	Transformer Car, O, gray die-cast frame, four sets of trucks, black transformer.......36		60	120
6519					
	1958	Allis Chalmers Car, O, orange car, gray reactor 27		45	90
6520					
	1949	Operating Searchlight, O, gray die-cast base, green.......132		225	450
6520					
	1949	Operating Searchlight, O, orange or maroon generator 20		32	65
6530					
	1960	Fire Prevention Car, O, red shell, white lettering...............21		35	70
6536					
	1958	Hopper, O, M&StL, red w/white lettering....................17		27	55
6544					
	1960	Missile Firing Car, O, blue frame, gray launch platform, red firing control w/four white rockets, white console...27		45	90
6555					
	1949	Tank, O, "Sunoco," silver, single dome, metal tank 18		30	60
6556					
	1958	Stock, O, M.K.T., Katy, red shell, white lettering and doors..51		85	170
6557					
	1958	Smoking Caboose, O, "Lionel," SP-type, Tuscan brown w/smoke unit, liquid type 59		98	195
6560					
	1955	Crane, O, "Bucyrus Erie," black frame, gray cab..............27		45	90
6560					
	1955	Crane, O, "Bucyrus Erie," red cab 17		28	55
6560-25					
	1961	Crane, O, "Bucyrus Erie," black frame, red cab 6560-25.....................................25		41	82
6561					
	1953	Cable Car, O, gray die-cast frame w/two orange or gray spools wrapped w/aluminum wire...18		30	60
6562					
	1956	Gondola, O, NYC, black 4		6	12
6562					
	1956	Gondola, O, NYC, gray.............14		23	45
6562					
	1956	Gondola, O, NYC, red.................4		7	14
6630					
	1960	IRBM Missile Launcher			

No.	Year	Description	C6	C8	C10
		Car, O, black frame, blue ramp, w/red and white missile	23	38	75
6636	1959	Hopper, O, Alaska, black w/orange lettering	21	35	70
6640	1960	U.S.M.C. Missile Launcher, olive frame, black ramp, w/white missile	40	68	135
6646	1957	Stock, O, "Lionel Lines," orange shell, black lettering	17	29	58
6650	1959	IRBM Missile Car, O, red frame, blue support, black ramp w/red and white missile	28	48	95
6650-80	1959	Missile for 6650-0, five white missiles	5	8	16
6651	1960	Marine Cannon Car, O, olive frame and cannon w/four cannon loads, uncataloged	63	105	210
6656	1950	Stock, O, yellow shell, black lettering	8	13	26
6657	1957	Caboose, O, D.R.G.W., SP type, yellow cab w/silver lower stripe, black lettering	50	83	165
6660	1958	Flat, O, car w/boom, red flat, yellow crane, turn control	24	40	80
6670	1959	Flat, O, car w/derrick, red flat, yellow crane, no turn control	18	30	60
6672	1954	Refrigerator, O, "Santa Fe," reefer, white shell, brown roof, black lettering	24	40	80
6672	1954	Refrigerator, O, blue lettering	18	30	60
6736	1960	Hopper, O, Detroit & Mackinac, red shell, white lettering	17	28	55
6800	1957	Flat, O, w/airplane, red frame w/black and yellow plane	54	70	140

No. 6804 Flat with two gray trucks, O, 1958, $160

No.	Year	Description	C6	C8	C10
6801	1957	Flat, O, w/white boat, red flat	23	38	75
6801-50	1957	Flat, O, w/yellow boat, red flat	21	35	70
6801-75	1957	Flat, O, w/blue boat, red flat	48	80	160
6802	1958	Flat, O, w/bridge, red flat w/black bridge	14	24	48
6803	1958	Flat, O, w/tank and sound truck, red frame, two gray vehicles	45	75	150
6804	1958	Flat, O, w/sound truck, red frame, two gray trucks	45	75	150
6805	1958	Atomic Energy Car, O, red frame, two gray radioactivity containers, lights under containers	48	80	160
6806	1958	Flat, O, w/radar and medical truck, red frame, two gray vehicles	45	75	150
6807	1958	Flat, O, w/duck, amphibian boat, red frame, one gray boat	30	50	100
6808	1958	Flat, O, w/tank and searchlight, red flat w/two gray vehicles	45	75	150
6809	1958	Flat, O, w/medical trucks, red frame, two gray vehicles	45	75	150
6810	1958	Flat, O, w/piggyback van, red frame, one trailer container, "Cooper Jarretting"	15	25	50

No.	Year	Description	C6	C8	C10
6812					
	1959	Track Maintenance Car, O, red frame, gray, blue or yellow platform, w/two blue men 33		55	110
6814					
	1959	First Aid Caboose, O, "Rescue Unit," white frame, cab and tool boxes, two stretchers, oxygen tank and man 37		63	125
6816					
	1959	Flat, O, w/bulldozer, "Allis-Chalmers," orange bulldozer, red flat 135		225	450
6816-100					
	1959	Bulldozer, O 75		125	250
6817					
	1959	Flat, O, w/scraper, same as 6816, except bulldozer replaced by scraper 54		90	180
6817-100					
	1959	Scraper, O 27		45	90
6818					
	1958	Flat, O, w/transformer, red frame, black transformer 15		25	50
6819					
	1959	Flat, O, w/helicopter, red frame w/gray helicopter 30		50	100
6820					
	1960	Aerial Missile Car, O, blue frame, navy helicopter............ 90		150	300
6821					
	1959	Flat, O, w/crates, red frame, tan crates 12		20	40
6822					
	1961	Searchlight Car, O, red frame, gray searchlight, black housing w/blue man 13		21	42
6823					
	1959	IRBM Missile Car, O, red frame, gray supports, two white missiles.................. 22		38	75
6824					
	1960	First Aid Caboose, O, "Rescue Unit," olive frame, cab, tool boxes, w/two stretchers, oxygen tank and man 63		105	210
6825					
	1959	Flat, O, w/arch bridge, red frame, black bridge, or gray bridge 20		32	65
6826					
	1959	Flat, O, w/trees, red frame w/bundles of life-like Christmas trees 33		55	110
6827					
	1960	Flat, O, w/power shovel,			

No.	Year	Description	C6	C8	C10
		black frame, yellow and black steam shovel 50		88	175
6828					
	1960	Flat, O, w/construction crane, black frame, yellow and black crane 45		70	140
6828-100					
	1960	Construction Crane, O 24		40	80
6830					
	1960	Submarine Car, O, blue frame, gray sub, "U.S. Navy" 36		60	120
6O27					
	1959	Caboose, O27, Alaska, blue 21		35	70
HO-039					
	1961	Track Cleaning Car, HO 36		60	120
HO-050					
	1959	Gang Car, HO 30		50	100
HO-055					
	1961	Loco, HO, M&StL switcher 30		50	100
HO-056					
	1959	Loco, HO, A.E.C. Switcher 45		75	150
HO-057					
	1959	Loco, HO, U.P. Switcher 30		50	100
HO-058					
	1960	Loco, R.I. Switcher 24		40	80
HO-068					
	1961	Inspection Car, HO................... 30		50	100
HO-59					
	1960	Loco, HO, U.S. Air Force Switcher........................ 30		50	100
HO-100					
	1961	Power Pack, HO 10		15	20
HO-101					
	1961	Power Pack, HO 10		15	20
HO-103					
	1959	Power Pack, HO 10		15	20
HO-103-800					
	1961	Power Pack, HO 10		15	20
HO-104					
	1961	Power Pack, HO 10		15	20
HO-110					
	1958	Trestle Set, HO 10		15	20
HO-111					
	1959	Trestle Set, HO 10		15	20
HO-114					
	1958	Engine House, HO, w/horn....... 50		75	100
HO-115					
	1961	Kit, HO, engine house 35		52	70
HO-117					
	1959	Engine House, HO.................... 45		68	90
HO-118					
	1958	Engine House, HO, w/whistle ... 50		75	100
HO-119					
	1959	Tunnel, HO 7		11	15

TRAINS and ACCESSORIES

MODEL MOTOR RACING

LIONEL 1962

COMPLETE SCIENCE LABS

PHONOGRAPHS • TAPE RECORDERS

The 1962 Lionel Catalog is valued at $11

No.	Year	Description	C6	C8	C10
HO-140					
	1962	Banjo Signal, HO 22		33	45
HO-145					
	1959	Automatic Gateman, HO 30		45	60
HO-150					
	1958	Rectifier, HO 2		3	4
HO-181					
	1958	Cab Control, HO 7		13	25
HO-197					
	1958	Radar Antenna, HO 20		30	40
HO-214					
	1958	Girder Bridge, HO 5		10	15
HO-222					
	1961	Deck Bridge, HO 10		15	20
HO-224					
	1961	Girder Bridge, HO 7		11	14
HO-226					
	1961	Truss Bridge, HO 7		11	14
HO-245-200					
	1960	Contactor, HO 4		5	7
HO-252					
	1959	Crossing Gate, HO 20		30	40
HO-300					
	1960	Operating Lumber Car, HO 8		14	28
HO-301					
	1960	Operating Dump Car, HO 12		20	40
HO-301-16					
	1960	Cargo Bin, HO 4		5	7
HO-319					
	1960	Oper, HO, helicopter car 16		27	55
HO-337					
	1961	Operating Giraffe Car, HO 15		25	50
HO-349					
		Turbo Missile Firing Car, HO ... 30		50	100
HO-357					
	1962	Cop and Hobo Car, HO 12		20	40
HO-365					
	1962	Missile Launching Car, HO 12		20	40
HO-366					
	1961	Operating Milk Car, HO 18		30	60
HO-370					
	1962	Sheriff and Outlaw Car, HO 12		20	40
HO-410					
	1959	Suburban Ranch House, HO 10		15	20
HO-411					
	1959	Figure Set, HO 10		15	20
HO-412					
	1959	Farm Set, HO 10		15	20
HO-413					
	1959	Railroad Structure Set, HO 10		15	20
HO-414					
	1959	Village Set, HO 10		15	20
HO-425					
	1962	Figure Set, HO 7		11	14
HO-430					
	1959	Tree Assortment, HO 6		9	12
HO-431					
	1959	Landscape Set, HO 10		15	20
HO-432					
	1961	Tree Assortment, HO 7		11	14
HO-470					
	1960	Missile Launching Platform, HO 34		51	68
HO-480					
	1961	Missile Firing Range Set, HO 7		11	14
HO-530					
	1958	Loco, HO, diesel F-3 powered A, DRGW 20		32	65
HO-531					
	1958	Loco, HO, diesel F-3 powered A, C.M. St.P&P 20		32	65
HO-532					
	1958	Loco, HO, diesel F-3 powered A, B&O 20		32	65
HO-533					
	1958	Loco, HO, diesel F-3 powered A, New Haven 20		32	65
HO-535					
	1962	Loco, HO, diesel Alco, AB, Santa Fe 20		32	65
HO-536					
	1963	Loco, HO, diesel Alco, Sante Fe 20		32	65
HO-537					
	1966	Loco, HO, diesel Alco, AB Santa Fe 20		32	65
HO-540					
	1958	Loco, HO, diesel F-3, Dummy B, DRGW 15		25	50
HO-541					
	1958	Loco, HO, diesel F-3, Dummy B, CMST P&P 15		25	50
HO-550					
	1958	Loco, HO, diesel F-3, Dummy A, DRGW 15		25	50
HO-555					
	1963	Loco, HO, diesel F-3 powered A, Santa Fe 19		32	64
HO-561					
	1959	Rotary Snowplow, HO, MSTL .. 60		100	200
HO-564					
	1960	Loco, HO, diesel Alco, powered A, C&O 19		32	64
HO-565					
	1959	Loco, HO, diesel Alco, powered A, Santa Fe 19		32	64

No. Year	Description	C6	C8	C10
HO-566				
1959	Loco, HO, diesel Alco, powered A, Texas special 19		32	64
HO-567				
1959	Loco, HO, diesel Alco, powered A, Alaska 19		32	64
HO-568				
1962	Loco, HO, diesel Alco, powered A, Union Pacific 19		32	64
HO-569				
1963	Loco, HO, diesel Alco, powered A, Union Pacific 19		32	64
HO-571				
1963	Loco, HO, diesel Alco, powered A, PRR 19		32	64
HO-576				
1959	Loco, HO, diesel F-3, Dummy B, Texas special 19		32	64
HO-577				
1959	Loco, HO, diesel F-3, Dummy B, Alaska 19		32	64
HO-581				
1960	Loco, HO, rectifier, PRR............ 19		32	64
HO-586				
1959	Loco, HO, diesel F-3, Dummy A, Texas special 15		25	50
HO-587				
1959	Loco, HO, diesel F-3, Dummy A, Alaska 15		25	50
HO-591				
1959	Loco, HO, rectifier, New Haven............................... 19		32	64
HO-592				
1966	Loco, HO, diesel GP9, Santa Fe..................................... 19		32	64
HO-593				
1963	Loco, HO, diesel GP9, Northern Pacific 19		32	64
HO-594				
1963	Loco, HO, diesel GP9, Santa Fe..................................... 19		32	64
HO-595				
1959	Loco, HO, diesel F-3, Dummy A, Santa Fe 15		25	50
HO-596				
1959	Loco, HO, diesel GP9, NYC 19		32	64
HO-597				
1960	Loco, HO, diesel GP9, Northern Pacific 19		32	64
HO-598				
1961	Loco, HO, diesel GP7, NYC 19		32	64
HO-602				
1960	Loco, HO, steam 15		25	50
HO-605				
1959	Loco, HO, steam 20		32	64

No. Year	Description	C6	C8	C10
HO-625				
1959	Loco, HO, steam........................ 27		45	90
HO-626				
1963	Loco, HO, steam........................ 19		33	65
HO-635				
1961	Loco, HO, steam........................ 19		32	65
HO-636				
1963	Loco, HO, steam........................ 19		33	65
HO-642				
1961	Loco, HO, steam........................ 19		33	65
HO-643				
1963	Loco, HO, steam........................ 19		33	65
HO-645				
1962	Loco, HO, steam........................ 19		33	65
HO-646				
1963	Loco, HO, steam........................ 19		33	65
HO-647				
1966	Loco, HO 19		33	65
HO-704				
1959	Baggage, HO, Texas Special 18		30	60
HO-705				
1959	Pullman, HO, Texas Special....... 18		30	60
HO-706				
1959	Vista Dome, HO, Texas Special 18		30	60
HO-707				
1959	Observation, HO, Texas Special 18		30	60
HO-709				
1960	Vista Dome, HO, Pennsylvania 8		13	26
HO-710				
1960	Observation, HO, Pennsylvania 6		10	20
HO-711				
1960	Baggage, HO, Pennsylvania 6		10	20
HO-712				
1961	Baggage, HO, Santa Fe............... 14		22	45
HO-713				
1961	Pullman, HO, Santa Fe 14		22	45
HO-714				
1961	Vista Dome, HO, Santa Fe........... 8		13	26
HO-715				
1961	Observation, HO, Santa Fe.......... 6		10	20
HO-723				
1963	Pullman, Ho, Pennsylvania 6		10	20
HO-725				
1963	Observation, HO, Pennsylvania 6		10	20
HO-733				
1964	Pullman, HO, Santa Fe 6		10	20
HO-735				
1964	Observation, HO, Santa Fe.......... 6		10	20

No.	Year	Description	C6	C8	C10
HO-800					
	1958	Flat, HO, w/airplane 18	30	60
HO-801					
	1958	Flat, HO, w/boat 9	15	30
HO-805					
	1959	AEC Car, HO, w/light 12	20	40
HO-806					
	1959	Flat Car, HO, w/helicopter 15	25	50
HO-807					
	1959	Flat Car, HO, w/bulldozer 14	23	45
HO-808					
		Flat Car, w/tractor 14	23	45
HO-809					
	1961	Helium Transport Car, HO 1	19	38
HO-810					
	1961	Generator Transport Car, HO..... 8	13	26
HO-811-25					
	1958	Flat, HO, w/stakes 6	10	20
HO-813					
	1962	Mercury Capsule Car, HO 10	16	32
HO-814					
	1958	Auto Transport Car, HO 15	25	50
HO-815					
	1958	Tank, HO.................................... 11	18	35
HO-815-50					
	1964	Tank, HO...................................... 8	13	25
HO-815-75					
	1963	Tank, HO...................................... 8	13	25
HO-815-85					
	1964	Tank, HO...................................... 8	13	25
HO-816					
	1962	Rocket Fuel Tank Car, HO 8	13	25
HO-816-50					
	1962	Rock Fuel Tank Car, HO 8	13	25
HO-817					
	1958	Caboose, HO............................... 7	12	24
HO-817-150					
	1960	Caboose, HO, Santa Fe 6	10	20
HO-817-200					
	1959	Caboose, HO, AEC 6	10	20
HO-817-225					
	1959	Caboose, HO, Alaska 6	10	20
HO-817-250					
	1959	Caboose, HO, Texas Special 6	10	20
HO-817-300					
	1959	Caboose, HO, Southern Pacific.................................... 6	10	20
HO-817-350					
	1960	Caboose, HO, Rock Island 6	10	20
HO-819-1					
	1958	Work Caboose, HO, P.R.R........... 8	13	25
HO-819-100					
	1958	Work Caboose, HO, B&M 8	13	25
HO-819-200					
	1959	Work Caboose, HO, B&M........... 8	13	25
HO-819-225					
	1960	Work Caboose, HO, Santa Fe......8	13	25
HO-819-250					
	1960	Work Caboose, HO, NP 8	13	25
HO-819-275					
	1960	Work Caboose, HO, C&O 8	13	25
HO-819-285					
	1963	Work Caboose, HO, C&O 8	13	25
HO-821					
	1960	Pipe Car, HO 8	13	25
HO-821-100					
	1963	Pipe Car, HO 10	16	32
HO-821-50					
	1964	Pipe Car, HO 8	13	25
HO-823					
	1960	Twin Missile Car, HO 21	35	70
HO-824					
	1958	Flat, HO, w/two cars 14	22	45
HO-827					
	1961	Caboose, HO, Lionel.................... 6	10	20
HO-827-50					
	1963	Caboose, HO, AEC 6	10	20
HO-827-75					
	1963	Caboose, HO, Lionel.................... 6	10	20
HO-830					
	1958	Flat, HO, w/two vans 12	20	40
HO-834					
	1959	Poultry Car, HO 13	21	42
HO-836					
	1961	Hopper, HO 6	10	20
HO-836-100					
	1964	Hopper, HO, Lionel 6	10	20
HO-836-60					
	1966	Hopper, HO, Alaska.................... 6	10	20
HO-837					
	1961	Caboose, HO, M&StL 5	8	15
HO-837-100					
	1963	Caboose, HO, M&StL 6	10	20
HO-838					
	1961	Caboose, HO, Lackawanna.......... 6	10	20
HO-840					
	1961	Caboose, HO, NYC 6	10	20
HO-841					
	1961	Caboose, HO................................ 6	10	20
HO-841-175					
	1962	Caboose, HO, Santa Fe 6	10	20
HO-841-50					
	1962	Caboose, HO, Union Pacific..................................... 6	10	20
HO-842					
	1960	Culvert Pipe Car, HO.................. 8	12	25

No.	Year	Description	C6	C8	C10
HO-845					
	1962	Gold Bullion Car, HO 10	16	32
HO-847					
	1960	Exploding Target Car, HO...........6	9	18
HO-847-100					
	1960	Exploding Target Car, HO........17	29	58
HO-850					
	1960	Missile Launching Car, HO.......11	18	35
HO-850-100					
		Missile Launching Car, HO.......11	19	38
HO-860					
	1958	Derrick, HO 10	16	32
HO-861					
	1960	Timber Transport Car 6	10	20
HO-861-100					
	1961	Timber Transport Car, HO 8	13	26
HO-862-25					
	1958	Gondola, HO 3	5	10
HO-863					
	1960	Rail Truck Car, HO 8	13	26
HO-864-1					
	1958	Box, HO, Seaboard 6	10	20
HO-864-100					
	1958	Box, HO, New Haven 6	10	20
HO-864-125					
	1958	Box, HO, Rutland 6	10	20
HO-864-150					
	1958	Box, HO, M&StL 6	10	20
HO-864-175					
	1958	Box, HO, Timken........................6	10	20
HO-864-200					
	1958	Box, HO, Monon 6	10	20
HO-864-225					
	1958	Box, HO, Central of Georgia.......6	10	20
HO-864-25					
	1958	Box, HO, NYC.............................6	10	20
HO-864-250					
	1958	Box, HO, Wabash........................6	10	20
HO-864-275					
	1962	Box, HO, State of Maine.............6	10	20
HO-864-300					
	1959	Box, HO, Alaska..........................6	10	20
HO-864-325					
	1959	Box, HO, D.S.S.A. 6	10	20
HO-864-350					
	1959	Box, HO, State of Maine.............9	15	30
HO-864-400					
	1960	Box, HO, B&M 6	10	20
HO-864-50					
	1958	Box, HO, State of Maine.............6	10	20
HO-864-700					
	1961	Box, HO, Santa Fe......................6	10	20
HO-864-900					
	1959	Box, HO, NYC.............................6	10	20
HO-864-925					
	1964	Box, HO, NYC.............................6	10	20
HO-864-935					
	1963	Box, HO, NYC.............................6	10	20
HO-865					
	1958	Gondola, HO, w/canisters 10	16	32
HO-865-225					
	1960	Gondola, HO, w/scrap iron 8	13	25
HO-865-250					
	1960	Gondola, HO, w/crates 8	13	25
HO-865-300					
	1963	Gondola, HO, w/crates 8	13	25
HO-865-350					
	1963	Gondola, HO, NYC 6	10	20
HO-865-375					
	1963	Gondola, HO, NYC 6	10	20
HO-865-400					
	1963	Gondola, HO, NYC w/crates 6	10	20
HO-865-435					
	1964	Gondola, HO...............................6	10	20
HO-866-1					
	1958	Cattle, HO, M.K.T. 6	10	20
HO-866-200					
	1959	Circus Car, HO............................10	16	32
HO-866-25					
	1958	Cattle, HO, Santa Fe 6	10	20
HO-870					
	1959	Maintenance Car, HO, w/generator 9	15	30
HO-872-1					
	1958	Reefer, HO, Fruit Growers...........6	10	20
HO-872-200					
	1959	Reefer, HO, Railway Express........6	10	20
HO-872-25					
	1958	Reefer, HO, Illinois Central 6	10	20
HO-872-50					
	1958	Reefer, HO, El Capitan.................6	10	20
HO-873					
	1962	Rodeo Car, HO............................6	10	20
HO-874					
	1964	Box, HO, NYC.............................15	25	50
HO-874-25					
	1965	Box, HO, NYC.............................6	10	20
HO-874-60					
	1964	Box, HO, B&M 6	10	20
HO-875					
	1959	Flat Car, HO, w/missile..............10	17	34
HO-877					
	1958	Miscellaneous Car, HO...............6	10	20
HO-879					
	1958	Derrick, HO 8	13	26

No.	Year	Description	C6	C8	C10
HO-880					
	1959	Maintenance Car, HO, w/light	18	30	60
HO-900					
	1960	Operating Platform, HO	11	18	36
HO-903					
	1958	Track, HO, straight three-inch	—	—	1
HO-905					
	1958	Track, HO, straight 1-1/2"	—	—	1
HO-906					
	1968	Track, HO, straight six-inch	—	—	1
HO-909					
	1958	Track, HO, straight nine-inch	—	—	1
HO-922					
	1958	Remote Control Switch, HO, right	2	—	3
HO-923					
	1958	Remote Control Switch, HO, left	2	—	3
HO-925					
	1958	Straight Terminal Track, HO	1	—	2
HO-925-10					
	1960	Insulating Clip, HO	—	—	1
HO-929					
	1958	Upcoupling Track, HO, nine-inch	2	3	4
HO-930					
	1960	30 Degrees Crossing, HO	2	3	4
HO-939					
	958	Uncoupler, HO	2	—	3
HO-942					
	1958	Manual Switch, HO, right	2	—	3
HO-943					
	1958	Manual Switch, HO, left	2	—	3
HO-950					
	1958	Re-railer, HO	2	—	3
HO-960					
	1960	Bumper Track, HO	—	—	1
HO-961					
	1961	Bumper Track, HO, illuminated	—	—	1
HO-975					
	1958	Curved Terminal Track, HO	—	—	1
HO-983					
	1958	Curved Track, HO, eighteen-inch radius, three-inch	—	—	1
HO-984					
	1958	Curved Track, HO, eighteen-inch radius, 4-1/2"	—	—	1
HO-985					
	1958	Curved Track, HO, fifteen-inch radius, nine-inch	—	—	1
HO-986					
	1958	Curved Track, HO, fifteen-inch radius, 4-1/2"	—	—	1
HO-989					
	1958	Curved Track, HO, eighteen-inch radius, nine-inch	—	—	1
HO-990					
	1958	90 Degrees Crossing, HO	3	5	7

VEHICLES

Modern man has always had a love affair with machines that move. Partial evidence of this is the amazing number of toy vehicles that have been produced in the twentieth century. In fact it could be resonably argued that toy vehicles are collected more than any other type of toy.

With the dawn of the modern industrial age, the mass production of full-size automobiles and their toy counterparts seemed to go hand-in-hand. As cars rolled off assembly lines, their miniature replicas were not far behind.

Cars and trucks weren't the only toy vehicles, however. Any sort of vehicle—including boats, planes and harsedrawn wagons—was a natural for miniaturization. The types and manufacturers of toy vehicles were as varied as the real things too. Toy makers crafted them from everything from cast iron and tin to wood and plastic.

The earliest toy automobiles came along soon after their big daddy originals in the late nineteenth century and were produced in cast iron. But it wan't until World War I that toy production really began to hit its stride

The Early Days

Firms such as Arcade and Hubley are among the most well-known and sought-after manufacturers of early cast-iron vehicles.

Cars, trucks and buses produced by Arcade Manufacturing of Freeport, Illinois are highly valued to toy vehicle collectors. Arcade actually began producing toys in the late 1800s, but it wasn't until around 1920 when the company reportadly issued its first toy vehicle, a replica of a Chicago Yellow Cab. After that came more realistic models of actual cars, trucks and buses. The company's slogan was "They Look Real."

Hubley is another name associated with quality toy vehicles. This Pennsylvania company began manufacturing cast-iron toys in the 1890s, mostly horse-drawn wagons, trains and guns. Byt he 1930s, Hubley was producing the cast-iron cars that became their most well-known products. Many were patterned after actual automobiles of the day, while others were apparently looser interpretations of reality. Some of the Hubley vehicles also inlcuded company names, and some of the most interesting pieces had separate nickel-plated grilles.

One of the more skilled makers of smaller sclae cast-iron vehicles was A.C. Williams. The Ohio company began producing toys in the late 1800s. The smaller cars and airplanes produced by A.C Williams were intended for the five-and-dine market of the time. Williams toys are difficult for the novice collector to identify since the toys bear no markings.

Steel Takes Over

One of the most famous manufacturers of toy cars and trucks was Buddy "L." these large predded-steel toys were not the kind of toys bought for display or quiet play on the living room floor. These were big trucks (around two feet long) designed for tough play.

Buddy "L" toys grew out of the Moline Pressed Steel company of Moline, Illinois. The company was named for the son of the company's owner, reportedly for whom the first toys were produced. The Buddy "L" toys most sought by collectors were produced in the 1920s ans 1930s and were of very heavy-duty construction. Starting in the early 1930s, the company began to use lighter-weight materials.

The Buddy "L" name has remained, but its post world-War II toys are not considered in the same league as its early issues, which command high collecotr prices today.

Buddy "L" is best remembered for its heavy duty trucks, but another name that was synonymous with trucks was smith miller. Founded by Bob Smith and Matt Miller, the company specialized in "famous trucks in miniature." Smith-Miller wa later known as Miller-Ironson Corporation, but is more commanly referred to a Smitty Toys. They produced large cast-metal and aluminaum trucks.

Because of their outstanding quality, some of the Mack trucks made by Smith-Miller are very highly regarded amont toy collecotrs. The Smilth-Miller name continues today, with new limited-edition trucks produced for collectors.

Wyandotte is another company associated with pressed steel vehicles. Known as both Wyandotte Toys or All Metal Products, this Michigan company produced several large steel vehicles with baked enamel finishes in the 1930s. Not all Wyandotte toys are marked, which tends to cause some confusion among collecotrs, but the vehicles can aften be identified by their art-deco styling and wooden wheels.

Another company that produced large steel toys was Structo. The company originally produced metal construction sets, but developed a line of vehicles in the 1920s.

Slush Molds

Slush casting was a process simple enough to be done in tiny factories and even in home industries during the Depression. A few large manufacturers made toys in this way—most notably Barclay, Manoil, Savoye, Kansas Toy and Novelty and others, but many were made by anonymous, small, unidentifiable, local operations, using molds made and marketed by a few firms. Many slush-cast toys are of very little value today, but there are exceptions. Foremost among these were dealer promotional replicas of real cars, made by Banthrico and National Products. Other very accurate and detailed slush models, similar in size and scale to the contemporary Tootsietoys, can be valuable. Most notable among these are certain nicely cast models of the Reo Victoria, Packard, Chrysler Imperial, Cord coupe (late 1920s), Buick and Model A Ford. These, and others made with an extra mold part resulting in detailed radiator grilles, were made by the Lincoln White Metal Works. Other small accurate replicas, with the names cast on the door sides, were made by Tommy Toy.

Rubber Toy Vehicles

The Auburn Rubber Company of Auburn, Indiana was not the first to introduce rubber toys to the American market, but they were no doubt the largest and had the greatest impact on the toy field. After introducing some toy soldiers in 1935, Auburn brought out its first vehicle in 1936—a beautiful coffin-nosed Cord sedan. Today, the Auburn Cord is one of the most highly prized rubber toys and is seldom seen offered for sale.

Auburn followed the Cord with a wealth of vehicles, including trucks, farm tractors and implements, motorcycles, racers, fire engines, military vehicles, aircraft, ships, and trains. It seems that 1952 was Auburn's last year of marketing rubber toys exclusively. The 1953 Auburn catalog contained a vinyl motorcycle, believed to be their first vinyl toy. By 1955 their toy line was mostly vinyl with a few rubber varieties hanging on. The 1956 catalog was exclusively vinyl, except for two rubber fire engines, the last rubber toys to be marketed by Auburn.

The Sun Rubber Company of Barberton, Ohio, was the second largest producer of rubber toys. Like Auburn, they produced a full line of toys in addition to vehicles, including dolls, balls and baby squeak toys. Sun Rubber's 1936 catalog contains a large selection of cars, trucks and racers. In later years, they added a few airplanes and military. Among the most famous of the Sun Rubber vehicles are the Walt Disney characters—Mickey Mouse and Donald Duck driving a tractor, firetruck, roadster or airplane. By 1955, Sun's catalog line largely consisted of athletic balls, and the Disney toys were included as the only vehicle toys.

Auburn and Sun made the vast majority of rubber toys we see today, but there were a significant number of rubber toys made by other companies, mostly prior to World War II. Several companies from the rubber industry produced rubber toy vehicles, including Firestone, Seiberling, Barr and Rainbow. All of the Rainbow, Barr and Seiberling toys appear to have been made from 1935-1936, or at least based on real cars from those years. Most of the Seiberling or Barr toys are 1935 Fords; the Firestone toys include a 1935 Ford, a 1936 Ford and a 1939 Mercury. Rainbow's vehicles seem to be based on the 1935 Oldsmobile. Some of these toys were mass-marketed through dimestores, just like Auburn and Sun toys; although, some were sold or given away at expositions and exhibits. All of the Firestone toys seem to be marked with some significant event, like the Texas Centennial in 1936.

Many rubber toys were produced as promotionals for the automobile industry and are not marked to indicate who manufactured them. A number of Chrysler, DeSoto, Dodge and Plymouth promotionals were produced during the mid-1930s and are highly prized as collectibles.

A few rubber vehicles were produced as very inexpensive toys, perhaps sold in sets, and can take the form of either a solid rubber or hollow vehicle. These toys often had the wheels molded into the body, so they could not turn. Many of these solid rubber toys are two-dimensional and are referred to as "flat" toys. Although they were originally sold as inexpensive toys, they are actively sought by collectors and constitute a small but important segment of the field.

Die-Cast

Other popularly-collected vehicles are smaller die-cast models, generally three to six inches long. Probably the leading producer of this type of toy was Tootsietoy.

Although few toys were produced by Tootsietoy before 1920, it was during the 1920s when the name Tootsietoy began to appear regularly. By the 1930s, the company was producing a wide line of toys, many of which are highly prized by collectors today. Tootsietoy's Federal vans from the 1920s are among the most sought-after toys, particularly those with company logos.

Being mass produced and economically priced, Tootsietoys were widely available in the five-and-dime arena. The success of these products no doubt led to several competitors no doubt led to several competitors.

One of the competitors was Barclay, which also produced die-cast vehicles, although most were generally considered of lesser quality that Tootsietoys. The first Barclay vehciles had metal tires, but in the mid-1930s, white rubber tires on wooden axles were introduced. Metal axles soon replaced the wood, and black tires replaced white after World War II.

Another competitor soon emerged from Europe—Dinky Toys were manufactured from 1933 through the 1970s in England and France. Their vehicles were high quality die cast, at least until the mid-1960s, generally in 1:43 scale.

Another competitor in theis clasificatin of small die-cast vehicles is Corgi, which came on the scene in the late 1950s. Corgi was the trade name for the die-cast toys which were produced by ngland's Mettoy Company.

One of the best known series of toy cars today is Matchbox. These die-cast beauties are roughly three-inches in length. However Lesney, the company that produced them, did manufacture several larger scale cars before it began the Matchbox line. Some of these early Lesney vehicles are valued at up to $2,000 each.

Matchbox vehicles were immesely popular, so much so that in the United States, mattel introduced a similar line called Hot Wheels. The California-based company gave its cars a California-type appeal, focusing of colorful hot rods that appealed to youngsters.

In the head-to-head battle that followed, Lesney at one time was producing 5.5 million toys a week. Eventually, Lesney lost the battle and went into receivership. Matchbox was restructured and sold twice, eventually landing with Tyco Toys. In 1996, Mattel purchased Tyco, bringing matchbox cars into their company.

Tips on Grading

Demand and desirability are affected by a number of factors, one of which is nostalgia. As a guide to other factors affecting desirability, there are a few broad, easy clues. Accuracy of scale and proportion, the use of many different cast parts, cast-in or decal logos and details and hand-painting (by the original maker, but not by some later child or collector) all enhance the value. In most cases, a four-inch roadster with a separate chassis, separate nickel-plated radiator and headlights, and a separate cast figure will be worth much more than a two-piece vehicle with the halves riveted together. While any imperfections or scratches always lessen a vehicles value, such things are more likely to deflate prices on vehicles such as Hot Wheels or Matchbox cars. On the latter two, any defect will bring the value down about twenty-five percent.

A.C. WILLIAMS

A.C. Williams was founded in 1886 when Adam Clark Williams (1848-1932) bought the J.W. Williams Company from his father. Toy production began in 1893 after fire forced the firm to move from Chagrin Falls, Ohio, to Ravenna.

Small cast-iron toys were Williams' specialty. Banks, cars and aircraft were predominant. A.C. Williams retired in 1919, but the firm halted toy production in 1938.

Few, if any, A.C. Williams' toys are marked, although turned steel hubs and starred axle peens are characteristics of a Williams toy.

	C6	C8	C10
Car Carrier, w/tree Austins, 1920, 12-1/2" long	450	675	900
Coupe, two-piece body, 1936, 3" long	95	145	190
Coupe, rumble seat, side mounts, 1930, cast iron, rubber tires, 6-3/4" long	155	225	310
Delivery Van, 8" long	350	525	700
Dump Truck, 6-1/4" long	195	292	390
Car, four-casting nickeled radiator car, 4" long	75	112	150
Laundry Truck, 8" long	400	600	800
Lincoln Touring Car, 7" long	312	470	625
Mack Gas Tank Truck, 3-3/4" long	122	185	245

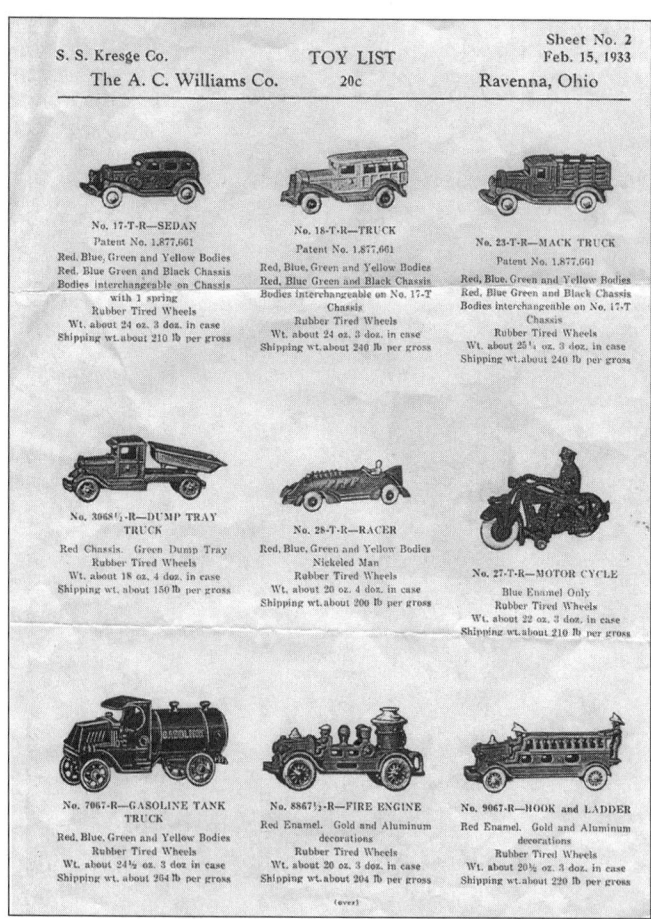

A 1933 advertisement for A.C. Williams vehicles from the S.S. Kresge Co.

Coupe, 1930, cast iron, A.C. Williams, 6-3/4" long, $310

Sedan, c. 1930, cast iron, streamlined rear fender, A.C. Williams, 6-1/2" long, $355

Mack Gas Tank Truck, 5-1/8" long	100	150	200
Mack Gas Tank Truck, 7-1/4" long	350	525	700
Mack Stake Truck, 3-1/2"	45	68	90
Mack Stake Truck, 4-1/4"	80	120	160
Mack Stake Truck, 5-1/8	112	170	225
Mack Stake Truck, 7" long	150	225	300
Mack Stake Truck, 8-1/2"	200	300	400
Mack Truck, 3-1/2" long	45	68	90
Mack Truck, 4-3/4" long	95	140	190
Mack Truck, 6-3/4" long	100	150	200
Model T Coupe, 6" long	180	270	360
Moving & Storage Truck, 3-1/2" long	112	168	225
Racer, boattailed, 6-1/2" long	262	395	525
Sedan, 5" long	75	112	150
Sedan, c. 1930, cast iron, streamlined rear fender, 6-1/2" long	175	265	355

Tank, A.C. Williams, 4" long, $145

	C6	C8	C10
Sedan, c. 1931, cast iron, interchangeable body, 6-3/4" long	350	525	700
Stake Truck, "C to C Co.," two pieces, 7" long	200	300	400
Steam Roller, 1930s, 5-1/2"	95	145	190
Studebaker, c. 1933-34, 2-tone sedan, approx. 4" long	110	165	220
Tank, 4" long	73	110	145
Taxi, 5-3/4" long	182	275	365
Touring Car, cast iron, 9-1/2" long	475	712	950
Touring Car w/driver, 5"	100	150	200
Wrecker, 6-1/2" long	250	375	500
Willys Knight, cast iron, 1920s, w/driver, 8" long	120	180	240

ALL AMERICAN TOY COMPANY

All American was founded by Clay Steinke in Salem, Oregon in 1948 and continued until 1955 in its location at the Jorgenson Building on Ferry Street. At their peak, All American employed forty-two people and sold a total of 26,000 toys. Their most popular toy was the Timber Toter, despite its formidable 1950 price of twenty dollars. Bill Hellie purchased the defunct company and all of their

Advertisement for All American the Scoop-A-Veyor, Play-Dozer and the Play-Loader.

C-5 Cattle Liner, All American Toy Company, 38" long, $1,150

D-3 Dyna-Dump, All American Toy Company, 20" long, $590

molds, dies, and parts. All American now sells parts and is producing new limited editions (see Leading Collectors and Dealers).

	C6	C8	C10
C-5 Cattle Liner, 38" long	500	800	1150
CL-8 Cargo Liner, 38" long	470	705	940
D-3 Dyna-Dump, 20" long	295	445	590
Hay Feed and Grain	275	410	550
HD-7 Play-Dozer, 9" long	338	505	675
HH-9 Heavy Hauler, 38" long	475	710	950
L-2 Timber Toter, w/logs, 38" extended length	275	415	555
LJ-4 Timber Toter, Jr., w/lumber, 20" long	212	318	425
MS Midget Skagit, battery-powered, 18" long	300	450	600
S-1 Scoop-a-Veyor, 16" long	237	355	475

AMERICAN METAL TOYS

	C6	C8	C10
Packard Coupe, steerable front wheels, 1920s, 54" long	3000	5000	7000
Pedal Car, dump truck, "Juvenile Auto," red and yellow tin, 57" long	2000	3500	5000
Pedal Car, Velie, c. 1918	1600	2500	3400
Tank, "22" on side	50	75	100
Tank, throwing flame, "No. 25"	60	90	120
Tank, throwing flame, flame not touching hull	45	67	90
Tank, throwing flame, flame touching hull	40	60	80

	C6	C8	C10
Tractor, "Baby Tractor," friction, marked "patented June 20, 1916"	100	150	200
Truck, Mack "Giant," 26-1/2" long	800	1400	2000

ARCADE MANUFACTURING COMPANY

In 1869 a foundry in Freeport, Illinois, was organized as a two-man partnership under the name of Novelty Iron and Brass Foundry. It was dissolved in 1885 when a new, larger factory was incorporated under the name of Arcade Manufacturing Co. Arcade made industrial castings and household items, but no toys. After a disastrous fire in 1892 and management changes in 1893, toys began to appear in its catalog, and by the early 1900s the line had become so extensive that a fifty-page catalog was issued showing a large line of notions and novelties, small stoves, banks and a few trains, including a unique pile-driver. But it was not until an enterprising young lawyer married the daughter of one of the officers and joined the firm in 1919 that the firm rapidly became one of the major makers of cast-iron toys. Struck by the large numbers of Yellow Cabs in the streets of Chicago, the young man approached the Yellow Cab Company with a novel proposition: in return for the sole right to make toy replicas of the cab, the Yellow Cab Company would have the exclusive right to use the toy in its advertising. Success was instantaneous.

Arcade went on to duplicate this pattern with miniature Buick, Chevrolet, Ford, Plymouth and Pontiac automobiles; and McCormack-Deering and International Harvester farm equipment; and several makes of trucks and buses.

In the booming 1920s, the company's sales swelled so much that a new and larger plant was built in 1927. Two years later, the stock market crash heralded the Great Depression, and hard times hit the small car business just as it did the large ones.

Cheap competition and dwindling demand for toys costing more than a dime had brought the company to the brink of bankruptcy by 1933. But once again the enterprising management gave the firm new life with an exclusive arrangement to provide souvenir replicas of the fairground buses made by G.M.C. for the Chicago Century of Progress. The Depression caused a cheapening of quality, but World War II gave the firm business in military material.

After the war, the company returned to making industrial and household hardware and a few toys, but cheaper toys of die-cast zamac, plastic, rubber and lithographed tin eclipsed the costlier cast-iron toys. In 1946 the firm was sold to Rockwell Manufacturing Co. of Pittsburgh. Death and retirement soon finished the change of the old firm, and it followed its guiding directors into oblivion when Rockwell moved to Alabama.

Arcade toys were meant to be played with and are exltremely rare in Mint condition. The year listed is the year the toy was introduced.

Contributor: Conrad Scwager, 10321 N. Trails Edge Dr., Peoria, IL 61615.

In 1994, an Arcade Brinks Express Truck was auctioned in Excellent condition for $20,000

	C6	C8	C10
A.C.F. Bus, 1927, 11-1/2" long	1200	2200	3500
Allis-Chalmers "WC" Tractor, 1941, 7-3/4" long	180	350	600
Allis-Chalmers Tractor and Dump Trailer, 1937, No. 2657, 12-3/4" long w/trailer	200	345	460
Allis-Chalmers Tractor and Dump Trailer, 1937, No. 2660, 8-1/4" long	150	200	300
Allis-Chalmers Tractor and Trailer, 1936, No. 2650, total length 13" long	175	300	400
Allis-Chalmers Tractor Trailer, 1937, No. 2650, 13" long w/trailer	250	375	500
Ambulance, 1932, No. 187, 7-3/4" long	400	700	1200
Ambulance, 1932, No. 188, 6" long	370	550	740
Ambulance, 1936, white-painted version of No. 2620 Chevrolet Panel Delivery Truck, 4" long	340	510	680
Anthony Dump Truck, 1927, 8-1/8" long	700	1500	2400
Austin "Roll-A-Plane," 8" long	450	675	900
Austin Autocrat Road Roller, 1928, No. 291, 7" long	200	300	450
Austin Delivery Truck, 1932, No. 173, 3-3/4" long	40	75	100
Austin Racer, 1932, No. 175X, 3-3/4" long	50	90	135
Austin Roadster, 1932, No. 174, 3-3/4" long	90	140	190
Austin Stake Truck, 1932, No. 176X, 3-3/4" long	90	140	200
Austin Wrecker, 1932, No. 177X, 3-3/4" long	100	150	225
Avery Tractor, 1923, stack, no hood, 4-1/2" long	50	75	110
Avery Tractor, 1926, has hood, no stack, 4-1/2" long	125	200	325
Borden's Milk Bottle Truck, 1936, No. 2640X, 6-1/4" long	750	1200	2500
Brinks Express Truck, 1932, 11-3/4" long, auctioned in Excellent condition, 1994			20,000
Buick Opera Coupe, 1927, 8-1/2" long	1900	2900	4900
Buick Sedan, 1927, 8-1/2" long	1500	2500	4000

Bus, Double-Decker, Arcade, 1936, No. 317, $900

Chevrolet Utility Coupe, Arcade, 1925, $900

	C6	C8	C10
Bus, Double-Decker, 1929, No. 316X, 8-1/2" long	350	600	900
Bus, Double-Decker, 1936, No. 317, "Chicago Motor Coach" stamp, 8-1/4" long	350	600	900
Car Carrier, 1930, No. 238, Ford AA truck w/5" Ford Model A cars or three 6" Ford Model A cars, 24-1/2" long	2000	3500	5000
Car Carrier, 1932, No. 296, Ford AA truck carries all options of 5" and 6" Ford Model A cars and trucks, 24-1/2" long	2000	3500	5000
Car Transport, 1937, No. 2977, holds two sedans and two trucks, 11-1/2" long	427	640	855
Car Transport, 1937, No. 3107, came w/two No. 1501 sedans, No. 1502 stake truck and No. 1503 wrecker, 18-1/2" long	900	1350	1800
Carry Car Truck and Trailer Set, 1934, No. 2970, carries three Austins, 14-1/4" long	650	1000	1500
Caterpillar Tractor, 1930, No. 271, 7-1/2" long	450	800	1300
Caterpillar Tractor, 1931, No. 266X, 3" long	50	75	100
Caterpillar Tractor, 1931, No. 267X, 3-7/8" long	150	250	400

	C6	C8	C10
Caterpillar Tractor, 1931, No. 268X 5-5/8" long	350	600	900
Caterpillar Tractor, 1931, No. 269X, 6-7/8" long	375	650	1100
Caterpillar Tractor, 1936, No. 270Y, later 2700Y, 7-3/4" long	700	1200	2200
Century of Progress Bus, 1933, No. 3220, 10-1/2" long	150	250	350
Century of Progress Bus, 1933, No. 3230, 7-5/8" long	100	175	250
Century of Progress Bus, 1933, No. 3250, 1934, 14-1/2" long	250	350	525
Century of Progress Bus, 1933, No. 3210, 12" long	200	300	400
Century of Progress Yellow Cab, 6-3/4" long	750	1000	1600
Checker Cab, 1932, No. 157, (came w/ and w/o "Checker" on visor), 9-1/4" long	5000	8000	12,000
Chevrolet Coupe, 1929, No. 121X, 8-1/4" long	700	1200	1800
Chevrolet Coupe, 1934, rumble seat, No. 1150X, 4-3/8" long	150	250	350

Century of Progress Bus, Arcade, 1933, No. 3220, $350

Checker Cab, 1932, Arcade, No. 157, $12,000

Fageol Bus, Arcade, 1925, 12" long, $500

	C6	C8	C10
Chevrolet Panel Delivery Truck, 1936, No. 2620X, 4" long	100	150	200
Chevrolet Sedan, 1929, No. 122X, 8-1/4" long	800	1300	2200
Chevrolet Sedan, 1934, No. 1170X, 4-1/4" long	70	110	180
Chevrolet Stake Truck, 1925, 9" long	800	1400	2300
Chevrolet Stake Truck, 1936, No. 2610, 4-1/4" long	90	120	200
Chevrolet Superior Roadster, 1925, 7" long	550	7500	1100
Chevrolet Superior Sedan, 1925, 7" long	450	650	950
Chevrolet Superior Touring Car, 1925, 7" long	500	700	1000
Chevrolet Utility Coupe, 1925, 7" long	500	700	900
Chevrolet Wrecker Truck, 1936, No. 2630X, 4-1/4" long	100	200	300
Chief Fire Chief Coupe, 1934, No. 1230, 6-3/4" long	1500	2500	3400
Chief Fire Chief Coupe, 1934, No. 1240, 5" long	500	800	1400
Coast to Coast GMC Transcontinental Bus, 1937, No. 4378X, 9" long	212	320	425
Corn Harvester, 1939, No. 4180, 5" long	100	175	250

	C6	C8	C10
Corn Harvester, 1939, No. 702, 6-1/2" long	150	250	400
Corn Planter, 1939, 4-1/2" long	40	80	125
Coupe, "1922" on spare tire, 9" long	800	1500	4000
Coupe, 1932, No. 109, no Arcade markings, rumble seat opens, 6" long	300	450	650
Coupe, like above, no 1922 date on spare	600	900	1500
Deluxe Sedan, 1941, No. 1590X, same as Yellow Cab No. 1590Y, but w/top lights and sun roof ground off, 8-1/2" long	500	825	1200
DeSoto Sedan, 1936, No. 1460X, 4" long	90	150	250
Double Decker Bus, 1939, No. 3180, 8" long	300	450	750
Dump Truck Trailer, 1931, No. 234, 12-7/8" long	700	1150	1900
Dump Truck, 1936, No. 2320, 4-1/2" long	90	130	200
Dump Truck, 1941, No. 3910X, 7" long	300	450	600
Dump Wagon, 1923, driver, no cab, 7" long	300	550	850
Express Truck, 1929, No. 207X, 8" long	300	600	900
Express Truck, 1929, No. 209X, 6" long	200	300	500
Express Truck, 1929, No. 214X, 5" long	150	250	400
Fageol Bus, 1925, 12" long	200	350	500
Fageol Bus, 5" long	80	150	300
Fageol Bus, 8" long	150	250	400
Farm Mower, 1939, No. 4210X, 4" long	40	70	100
Farmall "A" Tractor, 1941, No. 7050, 7-1/2" long	475	850	1200
Farmall "M" Tractor, 1941, No. 7070, 7-1/4" long	300	450	700
Farmall Tractor, 1929, No. 279, 6" long	225	400	800
Fire Chief Car, 1941, 5-5/8" long	160	300	450
Fire Engine, 1923, pumper, 7-1/2" long	200	375	500
Fire Engine, 1936, No. 1740, pumper, 9" long	400	700	1150
Fire Engine, 1936, No. 2340, 4-1/2" long	90	150	250
Fire Engine, 1941, No. 6990, 13-1/2" long	500	950	1525

Farmall Tractor, Arcade, 1929, No. 279, $800

Ford Model A Coupe, Arcade, 1928, No. 116X, rumble seat, $700

TOY WHITE DUMP TRUCK

No. 249. Length 11½ inches, width 4½ inches, height 5¼ inches bed down, 6¾ inches bed up.
Color: Black hood and front fenders with red body and red disc wheels.
Wheels: Nickel plated tires. Real rubber tires at small additional cost. Dual rear wheels.
Packed: 1 in a carton, 1 dozen in a case.
Case net weight 65 pounds, gross weight 75 pounds.
Case measurements 24x15½x13 inches.

TOY WHITE DELIVERY TRUCK

No. 252X. Length 8¼ inches, width 3 inches, height 3¼ inches.
Color: Light green trimmed in gold.
Wheels: Metal wheels, nickel plated tires, or real rubber tires at small additional cost.
Packed: 1 in a carton, 1 dozen in a case.
Case net weight 65 pounds, gross weight 40 pounds.

TOY WHITE MOVING VAN

No. 251. Length 13½ inches, width 4 inches, height 4¾ inches.
Color: Red hood and body stripes, rest of body cream.
Wheels: Metal red disc wheels with nickeled tires. Real rubber tires at small additional cost.
Packed: 1 in a carton, 1 dozen in a case.
Case net weight 65 pounds, gross weight 75 pounds.

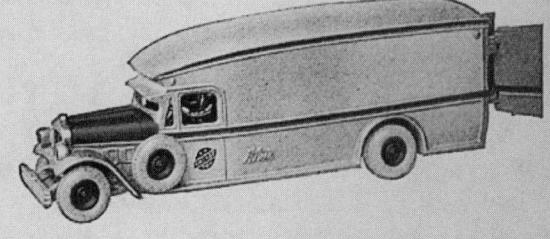

TOY PANEL DELIVERY TRUCK

No. 228X. Length 8¼ inches, width 3 inches, height 4 inches.
Color: Assorted, red, green, and blue, trimmed in gold.
Wheels: Disc wheels nickel plated tires. Real rubber tires at small additional cost.
Packed: 1 each in a carton, 1 dozen in a case.
Case net weight 37 pounds, gross weight 46 pounds.
Case measurements, 20x11x9 inches.

Top to Bottom: White Dump Truck, Arcade, 1929, No. 249, auctioned in Excellent condition in 1994 $23,000; White Moving Van, Arcade, 1929, No. 251, 13-1/2" long, auctioned in Excellent condition in 1994 for $13,200; White Delivery Truck, Arcade, 1929, No. 252X, 8-1/2" long, $6,000

Fire Trailer Truck, Arcade, 1934, No. 1940, $1,200

Greyhound Cruiser Coach Bus, Arcade, 1941, No. 4400, $450

	C6	C8	C10
Fire Ladder Truck, 1936, No. 1820, 7" long	150	250	400
Fire Trailer Truck, 1934, No. 1940, 16-1/4" long	600	900	1200
Ford Coupe, 1934, No. 1610X, rumble seat opens, 6-3/4" long	300	550	950
Ford Dump Truck, 1929, No. 219X, 7-1/2" long	285	425	700
Ford Express Truck, 1929, No. 210X, 8-1/4" long	700	1100	1900
Ford Model A Coupe, 1928, No. 113X, 4-1/8" long	200	300	400
Ford Model A Coupe, 1928, No. 106, rumble seat, 6-3/4" long	550	950	1400
Ford Model A Coupe, 1928, No. 116X, rumble seat, 5" long	350	550	700
Ford Model A Fordor, 1928, No. 207, 6-3/4" long	350	500	750
Ford Model A Tudor, 1928, No. 108, 6-3/4" long	550	850	1200
Ford Model A Wrecker, 1929, No. 215, w/"weaver" host	550	850	1400
Ford Model A Wrecker, 1930, No. 218, 4-1/2" long	125	200	300
Ford Model T Coupe, 1923, 6" long	175	300	450
Ford Model T Coupe, 1924, 6-1/2" long	290	435	750
Ford Model T Fordor Sedan, 1924, removable chauffeur, 6-1/2" long	250	350	650
Ford Model T Sedan, center door, 1923, 6-1/2" long	325	490	650
Ford Model T Stake Truck, 1927, 5-3/4" long	250	350	450

	C6	C8	C10
Ford Model T Stake Truck, 1927, 9" long	600	925	1250
Ford Model T Stake Truck, 1925, 8-3/4" long	800	1100	1600
Ford Model T Stake Truck, 1934, No. 2010X, 7" long	300	600	950
Ford Model T Touring Car Bank, 1923, 6-1/2" long	800	1100	1900
Ford Model T Touring Car, 1923, 6-1/2" long	250	300	700
Ford Model T Tudor, 1928, No. 118, 5" long	350	550	700
Ford Model T Wrecker, 1927, 11" long	700	1200	2000
Ford Sedan w/Trailer, 1937, "Covered Wagon," No. 1970, 12" long, trailer 5-1/2" long	650	120	2500
Ford Sedan, 1933, No. 1620X, 6-7/8" long	350	600	850
Ford Sedan, 1934, "Century of Progress," 6-7/8" long	800	1500	2400
Ford Sedan, 1934, "Century of Progress," 4-3/4" long	200	600	900
Ford Tractor and Plow, 1941, No. 7220, tractor 6-1/2" long, overall length 8-3/4"	350	550	850
Ford Truck, 1923, cab, one ton, 8-1/2" long	600	850	1500
Ford Tudor, 1937, 5-1/4" long	550	950	1500
Fordson Tractor, 1923, 5-3/4" long	138	225	325
Fordson Tractor, 1928, No. 273, 3-7/8" long	90	150	200
Fordson Tractor, 1928, No. 274, 4-3/4" long	112	190	250
Fordson Tractor, 1934, rubber wheels, No. 2730X, 3-1/2" long	75	125	175
Greyhound Cruiser Coach Bus, 1941, No. 4400, 9-1/8" long	200	325	450
Greyhound Lines Great Lakes Exposition, 1936, No. 436, 6-3/4" long	300	500	750
Greyhound Lines Bus, 1937, No. 3850 SP, 7-3/4" long	175	275	400
Greyhound Lines Bus, GMC, 1933, one-piece casting, 6"	100	200	300

Greyhound Super Coach, Arcade, 1937, No. 4380, $750

International Pickup Truck, Arcade, 1941, No. 7000, $1,280

Left to Right: Stake Truck, Arcade, 1929, No. 213, $325; International Dump Truck, Arcade, 1931, No. 236-0, $1,750

	C6	C8	C10
Greyhound Lines Great Lakes Exposition, 1936, No. 437, 11" long	375	650	1000
Greyhound Super Coach, 1937, No. 4380, 9" long	300	500	750
Ice Truck, circa 1941, No. 1933, 6-3/4" long	270	355	540
International Delivery Truck, 1936, No. 3020, 9-1/2" long	750	1900	1500
International Delivery Truck, 1932, No. 226, 9-3/4" long	1500	2400	3500
International Dump Truck, 1931, No. 236-0, 10-3/4" long	750	1200	1750
International Dump Truck, 1937, No. 3710, 9-1/2" long	400	550	950
International Dump Truck, 1940, No. 1670, chassis and dump box are steel, 11-5/8" long	500	1000	1650
International Dump Truck, 1941, No. 7100, 11-1/8" long	500	900	1400
International Dump Truck, 1936, No. 3030, 10-1/2" long	800	1600	2200
International Harvester, Trac Tractor, 1941, No. 7120, 7-1/2" long	800	1400	2000
International Pickup Truck, 1941, No. 7000, 9-1/2" long	450	850	1280
International Stake Truck, 1931, No. 237-0, 12" long	600	900	1400

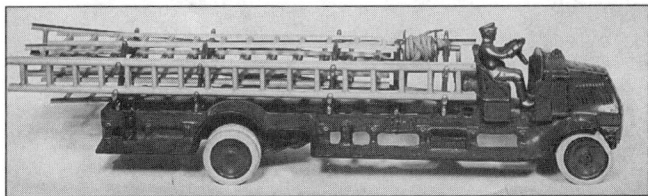

Mack Fire Apparatus Ladder Truck, Arcade, 1929, No. 242, $2,000

Mack Bus, Arcade, 1929, No. 318, $3,000

Left to Right: Mack Ice Truck, Arcade, 1932, No. 257, 10-3/4" long, $4,000; Mack Ice Truck, Arcade, 1930, No. 257, $1,000

	C6	C8	C10
International Stake Truck, 1936, No. 3090, 12" long	800	1100	2000
International Stake Truck, 1937, No. 2600, 9-1/2" long	700	1000	2800
International Stake Truck, 1941, No. 7090, 11-1/2" long	800	1100	2000
International Wrecker, 1940, No. 1650, wrecker crane body and crane are steel, 13" long	500	800	1100
Ladder Truck, 1936, No. 1700, w/ladders 12-1/2" long	475	715	950

International Delivery Truck, Arcade, 1936, No. 3020, $1,500

Mack Tank Truck, Arcade, 1925, "Lubrite," $2,800

Mack Tank Truck, Arcade, 1925, 13-1/4" long, $2,800

Mack Wrecker, Arcade, 1930, No. 255, $3,500

	C6	C8	C10
Ladder Truck, 1936, No. 2350, 4-3/4" long	90	150	200
Mack Bus, 1929, No. 318, 13-1/4" long	950	1500	3000
Mack Cement Mixer, 1931, 6-11/16" long, drum revolves	700	900	1200
Mack Chemical Truck, 1928, fire engine No. 245R, has ladders, 15" long	1500	2500	4000
Mack Chemical Truck, 1929, fire engine w/ladders, 10" long	350	650	100
Mack Chemical Truck, 1929, fire ladder truck, 15" long	800	1500	2000
Mack Dump Truck, 1925, 12" long	1400	2400	3400
Mack Dump Truck, 1929, No. 248X, 8-1/2" long	600	950	1600
Mack Fire Apparatus Truck, 1929, No. 242, ladder truck, 21" long	850	1350	2000

	C6	C8	C10
Mack High Dump Truck, 1931, No. 244X, 10" long	900	1600	2300
Mack High Dump Truck, 1931, No. 259X, 8-1/2" long	700	1150	1700
Mack Hoist Truck, 1932, No. 198, body 8" long	900	1500	2130
Mack Ice Truck, 1930, No. 257, w/driver, glass "ice" and tongs, 10-5/8" long	375	600	1000
Mack Ice Truck, 1931, No. 226, 8-1/2" long	300	500	800
Mack Ice Truck, 1932, No. 257, w/driver, glass "ice" and tongs, 10-3/4" long	1200	2500	4000
Mack Side Dump Truck, 1932, No. 1960, 9" long	1200	2000	2800
Mack Stake Truck, 1929, No. 246X, 12" long	1400	2800	4000
Mack Stake Truck, 1929, No. 253, 8-3/4" long	800	1600	2200
Mack Tank Truck, 1925, "American Gasoline," 13-1/4" long	1200	1850	2800
Mack Tank Truck, 1925, "Lubrite," 13-1/4" long	1200	1800	2800
Mack Tank Truck, 1925, 13-1/4" long	1000	1600	2800
Mack Tank Truck, 1930, No. 241, sheet metal tank, marked "Gasoline" and "Mack," 13" long	1200	1800	2800
Mack Wrecker, 1930 No. 255, 12-1/2" long	1500	2400	3500
McCormick-Deering Farmall Tractor, 1937, 6-1/4" long	250	400	600
McCormick-Deering Thresher, 1927, 12" long	250	400	600
McCormick-Deering Thresher, 1930, 9-1/2" long	200	300	400
McCormick-Deering Tractor, 1925, No.10-20, 6-3/4" long	300	425	600
Mullins Red Cap auto trailer	225	338	450
Nash Coupe, 1943, 4-1/2" long	250	400	650
Nash Panel Delivery, 1934, 4"	150	250	400
Nash Wrecker, 1936, 4-1/2" long	250	375	500

National Trailways Bus, Arcade, 1937, No. 3870, $1,700

McCormick-Deering Farmall Tractor, Arcade, 1937, $600

New York World's Fair Bus, Arcade, 1939, No. 3780, $900

	C6	C8	C10
National Trailways Bus, 1937, No. 3870, 9-1/4" long	650	1200	1700
New York World's Fair Bus, 1939, No. 3750, 7" long	150	200	300
New York World's Fair Bus, 1939, No. 3770, 8-1/2" long	300	400	550
New York World's Fair Bus, 1939, No. 3780, 10-1/2" long	450	650	900
New York World's Fair Tractor-Train, 1939, No. 7270, tractor and one car, tractor 3-1/4" long, car 4-1/4" long	200	300	450
New York World's Fair Tractor-Train, 1939, No. 7290, same as above w/three cars	350	600	900
Oliver Plow, 1923, 6-1/2" long	250	375	500
Oliver Plow, 1941, No. 4230X, 6-1/4" long	150	225	300
Oliver Superior Spreader, No 7140, 1941, 10-1/4" long	350	550	950
Oliver Tractor, 1937, No. 356, 7-1/2" long	300	500	675
Oliver Tractor, 1941, No. 3560, 7-1/2" long	300	500	700
Pierce "Silver Arrow," 1934, 7-1/4" long	300	450	750
Plymouth Coupe, 1933, No. 1340, 4-3/4" long	300	500	800
Plymouth Sedan, 1933, No. 1330, 4-3/4" long	300	450	750
Plymouth Stake Truck, 1933, No. 1840, 4-3/4" long	250	325	450
Plymouth Wrecker, 1933, No. 1830, 4-3/4" long	175	250	350
Pontiac Sedan, 1935, 6-1/2" long	350	525	800

	C6	C8	C10
Pontiac Sedan, 1935, No. 1350, 4-1/4" long	150	250	375
Pontiac Stake Truck, 1935, No. 2390, 6-1/4" long	300	450	600
Pontiac Stake Truck, 1936, No. 2780, 4-1/4" long	150	250	350
Pontiac Wrecker, 1936, No. 2000, 4-1/4" long	125	188	250
Racer, 1931, No. 138, 6-3/4" long	200	300	450
Racer, 1932, No. 137, 5-5/8" long	120	180	240
Racer, 1932, No. 140, 10-1/2" long, plastic or celluloid windshield, auctioned in 1994 in Excellent condition			11,500
Racer, 1937, No. 1457, 5-3/4" long	150	250	350
Racer, Bullet Racer, 1931, No. 139, 7-5/8" long	950	1500	2300
Racer, pre-1923, 7-3/4" long	400	600	800
Red Baby "Weaver" Wrecker, 1929, 12" long	900	1500	2300
Red Baby Dump Truck, 1923, No. 2, 10-3/4" long	900	1500	2500
Red Baby Dump Truck, 1923, No. 1, 10-3/4" long	900	1500	2500
Reo Coupe, 1931, 7-1/2"	1000	1700	3000
Reo Coupe, 1932, No. 1247, 9-3/8" long	1100	2500	4500
Sand Loading Shovel, 1932, No. 298 (later No. 299)	300	650	900
Scraper, 1929, No. 287, 8-1/4" long	100	200	300
Sedan and Trailer, 1937, No. 1497X, car 5-5/8" long, trailer 2-1/2" long	300	500	800
Sedan, 1937, No. 1501X, 4-3/4" long	100	200	300

Red Baby Dump Truck, Arcade, 1923, No. 2, $2,500

	C6	C8	C10
Side Dump Trailer, 1932, No. 290, fastens to trucks or tractors, 7" long	100	200	350
Stake Trailer Truck, 1931, No. 233, 11-5/16" long	200	450	600
Stake Truck, 1929, No. 208X, 6" long	220	330	440
Stake Truck, 1932, No. 208, no Arcade markings, 6" long	300	500	750
Stake Truck, 1937, No. 1502, 4-1/4" long	125	200	300
Stake Truck, 1929, No. 213, 5" long	125	200	325
Steam Shovel, 1932, No. 292 Industrial Derrick, body 6" long	500	750	1100
Tandem Disc Harrow, 1939, No. 704, 6-3/4" long	50	100	200
Tank, Army, 1937, No. 400, 8" long	400	700	950
Tank, Army, 1941, No. 3960, shoots, 4" long	100	200	300
Texas Centennial Bus, 1936, 10-3/4" long	1300	2200	3000
Tractor and Dump Trailer, 1941, No. 7300, 15-1/2" long	600	950	1300
Tractor, 1941, No. 4060, black rubber wheels, 6-1/4" long	180	300	450
Tractor, 1941, No. 7200, 6-1/2" long	180	270	360
Tractor, 1941, No. 7240, rubber wheels, 3-1/8" long	100	150	200
Tractor, 1941, No. 7341, wood wheels, 6-1/4" long	200	350	550
Trac-Tractor, 1937, No. 277, 8-1/4" long	600	950	1300
Trailer, Farm, 1929, No. 286, 6-3/8" long	150	200	325
Trailer, Farm, 1929, No. 288, 4-5/8" long	150	150	250
Trailer, Farm, 1929, No. 289, 3-3/4" long	75	150	250
Transport Trailer Truck, 1934, No. 1800, 7-1/2" long	385	580	770
Two-Wheeled Jack, 1932, No. 216, 5-1/2" long	75	125	200
W&K Truck Trailer, 1923, 8-1/2" long	200	300	450
White Bus, No. 319, 1928, 13-1/4" long	2800	5500	7400
White Delivery Truck, 1929, No. 252X, 8-1/4" long	2000	3000	6000
White Dump Truck, 1929, No. 249, 11-1/2" long, auctioned in 1994 in Excellent condition			23,000

Yellow Cab, Arcade, 1922, No. 1, $1,400

	C6	C8	C10
White Moving Van, 1929, No. 251, 13-1/2" long, auctioned in 1994 in Excellent condition			13,200
White Tank Truck, 1931, No. 254, "Gasoline," 14-1/8" long	850	1500	2000
Wrecker, 1929, No. 217, 1928, body 8" long	500	850	1400
Wrecker, 1932, No. 225, no Arcade markings	600	950	1500
Wrecker, 1934, No. 2020, 7" long	600	950	1500
Wrecker, 1937, No. 1493, 6-1/2" long	150	250	350
Wrecker, 1937, No. 1503, 4-3/4" long	100	150	200
Wrecker, 1941, No. 3900, 8-1/2" long	150	250	350
Yellow Baby Dump Truck, 1923, 10-1/2" long	900	1500	2500
Yellow Baby Wrecker, 1929, 12" long	650	1100	1600
Yellow Cab Bank, 1923, 8" long	700	1100	1500
Yellow Cab Bank, 1927, "Flat Top"	1200	2800	4000
Yellow Cab Panel Delivery Truck, 1925, 8-1/4" long, w/driver	900	1800	2500
Yellow Cab, 1922, No. 1, 9" long	600	900	1400
Yellow Cab, 1922, No. 2, 8" long	500	800	1200
Yellow Cab, 1925, No. 2, 8" long	600	900	1400
Yellow Cab, 1925, No. 3, 5-1/4" long	400	700	1100

White Bus, Arcade, 1928, No. 319, $7,400

'38 Olds, four-door sedan, Auburn Rubber, $60, Photo from Rubber Toy Vehicles *by Dave Leopard.*

Left to Right: '40 Olds, four-door sedan, fender skirts, Auburn Rubber, $50; '40 Olds, four-door sedan, open fenders, Auburn Rubber, $60, Photo from Rubber Toy Vehicles *by Dave Leopard.*

'39 Plymouth, two-door trunk back sedan, Auburn Rubber, $50, Photo from Rubber Toy Vehicles *by Dave Leopard.*

	C6	C8	C10
Yellow Cab, 1927, No. 5, 8-1/2" long	500	800	1000
Yellow Cab, 1934, Ford Sedan, 6-7/8" long	1200	2200	3500
Yellow Cab, 1936, No. 1580Y, 8-1/4" long	1400	2800	4000
Yellow Cab, 1941, No. 1590Y, 8-1/2" long	350	650	1000
Yellow Cab, No. 1350, 1935, 4-1/4" long	200	300	450
Yellow Coach Double-Decker Bus, 1925, 14" long	1500	2500	4000
Yellow Parlor Coach Bus, 1926, 13" long	800	1400	2200
Yellow Parlor Coach Bus, 1926, 9-1/2" long	325	550	750

AUBURN RUBBER

Contributor: Dave Leopard, 2507 Feather Run Trail, West Columbia, SC 29169-4915

	C6	C8	C10
'35 Ford Coupe, 4" long	27	41	55
'35 Ford, two-door slantback sedan, 4" long	27	41	55
'36 Cord, 4-door coffin-nose sedan, w/rounded bumper, minor variations, 6" long	25	35	50

'47 Chevy Cab Forward Box Truck, Auburn Rubber, $45. Photo from Rubber Toy Vehicles *by Dave Leopard.*

	C6	C8	C10
'36 Cord, four-door coffin-nose sedan, 6" long	65	98	130
'37 International Cabover Stake Truck, "US Army" decal, khaki, 5-3/8" long	30	40	55
'37 International Cabover Stake Truck, 3-3/4" long	20	30	40
'37 International Cabover Stake Truck, 4-1/4" long	20	30	40
'37 International Cabover Stake Truck, 5-3/8" long	25	35	50
'37 International Cabover Stake Truck, milk version, 4-1/4" long	60	80	100
'37 Olds, four-door sedan, 4-1/2" long	25	35	50
'38 GMC "Carry Car" Auto Transport, 11-1/2" long	45	65	100
'38 GMC Cab/Open Squared-off Trailer, 9" long	42	63	85
'38 Olds, four-door sedan, 5-3/4" long	30	45	60
'39 Plymouth, two-door trunk back sedan, 4-1/4" long	25	35	50
'40 Olds, four-door sedan, fender skirts, 6" long	30	40	50
'40 Olds, four-door sedan, open fenders, 6" long	35	45	60
'46 Lincoln convertible, two-door, round headlights, 4-1/2" long	20	30	40

'46 Lincoln convertible, two-door, round headlights, Auburn Rubber, $40. Photo from Rubber Toy Vehicles *by Dave Leopard.*

Cab-Forward Box Truck, smooth sides, futuristic, Auburn Rubber, $45. Photo from Rubber Toy Vehicles *by Dave Leopard.*

	C6	C8	C10
'46 Lincoln convertible, two-door, square headlights, 4-1/2" long	20	30	40
'47 Chevy Cab Forward Box Truck, 5-3/4" long	22	33	45
'48 Buick, two-door sedanette, fastback, 7-1/4" long	45	60	90
'50 Cadillac, four-door sedan, 7-1/4" long	40	60	80
'50 Pickup Truck, fender skirts, 4-1/2" long	20	30	40
'50 Pickup Truck, open fenders, 4-1/2" long	20	30	40
Ahrens-Fox Fire Engine, 5-1/2" long	75	112	150
Cab-Forward Box Truck, smooth sides, futuristic, 5-1/2" long	22	33	45
Cabover Box Truck, smooth sides, futuristic, 4-1/8" long	20	30	40
Cultipacker (Disc Harrows?), David Bradley, 4-3/8" long	22	33	45
Disc Harrows, 4-1/2" long	22	33	45
Farm Tractor, Graham-Bradley, 4-1/2" long	25	38	50
Farm Tractor, John Deere "A," 5" long	22	33	45
Farm Tractor, McCormick-Deering IH Farmall "M," 4" long	22	33	45

Farm Tractor, John Deere "A," Auburn Rubber, $45. Photo from Rubber Toy Vehicles *by Dave Leopard.*

	C6	C8	C10
Farm Tractor, Minneapolis-Moline "R," early style, 7-1/2" long	40	60	80
Farm Tractor, Minneapolis-Moline "R," later style, 7-1/4" long	40	60	80
Farm Tractor, Minneapolis-Moline "Z," 4" long	22	33	45
Farm Tractor, Oliver Row Crop "70," 8" long	45	65	85
Fire Engine, c. 1940s, hose and ladders, 7-3/4" long	27	41	55
Fire Engine, c. 1940s, ladders, no hose, 7-3/4" long	27	41	55
Harrow, 4-1/2" long	20	30	40
Harvester, open top, 5-1/2" long	35	50	75
International Cabover Stake Truck, khaki, w/rounded bumper, minor variations, 4-1/4" long	20	30	40
International Cabover Stake Truck, khaki, 4-1/4" long	20	30	40
Late '40s Futuristic Sedan, fin down back, 5" long	20	30	40
Manure Spreader, David Bradley, 4-3/4" long	20	30	40
Open Racer, boattail, 4-3/4" long	22	33	45

Late '40s Futuristic Sedan, fin down back, Auburn Rubber, $40. Photo from Rubber Toy Vehicles *by Dave Leopard.*

Open Racer, short, tapered tail, large tires, Auburn Rubber, $75. Photo from Rubber Toy Vehicles *by Dave Leopard.*

Open Racer, short, boattail, Auburn Rubber, $55. Photo from Rubber Toy Vehicles *by Dave Leopard.*

	C6	C8	C10
Open Racer, boattail, no side pipes, 4-3/4" long	22	33	45
Open Racer, no fenders, low fin, long back, 5-1/4" long	20	30	40
Open Racer, short, boattail 6-1/2" long	27	41	55
Open Racer, short, tapered tail, large tires, 10-1/2" long	37	56	75
Open Racer, small fin, 6-1/4" long	22	33	45
Open Racer, V-6, high fin, 10-1/2" long	55	82	110
Open Racer, V-6, low fin, 10-1/2" long	40	60	80
Pumper, c. 1940s, Boiler, 7-3/4" long	27	41	55
Reliable Front-Lift Seeder, 5" long	22	33	45
Side-Cutter Sickle Bar Mower, David Bradley, 3-3/4" long	20	30	40

Left to Right: Tank, Marmon-Harrington, Auburn Rubber, $45; Tank, Marmon-Harrington, Auburn Rubber, $30. Photo from Rubber Toy Vehicles *by Dave Leopard.*

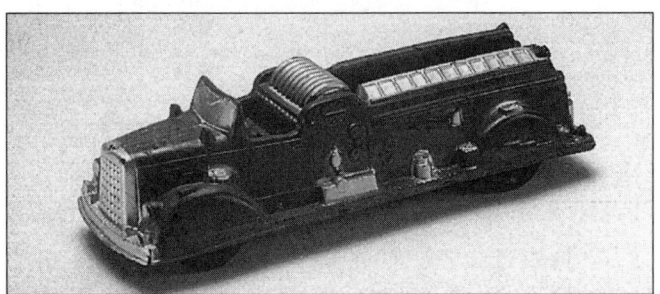

Pumper, c. 1940s, Boiler, Auburn Rubber, $55. Photo from Rubber Toy Vehicles *by Dave Leopard.*

	C6	C8	C10
Tank, Marmon-Harrington, 3-1/4" long	15	22	30
Tank, Marmon-Harrington, 4-1/2" long	22	33	45
Trailer, two wheel, Graham-Bradley, 5-3/4" long	22	33	45
Trailer, four wheel, Graham-Bradley, 4-3/4" long	22	33	45
Two Furrow Plow, David Bradley, 4-3/8" long	20	30	40
Updated Carry Car Transport, cab changed, trailer same, 11-3/4" long	45	65	100

BANNER

Banner was begun by Emanuel M. Pressner (1899-1974) and Bernard Schiller around 1945 at 150 Bruckner Blvd. in Bronx, New York. Pressner had been a toy importer before the war, and when the war cut off imports, he went to work for Columbia Protektosite, which, among other things, cast Beton's plastic toy soldiers. Schiller was eventually edged out.

Banner's original toys were small plastic cars and trucks, and the leading items for years were tea sets and metallic plastic forks, knives and spoons. Other items included plastic sand molds. The stamped steel Banner used was made up of "off-falls"—the blanks formed when holes were cut in steel to allow for car windows and television tubes.

The company, which at its peak periods had as many as 200 employees, went into Chapter 11 bankruptcy in 1965, came out of it, and was sold in 1967 to Tal-Cap, a toy conglomerate in Minnesota.

	C6	C8	C10
American Express Truck, tin, 10" long	100	200	350
American Express Truck, tin, 11" long	90	135	180
American Express Van	50	75	100
Carnation Milk Van	163	245	325
Dodge, 1950, plastic, 4" long	5	8	10
Dump Truck, plastic, 5-1/4" long	10	15	20

American Express Truck, tin, Banner, 11" long, $180

	C6	C8	C10
Garbage Truck, Ford, plastic, 1954, 4" long	15	22	30
Grocery Service Truck, 10" long	100	200	300
International Harvester Metro 1950 van, plastic, 4" long	12	18	25
Jewel Tea Van	155	232	310
LaFrance Fire Truck, plastic, 1950, 4" long	12	18	25
North American Van Lines Truck and Trailer, 15" long	110	165	220
Side Dump Truck, plastic, 1950s, 5-1/4" long	10	20	30
Service Station, cardboard, w/three plastic trucks, c. late 1940s-early 1950s	25	38	50
Stake Truck, GMC, plastic, 4" long	12	18	25
Station Wagon, 1948, Oldsmobile, plastic, 4" long	12	18	25
Tanker, plastic, 7" long	17	26	35
Toy Truck Van, 9" long	59	78	118
Tractor, Wheelhorse, plastic, 3" long	14	21	28
Wonder Bread Truck, c. 1950s, tin litho, 11" long	110	165	220

BARCLAY VEHICLES

Barclay vehicles can be roughly dated by their tires. The earliest are metal, and rubber tires on wooden hubs were introduced about 1934. Around 1936, nail axles began to replace the wooden hubs and it was after World War I that black tires appeared.

	C6	C8	C10
Ambulance, No. 194, large cross, 3-1/2" long	20	30	40
Ambulance, No. 194, small cross, 3-1/2" long	26	39	52
Ambulance, No. 50, 5" long	55	82	110

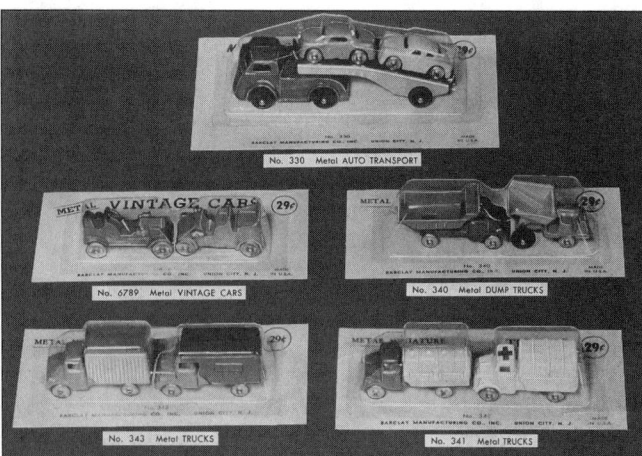

These Barclay blister packs are circa 1968. No. 330, the metal Auto Transport, is worth $70 in C10 condition. The other four sets are valued at $40.

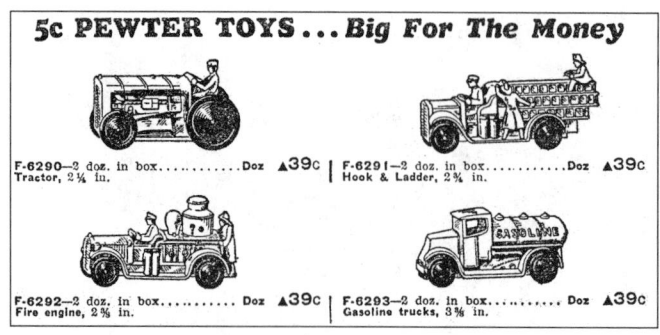

This ad from a Butler Bros. catalog is the earliest known appearance of Barclay vehicles.

	C6	C8	C10
Anti-Aircraft Gun Truck, No. 48, one man, 4" long	22	33	45
Anti-Aircraft Gun Truck, No. 48, two men, 4" long	16	24	32
Anti-Aircraft Gun Truck, No. 198, shown in 1931 Barclay catalog, 3-1/8" long	20	30	40
Armored Army Truck, No. 152, 2-7/8" long	8	13	17
Army Oil Truck, c. 1968, approx. 2" long	9	13	18
Army Tank Truck, No. 197, c. 1935-36, 3-1/8" long	11	16	22
Army Tractor (Minneapolis-Moline "Jeep"), 2-3/4" long	14	21	28
Army Truck w/Anti-Aircraft Gun, No. 151, 2-1/2" long	10	15	21
Army Truck w/Gun, No. 151, 2-3/4" long	13	19	27
Army Truck, open bed, c. 1968, approx. 2" long	7	11	15
Auburn Speeder, No. 58, c. 1931	17	26	35
Austin Coupe, c. 1931, No. 43, 2" long	30	45	60
Auto Transport Set, No. 330, two 1950s cars, 4-1/2" long	36	55	73
Beer Truck, c. 1940, No. 376, wood barrels, 4" long	27	41	55

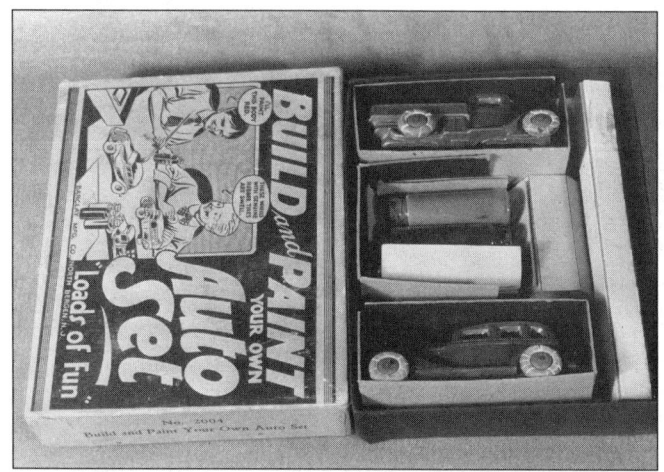

Build and Paint Set, $360

Convertible with vac-tioners, $100

	C6	C8	C10
Beer Truck, No. 377, w/barrels	35	52	70
Buick Sedan, 1929, 3" long	27	41	55
Build and Paint Set, truck, coupe, sedan, parts, paints, early	180	270	360
Bus, die cast, Coast to Coast, "Barclay Toy," two-piece, No. 405, 2-7/8" long	42	63	85
Bus, futuristic, "Made in U.S.A.," 3" long	34	51	68
Cannon Car, battery-powered headlight, in 1935 catalog, 3-1/2" long	80	130	225
Cannon Car, gunner low 3-5/16" long	13	21	27
Cannon Car, slight casting differences from headlight version, 3-1/4" long	19	28	38
Cannon Truck, moveable cannon, 4" long	37	56	75
Cannon Truck, w/moveable cannon, 4" long	20	30	40
Car Carrier, two small cars, early 1930s	25	38	50
Chief Police Car approx. 2" long	5	8	10
Chrysler Airflow Sedan, No. 1703, 1935, large	17	26	35
Chrysler Airflow, c. 1936, 4" long	30	45	60
Convertible w/vacationers	50	75	100
Cord Front Drive Coupe, c. 1931, No. 40 3-5/8" long	25	38	50
Coupe, 1930s, "Made in U.S.A.," 3" long	12	18	25
Coupe, 1934, 4-1/4" long	40	60	80
Coupe, c. 1935, 2-1/2" long	50	75	100
Coupe, cast rear tire, c. 1935, 200 series?, 3-1/8" long	21	31	42
Coupe, No. 51, c. 1931, 2-3/16" long	17	26	35

	C6	C8	C10
Coupe, removable spare tire, 1935, 4-1/2" long	30	45	60
Coupe, Streamline, No. 301, 3-1/4" long	50	75	100
Coupe, Streamline, No. 361	17	26	35
Coupe, two-piece, 1930s, "Barclay Toy," 2-7/8" long	42	63	85
Delivery Truck, No. 206, "Bakery Fine Cake Pies," c. 1934, 3-1/8" long	70	105	140
Delivery Truck, No. 309, 2-15/16" long	15	23	30
Delivery Truck, No. 309, c. 1936, 3-1/2" long	12	18	25
DeSoto Airflow, 1935, 5-3/16" long	17	26	35
Double Decker Bus, 4" long	60	90	120
Double Decker Bus, No. 56, c. 1931, 3-1/4" long	22	33	45
Double Transport Set No. 440, four cars on upper and lower racks, 1960s, hinged for unloading, 4-1/2" long	72	109	145
Dump Truck, c. 1960s, approx. 2" long	7	11	15
Dump Truck, spring action, ratchet, 1935, 4" long	20	30	40
Express stake truck, 1930s, 2-15/16" long	30	45	60
Field Kitchen, 2-1/4" long	35	52	70
Fire Engine No. 390?, moveable ladder, c. 1950s	15	22	30
Fire Engine, French-looking, 4" long	17	26	35
Fire Engine, two firemen, black metal wheels, 1930s, No. 41, 2-3/4" long	17	26	35

Left to Right: Coupe, removable spare tire, 1935, $60; Dump Truck, spring action, ratchet, 1935, $40

Left to Right: No. 302 Streamline Car, c. 1936, $50; Delivery Truck, No. 309, $30; Fire Engine, French-looking, $35

Coupe, 1934, 4-1/4" long, $80

Left to Right: No. 40 Cord Front Drive Coupe, c. 1931, 50; Parcel Delivery, slush lead, No. 45, $130; Golden Arrow Racer, $40

	C6	C8	C10
Fire Truck, No. 209 Fire Engine, c. 1934, 3-1/8" long 25		38	50
Fire Truck, No. 210, c. 1934, 3-1/8" long..... 25		38	50
Fire Truck, No. 368 Fire Truck, 1930s, "Fire Dept. No. 99," 5-3/4" long 20		30	40
Fire Truck, No. 50, c. 1931, 2-3/8" long....... 22		33	45
Ford, 1931, 2-1/4" long 15		22	30
Gas Truck, c. 1935, 200 series, four tank top, 3" long 25		38	50
Gasoline Truck, small, c. 1931, three tank top, 2-5/16" long 30		45	60
Golden Arrow Racer, 4-1/2" long 20		30	40
Hook and Ladder, No. 208, 1935, 3" long ... 16		24	32
Hospital Truck, c. 1968, 2" long................. 9		13	18
Imperial Chrysler Coupe, No. 39, c. 1931... 15		22	30
Large Streamline Coupe, 1930s 15		22	30
Large Streamline Racer, No. 363, in 1935 catalog, 6-7/8" long 45		68	90
Log Truck, c. 1960s, approx. 2" long 7		11	15
Mack Pickup Truck, 3-1/2" long............. 15		22	30
Milk & Cream Truck, stamped No. 377, white rubber tires, 3-5/8" long 81		122	163
Milk Truck in shape of bottle, No. 567...... 162		243	325
Milk Truck, No. 377, black rubber tires, 3-5/8" long 22		33	45
Milk Van Truck, bottle on side, 2-7/8" long 20		30	41
Motorcycle w/flat rider, full-dimensional sidecar, No. 55, 2-3/4" long 47		70	95
Moving Truck, c. 1960s, approx. 2" long....... 8		12	16
Officer's Car, w/megaphone on top, 2-1/2" long 22		33	44
Oil Truck, c. 1960s, approx. 2" long 9		13	18
Oil-Fuel Truck, No. 308, c. 1936, 3-9/16" long............ 12		18	25
Open Coupe w/driver in cab, early 1930s.... 15		22	30
Parcel Delivery, slush lead, No. 45, c. 1931, 3-5/8" long 65		98	130
Pepsi-Cola Truck, 1960s, 2" long 9		13	18
Police Car, 2" long 5		8	10
Police Car, No. 317, die cast, 3-5/8" long 15		22	30
Race Car, 3" long 12		18	24
Race Car, open, driver, 4" long 70		105	140
Racer w/tail fin, "Made U.S.A.," 3-1/2" long 17		26	35
Racer, closed cockpit, 5-1/2" long............... 17		26	35
Racer, closed cockpit, c. 1939, 7" long......... 30		45	60
Racer, No. 306, 1936.......................... 15		22	30
Racer, No. 5, 1931............................ 15		22	30
Racer, No. 53, early slush lead, 1920s-30s, approx. 2" long 24		36	48
Racer, Streamline, No. 303 Streamline, 4-3/8" long............ 15		22	30

	C6	C8	C10
Racer, two passengers, 4-1/4" long 55		82	110
Racing Car, c. 1968, approx. 2" long 5		8	10
Racing Car, c. 1968, no fenders, approx. 2" long 5		8	10
Racing Car, large, raised exhaust pipe, driver, 1935 catalog.................. 17		26	35
Racing car, No. 371, large, 1930s, 4-1/4" long......................... 16		24	32
Renault Tank, c. 1937, No. 47, 4" long 22		33	45
Searchlight Truck, second version 87		130	175
Searchlight Truck, white rubber tires, c. 1940, 4-1/16" long...................... 87		130	175
Sedan and "Tourist Trailer," "Made in U.S.A.," 1930s, 6-1/2" long 35		52	70
Sedan, c. 1934 37		56	75
Sedan, four-door, c. 1936, may be a Chrysler, 5" long 17		26	35
Sedan, No. 311, c. 1936 21		32	43
Sedan, streamline, No. 362, 1935, large 41		61	82
Sedan, two-door, 1960s, 1-5/8" long 2		3	5
Sedan, two-door, c. 1935, rubber wheels, 3-1/8" long 37		56	75
Sedan, two-piece, No. 401, 2-door, 1930s, "Barclay Toy," die cast, 2-7/8" long 42		63	85
Side Dump, 1-1/2" long 7		11	15
Silver Arrow Race Car, 5-1/2" long............. 22		33	45
Sport Coupe, removable spare tire, 1935, 2-7/8" long 32		48	65
Stake Truck, 1935, 4-3/8" long.................. 36		54	72
Stake truck, No. 207, 1935 catalog, 3-1/8" long 39		58	78
Station Wagon, No. 404, die-cast, 1930s, two-piece, "Barclay Toy," 2-15/16" long 37		56	75
Steam-Roller, traction type, slush lead w/tin roof, No. 44, c. 1931, 3-1/4" long..... 30		45	60
Streamline Car, c. 1936, No. 302, 3-1/8" long............ 25		38	50
Tank (based on U.S. M2 light tank), 2-1/4" long............ 20		31	41
Tank "4562," one man in turret, 3-7/8" long............ 17		26	35
Tank "4562," two men in turret, 3-7/8" long............ 21		31	42
Tank T41, 4-1/2" long 15		22	30
Tank, man in turret, die cast, black rubber tires, 2-5/8" long.................. 14		21	28
Taxi, c. 1940s, slush, 3-1/4" long................. 14		21	28
Taxi, No. 318, die cast, 3-1/4" long.............. 50		75	100
Tow Car, No. 205, 1935 catalog, 3-1/16" long............ 20		30	40
Tow Truck, "Towing Service," large............ 82		124	175

Left to Right: '35 Ford Coupe, Barr, $55; '35 Ford two-door slantback sedan, Barr, $55. Photo from Rubber Toy Vehicles *by Dave Leopard.*

Left to Right: '35 Ford Stake Body Truck, Barr, $4155; '35 Ford Army Truck, Barr, $65. Photo from Rubber Toy Vehicles *by Dave Leopard.*

	C6	C8	C10
Tow Truck, No. 312, "Towing" 1936 catalog, 3-3/8" long	17	26	35
Tractor, No. 203, peg hitch, 2-1/8" long	11	16	22
Tractor, caterpillar type, slush lead, 2-5/8" long	17	26	35
Tractor, No. 42, 1931, 2-3/16" long	12	18	25
Tractor, No. 7, c. late 1920s-early 1930s	15	22	30
Trailer Truck variously "Railway Express," or w/Moving Company name, c. 1950s	5	8	10
Transport Set No. 330, 2 cars, 1960s, 4-1/2" long	25	40	75
Transport Set, two car, 4-3/4" long	42	63	85
Truck, "Esso Gas," 1930s, 5" long	20	30	40
U.S. Army Truck, c. 1968, 2" long	7	11	15

'35 Ford Panel Truck/Ambulance, Barr, $55. Photo from Rubber Toy Vehicles *by Dave Leopard.*

Left to Right: Police car, Beaut $20; Taxi, Mfg. Co., $20.

	C6	C8	C10
U.S. Army Truck, No. 204, no hitch, red wood hubs, 2-1/2" long	19	28	38
U.S. Army Truck, white rubber wheels, wire or peg hitch, 2-1/2" long	12	18	25
U.S. Mail Truck, 1960s, 2" long	10	17	24
U.S. Motor Unit Truck, c. 1940, white rubber tires, three versions—no hitch, wire hitch, peg hitch, 3-1/4" long	17	26	35
Van, "White Horse" Van (some have sticker reading "Welcome I.C.M.A. compliments the White Motor Co."), approx. 3" long	55	82	110
Vintage Car, approx. 2" long	15	22	30
Volkswagen, 1960s, approx. 2" long	12	18	24
Wheel-A-Rific speedway track, two lead racers, black rubber wheels, 10' of plastic track, c. 1970	17	26	35
Wrecker, two piece, No. 403, die cast, 1930s, "Barclay Toy," 2-7/8" long	42	63	85
Wrecker, c. 1934, 3-15/16" long	30	45	60
Wrecker, No. 46, c. 1931, 3-1/2" long	22	33	45

BARR RUBBER

Contributor: Dave Leopard, 2507 Feather Run Trail, West Columbia, SC 29169-4915

	C6	C8	C10
'35 Ford Army Truck, 4-3/4" long	32	48	65
'35 Ford Coupe, 4" long	27	41	55
'35 Ford Panel Truck/Ambulance, 4-1/4"long	27	41	55
'35 Ford Stake Body Truck, 4-3/4" long	27	41	55
'35 Ford two-door slantback sedan, 4" long	27	41	55

BEAUT MFG. CO.

Beaut Mfg. Co., North Bergen, New Jersey, was founded in 1946 by Eugene Buhler and Irving Reader (former machinist and salesman, respectively) for Barclay Mfg. Co. The company put out five toys—a taxi cab, a police car, a fire engine, a sedan and a child's wagon. The company was successful at first, selling to Woolworth's and many overseas buyers. Beaut eased toymaking activities around 1950 because of competition from plastic toys, although they continued until 1982 as a general machine shop.

	C6	C8	C10
Fire car, No. 4, approx. 3-3/4" long	10	15	20
Police car, approx. 3-3/4" long	10	15	20
Sedan, approx. 3-3/4" long	10	15	20
Taxi, approx. 3-3/4" long	10	15	20

BEST TOY & NOVELTY FACTORY

Best Toy, founded by John M. Best in Manhattan Kansas in the 1930s, started as a family hobby for Best's children, relatives, friends and neighbors. From a hobby it grew into a respectable business, supplying toy distributors and dime stores. After several years of operation it was sold in 1939 to Ralstoy, a Ralston, Nebraska, company. Best toys are still found in today's toy markets.

At this point we are not certain when Best started or what number in the series was his first molding. In 1933, Best took over production from the toy line of Kansas Toy & Novelty of Clifton, Kansas. It's not known whether he introduced any new patterns, although with his experience it is likely that he did. Regardless, it was an important chapter in the story of those wandering molds. Best Toy and Novelty, along with the Kansas Toy molds, were acquired by Ralstoy of Ralston, Nebraska in 1939.

Best Toy reproductions can usually be distinguished by the rubber wheels and the marking "Made in USA." However, some of their toys used the metal wheels of the Kansas Toy originals or the later wood hubs with rubber tires. It is also possible that Best modified or rebuilt his molds to create variations.

The following abbreviations are for the details and variations useful in identification.	
HG	horizontal grille pattern
HL	horizontal hood louvers
HO	hood cap, Motometer or ornament
L	lacquer finish
LI	landau irons on convertibles
MDW	metal disc wheels
MDSW	metal disc solid spokes
MDWBT	wheels with black painted tires
MSW	metal open spoke wheels
MWW	metal simulated wire wheels
OW	open windows
RM	rearmount spare tire/wheel
SM	sidemounted spare
SP	string-pull knob in handcrank area
T	external trunk
UV	unnumbered version
VG	vertical grille pattern
VL	vertical hood louvers
WS, W/S	windshield
WV	windshield visor
WHRT	wooden hubs, rubber tires
WRDW	white hard rubber disc wheels
WRW	white soft rubber wheels (balloon tires)

For more information, see Kansas Toy.

Contributor: Fred Maxwell, 4722 N. 33 St., Arlington, VA 22207. Maxwell, a collector and occasional author, has been collecting antique aircraft and vehicle toys for over twenty-five years. He founded the Auto Collectors Club twenty-five years ago to promote interest in the central Atlantic states region.

	C6	C8	C10
Coupe, "93," Cadillac ?, Streamlined, hood similar to #91, grid pattern grille, two open windows, hard rubber wheels, 3-5/8" long	16	24	32
Larger Racer, "97," Bluebird record car, driver, large fin, twelve exhaust ports, hard rubber wheels, faired, 4-1/2" long	10	15	20
Oil Transport, "102," Streamlined "Gasoline" semi-trailer to #101, four tanks,four storage compartments, total length of cab-trailer 6-3/4", 4" long	47	70	95
Racer, "85," Record car w/large square fin, driver, HO, VG, 12 exhaust ports, WHRT, 4" long	10	15	20

Racer, "85," Record car, Best Toy & Novelty Factory, $20

BUDDY "L"

Buddy "L" toys, named after owner Fred Lundahl's son, Buddy, were first maufactured by the Moline Pressed Steel Company of Moiline, Illinois in 1921. Lundahl started the company eight years earlier in order to maufacture car and truck parts. The toys, originally made as special items for his son, caught the attention of other children and their fathers.

Buddy "L" toys are large, averaging twenty-one to twenty-six inches in length. The original toys were made of heavy steel and could support a grown man's weight, but lighter material was adopted in the 1930s. Wooden toys were produced during World War II when steel was in short supply.

Lundahl relinquished control of the company to J.W. Bettendorf in 1930 and died later that year. The named of the company has changed many times over the years, yet continues to make toys at the present time.

Because the early Buddy "L" toys were almost indestructible, fifty percent of the items found are either rusty or have been repainted which lowers the value considerably.

Contributor: Conrad Schwager, 10321 N. Trails Edge Rd., Peoria, IL 61615.

Baggage Truck, No. 203B, 1927-32, Buddy "L," $4,000

Coach, light green motorbus with gold stripes, No. 208, 1928-31, Buddy "L," $5,450

A 1954 advertisement for the Buddy "L" Hi-Lift Farm Supplies Dump Truck.

Large Trucks	C6	C8	C10
Auto Wrecker, No. 209, 1928-31	1800	2900	5000
Baggage Truck, No. 203B, 1927-32	1500	2500	4000
Coach, light green motorbus w/gold stripes, No. 208, 1928-31	2000	4000	5450
Coal Truck, No. 202, 1926-32	2500	4000	6200
Dump Truck (Ratchet), No. 201, 1923-29, 25"	600	900	1500
Express Truck, No. 200, 1921-31	800	1200	2000

Dump Truck (Ratchet), No. 201, 1923-29, 25", Buddy "L," $1,500

Ice Truck, No. 207, 1926-31, Buddy "L," $3,000

Stake Truck, No. 203, 1921-24, 1926-28, Buddy "L," $2,200

Oil Truck, No. 206A, 1925-30, Buddy "L," $2,175

	C6	C8	C10
Hydraulic Dump Truck, No. 201A			
1926-31 600	900	1500
Ice Truck, No. 207, 1926-31 1200	1800	3000
Lumber Truck, No. 203A, 1925-30 1500	2500	3500
Moving Van, No. 204, 1924-30 900	1500	2500
Oil Truck, No. 206A, 1925-30 900	1450	2175
Railway Express, No. 204A, 1926-31, 25" 1150	2500	3500
Sand & Gravel Truck, No. 202A			
1926-32 1800	4500	6500
Stake Truck, No. 203, 1921-24, 1926-28 800	1350	2200
Street Sprinkler Truck, No. 206, 206B,			
1924-31 1200	1800	3200

Fire Trucks

	C6	C8	C10
Aerial Ladder, w/three ladders,			
No. 205B, 1926-30 800	1350	2000
Hook & ladder, No. 205, 1923-32 800	1800	2800
Insurance Patrol, No. 205C, 1925-30 800	1300	2000
Pumper (Working), No. 205AB, 1930-31 950	2000	3000
Pumper, No. 205A, 1925-30 900	1800	2500
Water Tower Truck, No. 205D,			
(Working), 1929-32 2500	4200	7000

Hook & ladder, No. 205, 1923-32, Buddy "L," $2,800

Concrete Mixer, No. 280, 1926-30, Buddy "L," $1,000

Hook & ladder, No. 205, 1923-32, Buddy "L," $2,800

Model T Series

	C6	C8	C10
Flivver Coupe, No. 210B, 1924-30 900	1200	1600
Flivver Roadster, No. 210A, 1924-26 1000	1600	2200
Flivver Truck, No. 210, 1924-30 1100	1800	2600
Ford Dump Cart, No. 211, 1926-30 700	1400	2000
Ford Dump Truck, No. 211A, 1926-30 900	1600	2200
Ford Express Truck, No. 212, 1927-30 1400	2300	3225
One-Ton Ford Delivery Truck,			
No. 212A, 1927-30 2000	3500	5000

Construction Equipment

	C6	C8	C10
Aerial Tramway, No. 360, 1929-30 1500	2400	3300
Concrete Mixer, No. 280, 1926-30 400	650	1000
Dredge (Clamshell), No. 270, 1926-30 500	1000	1500
Heavy Shovel (on Treads), No. 220AB,			
1929-30 2000	4000	7000
Heavy Steam Shovel, No. 220A, 1929-30 ... 300	500	800
Hoisting Tower, No. 350, 1929-31 400	700	1250
Large Derrick, No. 241, 1922-31 200	300	500
Mixer (on Treads), No. 280A, 1929-31 ... 1100	1700	2600

Army Transport, with towed cannon, six-spoke wheels, 1954-57, 27" long, Buddy "L," $450

Army Truck, wood, Buddy "L," $200

	C6	C8	C10
Overhead Crane, No. 250, 1924-27	450	850	1000
Pile Driver, No. 260, 1926-28	450	800	900
Road Roller, No. 290, 1929-31	950	1500	2500
Sand Loader, No. 230, 1925-31	165	250	330
Sand Screener, No. 300, 1929-30	500	750	1200
Small Derrick, No. 240, 1922-31	175	300	450
Steam Shovel, No. 220, 1921-31	265	400	530
Tractor Dredge (on Treads), No. 270A, 1929-30	2500	5000	7500
Traveling Crane, No. 250A, 1928-30	800	1600	2300
Trencher, No. 400, 1928-31	950	1400	2100

Buddy "L" post-1932

	C6	C8	C10
Allied Van Lines Moving Van, No. 366, 31" long	338	600	950
Allied Van Lines, No. 910	600	1000	1500

	C6	C8	C10
Army Signal Corps Truck, 1941-42, 12" long	140	210	280
Army Tank, wood, 1943, 13" long	85	130	175
Army Transport, w/towed cannon, six-spoke wheels, 1954-57, 27" long	180	300	450
Army Truck 21, c. 1940, cloth top	150	200	300
Army Truck, No. 506, 20-1/2" long	150	200	300
Army Truck, wood	100	150	200
Automatic Tail-Gate Loader w/steering handle	150	250	350
Baggage Truck, No. 11, 1933, 26-1/2" long	300	450	650
Baggage Truck, No. 401, 1945-48, 17-1/2"	250	350	475
Big Show Circus Truck, wood, 1947, No. 484, 25-1/2" long	605	908	1210
City Baggage Dray, No. 439, 1934-37, 19" long	250	450	700
City Baggage Dray, No. 839, 1938, 20-3/4" long	200	350	550
Coca-Cola Truck, No. 5536, 1955-56 15" long	300	450	650
Coca-Cola Truck, No. 5426, 1960-61	150	250	400
Coca-Cola Truck, No. 5646, 1957-59	200	300	450
Concrete Mixer w/Truck, No. 54, 1937, 34-1/2" long	400	550	750
Concrete Mixer, No. 832, 1950-51, w/motor sound, 10-3/4" long	200	350	550
Country Squire Station Wagon, No. 53051, 1963-64, 15" long	150	250	375

Steam Shovel, No 220, 1921-31, Buddy "L," $530

Automatic Tail-Gate Loader with steering handle, Buddy "L," $350

Mister Buddy Ice Cream Van, 1964-65, Buddy "L," $275

Wrigley's Spearmint Railway Express Truck, No. 435, 1935, 23-1/8" long, Buddy "L," $2,200

	C6	C8	C10
Curtiss Candy Truck	175	350	465
Dairy Truck, No. 2002 (Junior Line) 1930-32, 24" long	1100	1800	2700
Dandy Digger, No. 33 and No. 2025, 1931-37	100	175	250
Delivery Truck, Deluxe Rider, No. 803, 1945-48, 22-3/4" long	260	450	650
Double Hydraulic Self-Loader-N-Dump Truck, No. 5892, 1956-57, 29" long	200	350	450
Dump Truck, No. 434, 1936, 20" long	350	500	700
Dump Truck, No. 634, 1948, 22-1/2" long	250	350	475
Emergency Auto Wrecker, No. 3317	175	275	375
Engine, No. 29, 1933-34, 25-1/2" long	350	500	650
Excavator Truck and Shovel Set No. 948, 1940, 27-1/2" long	288	532	575
Express Trailer Truck, No. 35, 1933-34	475	950	1400
Fast Delivery Truck, No. 3313	150	250	350
Fire Chief's Car w/Siren, No. 483, wood, 1949, 19-1/2" long	150	350	550
Fire Ladder Truck, semi, rounded trailer fenders, 1960	200	300	450
Greyhound Bus w/Bell, No. 481, wooden, 1948-49, 18-1/2" long	350	675	900

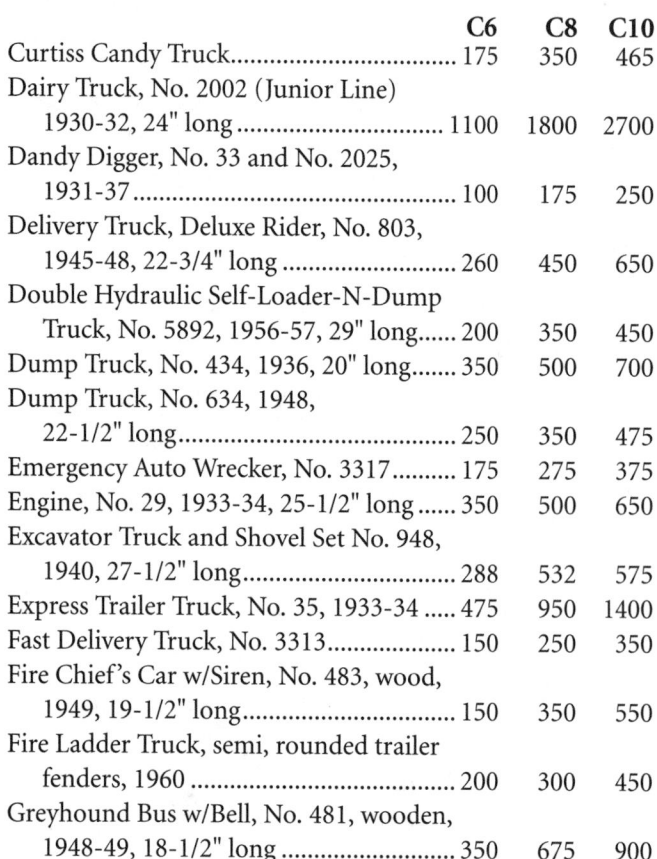

Riding Academy, No. 5455 Truck, with three horses, Buddy "L," $300

	C6	C8	C10
Greyhound Bus, winds up, 1938-40, 16" long	250	375	550
Hi-Lift Scoop-A-Dump	75	112	150
Hook and Ladder Truck, wooden, No. 859, 21-1/2" long	200	300	450
Hose Truck, No. 38, 1933, 21-3/4" long	250	400	650
Hydraulic Aerial Truck, No. 27, 1933-34, 40" long w/ladders down	550	850	1400
Hydraulic Dump Truck, No. 10, 1933-34, 24-3/4" long	600	950	1400
Ice Truck, No. 12, 1933-34, 26-1/2" long	700	1100	1600
International Delivery Truck, No. 51, 1935, 24-1/2" long	400	600	900
Merry-Go-Round Truck, No. 5429	100	150	250
Mister Buddy Ice Cream Van, 1964-65	100	175	275
Railway Express Truck, No. 480, wooden, 1947, 16-1/4" long	300	450	600
Railway Express Truck, No. 435, 1935, 23" long	1000	1600	2500
Railway Express Truck, No. 763, 1952, 25" long	600	1000	2000
Ride-N-Dump Truck	200	300	450
Riding Academy, No. 5455 Truck, w/three horses	125	200	300
Robotoy Dump Truck w/driver, operates on remote control	500	750	1050
Sand & Gravel Truck, No. 312, 13-1/2"	150	300	500
Scarab, No. 211, no wind-up mechanism, 1941, 10-1/2" long	200	300	400
Scarab, No. 711, wind-up, 1936-40, 10-1/2"	250	400	550
Service Truck, No. 5409, 1960	120	180	300
Siren Pull-n-Ride, No. 3722, 1953	200	250	350
Shell Truck, 13-1/2" long	300	650	900
Steam Shovel and International Truck, No. 16, 1937, 29-1/2" long, 36" extended	150	250	375
Steam Shovel on Treads (Junior Line) No. 2005, 1930-32, 24" long	300	450	700

Texaco Tanker, promo sold at gas stations, No. 5603, 25" long, Buddy "L," $300

	C6	C8	C10
Steam Shovel, mechanical, No. 30, 1935, 17-1/2" long, 13-1/2" high	175	275	400
Tank Truck, "Shell," No. 438, 1935, 19-1/4" long	450	750	1200
Tank Truck, No. 938, 1941, 21-1/2" long	350	500	850
Texaco Tanker, promo sold at gas stations, No. 5603, 25" long	150	225	300
Traveling Zoo, No. 5420, 1965-66	100	175	250
Utility Delivery Truck, No. 946, 1941-42, 25" long	175	250	350
Victory Jeep and Cannon, wood, No. 353	50	100	175
Water Tower, No. 28, 1936	1200	2000	3500
Wrecker, "Repair-It," No. 3667, 1953, 24" long	150	225	300
Wrecker, "Emergency Towing Rider" No. 903, 1949, 33" long	750	1100	1700
Wrecker, No. 13, 1933-37, 31" long	850	1500	3000
Wrecker, No. 37, 1933, 24" long	350	500	700
Wrecker, No. 437, 1934-37, 24" long	375	527	750
Wrecker, No. 503, 1940, 1941-42, 19-1/4" long	150	225	300
Wrecker, No. 813, 1938, 32" long	800	1400	2000
Wrecker, No. W37, 1939, 25-1/4 long	150	225	300
Wrecker, two-tone horizontal, No. 937, 1941-42, 25" long	200	300	425
Wrecker, two-tone slant, No. 937, 1939, 25-1/4" long	300	400	550
Wrigley's Spearmint Railway Express Agency Truck, No. 953, 1940	600	1100	1850

	C6	C8	C10
Wrigley's Spearmint Railway Express Truck, No. 435, 1935, headlights light up, 23-1/8" long	700	1400	2200
Wrigley's Spearmint Railway Express Truck, No. 835, 1938, 25" long	500	1000	1700

C.A.W. NOVELTY COMPANY

Charles A. Wood, founder of C.A.W. Novelty Company, not only ran a substantial operation but made some of the finest replica toys in the slush mold industry. Founded about 1925, Wood's company was active until about 1940, when lead casting came to a halt due to World War II.

All of Wood's output showed artistry, ingenuity and meticulous craftsmanship. The toys are smooth and crisp, with detailed moldings and extra touches such as open windshields and multiple colors. Early products had metal disk wheels with painted black tires or metal-spoked wheels. Other details included, open V-shaped, divided windshields; drivers inside cabs; and tri-motored aircraft with the outboard engines mounted on the landing gear struts. Wood once told a reporter that it sometimes took three or four years to make a mold—just one example of how much pride Wood took in his work.

Charles Wood was born in 1891. He lived and worked in Topeka, Kansas and in nearby Clifton before moving to Clay Center. He was known for his civic boosterism and good works. After he helped establish the local airport, he built and operated his own aircraft maintenance hangar. A master machinist, he produced all of his toy molds, production tools, toy parts, and even plastic wheels.

The C & H Mfg. Co., formed in 1940 by Rod Hemphill, the last C.A.W. employee, and Howard Clevenger, made toys using original C.A.W. molds. These reproductions are heavier than C.A.W.'s and have black rubber wheels.

The seldom found C.A.W. trademark, consists of unique, lead blind hubs fitted over a wire axle. They are sometimes found with ordinary nail axles piercing the hubs.

Contributor: Fred Maxwell, 4722 N. 33 St., Arlington, VA 22207.

Streamline Coupe, No. 30, Airflow, V-pattern grille, C.A.W. Novelty Company, $32

A mold used by C.A.W. The very elaborate mold is water cooled with a spring-actuated closure.

The following abbreviations are for the details and variations useful in identification.

HG	horizontal grille pattern
HL	horizontal hood louvers
HO	hood cap, Motometer or ornament
L	lacquer finish
LI	landau irons on convertibles
MDW	metal disc wheels
MDSW	metal disc solid spokes
MDWBT	wheels with black painted tires
MSW	metal open spoke wheels
MWW	metal simulated wire wheels
OW	open windows
RM	rearmount spare tire/wheel
SM	sidemounted spare
SP	string-pull knob in handcrank area
T	external trunk
UV	unnumbered version
VG	vertical grille pattern
VL	vertical hood louvers
WS, W/S	windshield
WV	windshield visor
WHRT	wooden hubs, rubber tires
WRDW	white hard rubber disc wheels
WRW	white soft rubber wheels (balloon tires)

Wonder Special, No. 33, Airflow coupe, C.A.W. Novelty Company, $32

Fuel Tanker, Ford? Truck, cab with driver inside, 3-3/4" long, C.A.W. Novelty Company, $40

	C6	C8	C10
Fuel Tanker, Ford? Truck, cab w/driver inside, no W/S, HG, three tanks, hose compartment, MSW, 3-3/4" long	20	30	40
Sport Roadster, Open Packard, driver w/cap (gilt or silver), no W/S, HG, VL, no headlamps, rear-mount, MDW, 3-1/2" long	20	30	40
Sport Roadster, similar to above, Buick?, no w/s, plain grille, VL, RM, right SM, MDW, also spoked version (MSW) 3-1/2" long	22	33	44

	C6	C8	C10
Streamline Coupe, No. 30, Airflow, V-patterngrille, HO, four OW, small rear fin, small winged design on rear-wheel skirts,MDW also WRW, bottom pan goes over rear axle, not under, 3" long	16	24	32
Three-Piece Auto Set, No. 40 as follows—			
Midget Coupe Racer, HG, HL, divided open W/S, two OW, two colored body, MDW, headlamps and cowl ventilators, 2-1/16"	10	15	20

Austin Bantam, two-door sedanette, part of No. 40 three-piece Auto Set, C.A.W. Novelty Company, $20

Mack Dump Truck, c. 1930s, 7" long, C.A.W. Novelty Company, $365

	C6	C8	C10
Midget Racer, gilt driver, VL, HG, MDW(easily confused w/Barclay No. 53), 2-1/8"	10	15	20
Austin Bantam, two-door sedanette, five OW, HL, plain grille, RM, MDW (easily confused w/other makers' Bantams), 2"	10	15	20
Wonder Special, No. 33, Airflow coupe, three-wheeled companion to No. 30 above, VG, 4 OW, WRW, front wheel skirts, pan goes over front axle, 3-3/8" long	16	24	32

Motorcycle and rider, "Champion," 4-3/4" long, Champion, $300

CHAMPION

The Champion Hardware Co., though in business from 1883 to 1954, produced toys only from 1930 to 1936, as a Depression stopgap. As might be expected from a hardware firm, the toys were cast iron. During its toy years the Geneva, Ohio outfit was headed by C.I. Chamberlin.

	C6	C8	C10
Car, four-casting nickeled radiator car, approx. 4" long	175	262	350
Coupe, Reo type, 7-1/2" long	212	318	425
Gas and Motor Oil Truck, cast iron, c. 1930s, 8" long	380	570	760
Mack Dump Truck, c. 1930s, 7" long	183	275	365
Mack Stake Truck, 7-1/2" long	175	265	350
Mack Stake Truck, c. 1930, 4-1/2" long	90	135	180
Motorcycle and rider, "Champion," 4-3/4" long	150	225	300
Panel Delivery, 7-3/4" long	495	745	990
Policeman on Motorcycle, rubber tires, 7" long	235	355	470

Panel Delivery, 7-3/4" long, Champion, $990

Bus, "Royal Blue Line Coast to Coast Service," Champion, $1,280

Wrecker, "Champion," 7-1/2" long, Champion, $615

Hercules Mack Dump Truck, 20" long, Chein, $850

Hercules Mack Tanker Truck, c. 1928, 19" long, Chein, $1,200

Hercules Mack, Motor Express, 19-1/2" long, Chein, $1,060

	C6	C8	C10
Race Car, 2 riders, 5-1/2"	125	188	250
Race Car, c. 1930s, 9" long	250	375	500
Race Car, cast iron, detachable driver, 6" long	150	225	300
Sedan, 5-1/4" long	112	188	225
Wrecker, "Champion," cast iron, 7-1/2" long	308	463	615

CHEIN

	C6	C8	C10
Army Truck, cannon on back, tin, early, 8-1/2" long	135	202	270
Army Truck, open bed, tin, early, 8-1/2" long	135	202	270
Bus, "Royal Blue Line Coast to Coast Service"	640	960	1280
Hercules Mack Dump Truck, tin, 20" long	425	638	850
Hercules Mack Motor Express, tin litho, Mack, 19-1/2" long	530	795	1060
Hercules Mack Tanker Truck, c. 1928, 19" long	500	750	1200

Transitional Taxi, clockwork, 10-1/2" long, Converse, $1,050

	C6	C8	C10
Hercules Roadster	300	450	600
Hercules Wrecker Truck, 20" long	500	750	1200
Sedan, tin wind-up, six-window, c. 1920s, 8-1/2" long	250	475	675
Truck, "Junior Oil Tank," 1920s, 8-1/2" long	62	93	125
Touring Car, tin litho, 7" long	250	375	500

CONVERSE

	C6	C8	C10
Auto w/fringe on top, three-seat, 1905, painted, pressed steel, clockwork, rubber tires	600	900	1200
Fire Engine Ladder Truck, bell, wooden headlight, 1915, 10" long	1250	1875	2500
Parcel Post Van, 1920s, 15" long	1500	2500	3700
Pick-up Truck, very early, open cab	500	750	1000
Roadster, 1908, wind-up, open cab, 15-1/2" long	1100	1600	3000
Touring Auto, 1910, pressed steel, canvas roof	900	1400	2300
Transitional Taxi, clockwork, 10-1/2" long	525	770	1050

Hercules Roadster, red (right) or yellow (left), Chein, $600

COR-COR

Formed in 1926 in Washington, Indiana by Louis A. Corcoran. At its peak it employed 590 people. Corcoran retired in 1941 and died in 1945.

	C6	C8	C10
Airflow windup, electric lights, 16" long	1000	1700	2265
Bus, 23" long	425	638	850
Dump Truck, dumps back or side to side, 23" long	225	338	450
Graham Paige Sedan, electric, 20" long	900	1450	1950
Van, painted metal, c. 1928, 23" long	363	445	725

COURTLAND (WALT REACH)

Non-Powered Vehicles

	C6	C8	C10
Courtland Side Dump Tractor-Trailer, No. 1200, 13" long, 3" wide, 3-1/4" high	175	250	375
Courtland Tractor-Trailer, same tractor as No. 2000 except marked, "Loft-Fresh Candies"	350	550	850

Courtland Side Dump Tractor-Trailer, No. 1200, Courtland, $375

Easter Greetings Rabbit Truck, No. 800, Courtland, $750

A Courtland advertisement for the No. 900 Truck assortment from the July 1946 issue of Playthings magazine.

Left to Right: Fire Patrol No. 2 Truck, 1946, No. 900, Courtland, $275; Moving and Storage Truck, 1946, No. 900, Courtland, $350

	C6	C8	C10
Easter Greetings Rabbit Truck, No. 800, 9" long	325	525	750
Express and Hauling Truck, 1946, No. 900, 9" long, 3" wide, 2-3/4" high	100	175	275
Fire Patrol No. 2 Truck, 1946, No. 900, L 9", W 3", H 2-3/4"	100	175	275
Ice Cream Truck, 1946, No. 900, 9" long, 3" wide, 2-3/4" high	125	200	300
Log Truck Tractor-Trailer, 1946, No. 620, 13" long, 3" wide, 3-1/4" high	150	225	350
Moving and Storage Truck, 1946, No. 900, 9" long, 3" wide, 2-3/4" high	150	225	350

Log Truck Tractor-Trailer, 1946, No. 620, Courtland, $350

Open Van Tractor-Trailer, 1946, No. 600, Courtland, $300

	C6	C8	C10
Open Van Tractor-Trailer, 1946, No. 600, 13" long, 3" wide, 3-1/4" high	125	200	300
Side Dump Tractor-Trailer, 1946, No. 610, 13" long, 3" wide, 3-1/4" high	100	175	275
Side Dump Tractor-Trailer, 1946, No. 700, 13" long, 3" wide, 3-1/4" high	125	200	325

Friction-Powered Vehicles

	C6	C8	C10
Dump Truck w/dual rear wheels, 10-1/2" long, 3" wide, 3-3/8" high	250	350	475
FBI Riot Squad Car, No. 4050, similar to 7600 FBI Riot Squad Car	100	125	150
FBI Riot Squad Car, No. 7600, 7-1/4" long, 3-1/4" wide, 2-3/4" high	175	200	250
Fire Chief Car, No. 4000, 7-1/4" long, 3-1/4" wide, 2-3/4" high	75	125	150
Fire Chief Car, No. 4000, sparking motor and red plastic bubble on hood, 7-1/4" long,3-1/4" wide, 2-3/4" high	100	125	150

Fire Chief Car, No. 4000, sparking motor and red plastic bubble on hood, Courtland, $150

Mechanical "Gulf" Gasoline Tractor-Trailer, No. 3875, Courtland, $475

	C6	C8	C10
Mechanical "Gulf" Gasoline Tractor-Trailer, No. 3875, 13" long, 3" wide, 3-1/4" high	225	350	475
Mechanical Fire Chief Car w/siren, No. 7500, 7-1/4" long, 3-1/4" wide, 3-1/4" high	150	200	250
Mechanical Military Gun Car, lithographed gun shield, 7-1/2" long, 3-1/4" wide, 2-1/2" high	275	375	500
Mechanical Military Gun Car, painted gun shield, 7-1/2" long, 3-1/4" wide, 2-1/2" high	250	350	475
Mechanical State Police Car w/siren, No. 7500, 7-1/4" long, 3-1/4" wide, 2-3/4" high	150	200	250
Mechanical Tractor w/tin wheels, w/o scraper, 7-1/2" long, 4-3/4" wide, 4-1/2" high	250	350	450
Mechanical Truck Terminal set, two trucks, No. 600	450	750	1100
Pop-Up Ladder Fire Truck, No. 5450, 13" long, 3" wide, 3-1/4" high	250	350	450
Space Rocket Patrol Car, No. 4060, 1952, 7-1/4" long, 3-1/4" wide, 2-3/4" high	150	200	250

Pop-Up Ladder Fire Truck, No. 5450, Courtland, $450

Space Rocket Patrol Car, No. 4060, 1952, Courtland, $250

	C6	C8	C10
Woody Sedan, blue and tan, No. 4000, stamped "A Walt Reach Toy by Courtland Toy Co. Philadelphia, Pa. Made in U.S.A."7-1/4" long, 3-1/4" wide, 2-3/4" high	65	75	100
Woody Sedan, red and tan, No. 4000, marked stamped "A Walt Reach Toy by Courtland Toy Co. Philadelphia, Pa. Made in U.S.A," 7-1/4" long, 3-1/4" wide, 2-3/4" high	65	75	100

CRAFTOY

Little is known about Craftoy, a small Omaha, Nebraska firm. Their brief career casting slush-mold vehicles ended when the pot-metal era was ended by the need for lead during Workd War II. It is known that Craftoy acquired some Ralston Toy & Novelty's molds when that company reorganized in 1940.

The No 92 sedan has the same number as a Best Toy coupe, but they are not the same car. The No. 100 racer is obviously not the same as the Best No. 100 sedan. Older molds were also used for No. 78 mixer, No. 81 racer, No. 102 gasoline semi-tanker, No. 101 fire truck, No. 103 speed car, No. 104 oil truck. The No. 105 station wagon possibly came from Ralston Toy. The ancestry of Kansas Toy is evident in the No. 17 tractor and the freight train set. The designs of the railroad coal car, stockcar and tank car are recent or new.

Black rubber wheels are characteristic of this line, but they are not exclusive to Craftoy.

Contributor: Fred Maxwell, 4722 N. 33 St., Arlington, VA 22207.

	C6	C8	C10
Cement Mixer, "78," 2 open windows, "Made in USA," 3-3/4"	8	12	16
Freight Train, "3600," 16-1/2" Locomotive, 0-6-4, 4-1/2", "KT&N RR," cars 3-1/4", caboose 2-3/4", "Made in USA," value of individual cars	6	9	12
Racer, "81," Miller FWD Indy racer, "Made in USA," 4-1/2"	10	15	20

	C6	C8	C10
Tractor, "17," "Fordson," "Made in USA," farm tractor, driver, rear wheels larger, visible engine, 2-1/2"	8	12	16

DAYTON FRICTION WORKS

Dayton was owned by D.P. Clark of Dayton, Ohio. Clark's wood and metal "Hill Climber" friction toys were his best known. In business from 1898, Dayton was one of the first to use a friction motor. William Schieble, who joined the company in the early 1900s, left in 1909 and formed the Schieble Toy and Novelty Company, using the "Hill Climber" name, which he felt was legally his. Clark continued to use the name despite Schieble's lawsuits, thus the parentage of some "Hill Climbers" is uncertain.

	C6	C8	C10
Armored Car, flywheel drive, sheet metal, red and gold, 1909, 11"	250	450	600
Coal and Ice Truck, tin, friction, c. 1920	200	300	400
Coupe, 1928, pressed steel, 12"	450	675	900

Armored Car, flywheel drive, sheet metal, red and gold, 1909, Dayton Friction Works, $600

Touring Car, open, dated 1909, friction motor, with driver, Dayton Friction Works, $500

American Oil Co. truck, 10-1/2" long, Dent Hardware Company, $1,500

Freeman's Dairy Truck, 6" long. Dent Hardware Company, $800

Valley View Dairy, 8" long, Dent Hardware Company, $1,500

Police Patrol, 8-3/4" long, Dent Hardware Company, $1,500

Touring Car, driver and passenger, 12" long, Dent Hardware Company, $710

	C6	C8	C10
Coupe, c. 1920, 12-1/2" long 600		900	1200
Dayton Friction, pressed steel, rubber			
tires, 1920s, 14-1/4" long 250		375	500
Dump Truck 200		300	400
Fire Ladder Truck, 18" long 275		365	550
Fire Pumper, 1920 500		750	1000
Ladder Truck, 1920s 350		525	700
Touring Car, friction motor, 13-1/2" long.... 500		750	1000
Touring Car, open, dated 1909, friction			
motor, driver 250		375	500
Touring Car, unpowered, 13-1/2" long 350		525	700

DENT HARDWARE COMPANY

Dent, of Fullerton, Pennsylvania, was in business from 1895 to 1973. Henry H. Dent, with four partners, was the owner and Dent cast-iron toys seem to have first appeared in 1898. In the 1920s it was one of the first manufacturers to try aluminum toys (with little success). Dent phased out toys during the hard times of the Depression.

	C6	C8	C10
American Oil Co., cast-iron truck,			
10-1/2" long... 750		1125	1500
Bus, cast iron, 6-1/4" long.......................... 375		563	750
Bus Line, 9" long.. 400		600	800
Bus, 10-1/2" long....................................... 500		800	1200
Coast to Coast Bus, 7-1/2" long................. 125		187	250

Public Service Bus, c. 1926, 13-1/2" long, Dent Hardware Company, $2,400

	C6	C8	C10
Coast to Coast Bus, 10" long...................... 450		675	900
Coast to Coast Bus, c. 1925, 15" long...... 1100		1700	2500
Contractors Mack Dump, open cab,			
10-1/2" long.. 1200		1800	2700
Coupe, 5" long... 125		188	250
Express J & B Stakebed Truck, 1915,			
driver, 14-1/2" long.............................. 500		800	1100

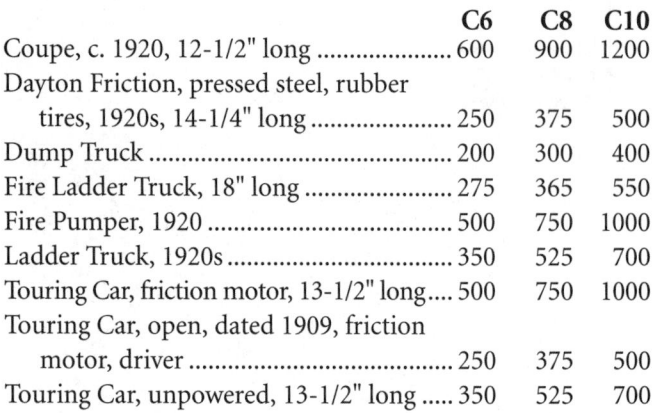

A series of original Dinky Toy Catalogs

Left to Right: 157 Jaguar XK 120, Dinky, $70; 344 Estate Car, Dinky, $70

	C6	C8	C10
Fire Truck, cast iron, 7" long	150	225	300
Fire Ladder Truck w/driver, 8-1/2" long	450	675	900
Fire Truck w/ladder and men, cast iron, 18" long	900	1350	1800
Freeman's Dairy Truck, sliding doors, milkman, 6" long	400	600	800
Hose Reeler w/men, cast iron, large	500	750	1000
Interurban Bus, cast iron, 9" long	417	625	835
LaSalle, approx. 4" long	200	300	400
Ladder Truck, two drivers, 10" long	250	375	500
Mack Dump Truck, c. 1925, iron wheels, 4-1/2" long	55	82	110
Model T 2-door sedan, iron wheels, c. 1925	125	187	250
Patrol, c. 1920s, 6-1/2" long	125	187	250
Police Patrol, 8-3/4" long	750	1125	1500
Public Service Bus, c. 1926, 13-1/2" long	1100	1700	2400
Sedan, spare tire, has stop and go light, full bumpers on front, 7-1/2"	900	1350	1800
Steam Roller, cast iron, 6" long	45	68	90
Touring Car, driver and passenger, 12" long	355	535	710
Valley View Dairy, 8" long	700	1100	1500
Yellow Cab, approx. 7-3/4" long	500	750	1150

DINKY

Dinky toys were first made in England in 1932 under the name "Modeled Miniatures," later "Meccano Miniatures," and in 1934, "Dinky," which in England means "fetching."

Left to Right: 174 Hudson Hornet Sedan, Dinky, $110; 172 Studebaker Land Cruiser, Dinky, $105

	C6	C8	C10
14c Coventry Fork Lift	42	63	85
23h Ferrari Racer	17	26	35
25c Flat Truck	83	125	165
27f 1948 Plymouth Station Wagon	60	90	120
29c Double Decker Bus	75	112	150
30r Fordson Truck	40	60	80
32c/576 Panhard Esso	60	90	120
33 "Bailly" Van	50	75	100
34 Royal Mail Van	45	68	90
36b Bentley	95	143	190
36c Humber, 1936	100	150	200
36d Rover	85	127	170
38c Lagonda	93	140	185
38d Alvis	105	158	210
39c Lincoln Zephyr	138	205	275
40a Riley 4DS	85	127	170
45 Vauxhall Victor	15	22	30
97 Euclid Truck	11	16	22
106 Thunderbird 2 space	60	90	120
112 Triumph Purdey	25	38	50
130 Ford Corsair	40	60	80
134 Triumph Vitesse	22	33	45
135 Triumph 2000	20	30	40
137 Plymouth, 1963	48	72	95
151 Austin Devon	17	26	35
154 Ford Taurus	17	26	35
157 Jaguar XK 120	35	53	70
168 Ford Escort	17	26	35
170 Ford Sedan, 1950	35	53	70
172 Studebaker Land Cruiser	52	78	105
174 Hudson Hornet Sedan	55	83	110
181 Volkswagen MBD	42	63	85
197 Morris Mini	32	48	65
198 Rolls Royce Phantom V	30	45	60
200 Matra 630	16	24	32
201 Plymouth Rally, 1976	17	26	35
207 Triumph TR7 Leyland	17	26	35
227 Beach Buggy	17	26	35
241 Austin Taxi	25	38	50
252 1968 Pontiac	32	48	65
254 Taxi	37	56	75
261 Telephone Van	62	93	125
267 Dodge Fire Rescue	27	41	55
267 Bedford Dump	9	13	18
308 Leyland Tractor	25	38	50
344 Estate Car	35	52	70

DOEPKE "MODEL TOYS"

Charles Wm. Doepke Mfg. Co., Inc, also known as Doepke, was located in Rossmoyne, Ohio. Each of their toys was an authorized replica of the actual vehicle, right down to the decals. The exception was the manufacturer's own "Model Toys" design. Doepke "Model Toys" advertised their toys as outlasting all othersthree to one.

At the end of World War II, Doepke hit the market with five models, the first in a line of heavy-duty metal operating replicas employing metal tread or authentic miniature tires. The tires were either Goodyear or Firestone, with authentic tread and name and tire sizes.

The first five numbers in the toy series were 2000, 2001, 2002, 2006, 2007. Following is a list of the Doepke vehicles.

No. 2000: Wooldridge H.D. Earth hauler, bright yellow, four large tires, twenty-five inches long, ten pounds. Two long doors, the length of the bottom of the dirt-hauling area, could be released to deposit a load.

No. 2001: The Barber-Greene high-capacity bucket loader, thirteen inches high, ten pounds, dark green, all steel and rolling on steel tread, was designed as a toy to lead earth haulers; hand crank.

No. 2002: Jaeger Concrete Mixer, bright yellow, fifteen inches long, eight pounds on four wheels, steerable via draw. Though perhaps the best-detailed, it did not sell well.

No. 2006: The Adams Diesel Roadgrader, dark orange, tweny-six inches long, fourteen pounds, all six wheels, three axles, and blade adjustable to all angles, exactly like the real thing, steerable via steering wheel.

No. 2007. The Unit Mobile Crane, dark orange, 11-1/2" long, 19-1/2" boom, eight pounds, eight ounces, with adjustable side jacks, steered via drawbar. It boasted a block and tackle and a removable operating clam shell as a standard accessory.

No. 2009: The Euclid Earth-Hauler Truck with uncoupling four-wheel tractor to use to tow other toys. It was twenty-seven inches long, eleven pounds, Euclid green or light roadgrader orange, and the trailer dumped in the same way as the Wooldridge.

No. 2010: The American LaFrance Pumper Fire Truck, eighteen inches long, seven pounds, was bright red with chrome trim, ladder, bell, fire extinguisher, hoses and nozzle, and had a reservoir that held water for hand-operated pressure pump.

No. 2011. The Heiliner Earth Scraper, twenty-nine inches long, thirteen pounds, bright dark red, loaded and dumped and operated on four wheels as the Wooldridge did.

No. 2012. The Caterpillar D6 Tractor and Bulldozer, caterpillar yellow, fifteen inches long, seven pounds, with real bulldozer treads for sharp realistic turning and adjustable bulldozer blade, plus heavy draw bar. Diesel motor was cast metal.

No. 2013 eliminated and replaced No. 2001. A Barber-Green mobile high-capacity bucket loader, twenty-two inches long, twelve inches high, and ten pounds, it had buckets on chains and rubber conveyor belt, and was adjustable and steered by steering wheel.

No. 2014. The American LaFrance Aerial Ladder Truck,

twenty-three inches long, forty-two inches long extended ladder height, eleven pounds, bright red and chrome, with bell, red light, adjustable side jacks, was a single unit truck steered by steering wheel.

Doepke "Model Toys" were doomed to extinction by lower-priced, lightweight imitators of lesser quality, some of which were started in the 1920s. No company ever matched the heavy-duty construction and realistic operating qualities of the one and only "Model Toys."

Of the Doepke "Model Toys" that were mass produced, several had variations in their basic construction from time to time. Usually these changes were an elimination of the more intricate operating procedures and had little or no effect on the toy's overall appearance.

Doepke accepted orders to make models of actual vehicles for various companies, but the toys with the most allure, playability, feasible mass production design, and greatest entertainment value were mass produced. The others, those that would not withstand rough handling by young hands or were too expensive, were only manufactured in low numbers, sometimes only one. This is no doubt the explanation for the number gaps between the marketed items.

An advertisement for Doepke Model Toys.

	C6	C8	C10
No. 2000 Wooldridge H.D. Earth Hauler, 25" long	100	150	200
No. 2001 Barber-Greene high-capacity loader, tracks, 13" high	190	285	380
No. 2002 Jaeger Concrete Mixer, 15" long	140	210	280
No. 2006 Adams Diesel Road Grader, 26" long	118	177	235

No. 2001 Barber-Greene high-capacity loader, Doepke, $380

No. 2002 Jaeger Concrete Mixer, Doepke, $280

No. 2009 Euclid Earth Hauler Truck, Doepke, $300

No. 2018 Jaguar, 1955, Doepke, $590

No. 2011 Heiliner Earth Scraper, Doepke, $380

No. 2012 Caterpillar D6 Tractor and Bulldozer, Doepke, $575

	C6	C8	C10
No. 2007 Unit Mobile Crane, 11-1/2" long	155	232	310
No. 2008 American LaFrance Aerial Ladder Truck	200	300	400
No. 2009 Euclid Earth Hauler Truck, 27" long	150	225	300
No. 2020 American LaFrance Pumper Fire Truck, 18" long	185	278	370
No. 2011 Heiliner Earth Scraper, 29" long	190	285	380
No. 2012 Caterpillar D6 Tractor and Bulldozer, 15" long	287	430	575
No. 2013 Barber-Greene Mobile high-capacity bucket loader, wheels, 22" long	145	218	290

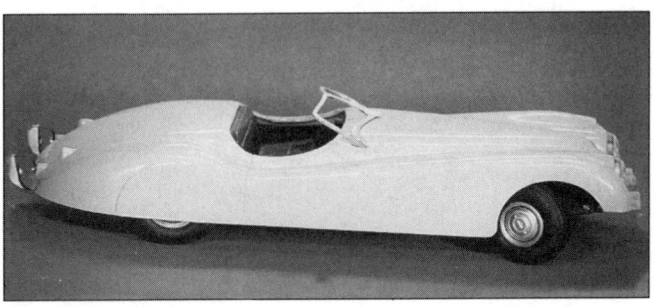

No. 2018 Jaguar, 1955, Doepke, $590

	C6	C8	C10
No. 2014 American LaFrance Aerial Ladder Fire Truck, 23" long	205	308	410
No. 2015 Clark Airport Tractor and Baggage Trailers	300	450	600
No. 2015 MG, 1954, 15" long	205	308	410
No. 2018 Jaguar, 1955	295	442	590
No. 2023 Searchlight Truck 1955	400	600	800

DUNWELL

Dunwell was the trade name given to its toys by Metal Products Co. of Clifton, New Jersey. Its trucks seem to have been sold c. 1953-1958. Their line closely resembles Tonka's and is rare.

	C6	C8	C10
Auto Transport	162	243	325
Cattle Semi	90	135	180
Dump Truck	100	150	200
Grain Hauler	50	75	100
Log Truck	110	165	220
Red Star Express Lines Truck	300	450	600
Snowcrop Refrigerator Semi	350	525	700
Steel Carrier Co. Semi	170	255	340
Wrecker	168	254	335

DYNA-MODEL PRODUCTS COMPANY

Dyna-Model Products Co. may have pioneered the scale model industry of today's markets with their "Dyna-Mo" brand of HO toys. They produced pot-metal toys, identified by their method of assembling body parts (clamping axles between small posts) and by the standardized appearance of the undersides of the whole line.

Produced in the 1930s, and perhaps into the post-war era, the toys were made by a coarse die-casting process. The earlier vintage cars were made in two to five parts, exclusive of wheels and axles, to be pinned, clamped or glued together, including body, frame, steering wheel, top and windshield. Some were packaged as kits with instructions printed on the box. The toys were factory painted in as many as four colors.

Contributor: Fred Maxwell, 4722 N. 33 St., Arlington, VA 22207.

	C6	C8	C10
Convertible, Cadillac two-door Sedan, late 1930s, 2-3/8"	6	9	12
Delivery Van, Pontiac, late 1930s, open windshield and door windows, 2-3/8"	4	6	8
Dump Truck, Open windows, hinged body w/realistic load of coal, three-piece, two colors, dual rear wheels, 2-3/4"	8	12	16
Limousine, Cadillac, late 1930s, open windows and windows, 2-1/2"	6	9	12
Pickup Truck, GMC?, 1930s, one-piece, open windows, one color, 2"	4	6	9
Pickup Truck, Mack?, "US Army," Air Corps star decals, late 1930s, two-piece body, two colors, 2"	4	6	8
Pickup Truck. GMC?, late 1930s, open windows, spoked wheels, two-piece, three colors, 2-1/2"	4	6	8
R-26 HO Buick Convertible, late 1930s, open, two-door sedan, top down, one-piece body, solid cast windshield, disc wheels, 2-3/8"	6	9	12
R-26 HO Surrey, Horseless carriage, tiller steering, three colors, three-piece body, kit, 1-3/4"	4	6	8
R-61 HO Model T Ford 1914 touring w/top, one-piece body, top up, three colors, "cut plastic windshield to fit, darken edges w/ink or paint and glue top and windshield in place, in slots provided," 1-5/8"	4	6	8
Roadster, 1920s Packard convertible, top down, rumble seat, one-piece body, glued windshield, spoked wheels, three colors, 2"	6	9	12
Roadster, Antique Buick?, open, right-hand steering, four-piece, three colors, 1-7/8"	4	6	8
Roadster, Model A Ford? top down, open rumble seat, disc wheels, one-piece body, unpainted, 2"	2	3	4
Roadster, Packard, same as above, top up, three colors, 2"	6	9	12
Sedan, Buick Sedan, 1930s, open windshield and windows, two colors, 2"	4	6	8
Sedan, Buick two-door airflow, open windshield and windows, 2-3/8"	6	9	12
Sedan, Cadillac two-door Sedan, open windshield and windows, late 1930s, 2-3/8"	6	9	12
Sedan, Pontiac four-door airflow, open windshield and windows incl. rear, 2-3/8"	6	9	12

	C6	C8	C10
Speedster, Antique Mercer, right-hand steering, four colors, three-piece, 2" 4		6	8
Taxi, Cadillac Sedan, late 1930s, open windshield and windows including rear, two colors, 2-3/8" 6		9	12
Taxi. Buick Sedan, late 1930s, open windshield and windows, two colors, 2-3/8" 6		9	12
Touring Car, 1914 Ford, top down cast in one-piece body, glued windshield, three colors, 1-3/4" 4		6	8
Touring Car, Antique Stanley Steamer, open tonneau, right-hand steering, four colors, four-piece, 2" 4		6	8
Touring Car, Antique, realistic folded top attachable w/hinge pins, left hand steering, five-piece, two colors, 1-7/8" 4		6	8
Touring, Packard, same as above, top down, three colors, 2" 6		9	12
Truck, Mack? same chassis as above, but tarpaulin-covered, two-piece body, 2" 4		6	8
Wrecker, GMC?, late 1930s, open windows, three-piece, four colors, 2-3/4" 6		9	12

ERIE

According to James Apthorpe, Erie toys were made by Parker White Metal Company, which apparently began in Erie, Pennsylvania, but moved to Fairview (West of Erie), Pennsylvania in the early 1960s. However, according to company officials he contacted, the firm made toys only prior to World War II. No catalogs were printed for Erie toys.

	C6	C8	C10
Lincoln Zephyr Sedan, 1936, painted, 5-1/2" long.. 40		50	60
Lincoln Zephyr Sedan, 1936, plated, 5-1/2" long.. 45		55	65
Lincoln Zephyr Sedan, 1936, painted, 3-1/2" long.. 25		30	35
Lincoln Zephyr Sedan, 1936, plated, 3-1/2" long.. 30		35	40
Packard Roadster, 1936, painted, 6" long.... 40		50	60
Packard Roadster, 1936, plated, 6" long 45		55	65
Packard Roadster, 1936, painted, 3-1/2" long.. 25		30	35
Packard Roadster, 1936, plated, 3-1/2" long.. 30		35	40
Ford Pickup Truck, 1935, low sides, painted, 5" long 45		60	75
Ford Pickup Truck, 1935, low sides, plated, 5" long 55		70	85
Ford Pickup Truck, 1935, high sides, large rear window, 5" long 40		50	60
Ford Pickup Truck, 1935, high sides, small rear window, 5" long 40		50	60

Sedan, c. 1939, sharknose, Erie, 4-1/4" long, $40

	C6	C8	C10
Ford Ice Truck, 1935, "Pure Ice Co.," 5" long 60		80	100
Ford Tow Truck, 1935, "Servel Body," 5" long 60		80	100
Cabover Truck, c. 1937, no tailgate, 3-1/4" 20		25	30
Cabover Truck, c. 1937, tailgate, updated, 3-1/4" long.. 20		25	30
Tow Truck, c. 1939, no chassis, 4-1/4" long.... 30		35	40
Sedan, c. 1939, futuristic, fin on trunk, no chassis, 4-1/4" long........................... 30		35	40
Coupe, c. 1939, futuristic, no chassis, 4-1/4" long.. 30		35	40
Sedan, c. 1939, sharknose, no chassis, 4-1/4" long.. 30		35	40

ERTL

Ertl was started by Fred Ertl Sr. in 1945, working out of his Dubuque, Iowa home. As business expanded, the firm moved to Dyersville. Ertl had learned to use sand molds in his native Germany, and very early in the company's history he began working directly from the original blueprints to make his toy tractors, trucks and other wheeled toys. Ertl's specialty is farm toys, with rights obtained from such manufacturers as International Harvester and John Deere. Today Ertl is the largest manufacturer of toy farm equipment in the world and in addition makes a number of other toys, such as cars, trucks and airplanes.

	C6	C8	C10
Case "L" Tractor 42		63	85
Caterpillar D-6 93		140	195
Fleetstar 10-wheel Dump Truck, red.......... 85		128	170
Ford 7500 Backhoe 37		56	75
GMC Dump 100		150	200
Grader 225		338	450
Hydraulic Dump Truck No. 1645............... 20		30	40
International Backhoe................................. 50		75	100
International Dump 100		150	200
Iron Horse Van 35		52	70
John Deere 440 Bulldozer 20		30	40
John Deere 500 Bulldozer w/blade.............. 50		75	100
John Deere 6600 Combine 70		105	140
John Deere Tilt Bed.................................... 92		138	185
Loadstar Dump Truck................................ 132		198	265

	C6	C8	C10
Loadstar Grain/Cattle Stake Truck	60	90	120
Loadstar Tilt Bed, green/gray	85	128	170
Loadstar Tow Truck, white/red	100	150	200
Mary Kay Cosmetics Trailer Truck	75	112	150
Mobile Tanker	42	63	85
Picker	30	45	60
Tractor and Wagon 8600	44	66	88
Transtar Rowe Furniture Truck	27	41	55
Transtar Texaco Tanker	45	68	90
Velveeta Semi	25	38	50

FIRESTONE

	C6	C8	C10
'35 Ford two-door humpback sedan, 4-7/8" long	75	100	150
'36 Ford two-door humpback sedan, 4-7/8" long	75	100	150
'39 Mercury fastback four-door sedan, 4-3/4" long	100	125	165

FREIDAG

	C6	C8	C10
Bus, cast iron, 6-3/4" long	225	338	450
Coupe, cast iron, 5-3/4" long	290	435	580
Racer, driver and passenger, 6-1/2" long	550	900	1300

GIRARD

	C6	C8	C10
Coupe, battery-operated headlights, 14" long	290	435	580
Fire Chief Car, 15" long	175	262	350
Fire Chief Siren Coupe, 14-1/2" long	350	525	700
Fire Truck, 1920s, 12" long	125	188	250
Pump Truck, battery-operated, headlights, 10" long	100	150	200
Roadster, electrified, 14-1/2" long	195	292	390
Side Dump, 11-1/2" long	97	145	195

Fire Chief Car, Girard, 15" long, $350

	C6	C8	C10
Stake Truck, electric, headlights, 10" long	200	300	400
Tank Truck, wood wheels, 11-1/2" long	70	105	140
Touring Bus, painted tin, c. 1920, 12" long	125	188	250
Truck w/Trailer, 1930s, 17" long	107	160	215

GREY IRON

	C6	C8	C10
Convertible Midget, 1-1/2"	20	30	40
Coupe Midget, 1-1/2" long	20	30	40
Delivery Truck, Midget, 1-1/2" long	20	30	40
Ford Coupe, 8-3/8" long	475	715	950

Part of page 85 from Grey Iron's No. 24 catalog.

'36 Ford two-door humpback sedan, Firestone, in yellow (left) or blue (right), $150

Ford Coupe, Grey Iron, 8-3/8" long, $950

	C6	C8	C10
Racer, Midget, 1-1/2" long	20	30	40
Sedan, 1927, 9" long	1000	1500	2000
Sedan, Airflow Type, Midget, 1-1/2" long	20	30	40
Sedan, older, Midget, 1-1/2" long	20	30	40

HESS

The Hess Service Stations first staked a claim in the toy world in the mid-1960s, collaborating with the Louis Marx Co., in producing a $1.29 Christmas-time toy that would promote the East-coast service station chain. The B-Line Mack Tanker, with battery-operated lights, inaugurated a series that would become a mainstay of the collecting world. Hess released a new model yearly, usually a tanker truck or tractor-trailer. It varied the line in 1966 with the Voyager tanker ship, in 1970 with an American LaFrance fire pumper truck, and in 1980 with the GMC Motorhome Training Van. Emergency vehicles reurned in 1986 and became a mainstay of the line-up into the 1990s. Race-car transporters became part of the line in 1988. Since collectors emphasize Mint-in-Box toys almost to the exclusion of played-with toys, the following prices are for MIB examples.

Contributor: Mark Rich, P.O. Box 971, Stevens Point, WI 54481-0971

1966 Voyager Tanker Ship, Hess, $2,400

1967 Tanker Truck, green and white trailer, red velvet box, Hess, $2,200

1975 Tractor-Box Trailer with oil barrels, Hess, $200

1980 GMC Training Van, Hess, $250

	C10
1964-5 B-Line Mack Tanker Truck, white trailer	2000
1966 Voyager Tanker Ship	2400
1967 Tanker Truck, green and white trailer, red velvet box	2200
1968-69 Tanker Truck, green and white trailer, Hong Kong	550
1969 Amerada Hess Tanker Truck (replica alert)	2000
1970-1 Pumper Fire Truck, Amerada Hess	695
1972-4 Amerada Hess Tanker Truck (reissue of 1968 model)	325
1975 Tractor-Box Trailer w/oil barrels, paper labels	200
1976 Tractor-Box Trailer w/oil barrels, no labels	200
1977 Tanker Truck, large rear label	150
1978-79 Tanker Truck, small rear label	95
1980 GMC TrainingVan	250
1982-83 "First Hess Truck," '34 Chevy Tanker	65
1983-85 "First Hess Truck" bank	65
1984-85 Tanker Truck Bank	65
1986 Ladder Truck	75

C10

1987 Tractor-Box Trailer bank, w/oil barrels	50
1988 Race Car Transporter	50
1989 Ladder Fire Truck, white	35
1990 Tanker Truck w/"Hess 1990" license plate	30
1991 Race Car Transporter	50

C10

1992 Tractor-Box Trailer w/window and Porsche	35
1993 Patrol Car	20
1993 Tanker Truck, limited edition "New Premium Diesel"	1500
1994 Fire Rescue Pickup Truck	15

1986 Ladder Truck, Hess, $75

1982-83 "First Hess Truck," '34 Chevy Tanker, Hess, $65

1970-1 Pumper Fire Truck, Amerada Hess, $695

1988 Race Car Transporter, Hess, $50

1991 Race Car Transporter, Hess, $50

1993 Patrol Car, Hess, $20

	C10
1995 Helicopter Transporter	35
1996 Emergency Ladder Truck	25
1997 Tractor-Box Trailer w/two race cars	25
1998 Mini Hess Tanker Truck	30

HOT WHEELS, VINTAGE

	C8	C10
'31 Doozie, orange, redline, 9649, 1977	15	60
'31 Doozie, orange, blackwall, 9649, 1977	8	15
'56 Hi Tail Hauler, orange, blackwall, 9647, 1977	10	35
'56 Hi Tail Hauler, orange, redline, 9647, 1977	15	60
'57 Chevy, red, redline, 9638, 1977	20	85
'57 Chevy, red, blackwall, 9638, 1977	10	30
Alive '55, blue, 6968, 1974	90	350
Alive '55, assorted, 6968, 1973	75	500
Alive '55, green, 6968, 1974	50	110
Alive '55, chrome, redline, 9210, 1977	15	55
Alive '55, chrome, blackwall, 9210, 1977	15	30
Ambulance, assorted, 6451, 1970	30	50
American Hauler, blue, 9118, 1976	20	50
American Tipper, red, 9089, 1976	20	50
American Victory, light blue, 7662, 1975	20	60
AMX/2, assorted, 6460, 1971	30	100
Aw Shoot, olive, 9243, 1976	15	25
Backwoods Bomb, light blue, 7670, 1975	40	125

Vintage Hot Wheels were packaged with pins featuring a picture of a Hot Wheels car.

	C8	C10
Backwoods Bomb, green, redline or blackwall, 7670, 1977	30	120
Baja Bruiser, orange, 8258, 1974	30	75
Baja Bruiser, yellow, blue in tampo, 8258, 1974	200	900
Baja Bruiser, yellow, magenta in tampo, 8258, 1974	200	900
Baja Bruiser, blue, redline or blackwall, 8258, 1977	25	85
Baja Bruiser, light green, 8258, 1976	300	1000
Beatnik Bandit, assorted, 6217, 1968	15	45
Boss Hoss, assorted, 6406, 1971	75	175
Boss Hoss, chrome, Club Kit, 6499, 1970	50	160
Brabham-Repco F1, assorted, 6264, 1969	10	25
Bronco 4-Wheeler, Toys R Us, 1690, 1981	50	120
Bugeye, assorted, 6178, 1971	30	75
Buzz Off, gold plated, redline or blackwall, 6976, 1977	15	30
Buzz Off, assorted, 6976, 1973	75	400
Buzz Off, blue, 6976, 1974	30	90
Bye Focal, assorted, 6187, 1971	90	375
Bywayman, Toys R Us, 2509, 1979	50	100
Bywayman, blue, red interior, 2196, 1989	40	50
Captain America, white, Scene Machine, 2879, 1979	40	100
Carabo, yellow, 7617, 1974	400	1200
Carabo, light green, 7617, 1974	25	70
Carabo, assorted, 6420, 1970	20	60
Cement Mixer, assorted, 6452, 1970	20	45
Chapparal 2G, assorted, 6256, 1969	15	35
Chevy Monza 2+2, light green, 9202, 1975	200	600
Chevy Monza 2+2, orange, 7671, 1975	40	110

The cover from the 1968 Mattel catalog featuring Hot Wheels.

Boss Hoss, chrome, Club Kit, 6499, Hot Wheels, 1970, $160

Classic '36 Ford Coupe, assorted, 6253, Hot Wheels, 1969, $50

	C8	C10
Chief's Special Cruiser, red, 7665, 1975	30	75
Chief's Special Cruiser, red, redline, 7665, 1977	25	65
Chief's Special Cruiser, red, blackwall, 7665, 1977	10	20
Circus Cats, white 60, 3303, 1981	50	120
Classic '31 Ford Woody, assorted, 6251, 1969	20	70
Classic '32 Ford Vicky, assorted, 6250, 1969	20	50
Classic '36 Ford Coupe, blue, 6253, 1969	10	25
Classic '36 Ford Coupe, assorted, 6253, 1969	15	50
Classic '57 T-Bird, assorted, 6252, 1969	25	70
Classic Caddy, red/white/blue, Museum Exhibit car, 2529, 1992	15	35
Classic Nomad, assorted, 6404, 1970	30	110
Cockney Cab, assorted, 6466, 1971	30	100
Continental Mark III, assorted, 6266, 1969	20	60
Cool One, plum, blackwall, 9120, 1977	20	40
Corvette Stingray, chrome, blackwall set only, 9506, 1977	55	70
Corvette Stingray, red, 9241, 1976	30	80
Corvette Stingray, chrome, 9506, 1976	20	50
Custom AMX, assorted, 6267, 1969	25	80
Custom Barracuda, assorted, 6211, 1968	35	325
Custom Camaro, white enamel, 6208, 1968	300	2000
Custom Camaro, assorted, 6208, 1968	50	375
Custom Charger, assorted, 6268, 1969	50	190
Custom Corvette, assorted, 6215, 1968	50	250
Custom Cougar, assorted, 6205, 1968	60	275
Custom El Dorado, assorted, 6218, 1968	25	100
Custom Firebird, assorted, 6212, 1968	45	220
Custom Fleetside, assorted, 6213, 1968	60	250
Custom Mustang, assorted, 6206, 1968	75	425
Custom Mustang, assorted w/open hood scoops or ribbed windows, 6206, 1968	400	1200
Custom Police Cruiser, assorted, 6269, 1969	55	200
Custom T-Bird, assorted, 6207, 1968	50	165
Custom VW Bug, assorted, 6220, 1968	15	60
Datsun 200SX, maroon, Canada, 3255, 1982	75	175
Demon, assorted, 6401, 1970	15	35
Deora, assorted, 6210, 1968	60	375
Double Header, assorted, 5880, 1973	120	450
Double Vision, assorted, 6975, 1973	110	400
Dune Daddy, assorted, 6967, 1973	110	400
Dune Daddy, light green, 6967, 1975	25	75

	C8	C10
Dune Daddy, orange, 6967, 1975	175	450
El Rey Special, light green, 8273, 1974	95	300
El Rey Special, light blue, 8273, 1974	200	650
El Rey Special, dark blue, 8273, 1974	225	450
El Rey Special, green, 8273, 1974	40	75
Emergency Squad, red, 7650, 1975	15	50
Evil Weevil, assorted, 6471, 1971	40	85
Ferrari 312P, red, 6973, 1974	40	80
Ferrari 312P, assorted, 6417, 1970	20	30
Ferrari 312P, assorted, 6973, 1973	300	1100
Ferrari 512-S, assorted, 6021, 1972	75	250
Fire Chief Cruiser, red, 6469, 1970	10	25
Fire Engine, red, 6454, 1970	25	60
Ford J-Car, assorted, 6214, 1968	10	60
Ford MK IV, assorted, 6257, 1969	10	35
Formula 5000, white, 9119, 1976	20	45
Formula 5000, chrome, 9511, 1976	30	65
Fuel Tanker, assorted, 6018, 1971	60	175
Funny Money, magenta, 7621, 1974	30	80
Funny Money, gray, blackwall, 7621, 1977	20	65
Funny Money, gray, redline, 7621, 1977	25	75
Funny Money, gray, 6005, 1972	60	325
GMC Motorhome, orange, redline, 9645, 1977	200	600
GMC Motorhome, orange, blackwall, 9645, 1977	10	25
Grass Hopper, light green, no engine, 7622, 1975	90	350
Grass Hopper, light green, 7621, 1974	30	90
Grass Hopper, assorted, 6461, 1971	25	55
Gremlin Grinder, chrome, blackwall, 9201, 1977	15	30
Gremlin Grinder, green, 7652, 1975	25	60
Gun Bucket, olive, 9090, 1976	25	60
Gun Bucket, olive, blackwall, 9090, 1977	25	60
Gun Slinger, olive, blackwall, 7664, 1976	15	30
Gun Slinger, olive, 7664, 1975	25	50
Hairy Hauler, assorted, 6458, 1971	20	50
Hammer Down, red set only, 1980		125
Heavy Chevy, light green, 7619, 1974	200	750
Heavy Chevy, chrome, Club Kit, 6189, 1970	50	175
Heavy Chevy, yellow, 7619, 1974	75	175
Heavy Chevy, chrome, redline or blackwall, 9212, 1977	40	120

Carabo, assorted, 6420, Hot Wheels, 1970, $60

Custom Fleetside, assorted, 6213, Hot Wheels, 1968, $250

Mongoose, red/blue, 6970, Hot Wheels, 1973, $1,400

	C8	C10
Heavy Chevy, assorted, 6408, 1970	25	55
Hiway Robber, assorted, 6979, 1973	75	250
Hood, assorted, 6175, 1971	15	90
Hot Bird, blue, 1980	40	100
Hot Bird, brown, 1980	45	120
Hot Heap, assorted, 6219, 1968	10	35
Human Torch, black, 2881, 1979	10	25
Ice T, light green, blackwall, 6980, 1977	20	35
Ice T, yellow, 6184, 1971	40	200
Ice T, assorted, 6980, 1973	200	650
Ice T, yellow w/hood tampo, 6980, 1974	200	525
Ice T, light green, 6980, 1974	30	75
Incredible Hulk Van, white, Scene Machine, 2850, 1979	45	100
Indy Eagle, gold, 6263, 1969	50	200
Indy Eagle, assorted, 6263, 1969	10	25
Inferno, yellow, 9186, 1976	30	60
Jack Rabbit Special, white, 6421, 1970	10	55
Jack-in-the-Box Promotion, white, Jack rabbit w/decals, 6421, 1970,	25	45
Jet Threat, assorted, 6179, 197	145	160
Jet Threat II, magenta, 8235, 1976	35	80
Khaki Kooler, olive, 9183, 1976	15	30
King Kuda, assorted, 6411, 1970	25	100
King Kuda, chrome, Club Kit, 6411, 1970	30	120
Large Charge, green, 8272, 1975	25	60
Letter Getter, white, redline, 9643, 1977	175	550
Letter Getter, white, blackwall, 9643, 1977	5	10
Light My Firebird, assorted, 6412, 1970	20	55
Lola GT 70, assorted, 6254, 1969	10	30
Lotus Turbine, assorted, 6262, 1969	10	30
Lowdown, light blue, 9185, 1976	30	75

	C8	C10
Lowdown, gold plated, redline or blackwall, 9185, 1977	15	30
Mantis, assorted, 6423, 1970	15	40
Masterati Mistral, assorted, 6277, 1969	50	125
Maxi Taxi, yellow, blackwall, 9184, 1977	20	60
Maxi Taxi, yellow, 9184, 1976	25	60
McClaren M6A, assorted, 6255, 1969	10	40
Mercedes 280SL, assorted, 6962, 1973	100	450
Mercedes 280SL, assorted, 6275, 1969	10	40
Mercedes C-111, assorted, 6978, 1973	300	1200
Mercedes C-111, red, 6978, 1974	40	90
Mercedes C-111, assorted, 6169, 1972	80	250
Mighty Maverick, light green, 9209, 1975	200	400
Mighty Maverick, blue, 7653, 1975	30	65
Mighty Maverick, assorted, 6414, 1970	35	85
Mighty Maverick, chrome, blackwall, 9209, 1977	25	50
Mod-Quad, assorted, 6456, 1970	15	40
Mongoose, red/blue, 6970, 1973	400	1400
Mongoose Funny Car, red, 6410, 1970	50	160
Mongoose II, metallic blue, 5954, 1971	75	350
Mongoose Rail Dragster, blue, two pack, 5952, 1971	75	600
Monte Carlo Stocker, yellow, 7660, 1975	45	90
Monte Carlo Stocker, yellow, blackwall, 7660, 1977	20	50
Motocross I, red, 7668, 1975	50	160
Motorcross Team Van, red, Scene Machine, 2853, 1979	50	125
Movin' On, white set only, 1980	125	
Moving Van, assorted, 6455, 1970	50	125
Mustang Stocker, chrome, 9203, 1976	40	90
Mustang Stocker, yellow w/red in tampo, 9203, 1975	300	900

Custom Mustang, assorted with open hood scoops or ribbed windows, 6206, Hot Wheels, 1968, $1,200

Mongoose Rail Dragster, blue, available in two pack, 5952, Hot Wheels, 1971, $600

Left to Right: TwinMill, $35; Carabo, $60; Red Baron, $40

Left to Right: Classsic ' 32 Ford Vicky, $50; Classic Cord, metallic blue, $400; Classic '31 Woody, $70

Custom AMX, $80; Custom Barracuda, $325; Custom Cougar, $275

Noodle Head, assorted, 6000, Hot Wheels, 1971, $150

Race Ace, white, 2620, Hot Wheels, 1986, $30

	C8	C10
Mustang Stocker, yellow w/magenta tampo, 7664, 1975	90	300
Mustang Stocker, chrome, redline or blackwall, 9203, 1977	40	90
Mustang Stocker, white, 7664, 1975	400	1200
Mutt Mobile, assorted, 5185, 1971	75	175
Neet Streeter, blue, 9244, 1976	20	60
Neet Streeter, chrome, blackwall set only, 9510, 1977	40	
Neet Streeter, chrome, 9510, 1976	20	40
Neet Streeter, blue, blackwall, 9244, 1977	15	30
Nitty Gritty Kitty, assorted, 6405, 1970	25	65
Noodle Head, assorted, 6000, 1971	40	150
Odd Job, assorted, 6981, 1973	100	600
Odd Rod, yellow, redline, 9642, 1977	30	50
Odd Rod, yellow, blackwall, 9642, 1977	20	40
Odd Rod, plum, blackwall or redline, 9642, 1977	200	400
Old Number 5, red, no louvers, 1695, 1982	10	20
Olds 442, assorted, 6467, 1971	275	625
Open Fire, 5881, 1972	100	400
Paddy Wagon, blue, 6966, 1973	30	120
Paddy Wagon, blue, blackwall, 6966, 1977	10	20
Paddy Wagon, blue, 6402, 1970	15	30
Paramedic, yellow, 7661, 1976	25	45
Paramedic, yellow, blackwall or redline, 7661, 1977	25	45
Paramedic, white, 7661, 1975	25	55
Peepin' Bomb, assorted, 6419, 1970	10	25
Pepsi Challenger, yellow funny car, 2023, 1982	15	20
Pit Crew Car, white, 6183, 1971	50	450
Poison Pinto, green, blackwall, 9240, 1977	10	20
Poison Pinto, chrome, blackwall set only, 9508, 1977	50	65
Poison Pinto, light green, 9240, 1976	25	60
Poison Pinto, chrome, 9508, 1976	20	40
Police Cruiser, white w/blue light, 6963, 1977	30	65
Police Cruiser, white, 6963, 1974	35	90
Police Cruiser, white, blackwall, 6963, 1977	25	45
Police Cruiser, white, 6963, 1973	250	600
Porsche 911, yellow, 7648, 1975	40	75

	C8	C10
Porsche 911, black, six pack blackwall, 7648, 1977	175	350
Porsche 911, chrome, redline or blackwall, 9206, 1977	20	40
Porsche 911, orange, 6972, 1975	25	60
Porsche 917, assorted, 6416, 1970	15	40
Porsche 917, red, 6972, 1974	175	500
Porsche 917, orange, 6972, 1974	40	75
Porsche 917, orange, blackwall, 6972, 1977	15	25
Porsche 917, assorted, 6972, 1973	300	950
Power Pad, assorted, 6459, 1970	25	65
Prowler, chrome, blackwall, 9207, 1977	35	70
Prowler, assorted, 6965, 1973	200	1000
Prowler, light green, 6965, 1974	500	1000
Prowler, orange, 6965, 1974	35	75
Python, assorted, 6216, 1968	10	55
Race Ace, white, 2620, 1986	15	30
Racer Rig, red/white, 6194, 1971	100	375
Ramblin' Cruiser, white w/o phone number, 7659, 1977	15	20
Ramblin' Wrecker, white, 7659, 1975	20	45
Ramblin' Wrecker, white, blackwall, 7659, 1977	10	20
Ranger Rig, green, 7666, 1975	20	65
Rash I, blue, 7616, 1974	300	800
Rash I, green, 7616, 1974	35	65
Rear Engine Mongoose, red, 5699, 1972	200	600
Rear Engine Snake, yellow, 5856, 1972	200	600
Red Baron, red, blackwall, 6964, 1977	10	20
Red Baron, red, 6964, 1973	30	200

S'Cool Bus, yellow, 6468, Hot Wheels, 1971, $750

Classic Cord, metallic green, $400

Mighty Maverick, $85

Show-Off, $400

Left to Right: Swinging Wing, 1970-71, $40; Splittin' Image, $35; Swinging Wing, 1973, $100

Seasider, assorted, 6413, Hot Wheels, 1970, $120

Snake, white/yellow, 6969, Hot Wheel, 1973, $1,500

	C8	C10
Red Baron, red, 6400, 1970	15	40
Rescue Squad, red, Scene Machine, 3304, 1982	50	90
Road King Truck, yellow set only, 7615, 1974	400	1000
Rock Buster, chrome, 9507, 1976	15	30
Rock Buster, yellow, blackwall, 9088, 1977	10	15
Rock Buster, chrome, blackwall set only, 9507, 1977	45	
Rock Buster, yellow, 9088, 1976	20	35
Rocket Bye Baby, assorted, 6186, 1971	60	200
Rodger Dodger, gold plated, blackwall or redline, 8259, 1977	25	70
Rodger Dodger, magenta, 8259, 1974	40	90
Rodger Dodger, blue, 8259, 1974	200	550
Rolls-Royce Silver Shadow, assorted, 6276, 1969	25	45
S'Cool Bus, yellow, 6468, 1971	175	750
S.W.A.T. Van, blue, Scene Machine, 2854, 1979	70	110
Sand Crab, assorted, 6403, 1970	10	40
Sand Drifter, green, 7651, 1975	150	375
Sand Drifter, yellow, 7651, 1975	20	50
Sand Witch, assorted, 6974, 1973	100	400
Scooper, assorted, 6193, 1971	100	325
Seasider, assorted, 6413, 1970	50	120
Second Wind, white, blackwall or redline, 9644, 1977	35	75
Shelby Turbine, assorted, 6265, 1969	10	25
Short Order, assorted, 6176, 1971	35	100
Show Hoss II, yellow, redline, 9646, 1977	300	600
Show Hoss II, yellow, blackwall, 9646, 1977	35	60
Show-Off, assorted, 6982, 1973	140	400
Sidekick, assorted, 6022, 1972	80	200

	C8	C10
Silhouette, assorted, 6209, 1968	20	90
Sir Rodney Roadster, yellow, blackwall, 8261, 1977	25	40
Sir Sidney Roadster, yellow, 8261, 1974	25	65
Sir Sidney Roadster, light green, 8261, 1974	325	650
Sir Sidney Roadster, orange/brown, 8261, 1974	375	700
Six Shooter, assorted, 6003, 1971	75	225
Sky Show Fleetside (Aero Launcher), assorted, 6436, 1970	400	850
Snake, white/yellow, 6969, 1973	600	1500
Snake Funny Car, assorted, 6409, 1970	60	300
Snake II, white, 5953, 1971	60	275
Snorkel, assorted, 6020, 1971	60	150
Space Van, gray, Scene Machine, 2855, 1979	45	100
Special Delivery, blue, 6006, 1971	45	150
Spider-Man, black, 2852, 1979	10	30
Spider-Man Van, white, Scene Machine, 2852, 1979	50	125
Splittin' Image, assorted, 6261, 1969	10	35
Spoiler Sport, light green, blackwall, 9641, 1977	5	10
Spoiler Sport, light green, redline, 9641, 1977	15	25
Staff Car, olive, blackwall, 9521, 1977	500	750
Staff Car, olive, six-pack only, 9521, 1977	400	750
Steam Roller, chrome, redline or blackwall, 9208, 1977	20	40
Steam Roller, chrome w/seven stars, 9208, 1977	100	300
Steam Roller, white, 8260, 1974	25	70
Steam Roller, white w/seven stars, 8260, 1974	100	300
Street Eater, black, 7669, 1975	30	50
Street Rodder, black, blackwall, 9242, 1977	20	45

Silhouette, assorted, 6209, Hot Wheels, 1968, $90

Sky Show Fleetside (Aero Launcher), assorted, 6436, Hot Wheels, 1970, $850

	C8	C10
Street Rodder, black, 9242, 1976	40	85
Street Snorter, assorted, 6971, 1973	110	400
Strip Teaser, assorted, 6188, 1971	65	200
Sugar Caddy, assorted, 6418, 1971	20	70
Super Chromes, chrome, blackwall six-pack, 9505, 1977		375
Super Van, Toys-R-Us, 7649, 1975	100	350
Super Van, chrome, 9205, 1976	20	40
Super Van, black, blackwall, 7649, 1977	15	25
Super Van, blue, 7649, 1975		650
Super Van, plum, 7649, 1975	90	250
Superfine Turbine, assorted, 6004, 1973	300	1100
Sweet "16," assorted, 6007, 1973	90	375
Swingin' Wing, assorted, 6422, 1970	15	40
T-4-2, assorted, 6177, 1971	35	165
T-Totaller, brown, blackwall, 9648, 1977	10	30
T-Totaller, black, Red Line, six-pack only, 9648, 1977	500	1000
T-Totaller, black, blackwall, 9648, 1977	10	30
Team Trailer, white/red, 6019, 1971	95	225
Thing, The, dark blue, 2882, 1979	15	35
Thor, yellow, 2880, 1979	10	30
Thrill Driver Torino, red/white, blackwall, set of two, 9793, 1977		275
TNT-Bird, assorted, 6407, 1970	25	70
Top Eliminator, blue, 7630, 1974	50	165
Top Eliminator, gold plated, redline or blackwall, 7630, 1977	25	45
Torero, assorted, 6260, 1969	10	60
Torino Stocker, gold plated, redline or blackwall, 7647, 1977	30	70
Torino Stocker, red, 7647, 1975	35	70
Tough Customer, olive, 7655, 1975	15	55
Tow Truck, assorted, 6450, 1970	30	80
Tri-Baby, assorted, 6424, 1970	15	40
Turbofire, assorted, 6259, 1969	10	45
Twinmill, assorted, 6258, 1969	10	35
Twinmill II, orange, blackwall, 8240, 1977	10	25
Twinmill II, chrome, 9509, 1976	20	45
Twinmill II, orange, 8240, 1976	10	35
Vega Bomb, green, 7658, 1975	250	800
Vega Bomb, orange, blackwall, 7654, 1977	25	55
Vega Bomb, orange, 7658, 1975	40	85
Volkswagen, orange w/bug on roof, 7620, 1974	30	60

Sweet "16," assorted, 6007, Hot Wheels, 1973, $375

Volkswagen Beach Bomb, surf boards on side raised panels, 6274, Hot Wheels, 1969, $275

	C8	C10
Volkswagen, orange w/stripes on roof, 7620, 1974	100	400
Volkswagen Beach Bomb, surfboards on side raised panels, 6274, 1969	50	275
Volkswagen Beach Bomb, surfboards in rear window, 6274, 1969		4500
Warpath, white, 7654, 1975	50	110
Waste Wagon, assorted, 6192, 1971	90	325
What-4, assorted, 6001, 1971	50	150
Whip Creamer, assorted, 6457, 1970	15	40
Winnipeg, yellow, 7618, 1974	90	300
Xploder, assorted, 6977, 1973	100	500
Z Whiz, white, redline, 9639, 1977		1500
Z Whiz, gray, blackwall, 9639, 1977	10	20
Z Whiz, gray, redline, 9639, 1977	25	55
Z Whiz, blue, 9639, 1982	20	55

HUBLEY

The Hubley manufacturing company was founded as early as 1892 by John Hubley and made iron toys from the start at its plant in Lancaster, Pennsylvania. Early toys included coal ranges, circus wagons and mechanical banks. Hubley's cast-iron toys were popular almost from the start and have long been collectors items, as they were well made and attractive.

By 1940, however, the cast-iron toy, due to the increased cost of freight and foreign competition, was becoming a thing of the past. At this time, when Hubley was the largest producer of cast-iron toys and cap pistols in the world, it began to introduce die-cast zinc alloy toys. During World War II Hubley was ninety-eight-percent engaged in war production, turning out over five million M-74 bomb fuses, which the Hubley engineers had played a large part in developing.

Since the war, Hubley has manufactured die-cast toys and plastic toys exclusively. In 1952, Hubley manufactured 9,763,610 toys and 11,184,878 cap pistols, about ten times the amount of toys and pistols they produced in 1930 but with a line of toys eighty percent smaller than in 1930. Hubley was acquired by Gabriel Industries in late 1965 and puts

A Hubley advertisement from Woolworth's 1954 Christmas catalog.

out holster sets, cap pistols, vehicles, hobby kits and a number of other toys.

	C6	C8	C10
Air Compress Truck, c. 1950s, 7" long	50	75	100
Airflow-type car, "Hubley U.S.A.," c. 1937, approx. 3-1/2" long	20	30	40
Army Motor Truck No. 807 w/driver, 15" long	1100	1700	2500
Auto Carrier, w/three cars and one pickup truck, c. 1939, 10" long	262	395	525
Auto Express, cast iron, 9"	900	1400	1900
Auto, 1922, Chevy?, 9" long	400	600	800
Auto, 6-1/2" long	80	120	160
Auto, c. 1950s, black plastic wheels, die-cast	12	18	25
Avery Tractor, very early, 4-3/4" long	112	168	225
Bell Telephone Truck, implements, 9" long	600	1000	1350
Bell Telephone Truck, 1931, w/derrick and windlass, auger, trailer w/10" pole, three digging tools, and two loose ladders, 10"	500	750	1040
Bell Telephone Truck, 1940s, 12-1/2" long	75	112	150

Bell Telephone Truck, post-WWII, 24" long, $175

	C6	C8	C10
Bell Telephone Truck, 3-3/4" long	150	225	300
Bell Telephone Truck, 5-1/4" long	175	262	350
Bell Telephone Truck, 7" long	600	950	1300
Bell Telephone Truck, just ladders as equipment, 13" long	250	375	500
Bell Telephone Truck, post-WWII, 24" long	87	130	175
Bell Telephone Truck, tools and ladders, 8-1/4" long	425	638	850
Bell Telephone Truck, w/tools, 12" long	500	800	1100
Black & White Cab, 1920s	1200	2000	3000
Bulldozer, die-cast, front scoop, c. 1950, rubber treads, 10-1/4"	62	93	125
Bus, (futuristic type), c. 1935, 3-1/2" long	50	75	100
Bus, "Coast to Coast" Bus, cast iron, 1927, 13" long	1000	1600	2200
Bus, 1930s, 8" long	60	90	120

An Ad for Hubley automobiles from the 1934 Butler Bros. catalog.

Bus, (futuristic type), c. 1935, Hubley, 3-1/2" long, $100

Coal Truck, c. 1922, Hubley, 9-1/2" long, $875

	C6	C8	C10
Bus, c. 1938, rubber wheels, 5-1/2" long	50	75	100
Cadillac, die-cast, 7" long	40	60	80
Car and House Trailer, Nos. 2278 and 2279, c. 1939	150	225	300
Caterpillar Tractor, 9" long	62	93	125
Caterpillar Tractor, driver in cab, 3-1/4" long	92	138	185
Cattle Truck, post-war	85	128	170
Cement Mixer, "Jaeger"	185	278	370
Cement Mixer, 18" long	400	600	800
Champion Stake Truck, 1930s, white rubber tires, 8-1/2" long	140	210	280
Chemical Truck w/ladders, 13" long	200	300	400
Chevrolet 1932 Coupe, kit	25	38	50
Chevrolet 1932 Phaeton kit, 1960s	40	60	80
Chevrolet 1932 Roadster kit, 1960s	25	38	50
Chrysler Airflow Racing Car, c. 1938	100	150	200
Chrysler Airflow, electrified, white rubber tires on wood hubs, 8" long	1200	2000	3240
Chrysler Airflow, take-apart body, 4-1/2" long	117	175	235
Chrysler Airflow, take-apart body, 6-3/4" long	425	638	850
Coal Truck, c. 1922, cast iron, 9-1/2" long	438	655	875
Coal Truck, cast iron, w/driver, 16-3/4" long	1200	1800	2500
Corvette, 13-1/2" long	255	380	510
Coupe Roadster, rumble seat, rubber tires, 11" long	212	318	425
Coupe, 1933 Ford	140	210	280

	C6	C8	C10
Crash Car, 3-wheel motorcycle, chrome wheels, 11-1/2" long	2400	4200	6365
Crash Car, c. 1937, white rubber tires, 4-3/4" long	100	150	200
Digger, Mack, General, 10" long	450	700	1000
Duesenberg Town Car, build-it model, 9" long	30	45	60
Dump Truck, 5-1/2" long	87	130	175
Dump Truck, c. 1938, 7-1/2" long	295	442	590
Dump Truck, Mack, 1930s, 6 tires, 10-3/4" long	650	1000	1500
Fire Engine No. 526, c. 1936, 10-1/2" long	175	263	350
Fire Engine Pumper, c. 1920, cast iron, black rubber tires, driver, boiler-tender, 12-1/2" long	350	525	700
Fire Engine Pumper, early, No. 504	350	525	700
Fire Engine, die-cast, white rubber tires w/wooden rims, c. 1941	112	168	225
Fire Ladder Truck, 19-1/2" long	600	950	1450
Fire Ladder Truck, c. 1920, two wood ladders, 15-1/2" long	300	450	600
Fire Ladder Truck, early, 8-1/2"	350	525	700
Fire Truck w/searchlight, white rubber tires w/wooden rims	55	82	110
Fire Truck, 5" long	120	180	240
Ford Coupe, 1936	40	60	80
Ford Model A Coupe Kit, 1960s	27	41	55
Ford Model A Phaeton Kit, 1960s	32	48	65
Ford Model A Pickup Kit, 1960s	32	48	65
Ford Model A Station Wagon Kit, 1960s	37	56	75
Ford Model A Town Car Kit, 1960s	32	48	65
Ford Model A Victoria Kit, 1960s	40	60	80
Fordson Front-End Loader, cast iron, c. early 1930s, 9" long	800	1400	2000
Hook & Ladder No. 463	28	42	56
Hook & Ladder Truck, cast iron, 19-1/2" long	200	300	400
Huber Road Roller, 13" long	2200	3300	5000

Bus, "Coast to Coast" Bus, 1927, Hubley, 13" long, $2,200

Life Saver Truck, c. 1930, Hubley, 4-1/4" long, $1,650

	C6	C8	C10
Huber Road Roller, 15" long	2500	3700	6000
Huber Road Roller, 4-1/2" long	110	165	220
Huber Road Roller, 8" long	382	575	765
Huber Road Roller, tractor-like, 7-3/4" long	257	385	515
Hubley Life Saver Truck, small hole in rear	400	600	800
Hubley Road Grader, 12" long	60	90	120
Jaguar Roadster, 1950s, 9"	55	82	110
Kiddietoy "Patrol" Stake Truck, c. 1937	27	41	55
Kiddietoy No. 432 MGTD Roadster, 6" long	110	165	220
Kiddietoy No. 457 Racer, die-cast, rubber tires, 6-1/2" long	27	41	55
Kiddietoy No. 510 series Dump Truck	125	188	250
Ladder Truck c. late 1930s, 5" long	45	68	90
Ladder Truck, 1930s, 10" long	110	165	225
Ladder Truck, c. 1940, 13-1/2" long	350	525	700
Ladder Truck, Terraplane front, 1930s, 6" long	312	468	625
Life Saver Truck, c. 1930, hole in rear is large enough to hold pack of Life Savers, 4-1/4" long	675	1100	1650
Limousine, 6-door, 1920s, 7" long	138	205	275
Lincoln Zephyr and House Trailer, cast iron, 14" overall	375	563	750
Lincoln Zephyr, 7-1/4" long	240	360	480
Log Truck No. 469	55	83	110
Log Truck w/five chained logs, black rubber tires, die-cast, approx. 19" long	138	205	275
Low Boy Truck, trailer, tractor	200	300	400
Mack Dump Truck, w/driver, 11-1/2" long	650	1100	1600
Mack Truck Steam Shovel-Digger, c. 1920, nickel wheels and scoop, 7" long	1300	2200	3200
Merchants Delivery, 1920s, approx. 6" long	400	600	800
MG, 5-3/4" long	55	82	110
MG, 8-3/4" long	112	168	225

Motorcycle, "Harley-Davidson," civilian rider, Hubley, 6-1/4" long, $775

	C6	C8	C10
Model T Coupe, 4" long	100	150	200
Monarch Tractor, 5-1/2" long	600	900	1200
Motor Express Tractor and Trailer, blackrubber tires, 500 series, approx. 19" long	95	143	190
Motorcycle "Traffic Car," four cylinder Indian w/stake sides on two-wheel cart, 11-1/2" long	1500	2500	3500
Motorcycle and rider, 4" long	110	165	220
Motorcycle Hill Climber, 1936, No. 649, 6-3/4" long	400	600	800
Motorcycle w/detachable cop, cast iron, "Made USA," c. mid-1930s, 4-1/4" long	60	90	120
Motorcycle w/sidecar, battery-operated headlight, cop driver, passenger, 8" long	1150	1900	2650
Motorcycle w/sidecar, No. 46-F, two demountable policemen, 8-1/2" long	700	1200	1600
Motorcycle, "Harley-Davidson," civilian rider, 6-1/4" long	382	575	775

Nite Coach, metal wheels, went on Nucar carrier, Hubley, 1930s, 3-1/2" long, $60

The cover of the 1936 Hubley Catalog

Nucar Transport with trailer, four cars, 17" long, $980

Panama Digger, Mack, Hubley, 13" long, $2,100

	C6	C8	C10
Motorcycle, "U.S. Air Mail," 9-1/2" long	1100	2000	2700
Motorcycle, Armored, w/sidecar and removable riders, 9" long	1200	2000	2750
Motorcycle, Harley-Davidson, Police, w/sidecar and rider, 5-1/4" long	250	350	500
Motorcycle, Harley-Davidson, w/policeman, 1930s, swivel head, small wheels near feet, 7-1/4" long	700	1200	1600
Motorcycle, Harley-Davidson, w/policeman, white rubber wheels, 5-1/2" long	275	363	550
Motorcycle, has light in front and place for battery, 6" long	300	450	600
Motorcycle, Indian, policeman rider, nickel-plated cylinder, 9-1/4" long	800	1300	1800
Motorcycle, Kiddietoy, plastic, 5" long	15	22	30
Motorcycle, Parcel Post Delivery, w/two-wheel cart, 9-1/4" long	1300	2200	2900
Motorcycle, policeman, "Cop," 1920s, 4" long	50	75	100
Motorcycle, two-cylinder Indian, w/sidecar, two cops, 9" long	600	900	1200
Motorized Steam Pumper, c. 1930s, 4" long	50	75	100

	C6	C8	C10
Nite Coach, metal wheels, went on Nucar carrier, 1930s, 3-1/2" long	30	45	60
Nucar Transport w/trailer, four cars, 17" long	490	735	980
Packard Roadster Kit	50	75	100
Packard, fifteen parts, 1929, 11" long, straight eight, auctioned in 1994 in Excellent condition			16,000
Packard, 1930 "Phaeton" kit	50	75	100
Panama Digger, 9-1/2" long	800	1300	1800
Panama Digger, 3-1/2" long	162	243	325
Panama Digger, Mack, 13" long	800	1400	2100
Parcel Post Motorcycle and sidecar, Harley-Davidson, 9-1/2"	1600	2800	4000
Patrol, driver, policeman, 15-1/2" long	1400	2100	2800
Pipe Truck No. 803, c. 1950s, 9-1/2" long	35	52	70
Power Shovel, 14"	105	158	210
Pumper, c. late 1930s	115	172	230
Pumper, Terraplane front, 1930s, 6-1/4" long	150	225	300
Racer "No. 1," 8" long	250	375	500
Racer 629, 1936, 6-3/4" long	142	215	285
Racer No. 5, painted and nickeled iron and aluminum, hood opens, 9-1/2" long	900	1600	2290

Motorcycle, has light in front and place for battery, Hubley, 6" long, $600

In 1994 this Hubley 1929 Packard was auctioned in Excellent condition for $16,000

Racer No. 5, Hubley, 9-1/2" long, $2,290

	C6	C8	C10
Racer, "1790," 5" 100		150	200
Racer, 1930s, two passengers, 5-1/2" long 130		195	260
Racer, 2241, 1930s, 7-1/2" long..................... 55		83	110
Racer, animated exhaust stacks, driver,			
8" long.. 600		1000	1400
Racer, die-cast, black rubber tires, 4" long.. 80		120	160
Racer, driver, large tail fin, 7" long............. 165		248	330
Racer, driver, rubber tires, 8" 250		375	500
Racer, plastic, 6-1/2" long 48		72	95
Railway Express Truck, rubber tires,			
5" long... 150		225	300
Road Roller, late 1920s, w/driver, 8" long..... 300		450	600
Road Scraper No. 481.................................... 60		90	120
Say it with Flowers, 10-1/2" long,			
auctioned 1994 in Excellent condition			18,000
Sedan, 1920, cast iron, 7" long.................. 100		150	200
Sedan, 1928, cast iron, 7" long.................. 150		225	300

Streetsweeper, "The Elgin," Hubley, 1931, 8" long.

	C6	C8	C10
Sedan, c. 1938, two-door, looks like Ford,			
rubber wheels, 3-1/2"............................... 70		105	140
Service Car, 4-1/4" long 60		90	120
Service Car, cast iron, including			
wheels, 5" long 200		300	400
Sport Car No. 485 70		105	140
Stake Bed Truck, 7" long............................. 100		150	200
Stake Bed Truck, cast iron, 3-1/2" long 25		38	50
Stake Truck w/trailer, No. 927, two-piece,			
21" long 100		150	200
Stake Truck, c. late 1930s 165		248	330
Stake Truck, No. 614, c. 1930s 75		112	150
Stake-type Truck, No. 452, black, rubber			
tires, c. post-WWII 55		82	110
Station Wagon, c. 1940s, 1950s,			
8-1/2" long 75		112	150
Steam Roller, 5" long................................... 100		150	200
Steam Shovel, "General," 15" long............. 450		700	1000
Steam Shovel, "General," 7" long.............. 238		357	575
Steam Shovel, "General," rubber tires on			
hubs, 9" long 375		563	750

Racer, "1790," Hubley, 5", $200

Road Roller, late 1920s, with driver, Hubley, 8" long, $600

Yellow Cab, c. 1939, 8" long, $1,600

XP-600 FIX-IT CAR OF TOMORROW

Molded and distributed by Ideal Toy Corporation, 200 Fifth Avenue, New York 10, New York. Available in blue body with ivory trim and black wheels and chassis; 15½" long, 6½" wide, 4" high.

APPROXIMATE RETAIL PRICE........$6.00

A 1954 advertisement for Ideal's XP-600 Fix-it Convertible.

	C6	C8	C10
Streetsweeper, "The Elgin," cast iron, 1931, 8" long	1550	2800	4350
Studebaker Roadster, frame and body separate	300	450	600
Studebaker Touring Car, cast iron	325	518	650
Telephone Truck, plastic	25	38	50
Touring Auto, cast iron, chauffeur and rider, 1915, 9-1/2" long	700	1300	1750
Tow Truck, cast iron, c. 1930s, 8-3/4" long	180	270	360
Tractor Loader No. 501, 1950s, 11" long	77	115	155
Tractor Trailer and Road Scraper, No. 506	100	150	200
Tractor, 1930s, 5" long	362	545	725
Tractor, Ford 6000	150	225	300
Tractor, No. 472	30	45	60
Tractor, steam boiler in front, c. early 1920s, 4-3/4" long	125	188	250
Trailer Truck, c. 1936-38	100	150	200
Transitional Fire Patrol, cast iron, driver, firemen, 1920, 12"	800	1300	2000
Truck and Trailer, "Motor Express," No. 2287, 8" long	162	243	325
Truck, "5 Ton Truck," eight wooden barrels, c. 1920, 17" long	700	1150	1760

	C6	C8	C10
Truck, "Borden's Milk Cream," standard version, 6" long	475	715	950
Truck, "Borden's Milk Cream," deluxe version, rubber tires, clicker, 7-1/2"	2000	3500	5500
Truck, Milk Cream Truck, 1930s, cast iron, white rubber tires, 3-1/2"	400	600	800
Wrecker, 3-1/2"	32	48	65
Wrecker, 4-3/4" long	115	172	230
Wrecker, c. 1940, white wheels on large hubs, 6" long	65	98	130
Wrecker, chrome wheels, service car	45	68	90
Wrecker, rubber wheels, 1930, 4-1/2" long	65	98	130
Wrecking Truck, 1930, cast iron, rubber tires, 7-1/2" long	150	225	300
Yellow Cab, c. 1939, 8" long	650	1150	1600

IDEAL

	C6	C8	C10
American LaFrance Fire Truck	72	108	145
Barracuda Coupe, 1964, plastic, 4" long	15	22	30
Cadillac, four-door, 1948, plastic, 4" long	25	38	50
Car Trailer, four cars, plastic, 27" long	40	60	80
Car Trailer, c. 1945, plastic, 3" long	20	30	40
Corvette	50	75	100
Dream Car Convertible, metal, 16" long	200	300	400
Fix-it Convertible	65	98	130
Ford Sunliner, plastic friction, 9"	88	132	175
Ice Cream Truck, plastic, 15" long	42	63	85
Jaguar Roadster, 6" long	35	52	70
Mercedes Sedan, plastic, 9" long	35	52	70
Pickup Truck, American, 1948, plastic, 4" long	7	10	14
Pickup Truck, Ford, 1940, plastic, 4" long	20	30	40
Semi, 12" long	35	52	70
Tow Truck, plastic and metal, 17" long	48	72	95
Tractor, 1948, plastic, 4" long	20	30	40
Truck, "Television Repair"	50	75	100

JANE FRANCIS TOYS

Jane Francis, located in Pittsburgh, Pennsylvania, produced die-cast vehilce during the early post-war period.

Contributor: Dave Leopard, 2507 Feather Run Trail, West Columbia, SC 29169-4915

	C6	C8	C10
Pickup Truck, 6-1/2" long	30	40	50
Pickup Truck, No. 347, 5" long	20	25	30
Pickup Truck, No. 447, 5" long	20	25	30
Tow Truck, No. 447, 5" long	30	35	40
Gulf Truck, tin cover, No. 447, 5" long	35	52	70
Sedan, fastback, futuristic, 6-1/2" long	42	63	85

Gulf Truck, tin cover, No. 447, Jane Francis, 5" long, $70

Tow Truck, No. 447, Jane Francis, 5" long, $40

	C6	C8	C10
Sedan, fastback, futuristic, w/wind-up motor, 6-1/2" long	70	105	140
Jane Francis "Gulf" Service Station, eight pieces	375	562	750

THE JUDY COMPANY

The Judy Company of Minneapolis, Minnesota, made educational toys, including a farm set called Happy's Farm Family (patented in 1945), which included a solid rubber car, pickup truck, and tractor, along with human and animal figures.

Contributor: Dave Leopard, 2507 Feather Run Trail, West Columbia, SC 29169-4915

	C6	C8	C10
Sedan, two dimensional, (part of set), solid rubber, 5-1/4" long	15	20	25

Pickup Truck, No. 347, Jane Francis, 5" long, $30. Photo from Rubber Toy Vehicles by Dave Leopard.

Left to Right: Sedan, two dimensional, solid rubber, part of set, The Judy Company, 5-1/4" long, $25; Pickup Truck, two dimensional, solid rubber, part of set, 5-1/4" long, $25. Photo from Rubber Toy Vehicles by Dave Leopard.

	C6	C8	C10
Pickup Truck, two dimensional (part of set), solid rubber, 5-1/4" long	15	20	25
Farm Tractor, two dimensional (part of set), solid rubber, 3-1/2" long	15	20	25

KANSAS TOY & NOVELTY COMPANY

Arthur L. Haynes, an auto mechanic, began molding toys in a shed in Clifton, Kansas in 1923. With clever hands and an artist's eye, he charmed his friends and local townspeople with his bright-colored toys. His patterns were made from advertising pictures, from local vehicles, and probably from other toys. He made his own production tools. His range was diverse.

This was a town enterprise from the beginning. Jess Foster, the newspaper editor, helped with alloy mixtures; Mr. Hadsell, the Union Pacific agent, suggested they send samples to Woolworths in New York. Clayton D. Young, a traveling salesman, saw the toys, joined the company, and built a profitable business with the chain stores, including Kress, Kresge, and Sears-Roebuck. He eventualy became a partner. At its peak of international sales in the late 1920s, the company employed as many as sixty-five people in two shifts during the Christmas order season.

They were young people who had grown up together. This informality was reflected in the local name, "the Hoopie Factory." Two or three of their early toys, and No. 26 and No. 33, were stripdowns—hoopies—probably raced locally. Whether "Whoopee," tractor toy No. 48, was a local spelling of this or whether it celebrated a fat cheering order is not known.

Haynes believed that he invented hollow-casting of metal toys. The process of making the slush or hollow-cast toys was a very simple one. The metal was melted down to a molten state and poured into a mold. After a few seconds, the liquid metal was poured off leaving a thin shell of metal solidified against the walls of the mold. The thickness of the shell varied depending on mold temperature, the alloy used and the length of time the molten metal was allowed to remain in the mold.

During its good years, Kansas Toy & Novelty produced more toys than any in the industry except Barclay. Mr. Young left the company in the late 1920s. Whether it was the loss of his talents and assets or the onset of the Great Depression, the company was in trouble by 1930. George Hoeffer reorganized the company and moved it across town, but this effort lasted only a few months. Although

KT&N continued until 1935, Best Toy & Novelty Company acquired the Kansas Toy molds in 1933.

Because Kansas Toy created a dynasty of at least four other toy companies using original Kansas Toy molds, many of which are in use today, collectors and dealers may be confused. The following has been included to try and clear the confusion surrounding the Kansas Toy models.

Metal wheels of several sizes and styles—disk, simulated wire, and spoked—were characteristic of early Kansas Toy & Novelty toys. Rubber tires on wood hubs, which were popularized by Tootsietoy Grahams, were introduced on the No. 75 mold in 1932. These were followed by white soft-rubber wheels (simulating balloon tires) and realistic white hard-rubber disc wheels sometimes painted black. Several Kansas Toys were made in two or three sizes (5¢, 10¢ and 15¢). Bottom-pans were not cast until high numbers (#76). Many were made with string-pull loops or knobs in the handcrank position. All colors were used, including gold, silver, and pink; the few found with two-colored bodies may have been salesman samples. Many early toys were finished in Egyptian lacquer, a japanning applied thinly so the bright metal showed through with a glittery look. A Mint toy with this finish has a modern look, and later toys were enameled. A mark of "Made in USA" is a sure clue to reproductions because this copyright law went into effect in the late 1930s. Black rubber wheels also signal a reproduction.

Clayton Stevenson, a toymaker in his own right (Lincoln White Metal Works and Midwest Toy), had been furnishing some molds and patterns as a subcontractor since the mid 1920s. He must have originated those handsome designs from three-piece molds, such as No. 8, No. 58, No. 60, No. 80, No.

88 and No. 91, with their intricate, realistic front ends. Some higher numbers have Stevenson-type patterned pans. These features slowed production and added to costs while blurring the difference between Kansas and Lincoln toys.

Among its many designs it is not surprising to find toys reflecting familiar vehicles—hoopies, stripdowns, midget racers, trucks, tractors, and farm implements. But Kansas Toy also made miniatures of record-setting aircraft and landspeed record cars.

Collectors should note that not all slush molds with numbers are Kansas Toy & Novelty Company and many were not numbered. Because these were unlabeled, unboxed bin-toys, the number may have been a convenience to certain wholesale buyers.

All cast numbers are shown in quotes.

Contributor: Fred Maxwell, 4722, N. 33 St., Arlington, VA 22207

	C6	C8	C10
Coupe, "35," Convertible, LI, VL, HG, HO, RM, MWW, also an UV, 2-1/4" long	20	30	40
Coupe, "8," Convertible, LI, VL, HG, WV, SP, RM, MWW, no HO, no headlamps, enamel finish, also UVs w/"Chrysler," headlamps and HO, or /MDSW, 3-1/8" long.................................	20	30	40
Coupe, Convertible, LI, VL, HG, WV, SP, MDSW, lacquer, 2-7/8"...........................	30	45	60
Coupe, crude, slant roof, shallow rear body, no fenders, hood similar to first racer above, lacquer; possibly the first "hoopie" or stripdown made?, 3-1/8" long, rare	32	48	64
Dirt Tumble, "64," adjustable dumping scoop, 1-1/2" wide on same frame as No. 62, six pieces, four colors, 4" long ...	35	52	70
Disk Harrow, "62," 8 disk on same 1-5/8" wide frame as #61, thirteen pieces, incl. disks and wheels, four colors, 4" long....	35	52	70

The following abbreviations are for the details and variations useful in identification.

HG	horizontal grille pattern
HL	horizontal hood louvers
HO	hood cap, Motometer or ornament
L	lacquer finish
LI	landau irons on convertibles
MDW	metal disc wheels
MDSW	metal disc solid spokes
MDWBT	wheels with black painted tires
MSW	metal open spoke wheels
MWW	metal simulated wire wheels
OW	open windows
RM	rearmount spare tire/wheel
SM	sidemounted spare
SP	string-pull knob in handcrank area
T	external trunk
UV	unnumbered version
VG	vertical grille pattern
VL	vertical hood louvers
WS, W/S	windshield
WV	windshield visor
WHRT	wooden hubs, rubber tires
WRDW	white hard rubber disc wheels
WRW	white soft rubber wheels (balloon tires)

Back row, left to right: Coupe, "8," Convertible, Kansas Toy & Novelty, 3-1/8" long, $40; Roadster, "14," open, "Chrysler," Kansas Toy & Novelty, 3-1/8" long, $36. Front row, left to right: Sedan, "60," 1930 Reo Royale? or Chrysler two-door Brougham, Kansas Toy & Novelty, $48; Coupe, "80," convertible, top up, Kansas Toy & Novelty, 3-1/2" long, $60.

Top row: Two versions of Kansas Toy's Farm Tractor, "17," "Fordson," with driver, 2-7/8" long, $40. Bottom row, left to right: Separator-Thresher, "27," Kansas Toy & Novelty, 3" long, $40; Steam Tractor, "25," "Case," Kansas Toy & Novelty, 3" long, $50

Overland Bus, "9," "Fageol," Kansas Toy & Novelty, 3-1/2" long, $60

	C6	C8	C10
Dump Truck, "42," Ford?, driver, no cab, diamond emblem on hinged body, LV, HG, SP, MWW, 3-1/2"	35	52	70
Farm Tractor, "17," "Fordson," driver, HG, crank, no tow hook, large 1-1/4" and 3/4"MDW w/four holes in disks, also found w/same size six spoke wheels, 2-7/8" long	20	30	40
Indy Racer, "10," driver, boattail, exhaust right, VL, HG, HO, SP, MSW or MWW, also UV, 3-1/8"	10	15	20
Locomotive-Tender, "36," "KT & N RR," 6 MSW, 4 MDW, 0-6-4, 4-3/8" long	7	10	14
Midget Racer, "31," driver, torpedo tail, VL, HG, HO, MWW, lacquer, also UV, 2-1/8"	14	21	28
Midget Racer, "67," driver, torpedo-tail, VL, HG, HO, MDW, smaller version of #31, also an UV, 1-1/2" long	44	66	88

Roadster, "14," open, "Chrysler," Kansas Toy & Novelty, 3-1/8" long, $36.

	C6	C8	C10
Midget Racer, no driver, torpedo tail, HO, SP, VL, HG, 5/8" MDW w/simulatedlug nuts, lacquer finish, 3" long	20	30	40
Midget Racer, same as above, w/driver, plain MDW, lacquer; easily confused w/another maker's copy; 3" long	20	30	40
Overland Bus, "9," "Fageol," solid windows, 3-1/2" long	30	45	60
Overland Bus, "Fageol," nine male passengers, driver and "baggage" cast-on windows, HG, RM, MDW, also an UV w/various family passengers on windows, 3-1/2"	26	39	52
Planter, "KTN No. 61," V-blade plough w/seed hopper, four pieces incl. wheels and three colors, 4" long	35	52	70
Plough, "63," single blade on same shaft as No. 61, 4" long	35	52	70
Racer, "46," 1929 Golden Arrow record car, driver, large tail fin, MWW, 2-7/8" long	12	18	24
Roadster, "14," open, "Chrysler," solid W/S, plain grille, HO, VL, SP, RM, MDSW, 3-1/8" long	18	27	36
Roadster, "54," Buick, driver w/cap, rumble seat, T, plain hood and grille, no headlamps, SM, MWW, also an UV, 2-3/8" long	20	30	40

Top row, left tot right: Midget Racer, no driver, torpedo tail, Kansas Toy & Novelty, 3" long, $40; Midget Racer, same as above, with driver, torpedo tail, Kasnas Toy & Novelty, 3" long, $40. Bottom row, left to right: Indy Racer, "10," driver, boattail, Kansas Toy & Novelty, 3-1/8", $20; Midget Racer, "31," driver, torpedo tail, Kansas Toy & Novelty, 2-1/8", $28; Midget Racer, "67," driver, torpedo-tail, Kansas Toy & Novelty, 1-1/2" long, $88.

Truck, "20," Ford?, Kansas Toy & Novelty, 3-1/8" long, $72

	C6	C8	C10
Roadster, "54," Buick, driver w/cap, rumble seat, T, plain hood and grille, no headlamps, no trunk, SM, MWW, also an UV, 2-1/4" long 25	38	50
Sedan, "60," 1930 Reo Royale? or Chrysler two-door Brougham, plain hood, vee-VG, square rear deck, MDW, MDWSM, also an UV w/MWW and MWWSM, 3-1/2" 24	36	48
Sedan, "Chevrolet," six windows, LI, WV, VL, SP, RM, MWW, 2-7/8" long 16	24	32
Separator-Thresher, "27," tow hook, auto-type MSW (not tractor rims), lacquer or enamel, also UV, 3" long 20	30	40
Steam Road Roller, "43," driver, SP, boiler, wooden rollers, 3-1/4" 20	30	40
Steam Tractor, "25," "Case," crew of two, tow loop, large front, small rear MSW andflywheel, 3" 25	38	50
Steam Tractor, "71," crew of two, tow-loop,small version of No. 25, 2-1/2" long... 10	15	20
Tour Bus, "59," 1928 Pickwick COE double-deck night-coach, screen grille, larger version of #49 above, also an UVw/dual wheels, 3-3/8" long... 50	75	100

Warehouse Tractor, "48," "Caterpillar," "Whoopee," driver, Kansas Toy & Novelty, 3" long, $50

	C6	C8	C10
Truck, "20," Ford?, solid W/S, two open windows, three tanks, VL, HG, rear faucet, MWW, versions w/ and w/o driver, also an UV, 3-1/8" long 36	54	72
Warehouse Tractor, "48," "Caterpillar," "Whoopee," driver, VL, HG, HO, SP, tow loop, MWW, also an UV, 3" long.... 25	38	50

Kansas Toy Transitional Vehicles

Kansas Toy & Novelty was reorganized in 1931 by George Hoeffer and, according to local accounts, did not cease operations until 1935. If this is true (there is some debate), some numbers from No. 75 to at least No. 100 were made by Kansas Toy.

Starting with No. 75, the new issues used wooden wheels, or hubs, and white rubber tires. The black painted tires have been found on numbers from 59 to 97. They may have also been used on the early Best Toy models.

	C6	C8	C10
Coupe, "80," convertible, top up, LI, two open windows, VG, T, MWW w/MWW SM,3-1/2" long 30	45	60
Coupe, "80," same as above except HRDW w/MDW, 3-1/2" long................. 40	60	80
Racer, "76," Auburn speedster, low driver, headrest fairing, SP, HG, slanted louvers, large oval fin, kickplates, HWRWor WHRT, 4-1/4".................... 25	38	50

The following abbreviations are for the details and variations useful in identification.

HG	horizontal grille pattern
HL	horizontal hood louvers
HO	hood cap, Motometer or ornament
L	lacquer finish
LI	landau irons on convertibles
MDW	metal disc wheels
MDSW	metal disc solid spokes
MDWBT	wheels with black painted tires
MSW	metal open spoke wheels
MWW	metal simulated wire wheels
OW	open windows
RM	rearmount spare tire/wheel
SM	sidemounted spare
SP	string-pull knob in handcrank area
T	external trunk
UV	unnumbered version
VG	vertical grille pattern
VL	vertical hood louvers
WS, W/S	windshield
WV	windshield visor
WHRT	wooden hubs, rubber tires
WRDW	white hard rubber disc wheels
WRW	white soft rubber wheels (balloon tires)

Ambulance, cast iron, Kenton, 7" long, $1,700

Bus, Double-Decker, Kenton, 9-1/2", $1,550

	C6	C8	C10
Roadster, "77," open sport Duesenberg, W/S down, driver, VG, slanted louvers, SM, T, WHRT, 4" long	25	38	50
Sedan "84," DeSoto?, airflow, four open windows, HO, HG, HL, HRDW, 1934 issue, 3-5/8" long	30	45	60
Sedan, "79," 2-door, Graham-like, four open windows, VG, HL, RM, WHRT w/five removable tires, found both w/ and w/o bottom pan, 4-1/4"	20	30	40

KENTON

	C6	C8	C10
Ambulance, cast iron, 7" long	750	1300	1700

Army Motortruck 807, cast iron, Kenton, 14" long, $1,300

Buckeye Ditcher, Kenton, 9" long, $940

	C6	C8	C10
Army Motor Truck 807, cast iron, 14" long	600	950	1300
Auto, cast iron, early, 6" long	250	375	500
Boattail Cut-Down Speedster, 1910, 7" long	120	180	240
Buckeye Ditcher, 9" long	470	705	940
Bus, "Coast-to-Coast"	350	525	700
Bus, 1920s, 10-3/4" long	375	525	750
Bus, cast iron, 8" long	175	262	350
Bus, Double-Decker, 1920, 7-1/4" long	1100	1650	2200
Bus, Double-Decker, 1920s, 6" long	312	470	625
Bus, Double-Decker, 9-1/2"	650	1050	1550
Cattle Truck, cast iron, c. 1938, 8" long	150	225	300
Cement Mixer, 7" long	423	635	845
Circus Truck, 10" long	1500	2500	3900
Coal Dump Truck, 8-1/2" long	300	450	600
Coupe, 1926, 10" long	3000	5500	9500
Coupe, 5" long	230	345	460
Coupe, 6-1/2" long	425	638	850
Coupe, 8" long	700	1100	1600
Dump Truck, 6" long	170	255	340
Dump Wagon, "Contractors," cast iron, 9-3/4" long	500	750	1000
Emergency Truck, c. 1930s, black rubber tires	180	270	360
Fire Apparatus Truck	400	600	800
Fire Pump Truck, early w/driver, 10" long	220	330	440

Dump Wagon, "Contractors," Kenton, 9-3/4" long, $1,000

Fire Pumper, c. 1920s, with gong, Kenton, 18" long, $700

	C6	C8	C10
Fire Pumper, 1920s, 14-1/2" long	500	850	1260
Fire Pumper, c. 1920s, w/gong, 18" long ...	350	525	700
Fire Truck, w/pumper, 15" long	1200	2000	2800
Franklin, air-cooled, 8-1/2"	1300	1950	2600
Hose Truck, 9" long	500	750	1050
Hose Truck, open cab, c. 1920s, green, driver, rider, hose, ladders, 6-3/4" long	285	430	570
Ice Truck, tongs and glass ice, 7-1/2" long	400	600	800
Jaeger "Mixer," cast- iron cement truck, 9" long	1100	1900	2600
Jaeger Cement Mixer, 6-1/2" long	365	545	730
Jaeger Cement Mixer, 8" long	1100	1700	2500
Ladder Truck, 17-1/4" long	750	1200	1700
Ladder Truck, cast iron, approx. 7-1/2" long	310	465	620

Patrol Wagon, marked "Patrol" on side, c. 1920s-30s, 9" long, $1,030

Pickwick Nite Coach, Kenton, 14" long, $3,800

Stake Truck, "Speed," Kenton, c. 1927, 5-1/2" long, $815

	C6	C8	C10
Ladder Truck, pressed-steel ladders, 16" long	325	488	650
Overland Circus Cage Truck w/driver, 7-1/2" long.................................	800	1300	2000
Overland Circus w/lion, 9" long	800	1300	2000
Patrol Wagon, marked "Patrol" on side, c. 1920s-30s, 9" long	500	750	103
Phaeton Touring Car, 12" long	350	562	700
Pickwick Nite Coach, cast iron, 14" long ...	1500	2500	3800
Pontiac, approx. 4" long..........................	150	225	300
Racer, early, 7-1/2" long	175	262	350
Racer, early, cast iron, 9" long..................	600	1000	1400
Red Devil w/driver, 6" long........................	200	300	400
Road Grader, cast iron, rubber tires, nickel-plated moveable blade, 7-1/2" long	212	318	425
Roadster, driver, c. 1908, 6" long	300	450	600
Runabout Auto, 1900, 5" long	170	255	340
Runabout Auto, cast iron, resembles a 1910 Franklin, w/driver, 7" long........	175	262	350
Sedan, 4" long..	110	165	225
Sedan, late 1930s, rubber tires, take-apart body, 7" long	1200	2000	2800
Sprinkler Truck, early, 8"	425	638	850
Stake Truck, "Speed," c. 1927, 5-1/2" long	408	612	815
Stake Truck, 6" long	235	352	470
Steam Roller, "Galion Master" 6-1/2" long	225	338	450
Steam Shovel, Marion, 7-1/4".....................	600	900	1200
Tank, cast iron 2-1/2" long..........................	80	120	160
Touring Car, open, driver and passenger, 8-1/2" long..........................	650	975	1300
Tow Auto, 1920s, 9-1/2" long..................	1100	1800	2700
Yellow Cab, 1950s, 6-3/8" long	470	705	940

Touring Car, open, driver and passenger, Kenton, 8-1/2" long, $1,300

KEYSTONE

Keystone of Boston, Massachusetts, had an odd assortment of products—movie projectors, steel trucks, wooden boats, and pressed wood forts and garages. Founded in June of either 1922 or 1923 by Chester Rimmer and Arthur Jackson, it was first located in a small shop in Malden, Massachusetts, under the name Jacrim. Rimmer retired in 1958 and sold out to various companies. Number and names are from a Keystone catalog.

	C6	C8	C10
No. 41 Dump Truck, 26-1/2" long	500	750	1050
No. 43 American Railway Express, 26" long	700	1200	1690
No. 44 Truck Loader, 17-3/4" high	175	263	350
No. 45 U.S. Mail Truck, 26" long	900	1450	2100
No. 46 Steam Shovel, when arm is extended 26" long	243	365	485
No. 47 Steam Shovel, when arm is extended 34-1/2" long	195	295	390

An early Keystone catalog.

	C6	C8	C10
No. 48 U.S. Army Truck, 26" long	500	800	1200
No. 49 Fire Truck, 27-1/2" long	1100	1800	2700
No. 51 Police Patrol, 27-1/2" long	800	1400	1900
No. 52 Fire Truck, 27-1/2" long	645	968	1290
No. 53 Sprinkler Truck, tank 12" long	1000	1600	2400

No. 44 Truck Loader, Keystone, 17-3/4" high, $350

No. 43 American Railway Express, Keystone, 26" long, $1,690

No. 58 Moving Van, Keystone, 26" long, $1,650

	C6	C8	C10
No. 54 Koaster Truck, w/skids, hoist cable, windlass, 26" long when skids retracted	800	1300	1800
No. 55 Koaster Truck, w/o skids and windlass	478	720	955
No. 56 Water Pump Tower, 29" long	700	1100	1600
No. 57 Chemical Pump Engine, 27-1/2" long	1000	1550	2100
No. 58 Moving Van, 26" long	700	1200	1650
No. 60 Riding Steam Roller	300	450	600
No. 62 Hydraulic Dump Truck, 26" long	500	800	1100
No. 73 Ambulance, military, 27" long	800	1300	1800
No. 78 Wrecking Car, 27" long	850	1350	1880
No. 79 Aerial Ladder, 30-1/2" long	700	1100	1550

KILGORE

Kilgore of Westerville, Ohio began making toys in the 1920s. Its toys were cast iron and low-priced, with cap pistols its most popular line. But it also did well with a number of attractive trucks, fire engines and cars, as well as scattered aircraft and ships. Some subsidiary manufacturing was done in Lancaster, Pennsylvania and Canada. In 1937, Kilgore began making plastic cars, trucks, planes and buses, and later added plastic cap pistols, placing it among the first companies to produce plastic toys. Kilgore remained in business until at least 1978.

	C6	C8	C10
Auto, "LF 1300A," w/driver	180	270	360

Livestock Truck, Kilgore, 9" long, $1,200

Pontiac, cast iron, Kilgore, 1930, 10", $2,700

Truck, "Arctic Ice Cream Truck," Kilgore, 8" long, $1,800

	C6	C8	C10
Bus, plastic, advertised in 1937, 4" long	20	25	30
Convertible w/rumble seat, early 1930s, w/driver, 7" long	160	240	320
Coupe, streamlined, plastic, advertised in 1937, 4" long	20	25	30
Double-Decker Bus, c. 1930, 6" long	450	675	900
Dump Truck, 1930s, 7" long	175	262	350
Dump Truck, cast iron, c. 1934, 5-3/4" long	160	240	320
Dump Truck, cast iron, c. 1934, 8-1/2" long	450	675	900
Fire Chief Sedan, plastic, advertised in 1937, 4" long	20	25	30
Fire Truck w/ladders, 1929, 6-3/4" long	188	282	375
Livestock Truck, 1930s, 7" long	275	365	550
Livestock Truck, 9" long	500	800	1200
Motorcycle, "Special Delivery," 4-1/4" long	150	225	350
Motorcycle, single rider, 4"	112	168	225
Police Car, plastic, 1937, 4"	20	25	30
Pontiac, cast iron, 1930, 10"	1200	1800	2700
Roadster, driver, rumble seat, 6" long	250	375	500
Roadster, Pierce-Arrow, take-apart body, 6-1/8" long	250	375	500
Sedan, 3-1/4" long	65	98	130
Sedan, Packard Luxury, take-apart body, 8-1/4" long	700	1300	1600
Stutz Roadster, thirteen parts	1100	1500	2500
Taxi, plastic, 4" long	20	25	30

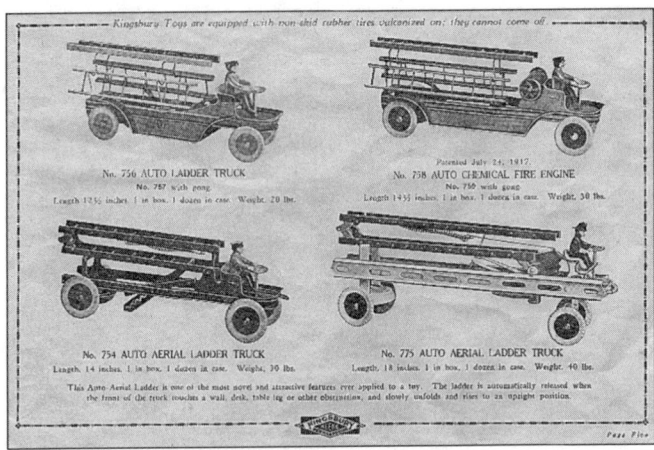

A page from a 1922 Kingsbury catalog.

Fire Chief Coupe, 1930s, Kingsbury, 14" long, $650

	C6	C8	C10
Truck, "Arctic Ice Cream Truck," 8" long ..	800	1300	1800
Truck, "Arctic Ice Cream Truck," 9" long ..	500	750	1000
Truck, "Express," plastic, advertised in 1937, 4" long..............................	20	25	30
Truck, "Toy Town Delivery," 6-1/8" long ..	445	668	890

KINGSBURY

Kingsbury, founded in 1886 in Keene, New Hampshire, was owned by Harry T. Kingsbury. Kingsbury apparently bought the Wilkins Toy Company, but didn't change the firm's name until after World War I.

Steel and spring motors characterize Kingsbury's toys. Cars, fire engines, farm equipment, and racing cars comprised its primary output. Kingsbury is still in business but apparently ended toy production in 1942.

	C6	C8	C10
Aerial Ladder Truck, pressed steel wind-up, c. 1941, ladder rises automaticallyto height of 38" when the truck runs into any obstruction, fireman on ladder climbs upand down by turning crank at base of ladder, 24" long...................................	180	270	360

	C6	C8	C10
Aerial Ladder Truck, pressed steel wind-up, c. 1905, ladder rises automaticallyto height of 38" when the truck runs into any obstruction, fireman on ladder climbs upand down by turning crank at base of ladder	425	638	850
Airflow, c. 1934, pressed steel, rubber tires, 14" long	310	465	620
Airflow, clockwork, 14" long	500	750	1060
Auto, very early, steel wind-up, 9-3/4" long.............................	250	375	500
Bluebird Racer, 18" long	1000	1500	2100
Brougham Sedan, pressed steel wind-up, 13" long	1100	1700	2425
Bus, pressed steel, 18" long	390	585	780
Cannon Truck, very early, clockwork, 11" long	210	315	420
Cannon Truck, c. 1939, wind-up, 15" long	125	188	250
Caterpillar, wind-up, 8-1/2"	225	338	450
Cattle Truck, 1930s, 19" long....................	212	318	425
DeSoto, pressed steel wind-up, c. 1938, 14-1/2" long.............................	218	327	435
Dump Truck, tin, driver, 10" long	450	675	900
Dump Truck, early 1930s, clockwork, 16" long	350	525	700
Fire Chief Coupe, 1930s, 14" long.............	325	438	650
Fire Pumper, very early, clockwork iron and steel, 11" long	363	545	725

Cannon Truck, c. 1939, wind-up, Kingsbury, 15" long, $250

Greyhound Bus, wind-up, Kingsbury, 18" long, $525

	C6	C8	C10
Fire Pumper, 1920s, 23" long	225	338	450
Fire Truck, 18" long	250	375	500
Ford Sedan & House Trailer, 1937, pressed steel, 23" long	450	675	900
Golden Arrow Racer, pressed steel wind-up, 20" long	600	1000	1375
Greyhound Bus, wind-up, 18" long	262	395	525
Ladder Truck, steel, driver, 22" long	187	280	375
Ladder Truck, c. 1930, 35" long	1200	2100	3100
Ladder Wagon Fire Truck, tin, rubber tires, 23-1/2" long	165	250	330
Phaeton Auto, 1900, rubber slip tires, 9-1/2" long	1400	2700	3500
Rack Truck, pressed steel wind-up, 16" long	350	525	700
Roadster, No. 242, electric headlights, spring motor, luggage rack, 13" long	375	563	750
Sunbeam Racer, sheetmetal, red w/rubber tires on steel wheels, clockwork motor, 19" long	800	1300	1725
Tractor, mechanical w/driver, 8" long	250	375	500
Tractor and Cart, tin, w/iron driver, white rubber wheels, c. 1930s, 11-1/2" long	195	292	390
Transit Truck, 1930s, 19" long	100	150	200
Truck w/C Cap, tin, 10" long	175	262	350
Wind-up Car, curved dash, driver, 9" long	225	338	450
Wrecker, pressed steel wind-up, 13" long	1000	1600	2300

LANSING SLIK-TOYS

Lansing Slik-Toys, made in Lansing, Iowa, sometimes bear the name "Kipp," in addition to the Lansing and Slik-Toy trademarks. Most Slik-Toys are made of aluminum in a single casting, although some were made of hard plastic. The company made many farm and construction toys, but the list below is confined to cars and trucks. Many Slik-Toys bear a four-digit number beginning with "9." If a toy bears such a number, even if it has no other markings, it is likely a Slik-Toy.

Contributor: Dave Leopard, 2507 Feather Run Trail, West Columbia, SC 29169-4915.

	C6	C8	C10
Fire Truck, No. 9606, 6" long	20	25	35
Fire Truck, No. 9700, 3-1/2" long	20	25	35
Fire Truck, No. 9706, plastic, 4" long	20	25	35
Metro Van, No. 9618, 5" long	20	25	35
Open Stake Truck, No. 9602, 7" long	40	50	60
Pickup Truck, No. 9601, 7" long	40	50	60
Pickup Truck, No. 9605, 6" long	25	30	40
Pickup Truck, plastic, No. 9703, 4" long	20	25	35
Roadster, No. 9701, 3-1/2" long	20	25	35
Sedan, Fastback, No. 9600, 7" long	40	50	60
Sedan, Fastback, No. 9600, taxi version, 7" long	45	55	65

A 1946 ad for Lansing Slik-Toys from Toys and Novelty.

	C6	C8	C10
Sedan, four-door, No. 9604, 6" long	20	25	35
Sedan, No. 9702, plastic, 4" long	20	25	35
Stake Truck, No. 9616, 6" long	20	25	35
Stakebody Truck, No. 9500, 11" long	40	50	60
Station Wagon, No. 9704, plastic, 4" long	20	25	35
Tank Truck, No. 9603, 7" long	40	50	60
Tank Truck, No. 9607, 6" long	20	25	35
Tank Truck, No. 9705, plastic, 4" long	20	25	35
Tractor/Trailer rig (flatbed trailer), No. 9613, 8" long	25	35	50
Tractor/Trailer rig (grain trailer), No. 9611, 8" long	25	35	50
Tractor/Trailer rig (log trailer), 8" long	25	35	50
Tractor/Trailer rig (milk tanker), No. 9610, 8" long	30	40	55
Wrecker, No. 9617, 5" long	20	25	35

Pickup Truck, plastic, No. 9703, Lansing Slik-Toys, 4" long, $35

LINCOLN WHITE METAL WORKS

This company, located in Lincoln, Nebraska, was formed by Clayton E. Stevenson, the manufacturer of many high-quality slush-mold vehicles. Stevenson made toys out of his home for many years and, as a salesman for Western Diecasting Co., even sold molds to Kansas Toy & Novelty company, Tip Top Toy Co. and others. His specialty was the three-piece mold, there is even some speculation that he was the inventor of this complex mold.

Stevenson's was a remarkably long toy-making career, about fifteen years, through the Great Depression. An auto mechanic, Stevenson was born in 1896 and raised in Axtell, Kansas. He and his wife, Esther, moved to Lincoln in 1931 where they began selling toys in his name. His new business grew rapidly, and he made upwards of 800,000 toys in three months. As his business grew, he moved to a larger facility at 2204 Y Street and in 1935 the company address was listed as 3433 J Street.

Lincoln White Metal Works toys were sold across the United States at Woolworth, Kress, Kresge and Schwartz Paper Co. stores, some were even abroad.

After nine years of production, the factory was sold in 1940 due to shortages of lead and rubber and the rising costs of labor. It is not certain who aquired the remaing molds and inventory, although many indications point to Ralstoy.

A variety of toys were made, including airplanes, midget racers, larger speed sedans, small coupes, tri-motor plane models and miniature sawmills. Most range in size from three-to-seven-inches in length. Stevenson designed his molds using photographs from magazines as guides. The midget racer was based on a Miller special, and the sedan is a replica of the front-drive Cord. A Nash was the basis for Lincoln White Metal's coupe.

Lincoln White Metal toys had a few distinct characteristics—early toys had metal wheels and tin propellers with patterned bottom-pans; later toys had rubber wheels. These distinctions can assist collectors in identifying their toys.

The following list is incomplete because of the rarity of these cars.

Contributors: Fred Maxwell, 4722 N. 33 St., Arlington, VA 22207; Perry Eichor, 703 North Almond Dr., Simpsonville, SC 29681.

Brougham, Graham?, Lincoln White Metal, 3-1/2" long, $60

Bluebird, record car, driver, V-8 engine with intake ports, triangular fin with wing design, Lincoln White Metal, 4" long, $40

	C6	C8	C10
Bluebird, record car, driver, V-8 engine w/intake ports, triangular fin w/wing design, 4" long	20	30	40
Brougham, Graham?, vertical vee-grille, SM, four open windows, T, from three-piece mold, 3-1/2" long	30	45	60
Sedan, Pierce-Arrow Silver Arrow, vertical vee-grille, headlamps and front fenders faired, six open windows, divided windshield, plain pan, 3-1/2" long	20	30	40
Speed Car, A V-12 version of Bluebird w/triangular fin, Lincoln?, 4-5/8" long	20	30	40

LINDSTROM

The Lindstrom Tool & Toy Company made wind-ups of light pressed steel as well as tin. It was located in Bridgeport, Connecticut, and began making toy cars about 1913. It seems to have ceased production sometime in the 1940s.

	C6	C8	C10
Lumber Truck, No. 160, steerable front wheels, tin, w/driver, 10" long	125	187	250
Steam Roller, No. 181, mechanical, 12" long	50	75	100

M&L TOY CO. INC.

M&L was incorporated October 21, 1947. Located on Paterson Plank Road in Union City, New Jersey, M&L got its name from Morris and Louis (last name unknown), the father and son team owners. The company seems to have begun in 1946, lasting until at least 1948. It made vehicles, trains, jeweled swords, water guns, mechanical toys and plastic horns. Most of M&L's were sold unpainted with plastic wheels. Most of their toys were copies.

	C6	C8	C10
Racer, 2-3/4" long 10	15	20
Cabin Racer 12	18	25

MANOIL

Numbers and names are from a Manoil catalog.

	C6	C8	C10
70 Soup Kitchen, large number 7	11	15
70A Soup Kitchen, small number................... 9	13	18
71 Shell Carrier w/Soldier on Shell Box, has loop 12	18	24
71A Shell Carrier w/Soldier on Shell Box 8	12	17
72 Water Wagon, large number 11	16	22
73 Tractor, loop front 12	18	25
73A Tractor, plain front 12	18	25
74 Armored Car w/Anti-Tank Gun 20	30	41
75A Armored Car w/Siren, siren cast separately 25	38	50
75 Armored Car w/Anti-Aircraft Gun 27	41	55
75A Armored Car w/Siren, siren cast w/vehicle 34	51	68
95 Tank.. 11	16	22
96 Large Shell on Truck............................ 11	16	22
97 Pontoon on Wheels 17	26	35
98 Torpedo on Wheels 9	14	19
103 Gasoline Truck.................................. 11	16	22
104 Chemical Truck 11	16	23
105 Five Barrel Gun on Wheels 12	18	24
701 Sedan, futuristic................................ 50	75	100
700 Sedan, futuristic................................ 57	85	115
702 Coupe, futuristic................................ 67	100	135
703 Wrecker, futuristic 75	112	150
706 Rocket, futuristic bus-like vehicle, Pat. No. 95793 50	75	100
705 Sedan, futuristic, Pat. No. 95792 40	60	80
704 Roadster, futuristic, Pat. No. 95791 54	81	108

Manoil Post-War Vehicles

	C6	C8	C10
707 Sedan.. 31	46	62
708 Roadster, horizontal radiator................ 27	41	54
708A Roadster, vertical radiator 32	48	64
709 Fire Engine 16	24	33
710 Oil Tanker 13	20	27
711 Aerial Ladder 200	300	400
712 Pumper 200	300	400
713 Bus... 12	18	24
714 Towing Truck................................... 10	15	20
715 Commercial Truck 10	15	20
716 Sedan... 10	15	20
717 Hard Top convertible 25	38	50
718 Convertible 10	15	20
719 Sport Car 10	15	20
720 Ranch Wagon 10	15	20

Manoil Plastic Vehicles

	C6	C8	C10
P-7 Roadster 7	11	14
P-8 Sedan 7	11	14
P-9 Pick-Up 7	11	14
P-10 Towing Truck 7	11	14
P-11 Road Scraper 7	11	14
P-12 Tractor 7	11	14
P-13 Dump Cart....................................... 7	11	14

LOUIS MARX CO.

	C6	C8	C10
Air Force Truck, "Air Defense Group," ride'm toy, No. 3290, 32" 125	188	250
Air Force Truck, canvas top, 20" 105	158	210
Ambulance, "M.D. War Dept.," 1930s 650	975	1300
Ambulance, No. 8500, 1930s, 14" long 250	375	500
Ambulance, No. 8600, 1930s, 14" long 240	360	480
Army Corps of Engineers, canvas top, 20" long 87	130	175
Army Jeep w/Searchlight Trailer, steel....... 87	130	175
Army Staff Car, plastic friction, 9" 12	18	25

712 Pumper, Manoil, $400

711 Aerial Ladder, Manoil, $400

Coca-Cola Truck, Sprite decal, Marx, 20" long, $365

Ice Truck with Tongs and Ice, Marx, $470

	C6	C8	C10
Auto Transport, 1950s, w/two tin litho cars, 34" long	175	205	350
Candy Truck, "Fanny Farmer," plastic	100	150	200
Cannon Truck, "Big Shot," plastic, fires cap-loaded missile, 22" long	75	112	150
Car Carrier, "Auto Transwalk" No. T-50447B, 1930s truck w/three cars	200	300	400
Car Carrier, Big Boss, 42" long	90	135	180
Chief-Fire Dept. No. 1, "Friction Drive," c. 1948	75	112	150
Coal Truck, electric motor and lights, early	280	420	564
Coca-Cola Truck, Linemar, tin, friction, 3" long	50	75	100
Coca-Cola Truck, Sprite decal, stamped steel, late 1940s to early 1950s, 20" long	182	275	365
Cord Convertible, 11" long	250	375	500
Corvette Coupe, plastic, friction, 8"	30	45	60
Crane, Lumar Contractors	120	180	240
Dairy Truck, "Pure Milk," w/glass bottles, pressed steel, tin wheels, c. 1940	100	150	200
Delivery Truck, Pet Shop, 1950s, 10"	80	120	160
Dump Truck, "Sand & Gravel" 1940s, 10" long	60	90	120
Dump Truck, Lumar Contractors, No. 962	480	720	960

	C6	C8	C10
Dump Truck, No. 1084	30	45	60
Dump Truck, No. 695B, 17" long	120	180	240
Dump Truck, two-color, No. T751, c. 1930s	85	128	170
Easter Stake Truck, 1938, 10-1/2" long	190	275	380
Falcon w/plastic bubble top, black rubber tires	145	218	290
Fire Truck, friction, 25" long	225	338	450
Gang Buster Car, No. 7200, 1930s, 14" long	550	825	1100
Grader, Lumar Power	35	52	70
Hi-Way Express Truck	123	185	245
Hydraulic Dump	55	83	110
Ice Truck w/Tongs and Ice	235	352	470
Jaguar, "Fix-It," Jaguar, plastic, 12" long	65	98	130
Lumar Scoop-A-Dump	100	150	200
Milk Truck "Cloverdale Farms"	135	202	270
Mechanical Coupe, tin wind-up, 1933, 8" long	275	400	575
Merchants Transfer Truck, tin wind-up, 1929, 10" long	275	400	700

Hi-Way Express Truck, Marx, $245

Pickup Truck, Marx, 11" long, $200

Siren Fire Chief, Marx, c. 1930, 15" long, $660

	C6	C8	C10
Moving Truck, "American Truck Co.," No. 65, friction	65	98	130
Mystery Taxi, c. 1930s, press down to operate	80	120	165
Navy Jeep, No. 1078	65	98	130
Navy Jeep, w/Searchlight Trailer	100	150	200
No. 1016 Machinery Moving Truck	262	395	525
Nutty Mad Cars, friction, c. 1965, each, 4" long	135	205	270
Panel Wagon	40	60	80
Pepsi-Cola Truck, 1950s, 11" long	35	52	70
Pickup Truck, 11" long, electric lights	100	150	200
Power Grader No. 1759, black or white wheels, 17-1/2" long	40	60	80
Road Grader, Heavy-duty	48	72	95
Roadster, convertible, 1930s, nickel-plated tin, 11" long	200	300	400
Rocker Dump No. 1752, 17-1/2"	60	90	120
Searchlight Truck	150	225	300
Siren Fire Chief, c. 1930, "F.D. 1st. Batt.," 15" long	330	495	660
Siren Police Car, No. 8300, 1930s, 14" long	200	300	400
Sparkling Hot Rod Racer, 1950s plastic wind-up, 8" long	37	52	75
Sports Coupe, 1930s, 15" long	200	300	400
Stake Truck, "Dairy Stake Truck"	163	245	325

Siren Police Car, No. 8300, Marx, 1930s, 14" long, $400

Tricky Taxi, friction, Marx, 4-1/2", $100

	C6	C8	C10
Stake Truck, c. 1941, 15" long	83	125	165
Stake-type Truck, three-color, No. E-271, c. 1941	95	145	190
Steam Shovel, Lumar Contractors	132	198	265
Tractor, "Heavy Gauge Tractor," No. 926	100	150	200
Tractor, "High-Boy Climbing Tractor," No. 950, 10-1/2" long	75	112	150
Trailer and Convertible Sedan, Lonesome Pine, 1930s, 19" long	462	695	925
Tricky Taxi, friction, 4-1/2"	50	75	100
Truck and Trailer, "Electrically Lighted Truck and Trailer Set," No. T-5715, c. 1930s, 15"	150	225	300
Truck and Trailer, Lazy-Dazy Dairy Farm, 22" long	95	142	190
Truck Train, "Mammoth," No. T-50-12345, c. 1930s, truck w/five trailers	175	262	350
Truck, "American Railroad Express Agency Inc.," early 1930s, open cab, 7" long	120	180	240
Truck, "City Sanitation Dept. Help Keep Your City Clean," c. 1940, 12-3/4" long	115	172	230
Truck, "Deluxe Delivery"	75	112	150
Truck, "Gravel," 13" long	112	168	225
Truck, "Gravel," 9" long	68	102	135
Truck, "REA Express," No. 1021	220	330	440
Truck, Grocery, 1950s, 14-1/2"	62	93	125
Truck, Guided Missile, No. 4488	220	330	440
Truck, Sinclair Fuel, steel	175	263	350
U.S. Army Truck w/Searchlight Trailer, 1950s, 27" total length	130	195	260
U.S. Mail Truck, 14" long	125	188	250
U.S. Navy Jeep w/Searchlight Trailer, 1950s, 21" total length	125	188	250
USA 41573147 Army Truck, c. 1952, 13-3/4" long	100	150	200

U.S. Mail Truck, Marx, 14" long, $250

	C6	C8	C10
Willys Jeep and Trailer, c. 1940s................ 133		200	265
Willys Jeep, steel, c. 1938, hood opens,			
windshield folds down, 12" 90		135	180
Willys Jeepster, plastic, wind-up 75		112	150
Wrecker and Covertible, "Fix-All," set 125		188	250
Wrecker Truck No. T-16, c. 1930s 150		225	300
Wrecker Truck, 1920s, 10" long 100		150	200
Wrecker, "Cities Service," 4-1/2",			
Linemar 65		98	130

MATCHBOX

Matchbox Toys grew out of a company begun in 1947 by two Navy friends, Leslie Smith and Rodney Smith (no relation). Manufacturing toys was not even in the plan at the beginning. On June 19, 1947, the two partners combined portions of their first names, and the name Lesney was born. In 1948 Lesney Products made their first toy—a 4-1/2-inch Aveling Barford Road Roller. Encouraged by the brisk sales, they produced three other toys that year—a 4-1/2-inch Caterpillar Bulldozer, a 3-3/4-inch Caterpillar Tractor, and a 3-3/4-inch Cement Mixer. It was decided to package the toys in a matchbox-type box, and thereafter the toys would be known as "Matchbox."

These small vehicles quickly became very popular and all other Lesney toy lines were discontinued. These first small vehicles had metal wheels but these were quickly changed to plastic. These type of wheels are now known to collectors as "Regular" wheels, not to be confused with the "Superfast" wheels that were introduced in 1969. Value on these rare early Lesney toys today ranges up to $1,000.

It is not uncommon to find slight color and style variations for the same vehicle. These variations were often due to paint or part shortages and are highly sought after by collectors.

The "Models of Yesteryear" line was introduced in 1956. The king-size line, known as Major Packs, was first developed and marketed in 1957.

Matchbox toys were first marketed in the United States in 1958, and by the early 1960s had become a household standard. Today these small vehicles are rapidly gaining popularity and value among collectors. Listed in the following pages are all of the basic models and some important variations. The C10 prices are for **unboxed** Matchboxes.

Contributor: Reid Covey, Box 2D Highmarket Rd., Constableville, NY, 13325. Covey lives in the heart of snow country with his wife Melissa, and works at the Boonville Ethan Allen plant.

An avid collector, Covey boasts of a collection that includes more than 1,500 Hot Wheels, 200 Matchbox cars and a vast collection of Jeff Gordon items. His wife's collection of #97 Chad Little items complements Covey's items and her 300-plus salt-and-pepper shakers.

Covey would like to thank Mark McManus, former Matchbox consultant, for his previous years of pricing and input.

	C6	C8	C10
No. 1 Diesel Road Roller, 1953 15		21	44
No. 1 Aveling Barford Road Roller, 1964 17		26	39
No. 1 Mercedes Benz Lorry, 1968 6		11	18
No. 1 Mod Rod, 1971 8		12	20
No. 1 Dodge Challenger, 1976 4		6	8
No. 2 Dumper, 1953 22		37	45
No. 2 Muir-Hill Dumper, 1962 9		15	24
No. 2 Mercedes Trailer, 1968 5		7	12
No. 2 Hot Rod Jeep, 1971 5		7	12
No. 2 Hovercraft, 1976 5		7	12
No. 3 Cement Mixer, 1953 25		36	48
No. 3 Bedford Ton Tipper, 1961 6		12	17
No. 3 Mercedes Benz Ambulance, 1968 5		10	15
No. 3 Monteverdi Hai, 1973 5		8	12
No. 3 Porsche Turbo, 1978............................. 4		7	10
No. 4 Tractor, 1954 34		45	60
No. 4 Triumph Motorcycle and sidecar,			
1959 22		35	47
No. 4 Stake Truck, 1967 4		7	12
No. 4 Gruesome Twosome, 1971 3		6	10
No. 4 Pontiac Firebird, 1976 3		6	10
No. 4 '57 Chevy, 1981.................................... 3		5	8

Different versions of Matchbox boxes

No. 12 Land Rover, $35

	C6	C8	C10
No. 5 London Bus, 1954	23	35	45
No. 5 Lotus Europea Sports Car, 1969	10	20	28
No. 5 Seafire, 1976	3	7	10
No. 5 U.S. Mail Truck, 1981	4	6	10
No. 6 Quarry Truck, 1955	17	24	35
No. 6 Euclid 10 Wheel Quarry, 1964	20	30	40
No. 6 Ford Pickup, 1969	8	13	20
No. 6 Mercedes Tourer, 1974	5	8	12
No. 7 Horse Drawn Milk Cart, 1955	55	70	100
No. 7 Ford Anglia, 1961	14	24	34
No. 7 Ford Refuse Truck, 1967	7	10	15
No. 7 Hairy Hustler, 1971	5	8	12
No. 7 VW Golf, 1976	4	6	9
No. 8 Caterpillar Tractor, 1955	25	40	57

No. 9 Merryweather Marquis Fire Engine, $30

	C6	C8	C10
No. 8 Ford Mustang Fastback, 1966	9	13	19
No. 8 Wildcat Dragster, 1971	7	12	16
No. 8 De Tomaso Pantera, 1975	15	22	38
No. 9 Dennis Fire Engine, 1955	33	50	67
No. 9 Merryweather Marquis Fire Engine, 1959	16	23	30
No. 9 Boat and Trailer, 1967	6	9	11
No. 9 Javelin, 1972	5	9	11
No. 9 Ford Escort RS2000, 1978	3	5	7
No. 10 Mechanical Horse and Trailer, 1955	35	52	67
No. 10 Sugar Container Truck, 1961	27	40	55
No. 10 Pipe Truck, 1967	10	17	22
No. 10 Piston Popper, 1973	5	8	14
No. 10 Plymouth "Gran Fury" Police Car, 1980	3	4	5
No. 11 Petrol Tanker (Esso decal), 1955	22	35	48
No. 11 Petrol Tanker, green body, no number on bottom	140	200	350
No. 11 Jumbo Crane (Taylor), 1964	7	12	17
No. 11 Scaffolding Truck (Mercedes), 1969	5	9	14
No. 11 Flying Bug, 1972	5	8	13
No. 11 Car Transporter, 1977	5	8	10
No. 12 Land Rover, 1953	17	23	35
No. 12 Safari Land Rover, 1965	11	18	30
No. 12 Setra Coach, 1971	8	14	18
No. 12 Big Bull, 1975	5	8	11
No. 12 Citroen CX, 1981	5	7	12
No. 13 Bedford Wreck Truck, 1955	22	39	57
No. 13 Thames Wreck Truck (MB Garages), 1959	22	35	47
No. 13 Dodge Wreck Truck (BP Label), 1961, yellow cab, green body	18	23	30

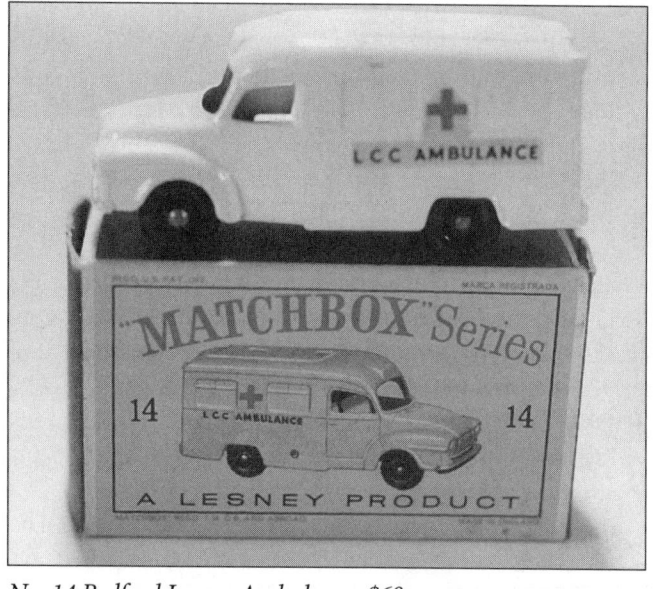

No. 14 Bedford Lomas Ambulance, $60

No. 19 MGA Sports Car, $69

No. 25 Bedford "Dunlop" Van, 1956

	C6	C8	C10
No. 13 Dodge Wreck Truck, green cab, yellow body (rare) 300	490	750
No. 13 Baja Buggy, 1971 8	10	15
No. 13 Snorkel Fire Engine, 1977 4	5	6
No. 14 Daimler Ambulance, 1955 17	25	41
No. 14 Bedford Lomas Ambulance 25	50	60
No. 14 Iso Grifo Sports Car, 1968 5	9	15
No. 14 Mini Ha Ha, 1975 6	9	15
No. 15 Prime Mover, 1955 27	38	52
No. 15 Dennis Refuse Truck, 1963 14	20	29
No. 15 Volkswagen 1500 Saloon, 1968 8	17	27
No. 15 Fork Lift Truck, 1972 5	7	11
No. 16 Low-Loading Trailer, 6 wheels, 1955 18	26	36
No. 16 Low-Loading Trailer, 8 wheels, 1955 18	26	36
No. 16 Scammel Mountaineer Dump w/plow, 1961 15	24	35
No. 16 Case Tractor Bulldozer, 1969 6	11	18
No. 16 Badger, 1974 5	8	13
No. 16 Pontiac, 1981 2	4	6
No. 17 Bedford Removal Van, 1955 33	60	90
No. 17 Austin Taxi, 1960 27	44	61
No. 17 8 Wheel Tipper "Hoveringham," 1964 7	13	18
No. 17 Horse Box "Ergomatic Cab," 1969 5	8	13
No. 17 Londoner, 1973 8	12	18
No. 18 Caterpillar Bulldozer, 1955 20	24	46
No. 18 Field Car, 1969 7	10	15
No. 18 Field Car, green plastic tires (rare) .. 55	133	165
No. 18 Hondarora, 1975 5	9	14
No. 19 MG Midget Sports Car, 1955 26	37	48
No. 19 MGA Sports Car, 1959 27	44	69
No. 19 Aston-Martin F.I., 1961 21	33	46
No. 19 Lotus Racing Car, 1965 6	8	11

	C6	C8	C10
No. 19 Road Dragster, 1971 4	6	10
No. 19 Cement Truck, 1976 5	7	9
No. 20 E.R.F. Lorry Truck, 1955 30	48	66
No. 20 Taxi Cab (Chevrolet Impala), 1965 15	25	34
No. 20 Lamborghini Marzel, 1969 9	13	16
No. 20 Police Patrol, 1975 4	6	10
No. 21 Long Distance Coach "London to Glasgow," 1955 24	39	54
No. 21 Commer Milk Truck, 1961 30	49	58
No. 21 Foden Concrete Truck, 1969 8	12	18
No. 21 Road Roller, 1973 6	8	14
No. 22 Vauxhall Cresta, 1955 35	45	54
No. 22 Pontiac "Grand Prix" Sports Coupe, 1964 10	14	18
No. 22 Freeman Inter City Commuter, 1970 6	9	14
No. 22 Blaze Buster, 1975 4	6	10
No. 23 Caravan Trailer, 1956 6	9	12
No. 23 House Trailer Caravan, 1967 16	28	40
No. 23 Volkswagen Camper, 1970 6	8	11
No. 23 Atlas, 1975 5	7	12
No. 24 Excavator, 1956 17	24	33
No. 24 Rolls Royce Silver Shadow, 1967 8	10	13
No. 24 Team "Matchbox," 1973 8	13	19
No. 24 Diesel Shunter, 1979 3	5	7
No. 25 Bedford "Dunlop" Van, 1956 30	48	64
No. 25 Volkswagen 1200 Sedan, 1958 38	56	70
No. 25 B.P. Tanker, 1960 19	29	42
No. 25 Ford Cortina G.T., 1968 6	8	10
No. 25 Mod Tractor, 1972 9	12	19
No. 25 Flat Car & Container, 1979 3	5	7
No. 26 Ready Mix Concrete Truck, 1956 18	26	36
No. 26 GMC Tipper Truck, 1968 7	10	12

No. 28 Bedford Compressor Truck, Matchbox, $48

	C6	C8	C10
No. 26 Big Banger, 1972	4	6	9
No. 26 Site Dumper, 1976	3	5	8
No. 27 Bedford Low-Loader, 1956	30	42	60
No. 27 Bedford Low-Loader, metal wheels (rare)	200	300	415
No. 27 Cadillac Sedan, 1960	38	55	77
No. 27 Mercedes Benz, 230SL, 1965	6	8	12
No. 27 Lamborghini Countach, 1974	5	7	10
No. 28 Bedford Compressor Truck, 1956	24	36	48
No. 28 Thames Compressor Truck, 1959	18	24	30
No. 28 Mack Ten Jaguar, 1964	33	49	66
No. 28 Mack Dump Truck, 1968	6	10	15
No. 28 Stoat, 1974	7	12	19
No. 28 Lincoln Continental, 1980	8	12	15
No. 29 Bedford Milk Delivery Van, 1956	18	27	36
No. 29 Austin A55 Cambridge, 1961	16	27	36
No. 29 Fire Pumper Truck, 1965	9	11	16
No. 29 Racing Mini, 1971	4	7	9
No. 29 Shovel Nose Tractor, 1976	5	8	12
No. 30 Ford Prefect w/towbar, 1956	30	42	55
No. 30 German Crane Truck, 1961	25	39	50
No. 30 Favin Crane, eight-wheel, 1965	11	16	22
No. 30 Beach Buggy, 1971	4	6	9
No. 30 Swamp Rat, 1977	4	6	8
No. 30 Articulated Truck, 1981	4	6	8
No. 31 Ford Customline Station Wagon, 1956	26	40	49
No. 31 Ford Fairlane Station Wagon, 1959	24	41	60
No. 31 Lincoln Continental, 1964	7	12	17
No. 31 Volks Dragon, 1971	5	7	10
No. 31 Caravan, 1977	4	6	8
No. 32 Jaguar XK 140 Coupe, 1956	30	41	54
No. 32 Leyland Tanker, 1968	16	24	34
No. 32 Excavator, 1981	10	18	24

	C6	C8	C10
No. 33 Ford Zodiac MKII, 1956	24	38	54
No. 33 Ford Zephyr 6 MKIII, 1963	19	27	38
No. 33 Lamborghini Muira P400, 1969	9	15	22
No. 33 Datsun 126X, 1973	5	8	12
No. 33 Police Motorcyclist, 1977	4	6	8
No. 34 Volkswagen Microvan "Matchbox" Express, 1956	30	44	60
No. 34 Volkswagen Camper, 1961	14	21	28
No. 34 Formula 1 Racing Car, 1971	7	11	14
No. 34 Vantastic, 1976	4	7	12
No. 34 Chevy Pro Stocker, 1981	2	4	6
No. 35 Marschall Horse Box, 1956	41	66	82
No. 35 Sno-Trac Tractor, 1961	13	20	29
No. 35 Merryweather Marquis Fire Engine, 1970	5	10	14
No. 35 Fandango, 1975	5	7	10
No. 36 Austin A50 w/towbar, 1956	18	30	40
No. 36 Lambretta and Sidecar, 1960	36	54	71
No. 36 Opel Diplomant, 1966	8	13	19
No. 36 Hot Rod Draguar, 1971	5	8	19
No. 36 Formula 5000, 1975	4	6	8
No. 36 Refuse Truck, 1981	3	5	8

No. 36 Lambretta and Sidecar, Matchbox, $71

No. 37 Coca-Cola Truck, Matchbox, $80

No. 38 Darrier Refuse Collectorm Matchbox, $38

No. 42 Bedford "Evening News" Van, Matchbox, $57

	C6	C8	C10
No. 37 Coca-Cola Truck, 1956	45	62	80
No. 37 Cattle Truck (Dodge), 1967	7	9	11
No. 37 Soopa Coopa, 1973	5	7	11
No. 37 Skip Truck, 1976	4	6	8
No. 38 Darrier Refuse Collector	20	29	38
No. 38 Vauxhall Estate, 1963	11	20	27
No. 38 Honda Motorcycle w/Trailer, 1968	11	16	22
No. 38 Stingeroo, 1973	6	8	11
No. 38 Armored Jeep, 1976	5	9	13
No. 38 Camper, 1981	3	5	7
No. 39 Ford Zodiac Convertible, 1956	28	41	56
No. 39 Pontiac Convertible, 1962	35	51	65
No. 39 Ford Tractor, 1967	6	10	16
No. 39 Clipper, 1973	6	8	12
No. 39 Rolls-Royce Silver Shadow MKII	4	6	8
No. 40 Bedford Seven-Ton Tipper, 1956	24	34	47
No. 40 Hay Trailer, 1967	4	8	12
No. 40 Leyland "Royal Tiger" Coach/Long Distance, 1961	11	18	26
No. 40 Guildsman, 1971	5	8	12
No. 40 Horse Box, 1977	4	6	8
No. 41 "D" Type Jaguar Racing Car, 1956	80	115	150
No. 41 Ford G.T. 40 (Sports Racer), 1965	14	21	30
No. 41 Siva Spyder, 1972	6	9	13
No. 41 Ambulance, 1978	4	6	8
No. 42 Bedford "Evening News" Van, 1956	30	42	57
No. 42 Studebaker Lark Wagonaire, 1965	12	19	27
No. 42 Iron Fairy Crane, 1969	7	11	18
No. 42 Iron Fairy Crane, (spoke wheels), 1970	30	42	54
No. 42 Tyre Fryer, 1972	4	8	12
No. 42 Container Truck, 1977	4	6	8
No. 43 Hillman Minx, 1957	30	46	54
No. 43 Aveling-Barford Shovel, 1962	11	19	27

	C6	C8	C10
No. 43 Pony Trailer, 1968	9	13	19
No. 43 Dragon Wheels, 1972	5	7	10
No. 43 Steam Loco, 1978	4	6	8
No. 44 Rolls-Royce Silver Cloud, 1957	19	26	37
No. 44 Refrigerator Truck, GMC, 1967	8	12	18
No. 44 Boss Mustang, 1972	3	5	8
No. 44 Passenger Coach, 1978	3	5	7
No. 45 Vauxhall Victor, 1957	14	24	33
No. 45 Ford Corsair w/green boat, 1959	11	15	20
No. 45 Ford Group Six, 1970	6	9	11
No. 45 BMW, 1976	5	8	11
No. 46 Morris Minor 1000, 1957	30	48	60
No. 46 Pickfords Removal Van, 1960	18	31	45
No. 46 Mercedes-Benz 300SE, 1968	6	11	16
No. 46 Stretcha Fetcha, 1972	5	9	15
No. 46 Ford Tractor, 1978	5	7	9
No. 47 Trojan "Brooke Bond" Van, 1957	38	55	70
No. 47 Neilson Ice Cream Van, 1963	30	46	60
No. 47 Daf Tipper Container Truck, 1968	8	12	16

No. 46 Morris Minor 1000, Matchbox, $60

No. 49 Army Half Track MKIII, Matchbox, $41

No. 55 Ford Police Car, Matchbox, $105

	C6	C8	C10
No. 47 Beach Hopper, 1973 5		7	10
No. 47 Pannier Loco, 1980 3		5	7
No. 48 Sports Boat & Trailer, 1957 28		39	53
No. 48 Dodge Dumper Truck, 1967 11		16	22
No. 48 Pi-Eyed Piper, 1973 4		6	10
No. 48 Sambron Jack Lift, 1977 4		6	8
No. 49 Army Half Track MKIII, 1958 19		30	41
No. 49 Mercedes Unimog Truck, 1967 11		18	24
No. 49 Chop Suey, 1973 5		7	10
No. 49 Chop Suey, chrome handle bar........ 30		45	70
No. 49 Crane Truck, 1976 3		5	8
No. 50 Commer Pickup Truck, 1958........... 22		34	45
No. 50 John Deere-Lanz Tractor, 1963........ 14		22	32
No. 50 Ford Kennel Truck, 1969.................. 10		15	20
No. 50 Articulated Truck, 1973...................... 6		11	16
No. 50 Harley Davidson Motorcycle, 1981 ... 2		3	5

	C6	C8	C10
No. 51 Albion Truck "Portland Cement," 1958 16		24	33
No. 51 Tipping Farm Trailer, 1963 8		10	12
No. 51 8 Wheel Tipper Truck, 1969 7		10	13
No. 51 Citroen SM, 1972 5		7	10
No. 51 Combine Harvester, 1979 4		6	8
No. 52 Maserati 4 CLT, 1958........................ 34		44	61
No. 52 BRM Racing Car, 1965....................... 9		13	18
No. 52 Dodge Charger MKIII, 1970.............. 4		8	11
No. 52 Police Launch, 1976 3		5	7
No. 53 Aston-Martin DB2/4, 1959 19		26	35
No. 53 Mercedes-Benz 220SE, 1968 16		24	34
No. 53 Ford Zodiac MKIV, 1968 10		13	18
No. 53 Tanzara, 1972...................................... 3		7	10
No. 53 C.J. 6 Jeep, 1977 4		6	8

No. 47 Trojan "Brooke Bond" Van, Matchbox, $70

No. 54 Army Saracen Personnel Carrier, Matchbox, $30

No. 56 Fiat 1500, Matchbox, $17

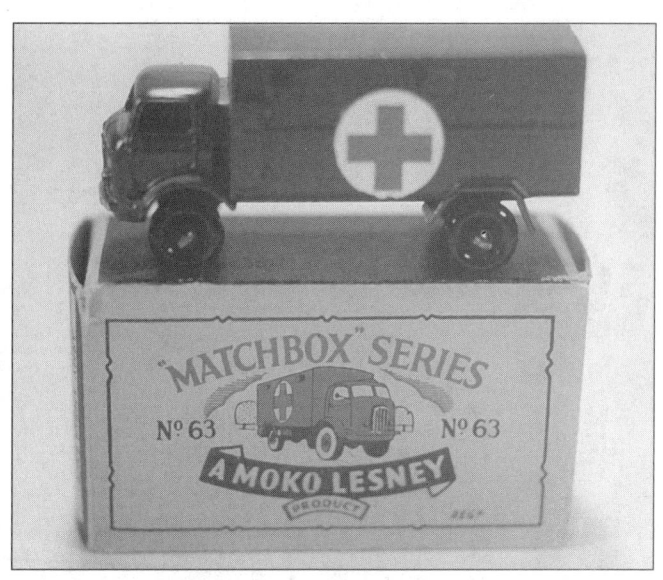

No. 63 Army Ambulance, Matchbox, $48

	C6	C8	C10
No. 54 Army Saracen Personnel Carrier, 1959 14		20	30
No. 54 Cadillac Ambulance, 1965 16		25	34
No. 54 Ford Capri, 1971.................................. 4		7	9
No. 54 Personnel Carrier, 1976..................... 5		7	10
No. 54 Mobile Home, 1981............................ 3		5	7
No. 55 D.U.K.W. (Army Amphibian), 1959 25		34	47
No. 55 Ford Police Car, 1963 52		77	105
No. 55 Mercury Parkland Police Car, 1969 13		20	26
No. 55 Mercury Police Car (Station Wagon), 1970 5		10	14
No. 55 Hell Raiser, 1975 4		6	8
No. 55 Ford Cortina, 1980 5		9	11

	C6	C8	C10
No. 56 London Trolley Bus, 1959 34		51	72
No. 56 Fiat 1500, 1965 9		12	17
No. 56 BMC 1800 Pininfarina, 1970 7		10	13
No. 56 Hi Trailer, 1975 4		6	9
No. 56 Mercedes 450SEL, 1980..................... 4		6	8
No. 57 Wolseley 1500, 1959 19		26	34
No. 57 Chevrolet Impala, 1966.................... 21		30	39
No. 57 Eccles Caravan, 1970 5		9	14
No. 57 Wild Life Truck, 1973....................... 7		9	11
No. 58 British European Airways Coach, 1959 16		24	32
No. 58 Drott Excavator, 1963..................... 25		28	51
No. 58 Daf Girder Truck, 1968 9		12	16
No. 58 Woosh-N-Push, 1972 6		10	13
No. 58 Faun Dumper, 1976 5		9	15
No. 59 Ford "Singer" Van, 1959 44		61	83

No. 59 Ford "Singer" Van, Matchbox, $83

No. 60 Morris Omnitruck J2 Pickup, Matchbox, $35

No. 68 Army Austin MKII Radio Truck, Matchbox, $22

	C6	C8	C10
No. 59 Ford Fairlane Fire Car, 1964	27	42	68
No. 59 Fire Chief Car, 1966...........................	73	99	137
No. 59 Planet Scout, 1975	13	18	27
No. 59 Porsche 928, 1981	5	7	9
No. 60 Morris Omnitruck J2 Pickup...........	17	26	35
No. 60 Truck w/Site Office, 1967	8	11	15
No. 60 Lotus Super Seven, 1971	6	9	12
No. 60 Holden Pickup, 1977	8	11	15
No. 61 Military Scout Car (Ferret), 1959	16	23	32
No. 61 Alvis Stalwart, 1967	20	30	44
No. 61 Blue Shark, 1971.................................	4	6	10
No. 61 Wreck Truck, 1978.............................	3	5	7
No. 62 General Army Lorry, 1959	17	22	28
No. 62 TV Service Van, 1964	30	50	65

No. 64 Scammel Army Wreck Truck, Matchbox, $38

No. 73 RAF 10 Ton Pressure Refueler Tanker, Matchbox, $45

No. 69 Commer 30 Cwt. Van "Nestle's," Matchbox, $49

	C6	C8	C10
No. 62 Mercury Cougar, 1969	8	10	14
No. 62 Rat Rod Dragster, 1971	4	7	11
No. 62 Renault 17 TL, 1974	5	7	10
No. 62 Chevrolet Corvette, 1980	2	4	6
No. 63 Army Ambulance, 1959	24	37	48
No. 63 Airport Fire Fighting Crash Tender, 1964	16	23	32
No. 63 Dodge Crane Truck, 1968	10	14	20
No. 63 Freeway Gas Tanker, 1973	9	14	19
No. 64 Scammell Army Wreck Truck, 1959	17	30	38
No. 64 MG 1100, 1966	8	12	16
No. 64 Slingshot Dragster, 1971	5	9	15
No. 64 Fire Chief Car, 1976...........................	3	5	8
No. 64 Caterpillar Tractor, 1981	3	5	7
No. 65 Jaguar 3.4 Litre Saloon, 1959	11	16	19
No. 65 Claas Combine Harvester, 1968	8	11	15

	C6	C8	C10
No. 65 Saab Sonnet, 1973 5		8	10
No. 65 Airport Coach, 1977 6		9	14
No. 66 Citroen DS19, 1959 18		22	30
No. 66 Harley Davidson Motorcycle and Sidecar, 1963 41		63	80
No. 66 Greyhound Bus, 1967 22		28	37
No. 66 Mazda RX500, 1972 5		8	10
No. 66 Ford Transit, 1977 5		9	16
No. 67 "Saladin" Armored Car, 1959 20		30	39
No. 67 Volkswagen 1600 T.L., 1968 7		10	12
No. 67 Hot Rocker, 1973 4		6	9
No. 67 Datsun 260Z, 1978 4		6	8
No. 68 Army Austin MKII Radio Truck, 1959 12		17	22
No. 68 Mercedes Coach, 1965 19		27	36
No. 68 Porsche 910, 1970 7		10	12
No. 68 Cosmobile, 1975 16		28	40
No. 69 Chevrolet Van, 1980 12		18	26
No. 69 Commer 30 Cwt. Van "Nestle's," 1959 27		38	49
No. 69 Hatra Tractor Shovel, 1965 13		17	24
No. 69 Rolls-Royce Silver Shadow, 1970 10		19	26
No. 69 Turbo Fury, 1973 6		8	12
No. 69 Wells Fargo security, 1978 5		9	14
No. 70 Ford Thames Estate Car, 1959 20		28	36
No. 70 Atkinson Grit-Spreading Truck, 1965 7		11	16
No. 70 Dodge Dragster, 1971 7		11	16
No. 70 S.P. Gun, 1977 3		6	10
No. 70 Ferrari, 1981 2		3	6
No. 71 Army Water Truck, 1959 15		24	33
No. 71 Jeep Pickup Truck, 1964 15		24	36
No. 71 Ford Heavy Wreck Truck, 1968 8		15	21
No. 71 Ford Heavy Wreck Truck, amber windows, light and white bumper 55		83	110
No. 71 Jumbo Jet, 1973 3		5	8
No. 71 Cattle Truck, 1976 4		6	8
No. 72 Fordson Tractor (Power Major), 1959 22		32	45
No. 72 Standard Jeep, 1967 8		13	18
No. 72 Hovercraft SRN6, 1972 7		11	19
No. 72 Bomag Road Roller, 1980 4		6	8
No. 73 RAF 10-Ton Pressure Refueler Tanker, 1959 22		32	45
No. 73 Ferrari Racing Car, 1963 15		27	36
No. 73 Mercury Station Wagon (Commuter), 1969 8		13	17
No. 73 Weasel, 1974 2		4	7
No. 73 Model "A" Ford, 1981 2		4	6
No. 74 Mobile Refreshment Bar (Canteen), 1959 24		37	51
No. 74 Daimler Bus, 1966 13		19	27
No. 74 Toe Joe, 1972 4		6	10

	C6	C8	C10
No. 74 Cougar Villager, 1978 4		6	8
No. 75 Ford Thunderbird, 1959 48		71	96
No. 75 Ferrari Berlinetta, 1965 11		16	22
No. 75 Alfa Carabo, 1971 6		9	13
No. 75 Helicopter, 1976 4		6	9

Models of Yesteryear

With year of introduction

	C6	C8	C10
Y-1 1925 Allchin 7 N.H.P. Traction Engine, 1955 38		55	77
Y-1 1911 Model "T" Ford, 1964 14		22	30
Y-1 1936 Jaguar SS100, 1977 14		22	32
Y-2 1911 "B" Type London Bus, 1955 49		75	104
Y-2 1911 Renault two-seater, 1963 11		19	31
Y-2 Prince Henry Vauxhall, 1970 10		16	22
Y-3 1907 London "E" Class Tramcar, 1955 55		87	115
Y-3 1910 Benz Limousine, 1965 13		22	29
Y-3 1934 Riley MPH, 1972 11		15	21
Y-4 Sentinel Steam Wagon, 1955 53		73	99

Y-6 1913 Cadillac, Models of Yesteryear, Matchbox, $58

Y-5 1927 Talbot Van, Models of Yesteryear, Matchbox, $39

Y-12 1912 Model "T" Ford, Models of Yesteryear, Matchbox, $25

Y-14 1931 Stutz Bearcat, Matchbox, $20

	C6	C8	C10
Y-4 1905 Shank-Mason Horse-Drawn Fire Engine, 1960	104	148	203
Y-4 1909 Opel Coupe, 1966	15	27	44
Y-4 1930 Dusenberg Model J, 1976	15	25	35
Y-5 1929 LeMans Bentley, 1955	48	64	87
Y-5 1929 Supercharged 4-1/2 Litre Bentley, 1960	16	25	33
Y-5 1907 Peugeot, 1968	17	29	36
Y-5 1927 Talbot Van, 1978	20	28	39
Y-6 1916 A.E.C. "Y" type Lorry Truck, 1955	32	43	55
Y-6 1926 Type "35" Bugatti, 1961	22	33	44
Y-6 1913 Cadillac, 1967	27	42	58
Y-6 1920 Rolls-Royce Fire Engine, 1978	18	29	44
Y-7 1914 4-Ton Leyland, 1955	37	54	74
Y-7 1913 Mercer Raceabout Sportcar, 1961	28	44	57
Y-7 1912 Rolls-Royce, 1967	25	39	48
Y-8 1926 Morris Cowley "Bullnose," 1955	66	93	121
Y-8 1914 Sunbeam Motorcycle w/sidecar, 1962	23	37	53
Y-8 1914 Stutz Roadster, 1968	12	19	33
Y-8 1945 MC TC Sports Car, 1978	7	11	15
Y-9 1924 Fowler "Big Lion" Showman Engine, 1955	58	78	100
Y-9 1912 Simplex, 1967	25	41	56
Y-10 1908 Grand Prix Mercedes Racing Car, 1957	40	60	80
Y-10 1928 Mercedes-Benz 36/220, 1963	24	38	50
Y-10 1906 Rolls-Royce Silver Cloud, 1968	12	17	25
Y-11 1920 Aveling and Porter Steam Roller, 1957	39	57	76
Y-11 1912 Packard Landaulet, 1963	19	29	37
Y-11 1938 Lagonda Drophead Coupe, 1972	15	22	32
Y-12 1899 Horse-Bus (London), 1957	81	113	150

	C6	C8	C10
Y-12 1909 Thomas Flyabout, 1967	22	33	44
Y-12 1912 Model "T" Ford, 1979	12	19	25
Y-13 1862 American 4-4-0 Locomotive	33	49	66
Y-13 1911 Daimler, 1965	17	26	32
Y-13 1918 Crossley Truck, 1972	20	33	42
Y-14 1903 "Duke of Connaught" Locomotive, 1957	85	122	159
Y-14 1911 Maxwell Roadster, 1965	25	38	54
Y-14 1931 Stutz Bearcat, 1972	10	15	20
Y-15 1907 Rolls-Royce "Silver Ghost," 1960	20	32	44
Y-15 1930 Packard Victoria, 1969	10	16	22
Y-16 1904 Spyker Veteran Auto, 1961	29	43	58
Y-16 1928 Mercedes SS, 1971	10	16	22
Y-17 1938 Hispano Suiza, 1972	11	17	26
Y-18 1937 Cord 812, 1979	8	10	12
Y-19 1935 Auburn 851, 1980	5	8	11
Y-20 1938 Mercedes 540K, 1981	6	8	10
Y-21 1929 Woody Wagon, 1981	7	11	17

METAL CAST PRODUCTS COMPANY

Metal Cast Products was formed when S. Sachs was reorganized in 1925. The producer of slush molds for small business and hobbyists, Metal Cast's molds were used by so many different franchises it is difficult to identify the actual makers unless they engraved their names on the model, Fred Green Toys was one such maker. Metal Cast objective was to offer any or all support materials and services to slush-mold entrepreneurs.

A variety of wheels may be found on Metal Cast vehicles—metal disk wheels, metal spoke wheels, wood wheels with rubber tires, and white or black rubber wheels.

Contributor: Fred Maxwell, 4722 No. 33 St., Arlington, VA 22207

	C6	C8	C10
Fire Engine, No. 61, hook and ladder truck, crew of two, 4-1/2"	6	10	14
Fire Engine, similar to No. 65 w/o watercannon, 3-3/8"	6	10	14
Open Rack Truck, No. 01-04, COE cab, stake semi-trailer, 6"	8	12	16
Packard Convertible, No. 41, two-door, top down, 5-1/4"	10	15	20

Packard Convertible, No. 41, two-door, top down, Metal Cast Products, 5-1/4", $20

A page from a 1949 Metal Cast Products catalog.

	C6	C8	C10
Streamline Sedan, No. 60, DeSoto? Airflow, eight open windows, spoke wheels, rubber tires, 4"	10	15	20
Tank Truck, No. 01-03, same COE cab, semi-fuel tanker, "FRED GREEN TOYS," "Made in U.S.A.," 6"	4	6	8
War Tank, No. 08, early heavy Sherman Tank, 4"	33	49	66

METAL MASTERS

	C6	C8	C10
Bus, c. 1938, 7-1/4" long	23	35	47
Fire Truck version of pickup, c. 1938, 7" long	30	40	50

Coca-Cola Truck, pressed steel, Metalcraft, 11" long, $1,000

	C6	C8	C10
Fire Truck, c. 1940, ladders, wind-up motors, 10" long	50	65	80
Fire Truck, c. 1940, removable ladders, 10" long	30	45	60
Jeep, c. 1947, 5-1/2" long	9	13	18
Pickup Truck, c. 1938, 7" long	20	30	40
Roadster, c. 1938, 7" long	20	30	40
Station Wagon, c. 1940, 8-1/2"	40	55	65
Station Wagon, c. 1940, ambulance version, 8-1/2" long	75	112	150
Station Wagon, c. 1940, wind-up motor, 8-1/2"	45	55	70
Tow Truck version of pickup, c. 1938, 7" long	30	40	50
Tow Truck, c. 1940, "ABC Towing Service," 10" long	40	50	65
Tow Truck, c. 1940, wind-up motor, 10" long	19	28	38

METALCRAFT

Metalcraft of St. Louis, Missouri, began producing its pressed steel trucks in 1928. About a million were sold, most as advertising premium toys. In 1937, the Depression caused Metalcraft to close.

Coca-Cola Truck, stamped metal, Metalcraft, 12" long, $1,000

CW Coffee Dump Truck, Metalcraft, 11" long, $700

Meadow Gold Butter Truck, battery-operated lights, 1935, 13" long, $550

	C6	C8	C10
Acme Stores Truck, heart-shaped grille, 1935, 13" long	200	300	500
Bunte Candies Truck, 1933, 12-1/2" long	250	350	600
Clover Farm Stores Truck	300	500	700
Coca-Cola Truck, ten bottles in racks, "Every Bottle Sterilized," c. 1928, 11" long	450	700	1100
Coca-Cola Truck, pressed steel, rubber tires, early 1930s, ten bottles in rack, "Every Bottle Sterilized," 11" long	450	700	1000
Coca-Cola Truck, ten bottles, late 1930s, long nose, stamped metal, 12" long	450	675	1000

Plee-Zing Quality Products, Metalcraft, 11" long, $550

Pure Oil Truck, Metalcraft, 1935, $1,100

	C6	C8	C10
CW Coffee Dump Truck, 1928, 11" long	300	500	700
CW Coffee Wrecker, 11-1/2"	300	500	700
Decker's Iowana Truck, heart-shaped grille, 1935	350	500	800
Delivery Truck Van, steel, 1928, 11" long	250	350	500
Drink Smile Truck, w/electric lights and spare tire, 1933, 12-1/2" long	300	450	650
Goodrich Silvertone Tires wrecker, w/three spare tires, 1931, 12" long	240	450	650
Heinz Truck, spare tire, elect lights, "Baked Beans," "Bottled Vinegar," "Rice Flakes," c. 1932, 12" long	350	500	850
Kroger Food Express Truck, open w/food packages, 10" long	300	500	700
Kroger Food Express Truck, closed, 1929, 11" long	325	450	650
Krug Bakery Truck, 1933, 12-1/2" long	450	600	900
Machinery Hauling Truck, 14-1/2" long	500	750	1000
Meadow Gold Butter Truck, battery-operated lights, 1935, 13" long	275	400	550
Plee-Zing Quality Products, 1928, 11" long	275	400	550
Pure Oil Truck, 1935	500	700	1100
Sand-Gravel Dump Truck, No. 150, 1928, 11" long	300	400	550
Shell Motor Oil Truck, eight barrels, 1933, 12" long	450	650	1000
St. Louis Truck, c. 1930, 11" long	250	400	550
Steam Shovel, No. 4, 8"	100	150	250
Sunshine Biscuits Truck, 1933, 12-1/2"	250	450	800
Towing & Repairs, 1928, 11-1/2"	250	375	550
Toy Town Grocery	250	375	550
Waldorf Lager, white	400	600	900
Waldorf Logan Truck, heart-shaped grille, 1935	300	500	700
Werks Tag Soap Truck	300	400	500
Weston's Biscuits	300	400	500
White King Delivery Truck, 12" long	300	400	500

MIDGETOY

Midgetoy was one of dozens of small toy companies that sprang up in the aftermath of World War II. The parent company, A & E Tool & Gage Co. of Rockford, Illinois, had been involved in the precision gage business since 1943. Owners Alvin and Earl Herdklotz, afraid they might need to lay off workers as things slowed down after the war, started a side-line of producing die-cast toys for the dime-store market. The Herdklotz brothers began with a Chevy truck set in 1946, consisting of a truck cab and chassis that could be transformed into a stake, oil, or dump truck by switching parts. Within a few years they would be employing more people to make toys than gages. In its heyday the company was second only to Tootsietoy in the production of die-cast toy vehicles.

In 1981, the Herdklotz brothers sold the company to a group of investors. The new owners unfortunately let the business languish, introducing no new toy designs and only producing such existing toy models as the popular train sets. The new Midgetoy company also packaged items produced by other toy companies. After one of the investors suffered a fatal heart attack, the Herdklotz brothers bought back the company in 1985 to shut it down.

The 1981 purchase of Midgetoy had not included the company's back inventory, which the Herdklotz brothers have been releasing to the public in recent years. The result is a plentiful supply of later, plastic-wheeled versions of its toys in excellent condition—a boon to collectors.

Midgetoys are simple, stylized vehicles, sturdily built—so much so that the Herdklotz brothers had people stand on them at trade shows to demonstrate their durability. The axle arrangement was patented by Midgetoy in 1957. The hidden wheels gave the toys their distinctive look until the 1970s, when the company turned to producing smaller toys akin to Tootsietoy's Jam-Pac vehicles because of the rising costs of metal.

In the listings below, dates refer to the year of first release of the model. Some toys were then produced for years or even decades. Later versions tend to be worth sixty to seventy percent of the first version. The abbreviations "brt" and "bpt" refer to tires made of black rubber and black plastic, respectively.

Contributor: Mark Rich, P.O. Box 971, Stevens Point, WI 54481-0971.

Midgetoy Pee-Wee Series (1969), 2" mini vehicles

	C6	C8	C10
American LaFrance Fire Truck	1	2	3
MG Sports Roadster	1	2	3
Jeep, race cars, sports cars and hot rods	—	1	2

Midgetoy Junior Series, 2 1/2" to 3 1/2" vehicles

	C6	C8	C10
American LaFrance Pumper, closed cab, 3-1/2", brt, early 1950s	10	15	20
American LaFrance Pumper, open cab, 2-3/4", brt, late 1950s	6	9	13
Army Amphibious "Battle Bug," 1949?	5	9	14
Army Howitzer, bpt	2	5	7
Army Howitzer, brt, 1949?	4	8	12
Army Jeep, brt, 1950	4	7	10
Buck Rogers Spaceship, bpt	8	13	22
Buck Rogers Spaceship, no front window, three black rubber tires, 1947	30	45	60
Buck Rogers Spaceship, punched front window, two black rubber tires and rear peg, 1947	20	32	45
Cadillac Convertible, brt, 1949	8	12	17
Corvette Convertible, brt, late 1950s	5	8	10
Ford Hot Rod, 2-1/2", br	5	8	10
Ford V-8 Hot Rod, bpt	5	9	12
Ford V-8 Hot Rod, brt, 1948	8	14	22
Ford Wrecker Truck, brt, late 1950s	10	15	20
Futuristic Rear-Engine Dream Car, no rear window, brt, 1948	12	25	35
Futuristic Rear-Engine Dream Car, rear window outlined, bpt	8	12	17
Greyhound Bus, brt, 1955	6	10	15
Interchangeable Truck Set Chevy cab w/Stake, Oil Tanker and Dump options, 1946	12	25	35
Interchangeable Truck Set	12	25	45
MG Sports Roadster, brt, 1958	6	9	13
Open Cockpit Indy Curtis Craft Race Car, brt, 1950	8	14	22
Sunbeam Racer, bpt	5	8	12
Sunbeam Racer, brt, 1950	8	14	22
Volkswagen Beetle, bpt, 1960	6	9	12

Midgetoy New Junior Series (1970), 2-1/2" to 3" vehicles

	C6	C8	C10
'68 Corvette L88 Stingray, 1971	2	3	4
Cadillac Ambulance, 1971	3	4	5
Ford 1971 Pickup Truck	2	3	4
Ford Mark IV, 1971	1	2	3
Ford Mustang	1	2	3

American La France Pumper Truck, Midgetoy Jumbo series, $30

Scenicruiser Bus, Midgetoy Jumbo series, $30

	C6	C8	C10
Ford Ranchero Pickup	2	3	4
Ford Torino Fire Chief Car, 1971	1	2	3
Ford Torino Police Car, 1971	1	2	3
Ford Torino, 1971	1	2	3
Ford Wrecker Truck, 1971	2	3	5
Jaguar XKE, 1971	2	4	6

Midgetoy King-Size Series, 4" vehicles

	C6	C8	C10
American La France Pumper, brt, early 1950s	11	18	24
Army Half-Track, brt, late 1950s	8	15	20
Army Personnel Carrier, brt, late 1950s	8	15	20
Army Tank, brt, late 1940s or early 1950s	8	15	20
Cadillac Four-Door Sedan, brt, late 1950s	10	15	20
Cadillac Four-Door Sedan, military, brt	8	13	18
Cadillac Two-Door Coupe, brt, early 1950s	11	18	24
Chrysler-style Convertible Roadster, brt	10	16	22
Ford Pickup Truck, brt, early 1950s	13	20	26
Ford Pickup Truck, brt, late 1950s	10	16	22
Oil Tanker Truck, brt, late 1950s	12	18	24
Oil Tanker Truck, military, brt	10	15	20
Van-style Streamlined Ambulance, Red-Cross, brt, late 1950s	8	12	16
Van-style Streamlined Station Wagon, brt, late 1950s	8	12	16

Midgetoy Jumbo Series, 6" vehicles

	C6	C8	C10
American La France Pumper Truck, brt	16	24	30
Cadillac Four-Door Convertible, brt	13	19	25
Mobile Artillery, brt, 1957	13	19	25
Oil Tanker, "Midgetoy Oil Co."	13	19	25
Oil Tanker, brt, 1957	13	19	25
Scenicruiser Bus, brt, late 1950s	16	24	30
Scenicruiser Bus, late version, "Midgetoy Bus Line"	14	20	28
Utility Truck	15	22	28

Midgetoy Chevrolet Tractor-Trailer Series, 8" vehicles

	C6	C8	C10
Auto Transporter w/loading ramp, 1962	12	20	27

1946 Chevrolet Truck, Midgetoy set, $20

	C6	C8	C10
Hook and Ladder Aerial Fire Truck, 1963	12	20	27
Kenworth Sleeper Cab, 1980	2	4	8
Oil Tanker Trailer, 1962	12	20	27
Oil Tanker, "Midgetoy Oil Co."	16	23	30
Shipping Van Trailer, 1962	12	20	27
Shipping Van, "Midgetoy Van Lines, Inc."	16	23	30

Midgetoy Sets

	C6	C8	C10
Dixie Chargers, three-car set, 1981	4	7	10
1860 Western Train,	6	12	25
1860 Western Train, "Train That Won the West," bpt	8	14	20
1920 Passenger Train	6	12	25
1920 Passenger Train, bpt	8	14	20
1940 Diesel Train, late version, "Amtrak", bpt	8	14	20
1940 Diesel Train	6	12	25
1946 Chevrolet Truck	6	12	20
1950 Freight Train	6	12	25
1950 Freight Train, bpt	8	14	20

NEFF-MOON TOY COMPANY

Located in Sandusky, Ohio, Neff-Moon was owned by William Moon and Charles Neff. Production of their pressed-steel toys began in 1923. The firm was one of the many toy companies to close during the Depression.

	C6	C8	C10
Groceries Van	300	450	600
Taxi, 12" long	350	525	700
Tow Truck, c. 1925, 16" long	200	300	400

NONPAREIL

	C6	C8	C10
Ambulance	30	45	60
Dry Goods	30	45	60
Police Patrol	30	45	60
Toyville Express	30	45	60

NYLINT

The Nylint Tool and Manufacturing Company was

formed in 1937 by Bernard C. Klint and David Nyberg in Rockford, Illinois, and toy production began in the spring of 1946. Since 1951, the firm has concentrated on the production of steel reproductions of earth-moving equipment and over-the-road trucks.

	C6	C8	C10
Airport Courtesy Van, No. 6900, "Holiday Inn," 12" long	275	332	550
Amazing Car, 1946-49, No. 600, windup, 13-3/4" long	100	150	200
Ambulance, No. 6700, 12" long	100	150	200
American Oil Emergency Truck, No. 6000, 11-1/4" long	100	150	200
Army Ambulance, No. 7300, 12" long	60	90	120
Bronco, No. 8200, 12-1/2" long	75	112	150
Bulldozer, No. 4200, 14" long	65	98	130
Camper on Pickup, No. 4400, 13-1/2" long	70	105	140
Construction Four-Wheel Platform Dump, No. 4600, 15-3/4" long	88	132	175
Countdown Rocket Launcher, 1959-61, No. 3500, 21" long	125	188	250
Custom Camper on above w/boat, No. 5400, 23-1/2" long	120	180	240
Custom Camper on above, No. 5300, 12-1/2" long	75	112	150
Deliverall, 1948-51, No. 1000, windup, 10" long	300	450	600
Dump Truck w/Cement Mixer, No. 5000, 20-1/2" long	125	188	250
Dump Truck, No. 5100, 13-1/2"	75	112	150
Electronic Cannon, 1956, No. 2400, has no radar antenna	100	150	200
Electronic Cannon, 1956, No. 2400, w/radar antenna, 22-1/2" long	88	132	175
Elgin Street Sweeper, 1950-52, No. 1100, windup, 8-1/4" long	250	375	500

	C6	C8	C10
Elgin Street Sweeper, 1956-57, No. 2300, battery-operated version, closed cab	120	180	240
Ford Econoline Van, No. 5800, 12" long	72	105	145
Ford Pickup & U-Haul Box Trailer, No. 4100	110	165	220
Ford Platform Tilt Truck, No. 3900, 15-3/4" long	125	188	250
Ford Rapid Delivery, No. 3600, 18-1/4" long	163	245	325
Ford Sales & Service, No. 3800, 13-5/8" long	140	210	280
Ford Speedway Truck w/Racer, No. 4000, 24-3/4" long	122	185	245
Ford U-Haul Rental Fleet, No. 4300, three pieces	175	263	350
Fun on Farm Econoline Truck, No. 7100, twenty-nine pieces, 11-1/4" long	87	130	175
Grader-Loader, 1959-61, No. 3000, 23-3/4" long	92	138	185
Guided Missile Carrier, first version (1958), No. 2800, nose cone of missile doesn't fire, 15-1/2" long	150	225	300
Guided Missile Carrier, later (through 1960), No. 2800, cone of missile fires	75	112	150
Happy Acres Truck w/horses, No. 4700, 14" long	65	98	130
Horse Van, No. 6300, 23-1/2"	78	117	155
Jack Hammer, 1958-60, No. 2900, 19-1/2" long, w/box	150	225	300
Jalopy, No. 6800, 9-5/8" long	30	45	60
Kennel Truck w/dogs, No. 6200, 11-1/2" long	88	132	175
Lift Truck (fork lift), 1947-49, No. 700, windup	75	112	150
Michigan Shovel, 1955-65, No. 2200, 31-1/2" long	78	117	155
Missile Launcher, 1957-60, No. 2600, 31-1/2" long	125	188	250
Mobile Home, Semi type, No. 6600, 30" long, 1964	125	188	250

Guided Missile Carrier, later (through 1960), No. 2800, cone of missile fires, Nylint, $150

Payloader, 1951-54, No. 1600, red, Nylint, 18" long, $150

Ranch Truck, No. 4500, Nylint, 14" long, $150

	C6	C8	C10
No. 3400 Highway Emergency Unit, 1959-63, 18-5/8" long	72	108	145
No. 8300 Texaco Service van, 12" long	150	225	300
Payloader Tractor-Shovel, 1959-61, No. 3100, 17-5/8" long	100	150	200
Payloader, 1951-54, No. 1600, red, 18" long	75	112	150
Payloader, 1955, No. 1600, tan	125	188	250
Payloader, 1956-57, No. 1600, light green	100	150	200
Payloader, 1958, No. 1600, dark green	100	150	200
Payloader, 1958, No. 1600, yellow	120	180	240
Pepsi Truck, No. 5500, 16-1/2"	125	188	250
Pickup Truck (Econoline), No. 5200, 11-1/4" long	80	120	160
Pony Farm Van, No. 8000, seven-piece set, 11-1/4" long	135	198	270
Power & Light Lineman Truck, 1959-61, No. 3200, 35-3/4" long	150	225	300
Power & Light Posthole Digger, 1959-61, No. 3300, 35-3/4" long	150	225	300
Pumpmobile, 1950-52, No. 1200, windup, 8-5/8" long	125	188	250
Ranch Truck, No. 4500, 14" long	75	112	150

	C6	C8	C10
Road Grader, 1951, No. 1400, small wheels, 19-1/4" long	65	98	130
Road Grader, 1952-58, No. 1400, larger wheels	70	105	140
Road Grader, No. 7900, 15" long	62	93	125
Scootcycle, 1948-50, No. 800, windup, 7-1/4" long	200	300	400
Speed Swing, 1955-58, No. 2000, 19" long	100	150	200
Street Sprinkler Truck, No. 3700, 18" long	140	210	280
Suburban Fire Pumper, No. 8100, 12-1/2" long	100	150	200
Telescoping Crane, 1957-60, No. 2500, 27" long	128	188	250
Tournadozer, 1956-59, No. 2100, 20" long	110	165	220
Tournahauler, 1953-56, No. 1700, 30-1/4" long	70	105	140
Tournahopper, 1951-56, No. 1500, 22-1/2" long	175	263	350
Tournarocker, 1951-52, No. 1300, open tractor w/driver, 18" long	62	93	125
Tournarocker, 1953-57, No. 1300, closed cab, no driver, 18" long	105	158	210
Tournatractor, 1954-55, No. 1900, 14-3/4" long	150	225	300
Traveloader, 1953-55, No. 1800, 30" long	113	170	225
U-Haul Cube Van, No. 8400, 1965, 22" long	87	130	175
U-Haul Trailer, No. 4800, 8" long	50	75	100
U-Haul Trailer, No. 4900, 9" long	50	75	100
U-Haul Truck & Trailer, No. 8410, 1974, 22" long	75	112	150
U-Haul Truck, Chevy, No. 8411	75	112	150
Uranium Hauler, 1958-59, No. 2700, 22-1/2" long	125	188	250

Tournarocker, 1951-52, No. 1300, open tractor with driver, Nylint, 18" long, $125

Traveloader, 1953-55, No. 1800, Nylint, 30" long, $225

Pedal Cars

	C6	C8	C10
'35 Pontiac Slantback Sedan, Perfect Rubber Co., 3-3/4" long	35	52	70
Auburn streamliner, Steelcraft	3000	5500	8000
Buick, Steelcraft late 1920s, 36" long	4000	7000	12,000
Cadillac, c. 1915, Toledo Metal Wheel Co., lithographed dashboard	500	750	1000
Cadillac, early, 40-1/2"	800	1200	1600
Car, c. 1905, chain driver, wooden spoke wheels	1250	1875	2500
Chrysler Airflow, 1937	1400	2500	3200
Chrysler Airflow, Steelcraft	1500	2500	4000
Coupe, Boycraft, 1925	2000	3500	6000
Coupe, open, 1920s or early 1930s, Gendron, 36" long	1200	1800	2400
DeSoto, 1939	1250	1875	2500
Dump Truck, American National "Big Boy"	6000	10,000	22,000
Essex, 1927	1100	1650	2200
Fire Truck, Mack, Steel-Craft	2500	4000	7000
Ford, "1896," tubular frame w/wire wheels, sheet metal seat w/wooden back rest and steering lever, plate under seat has diagram of motor, 9" long	1000	1500	2000
Ford, 1937, painted steel	750	1125	1500

	C6	C8	C10
Garton "Hot Rod"	410	615	825
Hook and Ladder, "AMF," late 1970s	200	300	400
Hudson, wood and steel, folding windshield, tilt-up steering wheel	400	600	800
Jewett open coupe, Steelcraft, 55" long	2500	5000	7500
Kidillac, c. 1950s	800	1400	2000
Lincoln 1921, Toledo	2500	5000	7500
Lincoln Zephyr, Steelcraft 1939	1700	2600	4000
Lincoln, 1937	1500	2400	3500
Lincoln, Gendron	1500	2500	4000
Mercer Raceabout, 1920	2000	3000	4000
Murray "Champion," 1955	500	800	1100
Murray "Earth Mover"	600	950	1300
Nash Sideway, 1920s, 34" long	1000	1500	2000
Packard Dual Cowl Phaeton, American National, 6' long	3000	4500	6000
Packard Roadster, 1920s, American National, 45" long	3000	5500	8000
Packard, early, wire wheels	300	450	600
Race car, "Pioneer," metal and wood	700	1050	1400
Skippy, Gendron, 1940	1200	2200	3500
Terraplane, 1934	1500	2250	3000
Winner, c. 1906	1000	1500	2000

Pyro

Pyro began in 1939 in Pyro Park, Union City, New Jersey. The owner was William Lester. At its height, the company had 400 employees.

	C6	C8	C10
Race Car, 4" long	17	26	35
Range Patrol Truck	10	15	20
Road Roller	12	18	25
"U.S. Army" Truck	5	8	10
"U.S.M.C." Truck	10	15	20
"U.S. Navy" Truck	10	15	20
Car, cast iron, 9" long	235	352	470

Rainbow

Contributor: Dave Leopard, 2507 Feather Run Trail, West Columbia, SC 29169-4915

	C6	C8	C10
'35 Oldsmobile Coupe, 3-3/4"	35	55	70
'35 Oldsmobile 4-door Sedan, 3-1/4" long	35	55	75
RA03 '35 Oldsmobile 4-door Sedan, 5" long	50	75	100
RT01 '35 Studebaker (?) stake side pickup, 5-1/4" long	45	65	85
RR01 Open Racer, tapered tail, 4" long	25	38	50

Ralston Toy & Novelty Company

Ralston Toy & Novelty Co., also known as Ralstoy, was formed in July of 1939, by Dr. Felix Despecher, former Mayor of Ralston, Nebraska, A.M. Erickson, and Henry C. Nestor. These three men acquired the molds of Best Toy Co. of Manhattan,

Top: An early Cadillac pedal car valued at from $800-1,600. Bottom: A close-up view of the grille.

Kansas and the surviving molds of Kansas Toy Co. Included in the acquisition was the temporary services of John M. Best, his molder Conrad Morsch and about 140 molds from these pioneering slush mold companies. Located in a building formerly occupied by the American Legion, they continued a low-cost toy line that had been familiar to collectors since Kansas Toy was founded in 1923.

With the death of founder Dr. Despecherin in 1940, the young company was forced into reorganization. Lawyer Paul Massey took over control but was forced to give up the use of pot metal item due to the need for lead during World War II. To survive, Ralstoy turned to making wooden toys, including a replica of an Army Jeep, selling almost two million through dime stores such as Woolworth and Kresge. Other wooden toys included an Army tank and a Navy PT boat.

After World War II, Ralstoy turned to die-cast toys and novelties. As the business expanded it moved to 5707 So. 77th St., where it is today producing a well-known line of promotional trucks under Art Massey.

Ralstoy did label a few of its toys. The bottom pans, introduced by Best Toy, provided a surface to emboss with "Ralstoy" and "Made in USA." Unlike other slush-mold toys, wheels are not a good clue.

Contributor: Fred Maxwell. 4722 N. 33 St., Arlington, VA 22207

	C6	C8	C10
Army Jeep, wooden, WWII issue	20	30	40
Army Tank, "107," "US Army," wood grooved 3/4" track-laying wheels, two gunturret, larger version of No. 74 above, also version w/black rubber wheels, 3-1/8"	13	20	26

Army tank, "74," "US Army," two-gun turret, Ralston Toy & Novelty, 2-1/4".

Sedan, large, "2R," die-cast, Cadillac?, "Ralstoy," "Made in USA," Ralston Toy & Novelty, 5-5/8", $75

Army Tank, wooden, "USA W356," "Ralstoy" on bottom, Ralston Toy & Novelty, WWII issue, $60

	C6	C8	C10
Army tank, "74," "US Army," two-gun turret, entirely different tank than Kansas Toy No. 74, 2-1/4"	13	20	26
Army Tank, wooden, "USA W356," "Ralstoy" on bottom, WWII issue	30	45	60
Ford Tractor, 1948, w/trailer, overall 9" long	30	45	60
Gun Truck, Large, "US Army Anti-Aircraft Unit," three axle carrier, AA gun, searchlight and crew of three, 5-5/8"	28	42	56
Mayflower Moving Van	20	30	40
Railway ? Gun, "108," version of No. 23 muzzle-loading cannon on wheeled platformw/hook and loop connectors, perhaps addition to No. 3600 toy train, 3-1/4"	12	18	25
Sedan, large, "2R," die-cast, Cadillac?, "Ralstoy," "Made in USA," four open vent windows, divided open windshield, three open rear windows, long fenders, rear-wheel skirts, bumper guard, black rubber wheels, early postwar issue?, 5-5/8"	37	56	75
Tanker Truck, "No. 102," "Ralstoy" International? sleeper cab, 3-3/8", two open windows, vertical grille w/"Gasoline" semi-trailer, "No. 102," four tanks, storage compartments, 6-3/4"	30	45	60
Transporter, Large, "Ralstoy" cab unit in RAV4 above, steel semi-trailer w/No. 74 tank, No. 34 muzzle-loading cannon and No. 32 aircraft, olive drab color, not known if Ralstoy issued them as a set (some stamped No. 108, some No. 101), 9"	40	60	80

RENWAL

The Renwal Manufacturing Company, founded in 1939 by either Irving Rosenblum or Irving Lawner (accounts vary), began by manufacturing a glass knife, later to be replaced by a plastic knife. It was this plastic knife that lead to the production of plastic toys in 1945.

Chein purchased Renwal's tooling when Renwal went out of business in the 1970s, Chein, in turn sold them to Revell.

	C6	C8	C10
Cadillac Hardtop Convertible, 5-1/2"	40	60	80
Cement Truck, 1940s, 6-1/2"	50	75	100

	C6	C8	C10
Fire Ladder Truck, plastic	40	60	80
Gasoline Truck No. 49, plastic	32	48	65
Hardtop Convertible, 1940s, 6-1/2"	22	33	45
Pickup Truck, die-cast, black rubber tires, 7" long	12	18	25
Racer No. 173, w/driver, 9-1/2"	85	128	170

Cement Truck, Renwal, 1940s, 6-1/2", $100

A page from a 1955 Renwal catalog.

'35 Chrysler two-door Airflow Sedan, 5-1/8" long, $100

'36 Plymouth four-door Trunkback Sedan, 4-7/8" long, $150

'35 DeSoto four-door Airflow Sedan, 5" long, $100

Gasoline Truck No. 49, plastic, Renwal, $65

	C6	C8	C10
Speed King Racer, 6-1/2" long	32	48	65
TV Truck No. 260, w/camera, mike, working spotlight, 18" long	75	112	150
Visible Auto Chassis	225	338	450

RUBBER VEHICLES
(UNKNOWN MANUFACTURERS)

Contributor: Dave Leopard, 2507 Feather Run Trail, West Columbia, SC 29169-4915

	C6	C8	C10
'35 DeSoto four-door Airflow Sedan, 5" long	50	75	100
'35 Chrysler two-door Airflow Sedan, 5-1/8" long	50	75	100
'36 Plymouth four-door Trunkback Sedan, 4-7/8" long	75	115	150
'37 Plymouth four-door Trunkback Sedan, 4-7/8" long	75	115	150
'46 Nash, two-door Fastback Sedan, hollow, molded tires, 4" long	12	18	25

'37 Plymouth four-door Trunkback Sedan, 4-7/8" long, $150. Photo from Rubber Toy Vehicles *by Dave Leopard.*

Open Racer, left side header pipes, solid rubber, 3-1/2" long, $50. Photo from Rubber Toy Vehicles *by Dave Leopard.*

	C6	C8	C10
Open Racer, left side header pipes, solid rubber, 3-1/2" long	20	35	50
Open Racer, V-8, solid, large tires on wood hubs, 4" long	25	40	60

SAVOYE PEWTER TOY COMPANY

Savoye Pewter Toy Co., manufacturer of slush-mold toys was incorporated August 1930. In 1931, Savoye Pewter Toy Co. was listed in a directory at 69 Paterson Plank Road in North Bergen, New Jersey, with nine employees.

Savoye vehicle toys are often identified by their somewhat coarse appearance, heavy slush mold body, and white rubber tires on oversized red wooden hubs that are smooth on the outside surface. These red hubs and rubber tires are consistent with industry styles of the early 1930s, although the style of some vehicles dates back to an earlier era.

Nearby Tommy Toy produced some Savoye-like vehicles, it is possible that Savoye sold its molds to Tommy Toy.

Contributor: Fred Maxwell, 4722 N. 33 St., Arlington, VA 22207

	C6	C8	C10
Bus, Cross-Country, partial upper deck, twelve open windows, rearmount spare, 3-3/8"	20	30	40
Bus, Heavy 5th Ave. Sight-Seeing, open overhanging upper deck, twelve open windows, gilt or silver trim, 4-3/4"	62	93	125

Tank Car Set, tow cab, 3-1/4" two tank cars 3-1/2", marked "Oil" "Cap. 80000" (RR type), Savoye, 10-1/4", $80. Photo from Rubber Toy Vehicles *by Dave Leopard.*

Tractor, Caterpillar? tractor with stack, Savoye, 2-3/4" long, $20

	C6	C8	C10
Coupe, similar to above, slanted louvers, fantasy grille and large black rubber wheels, 3-3/8" long	14	21	28
Coupe, two open windows, silver vertical grille, (Graham like), vertical louvers, 3-3/8" long	20	30	40
Fire Truck, driver and steersman w/high style gilt helmets, bell on hood, two glued ladders, oversized wheel wells w/oversized tires, 4-1/4" long	30	50	70
Roadster, driver, open rumble seat, silver vertical grille, (reminiscent of Tootsietoy Graham), vertical louvers, 3-1/2" long	20	35	50
Tank Car Set, tow cab, 3-1/4" two tank cars 3-1/2"; marked "Oil" "Cap. 80000" (RR type), not known whether Savoye sold these as a set; no known Savoye train, either, 10-1/4"	40	60	80
Tractor, Caterpillar? tractor w/stack, 2-3/4" long	10	15	20
Truck, Heavy "Beer Truck," six wood barrels set in cast depressions, 4-3/8" long	40	60	80

Left to Right: '35 Ford two-door slantback sedan, Seiberling, 5" long, $65; '35 Ford two-door slantback sedan, Seiberling, 4" long, $55

	C6	C8	C10
Truck, stake body, 4-1/2" long	12	18	24
Van, "Milk Grade A," two open windows, sidemounts, 3-1/4" long	20	30	40
Van, "Police Patrol," policeman on rear step, six open windows, gilt trim, sidemounts, 4" long	30	50	75

SCHIEBLE TOY AND NOVELTY

Schieble, located in Dayton, Ohio, was formed when William Schieble bought out his partner D.P. Clark in 1909. Clark then formed the Dayton Friction Works, where he continued to use Schieble's patents as well as the Hillclimber name, and protracted lawsuits followed.

	C6	C8	C10
Racer, team, c. 1910, steel windup, 12" long	450	675	900
Roadster, spare tire on back, 18-1/4" long	362	543	725
Sedan, 17" long	305	458	610
Touring Car, c. 1909, 14" long	300	450	600

SEIBERLING RUBBER

	C6	C8	C10
'35 Ford two-door slantback sedan, 5" long	32	48	65
'35 Ford two-door slantback sedan, 4" long	27	41	55

SMITH-MILLER TOYS

Smith Miller trucks entered an already competitive market in 1945. These cast-metal and aluminum trucks, produced in Santa Monica, California, should have failed—who would've thought that a new toy vehicle company could compete with such toy giants as Buddy "L," Structo, Marx and Hubley. Despite the stiff competition, Smith-Miller Toys stayed on the market for a full ten years outclassing virtually all toy trucks.

Their first trucks had two different classes, expensive replicas or smaller, no-name trucks that looked like half-breed Fords. During their last year they changed their profile from Mack Trucks to Auto-Car diesels with opening doors and working steering wheels.

Smith-Miller is once again in operation using original and new parts.

	C6	C8	C10
Aerial Ladder Semi, No. 410, six-wheel tractor and four-wheel trailer, "SMFD," 36" long	415	622	830
Arden Milk Truck, No. 204-A, twelve milk cans, four cases, four wheels, 14" long	300	450	600
"B" Mack Jr. Fire Truck, warning light, battery-operated, four wheels	495	742	990
"B" Mack Orange Dump, ten wheels	400	600	800
"B" Mack P.I.E., eighteen wheels	500	750	1000

Coca-Cola Truck, No. 206-C, sixteen Coca-Cola cases, Smith-Miller, 14" long, $1,400

GMC Bank of America, No. 404-B, Smith-Miller, $360

"B" Mack Orange Dump, ten wheels, Smith-Miller, $800

	C6	C8	C10
Bekins Van, No. 406, six-wheel tractor and four-wheel trailer, 29" long	338	528	675
Bekins Vanliner, No. 208-B, fourteen wheels, 22-1/2" long	650	1050	1600
Blue Diamond, ten-wheel dump truck, No. 408, 18-1/2" long	1225	1840	2450
Chevy Bekins Van, fourteen wheels, plain tires, hubcaps, 1945-46	200	300	400
Chevy Coca-Cola, four wheels, plain tires, early, 1945-46	450	675	900
Chevy Flatbed Tractor-Trailer, fourteen wheels, unpainted wood trailer, plain tires, hub caps, early, 1945	280	420	560
Chevy Milk Truck, four wheels, plain tires, hub caps, early, 1945-46	200	300	400
Coca-Cola Truck, No. 206-C, sixteen Coca-Cola cases, four wheels, 14" long	600	1000	1400
Coca-Cola Truck, twenty-four plastic bottles in six cases, four wheels, 1954-55	262	393	525
Dump Truck, No. 402, 11-1/2"	185	278	370

	C6	C8	C10
Ford Bekins Van, fourteen-wheeler, plain tires, hub, possibly earliest Smith-Miller,1944	200	300	400
Ford Coca-Cola, four wheels, wood soda cases, early, 1944	300	450	600
GMC "Drive-O" Steerable Dump, six wheels, cable w/hand control, 1946	212	318	425
GMC "Furniture Mart" Pickup, four wheels	155	232	310
GMC Bank of America, No. 404-B, lock and key, four wheels	180	270	360
GMC Be Mac fourteen wheel T-Trailer, 1949	185	278	370
GMC Coca-Cola, No. 306-C, four wheels, 16 Coke cases	275	362	550
GMC Heinz Grocery Truck	200	300	400
GMC Hi-Way Freighter Tractor-Trailer, No. 310-H, fourteen wheels	150	225	310
GMC Kraft Foods, No. 304-K, four wheels	425	638	850
GMC Lumber Tractor-Trailer, No. 406-L, fourteen wheels, eight timbers	212	318	425
GMC Lyon Van Tractor-Trailer, No. 308-V, fourteen wheels	275	410	550

GMC Lyon Van Tractor-Trailer, No. 407-V, ten wheels, Smith-Miller, $400

GMC Mobilgas Tanker, No. 409-G, Smith-Miller, $500

	C6	C8	C10
GMC Lyon Van Tractor-Trailer, No. 407-V, ten wheels	200	300	400
GMC Machinery Hauler, No. 408-H, thirteen wheels	212	318	425
GMC Machinery Hauler, ten wheels	388	582	775
GMC Marshall Field & Company Tractor-Trailer, ten-wheel T-Trailer	500	750	1000
GMC Material Truck, No. 402-M, four barrels, two timbers	210	315	420
GMC Materials Truck, No. 302-M, four barrels, three timbers	200	300	400
GMC Mobilgas Tanker, No. 409-G, fourteen wheels, two hoses	250	375	500
GMC Pacific Inter-Mountain Express (P.I.E.), No. 412-P, fourteen wheels	300	450	600
GMC P.I.E. Tractor-Trailer, No. 312-P	250	375	500
GMC Peoples First National Bank and Trust Company armored Truck, lock and key, 1951	262	393	525
GMC Rack Truck, No. 303-R, six wheels	140	210	280

GMC P.I.E. Tractor-Trailer, No. 312-P, Smith -Miller, $500

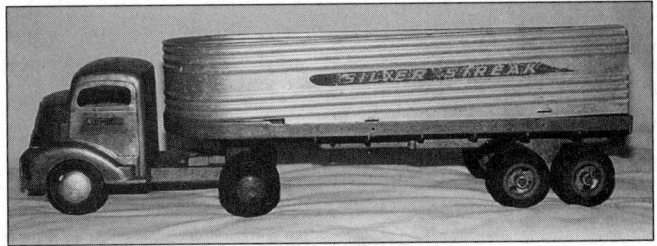

GMC Silver Streak Express Tractor-Trailer, No. 311-E, Smith-Miller, $485

	C6	C8	C10
GMC Rack Truck, No. 403-R, six wheels	175	262	350
GMC Redwood Logger Tractor-Trailer, No. 307-L, three logs	225	338	450
GMC Rexall Drug, four wheels	350	525	700
GMC Searchlight Truck, "Hollywood Film Ad" w/trailer, 1953	600	1000	1400
GMC Silver Streak Express Tractor-Trailer, No. 311-E, fourteen wheels	243	365	485
GMC Silver Streak Tractor-Trailer, No. 411-E, fourteen wheels	219	328	438
GMC Super Cargo Tractor-Trailer, No. 309-S, fourteen wheels, ten barrels	250	375	500
GMC Transcontinental Tractor-Trailer, No. 410-F, 14 wheels	165	255	370
GMC Triton Oil, No. 305-T, three drums	175	263	350
GMC Triton Oil, No. 405-T, six wheels, three drums	175	262	350
GMC U.S. Treasury Truck, armored truck, w/lock and key, 1952	250	375	500
GMC Wrecker, No. 301-W, four-wheeler	175	262	350
GMC Wrecker, No. 401-W, six wheels	85	128	170
Heinz Grocery Truck, No. 203-H, six wheels, 14" long	317	475	635
"L" Mack "Sibley's" Van, six wheels, rare	450	675	900
"L" Mack Aerial Ladder, "SMFD," eight wheels	390	585	780
"L" Mack Army Materials Truck, three barrels, two boards, one large crate, one small crate, ten wheels	383	575	765
"L" Mack Army Personnel Carrier, ten wheels	312	468	625
"L" Mack Bekins Van, all white, ten wheels	800	1350	1950
"L" Mack Blue Diamond Dump, ten wheels	788	1180	1575

MIC Tow Truck, "Official Tow Car," Smith-Miller, $1,600

"L" Mack Merchandise Van, Smith-Miller, $750

	C6	C8	C10
"L" Mack International Paper Co., 10 wheels	1000	1500	2000
"L" Mack Lyon Van, six wheels	1000	1500	2080
"L" Mack Material Truck, two barrels, six timbers, six wheels	500	750	1000
"L" Mack Merchandise Van and Trailer, twelve wheels	1050	1550	2200
"L" Mack Merchandise Van, six wheels	375	562	750
"L" Mack Mobil Tandem Tanker, twelve wheels	1000	1500	2000
"L" Mack Orange Hydraulic Dump, ten wheels	900	1400	1900
"L" Mack Orange Material Truck, three barrels, two boards, one large crate, one small, ten wheels	500	750	1000
"L" Mack P.I.E., fourteen wheels	600	900	1260
"L" Mack Tandem Timber, eighteen or twenty-four timbers, six wheels	600	950	1300
"L" Mack Telephone Truck, six wheels	700	1150	1500
"L" Mack West Coast Transport, six wheels	900	1400	1900
Lumber Trailer, No. 404T, 17"	500	750	1000
Lumber Truck, No. 201-L, 60 boards, six wheels, 14" long	500	800	1140
Lumber Truck, No. 404, 19"	300	450	600

Material Truck, No. 202-M, Smith-Miller, 14" long, $900

	C6	C8	C10
Material Truck, No. 202-M, three barrels, three cases, eighteen boards, four wheels, 14" long	450	675	900
MIC "Fruehauf Road Star" Tractor-Trailer, fourteen wheels	500	800	1200
MIC "Teamsters" Hydraulic Dump, ten wheels	650	1000	1500
MIC "Teamsters" Tractor-Trailer, fourteen wheels	462	695	925
MIC Aerial Ladder	383	575	765
MIC House Trailer	400	600	800
MIC Hydraulic Dump, ten wheels	700	1100	1675
MIC Lift-O-Matic, two barrels, six wheels	500	800	1100
MIC Lincoln Capri (for MIC House Trailer), steerable	450	675	900
MIC Lumber Truck, nine timbers, six wheels	338	505	675
MIC P.I.E. Tractor-Trailer, fourteen wheels	500	800	1100
MIC Tow Truck, "Official Tow Car," six wheels	700	1100	1600
MIC Tow Truck, unpainted, polished, six wheels	475	700	950
MIC Tractor-Trailer, polished aluminum trailer, no decals, fourteen wheels	450	675	900
Oil Truck, No. 205-P, four drums, six wheels, 14" long	225	338	450
Red Ball, No. 212-R, fourteen wheels, 23-1/2" long	150	250	375
Scoop Dump, No. 403, 14" long	275	410	550
Searchlight Truck, No. 407, "Hollywood Filmad," 18-1/2" long	450	675	900
Silver Streak, No. 405, six-wheel tractor, 28" long	110	165	220
Stake Truck, No. 210-S, fourteen wheels, 23-1/2" long	250	375	500
Sunkist Special, No. 211-L, fourteen wheels, 23-1/2" long	150	250	375
Timber Giant, No. 209-T, three logs, fourteen wheels, 23-1/2" long	250	375	500
Tow Truck, No. 401, 15" long	125	188	250

STEELCRAFT

	C6	C8	C10
Army Truck, Mack, c. 1930, 22" long	420	630	840
Coca-Cola Truck, 12 bottles on side	400	600	800
Dump Truck, Airflow	2000	3500	5000
Dump Truck, Mack	600	900	1300
Fire Truck, 25" long	600	900	1300
GMC Scissor Dump Truck	500	800	1250
Inter City Bus, 24" long	330	495	660
Little Jim Fire Truck	500	850	1200

	C6	C8	C10
Model T Roadster Pedal Car, license number "65-287," 50" long	325	488	650
Railway Express Truck, 26" long	1100	1600	2600
Road Roller, 16" long	200	300	400
Shell Motor Oil Truck, w/oil barrels	300	450	600
Steam Shovel	143	215	285
Steam Shovel, "Marion"	143	215	285
Tank Truck, sheet metal, 25-1/2" long	600	1000	1430
Truck, "City Delivery"	270	405	540
Truck, "City Milk Co.," 18" long	283	425	575
Truck, "Cream Crest"	450	675	900
Truck, "Fro-Joy" Ice Cream, c. 1930s	350	525	700
Truck, "Sheffield Farms," 1930s, 21" long	600	900	1300
Truck, "U.S. Mail," c. 1928, 27-1/4" long	800	1300	1800

Truck, "Cream Crest," Steelcraft, $900

Truck, "Sheffield Farms," Steelcraft, 1930s, 21" long, $1,300

Truck, "U.S. Mail," Steelcraft, c. 1928, 27-1/4" long, $1,800

STRUCTO

Structo of Freeport, Illinois, was founded in 1908 by brothers Louis and Edward Strohacker, and C.C. Thompson. They initially manufactured Erector Construction Kits, and in 1919 they started making toy vehicles. In 1935, J.G. Cokey bought a majority of the business, and when he died in 1975, the toy patents and designs were taken over by the Ertl Company.

	C6	C8	C10
Aerial Fire Truck, c. 1950s	100	150	200
Army Ambulance No. 416, 17" long	175	263	350
Army Truck w/canvas top, 21" long	250	375	500
Army Van, pressed steel and canvas, No. 415, 17-1/2" long	170	255	340
Auto Transport Trailer, No. 706, w/cars, 1953-54,	90	138	180
Barrel Truck, No. 609, early 1950s	115	173	230
Barrel Truck, windup, No. 811, early to mid-1950s	65	98	130
Bearcat Racer, clockwork, 12-1/4" long	325	490	650
Camper w/cloth top, 12" long	25	38	50
Caterpillar Tractor w/trailer, heavy spring clockwork motor, steel treads, No. 46	225	338	450
Cattle Trailer, No. 708	75	112	150
Cement Mixer, c. 1950s, 20" long	112	168	225
Communications Center Truck, 21" long	70	105	140
Coupe, convertible, c. 1920s	550	850	1200
Delivery Truck, tin, electric lights	150	225	300
Dump Truck, early, Mack type	200	300	400
Fire Dept. Emergency Patrol Truck, red bubble light, 1950s, 12" long	90	135	180
Garbage Truck, "Sanitation Dept."	112	168	225
Garbage Truck, 21" long	123	185	245
Gasoline Truck, No. 912, 1950s, 13" long	75	112	150
Gasoline Truck, windup, No. 866, early 1950s	130	195	260
Grain Trailer, No. 704, early and mid-1950s	100	150	200
Guided Missile Launcher, No. 906 w/plastic launcher, missiles of wood and vinyl, 13" long	70	105	140

Package Delivery, No. 603, Structo, early 1950s, $145

Police Patrol Truck, No. 426, Structo, 17" long, $1,100

	C6	C8	C10
Guided Missile Launching Truck, truck metal, missiles, etc., plastic, rubber tires 50	75	100
Hi-Lift Dump, windup, No. 844, early 1950s 110	165	220
Ladder Truck, 1950s 145	220	290
Machinery Hauler, 1940s 120	180	240
Machinery Truck, No. 607, early 1950s 170	255	340
Motor Express Stake Truck, No. 601, early 1950s 55	83	110
Moving Van, open cab, c. 1920, No. 427, 16" long 238	358	475
Overland Freight Trailer, No. 704, early 1950s 60	90	120
Package Delivery, No. 603, early 1950s 73	110	145
Packard Dump Truck, No. 405, c. 1930, 18" long 600	950	1400
Pickup Truck, 13" long 90	135	180
Pile Driver, 13" high 175	262	350
Police Patrol Truck, No. 426, 17" long 500	800	1100
Renault Tank, clockwork, green w/red turret 225	338	450
Roadster, 1920s, clockwork, 16" long 450	675	900

Machinery Hauler, Structo, 1940s, $240

Army Truck with canvas top, Structo, 21" long, $500

	C6	C8	C10
Sand Loader, c. 1928, 12" high 44	66	88
Searchlight Truck, metal, light and generator plastic, uses batteries, has rubber tires 132	198	265
Shovel Dump, No. 605, early 1950s 100	150	200

	C6	C8	C10
Stake Truck, lights work, 1930s, 21" long.. 212	318	425
Steam Shovel, 14" x 11" 200	300	400
Steam Shovel, 16" 57	87	115
Steam Shovel, 21" x 18" 50	75	100
Steel Cargo Trailer, No. 702, early to mid-1950s 187	280	375
Tank, No. 48, 11" long 225	338	450
Tank, olive drab w/orange turret, ten metal wheels, 12-1/2" 150	225	300
Tractor w/cast-iron driver, early, caterpillar type, 8-1/2" long 200	300	400
Transport Trailer, No. 700, early 1950s 90	135	180
Truck Assortment No. 317: Dump Truck, blue, Stake Truck, Lumber Truck, each 9" long, 3-1/2" wide, 3-1/2" tall, heavy gauge metal, rubber wheels, original box folds to form garage, 1920s, price per set . 75	112	150
Truck, "Structo Telephone Co.," c. 1948, 12" long 38	56	75
U.S. Mail Delivery Truck, No. 428, 17" long 187	280	375
Whippet Tank, heavy spring clockwork motor enameled green, red and black, may read "Patented 1920," 1929, No. 48, 12" 300	450	600
Wrecker Truck, windup, No. 822, early to mid-1950s 90	135	180
Wrecker, "Toyland Garage" 50	75	100

STURDITOY

	C6	C8	C10
Ambulance, open cab, c. 1929, 26" long... 2000	3500	5000

	C6	C8	C10
American Railway Express Truck, c. 1920s, 26" long	800	1300	1800
Armored truck, "Wells Fargo," c. 1927, 24" long	1000	1600	2700
Coal Dump Truck, 1920s, 25" long	1300	2100	2900

Pumper, Sturditoy, c. 1930, 26" long, $2,000

Truck, "Sturditoy Oil Company," Sturditoy, c. 1929, 27" long, $2,000

Traveling Store, Sturditoy, 26" long, $5,200

Coal Dump Truck, Sturditoy, 1920s, 25" long, $2,900

Wrecker, Sturditoy, 30" long, $2,750

	C6	C8	C10
Dump Truck, 1920s, 25" long	800	1300	1900
Dump Truck, 1920s, 26-1/2"	600	950	1300
Pumper, c. 1930, 26" long	800	1350	2000
Traveling Store, 26" long	2000	3500	5200
Truck, "Sturditoy Oil Company," c. 1929, 27" long	800	1350	2000
U.S. Mail Screenside Truck	800	1300	2000
Water Tower	850	1350	2150
Wrecker, 30" long	1000	1650	2750

SUN RUBBER

Sun Rubber of Barberton, Ohio, was founded in 1923and began making toys in 1924, automobiles were introduced in April 1935. The owner was Tom W. Smith, Jr.

All Sun Rubber Photos are from *Rubber Toy Vehicles* by Dave Leopard.

Contributor: Dave Leopard, 2507 Feather Run Trail, West Columbia, SC 29169-4915

	C6	C8	C10
'34 DeSoto Airflow, four-door sedan, No. 500, 4" long	20	30	50
'36 White Bus, streamlined, 1936, No. 520, 4-1/4" long	20	30	50
'40 Dodge, four-door sedan, No. 12001, 4-1/2" long	20	30	50
Ambulance, c. late 1930s, No. 12006, 3-3/4" long	20	30	50
Art Deco Housetrailer, No. 1025, 4-3/8" long	60	80	250

'34 DeSoto Airflow, four-door sedan, No. 500, Sun Rubber, 4" long, $50. Photo from Rubber Toy Vehicles by Dave Leopard.

*Town Car, Brewster-type limo, No. 1015, Sun Rubber, 5-3/8",
$95. Photo from* Rubber Toy Vehicles *by Dave Leopard.*

	C6	C8	C10
Coupe, external exhaust pipes, from 1936, No. 515, 4" long	20	30	50
Open Racer, boattail, "Super" racer, No. 12012, 6-3/4" long	30	45	65
Open Racer, full fenders on rear, 1936, No. 1000, 6-1/2" long	40	60	80
Open Racer, two drivers, 1936, No. 505, 4-3/8" long	20	30	50
Pickup Truck, stake sides, streamlined, No. 510, 4-1/2" long	25	35	55
Scout Car, four gunners, 1946, No. 12014, 6" long	45	65	100
Sedan, "Teardrop," c. 1936, No. 1010 (1936), 5-1/2" long	25	40	65
Station Wagon, Woody, mid-1930s, No. 12007, 3-3/4" long	20	30	50
Tank, revolving turret and gunner, 1946, No. 12015, 6" long	45	65	100
Town Car, Brewster-type limo, exposed driver, No. 1015, 5-3/8"	40	60	95
Tractor/Trailer, one piece, three axles, futuristic, No. 12013, 5-1/8" long	20	30	55
Truck, open "Master," futuristic, No. 12111, 5-5/8" long	25	35	55
Truck, open, futuristic, No. 12003, 4-1/2" long	20	30	50

*Art Deco Housetrailer, No. 1025, Sun Rubber, 4-3/8" long, $250.
Photos from* Rubber Toy Vehicles *by Dave Leopard.*

*Open Racer, full fenders on rear, 1936, No. 1000, Sun Rubber,
6-1/2" long, $80. Photos from* Rubber Toy Vehicles *by Dave
Loepard.*

	C6	C8	C10
Truck, open, stake sides, streamlined, No. 1005, 5-1/4"	25	40	55

THOMAS TOYS

Thomas Toys was founded by Islyn Thomas in 1944. Located at 80 Clinton Street, Newark, New Jersey, at its peak it had 350 employees. The company's first toys were plastic jeeps, planes and vinyl dolls. Thomas sold the firm in 1960 to Banner.

	C6	C8	C10
Buick Torpedo Sedan, plastic, No. 133, 11" long	20	30	40
Harley-Davidson w/removable rider, 3" long	75	112	150
No. 140 Loudspeaker Van, plastic, 4" long	20	25	30
Wrecker, 4-1/2" long	12	18	24

TIP TOP TOY CO.

The Tip Top Toy Co. was located in San Francisco, and produced die-cast and slush-cast vehicles through most of the 1920s and 1930s. The firm embossed its name inside some, but not all, of its toys. All Tip Top vehicles are extremely scarce.

	C6	C8	C10
Coupe, 1923 Dodge, 3-1/8"	16	24	32
Tow Truck, 3-5/16" long	16	24	32

TOLEDO METAL WHEEL COMPANY

The Toledo Metal Wheel Company was located in Toledo, Ohio, during at least the early and late 1920s. It manufactured a large range of pedal cars as well as toy trucks. The trade name for its products was "Blue Streak."

	C6	C8	C10
Truck, "Bull Dog", open cab, No. 45, 26" long	500	1000	1500
Dump Truck, "Bull Dog," No. 46, 26-1/2" long	600	1000	1475

	C6	C8	C10
Sprinkler Truck, "Bull Dog," No. 47, 27-1/2" long	600	1100	1510
Moving Van, "Bull Dog," No. 48, 26" long	550	1050	1550
Coal Truck, "Bull Dog," No. 50, 25" long	800	1350	1875
Fire Pumper Pedal Car, red painted, 59" long	1250	1875	2500

TOMMY TOY

Tommy Toy was in business in Union City, New Jersey, from November 13, 1935, to 1938-1939. The following vehicles have been identified by Charles E. Weldon, Jr., son of one of the owners of Tommy Toy.

Many of Tommy Toy vehicles look like other slush-mold items, such Metal Cast and Savoye. Since slush molds did tend to change hands, production of a vehicle by one company would not preclude later manufacture of the same toy by another company. The only vehicle known to bear the Tommy Toy trademark is the 810 Cord.

	C6	C8	C10
Aerial Ladder Truck (like Savoye), late 1920s type	20	30	40
Airflow-type Auto (like Kansas Toy), c. 1935	32	48	65
Ambulance, late 1920s-early 1930s type	16	24	32
Cannon Truck, mid-1930s (like Barclay; Barclay's had wooden hubs)	17	25	34
Convertible, 1935 Oldsmobile, w/driver, mid-to-late 1930s	20	30	40
Convertible, no driver, mid to late 1930s	8	12	16
Cord, 810, 1935	40	60	80
Coupe "Packard," mid-1930s	17	26	35
Delivery truck, "Delivery Deluxe," (like Savoye), late 1930s	18	27	36
Double-Decker Bus, closed top, early 1930s	16	24	32
Double-Decker Bus, open top, extended hood (like Savoye), late 1920s	35	52	70
Double-Decker Bus, open top, no hood (like Barclay), late 1930s	16	24	32
Dump Truck, late 1930s, (resembles Kansas Toy, Best Toy, Manhattan Toys)	16	24	32
Ladder Truck, mid-1930s	20	30	40
Police Patrol, open windows, late 1920s-early 1930s type	40	60	80
Police Patrol, solid windows, late 1920s-early 1930s type	35	52	70
Pumper, large, red hubs, late 1930s	11	16	22
Pumper, mid-1930s	12	18	25
Pumper, small, late 1930s	8	12	16
Racing Car, large, c. mid-1930s	16	24	32
Racing Car, small, c. mid-1930s	12	18	25
Sedan towing "Tourist" trailer, c. 1936-37	60	90	120
Sedan, four-door, c. 1935	17	26	35
Towing Car Coupe (like Savoye), early 1930s type	16	24	32

	C6	C8	C10
Truck, "Beer Truck," w/wooden barrels, late 1930s	14	21	28
Truck, "General Trucking," late 1930s	12	18	25
Truck, "Milk Truck," grilled window, c. late 1930s	20	30	40
Truck, "Milk Truck," smooth window, c. late 1930s	20	30	40
Truck, "Milk," late 1930s	20	30	40
Truck, "Oil," "Cap 80000" (like Metal Cast, which has different capacity number), 1930s, attaches to Tommy Toy Towing Car Coupe	8	12	16
Wrecker, late 1930s	10	15	20

TONKA

Tonka was incorporated in Mound, Minnesota, in September of 1946. The firm had secured the tooling for a steam shovel and crane and clam from Streator Industries, which had unsuccessfully introduced these toys at the The American International Toy Fair in February 1946. Tonka, which means "great" in Sioux-French, was located on the banks of Lake Minnetonka (and is now situated in Minnetonka itself). In 1948, Tonka introduced a forklift with trailer, and in 1949 premiered its line of trucks, including a dump and wrecker. The firm had originally been incorporated as Mound Metal Crafts, with a line of tie racks and garden tools.

	C6	C8	C10
1947			
No. 50 Steam Shovel, 20-3/4" long	115	172	230
No. 150 Crane and Clam, 24" long	88	132	175
1948			
No. 200 Lift Truck and Cart	350	525	750
1949			
No. 100 Steam Shovel Deluxe, 22" long	83	125	165
No. 120 Tractor and Carry-All Trailer w/No. 50 Steam Shovel	175	262	350
No. 125 Tractor and Carry-All Trailer w/No. 100 Steam Shovel	175	262	350
No. 130 Tractor and Carry-All Trailer, 30-1/2" long	125	188	250
No. 140 "Tonka Toy Transport Van," 22-1/4" long	185	275	370
No. 170 Tractor and Carry-All Trailer w/No. 150 Crane and Clam	200	300	400
No. 180 Dump Truck, 12" long	150	225	300
No. 250 Wrecker Truck, 12-1/2" long	100	150	250
1950			
No. 145 Steel Carrier Semi, 22" long	175	262	350
No. 175 Utility Hauler, 12" long	100	150	200

No. 700 Aerial Ladder Semi Fire Truck, Tonka, 32-1/2" long, $375

Steel Carrier Truck, Tonka, $230

	C6	C8	C10
1951			
No. 400 Allied Van Lines Semi, 23-1/2" long	150	225	300
1952			
No. 500 Livestock Hauler Semi, 22-1/4" long	140	210	280
No. 550 Grain Hauler Semi, 22-1/4" long	138	205	275
1953			
No. 575 Logger Semi, 22-1/4"	150	225	300
No. 575 Logger Semi, wood flat bed	125	188	250
No. 600 Road Grader, 17" long	80	120	160
No. 650 Green Giant Transport Semi, 22-1/4" long	155	235	310
No. 675 Trailer Fleet Set, two tractors (five interchangeable trailers), per set	350	580	775
Wrecker	125	188	250
1954			
No. 580 Pickup Truck	125	188	250
No. 700 Aerial Ladder Semi Fire Truck, 32-1/2" long	187	280	375
No. 725 Minute Maid Delivery Van, 14-1/2" long	275	362	550
No. 725 Star Kist Van, 14-1/2"	150	225	300
No. 750 Carnation Milk Step Van, 11-3/4" long	168	290	335

	C6	C8	C10
No. 750 Parcel Delivery Van, 11-3/4" long	180	270	360
No. 775 Road Builder Set, five-piece set, Road Grader (semi T&T crane and dump truck)	350	525	700
Steel Carrier Truck	115	172	230
Wrecker	140	210	280
Utility Truck	112	168	225
1955			
Allied Van Lines	188	280	375
Dump	108	162	215
Freighter	138	210	275
Hook and Ladder	165	250	330
Livestock Truck	120	180	240
Loboy and Shovel	213	320	425
No. 65 Trailer, stake side	30	45	60
No. 600 Grader	75	112	150
No. 725 Minute Maid Orange Juice Van	275	415	550
No. 750 Carnation Milk Delivery Van	163	245	325
No. 880 Pickup Truck	132	200	265
No. 0850 Lumber Truck, six wheels	225	338	450
No. 0860 Stake Truck, six wheels	210	315	420
Rescue Van	180	270	360
Wrecker	100	150	200
1956			
Green Giant Semi Reefer	200	300	400
No. 120 Shovel and Carry-All (Loboy), 33" long total	125	188	250
No. 180 Dump Truck, 13" long	113	170	225
No. 600 Road Grader, 17" long	50	75	100
No. 700 Aerial Ladder, 32-1/2" long	210	315	420
No. 880 Pickup Truck, 13-3/4"	155	235	310

No. 750 Carnation Milk Step Van, Tonka, 11-3/4" long, $335

No. 950 Pumper, Tonka, 17" long, $255

	C6	C8	C10
No. 950 Pumper, 17" long	128	185	255
No. 980 Hi-Way Dump Truck, 13" long....	120	180	240
No. 990 Suburban Pumper, 17"	175	262	350
No. 991 Farm Stake Truck, 13" long	138	210	275
No. 992 Aerial Sand Loader Set, Loader and Dump Truck	225	338	450
No. 994 Sand Loader Set, Loader and Dump Truck	90	135	180
No. 996 Wrecker (white color), (AAA), 12" long	125	188	250
No. 998 Lumber Truck, 18-3/4" long	80	120	160
Rescue Squad Van, 11-3/4"	175	263	350

1957

	C6	C8	C10
Aerial Ladder Truck	158	235	315
Big Mike Dual Hydraulic Dump Truck, 14" long	380	570	760
Farms Stake Truck	195	292	390
Gasoline Truck, 15" long	450	675	900
Hook and Ladder	150	225	300
Parcel Delivery Van, 12" long	130	195	260
Pickup w/Stake Trailer, 20-1/2" long	150	225	300
Stake Trailer alone	27	41	55
Stock Rack Truck w/Animals, 16-1/4" long	225	338	450
Three-in-One Hi-Way Service Truck, w/two snowblades, 13" long	190	285	380
Thunderbird Express Semi, 24" long	200	300	400
Wrecker	125	188	250

1958, Next Generation Cars

	C6	C8	C10
No. 02 Pickup Truck	80	120	160
No. 03 Utility Truck	150	225	300
No. 04 Farm Stake Truck	193	275	385
No. 05 Sportsman Pickup w/Topper, 12-3/4" long	142	215	285
No. 06 Dump Truck	123	185	245
No. 12 Road Grader	98	148	195
No. 18 Wrecker Truck	143	215	285
No. 20 Hydraulic Dump Truck	200	300	400
No. 28 Pickup w/Stake Trailer and Animal	150	225	300

No. 46 Suburban Pumper, Tonka, $300

	C6	C8	C10
No. 29 Sportsman Truck w/Box Trailer	150	225	300
No. 32 Stock Rack Truck	150	225	300
No. 33 "Gasoline" Truck, hinged back door, hose and nozzle	323	485	645
No. 34 Deluxe Sportsman w/Boat Trailer, 22-3/4" long	150	225	300
No. 35 Farm Stake w/two-Horse Trailer, 21-3/4" long	90	135	180
No. 36 Livestock Van	163	245	325
No. 37 Thunderbird Express	170	255	340
No. 39 Nationwide Moving Van, 24-1/2" long	185	280	370
No. 41 Hi-Way Service Truck	115	175	230
No. 43 Shovel & Carry-All Trailer	123	185	245
No. 45 Big Mike Dual Hydraulic Dump Truck w/Snow Plow	275	362	550
No. 46 Suburban Pumper	150	225	300
No. 48 Hydraulic Aerial Ladder	135	203	270

1959

	C6	C8	C10
No. 01 Service Truck, 12-3/4"	95	143	190
No. 05 Sportsman	95	143	190
No. 14 Dragline, 20" long	90	135	180
No. 16 Air Express	150	225	300
No. 22 Deluxe Sportsman	150	225	300
No. 30 Tandem Platform Stake, 28-1/4" long	218	327	435

No. 06 Dump Truck, Tonka, $200

No. 01 Service Truck, Tonka, $235

	C6	C8	C10
No. 36 Tandem Air Express, w/Trailer, 24-3/4" long	225	338	450
No. 40 Car Carrier	85	128	170
No. 41 Boat Transport, 38"	175	263	350
No. 42 Hydraulic Land Rover, 15" long	350	525	700
No. 44 Dragline & Trailer, 26-1/4" long	165	250	330
Sanitary Truck, square back	250	375	500

1960

The two center ribs on truck cabs were replaced by one rib.

	C6	C8	C10
No. 01 Service Truck	118	175	235
No. 02 Pickup	68	105	135
No. 04 Farm Stake Truck	90	135	180
No. 05 Sportsman	75	112	150
No. 06 Dump Truck	100	150	200
No. 08 Logger	110	165	220
No. 18 Wrecker, white sidewalls	75	112	150
No. 20 Hydraulic Dump	70	105	140
No. 22 Deluxe Sportsman	70	105	140
No. 28 Pickup and Trailer	145	220	290
No. 35 Farm Stake and Horse Trailer	100	150	200
No. 37 Thunderbird Express	175	263	350
No. 40 Car Carrier	75	112	150
No. 41 Boat Transport, 38" long	128	190	255
No. 46 Surburban Pumper	115	170	230
No. 48 Aerial Ladder	120	180	240
No. 100 Bulldozer, (plated roller wheels only in 1960), 8-7/8"	37	56	75
No. 105 Rescue Squad, 13-3/4" long	140	210	280
No. 110 Fisherman Pickup w/Sportsman cover, 14" long	83	125	165
No. 115 Power Boom Loader (1960 only), 18-1/2" long	275	363	550
No. 120 Cement Mixer, 15-1/2" long	105	158	210
No. 125 Loboy & Bulldozer, 26-1/4" long	190	275	380
No. 130 Deluxe Fisherman (also new boat and trailer)	175	263	350
No. 135 Mobile Dragline	85	128	170
No. 140 Sanitary Truck	300	450	600
No. 145 Tanker (first Tonka w/major use of plastic), 28" long	185	280	370
Tonka Ford Falcon (from set)	50	75	100
Tonka "Jolly Green Giant" Special, white, green stake racks	150	225	300
Tonka "Standard" Oil Company Wrecker Special	250	375	500

1961

The "T" in grille's center was eliminated.

	C6	C8	C10
No. 02 Pickup	110	165	220
No. 04 Farm Stake	65	98	130
No. 05 Sportsman	80	120	160
No. 06 Dump	93	140	185

No. 145 Tanker, Tonka, $400

	C6	C8	C10
No. 12 Road Grader, yellow	50	75	100
No. 14 Dragline, yellow	62	93	125
No. 18 Wrecker	125	188	250
No. 20 Hydraulic Dump	60	90	120
No. 22 Deluxe Sportsman	125	188	250
No. 35 Farm Stake Truck and Horse Trailer	95	143	190
No. 39 Allied Van	80	120	160
No. 40 Car Carrier	120	180	240
No. 41 Boat Transport Truck	275	363	550
No. 48 Aerial Ladder	138	185	275
No. 116 Dump Truck w/Sandloader, 23-1/4" long	105	158	210
No. 117 Boat Service Truck (1961 only)	125	188	250
No. 118 Giant Dozer, 12-1/2" long	50	75	100
No. 120 Cement Mixer	50	75	100
No. 130 Deluxe Fisherman	150	225	300
No. 134 Grading Service Truck, Trailer and Bulldozer, 25-1/2" long	163	245	325
No. 135 Mobile Dragline	133	200	265
No. 136 Houseboat Set, 29" long total	250	375	500
No. 142 Mobile Clam, 27-1/4" long	110	165	220
No. 145 Tanker	200	300	400

1962

Changes for this year—(New Tonka logo; "Tonka" above wavy line, "Mound, Minnesota," below)

	C6	C8	C10
No. 200 Jeep Dispatcher, 9-3/4" long	40	60	80
No. 201 "Serv-I-Car" 9-1/8" long	60	90	120
No. 249 Jeep Universal	37	56	75
No. 250 Tractor, 8-5/8" long	50	75	100
No. 300 Bulldozer	73	110	145
No. 301 Utility Dump, (revised Golf Club Tractor, 1961 only) 12-1/2" long	108	162	215
No. 302 Pickup	35	50	100
No. 308 Stake Pickup, 12-5/8" long	75	112	150
No. 350 Jeep Surrey, fringe top, 10-1/2" long	55	83	110
No. 402 "Loader," yellow and green	40	60	80
No. 404 Farm Stake Truck	150	225	300
No. 405 Sportsman	55	82	110
No. 406 Dump Truck	50	75	100
No. 410 "Jet Delivery" Truck, (1962 only) 14" long	100	150	200

	C6	C8	C10
No. 420 Airlines Luggage Service, 16-5/8" long...... 108	160	215
No. 512 Road Grader 45	68	90
No. 514 Dragline 85	128	170
No. 516 Jeep Runabout, Trailer, Boat, 25-5/8" long...... 80	120	160
No. 518 Wrecker 63	95	125
No. 520 Hydraulic Dump 60	90	120
No. 524 Dozer Packer, Packer has eleven tires, sold only in 1962, total 18-1/4" long...... 100	150	200
No. 528 Pickup and Trailer 125	188	250
No. 530 Camper, 14" long...... 93	140	185
No. 616 Dump Truck and Sand Loader 70	105	140
No. 618 Giant Dozer 100	150	200
No. 620 Cement Mixer 130	195	260
No. 735 Farm Stake and Horse Trailer 102	153	205
No. 739 Allied Van...... 95	140	190
No. 834 Grading Service Truck...... 70	105	140
No. 840 Car Carrier...... 100	150	200
No. 926 Pumper Truck...... 83	125	165
No. 942 Mobile Clam 88	132	175
No. 1348 Aerial Ladder 125	188	250

1963

Faceted headlights introduced this year.

	C6	C8	C10
No. 50 Mini-Tonka Jeep Pickup, 9-1/4" long...... 35	52	70
No. 56 Mini-Tonka Stake Truck, 9-1/4" long...... 35	52	70
No. 60 Mini-Tonka Dump 9-3/4" long 75	112	150
No. 68 Mini-Tonka Wrecker, 9-1/2" long...... 17	26	35
No. 70 Mini-Tonka Camper, 9-5/8" long...... 75	112	150
No. 201 "Servi-I-Car" 75	112	150
No. 250 Tractor, yellow w/red seat...... 75	112	150
No. 251 Military Jeep Universal, 10-1/2" long...... 50	75	100
No. 300 Bulldozer 55	82	110
No. 302 Pickup 50	75	100
No. 308 Stake Pickup 60	90	120
No. 350 Jeep Surrey 60	90	120
No. 352 Loader 40	60	80
No. 354 Style-Side Pickup, 14" long 40	60	80
No. 404 Farm Stake Truck...... 60	90	120
No. 406 Dump Truck 45	68	90
No. 422 Back Hoe, 17-1/8" long 80	120	160
No. 425 Jeep Pumper 10-3/4" long...... 105	158	210
No. 514 Dragline 60	90	120
No. 516 Jeep Runabout, Trailer and Boat ... 73	108	145
No. 518 Wrecker 75	112	150
No. 520 Hydraulic Dump Truck...... 105	158	210
No. 524 Dozer Packer, yellow...... 200	300	400

	C6	C8	C10
No. 530 Camper 82	125	165
No. 536 Giant Dozer 112	168	225
No. 616 Dump Truck and Sand Loader, yellow...... 90	135	180
No. 620 Cement Mixer...... 85	130	170
No. 625 Stake Pickup and Horse Trailer, 21-3/4" long overall 110	165	220
No. 640 Ramp Hoist, red and white, 19-1/4" long...... 200	300	400
No. 720 Terminal Train, fifteen suitcases, 33-5/8" long total 105	158	210
No. 739 Allied Van 118	175	235
No. 840 Car Carrier...... 35	52	70
No. 926 Pumper 130	195	260
No. 942 Mobile Clam 95	140	190
No. 1001 Trencher & Loboy, 28-1/2" long 140	210	280
No. 1348 Aerial Ladder Truck...... 100	150	200
No. 2100 Airport Service Set 138	210	275

1964

Futuristic cab introduced in 1964.

	C6	C8	C10
No. 77 Mini-Tonka Mixer, 9"...... 50	75	100
No. 86 Mini-Tonka Van, 16"...... 35	52	70
No. 90 Mini-Tonka Livestock Van, 16" long...... 50	75	100
No. 96 Mini-Tonka Car Carrier, two cars, 18-1/2" long...... 75	112	150
No. 250 Military Tractor, black seat 73	110	145
No. 251 Military Jeep Universal...... 37	56	75
No. 304 Jeep Commander, canvas top, 10-1/2" long...... 30	45	60
No. 315 Dump Truck, 13-1/2"...... 63	95	125
No. 375 Jeep Wrecker, 11"...... 75	112	150
No. 380 Troop Carrier, 14" 87	130	175
No. 384 Military Jeep and Box Trailer, 19-3/8" overall...... 75	112	150
No. 404 Stake Truck, red...... 85	128	170
No. 425 Jeep Pumper, black steering wheel...... 87	130	175
No. 504 Stake Pickup & Trailer, 21-5/8" long...... 75	112	150
No. 525 Jeep & Horse Trailer, two horses, 19-1/4" long total 62	93	125
No. 616 Dump Truck and Sandloader, orange and yellow 87	130	175
No. 640 Ramp Hoist, park green and white, very rare 300	450	600
No. 739 Allied Van Lines, black knob on door 87	130	175
No. 900 Mighty Tonka Dump Truck...... 65	98	130
No. 942 Mobile Clam, yellow 50	75	100
No. 998 Aerial Ladder, two auxiliary ladders 50	75	100

TOOTSIETOY

Tootsietoy is one of the best-known names in the world of the toy collecting, and for good reason.

The toys, products of a Chicago concern that now has a century of manufacturing behind it, have long appealed to parents because of their cheap price, and to kids because of their high play value. The Tootsietoy line through the years has included toy cars, trucks, trains, dollhouse furniture, airplanes and toy soldiers. During the company's heyday, roughly from the 1930s through 1960s, a person would have had to search long and hard to find a child with no knowledge of the trademark.

Dowst and Company started in 1876 in the publishing trade, and moved into manufacturing after the 1893 Columbian World Exposition in Chicago, where the new die-casting technology was introduced to the public. By then named Dowst Brothers, the company released its first die-cast-body, free-axle toy car in 1911, the generic Limousine. The first specific-model car, the Model T Ford touring car, followed in 1914. The name Tootsietoy was adopted in the early 1920s and was registered in 1924 as the company's trademark. Theodore Dowst, who joined the firm in 1906, is generally seen as the guiding force behind the growth of toy production at Dowst Brothers. He remained with the company even after its purchase by Nathan Shure in 1926, until 1945. For most collectors, the toys of the Ted Dowst period are the most noteworthy.

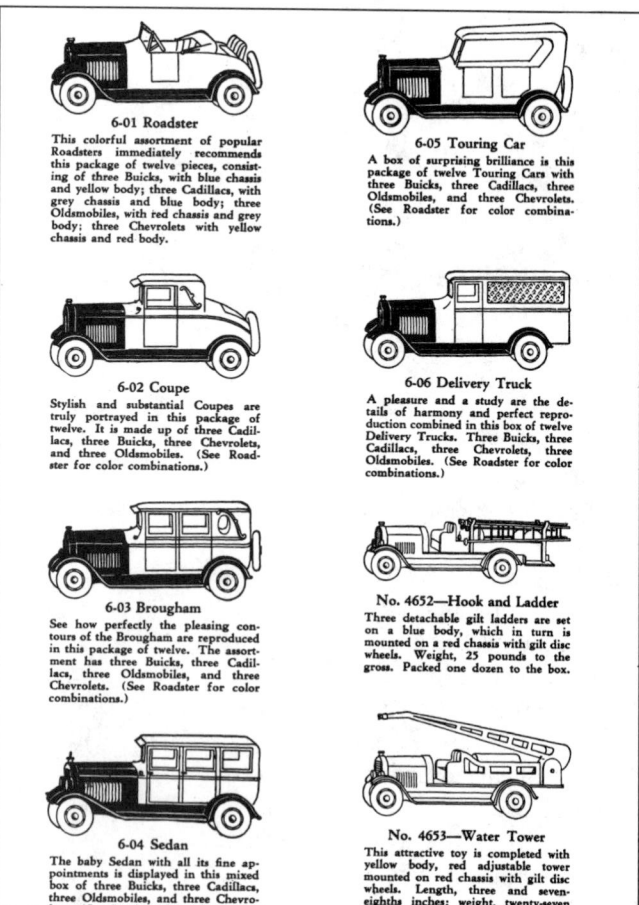

An advertisement for Tootsietoys.

High points in the world of Tootsietoy collecting include the 1933 Graham series, notable for its use of three-piece construction, with separately die-cast bodies, chassis and radiator grilles, and the 1935 LaSalles, which used four-piece construction, adding a casting for the rear bumpers. Collectors also avidly seek the 1932-33 Funnies series cars, which featured such comic figures as Andy Gump, Uncle Walt and Moon Mullins.

Interest seems to be growing in the various advertising toys Tootsietoy produced through the years, ranging from the 1932 Wrigley's Railroad Express truck to more recent U-Haul and Coast-to-Coast vehicles. Collector demand for post-war toys remains stable at a fairly low level; and it may not grow stronger any time soon, given the heavy contemporary interest in detailed scale models as opposed to made-for-play toys. On the other hand, interest in the post-Vietnam toys is inching upward, reflecting the maturing of the later Baby Boomers.

In the listings below, dates in parentheses refer to the years of original issue. In the case of series, the date refers to the year the series began. Many individual toys were produced for years or decades, making the dating of toys a sometimes puzzling matter.

Pre-war

	C6	C8	C10
Ford Model A Delivery Van, "US Mail," (1931) sold in sets only	38	56	75
23 Racer w/Driver (1927)	35	60	80
4528 Limousine (1911)	24	32	40
4570 Ford Model T Tourer, (1914)	35	50	65
4610 Ford Model T Pickup (1916)	35	50	70
4629 Sedan "Yellow Cab," (1923)	15	25	60
4636 Buick Coupe, (1924)	23	34	45
4641 Buick Touring Car (1925)	28	42	55
4642 Army Long-Range Cannon, (1931)	13	18	25
4646 Caterpillar Tractor w/treads (1931)	27	41	55
4651 Fageol Safety Coach (1927)	30	45	65
4652 Hook & Ladder Fire Engine (1927)	39	52	75
4653 Water Tower Fire Engine (1927)	38	56	75
4654 Huber Star Farm Tractor (1927)	40	65	95
4655 Ford Model A Coupe (1928)	20	30	40
4665 Ford Model A Sedan (1929)	20	30	40
4680 Overland Bus Lines (1929)	45	65	95

Federal Delivery Van Series (1924)

	C6	C8	C10
4630 "Grocery"	35	55	85
4631 "Bakery"	50	80	105
4632 "Market"	35	60	75
4633 "Laundry"	45	65	95
4634 "Milk" (most common in series)	25	40	55
4635 "Florist" (rarest in series)	95	175	225

Mack Trucks 1:72 scale (1925)

	C6	C8	C10
170 Interchangeable Truck Set (1925-31)	50	65	80

	C6	C8	C10
4638 Stake Truck, 1925, revised (1928)....... 23		34	45
4639 Coal Truck, 1925, revised (1928)........ 23		34	45
4640 Tank Truck, 1925, revised (1928) 23		34	45
4643 Anti-Aircraft Gun Army Truck,			
(1931) 25		38	50
4644 Searchlight Army Truck (1931) 25		40	55
4645 US Mail Air Mail Service (1931)........ 35		55	75
4670 A&P Trailer Truck, (1929) 100		150	200
4670 Amerian Railway Express			
Trailer Truck (1929)............................ 115		170	225

Depression-Years Miniatures (1931)

Two to three inches long. Initially Numbers 101, 103 and 104 were sold w/tin garages, which can greatly increase their value. These toys originally cost half the price of regular Tootsietoys.

4635 "Florist," Federal Delivery Van Series, Tootsietoy, $225

4670 A&P Trailer Truck, 1929, Mack Trucks, 1:72 scale, Tootsietoy, $200

4680 "Overland Bus," issued 1929 (later Diesteel wheels), Tootsietoy, $95

6105 Cadillac Touring Car, GM Series, Tootsietoy, $120

	C6	C8	C10
101/4656 Buick Marquette Coupe			
(1931) 10		15	20
102 Buick Marquette Roadster			
(1932?) 13		19	25
103/4657 Buick Marquette Sedan			
(1931) 10		15	20
104/4658 Mack Insurance Patrol fire			
truck (1931) 25		35	45
105 Mack Tank Truck (1932)..................... 25		40	55
106 Low Wing Monoplane (1932)			
w/prop, tin wings 35		55	70
107 High Wing Monoplane (1932)			
w/prop, tin wings 35		55	70
108 Caterpillar tractor (1932) w/tread........ 23		34	45
109 Ford Stake Truck (1932) 20		30	40
110 Bluebird Dayton Racer (1932)............. 25		40	55

5091 Funnies Series (1932)

These vehicles appeared in both simple and mechanical versions, in which the comic characters bobbed.

	C6	C8	C10
5101 Andy Gump roadster 175		265	350
5101 Andy Gump roadster,			
mechanical 225		340	450
5102 Uncle Walt roadster........................... 175		265	350
5102 Uncle Walt roadster,			
mechanical 225		340	450

5105 Kayo Ice Wagon, Funnies Series, Tootsietoy, $350

	C6	C8	C10
5103 Smitty Motorcyle............ 175		265	350
5103 Smitty Motorcyle, mechanical......... 225		340	450
5104 Moon Mullins Police Wagon 175		265	350
5104 Moon Mullins Police Wagon, mechanical...................... 225		340	450
5105 Kayo Ice Wagon 175		265	350
5105 Kayo Ice Wagon, mechanical 225		340	450
5106 Uncle Willie rowboat..................... 175		265	350
5106 Uncle Willie rowboat, mechanical 225		340	450

GM Series (1927)

The cars, pieced together from interchangeable parts, are distinguished chiefly by the names over the grilles. The numbers on the 1933 "no-name" series are invented, since Tootsietoy apparently never assigned any. They are added for convenience.

	C6	C8	C10
6001 Buick Roadster..................... 30		45	60
6002 Buick Coupe 28		41	55
6003 Buick Brougham.................... 28		41	55
6004 Buick Sedan 28		41	55
6005 Buick Touring Car 50		75	100
6006 Buick Screenside Delivery truck 35		53	70
6101 Cadillac Roadster................... 40		60	80
6102 Cadillac coupe 40		60	80
6103 Cadillac Brougham.................. 40		60	80
6104 Cadillac Sedan 40		60	80
6105 Cadillac Touring Car 60		90	120
6106 Cadillac Screenside Delivery Truck 48		71	95
6201 Chevrolet Roadster.................. 33		50	65
6202 Chevrolet Coupe 33		50	65
6203 Chevrolet Brougham................ 33		50	65
6204 Chevrolet Sedan 33		50	65
6205 Chevrolet Touring Car 55		83	110
6206 Chevrolet Screenside Delivery Truck 35		53	70
6301 Oldsmobile Roadster............... 38		55	75
6302 Oldsmobile Coupe 35		53	70
6303 Oldsmobile Brougham............. 35		53	70
6304 Oldsmobile Sedan 35		53	70
6305 Oldsmobile Touring Car 55		83	110
6306 Oldsmobile Screenside Delivery Truck 45		68	90
6401 "No-Name" Roadster............ 55		83	110
6402 "No-Name" Coupe 55		83	110
6403 "No-Name" Brougham 55		83	110
6404 "No-Name" Sedan 55		83	110
6405 "No-Name" Touring Car 75		113	150
6406 "No-Name" Screenside Delivery Truck 65		95	125

Mack Tractor-Trailers 1:43-scale (1931)

	C6	C8	C10
190 Auto Transport three-car Hauler (1931) w/101-103 Buicks..................... 105		140	175
190 Auto Transport four-car Hauler (1933) w/101-103 Buicks and 109 Ford 115		170	225
191 Contractor Set, w/Mack AC hauling three spoke-wheeled tipper trailers (1933) 75		100	150
192 "Tootsietoy Dairy" tanker, two-piece cab, three trailers (1933) 120		160	200
192 "Tootsietoy Dairy" tanker, one-piece cab, three trailers 75		115	150
198 Auto Transport, one-piece cab, three '35 Fords 125		200	275
198 Auto Transport, two-piece cab, three '35 Fords 150		250	350
187 Auto Transport, trailer holds three 1940s Buicks in tilted position (1941) 275		415	550
801 "Express" Stake Semi-Trailer, one-piece cab (1933) 55		80	105
801 "Express" Stake Semi-Trailer, two-piece cab 80		105	135
802 "Domaco" tank Semi-Trailer, one-piece cab (1933) 60		90	120
802 "Domaco" tank Semi-Trailer, two-piece cab 90		120	150
803 "Long Distance Hauling" Semi-Trailer (1933) 85		130	175

	C6	C8	C10

804 "City Fuel Company" Coal Truck, Mack Delivery Trucks and Vans, Tootsietoy, $130

801 "Express," Stake Semi-Trailer, one-piece cab, Mack Tractor-Trailers, Tootsietoy, $105

803 "Long Distance Hauling," Semi-Trailer, Mack Tractor-Trailers, Tootsietoy, $175

805 "Tootsietoy Dairy" Semi-Trailer, Semi-Trailer, Mack Tractor-Trailers, Tootsietoy, $140

	C6	C8	C10
805 "Tootsietoy Dairy" Semi-Trailer, dual tires (1933)	70	105	140
805 "Tootsietoy Dairy" Semi-Trailer, single tires	60	90	120

Mack Delivery Trucks and Vans (1933), 4"

	C6	C8	C10
804 "City Fuel Company" Coal Truck, four-wheel (1937)	60	95	130
804 "City Fuel Company" Coal Truck, ten-wheel (1933)	75	115	150
807 Delivery Motorcycle (1933, adapted from 5103)	85	125	175
810 "Commercial Tire & Supply Co." Van	112	168	225
810 "Railway Express Co., Wrigley's Gum," one-piece cab (1935)	70	105	150

804 "City Fuel Company" Coal Truck, ten-wheel, Mack Delivery Trucks and Vans, Tootsietoy, $150

	C6	C8	C10
810 "Railway Express Co., Wrigley's Gum," two-piece cab	75	115	165

Graham Series (1933), 4"

	C6	C8	C10
"Commercial Tire & Supply Co." Van	75	110	150
511 Roadster, five wheels	80	125	165
512 Coupe, five wheels	70	110	145
513 Sedan, five wheels	70	110	145
514 Convertible Coupe, five wheels	80	120	160
515 Convertible Sedan, five wheels	80	120	160
516 Towncar, five wheels	88	130	175
611 Roadster, six wheels	80	125	165
612 Coupe, six wheels	72	110	145
613 Sedan, six wheels	70	110	145
614 Convertible Coupe, six wheels	80	120	160
615 Convertible Sedan, six wheels	80	120	160
616 Towncar, six wheels	75	110	150
806 Wrecker	75	110	150
808 "Tootsietoy Dairy" Delivery Van	75	110	150
809 Army Ambulance	75	110	150
Bild-A-Car Coupe, four wheels	65	95	130
Bild-A-Car Roadster, four wheels	85	130	175
Bild-A-Car Sedan, four wheels	65	95	130

616 Towncar, Graham Series, Tootsietoy, $150

"Commercial Tire & Supply Co." Van, Graham Series, Tootsietoy, $150

716 Briggs-Lincoln prototype, "Doodlebug, Lincoln Series, Tootsietoy, $125

LaSalle Series (1935), 4"

	C6	C8	C10
712 Coupe	115	180	240
713 Sedan	115	180	240
714 Convertible Coupe	125	205	265
715 Convertible Sedan	125	205	265

Lincoln Series (1935), 4"

	C6	C8	C10
180 Zephyr and Roamer House Trailer	555	740	925
180 Zephyr and Roamer House Trailer, wind-up	660	880	1100
716 Briggs-Lincoln prototype, "Doodlebug"	75	95	125
6015 Zephyr	165	245	325
6015 Zephyr, wind-up version	240	365	485
6016 Wrecker	250	230	350
6016 Wrecker, wind-up version	350	525	700

Ford V8 Series (1935), 3"

	C6	C8	C10
111 '34 Sedan	30	45	60
111 '35 Sedan	15	23	30
112 '34 Coupe	33	49	65
112 '35 Coupe	18	26	35
113 '34 Wrecker	38	56	75
113 '35 Wrecker	33	49	65
114 '34 Convertible Coupe	40	60	80
114 '35 Convertible Coupe	30	45	60
115 '34 Convertible Sedan	40	60	80
115 '35 Convertible Sedan	30	45	60
116 '35 Roadster	23	34	45
117 '35 Roadster Fire Chief Car	50	75	100
118 DeSoto Airflow Sedan (1935), 3"	27	40	55

Midget Series/Cracker Jacks (1936), 1" vehicles

	C6	C8	C10
120 Oil Tank truck (1936), 3"	23	34	45
121 Ford Pickup Truck (1936) 3"	18	26	35
510 Boxed Set (eight-piece)	75	100	150
510 Boxed Set (ten-piece)	90	130	175

	C6	C8	C10
610 Boxed Set (twelve-piece, 1941?)	100	150	200
1628 Bus	6	9	12
1629 Wrecker	7	10	14
1630 Racer	5	7	10
1631 DeSoto Airflow Sedan	5	7	10
1632 Zephyr Railcar	7	10	14
1634 Fire Engine	7	10	14
1635 Delivery Van	6	9	12
1666 Army Tank	4	6	8
1667 Armored Car	6	9	12

Camelback Delivery Van Series (1937), 3"

	C6	C8	C10
123 "Special Delivery"	25	38	50
123 "Wieboldt's"	145	215	285
123 "Lewis's"	135	205	275
123 "Miller & Rhoads"	145	215	285
123 "McLeans"	145	215	285
123 "Shepards"	145	215	285

Reo Oil Truck Series (1938), distinctive 6" trucks

	C6	C8	C10
1006 Standard	35	55	80
1007 Sinclair	35	55	80
1008 Texaco	35	55	80
1009 Shell	40	60	90

Jumbo Series (1936), 6"

	C6	C8	C10
1016 Auburn Torpedo Roadster	23	34	45
1017 Torpedo Coupe	20	30	40
1018 Torpedo Sedan	20	30	40
1019 Torpedo Pickup truck	20	30	40
1027 Torpedo Wrecker	23	34	45
1026/1045 Torpedo Cross-Country "Greyhound" Bus	25	55	80
1045 "Greyhound" Bus w/tin bottom	55	50	70
1045 "Trans-America" Bus (1941), sold only in sets	90	130	175

Mack Fire Truck Series (1937), 4"

	C6	C8	C10
1040 Hook and Ladder	35	50	70

1040 Hook and Ladder, Mack Fire Truck Series, Tootsietoy, $70

	C6	C8	C10
1041 Hose Car	35	55	75
1042 Insurance Patrol, open end	30	45	60
1042 Insurance Patrol w/ladder and rear fireman	35	55	75

1940 3" Vehicles

Most if not all of these were reissued in the post-war period.

	C6	C8	C10
230 LaSalle Sedan	15	20	30
231 Chevy Coupe	15	20	30
232 Buick Roadmaster Touring Coupe	15	20	30
233 Boattail Roadster	15	20	30

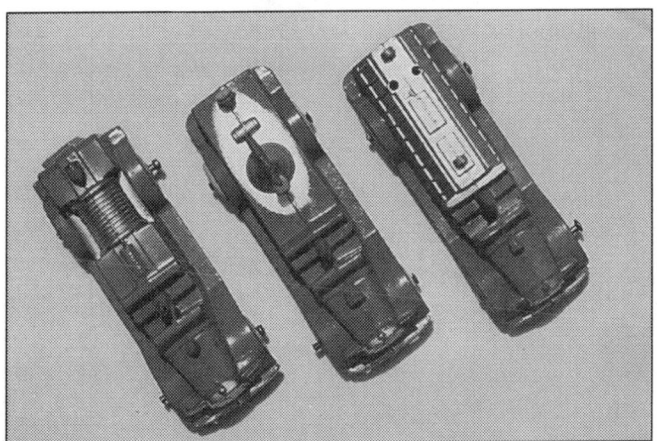

Left to Right: 237 Insurance Patrol Fire Engine, 1940, 3" Vehicles, Tootsietoy, $35; 236 Hook & Ladder Fire engine, 1940 3" Vehicles, Tootsietoy, $40; 238 Hose Wagon Fire Engine, 1940 3" Vehicles, Tootsietoy, $40

1010 "Wrigley" GMC Box Truck, 1940, Tootsietoy, 4", $110

1011 "Massey-Ferguson" Farm Tractor, 1941, Tootsietoy, 4", $400

	C6	C8	C10
234 GMC Box Truck	15	20	30
235 Oil Tank Truck	13	18	25
236 Hook and Ladder Fire engine	20	30	40
237 Insurance Patrol Fire Engine	15	25	35
238 Hose Wagon Fire Engine	20	30	40
239 '38 Ford Paneled Station Wagon	20	30	40

Other Pre-War Tootsietoys

	C6	C8	C10
1010 "Wrigley" GMC Box Truck (1940), 4"	55	80	110
1011 "Massey-Ferguson" Farm Tractor w/driver (1941), 4"	200	300	400
1043 Small Ford Sedan or Coupe, 111 or 112, and Camping Trailer (1937)	35	53	70
1044 Roamer House Trailer w/door and tin bottom (1937)	275	415	550
1046 Paneled Station Wagon (1940), 4"	43	64	85
4634 Army Supply Truck (1939), 4"	33	50	65
4635 Armored Car (1938), 4"	33	50	65
4647 Renault Tank w/treads (1931), 3"	23	34	45
4648 Steamroller (1931), 3"	65	95	125
4654 Farm Tractor, Army Field Battery Set #5071	58	86	115
4666 Bluebird Dayton Record Car (1932), 4"	30	45	55
7003 Farm Set, w/Ford Truck and Tractor, Huber StarBox Trailer, and Huber Star Scraper-Raker (1928)	135	205	275

1044 Roamer House Trailer, 1937, Tootsietoy, $550

1046 Paneled Station Wagon, 1940, Tootsietoy, 4", $85

Post-war Tootsietoys

Tootsietoy 3" Vehicles

	C6	C8	C10
'31 Ford B Hot Rod (1960)	8	12	20
'47 Studebaker Champion Coupe, rare	25	35	55
'47 Willys Jeepster	10	15	20
'49 Ford Custom Convertible	10	15	25
'49 Ford Custom Four-door Sedan	10	15	25
'49 Ford F1 Pickup	10	15	25
'49 Indianapolis No. 3 Race Car	10	15	25
'50 Chevrolet Deluxe Panel Truck	10	15	25
'50 Chevrolet Fleetline Deluxe Two-door Sedan	10	15	25
'50 Jeep CJ3	5	7	14
'50 Plymouth Special Deluxe Four-door Sedan	10	15	25
'50 Twin Coach Bus	12	21	30
'52 Ford Mainline Four-door Sedan	12	21	32
'54 American La France Pumper	10	15	25
'54 Ford Ranch Wagon	8	12	20
'54 Jaguar XK120 Roadster	8	12	20
'54 MG Roadster	8	12	20
'54 Nash Metropolitan Convertible	25	35	50
'55 Chevrolet Bel Air Four-door Sedan	8	12	20
'55 Ford Customline V-8 Two-door Sedan	8	12	20
'55 Ford Thunderbird Coupe	7	11	18
'56 Ford C600 Oil Tanker	8	12	20
'56 Triumph TR3 Roadster	7	11	18
'57 Ford F100 Styleside Pickup	5	7	14
'57 Ford Fairlane 500 Convertible	8	12	20
'57 Jaguar Type D	8	12	20
'57 Plymouth Belvedere Two-door Hardtop	8	12	20
'60 Ford Country Sedan Station Wagon	8	12	20
'60 Ford Falcon Two-door Sedan	5	8	15
'60 Studebaker Lark Custom Convertible	9	16	22
'60 Volkswagen Bug	7	11	18
U-Haul Trailer	4	6	8

4" Vehicles

	C6	C8	C10
'38 Buick Y Experimental Convertible	20	30	40
'41 Chrysler Windsor Convertible	20	30	40
'41 International Army Ambulance	24	34	50
'41 International K1 Panel Truck	22	32	45
'41 White Army Half Track	10	16	25
'47 Chevrolet Fleetmaster Coupe	13	19	25
'47 Hudson Streamlined Pickup	22	32	45
'47 Offenhauser Race Car	13	19	25
'47 Offenhauser Race Car, on trailer	15	22	30
'49 Ford F6 Oil Tanker	13	19	25

	C6	C8	C10
'49 Ford F6 Stake Truck	15	22	30
'49 Mercury Fire Chief Sedan	22	32	45
'49 Mercury Four-door Sedan	15	24	35
'49 Oldsmobile 88 Convertible	20	30	40
'50 Chevrolet Army Ambulance	15	24	35
'50 Chevrolet Deluxe Panel	14	21	28
'50 Dodge Pickup	15	22	30
'50 Jeep CJ3 Army	9	15	22
'50 Pontiac Cheftain Deluxe Coupe Sedan	20	30	40
'50 Pontiac Fire Chief chieftain Sedan	22	32	45
'52 Mercury Custom Four-door Sedan	15	22	30
'54 Ford Ranch Wagon	15	24	35
'54-55 Chevrolet Corvette Roadster	15	22	30
'55 Ford Thunderbird Coupe	20	30	40
'55 Oldsmobile 98 Holiday Two-door Hardtop	15	24	35
'56 Chevrolet Cameo Pickup	13	19	25
'59 Pontiac Star Chief Four-door Sedan	10	16	25
'60 Chrysler Windsor Convertible	13	19	25
'60 Rambler Super Cross-Country Wagon	15	24	35
'69 Ford LTD Two-door Hardtop (last of the larger-size die-cast Tootsietoys)	13	19	25
Army Cannon, four-wheel	10	15	25
Army Cannon, six-wheel	12	21	30
U-Haul Trailer	5	10	15

6" Series

	C6	C8	C10
'40 Ford Special Deluxe Convertible (1960)	20	30	40
'40 Ford V-8 Hot Rod (1960)	15	22	30
'42 Chrysler Thunderbolt Experimental Roadster	22	32	40

'42 Chrysler Thunderbolt Experimental Roadster, various color, 6" Series, post-war, Tootsietoy, $40

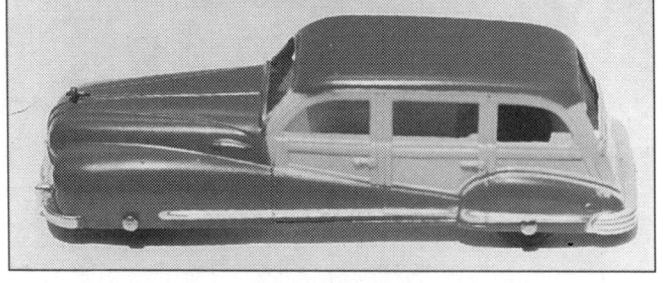

'48 Buick Super Estate Wagon, 6" Series, post-war, Tootsietoy,

	C6	C8	C10
'46 International K11 Oil Tanker:			
Standard	25	35	55
'46 International K11 Oil Tanker: Shell	25	40	65
'46 International K11 Oil Tanker:			
Sinclair	25	35	55
'46 International K11 Oil Tanker:			
Texaco	25	40	65
'47 Kaiser Sedan	28	37	50
'47 Mack L-Line Dump Truck	14	25	35
'47 Mack L-Line Fire Pumper	25	40	65
'47 Mack L-Line Stake Truck	22	32	45
'47 Mack L-Line Wrecker	14	25	35
'48 Buick Super Estate Wagon	27	42	65
'48 Cadillac 60 Special Four-door			
Sedan	18	26	35
'48 GMC 3751 Greyhound Diesel Bus	25	35	55
'49 Buick Roadmaster Four-door			
Sedan	20	34	45
'49 Ford F6 Oil Tanker: Shell	25	35	55
'49 Ford F6 Oil Tanker: Sinclair	25	35	55
'49 Ford F6 Oil Tanker: Standard	25	35	55
'49 Ford F6 Oil Tanker: Texaco	25	35	55
'50 Chrysler Windsor Convertible	70	95	125
'51 Buick Le Sabre Experimental			
Roadster	25	38	55
'52 Lincoln Capri Two-door Hardtop	28	37	50
'53 Chrysler New Yorker Four-door			
Sedan	18	28	45
'54 Buick Century Estate Wagon	20	34	45
'54 Buick Special Experimental Coupe	23	38	50
'54 Cadillac 62 Four-door Sedan	20	30	40
'54 MG Roadster	10	20	30
'55 Mack B-Line Cement Mixer	22	32	45
'55 Mack B-Line Cement Mixer, axle-driven			
drum	30	40	55
'55 Mack L-Line Stake Truck			
w/"Tootsietoy" tin cover (1958)	50	75	100
'56 Austin-Healey 100-5 Roadster	20	30	40
'56 Caterpillar Bulldozer	20	30	40
'56 Caterpillar Road Scraper	18	26	35
'56 Dodge D100 Panel Truck	23	38	50
'56 Ferrari Racer	18	28	45
'56 Jaguar XK140 Coupe	15	22	30
'56 Lancia Racer	18	27	45
'56 Mercedes 190SL Coupe	10	20	30
'56 Packard Patrician Four-door Sedan	28	37	50
'56 Porsche Spyder Roadster	10	20	30
'57 GMC Greyhound Scenicruiser Bus	22	32	45
'59 Ford Country Sedan Station Wagon	10	20	30
'59 Oldsmobile Dynamic 88			
Convertible	14	25	35
'60 Chevrolet El Camino Pickup			
w/Camper and Boat	17	32	50

	C6	C8	C10
'60 Chevrolet El Camino Pickup	12	22	30
'60 International Metro Van (rare)	100	125	150
'60 Jeep CJ5	9	18	25
'60 Jeep CJ5 w/snow-plow	25	35	55
'60 Volkswagen 113	10	20	30
'62 Ford C600 Oil Tanker Truck	20	30	40
'62 Ford Country Sedan Station Wagon	8	18	25
'62 Ford Econoline Pickup	20	30	40

Tractor-Trailer Trucks scaled to match 6" series

	C6	C8	C10
'47 International K5 Tractor-Trailers			
Auto Transporter	30	42	55
Machinery Hauler	30	42	55
Shipping Van, "Tootsietoy Trucking"	27	37	50
Utility Truck	27	37	50
'47 Mack L-Line Tractor-Trailers (1954)			
Hook and Ladder	35	55	75
Log Hauler	35	55	75
Machinery Hauler	35	55	75
Oil Tanker	32	50	70
Oil Tanker, "Tootsietoy Line"	50	75	125
Pipe Truck	35	55	75
Shipping Van, "Tootsietoy Line"	50	50	75
Shipping Van, "Tootsietoy Coast to			
Coast"	37	57	80
Stake Truck, open sides	50	70	115
Stake Truck, closed sides	35	55	75
'55 Mack B-Line Tractor-Trailers (1960)			
Auto Transport	30	42	65
Boat Transport	28	40	60
Hook and Ladder	28	40	60
Log Hauler	28	40	60
Machinery Hauler	28	40	60
Oil Tanker, "Mobil"	32	50	70
Oil Tanker, "Tootsietoy Line"	40	60	80
Pipe Truck	28	40	60
Shipping Van	28	40	60
Stake Truck, closed sides	28	40	60
Utility Truck	25	35	55
'58 International RC180			
Tractor-Trailers (1962)			
Auto Transport, metal trailer	42	65	85
Auto Transport, plastic trailer	24	32	45
Boat Transport, plastic trailer	24	32	45
Machinery Hauler	25	35	55
Shipping Van, "Dean Van Lines,"			
plastic trailer	40	60	80
'59 Chevrolet Tractor-Trailers (1965)			
Auto Transport	50	75	125
Hook and Ladder	50	75	125
Log Hauler	45	70	100
Machinery Hauler	45	70	100
Oil Tanker	45	70	100

HO Pocket Series (1960)

	C6	C8	C10
Cadillac	8	15	20
Dump Truck	10	15	22
Ford Sunliner Convertible w/Boat Trailer	10	18	30
Ford Sunliner Convertible w/Midget Racer Trailer	12	22	35
Ford Wrecker Truck	10	15	22
Metro Van, "Railway Express"	10	17	25
Metro Van, various	8	15	20
Rambler Station Wagon w/U-Haul Trailer	10	18	30
"Township School Bus"	10	17	25

Classic Series (1960)

	C6	C8	C10
4" vintage cars w/plastic wheels			
1906 Cadillac Coupe	8	12	18
1907 Stanley Steamer Runabout	8	12	18
1912 Ford Model T Touring Car	8	12	18
1919 Stutz Bearcat	8	12	18
1921 Mack Dump Truck	10	15	25
1929 Ford Model A Coupe	8	12	18

Little Toughs/Midget Series (1970)

	C6	C8	C10
"Coast to Coast" Shipping Semi-cab and Van	12	17	25
"Mobil" Semi-cab and Tanker	10	15	20
American La France Aerial Ladder Truck	5	8	12
American La France Ladder Truck	4	6	10
Auto Transport Semi-Cab and Trailer	12	17	25
Cement Truck	6	8	12
Dump Truck	6	8	12
Heavy duty Hydraulic Crane	8	12	17
Logging Semi-cab and Trailer	6	5	12
Miscellaneous 2" vehicles	1	2	3
Shipping Semi-cab and Van	6	8	12
Shuttle Truck (1967)	2	3	4

Airplanes

	C6	C8	C10
106 Lockheed Sirius, tin low wing, 1932	30	60	90
107 Bellanca, high tin wing monoplane, 1932	30	60	90
119 U.S. Army Northrup Alpha Pursuit plane, 1936	25	50	75
125 Lockheed Electra twin-engine, 1937	25	50	75
717 TWA DC-2, 1937	30	60	90
718 U.S. Navy Waco C-Model Biplane, 1937	45	85	125
719 Crusader, twin boom, twin engine, 1937	35	70	100

	C6	C8	C10
720 Fly-N-Giro, small-version auto-gyro, 1938	70	140	200
721 Curtis P-40 Pursuit, 1941, silver	70	140	200
721 Curtis P-40 Pursuit, olive	85	170	250
1030 USN Los Angeles Dirigible, 1937	45	85	125
1353 High Wing Monoplane, midget series	5	10	16
1407 Air Defense set of ten, die-cast midget series	50	100	150
1636 DC-2 TWA, midget series	4	8	12
1637 Atlantic Clipper, midget series	4	8	12
1638 P-38, midget series	10	20	30
1743 Aeroplane whistle tin-litho, Crackerjack	15	25	40
1744 High Wing Monoplane, tin-litho, Crackerjack	15	25	40
1746 Aerodawn, tin-litho, Crackerjack	15	25	40
1747 Low Wing Monoplane, tin-litho, Crackerjack	15	25	40
1812 Sky fleet, set of four, die-cast midget series	25	50	75
2220 Scorpion Helicopter, 1977-79	2	5	8
2552 Rescue Helicopter, four-blade	8	16	25
2552 Rescue Helicopter, two-blade, 1975-79	6	12	18
4482 Bleriot Plane, 1910	40	80	120
4550 DC-4, diecast charm	1	3	5
4649 Ford Tri-Motor, 1932	45	85	125
4650 Biplane, open-spoke tires, 1926	45	85	125
4659 Autogyro, 1934	40	80	120
4660 Aerodawn Seaplane	30	60	85
4660 Aerodawn, 1928, metal tires	30	60	85
4660 Aerodawn, 1928, rubber tires	30	55	80
4675 Bi-Wing Plane, closed metal tires	25	50	75
4675 Bi-Wing Seaplane	25	50	75
Airport hanger, two planes, box set	300	600	900

4659 Autogyro, 1934, Tootsietoy, $120

	C6	C8	C10
Army Cutlass, 1958-60 8		16	25
Army DC-4 Transport, 1941 40		75	110
Beechcraft Bonanza, 1948 8		16	25
Boeing 707, 1958 18		35	55
Boeing Stratocruiser, 1951-54 35		70	105
Coast guard Seaplane, 1950 50		100	150
Delta, 1954-55 15		25	40
Delta, two-piece casting 20		40	60
Dive-Bomber Waco Biplane, 1937 50		95	140
F-40 Skyway, 1956-69 7		13	20
F-86 Sabre Jet, single casting, 1956 7		13	20
F-86 Sabre Jet, two-casting body, 1950 8		16	25
F-94 Army Jet, 1956-69 8		16	25
F-94 Starfire Jet, 1956-69 7		13	20
High Wing Monoplane, early, two-color tin-litho, CJ 18		35	55
Hiller Helicopter, 1968-69 15		30	45
Lockheed Constellation, 1951 45		90	135
Navion, 1948-53 10		20	30
Navy Cutlass, 1956-69 7		13	20
P-38 Fighter, twin boom, twin engine, 1950 40		75	110
P-39 Fighter, 1947 50		100	150
P-80, Shooting Star, 1948 10		20	30
Panther Jet, single casting, 1956-69 7		13	20
Panther Jet, two-casting body, 1953-55 15		25	40
Piper Cub, 1948-52 8		16	25
Sikorsky S-58 Helicopter, 1958-69 30		55	85
Twin-Engine Convair, twin engine, 1950 ... 35		65	95
United DC-4 Supre Mainliner, 1941 35		65	95

Ships

	C6	C8	C10
127 Destroyer, 4" 9		12	15
128 Submarine, 4" 9		12	15
129 Tender, 4" 10		15	20
130 Yacht, 4" 18		24	30
1034 Battleship, 6" 15		20	25
1035 Cruiser, 5-1/2" 15		20	25
1036 Aircraft Carrier, 6" 14		21	28
1037 Transport, 6" 15		20	25
1038 Freighter, 5-1/2" 15		20	25
1039 Tanker, 5-1/2" 15		20	25

Miniature Ships

	C6	C8	C10
196 Battleship 4		6	8
1405 Fleet, nine-piece carded battleship assortment (1941): USS Idaho, USS Indiana, USS Tennessee, USS Texas, USS New Mexico, USS Maryland, USS Arizona, USS New York, USS Pennsylvania 50		75	100
1408 Naval Defense, fourteen-piece carded assortment (1941) 70		105	140

	C6	C8	C10
1612 Cruiser 3		4	6
1613 Destroyer 3		4	6
1614 Submarine (smaller) 2		3	4
1618 Submarine 3		4	6
1619 Destroyer 3		4	6
1620 Aero Carrier 4		6	8
1638 Battleship 4		6	8
1811 Sea Champions, five-piece carded set (1946) contains two No. 1638 battleships, one No. 1618 submarine, one No. 1619 destroyer, and one No. 1620 aero carrier 30		45	60
4519 Battleship 8		12	16
4538 Tugboat 2		3	4
4539 Speedboat 2		3	4

TURNER

	C6	C8	C10
Bulldog Mack, closed cab dump truck, red and green steel, 23" long 263		395	525
Dump Truck, 26" long 575		860	1150

An advertisement for Turner Toys from John C. Turner Corp. of Wapakoneta, Ohio.

	C6	C8	C10
Dump Truck, C-cab, 22" long	335	500	670
Dump Truck, friction, c. early 1930s, 15-1/2" long	1000	1700	2500
Fire Engine Pumper, 15" long	600	950	1400
Hook and Ladder, c. 1930s, 15" long	170	255	340
Lincoln Sedan, 26" long	1500	2800	4300
Packard (?) Roadster, friction, 26" long	700	1200	1700
Packard Roadster, 1920s, 16-1/2" long	800	1300	1900
Speedster, c. late 1920s, early 1930s, 17" long	500	750	1000
Steam Shovel	105	158	210
Turner Water Truck w/Copper Tank	150	225	300

Hay Loader, Case, Vindex, $5,600

This Mint condition Vindex Coast to Coast Bus was auctioned in 1994 for $18,000.

Power shovel, "P&H," Vindex, $8,000

VINDEX

Contributor: Kent M. Comstock, 532 Pleasant St. Ashland, OH 44805

	C6	C8	C10
Coast to Coast Bus, cast iron, c. 1929, Salesman's sample, 12" long, Mint condition, auctioned 1994			18,000
Hay Loader, Case, 9" long	2000	3500	5600
Thresher, "John Deere," 15" long	1400	2300	3900
Power shovel, "P&H," cast iron, wheels in caterpillar base, handle revolves rig, 12", 17" extended	2700	4100	8000
Racer, cast iron, "2," c. 1920s, 11-1/2" long	1000	1600	2500
Motorcycle w/detachable cop, "Henderson,"red or green, 9", auctioned in 1994 in Excellent condition for			3500
Motorcycle w/sidecar, two detachable cops, "Henderson," red or green, 9" long, Near Mint condition, auctioned in 1994			7500

Motorcycle with package truck, "Henderson PDQ Delivery," Vindex, $3,500

	C6	C8	C10
Motorcycle w/package truck, "HendersonPDQ Delivery," w/detachable blue rider, red or green, 9" long	1800	2500	3500

WANNATOY

	C6	C8	C10
Cadillac, plastic, 9" long	7	11	15
Convertible, 6" long	7	11	14
Delivery Truck, 4" long	3	4	6
Tank Truck, 5" long	7	11	14

WEEDEN

	C6	C8	C10
Auto, live steam, early, 8-3/4"	1500	3000	4500
Steam Fire Pumper	1300	2200	3500
Steam Road Roller, 1920s, brass, tin, cast iron, steam toy fired by alcohol, 7" long	250	375	500
Steam Tractor, 9" long	250	375	500

WILKINS

	C6	C8	C10
Aerial Ladder Truck, 1910, wind-up, 18" long	325	488	650
Dray, driver, barrels, tiller	400	600	800
Fire Engine, c. 1900 w/driver, steam boiler, 9" long	210	315	420
Hook and Ladder open truck, steel, wind-up motor, 9-1/4" long	238	360	475
Olds, 1904, curved dash, wind-up, 10"	400	600	800
Truck, open cab, very early, clockwork, 11" long	450	675	900

WOLVERINE

	C6	C8	C10
Car and Trailer, press down to operate, 27" long	200	300	400
Mystery Car, press down to make car move, c. 1938, 13" long	150	225	300
Speeding Bus "5 Via Main St.," tin litho, driver and occupants, "19302," press down on rear to move, 14" long	100	150	200
White Mustang dump truck, 14" long	70	105	140

WYANDOTTE

Wyandotte was formed in the fall of 1921 with toy pistols and rifles being their main product. But by 1935 the Wyandotte, Michigan, firm became known for its simple, streamlined, art deco steel cars and trucks with wooden wheels. During World War II Wyandotte made clips for the M-1 rifle and after the war moved the company to Piqua, Ohio.

In an attempt to diversify, it bought the Hafner Trains line, but went out of business in 1956. Wyandotte's heavy gauge steel toys with baked enamel finish also included aircraft, doll buggies, musical toys, wagons and games.

	C6	C8	C10
Ambulance, swinging rear door, No. 340, 11-1/4" long	112	168	225
Army Truck, steel w/wood wheels, 10" long	75	112	150
Army Truck, 22" long	100	150	200
Auto Transport, c. 1950s	75	112	150
Bank Truck, 6-1/2" long	37	56	75
Boattail Racer, steel, red w/white rubber tires, electric headlamps, 8-1/2" long	100	150	200
Car Carrier, early 1930s	125	188	250
Car Carrier, late, 22" long	150	225	300
Circus Truck, 10-3/4" long	250	375	500
Circus Truck, No. 503, 11" long	250	375	500

Auto Transport, Wyandotte, $150

Circus Truck with trailer, Wyandotte, $875

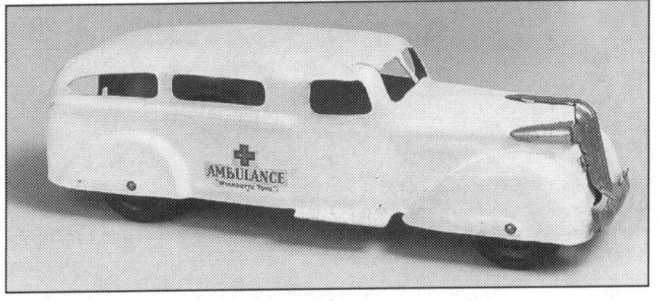

Ambulance, swinging rear door, No. 340, Wyandotte, $225

Wyandotte Advertisement from the February 1936 issue of Toys and Novelties

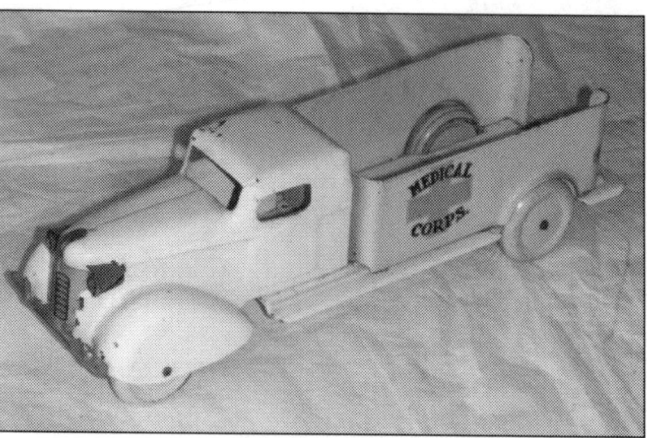

"Medical Corps" open truck, Wyandotte, $200

	C6	C8	C10
Circus Truck w/trailer, 19" long	438	655	875
City Delivery Truck, c. 1940	225	338	450
Convertible (open) Roadster, 1930s, 10" long	143	215	285
Cord, pressed steel, rubber tires, 13" long	283	425	565
Cord, Fire Dept. version, red, wind-up motor	365	548	730
Coupe, two-door, about 1930, 6" long	45	68	90
Coupe, c. 1940, 6" long	75	112	150
Coupe, c. 1930s, 7-1/2"	107	160	215
Coupe w/rumble seat, early 1930s, 8" long	125	188	250

	C6	C8	C10
Coupe, c. 1935, red w/white rubber tires, electric headlight, 8-1/2" long	100	150	200
Dairy Truck, 1930s, 12"	95	142	190
Deluxe Delivery Truck, c. 1936, 11" long	50	75	100
Dump Truck, No. 122	45	68	90
Dump Truck, No. 124	50	75	100
Dump Truck, No. 326, 1931	178	225	345
Dump Truck, 1930s, 6"	65	100	130
Dump Truck, pressed steel, c. 1940, 6-1/2" long	100	150	200
Dump Truck, steel, c. 1937, 7" long	45	68	90
Dump Truck, 12" long	52	78	105
Dump Truck, c. mid-1930s, white rubber tires, 15" long	67	100	135
Dump Truck, 1930s, 12-1/2"	57	85	115
Dump w/Sand Loader, c. 1941	300	450	600
Dump w/Scoop, post-war	55	83	110
Trailer Truck, "Express," tin wheels	102	153	205
Fire Truck w/ladder, ringing bell, 1939, 12" long	300	450	600
Grey Van, late, 24" long	173	215	355
Hydraulic Dump Truck, rear and side tip, 20" long	150	225	300

LaSalle Sedan with trailer, Wyandotte, $840

Oil Tanker, Wyandotte, $370

Side Dump, Wyandotte, $250

	C6	C8	C10
Ice Truck, marked "ICE" in sides, No. 348, c. 1940	250	375	500
LaSalle Sedan, 1930s	188	293	375
LaSalle Sedan w/trailer, 1930s, 25-1/2" long	420	630	840
"Medical Corps" open truck, c. 1939, 12" long	100	150	200
Motor Express Trailer Truck, c. 1950s	67	100	135
"Official AAA Service Car," 1930s, 12" long	238	305	475
Oil Tanker, 1930s	185	250	370
Pickup Truck, c. late 1930s, 6" long	30	45	60
Livestock Truck, "Pickway Pastures"	105	158	210
Race Car, pressed steel, rubber tires, c. 1937, 8-1/2" long	132	200	265
Railway Express Truck, c. 1939, 12" long	60	90	120
School Bus, 1930s, 24"	100	150	200
Sedan, c. 1940, 4" long	42	63	85
Sedan, c. 1940, 6" long	50	75	100
Semi, Grey Lines, cast wheels	200	300	400
Semi-Trailer Stake Truck "Valley Farms Livestock Produce," two-piece, 1940s, 8-1/2" long	52	78	105

Railway Express Truck, Wyandtte, $120

	C6	C8	C10
Side Dump, 1930s, 20"	125	188	250
Soap Box Derby Racer	200	300	400
Stake Truck, rubber wheels, 5-1/2" long	42	63	85
Stake Truck about 1930, 6-3/4" long	60	90	120
Stake Truck 1930s, white rubber wheels, 7-1/2" long	115	170	230
Stake Truck, 1931, No. 325, 9-3/4" long	134	200	268
Stake Truck, battery-operated headlights, 10" long	150	225	300
Stake Truck, c. 1930s, 12" long	88	132	175
Stake Truck, 1930s, 15"	300	450	600
Stake Truck, 20" long	90	135	180
Station Wagon, Cadillac, 1941, Woody model, No. 1007, metal, 21" long	188	280	375
Steam Shovel, 16" long	138	205	275
Sunshine Dairy Truck, 12"	60	90	120
Tow Truck, late	100	150	200
Town & Country Chrysler Convertible, 1940s, 12" long	105	158	210
Truck, "Toytown Delivery," 1941, 21" long	200	300	400
Station Wagon, "Toytown Estate"	125	188	250
Truck, "Toytown Ice Co.," c. 1941	100	150	200
Trailer Truck, plastic cab	65	98	130
Trailer Truck, 1950, extruded aluminum trailer	100	150	200
Valley Farms, 8-1/2"	85	128	170
Woody Convertible, top converts, 12" long	162	243	325
Wrecker, 1930s, wooden wheels, 10" long	75	112	150
Stake Van, "Wyandotte Truck Lines"	95	143	190
Sedan, "Wyandottey," pressed steel, two-door, sweeping long fenders, c. WWII, black plastic wheels	30	45	60

MISCELLANEOUS VEHICLES

	C6	C8	C10
Aerial Ladder Truck, Kelmet, 30" long	605	908	1210
Aerocar PT 560 Made in U.S.A. Plas-Tex, plastic, 7-1/2"	30	45	60
Ambulance, very early, Hillclimber, 10-1/2" long	500	800	1100
Anti-Aircraft Truck, "USA 1120," Sonny	600	900	1200
Armored Truck, pressed steel, Hillclimber, friction, 11" long	500	800	1100
Army Tank No. ST, cast iron, Big Bang, 8-1/8" long	35	50	100
Army Truck "U.S.A. 1120," Sonny	350	525	700
Artillery Truck, "US 1120," Sonny, 26" long	350	525	700
Auto, woman driver, friction, very early, Hillclimber, 6" long	500	750	1000
Boattail Speedster, cast iron, blue w/nickel wheels, driver, c. 1920s 5" long	100	150	200

	C6	C8	C10
Brinks Truck Bank, lead alloy, 9" long....... 175	263	350
Buick, 1947, plastic, 5-3/8" long 5	8	10
Cadillac, four-door, Lapin, 1948, 6" long.... 10	15	20
Caterpillar D-7, Reuhl........................... 312	468	625
Chrysler Airflow, heavy sheet metal w/wind-up motor, tin grille, headlightsand bumper, wooden wheels, 4" long 1200	2200	3000
City Fire Dept. Truck, 1930, pressed steel, rubber tires, 26" long 450	675	900
Comet Race Car, "3," fuel-powered, Hiller, c. 1940-42 1200	2000	2800
Corvette, Eldon, 14" long...................... 37	56	75
Coupe, plastic, Lapin, 1939...................... 15	20	30
Delivery Truck w/driver, friction, 10-1/2" long 100	150	200
Delivery Truck, "Holmes Coal Co.," pressed steel, 17-1/2" long 400	600	800
Delivery Truck, cast iron, 3-1/2" long 60	90	120
Delivery Truck, Packard, steel, 28" long.... 400	600	800
Delivery Van, wooden, "John Wanamaker," Laketoy, 10-1/2" long 180	270	360
Duesenberg electric w/transformer and steel track, Kingston Producers, Kokomo, 12" long 1200	2500	3700
Dump Truck (Beck), steers via horn on topof cab, late 1940s, large...................... 60	90	120
Dump Truck, "Dept. of Street Cleaning," c. 1935, 10-1/2" long 105	158	210
Dump Truck, cast iron, "2205," 4-1/2" long.................................. 90	135	180
Dump Truck, cast iron, driver, 7" long........ 90	135	180
Dump Truck, pressed steel, c. 1939, 6" long.. 50	75	100
Dump Truck, Richmond........................... 62	93	125
Dump Truck, Sonny, 26" long 400	600	800
Dump Truck, steel windup, 4-1/2" long...... 20	30	40
Dump Truck, tin, wooden wheels, 5-3/4" long.................................. 20	30	40
Dump Truck, white, Kelmet No. 501, 25" long.. 900	1500	2200
Electric Automobile, c. 1903, pressed steel, battery-activated, Knapp, c. 1903, 11" long.............................. 1100	1750	2600
Electric Racing Automobile set, Lionel ... 1000	1700	2400

	C6	C8	C10
Electricar, the Red Arrow, Kingston Producers, 1930s, 15" long 150	225	300
Fire Chief Car, friction, siren, Lupor, 7" long 50	75	100
Fire Chief Car, Hoge, 15" long................... 335	500	670
Fire Truck, siren, Saunders, 13" long.......... 50	75	100
Fire Truck, white, w/ladder, Kelmet 1000	1650	2400
Ford coupe, blue, chrome wheels, 5" long .. 80	120	160
Ford coupe, cast iron, black, chrome wheels, c. 1920s, 5" long 80	120	160
Frederick & Henry Horseless Carriage w/driver, cast iron and tin, Fallows Toys, c. 1905, 8"... 1500	2500	3900
Friction auto, c. 1894, wood, iron and tin, Clark, 10-1/2" long..................... 315	472	630
Friction auto, c. 1901, wood body covered w/steel, Clark................... 600	950	1300
Hook and Ladder wagon, aluminum, w/driver, 13" long........................... 100	150	200
Hook and Ladder Wagon, painted pressed steel, friction, driver, Hillclimber, 20" long...................... 300	450	600
Hook and Ladder wagon, tin friction, 21" long 100	150	200
Horseless carriage runabout, Ives, 6-1/2" long, 6" high to the top of jockey....... 2500	3750	5000
Horseless Carriage, woman driver, cast iron and wood, very early, Hillclimber, 7" long.......................... 350	525	700
Hose Wagon, 1897, two riders, friction toy.................................... 125	187	250
Jeepster, rubber tires, 14-1/4" long.............. 20	30	40
Ladder Truck, driver front and rear, cast iron, 5" long 45	68	90
Mack Dump Truck, cast iron, 1930s, 8-1/2" long 275	362	550
Mack Ladder Truck, cast iron, 18" long 300	450	600
Mack Stake Truck, cast iron, 7" long........... 70	105	140
Motor Tank No. ST, cast iron, Big Bang, 9-1/2" long................................ 75	250	500

Dump Truck, Sonny, 26" long, $800

Moving Van, "David," Rehrberger, c. 1924, 7-1/4" long, $4,800

	C6	C8	C10
Motorcyle, "Patrol," w/rider, c. 1940, cast iron, 6-1/4" long ... 160		240	320
Moving Van, "David," Rehrberger, c. 1924, 7-1/4" long ... 1800		3000	4800
Oil and Gas Truck, cast iron, 8" ... 200		300	400
Oil Truck, c. 1936, pressed steel, 10-3/4" long ... 100		150	200
Olds, clockwork, pressed steel, curved dash, Hafner, c. 1903, 10" long ... 500		750	1000
Police Car, 1949 Ford, Lupor ... 90		135	180
Race set, Midget, aluminum body, rubber tires, Ohlsson & Rice, c. 1940s 325		488	650
Racer "Parker Special," heavy steel body w/steel wheels, 11" ... 75		112	150
Racer w/track, Hillclimber, 7-1/2" long 375		562	750
Racer, pull toy, w/two riders, Ted Toys ... 125		188	250
Racer, Racer, steel wheels, Cleveland Toy, c. 1935, 13" long ... 175		262	350
Racer, Silver Bullet, Buffalo Toys, 26" long ... 350		525	700
Racing Car, cast iron, 7-1/4" long ... 260		390	520
Racing Car, cast iron, w/driver, full figure, spiked wheels, early 1920s ... 75		112	150
Racing Car, friction, w/driver, c. 1925 ... 150		225	300
Racing Car, pressed steel w/driver, white rubber tires, rubberband and gear powered, 7-1/2" long ... 17		26	35
Racing Car, tin litho, "Star Brand Shoes Are Better," "The Winner," 8-1/2" long ... 1200		1900	2800
Racing Set, 1930s, three tin racing cars, small tin garage ... 125		187	250
Roadster, Republic, 1920s, 10" long ... 140		210	280
Rock Crusher, "Cedar Rapids," Reuhl ... 600		900	1230
Rocket-Firing Tank, Eldon, 8" long ... 19		28	38
Roundabout w/upholstered drivers seat, clockwork, steel, Hafner, 7" ... 450		675	900
Sedan, six side windows, plastic, Lapin 1939 ... 15		20	30
Slot Car set, Road Race, Eldon, 1965 ... 32		48	65
Stake Truck, Chevrolet, plastic, Lapin, 1947, 4" long ... 10		15	20

	C6	C8	C10
Steam Pumper Fire Truck, cast iron, 5" ... 45		68	90
Steam Pumper Truck, cast iron, hard rubber wheels, driver, 12" long ... 150		225	300
Steam Pumper, "Boston," w/lamp, cast-iron wheels, 15-1/2" long ... 2500		3750	5000
Steam Pumper, tin and wooden friction drive, 11" long ... 70		105	140
Steam Pumper, tin and wooden chain, friction drive w/driver, "National," 10" long ... 200		300	400
Steam Roller, cast iron, c. early 1930s, 4-3/4" long ... 75		112	150
Steam Roller, steam-engine powered ... 200		300	450
Steam Shovel, "Sand Digger," 28" ... 150		225	300
Steamer, cast iron, two drivers, Ives, 19-1/2" long ... 500		750	1000
Tanker, Kelmet, 27" long ... 1800		3000	4100
Taxi Cab w/driver, sheet-metal, friction motor, Republic, c. 1926 ... 287		430	575
Texaco Tank Truck, 24" long ... 35		52	70
Touring Car, clockwork, pressed steel, Hafner, 10" long ... 1200		2000	2800
Touring Car, Hillclimber, 11" long ... 475		715	950
Tow Truck, cast iron, rubber wheels, 7-1/2" long ... 125		187	250
Tow Truck, plastic, Eldon, 18" long ... 50		75	100
Tractor, "Fordson," w/driver, cast iron, 5-3/4" long ... 140		210	280
Truck, "Express J & B," Jones & Bixler, 15-1/2" long ... 800		1300	1900
Truck, "Gibbs No. 701," Gibbs ... 150		250	350
Truck, "Railway Express," cast iron, early 1930s, 5" long ... 110		165	220
Truck, clockwork, steel "Auto Express Co.," Hafner, 8-1/2" long ... 450		675	900
Truck, friction, pressed steel and plastic, "Rocket Launcher" "U.S.A.F.," c. 1960 .. 60		90	120
Truck, Plumber's, plastic, Revell, 10" long .. 50		75	100
U.S. Army Shooting Tank, wood, pre WWII, metal action, 6" long ... 22		33	45

WHITE KNOB WIND-UPS

White knob wind-ups are small, plastic mechanical toys that came on the market around the mid-to-late 1970s. They get their name from the little white (sometimes colored on newer toys) ridged knob at the end of a metal rod which extends from the body and winds the motor when rotated.

Most wind-ups offer a single basic movement or action. "Walkers," "hoppers," "climbers," "rollers," "flip-overs," or "pop-overs" perform on a flat surface, while toys intended to be pinned on clothing may have eyes that move up and down or ears that wiggle back and forth. Swimmers move in water. A few of the most desirable white knob wind-ups have multiple movements occurring at the same time or in sequence. Wind-ups were (and are) typically sold loose or in bubble packaging. A few came boxed in sets with other figures or with accessories. Production originally was in Japan, Macao, Singapore and Taiwan, but more recently is centered in China.

White knob wind ups come in a variety of themes—transportation, tools and utensils, sports, space, popular culture, novelty, musical, movies and television, holidays and seasons, foods, fast-food giveaways, fairy tales, Disney, cartoon and comic characters, animals, and anatomical parts. Some white knob wind-ups have been produced by well-known companies such as Tomy, Galoob, Russ and Mattel, while others seem to be sold by small companies or importers with no reference as to manufacturer.

The following list is only representative of the many hundreds of wind-ups that have been produced. Color, structural, and decorating variations exist in many examples, and toys originally issued by one company (e.g., Tomy) may be released later by another company (e.g., Playskool). Prices quoted below reflect the original releases that are often marked as to manufacturer. As with other toys, white knob wind-ups in original packaging are more valuable. C10 values reflect Mint, working wind-ups with all accessories.

Contributor: M. Aaron Roy, Lake Erie Toy Museum, 817 Edgehill, Ashland, OH. Roy is a professor of psychology at Ashland University in Ashland, Ohio, and owner of the Lake Erie Toy Museum on Kelleys Island near Marblehead, Ohio. Included in the museum is his personal collection of toys from 1870 to 1980 is on display. Roy has collected a wide range of toys for over thirty years and is the author of numerous professional and hobby-related articles.

CHARACTERS

	C6	C8	C10
Barbie Microwave Oven, Sewing Machine, Radio/Tape Deck, VCR, Camera, Telephone, Computer, Mantel Clock, Stereo, Mixer; Mattel, 1986 and Arco, 1988, each	1	2	3
Cabbage Patch Kids, Tomy, 1985			
Crawler: boy or girl, each	4	6	8
Girl in walker	4	6	8
Boy with basketball	6	9	12
Boy on stick horse	6	9	12
Girl Cheerleader	6	9	12
Girl Baton Twirler	6	9	12
Rocking Babies: Basinette, Swing, Rocking Horse, each	10	15	20
The Chipmunks Hoppers (Imperial, 1983)			
Alvin w/harmonica	6	9	12
Simon w/guitar	6	9	12
Theodoor w/drums	6	9	12
E.T. Walker, LJN, 1982	6	9	12
Pop-up Space Ship	9	12	15
Garfield, playing guitar, saxophone or xylophone, Kat's Meow, 1985, each	9	12	15

Get Along Gang, Zipper the Cat, Tomy, $16

	C6	C8	C10
Get Along Gang, Dotty Dog, Montgomery Moose, Zipper the Cat, Bet-it-All Beaver, Woolma Lamb and Portia Porcupine on various vehicles, eleven different combinations; Tomy, 1981, each	10	13	16
Mickey Mouse			
Smile with white dots on pants, Tomy	5	10	15
No smile or dots, Durham Ind.	20	30	40

Nintendo, Super Mario 2 (left) and Zelda (right), Nasta, $20

Pluto, ears, collar, tail are part of body mold, Tomy, $10

	C6	C8	C10
Muppets, Tomy, 1983			
Pop-Ups: Animal Drummer or Great Gonzo's Shark Escape, each ... 8		12	16
Pop-Overs: Miss Piggy or Great Gonzo, each ... 8		12	16
Flip-Floppers: Animal Jalopy or Miss Piggy Swinetrek, each ... 8		12	16
Swimmers: Kermit the Frog, Miss Piggy, Fozzie the Bear, each ... 7		10	14
Nintendo, Zelda or Super Mario 2, Nasta ... 10		15	20
Pac Man rollers, Tomy, 1982			
Mr. or Ms., each ... 4		6	8
Inky Ghost, blue ... 10		15	20
Blinky Ghost, red ... 10		15	20

	C6	C8	C10
Pink Panther, Bandai-America, 1981			
Pink Panther Walker ... 15		20	30
Inspector Walker ... 20		30	40
Pluto			
Separate pieces for ears, collar and tail, Durham, 1977 ... 15		20	25
Ears, collar, tail are part of body mold, Tomy, 1977 ... 6		8	10
Popeye or Brutus Walker, Durham, 1980, each ... 20		25	30
Q*Bert Hopper, Kenner, 1983 ... 6		9	12
Smurfs Walkers, Galoob, 1982			
Musicians: trumpet, guitar, drum ... 2		4	6
Figures: Jokey holding present, Smurfette, papa Smurf, Flying Smurf, Gargomel, each ... 4		6	8

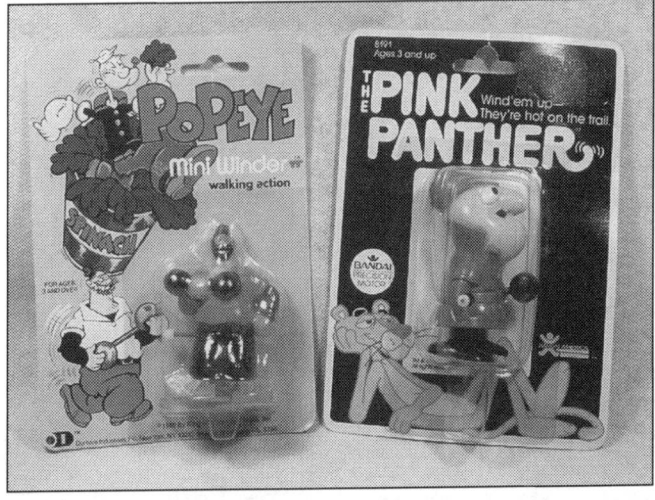

Left to Right: Brutus Walker, Durham, $30; Pink Panther, Inspector, $40

*Q*Bert hopper, Kenner, $12*

Left to Right: Spot 7-Up, Nasta, $12; Tang Trio Walker, Nasta, $12

	C6	C8	C10
Plain Walker, blue knob	10	15	20
Smurf on Swing	6	9	12
Smurfs on Teeter Totter	6	9	12
Smurfs Jumping Rope	6	9	12
Smurf Fun House, mushroom	10	15	20
Snoopy, Aviva			
Swimmer or walker	6	9	12
Walkers: Snoopy w/Top Hat, Snoopy Matador, Snoopy Tennis Player, Snoopy as Red Baron, Snoopy as Bull Fighter, Belle, Woodstock, each	3	5	7

Spiderman riding cycle with wrist-mounted ramp, Buddy L, $25

Birthday Cake Hoppers, yellow, Russ, $8

	C6	C8	C10
Snorks, Tomy, 1984			
Swimmers: five different, each	6	9	12
Walkers: five different, each	6	9	12
Spiderman Riding Cycle, Buddy L, 1981	15	20	25
Spot 7-Up, Nasta, 1988	4	8	12
Tang Trio walker, Nasta, 1988	4	8	12
Tom and Jerry Walkers, 1989, Multitoys			
Tom or Jerry	4	6	8
Spike, Tyke, Droopy, Quacker, each	5	8	10
Wizard of Oz Walkers, Multitoys, 1988			
Scarecrow, Alice, Witch, each	4	6	8

NON-CHARACTERS

	C6	C8	C10
Babies, Crawler or Walker, Tomy, 1977, each	4	6	8
Bathtubbies, Swimming Whale, Frog, Bear, Seal, Penguin, Turtle, Goldfish, and Duck, Tomy, 1983, each	2	3	4

Left to Right: Box Pops, Looney Bird, Tomy, $22; Minimals, hippopotamus, Tomy, $30; Major League Football helmet, Cleveland Browns, Russ, $8

Bumbling Boxing Game, Tomy, $30

Fruits and Vegetables, pepper, pear, pineapple and strawberry, $10 each

	C6	C8	C10
Birthday Cake hoppers, yellow or blue, Russ, 1989	4	6	8
Box Pops, rolling box stops and "Wacky Clown," "Funny Face" or "Looney Bird" pops out of the top, Tomy, 1981, each	10	16	22
Bumbling Boxing Game, two walking boxers on ring, Tomy, 1982	15	22	30
Burger King hoppers, burger, shake, fries, Talbot, 1983, each	4	6	8
Christmas, Russ			
Santa Hopper	4	6	8
Tree Hopper	4	6	8
Snowball on Skis Roller	6	8	10
Chubbles, walkers that hold gumballs, includes a boxer, dancer, robot and monster, Arrow, 1983, each	20	25	30
Curious Critters, (Rollers that are directed by a magnetic wand), Tomy, 1984			
Dogs: two different ones, each	8	12	16
Cats: two different ones, each	8	12	16
Dinosaurs, motorized kit, five different kits w/cream colored pieces on a sprue, Tomy, 1987, each	20	30	40
Flip Floppers, bus, plane, car, racer, space ship, helicopter, train, dune buggy, Tomy, 1983, each	2	3	4
Flopovers, flip-flop walkers that include a crab, bug, frog and gorilla, Tomy, 1983, each	8	10	12
Funny Football Game, Tomy, 1982	20	30	40
Fruits and Vegetables, rollers w/opening tops, paper stickers, includes pinapple, pepper, strawberry and pear, each	6	8	10

Flopovers, gorilla, Tomy, $12

	C6	C8	C10
Get Along Gadgets Rollers, toaster, clock, phone, coffee pot, record player, Tomy, 1983, each	6	8	10
Get Along Gang Rollers, Tomy, 1984			
Zipper Cat or Dotty Dog on a handcar, each	6	9	12
Lamb or Moose on a raft, each	6	9	12
Porcupine or Moose on a skateboard, each	6	9	12
Hamburgers			
Hopper, Russ	8	10	12
Roller	3	5	7
Walker	2	4	6
Home Run Homer Game, baseball hopper on green playing field, Tomy, 1982	15	22	30
Hop-A-Long Hoopster Game, hopping basketball on court, Tomy, 1982	15	22	30
Hilarious Hats Walkers, cowboy, football, police, Tomy, 1983, each	8	12	16
Inch-A-Longs, dog, crocodile, locomotive and truck crawling rollers, Bandai-America, 1981, each	6	9	12
Kid-A-Long Kids, boy on skateboard, girl on skates or tricycle, boy on wagon and cowboy or cowgirl on stick, Tomy, 1979, each	10	15	20
Lil' Big Toppers, Tomy, 1983			
Elephant roller, multi-actions	10	15	20

Kind-A-Long Kids, cowboy, girl on skates and boy on skateboard, Tomy, $20 each

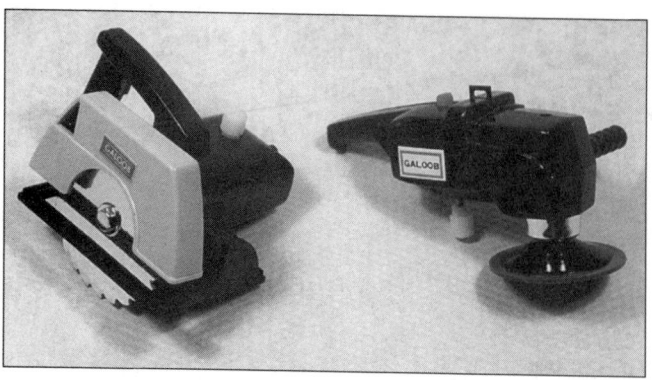

Mini-Tools, circular saw, sander, Galoob, $8

	C6	C8	C10
Clown in Car or Bear, each 5		8	10
Mad Balls Rollers, Screamin Meemie, Horn Head, Skull Face, Slobulus; each had heads w/moving tongues, Spearhead, 1986, each 2		3	4
Major League Baseballs, Baseball Hoppers w/colors and logos of each team, Russ, 1989, each 4		6	8
Major League Football Helmet, hoppers w/colors and logos of each team, Russ, 1989, each 4		6	8
Mini-Appliances, Floor Buffer, stereo and speakers, sewing machine, blender, mixer, food processor, Galoob, 1979, each 3		5	7
Mini-Tools, circular saw, jigsaw, sander, drill, chain saw, Galoob, 1980, each 4		6	8
Mini-Tools, chain saw, drill, jigsaw and circular saw, Imperial, 1988, each 2		3	4
Minimals, dog, duck, elephant, hippopotamus, horse, giraffe rollers about 1-1/2" long w/exterior wheels and back hole "hook," Tomy, 1982, each 15		23	30
Mity Machines, pile driver, pounder, bulldozer and backhoe, Galoob, 1984, each 5		7	9
Pecks Abouts, two-tone blue or red/yellow woodpeckers w/suction cups for feet, Tomy, 1982, each 8		12	16

Prancing Pony, Arabian (left) and Pinto (right), Tomy, $16 each

Robo Strux, Tomy, $40

	C6	C8	C10
Pillow People, boy, girl or baby w/pillow-shaped body, Nasta, 1988, each 8		10	12
Pocket Pets Hoppers, goose, squirrel, penguin, turtle, frog, toucan, beetle, rabbit, dog, owl, duck, and chicken, Tomy, 1983, each 2		3	4
Prancing Ponys, Pinto, Arabian Stallion, Palomino, Appaloosa w/accessories of a saddle, bridle, bucket, and brush, Tomy, 1983, each 8		12	16
Rascal Robots or Pocket 'Bots, three different walkers, Tomy, 1977 4		6	8
Robo Strux, kits w/two different colors of plastic on spue which make a robot-like creature, ten different robots, Tomy, 1985, each 20		30	40

Storybook Wind-ups, Mrs. Bunny pushing wheelbarrow (left) and Mrs. Goose with basket and Baby Quackers (right), Tomy, $60

Ugh-A-Bugs, beetle, $12

	C6	C8	C10
Robot Lion Force, black, red, green, yellow robot, LJN, 1984	5	10	15
Robot Star Mission, Durham, 1978	5	10	15
Roving Eyes, camera or binoculars w/moving eyes, Tomy, 1982, each	6	8	10

	C6	C8	C10
Scurry Furries, rabbit, dog, raccoon, owl, and green dragon, hoppers or rollers that are "fur" covered, Tomy, 1982	7	10	14
Silvia and Silvan, white or black cat w/fur and felt ears, Japan Artist Society, each	10	15	20
Snow Funnies Rollers, bear or rabbit on skis, Tomy, 1981, each	2	4	6
Storybook Winpups, Mrs. Goose w/basket and Baby Quackers or Mrs. Bunny pushing wheelbarrow and Baby Bouncy w/small paper storybook, Tomy, 1983, each	20	40	60
Strolling Bowling Game, hopper bowling ball knocks pins over on lane, Tomy, 1982	15	22	30
Ugh-A-Bugs Crawlers, stag beetle, tarantula, and atlas beetle, Tomy, 1981, each	6	9	12

WOOD &
COMPOSITION TOYS

See also Comic Character, Disney, Miscellaneous and Movie, Radio and TV

What is composition? Composition is a mixture of sawdust, glue and various materials that is heated and placed into molds to produce varied pieces. These pieces are then sanded, painted and made into many types of toys.

The toys in this chapter represent the years 1900-1950. Many of the pieces are made from a combination of composition heads, wood jointed bodies and string components, such as the Hotpoint Man, the RCA Radiotron Man and Pete the Pup by The Cameo Doll Company.

A little known company, Hatler Toy Company, a subsidiary of Franz Manufacturing Co., produced wood toys from their factory in Sterling, Illinois. They produced mainly pull toys of Blacks between the years of 1920-1936.

Fictional and playful characters were widely depicted in wood toys. The W.D. Reed Company of Leominister, Massachusetts, a producer of wood toys from 1875-1910, made such familiar toys as Gigantic Circus and Mammoth Hippodrome. Other interesting pieces of the time include composition and wood Punch and Judy puppets and Noah's Ark which came with several carved wood animals.

The Jaymar Company of New York was known for their small wood-jointed figures. Sears distributed Jaymar toys such as Moon Mullins, Little Orphan Annie, the Popeye family, and Amos and Andy. Easily affordable for most of today's collectors, the majority of the pieces can be found in the $50-$75 price range with the more popular character pieces ranging from $150-$200.

Kohner Brothers produced the fun push-up puppets that can be found in both plastic and wood variations. They used many Disney and licensed characters in their products including Howdy Doody, The Lone Ranger, Peter Pan and Donald Duck. Some were made of all wood, while others had a wood figure with plastic base.

There are several manufacturers that stand out as a leader of wood toys in the early 1900s not listed above. The number of companies that dabbled in wood toys is astronomical, this is the main reason many of these toys are so hard to identify. Companies would produce small, often unmarked samplings of wood toys and then, for no apparent reason, quit making them.

The market for wood toys will continue to grow due to the workmanship, durability and personalities of the marvelous pieces produced.

Condition is a major component when pricing composition and wood dolls and toys. Over time, elements such as heat, dust and humidity can destroy a toy. Excellent condition—C-8 to C-10—would describe an item with the smooth composition and good coloring. Good Condition—C-6 to C-8—would describe an without any obvious cracking and few of the small lines often found on composition toys or "crazing." Although, crazing, if minor, does not take away from the price of the item and is considered acceptable for an older piece. Poor Condition—C-5 or worse—describes an item with cracks, missing pieces, composition that has been lifted away from the body, or missing of faded paint. Do note, however, that the value of a doll will not go down if it had been restrung. A loosely or unstrung doll or toy can be easily repaired at a doll hospital.

Contributor: Michele Karl, P.O. Box 549, Port Richey, FL 34673. Karl is a collector who has written over 100 articles on dolls, toys and collectibles, including *Composition & Wood Dolls and Toys.* She is currently working on two more titles—*What Celebrities Collect* and *Plastic Dolls of the '50s and '60s.*

*Pete the Pup,
Cameo Doll Co.,
12", $275*

Mexican Man, possibly Jaymar, $50

Hustler Twins, Hustler, $150

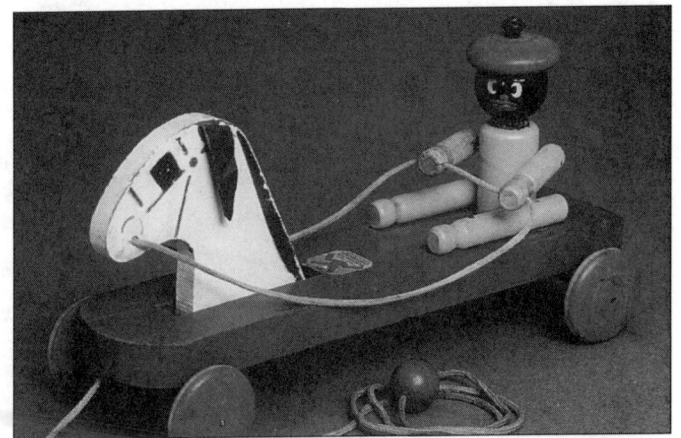

Hustler Sambo, $250

Betty Roll Duck, Hustler Doll Co., $75

Hustler Poncho, $200

Soldiers on Horses, possibly Reed, $300

HUSTLER DOLL COMPANY

	C6	C8
Betty Roll Duck	50	75
Hustler Twins, add $75 for box	100	150
Hustler Watch Dog	125	150
Hustler Poncho	150	200
Hustler Sambo	200	250

CAMEO DOLL COMPANY

	C6	C8
Bandy (Bandmaster)	1000	1500
Hotpoint Man	1000	1500
Jeep, 7-1/4"	500	600
Jeep, 9	600	750
Jeep, 12-1/2"	750	900
Pete the Pup, 9-10"	150	225
Pete the Pup, 12"	200	275
Pete the Pup, 15"	275	350
Pete the Pup, 17"	350	400
RCA Radiotron Man	1000	1500

Denny Dimwit, 1948, $350

Reed Circus, $2000

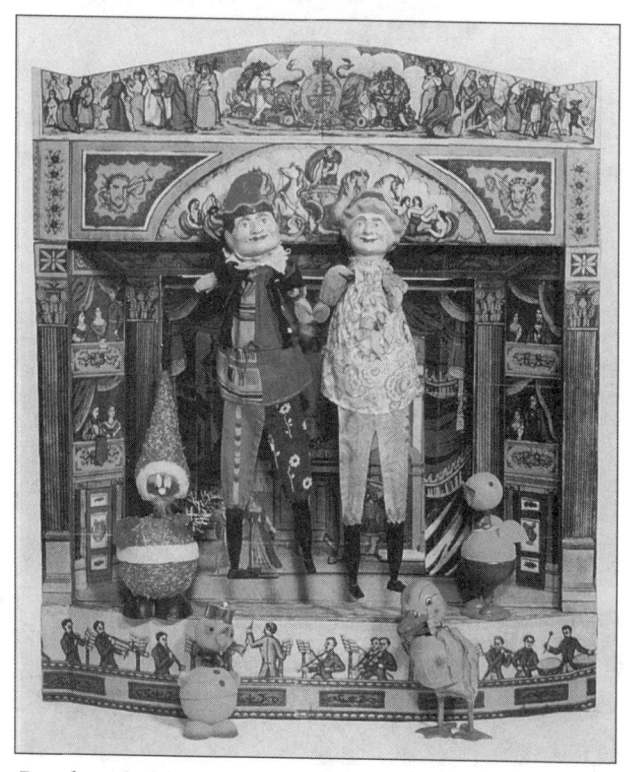

Punch and Judy Theater, $650

JAYMAR

	C6	C8
China Man	50	75
Ed Wynn	125	150
Indian	100	125
Jester	25	50
Policeman	50	75
Sandy (Little Orphan Annie)	50	75
Soldier	50	75
Mexican man, unmarked, believed to be made by Jaymar	25	50

KOHNER

	C6	C8
Bronco Bill, No. 125	25	50
Donald Duck at Wheel, No. 125	75	125
Howdy Doody, No. 180	75	100
Indian Chief, No. 176	35	50

	C6	C8
Lone Ranger, No. 182	50	75
Peter Pan, No. 141	50	75
Princess Summerfall Winterspring, No. 136	50	75

MISCELLANEOUS

	C6	C8
Soldiers on Horses, possibly Reed, early 1900s	200	300
Reed Circus, complete w/original box and paperwork	1500	2000
Denny Dimwit, marked "He wiggles, He Waggles, He's Smart, He's Friendly," 1948	250	350
Noah's Ark, wood w/painted figures, top opens to hold animals, late 1800s-early 1900s, 27" long	600	750+
Punch and Judy Theater, composition heads w/cloth bodies	500	650

Yo-Yos

Yo-yo history goes back far into the misty reaches of history. If you don't believe me, page through the *Oxford English Dictionary* to the word "bandalore," the yo-yo term of a prior age. According to the venerable OED, the bandalore even back in the early 1800s was regarded as the toy of a bygone era.

It may have originated in ancient Greece, ancient Egypt, or even the Philippines, where the items were not toys but weapons of the hunt.

The yo-yo of today, however, is most definitely a toy. It is one, moreover, that toy collectors are finding of increasing interest.

Toy yo-yos in the United States have been made primarily of tin, wood or plastic. There are desirable yo-yos to be found in all three materials.

Yo-yo collectors assign value to the toys on the basis of manufacturer, age, type and condition, just as do other toy collectors. Desirable yo-yo manufacturers include not only Duncan but Flores, Goody, Cheerio and Chico. Yo-yo manufacturers familiar to collectors of other varieties of toys include Lumar and Kusan.

American yo-yos seem to go back to the 1920s, when the country went through its first craze for the ancient toy. Flores, Duncan, and Cheerio, the last one a Canadian company, all started in that decade. Each subsequent decade seems to have seen the arrival of at least one new yo-yo manufacturer.

Many of the normal considerations go into evaluating the condition of an old yo-yo, with the addition of a few special ones. Since some early wooden yo-yos were fairly generic in appearance, the survival of the paper label or decal is of more than modest concern. Similarly, since others were never given labels at all, packaging becomes of paramount importance in identifying types. In die-stamped wood yo-yos, the condition of the stamp matters most. Edge-wear from "walking the dog" tends to be more acceptable than wear to the sides.

There is, of course, that element of how well the toy works. I have no idea if other yo-yo aficionados operate the same way, but unless the yo-yo in question has unwound and wound down and up a string a few times, it seems somehow ... Well, somehow less like a yo-yo.

If that makes any sense to you at all, then you will soon be searching for some of the items below.

Unless otherwise noted, the presence of the word "Junior" in the name or description refers to a toy slightly smaller than standard. Please also note that prices are highly volatile at present. Some of the prices below represent auction prices which reflect truly heightened collector interest, spurred on by truly Excellent condition examples coming into the market. Although I have tried to fairly break down prices for lesser-condition examples, poorer condition yo-yos will usually command considerably less than Mint examples, no matter the rarity. Keep in mind that in a volatile market such as this, prices may rise—or drop!—unpredictably.

Contributor: Mark Rich, P.O. Box 971, Stevens Point WI 54481. Rich is a collector, dealer and free-lance writer who has a penchant for yo-yos.

Bob Allen

	C6	C8	C10
Sidewinder Return Top, plastic, 1960s 12		18	28
Sidewinder Return Top, tin whistler, 1960s 22		34	45
Sidewinder Return Top, wood, 1960s 15		25	35

Cayo Manufacturing Company

	C6	C8	C10
Musical Ka-Yo, tin whistler, 1930s 110		160	200
Whistling Ka-Yo, tin whistler 125		175	225

Cheerio Toys and Games Inc.

	C6	C8	C10
#25 Tournament Practice Return Top, wood, foil decal, 1940s-50s.................... 25		37	50
#33 Beginners, wood, die-stamped, 1950s 20		32	45
#54 Special Yo-Yo, wood 25		37	50
#55 Beginner's Return Top, wood, foil decal 30		45	65
"Cheerio Yo-Yo, Kitchener Buttons, Ltd." wood, decal, 1920s-40s 75		115	150

	C6	C8	C10
Glitter Spin, wood, die-stamped, four jewels each side, 1950s	65	100	135
Glitter Spin, wood, foil decal, four jewels each side, 1947	75	115	150
Official Pro 99, wood, foil decal	30	45	65
Tournament Practice 99, wood, foil decal	45	70	90

Chico Toys Company

	C6	C8	C10
Olympic Tournament Yo-Yo Tops, wood, foil decal	20	32	45
Super Deluxe, wood, die-stamped plus label	15	25	35
Super Tournament top, wood, label	15	25	35
Superb Junior Top, wood, die-stamped	15	25	35

Dell Plastics

	C6	C8	C10
Big "D" Astronaut, plastic, spherical sides, 1960s	7	18	28
Big "D" Sleeper King, plastic	4	10	18
Big "D" Trickster, plastic, swirled	5	12	20
Fireball, plastic, spherical sides	7	16	25

Donald F. Duncan, Inc.

In the following listings, YYT = Yo-Yo Tops, and YYRT = Yo-Yo Return Top

Duncan Wood Yo-Yos

	C6	C8	C10
Disney's Wonderful World of Color, 1960s	7	16	25
Duncan Autograph Yo-Yo, late 1950s	20	32	45

Chico Superb Standard Top, $35

Duncan Beg. Yo-Yo, wood, $30

	C6	C8	C10
Duncan Autograph Yo-Yo, spherical, late 1950s	20	32	45
Duncan Award Yo-Yo, yellow Mr. Yo-Yo label, late 1950s, 5"dia.	50	75	100
Duncan Beg. Yo-Yo, Yo-Yo Man's head die-stamped	8	19	30
Duncan Beg. Yo-Yo	8	19	30
Duncan Brand Yo-Yo, wood-grain design, w/indented cattle-brands, 1977	4	9	15
Duncan Chief YYRT #44, foil label w/Indian, 1950s	32	55	75
Duncan Day-Glo Tournament Yo-Yo #77, Mr. Yo-Yo decal, fluorescent paint, 1950s	25	37	50
Duncan Dukes of Hazzard General Lee Yo-Yo, 1981	3	8	12
Duncan Eagle YYRT #999, oversized, paper label, 1950s	50	75	100
Duncan Expert Award Yo-Yo, pearlessence paint, 1950s	20	32	45
Duncan Gen. Beg. Yo-Yo Tops, 1930s	15	25	35
Duncan Hoot Mon!, 1960s	8	19	30
Duncan Imperial Jr. YYRT, w/Mickey Mouse or Yo-Yo Man paper inserts, 1960s	7	16	25
Duncan Imperial Yo-Yo, die-stamped fleur-de-lis, 1960s	3	8	12
Duncan Imperial Yo-Yo, fleur-de-lis, swirled plastic	7	16	25
Duncan Imperial YYT, Chevron logo, 1960s	7	16	25
Duncan Jeweled Cat's Eye	5	12	20

Duncan Gen. Beg. Yo-Yo Tops, wood, 1930s, $35

	C6	C8	C10
Duncan Jeweled Pearlessence Tournament YYRT	25	37	50
Duncan Jeweled Super Yo-Yo	30	45	65
Duncan Jeweled Tourn. YYT #101, four jewels, 1940s-50s	20	32	45
Duncan Junior Yo-Yo, wood, die-stamped, late 1950s	15	25	35
Duncan Litening YYRT, crackle paint, foil label, 1950s	32	55	75
Duncan Little Ace Yo-Yo Return Top, 1960s	6	14	22
Duncan Mardi Gras YYRT, imbedded glitter	32	55	75
Duncan Master Tops, die-stamped w/"Mr. Yo-Yo"	15	25	35
Duncan mini-yo-yo, late 1950s	15	25	35
Duncan O-Boy Junior, 1930s	20	32	45
Duncan O-Boy Yo-Yo Pat Pend., silver stamped, 1930s	25	37	50
Duncan Pearlessence Tournament YYRT #888, late 1950s	20	32	35
Duncan Satellite	15	25	35

DUNCAN PLASTIC YO-YOS

	C6	C8	C10
Duncan Pony Boy YYT #22, Jr. size, w/rattling BBs	20	32	45
Duncan Rainbow Tournament YYRT, die-stamped, 1950s	15	25	35
Duncan Rainbow YYRT #77, foil label, late 1950s	25	37	50
Duncan Satellite Yo-Yo, die-stamped w/stars, 1960s	15	25	35

	C6	C8	C10
Duncan Small Fry, wood, 1960s	15	25	35
Duncan Special 44 Yo-Yo top, 1950s	15	25	35
Duncan Spin Master, wood, 1960s	17	29	40
Duncan Suede Tournament YYT, flock covering, 1950s	20	32	45
Duncan Super Heroes Yo-Yo, Magic Motion, 1970s	6	14	22
Duncan Super Heroes Yo-Yo: Superman, Batman, Wonder Woman, Spiderman, Hulk, 1970s	4	10	18
Duncan Super Tournament YYRT #77, 1950s	20	32	45
Duncan Super Yo-Yo Practice Return Tops, late 1950s	25	37	50
Duncan Super Yo-Yo Tournament Tops #77, 1950s-60s	15	25	35
Duncan Tenite Imperial Yo-Yo, chevron logo, 1950s	8	19	30

DUNCAN TIN-LITHO YO-YOS

	C6	C8	C10
Duncan Tourn. Yo-Yo, die-stamped pennant logo	8	19	30
Duncan Tourn. Yo-Yo, pennant logo, four jewels, 1960s	32	55	75
Duncan Trickster Yo-Yo, 1960s	6	14	22
Duncan Yo-Yo Champion, pearlessence paint, silver foil sticker w/eagle, late 1950s	50	75	100
Duncan Yo-Yo Glow Imperial, indented logo, 1960s	5	12	20

Duncan Satellite, wood, $35

	C6	C8	C10
Duncan YYRT, M1 Satellite, die-stamped, 1960s	15	25	35
Duncan YYRT, M1 Satellite, whistling model, 1960s	15	25	35
Genuine Duncan Beg. Yo-Yo No. 33 and No. 44, jr. size, 1940s-50s	8	19	30
Genuine Duncan Beginner's YYT No. 44, die-stamped	15	25	35
Genuine Duncan Jeweled Yo-Yo, die-stamped, five jewels	32	55	75
Genuine Duncan Jr. YYT, full-sized, die-stamped	15	25	35
Genuine Duncan Junior YYT No. 33, die-stamped, 1930s	15	25	35
Genuine Duncan Tournament YYT No. 77, die-stamped, 1930s	15	25	35
Genuine Duncan Tournament YYT, yellow label, 1940s	20	32	45
Genuine Duncan Tournament YYT, die-stamped, 1940s	8	19	30
Genuine Duncan Tournament YYT, foil decal, 1930s	25	37	50
Genuine Duncan Yo-Yo Tournament Top No. 77, Mr. Yo-Yo on yellow decal, 1940s	20	32	45
Genuine Deluxe Duncan Tournament Yo-Yo	5	12	20
Genuine Duncan Rainbo Yo-Yo, separate inside yo-yo	215	325	525
Genuine Duncan Tournament YYT, opaque, die-stamped	8	19	30

Bosco Bear, wood, die-stamped, 1950s, $20

	C6	C8	C10
Genuine Duncan Whistling Yo-Yo No. 88, in various geometric patterns/colors, 1930s	150	200	280
Genuine Duncan Whistling YYT, solid color, 1940s	32	55	75
Luck-E JA-DO Contest Top, four-leaf clover logo, 1950s	25	37	50
Mickey Mouse Club Duncan YYRT, metal discs in string groove, 1960s	12	20	32
O-Boy Duncan Whistling Yo-Yo, 1930s	190	275	450
O-Boy Duncan Yo-Yo, die-stamped, 1930s	20	32	45
O-Boy Yo-Yo, 1929	32	55	75
Oversized version	50	75	100
Seattle Space Needle Duncan YYRT, 1962	32	55	75

DUNCAN "BUTTERFLY" YO-YOS

	C6	C8	C10
Duncan Butterfly Yo-Yo, wood, metal-fleck paint, die-stamped w/butterfly, mid-1950s	15	25	35
Duncan Butterfly, wood, die-stamped "butterfly" letters forming butterfly shape, late 1950s	20	32	45
Duncan Expert Award Yo-Yo, wood, metal-fleck paint, die-stamped w/eagle, late 1950s	20	32	45
Duncan Flat Top Return Top, wood, die-stamped, 1950s	32	55	75
Duncan Long Spin Wheels Butterfly Yo-Yo, plastic	7	16	25
Duncan Mardi Gras YYRT, 1960s	20	32	45
Duncan Tops, wood, die-stamped w/Mr. Yo-Yo, 1950s	20	32	45

Duncan Long Spin Wheels Butterfly Yo-Yo, plastic, $25

	C6	C8	C10
Genuine Duncan Beg. Yo-Yo, wood, junior size, die-stamped, 1960s 7		16	25
Genuine Duncan Butterfly Yo-Yo, plastic, each half a different color, indented logo, 1960s 7		16	25

DUNCAN ADVERTISING YO-YOS

	C6	C8	C10
7-Up, wood, die-stamped, 1950s 7		16	25
Amflite Bowling Balls, plastic, 1960s 4		10	18
Bosco Bear, wood, die-stamped, 1950s 5		12	20
Chrysler Corp, wood, die-stamped, 1950s.... 8		19	30
Coca-Cola, wood, die-stamped, 1950s 9		20	32
Coca-Cola, Sprite Boy, plastic, 1950s 65		90	120
Coca-Cola, plastic Imperial, 1970s 4		9	15
Delta Air Lines, plastic Imperial 2		5	10
Dr. Pepper, wood, die-stamped, 1950s 8		19	30
Hires Root Beer, red plastic 6		14	22
Honey & Nut Corn Flakes, butterfly, plastic 4		10	18
Kist Beverages, wood, die-stamped, 1950s.... 7		16	25
Kitty Clover Potato Chips, wood, die-stamped, 1950s 7		16	25
Rice Krispies, plastic Glow Imperial 4		9	15
Wendy's, plastic Imperial 2		5	10
Whirlpool, wood, die-stamped, 1950s 7		16	25

DUNCAN YO-YO PUBLICATIONS

	C6	C8	C10
How To Master Championship Tricks, 1947 6		14	22
The Art of Yo-Yo Playing, 1950 6		14	22
The Duncan Yo-Yo Book of Tricks, 1960 4		9	15
The Duncan Yo-Yo Book of Tricks, 1961 3		8	12
The Duncan Yo-Yo Trick Book, 1962 3		8	12

FESTIVAL PRODUCTS COMPANY

	C6	C8	C10
Festival Screamer Yo-Yo, tin litho, checkered or swirled pattern, paper label, 1960s 30		43	65
Festival Big Zapper Yo-Yo, wood, die-stamped 4		9	15
Festival Little Zapper Yo-Yo, wood, junior sized 4		9	15
Festival Tennis Ball Yo-Yo (or Bowling Ball, Baseball, Golf Ball, Football, Eight Ball, or Basket Ball), plastic, 1970s 3		7	12
Festival Official Harlem Globetrotters Basketball Yo-Yo, plastic, 1970s 4		9	15
Festival Joe Namath Football Signature Yo-Yo, plated plastic (gold or silver), 1970s 8		19	30
Festival Official National Hockey League Yo-Yo, various team stickers, plastic, 1970s 6		14	22

	C6	C8	C10
Festival Mickey Mouse Yo-Yo (or Donald Duck, Pluto, Goofy, or Mickey Mouse Club), plastic 5		12	20

FLI-BACK COMPANY, INC.

	C6	C8	C10
Fli-Back 45, 55, or 65 Yo-Yo, wood, die-stamped 7		16	25
Fli-Back 55 Yo-Yo, plastic, junior-size 4		9	15
Fli-Back Genuine Tournament Championship Return Top, wood, foil decal w/eagle 20		32	45
Fli-Back Orbit Away Yo-Yo, plastic 4		9	15
Fli-Back Top, wood, die-stamped w/eagle .. 15		25	35
Fli-Back Top, wood, die-stamped, no eagle .. 7		16	25
Fli-Back Yo-Yo, wood 3		8	12
Orbit Away, wood butterfly 7		16	25
Orbit, wood, space capsule logo, junior-size 7		16	25

FLORES, AKA THE YO-YO MANUFACTURING COMPANY

Flores is the original owner of the "yo-yo" trademark

	C6	C8	C10
Flores Yo-Yo, "pat. pend.," wood, regular or junior size 190		275	450
Flores Yo-Yo, wood, black paper sticker 190		275	450
Genuine Flores Yo-Yo, wood, stamped 175		250	425
Original Flores Yo-Yo Top, wood, oversize . 20		32	45

GOODY MANUFACTURING COMPANY

	C6	C8	C10
Genuine Goody Atomic Filipino Twirler, wood 32		55	75
Genuine Goody Champion Filipino Twirler, three jewels 32		55	75
Genuine Goody Master Filipino Twirler, wood 25		37	50
Genuine Goody Master Filipino Twirler, wood w/jewel 30		45	65
Genuine Goody Winner Filipino Twirler, wood w/jewel 32		55	75
Goody Joy-O-Top, wood 32		55	75
Goody Rainbow Filipino Twirler, wood, seven jewels 50		75	100

HI-KER, W.H. SCHLEE, INC.

	C6	C8	C10
Hi-Ker Beginners Top, wood, green/black.. 15		25	35
Hi-Ker Flat Top, wood, butterfly 15		25	35
Hi-Ker Professional Top, wood, 1950s 15		25	35
Hi-Ker Sparkle Master, wood, four jewels .. 50		75	100

	C6	C8	C10
Medalist Yo-Yo, wood 8		19	30
Pee-Wee Herman Yo-Yo, Spectra Star, 1988 2		5	10
Pez Yo-Yo, plastic 6		14	22
Pez Yo-Yo, tin 125		200	400
Phillips 66, plastic 2		5	10
Raggedy Ann & Andy, plastic, Hong Kong, 1980 7		16	25
Roy Rogers & Trigger, All Western Plastics ... 4		9	15
Smothers Brothers/Eastman Kodak, plastic, 1980s 2		5	10
Towle, silver-plated 28		40	55
Whirl-King Top, Standard Model, wood 5		12	20
Wooden yo-yo, Japan 2		5	10
Woody Woodpecker, Fox Kids Network, plastic 2		5	10
Yogi Bear, features in relief, plastic, Hong Kong 4		9	15

'56 Chevrolet, wood, $50

LUMAR (LOUIS MARX CO.)

	C6	C8	C10
Genuine Lumar 33 or 34 Beginner's Yo-Yo, tin-litho 50		75	100
Genuine Lumar Whistling Yo-Yo, tin-litho, 1930s 50		75	100
Magic Marxie Majestic, plastic 5		12	20

MISCELLANEOUS YO-YOS, INCLUDING CHARACTER YO-YOS

	C6	C8	C10
'56 Chevrolet, wood, two colors 25		37	50
'57 Chevy, plastic, Spectra Star, 1989 2		6	11
Alox Flying Disc, wood 5		12	20
Alvin, sterling silver over plastic 28		40	55
Amoco, recycled plastic 2		5	10
Bullwinkle Hand Caster, plastic, 1973 4		10	18
Buster Brown Yo-Yo, tin-litho, Japan 8		19	30
Citgo, plastic 2		4	6
Co-Co Puffs, plastic, butterfly 2		5	10
Davy Crockett Yo-Yo, wood, green/black, die-stamped 85		125	185
Edwards, "Drink Coca-Cola in Bottles," wood, 1930s 32		55	75
Fred Flinstone, features in relief, plastic, Hong Kong 4		9	15
General Electric "New Harvest," wood 7		16	25
Gorham Sterling Silver Yo-Yo, 1971 30		50	70
Gumby Yo-Yo, Prima Toy, plastic, 1988 4		10	18
Hallmark Peanuts Yo-Yos, 1970s 4		9	15
Kaysons Genuine Streamline Top, wood, decal 30		45	65
Kusan Twin Twirler, plastic, 1960s 8		19	30
Linda Sengpiel Supersonic Yo-Yo, MOC 15		25	35

ROYAL TOPS MANUFACTURING COMPANY

	C6	C8	C10
Royal Champion Filipino Sport Top, wood, junior size 15		25	35
Royal King Size Yo-Yo, wood, oversize 25		37	50
Royal Master Official Championship top, wood 20		32	45
Royal Master Tops, wood 20		32	45
Royal Master, plastic 5		12	20
Royal Monarch Yo-Yo, plastic 5		12	20
Royal Special Official Tournament Top, wood, decal, three jewel 150		200	300
Royal Special Yo-Yo Tops, wood, 1960s 15		25	35
Royal Spirit of '76 Yo-Yo, plastic 3		8	12
Royal Tournament Yo-Yo Tops, wood, four jewels 25		37	50
Royal Yo-Yo tops, butterfly, plastic 7		16	25
Royal Yo-Yo Tops, plastic 5		12	20
Royal Yo-Yo Tops, wood 15		25	35
Royal Yo-Yo Tops, wood, junior size 15		25	35

JACK RUSSELL COMPANY

	C6	C8	C10
Russell Galaxy 200, Sprite 2		5	10
Russell Genuine Galaxy Yo-Yo, Coca-Cola, plastic 2		5	10
Russell Ronald MacDonald Championship, plastic, 1970s 20		32	45
Russell Royale Galaxy 200, "Drink Coca-Cola," plastic 2		5	10
Russell Yo-Yo, Wood, 1950s 32		55	75

MISCELLANEOUS

Miscellaneous chapters are never easy to use; hopefully this one is different. Most items have been separated by manufacturer, although you will find a few listed by type of toy; please refer to the Table of Contents for a complete list.

Unfortunately, some toys and toy companies did not warrant separation. These toys will be found at the end of this chapter under name "Various Toys."

ARCADE

	C6	C8	C10
Bathroom Set, three-piece, cast-iron tub, stool, sink	425	638	850
Dining Room Table w/two chairs	245	368	490
Firehouse, "Engine Co. No. 99," 12-1/2" long	450	675	900
Gas Station, "Arcade Service" No. 900, 1941	400	600	800
Grand Piano and Bench, 3"	400	600	800
Highway sign, "Curve," cast iron	42	63	85
Highway Sign, "Men Working Ahead," cast iron	42	63	85
Highway Sign, "Road Closed," cast iron	42	63	85
Highway Sign, "Slow," cast iron	42	63	85
Highway Sign, "U.S. 30"	42	63	85
Kitchen Set, range, dinette, sink, refrigerator	500	750	1000
Lawnmower, c. 1920, iron and wood, 26-1/2" long	162	243	325
Pump and Tub	188	290	375
Sign, "Don't Park Here," cast iron, 4-1/2" high	42	63	85
Sign, "Stop," cast iron	42	63	85

	C6	C8	C10
Tools, cast iron, No. 779N, small, nickel finish, screwdriver, hammer, monkey wrench, pipe wrench, crescent wrench and S wrench, 1938, set of six, each	7	11	15
Weapons, cast iron No. 778N, small, nickel finish, cutlass, pistol, automatic, aerial bomb, tommy gun, airplane, 1938, set of 6, each	5	8	10
Windmill, cast iron, 15-1/4" high	100	150	200

AUBURN

	C6	C8	C10
Calf, rubber, c. 1937	6	9	12
Chicken, c. 1937	4	6	8
Collie, rubber, c. 1937	7	11	15
Colt, rubber, c. 1937	5	8	10

A grouping of Arcade cast-iron tools and signs. Each sign is valued at $85, the tools at $15 each

Pump and Tub, Arcade, $375

	C6	C8	C10
Cast iron w/turned barrel, "Hotchkiss," 9-1/2" long			
Cast iron, 15-1/2" long	100	150	200
Cast iron, Kilgore, 17" long	100	150	200
Cast iron, on four-wheel platform, 14" long	150	225	300
Coast Defense Gun, litho tin, camouflaged, 5" long	75	112	150
Coast Defense Gun, No. 830, wood and metal, Baldwin	44	66	88
Dainty cast iron, on wood base, 10" long	39	60	78
David Carlin mortar, c. WWI, cast iron, 15" long	175	263	350
Disappearing Coast Defense Gun, wood and steel, Thomas and Skinner, Indianapolis, 15"	60	90	120
Field-type, World War I, cast iron, 15-3/4" long	40	60	80
Firecracker mortar, cast-iron and rubber, Kilgore, 2"	32	48	65
Firecracker, cast iron, "Pat. Apr. 23, 1895," 4" long	105	158	210
Firecracker, cast-iron, firecracker cannon, rubber cannon ball, Kilgore, 4-1/2"	40	60	80
Firecracker-type, Kenton,	30	45	60
Howitzer type, die-cast, shoots, spring mechanism, pre-WWII, 5" long	40	60	80
Howitzer, Arcade, c. 1941, 4" long	12	18	25
Howitzer, c. 1930, double barreled, wood-handled firing lever, 9" long	40	50	75
Howitzer, plastic, Marx, c. 1960s, 12" long	15	22	30
Jolly Roger, metal, 1950s	37	56	75
Lead, "23," Kansas Toy, 3-1/4" long	8	12	16
Lead, "34," Kansas Toy, 2-1/4" long	10	15	20
Metal Action Cannon, Manoil, No. 200, marked "Made is USA"	12	18	24

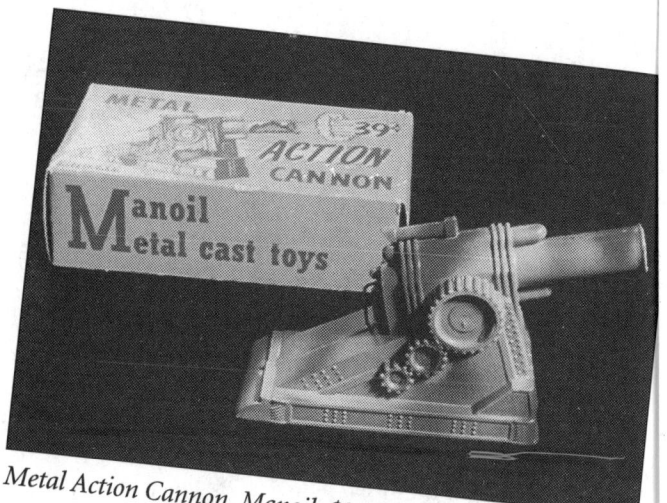

Metal Action Cannon, Manoil, $24

...tzer, plastic, Marx, c. 1960s, $75

	C6	C8	C10
Metal action, Manoil 19, marked "USA," early version,	10	15	20
Muzzleloader, cast iron, two wheels, Ives, 1900	150	225	300
Phoenix, brass barrel w/touch hole, 8" long	100	150	200
Premier, large thick barrel, large wheels, cast iron	20	30	40
Pressed steel base, 9-1/2"	15	22	30
Ralstoy No. 23	8	12	16
Ralstoy No. 34	8	12	16
Ralstoy, 3-3/4" long	8	12	16
Ranger Jr., cast iron, 10" long	125	188	250
Rapid fire, cast iron, embossed eagle	200	300	400
Remember the Maine, W.S. Hawkes Foundry, Dayton, Ohio, c. 1900, 13" long	250	375	500
Shell Shooting Long Tom Field Cannon, plastic, Marx, 1950s, 14" long	40	60	80
Sure Fire Cannon, Victory Toy Co., 1943, cardboard	37	56	75
Tin, camouflaged, early, 9"	45	68	90
Tin, pull lever for corks, 14" wood wheels	20	30	40
Tin, striped spring-loaded barrel w/lever	20	30	40
Tin, two-wheel, c. 1915, 7-1/4" long, 4" high	40	60	80
Tinplate, spring action, 1950s, Japan, 7" long	20	30	40
Tootsietoy, 155mm gun, pre-WWII	20	30	40
Tootsietoy, 155mm self-propelled howitzer, 1950s	20	30	40
Tootsietoy, 1930s, shoots, 5-1/2" long	30	45	60
Tootsietoy, 40mm AA gun, pre-WWII	17	26	35
Tootsietoy, pre-WWII, shoots, approx. 3-3/4" long	12	18	25
Twin Pom-Pom anti-aircraft cannon, Marx	50	75	100

ARCADE CAST IRON TOYS

No. 567 Lawn Mower

Steel metal parts. Wood handle and roller. Length 26½ inches, handle 22 inches, width 7¾ inches, height of wheel 3 inches, ¾ inch reel blades.
Color: Wheels yellow with red tread and red center discs. Reel blades yellow, frame green, handle brace green, handle yellow with red T-grip.
Notched gear on axle contacts steel spring inside the wheel causing a clicking noise.
Packed ½ dozen in a box, 3 dozen in a shipping case.
Case net weight 32 pounds. Case gross weight 35 pounds.
Case measurements: 16½x17x24 inches.

No. 564 Lawn Mower

Cast iron metal parts. Wood handle and roller.
Length overall 28 inches, T grip, handle 24 inches, width 8 inches, height of wheels 3¼ inches.
Color: Green wheels gold trimmed, red frame and braces, T grip handle and roller are plain wood. Gold bronzed reel.
The reel is three blade. Wheels, reel and roller revolve when in motion.
Packed 12 in a case.
Case net weight 25 pounds, case gross weight 31 pounds.
Case measurements: 8½x9x26 inches.

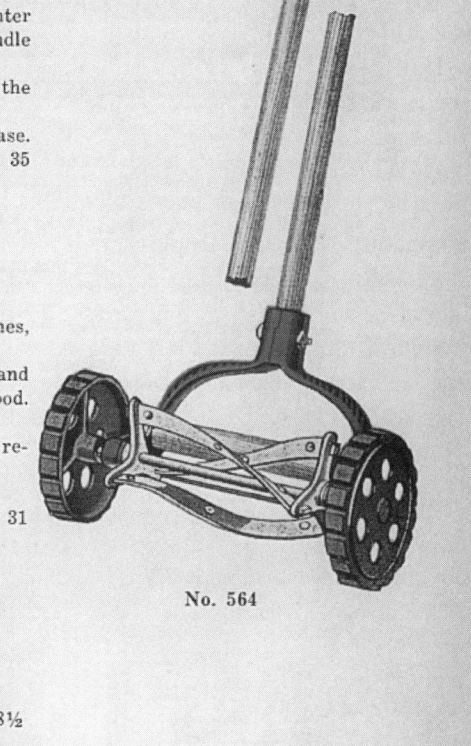

No. 567

No. 564

No. 570 Lawn Mower

Cast iron metal parts. Wood handle and roller.
Length overall 31 inches, handle 26 inches, width 8½ inches, height of wheels 4 inches.
Color: Green wheels gold trimmed. Red frame and braces, varnished wood T grip handle. Yellow reel.
The reel is four blade. Wheels, reel and roller revolve when in motion.
Packed ½ dozen in a case.
Case net weight 25 pounds, case gross weight 30 pounds.
Case measurements: 9x10x29 inches.

No. 569 Clipper Lawn Mower

Cast iron metal parts. Wood handle and roller.
Overall length 34½ inches, handle 28 inches, width 10 inches, height of wheels 4 inches.
Color: Green wheels gold trimmed. Red frame, green braces. Orange handle, red T grip. Gold bronzed reel.
The reel is four blade, and geared so that reel revolves faster than the wheels. Blades are set closer to cutter-bar than on other toy mowers.
Packed ½ dozen in a case.
Case net weight 39 pounds, case gross weight 46 pounds.
Case measurements: 10½x11½x33 inches.

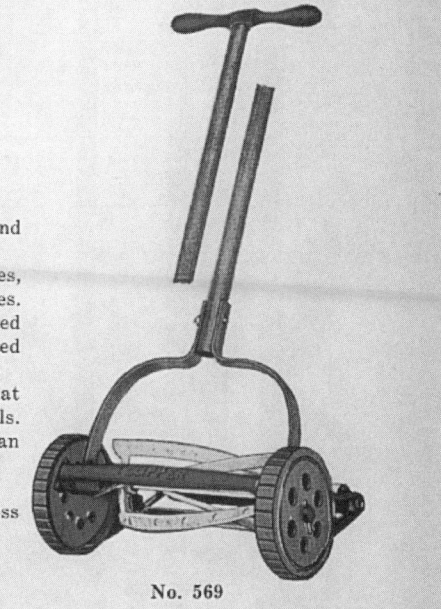

No. 570

No. 569

"THEY LOOK REAL"

26

Arcade Cast-Iron Toys catalog No. 51 featured several examples of their Lawnmowers. An Arcade lawnmower c. 1920 is valued at $325

	C6	C8	C10
Cow, rubber, c. 1937	7	11	15
Duck, rubber, c. 1937	4	6	8
Farm Set, rubber, forty-plus pieces, post WWII	70	105	140
Fence Section, rubber, c. 1937	4	6	8
Firehouse, rubber, Set No. 523	100	150	200
Horse, rubber, c. 1937	6	9	12
Piglet, rubber, c. 1937	4	6	8
Rubber Pig, rubber, c. 1937	4	6	8
Tomahawk, rubber	8	12	17

BALDWIN

	C6	C8	C10
Chicken on nest, marbles for eggs, pressed steel, 5" long	27	41	55
Kingpin, spring action bowling, pressed steel,	105	160	210
Little Red Hen, crank action, pressed steel, 1930s, 5" long	40	60	80

BARCLAY

	C6	C8	C10
Searchlight, swivels on base, 3"	20	30	40
Work Horse, No. 209	7	10	13
Horse, No. 210	5	8	10
Grazing Horse, No. 211	5	8	10
Standing Cow, No. 212	5	8	10
Grazing Cow, No. 213	6	8	11
Lying Cow, No. 214	6	9	12
Bull, No. 215	5	8	10
Grazing Sheep, No. 216?	5	8	10
Standing Sheep, No. 217	5	8	10
Resting Sheep, No. 218	6	9	12
Ram, No. 219	5	8	10
Pig, No. 220	5	8	10
Mess Table, two benches, wood	20	30	40

BLOCKS

	C6	C8	C10
American Logs, similar to Lincoln Logs, c. WWII	62	93	125
Auburn flexible building blocks, 1960s	7	10	14
Auburn Rubber building bricks, 1940s	17	25	34
Bill-Ding Clown, twenty-four blocks, 1950s	32	48	65
Bilt-E-Z Skyscraper, Scott Mfg., Chicago, c. 1925	45	68	90
Brownie, The, McLoughlin Bros., twenty litho blocks, 1891	400	600	800
Chautauqua Architectural Building No. 510, c. 1920s	75	112	150
Church building blocks, litho on wood, Bliss, c. 1900, 8-3/4" high	500	750	1000
Circus, The, Milton Bradley, c. 1910	262	393	525

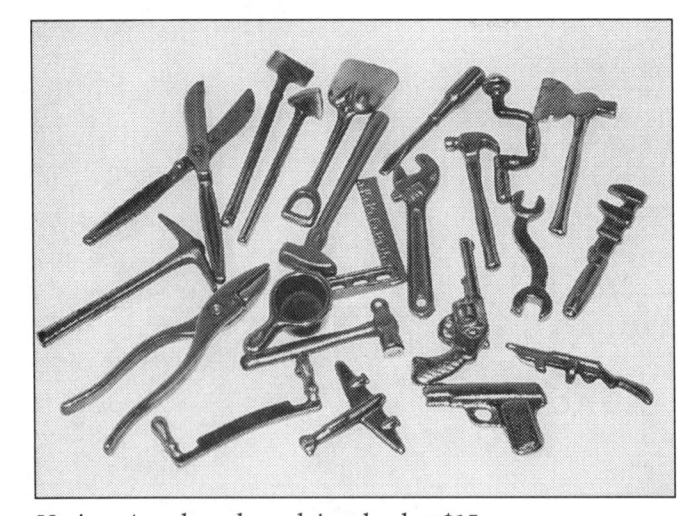

Various Arcade tools, each is valued at $15.

Church Building Blocks, Bliss, c. 1900, $1,000

The Circus, Milton Bradley, c. 1910, $525

	C6	C8	C10
Elgo American Plastic Bricks No. 705	17	26	35
Elgo American Plastic Bricks No. 715	22	33	45
Elgo American Plastic Bricks No. 725	32	48	65
Elgo American Plastic Bricks No. 735	62	93	125
Halsam American Blocks, wood, No. 60, 1939	27	41	55
Halsam American, Plastic Bricks No. 72	30	45	60
Halsam Block Wagon Pull Toy	22	33	45
Halsam Logs, Senior Size -3/4", No. 815	17	26	35
Halsam Logs, miniset, c. 1870s	37	56	75
Hill's Alphabet Blocks,			
Leecraft Circus Blocks, twelve wooden blocks, painted w/lion, tiger, letters and numbers, contained in wooden pull-toy cage, 1930s	35	52	70
Lincoln Bricks, Lincoln Logs	45	68	90
Lincoln Logs, 1923	10	15	20
Lincoln Logs, 1930	17	26	35
Lincoln Logs, 1947	17	26	35
Lincoln Logs, set 1C, post WWII	40	60	80
Lincoln Logs, set 2-L	45	68	90
Lincoln Logs, set 4 CF, 1950s, w/figures	150	225	300
Lincoln Logs, set No. 1A, John Wright, pat. 1920, complete	10	15	20
Lincoln Logs, set No. 29, early	60	90	120
Lincoln Logs, set S-C	7	11	15
Lincoln Timbers, pre-WWII, w/box, complete	30	45	60
Mother Goose Living Picture Blocks, c. 1890	325	487	650
Nesting-type, paper litho on cardboard, picturing children and animals, 1920, Cramer Publishing Co., set of six	150	225	300
Puzzle Blocks, depicting The Three Bears, Old Mother Hubbard, Little Bo-Peep, Puss in Boots, Jack the Giant Killer and Red Riding Hood, copyright 1892, set of six	35	52	70
Richter's Anchor Blocks, No. 11A	175	262	350
Richter's Anchor Blocks, No. 12	100	150	200
Richter's Anchor Blocks, No. 2-1/2	85	128	170
Richter's Anchor Blocks, No. 7	100	150	200

	C6	C8	C10
Stabuilt Blocks, The Embossing Co., 1916, 20" x 12"	42	63	85
Union Building Blocks, No. 7, early	75	112	150

CANNONS

	C6	C8	C10
Admiral Dewey, cast iron, c. 1890s, 11" long	200	300	400
Anti-Aircraft Gun, Marx, No. 617	37	56	75
Atomic Cannon, Ideal	50	75	100
Atomic Long Range Cannon, Marx 25" long	35	52	70
Big Parade, cast iron	25	38	50
Big Shot Canon, Marx	35	52	70
Big Victory, tin litho, 12" long	115	172	230
Big-Bang, Gas Cannon, 9"	75	250	500
Big-Bang, No. 60mm, 9"	15	30	60
Big-Bang, No. 6F, 9" long	15	30	60
Big-Bang, No. 7D, 8" long	35	50	150
Big-Bang, No. 7F, 9-3/4" long	75	125	200
Big-Bang, No. 8F, 12-1/2" long	75	125	200
Big-Bang, No. 105mm, 17-1/2"	20	40	80
Big-Bang, No. 10FC, 17-1/2" long	30	60	100
Big-Bang, No. 10W, 9" long	50	100	150
Big-Bang, No. 11D, 12-3/8" long	35	50	100
Big-Bang, No. 11F, 15" long	150	200	300
Big-Bang, No. 12F, 16-3/8" long	75	100	250
Big-Bang, No. 155mm, 24"	25	50	100
Big-Bang, No. 15AC, 16-1/4"	100	150	250
Big-Bang, No. 15FC, 24"	25	50	1..
Big-Bang, No. 16F, 22-1/4" long	150	250	
Big-Bang, The Artillery Game, 7" long	150	300	
Boy Ranger, fires marbles, cast iron, Kilgore, 17-1/2" long	180	270	
Boy Scout Machine Gun, 19" w/8-1/4" wheels	250	375	
Brass barrel, cast iron, Ives	200	300	
Brass Cannon, Cannon, red wheels, Ives, 7" long	150	2..	

Anti-Aircraft Gun, Marx, $75

	C6	C8	C10
Young America, cast iron,, "Rapid Fire Gun," 15-1/2" long	130	195	260

CHEIN

	C6	C8	C10
Cathedral Organ	100	150	200
Drum, 6" x 3-1/2"	30	45	60
Easter Egg w/chicken on top, opens up to hold candy, c. 1938, tin, 5-1/2"	15	22	30
Sand Chute, No. 45	80	120	160
Sand Pail, c. early 1940s, 7" diameter	26	39	52
Sand Loader	75	112	150
Sand Mill, 1930s, 7" wide, 11" high	50	75	100
Sand Toy, "Busy Mike," 1940s, 7-1/2" high	90	135	180
Sand Toy, monkey bends and twists, 7" high	20	30	40
Windmill sand toy, tin litho, 8" high	15	22	30

COURTLAND TOYS

	C6	C8	C10
800 Zylo-P-ano, 13-1/4" long, 5-1/2" wide	75	100	125
1000 Walt Reach Toys G-Man Pocket Siren Signal, 3-1/2" long, 2-3/8" wide, 1-3/4" high	75	100	150

Sand Toy, "Busy Mike," Chein, 1940s, $180

Mechanical Three-piece Train Set, Courtland, $200

	C6	C8	C10
1050 Halloween Pocket Siren Signal, 3-1/2" long, 2-3/8" wide, 1-3/4" high	125	150	225
1060 New Years Pocket Siren Signal, 3-1/2" long, 2-3/8" wide, 1-3/4" high	125	150	
2259000 Mechanical Three-piece Train Set, 24" long, 2-1/4" wide, 3-1/4" high	100	150	200
9050 Fire Department w/automatic garage door, nonpowered fire chief car w/the Courtland Toy Co., Phila. Pa., markings, 7-3/4" x 10-1/8" x 6-3/4"	75	125	175
9075 Private Garage w/automatic door, nonpowered car w/Courtland Toy Co., Phila. Pa. markings, 7-3/4" x 10-1/8" x 6-3/4"	75	125	175

CRANDALL

At age 16, Charles M. Crandall took over his family's wood-working business after the death of his father in 1849. Crandall made croquet sets after the Civil War. They were packed in thin wooden boxes with tongue-and-groove corners. When his sons were ill, Crandall took home a bag of the grooved scraps, and the buildings his sons made with them inspired "Crandall Building Blocks." The success of the interlocking blocks led to production of "Acrobats," with grooved parts. Crandall, who died in 1905, produced toys through the turn of the century.

	C6	C8	C10
Acrobats, four acrobats	250	375	500
Building Blocks No. 3, pat. 1867	250	375	500
Crandall's District School, c. 1875	600	950	1300
Crandall's Expression Blocks	288	435	575
Crandall's Heavy Artillery, soldiers, blocks	750	1250	2000
John Gilpin's Ride	500	800	1200
Man in Cap on Donkey, wheeled pull toy	275	413	550
Masquerade Blocks	320	528	976
Menagerie	550	900	1300

Acrobats, Crandall, $500

HUBLEY

	C6	C8	C10
Duck, pull toy, c. 1930s, 9-3/8" long	800	1400	2000
Ferris Wheel, early, cast iron, brass and tin, clockwork, 17" high	2000	4000	6500
Grasshopper, pull toy, cast iron	258	385	515
Gurdy, turn crank and play tune, shows animal playing cello	30	45	60
Jumbo the Elephant, on wheels	25	37	50
Marathon Rider (bicyclist) cast iron	300	450	600
Monkey Riding Tricycle, cast iron, aluminum, 6-1/4" long	2000	3500	5500

Crandall's District School, c. 1875, $1,300

Left to Right, Duck, pull toy, Hubley, $2,000; Grasshopper, pull toy, Hubley, $515

	C6	C8	C10
Old Dutch Cleanser Woman, cast iron	2200	3800	6000
Refrigerator, cast iron, Hubley, "GE," 7" high	150	225	300

IDEAL

	C6	C8	C10
Astronaut Space Helmet	37	56	75
Gas Station, 8" long, c. 1950s, w/cars	55	82	110
Mr. Machine, first version, can be taken apart and put together, 18" high	138	205	275
Mr. Machine, 1972 version, whistles, 17-1/2" high	32	48	65
Mr. Machine, 1977 version	27	41	55

Ferris Wheel, Hubley, $6,500

IVES

	C6	C8	C10
Acrobat, hand over hand, 10-1/2" high ...	2000	3000	4000
Automatic Toy Boxers, c. 1876, 11" high	4000	7000	12,000
Autoperipateticos walking doll	700	1050	1400
Barrel Walkers, c. 1890, wood and paper litho balance toy, acrobat, ballerina, monkey	200	300	400
Black Dancer, 1870s, clockwork	800	1300	1800
Black Dancer, c. 1873	2400	3600	4800
Black Dancer, clockwork, c. 1880, 11" high	800	1300	1800
Black Mechanical Walking Man, c. 1875, 9-1/2" high	1000	1600	2400
Blakesley & Williams, 1890, Mule Dancers, mechanical revolving, paper litho, painted tin, wooden box, clockwork, 8" tall................................	1600	2400	3200
Boy smoking cigar and holding stomach, cast iron	195	263	350
Chinese, "John Chinaman," wind-up walker, 9-1/2" high, auctioned in 1994 w/original box	7200		

Mechanical Bear, Ives, $760

	C6	C8	C10
Crawling Baby, 1893................................	1500	2250	3000
Crawling Baby, c. 1871	2000	3000	4000
Elephant Car, circus cage, cast iron, "serpent eggs" magic trick can be burnt in elephant'strunk, "Greatest Show on Earth......................................	790	1125	1500
Elephant Ramp Walker: See Ramp Walkers			
Fire Engine House, c. 1890, cast iron and wood, 16" long..............	2000	3000	5000
General Butler, wind-up walker, 9-1/2" high	2000	3500	5000
Hot Air Toy, c. 1870.................................	250	375	500
Jackass wind-up walker, 9-1/2" high, auctioned in 1994 in Very Good condition, missing left arm			12,000
Judge, clockwork, c. 1880.........................	1500	2300	3500
Juggler, clockwork early	1000	1500	2000
Mechanical Bear, patent 1872....................	380	570	760
Mechanical Performing Monkey, No. 49-10, 5-1/2" high	2250	3375	4500
Mule, articulated, cast iron, pull toy, 8" long	375	565	750
Old Mammy Washing Clothes, clockwork, 11" high, auctioned in 1993			13,800
Old Woman in a Shoe, pull toy, 9" long..	3000	4500	6000
Platform Horse, pull toy, 9-1/2" long......	1400	2100	2800
Preacher, clockwork, 10-1/2" high	1500	2400	3800
Rower, two-drive wheels protrude from bottom, wheel attached to rudder, 13" long	2500	5000	8000
Santa Claus, clockwork, c. 1875, 10" high	1800	3000	4400
Scottish Jigger	1250	1875	2500

Ives advertisement from the November 1908 issue of Playthings

Preacher, clockwork, Ives, $3,800

	C6	C8	C10
Struktiron set, 1915 100		150	200
Struktiron, 1916, non-motorized, w/box.. 275		363	550
Walking Horse, 6" long 375		562	750
Walking Horse, c. 1890s, 10" long 1000		1600	2400
Walking Santa, 9-3/4" high 1200		2200	3500
Zouave wind-up walker, 10-1/2" high..... 1500		2250	3000

KENNER

	C6	C8	C10
Baggage Cart, 6" 30		45	60
Drag Wagon, litho paper on sides, driver, 15-1/2" long.. 200		300	400
Easy Bake oven, 1960s 20		30	40
Give A Show Projector, 112 slides 35		52	70

KENTON

	C6	C8	C10
Elephant "Land-on-Roosevelt 1936" 80		120	160
Pull Toy, Clown on Elephant, Kenton, 1911 400		600	800

	C6	C8	C10
Pull Toy, Elephant, cast iron, on platform, Kenton, 5-1/2" long 210		315	420
Stove, cast iron, marked "Oak" on door 30		45	60
Stove, w/warming shelves and stove plates, high back for smokestack, "Royal" on door and shelves, 10" high .. 40		60	80

KEYSTONE

	C6	C8	C10
Bus Terminal... 92		138	189
Farm... 50		75	100
Firestone Station 112		168	225
Fort, "Exploding Fort with Shooting Tank" 46		69	92
Fort, " U.S. Coast Defense Fort," No. 523 ... 42		72	95
Fort, " U.S. Coast Defense Fort," w/accessories, No. 525, c. 1942.............. 40		55	80
Fort, "U.S. Coast Guard Defense Fort," w/accessories, No. 527, c. 1942.............. 40		70	100
Fort, No. 531, 12" long................................. 40		60	85
Fort, No. 533, same as 531, but two electric lights at entrance........................ 50		75	100

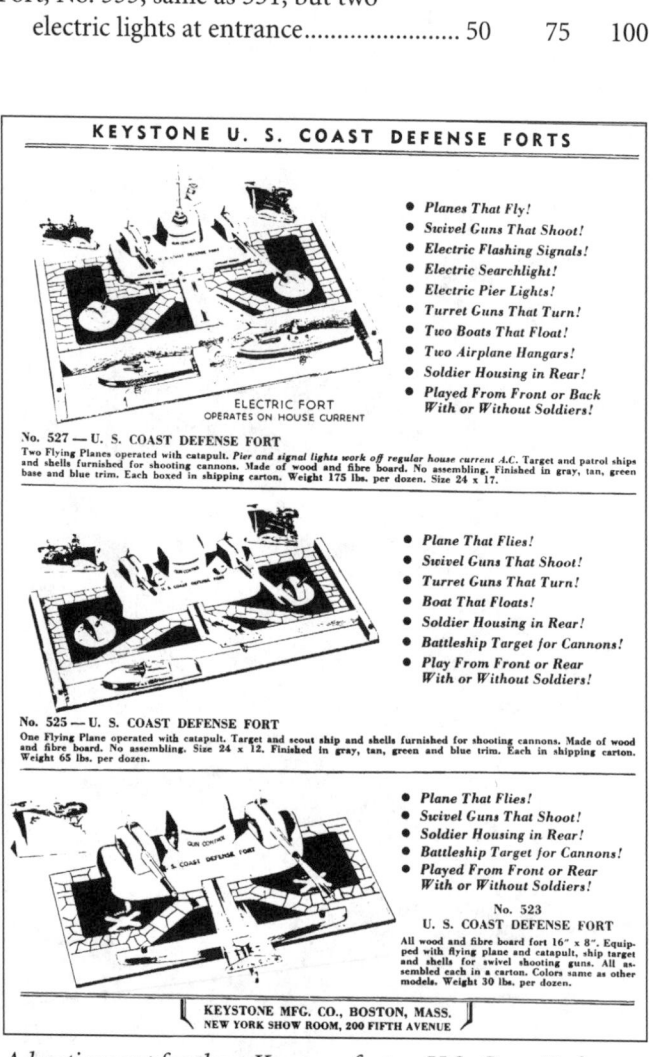

Advertisement for three Keystone forts—U.S. Coast Defense Fort Nos. 527, 525 and 523.

This catalog from Kenner highlights the many features of the Easy Bake Oven. Retailing at $15.95, an Easy Bake Oven from the 1960s is now valued at $40.

	C6	C8	C10
Fort, No. 535, w/two electric lights at entrance, 20" long 60	60	90	120
Keystone Fire Department 90	90	135	180
Keystone Garage, 1940s or 1950s, 8" x 8" x 6" 37	37	56	75
Kid Flyer boy on scooter, tin litho, string-wound, 8-1/2" long 300	300	450	600
Magic Lantern, Keystone, "Radioptocin" ... 40	40	60	80
Radiopticon, 1920s 75	75	112	150
Service Station 137	137	205	275
Warehouse 237	237	355	475

MARBLES

Marbles date back as far as ancient Rome, when they were made of clay and pottery. Marbles are divided into types, such as "Indian Swirls," "Clambroth" and "Lutz Type Swirls." Size numbers range from 000 (1/2-inch) to 8 (1-1/8-inch). There are estimated to be 40,000 to 50,000 current collectors of marbles in the United States, about 1,700 of whom belong to the Marble Collectors' Society of America (see Leading Collectors and Dealers).

	C10
Sulphide, bust of Jenny Lind, size 1-7/8"	900
Sulphide, Standing Bear, size 1-1/2"	125
Handmade Swirl, size 1-1/2"	175
Handmade Swirl, size 3/4"	20
Ribbon Lutz, size 3/4"	400
Clambroth, size 5/8"	150
Indian Swirls, size, 5/8"	100
Mica, size 3/4"	25

MARX

	C6	C8	C10
Air-Sea Power bombing set 110	110	165	220
Allstate Terminal & Warehouse, Sears, 1960s, 23" x 15" x 2" 150	150	225	300
Arcade Shooting Gallery 50	50	75	100
Army and Navy Mechanical Target, No. G169 20	20	30	40

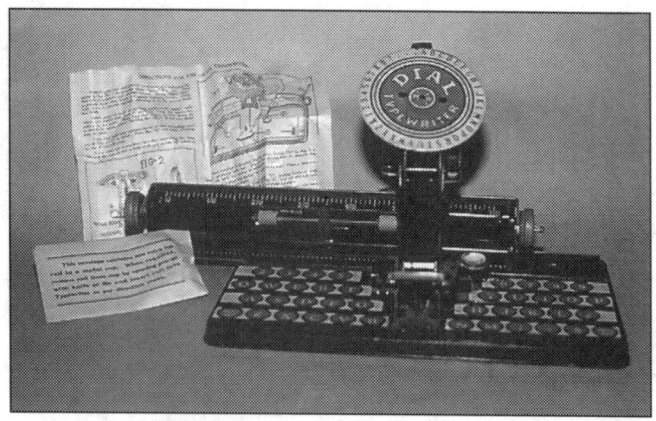

Dial Typewriter No. 1000A, Marx, $65

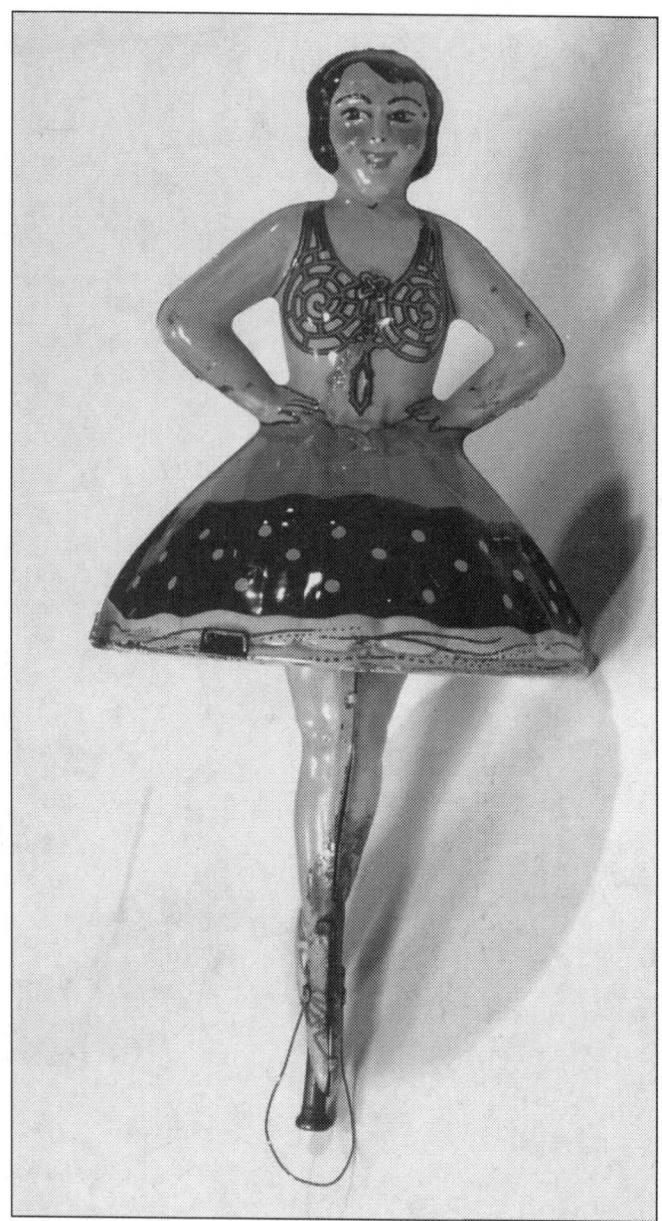

Ballerina, Marx, 1930s, $300

	C6	C8	C10
Army Code Sender, Morse key and phone, pressed steel, 9-1/2" 10	10	15	20
Ballerina, operated by sawtooth bar, pulled through, 1930s, 6" high 150	150	225	300
Bear Cyclist, metal, lever action 100	100	150	200
Bust 'Em Target Game, No. G38 20	20	30	40
Car Wash, "Minit" 175	175	262	350
Deluxe Dial Typewriter, 1930s 37	37	56	75
Dial Typewriter No. 1000A, 1930s 32	32	48	65
Dishwasher K54, c. 1950s 60	60	90	120
Gas Island, 1930s 200	200	300	400
General Alarm Fire House, 1940s, 17" long, 11" wide, 3" high 350	350	525	700
Headquarters, U.S. Army Training Center, tin litho, 5" x 8" x 11" 20	20	30	40

	C6	C8	C10
Hometown Drug Store, "F.W. Woolworth," tin litho, 5" x 2" x 3-1/2" 120	180	240
Hometown Favorite Store, "F.W. Woolworth," tin litho, 5" x 2" x 3-1/2" 120	180	240
Hometown Favorite Store, "S.S. Kresge Co.," tin litho 100	150	200
Hometown Firehouse, tin litho, 1930s, 5-1/2" x 2-1/2" x 3-1/2" 200	300	400
Hometown Grocery Store, tin litho, 1930s, 5" x 2-1/2" x 3-1/2" 60	90	120
Hometown Meat Market, tin litho, 1930s ... 60	90	120
Hometown Movie Theatre, tin litho, 1930s 62	93	125
Hometown Police Station 70	105	140
Hometown Savings Bank, tin litho 1930s, 5" x 2-1/2" x 3-1/2" 60	90	120
Honeymoon Cottage Village, tin litho, 1930s, 17" x 11" 133	200	266
Honeymoon Garage, 1930s, tin litho, 6-1/2" x 7" x 3" 45	68	90
Ice Skater, 1930s, operated by sawtooth bar, 5-1/2" high 150	225	300
Junior Dial Typewriter No. 2109, c. 1930s .. 20	30	40
King Arthur sword and shield, tin litho 37	56	75
Knockout Champs, celluloid, 1930s 418	627	835
Loop the Loop, 1930s, gravity toy, track 12" long, car 1-1/2" long 50	75	100
Magic Barn w/tractor 130	195	260

Roadside Rest, Marx, 1930, $675

	C6	C8	C10
Mechanical Gorilla 112	168	225
Newlywed Library, tin litho, 1930s, 5" x 2-1/2" x 3-1/2" long 75	112	150
Pathe News Movie Camera, tin litho 200	300	400
Practice Target Ranger, 1950s, 11" long 30	45	60
Pretty Maid Washing Machine, c. 1930s, 4-1/2" high 50	75	100
Refrigerator, K42, c. 1950s 15	22	30
Rex Mars Space Target Game, 1950s, 14" long 150	225	300
Roadside Rest, 1930 338	500	675
Rock'em, Sock'em Robots 30	45	60
Searchlight, tin litho, 3-1/2" high 20	30	40
Service Station, "Brightelite Filling Station" 283	425	565
Service Station, "Colonial Service Station," 1960s, 27" x 15" x 4" 90	135	180
Service Station, "Day & Nite Service Service Center" 75	112	150
Service Station, "Gulf" 300	450	600
Service Station, "Midtown" 112	168	225
Service Station, "Super Service" 175	263	350

Honeymoon Garage, Marx, 1930s, $90

Sunnyside Service Station, Marx, 1930s, $800

	C6	C8	C10
Service Station, "Universal Gas Service Station," 1940s, 6-1/2" high, base 12" long 150	225	300
Service Stattion, Happitime 85	128	170
Son of Garloo, plastic and tin wind-up 138	205	275
Stove K39, c. 1950s 20	30	40
Sunnyside Service Station, 1930s, complete 400	600	800
Tunnel, tin litho, depicts farm scene, rolling hills, houses, 8" x 10" x 7" 10	15	20
Typewriter No. 1110, metal and plastic, c. 1950s-1960s 10	15	20

MATTEL

	C6	C8	C10
Farmer in the Dell, tin, crank, 1951, 7" high 60	90	120
Four and 20 Blackbirds, 1950s, crank action, musical toy, 9" diameter 100	150	200
Jack in the Music Box, 1961 30	45	60
Mad Scientist Dissect An Alien 18	27	36
Mad Scientist Monster Lab 12	18	25
Mad Scientist Operating Room 10	15	20
Music Box Carousel 55	83	110
Musical Man on the Flying Trapeze 95	143	190
Thingmaker Creeple People Kit 37	56	75
Thingmaker Creepy Crawlers Pak, 1960s.... 18	27	37
Thingmaker Fang 'n Claw Kit, 1967 20	30	40
Thingmaker Fighting Man, 1964 50	75	100
Thingmaker Incredible Edibles Set 45	68	90
Thingmaker People Makers Pak 35	52	70
Thingmaker Slitherees Kit, 1967 45	68	90
Vacuform w/molds 35	52	70

Farmer in the Dell, Mattel, 1951, $120

Musical Man on the Flying Trapeze, Mattel, $190

OHIO ART

Founded by dentist H.S. Winzler in 1908, Ohio Art's original intent was to make metal picture frames, but in 1917 the firm bought C.E. Carter (Erie Toy Plant) and began producing metal toys, including a climbing monkey on a string for Ferdinand Strauss. Winzeler later sold the plant to Louis Marx, but continued making tin toys, while Marx, according to Ohio Art history, used the former Carter plant as the foundation of his own company. Ohio Art is still making toys in Bryan, Ohio.

	C6	C8	C10
Barrel Organ, musical, 5-1/2" tall 40	60	80
Beach Toy Water Pumper, c. 1939, signed "Elaine Ends Hileman," 8-1/2" high 17	26	35
Children's Tea Set, tin, 1950s, fourteen pieces 75	112	150
Drum, w/two sticks, 6" x 4" 10	15	20
Fido's Musical Dog House, 1960s, 8" high .. 36	54	72
Mini Farm Set, play set, 1960s, 12" long, 5" high 80	120	160
Realistic Farm Set, play set, No. 197, 1960s 16" long, 7" high 80	120	160
Sand Lift 50	75	100
Sandpail, 1940s, tin litho 42	63	85
Shooting Gallery, key wind, circus 48	72	95
Sunnyfield Farms Barn and Silo set w/animals, tin litho, 1950s 80	120	160
Toyland Band, drums, bass and snare, cymbals triangle and sticks, 7-1/2" high 20	30	40
Washtub, tin litho, wood and metal scrubboard, 1940s 16	24	32
Watering Can, tin litho, 1940s 15	22	30

No. 505a **ohio art**

Etch A Sketch®

PATENT NO. 3,055,113

Turn the knobs to design, draw or doodle on Etch A Sketch... the world's favorite drawing toy.

Pack, 1 dz. ctn. 19½ lbs.

Music

Music

Music

Music

Music

What is that?

It's my Etch A Sketch. Look, it's easy to do... you turn the knobs like this... And just like magic you make a line...

And turn this knob to make the line go up or down.

Here try it.

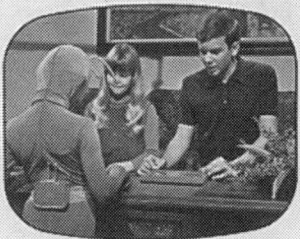
See how much fun it is? And it isn't messy... 'Cause the picture's on the inside.

Now hold it upside down and shake it.

Ohio Art's Etch A Sketch... much more than a toy!

It develops coordination and patience

And you do not have to be creative...

Pictures on the wall may be copied by almost everyone

Like these actually drawn on Etch A Sketch.

Already found in millions of homes around the world...

Bring wonderful fun for everyone

Another sensibly priced Fun-Time creation from The Ohio Art Company

Also makers of Bizzy Buzz Buzz®.

 THE OHIO ART COMPANY NEW YORK OFFICE: SUITE 901, 200 FIFTH AVENUE NORTH 10010 PHONE: 212/691-8000 HOME OFFICE: P.O. BOX 111, BRYAN, OHIO 43506 PHONE: 419/636-3141

12M TVS70

This Ohio Art insert shows scenes from an Etch-A-Scetch commercial. An Etch-A-Scetch from the 1970s is valued from $5-$10

An advertisement showing an assortment of Wolverine's toys, including the Sandy Andy toys.

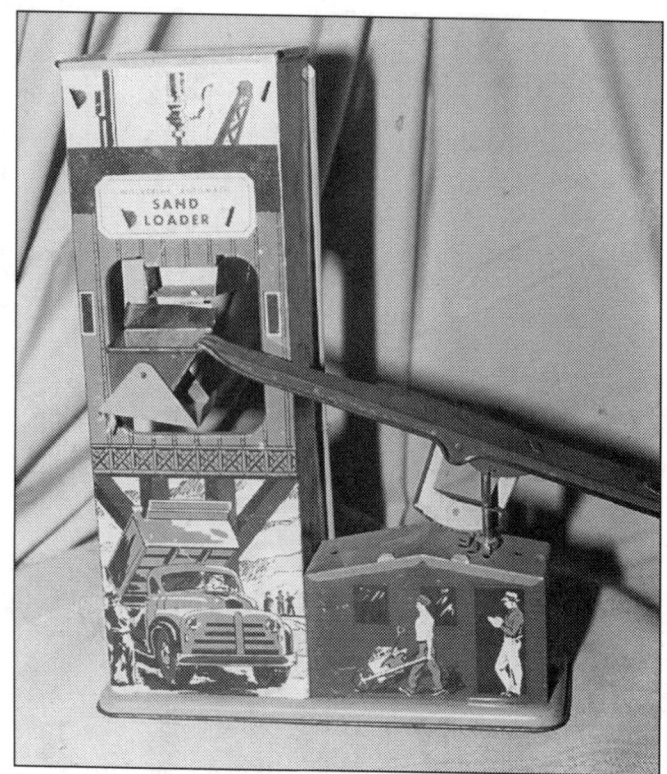

Automatic Sand Loader, Wolverine, 1947, $175

REMCO

	C6	C8	C10
B-52 Ball Turret	60	90	120
Drawbridge, plastic, two plastic autos, two boats, cardboard river scene, early 1950s, 27" long	79	119	158
Johnny Reb Cannon	88	132	175
Movieland Drive-In Theatre	90	135	180
Naval PomPom Gun	42	63	85
Space Commander Walkie Talkies	35	52	70

WOLVERINE

Founded by B.F. Bain in 1903, the Pittsburgh, Pennsylvania, company was named after Bain's hometown. In later years Wolverine became a subsidiary of Spang Industries, and in 1970 moved to Boonville, Arkansas. The Sandy Andy, in all its variations, was probably Wolverine's most successful and famous toy.

	C6	C8	C10
Adding Machine No. 39, 1940s, 7" long	25	38	50
Automatic Sand Loader, 1947, 11" high	87	130	175
Automatic Coal Loader, 1940s, 10" high	55	83	110
Automatic Sand Crane, tin	60	90	120
Bizzy Andy Trip Hammer, 1917	100	150	200
Bizzy Andy, sand toy, pat. 1914, steel and tin, 11" high	10	15	20

	C6	C8	C10
Captain Sandy Andy No. 63C sand toy, 1930s, 13" high	75	112	150
Corner Grocer, No. 182, 1930s, includes 16" tin counter, scale, phone, paper dispenser and groceries, 31" long opened; 15-3/4" closed	400	600	800
Corner Grocer, tin litho store	450	675	900
Dumping Sandy, 1916, 12" high	200	300	400
Farm Wagon, plastic wind-up, 10" long	40	60	80
General Grocery, 1930s, includes 10-1/4" tin counter, scale, phone, paper dispenser and groceries, 20-1/4" opened and 10-1/4" closed	375	565	750

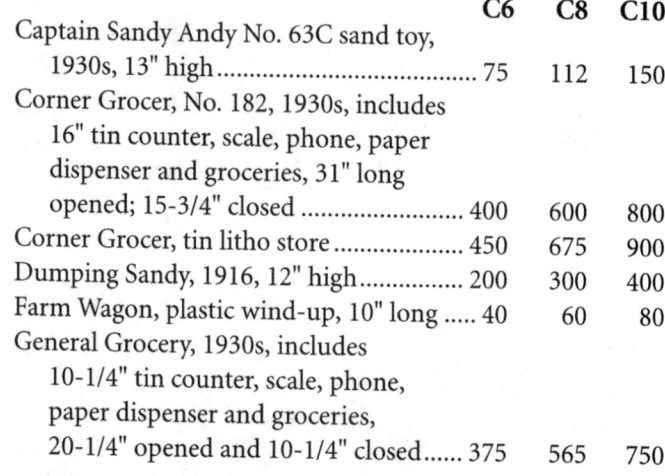

Automatic Coal Loader, Wolverine, $110

REMCO·TOYS·1961

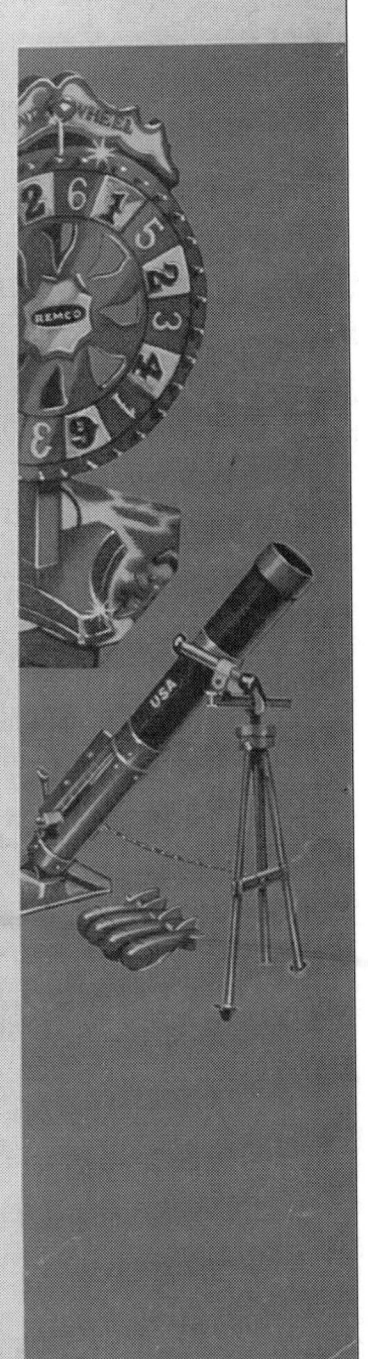

Remco's 1961 catalog includes such popular items at the Electronic B-52 Ball Turret Gun and the Johnny Reb Civil War Cannon.

Captain Sandy Andy, Wolverine, 1930s, $150

General Grocery, Wolverine, 1930s, $750

	C6	C8	C10
Kitchen Cabinet No. 178 39		58	78
Merry Masons sand toy, 16" high 70		105	140
Music Box, crank action, No. 38, 1930s,			
6" high 50		75	100
Organ, tin, crank action........................... 120		180	240
Panama Pile Driver, No. 54.......................... 85		128	170
Post Office w/cardboard accessories.......... 150		225	300
Sandy Andy Automatic Sand Toy, No. 60,			
patented 1909 and 1911...................... 80		120	160
Sandy Andy Full Back, 1920 375		565	750
Sandy Andy Sand Loader, 1912 65		98	130
Sandy Andy Trick Animals, seal, polar			
bear pull toy 350		525	700
Service Station, "Shell," w/three vehicles .. 175		263	350
Service Station, "Texaco Service Station,"			
1960s, 25" x 15" 90		135	180
Ski Jumper, catapult action, 1940s,			
18" long... 37		56	75

	C6	C8	C10
Skyscraper Elevator, w/"2000 lbs"			
counterweight, 1915, 24" high 150		225	300
State Capital Quiz, No. 43, 1940s, 7" long .. 40		60	80
Streamline Railway, pull toy, No. 129,			
17" long 150		225	300
Sunny Andy "Kiddie Kampers," action			
toy, color litho, three boy scouts and			
two girl scouts in backdrop camp			
setting, boys chop and saw wood and			
girls signal w/flags, marbles drop			
down chute, c. 1929, 5-5/8" x 3-1/2".... 250		375	500
Sunny Andy Cable Car Set, No. 53,			
c. 1920-30s, 12" high.............................. 80		120	160
Sunny Andy Fun Fair, action toy gravity			
activated by steel balls, No. 65, 1930s,			
14" long 195		286	390
Sunny Andy Rabbit Chase, 1930s, 9-1/2"			
diameter 150		225	300

WYANDOTTE

	C6	C8	C10
Air Raid Defense Target Game 52		78	105
Black Sambo target game, tin, has gun 70		105	140
Carnival, w/ferris wheel, carousel and			
airplane ride, metal............................... 700		1300	1860
Flash Strat-O-Wagon, 6" long 80		120	160
Hen, chubby, tin, lays egg when body			
pressed down, w/eight eggs,			
8-1/2" long.. 50		75	100
Musical push top, c. 1939 30		45	60
Posse Shooting Gallery, wind-up gallery,			
14" wide.. 90		135	180
Shooting Gallery, 1930s, wind-up,			
14" long, 11" high.................................... 65		98	130
Wagon, streamlined, steel, 1930s, 8" 150		225	300

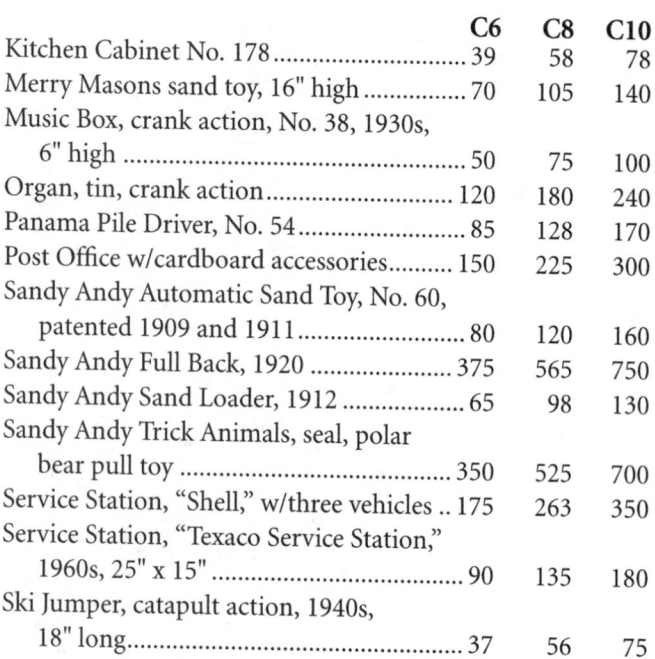

Corner Grocer, Wolverine, 1930s, $800

VARIOUS TOYS

	C6	C8	C10
Acrobatic Monkey John Henry Prod., 1950s, push toy, 10" long	60	90	120
Air Raid Warden Junior Kit, felt hat, arm band, gas mask, whistle, window sign, forms and street plan sheets, stethoscope, book of instructions, WWII era, rare	100	150	200
Artascope, optical toy, c. 1920, pressed steel, spin base w/multicolors, see-thru mirrors	60	90	120
Automaton Dancer, black dancer, 1800s, clockwork, I & W Co.	900	1500	2200
Baby Carriage, Kilgore, 4-7/8" high	250	375	500
Baby Carriage, tin, w/folding cloth top, 7-3/4" long	40	60	80
Badge, "Dick Steel News Service"	20	30	40
Badge, "Sheriff," six-pointed star, black oval insert and word "Oklahoma," nickeled metal	18	27	36
Bathroom Sink & Toilet, cast iron, Kilgore, each	45	68	90
Bones Player, Secor, 1880, cloth-dressed, cast iron, wood and tin figure w/hair, painted pot metal head, clockwork mechanism in body	1250	1875	2500
Bossy the Moo Cow, B & R Co., 1930s, 11" long	80	120	160
Bowling Alley, Ranger Steel	80	120	160
Boxers, Black, mechanical wind-up w/Ives clockwork mechanism	1000	1500	2000
Boy on Sled friction toy, rear wheels have spokes, Dayton, 9" long	262	393	525
Boy on Velocipede, papier-mâché, cloth and cast iron, wind-up, Stevens & Brown, or Althorp & Bergmann, c. 1870-1880, 10-3/4" long	1200	2000	2625

	C6	C8	C10
Boy Scout Five-In-One Mystery Hidden Compass	30	45	60
Bradley's Interchangeable Combination Circus in wooden box w/label, Pat. May 30, 1882, contains thirty five 3" x 5-1/4" interchangeable panels which makeup a changeable 15-3/4" x 9" circus scene	400	600	800
Brooklyn Bridge, paper litho and stained wood, mechanical, Bliss, 1880s, 4' x 11"	600	900	1200
Brownies Ten-Pin Set, early	650	1100	1600
Brownies, "Brownie Artillery," Brownies, cannon, etc., McLoughlin	650	1050	1500
Brownies, Brownie Glass Candy Container	500	750	1000
Buffalo Hunt, tin, Fallows, c. 1886, 9"	1200	2000	2700
Carousel, Althof Bergmann, 1870, painted tin, wood base, cloth canopy, clockwork, bisque head doll, wood body, tin arms, turns, cranks and gives motion, 20" tall	2500	4200	6000
Carousel, Marklin, c. 1909, 22" high, hand-cranked musical movement. Auctioned, w/some replacements, in 1994			55,000
Cash Register, "Uncle Sam's Cash Store Register," Durable Toy and Novelty, steel 5" high	26	39	52
Cash Register, Buddy L, steel, 9" x 10-1/2" x 9"	275	363	550
Cathedral Music Box, tin litho, of organ pipes and cherubs, plays loud or soft according to speed of cranking, no markings, German, 5" x 5" x 7"	325	488	650
Chemcraft Beginners Chemistry Set No. 602 by Porter, 1956	12	18	25
Chemistry set, Chemcraft No. 5, wooden box	37	56	75
Clever Clowns Trapeze Set, Grey Iron	275	363	550
Clever Clowns, Grey Iron, large set	500	750	1000
Consul, the educated monkey, tin hand toy, monkey automatically adds, subtracts, multiplies and divides, dated June 27, 1916, 5-1/2" x 6"	40	60	80
Dancers, clockwork, carved wood and jessobodies, clothes, black, Automatic Toy Works, New York City, 1870, 6-1/4" w x 10-1/4" t	600	900	1200
Davy Crockett Indian Target Set by Keystone Wood Company, David Crockett rifle, Wood stagecoach and horses, wood covered wagon and			

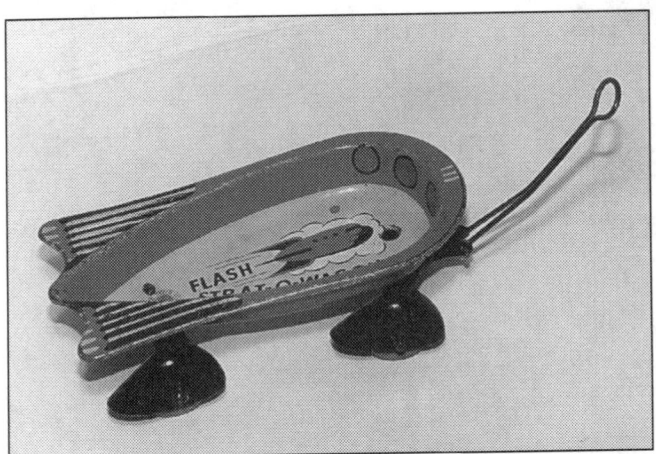

Flash Strat-O-Wagon, Wyandotte, $160

Tiny Tools, Arcade, $10 each

Windmill, Arcade, $200

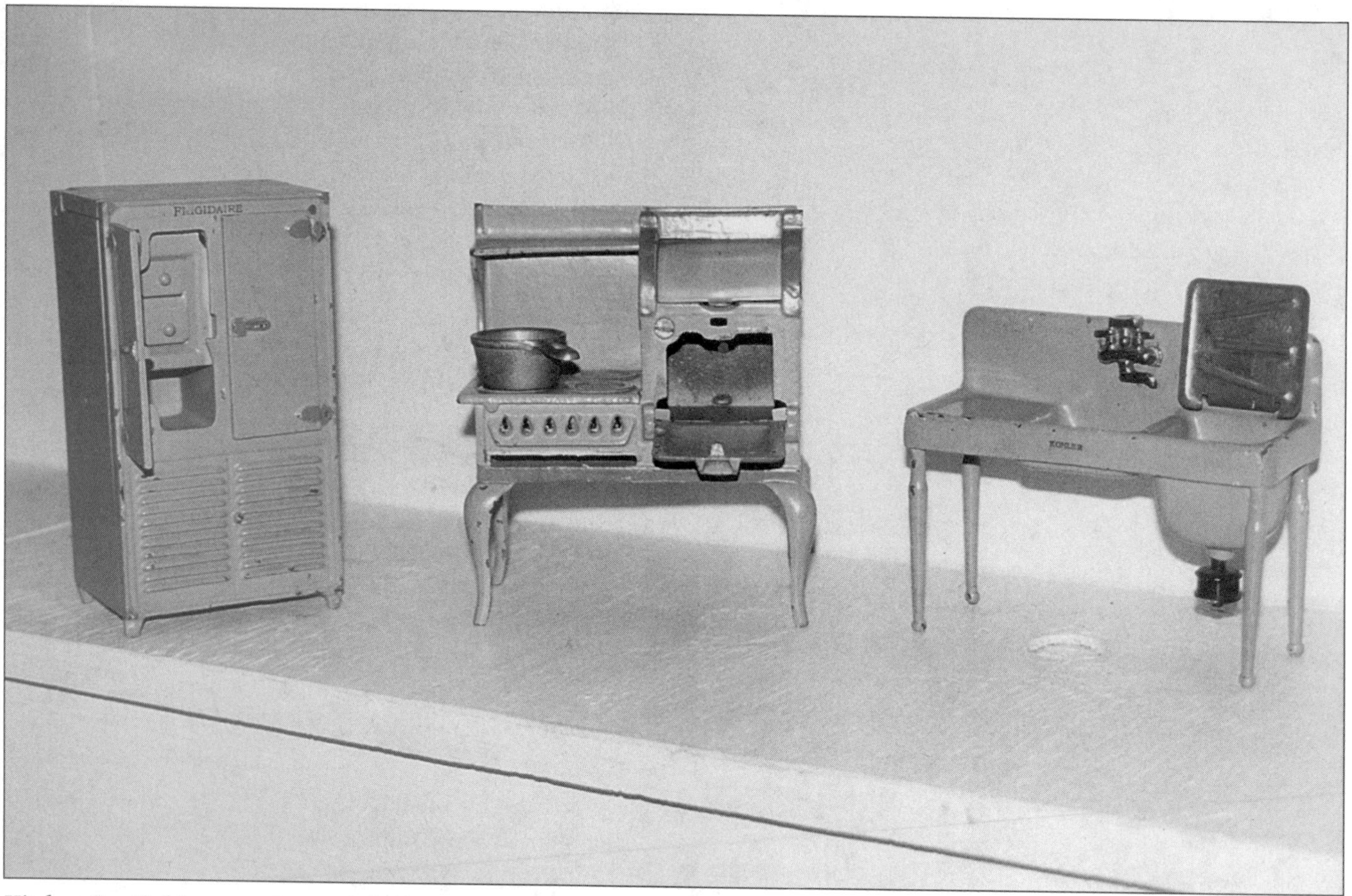

Kitchen Set, Refrigerator, Stove, Sink (dinette not shown), $1,000 for the set

horses, Indians, bear, etc.; all wood and hardboard litho set pre-dates Davy popularity of the 1950s, made c. 1949 40   60   80

Do-Do Toy Co. "Do-Do Clown," 1930s, squeeze toy, 5-1/2" long 70   105   140

Doctor's Set, Transogram, 1948, Little Country Doctor, full doctor set, chest and bag 32   48   65

Drive Safely set, Ranger Steel 112   168   225

Drum, Indian motif, tin litho, 11-3/4" diameter 175   263   350

Farm Set, cardboard and rubber, Judy Toys 62   93   125

Ferris Wheel, "DRGM," four figures, tin, 1895, 11-1/2" high 600   1000   1400

Fire House No. 8, Wilkins, tin, 18-1/2" long 600   900   1200

Fire Station, No. 8, clockwork bell and door, Kingsbury, 9" x 10" x 13" 150   225   300

Firehouse, heavy sheet metal, Turner, 12" x 15" x 21" 200   300   400

Fort, "Battle of the Toy Brigades," paper litho on wood, Bliss, c. 1880 600   1000   1400

Fort, Rich Toys No. 245, Siege Gun w/Stone Fort 25   40   75

Fort, Rich Toys No. 246, Siege Gun w/Stone Fort, two guns 30   50   80

Fort, Rich Toys No. 247, Siege Gun w/Stone Fort, three guns 40   60   80

	C6	C8	C10
Fort, Rich Toys No. 260, 26-3/4" long	35	50	75
Fort, Rich Toys No. 261, 26-1/2" long	50	75	100
Fort, Rich Toys No. 262, 27" long	100	200	300
Fort, Rich Toys No. 263, 29" long	275	363	550
Fort, Rich Toys, "Fort Washington"	112	168	225
Garage, heavy sheet metal, one window on each side, divided into four panes, Turner......................	100	150	200
Gas Station-Auto Laundry," Ranger Steel Co., 1940s, 3" x 5" x 13" long	130	195	260
Grocery Store, tin, scales, cash register, wrapping paper, order pad and pencil, "Little Toy Town Grocery Store," shelves w/small boxes of products, 14" long......................	100	150	200
Grocery Store, wood, "Pet's Grocery Store"......................................	400	600	800
H.K. Electric Engine, patented 1908, used DC current	50	75	100
Historoscope, rolled panorama, Milton Bradley, c. 1880	238	355	475

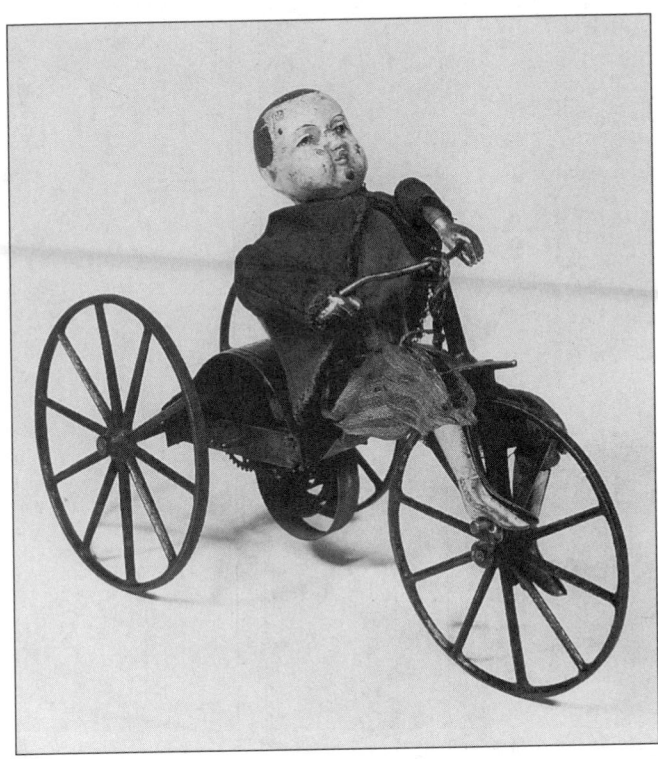

Boy on Velocipede, papier-mâché, cloth and cast iron, Stevens & Brown or Althorp & Bergmann, c. 1870-1880, $2,625

This c. 1909 carousel by Marklin auctioned in 1994 for $55,000.

	C6	C8	C10
Hobby Horse, "Black Beauty," wooden, 34" long 25	37	50
Horses in Hoops, Althof Bergmann, American painted tin, 1880, 4-1/2" diameter 800	1200	1600
Ice Box, "Alaska" cast iron, has glass cube of ice in top, 5" high 200	300	400
Junior Mechanic Construction Set, c. 1940 48	72	95
Junior WAC set, Hassenfeld Bros., hats, gas mask, bandages, etc. 40	60	80
Kaleidoscope "C. Bush, Prov. R.I., 1874," wood, brass & glass, 14" high 220	330	440
Kaleidoscope, Stevens, 1950s 10	15	20
Knife Sharpener, crank action, Girard 1930s, 8" high 60	90	120
Knockout Target Shooting Gallery, litho tin w/rifle, many targets 40	60	80
Laboratory, Chemcraft No. 418 Master Deluxe Laboratory, wooden box 175	263	350
Lindstrom's Little Show, cardboard and wood theatre w/seven show strips 250	375	500
Machine Gun, M101, fires caps, Buddy L ... 62	93	125
Magic Lantern Projector, tin, embossed deer on door and side, 8" long 60	90	120
Marky Maypo, rubber squeeze toy, 1960s ... 25	38	50
Merry-Go-Round, wind-up, litho paper and wood, w/four bisque figures riding four fur-skinned papier-mâché horses 600	900	1200
Merry-Go-Round, wood and litho paper, Jenny musical wind-up w/five horse-form seats 200	300	400
Monkey Riding Tricycle, cast iron, rubber tires, articulated legs, 7" long 1500	2700	3800
Monkey, mechanical, in red pants, red-checked shirt, squeeze metal lever attached to 34" spiral wire, monkey jumps alongside you, hitting cymbals, 10" high 62	93	125
Monkey, stuffed, red felt cap and jacket, glass eyes, moveable arms and legs, move his tail and head moves from side to side, and up and down, c. 1910, 9-1/2" high 60	90	120
Movie Projector, "Flip Movies," turn crank and flip cards from "Midgette" movies, w/film, c. early 1930s 56	84	112
Movie Projector, "Uncle Sam," hand cranks, c. 1920s 125	188	250
Mr. & Mrs. Potato Head Set, No. 2004, Hasbro 35	52	70

	C6	C8	C10
Mr. & Mrs. Potato Head Set, No. 2006, Hasbro 35	52	70
Mr. Potato Head No. 2000, Hasbro 19	28	38
Mr. Potato Head on the Farm, Hasbro 15	22	30
Mr. Potato Head, 1950s, plastic car and boat trailer, plus all the parts to create different faces, Hasbro 26	39	52
Mrs. Potato Head w/car, Hasbro 40	60	80
Mrs. Potato Head, Hasbro 50	75	100
Myrioptican, optical toy, Milton Bradley.. 300	450	600
Organ Grinder, monkey, push bottom, squeaks and dances, Kohner Bros., 6" wooden 20	30	40
Paddle Wheel and Tower on base, tin, 14" high 20	30	40
Phonograph, toy, Genola, cranks w/sound horn 100	150	200
Phonograph, toy, Nerona, cranks, sound comes from horn connected to needle, early 100	150	200
Play set, "Baby Haymaker," tin push toy, 1916, playset 125	188	250
Playstore Register, tin and brass, Durable Toy and Novelty Co., 4" high 18	27	36
Pull toy, Camel on Platform, tin, Althof-Bergmann 600	900	1200
Pull toy, Dog on Platform, animated, Fallows 1200	2000	4000
Pull toy, Elephant, tin, w/blanket, iron wheels, 4-1/2" long 170	255	340
Pull toy, Elephant w/saddle, tin, iron wheels, 4-1/2" long 75	112	150

Playstore Register, Durable Toy and Novelty Co., $36

	C6	C8	C10
Pull toy, Elephant with howdah, cast iron	600	900	1200
Pull toy, jockeys on horses, wood and paper litho, Gibbs, 10" long	750	1125	1500
Pull toy, Horse, leather reins, metal stirrups, felt saddle, c. 1880, 13-1/4" high	300	450	600
Pull toy, Horse and Animated Figure w/composition head and tin arms playing drum and cymbal, horse is tin, wheels, woodenplatform, 13-1/2"	500	750	1000
Pull toy, Horse and Polo Player on horse's back, tin, 4-1/4" long	75	112	150
Pull toy, Horse on Platform, tin and cast iron, 10" long	435	653	870
Pull toy, Horse on Platform, painted tin, George Brown, 1880, 6-1/2" long	250	375	500
Pull toy, Jockey on Dog, tin, early, Ives, 10-1/4" long	1000	1500	2000
Pull toy, Jockey on Goat, Ives, 9-1/2" long	3500	5200	7000
Pull toy, Jockey on Horse, tin, c. 1875, Fallows, 7" long	500	800	1200
Pull toy, Elephant on wheels, Gibbs, 10" long	200	300	400
Pull toy, Mary & Lamb, tin, Fallows, c. 1890, 6-1/2" long	1000	1600	2400
Pull toy, Rooster on Platform, painted tin, 1890, 4-3/4" long	100	150	200
Pull toy, Three Bears, Toycraft	30	45	60
Pull toy, Two Frogs, painted tin, Fallows, 1898, 7-1/2" long	900	1350	1800
Push Toy, Butterfly that flaps its wings	40	60	80

	C6	C8	C10
Push Toy, Clown on Log, bell toy, cast iron	500	750	1000
Push Toy, Gibbs, No. 29 Derby Rider	300	450	600
Push Toy, horse and rider, cast iron and wood, Wilkins, c. 1910, 29" long	262	395	525
Push Toy, large running horses, tin, Fallows, cast-iron wheels, 30" long	1000	1600	2300
Ripley's Believe It or Not Disk-O-Knowledge, round piece of cardboard w/another piece attached on top, turn to reveal questions and answers, 1932, 9-1/2" diameter	10	15	20
Rocket Space Ship No. 305, tin friction, sparks, Automatic Toy Co., 1930s, 8-1/2" long	80	120	160
Rolmonica, harmonica that plays rolls of tunes, "Blow, crank and play," w/three songs, 1930s	100	150	200
Roly Poly Clown, c. 1900, 13" high	412	618	825
Roly Poly, Boy on Horse, c. 1900	140	210	280
Round-Up Tex the Whirling Cowboy, plastic wind-up, Irwin, 1950s, 10" high	40	60	80
Sand Toy Set, 1942, includes tin litho frog, sailboat, shovel and round sieve, Chick Art Co.	36	54	78
Scales, cast iron, "Dayton," 3-1/2" high	40	60	80
Schieble Handcar, two men, tin, 9" long	350	525	700
Service Station, "Gulf Truck Service," Jane Francis	500	750	1000

Jockey on Horse, Fallows, c. 1875, Fallows, $1,200

Stove, marked "Eagle," cast iron, $100

	C6	C8	C10
Service Station, Superior Service Station Play set, 1950s	90	135	180
Sewing Machine, child's floor model, Stitchwell, c. 1920s	80	120	160
Shooting Gallery Chickens, cast iron, 10-1/4" long	75	112	150
Signal Jr. R-70 Twin Wireless Practice Set, two beginner's sending keys, and one advanced key, c. 1920	30	45	60
Slinky, 1947, w/box	12	18	25
Space Rocket Ship No. 306, 1930s, tin friction, sparks, siren, Automatic Toy Co., 8-1/2" long	150	225	300
Steve, Suzy Homemaker, 1968, Topper	18	27	37
Stove, "Daisy," cast white metal, 4-1/4" high	15	22	30
Stove, "Eagle," cast iron, 4-1/4" high	50	75	100
Stove, "Eagle, cast iron, 11-1/2" high	100	150	200
Stove, "Royal," cast iron, 4-1/2"	60	90	120
Stove, electric, one burner, two ovens, chrome-finished steel, porcelain on oven doors, 16" wide, 14" tall	80	120	160
Stove, wood-burning, cast iron, "The Queen"	45	67	90
Stove, wood-burning, cast iron, "The Triumph Range"	100	150	200
Stroller for baby, cast iron, Kilgore	40	60	80
Superior Space Port No. 75, 1950s, playset includes space drome, space cannon and plastic accessories, Cohn T. Inc. 17" long	350	525	700
Swing, animated, cast iron and pressed steel, for doll, w/eagle, wheel	600	900	1200
Swinging Clown, tin, base marked "C.D. Kenny Co.," 4-1/4" high	120	180	240

Zoetrope, wood and cardboard, Milton Bradley, $700

	C6	C8	C10
Symmetroscope, The, wood and tin type of kaleidoscope, F.P. Irving, Troy, N.Y., 6-1/4" high	60	90	120
Teeter-Totter, tin, when inverted, two children work their way down, Gibbs, 1910, 14-1/2" high	106	160	212
Tinker Toys No. 104	12	18	25
Tinker Toys No. 136	14	21	27
Tinker Toys, Electric ET-1	30	45	60
Tinker Toys, round box, 1940s, 12" high	12	18	24
Toledo Scales, cast iron, 4" x4"	25	37	50
Tom Thumb cash register, metal, by Western Stamping Co., 6-1/2" x 7-1/2" x 8-1/4"	25	38	50
Tool Chests, w/tools, four different, Buddy L, 1927-28, each	125	188	250
Tool Set, cast iron, steel and wood, Greycraft (Grey Iron), 1940	12	18	25
Tools, Grey Iron, 1933, per set	15	22	30
Top, Carnival Whistling Top, tin litho circus decor, spring-wound, Lupor, 1930s, 4" diameter	30	45	60
Top, wooden, c. 1940	4	6	8
Toy Town Garage, Parker Bros., 1910, three litho tin penny cars, paper lithogarage	1200	2000	3000
Toy Town Grocery Store, Parker Bros.	220	330	440
Tricycle, iron, Kilgore, 2-3/4"	30	45	60
Waffle Iron, cast iron, Wagner	25	37	50
Wagon, "Express" wood spoke wheels	250	375	500
Wagon, "Greyhound," full size, steel	80	120	160
Wagon, "Kiddie Kart," c. 1925, H.I. White, 20" long	50	75	100
Wagon, "Pioneer," tin, c. 1870, 25" long	312	468	625
Wagon, "Pony Express," 38" long	100	150	200
Wagon, "Radio Flyer, No. 94," 29" long	120	180	240
Wagon, Beaut Mfg. Co., No. 50	6	9	12
Wagon, Champion Express Coaster, 8" w/handle	65	98	130
Wagon, Express Flyer, cast iron	125	188	250
Wagon, wood, for child, 1900	175	263	350
Western Union telegraph key, battery powered, code printed on front	17	26	35
Whirligig of Life, McLoughlin, 1870s, illusion of motion	600	1000	1400
Wonder Clown, spinning top action, No. 110, 1950s, Nesco Co., 5-3/4" high	80	120	160
Wooden Music Maker, "Auto Phone Co. H.B. Horton's, Ithaca, N.Y.," uses player rolls, 9-1/2" high	100	150	200
Zoetrope, wood and cardboard, illusion of motion game, Milton Bradley	350	525	700

Appendix A

MUSEUMS

ANTIQUE TOY MUSEUM
Exit 230, I-44
P.O. Box 175
Stanton, MO 63079
(314) 927-5555

AUBURN-CORD-DUSENBERG MUSEUM
Auburn, IN 46706
Auburn toys and Cord and Dusenberg automobiles

BAUER TOY MUSEUM
 (Donald A. Bauer)
233 E. Main
Fredericksburg, TX
(512) 997-9394

DAISY GUN MUSEUM
U.S. 71 South
Rogers, AR
The world's most complete collection of air rifles, dating
    from the eighteenth century

ISLIP TOWN MUSEUM
Montauk Highway
Oakdale, NY

LAKE ERIE TOY MUSEUM (Aaron Roy)
P.O. Box 860
Kelleys Island, OH 43438
746-2451

LAWRENCE SCRIPPS WILKINSON COLLECTION
c/o Detroit Antique Toy Museum
6325 West Jefferson
Detroit, MI 48209
(383) 843-9775
Available only for traveling exhibitions

THE LONDON TOY & MODEL MUSEUM
23 Craven Hill
London, England

MARGARET WOODBURY STRONG MUSEUM
One Manhattan Square
Rochester, NY 14607

MUSEUM OF CHILDHOOD
8 Broad Street
Greensport, NY

MUSEUM OF THE CITY OF NEW YORK
5th Avenue and 103rd Street
New York, NY

NASHVILLE TOY MUSEUM
2613 McGavok Pike
Nashville, TN
Next to Opryland USA

REMEMBER WHEN TOY MUSEUM
Box 226A
Canton, MO 63435
288-3995 or 288-3176

SAN FRANCISCO INTERNATIONAL TOY MUSEUM
2801 Leavenworth Street
San Francisco, CA

SMITHSONIAN INSTITUTION
Public Inquiry Mail Service - MRC010
1000 Jefferson Drive SW
Washington, DC 20560
(202) 357-1300

THE STERLING COLLECTION
Stone Castle
804 North Third Street
Bardstown, KY

SULLIVAN-JOHNSON MUSEUM
223 North Main Street
Kenton, OH
Kenton Toys exhibit

THE TOY MUSEUM
42 Bridge St. Row
Chester, Cheshire
England

TOY TRAIN MUSEUM
Paradise Lane
Strasburg, PA

WASHINGTON DOLL'S HOUSE & TOY MUSEUM
5236 44th Street NW
Washington, DC 20015

Appendix B

AUCTION HOUSES

These are established firms experienced in auctioning large collections of toys.

REX & KATHY BARRETT (Mail)
P.O. Box 254
Medinah, IL 60157

BILL BERTOIA AUCTIONS
2413 Madison Ave.
Vineland, NJ 08360
(609) 692-1881
FAX: 609-692-8697

JEFF BUB
1658 Barbara Drive
Brunswick, OH 44212
(216) 225-1110

BUTTERFIELD & BUTTERFIELD
1244 Sutter Street
San Francisco, CA 94109

CHICAGO ANTIQUE TOY AUCTION
by Just Right, Inc.
6582 RFD
Long Grove, IL 60047
(708) 949-0059

CHRISTIE'S EAST
219 East 67th Street
New York, NY 10021
(212) 606-0400

CONTINENTAL AUCTIONS (Mail)
P.O. Box 193
Sheboygan, WI 53082

DEBBIE & MARTY KRIM'S NEW
    ENGLAND AUCTION GALLERY (Mail)
Box 2273-T
West Peabody, MA 01960
(508) 535-3140
Fax: (508) 535-7522

DUNNING'S AUCTION SERVICE
755 Church St.
Elgin, IL 60123-9302
Phone: (708) 741-3483
Fax: (708) 741-3589

GUERNSEY'S
108 East 73rd Street
New York, NY 10021
(212) 794-2280

HAKE'S AMERICANA & COLLECTIBLES
P.O. Box 1444N
York, PA 17405
(717) 848-1333
Sample catalog $3.00

JACKON'S AUCTIONEERS & APPRAISERS
James L. Jackson
2229 Lincoln St.
Cedar Falls, IA 50613
Phone: (319) 277-2256
Fax: (319) 277-1252
e-mail: jacksons@jacksonsauction.com

JAMES D. JULIA AUCTIONEERS, INC.
Rt. 201 Skowhegan Rd.
P.O. Box 830
Fairfield, ME 04937
Phone: (207) 453-7125; Fax: (207) 453-2502

HENRY KURTZ, Ltd.
163 Amsterdam Ave. Suite 136
New York, NY 10023
(212) 642-5904
FAX: 212-874-6018

LEWIS & LAMBRIGHT, INC.
112 N. Detroit St.
LaGrange, IN 46761
(413) 549-3775

JOY LUKE AUCTION GALLERY
300 E. Grove St.
Bloomington, IL 61701-5232
Phone: (309) 828-5533
Fax: (309) 829-2266

MAPES AUCTIONEERS & APPRAISERS
1600 Vestal Parkway West
Vestal, NY 13850
(607) 754-9193

TED MAURER
1003 Brookwood Dr.
Pottstown, PA 19646
323-1573 or 367-5024

MID-HUDSON AUCTION GALLERIES
One Idlewild Avenue
Croton-On-Hudson, NY 12520

NOEL BARRETT ANTIQUES & AUCTIONS
P.O. Box 300
Carversville, PA 18913

PHILIPS NEW YORK
406 E. 79th St.
New York, NY 10021

LLOYD W. RALSTON
173 Post Road
Fairfield, CT 06430
(203) 255-1233

RICHARD OPFER AUCTIONEERING, INC.
1919 Greenspring Drive
Timonium, MD 21093

SKINNER, Inc.
357 Main St.
Bolton, MA 01740-1104
Phone: (508) 779-6241
Fax: (508) 779-5144

SMITH HOUSE (mail)
P.O. Box 336
Eliot, ME 03903
(207) 439-4614

SOTHEBY'S
1334 York Avenue
New York, NY 10021
(212) 606-7000

TOY LOCATERS (mail)
5821 Diana Lane
Lake View, NY 14085
(716) 627-5840

WALLIS & WALLIS
West Street Auction Galleries
Glenn Butler Lewes
East Sussex BN7 2NJ
United Kingdom
Phone: 01273-480208
Fax: 01273-476562

WITHINGTON, Inc.
RD 2 Box 440
Hillsboro, NH 03244
Phone: (603) 464-3232

Appendix C
COLLECTORS AND DEALERS

It is suggested that, when writing to any of the following, you enclose a stamped, self-addressed envelope.

STAN ALEKNA
732 Aspen Lane
Lebanon, PA
Phone: (717) 228-2361
Fax: (717) 228-2362
Toy soldiers

STEVE BALKIN
Burlington Antique Toys
1082 Madison Avenue
New York, NY 10028
Toy soldiers including Warren

CHARLES W. BEST
11523 Pine Valley Drive
Franktown, CO 80116
budbest@aol.com
Old toy pistols, etc.

BOB LOWE'S TOONERVILLE JUNCTION
7 E. Church Street
Bethlehem, PA 18018
(215) 691-6736
Classic American and European Toys

BLYSTONE'S
2132 Delaware Ave.
Pittsburg, PA 15218
(412) 371-3511
FAX (412) 244-8028
Specialists in books on toys

RAY BRANDES
2964 Brookshire Way
Duluth, GA, 30136
(404) 476-8259
Big Bang cannons collector/dealer

LARRY BRUCH
P.O. Box 121
Mountaintop, PA 18707
(717) 474-9202
Old toys wanted and for sale

BUDDY K TOYS
Buddy L Toys, etc.
RD 9 Box 322
Bingen Road
Bethlehem, PA 18015

JIM BUSKIRK
c/o TGCA
3009 Oleander Avenue
San Marcos, CA 92069
Spring-Air BB guns, cast iron pistols

JIM & PATSY CARLSON
7939 Caberfae Trail
Clarkston, MI 48348-3708
Schoenhut collectors

ROD CARNAHAN
541 El Paso
Jacksonville, TX 75766
Buy, sell, trade old toys

CALVIN L. CHAUSSEE
Box 22
Calhan, CO 80808
(719) 347-2000
FAX: 719-347-2780
Antique toy buyer - any quantity

CLASSIC TOYS
69 Thompson St.
New York, NY 10012
New and old toys; military, vehicles, zoo, etc.

KENT M. COMSTOCK
532 Pleasant Street
Ashland, OH 44805
(419) 289-3308
Motorcycles, all types

CONTINENTAL HOBBY HOUSE
P.O. Box 193
Sheboygan, WI 53082
Toys and trains, regular catalogs

REID COVEY
Box 2D Highmarket Rd.
Constableville, NY 13325
(315) 397-8026
sullivan@northnet.org
Matchbox, Hot Wheels

DARROW'S FUN ANTIQUES
309 E. 61st Street
New York, NY 10021
(212) 838-0730
Old toys of all types

ROBERT A. DECENZO
P.O. Box 2266
Framingham, MA 01701
Marbles, tin wind-ups, paper litho, games, trains

DUTKINS' COLLECTABLES
1019 W. Route 70
Cherry Hill, NJ 08002
(609) 428-9559
Tin toys, soldiers, etc.

ECCLES BROTHERS
R.R. 1, Box 253-D
Burlington, IA 52601
Toy soldiers, comic figures and vehicles from original molds,
    catalog $3.00

PERRY R. EICHOR
703 North Almond Dr.
Simpsonville, SC 29681
Aircraft toys and literature

EXCALIBUR HOBBIES LTD
63 Exchange Street
Malden, MA 02148-5523
(617) 322-2959
Toy soldiers, all types

JUDY IZEN
P.O. Box 623
Lexington, MA 02173
jizenres@aol.com
Ideal dolls, Paper dolls

JOE FREEMAN - TIN TOY WORKS
1313 North 15th Street
Allentown, PA 18102
(610) 439-8268
FAX: (610) 439-1288
Repairs, parts made for tin toys

DANNY FUCHS
209-80 18th Avenue
Bayside, NY 11360
Superman toys, games, etc.

RAY FUNK
826 East 8th St.
Upland, CA 91786
Toys, bicycles

JOHN GIBSON
P.O. Box 40054
Washington, DC 20016
(301) 527-0076
Tootsietoy restoration, parts and services

TERRY GRAHAM
3083 Crescent Street
Long Island City, NY 11102
(718) 956-3382
Dealer in toy guns

TONY AND JACKI GRECCO
P.O. Box 3490
Poughkeepsie, NY 12603
(914) 462-8829
Toy soldiers and related items

A. (GUS) HANSEN
4645 Lilac Avenue
Glenview, IL 60025
Mignot, Dimestore, Britains, etc.

RAY HARADIN
Toys of Yesteryear
1039 Lakemont Drive
Pittsburgh, PA 15243-1817
(800) 349-8009
(Call for detailed catalog)
Mechanical banks, toy soldiers

JIM HARMON
634 S. Orchard Dr.
Burbank, CA 91506
Radio premiums and tapes, comic books and strips

W.S. (BILL) HARRISON III
223 Boa Vista St.
Punta Vista, FL 33983-5644

BILL HELLIE
All American Toy Company
P.O. Box 4266
Salem, OR 97302
American Toy Company parts and limited editions; buy sell,
    restore antique toys

JEFFREY L. HUBBARD
1770 4th Street South
Naples, FL 33940-7502
Doepke, Nylint collector

INSURANCE FOR COLLECTIBLE TOYS
Debbie Riley; Reeves & Melvin
P.O. Box 229
Millville, NJ 08332
(800) 298-4318

MICHELE KARL
P.O. Box 549
Port Richey, FL 34673
we2@gate.net
Wood and composition dolls

BRAD KREWSON
588 Lindford Drive
Bay Village, OH 44140
Beany & Cecil toys

BILL LANGO
127 74th Street
North Bergen, NJ 07047
Barclay vehicles, animals and soldiers from original and new
    molds; send for flyer

RICHARD LEACH
26146 Redfield Rd.
Edwardsburg, MI 49112
Old steam engine toys, literature

STEVE LEONARD
Box 127T
Albertson, LI, NY 11507
(516)742-0979
Antique mechanical toys, etc.

DAVID M. LEOPARD
2507 Feather Run Trail
West Columbia, SC 29169-4915
Old toy cars and trucks

CARL LOBEL
Box 74A
Warren, VT 05674
(802) 496-4025
Toys of all eras

LONDON BRIDGE COLLECTOR'S TOYS
East Penn Plaza
1325 Chestnut Street
Emmaus, PA 18049; (215) 967-6887
Britains soldiers, etc. and Britains replacement parts

RICHARD MacNARY
4727 Alpine Drive
Lilburn, GA 30247
Marx trains, Coca-Cola vehicles, wood, cardboard, paper
    toys, soldiers

MARBLE COLLECTORS SOCIETY OF AMERICA
P.O. Box 222
Trumbull, CT 06611

JOHN D. (JACK) MATTHEWS
13 Bufflehead Dr.
Kiawah Island, SC 29455
World War II toys, etc.

FRED MAXWELL
4722 No. 33 Street
Arlington, VA 22207
Collector/researcher; slush mold cars, planes, novelties, liter-
    ature, toys

K. WARREN MITCHELL
1008 Forward Pass
Pataskala, OH 43062
Soldiers of all types, regular lists at no charge

JOHN MURRAY
Box 29
Eden, NY 14057
Fisher-Price

NEW ERA TOYS
P.O. Box 10
Lambertville, NJ 08530
(609) 397-2113
Restorations service for pressed steel toy, pedal cars

BARBARA & JONATHAN NEWMAN
The Paper Soldier
8 McIntosh Lane
Clifton Park, NY 12065
Paper toys, old and new

TIM OEI - OEI ENTERPRISES, LTD.
241 Rowayton Ave.
Rowayton, CT 06853-1227
(203) 866-2470
Buys, sells, trades, restores old toys

DON PIELIN
1009 Kenilworth
Wheeling, IL 60090
Toy soldiers

PLYMOUTH ROCK TOY CO.
P.O. Box 1202
Plymouth, MA 02362
(508) 746-2842 or (508) 830-1180; FAX: (508) 830-0364
Toy pistols, etc., all eras

EDWARD K. POOLE
926 Terrace Mtn. Drive
Austin, TX 78746

Collectors and Dealers • 699

Toy soldiers, 1:36-scale ID vehicles and old wooden military
vehicle kits

HARVEY K. RAINESS
Rustic Ridge - N13
289 Mount Hope Avenue
Dover, NJ 07801
(201) 366-4677
Dealer in vehicles, tin, soldiers

MARK RICH
P.O. Box 971
Stevens Point, WI 54481
Tootsietoy, general toys

LEO RISHTY
Toydoc
2563 Jardin Lane
Weston, FL 33327
TOY1DOC@aol.com

SALUNGA (Don Eckel)
P.O. Box 369
Talmage, PA 17580
(717) 656-4857
Cast-iron parts for toys

PHIL SAVINO
Rt. 2, Box 76
Micanopy, FL 32667
Mail auctions in various toy categories - send SASE

CONRAD SCHWAGER
10321 N. Trails Edge Dr.
Peoria, IL 61615
Arcade, Buddy L, Metalcraft

SECOND CHILDHOOD
283 Bleecker Street
New York, NY
Antique toys

RONALD L. SIMKOFF
5171 Mayfield Rd.
Lyndhurst, OH 44124
(216) 461-2660
Holgate toys

JOHN K. SNYDER, JR.
Diamond International Galleries
1966 Greensprig Dr., Ste. 401
Timonium, MD 21093
Comic characters

SCOTT SMILES
848 S. Atlantic Dr., E.
Lantana, FL 33462
Tin wind-ups, etc.

BOB SMITH
62 West Ave.
Fairport, NY 14450
(716) 377-8394
Sells toys of all types, Toy shows

RON SMITH
33005 Arlesford
Solon, OH 44139
(216) 248-7006
Tin plate cars and planes, plastic promotional cars

MARK SUOZZI
Box 102
Ashfield, MA 01330
(413) 628-3241
Antique penny banks and toys

FRED THOMPSON
Smith-Miller Inc.
P.O. Box 139
Canoga Park, CA 91305
New designs of Smith-Miller vehicles

MARCIE TUBBS
6405 Mitchell Hollow Rd.
Charlotte, NC 28277
Dollhouses and Miniature Furniture
cardad@a01.com

DAVID WELCH
P.O. Box 714
Murphysboro, IL 62966
(618) 687-2282
PEZ, Cereal boxes, model kits, TV, Disney, premiums

RANDY WELCH
Raven' Tiques
27965 Peach Orchard Drive
Easton, MD 21601
(410) 822-5441
Ramp walkers, tin wind-ups, and sparklers

CHARLES FRANCIS WILDING
Secretary, Capitol Miniature Auto Collectors Club
10207 Greenacres Dr.
Silver Springs, MD 20903

FRED & MARGARET WILHELM
W & F Collectibles
Box 2054
Leucadia, CA 92024
Disney, Popeye, comic, Barclay, Manoil soldiers

FERDINAND ZEGEL
P.O. Box 589
Ft. Belvoir, VA 22060
Antique toys, postwar, Corgi, Dinky

RECOMMENDED READING

Periodicals

A.C. Gilbert Heritage Society Newsletter. Quarterly. Marion Designs, 594 Front St., Marion, MA 02738.

Antique Toy World. Monthly. Dale Kelley, P.O. Box 34509, Chicago, IL 60634.

Old Toy Soldier Newsletter. Bimonthly. Steve Sommers, 209 North Lombard, Oak Park, IL 60302.

Toy Cars & Vehicles. Monthly. Krause Publications, 700 E. State Street, Iola, WI 54990.

Toy Shop. Biweekly. Krause Publications, 700 E. State Street, Iola, WI 54990.

Toy Gun Collectors of America Newsletter. 16-page quarterly. Jim Buskirk, 3009 Oleander Avenue, San Marcos, CA 92069.

Toy Soldier Review. Vintage Castings Inc., 127-74th Street, North Bergen, NJ 07047.

U.S. Toy Collector. Vehicles only. Monthly. 231 S. Grove St., Missoula, MT 59801.

Books

Arcade Toys by Al Aune. 1990. Robert F. Mannella, 4441 Shari Ann Lane, Brooklyn Park, MN 55443.

The Barclay Catalog Book. Early Barclay catalogs, drawings, photos, etc. Richard O'Brien. (Out of print)

Big Bang Cannons. Raymond V. Brandes. Ray-Vin Publishing, 2964-R Brookshire Way, Duluth, GA 30136.

Cast Iron Toy Guns and Capshooter by Samuel H. Logan and Charles W. Best. Heavily illustrated book. $55. Sam Logan, 1200 Harvard Drive, Davis, CA 95616

Collecting American-Made Soldiers. Richard O'Brien. $45.95. Krause Publications, 700 East State Street, Iola, WI 54990.

Collecting Foreign-Made Soldiers. Richard O'Brien. $32.95. Krause Publications, 700 East State Street, Iola, WI 54990.

Collecting PEZ by David Welch. $43.95 in U.S., 350 pages. P.O. Box 714, Murphysboro, IL 62966. (618) 687-2282, FAX (618) 684-2243.

Collecting Toy Cars & Trucks, 2nd Edition. Richard O'Brien. $27.95. Krause Publications, 700 East State Street, Iola, WI 54990.

Fisher-Price 1931-1963. 1991 edition. $24.95. Krause Publications, 700 East State Street, Iola, WI 54990.

Marbles: Price and Identification Guide. Robert Black. P.O. Box 222, Trumbull, CT 06611.

Pictorial Guide to Weeden Steam Toys. Richard B. Leach. $10. 26146 Redfield Road, Edwardsburg, MI 49112.

Plastic Figure & Playset Collector. Bimonthly. $21 per year. Specialty Publishing Company, P.O. Box 1355, LaCrosse, WI 54602-1355.

Plastic Toys. Bill Hanlon. $72.90. All-color, 288 pages. Schiffer Publishing, 77 Lower Valley Road, Atglen, PA 19310.

Radio Mystery and Adventure. Jim Harmon. McFarland & Company, Inc., Jefferson, North Carolina & London.

Rubber Toy Vehicles. Dave Leopard. $26.95. Dave Leopard, 2507 Feather Run Trail, West Columbia, SC 29169-4915.

The Second Catalog Book. Reprints of catalogs by Manoil, Barclay, Warren, All-Nu, Authenticast, Belton, Grey Iron. $16. Richard O'Brien, 705 Greene Street, Beaufort, SC 29902.

The Story of American Toys by Richard O'Brien. 1990. $24.95. Abbeville Press. (Out of print)

Toys & Prices. Sharon Korbeck, editor. Krause Publications, 700 E. State St., Iola, WI 54490

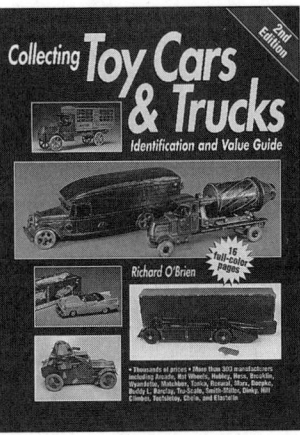
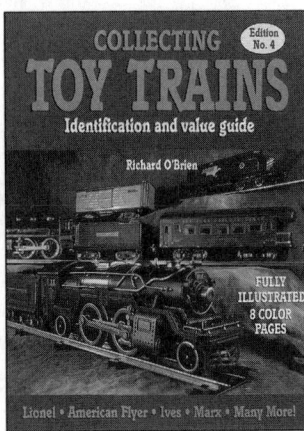

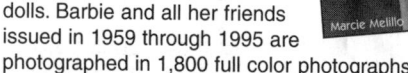

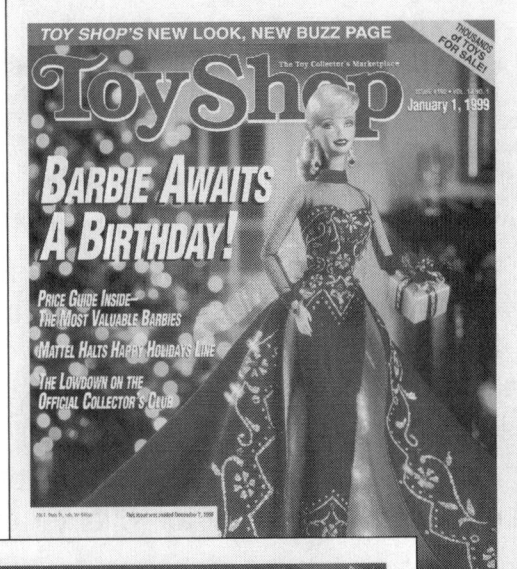